The Second World War

★

THE
Gathering
Storm

Winston S. Churchill

Published in association with
The Cooperation Publishing Company, Inc.

HOUGHTON MIFFLIN COMPANY BOSTON
The Riverside Press Cambridge
1948

The Riverside Press
CAMBRIDGE · MASSACHUSETTS
PRINTED IN U.S.A.

★

PREFACE

I MUST REGARD THESE VOLUMES of *The Second World War* as a continuation of the story of the First World War which I set out in *The World Crisis, The Eastern Front,* and *The Aftermath.* Together, if the present work is completed, they will cover an account of another Thirty Years' War.

I have followed, as in previous volumes, as far as I am able, the method of Defoe's *Memoirs of a Cavalier,* in which the author hangs the chronicle and discussion of great military and political events upon the thread of the personal experiences of an individual. I am perhaps the only man who has passed through both the two supreme cataclysms of recorded history in high Cabinet office. Whereas, however, in the First World War I filled responsible but subordinate posts, I was for more than five years in this second struggle with Germany the Head of His Majesty's Government. I write, therefore, from a different standpoint and with more authority than was possible in my earlier books.

Nearly all my official work was transacted by dictation to secretaries. During the time I was Prime Minister, I issued the memoranda, directives, personal telegrams, and minutes which amount to nearly a million words. These documents, composed from day to day under the stress of events and with the knowledge available at the moment, will no doubt show

iii

many shortcomings. Taken together, they nevertheless give a current account of these tremendous events as they were viewed at the time by one who bore the chief responsibility for the war and policy of the British Commonwealth and Empire. I doubt whether any similar record exists or has ever existed of the day-to-day conduct of war and administration. I do not describe it as history, for that belongs to another generation. But I claim with confidence that it is a contribution to history which will be of service to the future.

These thirty years of action and advocacy comprise and express my life-effort, and I am content to be judged upon them. I have adhered to my rule of never criticising any measure of war or policy after the event unless I had before expressed publicly or formally my opinion or warning about it. Indeed in the after-light I have softened many of the severities of contemporary controversy. It has given me pain to record these disagreements with so many men whom I liked or respected; but it would be wrong not to lay the lessons of the past before the future. Let no one look down on those honourable, well-meaning men whose actions are chronicled in these pages, without searching his own heart, reviewing his own discharge of public duty, and applying the lessons of the past to his future conduct.

It must not be supposed that I expect everybody to agree with what I say, still less that I only write what will be popular. I give my testimony according to the lights I follow. Every possible care has been taken to verify the facts; but much is constantly coming to light from the disclosure of captured documents or other revelations which may present a new aspect to the conclusions which I have drawn. This is why it is important to rely upon authentic contemporary records and the expressions of opinion set down when all was obscure.

One day President Roosevelt told me that he was asking publicly for suggestions about what the war should be called. I said at once "The Unnecessary War." There never was a war more easy to stop than that which has just wrecked what was left of the world from the previous struggle. The human tragedy reaches its climax in the fact that after all the exertions and sacrifices of hundreds of millions of people and of the victories of the Righteous Cause, we have still not found Peace or Security, and that we lie in the grip of even worse perils than those we have surmounted. It is my earnest hope that pondering upon the past may give guidance in days to come, enable a new generation to repair some of the errors of former years and thus govern, in accordance with the needs and glory of man, the awful unfolding scene of the future.

WINSTON SPENCER CHURCHILL

CHARTWELL
WESTERHAM
KENT
March 1948

★

ACKNOWLEDGMENTS

I HAVE BEEN GREATLY ASSISTED in the establishment of the story in its military aspect by Lieutenant-General Sir Henry Pownall; in naval matters by Commodore G. R. G. Allen; and on European and general questions by Colonel F. W. Deakin, of Wadham College, Oxford, who also helped me in my work *Marlborough: His Life and Times*. I have had much assistance from Sir Edward Marsh in matters of diction. I must in addition make my acknowledgments to the very large numbers of others who have kindly read these pages and commented upon them.

Lord Ismay has also given me his invaluable aid, and with my other friends will continue to do so in the future.

I record my obligations to His Majesty's Government for permission to reproduce the text of certain official documents of which the Crown copyright is legally vested in the Controller of His Majesty's Stationery Office.

★

Moral of the Work

In War: Resolution

In Defeat: Defiance

In Victory: Magnanimity

In Peace: Good Will

★

THEME OF THE VOLUME

How the English-speaking peoples
through their unwisdom,
carelessness, and good nature
allowed the wicked
to rearm

★

CONTENTS

Book One
FROM WAR TO WAR
1919–1939

Book Two

THE TWILIGHT WAR
September 3, 1939 — May 10, 1940

★

Maps and Diagrams

★

Book One

FROM WAR TO WAR

1919–1939

1

The Follies of the Victors

The War to End War — A Blood-Drained France — The Rhine Frontier — The Economic Clauses of the Versailles Treaty — Ignorance About Reparations — Destruction of the Austro-Hungarian Empire by the Treaties of St. Germain and of Trianon — The Weimar Republic — The Anglo-American Guarantee to France Repudiated by the United States — The Fall of Clemenceau — Poincaré Invades the Ruhr — The Collapse of the Mark — American Isolation — End of the Anglo-Japanese Alliance — Anglo-American Naval Disarmament — Fascism the Child of Communism — How Easy to Prevent a Second Armageddon — The One Solid Security for Peace — The Victors Forget — The Vanquished Remember — Moral Havoc of the Second World War — Failure to Keep Germany Disarmed the Cause.

AFTER THE END of the World War of 1914 there was a deep conviction and almost universal hope that peace would reign in the world. This heart's desire of all the peoples could easily have been gained by steadfastness in righteous convictions, and by reasonable common sense and prudence. The phrase "the war to end war" was on every lip, and measures had been taken to turn it into reality. President Wilson, wielding, as was thought, the authority of the United States, had made the conception of a League of Nations dominant in all minds. The British delegation at Versailles moulded and shaped his ideas into an instrument which will for ever constitute a milestone in the hard march of man. The victorious Allies were at that time all-powerful, so far as their outside enemies were concerned. They had to face grave internal difficulties and many

3

riddles to which they did not know the answer, but the Teutonic Powers in the great mass of Central Europe which had made the upheaval were prostrate before them, and Russia, already shattered by the German flail, was convulsed by civil war and falling into the grip of the Bolshevik or Communist Party.

*   *   *   *   *

In the summer of 1919, the Allied armies stood along the Rhine, and their bridgeheads bulged deeply into defeated, disarmed, and hungry Germany. The chiefs of the victor Powers debated and disputed the future in Paris. Before them lay the map of Europe to be redrawn almost as they might resolve. After fifty-two months of agony and hazards the Teutonic Coalition lay at their mercy, and not one of its four members could offer the slightest resistance to their will. Germany, the head and forefront of the offence, regarded by all as the prime cause of the catastrophe which had fallen upon the world, was at the mercy or discretion of conquerors, themselves reeling from the torment they had endured. Moreover, this had been a war, not of governments, but of peoples. The whole life-energy of the greatest nations had been poured out in wrath and slaughter. The war leaders assembled in Paris had been borne thither upon the strongest and most furious tides that have ever flowed in human history. Gone were the days of the Treaties of Utrecht and Vienna, when aristocratic statesmen and diplomats, victor and vanquished alike, met in polite and courtly disputation, and, free from the clatter and babel of democracy, could reshape systems upon the fundamentals of which they were all agreed. The peoples, transported by their sufferings and by the mass teachings with which they had been inspired, stood around in scores of millions to demand that retribution should be exacted to the full. Woe betide the leaders now perched on their dizzy pinnacles of triumph if they cast away at the conference table what the soldiers had won on a hundred blood-soaked battlefields.

France, by right alike of her efforts and her losses, held the leading place. Nearly a million and a half Frenchmen had perished defending the soil of France on which they stood against the invader. Five times in a hundred years, in 1814, 1815, 1870, 1914, and 1918, had the towers of Notre Dame seen the flash of Prussian guns and heard the thunder of their cannonade. Now for four horrible years thirteen provinces of France had lain in the rigorous grip of Prussian military rule. Wide regions had been systematically devastated by the enemy or pulverised in the encounter of the armies. There was hardly a cottage nor a family from Verdun to Toulon that did not mourn its dead or shelter its cripples. To those Frenchmen — and there were many in high authority — who had fought and suffered in 1870, it seemed almost a miracle that France should have emerged victorious from the incomparably more terrible struggle which had just ended. All their lives they had dwelt in fear of the German Empire. They remembered the preventive war which Bismarck had sought to wage in 1875; they remembered the brutal threats which had driven Delcassé from office in 1905; they had quaked at the Moroccan menace in 1906, at the Bosnian dispute of 1908, and at the Agadir crisis of 1911. The Kaiser's "mailed fist" and "shining armour" speeches might be received with ridicule in England and America. They sounded a knell of horrible reality in the hearts of the French. For fifty years almost they had lived under the terror of the German arms. Now, at the price of their life-blood, the long oppression had been rolled away. Surely here at last was peace and safety. With one passionate spasm the French people cried, "Never again!"

But the future was heavy with foreboding. The population of France was less than two-thirds that of Germany. The French population was stationary, while the German grew. In a decade or less the annual flood of German youth reaching the military age must be double that of France. Germany had fought nearly the whole world, almost single-handed, and she had almost conquered. Those who knew the most knew best the several occasions when the result of the Great War had trembled in the balance, and the accidents and chances which had turned the fateful scale. What prospect was there in the

future that the Great Allies would once again appear in their
millions upon the battlefields of France or in the East? Russia
was in ruin and convulsion, transformed beyond all semblance
of the past. Italy might be upon the opposite side. Great Britain and the United States were separated by the seas or oceans
from Europe. The British Empire itself seemed knit together
by ties which none but its citizens could understand. What
combination of events could ever bring back again to France
and Flanders the formidable Canadians of the Vimy Ridge;
the glorious Australians of Villers-Brettonneaux; the dauntless
New Zealanders of the crater-fields of Passchendaele; the stead-
fast Indian Corps which in the cruel winter of 1914 had held
the line by Armentières? When again would peaceful, careless,
anti-militarist Britain tramp the plains of Artois and Picardy
with armies of two or three million men? When again would
the ocean bear two millions of the splendid manhood of America to Champagne and the Argonne? Worn down, doubly deci-
mated, but undisputed masters of the hour, the French nation
peered into the future in thankful wonder and haunting dread.
Where then was that SECURITY without which all that had been
gained seemed valueless, and life itself, even amid the rejoicings of victory, was almost unendurable? The mortal need was
Security at all costs and by all methods, however stern or even
harsh.

*   *   *   *   *

On Armistice Day, the German armies had marched homeward in good order. "They fought well," said Marshal Foch,
Generalissimo of the Allies, with the laurels bright upon his
brow, speaking in soldierly mood: "let them keep their weapons." But he demanded that the French frontier should henceforth be the Rhine. Germany might be disarmed; her military
system shivered in fragments; her fortresses dismantled: Germany might be impoverished; she might be loaded with
measureless indemnities; she might become a prey to internal
feuds: but all this would pass in ten years or in twenty. The
indestructible might "of all the German tribes" would rise
once more and the unquenched fires of warrior Prussia glow

and burn again. But the Rhine, the broad, deep, swift-flowing Rhine, once held and fortified by the French Army, would be a barrier and a shield behind which France could dwell and breathe for generations. Very different were the sentiments and views of the English-speaking world, without whose aid France must have succumbed. The territorial provisions of the Treaty of Versailles left Germany practically intact. She still remained the largest homogeneous racial block in Europe. When Marshal Foch heard of the signing of the Peace Treaty of Versailles he observed with singular accuracy: "This is not Peace. It is an Armistice for twenty years."

* * * * *

The economic clauses of the Treaty were malignant and silly to an extent that made them obviously futile. Germany was condemned to pay reparations on a fabulous scale. These dictates gave expression to the anger of the victors, and to the belief of their peoples that any defeated nation or community can ever pay tribute on a scale which would meet the cost of modern war.

The multitudes remained plunged in ignorance of the simplest economic facts, and their leaders, seeking their votes, did not dare to undeceive them. The newspapers, after their fashion, reflected and emphasised the prevailing opinions. Few voices were raised to explain that payment of reparations can only be made by services or by the physical transportation of goods in wagons across land frontiers or in ships across salt water; or that when these goods arrive in the demanding countries, they dislocate the local industry except in very primitive or rigorously controlled societies. In practice, as even the Russians have now learned, the only way of pillaging a defeated nation is to cart away any movables which are wanted, and to drive off a portion of its manhood as permanent or temporary slaves. But the profit gained from such processes bears no relation to the cost of the war. No one in great authority had the wit, ascendancy, or detachment from public folly to declare these fundamental, brutal facts to the electorates; nor would

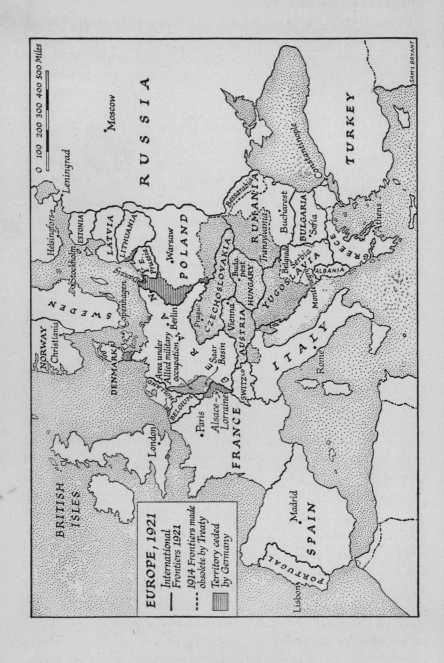

EUROPE, 1921

—— International Frontiers 1921

---- 1914 Frontiers made obsolete by Treaty

▥ Territory ceded by Germany

0 100 200 300 400 500 Miles

SAM'L BRYANT

RUSSIA

Moscow

Leningrad

Helsingfors

ESTONIA

LATVIA

LITHUANIA

N. E. Prussia

POLAND

Warsaw

SWEDEN

Stockholm

NORWAY

Christiania

DENMARK

Copenhagen

Danzig

BRITISH ISLES

London

HOLLAND

BELGIUM

Area under Allied military occupation

Berlin

Saar Basin

Paris

Alsace-Lorraine

FRANCE

SWITZ'L'D

Prague

CZECHOSLOVAKIA

Vienna

AUSTRIA

HUNGARY

Buda-pest

Bessarabia

RUMANIA

Transylvania

Bucharest

Belgrade

YUGO-SLAVIA

Serbia

Montenegro

ALBANIA

BULGARIA

Sofia

GREECE

Athens

Constantinople

TURKEY

ITALY

Rome

SPAIN

Madrid

PORTUGAL

Lisbon

anyone have been believed if he had. The triumphant Allies continued to assert that they would squeeze Germany "till the pips squeaked." All this had a potent bearing on the prosperity of the world and the mood of the German race.

In fact, however, these clauses were never enforced. On the contrary, whereas about one thousand million pounds of German assets were appropriated by the victorious Powers, more than one thousand five hundred millions were lent a few years later to Germany, principally by the United States and Great Britain, thus enabling the ruin of the war to be rapidly repaired in Germany. As this apparently magnanimous process was still accompanied by the machine-made howlings of the unhappy and embittered populations in the victorious countries, and the assurances of their statesmen that Germany should be made to pay "to the uttermost farthing," no gratitude or good will was to be expected or reaped.

Germany only paid, or was only able to pay, the indemnities later extorted because the United States was profusely lending money to Europe, and especially to her. In fact, during the three years 1926 to 1929 the United States was receiving back in the form of debt-instalment indemnities from all quarters about one-fifth of the money which she was lending to Germany with no chance of repayment. However, everybody seemed pleased and appeared to think this might go on for ever.

History will characterise all these transactions as insane. They helped to breed both the martial curse and the "economic blizzard," of which more later. Germany now borrowed in all directions, swallowing greedily every credit which was lavishly offered her. Misguided sentiment about aiding the vanquished nation, coupled with a profitable rate of interest on these loans, led British investors to participate, though on a much smaller scale than those of the United States. Thus, Germany gained the two thousand millions sterling in loans as against the one thousand million of indemnities which she paid in one form or another by surrender of capital assets and *valuta* in foreign countries, or by juggling with the enormous American loans.

All this is a sad story of complicated idiocy in the making of
which much toil and virtue was consumed.

*   *   *   *   *

The second cardinal tragedy was the complete break-up of
the Austro-Hungarian Empire by the Treaties of St. Germain
and Trianon. For centuries this surviving embodiment of the
Holy Roman Empire had afforded a common life, with advantages in trade and security, to a large number of peoples, none
of whom in our own time had the strength or vitality to stand
by themselves in the face of pressure from a revivified Germany
or Russia. All these races wished to break away from the federal or imperial structure, and to encourage their desires was
deemed a liberal policy. The Balkanisation of Southeastern
Europe proceeded apace, with the consequent relative aggrandisement of Prussia and the German Reich, which, though
tired and war-scarred, was intact and locally overwhelming.
There is not one of the peoples or provinces that constituted
the Empire of the Hapsburgs to whom gaining their independence has not brought the tortures which ancient poets and
theologians had reserved for the damned. The noble capital of
Vienna, the home of so much long-defended culture and tradition, the centre of so many roads, rivers, and railways, was left
stark and starving, like a great emporium in an impoverished
district whose inhabitants have mostly departed.

The victors imposed upon the Germans all the long-sought
ideals of the liberal nations of the West. They were relieved
from the burden of compulsory military service and from the
need of keeping up heavy armaments. The enormous American loans were presently pressed upon them, though they had
no credit. A democratic constitution, in accordance with all the
latest improvements, was established at Weimar. Emperors
having been driven out, nonentities were elected. Beneath this
flimsy fabric raged the passions of the mighty, defeated, but
substantially uninjured German nation. The prejudice of the
Americans against monarchy, which Mr. Lloyd George made
no attempt to counteract, had made it clear to the beaten Em-

pire that it would have better treatment from the Allies as a
republic than as a monarchy. Wise policy would have crowned
and fortified the Weimar Republic with a constitutional sovereign in the person of an infant grandson of the Kaiser, under
a council of regency. Instead, a gaping void was opened in the
national life of the German people. All the strong elements,
military and feudal, which might have rallied to a constitutional monarchy and for its sake respected and sustained the
new democratic and parliamentary processes, were for the time
being unhinged. The Weimar Republic, with all its liberal
trappings and blessings, was regarded as an imposition of the
enemy. It could not hold the loyalties or the imagination of
the German people. For a spell they sought to cling as in desperation to the aged Marshal Hindenburg. Thereafter mighty
forces were adrift; the void was open, and into that void after a
pause there strode a maniac of ferocious genius, the repository
and expression of the most virulent hatreds that have ever cor-
roded the human breast — Corporal Hitler.

* * * * *

France had been bled white by the war. The generation
that had dreamed since 1870 of a war of revenge had triumphed, but at a deadly cost in national life-strength. It was
a haggard France that greeted the dawn of victory. Deep fear
of Germany pervaded the French nation on the morrow of
their dazzling success. It was this fear that had prompted Marshal Foch to demand the Rhine frontier for the safety of France
against her far larger neighbour. But the British and American statesmen held that the absorption of German-populated
districts in French territory was contrary to the Fourteen Points
and to the principles of nationalism and self-determination
upon which the Peace Treaty was to be based. They therefore
withstood Foch and France. They gained Clemenceau by
promising: first, a joint Anglo-American guarantee for the defence of France; secondly, a demilitarised zone; and thirdly,
the total, lasting disarmament of Germany. Clemenceau accepted this in spite of Foch's protests and his own instincts.

The Treaty of Guarantee was signed accordingly by Wilson and Lloyd George and Clemenceau. The United States Senate refused to ratify the treaty. They repudiated President Wilson's signature. And we, who had deferred so much to his opinions and wishes in all this business of peacemaking, were told without much ceremony that we ought to be better informed about the American Constitution.

In the fear, anger, and disarray of the French people, the rugged, dominating figure of Clemenceau, with his world-famed authority, and his special British and American contacts, was incontinently discarded. "Ingratitude towards their great men," says Plutarch, "is the mark of strong peoples." It was imprudent for France to indulge this trait when she was so grievously weakened. There was little compensating strength to be found in the revival of the group intrigues and ceaseless changes of governments and ministers which were the characteristic of the Third Republic, however profitable or diverting they were to those engaged in them.

Poincaré, the strongest figure who succeeded Clemenceau, attempted to make an independent Rhineland under the patronage and control of France. This had no chance of success. He did not hesitate to try to enforce reparations on Germany by the invasion of the Ruhr. This certainly imposed compliance with the Treaties on Germany; but it was severely condemned by British and American opinion. As a result of the general financial and political disorganisation of Germany, together with reparation payments during the years 1919 to 1923, the mark rapidly collapsed. The rage aroused in Germany by the French occupation of the Ruhr led to a vast, reckless printing of paper notes with the deliberate object of destroying the whole basis of the currency. In the final stages of the inflation the mark stood at forty-three million millions to the pound sterling. The social and economic consequences of this inflation were deadly and far-reaching. The savings of the middle classes were wiped out, and a natural following was thus provided for the banners of National Socialism. The whole structure of German industry was distorted by the growth of mushroom trusts. The entire working capital of the country disappeared. The internal national debt and the debt of industry in the form of fixed capital charges and mortgages were, of course, simultaneously liquidated or repudiated. But this was no compensation for the loss of working capital. All led directly to the large-scale borrowings of a bankrupt nation abroad which were the feature of ensuing years. German sufferings and bitterness marched forward together — as they do today.

The British temper towards Germany, which at first had been so fierce, very soon went as far astray in the opposite direction. A rift opened between Lloyd George and Poincaré, whose bristling personality hampered his firm and far-sighted policies. The two nations fell apart in thought and action, and British sympathy or even admiration for Germany found powerful expression.

*   *   *   *   *

The League of Nations had no sooner been created than it received an almost mortal blow. The United States abandoned President Wilson's offspring. The President himself, ready to do battle for his ideals, suffered a paralytic stroke just as he was setting forth on his campaign, and lingered henceforward a futile wreck for a great part of two long and vital years, at the end of which his party and his policy were swept away by the Republican Presidential victory of 1920. Across the Atlantic on the morrow of the Republican success isolationist conceptions prevailed. Europe must be left to stew in its own juice, and must pay its lawful debts. At the same time tariffs were raised to prevent the entry of the goods by which alone these debts could be discharged. At the Washington Conference of 1921, far-reaching proposals for naval disarmament were made by the United States, and the British and American Governments proceeded to sink their battleships and break up their military establishments with gusto. It was argued in odd logic that it would be immoral to disarm the vanquished unless the victors also stripped themselves of their weapons. The finger of Anglo-American reprobation was presently to be pointed at

France, deprived alike of the Rhine frontier and of her treaty guarantee, for maintaining, even on a greatly reduced scale, a French Army based upon universal service.

The United States made it clear to Britain that the continuance of her alliance with Japan, to which the Japanese had punctiliously conformed, would constitute a barrier in Anglo-American relations. Accordingly, this alliance was brought to an end. The annulment caused a profound impression in Japan, and was viewed as the spurning of an Asiatic Power by the Western World. Many links were sundered which might afterwards have proved of decisive value to peace. At the same time, Japan could console herself with the fact that the downfall of Germany and Russia had, for a time, raised her to the third place among the world's naval Powers, and certainly to the highest rank. Although the Washington Naval Agreement prescribed a lower ratio of strength in capital ships for Japan than for Britain and the United States (5:5:3), the quota assigned to her was well up to her building and financial capacity for a good many years, and she watched with an attentive eye the two leading naval Powers cutting each other down far below what their resources would have permitted and what their responsibilities enjoined. Thus, both in Europe and in Asia, conditions were swiftly created by the victorious Allies which, in the name of peace, cleared the way for the renewal of war.

While all these untoward events were taking place, amid a ceaseless chatter of well-meant platitudes on both sides of the Atlantic, a new and more terrible cause of quarrel than the imperialism of czars and kaisers became apparent in Europe. The Civil War in Russia ended in the absolute victory of the Bolshevik Revolution. The Soviet armies which advanced to subjugate Poland were indeed repulsed in the Battle of Warsaw, but Germany and Italy nearly succumbed to Communist propaganda and designs. Hungary actually fell for a while under the control of the Communist dictator, Bela Kun. Although Marshal Foch wisely observed that "Bolshevism had never crossed the frontiers of victory," the foundations of European civilisation trembled in the early post-war years. Fascism was the shadow or ugly child of Communism. While Corporal Hitler was making himself useful to the German officer class in Munich by arousing soldiers and workers to fierce hatred of Jews and Communists, on whom he laid the blame of Germany's defeat, another adventurer, Benito Mussolini, provided Italy with a new theme of government which, while it claimed to save the Italian people from Communism, raised himself to dictatorial power. As Fascism sprang from Communism, so Nazism developed from Fascism. Thus were set on foot those kindred movements which were destined soon to plunge the world into even more hideous strife, which none can say has ended with their destruction.

*   *   *   *   *

Nevertheless, one solid security for peace remained. Germany was disarmed. All her artillery and weapons were destroyed. Her fleet had already sunk itself in Scapa Flow. Her vast army was disbanded. By the Treaty of Versailles only a professional long-service army not exceeding one hundred thousand men, and unable on this basis to accumulate reserves, was permitted to Germany for purposes of internal order. The annual quotas of recruits no longer received their training; the cadres were dissolved. Every effort was made to reduce to a tithe the officer corps. No military air force of any kind was allowed. Submarines were forbidden, and the German Navy was limited to a handful of vessels under ten thousand tons. Soviet Russia was barred off from Western Europe by a cordon of violently anti-Bolshevik states, who had broken away from the former Empire of the Czars in its new and more terrible form. Poland and Czechoslovakia raised independent heads, and seemed to stand erect in Central Europe. Hungary had recovered from her dose of Bela Kun. The French Army, resting upon its laurels, was incomparably the strongest military force in Europe, and it was for some years believed that the French air force was also of a high order.

Up till the year 1934, the power of the conquerors remained

unchallenged in Europe and indeed throughout the world.
There was no moment in these sixteen years when the three
former allies, or even Britain and France with their associates
in Europe, could not, in the name of the League of Nations
and under its moral and international shield, have controlled
by a mere effort of the will the armed strength of Germany.
Instead, until 1931 the victors, and particularly the United
States, concentrated their efforts upon extorting by vexatious
foreign controls their annual reparations from Germany. The
fact that these payments were made only from far larger American loans reduced the whole process to the absurd. Nothing
was reaped except ill-will. On the other hand, the strict enforcement at any time till 1934 of the disarmament clauses of
the Peace Treaty would have guarded indefinitely, without
violence or bloodshed, the peace and safety of mankind. But
this was neglected while the infringements remained petty,
and shunned as they assumed serious proportions. Thus the
final safeguard of a long peace was cast away. The crimes of
the vanquished find their background and their explanation,
though not, of course, their pardon, in the follies of the victors.
Without these follies crime would have found neither temptation nor opportunity.

*   *   *   *   *

In these pages I attempt to recount some of the incidents
and impressions which form in my mind the story of the
coming upon mankind of the worst tragedy in its tumultuous
history. This presented itself not only in the destruction of
life and property inseparable from war. There had been fearful slaughters of soldiers in the First World War, and much of
the accumulated treasure of the nations was consumed. Still,
apart from the excesses of the Russian Revolution, the main
fabric of European civilisation remained erect at the close of
the struggle. When the storm and dust of the cannonade
passed suddenly away, the nations despite their enmities could
still recognise each other as historic racial personalities. The
laws of war had on the whole been respected. There was a

common professional meeting-ground between military men who had fought one another. Vanquished and victors alike still preserved the semblance of civilised states. A solemn peace was made which, apart from unenforceable financial aspects, conformed to the principles which in the nineteenth century had increasingly regulated the relations of enlightened peoples. The reign of law was proclaimed, and a World Instrument was formed to guard us all, and especially Europe, against a renewed convulsion.

Now in the Second World War every bond between man and man was to perish. Crimes were committed by the Germans, under the Hitlerite domination to which they allowed themselves to be subjected, which find no equal in scale and wickedness with any that have darkened the human record. The wholesale massacre by systematised processes of six or seven millions of men, women, and children in the German execution camps exceeds in horror the rough-and-ready butcheries of Genghis Khan, and in scale reduces them to pigmy proportions. Deliberate extermination of whole populations was contemplated and pursued by both Germany and Russia in the Eastern war. The hideous process of bombarding open cities from the air, once started by the Germans, was repaid twentyfold by the ever-mounting power of the Allies, and found its culmination in the use of the atomic bombs which obliterated Hiroshima and Nagasaki.

We have at length emerged from a scene of material ruin and moral havoc the like of which had never darkened the imagination of former centuries. After all that we suffered and achieved, we find ourselves still confronted with problems and perils not less but far more formidable than those through which we have so narrowly made our way.

It is my purpose, as one who lived and acted in these days, first to show how easily the tragedy of the Second World War could have been prevented; how the malice of the wicked was reinforced by the weakness of the virtuous; how the structure and habits of democratic states, unless they are welded into larger organisms, lack those elements of persistence and conviction which can alone give security to humble masses; how, even in matters of self-preservation, no policy is pursued for even ten or fifteen years at a time. We shall see how the counsels of prudence and restraint may become the prime agents of mortal danger; how the middle course adopted from desires for safety and a quiet life may be found to lead direct to the bull's-eye of disaster. We shall see how absolute is the need of a broad path of international action pursued by many states in common across the years, irrespective of the ebb and flow of national politics.

It was a simple policy to keep Germany disarmed and the victors adequately armed for thirty years, and in the meanwhile, even if a reconciliation could not be made with Germany, to build ever more strongly a true League of Nations capable of making sure that treaties were kept or changed only by discussion and agreement. When three or four powerful Governments acting together have demanded the most fearful sacrifices from their peoples, when these have been given freely for the common cause, and when the longed-for result has been attained, it would seem reasonable that concerted action should be preserved so that at least the essentials would not be cast away. But this modest requirement the might, civilisation, learning, knowledge, science, of the victors were unable to supply. They lived from hand to mouth and from day to day, and from one election to another, until, when scarcely twenty years were out, the dread signal of the Second World War was given, and we must write of the sons of those who had fought and died so faithfully and well:

> "Shoulder to aching shoulder, side by side
> They trudged away from life's broad wealds of light." [1]

1 Siegfried Sassoon.

2

Peace at Its Zenith

1922–1931

DURING THE YEAR 1922, a new leader arose in Britain. Mr. Stanley Baldwin had been unknown or unnoticed in the world drama and played a modest part in domestic affairs. He had been Financial Secretary to the Treasury during the war and was at this time President of the Board of Trade. He became the ruling force in British politics from October, 1922, when he ousted Mr. Lloyd George, until May, 1937, when, loaded with honours and enshrined in public esteem, he laid down his heavy task and retired in dignity and silence to his Worcestershire home. My relations with this statesman are a definite part of the tale I have to tell. Our differences at times were serious, but in all these years and later I never had an unpleasant personal interview or contact with him, and at no time did I feel we could not talk together in good faith and understanding as man to man.

* * * * *

The party stresses which the Irish Settlement had created inside Mr. Lloyd George's Coalition were growing with the approach of an inevitable general election. The issue arose whether we should go to the country as a Coalition Government or break up beforehand. It seemed more in accordance with the public interest and the decencies of British politics that parties and ministers who had come through so much together and borne a mass of joint responsibilities should present themselves unitedly to the nation. In order to make this easy for the Conservatives, who were by far the larger and stronger party, the Prime Minister and I had written earlier in the year offering to resign our offices, and give our support from a private station to a new Government to be formed by Mr. Austen Chamberlain. The Conservative leaders, having considered this letter, replied firmly that they would not accept that sacrifice from us and that we must all stand or fall together. This chivalrous attitude was not endorsed by their followers in the party, which now felt itself strong enough to resume undivided power in the State.

By an overwhelming vote the Conservative Party determined to break with Lloyd George and end the National Coalition Government. The Prime Minister resigned that same afternoon. In the morning, we had been friends and colleagues of all these people. By nightfall, they were our party foes, intent on driving us from public life. With the solitary and unexpected exception of Lord Curzon, all the prominent Conservatives who had fought the war with us, and the majority of all the Ministers, adhered to Lloyd George. Those included Arthur Balfour, Austen Chamberlain, Robert Horne, and Lord Birkenhead, the four ablest figures in the Conservative Party. At the crucial moment I was prostrated by a severe operation for appendicitis, and in the morning when I recovered consciousness I learned that the Lloyd George Government had resigned, and that I had lost not only my appendix but my office as Secretary of State for the Dominions and Colonies, in which I conceived myself to have had some parliamentary and administrative success. Mr. Bonar Law, who had left us a year before for serious reasons of health, reluctantly became Prime Minister. He formed a Government of what one might call "The Second Eleven." Mr. Baldwin, the outstanding figure, was Chancellor of the Exchequer. The Prime Minister asked the King for a dissolution. The people wanted a change. Mr. Bonar Law, with Mr. Baldwin at his side, and Lord Beaverbrook as his principal stimulant and mentor, gained a majority of 120, with all the expectation of a five-year tenure of power. Early in the year 1923, Mr. Bonar Law resigned the Premiership and retired to die of his fell affliction. Mr. Baldwin succeeded him as Prime Minister, and Lord Curzon reconciled himself to the office of Foreign Secretary in the new Administration.

Thus began that period of fourteen years which may well be called "The Baldwin-MacDonald Régime." During all that time Mr. Baldwin was always, in fact if not in form, either at the head of the Government or leader of the Opposition, and as Mr. MacDonald never obtained an independent majority, Mr. Baldwin, whether in office or opposition, was the ruling political figure in Britain. At first in alternation but eventually in political brotherhood, these two statesmen governed the country. Nominally the representatives of opposing parties, of contrary doctrines, of antagonistic interests, they proved in fact to be more nearly akin in outlook, temperament, and method than any other two men who had been Prime Ministers since that office was known to the Constitution. Curiously enough, the sympathies of each extended far into the territory of the other. Ramsay MacDonald nursed many of the sentiments of the old Tory. Stanley Baldwin, apart from a manufacturer's ingrained approval of protection, was by disposition a truer representative of mild Socialism than many to be found in the Labour ranks.

* * * * *

Mr. Baldwin was by no means dazzled by his suddenly acquired political eminence. "Give me your prayers," he said,
when congratulations were offered. He was, however, soon
disquieted by the fear that Mr. Lloyd George would rally, upon
the cry of protection, the numerous dissentient Conservative
leaders who had gone out of office with the War Cabinet, and
thus split the Government majority and even challenge the
party leadership. He therefore resolved, in the autumn of
1923, to forestall his rivals by raising the protectionist issue
himself. He made a speech at Plymouth on October 25, which
could only have the effect of bringing the newly elected Parliament to an untimely end. He protested his innocence of any
such design; but to accept this would be to underrate his profound knowledge of British party politics. Parliament was
accordingly on his advice dissolved in October, and a second
general election was held within barely a twelvemonth.

The Liberal Party, rallying round the standard of free trade,
to which I also adhered, gained a balancing position at the
polls, and, though in a minority, might well have taken office
had Mr. Asquith wished to do so. In view of his disinclination,
Mr. Ramsay MacDonald, at the head of little more than two-
fifths of the House, became the first Socialist Prime Minister
of Great Britain, and lived in office for a year by the sufferance
and on the quarrels of the two older parties. The nation was
extremely restive under minority Socialist rule, and the political weather became so favourable that the two Oppositions —
Liberal and Conservative — picked an occasion to defeat the
Socialist Government on a major issue. There was another
general election — the third in less than two years. The Conservatives were returned by a majority of 222 over all other
parties combined.[1] At the beginning of this election Mr. Baldwin's position was very weak, and he made no particular contribution to the result. He had, however, previously maintained himself as party leader, and as the results were declared,
it became certain he would become again Prime Minister. He
retired to his home to form his second Administration.

[1] Conservatives 413, Liberal 40, Labour 151.

At this time I stood fairly high in Tory popularity. At the Westminster by-election six months before I proved my hold upon Conservative forces. Although I stood as a Liberal, great numbers of Tories worked and voted for me. In charge of each of my thirty-four committee rooms was a Conservative M.P. defying his leader Mr. Baldwin and the party machine. This was unprecedented. I was defeated only by forty-three votes out of twenty thousand cast. At the general election I was returned for Epping by a ten thousand majority, but as a "Constitutionalist." I would not at that time adopt the name "Conservative." I had had some friendly contacts with Mr. Baldwin in the interval; but I did not think he would survive to be Prime Minister. Now on the morrow of his victory, I had no idea how he felt towards me. I was surprised, and the Conservative Party dumbfounded, when he invited me to become Chancellor of the Exchequer, the office which my father had once held. A year later, with the approval of my constituents, not having been pressed personally in any way, I formally rejoined the Conservative Party and the Carlton Club, which I had left twenty years before.

*   *   *   *   *

My first question at the Treasury of an international character was our American debt. At the end of the war, the European Allies owed the United States about ten thousand million dollars, of which four thousand million were owed by Britain. On the other hand, we were owed by the other Allies, principally by Russia, seven thousand million dollars. In 1920, Britain had proposed an all-round cancellation of war debts. This involved, on paper at least, a sacrifice by us of about seven hundred and fifty million pounds sterling. As the value of money has halved since then, the figures could in fact be doubled. No settlement was reached. On August 1, 1922, in Mr. Lloyd George's day, the Balfour Note had declared that Great Britain would collect no more from her debtors, Ally or former enemy, than the United States collected from her. This was a worthy statement. In December of 1922, a British delegation, under

Government, visited Washington; and as the result Britain agreed to pay the whole of her war debt to the United States at a rate of interest reduced from five to three and one-half per cent, irrespective of receipts from her debtors.

This agreement caused deep concern in many instructed quarters, and to no one more than the Prime Minister himself. It imposed upon Great Britain, much impoverished by the war in which, as she was to do once again, she had fought from the first day to the last, the payment of thirty-five millions sterling a year for sixty-two years. The basis of this agreement was considered, not only in this island, but by many disinterested financial authorities in America, to be a severe and improvident condition for both borrower and lender. "They hired the money, didn't they?" said President Coolidge. This laconic statement was true, but not exhaustive. Payments between countries which take the form of the transfer of goods and services, or still more of their fruitful exchange, are not only just but beneficial. Payments which are only the arbitrary, artificial transmission across the exchange of such very large sums as arise in war finance cannot fail to derange the whole process of world economy. This is equally true whether the payments are exacted from an ally who shared the victory and bore much of the brunt or from a defeated enemy nation. The enforcement of the Baldwin-Coolidge debt settlement is a recognisable factor in the economic collapse which was presently to overwhelm the world, to prevent its recovery and inflame its hatreds.

The service of the American debt was particularly difficult to render to a country which had newly raised its tariffs to even higher limits, and had already buried in its vaults nearly all the gold yet dug up. Similar but lighter settlements were imposed upon the other European Allies. The first result was that everyone put the screw on Germany. I was in full accord with the policy of the Balfour Note of 1922, and had argued for it at the time; and when I became Chancellor of the Exchequer I reiterated it, and acted accordingly. I thought that if Great Britain were thus made not only the debtor, but the debt-collector of the United States, the unwisdom of the debt collection would become apparent at Washington. However, no such reaction followed. Indeed the argument was resented. The United States continued to insist upon its annual repayments from Great Britain.

It, therefore, fell to me to make settlements with all our Allies which, added to the German payments which we had already scaled down, would enable us to produce the thirty-five millions annually for the American Treasury. Severest pressure was put upon Germany, and a vexatious régime of international control of German internal affairs was imposed. The United States received from England three payments in full, and these were extorted from Germany by indemnities on the modified Dawes scale.

* * * * *

For almost five years I lived next door to Mr. Baldwin at Number 11 Downing Street, and nearly every morning on my way through his house to the Treasury, I looked in upon him for a few minutes' chat in the Cabinet Room. As I was one of his leading colleagues, I take my share of responsibility for all that happened. These five years were marked by very considerable recovery at home. This was a capable, sedate Government during a period in which marked improvement and recovery were gradually effected year by year. There was nothing sensational or controversial to boast about on the platforms, but measured by every test, economic and financial, the mass of the people were definitely better off, and the state of the nation and of the world was easier and more fertile by the end of our term than at its beginning. Here is a modest, but a solid claim.

It was in Europe that the distinction of the Administration was achieved.

* * * * *

Hindenburg now rose to power in Germany. At the end of February, 1925, Friedrich Ebert, leader of the pre-war German Social-Democrat Party, and first President of the German Republic after the defeat, died. A new President had to be chosen.

All Germans had long been brought up under paternal despotism, tempered by far-reaching customs of free speech and
parliamentary opposition. Defeat had brought them on its
scaly wings democratic forms and liberties in an extreme degree. But the nation was rent and bewildered by all it had
gone through, and many parties and groups contended for
precedence and office. Out of the turmoil emerged a strong
desire to turn to old Field-Marshal von Hindenburg, who was
dwelling in dignified retirement. Hindenburg was faithful to
the exiled Emperor, and favoured a restoration of the imperial
monarchy "on the English model." This, of course, was much
the most sensible though least fashionable thing to do. When
he was besought to stand as a candidate for the Presidency
under the Weimar Constitution, he was profoundly disturbed.
"Leave me in peace," he said again and again.

However, the pressure was continuous, and only Grand-
Admiral von Tirpitz at last was found capable of persuading
him to abandon both his scruples and his inclinations at the
call of Duty, which he had always obeyed. Hindenburg's opponents were Marx of the Catholic Centre and Thaelmann the
Communist. On Sunday, April 26, all Germany voted. The
result was unexpectedly close:

Hindenburg	14,655,766
Marx	13,751,615
Thaelmann	1,931,151

Hindenburg, who towered above his opponents by being illustrious, reluctant, and disinterested, was elected by less than a
million majority, and with no absolute majority on the total
poll. He rebuked his son Oskar for waking him at seven to tell
him the news: "Why did you want to wake me up an hour
earlier? It would still have been true at eight." And with this
he went to sleep again till his usual calling-time.

In France the election of Hindenburg was at first viewed as
a renewal of the German challenge. In England there was an
easier reaction. Always wishing as I did to see Germany recover
her honour and self-respect, and to let war-bitterness die, I was

not at all distressed by the news. "He is a very sensible old man," said Lloyd George to me when we next met; and so indeed he proved as long as his faculties remained. Even some of his most bitter opponents were forced to admit, "Better a Zero than a Nero." [2] However, he was seventy-seven, and his term of office was to be seven years. Few expected him to be returned again. He did his best to be impartial between the various parties, and certainly his tenure of the Presidency gave a sober strength and comfort to Germany without menace to her neighbours.

* * * * *

Meanwhile, in February, 1925, the German Government had addressed itself to M. Herriot, then French Premier. Their memorandum stated that Germany was willing to declare her acceptance of a pact by virtue of which the Powers interested in the Rhine, above all England, France, Italy, and Germany, would enter into a solemn obligation for a lengthy period towards the Government of the United States, as trustees, not to wage war against a contracting state. Furthermore, a pact expressly guaranteeing the existing territorial status on the Rhine would be acceptable to Germany. This was a remarkable event. The French Government undertook to consult their allies. Mr. Austen Chamberlain made the news public in the House of Commons on March 5. Parliamentary crises in France and Germany delayed the process of negotiation, but after consultation between London and Paris a formal Note was handed to Herr Stresemann, the German Minister, by the French Ambassador in Berlin on June 16, 1925. The Note declared that no agreement could be reached unless as a prior condition Germany entered the League of Nations. There could be no suggestion in any proposed agreement of a modification of the conditions of the Peace Treaty. Belgium must be included among the contracting Powers; and finally the natural complement of a Rhineland Pact would be a Franco-German Arbitration Treaty.

[2] Theodore Lessing, murdered by the Nazis, September, 1933.

The British attitude was debated in the House of Commons on June 24. Mr. Chamberlain explained that British commitments under the Pact would be limited to the West. France would probably define her special relationships with Poland and Czechoslovakia; but Great Britain would not assume any obligations other than those specified in the Covenant of the League. The British Dominions were not enthusiastic about a Western Pact. General Smuts was anxious to avoid regional arrangements. The Canadians were lukewarm, and only New Zealand was unconditionally prepared to accept the view of the British Government. Nevertheless, we persevered. To me the aim of ending the thousand-year strife between France and Germany seemed a supreme object. If we could only weave Gaul and Teuton so closely together economically, socially, and morally as to prevent the occasion of new quarrels, and make old antagonisms die in the realisation of mutual prosperity and interdependence, Europe would rise again. It seemed to me that the supreme interest of the British people in Europe lay in the assuagement of the Franco-German feud, and that they had no other interests comparable or contrary to that. This is still my view today.

Mr. Austen Chamberlain, as Foreign Secretary, had an outlook which was respected by all parties, and the whole Cabinet was united in his support. In July, the Germans replied to the French Note, accepting the linking-up of a Western Pact with the entry of Germany into the League of Nations, but stating the prior need for agreement upon general disarmament. M. Briand came to England and prolonged discussions were held upon the Western Pact and its surroundings. In August the French, with the full agreement of Great Britain, replied officially to Germany. Germany must enter the League without reservations as the first and indispensable step. The German Government accepted this stipulation. This meant that the conditions of the Treaties were to continue in force unless or until modified by mutual arrangement, and that no specific pledge for a reduction of Allied armaments had been obtained. Further demands by the Germans, put forward under intense nationalistic pressure and excitement, for the eradication from the Peace Treaty of the "war guilt" clause, for keeping open the issue of Alsace-Lorraine, and for the immediate evacuation of Cologne by Allied troops, were not pressed by the German Government, and would not have been conceded by the Allies.

On this basis the Conference at Locarno was formally opened on October 4. By the waters of this calm lake the delegates of Britain, France, Germany, Belgium, and Italy assembled. The Conference achieved: first, the Treaty of Mutual Guarantee between the five Powers; secondly, arbitration treaties between Germany and France, Germany and Belgium, Germany and Poland, Germany and Czechoslovakia. Thirdly, special agreements between France and Poland, and France and Czechoslovakia, by which France undertook to afford them assistance if a breakdown of the Western Pact were followed by an unprovoked resort to arms. Thus did the Western European Democracies agree to keep the peace among themselves in all circumstances, and to stand united against any one of their number who broke the contract and marched in aggression upon a brother land. As between France and Germany, Great Britain became solemnly pledged to come to the aid of whichever of the other two states was the object of unprovoked aggression. This far-reaching military commitment was accepted by Parliament and endorsed warmly by the nation. The histories may be searched in vain for a parallel to such an undertaking.

The question whether there was any obligation on the part of France or Britain to disarm, or to disarm to any particular level, was not affected. I had been brought into these matters as Chancellor of the Exchequer at an early stage. My own view about this two-way guarantee was that, while France remained armed and Germany disarmed, Germany could not attack her; and that, on the other hand, France would never attack Germany if that automatically involved Britain becoming Germany's ally. Thus, although the proposal seemed dangerous in theory — pledging us in fact to take part on one side or the other in any Franco-German war that might arise — there was little likelihood of such a disaster ever coming to pass; and this was the best means of preventing it. I was therefore always equally opposed to the disarmament of France and to the re-armament of Germany, because of the much greater danger this immediately brought on Great Britain. On the other hand, Britain and the League of Nations, which Germany joined as part of the agreement, offered a real protection to the German people. Thus there was a balance created in which Britain, whose major interest was the cessation of the quarrel between Germany and France, was to a large extent umpire and arbiter. One hoped that this equilibrium might have lasted twenty years, during which the Allied armaments would gradually and naturally have dwindled under the influence of a long peace, growing confidence, and financial burdens. It was evident that danger would arise if ever Germany became more or less equal with France, still more if she became stronger than France. But all this seemed excluded by solemn treaty obligations.

*   *   *   *   *

The Pact of Locarno was concerned only with peace in the West, and it was hoped that what was called "An Eastern Locarno" might be its successor. We should have been very glad if the danger of some future war between Germany and Russia could have been controlled in the same spirit and by similar measures as the possibility of war between Germany and France. Even the Germany of Stresemann was, however, disinclined to close the door on German claims in the East, or to accept the territorial treaty position about Poland, Danzig, the Corridor, and Upper Silesia. Soviet Russia brooded in her isolation behind the *cordon sanitaire* of anti-Bolshevik states. Although our efforts were continued, no progress was made in the East. I did not at any time close my mind to an attempt to give Germany greater satisfaction on her eastern frontier. But no opportunity arose during these brief years of hope.

*   *   *   *   *

There were great rejoicings about the treaty which emerged at the end of 1925 from the Conference at Locarno. Mr. Baldwin was the first to sign it at the Foreign Office. The Foreign Secretary, having no official residence, asked me to lend my dining-room at Number 11 Downing Street for his intimate friendly luncheon with Herr Stresemann. We all met together in great amity, and thought what a wonderful future would await Europe if its greatest nations became truly united and felt themselves secure. After this memorable instrument had received the cordial assent of Parliament, Sir Austen Chamberlain received the Garter and the Nobel Peace Prize. His achievement was the high-water mark of Europe's restoration, and it inaugurated three years of peace and recovery. Although old antagonisms were but sleeping, and the drumbeat of new levies was already heard, we were justified in hoping that the ground thus solidly gained would open the road to a further forward march.

At the end of the second Baldwin Administration, the state of Europe was tranquil, as it had not been for twenty years, and was not to be for at least another twenty. A friendly feeling existed towards Germany following upon our Treaty of Locarno, and the evacuation of the Rhineland by the French Army and Allied contingents at a much earlier date than had been prescribed at Versailles. The new Germany took her place in the truncated League of Nations. Under the genial influence of American and British loans Germany was reviving rapidly. Her new ocean liners gained the Blue Riband of the Atlantic. Her trade advanced by leaps and bounds, and internal prosperity ripened. France and her system of alliances also seemed secure in Europe. The disarmament clauses of the Treaty of Versailles were not openly violated. The German Navy was non-existent. The German air force was prohibited and still unborn. There were many influences in Germany strongly opposed, if only on grounds of prudence, to the idea of war, and the German High Command could not believe that the Allies would allow them to rearm. On the other hand, there lay before us what I later called the "economic blizzard."

Knowledge of this was confined to rare financial circles, and
these were cowed into silence by what they foresaw.

*   *   *   *   *

The general election of May, 1929, showed that the "swing
of the pendulum" and the normal desire for change were powerful factors with the British electorate. The Socialists had a
small majority over the Conservatives in the new House of
Commons. The Liberals, with about sixty seats, held the balance,
and it was plain that under Mr. Lloyd George's leadership they
would, at the outset at least, be hostile to the Conservatives. Mr.
Baldwin and I were in full agreement that we should not seek to
hold office in a minority or on precarious Liberal support. Accordingly, although there were some differences of opinion in the
Cabinet and the party about the course to be taken, Mr. Baldwin tendered his resignation to the King. We all went down to
Windsor in a special train to give up our seals and offices; and
on June 7, Mr. Ramsay MacDonald became for the second
time Prime Minister at the head of a minority Government
depending upon Liberal votes.

*   *   *   *   *

The Socialist Prime Minister wished his new Labour Government to distinguish itself by large concessions to Egypt, by
a far-reaching constitutional change in India, and by a renewed
effort for world, or at any rate British, disarmament. These
were aims in which he could count upon Liberal aid, and for
which he therefore commanded a parliamentary majority.
Here began my differences with Mr. Baldwin, and thereafter
the relationship in which we had worked since he chose me
for Chancellor of the Exchequer five years before became sen-
sibly altered. We still, of course, remained in easy personal
contact, but we knew we did not mean the same thing. My idea
was that the Conservative Opposition should strongly confront
the Labour Government on all great imperial and national
issues, should identify itself with the majesty of Britain as
under Lord Beaconsfield and Lord Salisbury, and should not

hesitate to face controversy, even though that might not immediately evoke a response from the nation. So far as I could see,
Mr. Baldwin felt that the times were too far gone for any
robust assertion of British imperial greatness, and that the hope
of the Conservative Party lay in accommodation with Liberal
and Labour forces, and in adroit, well-timed manoeuvres to
detach powerful moods of public opinion and large blocks of
voters from them. He certainly was very successful. He was
the greatest party manager the Conservatives had ever had. He
fought, as their leader, five general elections, of which he won
three. History alone can judge these general issues.

It was on India that our definite breach occurred. The
Prime Minister, strongly supported and even spurred by the
Conservative Viceroy, Lord Irwin, afterwards Lord Halifax,
pressed forward with his plan of Indian self-government. A
portentous conference was held in London, of which Mr.
Gandhi, lately released from commodious internment, was the
central figure. There is no need to follow in these pages the
details of the controversy which occupied the sessions of 1929
and 1930. On the release of Mr. Gandhi in order that he might
become the envoy of Nationalist India to the London Conference, I reached the breaking-point in my relations with Mr.
Baldwin. He seemed quite content with these developments,
was in general accord with the Prime Minister and the Viceroy,
and led the Conservative Opposition decidedly along this path.
I felt sure we should lose India in the final result and that
measureless disasters would come upon the Indian peoples. I
therefore after a while resigned from the Shadow Cabinet upon
this issue. On January 27, 1931, I wrote to Mr. Baldwin:

Now that our divergence of view upon Indian policy has become
public, I feel that I ought not any longer to attend the meetings of
your Business Committee, to which you have hitherto so kindly
invited me. I need scarcely add that I will give you whatever aid is
in my power in opposing the Socialist Government in the House
of Commons, and I shall do my utmost to secure their defeat at
the general election.

*   *   *   *   *

The year 1929 reached almost the end of its third quarter
under the promise and appearance of increasing prosperity,
particularly in the United States. Extraordinary optimism sustained an orgy of speculation. Books were written to prove
that economic crisis was a phase which expanding business
organisation and science had at last mastered. "We are apparently finished and done with economic cycles as we have known
them," said the President of the New York Stock Exchange in
September. But in October a sudden and violent tempest
swept over Wall Street. The intervention of the most powerful agencies failed to stem the tide of panic sales. A group of
leading banks constituted a milliard-dollar pool to maintain
and stabilise the market. All was vain.

The whole wealth so swiftly gathered in the paper values of
previous years vanished. The prosperity of millions of American homes had grown upon a gigantic structure of inflated
credit, now suddenly proved phantom. Apart from the nation-
wide speculation in shares which even the most famous banks
had encouraged by easy loans, a vast system of purchase by in-
stalment of houses, furniture, cars, and numberless kinds of
household conveniences and indulgences had grown up. All
now fell together. The mighty production plants were thrown
into confusion and paralysis. But yesterday, there had been the
urgent question of parking the motor-cars in which thousands
of artisans and craftsmen were beginning to travel to their daily
work. Today the grievous pangs of falling wages and rising unemployment afflicted the whole community, engaged till this
moment in the most active creation of all kinds of desirable
articles for the enjoyment of millions. The American banking
system was far less concentrated and solidly based than the
British. Twenty thousand local banks suspended payment.
The means of exchange of goods and services between man and
man was smitten to the ground; and the crash on Wall Street
reverberated in modest and rich households alike.

It should not, however, be supposed that the fair vision of
far greater wealth and comfort ever more widely shared, which
had entranced the people of the United States, had nothing be-

hind it but delusion and market frenzy. Never before had such immense quantities of goods of all kinds been produced, shared, and exchanged in any society. There is in fact no limit to the benefits which human beings may bestow upon one another by the highest exertion of their diligence and skill. This splendid manifestation had been shattered and cast down by vain imaginative processes and greed of gain which far outstripped the great achievement itself. In the wake of the collapse of the stock market came, during the years between 1929 and 1932, an unrelenting fall in prices and consequent cuts in production causing widespread unemployment.

The consequences of this dislocation of economic life became world-wide. A general contraction of trade in the face of unemployment and declining production followed. Tariff restrictions were imposed to protect the home markets. The general crisis brought with it acute monetary difficulties, and paralysed internal credit. This spread ruin and unemployment far and wide throughout the globe. Mr. MacDonald's Government, with all their promises behind them, saw unemployment during 1930 and 1931 bound up in their faces from one million to nearly three millions. It was said that in the United States ten million persons were without work. The entire banking system of the great Republic was thrown into confusion and temporary collapse. Consequential disasters fell upon Germany and other European countries. However, nobody starved in the English-speaking world.

*   *   *   *   *

It is always difficult for an administration or party which is founded upon attacking capital to preserve the confidence and credit so important to the highly artificial economy of an island like Britain. Mr. MacDonald's Labour-Socialist Government were utterly unable to cope with the problems which confronted them. They could not command the party discipline or produce the vigour necessary even to balance the budget. In such conditions a Government, already in a minority and deprived of all financial confidence, could not survive.

The failure of the Labour Party to face this tempest, the sudden collapse of British financial credit, and the break-up of the Liberal Party, with its unwholesome balancing power, led to a national coalition. It seemed that only a Government of all parties was capable of coping with the crisis. Mr. Mac-Donald and his Chancellor of the Exchequer, on a strong patriotic emotion, attempted to carry the mass of the Labour Party into this combination. Mr. Baldwin, always content that others should have the function so long as he retained the power, was willing to serve under Mr. MacDonald. It was an attitude which, though deserving respect, did not correspond to the facts. Mr. Lloyd George was still recovering from an operation — serious at his age; and Sir John Simon led the bulk of the Liberals into the all-party combination.

I was not invited to take part in the Coalition Government. I was politically severed from Mr. Baldwin about India. I was an opponent of the policy of Mr. MacDonald's Labour Government. Like many others, I had felt the need of a national concentration. But I was neither surprised nor unhappy when I was left out of it. Indeed, I remained painting at Cannes while the political crisis lasted. What I should have done if I had been asked to join, I cannot tell. It is superfluous to discuss doubtful temptations that have never existed. Certainly during the summer I had talked to MacDonald about a national administration, and he had shown some interest. But I was awkwardly placed in the political scene. I had had fifteen years of Cabinet office, and was now busy with my *Life of Marlborough*. Political dramas are very exciting at the time to those engaged in the clatter and whirlpool of politics, but I can truthfully affirm that I never felt resentment, still less pain, at being so decisively discarded in a moment of national stress. There was, however, an inconvenience. For all these years since 1905 I had sat on one or the other of the Front Benches, and always had the advantage of speaking from the box on which you can put your notes, and pretend with more or less success to be making it up as you go along. Now I had to find with some difficulty a seat below the Gangway on the Government side,

where I had to hold my notes in my hand whenever I spoke,
and take my chance in debate with other well-known ex-Cab-
inet Ministers. However, from time to time I got called.

*   *   *   *   *

The formation of the new Government did not end the
financial crisis, and I returned from abroad to find everything
unsettled in the advent of an inevitable general election. The
verdict of the electorate was worthy of the British nation. A
National Government had been formed under Mr. Ramsay
MacDonald, founder of the Labour-Socialist Party. They proposed to the people a programme of severe austerity and sacrifice. It was an earlier version of "Blood, sweat, toil, and tears,"
without the stimulus or the requirements of war and mortal peril. The sternest economy must be practised. Everyone would have his wages, salary, or income reduced. The mass
of the people were asked to vote for a régime of self-denial.
They responded as they always do when caught in the heroic
temper. Although contrary to their declarations, the Government abandoned the gold standard, and although Mr. Baldwin
was obliged to suspend, as it proved for ever, those very payments on the American debt which he had forced on the Bonar
Law Cabinet of 1923, confidence and credit were restored.
There was an overwhelming majority for the new Administration. Mr. MacDonald as Prime Minister was only followed by
seven or eight members of his own party; but barely a hundred
of his Labour opponents and former followers were returned
to Parliament. His health and powers were failing fast, and he
reigned in increasing decrepitude at the summit of the British
system for nearly four fateful years. And very soon in these
four years came Hitler.

3

Lurking Dangers

*My Reflections in 1928 — Annihilating Terrors of Future War —
Some Technical Predictions — Allied Hatred of War and Mili-
tarism — "Ease Would Retract" — The German Army — The
Hundred Thousand Volunteer Limit — General von Seeckt, His
Work and Theme — "A Second Scharnhorst" — The Withdrawal
of the Allied Mission of Control, January, 1927 — German
Aviation — Encroachment and Camouflage — The German Navy
— Rathenau's Munitions Scheme — Convertible Factories — The
"No Major War for Ten Years" Rule.*

IN MY BOOK, *The Aftermath*, I have set down some of the impressions of the four years which elapsed between the
Armistice and the change of Government in Britain at the
end of 1922. Writing in 1928, I was deeply under the impression of a future catastrophe.

It was not until the dawn of the twentieth century of the Christian Era that war began to enter into its kingdom as the potential
destroyer of the human race. The organisation of mankind into
great states and empires, and the rise of nations to full collective
consciousness, enabled enterprises of slaughter to be planned and
executed upon a scale and with a perseverance never before imagined. All the noblest virtues of individuals were gathered together
to strengthen the destructive capacity of the mass. Good finances,
the resources of world-wide credit and trade, the accumulation of
large capital reserves, made it possible to divert for considerable
periods the energies of whole peoples to the task of devastation.
Democratic institutions gave expression to the will-power of

millions. Education not only brought the course of the conflict
within the comprehension of everyone, but rendered each person
serviceable in a high degree for the purpose in hand. The press
afforded a means of unification and of mutual stimulation. Religion, having discreetly avoided conflict on the fundamental issues,
offered its encouragements and consolations, through all its forms,
impartially to all the combatants. Lastly, Science unfolded her
treasures and her secrets to the desperate demands of men, and
placed in their hand agencies and apparatus almost decisive in their
character.

In consequence many novel features presented themselves. Instead of fortified towns being starved, whole nations were
methodically subjected, or sought to be subjected, to the process
of reduction by famine. The entire population in one capacity or
another took part in the war; all were equally the object of attack.
The air opened paths along which death and terror could be
carried far behind the lines of the actual armies, to women, children, the aged, the sick, who in earlier struggles would perforce
have been left untouched. Marvellous organisation of railroads,
steamships, and motor vehicles placed and maintained tens of
millions of men continuously in action. Healing and surgery in
their exquisite developments returned them again and again to the
shambles. Nothing was wasted that could contribute to the process
of waste. The last dying kick was brought into military utility.

But all that happened in the four years of the Great War was
only a prelude to what was preparing for the fifth year. The
campaign of the year 1919 would have witnessed an immense accession to the powers of destruction. Had the Germans retained the
morale to make good their retreat to the Rhine, they would have
been assaulted in the summer of 1919 with forces and by methods
incomparably more prodigious than any yet employed. Thousands
of airplanes would have shattered their cities. Scores of thousands
of cannon would have blasted their front. Arrangements were
being made to carry simultaneously a quarter of a million men,
together with all their requirements, continuously forward across
country in mechanical vehicles moving ten or fifteen miles each day.
Poison gases of incredible malignity, against which only a secret
mask (which the Germans could not obtain in time) was proof,
would have stifled all resistance and paralysed all life on the hostile
front subjected to attack. No doubt the Germans too had their

plans. But the hour of wrath had passed. The signal of relief was given, and the horrors of 1919 remained buried in the archives of the great antagonists.

The war stopped as suddenly and as universally as it had begun. The world lifted its head, surveyed the scene of ruin, and victors and vanquished alike drew breath. In a hundred laboratories, in a thousand arsenals, factories, and bureaus, men pulled themselves up with a jerk, and turned from the task in which they had been absorbed. Their projects were put aside unfinished, unexecuted; but their knowledge was preserved; their data, calculations, and discoveries were hastily bundled together and docketed "for future reference" by the War Offices in every country. The campaign of 1919 was never fought; but its ideas go marching along. In every army they are being explored, elaborated, refined, under the surface of peace, and should war come again to the world, it is not with the weapons and agencies prepared for 1919 that it will be fought, but with developments and extensions of these which will be incomparably more formidable and fatal.

It is in these circumstances that we entered upon that period of exhaustion which has been described as Peace. It gives us, at any rate, an opportunity to consider the general situation. Certain sombre facts emerge, solid, inexorable, like the shapes of mountains from drifting mist. It is established that henceforward whole populations will take part in war, all doing their utmost, all subjected to the fury of the enemy. It is established that nations who believe their life is at stake will not be restrained from using any means to secure their existence. It is probable — nay, certain — that among the means which will next time be at their disposal will be agencies and processes of destruction wholesale, unlimited, and perhaps, once launched, uncontrollable.

Mankind has never been in this position before. Without having improved appreciably in virtue or enjoying wiser guidance, it has got into its hands for the first time the tools by which it can unfailingly accomplish its own extermination. That is the point in human destinies to which all the glories and toils of men have at last led them. They would do well to pause and ponder upon their new responsibilities. Death stands at attention, obedient, expectant, ready to serve, ready to shear away the peoples *en masse;* ready, if called on, to pulverise, without hope of repair, what is left of civilisation. He awaits only the word of command. He awaits it from a frail, bewildered being, long his victim, now — for one occasion only — his Master.

* * * * *

All this was published on January 1, 1929. Now, on another New Year's Day eighteen years later, I could not write it differently. All the words and actions for which I am accountable between the wars had as their object only the prevention of a second World War; and, of course, of making sure that if the worst happened we won, or at least survived. There can hardly ever have been a war more easy to prevent than this second Armageddon. I have always been ready to use force in order to defy tyranny or ward off ruin. But had our British, American, and Allied affairs been conducted with the ordinary consistency and common sense usual in decent households, there was no need for Force to march unaccompanied by Law; and Strength, moreover, could have been used in righteous causes with little risk of bloodshed. In their loss of purpose, in their abandonment even of the themes they most sincerely espoused, Britain, France, and most of all, because of their immense power and impartiality, the United States, allowed conditions to be gradually built up which led to the very climax they dreaded most. They have only to repeat the same well-meaning, short-sighted behaviour towards the new problems which in singular resemblance confront us today to bring about a third convulsion from which none may live to tell the tale.

* * * * *

I had written even earlier, in 1925, some thoughts and queries of a technical character which it would be wrong to omit in these days:

May there not be methods of using explosive energy incomparably more intense than anything heretofore discovered? Might not a bomb no bigger than an orange be found to possess a secret power to destroy a whole block of buildings — nay, to concentrate the force of a thousand tons of cordite and blast a township at a stroke? Could not explosives even of the existing type be guided automatically in flying machines by wireless or other rays, without a human pilot, in ceaseless procession upon a hostile city, arsenal, camp, or dockyard?

As for poison gas and chemical warfare in all its forms, only the first chapter has been written of a terrible book. Certainly every one of these new avenues to destruction is being studied on both sides of the Rhine with all the science and patience of which man is capable. And why should it be supposed that these resources will be limited to inorganic chemistry? A study of disease — of pestilences methodically prepared and deliberately launched upon man and beast — is certainly being pursued in the laboratories of more than one great country. Blight to destroy crops, anthrax to slay horses and cattle, plague to poison not armies only but whole districts — such are the lines along which military science is remorselessly advancing.

All this is nearly a quarter of a century old.

*   *   *   *   *

It is natural that a proud people vanquished in war should strive to rearm themselves as soon as possible. They will not respect more than they can help treaties exacted from them under duress.

> " . . . Ease would retract
> Vows made in pain, as violent and void."

The responsibility, therefore, of enforcing a continual state of military disarmament upon a beaten foe rests upon the victors. For this purpose they must pursue a twofold policy. First, while remaining sufficiently armed themselves, they must enforce with tireless vigilance and authority the clauses of the treaty which forbid the revival of their late antagonist's military power. Secondly, they should do all that is possible to reconcile the defeated nation to its lot by acts of benevolence designed to procure the greatest amount of prosperity in the beaten country, and labour by every means to create a basis of true friendship and of common interests, so that the incentive to appeal again to arms will be continually diminished. In these years I coined the maxim, "the redress of the grievances of the vanquished should precede the disarmament of the victors." As will be seen, the reverse process was, to a large extent, followed by Britain, the United States, and France. And thereby hangs this tale.

*　　*　　*　　*　　*

It is a prodigious task to make an army embodying the whole manhood of a mighty nation. The victorious Allies had at Mr. Lloyd George's suggestion limited the German Army to a hundred thousand men, and conscription was forbidden. This force, therefore, became the nucleus and the crucible out of which an army of millions of men was if possible to be re-formed. The hundred thousand men were a hundred thousand leaders. Once the decision to expand was taken, the privates could become sergeants, the sergeants officers. None the less, Mr. Lloyd George's plan for preventing the re-creation of the German Army was not ill-conceived. No foreign inspection could in times of peace control the quality of the hundred thousand men allowed to Germany. But the issue did not turn on this. Three or four millions of trained soldiers were needed merely to hold the German frontiers. To make a nation-wide army which could compare with, still more surpass, the French Army required not only the preparation of the leaders and the revival of the old regiments and formations, but the national compulsory service of each annual quota of men reaching the military age. Volunteer corps, youth movements, extensions of the police and constabulary forces, old-comrades associations, all kinds of non-official and indeed illegal organisations, might play their part in the interim period. But without universal national service the bones of the skeleton could never be clothed with flesh and sinew.

There was, therefore, no possibility of Germany creating an army which could face the French Army until conscription had been applied for several years. Here was a line which could not be transgressed without an obvious, flagrant breach of the Treaty of Versailles. Every kind of concealed, ingenious, elaborate preparation could be made beforehand, but the moment

must come when the Rubicon would have to be crossed and
the conquerors defied. Mr. Lloyd George's principle was thus
sound. Had it been enforced with authority and prudence,
there could have been no new forging of the German war
machine. The class called up for each year, however well
schooled beforehand, would also have to remain for at least two
years in the regimental or other units, and it was only after
this period of training that the reserves, without which no
modern army is possible, could be gradually formed and accumulated. France, though her manhood had been depleted
in a horrible degree by the previous war, had nevertheless
maintained a regular uninterrupted routine of training annual
quotas and of passing the trained soldiers into a reserve which
comprised the whole fighting man-power of the nation. For
fifteen years Germany was not allowed to build up a similar
reserve. In all these years the German Army might nourish
and cherish its military spirit and tradition, but it could not
possibly even dream of entering the lists against the long-established, unbroken development of the armed, trained, organised
man-power which flowed and gathered naturally from the
French military system.

*   *   *   *   *

The creator of the nucleus and structure of the future German Army was General von Seeckt. As early as 1921, Seeckt
was busy planning, in secret and on paper, a full-size German
army, and arguing deferentially about his various activities
with the Inter-Allied Military Commission of Control. His
biographer, General von Rabenau, wrote in the triumphant
days of 1940, "It would have been difficult to do the work of
1935/39 if from 1920 to 1934 the centre of leadership had corresponded to the needs of the small army." For instance, the
Treaty demanded a decrease in the officer corps from thirty-
four thousand to four thousand. Every device was used to overcome this fatal barrier, and in spite of the efforts of the Allied
Control Commission, the process of planning for a revived
German Army went forward.

The enemy [says Seeckt's biographer] did his best to destroy the General Staff, and was supported by the political parties within Germany. The Inter-Allied Control had rightly, from its standpoint, tried for years to make the training in higher staffs so primitive that there could be no General Staff. They tried in the boldest ways to discover how General Staff officers were being trained, but we succeeded in giving nothing away, neither the system nor what was taught. Seeckt never gave in, for had the General Staff been destroyed, it would have been difficult to re-create it. . . . Although the form had to be broken, the content was saved. . . .

In fact, under the pretence of being Departments of Reconstruction, Research, and Culture, several thousand staff officers in plain clothes and their assistants were held together in Berlin, thinking deeply about the past and the future.

Rabenau makes an illuminating comment:

Without Seeckt there would today [in 1940] be no General Staff in the German sense, for which generations are required and which cannot be achieved in a day, however gifted or industrious officers may be. Continuity of conception is imperative to safeguard leadership in the nervous trials of reality. Knowledge or capacity in individuals is not enough. In war the organically developed capacity of a majority is necessary, and for this decades are needed. . . . In a small hundred-thousand army, if the generals were not also to be small, it was imperative to create a great theoretical framework. To this end large-scale practical exercises or war games were introduced . . . not so much to train the General Staff, but rather to create a class of higher commanders.

These would be capable of thinking in full-scale military terms.

Seeckt insisted that false doctrines, springing from personal experiences of the Great War, should be avoided. All the lessons of that war were thoroughly and systematically studied. New principles of training and instructional courses of all kinds were introduced. All the existing manuals were rewritten, not for the hundred-thousand army, but for the armed might of the German Reich. In order to baffle the inquisitive Allies, whole sections of these manuals were printed in special type and made public. Those for internal consumption were secret. The main principle inculcated was the need for the closest co-operation of *all* vital arms. Not only the main services — infantry, motorised cavalry, and artillery — were to be tactically interwoven, but machine-gun, trench-mortar, tommy-gun units, and anti-tank weapons, army air squadrons, and much else were all to be blended. It is to this theme that the German war leaders attributed their tactical successes in the campaigns of 1939 and 1940. By 1924, Seeckt could feel that the strength of the German Army was slowly increasing beyond the hundred-thousand limit. "The fruits of this," said his biographer, "were born only ten years later." In 1925, the old Field-Marshal von Mackensen congratulated Seeckt on his building-up of the Reichswehr, and compared him, not unjustly, to the Scharnhorst who had secretly prepared the Prussian counter-stroke against Napoleon during the years of the French occupation of Germany after Jena. "The old fire burnt still, and the Allied Control had not destroyed any of the lasting elements of German strength."

In the summer of 1926, Seeckt conducted his largest military exercise for commanders with staffs and signals. He had no troops, but practically all the generals, commanding officers, and General Staff officers of the Army were introduced to the art of war and its innumerable technical problems on the scale of a German Army which, when the time came, could raise the German nation to its former rank.

For several years short-service training of soldiers beyond the official establishments was practised on a small scale. These men were known as "black," i.e., illegal. From 1925 onwards, the whole sphere of "black" was centralised in the Reichswehr Ministry and sustained by national funds. The General Staff plan of 1925 for an extension and improvement of the Army outside Treaty limits was to double and then to treble the existing legal seven infantry divisions. But Seeckt's ultimate aim was a minimum of sixty-three. From 1926 the main obstacle to this planning was the opposition of the Prussian Socialist Government. This was presently swept away. It was not till April, 1933, that the establishment of the hundred-thousand army was officially exceeded, though its strength had for some time been rising steadily above that figure.

* * * * *

Amid the good will and hopes following Locarno a questionable, though by no means irremediable, decision was taken by the British and French Governments. The Inter-Allied Control Commission was to be withdrawn, and in substitution there should be an agreed scheme of investigation by the League of Nations ready to be put into operation when any of the parties desired. It was thought that some such arrangement might form a complement to the Locarno Treaty. This hope was not fulfilled. Marshal Foch reported that effective disarmament of Germany had taken place; but it had to be recognised that the disarmament of a nation of sixty-five millions could not be permanent, and that certain precautions were necessary. In January, 1927, the Control Commission was nevertheless withdrawn from Germany. It was already known that the Germans were straining the interpretation of the Treaty in many covert and minor ways, and no doubt they were making paper plans to become a military nation once again. There were Boy Scouts, Cadet Corps, and many volunteer unarmed organisations both of youth and of veterans. But nothing could be done on a large scale in the Army or Navy which would not become obvious. The introduction of compulsory national service, the establishment of a military air force, or the laying-down of warships beyond the Treaty limits, would be an open breach of German obligations which could at any time have been raised in the League of Nations, of which Germany was now a member.

The air was far less definable. The Treaty prohibited a German military air force, and it was officially dissolved in May, 1920. In his farewell order Seeckt said he hoped that it would again rise and meanwhile its spirit would still live. He gave it every encouragement to do so. His first step had been to create within the Reichswehr Ministry a special group of experienced ex-air force officers, whose existence was hidden from the Allied Commission and protected against his own Government. This was gradually expanded until within the Ministry there were "air cells" in the various offices or inspectorates, and air personnel were gradually introduced throughout the cadres of the Army. The Civil Aviation Department was headed by an experienced wartime officer, a nominee of Seeckt's, who made sure that the control and development of civil aviation took place in harmony with military needs. This department, together with the German Civil Air Transport and various camouflaged military or naval air establishments, was to a great extent staffed by ex-flying officers without knowledge of commercial aviation.

Even before 1924, the beginnings of a system of airfields and civil aircraft factories and the training of pilots and instruction in passive air defence had come into existence throughout Germany. There was already much reasonable show of commercial flying, and very large numbers of Germans, both men and women, were encouraged to become "air-minded" by the institution of a network of gliding clubs. Severe limitations were observed, on paper, about the number of service personnel permitted to fly. But these rules, with so many others, were circumvented by Seeckt, who, with the connivance of the German Transport Ministry, succeeded in building up a sure foundation for an efficient industry and a future air arm. It was thought by the Allies, in the mood of 1926, derogatory to German national pride to go too far in curbing these German encroachments, and the victors rested on the line of principle which forbade a German military air force. This proved a very vague and shadowy frontier.

In the naval sphere similar evasions were practised. By the Versailles Treaty, Germany was allowed only to retain a small naval force with a maximum strength of fifteen thousand men. Subterfuges were used to increase this total. Naval organisations were covertly incorporated into civil ministries. The Army coastal defences, in Heligoland and elsewhere, were not destroyed as prescribed by the Treaty, and German naval artillerymen soon took them over. U-boats were illicitly built and their officers and men trained in other countries. Everything possible was done to keep the Kaiser's Navy alive, and to prepare for the day when it could openly resume a place upon the seas.

Important progress was also made in another decisive direction. Herr Rathenau had, during his tenure of the Ministry of Reconstruction in 1919, set on foot on the broadest lines the reconstruction of German war industry. "They have destroyed your weapons," he had told the generals, in effect. "But these weapons would in any case have become obsolete before the next war. That war will be fought with brand-new ones, and the army which is least hampered with obsolete material will have a great advantage."

Nevertheless, the struggle to preserve weapons from destruction was waged persistently by the German staffs throughout the years of control. Every form of deception and every obstacle baffled the Allied Commission. The work of evasion became thoroughly organised. The German police, which at first had interfered, presently became accessories of the Reichswehr in the amassing of arms. Under a civilian camouflage an organisation was set up to safeguard reserves of weapons and equipment. From 1926 this organisation had representatives all over Germany, and there was a network of depots of all kinds. Even more was ingenuity used to create machinery for future production of war material. Lathes which had been set up for war purposes and were capable of being reconverted to that use were retained for civil production in far greater numbers than were required for ordinary commercial use. State arsenals built for war were not closed down in accordance with the Treaty.

A general scheme had thus been put into action by which all the new factories, and many of the old, founded with American and British loans for reconstruction, were designed from the outset for speedy conversion to war, and volumes could be written on the thoroughness and detail with which this was planned. Herr Rathenau had been brutally murdered in 1922 by anti-Semite and nascent Nazi secret societies who

fastened their hatred upon this Jew — Germany's faithful servant. When he came to power in 1929, Herr Bruening carried
on the work with zeal and discretion. Thus, while the victors
reposed on masses of obsolescent equipment, an immense German potential of new munitions production was, year by year,
coming into being.

*   *   *   *   *

It had been decided by the War Cabinet in 1919 that as part
of the economy campaign the service departments should frame
their estimates on the assumption that "the British Empire will
not be engaged in any great war during the next ten years, and
that no expeditionary force will be required." In 1924, when
I became Chancellor of the Exchequer, I asked the Committee
of Imperial Defence to review this rule; but no recommendations were made for altering it. In 1927, the War Office suggested that the 1919 decision should be extended for the Army
only to cover ten years "from the present date." This was approved by the Cabinet and Committee of Imperial Defence.
The matter was next discussed on July 5, 1928, when I proposed, with acceptance, "that the basis of estimates for the
service departments should rest upon the statement that there
would be no major war for a period of ten years, and that this
basis should advance from day to day, but that the assumption
should be reviewed every year by the Committee of Imperial
Defence." It was left open for any service department or Dominion Government to raise the issue at their discretion if they
thought fit.

It has been contended that the acceptance of this principle
lulled the fighting departments into a false sense of security,
that research was neglected, and only short-term views prevailed, especially where expense was involved. Up till the time
when I left office in 1929, I felt so hopeful that the peace of the
world would be maintained that I saw no reason to take any
new decision; nor in the event was I proved wrong. War did
not break out till the autumn of 1939. Ten years is a long
time in this fugitive world. The ten-year rule with its day-to-

day advance remained in force until 1932 when, on March 23, Mr. MacDonald's Government rightly decided that its abandonment could be assumed.

All this time the Allies possessed the strength, and the right, to prevent any visible or tangible German rearmament, and Germany must have obeyed a strong united demand from Britain, France, and Italy to bring her actions into conformity with what the Peace Treaties had prescribed. In reviewing again the history of the eight years from 1930 to 1938, we can see how much time we had. Up till 1934 at least, German rearmament could have been prevented without the loss of a single life. It was not time that was lacking.

4

Adolf Hitler

The Blinded Corporal — The Obscure Fuehrer — The Munich Putsch, 1923 — "Mein Kampf" — Hitler's Problems — Hitler and the Reichswehr — The Schleicher Intrigue — The Impact of the Economic Blizzard — Chancellor Bruening — A Constitutional Monarchy! — Equality of Armaments — Schleicher Intervenes — The Fall of Bruening.

IN OCTOBER, 1918, a German corporal had been temporarily blinded by chlorine gas in a British attack near Comines. While he lay in hospital in Pomerania, defeat and revolution swept over Germany. The son of an obscure Austrian customs official, he had nursed youthful dreams of becoming a great artist. Having failed to gain entry to the Academy of Art in Vienna, he had lived in poverty in that capital and later in Munich. Sometimes as a house-painter, often as a casual labourer, he suffered physical privations and bred a harsh though concealed resentment that the world had denied him success. These misfortunes did not lead him into Communist ranks. By an honourable inversion he cherished all the more an abnormal sense of racial loyalty and a fervent and mystic admiration for Germany and the German people. He sprang eagerly to arms at the outbreak of the war, and served for four years with a Bavarian regiment on the Western Front. Such were the early fortunes of Adolf Hitler.

As he lay sightless and helpless in hospital during the winter of 1918, his own personal failure seemed merged in the disaster of the whole German people. The shock of defeat, the collapse

of law and order, the triumph of the French, caused this convalescent regimental orderly an agony which consumed his
being, and generated those portentous and measureless forces
of the spirit which may spell the rescue or the doom of mankind. The downfall of Germany seemed to him inexplicable
by ordinary processes. Somewhere there had been a gigantic
and monstrous betrayal. Lonely and pent within himself, the
little soldier pondered and speculated upon the possible causes
of the catastrophe, guided only by his narrow personal experiences. He had mingled in Vienna with extreme German
Nationalist groups, and here he had heard stories of sinister,
undermining activities of another race, foes and exploiters of
the Nordic world — the Jews. His patriotic anger fused with
his envy of the rich and successful into one overpowering hate.

When at length, as an unnoted patient, he was released from
hospital still wearing the uniform in which he had an almost
schoolboyish pride, what scenes met his newly unscaled eyes?
Fearful are the convulsions of defeat. Around him in the atmosphere of despair and frenzy glared the lineaments of Red
Revolution. Armoured cars dashed through the streets of
Munich scattering leaflets or bullets upon the fugitive way-
farers. His own comrades, with defiant red arm-bands on their
uniforms, were shouting slogans of fury against all that he
cared for on earth. As in a dream everything suddenly became
clear. Germany had been stabbed in the back and clawed down
by the Jews, by the profiteers and intriguers behind the front,
by the accursed Bolsheviks in their international conspiracy of
Jewish intellectuals. Shining before him he saw his duty, to
save Germany from these plagues, to avenge her wrongs, and
lead the master race to their long-decreed destiny.

The officers of his regiment, deeply alarmed by the seditious
and revolutionary temper of their men, were very glad to find
one, at any rate, who seemed to have the root of the matter in
him. Corporal Hitler desired to remain mobilised, and found
employment as a "political education officer" or agent. In this
guise he gathered information about mutinous and subversive
designs. Presently he was told by the security officer for whom

he worked to attend meetings of the local political parties of all complexions. One evening in September, 1919, the Corporal went to a rally of the German Workers' Party in a Munich brewery, and here he heard for the first time people talking in the style of his secret convictions against the Jews, the speculators, the "November criminals" who had brought Germany into the abyss. On September 16, he joined this party, and shortly afterwards, in harmony with his military work, undertook its propaganda. In February, 1920, the first mass meeting of the German Workers' Party was held in Munich, and here Adolf Hitler himself dominated the proceedings and in twenty-five points outlined the party programme. He had now become a politician. His campaign of national salvation had been opened. In April, he was demobilised, and the expansion of the party absorbed his whole life. By the middle of the following year, he had ousted the original leaders, and by his passion and genius forced upon the hypnotised company the acceptance of his personal control. Already he was "the Fuehrer." An unsuccessful newspaper, the *Voelkischer Beobachter,* was bought as the party organ.

The Communists were not long in recognising their foe. They tried to break up Hitler's meetings, and in the closing days of 1921 he organised his first units of storm troopers. Up to this point all had moved in local circles in Bavaria. But in the tribulation of German life during these first post-war years, many began here and there throughout the Reich to listen to the new gospel. The fierce anger of all Germany at the French occupation of the Ruhr in 1923 brought what was now called the National-Socialist Party a broad wave of adherents. The collapse of the mark destroyed the basis of the German middle class, of whom many in their despair became recruits of the new party and found relief from their misery in hatred, vengeance, and patriotic fervour.

At the beginning, Hitler had made clear that the path to power lay through aggression and violence against a Weimar Republic born from the shame of defeat. By November, 1923, "the Fuehrer" had a determined group around him, among whom Goering, Hess, Rosenberg, and Roehm were prominent. These men of action decided that the moment had come to attempt the seizure of authority in the State of Bavaria. General von Ludendorff lent the military prestige of his name to the venture, and marched forward in the *Putsch*. It used to be said before the war: "In Germany there will be no revolution, because in Germany all revolutions are strictly forbidden." This precept was revived on this occasion by the local authorities in Munich. The police fired, carefully avoiding the General, who marched straight forward into their ranks and was received with respect. About twenty of the demonstrators were killed; Hitler threw himself upon the ground, and presently escaped with other leaders from the scene. In April, 1924, he was sentenced to four years' imprisonment.

Although the German authorities had maintained order, and the German court had inflicted punishment, the feeling was widespread throughout the land that they were striking at their own flesh and blood, and were playing the foreigners' game at the expense of Germany's most faithful sons. Hitler's sentence was reduced from four years to thirteen months. These months in the Landsberg fortress were, however, sufficient to enable him to complete in outline *Mein Kampf*, a treatise on his political philosophy inscribed to the dead of the recent *Putsch*. When eventually he came to power, there was no book which deserved more careful study from the rulers, political and military, of the Allied Powers. All was there — the programme of German resurrection; the technique of party propaganda; the plan for combating Marxism; the concept of a National-Socialist State; the rightful position of Germany at the summit of the world. Here was the new Koran of faith and war: turgid, verbose, shapeless, but pregnant with its message.

The main thesis of *Mein Kampf* is simple. Man is a fighting animal; therefore the nation, being a community of fighters, is a fighting unit. Any living organism which ceases to fight for its existence is doomed to extinction. A country or race which ceases to fight is equally doomed. The fighting capacity of a race depends on its purity. Hence the need for ridding it of foreign defilements. The Jewish race, owing to its universality, is of necessity pacifist and internationalist. Pacifism is the deadliest sin; for it means the surrender of the race in the fight for existence. The first duty of every country is therefore to nationalise the masses; intelligence in the case of the individual is not of first importance; will and determination are the prime qualities. The individual who is born to command is more valuable than countless thousands of subordinate natures. Only brute force can ensure the survival of the race; hence the necessity for military forms. The race must fight; a race that rests must rust and perish. Had the German race been united in good time, it would have been already master of the globe. The new Reich must gather within its fold all the scattered German elements in Europe. A race which has suffered defeat can be rescued by restoring its self-confidence. Above all things the Army must be taught to believe in its own invincibility. To restore the German nation, the people must be convinced that the recovery of freedom by force of arms is possible. The aristocratic principle is fundamentally sound. Intellectualism is undesirable. The ultimate aim of education is to produce a German who can be converted with the minimum of training into a soldier. The greatest upheavals in history would have been unthinkable had it not been for the driving force of fanatical and hysterical passions. Nothing could have been effected by the bourgeois virtues of peace and order. The world is now moving towards such an upheaval, and the new German State must see to it that the race is ready for the last and greatest decisions on this earth.

Foreign policy may be unscrupulous. It is not the task of diplomacy to allow a nation to founder heroically, but rather to see that it can prosper and survive. England and Italy are the only two possible allies for Germany. No country will enter into an alliance with a cowardly pacifist state run by democrats and Marxists. So long as Germany does not fend for herself, nobody will fend for her. Her lost provinces cannot be regained by solemn appeals to Heaven or by pious hopes in the League of Nations, but only by force of arms. Germany must not repeat the mistake of fighting all her enemies at once. She must single out the most dangerous and attack him with all her forces. The world will only cease to be anti-German when Germany recovers equality of rights and resumes her place in the sun. There must be no sentimentality about Germany's foreign policy. To attack France for purely sentimental reasons would be foolish. What Germany needs is increase of territory in Europe. Germany's pre-war colonial policy was a mistake and should be abandoned. Germany must look for expansion to Russia and especially to the Baltic States. No alliance with Russia can be tolerated. To wage war together with Russia against the West would be criminal, for the aim of the Soviets is the triumph of international Judaism.

Such were the "granite pillars" of his policy.

* * * * *

The ceaseless struggles and gradual emergence of Adolf Hitler as a national figure were little noticed by the victors, oppressed and harassed as they were by their own troubles and party strife. A long interval passed before National Socialism or the "Nazi Party," as it came to be called, gained so strong a hold of the masses of the German people, of the armed forces, of the machinery of the State, and among industrialists not unreasonably terrified of Communism, as to become a power in German life of which world-wide notice had to be taken. When Hitler was released from prison at the end of 1924, he said that it would take him five years to reorganise his movement.

* * * * *

One of the democratic provisions of the Weimar Constitution prescribed biennial elections to the Reichstag. It was hoped by this provision to make sure that the masses of the German people should enjoy a complete and continuous control over their Parliament. In practice, of course, it only meant that they lived in a continual atmosphere of febrile political excitement and ceaseless electioneering. The progress of Hitler and his doctrines is thus registered with precision. In 1928, he had but twelve seats in the Reichstag. In 1930, this became 107; in 1932, 230. By that time the whole structure of Germany had been permeated by the agencies and discipline of the National-Socialist Party, and intimidation of all kinds and insults and brutalities towards the Jews were rampant.

It is not necessary in this account to follow year by year this complex and formidable development with all its passions and villainies, and all its ups and downs. The pale sunlight of Locarno shone for a while upon the scene. The spending of the profuse American loans induced a sense of returning prosperity. Marshal Hindenburg presided over the German State; and Stresemann was his Foreign Minister. The stable, decent majority of the German people, responding to their ingrained love of massive and majestic authority, clung to him till his dying gasp. But other powerful factors were also active in the distracted nation to which the Weimar Republic could offer no sense of security and no satisfactions of national glory or revenge.

Behind the veneer of republican governments and democratic institutions, imposed by the victors and tainted with defeat, the real political power in Germany and the enduring structure of the nation in the post-war years had been the General Staff of the Reichswehr. They it was who made and unmade presidents and cabinets. They had found in Marshal Hindenburg a symbol of their power and an agent of their will. But Hindenburg in 1930 was eighty-three years of age. From this time his character and mental grasp steadily declined. He became increasingly prejudiced, arbitrary, and senile. An enormous image had been made of him in the war, and patriots could show their admiration by paying for a nail to drive into it. This illustrates effectively what he had now become — "The Wooden Titan." It had for some time been clear to the generals that a satisfactory successor to the aged Marshal would have to be found. The search for the new man was, however, overtaken by the vehement growth and force of the National-Socialist Movement. After the failure of the 1923 *Putsch* in Munich, Hitler had professed a programme of strict legality within the framework of the Weimar Republic. Yet at the same time he had encouraged and planned the expansion of the military and para-military formations of the Nazi Party. From very small beginnings the S.A., the Storm Troops or "Brown Shirts," with their small disciplinary core, the S.S., grew in numbers and vigour to the point where the Reichswehr viewed their activities and potential strength with grave alarm.

At the head of the Storm Troops formations stood a German soldier of fortune, Ernst Roehm, the comrade and hitherto the close friend of Hitler through all the years of struggle. Roehm, Chief of the Staff of the S.A., was a man of proved ability and courage, but dominated by personal ambition, and sexually perverted. His vices were no barrier to Hitler's collaboration with him along the hard and dangerous path to power. The Storm Troops had, as Bruening complains, absorbed most of the old German Nationalist formations, such as the Free Companies which had fought in the Baltic and Poland against the Bolsheviks in the nineteen-twenties, and also the Nationalist Veterans' Organisation of the Steel Helmets (Stahlhelm).

Pondering most carefully upon the tides that were flowing in the nation, the Reichswehr convinced themselves with much reluctance that as a military caste and organisation in opposition to the Nazi Movement, they could no longer maintain control of Germany. Both factions had in common the resolve to raise Germany from the abyss and avenge her defeat; but while the Reichswehr represented the ordered structure of the Kaiser's Empire, and gave shelter to the feudal, aristocratic, landowning and well-to-do classes in German society, the S.A. had become to a large extent a revolutionary movement fanned by the discontents of temperamental or embittered subversives and the desperation of ruined men. They differed from the Bolsheviks whom they denounced no more than the North Pole does from the South.

For the Reichswehr to quarrel with the Nazi Party was to tear the defeated nation asunder. The Army chiefs in 1931 and 1932 felt they must, for their own sake and for that of the country, join forces with those to whom in domestic matters they were opposed with all the rigidity and severeness of the German mind. Hitler, for his part, although prepared to use any battering-ram to break into the citadels of power, had always before his eyes the leadership of the great and glittering Germany which had commanded the admiration and loyalty of his youthful years. The conditions for a compact between him and the Reichswehr were therefore present and natural on both sides. The Army chiefs had gradually realised that the strength of the Nazi Party in the nation was such that Hitler was the only possible successor to Hindenburg as head of the German nation. Hitler on his side knew that to carry out his programme of German resurrection an alliance with the governing élite of the Reichswehr was indispensable. A bargain was struck, and the German Army leaders began to persuade Hindenburg to look upon Hitler as eventual Chancellor of the Reich. Thus, by agreeing to curtail the activities of the Brown Shirts, to subordinate them to the General Staff, and ultimately, if unavoidable, to liquidate them, Hitler gained the allegiance of the controlling forces in Germany, official executive dominance, and the apparent reversion of the headship of the German State. The Corporal had travelled far.

*   *   *   *   *

There was, however, an inner and separate complication. If the key to any master-combination of German internal forces was the General Staff of the Army, several hands were grasping for that key. General Kurt von Schleicher at this time exercised a subtle and on occasions a decisive influence. He was the political mentor of the reserved and potentially dominating military circle. He was viewed with a measure of distrust by all sections and factions, and regarded as an adroit and useful political agent possessed of much knowledge outside the General Staff Manuals, and not usually accessible to soldiers. Schleicher had been long convinced of the significance of the Nazi Movement and of the need to stem and control it. On the other hand, he saw that in this terrific mob-thrust, with its ever-growing private army of S.A., there was a weapon which, if properly handled by his comrades of the General Staff, might reassert the greatness of Germany, and perhaps even establish his own. In this intention during the course of 1931 Schleicher began to plot secretly with Roehm, Chief of the Staff of the Nazi Storm Troopers. There was thus a major double process at work: the General Staff making their arrangements with Hitler, and Schleicher in their midst pursuing his personal conspiracy with Hitler's principal lieutenant and would-be rival, Roehm. Schleicher's contacts with the revolutionary element of the Nazi Party, and particularly with Roehm, lasted until both he and Roehm were shot by Hitler's orders three years later. This certainly simplified the political situation; and also that of the survivors.

* * * * *

Meanwhile, the economic blizzard smote Germany in her turn. The United States banks, faced with increasing commitments at home, refused to increase their improvident loans to Germany. This reaction led to the widespread closing of factories and the sudden ruin of many enterprises on which the peaceful revival of Germany was based. Unemployment in Germany rose to 2,300,000 in the winter of 1930. At the same time reparations entered a new phase. For the previous three years the American Commissioner, Mr. Young, had administered and controlled the German budgets and had collected the heavy payments demanded by the Allies, including the payments to Britain which I transmitted automatically to the United States Treasury. It was certain this system could not last. Already in the summer of 1929, Mr. Young had framed, proposed, and negotiated in Paris an important scheme of mitigation, which not only put a final limit to the period of reparation payments, but freed both the Reichsbank and the German railways from Allied control, and abolished the Reparations Commission in favour of the Bank for International Settlements. Hitler and his National-Socialist Movement joined forces with the business and commercial interests which were represented, and to some extent led, by the truculent and transient figure of the commercial magnate, Hugenberg. A vain but savage campaign was launched against this far-reaching and benevolent easement proffered by the Allies. The German Government succeeded by a dead-lift effort in procuring the assent of the Reichstag to the "Young Plan" by no more than 224 votes to 206. Stresemann, the Foreign Minister, who was now a dying man, gained his last success in the agreement for the complete evacuation of the Rhineland by the Allied armies, long before the Treaty required.

But the German masses were largely indifferent to the remarkable concessions of the victors. Earlier, or in happier circumstances, these would have been acclaimed as long steps upon the path of reconciliation and a return to true peace. But now the ever-present overshadowing fear of the German masses was unemployment. The middle classes had already been ruined and driven into violent courses by the flight from the mark. Stresemann's internal political position was undermined by the international economic stresses, and the vehement assaults of Hitler's Nazis and Hugenberg's capitalist magnates led to his overthrow. On March 28, 1930, Bruening, the leader of the Catholic Centre Party, became Chancellor.

*   *   *   *   *

Bruening was a Catholic from Westphalia and a patriot, seeking to re-create the former Germany in modern democratic guise. He pursued continuously the scheme of factory preparation for war which had been devised by Herr Rathenau before his murder. He had also to struggle towards financial stability amid mounting chaos. His programme of economy and reduction of civil service numbers and salaries was not popular. The tides of hatred flowed ever more turbulently. Supported by President Hindenburg, Bruening dissolved a hostile Reichstag, and the election of 1930 left him with a majority. He now made the last recognisable effort to rally what remained of the old Germany against the resurgent, violent, and debased nationalist agitation. For this purpose he had first to secure the re-election of Hindenburg as President.

Chancellor Bruening looked to a new but obvious solution. He saw the peace, safety, and glory of Germany only in the restoration of an emperor. Could he then induce the aged Marshal Hindenburg, if and when re-elected, to act for his last term of office as regent for a restored monarchy to come into effect upon his death? This policy, if achieved, would have filled the void at the summit of the German nation towards which Hitler was now evidently making his way. In all the circumstances this was the right course. But how could Bruening lead Germany to it? The conservative element, which was drifting to Hitler, might have been recalled by the restoration of Kaiser Wilhelm; but neither the Social Democrats nor the trade-union forces would tolerate the restoration of the old Kaiser or the Crown Prince. Bruening's plan was not to re-create a Second Reich. He desired a constitutional monarchy on English lines. He hoped that one of the sons of the Crown Prince might be a suitable candidate.

In November, 1931, he confided his plans to Hindenburg, on whom all depended. The aged Marshal's reaction was at once vehement and peculiar. He was astonished and hostile. He said that he regarded himself solely as trustee of the Kaiser. Any other solution was an insult to his military honour. The monarchical conception, to which he was devoted, could not be reconciled with picking and choosing among royal princes. Legitimacy must not be violated. Meanwhile, as Germany would not accept the return of the Kaiser, there was nothing left but he, himself, Hindenburg. On this he rested. No compromise for him! *"J'y suis, j'y reste."* Bruening argued vehemently and perhaps over-long with the old veteran. The Chancellor had a strong case. Unless Hindenburg would accept this monarchical solution, albeit unorthodox, there must be a revolutionary Nazi dictatorship. No agreement was reached. But whether or not Bruening could convert Hindenburg, it was imperative to get him re-elected as President, in order at least to stave off an immediate political collapse of the German State. In its first stage Bruening's plan was successful. At the Presidential elections held in March, 1932, Hindenburg was returned, after a second ballot, by a majority over his rivals, Hitler and the Communist Thaelmann. Both the economic position in Germany and her relations with Europe had now to be faced. The Disarmament Conference was sitting in Geneva, and Hitler throve upon a roaring campaign against the humiliations of Germany under Versailles.

In careful meditation Bruening drafted a far-reaching plan of Treaty revision; and in April, 1932, he went to Geneva and found an unexpectedly favourable reception. In conversations between him and MacDonald, Stimson, and Norman Davis, it seemed that agreement could be reached. The extraordinary basis of this was the principle, subject to various reserved interpretations, of "equality of armaments" between Germany and France. It is indeed surprising, as future chapters will explain, that anyone in his senses should have imagined that peace could be built on such foundations. If this vital point were conceded by the victors, it might well pull Bruening out of his plight; and then the next step — and this one wise — would be the cancelling of reparations for the sake of European revival. Such a settlement would, of course, have raised Bruening's personal position to one of triumph.

Norman Davis, the American Ambassador-at-Large, telephoned to the French Premier, Tardieu, to come immediately from Paris to Geneva. But unfortunately for Bruening, Tardieu had other news. Schleicher had been busy in Berlin, and had just warned the French Ambassador not to negotiate with Bruening because his fall was imminent. It may well be also that Tardieu was concerned with the military position of France on the formula of "equality of armaments." At any rate Tardieu did not come to Geneva, and on May 1 Bruening returned to Berlin. To arrive there empty-handed at such a moment was fatal to him. Drastic and even desperate measures were required to cope with the threatened economic collapse inside Germany. For these measures Bruening's unpopular Government had not the necessary strength. He struggled on through May, and meanwhile Tardieu, in the kaleidoscope of French parliamentary politics, was replaced by M. Herriot.

The new French Premier declared himself ready to discuss the formulas reached in the Geneva conversations. Mr. Norman Davis was instructed to urge the German Chancellor to go to Geneva without a moment's delay. This message was received by Bruening early on May 30. But meanwhile Schleicher's influence had prevailed. Hindenburg had already been persuaded to dismiss the Chancellor. In the course of that very morning, after the American invitation, with all its hope and imprudence, had reached Bruening, he learned that his fate was settled, and by midday he resigned to avoid actual dismissal. So ended the last Government in post-war Germany which might have led the German people into the enjoyment of a stable and civilised constitution, and opened peaceful channels of intercourse with their neighbours. The offers which the Allies had made to Bruening would, but for Schleicher's intrigue and Tardieu's delay, certainly have saved him. These offers had presently to be discussed with a different system and a different man.

5

The Locust Years[1]

1931–1935

The MacDonald-Baldwin Coalition — The Indian Collapse — All Germany Astir — Hindenburg and Hitler — Schleicher Fails as a Stopgap — Hitler Becomes Chancellor — The Burning of the Reichstag, February 27, 1933 — Hitler Wins a Majority at the Elections — The New Master — Qualitative Disarmament — 1932 in Germany — British Air Estimates of 1933 — Equality of Status in Armaments — "The MacDonald Plan" — "Thank God for the French Army" — Hitler Quits the League of Nations — A New York Adventure — Peace at Chartwell — Some Wise Friends — The Marlborough Battlefields — "Putzi" — The Attitude of the Conservative Party — Dangers in the Far East — Japan Attacks China — Accountability.

THE BRITISH GOVERNMENT which resulted from the general election of 1931 was in appearance one of the strongest, and in fact one of the weakest, in British records. Mr. Ramsay MacDonald, the Prime Minister, had severed himself, with the utmost bitterness on both sides, from the Socialist Party which it had been his life's work to create. Henceforward he brooded supinely at the head of an administration which, though nominally National, was in fact overwhelmingly Conservative. Mr. Baldwin preferred the substance to the form of power, and reigned placidly in the background. The Foreign Office was

---

[1] Four years later, Sir Thomas Inskip, Minister for Co-ordination of Defence, who was well-versed in the Bible, used the expressive phrase about this dismal period, of which he was the heir: "The years that the locust hath eaten." — Joel, 2:25.

filled by Sir John Simon, one of the leaders of the Liberal contingent. The main work of the Administration at home was
done by Mr. Neville Chamberlain, who soon succeeded Mr.
Snowden as Chancellor of the Exchequer. The Labour Party,
blamed for its failure in the financial crisis and sorely stricken
at the polls, was led by the extreme pacifist, Mr. George Lansbury. During the period of almost five years of this Administration, from January, 1931, to November, 1935, the entire
situation on the Continent of Europe was reversed.

*   *   *   *   *

On the first return of the new Parliament, the Government
demanded a vote of confidence upon their Indian policy. To
this I moved an amendment as follows:

Provided that nothing in the said policy shall commit this House
to the establishment in India of a Dominion Constitution as defined
by the Statute of Westminster. . . . And that no question of self-
government in India at this juncture shall impair the ultimate
responsibility of Parliament for the peace, order, and good government of the Indian Empire.

On this occasion I spoke for as much as an hour and a half,
and was heard with attention. But on this issue, as later on
upon defence, nothing that one could say made the slightest
difference. We have now along this subsidiary Eastern road
also reached our horrible consummation in the slaughter of
hundreds of thousands of poor people who only sought to earn
their living under conditions of peace and justice. I ventured
to tell the ignorant Members of all parties:

As the British authority passes for a time into collapse, the old
hatreds between the Moslems and the Hindus revive and acquire
new life and malignancy. We cannot easily conceive what these
hatreds are. There are in India mobs of neighbours, people who
have dwelt together in the closest propinquity all their lives, who
when held and dominated by these passions will tear each other
to pieces, men, women, and children, with their fingers. Not for a
hundred years have the relations between Moslems and Hindus
been so poisoned as they have been since England was deemed to

be losing her grip, and was believed to be ready to quit the scene if told to go.

We mustered little more than forty in the lobby against all the three parties in the House of Commons. This must be noted as a sad milestone on the downward path.

*   *   *   *   *

Meanwhile, all Germany was astir and great events marched forward.

Much had happened in the year which followed the fall of the Bruening Cabinet in May, 1932. Papen and the political general, Schleicher, had hitherto attempted to govern Germany by cleverness and intrigue. The time for these had now passed. Papen, who succeeded Bruening as Chancellor, hoped to rule with the support of the entourage of President Hindenburg and of the extreme Nationalist group in the Reichstag. On July 20, a decisive step was taken. The Socialist Government in Prussia was forcibly ousted from office. The question put to the Prime Minister of Prussia when he said he would only yield to physical force was: "How much force do you require?" He was then carried away from his desk. But Papen's rival was eager for power. In Schleicher's calculations the instrument lay in the dark hidden forces storming into German politics behind the rising power and name of Adolf Hitler. He hoped to make the Hitler Movement a docile servant of the Reichswehr, and in so doing to gain the control of both himself. The contacts between Schleicher and Roehm, the leader of the Nazi Storm Troopers, which had begun in 1931, were extended in the following year to more precise relations between Schleicher and Hitler himself. The road to power for both men seemed to be obstructed only by Papen and by the confidence displayed by Hindenburg in him.

In August, 1932, Hitler came to Berlin on a private summons from the President. The moment for a forward step seemed at hand. Thirteen million German voters stood behind the Fuehrer. A vital share of office must be his for the asking. He was now in somewhat the position of Mussolini on the eve of the march on Rome. But Papen did not care about recent Italian history. He had the support of Hindenburg and had no intention of resigning. The old Marshal saw Hitler. He was not impressed. "*That* man for Chancellor? I'll make him a postmaster and he can lick stamps with my head on them." In palace circles Hitler had not the influence of his competitors.

In the country the vast electorate was restless and adrift. In November, 1932, for the fifth time in a year, elections were held throughout Germany. The Nazis lost ground and their 230 seats were reduced to 196, the Communists gaining the balance. The bargaining power of the Fuehrer was thus weakened. Perhaps General Schleicher would be able to do without him after all. The General gained favour in the circle of Hindenburg's advisers. On November 17, Papen resigned and Schleicher became Chancellor in his stead. But the new Chancellor was found to have been more apt at pulling wires behind the scenes than at the open summit of power. He had quarrelled with too many people. Hitler together with Papen and the Nationalists now ranged themselves against him; and the Communists, fighting the Nazis in the streets and the Government by their strikes, helped to make his rule impossible. Papen brought his personal influence to bear on President Hindenburg. Would not after all the best solution be to placate Hitler by thrusting upon him the responsibilities and burdens of office? Hindenburg at last reluctantly consented. On January 30, 1933, Adolf Hitler took office as Chancellor of Germany.

The hand of the Master was soon felt upon all who would or might oppose the New Order. On February 2, all meetings or demonstrations of the German Communist Party were forbidden, and throughout Germany a round-up of secret arms belonging to the Communists began. The climax came on the evening of February 27, 1933. The building of the Reichstag broke into flames. Brown Shirts, Black Shirts, and their auxiliary formations were called out. Four thousand arrests, including the Central Committee of the Communist Party, were made overnight. These measures were entrusted to Goering,

now Minister of the Interior of Prussia. They formed the preliminary to the forthcoming elections and secured the defeat of
the Communists, the most formidable opponents of the new
régime. The organising of the electoral campaign was the task
of Goebbels, and he lacked neither skill nor zeal.

But there were still many forces in Germany reluctant, obstinate, or actively hostile to Hitlerism. The Communists, and
many who in their perplexity and distress voted with them,
obtained 81 seats; the Socialists 118; and the Nationalists of
Papen and Hugenberg 52. Against these Hitler secured a
Nazi vote of 17,300,000 votes with 288 seats. Thus, and thus
only, did Hitler obtain by hook and crook a majority vote from
the German people. He had 288 against the other parties numbering 251; a majority of 37 only. Under the ordinary processes
of civilised parliamentary government, so large a minority
would have had great influence and due consideration in the
State. But in the new Nazi Germany minorities were now to
learn that they had no rights.

On March 21, 1933, Hitler opened, in the garrison church at
Potsdam, hard-by the tomb of Frederick the Great, the First
Reichstag of the Third Reich. In the body of the church sat
the representatives of the Reichswehr, the symbol of the continuity of German might, and the senior officers of the S.A. and
S.S., the new figures of resurgent Germany. On March 24, the
majority of the Reichstag, overbearing or overaweing all opponents, confirmed by 441 votes to 94 complete emergency
powers to Chancellor Hitler for four years. As the result was
announced, Hitler turned to the benches of the Socialists and
cried, "And now I have no further need of you."

Amid the excitement of the election the exultant column
of the National Socialist Party filed past their leader in the
pagan homage of a torchlight procession through the streets
of Berlin. It had been a long struggle, difficult for foreigners,
especially those who had not known the pangs of defeat, to
comprehend. Adolf Hitler had at last arrived; but he was not
alone. He had called from the depths of defeat the dark and
savage furies latent in the most numerous, most serviceable,

ruthless, contradictory, and ill-starred race in Europe. He had conjured up the fearful idol of an all-devouring Moloch of which he was the priest and incarnation. It is not within my scope to describe the inconceivable brutality and villainy by which this apparatus of hatred and tyranny had been fashioned and was now to be perfected. It is necessary, for the purpose of this account, only to present to the reader the new and fearful fact which had broken upon the still-unwitting world: GERMANY UNDER HITLER, AND GERMANY ARMING.

* * * * *

While these deadly changes were taking place in Germany, the MacDonald-Baldwin Government felt bound to enforce for some time the severe reductions and restrictions which the financial crisis had imposed upon our already modest armaments, and steadfastly closed their eyes and ears to the disquieting symptoms in Europe. In vehement efforts to procure a disarmament of the victors equal to that which had been enforced upon the vanquished by the Treaty of Versailles, Mr. MacDonald and his Conservative and Liberal colleagues pressed a series of proposals forward in the League of Nations and through every other channel that was open. The French, although their political affairs still remained in constant flux and in motion without particular significance, clung tenaciously to the French Army as the centre and prop of the life of France and of all her alliances. This attitude earned them rebukes both in Britain and in the United States. The opinions of the press and public were in no way founded upon reality; but the adverse tide was strong.

When in May, 1932, the virtues of disarmament were extolled in the House of Commons by all parties, the Foreign Secretary opened a new line in the classification of weapons which should be allowed or discouraged. He called this "qualitative disarmament." It was easier to expose the fallacy than to convince the Members. I said:

The Foreign Secretary told us that it was difficult to divide weapons into offensive and defensive categories. It certainly is,

because almost every conceivable weapon may be used in defence
or offence; either by an aggressor or by the innocent victim of his
assault. To make it more difficult for the invader, heavy guns,
tanks, and poison gas are to be relegated to the evil category of
offensive weapons. The invasion of France by Germany in 1914
reached its climax without the employment of any of these weapons.
The heavy gun is to be described as "an offensive weapon." It is all
right in a fortress; there it is virtuous and pacific in its character;
but bring it out into the field — and, of course, if it were needed, it
would be brought out into the field — and it immediately becomes
naughty, peccant, militaristic, and has to be placed under the ban
of civilisation. Take the tank. The Germans, having invaded
France, entrenched themselves; and in a couple of years they shot
down 1,500,000 French and British soldiers who were trying to
free the soil of France. The tank was invented to overcome the fire
of the machine-guns with which the Germans were maintaining
themselves in France, and it saved a lot of lives in clearing the soil
of the invader. Now, apparently, the machine-gun, which was the
German weapon for holding on to thirteen provinces of France, is
to be the virtuous, defensive machine-gun, and the tank, which was
the means by which these Allied lives were saved, is to be placed
under the censure and obloquy of all just and righteous men. . . .

A truer classification might be drawn in banning weapons which
tend to be indiscriminate in their action and whose use entails
death and wounds, not merely on the combatants in the fighting
zones, but on the civil population, men, women, and children, far
removed from those areas. There, indeed, it seems to me would be
a direction in which the united nations assembled at Geneva might
advance with hope. . . .

At the end I gave my first formal warning of approaching
war:

I should very much regret to see any approximation in military
strength between Germany and France. Those who speak of that
as though it were right, or even a question of fair dealing, altogether underrate the gravity of the European situation. I would say
to those who would like to see Germany and France on an equal
footing in armaments: "Do you wish for war?" For my part, I
earnestly hope that no such approximation will take place during
my lifetime or that of my children. To say that is not in the least

to imply any want of regard or admiration for the great qualities
of the German people, but I am sure that the thesis that they should
be placed in an equal military position with France is one which, if
it ever emerged in fact, would bring us within practical distance of
almost measureless calamity.

The British air estimates of March, 1933, revealed a total
lack of comprehension alike by the Government and the Oppositions, Labour and Liberal, of what was going on. I had to
say (March 14, 1933) :

I regretted to hear the Under-Secretary say that we were only the
fifth air power, and that the ten-year programme was suspended
for another year. I was sorry to hear him boast that the Air
Ministry had not laid down a single new unit this year. All these
ideas are being increasingly stultified by the march of events, and
we should be well advised to concentrate upon our air defences with
greater vigour.

*   *   *   *   *

Under the so-called National Government, British public
opinion showed an increasing inclination to cast aside all care
about Germany. In vain the French had pointed out correctly
in a memorandum of July 21, 1931, that the general assurance
given at Versailles that a universal limitation of armaments
should follow the one-sided disarmament of Germany did not
constitute a Treaty obligation. It certainly was not an obligation enforceable apart from time and circumstance. Yet, when
in 1932 the German delegation to the Disarmament Conference categorically demanded the removal of all restrictions
upon their right to rearm, they found much support in the
British press. *The Times* spoke of "the timely redress of inequality," and *The New Statesman* of "the unqualified recognition of the principle of the equality of states." This
meant that the seventy million Germans ought to be allowed to
rearm and prepare for war without the victors in the late fearful struggle being entitled to make any objection. Equality of
status between victors and vanquished; equality between a
France of thirty-nine millions and a Germany of nearly double
that number!

The German Government were emboldened by the British
demeanour. They ascribed it to the fundamental weakness
and inherent decadence imposed even upon a Nordic race by
the democratic and parliamentary form of society. With all
Hitler's national drive behind them, they took a haughty line.
In July, their delegation gathered up its papers and quitted
the Disarmament Conference. To coax them back then became the prime political objective of the victorious Allies. In
November, the French, under severe and constant British pressure, proposed what was somewhat unfairly called "The
Herriot Plan." The essence of this was the reconstruction of all
European defence forces as short-service armies with limited
numbers, admitting equality of status but not necessarily accepting equality of strength. In fact and in principle, the
admission of equality of status made it impossible ultimately
not to accept equality of strength. This enabled the Allied
Governments to offer to Germany: "Equality of rights in a
system which would provide security for all nations." Under
certain safeguards of an illusory character the French were
reduced to accepting this meaningless formula. On this the
Germans consented to return to the Disarmament Conference.
This was hailed as a notable victory for peace.

Fanned by the breeze of popularity, His Majesty's Government now produced on March 16, 1933, what was called, after
its author and inspirer, "The MacDonald Plan." It accepted
as its starting-point the adoption of the French conception of
short-service armies — in this case of eight months' service —
and proceeded to prescribe exact figures for the troops of each
country. The French Army should be reduced from its peace-
time establishment of five hundred thousand men to two hundred thousand and the Germans should increase to parity at
that figure. By this time the German military forces, though
not yet provided with the mass of trained reserves which only a
succession of annual conscripted quotas could supply, may well
have amounted to the equivalent of over a million ardent volunteers, partially equipped, and with many forms of the latest
weapons coming along through the convertible and partially
converted factories to arm them.

At the end of the First World War, France, like Great Britain, had an enormous mass of heavy artillery, whereas the cannon of the German Army had in fact been blown to bits according to Treaty. Mr. MacDonald sought to remedy this evident inequality by proposing to limit the calibre of mobile artillery guns to 105 mm. or 4.2 inches. Existing guns up to six inches, could be retained, but all replacements were to be limited to 4.2 inches. British interests, as distinct from those of France, were to be protected by the maintenance of the Treaty restrictions against German naval armaments until 1935, when it was proposed that a new Naval Conference should meet. Military aircraft were prohibited to Germany for the duration of the agreement; but the three Allied Powers should reduce their own air forces to five hundred planes apiece.

I viewed this attack upon the French armed forces and the attempt to establish equality between Germany and France with strong aversion; and on March 23, 1933, I had the opportunity of saying to Parliament:

I doubt the wisdom of pressing this plan upon France at the present time. I do not think the French will agree. They must be greatly concerned at what is taking place in Germany, as well as at the attitude of some others of their neighbours. I dare say that during this anxious month there are a good many people who have said to themselves, as I have been saying for several years: "Thank God for the French Army." When we read about Germany, when we watch with surprise and distress the tumultuous insurgence of ferocity and war spirit, the pitiless ill-treatment of minorities, the denial of the normal protections of civilised society, the persecution of large numbers of individuals solely on the ground of race — when we see all that occurring in one of the most gifted, learned, and scientific and formidable nations in the world, one cannot help feeling glad that the fierce passions that are raging in Germany have not yet found any other outlet but upon themselves. It seems to me that at a moment like this to ask France to halve her Army while Germany doubles hers, to ask France to halve her air force while the German air force remains whatever it is, is a proposal likely to be considered by the French Government, at present at any rate, as somewhat unseasonable. The figures that are given in the plan of the strength of armies and airplanes secure to France only as many airplanes as would be possessed by Italy, leaving any air power possessed by Germany entirely out of consideration.

And again in April:

The Germans demand equality in weapons and equality in the organisation of armies and fleets, and we have been told: "You cannot keep so great a nation in an inferior position. What others have, they must have." I have never agreed. It is a most dangerous demand to make. Nothing in life is eternal, but as surely as Germany acquires full military equality with her neighbours while her own grievances are still unredressed and while she is in the temper which we have unhappily seen, so surely should we see ourselves within a measureable distance of the renewal of general European war.

. . . One of the things which we were told after the Great War would be a security for us was that Germany would be a democracy with parliamentary institutions. All that has been swept away. You have most grim dictatorship. You have militarism and appeals to every form of fighting spirit, from the reintroduction of duelling in the colleges to the Minister of Education advising the plentiful use of the cane in the elementary schools. You have these martial or pugnacious manifestations, and also this persecution of the Jews of which so many Members have spoken. . . .

I will leave Germany and turn to France. France is not only the sole great surviving democracy in Europe; she is also the strongest military power, I am glad to say, and she is the head of a system of states and nations. France is the guarantor and protector of the whole crescent of small states which runs right round from Belgium to Yugoslavia and Rumania. They all look to France. When any step is taken, by England or any other Power, to weaken the diplomatic or military security of France, all these small nations tremble with fear and anger. They fear that the central protective force will be weakened, and that then they will be at the mercy of the great Teutonic Power.

When one considers that the facts were hardly in dispute, the actions of a responsible government of respectable men and the public opinion which so flocculently supported them are scarcely comprehensible. It was like being smothered by a feather bed. I remember particularly the look of pain and aversion which I saw on the faces of Members in all parts of the House when I said, "Thank God for the French Army." Words were vain.

However, the French had the hardihood to insist that there should be a delay of four years before the destruction of their heavy war material. The British Government accepted this modification, provided that the French agreement about the destruction of their artillery was specified in a document for immediate signature. France bowed to this, and on October 12, 1933, Sir John Simon, after complaining that Germany had shifted her ground in the course of the preceding weeks, brought these draft proposals before the Disarmament Conference. The result was unexpected. Hitler, now Chancellor and Master of all Germany, having already given orders on assuming power to drive ahead boldly on a nation-wide scale, both in the training-camps and the factories, felt himself in a strong position. He did not even trouble to accept the Quixotic offers pressed upon him. With a gesture of disdain he directed the German Government to withdraw both from the Conference and from the League of Nations. Such was the fate of the MacDonald Plan.

*　　*　　*　　*　　*

It is difficult to find a parallel to the unwisdom of the British and weakness of the French Governments, who none the less reflected the opinion of their Parliaments in this disastrous period. Nor can the United States escape the censure of history. Absorbed in their own affairs and all the abounding interests, activities, and accidents of a free community, they simply gaped at the vast changes which were taking place in Europe, and imagined they were no concern of theirs. The considerable corps of highly competent, widely trained professional American officers formed their own opinions, but these produced no noticeable effect upon the improvident aloofness of American foreign policy. If the influence of the United States had been exerted, it might have galvanised the

French and British politicians into action. The League of
Nations, battered though it had been, was still an august instrument which would have invested any challenge to the new
Hitler war-menace with the sanctions of international law.
Under the strain the Americans merely shrugged their shoulders, so that in a few years they had to pour out the blood and
treasures of the New World to save themselves from mortal
danger.

Seven years later, when at Tours I witnessed the French
agony, all this was in my mind, and that is why, even when
proposals for a separate peace were mentioned, I spoke only
words of comfort and reassurance which I rejoice to feel have
been made good.

*   *   *   *   *

I had arranged at the beginning of 1931 to undertake a considerable lecture tour in the United States, and travelled to New
York immediately after this speech. Here I suffered a serious
accident which nearly cost me my life. On December 13, when
on my way to visit Mr. Bernard Baruch, I got out of my car
on the wrong side and walked across Fifth Avenue without
bearing in mind the opposite rule of the road which prevails
in America, or the red lights, then unused in Britain. There
was a shattering collision. For two months I was a wreck. I
gradually regained at Nassau in the Bahamas enough strength
to crawl around. In this condition I undertook a tour of forty
lectures throughout the United States, living all day on my
back in a railway compartment, and addressing in the evening
large audiences. On the whole I consider this was the hardest
time I have had in my life. I lay pretty low all through this
year; but in time my strength returned.

Meanwhile, at home our life flowed placidly downstream.
At Westminster Mr. Baldwin adopted and espoused the main
principles of Mr. MacDonald's India Bill, the conduct of which
in the Commons was entrusted to the new Secretary of State
for India, Sir Samuel Hoare. The report of the Simon Commission was ignored, and no opportunity of debating it was

given to Parliament. With about seventy other Conservatives I formed a group called "The India Defence League," which during the next four years resisted the Government's policy on India in so far as it went beyond the recommendations of the Commission. We fought the matter out at party conferences with a considerable measure of support, sometimes running very close, but always in a minority. The Labour Opposition voted in Parliament with the Government on the Indian issue, and it became, like disarmament, a link between the two Front Benches. Their followers presented an overwhelming majority against our group, and derided us as "die-hards." The rise of Hitler to power, the domination of the Nazi Party over all Germany, and the rapid, active growth of German armed power, led to further differences between me and the Government and the various political parties in the State.

The years from 1931 to 1935, apart from my anxiety on public affairs, were personally very pleasant to me. I earned my livelihood by dictating articles which had a wide circulation, not only in Great Britain and the United States, but also, before Hitler's shadow fell upon them, in the most famous newspapers of sixteen European countries. I lived in fact from mouth to hand. I produced in succession the various volumes of the *Life of Marlborough*. I meditated constantly upon the European situation and the rearming of Germany. I lived mainly at Chartwell, where I had much to amuse me. I built with my own hands a large part of two cottages and extensive kitchen-garden walls, and made all kinds of rockeries and waterworks and a large swimming-pool which was filtered to limpidity and could be heated to supplement our fickle sunshine. Thus I never had a dull or idle moment from morning till midnight, and with my happy family around me dwelt at peace within my habitation.

During these years I saw a great deal of Frederick Lindemann, Professor of Experimental Philosophy at Oxford University. Lindemann was already an old friend of mine. I had met him first at the close of the previous war, in which he had distinguished himself by conducting in the air a number of

experiments, hitherto reserved for daring pilots, to overcome
the then almost mortal dangers of a "spin." We came much
closer together from 1932 onwards, and he frequently motored
over from Oxford to stay with me at Chartwell. Here we had
many talks into the small hours of the morning about the dangers which seemed to be gathering upon us. Lindemann, "the
Prof," as he was called among his friends, became my chief
adviser on the scientific aspects of modern war and particularly
of air defence, and also on questions involving statistics of all
kinds. This pleasant and fertile association continued throughout the war.

Another of my close friends was Desmond Morton.[2] When,
in 1917, Field-Marshal Haig filled his personal staff with young
officers fresh from the firing-line, Desmond was recommended
to him as the pick of the artillery. He had commanded the
most advanced field battery in Arras during the severe spring
fighting of that year. To his Military Cross he added the
unique distinction of having been shot through the heart, and
living happily ever afterwards with the bullet in him. When I
became Minister of Munitions in July, 1917, I frequently visited the front as the Commander-in-Chief's guest, and he
always sent his trusted Aide-de-Camp, Desmond Morton, with
me. Together we visited many parts of the line. During these
sometimes dangerous excursions, and at the Commander-in-
Chief's house, I formed a great regard and friendship for this
brilliant and gallant officer, and in 1919, when I became Secretary of State for War and Air, I appointed him to a position in the Intelligence, which he held for many years.
He was a neighbour of mine, dwelling only a mile away from
Chartwell. He obtained from the Prime Minister, Mr. Mac-
Donald, permission to talk freely to me and keep me well informed. He became, and continued during the war to be, one
of my most intimate advisers till our final victory was won.

I had also formed a friendship with Ralph Wigram, then the
rising star of the Foreign Office and in the centre of all its
affairs. He had reached a level in that department which en-

[2] Now Major Sir Desmond Morton, K.C.B., M.C.

titled him to express responsible opinions upon policy, and to use a wide discretion in his contacts, official and unofficial. He was a charming and fearless man, and his convictions, based upon profound knowledge and study, dominated his being. He saw as clearly as I did, but with more certain information, the awful peril which was closing in upon us. This drew us together. Often we met at his little house in North Street, and he and Mrs. Wigram came to stay with us at Chartwell. Like other officials of high rank, he spoke to me with complete confidence. All this helped me to form and fortify my opinion about the Hitler Movement. For my part, with the many connections which I now had in France, in Germany, and other countries, I had been able to send him a certain amount of information which we examined together.

From 1933 onwards, Wigram became keenly distressed at the policy of the Government and the course of events. While his official chiefs formed every day a higher opinion of his capacity, and while his influence in the Foreign Office grew, his thoughts turned repeatedly to resignation. He had so much force and grace in his conversation that all who had grave business with him, and many others, gave ever-increasing importance to his views.

* * * * *

It was of great value to me, and it may be thought also to the country, that I should have the means of conducting searching and precise discussions for so many years in this very small circle. On my side, however, I gathered and contributed a great deal of information from foreign sources. I had confidential contacts with several of the French Ministers and with the successive chiefs of the French Government. Mr. Ian Colvin, the son of the famous leader-writer of the *Morning Post,* was the *News Chronicle* correspondent in Berlin. He plunged very deeply into German politics, and established contacts of a most secret character with some of the important German generals, and also with independent men of character and quality in Germany who saw in the Hitler Movement the

approaching ruin of their native land. Several visitors of consequence came to me from Germany and poured their hearts
out in their bitter distress. Most of these were executed by
Hitler during the war. From other directions I was able to
check and furnish information on the whole field of our air
defence. In this way I became as well-instructed as many Ministers of the Crown. All the facts I gathered from every source,
including especially foreign connections, I reported to the Government from time to time. My personal relations with Ministers and also with many of their high officials were close and
easy, and, although I was often their critic, we maintained a
spirit of comradeship. Later on, as will be seen, I was made
officially party to much of their most secret technical knowledge. From my own long experience in high office I was also
possessed of the most precious secrets of the State. All this
enabled me to form and maintain opinions which did not depend on what was published in the newspapers, though these
brought many items to the discriminating eye.

*   *   *   *   *

At Westminster I pursued my two themes of India and the
German menace, and went to Parliament from time to time to
deliver warning speeches, which commanded attention, but
did not, unhappily, wake to action the crowded, puzzled
Houses which heard them. On the German danger, as on
India, I found myself working in Parliament with a group of
friends. It was to a large extent composed differently from the
India Defence League. Sir Austen Chamberlain, Sir Robert
Horne, Sir Edward Grigg, Lord Winterton, Mr. Bracken, Sir
Henry Croft, and several others formed our circle. We met
regularly, and, to a large extent, pooled our information. The
Ministers eyed this significant but not unfriendly body of their
own supporters and former colleagues or seniors with respect.
We could at any time command the attention of Parliament
and stage a full-dress debate.

*   *   *   *   *

The reader will pardon a personal digression in a lighter vein.

In the summer of 1932, for the purposes of my *Life of Marlborough* I visited his old battlefields in the Low Countries and Germany. Our family expedition, which included "the Prof," journeyed agreeably along the line of Marlborough's celebrated march in 1705 from the Netherlands to the Danube, passing the Rhine at Coblenz. As we wended our way through these beautiful regions from one ancient, famous city to another, I naturally asked questions about the Hitler Movement, and found it the prime topic in every German mind. I sensed a Hitler atmosphere. After passing a day on the field of Blenheim, I drove into Munich and spent the best part of a week there.

At the Regina Hotel a gentleman introduced himself to some of my party. He was Herr Hanfstaengl, and spoke a great deal about "the Fuehrer," with whom he appeared to be intimate. As he seemed to be a lively and talkative fellow, speaking excellent English, I asked him to dine. He gave a most interesting account of Hitler's activities and outlook. He spoke as one under the spell. He had probably been told to get in touch with me. He was evidently most anxious to please. After dinner he went to the piano and played and sang many tunes and songs in such remarkable style that we all enjoyed ourselves immensely. He seemed to know all the English tunes that I liked. He was a great entertainer, and at that time, as is known, a favourite of the Fuehrer. He said I ought to meet him, and that nothing would be easier to arrange. Herr Hitler came every day to the hotel about five o'clock, and would be very glad indeed to see me.

I had no national prejudices against Hitler at this time. I knew little of his doctrine or record and nothing of his character. I admire men who stand up for their country in defeat, even though I am on the other side. He had a perfect right to be a patriotic German if he chose. I always wanted England, Germany, and France to be friends. However, in the course of conversation with Hanfstaengl, I happened to say, "Why is

your chief so violent about the Jews? I can quite understand
being angry with Jews who have done wrong or are against
the country, and I understand resisting them if they try to
monopolise power in any walk of life; but what is the sense of
being against a man simply because of his birth? How can any
man help how he is born?" He must have repeated this to
Hitler, because about noon the next day he came round with
rather a serious air and said that the appointment he had made
with me to meet Hitler could not take place, as the Fuehrer
would not be coming to the hotel that afternoon. This was the
last I saw of "Putzi" — for such was his pet name — although
we stayed several more days at the hotel. Thus Hitler lost his
only chance of meeting me. Later on, when he was all-powerful, I was to receive several invitations from him. But by that
time a lot had happened, and I excused myself.

*   *   *   *   *

All this while the United States remained intensely preoccupied with its own vehement internal affairs and economic
problems. Europe and far-off Japan watched with steady gaze
the rise of German warlike power. Disquietude was increasingly expressed in Scandinavian countries and the states of the
"Little Entente" and in some Balkan countries. Deep anxiety
ruled in France, where a large amount of knowledge of Hitler's
activities and of German preparations had come to hand. There
was, I was told, a catalogue of breaches of the Treaties of
immense and formidable gravity; but when I asked my French
friends why this matter was not raised in the League of Nations,
and Germany invited, or even ultimately summoned, to explain
her action and state precisely what she was doing, I was
answered that the British Government would deprecate such
an alarming step. Thus, while Mr. MacDonald, with Mr.
Baldwin's full authority, preached disarmament to the French,
and practised it upon the British, the German might grew by
leaps and bounds, and the time for overt action approached.

In justice to the Conservative Party it must be mentioned
that at each of the Conferences of the National Union of

Conservative Associations from 1932 onwards, resolutions proposed by such worthies as Lord Lloyd and Sir Henry Croft in
favour of an immediate strengthening of our armaments to
meet the growing danger from abroad were carried almost
unanimously. But the parliamentary control by the Government Whips in the House of Commons was at this time so
effective, and the three parties in the Government, as well as
the Labour Opposition, so sunk in lethargy and blindness, that
the warnings of their followers in the country were as ineffective
as were the signs of the times and the evidence of the Secret
Service. This was one of those awful periods which recur in
our history, when the noble British nation seems to fall from
its high estate, loses all trace of sense or purpose, and appears to
cower from the menace of foreign peril, frothing pious platitudes while foemen forge their arms.

In this dark time the basest sentiments received acceptance
or passed unchallenged by the responsible leaders of the
political parties. In 1933, the students of the Oxford Union,
under the inspiration of a Mr. Joad, passed their ever-
shameful resolution, "That this House refuses to fight for King
and country." It was easy to laugh off such an episode in
England, but in Germany, in Russia, in Italy, in Japan, the
idea of a decadent, degenerate Britain took deep root and
swayed many calculations. Little did the foolish boys who
passed the resolution dream that they were destined quite soon
to conquer or fall gloriously in the ensuing war, and prove
themselves the finest generation ever bred in Britain. Less
excuse can be found for their elders, who had no chance of
self-repudiation in action.[3]

[3] I cannot resist telling this story. The Oxford Union invited me to address
them. I declined to do so, but said I would give them an hour to ask me
questions. One of the questions was, "Do you think Germany was guilty of
making the last war?" I said, "Yes, of course." A young German Rhodes
scholar rose from his place and said, "After this insult to my country I will not
remain here." He then stalked out amid roars of applause. I thought him a
spirited boy. Two years later it was found out in Germany that he had a
Jewish ancestor. This ended his career in Germany.

*   *   *   *   *

In November, 1933, we had another debate in the House of Commons. I returned to my main theme:

We read of large importations of scrap iron and nickel and war metals, quite out of the ordinary. We read all the news which accumulates of the military spirit which is rife throughout the country; we see that a philosophy of blood-lust is being inculcated into their youth to which no parallel can be found since the days of barbarism. We see all these forces on the move, and we must remember that this is the same mighty Germany which fought all the world and almost beat the world; it is the same mighty Germany which took two and a half lives for every German life that was taken.[4] No wonder, when you have these preparations, these doctrines, and these assertions openly made, that there is alarm throughout the whole circle of nations which surround Germany. . . .

*   *   *   *   *

While this fearful transformation in the relative war-power of victors and vanquished was taking place in Europe, a complete lack of concert between the non-aggressive and peace-loving states had also developed in the Far East. This story forms a counterpart to the disastrous turn of events in Europe, and arose from the same paralysis of thought and action among the leaders of the former and future Allies.

The economic blizzard of 1929 to 1931 had affected Japan not less than the rest of the world. Since 1914 her population had grown from fifty to seventy millions. Her metallurgical factories had increased from fifty to one hundred and forty-eight. The cost of living had risen steadily. The production of rice was stationary, and its importation expensive. The need for raw material and for external markets was clamant. In the violent depression Britain and forty other countries felt increasingly compelled, as the years passed, to apply restrictions or tariffs against Japanese goods produced under labour conditions unrelated to European or American standards. China was more than ever Japan's principal export market for cotton and other manufactures, and almost her sole source of coal and

4 This excluded the Russian losses.

iron. A new assertion of control over China became, therefore, the main theme of Japanese policy.

In September, 1931, on a pretext of local disorders, the Japanese occupied Mukden and the zone of the Manchurian Railway. In January, 1932, they demanded the dissolution of all Chinese associations of an anti-Japanese character. The Chinese Government refused, and on January 28, the Japanese landed to the north of the International Concession at Shanghai. The Chinese resisted with spirit, and, although without airplanes or anti-tank guns or any of the modern weapons, maintained their resistance for more than a month. At the end of February, after suffering very heavy losses, they were obliged to retire from their forts in the Bay of Wu-Sung, and took up positions about twelve miles inland. Early in 1932, the Japanese created the puppet State of Manchukuo. A year later, the Chinese province of Jehol was annexed to it, and in March, 1933, Japanese troops, penetrating deeply into defence-less regions, had reached the Great Wall of China. This aggressive action corresponded to the growth of Japanese power in the Far East and her new naval position on the oceans.

From the first shot the outrage committed upon China aroused the strongest hostility in the United States. But the policy of isolation cut both ways. Had the United States been a member of the League of Nations, she could undoubtedly have led that Assembly into collective action against Japan, of which the United States would herself have been the principal mandatory. The British Government on their part showed no desire to act with the United States alone; nor did they wish to be drawn into antagonism with Japan further than their obligations under the League of Nations Charter required. There was a rueful feeling in some British circles at the loss of the Japanese Alliance and the consequential weakening of the British position with all its long-established interests in the Far East. His Majesty's Government could hardly be blamed if, in their grave financial and growing European embarrassments, they did not seek a prominent rôle at the side of the United States in the Far East without any hope of corresponding American support in Europe.

China, however, was a member of the League, and although
she had not paid her subscription to that body, she appealed
to it for what was no more than justice. On September 30,
1931, the League called on Japan to remove her troops from
Manchuria. In December, a Commission was appointed to
conduct an inquiry on the spot. The League of Nations entrusted the chairmanship of the Commission to the Earl of
Lytton, the worthy descendant of a gifted line. He had had
many years' experience in the East as Governor of Bengal and
as Acting Viceroy of India. The Report, which was unanimous,
was a remarkable document, and forms the basis of any serious
study of the conflict between China and Japan. The whole
background of the Manchurian affair was carefully presented.
The conclusions drawn were plain: Manchukuo was the artificial creation of the Japanese General Staff, and the wishes of
the population had played no part in the formation of this
puppet state. Lord Lytton and his colleagues in their Report
not only analysed the situation, but put forward concrete proposals for an international solution. These were for the
declaration of an autonomous Manchuria. It would still remain
part of China, under the aegis of the League, and there would
be a comprehensive treaty between China and Japan regulating
their interests in Manchuria. The fact that the League could
not follow up these proposals in no way detracts from the value
of the Lytton Report. The American Secretary of State,
Stimson, wrote of the document: "It became at once and remains today the outstanding impartial authority upon the
subject which it covers." In February, 1933, the League of
Nations declared that the State of Manchukuo could not be
recognised. Although no sanctions were imposed upon Japan,
nor any other action taken, Japan, on March 27, 1933, withdrew from the League of Nations. Germany and Japan had
been on opposite sides in the war; they now looked towards
each other in a different mood. The moral authority of the
League was shown to be devoid of any physical support at a
time when its activity and strength were most needed.

*   *   *   *   *

We must regard as deeply blameworthy before history the conduct, not only of the British National and mainly Conservative Government, but of the Labour-Socialist and Liberal Parties, both in and out of office, during this fatal period. Delight in smooth-sounding platitudes, refusal to face unpleasant facts, desire for popularity and electoral success irrespective of the vital interests of the State, genuine love of peace and pathetic belief that love can be its sole foundation, obvious lack of intellectual vigour in both leaders of the British Coalition Government, marked ignorance of Europe and aversion from its problems in Mr. Baldwin, the strong and violent pacifism which at this time dominated the Labour-Socialist Party, the utter devotion of the Liberals to sentiment apart from reality, the failure and worse than failure of Mr. Lloyd George, the erstwhile great wartime leader, to address himself to the continuity of his work, the whole supported by overwhelming majorities in both Houses of Parliament: all these constituted a picture of British fatuity and fecklessness which, though devoid of guile, was not devoid of guilt, and, though free from wickedness or evil design, played a definite part in the unleashing upon the world of horrors and miseries which, even so far as they have unfolded, are already beyond comparison in human experience.

6

The Darkening Scene

1934

Spring Warnings — The German Blood Purge of June 30 — The End of Disarmament — The Murder of Doctor Dollfuss, July 25 — The Death of Hindenburg — Hitler Head of the German State, August 1 — The Italian Dilemma — The Murder of King Alexander and M. Barthou at Marseilles, October 9 — M. Laval, French Foreign Minister, November — Italian Abyssinian Clash at Wal-Wal, December — Franco-Italian Agreement, January 6, 1935 — The Saar Plebiscite, January 13, 1935.

HITLER'S ACCESSION to the Chancellorship in 1933 had not been regarded with enthusiasm in Rome. Nazism was viewed as a crude and brutalised version of the Fascist theme. The ambitions of a Greater Germany towards Austria and in Southeastern Europe were well known. Mussolini foresaw that in neither of these regions would Italian interests coincide with those of the new Germany. Nor had he long to wait for confirmation.

* * * * *

The acquisition of Austria by Germany was one of Hitler's most cherished ambitions. The first page of *Mein Kampf* contains the sentence, "German Austria must return to the great German Motherland." From the moment, therefore, of the acquisition of power in January, 1933, the Nazi German Government cast its eyes upon Vienna. Hitler could not afford as yet to clash with Mussolini, whose interest in Austria had been loudly proclaimed. Even infiltration and underground activities had to be applied with caution by a Germany as yet militarily weak. Pressure on Austria, however, began in the first few months. Unceasing demands were made on the Austrian Government to force members of the satellite Austrian Nazi Party both into the Cabinet and into key posts in the Administration. Austrian Nazis were trained in an Austrian legion organised in Bavaria. Bomb outrages on the railways and at tourist centres, German airplanes showering leaflets over Salzburg and Innsbruck, disturbed the daily life of the Republic. The Austrian Chancellor Dollfuss was equally opposed both by Socialist pressure within and external German designs against Austrian independence. Nor was this the only menace to the Austrian State. Following the evil example of their German neighbours, the Austrian Socialists had built up a private army, with which to override the decision of the ballot box. Both dangers loomed upon Dollfuss during 1933. The only quarter to which he could turn for protection and whence he had already received assurance of support was Fascist Italy. In August, 1933, Dollfuss met Mussolini at Riccione. A close personal and political understanding was reached between them. Dollfuss, who believed that Italy would hold the ring, felt strong enough to move against one set of his opponents — the Austrian Socialists.

In January, 1934, Suvich, Mussolini's principal adviser on foreign affairs, visited Vienna as a gesture of warning to Germany. On January 21, he made the following public statement:

The importance of Austria, due to her position in the heart of Central Europe and in the Danube Basin, far exceeds, as is well known, her territorial and numerical size. If she is to fulfil in the interests of all the mission accorded her by centuries-old tradition and geographical situation, the normal conditions of independence and peaceful life must first of all be secured. That is the standpoint which Italy has long maintained in regard to both political and economic conditions on the basis of unchangeable principles.

Three weeks later, the Dollfuss Government took action against the Socialist organisations of Vienna. The Heimwehr

under Major Fey, belonging to Dollfuss's own party, received
orders to disarm the equivalent and equally illegal body controlled by the Austrian Socialists. The latter resisted forcibly,
and on February 12 street fighting broke out in the capital.
Within a few hours the Socialist forces were broken. This
event not only brought Dollfuss closer to Italy, but strengthened him in the next stage of his task against the Nazi penetration and conspiracy. On the other hand, many of the defeated
Socialists or Communists swung over to the Nazi camp in their
bitterness. In Austria as in Germany the Catholic-Socialist feud
helped the Nazis.

*   *   *   *   *

Until the middle of 1934, the control of events was still
largely in the hands of His Majesty's Government without the
risk of war. They could at any time, in concert with France
and through the agency of the League of Nations, have brought
an overwhelming power to bear upon the Hitler Movement,
about which Germany was profoundly divided. This would
have involved no bloodshed. But this phase was passing. An
armed Germany under Nazi control was approaching the
threshold. And yet, incredible though it may seem, far into
this cardinal year Mr. MacDonald, armed with Mr. Baldwin's
political power, continued to work for the disarmament of
France. I cannot but quote the unavailing protest which I
made in Parliament on February 7:

What happens, for instance, if, after we have equalised and
reduced the army of France to the level of that of Germany, and
got an equality for Germany, and with all the reactions which
will have followed in the sentiment of Europe upon such a change,
Germany then proceeds to say, "How can you keep a great nation
of seventy millions in a position in which it is not entitled to have
a navy equal to the greatest of the fleets upon the seas?" You will
say, "No; we do not agree. Armies — they belong to other people.
Navies — that question affects Britain's interests and we are bound
to say, 'No.' " But what position shall we be in to say that "No"?

Wars come very suddenly. I have lived through a period when
one looked forward, as we do now, with great anxiety and uncer-

tainty to what would happen in the future. Suddenly something
did happen — tremendous, swift, overpowering, irresistible. Let me
remind the House of the sort of thing that happened in 1914. There
was absolutely no quarrel between Germany and France. One July
afternoon the German Ambassador drove down to the Quai d'Orsay
and said to the French Prime Minister: "We have been forced to
mobilise against Russia, and war will be declared. What is to be
the position of France?" The French Premier made the answer
which his Cabinet had agreed upon, that France would act in
accordance with what she considered to be her own interests. The
Ambassador said, "You have an alliance with Russia, have you not?"
"Quite so," said the French Premier. And that was the process by
which, in a few minutes, the area of the struggle, already serious
in the East, was enormously widened and multiplied by the
throwing-in of the two great nations of the West on either side. But
sometimes even a declaration of neutrality does not suffice. On
this very occasion, as we now know, the German Ambassador was
authorised by his Government, in case the French did not do their
duty by their Russian ally, in case they showed any disposition to
back out of the conflict which had been resolved on by Germany,
to demand that the fortresses of Toul and Verdun should be handed
over to German troops as a guarantee that the French, having
declared neutrality, would not change their mind at a subsequent
moment. . . .

We may ourselves, in the lifetime of those who are here, if we are
not in a proper state of security, be confronted on some occasion
with a visit from an Ambassador, and may have to give an answer,
and if that answer is not satisfactory, within the next few hours
the crash of bombs exploding in London and the cataracts of
masonry and fire and smoke will warn us of any inadequacy which
has been permitted in our aerial defences. We are vulnerable as we
have never been before. I have often heard criticisms of the Liberal
Government before the war. . . . A far graver case rests upon those
who now hold power if, by any chance, against our wishes and
against our hopes, trouble should come.

Not one of the lessons of the past has been learned, not one of
them has been applied, and the situation is incomparably more
dangerous. Then we had the Navy and no air menace. Then the
Navy was the "sure shield" of Britain. . . . We cannot say that now.
This cursed, hellish invention and development of war from the

air has revolutionised our position. We are not the same kind of country we used to be when we were an island, only twenty years ago.

I then asked for three definite decisions to be taken without delay. For the Army: the reorganisation of our civil factories, so that they could be turned over rapidly to war purposes, should be begun in Britain, as all over Europe. For the Navy we should regain freedom of design. We should get rid of this London Treaty which had crippled us in building the kind of ships we wanted, and had stopped the United States from building a great battleship which she probably needed, and to which we should not have had the slightest reason to object. We should be helped in doing this by the fact that another of the parties to the Treaty [1] was resolved to regain her freedom too. Thirdly, the air. We ought to have an air force as strong as the air force of France or Germany, whichever was the stronger. The Government commanded overwhelming majorities in both branches of the Legislature, and nothing would be denied to them. They had only to make their proposals with confidence and conviction for the safety of the country, and their countrymen would sustain them.

*   *   *   *   *

There was at this moment a flicker of European unity against the German menace. On February 17, 1934, the British, French, and Italian Governments made a common declaration upon the maintenance of Austrian independence. On March 14, I spoke again in Parliament:

The awful danger of our present foreign policy is that we go on perpetually asking the French to weaken themselves. And what do we say is the inducement? We say, "Weaken yourselves," and we always hold out the hope that if they do it and get into trouble, we will then in some way or other go to their aid, although we have nothing with which to go to their aid. I cannot imagine a more dangerous policy. There is something to be said for isolation; there is something to be said for alliances. But there is nothing to be said

[1] Japan.

for weakening the Power on the Continent with whom you would
be in alliance, and then involving yourself more [deeply] in Continental tangles in order to make it up to them. In that way you
have neither the one thing nor the other; you have the worst of
both worlds.

The Romans had a maxim, "Shorten your weapons and lengthen
your frontiers." But our maxim seems to be, "Diminish your
weapons and increase your obligations." Aye, and diminish the
weapons of your friends.

* * * * *

Italy now made a final attempt to carry out the aforesaid
Roman maxim. On March 17, Italy, Hungary, and Austria
signed the so-called Rome Protocols, providing for mutual consultation in the event of a threat to any of the three parties. But
Hitler was growing steadily stronger, and in May and June
subversive activities increased throughout Austria. Dollfuss
immediately sent reports on these terrorist acts to Suvich with
a note deploring their depressive effect upon Austrian trade
and tourists.

It was with this dossier in his hand that Mussolini went to
Venice on June 14 to meet Hitler for the first time. The
German Chancellor stepped from his airplane in a brown
mackintosh and Homburg hat into an array of sparkling Fascist
uniforms, with a resplendent and portly Duce at their head.
As Mussolini caught sight of his guest, he murmured to his aide,
"Non mi piace." ("I don't like the look of him.") At this
strange meeting, only a general exchange of ideas took place,
with mutual lectures upon the virtues of dictatorship on the
German and Italian models. Mussolini was clearly perplexed
both by the personality and language of his guest. He summed
up his final impression in these words, "A garrulous monk."
He did, however, extract some assurances of relaxation of
German pressure upon Dollfuss. Ciano told the journalists
after the meeting, "You'll see. Nothing more will happen."

But the pause in German activities which followed was due
not to Mussolini's appeal, but to Hitler's own internal preoccupations.

* * * * *

The acquisition of power had opened a deep divergence between the Fuehrer and many of those who had borne him forward. Under Roehm's leadership the S.A. increasingly represented the more revolutionary elements of the party. There were senior members of the party, such as Gregor Strasser, ardent for social revolution, who feared that Hitler in arriving at the first place would simply be taken over by the existing hierarchy, the Reichswehr, the bankers, and the industrialists. He would not have been the first revolutionary leader to kick down the ladder by which he had risen to exalted heights. To the rank and file of the S.A. (Brown Shirts) the triumph of January, 1933, was meant to carry with it the freedom to pillage, not only the Jews and profiteers, but also the well-to-do, established classes of society. Rumours of a great betrayal by their Leader soon began to spread in certain circles of the party. Chief-of-Staff Roehm acted on this impulse with energy. In January, 1933, the S.A. had been four hundred thousand strong. By the spring of 1934, he had recruited and organised nearly three million men. Hitler in his new situation was uneasy at the growth of this mammoth machine, which, while professing fervent loyalty to his name, and being for the most part deeply attached to him, was beginning to slip from his own personal control. Hitherto he had possessed a private army. Now he had the national army. He did not intend to exchange the one for the other. He wanted both, and to use each, as events required, to control the other. He had now, therefore, to deal with Roehm. "I am resolved," he declared to the leaders of the S.A. in these days, "to repress severely any attempt to overturn the existing order. I will oppose with the sternest energy a second revolutionary wave, for it would bring with it inevitable chaos. Whoever raises his head against the established authority of the State will be severely treated, whatever his position."

In spite of his misgivings Hitler was not easily convinced of the disloyalty of his comrade of the Munich *Putsch,* who, for the last seven years, had been the Chief of Staff of his Brown Shirt Army. When, in December, 1933, the unity of the party with the State had been proclaimed, Roehm became a member of the German Cabinet. One of the consequences of the union of the party with the State was to be the merging of the Brown Shirts with the Reichswehr. The rapid progress of national rearmament forced the issue of the status and control of all the German armed forces into the forefront of politics. In February, 1934, Mr. Eden arrived in Berlin, and in the course of conversation, Hitler agreed provisionally to give certain assurances about the non-military character of the S.A. Roehm was already in constant friction with General von Blomberg, the Chief of the General Staff. He now feared the sacrifice of the party army he had taken so many years to build, and in spite of warnings of the gravity of his conduct, he published on April 18 an unmistakable challenge:

The Revolution we have made is not a national revolution, but a National-*Socialist* Revolution. We would even underline this last word, "Socialist." The only rampart which exists against reaction is represented by our assault groups, for they are the absolute incarnation of the revolutionary idea. The militant in the Brown Shirt from the first day pledged himself to the path of revolution, and he will not deviate by a hairbreadth until our ultimate goal has been achieved.

He omitted, on this occasion, the "Heil Hitler!" which had been the invariable conclusion of Brown Shirt harangues.

During the course of April and May, Blomberg continually complained to Hitler about the insolence and activities of the S.A. The Fuehrer had to choose between the generals who hated him and the Brown Shirt thugs to whom he owed so much. He chose the generals. At the beginning of June, Hitler, in a five-hour conversation, made a last effort to conciliate and come to terms with Roehm. But with this abnormal fanatic, devoured by ambition, no compromise was possible. The mystic hierarchic Greater Germany, of which Hitler dreamed, and the Proletarian Republic of the People's Army, desired by Roehm, were separated by an impassable gulf.

Within the framework of the Brown Shirts, there had been formed a small and highly trained élite, wearing black uniforms

and known as the S.S., or later as Black Shirts. These units
were intended for the personal protection of the Fuehrer and
for special and confidential tasks. They were commanded by
an ex-unsuccessful poultry farmer, Heinrich Himmler. Fore-
seeing the impending clash between Hitler and the Army on
the one hand, and Roehm and the Brown Shirts on the other,
Himmler took care to carry the S.S. into Hitler's camp. On the
other hand, Roehm had supporters of great influence within
the party, who, like Gregor Strasser, saw their ferocious plans
for social revolution being cast aside. The Reichswehr also had
its rebels. Ex-Chancellor von Schleicher had never forgiven his
disgrace in January, 1933, and the failure of the Army Chiefs
to choose him as successor to Hindenburg. In a clash between
Roehm and Hitler, Schleicher saw an opportunity. He was imprudent enough to drop hints to the French Ambassador in
Berlin that the fall of Hitler was not far off. This repeated the
action he had taken in the case of Bruening. But the times had
become more dangerous.

It will long be disputed in Germany whether Hitler was
forced to strike by the imminence of the Roehm plot, or
whether he and the generals, fearing what might be coming,
resolved on a clean-cut liquidation while they had the power.
Hitler's interest and that of the victorious faction was plainly
to establish the case for a plot. It is improbable that Roehm
and the Brown Shirts had actually got as far as this. They were
a menacing movement rather than a plot, but at any moment
this line might have been crossed. It is certain they were
drawing up their forces. It is also certain they were forestalled.

Events now moved rapidly. On June 25, the Reichswehr
was confined to barracks, and ammunition was issued to the
Black Shirts. On the opposite side the Brown Shirts were
ordered to stand in readiness, and Roehm with Hitler's consent
called a meeting for June 30 of all their senior leaders to
meet at Wiessee in the Bavarian Lakes. Hitler received warning of grave danger on the twenty-ninth. He flew to Godesberg,
where he was joined by Goebbels who brought alarming news
of impending mutiny in Berlin. According to Goebbels,

Roehm's adjutant, Karl Ernst, had been given orders to attempt a rising. This seems unlikely. Ernst was actually at Bremen, about to embark from that port on his honeymoon.

On this information, true or false, Hitler took instant decisions. He ordered Goering to take control in Berlin. He boarded his airplane for Munich, resolved to arrest his main opponents personally. In this life-or-death climax, as it had now become, he showed himself a terrible personality. Plunged in dark thought, he sat in the co-pilot's seat throughout the journey. The plane landed at an airfield near Munich at four o'clock in the morning of June 30. Hitler had with him, besides Goebbels, about a dozen of his personal bodyguard. He drove to the Brown House in Munich, summoned the leaders of the local S.A. to his presence, and placed them under arrest. At six o'clock, with Goebbels and his small escort only, he motored to Wiessee.

Roehm was ill in the summer of 1934 and had gone to Wiessee to take a cure. The establishment he had selected was a small châlet belonging to the doctor in charge of his case. No worse headquarters could have been chosen from which to organise an immediate revolt. The châlet stands at the end of a narrow cul-de-sac lane. All arrivals and departures could be easily noted. There was no room large enough to hold the alleged impending meeting of Brown Shirt leaders. There was only one telephone. This ill accords with the theory of an imminent uprising. If Roehm and his followers were about to revolt, they were certainly careless.

At seven o'clock the Fuehrer's procession of cars arrived in front of Roehm's châlet. Alone and unarmed Hitler mounted the stairs and entered Roehm's bedroom. What passed between the two men will never be known. Roehm was taken completely by surprise, and he and his personal staff were arrested without incident. The small party, with its prisoners, now left by road for Munich. It happened that they soon met a column of lorries of armed Brown Shirts on their way to acclaim Roehm at the conference convened at Wiessee for noon. Hitler stepped out of his car, called for the commanding officer, and, with confident authority, ordered him to take his men home. He was instantly obeyed. If he had been an hour later, or they had been an hour earlier, great events would have taken a different course.

On arrival at Munich, Roehm and his entourage were imprisoned in the same gaol where he and Hitler had been confined together ten years before. That afternoon the executions began. A revolver was placed in Roehm's cell, but, as he disdained the invitation, the cell door was opened within a few minutes, and he was riddled with bullets. All the afternoon the executions proceeded in Munich at brief intervals. The firing parties of eight had to be relieved from time to time on account of the mental stress of the soldiers. But for several hours the recurrent volleys were heard every ten minutes or so.

Meanwhile, in Berlin, Goering, having heard from Hitler, followed a similar procedure. But here, in the capital, the killings spread beyond the hierarchy of the S.A. Schleicher and his wife, who threw herself in front of him, were shot in their house. Gregor Strasser was arrested and put to death. Papen's private secretary and immediate circle were also shot; but for some unknown reason he himself was spared. In the Lichtefelde Barracks in Berlin, Karl Ernst, clawed back from Bremen, met his fate; and here, as in Munich, the volleys of the executioners were heard all day. Throughout Germany, during these twenty-four hours, many men unconnected with the Roehm plot disappeared as the victims of private vengeance, sometimes for very old scores. Otto von Kahr, for instance, who as head of the Bavarian Government had broken the 1923 *Putsch,* was found dead in the woods near Munich. The total number of persons "liquidated" is variously estimated as between five and seven thousand.

Late in the afternoon of this bloody day, Hitler returned by air to Berlin. It was time to put an end to the slaughter, which was spreading every moment. That evening a certain number of the S.S., who through excess of zeal had gone a little far in shooting prisoners, were themselves led out to execution. About one o'clock in the morning of July 1, the sounds of firing ceased.

Later in the day the Fuehrer appeared on the balcony of the Chancellery to receive the acclamations of the Berlin crowds, many of whom thought that he had himself been the victim. Some say he looked haggard, others triumphant. He may well have been both. His promptitude and ruthlessness had saved his purpose and no doubt his life. In that "Night of the Long Knives," as it was called, the unity of National-Socialist Germany had been preserved to carry its curse throughout the world.

A fortnight later the Fuehrer addressed the Reichstag, who sat in loyalty or awe before him. In the course of two hours he delivered a reasoned defence of his action. The speech reveals his knowledge of the German mind and his own undoubted powers of argument. Its climax was:

The necessity for acting with lightning speed meant that in this decisive hour I had very few men with me. . . . Although only a few days before I had been prepared to exercise clemency, at this hour there was no place for any such consideration. Mutinies are suppressed in accordance with laws of iron which are eternally the same. If anyone reproaches me and asks why I did not resort to the regular courts of justice for conviction of the offenders, then all that I can say to him is this: In this hour I was responsible for the fate of the German people, and thereby I became the Supreme Justiciar of the German people. . . . I did not wish to deliver up the Young Reich to the fate of the Old Reich. I gave the order to shoot those who were the ringleaders in this treason. . . .

Then followed this mixed but expressive metaphor:

And I further gave the order to burn out down to the raw flesh the ulcers of this poisoning of the wells in our domestic life, and of the poisoning of the outside world.

This massacre, however explicable by the hideous forces at work, showed that the new Master of Germany would stop at nothing, and that conditions in Germany bore no resemblance to those of a civilised state. A dictatorship based upon terror and reeking with blood had confronted the world. Anti-Semitism was ferocious and brazen, and the concentration-camp

system was already in full operation for all obnoxious or politically dissident classes. I was deeply affected by the episode,
and the whole process of German rearmament, of which there
was now overwhelming evidence, seemed to me invested with a
ruthless, lurid tinge. It glittered and it glared.

*   *   *   *   *

We may now return for a moment to the House of Commons.
In the course of June, 1934, the Standing Committee of the
Disarmament Conference at Geneva was adjourned indef-
initely. On July 13, I said:

I am very glad that the Disarmament Conference is passing out
of life into history. It is the greatest mistake to mix up disarmament
with peace. When you have peace you will have disarmament. But
there has been during these recent years a steady deterioration in
the relations between different countries, a steady growth of ill-will,
and a steady, indeed a rapid increase in armaments that has gone
on through all these years in spite of the endless flow of oratory, of
perorations, of well-meaning sentiments, of banquets, which have
marked this epoch.

Europe will be secure when nations no longer feel themselves in
great danger, as many of them do now. Then the pressure and the
burden of armaments will fall away automatically, as they ought to
have done in a long peace; and it might be quite easy to seal a
movement of that character by some general agreement. I hope,
indeed, that we have now also reached the end of the period of the
Government pressing France — this peaceful France with no militarism — to weaken her armed forces. I rejoice that the French have
not taken the advice which has been offered to them so freely from
various quarters, and which the leader of the Opposition [Mr.
Lansbury] no doubt would strongly endorse.

This is not the only Germany which we shall live to see, but we
have to consider that at present two or three men, in what may
well be a desperate position, have the whole of that mighty country
in their grip, have that wonderful scientific, intelligent, docile,
valiant people in their grip, a population of seventy millions; that
there is no dynastic interest such as the monarchy bring as a
restraint upon policy, because it looks long ahead and has much

to lose; and that there is no public opinion except what is manufactured by those new and terrible engines — broadcasting and a
controlled press. Politics in Germany are not as they are over here.
There, you do not leave office to go into Opposition. You do not
leave the Front Bench to sit below the Gangway. You may well
leave your high office at a quarter of an hour's notice to drive to
the police station, and you may be conducted thereafter very rapidly
to an even graver ordeal.

It seems to me that men in that position might very easily be
tempted to do what even a military dictatorship would not do,
because a military dictatorship, with all its many faults, at any rate
is one that is based on a very accurate study of the real facts; and
there is more danger in this kind of dictatorship than there would
be in a military dictatorship, because you have men who, to relieve
themselves from the great peril which confronts them at home,
might easily plunge into a foreign adventure of the most dangerous
and catastrophic character to the whole world.

*   *   *   *   *

The first temptation to such an adventure was soon to be
revealed.

During the early part of July, 1934, there was much coming
and going over the mountain paths leading from Bavaria into
Austrian territory. At the end of July, a German courier fell
into the hands of the Austrian frontier police. He carried documents, including cipher keys, which showed that a complete
plan of revolt was reaching fruition. The organiser of the
coup d'état was to be Anton von Rintelen, at that time Austrian
Minister to Italy. Dollfuss and his Ministers were slow to
respond to the warnings of an impending crisis and to the signs
of imminent revolt which became apparent in the early hours
of July 25. The Nazi adherents in Vienna mobilised during the
morning. Just before one o'clock in the afternoon, a party of
armed rebels entered the Chancellery, and Dollfuss, hit by two
revolver bullets, was left to bleed slowly to death. Another
detachment of Nazis seized the broadcasting station and announced the resignation of the Dollfuss Government and the
assumption of office by Rintelen.

But the other members of the Dollfuss Cabinet reacted with firmness and energy. President Doctor Miklas issued a formal command to restore order at all costs. The Minister of Justice, Doctor Schuschnigg, assumed the Administration. The majority of the Austrian Army and police rallied to his Government, and besieged the Chancellery building where, surrounded by a small party of rebels, Dollfuss was dying. The revolt had also broken out in the provinces, and parties from the Austrian legion in Bavaria crossed the frontier. Mussolini had by now heard the news. He telegraphed at once to Prince Starhemberg, the head of the Austrian Heimwehr, promising Italian support for Austrian independence. Flying specially to Venice, the Duce received the widow of Doctor Dollfuss with every circumstance of sympathy. At the same time three Italian divisions were dispatched to the Brenner Pass. On this Hitler, who knew the limits of his strength, recoiled. The German Minister in Vienna, Rieth, and other German officials implicated in the rising, were recalled or dismissed. The attempt had failed. A longer process was needed. Papen, newly spared from the blood-bath, was appointed as German Minister to Vienna, with instructions to work by more subtle means.

Papen had been appointed German Minister to Vienna for the explicit purpose of organising the overthrow of the Austrian Republic. He had a double task: the encouragement of the underground Austrian Nazi Party, which received henceforth a monthly subsidy of two hundred thousand marks, and the undermining or winning over of leading personalities in Austrian politics. In the early days of his appointment, he expressed himself with frankness verging upon indiscretion to his American colleague in Vienna.

In the boldest and most cynical manner [says the American Minister] Papen proceeded to tell me that all Southeastern Europe to the borders of Turkey was Germany's natural hinterland, and that he had been charged with the mission of effecting German economic and political control over the whole of this region. He blandly and directly said that getting control of Austria was to be the first step. He intended to use his reputation as a good Catholic to gain influence with Austrians like Cardinal Innitzer. The German Government was determined to gain control of Southeastern Europe. There was nothing to stop them. The policy of the United States, like that of France and England, was not "realistic."

Amid these tragedies and alarms, the aged Marshal Hindenburg, who had, for some months, been almost completely senile and so more than ever a tool of the Reichswehr, expired. Hitler became the head of the German State while retaining the office of Chancellor. He was now the Sovereign of Germany. His bargain with the Reichswehr had been sealed and kept by the blood-purge. The Brown Shirts had been reduced to obedience and reaffirmed their loyalty to the Fuehrer. All foes and potential rivals had been extirpated from their ranks. Henceforward they lost their influence and became a kind of special constabulary for ceremonial occasions. The Black Shirts, on the other hand, increased in numbers and strengthened by privileges and discipline, became under Himmler a Praetorian Guard for the person of the Fuehrer, a counterpoise to the Army leaders and military caste, and also political troops to arm with considerable military force the activities of the expanding secret police or Gestapo. It was only necessary to invest these powers with the formal sanction of a managed plebiscite to make Hitler's dictatorship absolute and perfect.

* * * * *

Events in Austria drew France and Italy together, and the shock of the Dolfuss assassination led to General Staff contacts. The menace to Austrian independence promoted a revision of Franco-Italian relations, and this had to comprise not only the balance of power in the Mediterranean and North Africa, but the relative positions of France and Italy in Southeastern Europe. But Mussolini was anxious, not only to safeguard Italy's position in Europe against the potential German threat, but also to secure her imperial future in Africa. Against Germany, close relations with France and Great Britain would be useful; but in the Mediterranean and Africa, disagreements with both these Powers might be inevitable. The Duce wondered whether

the common need for security felt by Italy, France, and Great
Britain might not induce the two former allies of Italy to accept
the Italian imperialist programme in Africa. At any rate, this
seemed a hopeful course for Italian policy.

*   *   *   *   *

In France, after the Stavisky scandal and the riots of
February, M. Daladier had been succeeded as Premier by a
Government of the Right Centre under M. Doumergue with
M. Barthou as Foreign Minister. Ever since the signature of
the Locarno Treaties, France had been anxious to reach formal
agreement on security measures in the East. British reluctance
to undertake commitments beyond the Rhine, the German
refusal to make binding agreements with Poland and Czechoslovakia, the fears of the Little Entente as to Russian intentions,
Russian suspicion of the capitalist West, all united to thwart
such a programme. In September, 1934, however, Louis
Barthou determined to go forward. His original plan was to
propose an Eastern Pact, grouping together Germany, Russia,
Poland, Czechoslovakia, and the Baltic States on the basis of a
guarantee by France of the European frontiers of Russia, and
by Russia of the eastern borders of Germany. Both Germany
and Poland were opposed to an Eastern Pact; but Barthou succeeded in obtaining the entry of Russia into the League of
Nations on September 18, 1934. This was an important step.
Litvinov, who represented the Soviet Government, was versed
in every aspect of foreign affairs. He adapted himself to the
atmosphere of the League of Nations and spoke its moral
language with so much success that he soon became an outstanding figure.

In her search for allies against the new Germany that had
been allowed to grow up, it was natural that France should
turn her eyes to Russia and try to re-create the balance of
power which had existed before the war. But in October a
tragedy occurred. In pursuance of French policy in the Balkans,
King Alexander of Yugoslavia had been invited to pay an
official visit to Paris. He landed at Marseilles, was met by

M. Barthou, and drove with him and General Georges through the welcoming crowds who thronged the streets gay with flags and flowers. Once again from the dark recesses of the Serbian and Croat underworld a hideous murder plot sprang upon the European stage, and, as at Sarajevo in 1914, a band of assassins, ready to give their lives, were at hand. The French police arrangements were loose and casual. A figure darted from the cheering crowds, mounted the running-board of the car, and discharged his automatic pistol into the King and its other occupants, all of whom were stricken. The murderer was immediately cut down and killed by the mounted Republican guardsman behind whom he had slipped. A scene of wild confusion occurred. King Alexander expired almost immediately. General Georges and M. Barthou stepped out of the car streaming with blood. The General was too weak to move, but soon received medical aid. The Minister wandered off in the crowd. It was twenty minutes before he received attention. He was made to walk upstairs to the Prefect's office before he could receive medical attention; the doctor then applied the tourniquet *below* the wound. He had already lost much blood: he was seventy-two, and he died in a few hours. This was a heavy blow to French foreign policy, which under him was beginning to take a coherent form. He was succeeded as Foreign Secretary by Pierre Laval.

Laval's later shameful record and fate must not obscure the fact of his personal force and capacity. He had a clear and intense view. He believed that France must at all costs avoid war, and he hoped to secure this by arrangements with the dictators of Italy and Germany, against whose systems he entertained no prejudice. He distrusted Soviet Russia. Despite his occasional protestations of friendship, he disliked England and thought her a worthless ally. At that time, indeed, British repute did not stand very high in France. Laval's first object was to reach a definite understanding with Italy, and he deemed the moment ripe. The French Government was obsessed by the German danger, and was prepared to make solid concessions to gain Italy. In January, 1935, M. Laval went to

Rome and signed a series of agreements with the object of
removing the main obstacles between the two countries. Both
Governments were united upon the illegality of German rearmament. They agreed to consult each other in the event of
future threats to the independence of Austria. In the colonial
sphere France undertook to make administrative concessions
about the status of Italians in Tunisia, and handed over to
Italy certain tracts of territory on the borders both of Libya
and of Somaliland, together with a twenty per cent share in
the Jibuti-Addis-Ababa Railway. These conversations were
designed to lay the foundations for more formal discussions
between France, Italy, and Great Britain about a common front
against the growing German menace. Across them all there
cut in the ensuing months the fact of Italian aggression in
Abyssinia.

*   *   *   *   *

In December, 1934, a clash took place between Italian and
Abyssinian soldiers at the wells of Wal-Wal on the borders of
Abyssinia and Italian Somaliland. This was to be the pretext
for the ultimate presentation before the world of Italian claims
upon the Ethiopian Kingdom. Thus the problem of containing Germany in Europe was henceforth confused and distorted
by the fate of Abyssinia.

*   *   *   *   *

There is one more incident at this juncture which should
be mentioned. Under the terms of the Treaty of Versailles, the
Saar Valley, a small strip of German territory, possessing rich
coal mines and important iron works, was to decide at the end
of fifteen years by a plebiscite whether the population wished
to return to Germany or not. The date fixed for this event
was in January, 1935. There could be no doubt of the outcome.
The majority would certainly vote for reincorporation into
the German Fatherland; and to make assurance doubly sure,
the Valley, though nominally governed by a League of Nations
Commission, was in fact under the control of the local Nazi
Party centre. Barthou realised that ultimately the Saar was

bound to return to Germany, but was inclined to insist upon some guarantees to those who might vote against immediate incorporation with Germany. His assassination changed the tone of the French policy. On December 3, 1934, Laval made a direct bargain with the Germans over the coal mines, and three days later announced publicly before the League Council that France would not oppose the return of the Saar to Germany. The actual plebiscite was held on January 13, 1935, under international supervision, in which a British brigade took part; and this little enclave, except Danzig, the only territorial embodiment of League sovereignty, voted by 90.3 per cent for return to Germany. This moral triumph for National Socialism, although the result of a normal and inevitable procedure, added to Hitler's prestige, and seemed to crown his authority with an honest sample of the will of the German people. He was not at all conciliated, still less impressed, by the proof of the League's impartiality or fair play. No doubt it confirmed his view that the Allies were decadent fools. For his own part he proceeded to concentrate on his main objective, the expansion of the German forces.

7

Air Parity Lost

1934–1935

The German Short Cut — The East Fulham Election, October 25, 1933 — Debate of February 7, 1934 — Mr. Baldwin's Pledge of Air Parity — The Labour Vote of Censure Against Air Increases — Liberal Hostility — My Precise Warning, November 28, 1934 — Mr. Baldwin's Contradiction — Hitler Claims Germany Has Air Parity, March, 1935 — Mr. MacDonald's Alarm — Mr. Baldwin's Confession, May 22 — The Labour and Liberal Attitudes — The Air Ministry View — Lord Londonderry Presently Succeeded by Sir Philip Cunliffe-Lister.

THE GERMAN GENERAL STAFF did not believe that the German Army could be formed and matured on a scale greater than that of France, and suitably provided with arsenals and equipment, before 1943. The German Navy, except for U-boats, could not be rebuilt in its old state under twelve or fifteen years, and in the process would compete heavily with all other plans. But owing to the unlucky discovery by an immature civilisation of the internal-combustion engine and the art of flying, a new weapon of national rivalry had leapt upon the scene capable of altering much more rapidly the relative war power of states. Granted a share in the ever-accumulating knowledge of mankind and in the march of Science, only four or five years might be required by a nation of the first magnitude, devoting itself to the task, to create a powerful, and perhaps a supreme, air force. This period would, of course, be shortened by any preliminary work and thought.

As in the case of the German Army, the re-creation of the German air power was long and carefully prepared in secret. As early as 1923, Seeckt had decided that the future German air force must be a part of the German war machine. For the time being he was content to build inside the "air-forceless army" a well-articulated air-force skeleton which could not be discerned, or at any rate was not discerned in its early years, from without. Air power is the most difficult of all forms of military force to measure, or even to express in precise terms. The extent to which the factories and training-grounds of civil aviation have acquired a military value and significance at any given moment cannot easily be judged and still less exactly defined. The opportunities for concealment, camouflage, and treaty evasion are numerous and varied. The air, and the air alone, offered Hitler the chance of a short cut, first to equality and next to predominance in a vital military arm over France and Britain. But what would France and Britain do?

By the autumn of 1933, it was plain that neither by precept nor still less by example would the British effort for disarmament succeed. The pacifism of the Labour and Liberal Parties was not affected even by the grave event of the German withdrawal from the League of Nations. Both continued in the name of peace to urge British disarmament, and anyone who differed was called "warmonger" and "scaremonger." It appeared that their feeling was endorsed by the people, who, of course, did not understand what was unfolding. At a by-election which occurred in East Fulham on October 25, a wave of pacifist emotion increased the Socialist vote by nearly nine thousand, and the Conservative vote fell by over ten thousand. The successful candidate, Mr. Wilmot, said after the poll that "British people demand . . . that the British Government shall give a lead to the whole world by initiating immediately a policy of general disarmament." And Mr. Lansbury, then leader of the Labour Party, said that all nations must "disarm to the level of Germany as a preliminary to total disarmament." This election left a deep impression upon Mr. Baldwin, and he referred to it in a remarkable speech three years later. In

November came the Reichstag election, at which no candidates except those endorsed by Hitler were tolerated, and the Nazis obtained ninety-five per cent of the votes polled.

It would be wrong in judging the policy of the British Government not to remember the passionate desire for peace which animated the uninformed, misinformed majority of the British people, and seemed to threaten with political extinction any party or politician who dared to take any other line. This, of course, is no excuse for political leaders who fall short of their duty. It is much better for parties or politicians to be turned out of office than to imperil the life of the nation. Moreover, there is no record in our history of any Government asking Parliament and the people for the necessary measures of defence and being refused. Nevertheless, those who scared the timid MacDonald-Baldwin Government from their path should at least keep silent.

The air estimates of March, 1934, totalled only twenty millions, and contained provision for four new squadrons, or an increase in our first-line air strength from 850 to 890. The financial cost involved in the first year was £130,000.

On this I said:

We are, it is admitted, the fifth air Power only — if that. We are but half the strength of France, our nearest neighbour. Germany is arming fast and no one is going to stop her. That seems quite clear. No one proposes a preventive war to stop Germany breaking the Treaty of Versailles. She is going to arm; she is doing it; she has been doing it. I have no knowledge of the details, but it is well known that those very gifted people, with their science and with their factories — with what they call their "Air-Sport" — are capable of developing with great rapidity the most powerful air force for all purposes, offensive and defensive, within a very short period of time.

I dread the day when the means of threatening the heart of the British Empire should pass into the hands of the present rulers of Germany. We should be in a position which would be odious to every man who values freedom of action and independence, and also in a position of the utmost peril for our crowded, peaceful population engaged in their daily toil. I dread that day, but it is not perhaps far distant. It is perhaps only a year, or perhaps eighteen months distant. It has not come yet — at least so I believe or I hope and pray; but it is not far distant. There is time for us to take the necessary measures, but it is the measures we want. We want the measures to achieve parity. No nation playing the part we play and aspire to play in the world has a right to be in a position where it can be blackmailed. . . .

None of the grievances between the victors and the vanquished have been redressed. The spirit of aggressive Nationalism was never more rife in Europe and in the world. Far away are the days of Locarno, when we nourished bright hopes of the reunion of the European family. . . .

I called upon Mr. Baldwin as the man who possessed the power for action. His was the power, and his the responsibility.

In the course of his reply Mr. Baldwin said:

If all our efforts for an agreement fail, and if it is not possible to obtain this equality in such matters as I have indicated, then any Government of this country — a National Government more than any, and *this* Government — will see to it that in air strength and air power this country shall no longer be in a position inferior to any country within striking distance of its shores.

Here was a most solemn and definite pledge, given at a time when it could almost certainly have been made good by vigorous action on a large scale.

*   *   *   *   *

Although Germany had not yet openly violated the clauses of the Treaty which forbade her a military air force, civil aviation and an immense development of gliding had now reached a point where they could very rapidly reinforce and extend the secret and illegal military air force already formed. The blatant denunciations of Communism and Bolshevism by Hitler had not prevented the clandestine sending by Germany of arms to Russia. On the other hand, from 1927 onwards a number of German pilots were trained by the Soviets for military purposes. There were fluctuations, but in 1932 the British Ambassador in Berlin reported that the Reichswehr had

close technical liaison with the Red Army. Just as the Fascist
Dictator of Italy had, almost from his accession to power, been
the first to make a trade agreement with Soviet Russia, so now
the relations between Nazi Germany and the vast Soviet State
appeared to be unprejudiced by public ideological controversy.

*   *   *   *   *

Nevertheless, when on July 20, 1934, the Government
brought forward some belated and inadequate proposals for
strengthening the Royal Air Force by forty-one squadrons or
about 820 machines *only to be completed in five years,* the
Labour Party, supported by the Liberals, moved a vote of
censure upon them in the House of Commons.

The motion regretted that

His Majesty's Government should enter upon a policy of rearmament neither necessitated by any new commitment nor calculated
to add to the security of the nation, but certain to jeopardise the
prospects of international disarmament and to encourage a revival
of dangerous and wasteful competition in preparation for war.

In support of this complete refusal by the Opposition to take
any measures to strengthen our air power, Mr. Attlee, speaking
in their name, said: "We deny the need for increased air
armaments. . . . We deny the proposition that an increased
British air force will make for the peace of the world, and we
reject altogether the claim to parity." The Liberal Party supported this censure motion, although they would have preferred their own, which ran as follows:

That this House views with grave concern the tendency among
the nations of the world to resume the competitive race of armaments which has always proved a precursor of war; it will not
approve any expansion of our own armaments unless it is clear
that the Disarmament Conference has failed and unless a definite
case is established; and these conditions not being present as regards
the proposed additional expenditure of £20,000,000 upon air
armaments, the House declines its assent.

In his speech the Liberal leader, Sir Herbert Samuel, said:
"What is the case in regard to Germany? Nothing we have so

far seen or heard would suggest that our present air force is not adequate to meet any peril at the present time from this quarter."

When we remember that this was language used after careful deliberation by the responsible heads of parties, the danger of our country becomes apparent. This was the formative time when by extreme exertions we could have preserved the air strength on which our independence of action was founded. If Great Britain and France had each maintained quantitative parity with Germany, they would together have been double as strong, and Hitler's career of violence might have been nipped in the bud without the loss of a single life. Thereafter it was too late. We cannot doubt the sincerity of the leaders of the Socialist and Liberal Parties. They were completely wrong and mistaken, and they bear their share of the burden before history. It is indeed astonishing that the Socialist Party should have endeavoured in after years to claim superior foresight and should have reproached their opponents with failing to provide for national safety.

*   *   *   *   *

I now enjoyed for once the advantage of being able to urge rearmament in the guise of a defender of the Government. I therefore received an unusually friendly hearing from the Conservative Party.

One would have thought that the character of His Majesty's Government and the record of its principal Ministers would have induced the Opposition to view the request for an increase in the national defence with some confidence and some consideration. I do not suppose there has ever been such a pacifist-minded Government. There is the Prime Minister, who in the war proved in the most extreme manner and with very great courage his convictions and the sacrifices he would make for what he believed was the cause of pacifism. The Lord President of the Council is chiefly associated in the public mind with the repetition of the prayer, "Give peace in our time." One would have supposed that when Ministers like these come forward and say that they feel it their duty to ask for some small increase in the means they have of guaranteeing the public safety, it would weigh with the Opposition and would be considered as a proof of the reality of the danger from which they seek to protect us.

Then look at the apologies which the Government have made. No one could have put forward a proposal in more extremely inoffensive terms. Meekness has characterised every word which they have spoken since this subject was first mooted. We are told that we can see for ourselves how small is the proposal. We are assured that it can be stopped at any minute if Geneva succeeds. And we are also assured that the steps we are taking, although they may to some lower minds have associated with them some idea of national self-defence, are really only associated with the great principle of collective security.

But all these apologies and soothing procedures are most curtly repulsed by the Opposition. Their only answer to these efforts to conciliate them is a vote of censure, which is to be decided tonight. It seems to me that we have got very nearly to the end of the period when it is worth while endeavouring to conciliate some classes of opinion upon this subject. We are in the presence of an attempt to establish a kind of tyranny of opinion, and if its reign could be perpetuated, the effect might be profoundly injurious to the stability and security of this country. We are a rich and easy prey. No country is so vulnerable, and no country would better repay pillage than our own. . . . *With our enormous metropolis here, the greatest target in the world, a kind of tremendous, fat, valuable cow tied up to attract the beast of prey,* we are in a position in which we have never been before, and in which no other country is at the present time.

Let us remember this: our weakness does not only involve ourselves; our weakness involves also the stability of Europe.

I then proceeded to argue that Germany was already approaching air parity with Britain:

I first assert that Germany has already, in violation of the Treaty, created *a military air force which is now nearly two-thirds as strong as our present home defence air force.* That is the first statement which I put before the Government for their consideration. The second is that Germany is rapidly increasing this air force, not only by large sums of money which figure in her estimates, but also by public subscriptions — very often almost forced subscriptions —

which are in progress and have been in progress for some time all over Germany. *By the end of* 1935, *the German air force will be nearly equal in numbers and efficiency to our home defence air force at that date even if the Government's present proposals are carried out.*

The third statement is that if Germany continues this expansion and if we continue to carry out our scheme, then some time in 1936 Germany will be definitely and substantially stronger in the air than Great Britain. Fourthly, and this is the point which is causing anxiety, once they have got that lead we may never be able to overtake them. If these assertions cannot be contradicted, then there is cause for the anxiety which exists in all parts of the House, not only because of the physical strength of the German air force, but I am bound to say also because of the character of the present German dictatorship. *If the Government have to admit at any time in the next few years that the German air forces are stronger than our own, then they will be held, and I think rightly held, to have failed in their prime duty to the country.*

I ended as follows:

The Opposition are very free-spoken, as most of us are in this country, on the conduct of the German Nazi Government. No one has been more severe in criticism than the Labour Party or that section of the Liberal Party which I see opposite. And their great newspapers, now united in the common cause, have been the most forward in the severity of their strictures. But these criticisms are fiercely resented by the powerful men who have Germany in their hands. So that we are to disarm our friends, we are to have no allies, we are to affront powerful nations, and we are to neglect our own defences entirely. That is a miserable and perilous situation. Indeed, the position to which they seek to reduce us by the course which they have pursued and by the vote which they ask us to take is one of terrible jeopardy, and in voting against them tonight we shall hope that a better path for national safety will be found than that along which they would conduct us.

The Labour Party's vote of censure was, of course, defeated by a large majority, and I have no doubt that the nation, had it been appealed to with proper preparation on these issues, would equally have sustained the measures necessary for national safety.

*   *   *   *   *

It is not possible to tell this story without recording the milestones which we passed on our long journey from security to the jaws of Death. Looking back, I am astonished at the length of time that was granted to us. It would have been possible in 1933, or even in 1934, for Britain to have created an air power which would have imposed the necessary restraints upon Hitler's ambition, or would perhaps have enabled the military leaders of Germany to control his violent acts. More than five whole years had yet to run before we were to be confronted with the supreme ordeal. Had we acted even now with reasonable prudence and healthy energy, it might never have come to pass. Based upon superior air power, Britain and France could safely have invoked the aid of the League of Nations, and all the states of Europe would have gathered behind them. For the first time the League would have had an instrument of authority.

When the Winter Session opened on November 28, 1934, I moved in the name of some of my friends [1] an amendment to the Address, declaring that "the strength of our national defences, and especially of our air defences, is no longer adequate to secure the peace, safety, and freedom of Your Majesty's faithful subjects." The House was packed and very ready to listen. After using all the arguments which emphasised the heavy danger to us and to the world, I came to precise facts:

I assert, first, that Germany already, at this moment, has a military air force — that is to say, military squadrons, with the necessary ground services, and the necessary reserves of trained personnel and material — which only awaits an order to assemble in full open combination; and that this illegal air force is rapidly approaching equality with our own. Secondly, by this time next year, if Germany executes her existing programme without acceleration, and if we execute our existing programme on the basis which now lies before us without slowing down, and carry out the increases announced to Parliament in July last, the German military air force will this time next year be in fact at least as strong as our

1 The amendment stood in the names of Mr. Churchill, Sir Robert Horne, Mr. Amery, Captain F. E. Guest, Lord Winterton, and Mr. Boothby.

own, and it may be even stronger. Thirdly, on the same basis — that is to say, both sides continuing with their existing programmes as at present arranged — by the end of 1936, that is, one year farther on, and two years from now — the German military air force will be nearly fifty per cent stronger, and in 1937 nearly double. All this is on the assumption, as I say, that there is no acceleration on the part of Germany, and no slowing-down on our part.

Mr. Baldwin, who followed me at once, faced this issue squarely, and on the case made out by his Air Ministry advisers, met me with direct contradiction:

It is not the case that Germany is rapidly approaching equality with us. I pointed out that the German figures are total figures, not first-line strength figures, and I have given our own first-line figures and said they are only first-line figures, with a considerably larger reserve at our disposal behind them, even if we confine the comparison to the German air strength and the strength of the Royal Air Force immediately available in Europe. Germany is actively engaged in the production of service aircraft, but her real strength is not fifty per cent of our strength in Europe today. As for the position this time next year, if she continues to execute her air programme without acceleration, and if we continue to carry out at the present approved rate the expansion announced to Parliament in July, *so far from the German military air force being at least as strong as, and probably stronger than, our own, we estimate that we shall still have a margin in Europe alone of nearly fifty per cent.* I cannot look farther forward than the next two years. Mr. Churchill speaks of what may happen in 1937. Such investigations as I have been able to make lead me to believe that his figures are considerably exaggerated.

*   *   *   *   *

This sweeping assurance from the virtual Prime Minister soothed most of the alarmed, and silenced many of the critics. Everyone was glad to learn that my precise statements had been denied upon unimpeachable authority. I was not at all convinced. I believed that Mr. Baldwin was not being told the truth by his advisers, and anyhow that he did not know the facts.

*   *   *   *   *

Thus the winter months slipped away, and it was not till the spring that I again had the opportunity of raising the issue. I gave full and precise notice.

Mr. Churchill to Mr. Baldwin.   17.3.35.

On the air estimates on Tuesday, I propose to renew our discussion of last November and to analyse as far as I can your figures of British and German air strength for home defence at the various dates in question, viz.: then, now, at the end of the year 1935, calendar and financial, etc. I believe that the Germans are already as strong as we are and possibly stronger, and that if we carry out our new programme as prescribed, Germany will be fifty per cent stronger than we by the end of 1935 or the beginning of 1936. This, as you will see, runs counter to your statement of November, that we should have a fifty-per-cent superiority at that date. I shall, of course, refer to your undertaking of March, 1934, that "this country shall no longer be in a position inferior to any country within striking distance of our shores," and I shall argue that, according to such knowledge as I have been able to acquire, this is not being made good, as will rapidly be proved by events.

I thought it would be convenient to you if I let you know beforehand, as I did on the last occasion, what my general line will be, and if whoever speaks for the Government is able to prove the contrary, no one will be better pleased than I.

On March 19, the air estimates were presented to the House. I reiterated my statement of November, and again directly challenged the assurances which Mr. Baldwin had then given. A very confident reply was made by the Under-Secretary for Air. However, at the end of March, the Foreign Secretary and Mr. Eden paid a visit to Herr Hitler in Germany, and in the course of an important conversation, the text of which is on record, they were told personally by him that the German air force had already reached parity with Great Britain. This fact was made public by the Government on April 3. At the beginning of May, the Prime Minister wrote an article in his own organ, *The Newsletter,* in which he emphasised the dangers of German rearmament in terms akin to those which I had so often expressed since 1932. He used the revealing word "ambush," which must have sprung from the anxiety of his heart. We had indeed fallen into an ambush. Mr. MacDonald himself opened the debate. After referring to the declared German intention to build a navy beyond the Treaty and submarines in breach of it, he came to the air position:

In the debate last November certain estimates were put forward on the basis of our then estimates as to the strength of the German air force, and the assurance was given by the Lord President, on behalf of the Government, that in no circumstances would we accept any position of inferiority with regard to whatever air force might be raised in Germany in the future. If it were not so, that would put us in an impossible position of which the Government and the Air Ministry are fully aware. In the course of the visit which the Foreign Secretary and the Lord Privy Seal paid to Berlin at the end of March, the German Chancellor stated, as the House was informed on April 3, that Germany had reached parity with Great Britain in the air. Whatever may be the exact interpretation of this phrase in terms of air strength, it undoubtedly indicated that the German force has been expanded to a point considerably in excess of the estimates which we were able to place before the House last year. That is a grave fact, with regard to which both the Government and the Air Ministry have taken immediate notice.

When in due course I was called, I said:

Even now, we are not taking the measures which would be in true proportion to our needs. The Government have proposed these increases. They must face the storm. They will have to encounter every form of unfair attack. Their motives will be misrepresented. They will be calumniated and called warmongers. Every kind of attack will be made upon them by many powerful, numerous, and extremely vocal forces in this country. They are going to get it anyway. Why, then, not fight for something that will give us safety? Why, then, not insist that the provision for the air force should be adequate, and then, however severe may be the censure and however strident the abuse which they have to face, at any rate there will be this satisfactory result — that His Majesty's Government will be able to feel that in this, of all matters the prime responsibility of a Government, they have done their duty.

Although the House listened to me with close attention, I felt a sensation of despair. To be so entirely convinced and

vindicated in a matter of life and death to one's country, and
not to be able to make Parliament and the nation heed the
warning, or bow to the proof by taking action, was an experience most painful. I went on:

I confess that words fail me. In the year 1708, Mr. Secretary
St. John, by a calculated Ministerial indiscretion, revealed to the
House the fact that the battle of Almanza had been lost in the
previous summer because only eight thousand English troops were
actually in Spain out of the twenty-nine thousand that had been
voted by the House of Commons for this service. When a month
later this revelation was confirmed by the Government, it is recorded that the House sat in silence for half an hour, no Member
caring to speak or wishing to make a comment upon so staggering
an announcement. And yet how incomparably small that event
was to what we have now to face! That was merely a frustration
of policy. Nothing that could happen to Spain in that war could
possibly have contained in it any form of danger which was potentially mortal.

                    *   *   *   *   *

There is a wide measure of agreement in the House tonight upon
our foreign policy. We are bound to act in concert with France
and Italy and other Powers, great and small, who are anxious to
preserve peace. I would not refuse the co-operation of any Government which plainly conformed to that test, so long as it was willing
to work under the authority and sanction of the League of Nations.
Such a policy does not close the door upon a revision of the
Treaties, but it procures a sense of stability, and an adequate gathering together of all reasonable Powers for self-defence, before any
inquiry of that character [i.e., Treaty revision] can be entered upon.
In this august association for collective security we must build up
defence forces of all kinds and combine our action with that of
friendly Powers, so that we may be allowed to live in quiet ourselves and retrieve the woeful miscalculations of which we are at
present the dupes, and of which, unless we take warning in time,
we may some day be the victims.

There lay in my memory at this time some lines from an
unknown writer about a railway accident. I had learnt them

from a volume of *Punch* cartoons which I used to pore over
when I was eight or nine years old at school at Brighton.

"Who is in charge of the clattering train?
The axles creak and the couplings strain;
And the pace is hot, and the points are near,
And Sleep has deadened the driver's ear;
And the signals flash through the night in vain,
For Death is in charge of the clattering train."

However, I did not repeat them.

*   *   *   *   *

It was not until May 22 that Mr. Baldwin made his celebrated confession. I am forced to cite it:

First of all, with regard to the figure I gave in November of
German aeroplanes, nothing has come to my knowledge since that
makes me think that figure was wrong. I believed at that time it
was right. *Where I was wrong was in my estimate of the future.
There I was completely wrong. We were completely misled on that
subject. . . .*
I would repeat here that there is no occasion, in my view, in
what we are doing, for panic. But I will say this deliberately, with
all the knowledge I have of the situation, that I would not remain
for one moment in any Government which took less determined
steps than we are taking today. I think it is only due to say that
there has been a great deal of criticism, both in the press and
verbally, about the Air Ministry as though they were responsible
for possibly an inadequate programme, for not having gone ahead
faster, and for many other things. I only want to repeat that whatever responsibility there may be — and we are perfectly ready to
meet criticism — *that responsibility is not that of any single
Minister; it is the responsibility of the Government as a whole, and
we are all responsible, and we are all to blame.*

I hoped that this shocking confession would be a decisive
event, and that at the least a parliamentary committee of all
parties would be set up to report upon the facts and upon our
safety. The House of Commons had a different reaction. The
Labour and Liberal Oppositions, having nine months earlier
moved or supported a vote of censure even upon the modest

steps the Government had taken, were ineffectual and undecided. They were looking forward to an election against "Tory
Armaments." Neither the Labour nor the Liberal spokesmen
had prepared themselves for Mr. Baldwin's disclosures and admission, and they did not attempt to adapt their speeches to
this outstanding episode. Mr. Attlee said:

> As a party we do not stand for unilateral disarmament. . . . We
> stand for collective security through the League of Nations. We
> reject the use of force as an instrument of policy. We stand for the
> reduction of armaments and pooled security. . . . We have stated
> that this country must be prepared to make its contribution to
> collective security. Our policy is not one of seeking security through
> rearmament, but through disarmament. Our aim is the reduction
> of armaments, and then the complete abolition of all national
> armaments and the creation of an international police force under
> the League.

What was to happen if this spacious policy could not be immediately achieved or till it was achieved, he did not say. He
complained that the White Paper on Defence justified increases
in the Navy by references to the United States, and increases in
our air force by references to the air forces of Russia, Japan,
and the United States. "All that was old-fashioned talk and
right outside the collective system." He recognised that the fact
of German rearmament had become dominating, but "The
measure of the counterweight to any particular armed forces
is not the forces of this country or of France, but the combined
force of all loyal Powers in the League of Nations. An aggressor must be made to realise that if he challenges the world, he
will be met by the co-ordinated forces of the world, not by a
number of disjointed national forces." The only way was to
concentrate all air power in the hands of the League, which
must be united and become a reality. Meanwhile, he and his
party voted against the measure proposed.

For the Liberals, Sir Archibald Sinclair asked the Government to summon

a fresh economic conference, and to bring Germany not only
within the political comity of nations, but also into active

co-operation with ourselves in all the works of civilisation and in raising the standards of life of both peoples. . . . Let the Government table detailed and definite proposals for the abolition of military air forces and the control of civil aviation. If the proposals are resisted, let the responsibility be cleared and properly fixed.

Nevertheless [he said], while disarmament ought vigorously to be pursued as the chief objective of the Government, a situation in which a great country not a member of the League of Nations possesses the most powerful army and perhaps the most powerful air force in Western Europe, with probably a greater coefficient of expansion than any other air force . . . cannot be allowed to endure. . . . The Liberal Party would feel bound to support measures of national defence when clear proof was afforded of their necessity. . . . I cannot therefore agree that to increase our national armaments is necessarily inconsistent with our obligations under the collective peace system.

He then proceeded to deal at length with "the question of private profits being made out of the means of death," and quoted a recent speech by Lord Halifax, Minister of Education, who had said that the British people were "disposed to regard the preparation of instruments of war as too high and too grave a thing to be entrusted to any hands less responsible than those of the State itself." Sir Archibald Sinclair thought that there ought to be national factories for dealing with the rapid expansion in air armaments, for which expansion, he said, a case had been made out.

The existence of private armament firms had long been a bugbear to Labour and Liberal minds, and it lent itself readily to the making of popular speeches. It was, of course, absurd to suppose that at this time our air expansion, recognised as necessary, could be achieved through national factories only. A large part of the private industry of the country was urgently required for immediate adaptation and to reinforce our existing sources of manufacture. Nothing in the speeches of the Opposition leaders was in the slightest degree related to the emergency in which they admitted we stood, or to the far graver facts which we now know lay behind it.

The Government majority for their part appeared captivated by Mr. Baldwin's candour. His admission of having been utterly wrong, with all his sources of knowledge, upon a vital matter for which he was responsible was held to be redeemed by the frankness with which he declared his error and shouldered the blame. There was even a strange wave of enthusiasm for a Minister who did not hesitate to say that he was wrong. Indeed, many Conservative Members seemed angry with me for having brought their trusted leader to a plight from which only his native manliness and honesty had extricated him; but not, alas, his country.

*   *   *   *   *

My kinsman, Lord Londonderry, a friend from childhood days, the direct descendant of the famous Castlereagh of Napoleonic times, was a man of unquestionable loyalty and patriotism. He had presided over the Air Ministry since the formation of the coalition. In this period the grave changes which have been described had overshadowed our affairs, and the Air Ministry had become one of the most important offices in the State. During the years of retrenchment and disarmament, he and his Ministry had tried to keep and get as much as they could from a severe and arbitrary Chancellor of the Exchequer. They were overjoyed when in the summer of 1934 an air programme of forty-one additional squadrons was conceded to them by the Cabinet. But in British politics the hot fits very quickly succeed the cold. When the Foreign Secretary returned from Berlin, profoundly startled by Hitler's assertion that his air force was equal to that of Britain, the whole Cabinet became deeply concerned. Mr. Baldwin had to face, in the light of what was now generally accepted as a new situation, his assertions of November, when he had contradicted me. The Cabinet had no idea they had been overtaken in the air, and turned, as is usually the case, inquisitorial looks upon the department involved and its Minister.

The Air Ministry did not realise that a new inheritance awaited them. The Treasury's fetters were broken. They had

but to ask for more. Instead of this, they reacted strongly
against Hitler's claim to air parity. Londonderry, who was
their spokesman, even rested upon the statement that *"when
Simon and Eden went to Berlin there was only one German
operational squadron in being. From their training establishments they hoped to form fifteen to twenty squadron formations by the end of the month."* [2] All this is a matter of nomen-
clature. It is, of course, very difficult to classify air forces,
because of the absence of any common "yardstick" and all the
variations in defining "First-line air strength" and "Operational Units." The Air Ministry now led its chief into an
elaborate vindication of their own past conduct, and in consequence were entirely out of harmony with the new mood of a
genuinely alarmed Government and public. The experts and
officials at the Air Ministry had given Mr. Baldwin the figures
and forecasts with which he had answered me in November.
They wished him to go into action in defence of these statements; but this was no longer practical politics. There seems
no doubt that these experts and officials of the Air Ministry at
this time were themselves misled and misled their chief. A
great air power, at least the equal of our own, long pent-up,
had at last sprung into daylight in Germany.

It was an odd and painful experience for Londonderry, as
his book describes, after having gone through several years of
asking for more, to be suddenly turned out for not asking
enough. But apart from all this, his political standing was not
sufficient to enable him to head a department, now at the very
centre and almost at the summit of our affairs. Besides, everyone could see that in such times the Air Minister must be in
the House of Commons. Accordingly, Mr. Ramsay MacDonald's vacation of the Premiership later in the year became also
the occasion for the appointment of Sir Philip Cunliffe-Lister,
then Secretary of State for the Colonies, as Air Minister, as part
of a new policy for vigorous air expansion. Lord Londonderry
with much reluctance became Lord Privy Seal and leader of
the House of Lords; but after the general election, Mr. Bald-

2 The Marquess of Londonderry, *Wings of Destiny*, 1943, page 128.

win dispensed with his services in both these capacities. The
great achievement of his period in office was the designing and
promotion of the ever-famous Hurricane and Spitfire fighters.
The first prototypes of these flew in November, 1935, and
March, 1936, respectively. Londonderry does not mention this
in his defence, but he might well have done so, since he took
the blame of so much that he had not done. The new Secretary
of State, wafted by favourable breezes and fresh tides, ordered
immediate large-scale production of these types, and they were
ready in some numbers none too soon. Cunliffe-Lister was a much
more potent political figure than his predecessor and had a better chance and a more inspiriting task. He brought an altogether more powerful force to bear upon our air policy and
administration, and set himself actively to work to make up for
the time lost by the Cabinet from 1932 to 1934. He, however,
made the serious mistake of quitting the House of Commons
for the House of Lords in November, 1935, thus stultifying one
of the arguments for his transfer to the Secretaryship of State
for Air. This was to cost him his office a few years later.

*   *   *   *   *

A disaster of the first magnitude had fallen upon us. Hitler
had already obtained parity with Great Britain. Henceforward
he had merely to drive his factories and training-schools at full
speed, not only to keep his lead in the air, but steadily to improve it. Henceforward all the unknown, immeasurable threats
which overhung London from air attack would be a definite
and compelling factor in all our decisions. Moreover, we could
never catch up; or at any rate, the Government never did catch
up. Credit is due to them and to the Air Ministry for the high
efficiency of the Royal Air Force. But the pledge that air parity
would be maintained was irrevocably broken. It is true that
the immediate further expansion of the German air force did
not proceed at the same rate as in the period when they gained
parity. No doubt a supreme effort had been made by them to
achieve at a bound this commanding position and to assist and
exploit it in their diplomacy. It gave Hitler the foundation for

the successive acts of aggression which he had planned and which were now soon to take place. Very considerable efforts were made by the British Government in the next four years, and there is no doubt that we excelled in air quality; but quantity was henceforth beyond us. The outbreak of the war found us with barely half the German numbers.

8

Challenge and Response

1935

THE YEARS of underground burrowings, of secret or disguised preparations were now over, and Hitler at length
felt himself strong enough to make his first open challenge.
On March 9, 1935, the official constitution of the German air
force was announced, and on the sixteenth it was declared that
the German Army would henceforth be based on national compulsory service. The laws to implement these decisions were
soon promulgated, and action had already begun in anticipation. The French Government, who were well informed of
what was coming, had actually declared the consequential extension of their own military service to two years a few hours
earlier on the same momentous day. The German action was
an open, formal affront to the treaties of peace upon which the
League of Nations was founded. As long as the breaches had
taken the form of evasions or calling things by other names, it
was easy for the responsible victorious Powers, obsessed by

130

pacifism and preoccupied with domestic politics, to avoid the responsibility of declaring that the Peace Treaty was being broken or repudiated. Now the issue came with blunt and brutal force. Almost on the same day the Ethiopian Government appealed to the League of Nations against the threatening demands of Italy. When, on March 24, against this background, Sir John Simon with the Lord Privy Seal, Mr. Eden, visited Berlin at Hitler's invitation, the French Government thought the occasion ill-chosen. They had now themselves at once to face, not the reduction of their Army, so eagerly pressed upon them by Mr. MacDonald the year before, but the extension of compulsory military service from one year to two. In the prevailing state of public opinion this was a heavy task. Not only the Communists but the Socialists had voted against the measure. When M. Léon Blum said: "The workers of France will rise to resist Hitlerite aggression," Thorez replied, amid the applause of his Soviet-bound faction, "We will not tolerate the working classes being drawn into a so-called war in defence of democracy against fascism."

The United States had washed their hands of all concern in Europe, apart from wishing well to everybody, and were sure they would never have to be bothered with it again. But France, Great Britain, and also — decidedly — Italy, in spite of their discordances, felt bound to challenge this definite act of Treaty violation by Hitler. A conference of the former principal Allies was summoned under the League of Nations at Stresa, and all these matters were brought to debate.

*   *   *   *   *

Anthony Eden had for nearly ten years devoted himself almost entirely to the study of foreign affairs. Taken from Eton at eighteen to the World War, he had served for four years with distinction in the 60th Rifles through many of the bloodiest battles, and risen to the rank of Brigade-Major, with the Military Cross. Shortly after entering the House of Commons in 1925, he became Parliamentary Private Secretary to Austen Chamberlain at the Foreign Office during Mr. Bald-

win's second Administration. In the MacDonald-Baldwin Coalition of 1931, he was appointed Under-Secretary of State and
served under the new Foreign Secretary, Sir John Simon. The
duties of an under-secretary are often changed, but his responsibilities are always limited. He has to serve his chief in carrying out the policy settled in the Cabinet, of which he is not a
member and to which he has no access. Only in an extreme case
where conscience and honour are involved is he justified in
carrying any difference about foreign policy to the point of
public controversy or resignation.

Eden had, however, during all these years obtained a wide
view of the foreign scene, and he was intimately acquainted
with the life and thought of the great department upon which
so much depends. Sir John Simon's conduct of foreign affairs
was not in 1935 viewed with favour either by the Opposition
or in influential circles of the Conservative Party. Eden, with
all his knowledge and exceptional gifts, began therefore to
acquire prominence. For this reason, after becoming Lord
Privy Seal at the end of 1934, he had retained by the desire of
the Cabinet an informal but close association with the Foreign
Office; and thus had been invited to accompany his former
chief, Sir John Simon, on the inopportune, but not unfruitful,
visit to Berlin. The Foreign Secretary returned to London
after the interview with Hitler, bringing with him the important news, already mentioned, that according to Hitler, Germany *had now gained air parity with Britain.* Eden was sent
on to Moscow, where he established contacts with Stalin which
were to be revived with advantage after some years. On the
homeward journey, his airplane ran into a severe and prolonged storm, and when after a dangerous flight they landed,
he was almost in a state of collapse. The doctors declared that
he was not fit to go with Simon to the Stresa Conference, and
indeed for several months he was an invalid. In these circumstances the Prime Minister decided himself to accompany the
Foreign Secretary, although at this time his own health, eyesight, and mental powers were evidently failing. Great Britain
was, therefore, weakly represented at this all-important meet-

ing, which MM. Flandin and Laval attended on behalf of France, and Signors Mussolini and Suvich on behalf of Italy.

There was general agreement that open violation of solemn treaties, for the making of which millions of men had died, could not be borne. But the British representatives made it clear at the outset that they would not consider the possibility of sanctions in the event of Treaty violation. This naturally confined the Conference to the region of words. A resolution was passed unanimously to the effect that "unilateral" — by which they meant one-sided — breaches of treaties could not be accepted, and the Executive Council of the League of Nations was invited to pronounce upon the situation disclosed. On the second afternoon of the Conference, Mussolini strongly supported this action, and was outspoken against aggression by one Power upon another. The final declaration was as follows:

The three Powers, the object of whose policy is the collective maintenance of peace within the framework of the League of Nations, find themselves in complete agreement in opposing, by all practicable means, any unilateral repudiation of treaties which may endanger the peace of Europe, and will act in close and cordial collaboration for this purpose.

The Italian Dictator in his speech had stressed the words *"peace of Europe,"* and paused after "Europe" in a noticeable manner. This emphasis on Europe at once struck the attention of the British Foreign Office representatives. They pricked up their ears and well understood that, while Mussolini would work with France and Britain to prevent Germany from re-arming, he reserved for himself any excursion in Africa against Abyssinia on which he might later resolve. Should this point be raised or not? Discussions were held that night among the Foreign Office officials. Everyone was so anxious for Mussolini's support in dealing with Germany that it was felt undesirable at that moment to warn him off Abyssinia, which would obviously have very much annoyed him. Therefore, the question was not raised; it passed by default, and Mussolini felt, and in a sense had reason to feel, that the Allies had acquiesced in his

statement and would give him a free hand against Abyssinia.
The French remained mute on the point, and the Conference
separated.

In due course, on April 15/17, the Council of the League of
Nations examined the alleged breach of the Treaty of Versailles
committed by Germany in decreeing universal compulsory
military service. The following Powers were represented on
the Council: The Argentine Republic, Australia, Great Britain, Chile, Czechoslovakia, Denmark, France, Germany, Italy,
Mexico, Poland, Portugal, Spain, Turkey, and the U.S.S.R. All
these Powers voted for the principle that treaties should not be
broken by "unilateral" action, and referred the issue to the
Plenary Assembly of the League. At the same time the Foreign
Ministers of the three Scandinavian countries, Sweden, Norway, Denmark, and of Holland, being deeply concerned about
the naval balance in the Baltic, also met together in general
support. In all, nineteen countries formally protested. But
how vain was all their voting without the readiness of any
single Power or any group of Powers to contemplate the use
of *force*, even in the last resort!

*   *   *   *   *

Laval was not disposed to approach Russia in the firm spirit
of Barthou. But in France there was now an urgent need. It
seemed, above all, necessary to those concerned with the life of
France to obtain national unity on the two years' military service which had been approved by a narrow majority in March.
Only the Soviet Government could give permission to the important section of Frenchmen whose allegiance they commanded. Besides this, there was a general desire in France for
a revival of the old alliance, or something like it. On May 2,
the French Government put their signature to a Franco-Soviet
Pact. This was a nebulous document guaranteeing mutual
assistance in the face of aggression over a period of five years.

To obtain tangible results in the French political field, M.
Laval now went on a three days' visit to Moscow, where he was
welcomed by Stalin. There were lengthy discussions, of which

a fragment not hitherto published may be recorded. Stalin and Molotov were, of course, anxious to know above all else what was to be the strength of the French Army on the Western Front: how many divisions? what period of service? After this field had been explored, Laval said: "Can't you do something to encourage religion and the Catholics in Russia? It would help me so much with the Pope." "Oho!" said Stalin. "The Pope! How many divisions has *he* got?" Laval's answer was not reported to me; but he might certainly have mentioned a number of legions not always visible on parade. Laval had never intended to commit France to any of the specific obligations which it is the habit of the Soviets to demand. Nevertheless, he obtained a public declaration from Stalin on May 15, approving the policy of national defence carried out by France in order to maintain her armed forces at the level of security. On these instructions the French Communists immediately turned about and gave vociferous support to the defence programme and the two years' service. As a factor in European security, the Franco-Soviet Pact, which contained no engagements binding on either party in the event of German aggression, had only limited advantages. No real confederacy was achieved with Russia. Moreover, on his return journey the French Foreign Minister stopped at Cracow to attend the funeral of Marshal Pilsudski. Here he met Goering, with whom he talked with much cordiality. His expressions of distrust and dislike of the Soviets were duly reported through German channels to Moscow.

Mr. MacDonald's health and capacity had declined to a point which made his continuance as Prime Minister impossible. He had never been popular with the Conservative Party, who regarded him, on account of his political and war records and Socialist faith, with long-bred prejudice softened in later years by pity. No man was more hated or with better reason by the Labour-Socialist Party which he had so largely created and then laid low by what they viewed as his treacherous desertion in 1931. In the massive majority of the Government he had but seven party followers. The disarmament policy to which he had given his utmost personal efforts had now proved a disastrous failure. A general election could not be far distant, in which he could play no helpful part. In these circumstances there was no surprise when, on June 7, it was announced that he and Mr. Baldwin had changed places and offices, and that Mr. Baldwin had become Prime Minister for the third time. The Foreign Office also passed to another hand. Sir Samuel Hoare's labours at the India Office had been crowned by the passing of the Government of India Bill, and he was now free to turn to a more immediately important sphere. For some time past Sir John Simon had been bitterly attacked for his foreign policy by influential Conservatives closely associated with the Government. He now moved to the Home Office, with which he was well acquainted, and Sir Samuel Hoare became Secretary of State for Foreign Affairs.

At the same time Mr. Baldwin adopted a novel expedient. He appointed Mr. Eden, whose prestige was steadily growing and whose health was now restored, to be Minister for League of Nations Affairs. Mr. Eden was to work in the Foreign Office with equal status to the Foreign Secretary and with full access to the dispatches and the departmental staff. Mr. Baldwin's object was no doubt to conciliate the strong tide of public opinion associated with the League of Nations Union by showing the importance which he attached to the League and to the conduct of our affairs at Geneva. When about a month later, I had the opportunity of commenting on what I described as "the new plan of having two equal Foreign Secretaries," I drew attention to its defects:

I was very glad, indeed, that the Prime Minister said yesterday that this was only a temporary experiment. I cannot feel that it will last long or ever be renewed. . . . We need the integral thought of a single man responsible for Foreign Affairs, ranging over the entire field and making every factor and every incident contribute to the general purpose upon which Parliament has agreed. The Foreign Secretary, whoever he is, whichever he is, must be supreme in his department, and everyone in that great office ought to look to him, and to him alone. I remember that we had a discussion in the war about unity of command, and that Mr. Lloyd George said, "It is not a question of one general being better than another, but of one general being better than two." There is no reason why a strong Cabinet Committee should not sit with the Foreign Secretary every day in these difficult times, or why the Prime Minister should not see him or his officials at any time; but when the topic is so complicated and vast, when it is in such continued flux, it seems to me that confusion will only be made worse confounded by dual allegiances and equal dual responsibilities.

All this was certainly borne out by events.

* * * * *

While men and matters were in this posture, a most surprising act was committed by the British Government. Some at least of its impulse came from the Admiralty. It is always dangerous for soldiers, sailors, or airmen to play at politics. They enter a sphere in which the values are quite different from those to which they have hitherto been accustomed. Of course, they were following the inclination or even the direction of the First Lord and the Cabinet, who alone bore the responsibility. But there was a strong favourable Admiralty breeze. There had been for some time conversations between the British and German Admiralties about the proportions of the two navies. By the Treaty of Versailles the Germans were not entitled to build more than four battleships of ten thousand tons displacement, in addition to six ten-thousand-ton cruisers. The British Admiralty had recently found out that the last two pocket battleships being constructed, the *Scharnhorst* and the *Gneisenau*, were of a far larger size than the Treaty allowed, and of a quite different type. In fact they turned out to be twenty-six-thousand-ton light battle cruisers, or commerce-destroyers of the highest class.

In the face of this brazen and fraudulent violation of the Peace Treaty, carefully planned and begun at least two years earlier (1933), the Admiralty actually thought it was worth while making an Anglo-German naval agreement. His Majesty's Government did this without consulting their French

ally or informing the League of Nations. At the very time
when they themselves were appealing to the League and enlist-
ing the support of its members to protest against Hitler's violation of the military clauses of the Treaty, they proceeded by a
private agreement to sweep away the naval clauses of the same
treaty.

The main feature of the agreement was that the German
Navy should not exceed one-third of the British. This greatly
attracted the Admiralty, who looked back to the days before the
Great War when we had been content with a ratio of sixteen
to ten. For the sake of that prospect, taking German assurances
at their face value, they proceeded to concede to Germany the
right to build U-boats explicitly denied to her in the Peace
Treaty. Germany might build sixty per cent of the British submarine strength, and if she decided that the circumstances were
exceptional she might build to a hundred per cent. The Germans, of course, gave assurances that their U-boats would never
be used against merchant ships. Why, then, were they needed?
For clearly, if the rest of the agreement was kept, they could
not influence the naval decision, so far as warships were concerned.

The limitation of the German Fleet to a third of the British
allowed Germany a programme of new construction which
would set her yards to work at maximum activity for at least
ten years. There was, therefore, no practical limitation or restraint of any kind imposed upon German naval expansion.
They could build as fast as was physically possible. The quota
of ships assigned to Germany by the British project was, in
fact, far more lavish than Germany found it expedient to use,
having regard partly, no doubt, to the competition for armour-
plate arising between warship and tank construction. They
were authorised to build five capital ships, two aircraft carriers,
twenty-one cruisers, and sixty-four destroyers. In fact, however,
all they had ready or approaching completion by the outbreak
of war were two capital ships, no aircraft carriers, eleven cruisers, and twenty-five destroyers, or considerably less than half
what we had so complacently accorded them. By concentrating

their available resources on cruisers and destroyers at the expense of battleships, they could have put themselves in a more advantageous position for a war with Britain in 1939 or 1940. Hitler, as we now know, informed Admiral Raeder that war with England would not be likely till 1944/45. The development of the German Navy was therefore planned on a long-term basis. In U-boats alone did they build to the full paper limits allowed. As soon as they were able to pass the sixty-per-cent limit, they invoked the provision allowing them to build to one hundred per cent, and fifty-seven were actually constructed when war began.

In the design of new battleships, the Germans had the further advantage of not being parties to the provisions of the Washington Naval Agreement or the London Conference. They immediately laid down the *Bismarck* and *Tirpitz*, and, while Britain, France, and the United States were all bound by the thirty-five-thousand-tons limitation, these two great vessels were being designed with a displacement of over forty-five thousand tons, which made them, when completed, certainly the strongest vessels afloat in the world.

It was also at this moment a great diplomatic advantage to Hitler to divide the Allies, to have one of them ready to condone breaches of the Treaty of Versailles, and to invest the regaining of full freedom to rearm with the sanction of agreement with Britain. The effect of the announcement was another blow to the League of Nations. The French had every right to complain that their vital interests were affected by the permission accorded by Great Britain for the building of U-boats. Mussolini saw in this episode evidence that Great Britain was not acting in good faith with her other allies, and that, so long as her special naval interests were secured, she would apparently go to any length in accommodation with Germany, regardless of the detriment to friendly Powers menaced by the growth of the German land forces. He was encouraged by what seemed the cynical and selfish attitude of Great Britain to press on with his plans against Abyssinia. The Scandinavian Powers, who only a fortnight before had courageously sustained the protest against Hitler's introduction of compulsory service in the German Army, now found that Great Britain had behind the scenes agreed to a German Navy which, though only a third of the British, would within this limit be master of the Baltic.

Great play was made by British Ministers with the German offer to co-operate with us in abolishing the submarine. Considering that the condition attached to it was that all other countries should agree at the same time, and that it was well known there was not the slightest chance of other countries agreeing, this was a very safe offer for the Germans to make. This also applied to the German agreement to restrict the use of submarines so as to strip submarine warfare against commerce of inhumanity. Who could suppose that the Germans, possessing a great fleet of U-boats and watching their women and children being starved by a British blockade, would abstain from the fullest use of that arm? I described this view as "the acme of gullibility."

Far from being a step toward disarmament, the agreement, had it been carried out over a period of years, would inevitably have provoked a world-wide development of new warship-building. The French Navy, except its latest vessels, would require reconstruction. This again would react upon Italy. For ourselves, it was evident that we should have to rebuild the British Fleet on a very large scale in order to maintain our three-to-one superiority in modern ships. It may be that the idea of the German Navy being one-third of the British also presented itself to our Admiralty as the British Navy being three times the German. This perhaps might clear the path to a reasonable and overdue rebuilding of our Fleet. But where were the statesmen?

This agreement was announced to Parliament by the First Lord of the Admiralty, Sir Bolton Eyres-Monsell, on June 21, 1935. On the first opportunity, July 11, and again on July 22, I condemned it:

I do not believe that this isolated action by Great Britain will be found to work for the cause of peace. The immediate reaction is that every day the German Fleet approaches a tonnage which gives it absolute command of the Baltic, and very soon one of the deterrents of a European war will gradually fade away. So far as the position in the Mediterranean is concerned, it seems to me that we are in for very great difficulties. Certainly a large addition of new shipbuilding must come when the French have to modernize their Fleet to meet German construction and the Italians follow suit, and we shall have pressure upon us to rebuild from that point of view, or else our position in the Mediterranean will be affected. But worst of all is the effect upon our position at the other end of the world, in China and in the Far East. What a windfall this has been to Japan! Observe what the consequences are. The First Lord said, "Face the facts." The British Fleet, when this programme is completed, will be largely anchored to the North Sea. That means to say the whole position in the Far East has been very gravely altered, to the detriment of the United States and of Great Britain and to the detriment of China. . . .

I regret that we are not dealing with this problem of the resuscitation of German naval power with the Concert of Europe on our side, and in conjunction with many other nations whose fortunes are affected and whose fears are aroused equally with our own by the enormous developments of German armaments. What those developments are no one can accurately measure. We have seen that powerful vessels, much more powerful than we expected, can be constructed unknown even to the Admiralty. We have seen what has been done in the air. I believe that if the figures of the expenditure of Germany during the current financial year could be ascertained, the House and the country would be staggered and appalled by the enormous expenditure upon war preparations which is being poured out all over that country, converting the whole mighty nation and empire of Germany into an arsenal virtually on the threshold of mobilisation.

* * * * *

It is only right to state here the contrary argument as put forward by Sir Samuel Hoare in his first speech as Foreign Secretary on July 11, 1935, in response to many domestic and European criticisms:

The Anglo-German Naval Agreement is in no sense a selfish agreement. On no account could we have made an agreement that

was not manifestly in our view to the advantage of the other naval
Powers. On no account could we have made an agreement that we
did not think, so far from hindering general agreement, would
actually further it. The question of naval disarmament has always
been treated distinctively from the question of land and air disarmament. The naval question has always been treated apart, and
it was always the intention, so far as I know, of the naval Powers
to treat it apart.

Apart, however, from the juridical position, there seemed to us
to be, in the interests of peace — which is the main objective of the
British Government — overwhelming reasons why we should conclude the agreement. In the opinion of our naval experts, we were
advised to accept the agreement as a safe agreement for the British
Empire. Here again we saw a chance that might not recur of eliminating one of the causes that chiefly led to the embitterment before
the Great War — the race of German naval armaments. Incidentally, out of that discussion arose the very important statement
of the German Government that henceforth, so far as they were
concerned, they would eliminate one of the causes that made the
war so terrible, namely, the unrestricted use of submarines against
merchant ships. Thirdly, we came definitely to the view that there
was a chance of making an agreement that seemed on naval grounds
manifestly to the advantage of other naval Powers, including
France. . . . With the French Fleet at approximately its present
level as compared with our own Fleet, the agreement gives France
a permanent superiority over the German Fleet of forty-three
per cent, as compared with an inferiority of about thirty per cent
before the war. . . . I am therefore bold enough to believe that,
when the world looks more dispassionately at these results, the overwhelming majority of those who stand for peace and a restriction of
armaments will say that the British Government took not only a
wise course but the only course that in the circumstances was open
to them.

What had in fact been done was to authorise Germany to
build to her utmost capacity for five or six years to come.

*   *   *   *   *

Meanwhile, in the military sphere the formal establishment
of conscription in Germany on March 16, 1935, marked the

fundamental challenge to Versailles. But the steps by which the German Army was now magnified and reorganised are not of technical interest only. The whole function of the Army in the National-Socialist State required definition. The purpose of the law of May 21, 1935, was to expand the technical élite of secretly trained specialists into the armed expression of the whole nation. The name Reichswehr was changed to that of Wehrmacht. The Army was to be subordinated to the supreme leadership of the Fuehrer. Every soldier took the oath, not as formerly to the Constitution, but to the person of Adolf Hitler. The War Ministry was directly subordinated to the orders of the Fuehrer. Military service was an essential civic duty, and it was the responsibility of the Army to educate and to unify, once and for all, the population of the Reich. The second clause of the law reads: "The Wehrmacht is the armed force and the school of military education of the German people."

Here, indeed, was the formal and legal embodiment of Hitler's words in *Mein Kampf*:

The coming National-Socialist State should not fall into the error of the past and assign to the Army a task which it does not and should not have. The German Army is not to be a school for the maintenance of tribal peculiarities, but rather a school for the mutual understanding and adjustment of all Germans. Whatever may have a disruptive effect in national life should be given a unifying effect through the Army. It should furthermore raise the individual youth above the narrow horizon of his little countryside and place him in the German nation. He must learn to respect, not the boundaries of his birthplace, but the boundaries of his Fatherland; for it is these which he too must some day defend.

Upon these ideological bases the law also established a new territorial organisation. The Army was now organised in three commands, with headquarters at Berlin, Cassel, and Dresden, subdivided into ten (later twelve) *Wehrkreise* (military districts). Each *Wehrkreis* contained an army corps of three divisions. In addition a new kind of formation was planned — the armoured division, of which three were soon in being.

Detailed arrangements were also made regarding military

service. The regimentation of German youth was the prime task of the new régime. Starting in the ranks of the Hitler Youth, the boyhood of Germany passed at the age of eighteen on a voluntary basis into the S.A. for two years. By a law of June 26, 1935, the work battalions or *Arbeitsdienst* became a compulsory duty on every male German reaching the age of twenty. For six months he would have to serve his country, constructing roads, building barracks, or draining marshes, thus fitting him physically and morally for the crowning duty of a German citizen — service with the armed forces. In the work battalions, the emphasis lay upon the abolition of class and the stressing of the social unity of the German people; in the Army, it was put upon discipline and the territorial unity of the nation.

The gigantic task of training the new body and of expanding the cadres prescribed by the technical conception of Seeckt now began. On October 15, 1935, again in defiance of the clauses of Versailles, the German Staff College was reopened with formal ceremony by Hitler, accompanied by the chiefs of the armed services. Here was the apex of the pyramid whose base was now already constituted by the myriad formations of the work battalions. On November 7, 1935, the first class, born in 1914, was called up for service: 596,000 young men to be trained in the profession of arms. Thus, at one stroke, on paper at least, the German Army was raised to nearly seven hundred thousand effectives.

With the task of training came the problems of financing rearmament and expanding German industry to meet the needs of the new national Army. By secret decrees Doctor Schacht had been made virtual Economic Dictator of Germany. Seeckt's pioneer work was now put to its supreme test. The two major difficulties were first the expansion of the officer corps, and secondly the organisation of the specialised units, the artillery, the engineers, and the signals. By October, 1935, ten army corps were forming. Two more followed a year later, and a thirteenth in October, 1937. The police formations were also incorporated in the armed forces.

It was realised that after the first call-up of the 1914 class, in Germany as in France, the succeeding years would bring a diminishing number of recruits, owing to the decline in births during the period of the World War. Therefore, in August, 1936, the period of active military service in Germany was raised to two years. The 1915 class numbered 464,000, and with the retention of the 1914 class for another year, the number of Germans under regular military training in 1936 was 1,511,000 men, excluding the para-military formations of the party and the work battalions. The effective strength of the French Army, apart from reserves, in the same year was 623,000 men, of whom only 407,000 were in France.

The following figures, which actuaries could foresee with some precision, tell their tale:

TABLE OF THE COMPARATIVE FRENCH AND GERMAN FIGURES FOR THE CLASSES BORN FROM 1914 TO 1920, AND CALLED UP FROM 1934 TO 1940

Class	German	French
14	596,000 men	279,000 men
15	464,000	184,000
16	351,000	165,000
17	314,000	171,000
18	326,000	197,000
19	485,000	218,000
20	636,000	360,000
	3,172,000	1,574,000

Until these figures became facts as the years unfolded, they were still but warning shadows. All that was done up to 1935 fell far short of the strength and power of the French Army and its vast reserves, apart from its numerous and vigorous allies. Even at this time a resolute decision upon the authority, which could easily have been obtained, of the League of Nations might have arrested the whole process. Germany either could have been brought to the bar at Geneva and invited to give a full explanation and allow inter-Allied missions of inquiry to examine the state of her armaments and military formations in breach of the Treaty; or, in the event of refusal, the Rhine

bridgeheads could have been reoccupied until compliance with
the Treaty had been secured, without there being any possibility of effective resistance or much likelihood of bloodshed.
In this way the Second World War could have been prevented or
at least delayed indefinitely. Many of the facts and their whole
general tendency were well known to the French and British
Staffs, and were to a lesser extent realised by the Governments.
The French Government, which was in ceaseless flux in the fascinating game of party politics, and the British Government, which
arrived at the same vices by the opposite process of general
agreement to keep things quiet, were equally incapable of any
drastic or clear-cut action, however justifiable both by treaty
and by common prudence. The French Government had not
accepted all the reductions of their own forces pressed upon
them by their ally; but like their British colleagues they lacked
the quality to resist in any effective manner what Seeckt in his
day had called "The Resurrection of German Military Power."

9

Problems of Air and Sea

1935–1939

A Technical Interlude — German Power to Blackmail — Approaches to Mr. Baldwin and the Prime Minister — The Earth versus the Air — Mr. Baldwin's Invitation — The Air Defence Research Committee — Some General Principles — Progress of Our Work — The Development of Radar — Professor Watson-Watt and Radio Echoes — The Tizard Report — The Chain of Coastal Stations — Air-Marshal Dowding's Network of Telephonic Communications — The "Graf Zeppelin" Flies up Our East Coast: Spring of 1939 — I.F.F. — A Visit to Martlesham, 1939 — My Admiralty Contacts — The Fleet Air Arm — The Question of Building New Battleships — Calibre of Guns — Weight of Broadsides — Number of Turrets — My Letter to Sir Samuel Hoare of August 1, 1936 — The Admiralty Case — Quadruple Turrets — An Unfortunate Sequel — A Visit to Port Portland: the "Asdics."

TECHNICAL DECISIONS of high consequence affecting our future safety now require to be mentioned, and it will be convenient in this chapter to cover the whole four years which lay between us and the outbreak of war.

After the loss of air parity, we were liable to be blackmailed by Hitler. If we had taken steps betimes to create an air force half as strong again, or twice as strong, as any that Germany could produce in breach of the Treaty, we should have kept control of the future. But even air parity, which no one could say was aggressive, would have given us a solid measure of defensive confidence in these critical years, and a broad basis

147

from which to conduct our diplomacy or expand our air force.
But we had lost air parity. And such attempts as were made
to recover it were vain. We had entered a period when the
weapon which had played a considerable part in the previous
war had become obsessive in men's minds, and also a prime
military factor. Ministers had to imagine the most frightful
scenes of ruin and slaughter in London if we quarrelled with
the German Dictator. Although these considerations were not
special to Great Britain, they affected our policy, and by consequence all the world.

During the summer of 1934, Professor Lindemann wrote to
The Times newspaper, pointing out the possibility of decisive
scientific results being obtained in air defence research. In
August, we tried to bring the subject to the attention, not
merely of the officials at the Air Ministry who were already on
the move, but of their masters in the Government. In September, we journeyed from Cannes to Aix-les-Bains and had an
agreeable conversation with Mr. Baldwin, who appeared deeply
interested. Our request was for an inquiry on a high level.
When we came back to London, departmental difficulties arose,
and the matter hung in suspense. Early in 1935, an Air Ministry Committee composed of scientists was set up and instructed to explore the future. We remembered that it was
upon the advice of the Air Ministry that Mr. Baldwin had
made the speech which produced so great an impression in
1933 when he said that there was really no defence. "The
bomber will always get through." We had, therefore, no confidence in any Air Ministry departmental committee, and
thought the subject should be transferred from the Air Ministry to the Committee of Imperial Defence, where the heads of
the Government, the most powerful politicians in the country,
would be able to supervise and superintend its actions and also
to make sure that the necessary funds were not denied. At this
stage we were joined by Sir Austen Chamberlain, and we continued at intervals to address Ministers on the subject.

In February, we were received by Mr. MacDonald personally, and we laid our case before him. No difference of prin-

ciple at all existed between us. The Prime Minister was most sympathetic when I pointed out the peace aspect of the argument. Nothing, I said, could lessen the terrors and anxieties which overclouded the world so much as the removal of the idea of surprise attacks upon the civil populations. Mr. MacDonald seemed at this time greatly troubled with his eyesight. He gazed blankly out of the windows onto Palace Yard, and assured us he was hardening his heart to overcome departmental resistance. The Air Ministry, for their part, resented the idea of any outside or superior body interfering in their special affairs, and for a while nothing happened.

I therefore raised the matter in the House on June 7, 1935:

The point [I said] is limited, and largely scientific in its character. It is concerned with the methods which can be invented or adopted or discovered to enable the earth to control the air, to enable defence from the ground to exercise control — indeed domination — upon airplanes high above its surface. . . . My experience is that in these matters, when the need is fully explained by military and political authorities, Science is always able to provide something. We were told that it was impossible to grapple with submarines, but methods were found which enabled us to strangle the submarines below the surface of the water, a problem not necessarily harder than that of clawing down marauding airplanes. Many things were adopted in the war which we were told were technically impossible, but patience, perseverance, and, above all, the spur of necessity under war conditions, made men's brains act with greater vigour, and Science responded to the demands. . . .

It is only in the twentieth century that this hateful conception of inducing nations to surrender by terrorising the helpless civil population by massacring the women and children has gained acceptance and countenance among men. This is not the cause of any one nation. Every country would feel safer if once it were found that the bombing airplane was at the mercy of appliances directed from the earth, and the haunting fears and suspicions which are leading nations nearer and nearer to another catastrophe would be abated. . . . We have not only to fear attacks upon our civil population in our great cities, in respect of which we are more vulnerable than any other country in the world, but also attacks

upon the dockyards and other technical establishments without
which our Fleet, still an essential factor in our defence, might be
paralysed or even destroyed. Therefore, it is not only for the sake
of a world effort to eliminate one of the worst causes of suspicion
and of war, but as a means of restoring to us here in Great Britain
the old security of our island, that this matter should receive and
command the most vigorous thought of the greatest men in our
country and our Government, and should be pressed forward by
every resource that the science of Britain can apply and the wealth
of the country can liberate.

On the very next day, the Ministerial changes recorded in
the previous chapter took place and Mr. Baldwin became
Prime Minister. Sir Philip Cunliffe-Lister, Lord Swinton as
he soon afterwards became, succeeded Lord Londonderry as
Air Minister. One afternoon a month later, I was in the smoking-room of the House of Commons when Mr. Baldwin came
in. He sat down next to me and said at once: "I have a proposal to make to you. Philip is very anxious that you should
join the newly formed Committee of Imperial Defence on Air
Defence Research, and I hope you will." I said I was a critic
of our air preparations and must reserve my freedom of action.
He said: "That is quite understood. Of course you will be perfectly free except upon the secret matters you learn only at the
Committee."

I made it a condition that Professor Lindemann should at
least be a member of the Technical Sub-Committee, because I
depended upon his aid. A few days later, the Prime Minister
wrote:

8 *July,* 1935.

I am glad you have seen Hankey, and I take your letter as an
expression of your willingness to serve on that Committee.

I am glad, and I think you may be of real help in a most important investigation.

Of course, you are free as air [the correct expression in this case!]
to debate the general issues of policy, programmes, and all else
connected with the air services.

My invitation was not intended as a muzzle, but as a gesture of
friendliness to an old colleague.

Accordingly, for the next four years I attended these meetings and thus obtained a full view of this vital sphere of our air defence, and built up my ideas upon it year by year in close and constant discussion with Lindemann. I immediately prepared a memorandum for the Committee which embodied the thought and knowledge I had already gathered, without official information, in my talks and studies with Lindemann and from my own military conceptions. This paper is of interest because of the light which it throws on the position in July, 1935. No one at that time had considered the use of radio beams for guiding bombers. The difficulties of training large numbers of individual pilots were obvious, and it was generally held that at night large fleets of aircraft would be led by a few master-bombers. Great advances into new fields were made in the four years which were to pass before the life of the nation was to be at stake; and meanwhile the adoption of bombing guided by radio beams caused profound tactical changes. Hence much that was written then was superseded, but a good deal was tried by me when I had power — not all with success.

23 *July*, 1935.

The following notes are submitted with much diffidence, and in haste on account of our early meeting, in the hopes that they may be a contribution to our combined thought.

General tactical conceptions and what is technically feasible act and react upon one another. Thus, the scientist should be told what facilities the air force would like to have, and airplane design be made to fit into and implement a definite scheme of warfare.

At this stage we must assume a reasonable war hypothesis, namely, that Great Britain, France, and Belgium are allies attacked by Germany.

After the outbreak of such a war, the dominating event will be the mobilisation of the great Continental armies. This will take at least a fortnight, diversified and hampered by mechanised and motorised inroads. The French and German General Staffs' minds will be riveted upon the assembly and deployment of the armies. Neither could afford to be markedly behindhand at the first main shock. It may be hoped that Germany will not be ready for a war, in which the Army and Navy are to play an important part, for two or three years. Their Navy is at the moment exiguous; they have not yet obtained the command of the Baltic; and it would appear that their heavy artillery is still inadequate. To build a navy and to produce heavy artillery and train the men will take a time measured in years rather than in months.

A large part of German munitions production is concentrated in the Ruhr, which is easily accessible to enemy bombing. She must realise that she would be cut off from foreign supplies of many essential war materials (copper, tungsten, cobalt, vanadium, petrol, rubber, wool, etc.), and *even her iron supply will be reduced unless she dominates the Baltic,* so that she is scarcely yet in a position to undertake a war of long duration. Great efforts are of course being made to overcome these handicaps, such as the removal of certain factories from the frontier to Central Germany, the synthetic production of substances such as petrol and rubber, and the accumulation of large stocks. But it seems unlikely that Germany will be in a position before 1937 or 1938 to begin with any hope of success a war of the three services which might last for years, and in which she would have scarcely any allies.

It would appear in such a war the first task of the Anglo-French air force should be the breaking-down of enemy communications, their railways, motor roads, Rhine bridges, viaducts, etc., and the maximum disturbance of their assembly zones and munition-dumps. Next in priority come the most accessible factories for their war industry in all its forms. It seems fairly certain that if our efforts from zero hour were concentrated on these vital targets, *we should impose a similar policy on the enemy.* Otherwise, the French would have an unobstructed mobilisation, and command the initiative in the great land battle. Thus, any German aircraft used to commit acts of terror upon the British and French civil populations will be grudged and sparingly diverted.

Nevertheless, we must expect that even in a three-Service war, attempts will be made to burn down London, or other great cities within easy reach, in order to test the resisting will-power of the Government and people under these terrible ordeals. Secondly, the port of London, and the dockyards upon which the life of the Fleet depends, are also military targets of the highest possible consequence.

There is, however, always the ugly possibility that those in authority in Germany may believe that it would be possible to beat

a nation to its knees in a very few months, or even weeks, by violent
aerial mass attack. The conception of psychological shock tactics has
a great attraction for the German mind. Whether they are right or
wrong is beside the point. If the German Government believes that
it can force a country to sue for peace by destroying its great cities
and slaughtering the civilian population from the air before the
Allied armies have mobilised and advanced materially, this might
well lead it to commence hostilities with the air arm alone. It need
scarcely be added that England, if she could be separated from
France, would be a particularly apt victim for this form of aggression. For her main form of counter-attack apart from aerial
reprisals, namely, a naval blockade, only makes itself felt after a
considerable time.

If the aerial bombardment of our cities can be restricted or
prevented, the chance (which may in any case be illusory) that our
morale could be broken by "frightfulness" will vanish, and the
decision will remain in the long run with the armies and navies.
The more our defences are respected, the greater will be the
deterrent upon a purely air war.

*   *   *   *   *

I had two ideas to contribute, some explanation of which will
be found in the Appendix. It must be remembered that in
1935 we had still more than four years to run before any radio-
detection method came into play.

*   *   *   *   *

The Committee worked in secret, and no statement was ever
made of my association with the Government, whom I continued to criticise and attack with increasing severity in other
parts of the field. It is often possible in England for experienced politicians to reconcile functions of this kind in the same
way as the sharpest political differences are sometimes found
not incompatible with personal friendships. Scientists are,
however, a far more jealous society. In 1937, a considerable
difference on the Technical Sub-Committee grew between
them and Professor Lindemann. His colleagues resented the
fact that he was in constant touch with me, and that I pressed

his points on the main Committee, to which they considered
Sir Henry Tizard should alone explain their collective view.
Lindemann was, therefore, asked to retire. He was perfectly
right in arming me with the facts on which to argue; indeed,
this was the basis on which we had both joined in the work.
Nevertheless, in the public interest, in spite of his departure, I
continued with his full agreement to remain a member; and in
1938, as will presently be described, I was able to procure his
reinstatement.

*   *   *   *   *

The possibility of using radio waves scattered back from
aircraft and other metal objects seems to have occurred to a
very large number of people in England, America, Germany,
and France in the nineteen-thirties. We talked of them as
R.D.F. (Radio Direction-Finding) or later as *radar*. The practical aim was to discern the approach of hostile aircraft, not by
human senses, by eye or ear, but by the echo which they sent
back from radio waves. About seventy miles up there is a reflecting canopy (ionosphere), the existence of which prevents
ordinary wireless waves from wandering off into space, and
thus makes long-range wireless communication possible. The
technique of sending up very short pulses and observing their
echo had been actively developed for some years by our
scientists, and notably by Professor Appleton.

In February, 1935, a Government research scientist, Professor
Watson-Watt, had first explained to the Technical Sub-Committee that the detection of aircraft by radio echoes might be
feasible and had proposed that it should be tested. The Committee was impressed. It was assumed that it would take five
years to detect aircraft up to a range of fifty miles. On July 25,
1935, at the fourth meeting of the Air Defence Research Committee, and the first which I attended, Tizard made his report
upon radio-location. The preliminary experiments were held
to justify further executive action. The service departments
were invited to formulate plans. A special organisation was set
up, and a chain of stations established in the Dover-Orfordness
area for experimental purposes. The possibility of radio-location of ships was also to be explored.

By March, 1936, stations were being erected and equipped along the south coast, and it was hoped to carry out experimental exercises in the autumn. During the summer there were considerable delays in construction, and the problem of hostile jamming appeared. In July, 1937, plans were brought forward by the Air Ministry, and approved by the Air Defence Research Committee, to create a chain of twenty stations from the Isle of Wight to the Tees by the end of 1939 at the cost of over a million pounds. Experiments were now tried for finding hostile aircraft after they had come inland. By the end of the year we could track them up to a distance of thirty-five miles at ten thousand feet. Progress was also being made about ships. It had been proved possible to fix vessels from the air at a range of nine miles. Two ships of the Home Fleet were already equipped with apparatus for aircraft detection, and experiments were taking place for range-finding on aircraft, for fire control of anti-aircraft (A.A.) guns, and for the direction of searchlights. Work proceeded. By December, 1938, fourteen of the twenty new stations planned were operating with temporary equipment. Location of ships from the air was now possible at thirty miles.

By 1939, the Air Ministry, using comparatively long-wave radio (ten metres), had constructed the so-called coastal chain, which enabled us to detect aircraft approaching over the sea at distances up to about sixty miles. An elaborate network of telephonic communication had been installed under Air-Marshal Dowding, of Fighter Command, linking all these stations with a central command station at Uxbridge, where the movements of all aircraft observed could be plotted on large maps and thus the control in action of all our own air forces maintained. Apparatus called *I.F.F.* (Identification Friend or Foe) had also been devised which enabled our coastal chain radar stations to distinguish British aircraft which carried it from enemy aircraft. It was found that these long-wave stations did not detect aircraft approaching at low heights over the sea, and as a counter to this danger a supplementary set of stations called *C.H.L.* (Chain Stations Home Service Low Cover) was con-

structed, using much shorter waves (one and a half metres),
but only effective over a shorter range.

To follow enemy aircraft once they had come inland, we had
meanwhile to rely upon the Royal Observer Corps, which only
operated by ear and eye, but which, when linked up with all
the telephone exchanges, proved of high value, and in the early
part of the Battle of Britain was our main foundation. It was
not enough to detect approaching enemy aircraft over the sea,
though that gave at least fifteen to twenty minutes' warning.
We must seek to guide our own aircraft towards the attackers
and intercept them over the land. For this purpose a number
of stations with what were called *G.C.I.* (Ground Control of
Interception) were being erected. But all this was still embryonic at the outbreak of war.

*   *   *   *   *

The Germans were also busy, and in the spring of 1939, the
Graf Zeppelin flew up the east coast of Britain. General Mar-
tini, Director-General of Signals in the Luftwaffe, had arranged
that she carried special listening equipment to discover the existence of British radar transmissions, if any. The attempt
failed, but had her listening equipment been working properly,
the *Graf Zeppelin* ought certainly to have been able to carry
back to Germany the information that we had radar, for our
radar stations were not only operating at the time, but also
detected her movements and divined her intention. The Germans would not have been surprised to hear our radar pulses, for
they had developed a technically efficient radar system which
was in some respects ahead of our own. What would have surprised them, however, was the extent to which we had turned
our discoveries to practical effect, and woven all into our general air defence system. In this we led the world, and it was
operational efficiency rather than novelty of equipment that
was the British achievement.

The final meeting of the Air Defence Research Committee
took place on July 11, 1939. Twenty radar stations were at
that time in existence between Portsmouth and Scapa Flow,

able to detect aircraft flying above ten thousand feet, with ranges varying from fifty to one hundred and twenty miles. A satisfactory anti-jamming device and a simplified method of I.F.F. were now actually in production. Flight trials were taking place with experimental sets in aircraft to try to "home" on enemy machines. The experimental sets for the location of ships from the air had proved too bulky for air-service purposes, and were passed to the Admiralty for possible use by ships.

* * * * *

I add a final note. In June, 1939, Sir Henry Tizard, at the desire of the Secretary of State, conducted me in a rather disreputable airplane to see the establishments which had been developed on the east coast. We flew around all day. I sent my impressions to the Air Minister, and I print them here because they give a glimpse of where we were in this radar field on the eve of the task.

Mr. Churchill to Sir Kingsley Wood.

. . . I found my visit to Martlesham and Bawdsey under Tizard's guidance profoundly interesting, and also encouraging. It may be useful if I put down a few points which rest in my mind:

These vital R.D.F. (radio direction-finding) stations require immediate protection. We thought at first of erecting dummy duplicates and triplicates of them at little expense; but on reflection it seems to me that here is a case for using the smoke-cloud. . . .

A weak point in this wonderful development is, of course, that when the raid crosses the coast, it leaves the R.D.F., and we become dependent upon the Observer Corps. This would seem transition from the middle of the twentieth century to the early stone age. Although I hear that good results are obtained from the Observer Corps, we must regard following the raider inland by some application of R.D.F. as most urgently needed. It will be some time before the R.D.F. stations can look back inland, and then only upon a crowded and confused air theatre. . . .

The progress in R.D.F., especially applied to range-finding, must surely be of high consequence to the Navy. It would give power to engage an enemy irrespective of visibility. How different would have been the fate of the German battle cruisers when they attacked

Scarborough and Hartlepool in 1914, if we could have pierced the
mist! I cannot conceive why the Admiralty are not now hot upon
this trail. Tizard also pointed out the enormous value to destroyers
and submarines of directing torpedoes accurately, irrespective of
visibility by night or day. I should have thought this was one of
the biggest things that had happened for a long time, and all for
our benefit.

The method of discrimination between friend and foe is also
of the highest consequence to the Navy, and should entirely
supersede recognition signals with all their peril. I presume the
Admiralty knows all about it.

Finally, let me congratulate you upon the progress that has been
made. We are on the threshold of immense securities for our island.
Unfortunately, we want to go farther than the threshold, and time
is short.

I shall in a later volume explain the way in which, by these
and other processes, the German attack on Great Britain
was to a large extent parried in the autumn and winter of
1940. There is no doubt that the work of the Air Ministry and the Air Defence Research Committee, both under
Lord Swinton and his successor, played the decisive part in
procuring this precious reinforcement to our fighter aircraft.
When in 1940, the chief responsibility fell upon me and our
national survival depended upon victory in the air, I had the
advantage of a layman's insight into the problems of air warfare resulting from four long years of study and thought based
upon the fullest official and technical information. Although I
have never tried to be learned in technical matters, this mental
field was well lit for me. I knew the various pieces and the
moves on the board, and could understand anything I was told
about the game.

*   *   *   *   *

My contacts with the Admiralty during these years were also
constant and intimate. In the summer of 1936, Sir Samuel
Hoare became First Lord, and he authorised his officers to
discuss Admiralty matters freely with me; and as I took a keen
interest in the Navy, I availed myself fully of these opportuni-

ties. I had known the First Sea Lord, Admiral Chatfield, from
the Beatty days of 1914, and my correspondence with him on
naval problems began in 1936. I also had a long-standing acquaintance with Admiral Henderson, the Controller of the
Navy and Third Sea Lord, who deals with all questions of construction and design. He was one of our finest gunnery experts
in 1912, and as I used when First Lord often to go out and
see the initial firings of battleships before their gun-mountings
were accepted from the contractors, I was able to form a very
high opinion of his work. Both these officers at the summit
of their careers treated me with the utmost confidence, and
although I differed from them and criticised severely much
that was done or not done, no complaint or personal reproaches
ever disturbed our association.

The question of whether the Fleet air arm should be under
the Admiralty or the Air Ministry was hotly disputed between
the two departments and services. I took the Navy view, and
my advocacy of it in Parliament drew a cordial letter of thanks
from the First Sea Lord, in which he entered upon the whole
question of naval policy. Sir Thomas Inskip came down to
see me at Chartwell, and asked for my advice on this nicely
balanced issue. I drew up for him a memorandum which, as
it was eventually adopted almost word for word by His
Majesty's Government, may be printed in the Appendix.

*   *   *   *   *

When at last it was decided to begin building battleships
again, the question of their design caused me great concern.
Up to this moment practically all the capital ships of the Royal
Navy had been built or designed during my administration of
the Admiralty from 1911 to 1915. Only the *Nelson* and the
Rodney were created after the First World War. I have in
The World Crisis described all the process of rebuilding the
Navy and the designing of the *Queen Elizabeth* class of fast
battleships in my first tenure of the Admiralty, when I had at
my disposal so much of the genius and inspiration of Lord
Fisher. To this I was always able to apply my own thought

gathered from many other naval expert sources, and I still held strong opinions.

As soon as I heard that a battleship programme had been agreed to by the Cabinet, I was at once sure that our new ships should continue to mount the sixteen-inch gun, and that this could be achieved within thirty-five thousand tons displacement — the treaty limit, which we alone rigidly respected — by three triple sixteen-inch-gun turrets. I had several talks and some correspondence with Sir Samuel Hoare, and as I was not convinced by the arguments I heard, I began to ask questions in the House about the relative weight of broadsides from fourteen-inch- and sixteen-inch-gunned ships. For my private information the following figures were given:

> 14-inch 9 gun broadside   6.38 tons
> 16-inch 9 gun broadside   9.55 tons

The figure for the sixteen-inch gun is based, not on the existing sixteen-inch gun of H.M.S. *Nelson,* but on a hypothetical sixteen-inch gun of the type which the Americans have in mind for their new capital ships.

I was deeply impressed by the superior weight of the sixteen-inch broadside. I therefore wrote to Sir Samuel Hoare:

Mr. Churchill to Sir Samuel Hoare.   1.VIII.36.

It is very civil of you to attach any importance to my opinion, and *prima facie* there is a case. I cannot answer the argument about the long delay involved. Once again we alone are injured by treaties. I cannot doubt that a far stronger ship could be built with three triple sixteen-inch-gun turrets in a 35,000-ton hull, than any combination of fourteen-inch. Not only would she be a better ship, but she would be rated a better ship and a more powerful token of naval power by everyone, including those who serve in her. Remember, the Germans get far better results out of their guns per calibre than we do. They throw a heavier shell farther and more accurately. The answer is a big punch. Not only is there an enormous increase in the weight of broadside, but in addition the explosive charge of a sixteen-inch shell must be far larger than that of a fourteen-inch. If you can get through the armour, it is worth while doing something inside with the explosion.

Another aspect is the number of turrets. What a waste to have four turrets, which I suppose weigh two thousand tons each, when three will give a bigger punch! With three turrets the centralisation of armour against gun-fire and torpedoes can be much more intense, and the decks all the more clear for the anti-aircraft batteries. If you ask your people to give you a legend for a sixteen-inch-gun ship, I am persuaded they would show you decidedly better proportions than could be achieved at fourteen-inch. Of course, there may be an argument about gunnery control, the spread of shot, etc., with which I am not familiar. Still, I should have thought that the optimum gunnery effect could be reached with salvos of four and five alternately.

Nothing would induce me to succumb to fourteen-inch if I were in your shoes. The Admiralty will look rather silly if they are committed to two fourteen-inch-gun ships, and both Japan and the United States go in for sixteen-inch a few months later. I should have thought it was quite possible to lie back and save six months in construction. It is terrible deliberately to build British battle-ships costing £7,000,000 apiece that are not the strongest in the world! As old Fisher used to say, "The British Navy always travels first class."

However, these are only vaticinations! I went through all this in bygone years, or I would not venture to obtrude it on you. I will get in touch with Chatfield as you suggest.

The First Lord in no way resented my arguments and a considerable correspondence took place between us; and I also had several conversations with him and the First Sea Lord. Before leaving the Admiralty at the end of May, 1937, Sir Samuel Hoare sent me two memoranda prepared by the Naval Staff, one dealing with battleships and the other with cruisers. The Admiralty case about battleship design was that since the Washington Treaty Great Britain had continually pressed for a reduction in displacement and size of guns on grounds of economy. It had not been possible, when the new British battleships were at last sanctioned in 1936, to throw over the treaty limitations of the fourteen-inch gun or the 35,000-ton ship. The design of the battleships of the *King George V* class had to be started before it could become known whether other Powers would accept these limits as governing the immediate future. The turrets of the *King George V* class had in fact been ordered in May, 1936. Had the Admiralty delayed decision upon design until April, 1937, only two ships would be available by 1941, instead of five. Should foreign countries go beyond the Washington limits, the designs for the 1938 programme ships, which would be complete in 1942, could take a larger scope.

If, however, we should eventually be forced to go to fully balanced sixteen-inch-gun ships and not sacrifice any of the structural strength and other characteristics of the *King George V* class, there would be considerable increase in displacement. The resultant vessels could not pass through the Panama Canal and we should have to enlarge our docks as well as add to the cost of each ship. The Admiralty concurred with my preference for a ship of nine sixteen-inch-guns in three turrets, rather than one with ten fourteen-inch guns in four turrets. All their battleship designs were of ships having three "multi-gun turrets."

After studying this long and massive paper, I recognised that we could not face the delay involved in putting larger guns in the first five battleships. The decision was irrevocable. I urged, however, that the designs for the larger guns and turrets should be completed as a precaution and that the tools and appliances necessary to adapt the gun-plants, etc., to the larger calibre should actually be made, even at considerable expense.

In my discussions with the Admiralty about battleship design, I had not appreciated the fact that they had designed and were in process of drawing-out quadruple turrets for the fourteen-inch gun, thus achieving a total of twelve guns. Had I realised this, I should have been forced to reconsider my view. The expression "multi-gun turrets" led to this misunderstanding on my part. Three quadruple turrets would have avoided many of the evils which I saw in a four-turret ship, and twelve fourteen-inch guns, though not the equal of nine sixteen-inch, were a considerable improvement in weight of metal.

However, the sequel of the Admiralty policy was unfortunate. Serious delays took place in the designing of the entirely novel quadruple turret for the fourteen-inch gun. No sooner had work been started upon this than the Admiralty Board decided to change the third turret superposed forward for a two-gun turret. This, of course, meant redesigning the two or three thousand parts which composed these amazing pieces of mechanism, and a further delay of at least a year in the completion of the *King George V* and *Prince of Wales* was caused by this change of plan. Moreover, our new ships were now reduced to ten guns, and all my arguments about the inferiority of their broadsides compared to sixteen-inch gun ships resumed their force. Meanwhile, the Americans got round the problem of putting three triple sixteen-inch turrets into a 35,000-ton hull. The French and the Germans chose the fifteen-inch gun, the French mounting eight guns in two quadruple turrets, and the Germans eight in four twin turrets. The Germans, however, like the Japanese, had no intention of being bound by any treaty limitations, and the *Bismarck's* displacement exceeded 45,000 tons, with all the advantages which thus accrued. We alone, having after all these years at last decided to build five battleships on which the life of the Navy and the maintenance of sea power were judged to depend, went back from the sixteen-inch gun to the fourteen-inch, while others increased their calibres. We, therefore, produced a series of vessels, each taking five years to build, which might well have carried heavier gun-power.

* * * * *

On June 15, 1938, the First Sea Lord took me down to Portland to show me the "Asdics." This was the name which described the system of groping for submarines below the surface by means of sound waves through the water which echoed back from any steel structure they met. From this echo the position of the submarine could be fixed with some accuracy. We were on the threshold of this development at the end of the First World War.

We slept on board the flagship and had a long talk with Sir Charles Forbes, the Commander-in-Chief. All the morning was spent at the Anti-Submarine School, and in about four hours

I received a very full account. We then went to sea in a destroyer, and during the afternoon and evening an exercise of great interest was conducted for my benefit. A number of submarines were scattered about in the offing. Standing on the bridge of the destroyer which was using the Asdic, with another destroyer half a mile away, in constant intercourse, I could see and hear the whole process, which was the sacred treasure of the Admiralty, and in the culture of which for a whole generation they had faithfully persevered. Often I had criticised their policy. No doubt on this occasion I overrated, as they did, the magnitude of their achievement, and forgot for a moment how broad are the seas. Nevertheless, if this twenty years' study had not been pursued with large annual expenditure and thousands of highly skilled officers and men employed and trained with nothing to show for it — all quite unmentionable — our problem in dealing with the U-boat, grievous though it proved, might well have found no answer but defeat.

To Chatfield I wrote:

I have reflected constantly on all that you showed me, and I am sure the nation owes the Admiralty, and those who have guided it, an inestimable debt for the faithful effort sustained over so many years which has, as I feel convinced, relieved us of one of our great dangers.

What surprised me was the clarity and force of the [Asdic] indications. I had imagined something almost imperceptible, certainly vague and doubtful. I never imagined that I should hear one of those creatures asking to be destroyed. It is a marvellous system and achievement.

The Asdics did not conquer the U-boat; but without the Asdics the U-boat would not have been conquered.

10

Sanctions Against Italy

1935

WORLD PEACE now suffered its second heavy stroke. The loss by Britain of air parity was followed by the transference of Italy to the German side. The two events combined enabled Hitler to advance along his predetermined deadly course. We have seen how helpful Mussolini had been in the protection of Austrian independence, with all that it implied in Central and Southeastern Europe. Now he was to march over to the opposite camp. Nazi Germany was no longer to be alone. One of the principal Allies of the First World War would soon join her. The gravity of this downward turn in the balance of safety oppressed my mind.

Mussolini's designs upon Abyssinia were unsuited to the ethics of the twentieth century. They belonged to those dark ages when white men felt themselves entitled to conquer yellow, brown, black, or red men, and subjugate them by their superior strength and weapons. In our enlightened days, when crimes and cruelties have been committed from which savages of former times would have recoiled, or of which they would at least have been incapable, such conduct was at once obsolete and reprehensible. Moreover, Abyssinia was a member of the League of Nations. By a curious inversion it was Italy who had in 1923 pressed for her inclusion, and Britain who had opposed it. The British view was that the character of the Ethiopian Government and the conditions prevailing in that wild land of tyranny, slavery, and tribal war were not consonant with membership of the League. But the Italians had had their way, and Abyssinia was a member of the League with all its rights and such securities as it could offer. Here, indeed, was a testing case for the instrument of world government upon which the hopes of all good men were founded.

The Italian Dictator was not actuated solely by desire for territorial gains. His rule, his safety, depended upon prestige. The humiliating defeat which Italy had suffered forty years before at Adowa, and the mockery of the world when an Italian army had not only been destroyed or captured but shamefully mutilated, rankled in the minds of all Italians. They had seen how Britain had after the passage of years avenged both Khartoum and Majuba. To proclaim their manhood by avenging Adowa meant almost as much in Italy as the recovery of Alsace-Lorraine in France. There seemed no way in which Mussolini could more easily or at less risk and cost consolidate his own power or, as he saw it, raise the authority of Italy in Europe, than by wiping out the stain of bygone years, and adding Abyssinia to the recently built Italian Empire. All such thoughts were wrong and evil, but since it is always wise to try to understand another country's point of view, they may be recorded.

In the fearful struggle against rearming Nazi Germany which I could feel approaching with inexorable strides, I was most reluctant to see Italy estranged, and even driven into the opposite camp. There was no doubt that the attack by one member of the League of Nations upon another at this juncture, if not resented, would be finally destructive of the League as a factor for welding together the forces which could alone control the might of resurgent Germany and the awful Hitler menace. More could perhaps be got out of the vindicated majesty of the League than Italy could ever give, withhold, or transfer. If, therefore, the League were prepared to use the united strength of all its members to curb Mussolini's policy, it was our bounden duty to take our share and play a faithful part. There seemed in all the circumstances no obligation upon Britain to take the lead herself. She had a duty to take account of her own weakness caused by the loss of air parity, and even more of the military position of France, in the face of German rearmament. One thing was clear and certain. Half-measures were useless for the League and pernicious to Britain if she assumed its leadership. If we thought it right and necessary for the law and welfare of Europe to quarrel mortally with Mussolini's Italy, we must also strike him down. The fall of the lesser dictator might combine and bring into action all the forces — and they were still overwhelming — which would enable us to restrain the greater dictator, and thus prevent a second German war.

These general reflections are a prelude to the narrative of this chapter.

* * * * *

Ever since the Stresa Conference, Mussolini's preparations for the conquest of Abyssinia had been apparent. It was evident that British opinion would be hostile to such an act of Italian aggression. Those of us who saw in Hitler's Germany a danger, not only to peace but to survival, dreaded this movement of a first-class Power, as Italy was then rated, from our side to the other. I remember a dinner at which Sir Robert Vansittart and Mr. Duff Cooper, then only an under-secretary, were present, at which this adverse change in the balance of Europe was clearly foreseen. The project was mooted of some of us going out to see Mussolini in order to explain to him the inevitable effects which would be produced in Great Britain. Nothing came of this; nor would it have been of any good. Mussolini, like Hitler, regarded Britannia as a frightened, flabby old woman, who at the worst would only bluster and was, anyhow, incapable of making war. Lord Lloyd, who was on friendly terms with him, noted how he had been struck by the Joad Resolution of the Oxford undergraduates in 1933 refusing "to fight for king and country."

*   *   *   *   *

In Parliament I expressed my misgivings on July 11:

We seemed to have allowed the impression to be created that we were ourselves coming forward as a sort of bell-wether or fugleman to lead opinion in Europe against Italy's Abyssinian designs. It was even suggested that we would act individually and independently. I am glad to hear from the Foreign Secretary that there is no foundation for that. We must do our duty, but we must do it with other nations only in accordance with the obligations which others recognise as well. We are not strong enough to be the lawgiver and the spokesman of the world. We will do our part, but we cannot be asked to do more than our part in these matters. . . .

As we stand today there is no doubt that a cloud has come over the old friendship between Great Britain and Italy, a cloud which, it seems to me, may very easily not pass away, although undoubtedly it is everyone's desire that it should. It is an old friendship, and we must not forget, what is a little-known fact, that at the time Italy entered into the Triple Alliance in the last century she stipulated particularly that in no circumstances would her obligations under the alliance bring her into armed conflict with Great Britain.

*   *   *   *   *

In August, the Foreign Secretary invited me and also the Opposition Party leaders to visit him separately at the Foreign Office, and the fact of these consultations was made public by the Government. Sir Samuel Hoare told me of this growing anxiety about Italian aggression against Abyssinia and asked me how far I should be prepared to go against it. Wishing to know more about the internal and personal situation at the Foreign Office under dyarchy before replying, I asked about Eden's view. "I will get him to come," said Hoare, and in a few minutes Anthony arrived smiling and in the best of tempers. We had an easy talk. I said I thought the Foreign Secretary was *justified in going as far with the League of Nations against Italy as he could carry France;* but I added that he ought not to put any pressure upon France because of her military convention with Italy and her German preoccupations; and that in the circumstances I did not expect France would go very far. I then spoke of the Italian divisions on the Brenner Pass, of the unguarded southern front of France and other military aspects.

Generally I strongly advised the Ministers not to try to take a leading part or to put themselves forward too prominently. In this I was, of course, oppressed by my German fears and the condition to which our defences had been reduced.

* * * * *

In the early months of 1935, there was organised a Peace Ballot for collective security and for upholding the Covenant of the League of Nations. This scheme received the blessing of the League of Nations Union, but was sponsored by a separate organisation largely supported by the Labour and Liberal Parties. The following were the questions put:

THE PEACE BALLOT

1. Should Great Britain remain a member of the League of Nations?
2. Are you in favour of an all-round reduction of armaments by international agreement?
3. Are you in favour of the all-round abolition of national military and naval aircraft by international agreement?
4. Should the manufacture and sale of armaments for private profit be prohibited by international agreement?
5. Do you consider that if a nation insists on attacking another, the other nations should combine to compel it to stop by:
   (a) economic and non-military measures,
   (b) if necessary military measures?

It was announced on June 27 that over eleven million persons had subscribed their names affirmatively to this. The Peace Ballot seemed at first to be misunderstood by Ministers. Its name overshadowed its purpose. It, of course, combined the contradictory propositions of reduction of armaments and forcible resistance to aggression. It was regarded in many quarters as a part of the pacifist campaign. On the contrary, clause 5 affirmed a positive and courageous policy which could, at this time, have been followed with an overwhelming measure of national support. Lord Cecil and other leaders of the League of Nations Union were, as this clause declared, and as events soon showed, willing, and indeed resolved, to go to war in a righteous cause, provided that all necessary action was taken under the auspices of the League of Nations. Their evaluation of the facts underwent considerable changes in the next few months. Indeed, within a year I was working with them in harmony upon the policy which I described as "Arms and the Covenant."

*   *   *   *   *

As the summer drew on, the movement of Italian troopships through the Suez Canal was continuous, and considerable forces and supplies were assembled along the eastern Abyssinian frontier. Suddenly an extraordinary, and to me, after my talks at the Foreign Office, a quite unexpected, event occurred. On August 24, the Cabinet resolved and declared that Britain would uphold its obligation under its treaties and under the Covenant of the League. This produced an immediate crisis in the Mediterranean, and I thought it right, since I had been so recently consulted, to ask the Foreign Secretary to reassure me about the naval situation:

Mr. Churchill to Sir Samuel Hoare.   *August 25, 1935.*
I am sure you will be on your guard against the capital fault of letting diplomacy get ahead of naval preparedness. We took care about this in 1914.
Where are the fleets? Are they in good order? Are they adequate? Are they capable of rapid and complete concentration? Are they safe? Have they been formally warned to take precautions? Re-

member you are putting extreme pressure upon a Dictator who
may get into desperate straits. He may well measure your corn by
his bushel. He may at any moment in the next fortnight credit
you with designs far beyond what the Cabinet at present harbour.
While you are talking judicious, nicely graded formulas, he may
act with violence. Far better put temptation out of his way.

I see by the newspapers that the Mediterranean Fleet is leaving
Malta for the Levant. Certainly it is wise [for the Fleet] to quit
Malta, which, I understand, is totally unprovided with anti-aircraft
defence. The Mediterranean Fleet based at Alexandria, etc., is on
paper — that is all we are justified in going by — far weaker than
the Italian Navy. I spent some time today looking up the cruiser
and flotilla construction of the two countries since the war. It seems
to me that you have not half the strength of Italy in modern cruisers
and destroyers, and still less in modern submarines. Therefore, it
seems to me that very searching questions should be asked of the
Admiralty *now* as to the position of this British Fleet in the Levant.
It is enough to do us grievous loss. Is it enough to defend itself?
It is more than three thousand miles from reinforcement by the
Atlantic and Home Fleets. Much might happen before these could
effect a junction. I do not, indeed I dare not, doubt but that the
Admiralty have studied the dispositions with vigilance. I hope you
will satisfy yourself that their answers to these suggestions are
adequate.

I heard some time ago talk about a plan of evacuating the
Mediterranean in the event of a war with Italy and holding only
the Straits of Gibraltar and the Red Sea. The movement of the
Mediterranean Fleet to the Levant looks like a piece of this policy.
If so I hope it has been thought out. If we abandon the Mediterranean while in a state of war or quasi-war with Italy, there is
nothing to prevent Mussolini landing in Egypt in force and seizing
the Canal. Nothing but France. Is the Admiralty sure of France in
such a contingency?

George Lloyd, who is with me, thinks I ought to send you this
letter in view of the hazards of the situation. I do not ask you for
a detailed answer; but we should like your assurance that you
have been satisfied with the Admiralty dispositions.

The Foreign Secretary replied on August 27:

You may rest assured that all the points you have mentioned

have been, and are being, actively discussed. I am fully alive to the
kind of risks that you mention, and I will do my best to see that
they are not ignored. Please have no hesitation in sending me any
suggestions or warnings that you think necessary. You know as well
as anyone the risks of a situation such as this, and you also know
as well as anyone, at least outside the Government, the present state
of our imperial defences.

*   *   *   *   *

Mr. Eden, Minister for League of Nations Affairs and almost
co-equal of the Foreign Secretary, had already been for some
weeks at Geneva, where he had rallied the Assembly to a policy
of "sanctions" against Italy if she invaded Abyssinia. The peculiar office to which he had been appointed made him by its
very nature concentrate upon the Abyssinian question with
an emphasis which outweighed other aspects. "Sanctions"
meant the cutting-off from Italy of all financial aid and of
economic supplies, and the giving of all such assistance to
Abyssinia. To a country like Italy, dependent for so many commodities needed in war upon unhampered imports from overseas, this was indeed a formidable deterrent. Eden's zeal and
address and the principles which he proclaimed dominated
the Assembly. On September 11, the Foreign Secretary, Sir
Samuel Hoare, having arrived at Geneva, himself addressed
them:

I will begin by reaffirming the support of the League by the
Government I represent and the interest of the British people in
collective security. . . . The ideas enshrined in the Covenant and
in particular the aspiration to establish the rule of law in international affairs have become a part of our national conscience. It is
to the principles of the League and not to any particular manifestation that the British nation has demonstrated its adherence.
Any other view is at once an underestimation of our good faith
and an imputation upon our sincerity. In conformity with its
precise and explicit obligations the League stands, and my country
stands with it, for the collective maintenance of the Covenant in
its entirety, and particularly for steady and collective resistance to
all acts of unprovoked aggression.

In spite of my anxieties about Germany, and little as I liked the way our affairs were handled, I remember being stirred by this speech when I read it in Riviera sunshine. It aroused everyone, and reverberated throughout the United States. It united all those forces in Britain which stood for a fearless combination of righteousness and strength. Here at least was a policy. If only the orator had realised what tremendous powers he held unleashed in his hand at that moment, he might indeed for a while have led the world.

These declarations gathered their validity from the fact that they had behind them, like many causes which in the past have proved vital to human progress and freedom, the British Navy. For the first and the last time the League of Nations seemed to have at its disposal a secular arm. Here was the international police force, upon the ultimate authority of which all kinds of diplomatic and economic pressures and persuasion could be employed. When on September 12, the very next day, the battle cruisers *Hood* and *Renown*, accompanied by the Second Cruiser Squadron and a destroyer flotilla, arrived at Gibraltar, it was assumed on all sides that Britain would back her words with deeds. Policy and action alike gained immediate and overwhelming support at home. It was taken for granted, not unnaturally, that neither the declaration nor the movement of warships would have been made without careful expert calculation by the Admiralty of the fleet or fleets required in the Mediterranean to make our undertakings good.

At the end of September, I had to make a speech at the City Carlton Club, an orthodox body of some influence. I tried to convey a warning to Mussolini which I believe he read:

To cast an army of nearly a quarter of a million men, embodying the flower of Italian manhood, upon a barren shore two thousand miles from home, against the good will of the whole world and without command of the sea, and then in this position embark upon what may well be a series of campaigns against a people and in regions which no conqueror in four thousand years ever thought it worth while to subdue, is to give hostages to fortune unparalleled in all history.[1]

[1] See also my conversation with Count Grandi, Appendix A, Book I.

Sir Austen Chamberlain wrote to me agreeing with this speech, and I replied:

October 1, 1935.

I am glad you approve the line I took about Abyssinia; but I am very unhappy. It would be a terrible deed to smash up Italy, and it will cost us dear. How strange it is that after all these years of begging France to make it up with Italy, we are now forcing her to choose between Italy and ourselves! I do not think we ought to have taken the lead in such a vehement way. If we had felt so strongly on the subject we should have warned Mussolini two months before. The sensible course would have been gradually to strengthen the Fleet in the Mediterranean during the early summer, and so let him see how grave the matter was. Now what can he do? I expect a very serious rise of temperature when the fighting [in Abyssinia] begins.

* * * * *

In October, Mussolini, undeterred by belated British naval movements, launched the Italian armies upon the invasion of Abyssinia. On the tenth, by the votes of fifty sovereign states to one, the Assembly of the League resolved to take collective measures against Italy, and a committee of eighteen was appointed to make further efforts for a peaceful solution. Mussolini, thus confronted, made a clear-cut statement, marked by deep shrewdness. Instead of saying, "Italy will meet sanctions with war," he said: "Italy will meet them with discipline, with frugality, and with sacrifice." At the same time, however, he intimated that *he would not tolerate the imposition of any sanctions which hampered his invasion of Abyssinia*. If that enterprise were endangered, he would go to war with whoever stood in his path. "Fifty nations!" he said. "Fifty nations, led by one!" Such was the position in the weeks which preceded the dissolution of Parliament in Britain and the general election, which was now constitutionally due.

* * * * *

Bloodshed in Abyssinia, hatred of Fascism, the invocation of sanctions by the League, produced a convulsion within the

British Labour Party. Trade-unionists, among whom Mr. Ernest Bevin was outstanding, were by no means pacifist by temperament. A very strong desire to fight the Italian Dictator, to enforce sanctions of a decisive character, and to use the British Fleet, if need be, surged through the sturdy wage-earners. Rough and harsh words were spoken at excited meetings. On one occasion Mr. Bevin complained that "he was tired of having George Lansbury's conscience carted about from conference to conference." Many members of the Parliamentary Labour Party shared the trade-union mood. In a far wider sphere, all the leaders of the League of Nations Union felt themselves bound to the cause of the League. Clause 5 of their "Peace Ballot" was plainly involved. Here were principles in obedience to which lifelong humanitarians were ready to die, and if to die, also to kill. On October 8, Mr. Lansbury resigned his leadership of the Parliamentary Labour Party, and Major Attlee, who had a fine war record, reigned in his stead.

*   *   *   *   *

But this national awakening was not in accord with Mr. Baldwin's outlook or intentions. It was not till several months after the election that I began to understand the principles upon which "sanctions" were founded. The Prime Minister had declared that sanctions meant war; secondly, he was resolved there must be no war; and thirdly, he decided upon sanctions. It was evidently impossible to reconcile these three conditions. Under the guidance of Britain and the pressures of Laval, the League of Nations Committee, charged with devising sanctions, kept clear of any that would provoke war. A large number of commodities, some of which were war materials, were prohibited from entering Italy, and an imposing schedule was drawn up. But oil, without which the campaign in Abyssinia could not have been maintained, continued to enter freely, because it was understood that to stop it meant war. Here the attitude of the United States, not a member of the League of Nations and the world's main oil supplier, though benevolent, was uncertain. Moreover, to stop it to Italy involved also stopping it to Germany. The export of aluminium into Italy was strictly forbidden; but aluminium was almost the only metal that Italy produced in quantities beyond her own needs. The importation of scrap iron and iron ore into Italy was sternly vetoed in the name of public justice. But as the Italian metallurgical industry made but little use of them, and as steel billets and pig iron were not interfered with, Italy suffered no hindrance. Thus, the measures pressed with so great a parade were not real sanctions to paralyse the aggressor, but merely such half-hearted sanctions as the aggressor would tolerate, because in fact, though onerous, they stimulated Italian war spirit. The League of Nations, therefore, proceeded to the rescue of Abyssinia on the basis that nothing must be done to hamper the invading Italian armies. These facts were not known to the British public at the time of the election. They earnestly supported the policy of the sanctions, and believed that this was a sure way of bringing the Italian assault upon Abyssinia to an end.

Still less did His Majesty's Government contemplate the use of the Fleet. All kinds of tales were told of Italian suicide squadrons of dive-bombers which would hurl themselves upon the decks of our ships and blow them to pieces. The British Fleet which was lying at Alexandria had now been reinforced. It could by a gesture have turned back Italian transports from the Suez Canal, and would as a consequence have had to offer battle to the Italian Navy. We were told that it was not capable of meeting such an antagonist. I had raised the question at the outset, but had been reassured. Our battleships, of course, were old, and it now appeared that we had no aircraft cover and very little anti-aircraft ammunition. It transpired, however, that the Admiral commanding resented the suggestion attributed to him that he was not strong enough to fight a fleet action. It would seem that before taking their first decision to oppose the Italian aggression, His Majesty's Government should carefully have examined ways and means and also made up their minds.

There is no doubt on our present knowledge that a bold

decision would have cut the Italian communications with Ethiopia, and that we should have been successful in any naval battle which might have followed. I was never in favour of isolated action by Great Britain, but having gone so far it was a grievous deed to recoil. Moreover, Mussolini would never have dared to come to grips with a resolute British Government. Nearly the whole of the world was against him, and he would have had to risk his régime upon a single-handed war with Britain, in which a fleet action in the Mediterranean would be the early and decisive test. How could Italy have fought this war? Apart from a limited advantage in modern light cruisers, her navy was but a fourth the size of the British. Her numerous conscript army, which was vaunted in millions, could not come into action. Her air power was in quantity and quality far below even our modest establishments. She would instantly have been blockaded. The Italian armies in Abyssinia would have famished for supplies and ammunition. Germany could as yet give no effective help. If ever there was an opportunity of striking a decisive blow in a generous cause with the minimum of risk, it was here and now. The fact that the nerve of the British Government was not equal to the occasion can be excused only by their sincere love of peace. Actually it played a part in leading to an infinitely more terrible war. Mussolini's bluff succeeded, and an important spectator drew far-reaching conclusions from the fact. Hitler had long resolved on war for German aggrandisement. He now formed a view of Great Britain's degeneracy which was only to be changed too late for peace and too late for him. In Japan, also, there were pensive spectators.

* * * * *

The two opposite processes of gathering national unity on the burning issue of the hour and the clash of party interests inseparable from a general election moved forward together. This was greatly to the advantage of Mr. Baldwin and his supporters. "The League of Nations would remain as heretofore the keystone of British foreign policy," so ran the Government's election manifesto. "The prevention of war and the establishment of peace in the world must always be the most vital interest of the British people, and the League is the instrument which has been framed and to which we look for the attainment of these objects. We shall therefore continue to do all in our power to uphold the Covenant and to maintain and increase the efficiency of the League. In the present unhappy dispute between Italy and Abyssinia *there will be no wavering in the policy we have hitherto pursued.*"

The Labour Party, on the other hand, was much divided. The majority was pacifist, but Mr. Bevin's active campaign commanded many supporters among the masses. The official leaders, therefore, tried to give general satisfaction by pointing opposite ways at once. On the one hand they clamoured for decisive action against the Italian Dictator; on the other they denounced the policy of rearmament. Thus Mr. Attlee in the House of Commons on October 22: "We want effective sanctions, effectively applied. We support economic sanctions. We support the League system." But then, later in the same speech: "We are not persuaded that the way to safety is by piling up armaments. We do not believe that in this [time] there is such a thing as national defence. We think that you have to go forward to disarmament and not to the piling-up of armaments." Neither side usually has much to be proud of at election times. The Prime Minister himself was no doubt conscious of the growing strength behind the Government's foreign policy. He was, however, determined not to be drawn into war on any account. It seemed to me, viewing the proceedings from outside, that he was anxious to gather as much support as possible and use it to begin British rearmament on a modest scale.

*   *   *   *   *

The Conservative Party Conference was held at Bournemouth on the very day when Mussolini began his attack on Abyssinia and his bombs were falling on Adowa. In view of this, and not less of the now imminent general election, we all closed our ranks as party men.

I supported a resolution which was carried unanimously:

(1) To repair the serious deficiencies in the defence forces of the Crown, and, in particular, first, to organise our industry for speedy conversion to defence purposes, if need be.

(2) To make a renewed effort to establish equality in the air with the strongest foreign air force within striking distance of our shores.

(3) To rebuild the British Fleet and strengthen the Royal Navy, so as to safeguard our food and livelihood and preserve the coherence of the British Empire.

Hitherto in these years I had not desired office, having had so much of it, and being opposed to the Government on their Indian policy. But with the passage of the India Bill, which was to take some years to come into force, this barrier had fallen away. The growing German menace made me anxious to lay my hands upon our military machine. I could now feel very keenly what was coming. Distracted France and timid, peace-loving Britain would soon be confronted with the challenge of the European Dictators. I was in sympathy with the changing temper of the Labour Party. Here was the chance of a true National Government. It was understood that the Admiralty would be vacant, and I wished very much to go there should the Conservatives be returned to power. I was, of course, well aware that this desire was not shared by several of Mr. Baldwin's principal colleagues. I represented a policy, and it was known that I should strive for it whether from without or from within. If they could do without me, they would certainly be very glad. To some extent this depended upon their majority.

*　　*　　*　　*　　*

At the general election the Prime Minister spoke in strong terms of the need for rearmament, and his principal speech was devoted to the unsatisfactory condition of the Navy. However, having gained all that there was in sight upon a programme of sanctions and rearmament, he became very anxious to comfort the professional peace-loving elements in the nation, and allay any fears in their breasts which his talk about naval re-

quirements might have caused. On October 1, two weeks before the poll, he made a speech to the Peace Society at the
Guildhall. In the course of this he said, "I give you my word
there will be no great armaments." In the light of the knowledge which the Government had of strenuous German preparations, this was a singular promise. Thus the votes both of those
who sought to see the nation prepare itself against the dangers
of the future, and of those who believed that peace could be
preserved by praising its virtues, were gained.

*   *   *   *   *

I fought my contest in the Epping Division upon the need for
rearmament and upon a severe and *bona-fide* policy of sanctions. Generally speaking I supported the Government, and although many of my Conservative friends had been offended by
my almost ceaseless criticism of Government measures, I was
returned by an ample majority. Upon the declaration of the
poll I thought it right to safeguard my own position. "I take
it from your vote, in view of the speeches I have made, that you
desire me to exercise my independent judgment as a Member
of Parliament, and in accordance with the highest traditions
of that House, to give the fruits of my knowledge and experience freely and without fear." The result of the general election was a triumph for Mr. Baldwin. The electors accorded
him a majority of two hundred and forty-seven over all other
parties combined, and after five years of office he reached a position of personal power unequalled by any Prime Minister since
the close of the Great War. All who had opposed him, whether on
India or on the neglect of our defences, were stultified by this
renewed vote of confidence, which he had gained by his skilful
and fortunate tactics in home politics and by the esteem so
widely felt for his personal character. Thus an administration
more disastrous than any in our history saw all its errors and
shortcomings acclaimed by the nation. There was, however, a
bill to be paid, and it took the new House of Commons nearly
ten years to pay it.

*   *   *   *   *

It had been widely bruited that I should join the Government as First Lord of the Admiralty. But after the figures of his victory had been proclaimed, Mr. Baldwin lost no time in announcing through the Central Office that there was no intention to include me in the Government. In this way he paid some of his debt to the pacifist deputation which he had received in the last days of the election. There was much mocking in the press about my exclusion. But now one can see how lucky I was. Over me beat the invisible wings.

And I had agreeable consolations. I set out with my paint-box for more genial climes without waiting for the meeting of Parliament.

*   *   *   *   *

There was an awkward sequel to Mr. Baldwin's triumph, for the sake of which we may sacrifice chronology. His Foreign Secretary, Sir Samuel Hoare, travelling through Paris to Switzerland on a well-earned skating holiday, had a talk with M. Laval, still French Foreign Minister. The result of this was the Hoare-Laval Pact of December 9. It is worth while to look a little into the background of this celebrated incident.

The idea of Britain leading the League of Nations against Mussolini's Fascist invasion of Abyssinia had carried the nation in one of its big swings. But once the election was over and the Ministers found themselves in possession of a majority which might give them for five years the guidance of the State, many tiresome consequences had to be considered. At the root of them all lay Mr. Baldwin's "There must be no war," and also, "There must be no large rearmament." This remarkable party manager, having won the election on world leadership against aggression, was profoundly convinced that we must keep peace at any price.

Moreover, now from the Foreign Office came a very powerful thrust. Sir Robert Vansittart never removed his eyes for one moment from the Hitler peril. He and I were of one mind on that point. And now British policy had forced Mussolini to change sides. Germany was no longer isolated. The four Western Powers were divided two against two instead of three against one. This marked deterioration in our affairs aggravated the anxiety in France. The French Government had already made the Franco-Italian agreement of January. Following thereupon had come the military convention with Italy. It was calculated that this convention saved eighteen French divisions from the Italian front for transference to the front against Germany. In his negotiations it is certain that M. Laval had given more than a hint to Mussolini that France would not trouble herself about anything that might happen to Abyssinia. The French had a considerable case to argue with British Ministers. First, for several years we had tried to make them reduce their army, which was all they had to live upon. Secondly, the British had had a very good run in the leadership of the League of Nations against Mussolini. They had even won an election upon it; and in democracies elections are very important. Thirdly, we had made a naval agreement, supposed to be very good for ourselves, which made us quite comfortable upon the seas apart from submarine warfare.

But what about the French front? How was it to be manned against the ever-growing German military power? Two divisions to be sent only under many reservations was all the British could offer for the first six months; so really they should not talk too much. Now the British Government, in a fine flow of martial, moral and world sentiment, "fifty nations led by one," were making a mortal feud with Italy. France had much to worry about, and only very silly people, of whom there are extremely large numbers in every country, could ignore all this. If Britain had used her naval power, closed the Suez Canal, and defeated the Italian Navy in a general engagement, she would have had the right to call the tune in Europe. But on the contrary, she had definitely declared that whatever happened she would not go to war over Abyssinia. Honest Mr. Baldwin; a triumphant vote in the constituencies; a solid Tory majority for five more years; every aspect of righteous indignation, but no war, no war! The French, therefore, felt very strongly that they should not be drawn into permanent estrangement from Italy because of all the strong feeling which had suddenly

surged up in England against Mussolini. Especially did they
feel this when they remembered that Britain had bowed before
the Italian naval challenge in the Mediterranean, and when
two divisions of troops were all we could send at the outset to
help France if she were invaded by Germany. One can certainly understand Monsieur Laval's point of view at this
time.

Now in December a new set of arguments marched upon the
scene. Mussolini, hard pressed by sanctions, and under the very
heavy threat of "fifty nations led by one," would, it was whis-
pered, welcome a compromise on Abyssinia. Poison gas, though
effective against the native Ethiopians, would certainly not ele-
vate the name of Italy in the world. The Abyssinians were
being defeated. They were not, it was said, prepared to make
large concessions and wide surrenders of territory. Could not
a peace be made which gave Italy what she had aggressively
demanded and left Abyssinia four-fifths of her entire empire?
Vansittart, who happened to be in Paris at the time the Foreign
Secretary passed through, and was thus drawn into the affair,
should not be misjudged because he thought continuously of
the German threat, and wished to have Britain and France
organised at their strongest to face this major danger, with Italy
in their rear a friend and not a foe.

But the British nation from time to time gives way to waves
of crusading sentiment. More than any other country in the
world, it is at rare intervals ready to fight for a cause or a theme,
just because it is convinced in its heart and soul that it will not
get any material advantage out of the conflict. Baldwin and his
Ministers had given a great uplift to Britain in their resistance
to Mussolini at Geneva. They had gone so far that their only
salvation before history was to go all lengths. Unless they were
prepared to back words and gestures by action, it might have
been better to keep out of it all, like the United States, and let
things rip and see what happened. Here was an arguable plan.
But it was not the plan they had adopted. They had appealed
to the millions, and the unarmed, and hitherto unconcerned,
millions had answered with a loud shout, overpowering all

other cries, "Yes, we will march against evil, and we will march
now. Give us the weapons."

The new House of Commons was a spirited body. With all
that lay before them in the next ten years, they had need to be.
It was therefore with a horrible shock that, while tingling from
the election, they received the news that a compromise had
been made between Sir Samuel Hoare and M. Laval about
Abyssinia. This crisis nearly cost Mr. Baldwin his political
life. It shook Parliament and the nation to its base. Mr. Baldwin fell almost overnight from his pinnacle of acclaimed
national leadership to a depth where he was derided and despised. His position in the House during these days was pitiful.
He had never understood why people should worry about all
these bothersome foreign affairs. They had a Conservative
majority and no war. What more could they want? But the
experienced pilot felt and measured the full force of the storm.

The Cabinet, on December 9, had approved the Hoare-Laval
plan to partition Abyssinia between Italy and the Emperor.
On the thirteenth the full text of the Hoare-Laval proposals
was laid before the League. On the eighteenth the Cabinet
abandoned the Hoare-Laval proposals, thus entailing the resignation of Sir Samuel Hoare. In the debate on the nineteenth
Mr. Baldwin said:

I felt that these proposals went too far. I was not at all surprised
at the expression of feeling in that direction. I was not expecting
that deeper feeling that was manifest in many parts of the country
on what I may call the grounds of conscience and of honour. The
moment I am confronted with that, I know that something has
happened that has appealed to the deepest feelings of our countrymen, that some note has been struck that brings back from them
a response from the depths. I examined again all that I had done,
and I felt that . . . there could not be support in this country
behind those proposals even as terms of negotiation. It is perfectly
obvious now that the proposals are absolutely and completely
dead. This Government is certainly going to make no attempt to
resurrect them. If there arose a storm when I knew I was in the
right, I would let it break on me, and I would either survive it or
break. If I felt after examination of myself that there was in that

storm something which showed me that I had done something that was not wise or right, then I would bow to it.

The House accepted this apologia. The crisis passed. On his return from Geneva, Mr. Eden was summoned to 10 Downing Street by the Prime Minister to discuss the situation following Sir Samuel Hoare's resignation. Mr. Eden at once suggested that Sir Austen Chamberlain should be invited to take over the Foreign Office, and added that if desired he was prepared to serve under him in any capacity. Mr. Baldwin replied that he had already considered this and had informed Sir Austen himself that he did not feel able to offer the Foreign Office to him. This may have been due to Sir Austen's health. On December 22, Mr. Eden became Foreign Secretary.

*   *   *   *   *

My wife and I passed this exciting week at Barcelona. Several of my best friends advised me not to return. They said I should only do myself harm if I were mixed up in this violent conflict. Our comfortable Barcelona hotel was the rendezvous of the Spanish Left. In the excellent restaurant where we lunched and dined were always several groups of eager-faced, black-coated young men purring together with glistening eyes about Spanish politics, in which quite soon a million Spaniards were to die. Looking back, I think I ought to have come home. I might have brought an element of decision and combination to the anti-Government gatherings which would have ended the Baldwin régime. Perhaps a Government under Sir Austen Chamberlain might have been established at this moment. On the other hand, my friends cried: "Better stay away. Your return will only be regarded as a personal challenge to the Government." I did not relish the advice, which was certainly not flattering; but I yielded to the impression that I could do no good, and stayed on at Barcelona daubing canvases in the sunshine. Thereafter Frederick Lindemann joined me, and we cruised in a nice steamship around the eastern coasts of Spain and landed at Tangier. Here I found Lord Rothermere with a pleasant circle. He told me that Mr. Lloyd George was at

Marrakesh, where the weather was lovely. We all motored thither. I lingered painting in delightful Morocco, and did not return till the sudden death of King George V on January 20.

* * * * *

The collapse of Abyssinian resistance and the annexation of the whole country by Italy produced unhelpful effects in German public opinion. Even those elements which did not approve of Mussolini's policy or action admired the swift, efficient, and ruthless manner in which, as it seemed, the campaign had been conducted. The general view was that Great Britain had emerged thoroughly weakened. She had earned the undying hatred of Italy; she had wrecked the Stresa Front once and for all; and her loss of prestige in the world contrasted agreeably with the growing strength and repute of the new Germany. "I am impressed," wrote one of our representatives in Bavaria, "by the note of contempt in references to Great Britain in many quarters. . . . It is to be feared that Germany's attitude in the negotiations for a settlement in Western Europe and for a more general settlement of European and extra-European questions will be found to have stiffened."

An article in the *Muenchener Zeitung* (May 16, 1936) contains some illuminating passages:

The English like a comfortable life compared with our German standards. This does not indeed mean that they are incapable of sustained efforts, but they avoid them so far as they can, without impairing their personal and national security. They also control means and wealth which have enabled them, in contrast with us, for a century or so, to increase their capital more or less automatically. . . . After the war, in which the English after some preliminary hesitation showed certainly an amazing energy, the British masters of the world thought they had at last earned a little rest. They disarmed along the whole line — in civil life even more than on land and sea. They reconciled themselves to abandoning the two-power [naval] standard and accepted parity with America. . . . How about the Army? How about the air force? . . . For the land and air defence forces England needs above all men, not merely money, but also the lives of her citizens for Empire defence.

Indeed, of the eleven thousand men needed for the new air programme, seven thousand are lacking. Again, the small Regular Army shows a large deficiency, about one whole division, and the Territorial Army (a sort of Sunday-School for amateur soldiers) is so far below its authorised numbers that it cannot in any way be considered an effective combatant force. Mr. Baldwin himself said a short time ago that he had no intention of changing the system of recruiting by the introduction of conscription.

A policy which seeks to achieve success by postponing decisions can today hardly hope to resist the whirlwind which is shaking Europe and indeed the whole world. Few are the men who, upon national and not upon party grounds, rage against the spinelessness and ambiguous attitude of the Government, and hold them responsible for the dangers into which the Empire is being driven all unaware. The masses seem to agree with the Government that the situation will improve by marking time, and that by means of small adjustments and carefully thought-out manoeuvres the balance can once again be rectified. . . .

Today all Abyssinia is irrevocably, fully, and finally Italian alone. This being so, neither Geneva nor London can have any doubt that only the use of extraordinary force can drive the Italians out of Abyssinia. But neither the power nor the courage to use force is at hand.

All this was only too true. His Majesty's Government had imprudently advanced to champion a great world cause. They had led fifty nations forward with much brave language. Confronted with brute facts Mr. Baldwin had recoiled. Their policy had for a long time been designed to give satisfaction to powerful elements of opinion at home rather than to seek the realities of the European situation. By estranging Italy they had upset the whole balance of Europe and gained nothing for Abyssinia. They had led the League of Nations into an utter fiasco, most damaging if not fatally injurious to its effective life as an institution.

11

Hitler Strikes

1936

A New Atmosphere in Britain — Hitler Free to Strike — Ratification of the Franco-Soviet Pact — The Rhineland and the Treaties of Versailles and Locarno — Hitler Reoccupies the Rhineland, March 7 — French Hesitation — Flandin's Visit to London — British Pacifism — Flandin and Baldwin — Ralph Wigram's Grief — Hitler's Vindication and Triumph — A Minister of Co-ordination of Defence — Sir Thomas Inskip Chosen — A Blessing in Disguise — My Hopes of the League — Eden Insists on Staff Conversations with France — German Fortification of the Rhineland — My Warnings in Parliament — Mr. Bullitt's Post-War Revelations — Hitler's Pledge to Austria, July 11.

WHEN I RETURNED at the end of January, 1936, I was conscious of a new atmosphere in England. Mussolini's conquest of Ethiopia and the brutal methods by which it had been accomplished, the shock of the Hoare-Laval negotiations, the discomfiture of the League of Nations, the obvious breakdown of "collective security," had altered the mood, not only of the Labour and Liberal Parties, but of that great body of well-meaning but hitherto futile opinion represented by the eleven million votes cast in the Peace Ballot only seven months before. All these forces were now prepared to contemplate war against Fascist or Nazi tyranny. Far from being excluded from lawful thought, the use of force gradually became a decisive point in the minds of a vast mass of peace-loving people, and even of many who had hitherto been proud to be called pacifists. But

188

force, according to the principles which they served, could only
be used on the initiative and under the authority of the League
of Nations. Although both the Opposition parties continued
to oppose all measures of rearmament, there was an immense
measure of agreement open, and had His Majesty's Government risen to the occasion they could have led a united people
forward into the whole business of preparation in an emergency spirit.

The Government adhered to their policy of moderation, half-
measures, and keeping things quiet. It was astonishing to me
that they did not seek to utilise all the growing harmonies
that now existed in the nation. By this means they would
enormously have strengthened themselves and have gained the
power to strengthen the country. Mr. Baldwin had no such
inclinations. He was ageing fast. He rested upon the great
majority which the election had given him, and the Conservative Party lay tranquil in his hand.

*   *   *   *   *

Once Hitler's Germany had been allowed to rearm without
active interference by the Allies and former associated Powers,
a second World War was almost certain. The longer a decisive
trial of strength was put off, the worse would be our chances, at
first of stopping Hitler without serious fighting, and as a second stage of being victorious after a terrible ordeal. In the
summer of 1935, Germany had reinstituted conscription in
breach of the Treaties. Great Britain had condoned this, and
by a separate agreement her rebuilding of a navy, if desired,
with U-boats on the British scale. Nazi Germany had secretly
and unlawfully created a military air force which, by the
spring of 1935, openly claimed to be equal to the British. She
was now in the second year of active munitions production
after long covert preparations. Great Britain and all Europe,
and what was then thought distant America, were faced with
the organised might and will-to-war of seventy millions of the
most efficient race in Europe, longing to regain their national
glory, and driven — in case they faltered — by a merciless military, social, and party régime.

Hitler was now free to strike. The successive steps which he took encountered no effective resistance from the two liberal democracies of Europe, and, apart from their far-seeing President, only gradually excited the attention of the United States. The battle for peace which could, during 1935, have been won, was now almost lost. Mussolini had triumphed in Abyssinia, and had successfully defied the League of Nations and especially Great Britain. He was now bitterly estranged from us, and had joined hands with Hitler. The Berlin-Rome Axis was in being. There was now, as it turned out, little hope of averting war or of postponing it by a trial of strength equivalent to war. Almost all that remained open to France and Britain was to await the moment of the challenge and do the best they could.

There was, perhaps, still time for an assertion of collective security, based upon the avowed readiness of all members concerned to enforce the decisions of the League of Nations by the sword. The democracies and their dependent states were still actually and potentially far stronger than the dictatorships, but their position relatively to their opponents was less than half as good as it had been twelve months before. Virtuous motives, trammelled by inertia and timidity, are no match for armed and resolute wickedness. A sincere love of peace is no excuse for muddling hundreds of millions of humble folk into total war. The cheers of weak, well-meaning assemblies soon cease to echo, and their votes soon cease to count. Doom marches on.

*   *   *   *   *

Germany had, during the course of 1935, repulsed and sabotaged the efforts of the Western Powers to negotiate an Eastern Locarno. The new Reich at this moment declared itself a bulwark against Bolshevism, and for them, they said, there could be no question of working with the Soviets. Hitler told the Polish Ambassador in Berlin on December 18, that "he was resolutely opposed to any co-operation of the West with Russia." It was in this mood that he sought to hinder and undermine the French attempts to reach direct agreement with

Moscow. The Franco-Soviet Pact had been signed in May, but not ratified by either party. It became a major object of German diplomacy to prevent such a ratification. Laval was warned from Berlin that if this move took place there could be no hope of any further Franco-German rapprochement. His reluctance to persevere thereafter became marked; but did not affect the event.

In January, 1936, M. Flandin, the new French Foreign Minister, came to London for the funeral of King George V. On the evening of his visit he dined at Downing Street with Mr. Baldwin and Mr. Eden. The conversation turned to the future attitude of France and Britain in the event of a violation of the Locarno Treaty by Germany. Such a step by Hitler was considered probable, as the French Government now intended to proceed with the ratification of the Franco-Soviet Pact. Flandin undertook to seek the official views of the French Cabinet and General Staff. In February at Geneva, according to his account, he informed Mr. Eden that the armed forces of France would be put at the disposal of the League in the event of a treaty violation by Germany, and asked the British Minister for the eventual assistance of Great Britain in conformity with the clauses of Locarno.

On February 28, the French Chamber ratified the Franco-Soviet Pact, and the following day the French Ambassador in Berlin was instructed to approach the German Government and inquire upon what basis general negotiations for a Franco-German understanding could be initiated. Hitler, in reply, asked for a few days in which to reflect. At ten o'clock on the morning of March 7, Herr von Neurath, the German Foreign Minister, summoned the British, French, Belgian, and Italian Ambassadors to the Wilhelmstrasse to announce to them a proposal for a twenty-five-year pact, a demilitarisation on both sides of the Rhine frontier, a pact limiting air forces, and non-aggression pacts to be negotiated with Eastern and Western neighbours.

* * * * *

The "demilitarised zone" in the Rhineland had been estab-

lished by Articles 42, 43, and 44 of the Treaty of Versailles.
These articles declared that Germany should not have or
establish fortifications on the left bank of the Rhine or within
fifty kilometres of its right bank. Neither should Germany
have in this zone any military forces, nor hold at any time any
military manoeuvres, nor maintain any facilities for military
mobilisation. On top of this lay the Treaty of Locarno, freely
negotiated by both sides. In this treaty the signatory Powers
guaranteed individually and collectively the permanence of
the frontiers of Germany and Belgium and of Germany and
France. Article 2 of the Treaty of Locarno promised that Germany, France, and Belgium would never invade or attack across
these frontiers. Should, however, Articles 42 or 43 of the
Treaty of Versailles be infringed, such a violation would constitute "an unprovoked act of aggression," and immediate action would be required from the offended signatories because of
the assembling of armed forces in the demilitarised zone. Such
a violation should be brought at once before the League of
Nations, and the League, having established the fact of violation, must then advise the signatory Powers that they were
bound to give their military aid to the Power against whom
the offence had been perpetrated.

*   *   *   *   *

At noon on this same March 7, 1936, two hours after his proposal for a twenty-five-year pact, Hitler announced to the
Reichstag that he intended to reoccupy the Rhineland, and
even while he spoke, German columns, about thirty-five thousand
strong, streamed across the boundary and entered all the main
German towns. They were everywhere received with rejoicing,
tempered by the fear of Allied action. Simultaneously, in order
to baffle British and American public opinion, Hitler declared
that the occupation was purely symbolic. The German Ambassador in London handed Mr. Eden similar proposals to
those which Neurath in Berlin had given to the Ambassadors
of the other Locarno Powers in the morning. This provided
comfort for everyone on both sides of the Atlantic who wished

to be humbugged. Mr. Eden made a stern reply to the Ambassador. We now know, of course, that Hitler was merely using these conciliatory proposals as part of his design and as a cover for the violent act he had committed, the success of which was vital to his prestige and thus to the next step in his programme.

It was not only a breach of an obligation exacted by force of arms in war and of the Treaty of Locarno, signed freely in full peace, but the taking advantage of the friendly evacuation by the Allies of the Rhineland several years before it was due. This news caused a world-wide sensation. The French Government under M. Sarraut, in which M. Flandin was Foreign Minister, uprose in vociferous wrath and appealed to all its allies and to the League. At this time France commanded the loyalty of the "Little Entente," namely, Czechoslovakia, Yugoslavia, and Rumania. The Baltic States and Poland were also associated with the French system. Above all, France also had a right to look to Great Britain, having regard to the guarantee we had given for the French frontier against German aggression, and the pressure we had put upon France for the earlier evacuation of the Rhineland. Here if ever was the violation, not only of the Peace Treaty, but of the Treaty of Locarno; and an obligation binding upon all the Powers concerned.

* * * * *

In France there was a hideous shock. MM. Sarraut and Flandin had the impulse to act at once by general mobilisation. If they had been equal to their task, they would have done so; and thus compelled all others to come into line. It was a vital issue for France. But they appeared unable to move without the concurrence of Britain. This is an explanation, but no excuse. The issue was vital to France, and any French Government worthy of the name should have made up its own mind and trusted to the Treaty obligations. More than once in these fluid years French Ministers in their ever-changing Governments were content to find in British pacifism an excuse for their own. Be this as it may, they did not meet with any encouragement to resist the German aggression from the British. On the contrary, if they hesitated to act, their British allies did not hesitate to dissuade them. During the whole of Sunday there were agitated telephonic conversations between London and Paris. His Majesty's Government exhorted the French to wait in order that both countries might act jointly and after full consideration. A velvet carpet for retreat!

The unofficial responses from London were chilling. Mr. Lloyd George hastened to say, "In my judgment Herr Hitler's greatest crime was not the breach of a treaty, because there was provocation." He added that "He hoped we should keep our heads." The provocation was presumably the failure of the Allies to disarm themselves more than they had done. Lord Snowden concentrated upon the proposed non-aggression pact, and said that Hitler's previous peace overtures had been ignored, but the peoples would not permit *this* peace offer to be neglected. These utterances may have expressed misguided British public opinion at the moment, but will not be deemed creditable to their authors. The British Cabinet, seeking the line of least resistance, felt that the easiest way out was to press France into another appeal to the League of Nations.

*   *   *   *   *

There was also great division in France. On the whole, it was the politicians who wished to mobilise the army and send an ultimatum to Hitler, and the generals who, like their German counterparts, pleaded for calm, patience, and delay. We now know of the conflicts of opinion which arose at this time between Hitler and the German High Command. If the French Government had mobilised the French Army, with nearly a hundred divisions, and its air force (then still falsely believed to be the strongest in Europe), there is no doubt that Hitler would have been compelled by his own General Staff to withdraw, and a check would have been given to his pretensions which might well have proved fatal to his rule. It must be remembered that France alone was at this time quite strong

enough to drive the Germans out of the Rhineland, even without the aid which her own action, once begun, and the invocation of the Locarno Treaty would certainly have drawn from
Great Britain. In fact she remained completely inert and
paralysed, and thus lost irretrievably the last chance of arresting
Hitler's ambitions without a serious war. Instead, the French
Government were urged by Britain to cast their burden upon
the League of Nations, already weakened and disheartened by
the fiasco of sanctions and the Anglo-German Naval Agreement
of the previous year.

On Monday, March 9, Mr. Eden went to Paris accompanied
by Lord Halifax and Ralph Wigram. The first plan had been
to convene a meeting of the League in Paris, but presently
Wigram, on Eden's authority, was sent to invite Flandin to
come to London to have the meeting of the League in England,
as he would thus get more effective support from Britain. This
was an unwelcome mission for the faithful official. Immediately
on his return to London on March 11, he came to see me, and
told me the story. Flandin himself arrived late the same night,
and at about 8.30 on Thursday morning he came to my flat in
Morpeth Mansions. He told me that he proposed to demand
from the British Government simultaneous mobilisation of the
land, sea, and air forces of both countries, and that he had received assurances of support from all the nations of the Little
Entente and from other states. He read out an impressive list
of the replies received. There was no doubt that superior
strength still lay with the Allies of the former war. They had
only to act to win. Although we did not know what was passing between Hitler and his generals, it was evident that overwhelming force lay on our side. There was little I could do
in my detached private position, but I wished our visitor all
success in bringing matters to a head and promised any
assistance that was in my power. I gathered my principal
associates at dinner that night to hear M. Flandin's exhortations.

Mr. Chamberlain was at this time, as Chancellor of the Exchequer, the most effective member of the Government. His

able biographer, Mr. Keith Feiling, gives the following extract
from his diary: "March 12, talked to Flandin, emphasising that
public opinion would not support us in sanctions of any kind.
His view is that if a firm front is maintained, Germany will
yield without war. We cannot accept this as a reliable estimate
of a mad Dictator's reaction." When Flandin urged at least an
economic boycott, Chamberlain replied by suggesting an international force during negotiations, agreed to a pact for mutual
assistance, and declared that if by giving up a colony we could
secure lasting peace, he would consider it.[1]

Meanwhile, most of the British press, with *The Times* and
the *Daily Herald* in the van, expressed their belief in the sincerity of Hitler's offers of a non-aggression pact. Austen Chamberlain, in a speech at Cambridge, proclaimed the opposite
view. Wigram thought it was within the compass of his duty
to bring Flandin into touch with everyone he could think of
from the City, from the press, and from the Government, and also
with Lord Lothian. To all whom Flandin met at the Wigrams'
he spoke in the following terms: "The whole world and especially the small nations today turn their eyes towards England.
If England will act now, she can lead Europe. You will have a
policy, all the world will follow you, and thus you will prevent
war. It is your last chance. If you do not stop Germany now,
all is over. France cannot guarantee Czechoslovakia any more
because that will become geographically impossible. If you
do not maintain the Treaty of Locarno, all that will remain to
you is to await a rearmament by Germany, against which
France can do nothing. If you do not stop Germany by force
today, war is inevitable, even if you make a temporary friendship with Germany. As for myself, I do not believe that friendship is possible between France and Germany; the two countries will always be in tension. Nevertheless, if you abandon
Locarno, I shall change my policy, for there will be nothing
else to do." These were brave words; but action would have
spoken louder.

Lord Lothian's contribution was: "After all, they are only

[1] Keith Feiling, *Life of Neville Chamberlain*, page 279.

going into their own back-garden." This was a representative British view.

* * * * *

When I heard how ill things were going, and after a talk with Wigram, I advised M. Flandin to demand an interview with Mr. Baldwin before he left. This took place at Downing Street. The Prime Minister received M. Flandin with the utmost courtesy. Mr. Baldwin explained that, although he knew little of foreign affairs, he was able to interpret accurately the feelings of the British people. And they wanted peace. M. Flandin says that he rejoined that the only way to ensure this was to stop Hitlerite aggression while such action was still possible. France had no wish to drag Great Britain into war; she asked for no practical aid, and she would herself undertake what would be a simple police operation, as, according to French information, the German troops in the Rhineland had orders to withdraw if opposed in a forcible manner. Flandin asserts that he said that all that France asked of her ally was a free hand. This is certainly not true. How could Britain have restrained France from action to which, under the Locarno Treaty, she was legally entitled? The British Prime Minister repeated that his country could not accept the risk of war. He asked what the French Government had resolved to do. To this no plain answer was returned. According to Flandin, Mr. Baldwin then said: "You may be right, but if there is *even one chance in a hundred* that war would follow from your police operation, I have not the right to commit England." And after a pause he added: "England is not in a state to go to war." There is no confirmation of this. M. Flandin returned to France convinced, first, that his own divided country could not be united except in the presence of a strong will-power in Britain, and secondly, that, so far from this being forthcoming, no strong impulse could be expected from her. Far too easily he plunged into the dismal conclusion that the only hope for France was in an arrangement with an ever more aggressive Germany.

In view of what I saw of Flandin's attitude during these

anxious days, I felt it my duty, in spite of his subsequent lapses,
to come to his aid, so far as I was able, in later years. I used
all my power in the winter of 1943/44 to protect him when
he was arrested in Algeria by the De Gaulle Administration.
In this I invoked and received active help from President
Roosevelt. When after the war Flandin was brought to trial,
my son Randolph, who had seen much of Flandin during the
African campaign, was summoned as a witness, and I am glad
to think that his advocacy, and also a letter which I wrote for
Flandin to use in his defence, were not without influence in
procuring the acquittal which he received from the French
tribunal. Weakness is not treason, though it may be equally
disastrous. Nothing, however, can relieve the French Government of their prime responsibility. Clemenceau or Poincaré
would have left Mr. Baldwin no option.

*   *   *   *   *

The British and French submission to the violations of the
Treaties of Versailles and Locarno, involved in Hitler's seizure
of the Rhineland, was a mortal blow to Wigram. "After the
French Delegation had left," wrote his wife to me, "Ralph
came back, and sat down in a corner of the room where he had
never sat before, and said to me, 'War is now *inevitable*, and
it will be the most terrible war there has ever been. I don't
think I shall see it, but you will. Wait now for bombs on this
little house.' [2] I was frightened at his words, and he went on,
'All my work these many years has been no use. I am a failure.
I have failed to make the people here realise what is at stake.
I am not strong enough, I suppose. I have not been able to
make them understand. Winston has always, always understood, and he is strong and will go on to the end.' "

My friend never seemed to recover from this shock. He
took it too much to heart. After all, one can always go on doing what one believes to be his duty, and running ever greater
risks till knocked out. Wigram's profound comprehension
reacted on his sensitive nature unduly. His untimely death in

[2] It was actually smitten.

December, 1936, was an irreparable loss to the Foreign Office, and played its part in the miserable decline of our fortunes.

*   *   *   *   *

When Hitler met his generals after the successful reoccupation of the Rhineland, he was able to confront them with the falsity of their fears and prove to them how superior his judgment or "intuition" was to that of ordinary military men. The generals bowed. As good Germans they were glad to see their country gaining ground so rapidly in Europe and its former adversaries so divided and tame. Undoubtedly Hitler's prestige and authority in the supreme circle of German power was sufficiently enhanced by this episode to encourage and enable him to march forward to greater tests. To the world he said: "All Germany's territorial ambitions have now been satisfied."

France was thrown into incoherency amid which fear of war, and relief that it had been avoided, predominated. The simple English were taught by their simple press to comfort themselves with the reflection: "After all, the Germans are only going back to their own country. How should we feel if we had been kept out of, say, Yorkshire for ten or fifteen years?" No one stopped to note that the detrainment points from which the German Army could invade France had been advanced by one hundred miles. No one worried about the proof given to all the Powers of the Little Entente and to `Europe that France would not fight, and that England would hold her back even if she would. This episode confirmed Hitler's power over the Reich, and stultified, in a manner ignominious and slurring upon their patriotism, the generals who had hitherto sought to restrain him.

*   *   *   *   *

During this exciting period my own personal fortunes were, it now appears, discussed in high quarters. The Prime Minister, under constant pressure, had decided at last to create a new Ministry — not of Defence, but of the Co-ordination of Defence. Neville Chamberlain's biographer has given some account of this. Austen Chamberlain, whose influence with the Government stood high, thought and said that it was an "immense mistake" to exclude me. Sir Samuel Hoare had returned from convalescence, and in view of the docility with which he had accepted his dismissal after the Hoare-Laval crisis, he evidently had strong claims for re-employment. The Prime Minister thought it would be best for Neville Chamberlain to take the new office, and for Austen to go back to the Exchequer. Neville, who was certain to succeed Baldwin in the immediate future, declined this proposal. "The party," says Mr. Feiling, "would not have the immediate return of Hoare. If the new Ministry went to Churchill, it would alarm those Liberal and Central elements who had taken his exclusion as a pledge against militarism,[3] it would be against the advice of those responsible for interpreting the party's general will, and would it not when Baldwin disappeared raise a disputed succession?" For a whole month, we are told, "these niceties and gravities were well weighed."

I was naturally aware that this process was going on. In the debate of March 9, I was careful not to derogate in the slightest degree from my attitude of severe though friendly criticism of Government policy, and I was held to have made a successful speech. I did not consider the constitution of the new office and its powers satisfactory. But I would gladly have accepted the post, being confident that knowledge and experience would prevail. Apparently (according to Mr. Feiling) the German entry into the Rhineland on March 7 was decisive against my appointment. It was certainly obvious that Hitler would not like it. On the ninth, Mr. Baldwin selected Sir Thomas Inskip, an able lawyer, who had the advantages of being little known himself and knowing nothing about military subjects. The Prime Minister's choice was received with astonishment by press and public. To me this definite, and as it seemed final, exclusion from all share in our preparations for defence was a heavy blow.

[3] This was the reverse of the truth at this time. The signers of the Peace Ballot were at one with me upon armed collective security.

I had to be very careful not to lose my poise in the great discussions and debates which crowded upon us and in which I was often prominent. I had to control my feelings and appear serene, indifferent, detached. In this endeavour continuous recurrence to the safety of the country was a good and simple rule. In order to steady and absorb my mind, I planned in outline a history of what had happened since the Treaty of Versailles down to the date we had reached. I even began the opening chapter, and part of what I wrote then finds its place without the need of alteration in this present book. I did not, however, carry this project very far because of the press of events, and also of the current literary work by which I earned my pleasant life at Chartwell. Moreover, by the end of 1936, I became absorbed in my *History of the English-Speaking Peoples,* which I actually finished before the outbreak of war and which will some day be published. Writing a long and substantial book is like having a friend and companion at your side, to whom you can always turn for comfort and amusement, and whose society becomes more attractive as a new and widening field of interest is lighted in the mind.

Mr. Baldwin certainly had good reason to use the last flickers of his power against one who had exposed his mistakes so severely and so often. Moreover, as a profoundly astute party manager, thinking in majorities and aiming at a quiet life between elections, he did not wish to have my disturbing aid. He thought, no doubt, that he had dealt me a politically fatal stroke, and I felt he might well be right. How little can we foresee the consequences either of wise or unwise action, of virtue or of malice! Without this measureless and perpetual uncertainty, the drama of human life would be destroyed. Mr. Baldwin knew no more than I how great was the service he was doing me in preventing me from becoming involved in all the Cabinet compromises and shortcomings of the next three years, and from having, if I had remained a Minister, to enter upon a war bearing direct responsibility for conditions of national defence bound to prove fearfully inadequate.

This was not the first time — or indeed the last — that I have received a blessing in what was at the time a very effective disguise.

*   *   *   *   *

I still had the hope that the appeal which France had made to the League of Nations would result in bringing into being an international pressure upon Germany to carry out the decisions of the League.

France [I wrote on March 13, 1936] has taken her case before the Court, and she asks for justice there. If the Court finds that her case is just, but is unable to offer any satisfaction, the Covenant of the League of Nations will have been proved a fraud, and collective security a sham. If no means of lawful redress can be offered to the aggrieved party, the whole doctrine of international law and co-operation upon which the hopes of the future are based would lapse ignominiously. It would be replaced immediately by a system of alliances and groups of nations deprived of all guarantees but their own right arm. On the other hand, if the League of Nations were able to enforce its decree upon one of the most powerful countries in the world found to be an aggressor, then the authority of the League would be set upon so majestic a pedestal that it must henceforth be the accepted sovereign authority by which all the quarrels of people can be determined and controlled. Thus we might upon this occasion reach by one single bound the realisation of our most cherished dreams.

But the risk! No one must ignore it. How can it be minimised? There is a simple method: the assembly of an overwhelming force, moral and physical, in support of international law. If the relative strengths are narrowly balanced, war may break out in a few weeks, and no one can measure what the course of war may be, or who will be drawn into its whirlpools, or how, if ever, they will emerge. But if the forces at the disposal of the League of Nations are four or five times as strong as those which the aggressor can as yet command, the chances of a peaceful and friendly solution are very good. Therefore, every nation, great or small, should play its part according to the Covenant of the League.

Upon what force can the League of Nations count at this cardinal moment? Has she sheriffs and constables with whom to sustain her judgments, or is she left alone, impotent, a hollow mockery amid the lip-serving platitudes of irresolute or cynical devotees? Strangely

enough for the destiny of the world, there was never a moment or
occasion when the League of Nations could command such overwhelming force. The constabulary of the world is at hand. On
every side of Geneva stand great nations, armed and ready, whose
interests as well as whose obligations bind them to uphold, and in
the last resort enforce, the public law. This may never come to
pass again. The fateful moment has arrived for choice between
the New Age and the Old.

All this language was agreeable to the Liberal and Labour
forces with whom I and several of my Conservative friends
were at this time working. It united Conservatives alarmed
about national safety with trade-unionists, with Liberals, and
with the immense body of peace-minded men and women who
had signed the Peace Ballot of a year before. There is no doubt
that had His Majesty's Government chosen to act with firmness
and resolve through the League of Nations, they could have
led a united Britain forward on a final quest to avert war.

*   *   *   *   *

The violation of the Rhineland was not debated till March
26. The interval was partly filled by a meeting of the Council
of the League of Nations in London. As the result, Germany
was invited to submit to the Hague Court her case against the
Franco-Soviet Pact, about which Hitler had complained, and to
undertake not to increase her troops in the Rhineland pending further negotiations. If Germany refused this latter request, the British and Italian Governments undertook to carry
out the steps entailed by their obligations under the Treaty of
Locarno. Not much value could be assigned to the Italian
promise. Mussolini was already in close contact with Hitler.
Germany felt strong enough to decline any conditions limiting
her forces in the Rhineland. Mr. Eden, therefore, insisted that
staff conversations should take place between Great Britain,
France, and Belgium to enable any joint action which might
at some future time become necessary under the Treaty of
Locarno to be studied and prepared in advance. The youthful
Foreign Secretary made a courageous speech, and carried the

House with him. Sir Austen Chamberlain and I both spoke
at length in his support. The Cabinet was lukewarm, and it
was no easy task for Eden even to procure the institution of
staff conversations. Usually such conversations do not play any
part as diplomatic counters, and take place secretly or even
informally. Now they were the only practical outcome of three
weeks' parleyings and protestations, and the only Allied reply
to Hitler's breach of the Treaty and solid gain of the
Rhineland.

In the course of my speech I said:

We cannot look back with much pleasure on our foreign policy
in the last five years. They certainly have been disastrous years.
God forbid that I should lay on the Government of my own
country the charge of responsibility for the evils which have come
upon the world in that period. . . . But certainly we have seen the
most depressing and alarming change in the outlook of mankind
which has ever taken place in so short a period. Five years ago all
felt safe; five years ago all were looking forward to peace, to a
period in which mankind would rejoice in the treasures which
science can spread to all classes if conditions of peace and justice
prevail. Five years ago to talk of war would have been regarded
not only as a folly and a crime, but almost as a sign of lunacy. . . .

The violation of the Rhineland is serious because of the menace
to which it exposes Holland, Belgium, and France. I listened with
apprehension to what the Secretary of State said about the Germans
declining even to refrain from entrenching themselves during the
period of negotiations. When there is a line of fortifications, as I
suppose there will be in a very short time, it will produce reactions
on the European situation. *It will be a barrier across Germany's
front door which will leave her free to sally out eastwards and
southwards by the other doors.*

The far-reaching consequences of the fortification of the
Rhineland were only gradually comprehended in Britain and
the United States. On April 6, when the Government asked
for a vote of confidence in their foreign policy, I recurred to
this subject:

Herr Hitler has torn up the Treaties and has garrisoned the

Rhineland. His troops are there, and there they are going to stay. All this means that the Nazi régime has gained a new prestige in Germany and in all the neighbouring countries. But more than that, Germany is now fortifying the Rhine zone or is about to fortify it. No doubt it will take some time. We are told that in the first instance only field entrenchments will be erected, but those who know to what perfection the Germans can carry field entrenchments, like the Hindenburg Line, with all the masses of concrete and the underground chambers there included, will realise that field entrenchments differ only in degree from permanent fortifications, and work steadily up from the first cutting of the sods to their final and perfect form.

I do not doubt that the whole of the German frontier opposite to France is to be fortified as strongly and as speedily as possible. Three, four, or six months will certainly see a barrier of enormous strength. What will be the diplomatic and strategic consequences of that? . . . *The creation of a line of forts opposite to the French frontier will enable the German troops to be economised on that line, and will enable the main forces to swing round through Belgium and Holland.* . . . Then look East. There the consequences of the Rhineland fortifications may be more immediate. That is to us a less direct danger, but it is a more imminent danger. The moment those fortifications are completed, and in proportion as they are completed, the whole aspect of middle Europe is changed. *The Baltic States, Poland and Czechoslovakia, with which must be associated Yugoslavia, Rumania, Austria, and some other countries, are all affected very decisively the moment that this great work of construction has been completed.*

Every word of this warning was successively and swiftly proved true.

*　　*　　*　　*　　*

After the occupation of the Rhineland and the development of the line of fortifications against France, the incorporation of Austria in the German Reich was evidently to be the next step. The story that had opened with the murder of Chancellor Dollfuss in July, 1934, had soon another and a consequential chapter to unfold. With illuminating candour, as we now know, the German Foreign Minister Neurath told the American Ambassador in Moscow, Mr. Bullitt, on May 18, 1936, that it was the policy of the German Government to do nothing active in foreign affairs until the Rhineland had been digested. He explained that *until the German defences had been built on the French and Belgian frontiers,* the German Government would do everything to prevent rather than encourage an outbreak by the Nazis in Austria, and that they would pursue a quiet line with regard to Czechoslovakia. *"As soon as our fortifications are constructed," he said, "and the countries in Central Europe realise that France cannot enter German territory, all these countries will begin to feel very differently about their foreign policies, and a new constellation will develop."* Neurath further informed Mr. Bullitt that the youth of Austria was turning more and more towards the Nazis, and the dominance of the Nazi Party in Austria was inevitable and only a question of time. *But the governing factor was the completion of the German fortifications on the French frontier,* for otherwise a German quarrel with Italy might lead to a French attack on Germany.

On May 21, 1936, Hitler in a speech to the Reichstag declared that "Germany neither intends nor wishes to interfere in the internal affairs of Austria, to annex Austria, or to conclude an *Anschluss.*" On July 11, 1936, he signed a pact with the Austrian Government agreeing not to influence in any way the internal affairs of Austria, and especially not to give any active support to the Austrian National-Socialist Movement. Within five days of this agreement secret instructions were sent to the National-Socialist Party in Austria to extend and intensify their activities. Meanwhile, the German General Staff under Hitler's orders were set to draw up military plans for the occupation of Austria when the hour should strike.

12

The Loaded Pause—Spain

1936–1937

*The Foreign Policy of England — The New Dominator — The
League of Nations — Two Years' Interlude — My Memorandum
on Supply Organisation, June 6, 1936 (Appendix) — The Civil
War in Spain — Non-Intervention — The Anti-Comintern Pact
— Mr. Baldwin's "Frankness" Speech — Arms and the Covenant
— The Albert Hall Meeting — The Abdication of King Edward
VIII — Mr. Baldwin's Wisdom — The Coronation of King
George VI — A Letter from the King — Mr. Baldwin's Retire-
ment — Mr. Chamberlain Prime Minister — Ministerial Changes
— Baldwin and Chamberlain — A Talk with Ribbentrop.*

HERE IS THE PLACE to set forth the principles of British policy towards Europe which I had followed for many years
and follow still. I cannot better express them than in the words
which I used to the Conservative Members Committee on
Foreign Affairs, who invited me to address them in private at
the end of March, 1936.

For four hundred years the foreign policy of England has been
to oppose the strongest, most aggressive, most dominating Power
on the Continent, and particularly to prevent the Low Countries
falling into the hands of such a Power. Viewed in the light of
history, these four centuries of consistent purpose amid so many
changes of names and facts, of circumstances and conditions, must
rank as one of the most remarkable episodes which the records of
any race, nation, state, or people can show. Moreover, on all
occasions England took the more difficult course. Faced by Philip II
of Spain, against Louis XIV under William III and Marlborough,
against Napoleon, against William II of Germany, it would have

been easy and must have been very tempting to join with the
stronger and share the fruits of his conquest. However, we always
took the harder course, joined with the less strong Powers, made a
combination among them, and thus defeated and frustrated the
Continental military tyrant whoever he was, whatever nation he
led. Thus we preserved the liberties of Europe, protected the
growth of its vivacious and varied society, and emerged after four
terrible struggles with an ever-growing fame and widening Empire,
and with the Low Countries safely protected in their independence.
Here is the wonderful unconscious tradition of British foreign
policy. All our thoughts rest in that tradition today. I know of
nothing which has occurred to alter or weaken the justice, wisdom,
valour, and prudence upon which our ancestors acted. I know of
nothing that has happened to human nature which in the slightest
degree alters the validity of their conclusions. I know of nothing in
military, political, economic, or scientific fact which makes me feel
that we might not, or cannot, march along the same road. I venture
to put this very general proposition before you because it seems to
me that if it is accepted, everything else becomes much more simple.

Observe that the policy of England takes no account of which
nation it is that seeks the overlordship of Europe. The question is not
whether it is Spain, or the French Monarchy, or the French Empire,
or the German Empire, or the Hitler régime. It has nothing to do
with rulers or nations; it is concerned solely with whoever is the
strongest or the potentially dominating tyrant. Therefore, we
should not be afraid of being accused of being pro-French or anti-
German. If the circumstances were reversed, we could equally be
pro-German and anti-French. It is a law of public policy which we
are following, and not a mere expedient dictated by accidental
circumstances, or likes and dislikes, or any other sentiment.

The question, therefore, arises which is today the Power in
Europe which is the strongest, and which seeks in a dangerous and
oppressive sense to dominate. Today, for this year, probably for
part of 1937, the French Army is the strongest in Europe. But no
one is afraid of France. Everyone knows that France wants to be
let alone, and that with her it is only a case of self-preservation.
Everyone knows that the French are peaceful and overhung by fear.
They are at once brave, resolute, peace-loving, and weighed down
by anxiety. They are a liberal nation with free parliamentary
institutions.

Germany, on the other hand, fears no one. She is arming in a manner which has never been seen in German history. She is led by a handful of triumphant desperadoes. The money is running short, discontents are arising beneath these despotic rulers. Very soon they will have to choose, on the one hand, between economic and financial collapse or internal upheaval, and on the other, a war which could have no other object, and which, if successful, can have no other result, than a Germanised Europe under Nazi control. Therefore, it seems to me that all the old conditions present themselves again, and that our national salvation depends upon our gathering once again all the forces of Europe to contain, to restrain, and if necessary to frustrate, German domination. For, believe me, if any of those other Powers, Spain, Louis XIV, Napoleon, Kaiser Wilhelm II, had with our aid become the absolute masters of Europe, they could have despoiled us, reduced us to insignificance and penury on the morrow of their victory. We ought to set the life and endurance of the British Empire and the greatness of this island very high in our duty, and not be led astray by illusions about an ideal world, which only means that other and worse controls will step into our place, and that the future direction will belong to them.

It is at this stage that the spacious conception and extremely vital organisation of the League of Nations presents itself as a prime factor. The League of Nations is, in a practical sense, a British conception, and it harmonises perfectly with all our past methods and actions. Moreover, it harmonises with those broad ideas of right and wrong, and of peace based upon controlling the major aggressor, which we have always followed. We wish for the reign of law and freedom among nations and within nations, and it was for that, and nothing less than that, that those bygone architects of our repute, magnitude, and civilisation fought, and won. The dream of a reign of international law and of the settlement of disputes by patient discussion, but still in accordance with what is lawful and just, is very dear to the British people. You must not underrate the force which these ideals exert upon the modern British democracy. One does not know how these seeds are planted by the winds of the centuries in the hearts of the working people. They are there, and just as strong as their love of liberty. We should not neglect them, because they are the essence of the genius of this island. Therefore, we believe that in the fostering and

fortifying of the League of Nations will be found the best means
of defending our island security, as well as maintaining grand
universal causes with which we have very often found our own
interests in natural accord.

My three main propositions are: First, that we must oppose the
would-be dominator or potential aggressor. Secondly, that Germany
under its present Nazi régime and with its prodigious armaments,
so swiftly developing, fills unmistakably that part. Thirdly, that the
League of Nations rallies many countries, and unites our own
people here at home in the most effective way to control the would-
be aggressor. I venture most respectfully to submit these main
themes to your consideration. Everything else will follow from
them.

It is always more easy to discover and proclaim general principles
than to apply them. First, we ought to count our effective association with France. That does not mean that we should develop a
needlessly hostile mood against Germany. It is a part of our duty
and our interest to keep the temperature low between these two
countries. We shall not have any difficulty in this so far as France
is concerned. Like us, they are a parliamentary democracy with
tremendous inhibitions against war, and, like us, under considerable drawbacks in preparing their defence. Therefore, I say we
ought to regard our defensive association with France as fundamental. Everything else must be viewed in proper subordination
now that the times have become so sharp and perilous. Those who
are possessed of a definite body of doctrine and of deeply rooted
convictions upon it will be in a much better position to deal with

the shifts and surprises of daily affairs than those who are merely
taking short views, and indulging their natural impulses as they
are evoked by what they read from day to day. The first thing is
to decide where you want to go. For myself, I am for the armed
League of all Nations, or as many as you can get, against the
potential aggressor, with England and France as the core of it. Let
us neglect nothing in our power to establish the great international
framework. If that should prove to be beyond our strength, or if
it breaks down through the weakness or wrong-doing of others,
then at least let us make sure that England and France, the two
surviving free great countries of Europe, can together ride out any
storm that may blow with good and reasonable hopes of once again
coming safely into port.

If we add the United States to Britain and France; if we change the name of the potential aggressor; if we substitute the United Nations Organisation for the League of Nations, the Atlantic Ocean for the English Channel, and the world for Europe, the argument is not necessarily without its application today.

*   *   *   *   *

Two whole years passed between Hitler's seizure of the Rhineland in March, 1936, and his rape of Austria in March, 1938. This was a longer interval than I had expected. Everything happened in the order foreseen and stated, but the spacing between the successive blows was longer. During this period no time was wasted by Germany. The fortification of the Rhineland, or "The West Wall," proceeded apace, and an immense line of permanent and semi-permanent fortifications grew continually. The German Army, now on the full methodical basis of compulsory service and reinforced by ardent volunteering, grew stronger month by month, both in numbers and in the maturity and quality of its formations. The German Air Force held and steadily improved the lead it had obtained over Great Britain. The German munition plants were working at high pressure. The wheels revolved and the hammers descended day and night in Germany, making its whole industry an arsenal, and welding all its population into one disciplined war machine. At home in the autumn of 1936, Hitler inaugurated a Four Years' Plan to reorganise German economy for greater self-sufficiency in war. Abroad he obtained that "strong alliance" which he had stated in *Mein Kampf* would be necessary for Germany's foreign policy. He came to terms with Mussolini, and the Rome-Berlin Axis was formed.

Up till the middle of 1936, Hitler's aggressive policy and treaty-breaking had rested, not upon Germany's strength, but upon the disunion and timidity of France and Britain and the isolation of the United States. Each of his preliminary steps had been gambles in which he knew he could not afford to be seriously challenged. The seizure of the Rhineland and

its subsequent fortification was the greatest gamble of all. It
had succeeded brilliantly. His opponents were too irresolute
to call his bluff. When next he moved in 1938, his bluff was
bluff no more. Aggression was backed by force, and it might
well be by superior force. When the Governments of France
and Britain realised the terrible transformation which had
taken place, it was too late.

*   *   *   *   *

I continued to give the closest attention to our military
preparations. My relations with Sir Thomas Inskip, Minister
for Co-ordination of Defence, were friendly, and I did my
best to help him privately. At his request I wrote and sent
him a memorandum about the much-needed Ministry of Supply, which is dated June 6, 1936.[1] No effective action was, however, taken to create a Ministry of Supply until the spring of
1939, nearly three years later, nor was any attempt made to
introduce emergency conditions into our munitions production.

*   *   *   *   *

At the end of July, 1936, the increasing degeneration of the
parliamentary régime in Spain, and the growing strength of the
movements for a Communist, or alternatively an Anarchist,
revolution, led to a military revolt which had long been preparing. It is part of the Communist doctrine and drillbook,
laid down by Lenin himself, that Communists should aid all
movements towards the Left and help into office weak Constitutional, Radical, or Socialist Governments. These they
should undermine, and from their falling hands snatch absolute power, and found the Marxist State. In fact, a perfect
reproduction of the Kerensky period in Russia was taking
place in Spain. But the strength of Spain had not been shattered by foreign war. The Army still maintained a measure
of cohesion. Side by side with the Communist conspiracy there
was elaborated in secret a deep military counterplot. Neither
side could claim with justice the title-deeds of legality, and

1 See Appendix C, Book I.

Spaniards of all classes were bound to consider the life of Spain.

Many of the ordinary guarantees of civilised society had been already liquidated by the Communist pervasion of the decayed Parliamentary Government. Murders began on both sides, and the Communist pestilence had reached a point where it could take political opponents in the streets or from their beds and kill them. Already a large number of these assassinations had taken place in and around Madrid. The climax was the murder of Señor Sotelo, the Conservative leader, who corresponded somewhat to the type of Sir Edward Carson in British politics before the 1914 war. This crime was the signal for the generals of the Army to act. General Franco had a month before written a letter to the Spanish War Minister, making it clear that if the Spanish Government could not maintain the normal securities of law in daily life, the Army would have to intervene. Spain had seen many *pronunciamientos* by military chiefs in the past. When, after General Sanjurjo had perished in an air crash, General Franco raised the standard of revolt, he was supported by the Army, including the rank and file. The Church, with the noteworthy exception of the Dominicans, and nearly all the elements of the Right and Centre, adhered to him, and he became immediately the master of several important provinces. The Spanish sailors killed their officers and joined what soon became the Communist side. In the collapse of civilised Government, the Communist sect obtained control, and acted in accordance with their drill. Bitter civil war now began. Wholesale cold-blooded massacres of their political opponents, and of the well-to-do, were perpetrated by the Communists, who had seized power. These were repaid with interest by the forces under Franco. All Spaniards went to their deaths with remarkable composure, and great numbers on both sides were shot. The military cadets defended their college at the Alcazar in Toledo with the utmost tenacity, and Franco's troops, forcing their way up from the south, leaving a trail of vengeance behind them in every Communist village, presently achieved their relief. This episode deserves the notice of historians.

In this quarrel I was neutral. Naturally, I was not in favour
of the Communists. How could I be, when if I had been a
Spaniard they would have murdered me and my family and
friends? I was sure, however, that with all the rest they had
on their hands the British Government were right to keep out
of Spain. France proposed a plan of non-intervention, whereby
both sides would be left to fight it out without any external
aid. The British, German, Italian, and Russian Governments
subscribed to this. In consequence, the Spanish Government,
now in the hands of the most extreme revolutionaries, found
itself deprived of the right even to buy the arms ordered with
the gold it physically possessed. It would have been more
reasonable to follow the normal course, and to have recognised the belligerency of both sides as was done in the American Civil War from 1861 to 1865. Instead, however, the policy
of non-intervention was adopted and formally agreed to by all
the Great Powers. This agreement was strictly observed by
Great Britain; but Italy and Germany on the one side, and
Soviet Russia on the other, broke their engagement constantly
and threw their weight into the struggle one against the
other. Germany in particular used her air power to commit
such experimental horrors as the bombing of the defenceless
little township of Guernica.

The Government of M. Léon Blum, which had succeeded
the Flandin Ministry in May, was under pressure from its
Communist supporters in the Chamber to support the Spanish
Government with war material. The Air Minister, M. Cot,
without too much regard for the strength of the French air
force, then in a state of decay, was secretly delivering planes
and equipment to the Republican armies. I was perturbed at
such developments, and on July 31, 1936, I wrote to M. Corbin,
the French Ambassador:

One of the greatest difficulties I meet with in trying to hold on
to the old position is the German talk that the anti-Communist
countries should stand together. I am sure if France sent airplanes,
etc., to the present Madrid Government, and the Germans and
Italians pushed in from the other angle, the dominant forces here

would be pleased with Germany and Italy, and estranged from France. I hope you will not mind my writing this, which I do, of course, entirely on my own account. I do not like to hear people talking of England, Germany, and Italy forming up against European Communism. It is too easy to be good.

I am sure that an absolutely rigid neutrality, with the strongest protest against any breach of it, is the only correct and safe course at the present time. A day may come, if there is a stalemate, when the League of Nations may intervene to wind up the horrors. But even that is very doubtful.

*   *   *   *   *

There is another event which must be recorded here. On November 25, 1936, the Ambassadors of all the Powers represented in Berlin were summoned to the Foreign Office, where Herr von Neurath disclosed the details of the Anti-Comintern Pact, which had been negotiated with the Japanese Government. The purpose of the pact was to take common action against the international activities of the Comintern, either within the boundaries of the contracting states, or beyond them.

*   *   *   *   *

During the whole of 1936 the anxiety of the nation and Parliament continued to mount and was concentrated in particular upon our air defences. In the debate on the Address on November 12, I severely reproached Mr. Baldwin for having failed to keep his pledge that "any Government of this country — a National Government more than any, and *this* Government — will see to it that in air strength and air power this country shall no longer be in a position inferior to any country within striking distance of our shores." I said, "The Government simply cannot make up their minds, or they cannot get the Prime Minister to make up his mind. So they go on in strange paradox, decided only to be undecided, resolved to be irresolute, adamant for drift, solid for fluidity, all-powerful to be impotent. So we go on preparing more months and years — precious, perhaps vital, to the greatness of Britain — for the locusts to eat."

Mr. Baldwin replied to me in a remarkable speech, in which he said:

I want to speak to the House with the utmost frankness. . . . The difference of opinion between Mr. Churchill and myself is in the years 1933 onwards. In 1931/32, although it is not admitted by the Opposition, there was a period of financial crisis. But there was another reason. I would remind the House that not once but on many occasions in speeches and in various places, when I have been speaking and advocating as far as I am able the democratic principle, I have stated that *a democracy is always two years behind the dictator.* I believe that to be true. It has been true in this case. I put before the whole House my own views with an appalling frankness. You will remember at that time the Disarmament Conference was sitting in Geneva. You will remember at that time there was probably a stronger pacifist feeling running through this country than at any time since the war. You will remember *the election at Fulham in the autumn of 1933, when a seat which the National Government held was lost by about seven thousand votes on no issue but the pacifist.* . . . My position as the leader of a great party was not altogether a comfortable one. I asked myself what chance was there — when that feeling that was given expression to in Fulham was common throughout the country — what chance was there within the next year or two of that feeling being so changed that the country would give a mandate for rearmament? Supposing I had gone to the country and said that Germany was rearming, and that we must rearm, does anybody think that this pacific democracy would have rallied to that cry at that moment? *I cannot think of anything that would have made the loss of the election from my point of view more certain.*

This was indeed appalling frankness. It carried naked truth about his motives into indecency. That a Prime Minister should avow that he had not done his duty in regard to national safety because he was afraid of losing the election was an incident without parallel in our parliamentary history. Mr. Baldwin was, of course, not moved by any ignoble wish to remain in office. He was in fact in 1936 earnestly desirous of retiring. His policy was dictated by the fear that if the Socialists came into power, even less would be done than his Govern-

ment intended. All their declarations and votes against defence measures are upon record. But this was no complete
defence, and less than justice to the spirit of the British people.
The success which had attended the naïve confession of mis-
calculation in air parity the previous year was not repeated on
this occasion. The House was shocked. Indeed the impression produced was so painful that it might well have been fatal
to Mr. Baldwin, who was also at that time in failing health,
had not the unexpected intervened.

*   *   *   *   *

At this time there was a great drawing-together of men and
women of all parties in England who saw the perils of the
future, and were resolute upon practical measures to secure
our safety and the cause of freedom, equally menaced by both
the totalitarian impulsions and our Government's compla-
cency. Our plan was the most rapid large-scale rearmament
of Britain, combined with the complete acceptance and employment of the authority of the League of Nations. I called
this policy "Arms and the Covenant." Mr. Baldwin's performance in the House of Commons was viewed among us all
with disdain. The culmination of this campaign was to be a
meeting at the Albert Hall. Here on December 3 we gathered
many of the leading men in all the parties — strong Tories of
the Right Wing earnestly convinced of the national peril; the
leaders of the League of Nations Peace Ballot; the representatives of many great trade unions, including in the chair my old
opponent of the general strike, Sir Walter Citrine; the Liberal
Party and its leader, Sir Archibald Sinclair. We had the feeling that we were upon the threshold of not only gaining respect for our views, but of making them dominant. It was at
this moment that the King's passion to marry the woman he
loved caused the casting of all else into the background. The
abdication crisis was at hand.

Before I replied to the vote of thanks there was a cry, "God
Save the King"; and this excited prolonged cheering. I explained, therefore, on the spur of the moment my personal
position.

There is another grave matter which overshadows our minds tonight. In a few minutes we are going to sing "God Save the King." I shall sing it with more heartfelt fervour than I have ever sung it in my life. I hope and pray that no irrevocable decision will be taken in haste, but that time and public opinion will be allowed to play their part, and that a cherished and unique personality may not be incontinently severed from the people he loves so well. I hope that Parliament will be allowed to discharge its function in these high constitutional questions. I trust that our King may be guided by the opinions that are now for the first time being expressed by the British nation and the British Empire, and that the British people will not in their turn be found wanting in generous consideration for the occupant of the Throne.

It is not relevant to this account to describe the brief but intensely violent controversy that followed. I had known King Edward VIII since he was a child, and had in 1910 as Home Secretary read out to a wonderful assembly the proclamation creating him Prince of Wales at Carnarvon Castle. I felt bound to place my personal loyalty to him upon the highest plane. Although during the summer I had been made fully aware of what was going forward, I in no way interfered nor communicated with him at any time. However, presently in his distress he asked the Prime Minister for permission to consult me. Mr. Baldwin gave formal consent, and on this being conveyed to me, I went to the King at Fort Belvedere. I remained in contact with him till his abdication, and did my utmost to plead both to the King and to the public for patience and delay. I have never repented of this — indeed, I could do no other.

The Prime Minister proved himself to be a shrewd judge of British national feeling. Undoubtedly he perceived and expressed the profound will of the nation. His deft and skilful handling of the abdication issue raised him in a fortnight from the depths to the pinnacle. There were several moments when I seemed to be entirely alone against a wrathful House of Commons. I am not, when in action, unduly affected by hostile currents of feeling; but it was on more than one occasion al-

most physically impossible to make myself heard. All the forces
I had gathered together on "Arms and the Covenant," of
which I conceived myself to be the mainspring, were estranged
or dissolved, and I was myself so smitten in public opinion
that it was the almost universal view that my political life
was at last ended. How strange it is that this very House of
Commons, which had regarded me with so much hostility,
should have been the same instrument which hearkened to
my guidance and upheld me through the long adverse years of
war till victory over all our foes was gained! What a proof is
here offered that the only wise and safe course is to act from
day to day in accordance with what one's own conscience seems
to decree!

From the abdication of one King we passed to the coronation of another, and until the end of May, 1937, the ceremonial
and pageantry of a solemn national act of allegiance and the
consecration of British loyalties at home and throughout the
Empire to the new Sovereign filled all minds. Foreign affairs
and the state of our defences lost all claim upon the public
mood. Our island might have been ten thousand miles away
from Europe. However, I am permitted to record that on May
18, 1937, on the morrow of the Coronation, I received from
the new King, His present Majesty, a letter in his own hand-
writing:

> The Royal Lodge,
> The Great Park,
> Windsor, Berks.
> 18.V.37

My dear Mr. Churchill,

I am writing to thank you for your very nice letter to me. I
know how devoted you have been, and still are, to my dear brother,
and I feel touched beyond words by your sympathy and understanding in the very difficult problems that have arisen since he left us in
December. I fully realise the great responsibilities and cares that
I have taken on as King, and I feel most encouraged to receive your
good wishes, as one of our great statesmen, and from one who has
served his country so faithfully. I can only hope and trust that the

good feeling and hope that exists in the Country and Empire now
will prove a good example to other nations in the world.

>   Believe me,
>   Yours very sincerely,
>   GEORGE R.I.

This gesture of magnanimity towards one whose influence
at that time had fallen to zero will ever be a cherished experience in my life.

*   *   *   *   *

On May 28, 1937, after King George VI had been crowned,
Mr. Baldwin retired. His long public services were suitably
rewarded by an earldom and the Garter. He laid down the
wide authority he had gathered and carefully maintained, but
had used as little as possible. He departed in a glow of public
gratitude and esteem. There was no doubt who his successor
should be. Mr. Neville Chamberlain had, as Chancellor of the
Exchequer, not only done the main work of the Government
for five years past, but was the ablest and most forceful
Minister, with high abilities and an historic name. I had described him a year earlier at Birmingham in Shakespeare's
words as the "pack-horse in our great affairs," and he had accepted this description as a compliment. I had no expectation
that he would wish to work with me; nor would he have been
wise to do so at such a time. His ideas were far different from
mine on the treatment of the dominant issues of the day. But
I welcomed the accession to power of a live, competent, executive figure. While still Chancellor of the Exchequer he had
involved himself in a fiscal proposal for a small-scale national
defence contribution which had been ill-received by the Conservative Party and was, of course, criticised by the Opposition.
I was able, in the first days of his Premiership, to make a speech
upon this subject which helped him to withdraw, without any
loss of dignity, from a position which had become untenable.
Our relations continued to be cool, easy, and polite both in
public and in private.

Mr. Chamberlain made few changes in the Government. He

had had disagreements with Mr. Duff Cooper about War Office Administration, and much surprised him by offering him
advancement to the great key office of the Admiralty. The
Prime Minister evidently did not know the eyes through which
his new First Lord, whose early career had been in the Foreign
Office, viewed the European scene. In my turn I was astonished
that Sir Samuel Hoare, who had just secured a large expansion
of the naval programme, should wish to leave the Admiralty
for the Home Office. Hoare seems to have believed that prison
reform in a broad humanitarian sense would become the prevailing topic in the immediate future; and since his family
was connected with the famous Elizabeth Fry, he had a strong
personal sentiment about it.

*   *   *   *   *

I may here set down a comparative appreciation of these two
Prime Ministers, Baldwin and Chamberlain, whom I had
known so long and under whom I had served or was to serve.
Stanley Baldwin was the wiser, more comprehending personality, but without detailed executive capacity. He was largely
detached from foreign and military affairs. He knew little of
Europe, and disliked what he knew. He had a deep knowledge
of British party politics, and represented in a broad way some
of the strengths and many of the infirmities of our island race.
He had fought five general elections as leader of the Conservative Party and had won three of them. He had a genius for
waiting upon events and an imperturbability under adverse
criticism. He was singularly adroit in letting events work
for him, and capable of seizing the ripe moment when it came.
He seemed to me to revive the impressions history gives us of
Sir Robert Walpole, without, of course, the eighteenth-century
corruption, and he was master of British politics for nearly as
long.

Neville Chamberlain, on the other hand, was alert, business-
like, opinionated, and self-confident in a very high degree. Unlike Baldwin, he conceived himself able to comprehend the
whole field of Europe, and indeed the world. Instead of a

vague but none the less deep-seated intuition, we had now a
narrow, sharp-edged efficiency within the limits of the policy
in which he believed. Both as Chancellor of the Exchequer
and as Prime Minister, he kept the tightest and most rigid
control upon military expenditure. He was throughout this
period the masterful opponent of all emergency measures. He
had formed decided judgments about all the political figures
of the day, both at home and abroad, and felt himself capable
of dealing with them. His all-pervading hope was to go down
to history as the Great Peacemaker; and for this he was prepared to strive continually in the teeth of facts, and face great
risks for himself and his country. Unhappily, he ran into
tides the force of which he could not measure, and met hurricanes from which he did not flinch, but with which he could
not cope. In these closing years before the war, I should have
found it easier to work with Baldwin, as I knew him, than
with Chamberlain; but neither of them had any wish to work
with me except in the last resort.

*   *   *   *   *

One day in 1937, I had a meeting with Herr von Ribbentrop, German Ambassador to Britain. In one of my fortnightly
articles I had noted that he had been misrepresented in some
speech he had made. I had, of course, met him several times
in society. He now asked me whether I would come to see
him and have a talk. He received me in the large upstairs
room at the German Embassy. We had a conversation lasting
for more than two hours. Ribbentrop was most polite, and we
ranged over the European scene, both in respect of armaments
and policy. The gist of his statement to me was that Germany
sought the friendship of England (on the Continent we are still
often called "England"). He said he could have been Foreign
Minister of Germany, but he had asked Hitler to let him come
over to London in order to make the full case for an Anglo-
German entente or even alliance. Germany would stand guard
for the British Empire in all its greatness and extent. They
might ask for the return of the German colonies, but this was

evidently not cardinal. What was required was that Britain should give Germany a free hand in the East of Europe. She must have her *Lebensraum,* or living-space, for her increasing population. Therefore, Poland and the Danzig Corridor must be absorbed. White Russia and the Ukraine were indispensable to the future life of the German Reich of more than seventy million souls. Nothing less would suffice. All that was asked of the British Commonwealth and Empire was not to interfere. There was a large map on the wall, and the Ambassador several times led me to it to illustrate his projects.

After hearing all this, I said at once that I was sure the British Government would not agree to give Germany a free hand in Eastern Europe. It was true we were on bad terms with Soviet Russia and that we hated Communism as much as Hitler did, but he might be sure that, even if France were safeguarded, Great Britain would never disinterest herself in the fortunes of the Continent to an extent which would enable Germany to gain the domination of Central and Eastern Europe. We were actually standing before the map when I said this. Ribbentrop turned abruptly away. He then said: "In that case, war is inevitable. There is no way out. The Fuehrer is resolved. Nothing will stop him and nothing will stop us." We then returned to our chairs. I was only a private Member of Parliament, but of some prominence. I thought it right to say to the German Ambassador — in fact, I remember the words well: "When you talk of war, which, no doubt, would be general war, you must not underrate England. She is a curious country, and few foreigners can understand her mind. Do not judge by the attitude of the present Administration. Once a great cause is presented to the people, all kinds of unexpected actions might be taken by this very Government and by the British nation." And I repeated: "Do not underrate England. She is very clever. If you plunge us all into another Great War, she will bring the whole world against you like last time." At this, the Ambassador rose in heat and said, "Ah, England may be very clever, but this time she will not bring the world against Germany." We turned the conversation onto easier lines, and nothing more of note occurred. The incident, however, remains in my memory, and, as I reported it at the time to the Foreign Office, I feel it right to put it on record.

When he was on his trial for his life by the conquerors, Ribbentrop gave a distorted version of this conversation and claimed that I should be summoned as a witness. What I have set down about it is what I should have said had I been called.

13

Germany Armed

1936–1938

The "Over-all Strategic Objective" — German Expenditure on Armaments — Independent Inquiries — The Conservative Deputation to the Prime Minister, July 28, 1936 — My Statement of the Case — General Conclusions — My Fear — Our Second Meeting, November 23, 1936 — Lord Swinton Leaves the Air Ministry, May 12, 1938 — Debate in Parliament — Lindemann Rejoins the Air Defence Research Committee — My Correspondence with M. Daladier — The French Estimate of German Air Strength, 1938 — My Estimate of the German Army, June, 1938 — M. Daladier Concurs — The Decay of the French Air Force — The Careless Islanders.

ADVANTAGE IS GAINED in war and also in foreign policy and other things by selecting from many attractive or unpleasant alternatives the dominating point. American military thought had coined the expression "Over-all Strategic Objective." When our officers first heard this, they laughed; but later on its wisdom became apparent and accepted. Evidently this should be the rule, and other great business be set in subordinate relationship to it. Failure to adhere to this simple principle produces confusion and futility of action, and nearly always makes things much worse later on.

Personally I had no difficulty in conforming to the rule long before I heard it proclaimed. My mind was obsessed by the impression of the terrific Germany I had seen and felt in action during the years of 1914 to 1918 suddenly becoming again

possessed of all her martial power, while the Allies, who had
so narrowly survived, gaped idle and bewildered. Therefore,
I continued by every means and on every occasion to use what
influence I had with the House of Commons and also with
individual Ministers to urge forward our military preparations
and to procure allies and associates for what would before long
become again the Common Cause.

One day a friend of mine in a high confidential position
under the Government came over to Chartwell to swim with
me in my pool when the sun shone bright and the water was
fairly warm. We talked of nothing but the coming war, of the
certainty of which he was not entirely convinced. As I saw
him off, he suddenly on an impulse turned and said to me,
"The Germans are spending a thousand million pounds sterling a year on their armaments." I thought Parliament and
the British public ought to know the facts. I, therefore, set
to work to examine German finance. Budgets were produced
and still published every year in Germany; but from their
wealth of figures it was very difficult to tell what was happening. However, in April, 1936, I privately instituted two separate lines of scrutiny. The first rested upon two German refugees of high ability and inflexible purpose. They understood
all the details of the presentment of German budgets, the value
of the mark, and so forth. At the same time I asked my friend,
Sir Henry Strakosch, whether he could not find out what was
actually happening. Strakosch was the head of the firm called
"Union Corporation," with great resources, and a highly
skilled, devoted personnel. The brains of this City company
were turned for several weeks onto the problem. Presently
they reported with precise and lengthy detail that the German
war expenditure was certainly round about a thousand million
pounds sterling a year. At the same time the German refugees,
by a totally different series of arguments, arrived independently
at the same conclusion. One thousand million pounds sterling
per annum at the money values of 1936!

I had, therefore, two separate structures of fact on which
to base a public assertion. So I accosted Mr. Neville Chamber-

lain, still Chancellor of the Exchequer, in the lobby the day
before a debate and said to him, "Tomorrow I shall ask you
whether it is not a fact that the Germans are spending a thous-
and million pounds a year on warlike preparations, and I shall
ask you to confirm or deny." Chamberlain said: "I cannot
deny it, and if you put the point I shall confirm it." I must
quote my words:

Taking the figures from German official sources, the expenditure
on capital account, from the end of March, 1933, to the end of
June, 1935, has been as follows: in 1933 nearly five milliards of
marks; in 1934 nearly eight milliards; and in 1935 nearly eleven
milliards — a total of twenty-four milliards, or roughly two
thousand million pounds. Look at these figures, five, eight, and
eleven for the three years. They give you exactly the kind of
progression which a properly developing munitions industry
would make.

Specifically I asked the Chancellor:

Whether he is aware that the expenditure by Germany upon
purposes directly and indirectly concerned with military preparations, including strategic roads, may well have amounted to the
equivalent of eight hundred million pounds, during the calendar
year 1935; and whether this rate of expenditure seems to be continuing in the current calendar year.

Mr. Chamberlain: The Government have no official figures, but
from such information as they have, I see no reason to think that
the figure mentioned in my right hon. friend's question is necessarily excessive as applied to either year, although, as he himself
would agree, there are elements of conjecture.

I substituted the figure of eight hundred million for one
thousand million pounds to cover my secret information, and
also to be on the safe side.

*   *   *   *   *

I sought by several means to bring the relative state of
British and German armaments to a clear-cut issue. I asked for
a debate in secret session. This was refused. "It would cause
needless alarm." I got little support. All secret sessions are

unpopular with the press. Then on July 20, 1936, I asked the Prime Minister whether he would receive a deputation of Privy Councillors and a few others who would lay before him the facts so far as they knew them. Lord Salisbury requested that a similar deputation from the House of Lords should also come. This was agreed. Although I made personal appeals both to Mr. Atlee and Sir Archibald Sinclair, the Labour and Liberal Parties declined to be represented. Accordingly on July 28, we were received in the Prime Minister's House of Commons room by Mr. Baldwin, Lord Halifax, and Sir Thomas Inskip. The following Conservative and non-party notables came with me. Sir Austen Chamberlain introduced us.

THE DEPUTATION

House of Commons	*House of Lords*
Sir Austen Chamberlain	The Marquess of Salisbury
Mr. Churchill	Viscount FitzAlan
Sir Robert Horne	Viscount Trenchard
Mr. Amery	Lord Lloyd
Sir John Gilmour	Lord Milne
Captain Guest	
Admiral Sir Roger Keyes	
Earl Winterton	
Sir Henry Croft	
Sir Edward Grigg	
Viscount Wolmer	
Lieut.-Col. Moore-Brabazon	
Sir Hugh O'Neill	

This was a great occasion. I cannot recall anything like it in what I have seen of British public life. The group of eminent men, with no thought of personal advantage, but whose lives had been centred upon public affairs, represented a weight of Conservative opinion which could not easily be disregarded. If the leaders of the Labour and Liberal Oppositions had come with us, there might have been a political situation so tense as to enforce remedial action. The proceedings occupied three or four hours on each of two successive days.

I have always said Mr. Baldwin was a good listener. He certainly seemed to listen with the greatest interest and attention. With him were various members of the staff of the Committee of Imperial Defence. On the first day I opened the case in a statement of an hour and a quarter, of which some extracts, given in Appendix D, Book I, throw a fairly true light on the scene.

I ended as follows:

First, we are facing the greatest danger and emergency of our history. Secondly, we have no hope of solving our problem except in conjunction with the French Republic. The union of the British Fleet and the French Army, together with their combined air forces operating from close behind the French and Belgian frontiers, together with all that Britain and France stand for, constitutes a deterrent in which salvation may reside. Anyhow, it is the best hope. Coming down to detail, we must lay aside every impediment in raising our own strength. We cannot possibly provide against all possible dangers. We must concentrate upon what is vital and take our punishment elsewhere. . . . Coming to still more definite propositions, we must increase the development of our air power in priority over every other consideration. At all costs we must draw the flower of our youth into piloting airplanes. Never mind what inducements must be offered, we must draw from every source, by every means. We must accelerate and simplify our aeroplane production and push it to the largest scale, and not hesitate to make contracts with the United States and elsewhere for the largest possible quantities of aviation material and equipment of all kinds. We are in danger, as we have never been in danger before — no, not even at the height of the submarine campaign [1917]. . . .

This thought preys upon me: *The months slip by rapidly. If we delay too long in repairing our defences, we may be forbidden by superior power to complete the process.*

* * * * *

We were much disappointed that the Chancellor of the Exchequer could not be present. It was evident that Mr. Baldwin's health was failing, and it was well known that he

would soon seek rest from his burdens. There could be no
doubt who would be his successor. Unhappily, Mr. Neville
Chamberlain was absent upon a well-deserved holiday, and
did not have the opportunity of this direct confrontation with
the facts from members of the Conservative Party who included
his brother and so many of his most valued personal friends.

Most earnest consideration was given by Ministers to our
formidable representations, but it was not till after the recess,
on November 23, 1936, that we were all invited by Mr. Baldwin to receive a more fully considered statement on the whole
position. Sir Thomas Inskip then gave a frank and able account, in which he did not conceal from us the gravity of the
plight into which we had come. In substance this was to the
effect that our estimates and, in particular, my statements took
a too gloomy view of our prospects; that great efforts were being made (as indeed they were) to recover the lost ground; but
that no case existed which would justify the Government in
adopting emergency measures; that these would necessarily be
of a character to upset the whole industrial life of this country, would cause widespread alarm, and advertise any deficiencies that existed, and that within these limits everything
possible was being done. On this Sir Austen Chamberlain
recorded our general impression that our anxieties were not
relieved and that we were by no means satisfied. Thus we
took our leave.

I cannot contend that at this date, the end of 1936, the
position could have been retrieved. Much more, however,
could and ought to have been done by an intense conclusive
effort. And of course the fact and proof of this effort must
have had its immeasurable effect on Germany, if not on Hitler.
But the paramount fact remained that the Germans had the
lead of us in the air, and also over the whole field of munitions
production, even making allowance for our smaller military
needs, and for the fact that we had a right also to count upon
France and the French Army and air force. It was no longer
in our power to forestall Hitler or to regain air parity. Nothing could now prevent the German Army and the German air

force from becoming the strongest in Europe. By extraordinary and disturbing exertions we could improve our position. We could not cure it.

These sombre conclusions, which were not seriously disputed by the Government, no doubt influenced their foreign policy; and full account must be taken of them when we try to form a judgment upon the decisions which Mr. Chamberlain, when he became Prime Minister, took before and during the Munich crisis. I was at this time only a private Member of Parliament, and I bore no official responsibility. I strove my utmost to galvanise the Government into vehement and extraordinary preparation, even at the cost of world alarm. In these endeavours no doubt I painted the picture even darker than it was. The emphasis which I had put upon the two years' lag which afflicted us may well be judged inconsistent with my desire to come to grips with Hitler in October, 1938. I remain convinced, however, that it was right to spur the Government by every means, and that it would have been better in all the circumstances, which will presently be described, to fight Hitler in 1938 than it was when we finally had to do so in September, 1939. Of this more later.

*   *   *   *   *

Presently Mr. Baldwin, as we have seen, gave place to Mr. Neville Chamberlain; and we must now move on to 1938. Lord Swinton was a very keen and efficient Air Minister, and for a long time had great influence in the Cabinet in procuring the necessary facilities and funds. The anxiety about our air defences continued to grow, and reached its climax in May. The many great and valuable expansions and improvements which Lord Swinton had made could not become apparent quickly, and in any case the whole policy of the Government lacked both magnitude and urgency. I continued to press for an inquiry into the state of our air programme and found increasing support. Swinton had made the mistake of accepting a peerage. He was not, therefore, able to defend himself and his department in the House of Commons. The spokesman who

was chosen from the Government Front Bench was utterly
unable to stem the rising tide of alarm and dissatisfaction.
After one most unfortunate debate, it became obvious that the
Air Minister should be in the House of Commons.

One morning (May 12) at the Air Defence Research Committee we were all busily engaged — scientists, politicians, and
officials — on technical problems, when a note was brought in
to the Air Minister asking him to go to Downing Street. He
desired us to continue our discussions, and left at once. He
never returned. He had been dismissed by Mr. Chamberlain.

In the agitated debate which followed on the twenty-fifth, I
tried to distinguish between the exertions and capacity of the
fallen Minister and the general complaint against the Government:

The credit of Government statements has been compromised by
what has occurred. The House has been consistently misled about
the air position. The Prime Minister himself has been misled. He
was misled right up to the last moment, apparently. Look at the
statement which he made in March, when he spoke about our
armaments: "The sight of this enormous, this almost terrifying,
power which Britain is building up has a sobering effect, a steady-
ing effect, on the opinion of the world."

I have often warned the House that the air programmes were
falling into arrear. But I have never attacked Lord Swinton. I
have never thought that he was the one to blame — certainly not
the only one to blame. It is usual for the critics of a Government
to discover hitherto unnoticed virtues in any Minister who is forced
to resign. But perhaps I may quote what I said three months ago:
"It would be unfair to throw the blame on any one Minister, or
upon Lord Swinton, for our deficiency. He certainly represents an
extremely able and wholehearted effort to do the best he possibly
could to expand our air power, and the results which he achieved
would be bright, if they were not darkened by the time-table, and
if they were not outshone by other relative facts occurring elsewhere."

*   *   *   *   *

The hard responsibility for the failure to fulfil the promises
made to us rests upon those who have governed and guided this

island for the last five years, that is to say, from the date when
German rearmament in real earnest became apparent and known.
I certainly did not attempt to join in a man-hunt of Lord Swinton.
I was very glad today to hear the Prime Minister's tribute to him.
Certainly he deserves our sympathy. He had the confidence and
friendship of the Prime Minister, he had the support of an
enormous parliamentary majority; yet he has been taken from his
post at what, I think, is the worst moment in the story of air
expansion. It may be that in a few months there will be a considerable flow of aircraft arriving; yet he has had to answer for his
record at this particularly dark moment for him. I was reading the
other day a letter of the great Duke of Marlborough, in which
he said: "To remove a General in the midst of a campaign — that is
the mortal stroke."

I turned to other aspects of our defences:

We are now in the third year of openly avowed rearmament.
Why is it, if all is going well, there are so many deficiencies? Why,
for instance, are the Guards drilling with flags instead of machine-
guns? Why is it that our small Territorial Army is in a rudimentary
condition? Is that all according to schedule? Why, when you consider how small are our forces, should it be impossible to equip
the Territorial Army simultaneously with the Regular Army? It
would have been a paltry task for British industry, which is more
flexible and more fertile than German industry in every sphere
except munitions.

*   *   *   *   *

The other day the Secretary of State for War was asked about
the anti-aircraft artillery. The old three-inch guns of the Great War,
he said, had been modernised, and deliveries of the newer guns —
and there is more than one type of newer gun — were proceeding
"in advance of schedule." But what is the schedule? If your
schedule prescribes a delivery of half a dozen, ten, a dozen, twenty,
or whatever it may be, guns per month, no doubt that may easily
be up to schedule, and easily be in advance of it. But what is the
adequacy of such a schedule to our needs? A year ago I reminded
the House of the published progress of Germany in anti-aircraft
artillery — thirty regiments of twelve batteries each of mobile artillery alone, aggregating something between twelve and thirteen
hundred guns, in addition to three or four thousand guns in fixed

positions. These are all modern guns, not guns of 1915, but all
guns made since the year 1933.

Does not that give the House an idea of the tremendous scale of
these transactions? We do not need to have a gigantic army like
Continental countries; but in the matter of anti-aircraft defence we
are on equal terms. We are just as vulnerable, and perhaps more
vulnerable. Here is the government thinking of anti-aircraft
artillery in terms of hundreds where the Germans have it today
in terms of thousands.

*   *   *   *   *

We are thinking at the present time in terms of production for
three separate armed forces. In fact and in truth, the supply of
arms for all fighting forces resolves itself into a common problem
of the provision and distribution of skilled labour, raw materials,
plant, machinery, and technical appliances. That problem can only
be dealt with comprehensively, harmoniously, and economically
through one central dominating control. At the present time there
is inefficiency and overlapping, and there is certainly waste. Why is it
that this skilful aircraft industry of Britain requires ninety thousand
men, and that it produces only one-half to one-third of what is
being produced by about one hundred and ten thousand men in
Germany? Is that not an extraordinary fact? It is incredible that
we have not been able to produce a greater supply of aeroplanes
at this time. Given a plain office table, an empty field, money and
labour, we should receive a flow of aeroplanes by eighteen months;
yet this is the thirty-fourth month since Lord Baldwin decided that
the air force must be tripled.

*   *   *   *   *

The new Secretary of State for Air, Sir Kingsley Wood, invited me to remain on the Air Defence Research Committee.
The skies had now grown much darker, and I felt keenly the
need of Lindemann's interpretation of the technical aspects
and of his advice and aid. I, therefore, wrote to him, saying
that, unless he was associated with me, I would not continue.
After some tussling behind the scenes, Lindemann was placed
on the main Committee, and we resumed our joint work.

*   *   *   *   *

Always, up till the Armistice of June, 1940, whether in peace
or war, in a private station or as head of the Government, I
enjoyed confidential relations with the often-changing Premiers
of the French Republic and with many of its leading Ministers.
I was most anxious to find out the truth about German rearmament and to cross-check my own calculations by theirs. I
therefore wrote to M. Daladier, with whom I was personally
acquainted:

Mr. Churchill to M. Daladier. *May 3,* 1938.

Your predecessors, M.M. Blum and Flandin, were both kind
enough to give me the French estimates of the German air strength
at particular periods in recent years. I should be much obliged if
you could let me know what your view is now. I have several
sources of information which have proved accurate in the past, but
am anxious to have a cross-check from an independent source.

I am so glad that your visit here was so successful, and I hope
now that all those staff arrangements will be made, the need for
which I have pressed upon our Ministers.

In response M. Daladier sent me a document of seventeen
pages dated May 11, 1938, which "had been deeply thought
out by the French Air Staff." I showed this important paper
to my friends in the British departments concerned, who examined it searchingly and reported that "it agreed in every
essential with the independent opinions formed by the British
Air Staff on the basis of their own information." The French
estimate of the size of the German air force was slightly higher
than that of the British. Early in June I was in a position to
write to M. Daladier with a considerable amount of authoritative opinion behind me.

Mr. Churchill to M. Daladier. *June 6,* 1938.

I am very much obliged to you for the invaluable information
which I have received through the French Military Attaché. You
may be sure I shall use it only with the greatest discretion, and in
our common interests.

The general estimate of the German air force at the present time
agrees with the private views I have been able to form. I am

inclined to think, however, that the German aircraft industry is
turning out aircraft at a somewhat higher rate than is allowed, and
that the figure given is that for the actual deliveries of aircraft of
military types to the German air force, excluding deliveries for
export, and to General Franco. It is probable that the German
air force will consist of three hundred squadrons by April 1, 1939,
and four hundred squadrons by April 1, 1940.

I was also most anxious to cross-check my own estimates of
the German Army with those which I had been able to form
from English sources. Accordingly I added the following:

I venture to enclose a very short note of the information I have
been able to gather from various sources about the present and
prospective strength of the German Army. It would be a convenience to me to know whether this agrees broadly with your
estimates. It would be quite sufficient if the figures, as you understand them, could be pencilled in in any case where you think
I am in error.

NOTE

The German Army at this date, June 1, consists of thirty-six
regular divisions, and four armoured divisions, the whole at full
war-strength. The non-armoured divisions are rapidly acquiring
the power to triple themselves, and can at the present time be
doubled. The artillery beyond seventy divisions is markedly incomplete. The officer corps is thin over the whole force. Nevertheless,
by October 1, 1938, we cannot expect less than fifty-six plus four
armoured, equals sixty fully equipped and armed divisional formations. Behind these will stand a reservoir of trained men equal in
man-power to about another thirty-six divisions, for which skeleton
formations have been devised and for which armaments, small arms
and a very low complement of artillery, would be available if a
lower standard were accepted for part of the active army. This
takes no account of the man-power of Austria, which at the extreme
computation could provide twelve divisions without arms but
ready to draw on the general pool of German munitions industry.
In addition there are a number of men and formations of an
unbrigaded nature — frontier defence force, Landwehr divisions,
and so on, who are relatively unarmed.

On June 18, 1938, M. Daladier wrote:

I am particularly pleased to learn that the information enclosed in my letter of May 16 corresponds to yours.

I am entirely in accord with you in the facts relating to the German Army contained in the note annexed to your letter of June 6. It should be pointed out, however, that of the thirty-six ordinary divisions of which Germany actually disposes, four are entirely motorised and two are in the course of becoming so soon.

In fact, according to our post-war information from German sources, this epitome of the German Army in the summer of 1938 was remarkably accurate, considering that it was produced by a private person. It shows that in my long series of campaigns for British rearmament I was by no means ill-informed.

*   *   *   *   *

References have been made at various points in this tale to the French air power. At one time it was double our own and Germany was not supposed to have an air force at all. Until 1933, France had held a high place among the air fleets of Europe. But in the very year in which Hitler came into power, a fateful lack of interest and support began to be displayed. Money was grudged; the productive capacity of the factories was allowed to dwindle; modern types were not developed. The French forty-hour week could not rival the output of a Germany working harsh hours under wartime conditions. All this happened about the same time as the loss of air parity in Britain which has been so fully described. In fact the Western Allies, who had the right to create whatever air forces they thought necessary for their safety, neglected this vital weapon, while the Germans, who were prohibited by treaty from touching it, made it the spear-point of their diplomacy and eventual attack.

The French "Popular Front" Government of 1936 and later took many substantial measures to prepare the French Army and Navy for war. No corresponding exertion was made in the air. There is an ugly graph [1] which shows in a decisive

1 See Appendix D, Book I.

fashion the downward streak of French air power and its intersection in 1935 by the line of ever-rising German achievement. It was not until the summer of 1938, when M. Guy La Chambre became Air Minister, that vigorous steps were taken to revive the French air force. But then only eighteen months remained. Nothing that the French could do could prevent the German Army growing and ripening as each year passed and thus overtaking their own army. But it is astonishing that their air power should have been allowed to fall by the wayside. It is not for me to apportion responsibility and blame to the Ministers of friendly and Allied foreign countries. But when in France they are looking out for "guilty men," it would seem that here is a field which might well be searchingly explored.

*   *   *   *   *

The spirit of the British nation and of the Parliament they had newly elected gradually rose as consciousness of the German, and soon of the German-Italian, menace slowly and fitfully dawned upon them. They became willing, and even eager, for all kinds of steps which, taken two or three years earlier, would have prevented their troubles. But as their mood improved, the power of their opponents and also the difficulty of their task increased. Many say that nothing except war could have stopped Hitler after we had submitted to the seizure of the Rhineland. This may indeed be the verdict of future generations. Much, however, could have been done to make us better prepared and thus lessen our hazards. And who shall say what could not have happened?

14

Mr. Eden at the Foreign Office:
His Resignation

Foreign Secretary and Prime Minister — Eden and Chamberlain —
Sir Robert Vansittart — My Contacts with the Foreign Secretary
About Spain — The Nyon Conference — Our Correspondence —
A British Success — Divergence Between Prime Minister and
Foreign Secretary — Lord Halifax Visits Germany and Hitler —
I Decline an Invitation — Eden Feels Isolated — President Roose-
velt's Overture — The Prime Minister's Reply — The President
Rebuffed and Discouraged — Mr. Chamberlain's Grave Responsi-
bility — Final Breach Between Eden and Chamberlain About
Conversations in Rome — A Sleepless Night at Chartwell.

THE FOREIGN SECRETARY has a special position in a British
Cabinet. He is treated with marked respect in his high
and responsible office, but he usually conducts his affairs under
the continuous scrutiny, if not of the whole Cabinet, at least
of its principal members. He is under an obligation to keep
them informed. He circulates to his colleagues, as a matter
of custom and routine, all his executive telegrams, the reports
from our embassies abroad, the records of his interviews with
foreign Ambassadors or other notables. At least this has been
the case during my experience of Cabinet life. This supervision is, of course, especially maintained by the Prime Minister,
who personally or through his Cabinet is responsible for controlling, and has the power to control, the main course of foreign policy. From him at least there must be no secrets. No
Foreign Secretary can do his work unless he is supported constantly by his chief. To make things go smoothly, there must

239

not only be agreement between them on fundamentals, but also
a harmony of outlook and even to some extent of temperament.
This is all the more important if the Prime Minister himself
devotes special attention to foreign affairs.

Eden was the Foreign Secretary of Mr. Baldwin, who, apart
from his main well-known desire for peace and a quiet life,
took no active share in foreign policy. Mr. Chamberlain, on
the other hand, sought to exercise a masterful control in many
departments. He had strong views about foreign affairs, and
from the beginning asserted his undoubted right to discuss
them with foreign Ambassadors. His assumption of the
Premiership, therefore, implied a delicate but perceptible
change in the position of the Foreign Secretary.

To this was added a profound, though at first latent, difference of spirit and opinion. The Prime Minister wished to
get on good terms with the two European dictators, and believed that conciliation and the avoidance of anything likely
to offend them was the best method. Eden, on the other hand,
had won his reputation at Geneva by rallying the nations of
Europe against one dictator; and, left to himself, might well
have carried sanctions to the verge of war, and perhaps beyond.
He was a devoted adherent of the French Entente. He had
just insisted upon "staff conversations." He was anxious to
have more intimate relations with Soviet Russia. He felt and
feared the Hitler peril. He was alarmed by the weakness of
our armaments, and its reaction on foreign affairs. It might
almost be said that there was not much difference of view between him and me, except of course that he was in harness.
It seemed, therefore, to me from the beginning that differences
would be likely to arise between these two leading ministerial
figures as the world situation became more acute.

Moreover, in Lord Halifax the Prime Minister had a colleague who seemed to share his views of foreign affairs with
sympathy and conviction. My long and intimate associations
with Edward Halifax dated from 1922 when, in the days of
Lloyd George, he became my Under-Secretary at the Dominions and Colonial Office. Political differences — even as serious

and prolonged as those which arose between us about his policy as Viceroy of India — had never destroyed our personal relations. I thought I knew him very well, and I was sure that there was a gulf between us. I felt also that this same gulf, or one like it, was open between him and Anthony Eden. It would have been wiser, on the whole, for Mr. Chamberlain to have made Lord Halifax his Foreign Secretary when he formed his Government. Eden would have been far more happily placed in the War Office or the Admiralty, and the Prime Minister would have had a kindred spirit and his own man at the Foreign Office. This inauspicious situation developed steadily during the year that Eden and Chamberlain worked together.

* * * * *

Up to this time and during many anxious years Sir Robert Vansittart had been the official head of the Foreign Office. His fortuitous connection with the Hoare-Laval Pact had affected his position both with the new Foreign Secretary, Mr. Eden, and in wide political circles. The Prime Minister, who leaned more and more upon his chief industrial adviser, Sir Horace Wilson, and consulted him a great deal on matters entirely outside his province or compass, regarded Vansittart as hostile to Germany. This was indeed true, for no one more clearly realised or foresaw the growth of the German danger or was more ready to subordinate other considerations to meeting it. The Foreign Secretary felt he could work more easily with Sir Alexander Cadogan, a Foreign Office official also of the highest character and ability. Therefore, at the end of 1937, Vansittart was apprised of his impending dismissal, and on January 1, 1938, was appointed to the special post of "Chief Diplomatic Adviser to His Majesty's Government." This was represented to the public as promotion, and might well indeed appear to be so. In fact, however, the whole responsibility for managing the Foreign Office passed out of his hands. He kept his old traditional room, but he saw the Foreign Office telegrams only after they had reached the Foreign Secretary with the minutes of the department upon them. Vansittart, who refused the

Embassy in Paris, continued in this detached position for some
time.

                    *   *   *   *   *

Between the summer of 1937 and the end of that year, divergence, both in method and aim, grew between the Prime Minister and his Foreign Secretary. The sequence of events which
led to Mr. Eden's resignation in February, 1938, followed a
logical course.

The original points of difference arose about our relations
with Germany and Italy. Mr. Chamberlain was determined to
press his suit with the two dictators. In July, 1937, he invited
the Italian Ambassador, Count Grandi, to Downing Street. The
conversation took place with the knowledge, but not in the
presence, of Mr. Eden. Mr. Chamberlain spoke of his desire
for an improvement of Anglo-Italian relations. Count Grandi
suggested to him that as a preliminary move it might be well
if the Prime Minister were to write a personal appeal to Mussolini. Mr. Chamberlain sat down and wrote such a letter during the interview. It was dispatched without reference to the
Foreign Secretary, who was in the Foreign Office a few yards
away. The letter produced no apparent results, and our relations with Italy, because of the increasing Italian intervention
in Spain, got steadily worse.

Mr. Chamberlain was imbued with a sense of a special and
personal mission to come to friendly terms with the Dictators
of Italy and Germany, and he conceived himself capable of
achieving this relationship. To Mussolini he wished to accord
recognition of the Italian conquest of Abyssinia as a prelude to
a general settlement of differences. To Hitler he was prepared
to offer colonial concessions. At the same time he was disinclined to consider in a conspicuous manner the improvement
of British armaments or the necessity of close collaboration
with France, both on the staff and political levels. Mr. Eden,
on the other hand, was convinced that any arrangement with
Italy must be part of a general Mediterranean settlement,
which must include Spain, and be reached in close understanding with France. In the negotiation of such a settlement, our

recognition of Italy's position in Abyssinia would clearly be an important bargaining counter. To throw this away in the prelude and appear eager to initiate negotiations was, in the Foreign Secretary's view, unwise.

During the autumn of 1937 these differences became more severe. Mr. Chamberlain considered that the Foreign Office was obstructing his attempts to open discussions with Germany and Italy, and Mr. Eden felt that his chief was displaying immoderate haste in approaching the Dictators, particularly while British armaments were so weak. There was in fact a profound practical and psychological divergence of view.

*　　*　　*　　*　　*

In spite of my differences with the Government, I was in close sympathy with their Foreign Secretary. He seemed to me the most resolute and courageous figure in the Administration, and although as a private secretary and later as an Under-Secretary of State in the Foreign Office he had had to adapt himself to many things I had attacked and still condemn, I felt sure his heart was in the right place and that he had the root of the matter in him. For his part, he made a point of inviting me to Foreign Office functions, and we corresponded freely. There was, of course, no impropriety in this practice, and Mr. Eden held to the well-established precedent whereby the Foreign Secretary is accustomed to keep in contact with the prominent political figures of the day on all broad international issues.

On August 7, 1937, I wrote to him:

This Spanish business cuts across my thoughts. It seems to me most important to make Blum stay with us strictly neutral, even if Germany and Italy continue to back the rebels and Russia sends money to the Government. If the French Government takes sides against the rebels, it will be a godsend to the Germans and pro-Germans. In case you have a spare moment look at my article in the *Evening Standard* on Monday.

In this article I had written:

The worst quarrels only arise when both sides are equally in the right and in the wrong. Here, on the one hand, the passions of a

poverty-stricken and backward proletariat demand the overthrow
of Church, State, and property, and the inauguration of a Communist régime. On the other hand, the patriotic, religious, and
bourgeois forces, under the leadership of the Army, and sustained
by the countryside in many provinces, are marching to re-establish
order by setting up a military dictatorship. The cruelties and
ruthless executions extorted by the desperation of both sides, the
appalling hatreds unloosed, the clash of creed and interest, make it
only too probable that victory will be followed by the merciless
extermination of the active elements of the vanquished and by a
prolonged period of iron rule.

In the autumn of 1937, Eden and I had reached, though by
somewhat different paths, a similar standpoint against active
Axis intervention in the Spanish Civil War. I always supported
him in the House when he took resolute action, even though
it was upon a very limited scale. I knew well what his difficulties were with some of his senior colleagues in the Cabinet and
with his chief, and that he would act more boldly if he were
not enmeshed. We saw a good deal of each other at the end of
August at Cannes, and one day I gave him and Mr. Lloyd
George luncheon at a restaurant halfway between Cannes and
Nice. Our conversation ran over the whole field — the Spanish
struggle, Mussolini's persistent bad faith and intervention in
Spain, and finally, of course, the dark background of ever-
growing German power. I thought we were all three pretty
well agreed. The Foreign Secretary was naturally most guarded
about his relations with his chief and colleagues, and no reference was made to this delicate topic. Nothing could have
been more correct than his demeanour. Nevertheless, I was
sure he was not a happy man in his great office.

*   *   *   *   *

Soon in the Mediterranean a crisis arose which he handled
with firmness and skill, and which was accordingly solved in a
manner reflecting a gleam of credit upon our course. A number of merchant ships had been sunk by so-called Spanish submarines. Actually there was no doubt that they were not Span-

ish but Italian. This was sheer piracy, and it stirred all who knew about it to action. A conference of the Mediterranean Powers was convened at Nyon for September 10. To this the Foreign Secretary, accompanied by Vansittart and Lord Chatfield, the First Sea Lord, proceeded.

Mr. Churchill to Mr. Eden.   9.IX.37.

In your last letter you said that you would be very glad to see Lloyd George and me before you left for Geneva. We have met today, and I venture to let you know our views.

This is the moment to rally Italy to her international duty. Submarine piracy in the Mediterranean and the sinking of ships of many countries without any care for the lives of their crews must be suppressed. For this purpose all Mediterranean Powers should agree to keep their own submarines away from certain defined routes for commerce. In these routes the French and British Navies should search for all submarines, and any found by the detector apparatus should be pursued and sunk as a pirate. Italy should be asked in the most courteous manner to participate in this. If, however, she will not do so, she should be told, "That is what we are going to do."

At the same time, as it is very important to have the friendly concurrence of Italy, France should say that unless this concurrence is obtained, she will open the Pyrenees frontier to the import of munitions of all kinds. Thus, on the one hand, Italy would be faced by the fact that the sea routes through the Mediterranean are going to be cleared of pirate submarines whatever happens, while at the same time she will gain nothing by not joining in, because the French frontier will be open. This point we consider essential. This combination of pressure upon Italy to join with the other Mediterranean Powers, coupled with the fact that she would risk much and gain nothing by standing out, would almost certainly be effective provided Mussolini knows that France and England are in earnest.

It is not believed that Germany is ready for a major war this year, and if it is hoped to have good relations with Italy in the future, matters should be brought to a head now. The danger from which we suffer is that Mussolini thinks all can be carried off by bluff and bullying, and that in the end we shall only blether and withdraw. It is in the interests of European peace that a firm front should be shown now, and if you feel able to act in this sense, we wish to assure you of our support upon such a policy in the House of Commons and in the country however matters may turn.

Speaking personally, I feel that this is as important a moment for you as when you insisted upon the staff conversations with France after the violation of the Rhineland. The bold path is the path of safety.

Pray make any use of this letter privately or publicly that you may consider helpful to British interests and to the interests of peace.

P.S. — I have read this letter to Mr. Lloyd George who declares himself in full agreement with it.

The Conference at Nyon was brief and successful. It was agreed to establish British and French anti-submarine patrols, with orders which left no doubt as to the fate of any submarine encountered. This was acquiesced in by Italy, and the outrages stopped at once.

Mr. Eden to Mr. Churchill.   14.X.37.

You will now have seen the line which we have taken at Nyon, which, in part at least, coincides with that suggested in your letter. I hope you will agree that the results of the Conference are satisfactory. They seem so as viewed from here. The really important political fact is that we have emphasised that co-operation between Britain and France can be effective, and that the two Western Democracies can still play a decisive part in European affairs. The programme upon which we eventually agreed was worked out jointly by the French and ourselves. I must say that they could not have co-operated more sincerely, and we have been surprised at the extent of the naval co-operation which they have been ready to offer. It is fair to say that if we include their help in the air we shall be working on a fifty-fifty basis.

I agree that what we have done here only deals with one aspect of the Spanish problem. But it has much increased our authority among the nations at a time when we needed such an increase badly. The attitude of the smaller Powers of the Mediterranean was no less satisfactory. They played up well under the almost effusively friendly lead of Turkey. Chatfield has been a great success with everyone, and I feel that the Nyon Conference, by its brevity and success, has done something to put us on the map again. I hope that this may be your feeling too.

At least it has heartened the French and ourselves to tackle our immensely formidable task together.

Mr. Churchill to Mr. Eden.   20.IX.37.

It was very good of you, when so busy, to write to me. Indeed I congratulate you on a very considerable achievement. It is only rarely that an opportunity comes when stern and effective measures can be brought to bear upon an evil-doer without incurring the risk of war. I have no doubt that the House of Commons will be very much pleased with the result.

I was very glad to see that Neville has been backing you up, and not, as represented by the popular press, holding you back by the coat-tails. My hope is that the advantages you have gained will be firmly held on to. Mussolini only understands superior force, such as he is now confronted with in the Mediterranean. The whole naval position there is transformed from the moment that the French bases are at our disposal. Italy cannot resist an effective Anglo-French combination. I hope, therefore, that Mussolini will be left to find his own way out of the diplomatic ditch into which he has blundered. The crystallisation against him for an unassailable purpose which has taken place in the Mediterranean is the one thing above all that he should have laboured to avoid. He has brought it about. I hope that the Anglo-French naval co-operation which has now begun will be continued indefinitely, and that both navies and air forces will continue to use each other's facilities. This will be needed to prevent trouble arising about the Balearic Islands. The continued fortification of the Mediterranean by Italy against us will have to be dealt with in the future, as it is a capital danger to the British Empire. The more permanent the present arrangement becomes, the less loaded with danger will this situation be.

Bernard Baruch telegraphs he is writing the results of his interview with the President [after our talks in London]. I have little doubt that the President's speech against dictatorships has been largely influenced by our talk, and I trust that the ground on the tariff and currency side is also being explored.

Mr. Eden to Mr. Churchill.   25.IX.37.

Thank you so much for your letter of September 20, and for the generous things you have written about Nyon, which I much appreciate. I thought your summing up of the position at Nyon, "It is only rarely that an opportunity comes when stern and effective measures can be brought to bear upon an evil-doer without incurring the risk of war," effectively described the position. Mussolini has been unwise enough to overstep the limits, and he has had to pay the penalty. There is no doubt that the spectacle of eighty Anglo-French destroyers patrolling the Mediterranean assisted by a considerable force of aircraft has made a profound impression on opinion in Europe. From reports which I have received, Germany herself has not been slow to take note of this fact. It was a great relief, both to Delbos and me, to be able to assert the position of our respective countries in this way in the autumn of a year in which we have inevitably had to be so much on the defensive. There is plenty of trouble ahead, and we are not yet, of course, anything like as strong in the military sense as I would wish, but Nyon has enabled us to improve our position and to gain more time.

I also cordially agree with you on the importance of the Anglo-French co-operation which we have now created in the Mediterranean. The whole French attitude was, of course, fundamentally different from that which prevailed when Laval was in command. The French Naval Staff could not have been more helpful, and they really made a great effort to make an important contribution to the joint force. Our Admiralty were, I am sure, impressed. Moreover, the mutual advantages to which you refer in respect of the use of each other's bases are very valuable. Nor will Italian participation, whatever its ultimate form, be able to affect the realities of the situation.

The Nyon Conference, although an incident, is a proof of how powerful the combined influence of Britain and France, if expressed with conviction and a readiness to use force, would have been upon the mood and policy of the Dictators. That such a policy would have prevented war at this stage cannot be asserted. It might easily have delayed it. It is the fact that whereas "appeasement" in all its forms only encouraged their aggression and gave the Dictators more power with their own peoples, any sign of a positive counter-offensive by the Western Democracies immediately produced an abatement of tension.

This rule prevailed during the whole of 1937. After that, the scene and conditions were different.

*   *   *   *   *

Early in October, 1937, I was invited to a dinner at the Foreign Office for the Yugoslav Premier, M. Stoyadinovitch. Afterwards, when we were all standing about and I was talking to Eden, Lord Halifax came up and said in a genial way that Goering had invited him to Germany on a sports visit, and the hope was held out that he would certainly be able to see Hitler. He said that he had spoken about it to the Prime Minister, who thought it would be a very good thing, and therefore he had accepted. I had the impression that Eden was surprised and did not like it; but everything passed off pleasantly. Halifax, therefore, visited Germany in his capacity as a Master of Foxhounds. The Nazi press welcomed him as "Lord Halalifax," *Halali!* being a Continental hunting-cry, and after some sporting entertainment he was in fact bidden to Berchtesgaden and had an informal and none too ceremonious interview with the Fuehrer. This did not go very well. One could hardly conceive two personalities less able to comprehend one another. This High Church Yorkshire aristocrat and ardent peace-lover, reared in all the smiling good will of former English life, who had taken his part in the war as a good officer, met on the other side the demon-genius sprung from the abyss of poverty, inflamed by defeat, devoured by hatred and revenge, and convulsed by his design to make the German race masters of Europe or maybe the world. Nothing came of all this but chatter and bewilderment.

*   *   *   *   *

I may mention here that Ribbentrop twice tendered me an invitation to visit Herr Hitler. Long before, as Colonial Under-Secretary and a major in the Oxfordshire Yeomanry, I had been the guest of the Kaiser at the German manoeuvres in 1907 and in 1909. But now there was a different tune. Mortal quarrels were afoot; and I had my station in them. I would

gladly have met Hitler with the authority of Britain behind
me. But as a private individual I should have placed myself
and my country at a disadvantage. If I had agreed with the
Dictator-host, I should have misled him. If I had disagreed, he
would have been offended, and I should have been accused of
spoiling Anglo-German relations. Therefore I declined, or
rather let lapse, both invitations. All those Englishmen who
visited the German Fuehrer in these years were embarrassed or
compromised. No one was more completely misled than Mr.
Lloyd George, whose rapturous accounts of his conversations
make odd reading today. There is no doubt that Hitler had a
power of fascinating men, and the sense of force and authority
is apt to assert itself unduly upon the tourist. Unless the terms
are equal, it is better to keep away.

*   *   *   *   *

During these November days, Eden became increasingly
concerned about our slow rearmament. On the eleventh, he
had an interview with the Prime Minister and tried to convey
his misgivings. Mr. Neville Chamberlain after a while refused
to listen to him. He advised him to "go home and take an
aspirin." When Halifax returned from Berlin, he reported that
Hitler had told him the colonial question was the only outstanding issue between Britain and Germany. He believed the
Germans were in no hurry. There was no immediate prospect
of a peace deal. His conclusions were negative and his mood
passive.

In February, 1938, the Foreign Secretary conceived himself to
be almost isolated in the Cabinet. The Prime Minister had
strong support against him and his outlook. A whole band of
important Ministers thought the Foreign Office policy dangerous
and even provocative. On the other hand, a number of the
younger Ministers were very ready to understand his point of
view. Some of them later complained that he did not take them
into his confidence. He did not, however, contemplate anything
like forming a group against his leader. The Chiefs of Staff
could give him no help. Indeed, they enjoined caution and

dwelt upon the dangers of the situation. They were reluctant
to draw too close to the French lest we should enter into engagements beyond our power to fulfil. They took a gloomy
view of Russian military strength after the purge. They believed it necessary to deal with our problems as though we had
three enemies — Germany, Italy, and Japan — who might all
attack us together, and few to help us. We might ask for air
bases in France, but we were not able to send an army in the
first instance. Even this modest suggestion encountered strong
resistance in the Cabinet.

*   *   *   *   *

But the actual breach came over a new and separate issue.
On the evening of January 11, 1938, Mr. Sumner Welles, the
American Under-Secretary of State, called upon the British
Ambassador in Washington. He was the bearer of a secret and
confidential message from President Roosevelt to Mr. Chamberlain. The President was deeply anxious at the deterioration of
the international situation, and proposed to take the initiative
by inviting the representatives of certain Governments to Washington to discuss the underlying causes of present differences.
Before taking this step, however, he wished to consult the British Government on their view of such a plan, and stipulated
that no other Government should be informed either of the
nature or the existence of such a proposal. He asked that not
later than January 17 he should be given a reply to his message,
and intimated that only if his suggestion met with "the cordial
approval and wholehearted support of His Majesty's Government" would he then approach the Governments of France,
Germany, and Italy. Here was a formidable and measureless
step.

In forwarding this most secret message to London, the British Ambassador, Sir Ronald Lindsay, commented that in his
view the President's plan was a genuine effort to relax international tension, and that if His Majesty's Government withheld
their support, the progress which had been made in Anglo-
American co-operation during the previous two years would be

destroyed. He urged in the most earnest manner acceptance of
the proposal by the British Government. The Foreign Office
received the Washington telegram on January 12, and copies
were sent to the Prime Minister in the country that evening.
On the following morning, he came to London, and on his instructions a reply was sent to the President's message. Mr. Eden
was at this time on a brief holiday in the South of France. Mr.
Chamberlain's reply was to the effect that he appreciated the
confidence of President Roosevelt in consulting him in this
fashion upon his proposed plan to alleviate the existing tension
in Europe, but he wished to explain the position of his own
efforts to reach agreement with Germany and Italy, particularly
in the case of the latter. "His Majesty's Government would be
prepared, for their part, if possible with the authority of the
League of Nations, to recognise *de jure* the Italian occupation
of Abyssinia, if they found that the Italian Government on
their side were ready to give evidence of their desire to contribute to the restoration of confidence and friendly relations."
The Prime Minister mentioned these facts, the message continued, so that the President might consider whether his present proposal might not cut across the British efforts. Would
it not, therefore, be wiser to postpone the launching of the
American plan?

This reply was received by the President with some disappointment. He intimated that he would reply by letter to Mr.
Chamberlain on January 17. On the evening of January 15
the Foreign Secretary returned to England. He had been urged
to come back, not by his chief, who was content to act without
him, but by his devoted officials at the Foreign Office. The
vigilant Alexander Cadogan awaited him upon the pier at
Dover. Mr. Eden, who had worked long and hard to improve
Anglo-American relations, was deeply perturbed. He immediately sent a telegram to Sir Ronald Lindsay attempting to
minimise the effects of Mr. Chamberlain's chilling answer. The
President's letter reached London on the morning of January
18. In it he agreed to postpone making his proposal in view of
the fact that the British Government were contemplating direct

negotiations, but he added that he was gravely concerned at the suggestion that His Majesty's Government might accord recognition to the Italian position in Abyssinia. He thought that this would have a most harmful effect upon Japanese policy in the Far East and upon American public opinion. Mr. Cordell Hull, in delivering this letter to the British Ambassador in Washington, expressed himself even more emphatically. He said that such a recognition would "rouse a feeling of disgust, would revive and multiply all fears of pulling the chestnuts out of the fire; it would be represented as a corrupt bargain completed in Europe at the expense of interests in the Far East in which America was intimately concerned."

The President's letter was considered at a series of meetings of the Foreign Affairs Committee of the Cabinet. Mr. Eden succeeded in procuring a considerable modification of the previous attitude. Most of the Ministers thought he was satisfied. He did not make it clear to them that he was not. Following these discussions, two messages were sent to Washington on the evening of January 21. The substance of these replies was that the Prime Minister warmly welcomed the President's initiative, but was not anxious to bear any responsibility for its failure if American overtures were badly received. Mr. Chamberlain wished to point out that we did not accept in an unqualified manner the President's suggested procedure, which would clearly irritate both the Dictators and Japan. Nor did His Majesty's Government feel that the President had fully understood our position in regard to de jure recognition. The second message was in fact an explanation of our attitude in this matter. We intended to accord such recognition only as part of a general settlement with Italy.

The British Ambassador reported his conversation with Mr. Sumner Welles when he handed these messages to the President on January 22. He stated that Mr. Welles told him that "the President regarded recognition as an unpleasant pill which we should both have to swallow, and he wished that we should both swallow it together."

Thus it was that President Roosevelt's proposal to use Amer-

ican influence for the purpose of bringing together the leading
European Powers to discuss the chances of a general settlement,
this, of course, involving however tentatively the mighty power
of the United States, was rebuffed by Mr. Chamberlain. This
attitude defined in a decisive manner the difference of view
between the British Prime Minister and his Foreign Secretary.
Their disagreements were still confined to the circle of the
Cabinet for a little time longer; but the split was fundamental.
The comments of Mr. Chamberlain's biographer, Professor
Feiling, upon this episode, are not without interest: "While
Chamberlain feared the Dictators would pay no heed or else
*would use this line-up of the democracies as a pretext for a
break,* it was found on Eden's return that he would rather risk
that calamity than the loss of American good will. There was
the first breath of resignation. But a compromise was beaten
out. . . . " Poor England! Leading her free, careless life from
day to day, amid endless good-tempered parliamentary babble,
she followed, wondering, along the downward path which led
to all she wanted to avoid. She was continually reassured by
the leading articles of the most influential newspapers, with
some honourable exceptions, and behaved as if all the world
were as easy, uncalculating, and well-meaning as herself.

*   *   *   *   *

It was plain that no resignation by the Foreign Secretary
could be founded upon the rebuff administered by Mr. Chamberlain to the President's overture. Mr. Roosevelt was indeed
running great risks in his own domestic politics by deliberately
involving the United States in the darkening European scene.
All the forces of isolationism would have been aroused if any
part of these interchanges had transpired. On the other hand,
no event could have been more likely to stave off, or even
prevent, war than the arrival of the United States in the circle
of European hates and fears. To Britain it was a matter almost
of life and death. No one can measure in retrospect its effect
upon the course of events in Austria and later at Munich. We
must regard its rejection — for such it was — as the loss of the

last frail chance to save the world from tyranny otherwise than by war. That Mr. Chamberlain, with his limited outlook and inexperience of the European scene, should have possessed the self-sufficiency to wave away the proffered hand stretched out across the Atlantic leaves one, even at this date, breathless with amazement. The lack of all sense of proportion, and even of self-preservation, which this episode reveals in an upright, competent, well-meaning man, charged with the destinies of our country and all who depended upon it, is appalling. One cannot today even reconstruct the state of mind which would render such gestures possible.

*   *   *   *   *

I have yet to unfold the story of the treatment of the Russian offers of collaboration in the advent of Munich. If only the British people could have known and realised that, having neglected our defences and sought to diminish the defences of France, we were now disengaging ourselves, one after the other, from the two mighty nations whose extreme efforts were needed to save our lives and their own, history might have taken a different turn. But all seemed so easy from day to day. Now ten years later, let the lessons of the past be a guide.

*   *   *   *   *

It must have been with declining confidence in the future that Mr. Eden went to Paris on January 25 to consult with the French. Everything now turned upon the success of the approach to Italy, of which we had made such a point in our replies to the President. The French Ministers impressed upon Mr. Eden the necessity of the inclusion of Spain in any general settlement with the Italians; on this he needed little convincing. On February 10, the Prime Minister and the Foreign Secretary met Count Grandi, who declared that the Italians were ready in principle to open the conversations.

On February 15 the news came of the submission of the Austrian Chancellor, Schuschnigg, to the German demand for the introduction into the Austrian Cabinet of the chief Nazi agent, Seyss-Inquart, as Minister of the Interior and head of the Austrian police. This grave event did not avert the personal crisis between Mr. Chamberlain and Mr. Eden. On February 18 they saw Count Grandi again. This was the last business they conducted together. The Ambassador refused either to discuss the Italian position towards Austria, or to consider the British plan for the withdrawal of volunteers, or so-called volunteers — in this case five divisions of the regular Italian Army — from Spain. Grandi asked, however, for general conversations to be opened in Rome. The Prime Minister wished for these, and the Foreign Secretary was strongly opposed to such a step.

There were prolonged parleyings and Cabinet meetings. Of these the only authoritative account yet disclosed is in Mr. Chamberlain's biography. Mr. Feiling says that the Prime Minister "let the Cabinet see that the alternative to Eden's resignation might be his own." He quotes from some diary or private letter, to which he was given access, the following statement by the Prime Minister: "I thought it necessary to say clearly that I could not accept any decision in the opposite sense." "The Cabinet," says Mr. Feiling, "were unanimous, though with a few reserves." We have no knowledge of how and when these statements were made during the protracted discussions. But at the end Mr. Eden briefly tendered his resignation on the issue of the Italian conversations taking place at this stage and in these circumstances. At this his colleagues were astonished. Mr. Feiling says they were "much shaken." They had not realised that the differences between the Foreign Secretary and the Prime Minister had reached breaking-point. Evidently if Mr. Eden's resignation was involved, a new question raising larger and more general issues was raised. However, they had all committed themselves on the merits of the matter in dispute. The rest of the long day was spent in efforts to induce the Foreign Secretary to change his mind. Mr. Chamberlain was impressed by the distress of the Cabinet. "Seeing how my colleagues had been taken aback I proposed an adjournment until next day." But Eden saw no

use in continuing a search for formulas, and by midnight, on
the twentieth, his resignation became final. "Greatly to his
credit, as I see it," noted the Prime Minister.[1] Lord Halifax
was at once appointed Foreign Secretary in his place.[2]

It had, of course, become known that there were serious differences in the Cabinet, though the cause was obscure. I had
heard something of this, but carefully abstained from any communication with Mr. Eden. I hoped that he would not on any
account resign without building up his case beforehand, and
giving his many friends in Parliament a chance to draw out
the issues. But the Government at this time was so powerful
and aloof that the struggle was fought out inside the ministerial
conclave, and mainly between the two men.

*   *   *   *   *

Late in the night of February 20, a telephone message
reached me as I sat in my old room at Chartwell (as I often
sit now) that Eden had resigned. I must confess that my heart
sank, and for a while the dark waters of despair overwhelmed
me. In a long life I have had many ups and downs. During
all the war soon to come and in its darkest times I never had
any trouble in sleeping. In the crisis of 1940, when so much
responsibility lay upon me, and also at many very anxious,
awkward moments in the following five years, I could always
flop into bed and go to sleep after the day's work was done —
subject, of course, to any emergency call. I slept sound and
awoke refreshed, and had no feelings except appetite to grapple
with whatever the morning's boxes might bring. But now, on
this night of February 20, 1938, and on this occasion only, sleep
deserted me. From midnight till dawn I lay in my bed consumed by emotions of sorrow and fear. There seemed one
strong young figure standing up against long, dismal, drawling
tides of drift and surrender, of wrong measurements and feeble
impulses. My conduct of affairs would have been different from

[1] Feiling, op. cit., page 338.
[2] Ibid.

his in various ways; but he seemed to me at this moment to
embody the life-hope of the British nation, the grand old British race that had done so much for men, and had yet some more
to give. Now he was gone. I watched the daylight slowly creep
in through the windows, and saw before me in mental gaze the
vision of Death.

15

The Rape of Austria

February, 1938

USUALLY IN MODERN TIMES when states have been defeated in war they have preserved their structure, their identity, and the secrecy of their archives. On this occasion, the war being fought to an utter finish, we have come into full possession of the inside story of the enemy. From this we can check with some exactness our own information and performances. We have seen how in July, 1936, Hitler had instructed the German General Staff to draw up military plans for the occupation of Austria when the hour should strike. This operation was labelled "Case Otto." Now, a year later, on June 24, 1937, he crystallised these plans by a special directive. On November 5, he unfolded his future designs to the chiefs of his armed forces. Germany must have more "living space." This could best be

found in Eastern Europe — Poland, White Russia, and the
Ukraine. To obtain this would involve a major war, and incidentally the extermination of the people then living in those
parts. Germany would have to reckon with her two "hateful
enemies," England and France, to whom "a German Colossus
in the centre of Europe would be intolerable." In order to
profit by the lead she had gained in munitions production and
by the patriotic fervour aroused and represented by the Nazi
Party, she must therefore make war at the first promising opportunity, and deal with her two obvious opponents before
they were ready to fight.

Neurath, Fritsch, and even Blomberg, all of them influenced
by the views of the German Foreign Office, General Staff, and
officer corps, were alarmed by this policy. They thought that
the risks to be run were too high. They recognised that by the
audacity of the Fuehrer, they were definitely ahead of the Allies
in every form of rearmament. The Army was maturing month
by month, the internal decay of France and the lack of will-
power in Britain were favourable factors which might well run
their full course. What was a year or two when all was moving
so well? They must have time to complete the war machine,
and a conciliatory speech now and again from the Fuehrer
would keep these futile and degenerate democracies chatter-
ing. But Hitler was not sure of this. His genius taught him
that victory would not be achieved by processes of certainty.
Risks had to be run. The leap had to be made. He was flushed
with his successes, first in rearmament, second in conscription,
third in the Rhineland, fourth by the accession of Mussolini's
Italy. To wait till everything was ready was probably to wait
till all was too late. It is very easy for historians and other
people, who do not have to live and act from day to day, to say
that he would have had the whole fortunes of the world in his
hand if he had gone on growing in strength for another two
or three years before striking. However, this does not follow.
There are no certainties in human life or in the life of states.
Hitler was resolved to hurry, and have the war while he was
in his prime.

On February 4, 1938, he dismissed Fritsch, and himself
assumed the supreme command of the armed forces. Blomberg,
weakened with the officer corps by an inappropriate marriage,
also fell out. So far as it is possible for one man, however gifted
and powerful, however terrible the penalties he can inflict, to
make his will effective over spheres so vast, the Fuehrer assumed
direct control, not only of the policy of the State, but of the
military machine. He had at this time something like the
power of Napoleon after Austerlitz and Jena, without, of
course, the glory of winning great battles by his personal direction on horseback, but with triumphs in the political and
diplomatic field which all his circle and followers knew were
due alone to him and to his judgment and daring.

*   *   *   *   *

Apart from his resolve, so plainly described in *Mein Kampf*,
to bring all Teutonic races into the Reich, Hitler had two
reasons for wishing to absorb the Austrian Republic. It opened
to Germany both the door of Czechoslovakia and the more
spacious portals of Southeastern Europe. Since the murder of
Chancellor Dollfuss in July, 1934, by the Austrian section of
the Nazi Party, the process of subverting the independent Austrian Government by money, intrigue, and force had never
ceased. The Nazi Movement in Austria grew with every success that Hitler reaped elsewhere, whether inside Germany or
against the Allies. It had been necessary to proceed step by
step. Officially Papen was instructed to maintain the most
cordial relations with the Austrian Government, and to procure
the official recognition by them of the Austrian Nazi Party as a
legal body. At that time the attitude of Mussolini had imposed
restraint. After the murder of Doctor Dollfuss, the Italian Dictator had flown to Venice to receive and comfort the widow
who had taken refuge there, and considerable Italian forces
had been concentrated on the southern frontier of Austria. But
now in the dawn of 1938 decisive changes in European group-
ings and values had taken place. The Siegfried Line confronted France with a growing barrier of steel and concrete,

requiring as it seemed an enormous sacrifice of French manhood to pierce. The door from the West was shut. Mussolini
had been driven into the German system by sanctions so ineffectual that they had angered him without weakening his
power. He might well have pondered with relish on Mac-
chiavelli's celebrated remark, "Men avenge slight injuries, but
not grave ones." Above all, the Western Democracies had
seemed to give repeated proofs that they would bow to violence
so long as they were not themselves directly assailed. Papen
was working skilfully inside the Austrian political structure.
Many Austrian notables had yielded to his pressure and intrigues. The tourist trade, so important to Vienna, was im-
peded by the prevailing uncertainty. In the background, terrorist activity and bomb outrages shook the frail life of the
Austrian Republic.

It was thought that the hour had now come to obtain control of Austrian policy by procuring the entry into the Vienna
Cabinet of the leaders of the lately legalised Austrian Nazi
Party. On February 12, 1938, eight days after assuming the
supreme command, Hitler had summoned the Austrian Chancellor, Herr von Schuschnigg, to Berchtesgaden. He had
obeyed, and was accompanied by his Foreign Minister, Guido
Schmidt. We now have Schuschnigg's record, in which the following dialogue occurs.[1] Hitler had mentioned the defences of
the Austrian frontier. These were no more than might be
required to make a military operation necessary to overcome
them, and thus raise major issues of peace and war.

Hitler: I only need to give an order, and overnight all the ridicu-
lous scarecrows on the frontier will vanish. You don't really believe
that you could hold me up for half an hour? Who knows — perhaps
I shall be suddenly overnight in Vienna: like a spring storm. Then
you will really experience something. I would willingly spare the
Austrians this; it will cost many victims. *After the troops will
follow the S.A. and the Legion!* No one will be able to hinder the
vengeance, not even myself. Do you want to turn Austria into
another Spain? All this I would like if possible to avoid.

[1] Schuschnigg, *Ein Requiem in Rot-Weiss-Rot,* page 37 ff.

Schuschnigg: I will obtain the necessary information and put a stop to the building of any defence works on the German frontier. Naturally I realise that you can march into Austria, but, Mr. Chancellor, whether we wish it or not, that would lead to the shedding of blood. We are not alone in the world. That probably means war.

Hitler: That is very easy to say at this moment as we sit here in club armchairs, but behind it all there lies a sum of suffering and blood. Will you take the responsibility for that, Herr Schuschnigg? Don't believe that anyone in the world will hinder me in my decisions! Italy? I am quite clear with Mussolini: with Italy I am on the closest possible terms. England? England will not lift a finger for Austria. . . . And France? Well, two years ago when we marched into the Rhineland with a handful of battalions — at that moment I risked a great deal. If France had marched then, we should have been forced to withdraw. . . . But for France it is now too late!

This first interview took place at eleven in the morning. After a formal lunch, the Austrians were summoned into a small room, and there confronted by Ribbentrop and Papen with a written ultimatum. The terms were not open to discussion. They included the appointment of the Austrian Nazi Seyss-Inquart as Minister of Security in the Austrian Cabinet, a general amnesty for all Austrian Nazis under detention, and the official incorporation of the Austrian Nazi Party in the Government-sponsored Fatherland Front.

Later Hitler received the Austrian Chancellor. "I repeat to you, this is the very last chance. Within three days I expect the execution of this agreement." In Jodl's diary the entry reads, "Von Schuschnigg together with Guido Schmidt are again being put under heaviest political and military pressure. At 11 P.M. Schuschnigg signs the 'protocol.' " [2] As Papen drove back with Schuschnigg in the sledge which conveyed them over the snow-covered roads to Salzburg, he commented, "Yes, that is how the Fuehrer can be; now you have experienced it for yourself. But when you next come, you will have a much easier time. The Fuehrer can be really charming." [3]

2 *Nuremberg Documents* (H.M. Stationery Office), Part 1, page 249.
3 Schuschnigg, *op. cit.*, pages 51–52.

On February 20, Hitler spoke to the Reichstag:

I am happy to be able to tell you, gentlemen, that during the past few days a further understanding has been reached with a country that is particularly close to us for many reasons. The Reich and German Austria are bound together, not only because they are the same people, but also because they share a long history and a common culture. The difficulties which had been experienced in carrying out the Agreement of July 11, 1936, compelled us to make an attempt to clear out of the way misunderstandings and hindrances to a final conciliation. Had this not been done, it is clear that an intolerable situation might one day have developed, whether intentionally or otherwise, which might have brought about a very serious catastrophe. I am glad to be able to assure you that these considerations corresponded with the views of the Austrian Chancellor, whom I invited to come to visit me. The idea and the intention were to bring about a relaxation of the strain in our relations with one another by giving under the existing legislation the same legal rights to citizens holding National-Socialist views as are enjoyed by the other citizens of German Austria. In conjunction with this there should be a practical contribution towards peace by granting a general amnesty, and by creating a better understanding between the two states through a still closer friendly co-operation in as many different fields as possible — political, personal, and economic — all complementary to and within the framework of the Agreement of July 11. I express in this connection before the German people my sincere thanks to the Austrian Chancellor for his great understanding and the warmhearted willingness with which he accepted my invitation and worked with me, so that we might discover a way of serving the best interests of the two countries; for, after all, it is the interest of the whole German people, whose sons we all are, wherever we may have been born.[4]

One can hardly find a more perfect specimen of humbug and hypocrisy for British and American benefit. I print it only because of its unique quality in these respects. What is astounding is that it should have been regarded with anything but scorn by men and women of intelligence in any free country.

[4] *Hitler's Speeches* (N. H. Baynes, Editor), volume 2, pages 1407–08.

*   *   *   *   *

For a moment we must return to the serious British event which the last chapter has described. On the next day, February 21, there was an imposing debate in the House of Commons on the resignation of the Foreign Secretary and his Under-Secretary, Lord Cranborne — a man in whom "still waters run deep" — who acted with him in loyalty and conviction. Eden could, of course, make no open reference to President Roosevelt's overture and its discouragement. The differences about Italy were on a minor plane. Eden said:

I have spoken of the immediate difference which has divided me from my colleagues, and I should not be frank if I were to pretend that it is an isolated issue. It is not. *Within the last few weeks upon one most important decision of foreign policy which did not concern Italy at all the difference was fundamental.*

He concluded:

I do not believe that we can make progress in European appeasement if we allow the impression to gain currency abroad that we yield to constant pressure. . . . I am certain in my own mind that progress depends above all on the temper of the nation, and that temper must find expression in a firm spirit. That spirit I am confident is there. Not to give voice to it is I believe fair neither to this country nor to the world.

Mr. Attlee made a searching point. The resignation of Mr. Eden was being proclaimed in Italy as "another great victory for the Duce." "All over the world we hear the story, 'You see how great is the power of our Leader; the British Foreign Secretary has gone.'"

I did not speak till the second day, when I paid my tribute to both the resigning Ministers. I also sustained Mr. Attlee's accusation:

This last week has been a good week for the Dictators — one of the best they have ever had. The German Dictator has laid his heavy hand upon a small but historic country, and the Italian Dictator has carried his vendetta against Mr. Eden to a victorious conclusion. The conflict between them has been long. There can be no doubt whatever that Signor Mussolini has won. All the majesty, power, and dominion of the British Empire have not been able to secure the success of the causes which were entrusted to the late Foreign Secretary by the general will of Parliament and of the country. . . . So that is the end of this part of the story, namely, the departure from power of the Englishman whom the British nation and the British Parliament entrusted with a certain task; and the complete triumph of the Italian Dictator, at a moment when he desperately needed success for domestic reasons. All over the world, in every land, under every sky and every system of government, wherever they may be, the friends of England are dismayed and the foes of England are exultant. . . .

The resignation of the late Foreign Secretary may well be a milestone in history. Great quarrels, it has been well said, arise from small occasions but seldom from small causes. The late Foreign Secretary adhered to the old policy which we have all forgotten for so long. The Prime Minister and his colleagues have entered upon another and a new policy. The old policy was an effort to establish the rule of law in Europe, and build up through the League of Nations effective deterrents against the aggressor. Is it the new policy to come to terms with the totalitarian Powers in the hope that by great and far-reaching acts of submission, not merely in sentiment and pride, but in material factors, peace may be preserved?

The other day Lord Halifax said that Europe was confused. The part of Europe which is confused is that part ruled by parliamentary governments. I know of no confusion on the side of the great Dictators. They know what they want, and no one can deny that up to the present at every step they are getting what they want. The grave and largely irreparable injury to world security took place in the years 1932 to 1935. . . . The next opportunity when the Sibylline books were presented to us was the reoccupation of the Rhineland at the beginning of 1936. Now we know that a firm stand by France and Britain, under the authority of the League of Nations, would have been followed by the immediate evacuation of the Rhineland without the shedding of a drop of blood; and the effects of that *might have enabled the more prudent elements in the German Army to regain their proper position,* and would not have given to the political head of Germany that enormous ascendancy which has enabled him to move forward. Now we are at a moment when a third move is made, but when that opportunity does not present itself in the same favourable manner. Austria has been laid in thrall, *and we do not know whether Czechoslovakia will not suffer a similar attack.*

* * * * *

The Continental drama ran its course. Mussolini now sent a verbal message to Schuschnigg saying that he considered the Austrian attitude at Berchtesgaden to be both right and adroit. He assured him both of the unalterable attitude of Italy towards the Austrian question and of his personal friendship. On February 24, the Austrian Chancellor himself spoke to the Austrian Parliament, welcoming the settlement with Germany, but emphasising, with some sharpness, that beyond the specific terms of the Agreement, Austria would never go. On March 3, he sent a confidential message to Mussolini through the Austrian military attaché in Rome informing the Duce that he intended to strengthen the political position in Austria by holding a plebiscite. Twenty-four hours later he received a message from the Austrian military attaché in Rome describing his interview with Mussolini. In this the Duce expressed himself optimistically. The situation would improve. An imminent *détente* between Rome and London would ensure a lightening of the existing pressure. . . . As to the plebiscite, Mussolini uttered a warning: "E un errore [it's a mistake]. If the result is satisfactory, people will say that it is not genuine. If it is bad, the situation of the Government will be unbearable; and if it is indecisive, then it is worthless." But Schuschnigg was determined. On March 9, he announced officially that a plebiscite would be held throughout Austria on the following Sunday, March 13.

At first nothing happened. Seyss-Inquart seemed to accept the idea without demur. At 5.30, however, on the morning of March 11, Schuschnigg was rung up on the telephone from Police Headquarters in Vienna. He was told: "The German frontier at Salzburg was closed an hour ago. The German customs officials have been withdrawn. Railway communications have been cut." The next message to reach the Austrian Chan-

cellor was from his consul-general in Munich saying that the
German army corps there had been mobilised: supposed destination — Austria!

Later in the morning, Seyss-Inquart came to announce that
Goering had just telephoned to him that the plebiscite must
be called off within an hour. If no reply was received within
that time Goering would assume that Seyss-Inquart had been
hindered from telephoning, and would act accordingly. After
being informed by responsible officials that the police and
army were not entirely reliable, Schuschnigg informed Seyss-
Inquart that the plebiscite would be postponed. A quarter of
an hour later, the latter returned with a reply from Goering
scribbled on a message-pad:

> The situation can only be saved if the Chancellor resigns imme-
> diately and if within two hours Doctor Seyss-Inquart is nominated
> Chancellor. If nothing is done within this period, the German
> invasion of Austria will follow.[5]

Schuschnigg waited on President Miklas to tender his
resignation. While in the President's room, he received a deciphered message from the Italian Government that they could
offer no counsel. The old President was obstinate: "So in the
decisive hour I am left alone." He steadfastly refused to nominate a Nazi Chancellor. He was determined to force the Germans into a shameful and violent deed. But for this they were
well prepared. A vivid account of the German reaction is found
again in Jodl's diary for March 10:

> By surprise and without consulting his Ministers, von Schuschnigg
> ordered a plebiscite for Sunday, March 13, which should bring a
> strong majority for the legitimate party *in the absence of plan or
> preparation*. The Fuehrer is determined not to tolerate it. This
> very night, March 9/10, he calls for Goering. General von Reichenau
> is called back from the Cairo Olympic Committee, General von
> Schubert is ordered to come, as well as Minister Glaise-Horstenau,
> who is with the district leader [Gauleiter Burckel] in the Palatinate.
> General Keitel communicates the facts at 1.45. He drives to the
> Reichskanzlei at 10 o'clock. I follow at 10.15 to give him the old

5 Schuschnigg, *op. cit.*, pages 66–72.

draft, "Prepare Case Otto." 13.00 hours, General K. [Keitel] informs Chief of Operational Staff and Admiral Canaris; Ribbentrop is detained in London. Neurath takes over the Foreign Office. Fuehrer wants to transmit ultimatum to the Austrian Cabinet. A personal letter is dispatched to Mussolini, and the reasons are developed which forced the Fuehrer to take action.[6]

On the following day, March 11, orders were issued by Hitler to the German armed forces for the military occupation of Austria. "Operation Otto," so long studied, so carefully prepared, began. President Miklas confronted Seyss-Inquart and the Austrian Nazi leaders in Vienna with firmness throughout a hectic day. The telephone conversation between Hitler and Prince Philip of Hesse, his special envoy to the Duce, was quoted in evidence at Nuremberg, and is of interest:

Hesse: I have just come back from Palazzo Venezia. The Duce accepted the whole thing in a very friendly manner. He sends you his regards. He had been informed from Austria, von Schuschnigg gave him the news. He had then said it [i.e., Italian intervention] would be a complete impossibility; it would be a bluff; such a thing could not be done. So he [Schuschnigg] was told that it was unfortunately arranged thus, and it could not be changed any more. Then Mussolini said that Austria would be immaterial to him.

Hitler: Then please tell Mussolini I will never forget him for this.

Hesse: Yes.

Hitler: Never, never, never, whatever happens. I am still ready to make a quite different agreement with him.

Hesse: Yes, I told him that too.

Hitler: As soon as the Austrian affair has been settled, I shall be ready to go with him through thick and thin; nothing matters.

Hesse: Yes, my Fuehrer.

Hitler: Listen, I shall make any agreement — I am no longer in fear of the terrible position which would have existed militarily in case we had become involved in a conflict. You may tell him that I do thank him ever so much; never, never shall I forget that.

Hesse: Yes, my Fuehrer.

Hitler: I will never forget it, whatever may happen. If he should ever need any help or be in any danger, he can be convinced that

[6] *Nuremberg Documents,* Part 1, page 251.

I shall stick to him whatever might happen, even if the whole world
were against him.

Hesse: Yes, my Fuehrer.[7]

Certainly when he rescued Mussolini from the Italian Provisional Government in 1943, Hitler kept his word.

* * * * *

A triumphal entry into Vienna had been the Austrian Corporal's dream. On the night of Saturday, March 12, the Nazi
Party in the capital had planned a torchlight procession to
welcome the conquering hero. But nobody arrived. Three
bewildered Bavarians of the supply services who had come by
train to make billeting arrangements for the invading army
had, therefore, to be carried shoulder-high through the streets.
The cause of this hitch leaked out slowly. The German war
machine had lumbered falteringly over the frontier and come
to a standstill near Linz. In spite of perfect weather and good
conditions, the majority of the tanks broke down. Defects appeared in the motorised heavy artillery. The road from Linz
to Vienna was blocked with heavy vehicles at a standstill.
General von Reichenau, Hitler's special favourite, Commander
of Army Group IV, was deemed responsible for a breakdown
which exposed the unripe condition of the German Army at
this stage in its reconstruction.

Hitler himself, motoring through Linz, saw the traffic jam,
and was infuriated. The light tanks were disengaged from
confusion and straggled into Vienna in the early hours of Sunday morning. The armoured vehicles and motorised heavy
artillery were loaded onto the railway trucks, and only thus
arrived in time for the ceremony. The pictures of Hitler
driving through Vienna amid exultant or terrified crowds are
well known. But this moment of mystic glory had an unquiet
background. The Fuehrer was in fact convulsed with anger
at the obvious shortcomings of his military machine. He rated
his generals, and they answered back. They reminded him of

7 Schuschnigg, *op. cit.*, pages 102–03, and *Nuremberg Documents*, Part 1, pages
258–59.

his refusal to listen to Fritsch and his warnings that Germany
was not in a position to undertake the risk of a major conflict.
Appearances were preserved. The official celebrations and
parades took place. On the Sunday after large numbers of
German troops and Austrian Nazis had taken possession of
Vienna, Hitler declared the dissolution of the Austrian Republic and the annexation of its territory to the German Reich.

*   *   *   *   *

Herr von Ribbentrop was at this time about to leave London
to become Foreign Secretary in Germany. Mr. Chamberlain
gave a farewell luncheon in his honour at Number 10 Downing
Street. My wife and I accepted the Prime Minister's invitation
to attend. There were perhaps sixteen people present. My wife
sat next to Sir Alexander Cadogan near one end of the table.
About halfway through the meal, a Foreign Office messenger
brought him an envelope. He opened it and was absorbed in
the contents. Then he got up, walked round to where the
Prime Minister was sitting, and gave him the message.
Although Cadogan's demeanour would not have indicated that
anything had happened, I could not help noticing the Prime
Minister's evident preoccupation. Presently Cadogan came
back with the paper and resumed his seat. Later, I was told its
contents. It said that Hitler had invaded Austria and that the
German mechanised forces were advancing fast upon Vienna.
The meal proceeded without the slightest interruption, but
quite soon Mrs. Chamberlain, who had received some signal
from her husband, got up, saying, "Let us *all* have coffee in the
drawing-room." We trooped in there, and it was evident to me
and perhaps to some others that Mr. and Mrs. Chamberlain
wished to bring the proceedings to an end. A kind of general
restlessness pervaded the company, and everyone stood about
ready to say good-bye to the guests of honour.

However, Herr von Ribbentrop and his wife did not seem
at all conscious of this atmosphere. On the contrary, they
tarried for nearly half an hour engaging their host and hostess
in voluble conversation. At one moment I came in contact with

Frau von Ribbentrop, and in a valedictory vein I said, "I hope England and Germany will preserve their friendship." "Be careful you don't spoil it," was her graceful rejoinder. I am sure they both knew perfectly well what had happened, but thought it was a good manoeuvre to keep the Prime Minister away from his work and the telephone. At length Mr. Chamberlain said to the Ambassador, "I am sorry I have to go now to attend to urgent business," and without more ado he left the room. The Ribbentrops lingered on, so that most of us made our excuses and our way home. Eventually I suppose they left. This was the last time I saw Herr von Ribbentrop before he was hanged.

*   *   *   *   *

The outrage against Austria and the subjugation of beautiful Vienna, with all its fame, culture, and contribution to the story of Europe, hit me hard. On the morrow of these events, March 14, I said in the House of Commons:

The gravity of the event of March 12 cannot be exaggerated. Europe is confronted with a programme of aggression, nicely calculated and timed, unfolding stage by stage, and there is only one choice open, not only to us but to other countries, either to submit like Austria, or else take effective measures while time remains to ward off the danger, and if it cannot be warded off to cope with it. . . . If we go on waiting upon events, how much shall we throw away of resources now available for our security and the maintenance of peace? How many friends will be alienated, how many potential allies shall we see go one by one down the grisly gulf? How many times will bluff succeed until behind bluff ever-gathering forces have accumulated reality? . . . *Where are we going to be two years hence, for instance, when the German Army will certainly be much larger than the French Army,* and when all the small nations will have fled from Geneva to pay homage to the ever-waxing power of the Nazi system, and to make the best terms that they can for themselves?

And further:

Vienna is the centre of the communications of all the countries which formed the old Austro-Hungarian Empire, and of the

countries lying to the southeast of Europe. A long stretch of the
Danube is now in German hands. This mastery of Vienna gives to
Nazi Germany military and economic control of the whole of the
communications of Southeastern Europe, by road, by river, and by
rail. What is the effect of this on the structure of Europe? What is
the effect of it upon what is called the balance of power, such as
it is – upon what is called the "Little Entente"? I must say a word
about this group of Powers called the Little Entente. Taken singly,
the three countries of the Little Entente may be called Powers of
the second rank, but they are very powerful and vigorous states, and
united they are a Great Power. They have hitherto been, and are
still, united by the closest military agreement. Together they make
the complement of a Great Power and of the military machinery
of a Great Power. Rumania has the oil, Yugoslavia has the minerals
and raw materials. Both have large armies, both are mainly supplied with munitions from Czechoslovakia. To English ears, the
name of Czechoslovakia sounds outlandish. No doubt they are
only a small democratic state, no doubt they have an army only
two or three times as large as ours, no doubt they have a munitions
supply only three times as great as that of Italy, but still they are
a virile people, they have their rights, they have their treaty rights,
they have a line of fortresses, and they have a strongly manifested
will to live, a will to live freely.

Czechoslovakia is at this moment isolated, both in the economic
and in the military sense. Her trade outlet through Hamburg,
which is based upon the Peace Treaty, can of course be closed at
any moment. Now her communications by rail and river to the
south, and beyond the south to the southeast, are liable to be
severed at any moment. Her trade may be subjected to tolls of a
destructive character, of an absolutely strangling character. Here
is a country which was once the greatest manufacturing area in the
old Austro-Hungarian Empire. It is now cut off, or may be cut off
at once, unless out of these discussions which must follow arrangements are made securing the communications of Czechoslovakia.
She may be cut off at once from the sources of her raw materials in
Yugoslavia and from the natural markets which she has established
there. The economic life of this small state may be very largely
strangled as a result of the act of violence which was perpetrated
last Friday night. A wedge has been driven into the heart of what is
called the Little Entente, this group of countries which have as

much right to live in Europe unmolested as any of us have the right
to live unmolested in our native land.

*   *   *   *   *

It was the Russians who now sounded the alarm, and on
March 18 proposed a conference on the situation. They wished
to discuss, if only in outline, ways and means of implementing
the Franco-Soviet Pact within the frame of League action in the
event of a major threat to peace by Germany. This met with
little warmth in Paris and London. The French Government
was distracted by other preoccupations. There were serious
strikes in the aircraft factories. Franco's armies were driving
deep into the territory of Communist Spain. Chamberlain was
both sceptical and depressed. He profoundly disagreed with my
interpretation of the dangers ahead and the means of combating them. I had been urging the prospects of a Franco-
British-Russian alliance as the only hope of checking the Nazi
onrush.

Mr. Feiling tells us that the Prime Minister expressed his
mood in a letter to his sister on March 20:

The plan of the "Grand Alliance," as Winston calls it, had occurred to me long before he mentioned it. . . . I talked about it to
Halifax, and we submitted it to the Chiefs of Staff and F.O. experts.
It is a very attractive idea; indeed, there is almost everything to be
said for it until you come to examine its practicability. From that
moment its attraction vanishes. You have only to look at the map to
see that nothing that France or we could do could possibly save
Czechoslovakia from being overrun by the Germans, if they wanted
to do it. . . . I have, therefore, abandoned any idea of giving guarantee to Czechoslovakia, or to the French in connection with her
obligations to that country.[8]

Here was at any rate a decision. It was taken on wrong
arguments. In modern wars of great nations or alliances particular areas are not defended only by local exertions. The
whole vast balance of the war front is involved. This is still
more true of policy before war begins and while it may still be

8 Feiling, *op. cit.*, pages 347–48.

averted. It surely did not take much thought from the "Chiefs of Staff and F.O. experts" to tell the Prime Minister that the British Navy and the French Army could not be deployed on the Bohemian mountain front to stand between the Czecho-slovak Republic and Hitler's invading army. This was indeed evident from the map. But the certainty that the crossing of the Bohemian frontier line would have involved a general European war might well even at that date have deterred or delayed Hitler's next assault. How erroneous Mr. Chamber-lain's private and earnest reasoning appears when we cast our minds forward to the guarantee he was to give to Poland *within a year,* after all the strategic value of Czechoslovakia had been cast away, and Hitler's power and prestige had almost doubled!

* * * * *

On March 24, 1938, in the House of Commons, the Prime Minister gave us his view about the Russian move:

His Majesty's Government are of the opinion that the indirect but none the less inevitable consequence of such action as is pro-posed by the Soviet Government would be to aggravate the tendency towards the establishment of exclusive groups of nations which must in the view of His Majesty's Government be inimical to the prospects of European peace.

Nevertheless, the Prime Minister could not avoid facing the brutal fact that there existed a "profound disturbance of inter-national confidence," and that the Government would have, sooner or later, to decide upon a definition of Great Britain's obligations in Europe. What would be our obligations in Central Europe? "If war broke out, it would be unlikely to be confined to those who have assumed legal obligations. It would be quite impossible to say where it would end and what Governments might be involved." It must further be observed that the argument about the evils of "exclusive groups of na-tions" loses its validity if the alternative is being mopped-up one by one by the aggressor. Moreover, it overlooks all ques-tions of right and wrong in international relationships. There was, after all, in existence the League of Nations and its Charter.

The Prime Minister's course was now marked out: simultaneous diplomatic pressure on Berlin and Prague, appeasement in regard to Italy, a strictly restrained definition of our obligations to France. To carry out the first two moves, it was essential to be careful and precise about the last.

* * * * *

The reader is now invited to move westward to the Emerald Isle. "It's a long way to Tipperary," but a visit there is sometimes irresistible. In the interval between Hitler's seizure of Austria and his unfolding design upon Czechoslovakia, we must turn to a wholly different kind of misfortune which befell us.

Since the beginning of 1938 there had been negotiations between the British Government and that of Mr. de Valera in Southern Ireland, and on April 25 an agreement was signed whereby among other matters Great Britain renounced all rights to occupy for naval purposes the two Southern Irish ports of Queenstown and Berehaven, and the base in Lough Swilly. The two southern ports were a vital feature in the naval defence of our food supply. When in 1922, as Colonial and Dominions Secretary, I had dealt with the details of the Irish Settlement which the Cabinet of those days had made, I brought Admiral Beatty to the Colonial Office to explain to Michael Collins the importance of these ports to our whole system of bringing supplies into Britain. Collins was immediately convinced. "Of course you must have the ports," he said, "they are necessary for your life." Thus the matter was arranged, and everything had worked smoothly in the sixteen years that had passed. The reason why Queenstown and Berehaven were necessary to our safety is easy to understand. They were the fuelling-bases from which our destroyer flotillas ranged westward into the Atlantic to hunt U-boats, and protect incoming convoys as they reached the throat of the Narrow Seas. Lough Swilly was similarly needed to protect the approaches to the Clyde and Mersey. To abandon these meant

that our flotillas would have to start in the north from Lam-
lash and in the south from Pembroke Dock or Falmouth, thus
decreasing their radius of action and the protection they could
afford by more than four hundred miles out and home.

It was incredible to me that the Chiefs of Staff should have
agreed to throw away this major security, and to the last moment I thought that at least we had safeguarded our right to
occupy these Irish ports in the event of war. However, Mr.
de Valera announced in the Dail that no conditions of any
kind were attached to the cession. I was later assured that Mr.
de Valera was surprised at the readiness with which the British
Government had deferred to his request. He had included it
in his proposals as a bargaining-counter which could be dispensed with when other points were satisfactorily settled.

Lord Chatfield has in his last book devoted a chapter to explaining the course he and the other Chiefs of Staff took.[9] This
should certainly be read by those who wish to pursue the subject. Personally I remain convinced that the gratuitous surrender of our right to use the Irish ports in war was a major
injury to British national life and safety. A more feckless act
can hardly be imagined — and at such a time. It is true that in
the end we survived without the ports. It is also true that if
we had not been able to do without them, we should have re-
taken them by force rather than perish by famine. But this is
no excuse. Many a ship and many a life were soon to be lost as
the result of this improvident example of appeasement.

The whole Conservative Party, except the handful of Ulster
Members, supported the Prime Minister, and of course a step
like this was meat and drink to the Labour and Liberal Opposition. I was, therefore, almost entirely alone when on May 5 I
rose to make my protest. I was listened to with a patient air
of scepticism. There was even a kind of sympathetic wonder
that anyone of my standing should attempt to plead so hopeless
a case. I never saw the House of Commons more completely
misled. It was but fifteen months to the declaration of war.
The Members were to feel very differently about it when our
existence hung in the balance during the Battle of the Atlantic.

[9] Lord Chatfield, *It Might Happen Again*, chapter XVIII.

As my speech has been fully published in *Into Battle,* I do not
quote it here save on one point. The issue of Southern Irish
neutrality in time of war was not faced.

What guarantee [I asked] have you that Southern Ireland, or the
Irish Republic as they claim to be, will not declare neutrality if
we are engaged in war with some powerful nation? The first step
certainly which such an enemy would take would be to offer complete immunity of every kind to Southern Ireland if she would
remain neutral. . . . You cannot exclude this possibility of neutrality
as being one which may come within the immediate sphere of our
experience. The ports may be denied us in the hour of need, and
we may be hampered in the gravest manner in protecting the
British population from privation and even starvation. Who would
wish to put his head in such a noose? Is there any other country in
the world where such a step would even have been contemplated?
It would be an easy step for a Dublin Government to deny the
ports to us once we have gone. The cannon are there, the mines
will be there. But more important for this purpose, the juridical
right will be there. You had the rights; you have ceded them; you
hope in their place to have good will strong enough to endure
tribulation for your sake. Suppose you have it not. It will be no
use saying, "then we will retake the ports." You will have no right
to do so. To violate Irish neutrality should it be declared at the
moment of a Great War may put you out of court in the opinion of
the world, and may vitiate the cause by which you may be involved
in war. . . . You are casting away real and important means of
security and survival for vain shadows and for ease.

The comment of *The Times* newspaper was illuminating:

The agreement on defence . . . releases the Government of the
United Kingdom from the articles of the Anglo-Irish Treaty of
1921, by which they assumed the onerous and delicate task of defending the fortified harbours of Cork, Berehaven, and Lough
Swilly in the event of war.

Further releases might have been obtained by handing over
Gibraltar to Spain and Malta to Italy. Neither touched the
actual existence of our population more directly.

With that I leave this lamentable and amazing episode.

16

Czechoslovakia

An Unlikely Historical Controversy — Hitler's Next Objective — "No Evil Intentions Towards Czechoslovakia" — M. Blum's Pledge — My Visit to Paris, March, 1938 — M. Daladier Succeeds M. Blum — The Anglo-Italian Pact — An Interview with the Sudeten Leader — Misgivings and Reluctance of the German Generals — The Relations of Soviet Russia with Czechoslovakia — Stalin and Benes — Plot and Purge in Russia — M. Daladier's Declaration of June 12 — Hitler's Promise to Keitel — Captain Wiedemann's Mission to London — I Address My Constituents at Theydon Bois, August 27 — My Letter to Lord Halifax of August 31 — The Soviet Ambassador's Visit to Chartwell — My Report to the Foreign Office — "The Times" Leading Article of September 7 — M. Bonnet's Question and the British Answer — Hitler's Crisis Speech at Nuremberg.

FOR SOME YEARS it seemed that the question whether Britain and France were wise or foolish in the Munich episode would become a matter of long historical controversy. However, the revelations which have been made from German sources, and particularly at the Nuremberg Trials, have rendered this unlikely. The two main issues in dispute were: first, whether decisive action by Britain and France would have forced Hitler to recede or have led to his overthrow by a military conspiracy; secondly, whether the year that intervened between Munich and the outbreak of war placed the Western Powers relatively in a better or worse position, compared with Germany, than in September, 1938.

Many volumes have been written, and will be written, upon the crisis that was ended at Munich by the sacrifice of Czechoslovakia; and it is only intended here to give a few of the cardinal facts and establish the main proportions of events. These follow inexorably from Hitler's resolve to reunite all Germans in a Greater Reich and to expand eastwards, and his conviction that the men at the head of France and Britain would not fight owing to their love of peace and failure to rearm. The usual technique was employed against Czechoslovakia. The grievances, which were not unreal, of the Sudeten Germans were magnified and exploited. The public case was opened against Czechoslovakia by Hitler in his speech to the Reichstag on February 20, 1938. "Over ten million Germans," he said, "live in two of the states adjoining our frontier." It was the duty of Germany to protect those fellow Germans and secure to them "general freedom, personal, political, and ideological."

This public announcement of the intention of the German Government to interest themselves in the position of the German inhabitants of Austria and Czechoslovakia was intimately related to the secret planning of Germany's political offensive in Europe. The declared objectives of the Nazi German Government were twofold — the absorption by the Reich of all German minorities living beyond her frontiers, and thereby the extension of her living space in the East. The less publicised purpose of German policy was military in character — the liquidation of Czechoslovakia with its potentialities both as a Russian air base and as an Anglo-French military makeweight in event of war. As early as June, 1937, the German General Staff had been, on Hitler's instructions, busy at work drafting plans for the invasion and destruction of the Czechoslovak State.

One draft reads:

The aim and object of this surprise attack by the German armed forces should be to eliminate from the very beginning and for the duration of the war the threat from Czechoslovakia to the rear of the operations in the West, and to take from the Russian air force the most substantial portion of its operational base in Czechoslovakia.[1]

The acceptance by the Western Democracies of the German subjugation of Austria encouraged Hitler to pursue his designs more sharply against Czechoslovakia. The military control of Austrian territory was in fact intended to be the indispensable preliminary to the assault on the Bohemian bastion. While the invasion of Austria was in full swing, Hitler said in the motor-car to General von Halder: "This will be very inconvenient to the Czechs." Halder saw immediately the significance of this remark. To him it lighted up the future. It showed him Hitler's intentions, and at the same time, as he viewed it, Hitler's military ignorance. "It was practically impossible," he has explained, "for a German army to attack Czechoslovakia from the south. The single railway line through Linz was completely exposed, and surprise was out of the question." But Hitler's main political-strategic conception was correct. The West Wall was growing, and although far from complete, already confronted the French Army with horrible memories of the Somme and Passchendaele. He was convinced that neither France nor Britain would fight.

On the day of the march of the German armies into Austria, the French Ambassador in Berlin reported that Goering had given a solemn assurance to the Czech Minister in Berlin that Germany had *no evil intentions towards Czechoslovakia.* On March 14, the French Premier, M. Blum, solemnly declared to the Czech Minister in Paris that France would unreservedly honour her engagements to Czechoslovakia. These diplomatic reassurances could not conceal the grim reality. The whole strategic position on the Continent had changed. The German arguments and armies could now concentrate directly upon the western frontiers of Czechoslovakia, whose border districts were German in racial character, with an aggressive and active German Nationalist Party eager to act as a fifth column in event of trouble.

At the end of March, I went to Paris and had searching con-

1 *Nuremberg Documents,* Part 2, page 4.

versations with the French leaders. The Government were
agreeable to my going to vivify my French contacts. I stayed
at our Embassy and saw in a continued succession many of
the principal French figures, Premier Léon Blum, Flandin,
General Gamelin, Paul Reynaud, Pierre Cot, Herriot, Louis
Marin, and others. To Blum I said at one moment, "The German field howitzer is believed to be superior in range and of
course in striking power to the *soizante-quinze* even when re-
lined." He replied, "Is it from you that I am to learn the state
of the French artillery?" I said, "No, but ask your Ecole Poly-
technique, who are by no means convinced by the exposition
lately given to them of the relative power of the modernised
soizante-quinze." He was immediately genial and friendly.
Reynaud said to me, "We quite understand that England will
never have conscription. Why do you not, therefore, go in for
a mechanical army? If you had six armoured divisions, you
would indeed be an effective Continental force," or words to
that effect. It seemed that a Colonel de Gaulle had written a
much-criticised book about the offensive power of modern armoured vehicles. Here was one of the roots of the matter.

The Ambassador and I had a long luncheon alone with
Flandin. He was quite a different man from the one I had
known in 1936; then responsible and agitated; now out of office, cool, massive, and completely convinced that there was no
hope for France except in an arrangement with Germany. We
argued for two hours. Gamelin, who also visited me, was
rightly confident in the strength of the French Army at the
moment, but none too comfortable when I questioned him upon the artillery, about which he had precise knowledge. He
was always trying his best within the limits of the French political system. But the attention of the French Government
to the dangers of the European scene was distracted by the
ceaseless whirlpool of internal politics at the moment and by
the imminent fall of the Blum Government. It was all the
more essential that our common and mutual obligations in the
event of a general crisis should be established without any trace
of misunderstanding. On April 10, the French Government

was re-formed with M. Daladier as Premier and M. Bonnet as Minister for Foreign Affairs. These two men were to bear the responsibility for French policy in the critical months ahead.

In the hope of deterring Germany from a further aggression, the British Government, in accordance with Mr. Chamberlain's resolve, sought a settlement with Italy in the Mediterranean. This would strengthen the position of France, and would enable both the French and British to concentrate upon events in Central Europe. Mussolini, to some extent placated by the fall of Eden, and feeling himself in a strong bargaining position, did not repulse the British repentance. On April 16, 1938, an Anglo-Italian agreement was signed giving Italy in effect a free hand in Abyssinia and Spain in return for the imponderable value of Italian good will in Central Europe. The Foreign Office was sceptical of this transaction. Mr. Chamberlain's biographer tells us that he wrote in a personal and private letter, "You should have seen the draft put up to me by the F.O.; it would have frozen a Polar bear." [2]

I shared the misgivings of the Foreign Office at this move:

Mr. Churchill to Mr. Eden.   18.IV.38.

The Italian Pact is, of course, a complete triumph for Mussolini, who gains our cordial acceptance for his fortification of the Mediterranean against us, for his conquest of Abyssinia, and for his violence in Spain. The fact that we are not to fortify Cyprus without "previous consultation" is highly detrimental. The rest of it is to my mind only padding.

Nevertheless, I feel that considerable caution is necessary in opposing the agreement bluntly. It is a done thing. It is called a move towards peace. It undoubtedly makes it less likely that sparks from the Mediterranean should light a European conflagration. France will have to follow suit for her own protection, in order not to be divided from Britain. Finally, there is the possibility that Mussolini may be drawn by his interests to discourage German interference in the Danube Basin.

Before making up my mind, I should like to know your views and intentions. I think the Anglo-Italian Pact is only the first step, and that the second will be an attempt to patch up something even

2 Feiling, *op. cit.,* page 350.

more specious with Germany, which will lull the British public
while letting the German armed strength grow and German designs
in the East of Europe develop.

Chamberlain last week told the Executive of the National Union
[of Conservative Associations] in secret that he "had not abandoned
hopes of similar arrangements with Germany." They took this
rather coldly.

Meanwhile, our progress in the air is increasingly disappointing. . . .

Mr. Eden to Mr. Churchill.   28.IV.38.

. . . With regard to the Italian Pact, I agree with what you write.
Mussolini gives us nothing more than the repetition of promises
previously made and broken by him, except for the withdrawal of
troops from Libya, troops which were probably originally sent there
for their nuisance value. It has now become clear that, as I expected, Mussolini continued his intervention in Spain after the
conversations in Rome had opened. He must be an optimist,
indeed, who believes that Mussolini will cease increasing that intervention now, should it be required to secure Franco's victory.

As a diplomatic instrument the pact embodies a machinery which
is likely to be found very troublesome to work. It is not to come
into force until after the Italians leave Spain. It is almost certain,
however, that many months will elapse before that occurs, and
since what is important is not the presence of Italian infantry, but
the assertions of their experts and the Germans, it will be difficult
to establish with certainty that the withdrawal has taken place. But
maybe some do not mind much about that.

Then there is the Italian position in Abyssinia, which, from what
I hear, so far from improving grows steadily worse. I am afraid that
the moment we are choosing for its recognition will not benefit our
authority among the many millions of the King's coloured subjects.

None the less I equally agree as to the need for caution in any
attitude taken up towards the agreement. After all, it is not an
agreement yet, and it would be wrong certainly for me to say anything which could be considered as making its fruition more difficult. After all, this is precisely what I promised I would do in my
resignation speech and at Leamington.

The most anxious feature of the international situation, as I
see it, is that temporary relaxation of tension may be taken as a

pretext for the relaxation of national effort, which is already inadequate to the gravity of the times. . . .

Hitler was watching the scene with vigilance. To him also
the ultimate alignment of Italy in a European crisis was important. In conference with his Chiefs of Staff at the end of
April, he was considering how to force the pace. Mussolini
wanted a free hand in Abyssinia. In spite of the acquiescence
of the British Government, he might ultimately need German
support in this venture. If so, he should accept German action
against Czechoslovakia. This issue must be brought to a head,
and in the settling of the Czech question, Italy would be involved on Germany's side. The declarations of British and
French statesmen were, of course, studied in Berlin. The intention of these Western Powers to persuade the Czechs to be
reasonable in the interests of European peace was noted with
satisfaction. The Nazi Party of the Sudetenland, led by Henlein, now formulated their demands for autonomy in the Ger-
man-border regions of that country. Their programme had
been announced in Henlein's speech at Carlsbad on April 24.
The British and French Ministers in Prague called on the
Czech Foreign Minister shortly after this to "express the hope
that the Czech Government will go to the furthest limit in
order to settle the question."

During May, the Germans in Czechoslovakia were ordered to
increase their agitation. On May 12, Henlein visited London
to acquaint the British Government with the wrongs inflicted
upon his followers. He expressed a wish to see me. I therefore arranged a talk at Morpeth Mansions the next day, at
which Sir Archibald Sinclair was present, and Professor Lindemann was our interpreter.

Henlein's solution, as he described it, may be summed up
as follows:

There should be a central Parliament in Prague, which should
have control of foreign policy, defence, finance, and communications. All parties should be entitled to express their views there,
and the Government would act on majority decisions. The frontier

fortresses could be manned by Czech troops, who would of course
have unhindered access thereto. The Sudeten German regions, and
possibly the other minority districts, should enjoy local autonomy;
that is to say, they should have their own town and county councils,
and a diet in which matters of common regional concern could be
debated within definitely delimited frontiers. He would be prepared to submit questions of fact, e.g., the tracing of the boundary,
to an impartial tribunal, perhaps even appointed by the League
of Nations. All parties would be free to organise and offer themselves for election, and impartial courts of justice would function
in autonomous districts. The officials, i.e., postal, railway, and
police officers, in the German-speaking regions, would of course be
German-speaking, and a reasonable proportion of the total taxes
collected should be returned to these regions for their administration.

M. Masaryk, the Czech Minister in London, who was afterwards informed of this conversation, professed himself contented with a settlement on these lines. A peaceful solution of
admitted racial and minority quarrels compatible with the
independence of the Czech Republic was by no means impossible, if there were German good faith and good will. But on
this condition I had no illusions.

On May 17, negotiations about the Sudeten question began
between Henlein, who had visited Hitler on his return journey,
and the Czech Government. Municipal elections were due in
Czechoslovakia, and the German Government began a calculated war of nerves in preparation for them. Persistent rumours already circulated of German troop movements towards
the Czech frontier. On May 20, Sir Nevile Henderson was requested to make inquiries in Berlin on this matter. German
denials did not reassure the Czechs, who on the night of May
20/21 decreed a partial mobilisation of their army.

*   *   *   *   *

It is important at this stage to consider the German intentions. Hitler had for some time been convinced that neither
France nor Britain would fight for Czechoslovakia. On May 28,
he called a meeting of his principal advisers and gave instruc-

tions for the preparations to attack Czechoslovakia. He declared this later in public in a speech to the Reichstag on January 30, 1939:

> In view of this intolerable provocation . . . I resolved to settle once and for all, and this time radically, the Sudeten-German question. On May 28, I ordered (1) that preparations should be made for military action against this state by October 2; and (2) the immense and accelerated expansion of our defensive front in the West.[3]

His service advisers, however, did not share unanimously his overwhelming confidence. The German generals could not be persuaded, considering the still enormous preponderance of Allied strength except in the air, that France and Britain would submit to the Fuehrer's challenge. To break the Czech Army and pierce or turn the Bohemian fortress line would require practically the whole of thirty-five divisions. The German Chiefs of Staff informed Hitler that the Czech Army must be considered efficient and up-to-date in arms and equipment. The fortifications of the West Wall or Siegfried Line, though already in existence as field works, were far from completed. Thus, at the moment of attacking the Czechs only five effective and eight reserve divisions would be available to protect the whole of Germany's western frontier against the French Army, which could mobilise a hundred divisions. The generals were aghast at running such risks, when by waiting a few years the German Army would again be master. Although Hitler's political judgment had been proved correct by the pacifism and weakness of the Allies about conscription, the Rhineland, and Austria, the German High Command could not believe that Hitler's bluff would succeed a fourth time. It seemed so much beyond the bounds of reason that great victorious nations, possessing evident military superiority, would once again abandon the path of duty and honour, which was also for them the path of common sense and prudence. Besides all this, there was Russia, with her Slav affinities with Czecho-

---

[3] *Hitler's Speeches, op. cit.*, volume 2, page 1571.

slovakia, and whose attitude towards Germany at this juncture was full of menace.

The relations of Soviet Russia with Czechoslovakia as a state, and personally with President Benes, were those of intimate and solid friendship. The roots of this lay in a certain racial affinity, and also in comparatively recent events which require a brief digression. When President Benes visited me at Marrakesh in January, 1944, he told me this story. In 1935, he had received an offer from Hitler to respect in all circumstances the integrity of Czechoslovakia in return for a guarantee that she would remain neutral in the event of a Franco-German war. When Benes pointed to his treaty obliging him to act with France in such a case, the German Ambassador replied that there was no need to denounce the treaty. It would be sufficient to break it, if and when the time came, by simply failing to mobilise or march. The small Republic was not in a position to indulge in indignation at such a suggestion. Their fear of Germany was already very grave, more especially as the question of the Sudeten Germans might at any time be raised and fomented by Germany, to their extreme embarrassment and growing peril. They therefore let the matter drop without comment or commitment, and it did not stir for more than a year. In the autumn of 1936, a message from a high military source in Germany was conveyed to President Benes to the effect that if he wanted to take advantage of the Fuehrer's offer, he had better be quick, because events would shortly take place in Russia rendering any help he could give to Germany insignificant.

While Benes was pondering over this disturbing hint, he became aware that communications were passing through the Soviet Embassy in Prague between important personages in Russia and the German Government. This was a part of the so-called military and Old-Guard Communist conspiracy to overthrow Stalin and introduce a new régime based on a pro-German policy. President Benes lost no time in communicating all he could find out to Stalin.[4] Thereafter there followed

4 There is, however, some evidence that Benes' information had previously

the merciless, but perhaps not needless, military and political
purge in Soviet Russia, and the series of trials in January, 1937,
in which Vyshinsky, the Public Prosecutor, played so masterful
a part.

Although it is highly improbable that the Old-Guard Communists had made common cause with the military leaders,
or *vice versa,* they were certainly filled with jealousy of Stalin,
who had ousted them. It may, therefore, have been convenient
to get rid of them at the same time, according to the standards
maintained in a totalitarian state. Zinoviev, Bukharin, Radek,
and others of the original leaders of the Revolution, Marshal
Tukachevsky, who had represented the Soviet Union at the
Coronation of King George VI, and many other high officers
of the Army, were shot. In all not less than five thousand officers and officials above the rank of captain were "liquidated."
The Russian Army was purged of its pro-German elements at a
heavy cost to its military efficiency. The bias of the Soviet
Government was turned in a marked manner against Germany.
Stalin was conscious of a personal debt to President Benes; and
a very strong desire to help him and his threatened country
against the Nazi peril animated the Soviet Government. The
situation was, of course, thoroughly understood by Hitler; but
I am not aware that the British and French Governments were
equally enlightened. To Mr. Chamberlain and the British
and French General Staffs the purge of 1937 presented itself
mainly as a tearing to pieces internally of the Russian Army,
and a picture of the Soviet Union as riven asunder by ferocious
hatreds and vengeance. This was perhaps an excessive view;
for a system of government founded on terror may well be
strengthened by a ruthless and successful assertion of its power.
The salient fact for the purposes of this account is the close association of Russia and Czechoslovakia, and of Stalin and
Benes.

But neither the internal stresses in Germany nor the ties

---

been imparted to the Czech police by the Ogpu, who wished it to reach Stalin
from a friendly foreign source. This did not detract from Benes' service to
Stalin, and is therefore irrelevant.

between Benes and Stalin were known to the outside world, or appreciated by the British and French Ministers. The Siegfried Line, albeit unperfected, seemed a fearful deterrent. The exact strength and fighting power of the German Army, new though it was, could not be accurately estimated and was certainly exaggerated. There were also the unmeasured dangers of air attack on undefended cities. Above all there was the hatred of war in the hearts of the democracies.

Nevertheless, on June 12, M. Daladier renewed his predecessor's pledge of March 14, and declared that France's engagements towards Czechoslovakia "are sacred, and cannot be evaded." This considerable statement sweeps away all chatter about the Treaty of Locarno thirteen years before having by implication left everything in the East vague pending an Eastern Locarno. There can be no doubt before history that the treaty between France and Czechoslovakia of 1924 had complete validity, not only in law but in fact; and that this was reaffirmed by successive heads of the French Government in all the circumstances of 1938.

But on this subject, Hitler was convinced that his judgment alone was sound, and on June 18 he issued a final directive for the attack on Czechoslovakia, in the course of which he sought to reassure his anxious generals.

Hitler to Keitel:

I will decide to take action against Czechoslovakia only if I am firmly convinced, as in the case of the demilitarised zone and the entry into Austria, that France will not march, and that therefore England will not intervene.[5]

With the object of confusing the issue, Hitler at the beginning of July sent his personal aide, Captain Wiedemann, to London. This envoy was received by Lord Halifax on July 18, ostensibly without the knowledge of the German Embassy. The Fuehrer was, it was suggested, hurt at our lack of response to his overtures in the past. Perhaps the British Government would receive Goering in London for fuller discussions. The

[5] *Nuremberg Documents,* Part 2, page 10.

Germans might, in certain circumstances, be prepared to delay action against the Czechs for a year. A few days later, Chamberlain took up this possibility with the German Ambassador. To clear the ground in Prague, the British Prime Minister had already suggested to the Czechs the sending of an investigator to Czechoslovakia to promote a friendly compromise. The royal visit to Paris on July 20 gave Halifax the opportunity of discussing this proposal with the French Government, and in a brief interchange of views both Governments agreed to make this effort at mediation.

On July 26, 1938, Chamberlain announced to Parliament the mission of Lord Runciman to Prague with the object of seeking a solution there by arrangements between the Czech Government and Herr Henlein. On the following day, the Czechs issued a draft statute for national minorities to form a basis of negotiation. On the same day, Lord Halifax stated in Parliament: *"I do not believe that those responsible for the Government of any country in Europe today want war."* On August 3, Lord Runciman reached Prague, and a series of interminable and complicated discussions took place with the various interested parties. Within a fortnight these negotiations broke down; and from this point events moved rapidly.

On August 27, Ribbentrop, now Foreign Minister, reported a visit which he had received from the Italian Ambassador in Berlin, who "had received another written instruction from Mussolini asking that Germany would communicate in time the probable date of action against Czechoslovakia." Mussolini asked for such notification in order "to be able to take in due time the necessary measures on the French frontier."

*   *   *   *   *

Anxiety grew steadily during August. To my constituents I said on the twenty-seventh:

It is difficult for us in this ancient forest of Theydon Bois, the very name of which carries us back to Norman days — here, in the heart of peaceful, law-abiding England — to realise the ferocious passions which are rife in Europe. During this anxious month

you have no doubt seen reports in the newspapers, one week good,
another week bad; one week better, another week worse. But I
must tell you that the whole state of Europe and of the world is
moving steadily towards a climax which cannot be long delayed.

War is certainly not inevitable. But the danger to peace will
not be removed until the vast German armies which have been
called from their homes into the ranks have been dispersed. For
a country which is itself not menaced by anyone, in no fear of
anyone, to place fifteen hundred thousand soldiers upon a war
footing is a very grave step. . . . It seems to me, and I must tell it to
you plainly, that these great forces have not been placed upon a
war footing without an intention to reach a conclusion within a
very limited space of time. . . .

We are all in full agreement with the course our Government
have taken in sending Lord Runciman to Prague. We hope —
indeed, we pray — that his mission of conciliation will be successful,
and certainly it looks as if the Government of Czechoslovakia were
doing their utmost to put their house in order, and to meet every
demand which is not designed to compass their ruin as a state. . . .
But larger and fiercer ambitions may prevent a settlement, and then
Europe and the civilised world will have to face the demands of
Nazi Germany, or perhaps be confronted with some sudden violent
action on the part of the German Nazi Party, carrying with it the
invasion of a small country and its subjugation. Such an episode
would not be simply an attack upon Czechoslovakia; it would be
an outrage against the civilisation and freedom of the whole
world. . . .

Whatever may happen, foreign countries should know — and the
Government are right to let them know — that Great Britain and
the British Empire must not be deemed incapable of playing their
part and doing their duty as they have done on other great occasions
which have not yet been forgotten by history.

I was in these days in some contact with Ministers. My
relations with Lord Halifax were, of course, marked by the
grave political differences which existed between me and His
Majesty's Government, both in defence and foreign policy. In
the main Eden and I meant the same thing. I could not feel
the same about his successor. None the less, whenever there
was any occasion, we met as friends and former colleagues of

many years' standing, and I wrote to him from time to time. Now and then he asked me to go to see him.

Mr. Churchill to Lord Halifax.   31.VIII.38.

If Benes makes good, and Runciman thinks it a fair offer, yet nevertheless it is turned down, it seems to me there are two things which might have been done this week to increase the deterrents against violent action by Hitler, neither of which would commit you to the dread guarantee.

First, would it not be possible to frame a Joint Note between Britain, France, and Russia stating: (*a*) their desire for peace and friendly relations; (*b*) their deep anxiety at the military preparations of Germany; (*c*) their joint interest in a peaceful solution of the Czechoslovak controversy; and (*d*) that an invasion by Germany of Czechoslovakia would raise capital issues for all three Powers? This Note, when drafted, should be formally shown to Roosevelt by the Ambassadors of the three Powers, and we should use every effort to induce him to do his utmost upon it. It seems to me not impossible that he would then himself address Hitler, emphasising the gravity of the situation, and saying that it seemed to him that a world war would inevitably follow from an invasion of Czechoslovakia, and that he earnestly counselled a friendly settlement.

It seems to me that this process would give the best chance to the peaceful elements in German official circles to make a stand, and that Hitler might find a way out for himself by parleying with Roosevelt. However, none of these developments can be predicted; one only sees them as hopes. *The important thing is the Joint Note.*

The second step which might save the situation would be fleet movements, and the placing of the reserve flotillas and cruiser squadrons into full commission. I do not suggest calling out the Royal Fleet Reserve or mobilisation, but there are, I believe, five or six flotillas which could be raised to First Fleet scale, and also there are about two hundred trawlers which could be used for anti-submarine work. The taking of these and other measures would make a great stir in the naval ports, the effect of which could only be beneficial as a deterrent, and a timely precaution if the worst happened.

I venture to hope that you will not resent these suggestions from one who has lived through such days before. It is clear that speed is vital.

*   *   *   *   *

In the afternoon of September 2, I received a message from
the Soviet Ambassador that he would like to come down to
Chartwell and see me at once upon a matter of urgency. I had
for some time had friendly personal relations with M. Maisky,
who also saw a good deal of my son Randolph. I thereupon received the Ambassador, and after a few preliminaries he told
me in precise and formal detail the story set out below. Before
he had got very far, I realised that he was making a declaration
to me, a private person, because the Soviet Government preferred this channel to a direct offer to the Foreign Office which
might have encountered a rebuff. It was clearly intended that
I should report what I was told to His Majesty's Government.
This was not actually stated by the Ambassador, but it was implied by the fact that no request for secrecy was made. As the
matter struck me at once as being of the first importance, I was
careful not to prejudice its consideration by Halifax and Chamberlain by proceeding to commit myself in any way, or use language which would excite controversy between us.

Mr. Churchill to Lord Halifax   3.IX.38.

I have received privately from an absolutely sure source the
following information, which I feel it my duty to report to you,
although I was not asked to do so.

Yesterday, September 2, the French Chargé d'Affaires in Moscow
(the Ambassador being on leave) called upon M. Litvinov and, in
the name of the French Government, asked him what aid Russia
would give to Czechoslovakia against a German attack, having
regard particularly to the difficulties which might be created by the
neutrality of Poland or Rumania. Litvinov asked in reply what
the French would do themselves, pointing out that the French
had a direct obligation, whereas the Russian obligation was dependent on the action of France. The French Chargé d'Affaires did
not reply to this question. Nevertheless, Litvinov stated to him,
first, that the Russian Soviet Union had resolved to fulfil their
obligations. He recognised the difficulties created by the attitude
of Poland and Rumania, but he thought that in the case of
Rumania these could be overcome.

In the last few months the policy of the Rumanian Government
had been markedly friendly to Russia, and their relations had

greatly improved. M. Litvinov thought that the best way to over-come the reluctance of Rumania would be through the agency of the League of Nations. If, for instance, the League decided that Czechoslovakia was the victim of aggression and that Germany was the aggressor, that would probably determine the action of Rumania in regard to allowing Russian troops and air forces to pass through her territory.

The French Chargé d'Affaires raised the point that the Council might not be unanimous, and was answered that M. Litvinov thought a majority decision would be sufficient, and that Rumania would probably associate herself with the majority in the vote of the Council. M. Litvinov, therefore, advised that the Council of the League should be invoked under Article 11, on the ground that there was danger of war, and that the League Powers should consult together. He thought the sooner this was done the better, as time might be very short. He next proceeded to tell the French Chargé d'Affaires that staff conversations ought immediately to take place between Russia, France, and Czechoslovakia as to the means and measures of giving assistance. The Soviet Union was ready to join in such staff conversations at once.

Fourthly, he recurred to his interview of March 17, of which you no doubt have a copy in the Foreign Office, advocating consultation among the peaceful Powers about the best method of preserving peace, with a view, perhaps, to a joint declaration including the three Great Powers concerned, France, Russia, and Great Britain. He believed that the United States would give moral support to such a declaration. All these statements were made on behalf of the Russian Government as what they think may be the best way of stopping a war.

I pointed out that the news today seemed to indicate a more peaceful attitude on the part of Herr Hitler, and that I thought it was unlikely that the British Government would consider any further steps until or unless there was a fresh breakdown in the Henlein-Benes negotiations in which the fault could not on any account be attributed to the Government of Czechoslovakia. We should not want to irritate Herr Hitler, if his mind was really turning towards a peaceful solution.

All this may, of course, have reached you through other channels, but I considered the declarations of M. Litvinov so important that I ought not to leave this to chance.

I sent the report to Lord Halifax as soon as I had dictated it, and he replied on September 5 in a guarded manner, that he did not at present feel that action of the kind proposed under Article 11 would be helpful, but that he would keep it in his mind. "For the present, I think, as you indicated, we must review the situation in the light of the report with which Henlein has returned from Berchtesgaden." He added that the situation remained very anxious.

*   *   *   *   *

In its leading article of September 7, *The Times* stated:

If the Sudetens now ask for more than the Czech Government are ready to give in their latest set of proposals, it can only be inferred that the Germans are going beyond the mere removal of disabilities for those who do not find themselves at ease within the Czechoslovak Republic. In that case it might be worth while for the Czechoslovak Government to consider whether they should exclude altogether the project, which has found favour in some quarters, of making Czechoslovakia a more homogeneous state by the cession of that fringe of alien populations who are contiguous to the nation to which they are united by race.

This, of course, involved the surrender of the whole of the Bohemian fortress line. Although the British Government stated at once that this *Times* article did not represent their views, public opinion abroad, particularly in France, was far from reassured. During the course of the same day — September 7 — the French Ambassador in London called on Lord Halifax on behalf of his Government to ask for a clarification of the British position in event of a German attack on Czechoslovakia.

M. Bonnet, then French Foreign Minister, declares that on September 10, 1938, he put the following question to our Ambassador in Paris, Sir Eric Phipps: "Tomorrow Hitler may attack Czechoslovakia. If he does, France will mobilise at once. She will turn to you, saying, 'We march: do you march with us?' What will be the answer of Great Britain?"

The following was the answer approved by the Cabinet, sent by Lord Halifax through Sir Eric Phipps on the twelfth:

I naturally recognise of what importance it would be to the French Government to have a plain answer to such a question. But, as you pointed out to Bonnet, the question itself, though plain in form, cannot be dissociated from the circumstances in which it might be posed, which are necessarily at this stage completely hypothetical.

Moreover, in this matter it is impossible for His Majesty's Government to have regard only to their own position, inasmuch as in any decision they may reach or action they may take they would, in fact, be committing the Dominions. Their Governments would quite certainly be unwilling to have their position in any way decided for them in advance of the actual circumstances, of which they would desire themselves to judge.

So far, therefore, as I am in a position to give any answer at this stage to M. Bonnet's question, it would have to be that while His Majesty's Government would never allow the security of France to be threatened, they are unable to make precise statements of the character of their future action, or the time at which it would be taken, in circumstances that they cannot at present foresee.[6]

Upon the statement that "His Majesty's Government would never allow the security of France to be threatened," the French asked what aid they could expect if it were. The reply from London was, according to Bonnet, two divisions, not motorised, and one hundred and fifty airplanes during the first six months of the war. If M. Bonnet was seeking for an excuse for leaving the Czechs to their fate, it must be admitted that his search had met with some success.

On September 12 also, Hitler delivered at a Nuremberg Party rally a violent attack on the Czechs, who replied on the following day by the establishment of martial law in certain districts of the Republic. On September 14, negotiations with Henlein were definitely broken off, and on the fifteenth the Sudeten leader fled to Germany.

The summit of the crisis was now reached.

6 Printed in Georges Bonnet, *De Washington au Quai d'Orsay*, pages 360–61.

17

The Tragedy of Munich

MR. CHAMBERLAIN was now in complete control of British foreign policy, and Sir Horace Wilson was his principal confidant and agent. Lord Halifax, in spite of increasing doubts derived from the atmosphere of his department, fol-

lowed the guidance of his chief. The Cabinet was deeply perturbed, but obeyed. The Government majority in the House
of Commons was skilfully handled by the Whips. One man
and one man only conducted our affairs. He did not shrink
either from the responsibility which he incurred, or from the
personal exertions required.

During the night of September 13/14, M. Daladier got in
touch with Mr. Chamberlain. The French Government were
of the opinion that a joint approach to Hitler on a personal
basis by the French and British leaders might be of value.
Chamberlain, however, had been communing with himself.
On his own initiative he telegraphed to Hitler proposing to
come to see him. He informed the Cabinet of his action the
next day, and in the afternoon received Hitler's reply inviting
him to Berchtesgaden. Accordingly, on the morning of September 15, the British Prime Minister flew to the Munich airfield. The moment was not in all respects well chosen. When
the news reached Prague, the Czech leaders could not believe
it was true. They were astonished that at the very moment
when for the first time they had the internal situation in the
Sudeten areas in hand, the British Prime Minister should himself pay a direct visit to Hitler. This they felt would weaken
their position with Germany. Hitler's provocative speech of
September 12, and the German-sponsored revolt of Henlein's
adherents which had followed, had failed to gain local support.
Henlein had fled to Germany, and the Sudeten German Party,
bereft of his leadership, was clearly opposed to direct action.
The Czech Government in the so-called "Fourth Plan" had
officially proposed to the Sudeten German leaders administrative schemes for regional autonomy which not only exceeded
Henlein's Carlsbad requests of April, but also fully met Chamberlain's view expressed in his speech of March 24, and Sir
John Simon's statements in his speech of August 27. But even
Lord Runciman realised that the last thing the Germans
wanted was a satisfactory bargain between the Sudeten leaders
and the Czech Government. Chamberlain's journey gave them
an opportunity to increase their demands; and on instructions

from Berlin the extremists in the Sudeten Party now openly
claimed union with the Reich.

*   *   *   *   *

The Prime Minister's plane arrived at Munich airport in the
afternoon of September 16; he travelled by train to Berchtesgaden. Meanwhile, all the radio stations of Germany broadcast
a proclamation by Henlein demanding the annexation of the
Sudeten areas to the Reich. This was the first news that reached
Mr. Chamberlain when he landed. It was no doubt planned
that he should know it before meeting Hitler. The question
of *annexation* had never yet been raised either by the German
Government or by Henlein; and a few days earlier, the Foreign
Office had stated that it was not the accepted policy of the British
Government.

Mr. Feiling has already published such records as are extant
of the conversations between Chamberlain and Hitler. The
salient point we may derive from his account is this: "In spite
of the hardness and ruthlessness I thought I saw in his face, I
got the impression that *here was a man who could be relied
upon when he had given his word.*" [1] In fact, Hitler had for
months past, as we have seen, resolved and prepared for the
invasion of Czechoslovakia, which awaited only the final signal.
When the Prime Minister reached London on Saturday, September 17, he summoned the Cabinet. Lord Runciman had
now returned, and his report was assured of attention. He had
all this time been failing in health, and the violent stress to
which he had been exposed in his mission had reduced him to
the most modest dimensions. He now recommended "a policy
for immediate and drastic action," namely, "the transfer of predominantly German districts to Germany." This at least had
the merit of simplicity.

Both the Prime Minister and Lord Runciman were convinced that only the cession of the Sudeten areas to Germany

[1] Feiling, *op. cit.*, page 367.

would dissuade Hitler from ordering the invasion of Czechoslovakia. Mr. Chamberlain had been strongly impressed at his
meeting with Hitler "that the latter was in a fighting mood."
His Cabinet were also of the opinion that the French had no
fight in them. There could, therefore, be no question of resisting Hitler's demands upon the Czech State. Some ministers
found consolation in such phrases as "the rights of self-determination," "the claims of a national minority to just treatment";
and even the mood appeared of "championing the small man
against the Czech bully."

It was now necessary to keep in backward step with the
French Government. On September 18, Daladier and Bonnet
came to London. Chamberlain had already decided in principle to accept Hitler's demands as explained to him at Berchtesgaden. There only remained the business of drafting the
proposals to be presented to the Czech Government by the
British and French representatives in Prague. The French
Ministers brought with them a set of draft proposals which
were certainly more skilfully conceived. They did not favour
a plebiscite because, they observed, there might be demands
for further plebiscites in the Slovak and Ruthene areas. They
favoured an outright cession of the Sudetenland to Germany.
They added, however, that the British Government with
France, *and with Russia*, whom they had not consulted, should
guarantee the new frontiers of the mutilated Czechoslovakia.

Many of us, even outside Cabinet circles, had the sensation
that Bonnet represented the quintessence of defeatism, and
that all his clever verbal manoeuvres had the aim of "peace
at any price." In his book, written after the war, he labours
naturally to thrust the whole burden upon Chamberlain and
Halifax. There can be no doubt of what he had in his own
mind. At all costs he wished to avoid having to fulfil the solemn, precise, and so recently renewed obligations of France
to go to war in defence of Czechoslovakia. The British and
French Cabinets at this time presented a front of two overripe
melons crushed together; whereas what was needed was a gleam
of steel. On one thing they were all agreed: there should be

no consultation with the Czechs. These should be confronted with the decision of their guardians. The Babes in the Wood had no worse treatment.

In presenting their decision or ultimatum to the Czechs, England and France said: "Both the French and British Governments recognise how great is the sacrifice thus required of Czechoslovakia. They have felt it their duty jointly to set forth frankly the conditions essential to security. . . . The Prime Minister must resume conversations with Herr Hitler not later than Wednesday, or sooner if possible. We, therefore, feel we must ask for your reply at the earliest possible moment." Proposals involving the immediate cession to Germany of all areas in Czechoslovakia containing over fifty per cent of German inhabitants were, therefore, handed to the Czech Government in the afternoon of September 19.

Great Britain, after all, had no treaty obligation to defend Czechoslovakia, nor was she pledged in any informal way. But France had definitely bound herself by treaty to make war upon Germany if she attacked Czechoslovakia. For twenty years President Benes had been the faithful ally and almost vassal of France, always supporting French policies and French interests on the League of Nations and elsewhere. If ever there was a case of solemn obligation, it was here and now. Fresh and vivid were the declarations of MM. Blum and Daladier. It was a portent of doom when a French Government failed to keep the word of France. I have always believed that Benes was wrong to yield. He should have defended his fortress line. Once fighting had begun, in my opinion at that time, France would have moved to his aid in a surge of national passion, and Britain would have rallied to France almost immediately. At the height of this crisis (on September 20) I visited Paris for two days in order to see my friends in the French Government, Reynaud and Mandel. Both these Ministers were in lively distress and on the verge of resigning from the Daladier Cabinet. I was against this, as their sacrifice could not alter the course of events, and would only leave the French Government weakened by the loss of its two most capable and resolute men. I

ventured even to speak to them in this sense. After this painful
visit I returned to London.

*   *   *   *   *

At 2 A.M. on the night of September 20/21, the British and
French Ministers in Prague called on President Benes to inform him in effect that there was no hope of arbitration on
the basis of the German-Czechoslovak Treaty of 1925, and to
urge upon him the acceptance of the Anglo-French proposals
*"before producing a situation for which France and Britain
could take no responsibility."* The French Government at
least was sufficiently ashamed of this communication to instruct
its Minister only to make it verbally. Under this pressure on
September 21, the Czech Government bowed to the Anglo-
French proposals. There was in Prague at this moment a general of the French Army named Faucher. He had been in
Czechoslovakia with the French Military Mission since 1919,
and had been its chief since 1926. He now requested the
French Government to relieve him of his duties, and placed
himself at the disposal of the Czechoslovak Army. He also
adopted Czech citizenship.

The following French defence has been made, and it cannot
be lightly dismissed: If Czechoslovakia had refused to submit,
and war had resulted, France would have fulfilled her obligations; but if the Czechs chose to give in under whatever pressures were administered, French honour was saved. We must
leave this to the judgment of history.

*   *   *   *   *

On the same day, September 21, I issued a statement on the
crisis to the press in London:

The partition of Czechoslovakia under pressure from England
and France amounts to the complete surrender of the Western
Democracies to the Nazi threat of force. Such a collapse will bring
peace or security neither to England nor to France. On the contrary, it will place these two nations in an ever-weaker and more

dangerous situation. The mere neutralisation of Czechoslovakia means the liberation of twenty-five German divisions, which will threaten the Western Front; in addition to which it will open up for the triumphant Nazis the road to the Black Sea. It is not Czechoslovakia alone which is menaced, but also the freedom and the democracy of all nations. The belief that security can be obtained by throwing a small state to the wolves is a fatal delusion. The war potential of Germany will increase in a short time more rapidly than it will be possible for France and Great Britain to complete the measures necessary for their defence.

*   *   *   *   *

At the Assembly of the League of Nations on September 21, an official warning was given by Litvinov:

. . . at the present time, Czechoslovakia is suffering interference in its internal affairs at the hands of a neighbouring state, and is publicly and loudly menaced with attack. One of the oldest, most cultured, most hard-working of European peoples, who acquired their independence after centuries of oppression, today or tomorrow may decide to take up arms in defence of that independence. . . .

Such an event as the disappearance of Austria passed unnoticed by the League of Nations. Realising the significance of this event for the fate of the whole of Europe, and particularly of Czechoslovakia, the Soviet Government, immediately after the *Anschluss,* officially approached the other European Great Powers with a proposal for an immediate collective deliberation on the possible consequences of that event, in order to adopt collective preventive measures. To our regret, this proposal, which if carried out could have saved us from the alarm which all the world now feels for the fate of Czechoslovakia, did not receive its just appreciation . . . When, a few days before I left for Geneva, the French Government for the first time inquired as to our attitude in the event of an attack on Czechoslovakia, I gave in the name of my Government the following perfectly clear and unambiguous reply: "We intend to fulfil our obligations under the Pact, and together with France to afford assistance to Czechoslovakia by the ways open to us. Our War Department is ready immediately to participate in a conference with representatives of the French and Czechoslovak War Departments, in order to discuss the measures appropriate to the moment." . . . It was only two days ago that the Czechoslovak Government addressed a formal inquiry to my Government as to whether the Soviet Union is prepared, in accordance with the Soviet-Czech Pact, to render Czechoslovakia immediate and effective aid if France, loyal to her obligations, will render similar assistance, to which my Government gave a clear answer in the affirmative.

It is indeed astonishing that this public, and unqualified, declaration by one of the greatest Powers concerned should not have played its part in Mr. Chamberlain's negotiations, or in the French conduct of the crisis. I have heard it suggested that it was geographically impossible for Russia to send troops into Czechoslovakia and that Russian aid in the event of war would have been limited to modest air support. The assent of Rumania, and also to a lesser extent of Hungary, to allow Russian forces to pass through their territory was, of course, necessary. This might well have been obtained from Rumania at least, as indicated to me by M. Maisky, through the pressures and guarantees of a Grand Alliance acting under the aegis of the League of Nations. There were two railways from Russia into Czechoslovakia through the Carpathian Mountains, the northerly from Czernowitz through the Bukovina, the southerly through Hungary by Debreczen. These two railways alone, which avoid both Bukarest and Budapest by good margins, might well have supported Russian armies of thirty divisions. As a counter for keeping the peace, these possibilities would have been a substantial deterrent upon Hitler, and would almost certainly have led to far greater developments in the event of war. Stress has also been laid upon Soviet duplicity and bad faith, and the Soviet offer was in effect ignored. They were not brought into the scale against Hitler, and were treated with an indifference — not to say disdain — which left a mark in Stalin's mind. Events took their course as if Soviet Russia did not exist. For this we afterwards paid dearly.

* * * * *

Mussolini, speaking at Treviso on September 21, said — not

without some pith — "If Czechoslovakia finds herself today in
what might be called a 'delicate situation,' it is because she
was — one may already say 'was,' and I shall tell you why immediately — not just Czechoslovakia, but 'Czecho-Germano-
Polono-Magyaro-Rutheno-Rumano-Slovakia,' and I would emphasise that now that this problem is being faced, it is essential
it should be solved in a general manner." [2]

Under the humiliation of the Anglo-French proposals, the
Czech Government resigned, and a non-party Administration
was formed under General Syrovy, the commander of the
Czechoslovak legions in Siberia during the First World War.
On September 22, President Benes broadcast to the Czech nation a dignified appeal for calm. While Benes was preparing
his broadcast, Chamberlain had been flying to his second meeting with Hitler, this time at the Rhineland town of Godesberg.
The British Prime Minister carried with him, as a basis for
final discussion with the Fuehrer, the details of the Anglo-
French proposals accepted by the Czech Government. The two
men met in the hotel at Godesberg which Hitler had quitted
in haste four years earlier for the Roehm purge. From the first,
Chamberlain realised that he was confronted with what he
called, in his own words, "a totally unexpected situation." He
described the scene in the House of Commons on his return:

I had been told at Berchtesgaden that if the principle of self-
determination were accepted, Herr Hitler would discuss with me
the ways and means of carrying it out. He told me afterwards that
he never for one moment supposed that I should be able to come
back and say that the principle was accepted. I do not want the
House to think that he was deliberately deceiving me — I do not
think so for one moment — but, for me, I expected that when I got
back to Godesberg, I had only to discuss quietly with him the proposals that I had brought with me; and it was a profound shock to
me when I was told at the beginning of the conversation that these
proposals were not acceptable, and that they were to be replaced
by other proposals of a kind which I had not contemplated at all.
I felt that I must have a little time to consider what I was to do.

[2] Quoted in Ripka, *Munich and After,* page 117.

Consequently I withdrew, my mind full of foreboding as to the
success of my mission. I first, however, obtained from Herr Hitler
an extension of his previous assurance that he would not move his
troops pending the results of the negotiations. I, on my side, undertook to appeal to the Czech Government to avoid any action which
might provoke incidents.

Discussions were broken off until the next day. Throughout
the morning of September 23, Chamberlain paced the balcony
of his hotel. He sent a written message to Hitler after break-
fast stating that he was ready to convey the new German proposals to the Czech Government, but pointing out grave difficulties. Hitler's reply in the afternoon showed little signs of
yielding, and Chamberlain asked that a formal memorandum
accompanied by maps should be handed to him at a final meeting that evening. The Czechs were now mobilising, and both
the British and French Governments officially stated to their
representatives in Prague that they could no longer take the
responsibility of advising them not to. At 10.30 that night
Chamberlain again met Hitler. The description of the meeting
is best told in his own words:

The memorandum and the map were handed to me at my final
interview with the Chancellor, which began at half-past ten that
night and lasted into the small hours of the morning, an interview
at which the German Foreign Secretary was present, as well as Sir
Nevile Henderson and Sir Horace Wilson; and, for the first time, I
found in the memorandum a time limit. Accordingly, on this
occasion I spoke very frankly. I dwelt with all the emphasis at my
command on the risks which would be incurred by insisting on such
terms, and on the terrible consequences of a war, if war ensued. I
declared that the language and the manner of the documents, which
I described as an ultimatum rather than a memorandum, would
profoundly shock public opinion in neutral countries, and I bitterly
reproached the Chancellor for his failure to respond in any way to
the efforts which I had made to secure peace.
I should add that Hitler repeated to me with great earnestness
what he had said already at Berchtesgaden, namely, that this was
the last of his territorial ambitions in Europe and that he had no

wish to include in the Reich people of other races than Germans.
In the second place, he said, again very earnestly, that he wanted to
be friends with England and that, if only this Sudeten question
could be got out of the way in peace, *he would gladly resume conversations.* It is true, he said, "There is one awkward question, the
colonies; but that is not a matter for war."

On the afternoon of September 24, Mr. Chamberlain returned to London, and on the following day three meetings
of the Cabinet were held. There was a noticeable stiffening of
opinion both in London and in Paris. It was decided to reject
the Godesberg terms, and this information was conveyed to
the German Government. The French Cabinet agreed, and a
partial French mobilisation was carried out promptly and with
more efficiency than was expected. On the evening of September 25, the French Ministers came again to London and reluctantly accepted their obligations to the Czechs. During the
course of the following afternoon, Sir Horace Wilson was sent
with a personal letter to Hitler in Berlin three hours before
the latter was to speak in the Sports Palace. The only answer
Sir Horace was able to obtain was that Hitler would not depart
from the time limit set by the Godesberg ultimatum, namely,
Saturday, October 1, on which day he would march into the territories concerned unless he received Czech acquiescence by
2 P.M. on Wednesday, twenty-eighth.

That evening Hitler spoke in Berlin. He referred to England and France in accommodating phrases, launching at the
same time a coarse and brutal attack on Benes and the Czechs.
He said categorically that the Czechs must clear out of the
Sudetenland by the twenty-sixth, but once this was settled, he
had no more interest in what happened to Czechoslovakia.
"This is the last territorial claim I have to make in Europe."

*   *   *   *   *

As on similar occasions, my contacts with His Majesty's
Government became more frequent and intimate with the
mounting of the crisis. On September 10, I had visited the
Prime Minister at Downing Street for a long talk. Again on

September 26, he either invited me or readily accorded me an interview. At 3.30 in the afternoon of this critical day, I was received by him and Lord Halifax in the Cabinet Room. I pressed upon them the policy set forth in my letter to Lord Halifax of August 31, namely, a declaration showing the unity of sentiment and purpose between Britain, France, *and Russia* against Hitlerite aggression. We discussed at length and in detail a communiqué, and we seemed to be in complete agreement. Lord Halifax and I were at one, and I certainly thought the Prime Minister was in full accord. There was present a high official of the Foreign Office who built up the draft. When we separated, I was satisfied and relieved.

About eight o'clock that night, Mr. Leeper, then head of the Foreign Office Press Department, now Sir Reginald Leeper, presented to the Foreign Secretary a communiqué of which the following is the pith:

If, in spite of the efforts made by the British Prime Minister, a German attack is made upon Czechoslovakia, the immediate result must be that France will be bound to come to her assistance, and Great Britain *and Russia* will certainly stand by France.

This was approved by Lord Halifax and immediately issued.

When earlier I returned to my flat at Morpeth Mansions, I found about fifteen gentlemen assembled. They were all Conservatives: Lord Cecil, Lord Lloyd, Sir Edward Grigg, Sir Robert Horne, Mr. Boothby, Mr. Bracken, and Mr. Law. The feeling was passionate. It all focused on the point, "We must get Russia in." I was impressed and indeed surprised by this intensity of view in Tory circles, showing how completely they had cast away all thoughts of class, party, or ideological interests, and to what a pitch their mood had come. I reported to them what had happened at Downing Street and described the character of the communiqué. They were all greatly reassured.

The French Right press treated this communiqué with suspicion and disdain. The *Matin* called it "A clever lie." M. Bonnet, who was now very busy showing how forward in action

he was, told several Deputies that he had no confirmation of
it, leaving on them the impression that this was not the British
pledge he was looking for. This was no doubt not difficult for
him to convey.

I dined that night with Mr. Duff Cooper at the Admiralty.
He told me that he was demanding from the Prime Minister
the immediate mobilisation of the Fleet. I recalled my own
experiences a quarter of a century before when similar circumstances had presented themselves.

*   *   *   *   *

It seemed that the moment of clash had arrived and that the
opposing forces were aligned. The Czechs had a million and a
half men armed behind the strongest fortress line in Europe,
and equipped by a highly organised and powerful industrial
machine. The French Army was partly mobilised, and, albeit
reluctantly, the French Ministers were prepared to honour
their obligations to Czechoslovakia. Just before midnight on
September 27, the warning telegram was sent out from the Admiralty ordering the mobilisation of the Fleet for the following
day. This information was given to the British press almost
simultaneously (at 11.38 P.M.). At 11.20 A.M. on September 28,
the actual orders to the British Fleet to mobilise were issued
from the Admiralty.

*   *   *   *   *

We may now look behind the brazen front which Hitler
presented to the British and French Governments. General
Beck, the Chief of the Army General Staff, had become
profoundly alarmed about Hitler's schemes. He entirely dis-
approved of them, and was prepared to resist. After the invasion of Austria in March, he had sent a memorandum to
Hitler arguing by detailed facts that the continuance of a programme of conquest must lead to world-wide catastrophe and
the ruin of the now reviving Reich. To this Hitler did not reply. There was a pause. Beck refused to share the responsibility before history for the war plunge which the Fuehrer was

resolved to make. In July, a personal confrontation took place. When the imminence of an attack on Czechoslovakia became clear, Beck demanded an assurance against further military adventures. Here was a crunch. Hitler rejoined that the Army was the instrument of the State, that he was the head of the State, and that the Army and other forces owed unquestioning obedience to his will. On this Beck resigned. His request to be relieved of his post remained unanswered. But the General's decision was irrevocable. Henceforth he absented himself from the War Ministry. Hitler was, therefore, forced to dismiss him, and appointed Halder as his successor. For Beck there remained only a tragic but honourable fate.

All this was kept within a secret circle; but there now began an intense, unceasing struggle between the Fuehrer and his expert advisers. Beck was universally trusted and respected by the Army Staff, who were united, not only in professional opinion, but in resentment of civilian and party dictation. The September crisis seemed to provide all the circumstances which the German generals dreaded. Between thirty and forty Czech divisions were deploying upon Germany's eastern frontier, and the weight of the French Army, at odds of nearly eight to one, began to lie heavy on the Western Wall. A hostile Russia might operate from Czech airfields, and Soviet armies might wend their way forward through Poland or Rumania. Finally, in the last stage the British Navy was said to be mobilising, As all this developed, passions rose to fever heat.

First, we have the account, given by General Halder, of a definite plot to arrest Hitler and his principal associates. The evidence for this does not rest only on Halder's detailed statements. Plans were certainly made, but how far they were at the time backed by resolve cannot be judged precisely. The generals were repeatedly planning revolts, and as often drew back at the last moment for one reason or another. It was to the interest of the parties concerned after they were the prisoners of the Allies to dwell upon their efforts for peace. There can be no doubt, however, of the existence of the plot at this moment, and of serious measures to make it effective.

By the beginning of September [Halder says], we had taken the
necessary steps to immunize Germany from this madman. At this
time the prospect of war filled the great majority of the German
people with horror. We did not intend to kill the Nazi leaders —
merely to arrest them, establish a military Government, and issue
a proclamation to the people that we had taken this action only
because we were convinced they were being led to certain disaster.

The following were in the plot: Generals Halder, Beck,
Stuelpnagel, Witzleben (Commander of the Berlin garrison),
Thomas (Controller of Armaments), Brockdorff (Commander
of the Potsdam garrison), and Graf von Helldorf, who was in
charge of the Berlin police. The Commander-in-Chief, General
von Brauchitsch, was informed, and approved.

It was easy, as a part of the troop movements against Czechoslovakia and of ordinary military routine, to hold one Panzer
division so near to Berlin that it could reach the capital by a
night's march. The evidence is clear that the Third Panzer
Division, commanded by General Hoeppner, was at the time of
the Munich crisis stationed south of Berlin. General Hoeppner's secret mission was to occupy the capital, the Chancellery,
and the important Nazi Ministries and offices at a given signal.
For this purpose it was added to General Witzleben's command.
According to Halder's account, Helldorf, Chief of the Berlin
police, then made meticulous arrangements to arrest Hitler,
Goering, Goebbels, and Himmler. "There was no possibility
of a hitch. All that was required for a completely successful
coup was Hitler's presence in Berlin." He arrived there from
Berchtesgaden on the morning of September 14. Halder heard
of this at midday, and immediately went over to see Witzleben
and complete the plans. It was decided to strike at eight that
same evening. At 4 P.M., according to Halder, a message was
received in Witzleben's office that Mr. Chamberlain was going
to fly to see the Fuehrer at Berchtesgaden. A meeting was at
once held, at which he, Halder, told Witzleben that "if Hitler
had succeeded in his bluff, he would not be justified, as Chief
of Staff, in calling it." It was accordingly decided to defer action, and await events.

Such is the tale, which historians should probe, of this internal crisis in Berlin as told by General von Halder, at that time Chief of the Staff. It has since been confirmed by other generals — Mueller and Hillebrandt — and has been accepted as genuine by various authorities who have examined it. If it should eventually be accepted as historical truth, it will be another example of the very small accidents upon which the fortunes of mankind turn.

Of other less violent but earnest efforts of the General Staff to restrain Hitler there can be no doubt. On September 26, a deputation, consisting of General von Hanneken, Ritter von Leeb, and Colonel Bodenschatz, called at the Chancellery of the Reich and requested to be received by Herr Hitler. They were sent away. At noon on the following day, the principal generals held a meeting at the War Office. They agreed upon a memorial which they left at the Chancellery. This document was published in France in November, 1938.[3] It consisted of eighteen pages divided into five chapters and three appendices. Chapter I stresses the divergences between the political and military leadership of the Third Reich, and declares that the low morale of the German population renders it incapable of sustaining a European war. It states that in the event of war breaking out, exceptional powers must be given to the military authorities. Chapter II describes the bad condition of the Reichswehr and mentions that the military authorities have felt obliged "to shut their eyes in many serious cases to the absence of discipline." Chapter III enumerates the various deficiencies in German armaments, dwelling upon the defects in the Siegfried Line, so hurriedly constructed, and the lack of fortifications in the Aix-la-Chapelle and Saarbruecken areas. Fear is expressed of an incursion into Belgium by the French troops concentrated around Givet. Finally, emphasis is laid on the shortage of officers. No fewer than forty-eight thousand officers and one hundred thousand N.C.O.'s were necessary to bring the Army up to war strength, and in the event of a gen-

---

[3] Published by Professor Bernard Lavergne, in *L'Année Politique Française et Etrangère* in November, 1938. Quoted in Ripka, *op. cit.*, page 212 ff.

eral mobilisation, no fewer than eighteen divisions would find themselves devoid of trained subordinate commanders.

The document presents the reasons why defeat must be expected in any but a strictly local war, and affirms that less than a fifth of the officers of the Reichswehr believe in the possibility of a victory for Germany. A military appreciation about Czechoslovakia in the Appendix states that the Czechoslovak Army, even if fighting without allies, could hold out for three months, and that Germany would need to retain covering forces on the Polish and French frontiers as well as on the Baltic and North Sea coasts, and to keep a force of at least a quarter of a million troops in Austria to guard against popular risings and a possible Czechoslovak offensive. Finally, the General Staff believed that it was highly improbable that hostilities would remain localised during the three-month period.

The warnings of the soldiers were finally reinforced by Admiral Raeder, Chief of the German Admiralty. At 10 P.M. on September 27, Raeder was received by the Fuehrer. He made a vehement appeal, which was emphasised a few hours later by the news that the British Fleet was being mobilised. Hitler now wavered. At 2 A.M. the German radio broadcast an official denial that Germany intended to mobilise on the twenty-ninth, and at 11.45 the same morning a statement of the German official news agency was given to the British press, again denying the reports of the intended German mobilisation. The strain upon this one man and upon his astounding will-power must at this moment have been most severe. Evidently he had brought himself to the brink of a general war. Could he take the plunge in the face of an unfavourable public opinion and of the solemn warnings of the Chiefs of his Army, Navy, and air force? Could he, on the other hand, afford to retreat after living so long upon prestige?

*   *   *   *   *

While the Fuehrer was at grips with his generals, Mr. Chamberlain himself was preparing to broadcast to the English nation. On the evening of September 27, he spoke as follows:

How horrible, fantastic, incredible, it is that we should be digging
trenches and trying on gas-masks here because of a quarrel in a far-
away country between people of whom we know nothing! . . . I
would not hesitate to pay even a third visit to Germany, if I thought
it would do any good. . . . I am myself a man of peace to the
depths of my soul. Armed conflict between nations is a nightmare
to me; but if I were convinced that any nation had made up its
mind to dominate the world by fear of its force, I should feel that
it must be resisted. Under such a domination, life for people who
believe in liberty would not be worth living: but war is a fearful
thing, and we must be very clear, before we embark on it, that it is
really the great issues that are at stake.

After delivering this balancing broadcast, he received Hitler's
reply to the letter he had sent through Sir Horace Wilson.
This letter opened a chink of hope. Hitler offered to join in
a guarantee of the new frontiers of Czechoslovakia, and was
willing to give further assurances about the manner of carrying
out the new plebiscite. There was little time to lose. The German ultimatum contained in the Godesberg memorandum was
due to expire at 2 P.M. on the following day, Wednesday, September 28. Chamberlain, therefore, drafted a personal message to Hitler:

After reading your letter, I feel certain that you can get all essentials without war, and without delay. I am ready to come to
Berlin myself at once to discuss arrangements for transfer with you
and representatives of the Czech Government, together with representatives of France and Italy if you desire. I feel convinced that we
could reach agreement in a week.[4]

At the same time he telegraphed to Mussolini informing him
of this last appeal to Hitler:

I trust your Excellency will inform the German Chancellor that
you are willing to be represented, and urge him to agree to my
proposal, which will keep our peoples out of war.

It is one of the remarkable features of this crisis that no
close and confidential consultation seems to have existed be-

4 Feiling, *op. cit.*, page 372.

tween London and Paris. There was a broad coincidence of
view, but little or no personal contact. While Mr. Chamberlain, without consulting either the French Government or his
own Cabinet colleagues, was drafting these two letters, the
French Ministers were taking their own separate measures
along parallel lines. We have seen the strength of the forces
opposed to standing up to Germany in the French press, and
how the firm British communiqué, naming Russia, was suggested in Paris newspapers, inspired by the French Foreign
Office, to be a forgery. The French Ambassador in Berlin was
instructed on the night of the twenty-seventh to make yet further proposals extending the territory in the Sudetenland to be
handed over for immediate German occupation. While M.
François-Poncet was with Hitler, a message arrived from Mussolini advising that Chamberlain's idea of a conference should
be accepted and that Italy should take a part. At three o'clock
on the afternoon of September 28, Hitler sent messages to
Chamberlain and Daladier proposing a meeting at Munich on
the following day together with Mussolini. At that hour Mr.
Chamberlain was addressing the House of Commons, giving
them a general view of recent events. As he neared the end
of his speech, the message inviting him to Munich was passed
down to him by Lord Halifax, who was sitting in the Peers'
Gallery. Mr. Chamberlain was at that moment describing the
letter which he had sent to Mussolini and the results of this
move:

In reply to my message to Signor Mussolini, I was informed that
instructions had been sent by the Duce . . . that while Italy would
fulfil completely her pledges to stand by Germany, yet, in view of
the great importance of the request made by His Majesty's Government to Signor Mussolini, the latter hoped Herr Hitler would see
his way to postpone action, which the Chancellor had told Sir
Horace Wilson was to be taken at 2 P.M. today, for at least twenty-
four hours so as to allow Signor Mussolini time to re-examine the
situation and endeavour to find a peaceful settlement. In response,
Herr Hitler has agreed to postpone mobilisation for twenty-four
hours. . . . That is not all. I have something further to say to the

House yet. I have now been informed by Herr Hitler that he invites
me to meet him at Munich tomorrow morning. He has also invited
Signor Mussolini and M. Daladier. Signor Mussolini has accepted,
and I have no doubt M. Daladier will also accept. I need not say
what my answer will be. . . . I am sure that the House will be ready
to release me now to go and see what I can make of this last effort.

Thus, for the third time Mr. Chamberlain flew to Germany.

*   *   *   *   *

Many accounts have been written of this memorable meeting,
and it is not possible here to do more than emphasise some
special features. No invitation was extended to Russia. Nor
were the Czechs themselves allowed to be present at the meetings. The Czech Government had been informed in bald terms
on the evening of the twenty-eighth that a conference of the
representatives of the four European Powers would take place
the following day. Agreement was reached between "the Big
Four" with speed. The conversations began at noon and lasted
till two o'clock the next morning. A memorandum was drawn
up and signed at 2 A.M. on September 30. It was in essentials
the acceptance of the Godesberg ultimatum. The Sudetenland
was to be evacuated in five stages beginning on October 1 and
to be completed within ten days. An International Commission
was to determine the final frontiers. The document was placed
before the Czech delegates who had been allowed to come to
Munich to receive the decisions.

While the three statesmen were waiting for the experts to
draft the final document, the Prime Minister asked Hitler
whether he would care for a private talk. Hitler "jumped at
the idea." [5] The two leaders met in Hitler's Munich flat on
the morning of September 30 and were alone except for the
interpreter. Chamberlain produced a draft declaration which
he had prepared, as follows:

We, the German Fuehrer and Chancellor, and the British Prime
Minister, have had a further meeting today and are agreed in
recognising that the question of Anglo-German relations is of the
first importance for the two countries and for Europe.

[5] See Feiling, *op. cit.*, page 376.

We regard the Agreement signed last night, and the Anglo-German Naval Agreement, as symbolic of the desire of our two peoples never to go to war with one another again.

We are resolved that the method of consultation shall be the method adopted to deal with any other questions that may concern our two countries, and we are determined to continue our efforts to remove possible sources of difference, and thus to contribute to assure the peace of Europe.

Hitler read this note and signed it without demur.

Closeted with his Italian confederate he must have discussed less amiable solutions. A letter written by Mussolini to Hitler in June, 1940, and lately published, is revealing:

Fuehrer,   *Rome,* 26.VI.40.

Now that the time has come to thrash England, I remind you *of what I said to you at Munich about the direct participation of Italy in the assault of the Isle.* I am ready to take part in this with land and air forces, and you know how much I desire it. I pray you to reply in order that I can pass into the phase of action. Awaiting this day, I send you my salute of comradeship.

MUSSOLINI [6]

There is no record of any other meeting between Hitler and Mussolini *at Munich* in the interval.

Chamberlain returned to England. At Heston where he landed, he waved the joint declaration which he had got Hitler to sign, and read it to the crowd of notables and others who welcomed him. As his car drove through cheering crowds from the airport, he said to Halifax, sitting beside him, "All this will be over in three months"; but from the windows of Downing Street he waved his piece of paper again and used these words, "This is the second time there has come back from Germany to Downing Street peace with honour. I believe it is peace in our time."

*   *   *   *   *

We have now also Marshal Keitel's answer to the specific

[6] *Les lettres secrètes échangés par Hitler et Mussolini.* Introduction de André François-Poncet.

question put to him by the Czech representative at the Nuremberg Trials:

Colonel Eger, representing Czechoslovakia, asked Marshal Keitel:
"Would the Reich have attacked Czechoslovakia in 1938 if the
Western Powers had stood by Prague?"

Marshal Keitel answered: "Certainly not. We were not strong
enough militarily. The object of Munich [i.e., reaching an agreement at Munich] was to get Russia out of Europe, to gain time, and
to complete the German armaments." [7]

*   *   *   *   *

Hitler's judgment had been once more decisively vindicated.
The German General Staff was utterly abashed. Once again the
Fuehrer had been right, after all. He with his genius and intuition alone had truly measured all the circumstances, military
and political. Once again, as in the Rhineland, the Fuehrer's
leadership had triumphed over the obstruction of the German
military chiefs. All these generals were patriotic men. They
longed to see the Fatherland regain its position in the world.
They were devoting themselves night and day to every process
that could strengthen the German forces. They, therefore, felt
smitten in their hearts at having been found so much below
the level of the event, and in many cases their dislike and their
distrust of Hitler were overpowered by admiration for his commanding gifts and miraculous luck. Surely here was a star to
follow, surely here was a guide to obey. Thus did Hitler finally
become the undisputed master of Germany, and the path was
clear for the great design. The conspirators lay low, and were
not betrayed by their military comrades.

*   *   *   *   *

It may be well here to set down some principles of morals
and action which may be a guide in the future. No case of
this kind can be judged apart from its circumstances. The facts
may be unknown at the time, and estimates of them must be
largely guesswork, coloured by the general feelings and aims of

[7] Quoted in Paul Reynaud, *La France a sauvé l'Europe,* volume 1, page 561,
note.

whoever is trying to pronounce. Those who are prone by temperament and character to seek sharp and clear-cut solutions of difficult and obscure problems, who are ready to fight whenever some challenge comes from a foreign Power, have not always been right. On the other hand, those whose inclination is to bow their heads, to seek patiently and faithfully for peaceful compromise, are not always wrong. On the contrary, in the majority of instances they may be right, not only morally but from a practical standpoint. How many wars have been averted by patience and persisting good will! Religion and virtue alike lend their sanctions to meekness and humility, not only between men but between nations. How many wars have been precipitated by firebrands! How many misunderstandings which led to wars could have been removed by temporising! How often have countries fought cruel wars and then after a few years of peace found themselves not only friends but allies!

The Sermon on the Mount is the last word in Christian ethics. Everyone respects the Quakers. Still, it is not on these terms that Ministers assume their responsibilities of guiding states. Their duty is first so to deal with other nations as to avoid strife and war and to eschew aggression in all its forms, whether for nationalistic or ideological objects. But the safety of the State, the lives and freedom of their own fellow countrymen, to whom they owe their position, make it right and imperative in the last resort, or when a final and definite conviction has been reached, that the use of force should not be excluded. If the circumstances are such as to warrant it, force may be used. And if this be so, it should be used under the conditions which are most favourable. There is no merit in putting off a war for a year if, when it comes, it is a far worse war or one much harder to win. These are the tormenting dilemmas upon which mankind has throughout its history been so frequently impaled. Final judgment upon them can only be recorded by history in relation to the facts of the case as known to the parties at the time, and also as subsequently proved.

There is, however, one helpful guide, namely, for a nation to keep its word and to act in accordance with its treaty obligations to allies. This guide is called *honour*. It is baffling to reflect that what men call honour does not correspond always to Christian ethics. Honour is often influenced by that element of pride which plays so large a part in its inspiration. An exaggerated code of honour leading to the performance of utterly vain and unreasonable deeds could not be defended, however fine it might look. Here, however, the moment came when Honour pointed the path of Duty, and when also the right judgment of the facts at that time would have reinforced its dictates.

For the French Government to leave her faithful ally, Czechoslovakia, to her fate was a melancholy lapse from which flowed terrible consequences. Not only wise and fair policy, but chivalry, honour, and sympathy for a small threatened people made an overwhelming concentration. Great Britain, who would certainly have fought if bound by treaty obligations, was nevertheless now deeply involved, and it must be recorded with regret that the British Government not only acquiesced but encouraged the French Government in a fatal course.

18

Munich Winter

Poland and Hungary: Beasts of Prey — Stresses in English Life — Mr. Duff Cooper's Resignation Speech — The Munich Debate — Hitler's Speech of October 9 — The British Cabinet Dilemma: Rearmament or Peace — The Question of a General Election — Correspondence with Mr. Duff Cooper — The Mutilation of Czechoslovakia — The Prime Minister's Power and Responsibility — His Approaches to Italy and Visit to Paris, November, 1938 — M. Bonnet's Addresses to Germany — Consequences of Munich — Decline, Actual and Prospective, in the Relative Strength of the Anglo-French Combination — Improvement in the British Air Position — British and German Air Power, 1938–1940 — Germany's Population Increased by Ten Millions in 1938.

O<small>N</small> S<small>EPTEMBER</small> 30, Czechoslovakia bowed to the decisions of Munich. "They wished," they said, "to register their protest before the world against a decision in which they had no part." President Benes resigned because "he might now prove a hindrance to the developments to which our new State must adapt itself." He departed from Czechoslovakia and found shelter in England. The dismemberment of the Czechoslovak State proceeded in accordance with the Agreement. But the Germans were not the only vultures upon the carcass. Immediately after the Munich Agreement on September 30, the Polish Government sent a twenty-four-hour ultimatum to the Czechs demanding the immediate handing-over of the frontier district of Teschen. There was no means of resisting this harsh demand.

The heroic characteristics of the Polish race must not blind us to their record of folly and ingratitude which over centuries has led them through measureless suffering. We see them, in 1919, a people restored by the victory of the Western Allies after long generations of partition and servitude to be an independent Republic and one of the main Powers in Europe. Now, in 1938, over a question so minor as Teschen, they sundered themselves from all those friends in France, Britain, and the United States who had lifted them once again to a national, coherent life, and whom they were soon to need so sorely. We see them hurrying, while the might of Germany glowered up against them, to grasp their share of the pillage and ruin of Czechoslovakia. During the crisis the door was shut in the face of the British and French Ambassadors, who were denied even access to the Foreign Secretary of the Polish State. It is a mystery and tragedy of European history that a people capable of every heroic virtue, gifted, valiant, charming, as individuals, should repeatedly show such inveterate faults in almost every aspect of their governmental life. Glorious in revolt and ruin; squalid and shameful in triumph. The bravest of the brave, too often led by the vilest of the vile! And yet there were always two Polands; one struggling to proclaim the truth and the other grovelling in villainy.

We shall yet have to recount the failure of their military preparations and plans; the arrogance and errors of their policy; the awful slaughters and miseries to which they doomed themselves by their follies. Yet we shall never seek in vain for their perennial impulse to strike against tyranny and to suffer with invincible fortitude all the agonies they perpetually draw upon themselves.

* * * * *

The Hungarians had also been on the fringe of the Munich discussions. Horthy had visited Germany at the end of August, 1938, but Hitler had been very reserved in his attitude. Although he talked long with the Hungarian Regent on the afternoon of August 23, he did not reveal to him the date of his intended move against Czechoslovakia. "He himself did

not know the time. Whoever wanted to join the meal would
have to share in the cooking as well." But the hour of the meal
had not been disclosed. Now, however, the Hungarians arrived with their claims.

*   *   *   *   *

It is not easy in these latter days, when we have all passed
through years of intense moral and physical stress and exertion,
to portray for another generation the passions which raged in
Britain about the Munich Agreement. Among the Conservatives, families and friends in intimate contact were divided to
a degree the like of which I have never seen. Men and women,
long bound together by party ties, social amenities and family
connections, glared upon one another in scorn and anger. The
issue was not one to be settled by the cheering crowds which
had welcomed Mr. Chamberlain back from the airport or
blocked Downing Street and its approaches; nor by the re-
doubtable exertions of the Ministerial Whips and partisans.
We who were in a minority at the moment cared nothing for
the jokes or scowls of the Government supporters. The Cabinet was shaken to its foundations, but the event had happened,
and they held together. One Minister alone stood forth. The
First Lord of the Admiralty, Mr. Duff Cooper, resigned his great
office, which he had dignified by the mobilisation of the Fleet.
At the moment of Mr. Chamberlain's overwhelming mastery
of public opinion, he thrust his way through the exulting
throng to declare his total disagreement with its leader.

At the opening of the three days' debate on Munich, he
made his resignation speech. This was a vivid incident in our
parliamentary life. Speaking with ease and without a note, for
forty minutes he held the hostile majority of his party under
his spell. It was easy for Labour men and Liberals in hot opposition to the Government of the day to applaud him. This was
a rending quarrel within the Tory Party. Some of the truths
he uttered must be recorded here:

I besought my colleagues not to see this problem always in terms
of Czechoslovakia, not to review it always from the difficult strategic

position of that small country, but rather to say to themselves, "A moment may come when, owing to the invasion of Czechoslovakia, a European war will begin, and when that moment comes we must take part in that war, we cannot keep out of it, and there is no doubt upon which side we shall fight." Let the world know that, and it will give those who are prepared to disturb the peace reason to hold their hand.

*   *   *   *   *

Then came the last appeal from the Prime Minister on Wednesday morning. For the first time, from the beginning to the end of the four weeks of negotiations, Herr Hitler was prepared to yield an inch, an ell, perhaps, but to yield some measure to the representations of Great Britain. But I would remind the House that the message from the Prime Minister was not the first news that he had received that morning. At dawn he had learned of the mobilisation of the British Fleet. It is impossible to know what are the motives of men, and we shall probably never be satisfied as to which of these two sources of inspiration moved him most when he agreed to go to Munich; but we do know that never before had he given in, and that then he did. I had been urging the mobilisation of the Fleet for many days. I had thought that this was the kind of language which would be easier for Herr Hitler to understand than the guarded language of diplomacy or the conditional clauses of the civil service. I had urged that something in that direction might be done at the end of August and before the Prime Minister went to Berchtesgaden. I had suggested that it should accompany the mission of Sir Horace Wilson. I remember the Prime Minister stating it was the one thing that would ruin that mission, and I said it was the one thing that would lead it to success.

That is the deep difference between the Prime Minister and myself throughout these days. The Prime Minister has believed in addressing Herr Hitler through the language of sweet reasonableness. I have believed that he was more open to the language of the mailed fist.

*   *   *   *   *

The Prime Minister has confidence in the good will and in the word of Herr Hitler, although, when Herr Hitler broke the Treaty of Versailles, he undertook to keep the Treaty of Locarno, and when he broke the Treaty of Locarno, he undertook not to interfere

further, or to have further territorial claims in Europe. When he
entered Austria by force, he authorised his henchmen to give an
authoritative assurance that he would not interfere with Czechoslovakia. That was less than six months ago. Still the Prime Minister
believes that he can rely upon the good faith of Hitler.

*   *   *   *   *

The long debate was not unworthy of the emotions aroused
and the issues at stake. I well remember that when I said, "We
have sustained a total and unmitigated defeat," the storm
which met me made it necessary to pause for a while before
resuming. There was widespread and sincere admiration for
Mr. Chamberlain's persevering and unflinching efforts to maintain peace, and for the personal exertions which he had made.
It is impossible in this account to avoid marking the long series
of miscalculations, and misjudgments of men and facts, on
which he based himself; but the motives which inspired him
have never been impugned, and the course he followed required the highest degree of moral courage. To this I paid
tribute two years later in my speech after his death. The differences which arose between leading Conservatives, fierce though
they were, carried with them no lack of mutual respect, nor in
most cases did they sever, except temporarily, personal relations. It was common ground between us that the Labour and
Liberal Oppositions, now so vehement for action, had never
missed an opportunity of gaining popularity by resisting and
denouncing even the half-measures for defence which the Government had taken.

There was also a serious and practical line of argument, albeit
not to their credit, on which the Government could rest themselves. No one could deny that we were hideously unprepared
for war. Who had been more forward in proving this than I
and my friends? Great Britain had allowed herself to be far
surpassed by the strength of the German air force. All our
vulnerable points were unprotected. Barely a hundred anti-
aircraft guns could be found for the defence of the largest city
and centre of population in the world; and these were largely

in the hands of untrained men. If Hitler was honest and lasting peace had in fact been achieved, Chamberlain was right. If, unhappily, he had been deceived, at least we should gain a breathing-space to repair the worst of our neglects. These considerations, and the general relief and rejoicing that the horrors of war had been temporarily averted, commanded the loyal assent of the mass of Government supporters. The House approved the policy of His Majesty's Government, "by which war was averted in the recent crisis," by 366 to 144. The thirty or forty dissentient Conservatives could do no more than register their disapproval by abstention. This we did as a formal and united act.

In the course of my speech I said:

We really must not waste time after all this long debate upon the difference between the positions reached at Berchtesgaden, at Godesberg, and at Munich. They can be very simply epitomised, if the House will permit me to vary the metaphor. One pound was demanded at the pistol's point. When it was given, two pounds were demanded at the pistol's point. Finally, the Dictator consented to take £1 17s. 6d. and the rest in promises of good will for the future.

No one has been a more resolute and uncompromising struggler for peace than the Prime Minister. Everyone knows that. Never has there been such intense and undaunted determination to maintain and secure peace. Nevertheless, I am not quite clear why there was so much danger of Great Britain or France being involved in a war with Germany at this juncture if, in fact, they were ready all along to sacrifice Czechoslovakia. The terms which the Prime Minister brought back with him could easily have been agreed, I believe, through the ordinary diplomatic channels at any time during the summer. And I will say this, that I believe the Czechs, left to themselves and told they were going to get no help from the Western Powers, would have been able to make better terms than they have got after all this tremendous perturbation. They could hardly have had worse.

All is over. Silent, mournful, abandoned, broken, Czechoslovakia recedes into the darkness. She has suffered in every respect by her associations with France, under whose guidance and policy she has been actuated for so long.

* * * * *

I find unendurable the sense of our country falling into the
power, into the orbit and influence of Nazi Germany, and of our
existence becoming dependent upon their good will or pleasure. It
is to prevent that that I have tried my best to urge the maintenance
of every bulwark of defence — first, the timely creation of an air
force superior to anything within striking distance of our shores;
secondly, the gathering together of the collective strength of many
nations; and thirdly, the making of alliances and military conventions, all within the Covenant, in order to gather together forces
at any rate to restrain the onward movement of this power. It has
all been in vain. Every position has been successively undermined
and abandoned on specious and plausible excuses.

I do not grudge our loyal, brave people, who were ready to do
their duty no matter what the cost, who never flinched under the
strain of last week, the natural, spontaneous outburst of joy and
relief when they learned that the hard ordeal would no longer be
required of them at the moment; but they should know the truth.
They should know that there has been gross neglect and deficiency
in our defences; they should know that we have sustained a defeat
without a war, the consequences of which will travel far with us
along our road; they should know that we have passed an awful
milestone in our history, when the whole equilibrium of Europe
has been deranged, and that the terrible words have for the time
being been pronounced against the Western Democracies: "Thou
art weighed in the balance and found wanting." And do not suppose that this is the end. This is only the beginning of the reckoning. This is only the first sip, the first foretaste of a bitter cup
which will be proffered to us year by year unless, by a supreme
recovery of moral health and martial vigour, we arise again and
take our stand for freedom as in the olden time.

*   *   *   *   *

Hitler's gratitude for British good will and for the sincere
rejoicings that peace with Germany had been preserved at
Munich found only frigid expression. On October 9, less than
a fortnight after he had signed the declaration of mutual
friendship which Mr. Chamberlain had pressed upon him, he
said in a speech at Saarbruecken:

The statesmen who are opposed to us wish for peace . . . but they govern in countries whose domestic organisation makes it possible that at any time they may lose their position to make way for others who are not anxious for peace. And those others are there. It only needs that in England instead of Chamberlain, Mr. Duff Cooper or Mr. Eden or Mr. Churchill should come to power, and then we know quite well that it would be the aim of these men immediately to begin a new World War. They make no secret of the fact: they admit it openly. We know further that now, as in the past, there lurks in the background the menacing figure of that Jewish-international foe who has found a basis and a form for himself in a state turned Bolshevist. And we know further the power of a certain international press which lives only on lies and slander. That obliges us to be watchful and to remember the protection of the Reich. At any time ready for peace, but at every hour also ready to defend ourselves.

I have, therefore, decided, as I announced in my speech at Nuremberg, to continue the construction of our fortifications in the West with increased energy. I shall now also bring within the line of these fortifications the two large areas which up to the present lie in front of our fortifications — the district of Aachen [Aix-la-Chapelle] and the district of Saarbruecken.

He added:

It would be a good thing if in Great Britain people would gradually drop certain airs which they have inherited from the Versailles epoch. We cannot tolerate any longer *the tutelage of governesses.* Inquiries of British politicians concerning the fate of Germans within the frontiers of the Reich — or of others belonging to the Reich — are not in place. We for our part do not trouble ourselves about similar things in England. The outside world might often have reason enough to concern itself with its own national affairs or, for instance, with affairs in Palestine.

After the sense of relief springing from the Munich Agreement had worn off, Mr. Chamberlain and his Government found themselves confronted by a sharp dilemma. The Prime Minister had said, "I believe there will be peace for our time." But the majority of his colleagues wished to utilise "our time" to rearm as rapidly as possible. Here a division arose in the Cabinet. The sensations of alarm which the Munich crisis had aroused, the flagrant exposure of our deficiencies especially in anti-aircraft guns, dictated vehement rearmament. Hitler, on the other hand, was shocked at such a mood. "Is this the trust and friendship," he might have pretended, "of our Munich Pact? If we are friends and you trust us, why is it necessary for you to rearm? Let me have the arms, and you show the trust." But this view, though it would have been thoroughly justified on the data presented to Parliament, carried no conviction. There was a strong forward surge for invigorated rearmament. And this, of course, was criticised by the German Government and its inspired press. However, there was no doubt of the opinion of the British nation. While rejoicing at being delivered from war by the Prime Minister and cheering peace slogans to the echo, they felt the need of weapons acutely. All the service departments put in their claims and referred to the alarming shortages which the crisis had exposed. The Cabinet reached an agreeable compromise on the basis of all possible preparations without disturbing the trade of the country or irritating the Germans and Italians by large-scale measures.

*   *   *   *   *

It was to Mr. Chamberlain's credit that he did not yield to temptations and pressures to seek a general election on the morrow of Munich. This could only have led to greater confusion. Nevertheless, the winter months were anxious and depressing to those Conservatives who had criticised and refused to vote for the Munich settlement. Each of us was attacked in his constituency by the Conservative Party machine, and many there were, who a year later were our ardent supporters, who agitated against us. In my own constituency, the Epping Division, matters came to such a pass that I had to make it clear that if a resolution of censure were carried against me in my local Association, I should immediately resign my seat and fight a by-election. However, my ever-faithful and tireless champion and chairman, Sir James Hawkey, with a strong circle of determined men and women, fought the ground inch by inch and stood by me, and at the decisive meeting of the Association I received in this murky hour a vote of confidence of three to two. But it was a gloomy winter.

In November, we had another debate on national defence in which I spoke at length.

Mr. Duff Cooper to Mr. Churchill.   19.XI.38.

I am very distressed to hear that you resented the reference that I made to you in my speech in the House last Thursday. I cannot see why you should. I merely said that I thought that all the P.M. meant by his reference to 1914 was that any inquiry after mobilisation would always show up gaps and deficiencies, and that therefore he had hardly merited the rebuke you delivered to him. I might, of course, have omitted all reference to you, but I think it is always a good thing in debate to hang one's arguments on to previous speeches. Nor was my position on Thursday quite simple. Your great philippic, which I enjoyed immensely and admired still more, was an onslaught on the Government's record over a period of three years, during the whole of which, except the last six weeks, I was a member of the Government. You could hardly expect me, therefore, to say that I entirely agreed with you and to vote accordingly. However, I am not the less sorry to have hurt you, whether your reasons for feeling hurt are good or bad, and I hope you will forgive me because your friendship, your companionship, and your advice are very, very precious to me.

Mr. Churchill to Mr. Duff Cooper.   22.XI.38.

Thank you so much for your letter, which I was very glad to get. In the position in which our small band of friends now is, it is a great mistake ever to take points off one another. The only rule is: Help each other when you can, but never harm. – Never help the Bear. With your facility of speech it ought to be quite easy to make your position clear without showing differences from me. I will always observe this rule. Although there was nothing in what you said to which I could possibly object, yet the fact that you went out of your way to answer me led several of my friends to wonder whether there was not some purpose behind it; for instance, the desire to isolate me as much as possible from the other Conservatives who disagree with the Government. I did not credit this myself, and I am entirely reassured by your charming letter. We are so few, enemies so many, the cause so great, that we cannot afford to weaken each other in any way.

I thought the parts of your speech which I heard very fine indeed, especially the catalogue of disasters which we have sustained in the last three years. I don't know how you remembered them all without a note.

I am, of course, sorry about the debate. Chamberlain has now got away with everything. Munich is dead, the unpreparedness is forgotten, and there is to be no real, earnest, new effort to arm the nation. Even the breathing-space, purchased at a hideous cost, is to be wasted. It was my distress at these public matters that made me grumpy when you suggested supper, for I did not then know what you had said in the early part of your speech.

But anyway, count always upon your sincere friend.

*   *   *   *   *

On November 1, a nonentity, Doctor Hacha, was elected to the vacant Presidency of the remnants of Czechoslovakia. A new Government took office in Prague. "Conditions in Europe and the world in general," said the Foreign Minister of this forlorn administration, "are not such that we should hope for a period of calm in the near future." Hitler thought so too. A formal division of the spoils was made by Germany at the beginning of November. Poland was not disturbed in her occupation of Teschen. The Slovaks, who had been used as a pawn by Germany, obtained a precarious autonomy. Hungary received a piece of flesh at the expense of Slovakia. When these consequences of Munich were raised in the House of Commons, Mr. Chamberlain explained that the French and British offer of an international guarantee to Czechoslovakia, which had been given after the Munich Pact, did not affect the existing frontiers of that State, but referred only to the hypothetical question of unprovoked aggression.

What we are doing now [he said with much detachment] is witnessing the readjustment of frontiers laid down in the Treaty of Versailles. I do not know whether the people who were responsible for those frontiers thought they would remain permanently as they were laid down. I doubt very much whether they did. They probably expected that from time to time the frontiers would have to be adjusted. It is impossible to conceive that those people would be such supermen as to be able to see what would be the right frontiers for all time. The question is not whether those frontiers should be readjusted from time to time, but whether they should be readjusted by negotiation and discussion or be readjusted by war. Readjustment is going on, and in the case of the Hungarian frontier arbitration by Germany and Italy has been accepted by Czechoslovakia and Hungary for the final determination of the frontier between them. I think I have said enough about Czechoslovakia. . . .

There was, however, to be a later occasion.

* * * * *

I wrote on November 17, 1938:

Everyone must recognise that the Prime Minister is pursuing a policy of a most decided character and of capital importance. He has his own strong view about what to do, and about what is going to happen. He has his own standard of values; he has his own angle of vision. He believes that he can make a good settlement for Europe and for the British Empire by coming to terms with Herr Hitler and Signor Mussolini. No one impugns his motives. No one doubts his conviction or his courage. Besides all this, he has the power to do what he thinks best. Those who take a different view, both of the principles of our foreign policy and of the facts and probabilities with which our country has to deal, are bound to recognise that we have no power at all to prevent him, by the resources and methods which are at his disposal, from taking the course in which he sincerely believes. He is willing to take the responsibility; he has the right to take the responsibility; and we are going to learn, in a comparatively short time, what he proposes should happen to us.

The Prime Minister is persuaded that Herr Hitler seeks no further territorial expansion upon the Continent of Europe; that the mastering and absorption of the Republic of Czechoslovakia has satiated the appetite of the German Nazi régime. It may be that he wishes to induce the Conservative Party to return to Germany the mandated territories in British possession, or what is judged to be their full equivalent. He believes that this act of restoration will bring about prolonged good and secure relations between Great

Britain and Germany. He believes further that these good relations can be achieved without weakening in any way the fundamental ties of self-preservation which bind us to the French Republic, which ties, it is common ground between us all, must be preserved. Mr. Chamberlain is convinced that all this will lead to general agreement, to the appeasement of the discontented Powers, and to a lasting peace.

But all lies in the regions of hope and speculation. A whole set of contrary possibilities must be held in mind. He may ask us to submit to things which we cannot endure; he may be forced to ask us to submit to things which we cannot endure. Or again, the other side in this difficult negotiation may not act in the same spirit of good will and good faith as animates the Prime Minister. What we have to give, what we are made to give, may cost us dear, but it may not be enough. It may involve great injury and humbling to the British Empire, but it may not stay or even divert for more than a few months, if that, the march of events upon the Continent. *By this time next year we shall know whether the Prime Minister's view of Herr Hitler and the German Nazi Party is right or wrong. By this time next year we shall know whether the policy of appeasement has appeased, or whether it has only stimulated a more ferocious appetite.* All we can do in the meanwhile is to gather forces of resistance and defence, so that if the Prime Minister should unhappily be wrong, or misled, or deceived, we can at the worst keep body and soul together.

*   *   *   *   *

Whatever might be thought of "Peace in our time," Mr. Chamberlain was more than ever alive to the need for dividing Italy from Germany. He hopefully believed that he had made friends with Hitler; to complete his work he must gain Mussolini's Italy as a counterpoise to the dear-bought reconciliation with Germany. In this renewed approach to the Italian Dictator, he had to carry France with him. There must be love all round. We shall study the result of these overtures in the next chapter.

Late in November, the Prime Minister and Lord Halifax visited Paris. The French Ministers agreed without enthusiasm to Mr. Chamberlain's suggestion of his visit to Rome; but he and Lord Halifax were glad to learn that the French were now planning to imitate the British declaration on the future of Anglo-German relations signed by Chamberlain and Hitler at Munich. On November 27, 1938, M. Bonnet sent a message to the French Ambassador in Washington describing this intention of the French Government: "Mr. Neville Chamberlain and Lord Halifax, in the course of discussions held in Paris yesterday, clearly expressed their satisfaction at a declaration which they regarded as being of a character, like that of the Anglo-German declaration, which would constitute an immediate contribution to the work of international appeasement." [1] For the purpose of these discussions, Ribbentrop came to Paris, bringing with him Doctor Schacht. The Germans hoped, not only for a general statement of good intentions, but for a concrete economic agreement. They obtained the former, which was signed in Paris on December 6, but even M. Bonnet was not prepared to accept the latter, in spite of considerable temptation to pose as the architect of Franco-German understanding.

The mission of Ribbentrop to Paris had also a deeper motive. Just as Mr. Chamberlain hoped to split Rome from Berlin, so Hitler believed that he could divide Paris from London. M. Bonnet's version of his talk with Ribbentrop on this subject is not without interest:

In regard to Great Britain, I indicated to M. Ribbentrop the rôle which the improvement of Anglo-German relations must play in any developments of the policy of European appeasement, which was considered as the essential object of any Franco-German undertaking. The German Foreign Minister made efforts to throw upon the British Government the responsibility for the present state of affairs. The Government, and particularly the British press, after having appeared to show, on the morrow of Munich, a certain comprehension, had adopted the most disappointing attitude towards the Government of Berlin. . . . The manifestations multiplied in Parliament by Messrs. Duff Cooper, Churchill, Eden, and Morrison, and certain newspaper articles, have been strongly resented in

[1] *Livre Jaune Français,* pages 35–37.

Germany, where one had not been able to restrain the reactions
of the press. I emphasised anew the fundamental and unshakable
character of Anglo-French solidarity, indicating very clearly that a
real Franco-German *détente* could not be conceivable in the long-
run without a parallel Anglo-German *détente*.[2]

*   *   *   *   *

The question has been debated whether Hitler or the Allies
gained the more in strength in the year that followed Munich.
Many persons in Britain who knew our nakedness felt a sense
of relief as each month our air force developed and the Hurricane and Spitfire types approached issue. The number of
formed squadrons grew and the ack-ack guns multiplied. Also
the general pressure of industrial preparation for war continued to quicken. But these improvements, invaluable though
they seemed, were petty compared with the mighty advance in
German armaments. As has been explained, munition production on a nation-wide plan is a four years' task. The first year
yields nothing; the second very little; the third a lot, and the
fourth a flood. Hitler's Germany in this period was already in
the third or fourth year of intense preparation under conditions of grip and drive which were almost the same as those of
war. Britain, on the other hand, had only been moving on a
non-emergency basis, with a weaker impulse and on a far
smaller scale. In 1938/39, British military expenditure of all
kinds reached £304,000,000,[3] and German was at least £1,500,-
000,000. It is probable that in this last year before the outbreak, Germany manufactured at least double, and possibly
treble, the munitions of Britain and France put together, and
also that her great plants for tank production reached full
capacity. They were, therefore, getting weapons at a far higher
rate than we.

The subjugation of Czechoslovakia robbed the Allies of the
Czech Army of twenty-one regular divisions, fifteen or sixteen
second-line divisions already mobilised, and also their moun-

---

2 *Ibid.*, pages 43–44.
3 1937/38: £234,000,000. 1948/39: £304,000,000. 1939/40: £367,000,000.

tain fortress line which, in the days of Munich, had required the deployment of thirty German divisions, or the main strength of the mobile and fully trained German Army. According to Generals Halder and Jodl, there were but thirteen German divisions, of which only five were composed of first-line troops, left in the West at the time of the Munich arrangement. We certainly suffered a loss through the fall of Czechoslovakia equivalent to some thirty-five divisions. Besides this the Skoda Works, the second most important arsenal in Central Europe, the production of which between August, 1938, and September, 1939, was in itself nearly equal to the actual output of British arms factories in that period, was made to change sides adversely. While all Germany was working under intense and almost war pressure, French Labour had achieved as early as 1936 the long desired forty-hours week.

Even more disastrous was the alteration in the relative strength of the French and German Armies. With every month that passed, from 1938 onwards the German Army not only increased in numbers and formations, and in the accumulation of reserves, but in quality and maturity. The advance in training and general proficiency kept pace with the ever-augmenting equipment. No similar improvement or expansion was open to the French Army. It was being overtaken along every path. In 1935, France, unaided by her previous allies, could have invaded and reoccupied Germany almost without serious fighting. In 1936, there could still be no doubt of her overwhelmingly superior strength. We now know, from the German revelations, that this continued in 1938, and it was the knowledge of their weakness which led the German High Command to do their utmost to restrain Hitler from every one of the successful strokes by which his fame was enhanced. In the year after Munich which we are now examining, the German Army, though still weaker in trained reserves than the French, approached its full efficiency. As it was based upon a population double as large as that of France, it was only a question of time when it would become by every test the stronger. In morale also the Germans had the advantage. The desertion of an ally, espe-

cially from fear of war, saps the spirit of any army. The sense
of being forced to yield depresses both officers and men. While
on the German side confidence, success, and the sense of growing power inflamed the martial instincts of the race, the admission of weakness discouraged the French soldiers of every rank.

*   *   *   *   *

There is, however, one vital sphere in which we began to
overtake Germany and improve our own position. In 1938, the
process of replacing British biplane fighters, like the Gladiators,
by modern types of Hurricanes and later Spitfires had only just
begun. In September of 1938, we had but five squadrons remounted on Hurricanes. Moreover, reserves and spares for the
older aircraft had been allowed to drop, since they were going
out of use. The Germans were well ahead of us in remounting
with modern fighter types. They already had good numbers
of the M.E. 109 against which our old aircraft would have
fared very ill. Throughout 1939, our position improved as
more squadrons were remounted. In July of that year we had
twenty-six squadrons of modern eight-gun fighters, though
there had been little time to build up a full scale of reserves
and spares. By July, 1940, at the time of the Battle of Britain,
we had on the average forty-seven squadrons of modern fighters
available.

On the German side the figures of strength increased as
follows:

1938	Bombers	1,466
	Fighters	920
1939	Bombers	1,553
	Fighters	1,090
1940	Bombers	1,558
	Fighters	1,290

The Germans had in fact done most of their air expansion
both in quantity and quality before the war began. Our effort
was later than theirs by nearly two years. Between 1939 and
1940, they made a twenty per cent increase only, whereas our
increase in modern fighter aircraft was eighty per cent. The

year 1938 in fact found us sadly deficient in quality, and although by 1939 we had gone some way towards meeting the disparity, we were still relatively worse off than in 1940, when the test came.

We might in 1938 have had air raids on London, for which we were lamentably unprepared. There was, however, no possibility of a decisive Air Battle of Britain until the Germans had occupied France and the Low Countries, and thus obtained the necessary bases in close striking distance of our shores. Without these bases they could not have escorted their bombers with the fighter aircraft of those days. The German armies were not capable of defeating the French in 1938 or 1939.

The vast tank production with which they broke the French Front did not come into existence till 1940, and in the face of the French superiority in the West and an unconquered Poland in the East, they could certainly not have concentrated the whole of their air power against England as they were able to do when France had been forced to surrender. This takes no account either of the attitude of Russia or of whatever resistance Czechoslovakia might have made. I have thought it right to set out the figures of relative air power in the period concerned, but they do not in any way alter the conclusions which I have recorded.

For all the above reasons, the year's breathing-space said to be "gained" by Munich left Britain and France in a much worse position compared to Hitler's Germany than they had been at the Munich crisis.

*   *   *   *   *

Finally there is this staggering fact: that in the single year 1938, Hitler had annexed to the Reich, and brought under his absolute rule 6,750,000 Austrians and 3,500,000 Sudetens, a total of over ten millions of subjects, toilers, and soldiers. Indeed the dread balance had turned in his favour.

19

Prague, Albania, and the Polish Guarantee

January–April, 1939

Chamberlain's Visit to Rome — German Concentrations Towards Czechoslovakia — Ministerial Optimism — Hitler Invades Czechoslovakia — Chamberlain's Speech at Birmingham — A Complete Change of Policy — My Letter to the Prime Minister of March 31 — The Soviet Government's Proposal for a Six-Power Conference — The British Guarantee to Poland — A Word with Colonel Beck — The Italian Landing in Albania, April 7, 1939 — Faulty Disposition of the British Mediterranean Fleet — My Speech in the House of Commons of April 13 — My Letter to Lord Halifax — Meeting of Goering, Mussolini, and Ciano on War Measures — German Strategic Advantages of the Annexation of Czechoslovakia — The Government Introduces Conscription — Weak Attitude of the Labour and Liberal Oppositions — Agitation for a National Government in Britain — Sir Stafford Cripps' Appeals — Mr. Stanley's Offer to Resign.

M^R. CHAMBERLAIN continued to believe that he had only to form a personal contact with the Dictators to effect a marked improvement in the world situation. He little knew that their decisions were taken. In a hopeful spirit he proposed that he and Lord Halifax should visit Italy in January. After some delay an invitation was extended, and on January 11 the meeting took place. It makes one flush to read in Ciano's *Diary* the comments which were made behind the Italian scene about our country and its representatives.

Essentially [writes Ciano] the visit was kept in a minor key. . . . Effective contact has not been made. How far apart we are from

these people! It is another world. We were talking about it after
dinner to the Duce. "These men," said Mussolini, "are not made
of the same stuff as Francis Drake and the other magnificent
adventurers who created the Empire. They are after all the tired
sons of a long line of rich men." . . .

The British [noted Ciano] do not want to fight. They try to
draw back as slowly as possible, but they do not want to fight. . . .
Our conversations with the British have ended. Nothing was
accomplished. I have telephoned to Ribbentrop saying it was a
fiasco, absolutely innocuous. . . . Chamberlain's eyes filled with
tears as the train started moving and his countrymen started singing, "For he's a jolly good fellow." "What is this little song?"
asked Mussolini. . . .

And then a fortnight later:

Lord Perth has submitted for our approval the outlines of the
speech that Chamberlain will make in the House of Commons in
order that we may suggest changes if necessary. The Duce approved it, and commented: "I believe this is the first time that the
head of the British Government has submitted to a foreign Government the outlines of one of his speeches. It's a bad sign for them." [1]

However, in the end it was Ciano and Mussolini who went to
their doom.

Meanwhile, on January 18, Ribbentrop was at Warsaw to
open the diplomatic offensive against Poland. The absorption
of Czechoslovakia was to be followed by the encirclement of
Poland. The first stage in this operation would be the cutting-
off of Poland from the sea by the assertion of German sovereignty in Danzig and by the prolongation of the German
control of the Baltic to the vital Lithuanian port of Memel.
The Polish Government displayed strong resistance to this
pressure, and for a while Hitler watched and waited for the
campaigning season.

During the second week of March, rumours gathered of
troop movements in Germany and Austria, particularly in the
Vienna-Salzburg region. Forty German divisions were reported
to be mobilised on a war footing. Confident of German sup-

[1] Ciano, *Diary, 1939–43* (edited by Malcolm Muggeridge), pages 9–10.

port, the Slovaks were planning the separation of their territory
from the Czechoslovak Republic. Colonel Beck, relieved to see
the Teutonic wind blowing in another direction, declared publicly in Warsaw that his Government had full sympathy with
the aspirations of the Slovaks. Father Tiso, the Slovak leader,
was received by Hitler in Berlin with the honours due to a
Prime Minister. On the twelfth Mr. Chamberlain, questioned
in Parliament about the guarantee of the Czechoslovak frontier, reminded the House that this proposal had been directed
against unprovoked aggression. No such aggression had yet
taken place. He did not have long to wait.

*   *   *   *   *

A wave of perverse optimism had swept across the British
scene during these March days. In spite of the growing stresses
in Czechoslovakia under intense German pressure from without and from within, the Ministers and newspapers identified
with the Munich Agreement did not lose faith in the policy
into which they had drawn the nation. Even the secession of
Slovakia as a result of constant Nazi intrigue, and the troop
movements apparent in Germany, did not prevent the Home
Secretary from speaking to his constituents on March 10 about
his hopes of a Five Years' Peace Plan which would lead in
time to the creation of "a Golden Age." A plan for a
commercial treaty with Germany was still being hopefully
discussed. The famous periodical, *Punch*, produced a
cartoon showing John Bull waking with a gasp of relief from
a nightmare, while all the evil rumours, fancies, and suspicions
of the night were flying away out of the window. On the very
day when this appeared, Hitler launched his ultimatum to the
tottering Czech Government, bereft of their fortified line by
the Munich decisions. German troops, marching into Prague,
assumed absolute control of the unresisting State. I remember
sitting with Mr. Eden in the smoking-room of the House of
Commons when the editions of the evening papers recording
these events came in. Even those who, like us, had no illusions
and had testified earnestly were surprised at the sudden vio-

lence of this outrage. One could hardly believe that with all their secret information His Majesty's Government could be so far adrift. March 14 witnessed the dissolution and subjugation of the Czechoslovak Republic. The Slovaks formally declared their independence. Hungarian troops, backed surreptitiously by Poland, crossed into the eastern province of Czechoslovakia, or the Carpatho-Ukraine, which they demanded. Hitler, having arrived in Prague, proclaimed a German Protectorate over Czechoslovakia, which was thereby incorporated in the Reich.

On March 15, Mr. Chamberlain had to say to the House: "The occupation of Bohemia by German military forces began at six o'clock this morning. The Czech people have been ordered by their Government not to offer resistance." He then proceeded to state that the guarantee he had given Czechoslovakia no longer in his opinion had validity. After Munich, five months before, the Dominions Secretary, Sir Thomas Inskip, had said of this guarantee: "His Majesty's Government feel under a moral obligation to Czechoslovakia to keep the guarantee [as though it were technically in force]. . . . In the event, therefore, of an act of unprovoked aggression against Czechoslovakia, His Majesty's Government would certainly be bound to take all steps in their power to see that the integrity of Czechoslovakia is preserved." "That," said the Prime Minister, "remained the position until yesterday. But the position has altered since the Slovak Diet declared the independence of Slovakia. The effect of this declaration put an end by internal disruption to the State whose frontiers we had proposed to guarantee, and His Majesty's Government cannot accordingly hold themselves bound by this obligation."

This seemed decisive. "It is natural," he said, in conclusion, "that I should bitterly regret what has now occurred, but do not let us on that account be deflected from our course. Let us remember that the desire of all the peoples of the world still remains concentrated on the hopes of peace."

Mr. Chamberlain was due to speak at Birmingham two days later. I fully expected that he would accept what had happened

with the best grace possible. This would have been in harmony
with his statement to the House. I even imagined that he
might claim credit for the Government for having, by its foresight at Munich, decisively detached Great Britain from the
fate of Czechoslovakia and indeed of Central Europe. "How
fortunate," he might have said, "that we made up our minds
in September last not to be drawn into the Continental
struggle! We are now free to allow these broils between countries which mean nothing to us to settle themselves without
expense in blood or treasure." This would, after all, have been
a logical decision following upon the disruption of Czechoslovakia agreed to at Munich and endorsed by a majority of the
British people, so far as they understood what was going on.
This also was the view taken by some of the strongest supporters of the Munich Pact. I therefore awaited the Birmingham declaration with anticipatory contempt.

The Prime Minister's reaction surprised me. He had conceived himself as having a special insight into Hitler's character, and the power to measure with shrewdness the limits of
German action. He believed, with hope, that there had been
a true meeting of minds at Munich, and that he, Hitler, and
Mussolini had together saved the world from the infinite horrors of war. Suddenly as by an explosion his faith and all that
had followed from his actions and his arguments was shattered.
Responsible as he was for grave misjudgments of facts, having
deluded himself and imposed his errors on his subservient colleagues and upon the unhappy British public opinion, he none
the less between night and morning turned his back abruptly
upon his past. If Chamberlain failed to understand Hitler,
Hitler completely underrated the nature of the British Prime
Minister. He mistook his civilian aspect and passionate desire
for peace for a complete explanation of his personality, and
thought that his umbrella was his symbol. He did not realise
that Neville Chamberlain had a very hard core, and that he
did not like being cheated.

The Birmingham speech struck a new note. "His tone,"
says his biographer, "was very different. . . . Informed by fuller

knowledge and by strong representations as to opinion in the House, the public, and the Dominions, he threw aside the speech long drafted on domestic questions and social service, and grasped the nettle." He reproached Hitler with a flagrant personal breach of faith about the Munich Agreement. He quoted all the assurances Hitler had given: "This is the last territorial claim which I have to make in Europe." "I shall not be interested in the Czech State any more, and I can guarantee it. We don't want any Czechs any more."

I am convinced [said the Prime Minister] that after Munich the great majority of the British people shared my honest desire that that policy should be carried farther, but today I share their disappointment, their indignation, that those hopes have been so wantonly shattered. How can these events this week be reconciled with those assurances which I have read out to you?

Who can fail to feel his heart go out in sympathy to the proud, brave people who have so suddenly been subjected to this invasion, whose liberties are curtailed, whose national independence is gone? . . . Now we are told that this seizure of territory has been necessitated by disturbances in Czechoslovakia. . . . If there were disorders, were they not fomented from without? . . . Is this the last attack upon a small state or is it to be followed by another? Is this in fact a step in the direction of an attempt to dominate the world by force?

It is not easy to imagine a greater contradiction to the mood and policy of the Prime Minister's statement two days earlier in the House of Commons. He must have been through a period of intense stress. On the fifteenth he had said: "Do not let us be deflected from our course." But this was "Right-about-turn."

Moreover, Chamberlain's change of heart did not stop at words. The next "small state" on Hitler's list was Poland. When the gravity of the decision and all those who had to be consulted are borne in mind, the period must have been busy. Within a fortnight (March 31) the Prime Minister said in Parliament:

I now have to inform the House that . . . in the event of any action which clearly threatened Polish independence and which the Polish Government accordingly considered it vital to resist with their national forces, His Majesty's Government would feel themselves bound at once to lend the Polish Government all support in their power. They have given the Polish Government an assurance to this effect.

I may add that the French Government have authorised me to make it plain that they stand in the same position in this matter as do His Majesty's Government. . . . [And later] The Dominions have been kept fully informed.

This was no time for recriminations about the past. The guarantee to Poland was supported by the leaders of all parties and groups in the House. "God helping, we can do no other," was what I said. At the point we had reached, it was a necessary action. But no one who understood the situation could doubt that it meant in all human probability a major war in which we should be involved.

*   *   *   *   *

In this sad tale of wrong judgments formed by well-meaning and capable people, we now reach our climax. That we should all have come to this pass makes those responsible, however honourable their motives, blameworthy before history. Look back and see what we had successively accepted or thrown away: a Germany disarmed by solemn treaty; a Germany rearmed in violation of a solemn treaty; air superiority or even air parity cast away; the Rhineland forcibly occupied and the Siegfried Line built or building; the Berlin-Rome Axis established; Austria devoured and digested by the Reich; Czechoslovakia deserted and ruined by the Munich Pact; its fortress line in German hands; its mighty arsenal of Skoda henceforward making munitions for the German armies; President Roosevelt's effort to stabilise or bring to a head the European situation by the intervention of the United States waved aside with one hand, and Soviet Russia's undoubted willingness to join the Western Powers and go all lengths to save Czechoslovakia ignored on the other; the services of thirty-five Czech divisions against the still unripened German Army cast away, when Great Britain could herself supply only two to strengthen the front in France — all gone with the wind.

And now, when every one of these aids and advantages has been squandered and thrown away, Great Britain advances, leading France by the hand, to guarantee the integrity of Poland — of that very Poland which with hyena appetite had only six months before joined in the pillage and destruction of the Czechoslovak State. There was sense in fighting for Czechoslovakia in 1938 when the German Army could scarcely put half a dozen trained divisions on the Western Front, when the French with nearly sixty or seventy divisions could most certainly have rolled forward across the Rhine or into the Ruhr. But this had been judged unreasonable, rash, below the level of modern intellectual thought and morality. Yet now at last the two Western Democracies declared themselves ready to stake their lives upon the territorial integrity of Poland. History, which we are told is mainly the record of the crimes, follies, and miseries of mankind, may be scoured and ransacked to find a parallel to this sudden and complete reversal of five or six years' policy of easy-going placatory appeasement, and its transformation almost overnight into a readiness to accept an obviously imminent war on far worse conditions and on the greatest scale.

Moreover, how could we protect Poland and make good our guarantee? Only by declaring war upon Germany and attacking a stronger Western Wall and a more powerful German Army than those from which we had recoiled in September, 1938. Here is a line of milestones to disaster. Here is a catalogue of surrenders, at first when all was easy and later when things were harder, to the ever-growing German power. But now at last was the end of British and French submission. Here was decision at last, taken at the worst possible moment and on the least satisfactory ground, which must surely lead to the slaughter of tens of millions of people. Here was the righteous cause deliberately and with a refinement of inverted artistry committed to mortal battle after its assets and advantages had been

so improvidently squandered. Still, if you will not fight for
the right when you can easily win without bloodshed; if you
will not fight when your victory will be sure and not too costly;
you may come to the moment when you will have to fight with
all the odds against you and only a precarious chance of survival. There may even be a worse case. You may have to fight
when there is no hope of victory, because it is better to perish
than live as slaves.

*   *   *   *   *

The Birmingham speech brought me much closer to Mr.
Chamberlain:

I venture to reiterate the suggestion which I made to you in the
lobby yesterday afternoon, that the anti-aircraft defences should
forthwith be placed in full preparedness. Such a step could not be
deemed aggressive, yet it would emphasise the seriousness of the
action H.M. Government are taking on the Continent. The bringing together of these officers and men would improve their efficiency
with every day of their embodiment. The effect at home would
be one of confidence rather than alarm. But it is of Hitler I am
thinking mostly. He must be under intense strain at this moment.
He knows we are endeavouring to form a coalition to restrain his
further aggression. With such a man anything is possible. The
temptation to make a surprise attack on London, or on the aircraft
factories, about which I am even more anxious, would be removed
if it was known that all was ready. There could, in fact, be no
surprise, and therefore the incentive to the extremes of violence
would be removed and more prudent counsels might prevail.

In August, 1914, I persuaded Mr. Asquith to let me send the
Fleet to the North so that it could pass the Straits of Dover and the
Narrow Seas *before* the diplomatic situation had become hopeless.
It seems to me that manning the anti-aircraft defences now stands
in a very similar position, and I hope you will not mind my putting
this before you.

*   *   *   *   *

The Poles had gained Teschen by their shameful attitude
towards the liquidation of the Czechoslovak State. They were
soon to pay their own forfeits. On March 21, when Ribbentrop saw M. Lipski, the Polish Ambassador in Berlin, he

adopted a sharper tone than in previous discussions. The occupation of Bohemia and the creation of satellite Slovakia brought the German Army to the southern frontiers of Poland. Lipski told Ribbentrop that the Polish man-in-the-street could not understand why the Reich had assumed the protection of Slovakia, that protection being directed against Poland. He also inquired about the recent conversations between Ribbentrop and the Lithuanian Foreign Minister. Did they affect Memel? He received his answer two days later (March 23). German troops occupied Memel.

The means of organising any resistance to German aggression in Eastern Europe were now almost exhausted. Hungary was in the German camp. Poland had stood aside from the Czechs, and was unwilling to work closely with Rumania. Neither Poland nor Rumania would accept Russian intervention against Germany across their territories. The key to a Grand Alliance was an understanding with Russia. On March 21, the Russian Government, which was profoundly affected by all that was taking place, and in spite of having been left outside the door in the Munich crisis, proposed a Six-Power Conference. On this subject also Mr. Chamberlain had decided views. In a private letter he wrote on March 26:

I must confess to the most profound distrust of Russia. I have no belief whatever in her ability to maintain an effective offensive, even if she wanted to. And I distrust her motives, which seem to me to have little connection with our ideas of liberty, and to be concerned only with getting everyone else by the ears. Moreover, she is both hated and suspected by many of the smaller states, notably by Poland, Rumania, and Finland.[2]

The Soviet proposal for a Six-Power Conference was therefore coldly received and allowed to drop.

The possibilities of weaning Italy from the Axis, which had loomed so large in British official calculations, were also vanishing. On March 26, Mussolini made a violent speech asserting Italian claims against France in the Mediterranean. Secretly he was planning for the extension of Italian influence in the

[2] Feiling, op. cit., page 603.

Balkans and the Adriatic, to balance the German advance in Central Europe. His plans for invading Albania were now ready.

On March 29, Mr. Chamberlain announced in Parliament the planned doubling of the Territorial Army, including an increase on paper of 210,000 men (unequipped). On April 3, Keitel, Hitler's Chief of Staff, issued the secret "Directive for the Armed Forces, 1939/40," in regard to Poland — "Case White" was the code name. The Fuehrer added the following directions: "Preparations must be made in such a way that the operations can be carried out at any time from September 1 onwards."

* * * * *

On April 4, the Government invited me to a luncheon at the Savoy in honour of Colonel Beck, the Polish Foreign Minister, who had come upon an official visit of significance. I had met him the year before on the Riviera, when we had lunched alone together. I now asked him: "Will you get back all right in your special train through Germany to Poland?" He replied: "I think we shall have time for that."

* * * * *

A new crisis now opened upon us.

At dawn on April 7, 1939, Italian forces landed in Albania, and after a brief scuffle took over the country. As Czechoslovakia was to be the base for aggression against Poland, so Albania would be the springboard for Italian action against Greece and for the neutralising of Yugoslavia. The British Government had already undertaken a commitment in the interests of peace in Northeastern Europe. What about the threat developing in the Southeast? The vessel of peace was springing a leak from every beam.

On April 9, I wrote to the Prime Minister:

I am hoping that Parliament will be recalled at the latest on Tuesday, and I write to say how much I hope the statements which you will be able to make will enable the same united front to be presented as in the case of the Polish Agreement.

It seems to me, however, that hours now count. It is imperative for us to recover the initiative in diplomacy. This can no longer be done by declarations or by the denouncing of the Anglo-Italian Agreement or by the withdrawal of our Ambassador.

It is freely stated in the Sunday papers that we are offering a guarantee to Greece and Turkey. At the same time I notice that several newspapers speak of a British naval occupation of Corfu. Had this step been already taken, it would afford the best chance of maintaining peace. If it is not taken by us, of course with Greek consent, it seems to me that after the publicity given to the idea in the press and the obvious needs of the situation, Corfu will be speedily taken by Italy. Its recapture would then be impossible. On the other hand, if we are there first, an attack even upon a few British ships would confront Mussolini with beginning a war of aggression upon England. This direct issue gives the best chance to all the forces in Italy which are opposed to a major war with England. So far from intensifying the grave risks now open, it diminishes them. But action ought to be taken tonight.

What is now at stake is nothing less than the whole of the Balkan Peninsula. If these states remain exposed to German and Italian pressure while we appear, as they may deem it, incapable of action, they will be forced to make the best terms possible with Berlin and Rome. How forlorn then will our position become! We shall be committed to Poland, and thus involved in the East of Europe, while at the same time cutting off from ourselves all hope of that large alliance which once effected might spell salvation.

I write the above without knowledge of the existing position of our Mediterranean Fleet, which should, of course, be concentrated and *at sea,* in a suitable but not too close supporting position.

The British Mediterranean Fleet was in fact scattered. Of our five great capital ships, one was at Gibraltar, another in the Eastern Mediterranean, and the remaining three were lolling about inside or outside widely separated Italian ports, two of them not protected by their flotillas. The destroyer flotillas themselves were dispersed along the European and African shores, and a large number of cruisers were crowded in Malta Harbour without the protection of the powerful anti-aircraft batteries of battleships. At the very time that the Fleet was suffered to disperse in this manner, it was known

that the Italian Fleet was concentrated in the Straits of Otranto
and that troops were being assembled and embarked for some
serious enterprise.

I challenged these careless dispositions on April 13 in the
House of Commons:

The British habit of the week-end, the great regard which the
British pay to holidays which coincide with festivals of the Church,
is studied abroad. Good Friday was also the first day after Parliament had dispersed. It was known too that on that day the British
Fleet was carrying out in a routine manner a programme long
announced. It would therefore be dispersed in all quarters. . . . I
can well believe that if our Fleet had been concentrated and
cruising in the southern parts of the Ionian Sea, the Albanian
adventure would never have been undertaken. . . .

After twenty-five years' experience in peace and war, I believe
the British Intelligence Service to be the finest of its kind in the
world. Yet we have seen, both in the case of the subjugation of
Bohemia and on the occasion of the invasion of Albania, that
Ministers of the Crown had apparently no inkling, or at any rate
no conviction, of what was coming. I cannot believe that this is
the fault of the British Secret Service.

How was it that on the eve of the Bohemian outrage Ministers
were indulging in what was called "Sunshine talk" and predicting
"the dawn of a Golden Age"? How was it that last week's holiday
routine was observed at a time when clearly something of a quite
exceptional character, the consequences of which could not be
measured, was imminent? . . . It seems to me that Ministers run the
most tremendous risks if they allow the information collected by the
Intelligence Department and sent to them, I am sure, in good time,
to be sifted and coloured and reduced in consequence and importance, and if they ever get themselves into a mood of attaching
weight only to those pieces of information which accord with their
earnest and honourable desire that the peace of the world should
remain unbroken.

All things are moving at the same moment. Year by year, month
by month, they have all been moving forward together. While we
have reached certain positions in thought, others have reached
certain positions in fact. The danger is now very near, and a great
part of Europe is to a very large extent mobilised. Millions of men

are being prepared for war. Everywhere the frontier defences are
being manned. Everywhere it is felt that some new stroke is impending. If it should fall, can there be any doubt that we should be
involved? We are no longer where we were two or three months
ago. We have committed ourselves in every direction, rightly in my
opinion, having regard to all that has happened. It is not necessary
to enumerate the countries to which directly or indirectly we have
given or are giving guarantees. What we should not have dreamt of
doing a year ago, when all was so much more hopeful, what we
should not have dreamt of doing even a month ago, we are doing
now. Surely then when we aspire to lead all Europe back from
the verge of the abyss onto the uplands of law and peace, we must
ourselves set the highest example. We must keep nothing back.
How can we bear to continue to lead our comfortable easy lives here
at home, unwilling to pronounce even the word "Compulsion,"
unwilling to take even the necessary measures by which the armies
which we have promised can alone be recruited and equipped?
The dark bitter waters are rising fast on every side. How can we
continue — let me say with particular frankness and sincerity —
with less than the full force of the nation incorporated in the
governing instrument?

I reiterated my complaints about the Fleet a few days later
in a private letter to Lord Halifax:

The dispositions of our Fleet are inexplicable. First, on Tuesday
night, April 4, the First Lord showed that the Home Fleet was in
such a condition of preparedness that the men could not even leave
the anti-aircraft guns to come below. This was the result of a scare
telegram, and was, in my opinion, going beyond what vigilance
requires. On the other hand, at the same time, the Mediterranean
Fleet was, as I described to the House, scattered in the most vulnerable disorder throughout the Mediterranean; and as photographs published in the newspapers show, the *Barham* was actually
moored alongside the Naples jetty. Now the Mediterranean Fleet
has been concentrated and is at sea, where it should be. Therefore,
no doubt all is well in the Mediterranean. But the unpreparedness
is transferred to home waters. The Atlantic Fleet, except for a few
anti-aircraft guns, has been practically out of action for some days
owing to very large numbers of men having been sent on leave.
One would have thought at least the leave could be "staggered" in

times like these. All the minesweepers are out of action refitting. How is it possible to reconcile this with the statement of tension declared to be existing on Tuesday week? It seems to be a grave departure from the procedure of continuous and reasonable vigilance. After all, the conditions prevailing now are not in principle different from those of last week. The First Sea Lord is seriously ill, so I expect a great deal falls upon Stanhope.

I write this to you for your own personal information, and in order that you can check the facts for yourself. Pray, therefore, treat my letter as strictly private, as I do not want to bother the Prime Minister with the matter, but I think you ought to know.

*   *   *   *   *

On April 15, 1939, after the declaration of the German Protectorate of Bohemia and Moravia, Goering met Mussolini and Ciano in order to explain to the Italians the progress of German preparations for war. The minutes of this meeting have been found. One passage reads — it is Goering who is speaking:

The heavy armament of Czechoslovakia shows, in any case, how dangerous it could have been, even after Munich, in the event of a serious conflict. By German action, the situation of both Axis countries was ameliorated because, among other reasons, of the economic possibilities which resulted from the transfer to Germany of the great productive capacity of Czechoslovakia. That contributes toward a considerable strengthening of the Axis against the Western Powers. Furthermore, Germany now need not keep ready a single division of protection against that country in case of a bigger conflict. This, too, is an advantage by which both Axis countries will, in the last analysis, benefit. . . . The action taken by Germany in Czechoslovakia is to be viewed as an advantage for the Axis Powers. Germany could now attack this country from two flanks, and would be within only twenty-five minutes' flying distance from the new Polish industrial centre, which had been moved farther into the interior of the country, nearer to the other Polish industrial districts, because of its proximity to the border.[3]

"The bloodless solution of the Czech conflict in the autumn of 1938 and spring of 1939 and the annexation of Slovakia,"

[3] *Nuremberg Documents, op. cit.,* Part 2, page 106.

said General von Jodl in a lecture some years after, "rounded off the territory of Greater Germany in such a way that it now became possible to consider the Polish problem on the basis of more or less favourable strategic premises." [4]

On the day of Goering's visit to Rome, President Roosevelt sent a personal message to Hitler and Mussolini urging them to give a guarantee not to undertake any further aggression for ten "or even twenty-five years, if we are to look that far ahead." The Duce at first refused to read the document, and then remarked: "A result of infantile paralysis"! He little thought he was himself to suffer a worse affliction.

* * * * *

On April 27, the Prime Minister took the serious decision to introduce conscription, although repeated pledges had been given by him against such a step. To Mr. Hore-Belisha, the Secretary of State for War, belongs the credit of forcing this belated awakening. He certainly took his political life in his hands, and several of his interviews with his chief were of a formidable character. I saw something of him in this ordeal, and he was never sure that each day in office would not be his last.

Of course, the introduction of conscription at this stage did not give us an army. It only applied to the men of twenty years of age; they had still to be trained; and after they had been trained, they had still to be armed. It was, however, a symbolic gesture of the utmost consequence to France and Poland, and to other nations on whom we had lavished our guarantees. In the debate the Opposition failed in their duty. Both Labour and Liberal Parties shrunk from facing the ancient and deep-rooted prejudice which has always existed in England against compulsory military service. The leader of the Labour Party moved that:

Whilst prepared to take all necessary steps to provide for the safety of the nation and the fulfilment of its international obligations, this House regrets that His Majesty's Government in breach

[4] *Ibid.*, page 107.

of their pledges should abandon the voluntary principle which has
not failed to provide the man-power needed for defence, and is of
opinion that the measure proposed is ill-conceived, and, so far
from adding materially to the effective defence of the country, will
promote division and discourage the national effort, and is further
evidence that the Government's conduct of affairs throughout these
critical times does not merit the confidence of the country or this
House.

—— The leader of the Liberal Party also found reasons for opposing this step. Both these men were distressed at the course
they felt bound on party grounds to take. But they both took
it and adduced a wealth of reasons. The division was on party
lines, and the Conservatives carried their policy by 380 to 143
votes. In my speech I tried my best to persuade the Opposition
to support this indispensable measure; but my efforts were
vain. I understood fully their difficulties, especially when
confronted with a Government to which they were opposed.
I must record the event, because it deprives Liberal and Labour
partisans of any right to censure the Government of the day.
They showed their own measure in relation to events only too
plainly. Presently they were to show a truer measure.

*   *   *   *   *

—— Though Mr. Chamberlain still hoped to avert war, it was
plain that he would not shrink from it if it came. Mr. Feiling
says that he noted in his diary, "Churchill's chances [of entering
the Government] improve as war becomes more probable and
vice versa." [5] This was perhaps a somewhat disdainful epitome.
There were many other thoughts in my mind besides those of
becoming once again a Minister. All the same, I understood
the Prime Minister's outlook. He knew, if there was war,
he would have to come to me, and he believed rightly that I
would answer the call. On the other hand, he feared that Hitler would regard my entry into the Government as a hostile
manifestation, and that it would thus wipe out all remaining
chances of peace. This was a natural, but a wrong view.

[5] Feiling. *op. cit.*, page 406.

None the less, one can hardly blame Mr. Chamberlain for not wishing to bring so tremendous and delicate a situation to a head for the sake of including any particular Member of the House of Commons in his Government.

In March, I had joined Mr. Eden and some thirty Conservative Members in tabling a resolution for a National Government. During the summer, there arose a very considerable stir in the country in favour of this, or at the least for my, and Mr. Eden's, inclusion in the Cabinet. Sir Stafford Cripps, in his independent position, became deeply distressed about the national danger. He visited me and various Ministers to urge the formation of what he called an "All-in Government." I could do nothing; but Mr. Stanley, President of the Board of Trade, was deeply moved. He wrote to the Prime Minister offering his own office if it would facilitate a reconstruction.

Mr. Stanley to the Prime Minister.   *June 30, 1939.*

I hesitate to write to you at a time like this when you are overwhelmed with care and worry, and only the urgency of affairs is my excuse. I suppose we all feel that the only chance of averting war this autumn is to bring home to Hitler the certainty that we shall fulfil our obligations to Poland and that aggression on his part must inevitably mean a general conflagration. All of us, as well, must have been thinking whether there is any action we can take which, without being so menacing as to invite reprisal, will be sufficiently dramatic to command attention. I myself can think of nothing which would be more effective, if it were found to be possible, than the formation now of the sort of Government which inevitably we should form at the outbreak of war. It would be a dramatic confirmation of the national unity and determination and would, I imagine, not only have a great effect in Germany, but also in the United States. It is also possible that, if at the eleventh hour some possibility of a satisfactory settlement emerged, it would be much easier for such a Government to be at all conciliatory. You, of course, must yourself have considered the possibility and must be much more conscious of possible difficulties than I could be, but I thought I would write both to let you know my views and to assure you that, if you did contemplate such a possibility, I — as I am sure all the rest of our colleagues — would gladly serve in any position, however small, either inside or outside the Government.

The Prime Minister contented himself with a formal acknowledgment.

As the weeks passed by, almost all the newspapers, led by the *Daily Telegraph* (July 3), emphasised by the *Manchester Guardian,* reflected this surge of opinion. I was surprised to see its daily recurrent and repeated expression. Thousands of enormous posters were displayed for weeks on end on metropolitan hoardings, "Churchill Must Come Back." Scores of young volunteer men and women carried sandwich-board placards with similar slogans up and down before the House of Commons. I had nothing to do with such methods of agitation, but I should certainly have joined the Government had I been invited. Here again my personal good fortune held, and all else flowed out in its logical, natural, and horrible sequence.

20

The Soviet Enigma

Hitler Denounces the Anglo-German Naval Agreement — And the Polish Non-Aggression Pact — The Soviet Proposal of a Three-Power Alliance — Dilemma of the Border States — Soviet-German Contacts Grow — The Dismissal of Litvinov — Molotov — Anglo-Soviet Negotiations — Debate of May 19 — Mr. Lloyd-George's Speech — My Statement on the European Situation — The Need of the Russian Alliance — Too Late — The "Pact of Steel" Between Germany and Italy — Soviet Diplomatic Tactics.

WE HAVE REACHED THE PERIOD when all relations between Britain and Germany were at an end. We now know, of course, that there never had been any true relationship between our two countries since Hitler came into power. He had only hoped to persuade or frighten Britain into giving him a free hand in Eastern Europe; and Mr. Chamberlain had cherished the hope of appeasing and reforming him and leading him to grace. However, the time had come when the last illusions of the British Government had been dispelled. The Cabinet was at length convinced that Nazi Germany meant war, and the Prime Minister offered guarantees and contracted alliances in every direction still open, regardless of whether we could give any effective help to the countries concerned. To the Polish guarantee was added a Rumanian guarantee, and to these an alliance with Turkey.

We must now recall the sad piece of paper which Mr. Chamberlain had got Hitler to sign at Munich and which he waved triumphantly to the crowd when he quitted his airplane at

Heston. In this he had invoked the two bonds which he assumed existed between him and Hitler and between Britain and Germany, namely, the Munich Agreement and the Anglo-German Naval Treaty. The subjugation of Czechoslovakia had destroyed the first; Hitler now brushed away the second.

Addressing the Reichstag on April 28, he said:

Since England today, both through the press and officially, upholds the view that Germany should be opposed in all circumstances, and confirms this by the policy of encirclement known to us, the basis of the Naval Treaty has been removed. I have therefore resolved to send today a communication to this effect to the British Government. This is to us not a matter of practical material importance — for I still hope that we shall be able to avoid an armaments race with England — but an action of self-respect. Should the British Government, however, wish to enter once more into negotiations with Germany on this problem, no one would be happier than I at the prospect of still being able to come to a clear and straightforward understanding.[1]

The Anglo-German Naval Agreement, which had been so marked a gain to Hitler at an important and critical moment in his policy, was now represented by him as a favour to Britain, the benefits of which would be withdrawn as a mark of German displeasure. The Fuehrer held out the hope to the British Government that he might be willing to discuss the naval problem further with His Majesty's Government, and he may even have expected that his former dupes would persist in their policy of appeasement. To him it now mattered nothing. He had Italy, and he had his air superiority; he had Austria and Czechoslovakia, with all that implied. He had his Western Wall. In the purely naval sphere he had always been building U-boats as fast as possible irrespective of any agreement. He had already as a matter of form invoked his right to build a hundred per cent of the British numbers, but this had not limited in the slightest degree the German U-boat construction programme. As for the larger vessels, he could not nearly digest the generous allowance which had been accorded

[1] *Hitler's Speeches, op. cit.,* volume 2, page 1626.

to him by the Naval Agreement. He, therefore, made fine im-
pudent play with flinging it back in the face of the simpletons
who made it.

In this same speech Hitler also denounced the German-
Polish Non-Aggression Pact. He gave as his direct reason the
Anglo-Polish Guarantee,

which would in certain circumstances compel Poland to take
military action against Germany in the event of a conflict between
Germany and any other Power, in which England in her turn
would be involved. This obligation is contrary to the agreement
which I made with Marshal Pilsudski some time ago. . . . I therefore
look upon the agreement as having been unilaterally infringed by
Poland and thereby no longer in existence. I sent a communication
to this effect to the Polish Government. . . .

After studying this speech at the time, I wrote in one of my
articles:

It seems only too probable that the glare of Nazi Germany is now
to be turned onto Poland. Herr Hitler's speeches may or may not
be a guide to his intentions, but the salient object of last Friday's
performance was obviously to isolate Poland, to make the most
plausible case against her, and to bring intensive pressure upon her.
The German Dictator seemed to suppose that he could make the
Anglo-Polish Agreement inoperative by focusing his demands on
Danzig and the Corridor. He apparently expects that those elements in Great Britain which used to exclaim, "Who would fight
for Czechoslovakia?" may now be induced to cry, "Who would fight
for Danzig and the Corridor?" He does not seem to be conscious
of the immense change which has been wrought in British public
opinion by his treacherous breach of the Munich Agreement, and
of the complete reversal of policy which this outrage brought about
in the British Government, and especially in the Prime Minister.
The denunciation of the German-Polish Non-Aggression Pact of
1934 is an extremely serious and menacing step. That pact had
been reaffirmed as recently as last January, when Ribbentrop visited
Warsaw. Like the Anglo-German Naval Treaty, it was negotiated
at the wish of Herr Hitler. Like the Naval Treaty, it gave marked
advantages to Germany. Both agreements eased Germany's position
while she was weak. The Naval Agreement amounted in fact to a

condonation by Great Britain of a breach of the military clauses of
the Treaty of Versailles, and thus stultified both the decisions of
the Stresa front and those which the Council of the League were
induced to take. The German-Polish Agreement enabled Nazi attention to be concentrated first upon Austria and later upon Czechoslovakia, with ruinous results to those unhappy countries. It temporarily weakened the relations between France and Poland and
prevented any solidarity of interests growing up among the states
of Eastern Europe. Now that it has served its purpose for Germany,
it is cast away by one-sided action. Poland is implicitly informed
that she is now in the zone of potential aggression.

*   *   *   *   *

The British Government had to consider urgently the practical implications of the guarantees given to Poland and to
Rumania. Neither set of assurances had any military value
except within the framework of a general agreement with
Russia. It was, therefore, with this object that talks at last
began in Moscow on April 15 between the British Ambassador
and M. Litvinov. Considering how the Soviet Government had
hitherto been treated, there was not much to be expected
from them now. However, on April 16 they made a formal
offer, the text of which was not published, for the creation of
a united front of mutual assistance between Great Britain,
France, and the U.S.S.R. The three Powers, with Poland added
if possible, were furthermore to guarantee those states in Central and Eastern Europe which lay under the menace of German aggression. The obstacle to such an agreement was the terror of these same border countries of receiving Soviet help in
the shape of Soviet armies marching through their territories
to defend them from the Germans, and incidentally incorporating them in the Soviet-Communist system of which they
were the most vehement opponents. Poland, Rumania, Finland, and the three Baltic States did not know whether it was
German aggression or Russian rescue that they dreaded more.
It was this hideous choice that paralysed British and French
policy.

There can, however, be no doubt, even in the after light,

that Britain and France should have accepted the Russian offer, proclaimed the Triple Alliance, and left the method by which it could be made effective in case of war to be adjusted between allies engaged against a common foe. In such circumstances a different temper prevails. Allies in war are inclined to defer a great deal to each other's wishes; the flail of battle beats upon the front, and all kinds of expedients are welcomed which, in peace, would be abhorrent. It would not be easy in a grand alliance, such as might have been developed, for one ally to enter the territory of another unless invited.

But Mr. Chamberlain and the Foreign Office were baffled by this riddle of the Sphinx. When events are moving at such speed and in such tremendous mass as at this juncture, it is wise to take one step at a time. The alliance of Britain, France, and Russia would have struck deep alarm into the heart of Germany in 1939, and no one can prove that war might not even then have been averted. The next step could have been taken with superior power on the side of the Allies. The initiative would have been regained by their diplomacy. Hitler could afford neither to embark upon the war on two fronts, which he himself had so deeply condemned, nor to sustain a check. It was a pity not to have placed him in this awkward position, which might well have cost him his life. Statesmen are not called upon only to settle easy questions. These often settle themselves. It is where the balance quivers, and the proportions are veiled in mist, that the opportunity for world-saving decisions presents itself. Having got ourselves into this awful plight of 1939, it was vital to grasp the larger hope.

It is not even now possible to fix the moment when Stalin definitely abandoned all intention of working with the Western Democracies and of coming to terms with Hitler. Indeed, it seems probable that there never was such a moment. The publication in *Nazi-Soviet Relations, 1939–41,* by the American State Department of a mass of documents captured from the archives of the German Foreign Office gives us, however, a number of facts hitherto unknown. Apparently something happened as early as February, 1939; but this was almost

certainly concerned with trading and commercial questions
affected by the status of Czechoslovakia, after Munich, which
required discussion between the two countries. The incorporation of Czechoslovakia in the Reich in mid-March magnified
these issues. Russia had some contracts with the Czechoslovak
Government for munitions from the Skoda Works. What was
to happen to these contracts now that Skoda had become a
German arsenal?

On April 17, the State Secretary in the German Foreign
Office, Weizsaecker, records that the Russian Ambassador had
visited him that day for the first time since he had presented
his credentials nearly a year before. He asked about the Skoda
contracts, and Weizsaecker pointed out that "a favourable atmosphere for the delivery of war materials to Soviet Russia
was not exactly being created at present by reports of a Rus-
sian-British-French Air Pact and the like." On this the Soviet
Ambassador turned at once from trade to politics, and asked
the State Secretary what he thought of German-Russian relations. Weizsaecker replied that it appeared to him that "the
Russian press lately was not fully participating in the anti-
German tone of the American and some of the English papers."
On this the Soviet Ambassador said, "Ideological differences of
opinion had hardly influenced the Russian-Italian relationship,
and they need not prove a stumbling-block to Germany either.
Soviet Russia had not exploited the present friction between
Germany and the Western Democracies against her, nor did
she desire to do so. There exists for Russia no reason why
she should not live with Germany on a normal footing. And
from normal, relations might become better and better."

We must regard this conversation as significant, especially
in view of the simultaneous discussions in Moscow between the
British Ambassador and M. Litvinov and the formal offer of
the Soviet, on April 16, of a Three-Power Alliance with Great
Britain and France. It is the first obvious move of Russia from
one leg to the other. "Normalisation" of the relations between
Russia and Germany was henceforward pursued, step for step,
with the negotiations for a triple alliance against German aggression.

If, for instance, Mr. Chamberlain on receipt of the Russian offer had replied, "Yes. Let us three band together and break Hitler's neck," or words to that effect, Parliament would have approved, Stalin would have understood, and history might have taken a different course. At least it could not have taken a worse.

On May 4, I commented on the position in these terms:

Above all, time must not be lost. Ten or twelve days have already passed since the Russian offer was made. The British people, who have now, at the sacrifice of honoured, ingrained custom, accepted the principle of compulsory military service, have a right, in conjunction with the French Republic, to call upon Poland not to place obstacles in the way of a common cause. Not only must the full co-operation of Russia be accepted, but the three Baltic States, Lithuania, Latvia, and Esthonia, must also be brought into association. To these three countries of warlike peoples, possessing together armies totalling perhaps twenty divisions of virile troops, a friendly Russia supplying munitions and other aid is essential.

There is no means of maintaining an Eastern Front against Nazi aggression without the active aid of Russia. Russian interests are deeply concerned in preventing Herr Hitler's designs on Eastern Europe. It should still be possible to range all the states and peoples from the Baltic to the Black Sea in one solid front against a new outrage or invasion. Such a front, if established in good heart, and with resolute and efficient military arrangements, combined with the strength of the Western Powers, may yet confront Hitler, Goering, Himmler, Ribbentrop, Goebbels and Company with forces the German people would be reluctant to challenge.

*   *   *   *   *

Instead, there was a long silence while half-measures and judicious compromises were being prepared. This delay was fatal to Litvinov. His last attempt to bring matters to a clear-cut decision with the Western Powers was deemed to have failed. Our credit stood very low. A wholly different foreign policy was required for the safety of Russia, and a new exponent must be found. On May 3, an official communiqué from Moscow announced that "M. Litvinov had been released

from the office of Foreign Commissar at his request and that
his duties would be assumed by the Premier, M. Molotov."
The German Chargé d'Affaires in Moscow reported on May
4 as follows:

Since Litvinov had received the English Ambassador as late as
May 2 and had been named in the press of yesterday as guest of
honour at the parade, his dismissal appears to be the result of a
spontaneous decision by Stalin. . . . At the last Party Congress,
Stalin urged caution lest the Soviet Union should be drawn into
conflict. Molotov (no Jew) is held to be "the most intimate friend
and closest collaborator of Stalin." His appointment is apparently
the guarantee that the foreign policy will be continued strictly in
accordance with Stalin's ideas.

Soviet diplomatic representatives abroad were instructed
to inform the Governments to which they were accredited
that this change meant no alteration in Russian foreign policy.
Moscow radio announced on May 4 that Molotov would carry
on the policy of Western security that for years had been Litvinov's aim. The eminent Jew, the target of German antagonism, was flung aside for the time being like a broken tool,
and, without being allowed a word of explanation, was bundled
off the world stage to obscurity, a pittance, and police supervision. Molotov, little known outside Russia, became Commissar
for Foreign Affairs, in the closest confederacy with Stalin. He
was free from all encumbrance of previous declarations, free
from the League of Nations atmosphere, and able to move in
any direction which the self-preservation of Russia might seem
to require. There was in fact only one way in which he was
now likely to move. He had always been favourable to an arrangement with Hitler. The Soviet Government were convinced by
Munich and much else that neither Britain nor France would
fight till they were attacked, and would not be much good
then. The gathering storm was about to break. Russia must
look after herself.

The dismissal of Litvinov marked the end of an epoch. It
registered the abandonment by the Kremlin of all faith in a
security pact with the Western Powers and in the possibility

of organising an Eastern Front against Germany. The German press comments at the time, though not necessarily accurate, are interesting. A dispatch from Warsaw was published in the German newspapers on May 4, stating that Litvinov had resigned after a bitter quarrel with Marshal Voroshilov ("the Party Boy," as cheeky and daring Russians called him in moments of relaxation). Voroshilov, no doubt on precise instructions, had declared that the Red Army was not prepared to fight for Poland, and, in the name of the Russian General Staff, condemned "excessively far-reaching military obligations." On May 7, the *Frankfurter Zeitung* was already sufficiently informed to state that Litvinov's resignation was extremely serious for the future of Anglo-French "encirclement," and its probable meaning was that those in Russia concerned with the military burden resulting from it had called a halt to Litvinov. All this was true; but for an interval it was necessary that a veil of deceit should cover the immense transaction, and that even up till the latest moment the Soviet attitude should remain in doubt. Russia must have a move both ways. How else could she drive her bargain with the hated and dreaded Hitler?

*   *   *   *   *

The Jew Litvinov was gone, and Hitler's dominant prejudice placated. From that moment the German Government ceased to define its foreign policy, as anti-Bolshevism, and turned its abuse upon the "pluto-democracies." Newspaper articles assured the Soviets that the German *Lebensraum* did not encroach on Russian territory; that indeed it stopped short of the Russian frontier at all points. Consequently there could be no cause of conflict between Russia and Germany unless the Soviets entered into "encirclement" engagements with England and France. The German Ambassador, Count Schulenburg, who had been summoned to Berlin for lengthy consultations, returned to Moscow with an offer of an advantageous goods credit on a long-term basis. The movement on both sides was towards a compact.

This violent and unnatural reversal of Russian policy was

a transmogrification of which only totalitarian states are capable. Barely two years since, the leaders of the Russian Army, Tukhachevsky and several thousands of its most accomplished officers, had been slaughtered for the very inclinations which now became acceptable to the handful of anxious masters in the Kremlin. Then pro-Germanism had been heresy and treason. Now, overnight, it was the policy of the State, and woe was mechanically meted out to any who dared dispute it, and often to those not quick enough on the turn-about.

For the task in hand no one was better fitted or equipped than the new Foreign Commissar.

*   *   *   *   *

The figure whom Stalin had now moved to the pulpit of Soviet foreign policy deserves some description, not available to the British or French Governments at the time. Vyacheslav Molotov was a man of outstanding ability and cold-blooded ruthlessness. He had survived the fearful hazards and ordeals to which all the Bolshevik leaders had been subjected in the years of triumphant revolution. He had lived and thrived in a society where ever-varying intrigue was accompanied by the constant menace of personal liquidation. His cannon-ball head, black moustache, and comprehending eyes, his slab face, his verbal adroitness and imperturbable demeanour, were appropriate manifestations of his qualities and skill. He was above all men fitted to be the agent and instrument of the policy of an incalculable machine. I have only met him on equal terms, in parleys where sometimes a strain of humour appeared, or at banquets where he genially proposed a long succession of conventional and meaningless toasts. I have never seen a human being who more perfectly represented the modern conception of a robot. And yet with all this there was an apparently reasonable and keenly polished diplomatist. What he was to his inferiors I cannot tell. What he was to the Japanese Ambassador during the years when, after the Teheran Conference, Stalin had promised to attack Japan, once the German Army was beaten, can be deduced from his recorded conversations. One delicate, searching, awkward interview after another was conducted with perfect poise, impenetrable purpose, and bland, official correctitude. Never a chink was opened. Never a needless jar was made. His smile of Siberian winter, his carefully measured and often wise words, his affable demeanour, combined to make him the perfect agent of Soviet policy in a deadly world.

Correspondence with him upon disputed matters was always useless, and, if pushed far, ended in lies and insults, of which this work will presently contain some examples. Only once did I seem to get a natural, human reaction. This was in the spring of 1942, when he alighted in England on his way back from the United States. We had signed the Anglo-Soviet Treaty, and he was about to make his dangerous flight home. At the garden gate of Downing Street, which we used for secrecy, I gripped his arm and we looked each other in the face. Suddenly he appeared deeply moved. Inside the image there appeared the man. He responded with an equal pressure. Silently we wrung each other's hands. But then we were all together, and it was life or death for the lot. Havoc and ruin had been around him all his days, either impending on himself or dealt by him to others. Certainly in Molotov the Soviet machine had found a capable and in many ways a characteristic representative — always the faithful Party man and Communist disciple. How glad I am at the end of my life not to have had to endure the stresses which he had suffered; better never be born. In the conduct of foreign affairs, Sully, Talleyrand, Metternich, would welcome him to their company, if there be another world to which Bolsheviks allow themselves to go.

* * * * *

From the moment when Molotov became Foreign Commissar, he pursued the policy of an arrangement with Germany at the expense of Poland. It was not very long before the French became aware of this. There is a remarkable dispatch by the French Ambassador in Berlin, dated May 7, published in the French Yellow Book, which states that on his secret in-

formation he was sure that a Fourth Partition of Poland was
to be the basis of the German-Russian rapprochement. "Since
the month of May," writes M. Daladier in April, 1946, "the
U.S.S.R. had conducted two negotiations, one with France, the
other with Germany. She appeared to prefer to partition
rather than to defend Poland. Such was the immediate cause
of the Second World War." [2] But there were other causes too.

*   *   *   *   *

On May 8, the British Government at last replied to the
Soviet Note of April 16. While the text of the British document was not published, the Tass Agency on May 9 issued a
statement giving the main points of the British proposals. On
May 10, the official organ, *Isvestia,* printed a communiqué to
the effect that Reuter's statement of the British counter-proposals, namely, that "the Soviet Union must separately guarantee
every neighbouring state, and that Great Britain pledges herself
to assist the U.S.S.R. if the latter becomes involved in war
as a result of its guarantees," did not correspond to fact. The
Soviet Government, said the communiqué, had received the
British counter-proposals on May 8, but these did not mention
the Soviet Union's obligation of a separate guarantee to each
of its neighbouring states, whereas they did state that the
U.S.S.R. was obliged to render immediate assistance to Great
Britain and France in the event of their being involved in war
under their guarantees to Poland and Rumania. No mention,
however, was made of any assistance on their part to the Soviet
Union in the event of its being involved in war in consequence
of its obligations towards any Eastern European state.

Later on the same day, Mr. Chamberlain said that the Government had undertaken their new obligations in Eastern
Europe without inviting the direct participation of the Soviet
Government on account of various difficulties. His Majesty's
Government had suggested that the Soviet Government should
make, on their own behalf, a similar declaration, and express
their readiness to lend assistance, if desired, to countries which

[2] Quoted by Reynaud, *op. cit.,* volume 1, page 585.

might be victims of aggression and were prepared to defend their own independence.

Almost simultaneously the Soviet Government presented a scheme at once more comprehensive and more rigid which, whatever other advantages it might present, must in the view of His Majesty's Government inevitably raise the very difficulties which their own proposals had been designed to avoid. They accordingly pointed out to the Soviet Government the existence of these difficulties. At the same time they made certain modifications in their original proposals. In particular, they [H.M.G.] made it plain that *if the Soviet Government wished to make their own intervention contingent on that of Great Britain and France, His Majesty's Government for their part would have no objection.*

It was a pity that this had not been explicitly stated a fortnight earlier.

It should be mentioned here that on May 12, the Anglo-Turkish Agreement was formally ratified by the Turkish Parliament. By means of this addition to our commitments, we hoped to strengthen our position in the Mediterranean in the event of a crisis. Here was our answer to the Italian occupation of Albania. Just as the period of talking with Germany was over, so now we reached in effect the same deadlock with Italy.

The Russian negotiations proceeded languidly, and on May 19 the whole issue was raised in the House of Commons. The debate, which was short and serious, was practically confined to the leaders of parties and to prominent ex-Ministers. Mr. Lloyd George, Mr. Eden, and I all pressed upon the Government the vital need of an immediate arrangement with Russia of the most far-reaching character and on equal terms. Mr. Lloyd George began, and painted a picture of gloom and peril in the darkest hues:

The situation reminds me very much of the feeling that prevailed in the early spring of 1918. We knew there was a great attack coming from Germany, but no one quite knew where the blow would fall. I remember that the French thought it would fall on their front, while our generals thought it would fall on ours. The

French generals were not even agreed as to the part of their front
on which the attack would fall, and our generals were equally
divided. All that we knew was that there was a tremendous onslaught coming somewhere, and the whole atmosphere was filled
with I will not say fear, but with uneasiness. We could see the
tremendous activities behind the German lines, and we knew that
they were preparing something. That is more or less what seems
to me to be the position today . . . we are all very anxious; the
whole world is under the impression that there is something preparing in the nature of another attack from the aggressors. Nobody quite knows where it will come. We can see that they are
speeding up their armaments at a rate hitherto unprecedented, especially in weapons of the offensive — tanks, bombing airplanes, submarines. We know that they are occupying and fortifying fresh
positions that will give them strategic advantages in a war with
France and ourselves. . . . They are inspecting and surveying, from
Libya to the North Sea, all sorts of situations that would be of vital
importance in the event of war. There is a secrecy in the movements behind the lines which is very ominous.

There is the same kind of secrecy as in 1918, in order to baffle us
as to their objects. They are not preparing for defence. . . . They
are not preparing themselves against attack from either France,
Britain, or Russia. That has never been threatened. I have never
heard, either privately or publicly, any hint or suggestion that we
were contemplating an attack upon Italy or Germany in any
quarter, and they know it quite well. Therefore, all these preparations are not for defence. They are for some contemplated offensive
scheme against someone or other in whom we are interested.

*　　　*　　　*　　　*　　　*

Mr. Lloyd George then added some words of wisdom:

The main military purpose and scheme of the Dictators is to
produce quick results, to avoid a prolonged war. A prolonged war
never suits dictators. A prolonged war like the Peninsular War
wears them down, and the great Russian defence, which produced
no great military victory for the Russians, broke Napoleon.
Germany's ideal is now, and always has been, a war which is
brought to a speedy end. The war against Austria in 1866 did not
last more than a few weeks, and the war in 1870 was waged in such

a way that it was practically over in a month or two. In 1914, plans were made with exactly the same aim in view, and it was very nearly achieved; and they would have achieved it but for Russia. But from the moment they failed to achieve a speedy victory, the game was up. You may depend upon it that the great military thinkers of Germany have been working out the problem, what was the mistake of 1914, what did they lack, how can they fill up the gaps and repair the blunders or avoid them in the next war?

Mr. Lloyd George, pressing on from fact to fancy, then suggested that the Germans had already got "twenty thousand tanks" and "thousands of bomber airplanes." This was far beyond the truth. Moreover, it was an undue appeal to the fear motive. And why had he not been busy all these years with my small group ingeminating rearmament? But his speech cast a chill over the assembly. Two years before, or better still three, such statements and all the pessimism of his speech would have been scorned and derided; but then there was time. Now, whatever the figures, it was all too late.

The Prime Minister replied, and for the first time revealed to us his views on the Soviet offer. His reception of it was certainly cool, and indeed disdainful:

If we can evolve a method by which we can enlist the co-operation and assistance of the Soviet Union in building up that peace front, we welcome it; we want it; we attach value to it. The suggestion that we despise the assistance of the Soviet Union is without foundation. Without accepting any view of an unauthorised character as to the precise value of the Russian military forces, or the way in which they would best be employed, no one would be so foolish as to suppose that that huge country, with its vast population and enormous resources, would be a *negligible factor* in such a situation as that with which we are confronted.

This seemed to show the same lack of proportion as we have seen in the rebuff to the Roosevelt proposals a year before.

I then took up the tale:

I have been quite unable to understand what is the objection to making the agreement with Russia which the Prime Minister

professes himself desirous of doing, and making it in the broad
and simple form proposed by the Russian Soviet Government.

Undoubtedly, the proposals put forward by the Russian Government contemplate a triple alliance against aggression between
England, France, and Russia, which alliance may extend its benefits
to other countries if and when those benefits are desired. The
alliance is solely for the purpose of resisting further acts of aggression and of protecting the victims of aggression. I cannot see what
is wrong with that. What is wrong with this simple proposal? It
is said, "Can you trust the Russian Soviet Government?" I suppose
in Moscow they say, "Can we trust Chamberlain?" I hope we may
say that the answer to both questions is in the affirmative. I
earnestly hope so.

*   *   *   *   *

This Turkish proposal, which is universally accepted, is a great
consolidating and stabilising force throughout the whole of the
Black Sea area and the Eastern Mediterranean. Turkey, with whom
we have made this agreement, is in the closest harmony with Russia.
She is also in the closest harmony with Rumania. These Powers
together are mutually protecting vital interests.

*   *   *   *   *

There is a great identity of interests between Great Britain and
the associated Powers in the South. Is there not a similar identity
of interests in the North? Take the countries of the Baltic, Lithuania, Latvia, and Esthonia, which were once the occasion of the
wars of Peter the Great. It is a major interest of Russia that these
Powers should not fall into the hands of Nazi Germany. That is a
vital interest in the North. I need not elaborate the arguments
about [a German attack upon] the Ukraine, which means an
invasion of Russian territory. All along the whole of this eastern
front you can see that the major interests of Russia are definitely
engaged, and therefore it seems you could fairly judge that they
would pool their interests with other countries similarly affected.

*   *   *   *   *

If you are ready to be an ally of Russia in time of war, which is
the supreme test, the great occasion of all, if you are ready to join
hands with Russia in the defence of Poland, which you have

guaranteed, and of Rumania, why should you shrink from becoming the ally of Russia now, when you may by that very fact prevent
the breaking-out of war? I cannot understand all these refinements
of diplomacy and delay. If the worst comes to the worst, you are in
the midst of it with them, and you have to make the best of it with
them. If the difficulties do not arise, well, you will have had the
security in the preliminary stages.

*   *   *   *   *

His Majesty's Government have given a guarantee to Poland.
I was astounded when I heard them give this guarantee. I support
it, but I was astounded by it, because nothing that had happened
before led one to suppose that such a step would be taken. I want
to draw the attention of the Committee to the fact that the question
posed by Mr. Lloyd George ten days ago and repeated today has not
been answered. The question was whether the General Staff was
consulted before this guarantee was given as to whether it was safe
and practical to give it, and whether there were any means of implementing it. The whole country knows that the question has
been asked, and it has not been answered. That is disconcerting
and disquieting.

*   *   *   *   *

Clearly Russia is not going to enter into agreements unless she is
treated as an equal, and not only is treated as an equal, but has
confidence that the methods employed by the Allies — by the peace
front — are such as would be likely to lead to success. No one wants
to associate himself with indeterminate leadership and uncertain
policies. The Government must realise that none of these states in
Eastern Europe can maintain themselves for, say, a year's war unless
they have behind them the massive, solid backing of a friendly
Russia, joined to the combination of the Western Powers. In the
main, I agree with Mr. Lloyd George that if there is to be an
effective eastern front — an eastern peace front, or a war front as it
might become — it can be set up only with the effective support
of a friendly Soviet Russia lying behind all those countries.

Unless there is an eastern front set up, what is going to happen
to the West? What is going to happen to those countries on the
western front to whom, if we have not given guarantees, it is admitted we are bound — countries like Belgium, Holland, Denmark,

and Switzerland? Let us look back to the experiences we had in
1917. In 1917, the Russian front was broken and demoralised.
Revolution and mutiny had sapped the courage of that great disciplined army, and the conditions at the front were indescribable;
and yet, until the Treaty was made closing the front down, more
than one million five hundred thousand Germans were held upon
that front, even in its most ineffectual and unhappy condition.
Once that front was closed down, one million Germans and five
thousand cannon were brought to the West, and at the last moment
almost turned the course of the war and forced upon us a disastrous
peace.

It is a tremendous thing, this question of the eastern front. I am
astonished that there is not more anxiety about it. Certainly, I do
not ask favours of Soviet Russia. This is no time to ask favours of
countries. But here is an offer, a fair offer, and a better offer, in
my opinion, than the terms which the Government seek to get for
themselves; a more simple, a more direct, and a more effective offer.
Let it not be put aside and come to nothing. I beg His Majesty's
Government to get some of these brutal truths into their heads.
Without an effective eastern front, there can be no satisfactory
defence of our interests in the West, and without Russia there can
be no effective eastern front. If His Majesty's Government, having
neglected our defences for a long time, having thrown away Czechoslovakia with all that Czechoslovakia meant in military power,
having committed us, without examination of the technical aspects,
to the defence of Poland and Rumania, now reject and cast away
the indispensable aid of Russia, and so lead us in the worst of all
ways into the worst of all wars, they will have ill-deserved the confidence and, I will add, the generosity with which they have been
treated by their fellow-countrymen.

There can be little doubt that all this was now too late.
Attlee, Sinclair, and Eden spoke on the general line of the
imminence of the danger and the need of the Russian alliance.
The position of the leaders of the Labour and Liberal Parties
was weakened by the vote against compulsory national service
to which they had led their followers only a few weeks before.
The plea, so often advanced, that this was because they did not
like the foreign policy, was feeble; for no foreign policy can
have validity if there is no adequate force behind it and no

national readiness to make the necessary sacrifices to produce that force.

$$* \quad * \quad * \quad * \quad *$$

The efforts of the Western Powers to produce a defensive alignment against Germany were well matched by the other side. Conversations between Ribbentrop and Ciano at Como at the beginning of May came to formal and public fruition in the so-called "Pact of Steel," signed by the two Foreign Ministers in Berlin on May 22. This was the challenging answer to the flimsy British network of guarantees in Eastern Europe. Ciano in his *Diary* records a conversation with Hitler at the time of the signature of this alliance:

Hitler states that he is well satisfied with the Pact, and confirms the fact that Mediterranean policy will be directed by Italy. He takes an interest in Albania, and is enthusiastic about our programme for making of Albania a stronghold which will inexorably dominate the Balkans.[3]

Hitler's satisfaction was more clearly revealed when on the day following the signing of the Pact of Steel, May 23, he held a meeting with his Chiefs of Staff. The secret minutes of the conversation are on record:

We are at present in a state of patriotic fervour, which is shared by two other nations — Italy and Japan. The period which lies behind us has indeed been put to good use. All measures have been taken in the correct sequence and in harmony with our aims. The Pole is no "supplementary enemy." Poland will always be on the side of our adversaries. In spite of treaties of friendship, Poland has always had the secret intention of exploiting every opportunity to do us harm. Danzig is not the subject of the dispute at all. It is a question of expanding our living space in the East and of securing our food supplies. There is, therefore, no question of sparing Poland, and we are left with the decision: to attack Poland at the first suitable opportunity. We cannot expect a repetition of the Czech affair. There will be war. Our task is to isolate Poland. The success of the isolation will be decisive.

If it is not certain that a German-Polish conflict will not lead

[3] Ciano, *Diary, op. cit.,* page 90.

to war in the West, then the fight must be primarily against
England and France. If there were an alliance of France, England,
and Russia against Germany, Italy, and Japan, I should be constrained to attack England and France with a few annihilating
blows. I doubt the possibility of a peaceful settlement with
England. We must prepare ourselves for the conflict. England sees
in our development the foundation of a hegemony which would
weaken her. England is, therefore, our enemy, and the conflict
with England will be a life-and-death struggle. The Dutch and
Belgian air bases must be occupied by armed force. Declarations of
neutrality must be ignored.

If England intends to intervene in the Polish war, we must
occupy Holland with lightning speed. We must aim at securing
a new defence line on Dutch soil up to the Zuyder Zee. The idea
that we can get off cheaply is dangerous; there is no such possibility.
We must burn our boats, and it is no longer a question of justice or
injustice, but of life or death for eighty million human beings.
Every country's armed forces or government must aim at a short
war. The Government, however, must also be prepared for a war
of ten or fifteen years' duration.

England knows that to lose a war will mean the end of her world
power. England is the driving force against Germany.

The British themselves are proud, courageous, tenacious, firm
in resistance and gifted as organisers. They know how to exploit
every new development. They have the love of adventure and the
bravery of the Nordic race. The German average is higher. But
if in the First World War we had had two battleships and two
cruisers more, and if the battle of Jutland had begun in the
morning, the British Fleet would have been defeated [4] and England
brought to her knees. In addition to the surprise attack, preparations for a long war must be made, while opportunities on the
Continent for England are eliminated. The Army will have to hold
positions essential to the Navy and air force. If Holland and
Belgium are successfully occupied and held, and if France is also
defeated, the fundamental conditions for a successful war against
England will have been secured.[5]

[4] Hitler was evidently quite ignorant of the facts of Jutland, which was from
beginning to end an unsuccessful effort by the British Fleet to bring the Germans to a general action in which the overwhelming gun-fire of the British
line of battle would have soon been decisive.

[5] *Nuremberg Documents, op. cit.*, Part 1, pages 167–68.

On May 30, the German Foreign Office sent the following instruction to their Ambassador in Moscow: "Contrary to the policy previously planned we have now decided to undertake definite negotiations with the Soviet Union." [6] While the ranks of the Axis closed for military preparation, the vital link of the Western Powers with Russia had perished. The underlying discordance of view can be read into Foreign Commissar Molotov's speech of May 31 in reply to Mr. Chamberlain's speech in the Commons of May 19.

As far back [he said] as the middle of April, the Soviet Government entered into negotiations with the British and French Governments about the necessary measures to be taken. The negotiations started then are not yet concluded. It became clear some time ago that if there was any real desire to create an efficient front of peaceable countries against the advance of aggression, the following minimum conditions were imperative:

The conclusion between Great Britain, France, and the U.S.S.R. of an effective pact of mutual assistance against aggression, of an exclusively defensive character.

A guarantee on the part of Great Britain, France, and the U.S.S.R. of the states of Central and Eastern Europe, including without exception all the European countries bordering on the U.S.S.R., against an attack by aggressors.

The conclusion between Great Britain, France, and the U.S.S.R. of a definite agreement on the forms and extent of the immediate and effective assistance to be rendered to one another and to the guaranteed states in the event of an attack by aggressors.

The negotiations had come to a seemingly unbreakable deadlock. The Polish and Rumanian Governments, while accepting the British guarantee, were not prepared to accept a similar undertaking in the same form from the Russian Government. A similar attitude prevailed in another vital strategic quarter — the Baltic States. The Soviet Government made it clear that they would only adhere to a pact of mutual assistance if Finland and the Baltic States were included in a general guarantee. All four countries now refused, and per-

6 *Nazi-Soviet Relations*, page 15.

haps in their terror would for a long time have refused, such a
condition. Finland and Esthonia even asserted that they would
consider a guarantee extended to them without their assent
as an act of aggression. On the same day, May 31, Esthonia
and Latvia signed non-aggression pacts with Germany. Thus
Hitler penetrated with ease into the frail defences of the tardy,
irresolute coalition against him.

21

On the Verge

SUMMER ADVANCED, preparations for war continued throughout Europe, and the attitudes of diplomatists, the speeches of politicians, and the wishes of mankind counted each day for less. German military movements seemed to portend the settlement of the dispute with Poland over Danzig as a preliminary to the assault on Poland itself. Mr. Chamberlain expressed his anxieties to Parliament on June 10, and repeated his intention to stand by Poland if her independence were threatened. In a spirit of detachment from the facts, the Belgian Government, largely under the influence of their King, announced on June 23 that they were opposed to staff talks with England and France and that Belgium intended to maintain a strict neutrality. The tide of events brought with it a

closing of the ranks between England and France, and also at
home. There was much coming and going between Paris and
London during the month of July. The celebrations of the
Fourteenth of July were an occasion for a display of Anglo-
French union. I was invited by the French Government to at-
tend this brilliant spectacle.

As I was leaving Le Bourget after the parade, General Gamelin suggested that I should visit the French Front. "You have
never seen the Rhine sector," he said. "Come then in August,
we will show you everything." Accordingly a plan was made
and on August 15, General Spears and I were welcomed by
his close friend, General Georges, Commander-in-Chief of the
armies in France and *Successeur Eventuel* to the Supreme Commander. I was delighted to meet this most agreeable and competent officer, and we passed the next ten days in his company,
revolving military problems and making contacts with Gamelin,
who was also inspecting certain points on this part of the front.

Beginning at the angle of the Rhine near Lauterbourg, we
traversed the whole sector to the Swiss frontier. In England,
as in 1914, the carefree people were enjoying their holidays
and playing with their children on the sands. But here along
the Rhine a different light glared. All the temporary bridges
across the river had been removed to one side or the other.
The permanent bridges were heavily guarded and mined.
Trusty officers were stationed night and day to press at a signal
the buttons which would blow them up. The great river, swollen by the melting Alpine snows, streamed along in sullen, turgid flow. The French outposts crouched in their rifle-pits amid
the brushwood. Two or three of us could stroll together to the
water's edge, but nothing like a target, we were told, must
be presented. Three hundred yards away on the farther side,
here and there among the bushes, German figures could be
seen working rather leisurely with pick and shovel at their defences. All the riverside quarter of Strasbourg had already
been cleared of civilians. I stood on its bridge for some time
and watched one or two motor cars pass over it. Prolonged
examination of passports and character took place at either

end. Here the German post was little more than a hundred
yards away from the French. There was no intercourse with
them. Yet Europe was at peace. There was no dispute between Germany and France. The Rhine flowed on, swirling
and eddying, at six or seven miles an hour. One or two canoes
with boys in them sped past on the current. I did not see the
Rhine again until more than five years later in March, 1945,
when I crossed it in a small boat with Field-Marshal Mont-
gomery. But that was near Wesel, far to the north.

On my return I sent a few notes of what I had gathered to
the Secretary of State for War and perhaps to some other Ministers with whom I was in touch:

The French Front cannot be surprised. It cannot be broken at
any point except by an effort which would be enormously costly in
life, and would take so much time that the general situation would
be transformed while it was in progress. The same is true, though
to a lesser extent, of the German side.

The flanks of this front, however, rest upon two small neutral
states. The attitude of Belgium is thought to be profoundly unsatisfactory. At present there are no military relations of any kind
between the French and the Belgians.

At the other end of the line, about which I was able to learn a
good deal, the French have done everything in their power to
prepare against an invasion through Switzerland. This operation
would take the form of a German advance up the Aar, protected
on its right by a movement into or towards the Belfort Gap. I
personally think it extremely unlikely that any heavy German
attempt will be made either against the French Front or against
the two small countries on its flanks in the opening phase.

It is not necessary for Germany to mobilise before attacking
Poland. They have enough divisions already on a war footing to
act upon their eastern front, and would have time to reinforce
the Siegfried Line by mobilising simultaneously with the beginning
of a heavy attack on Poland. Thus, a German mobilisation is a
warning signal which may not be forthcoming in advance of war.
The French, on the other hand, may have to take extra measures
in the period of extreme tension now upon us.

As to date, it is thought Hitler would be wise to wait until the

snow falls in the Alps and gives the protection of winter to
Mussolini. During the first fortnight of September, or even earlier,
these conditions would be established. There would still be time
for Hitler to strike heavily at Poland before the mud period of
late October or early November would hamper a German offensive
there. Thus this first fortnight in September seems to be particularly critical, and the present German arrangements for the Nuremberg demonstration — propaganda, etc. — seem to harmonise with
such a conclusion.

* * * * *

What was remarkable about all I learned on my visit was
the complete acceptance of the defensive which dominated
my most responsible French hosts, and imposed itself irre-
sistibly upon me. In talking to all these highly competent
French officers, one had the sense that the Germans were the
stronger, and that France had no longer the life-thrust to
mount a great offensive. She would fight for her existence
— *voilà tout!* There was the fortified Siegfried Line, with all
the increased fire-power of modern weapons. In my own bones,
too, was the horror of the Somme and Passchendaele offensives.
The Germans were, of course, far stronger than in the days
of Munich. We did not know the deep anxieties which rent
their High Command. We had allowed ourselves to get into
such a condition, physically and psychologically, that no responsible person — and up to this point I had no responsibilities — could act on the assumption — which was true — that
only forty-two half-equipped and half-trained German divisions guarded their long front from the North Sea to Switzerland. This compared with thirteen at the time of Munich.

* * * * *

In these final weeks my fear was that His Majesty's Government, in spite of our guarantee, would recoil from waging war
upon Germany if she attacked Poland. There is no doubt that
at this time Mr. Chamberlain had resolved to take the plunge,
bitter though it was to him. But I did not know him so well
as I did a year later. I feared that Hitler might try a bluff

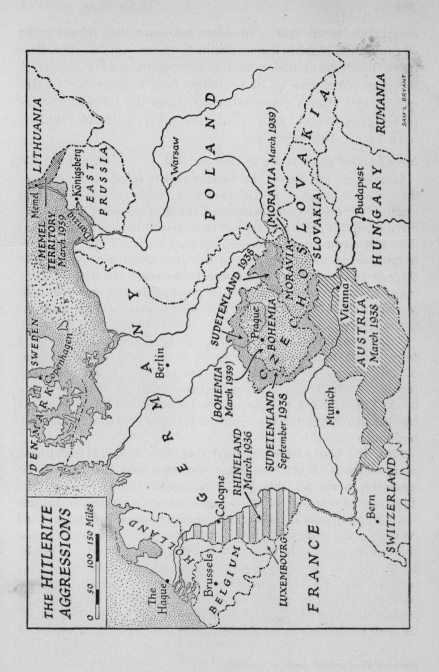

THE HITLERITE AGGRESSIONS

0 50 100 150 Miles

SAM'L. BRYANT

SWEDEN

DENMARK

Copenhagen

LITHUANIA

Memel
MEMEL TERRITORY March 1939

EAST PRUSSIA
Königsberg

Danzig March 1939

POLAND

Warsaw

G E R M A N Y

Berlin

HOLLAND
The Hague

Brussels
BELGIUM

Cologne

RHINELAND March 1936

LUXEMBOURG

SUDETENLAND September 1938

(BOHEMIA March 1939)

Prague
BOHEMIA
SUDETENLAND 1938

C Z E C H O S L O V A K I A

MORAVIA
(MORAVIA March 1939)

SLOVAKIA

FRANCE

Munich

Vienna
AUSTRIA March 1938

HUNGARY
Budapest

Bern
SWITZERLAND

RUMANIA

about some novel agency or secret weapon which would baffle
or puzzle the overburdened Cabinet. From time to time Professor Lindemann had talked to me about atomic energy. I
therefore asked him to let me know how things stood in this
sphere, and after a conversation, I wrote the following letter
to Kingsley Wood, with whom my fairly intimate relations
have been mentioned:

Mr. Churchill to Secretary of State for Air.   *August 5, 1939.*

Some weeks ago one of the Sunday papers splashed the story of
the immense amount of energy which might be released from
uranium by the recently discovered chain of processes which take
place when this particular type of atom is split by neutrons. At first
sight this might seem to portend the appearance of new explosives
of devastating power. *In view of this it is essential to realise that
there is no danger that this discovery, however great its scientific
interest, and perhaps ultimately its practical importance, will lead
to results capable of being put into operation on a large scale for
several years.*

There are indications that tales will be deliberately circulated
when international tension becomes acute about the adaptation
of this process to produce some terrible new secret explosive,
capable of wiping out London. Attempts will no doubt be made
by the Fifth Column to induce us by means of this threat to accept
another surrender. For this reason it is imperative to state the true
position.

First, the best authorities hold that only a minor constituent
of uranium is effective in these processes, and that it will be
necessary to extract this before large-scale results are possible.
This will be a matter of many years. Secondly, the chain process
can take place only if the uranium is concentrated in a large mass.
As soon as the energy develops, it will explode with a mild detona-
tion before any really violent effects can be produced.[1] It might
be as good as our present-day explosives, but it is unlikely to
produce anything very much more dangerous. Thirdly, these experiments cannot be carried out on a small scale. If they had been
successfully done on a big scale (i.e., with the results with which
we shall be threatened unless we submit to blackmail), it would be

[1] This difficulty was, of course, overcome later, but only by very elaborate
methods after several years of research.

impossible to keep them secret. Fourthly, only a comparatively small amount of uranium in the territories of what used to be Czechoslovakia is under the control of Berlin.

For all these reasons the fear that this new discovery has provided the Nazis with some sinister, new, secret explosive with which to destroy their enemies is clearly without foundation. Dark hints will no doubt be dropped and terrifying whispers will be assiduously circulated, but it is to be hoped that nobody will be taken in by them.

It is remarkable how accurate this forecast was. Nor was it the Germans who found the path. Indeed, they followed the wrong trail, and had actually abandoned the search for the atomic bomb in favour of rockets or pilotless airplanes at the moment when President Roosevelt and I were taking the decisions and reaching the memorable agreements, which will be described in their proper place, for the large-scale manufacture of atomic bombs.

I also wrote in my final paper for the Air Defence Research Committee:

August 10, 1939.

The main defence of England against air raids is the toll which can be extracted from the raiders. One-fifth knocked out each go will soon bring the raids to an end. . . . We must imagine the opening attack as a large affair crossing the sea in relays for many hours. But it is not the first results of the air attack which will govern the future of the air war. It is not child's play to come and attack England. A heavy proportion of casualties will lead the enemy to make severe calculations of profit and loss. As daylight raiding will soon become too expensive, we have chiefly to deal with random night-bombing of the built-up areas.

*   *   *   *   *

"Tell Chamberlain," said Mussolini to the British Ambassador on July 7, "that if England is ready to fight in defence of Poland, Italy will take up arms with her ally, Germany." But behind the scenes his attitude was the opposite. He sought at this time no more than to consolidate his interests in the Mediterranean and North Africa, to cull the fruits of his inter-

vention in Spain, and to digest his Albanian conquest. He did
not like being dragged into a European war for Germany to
conquer Poland. For all his public boastings, he knew the
military and political fragility of Italy better than anyone. He
was willing to talk about a war in 1942, if Germany would give
him the munitions; but in 1939 — No!

As the pressure upon Poland sharpened during the summer,
Mussolini turned his thoughts upon repeating his Munich
rôle of mediator, and he suggested a World Peace Conference.
Hitler curtly dispelled such ideas. On August 11, Ciano met
Ribbentrop at Salzburg. According to Ciano's *Diary:*

> The Duce is anxious for me to prove by documentary evidence
> that an outbreak of war at this time would be folly. . . . It would
> be impossible to localise it in Poland, and a general war would
> be disastrous for everyone. Never has the Duce spoken of the need
> for peace so unreservedly and with so much warmth. . . . Ribben-
> trop is evasive. Whenever I ask him for particulars about German
> policy, his conscience troubles him. He has lied too many times
> about German intentions towards Poland not to feel uneasy now
> about what he must tell me, and what they are really planning to
> do. . . . The German decision to fight is implacable. Even if they
> were given more than they ask, they would attack just the same,
> because they are possessed by the demon of destruction. . . . At times
> our conversation becomes very tense. I do not hesitate to express
> my thoughts with brutal frankness. But this does not move him.
> I am becoming aware how little we are worth in the opinion of
> the Germans.[2]

Ciano went on to see Hitler the next day. We have the
German minutes of this meeting. Hitler made it clear that he
intended to settle with Poland, that he would be forced to
fight England and France as well, and that he wanted Italy to
come in. He said, "If England keeps the necessary troops in
her own country, she can send to France at the most two infantry divisions and one armoured division. For the rest she
could supply a few bomber squadrons, but hardly any fighters
because the German air force would at once attack England,

2 Ciano, *op. cit.*, page 123.

and the English fighters would be urgently needed for its defence." About France he said that after the destruction of
Poland — which would not take long — Germany would be
able to assemble hundreds of divisions along the West Wall,
and France would thus be compelled to concentrate all her
available forces from the colonies and from the Italian frontier
and elsewhere on her Maginot Line for the life-and-death
struggle. Ciano in reply expressed his surprise at the gravity
of what he had been told. There had, he complained, never
been any previous sign from the German side that the Polish
quarrel was so serious and imminent. On the contrary, Ribbentrop had said that the Danzig question would be settled
in the course of time. The Duce, convinced that a conflict with
the Western Powers was unavoidable, had assumed that he
should make plans for this event during a period of two or
three years.

After these interchanges Ciano returned gloomily to report
to his master, whom he found more deeply convinced that the
Democracies would fight, and even more resolved to keep out
of the struggle himself.

*   *   *   *   *

A renewed effort to come to an arrangement with Soviet
Russia was made by the British and French Governments. It
was decided to send a special envoy to Moscow. Mr. Eden, who
had made useful contacts with Stalin some years before, volunteered to go. This generous offer was declined by the Prime
Minister. Instead, on June 12, Mr. Strang, an able official but
without any special standing outside the Foreign Office, was entrusted with this momentous mission. This was another mistake. The sending of so subordinate a figure gave actual offence. It is doubtful whether he was able to pierce the outer
crust of the Soviet organism. In any case all was now too late.
Much had happened since M. Maisky had been sent to see me
at Chartwell in August, 1938. Munich had happened. Hitler's
armies had had a year more to mature. His munition factories, reinforced by the Skoda Works, were all in full blast.

The Soviet Government cared much for Czechoslovakia; but Czechoslovakia was gone. Benes was in exile. A German Gauleiter ruled in Prague.

On the other hand, Poland presented to Russia an entirely different set of age-long political and strategic problems. Their last major contact had been the Battle of Warsaw in 1919, when the Bolshevik armies under Ensign Krylenko had been hurled back from their invasion by Pilsudski aided by the advice of General Weygand and the British Mission under Lord D'Abernon, and thereafter pursued with bloody vengeance. During these years Poland had been a spearpoint of anti-Bolshevism. With her left hand she joined and sustained the anti-Soviet Baltic States. But with her right hand, at Munich-time, she had helped to despoil Czechoslovakia. The Soviet Government were sure that Poland hated them, and also that Poland had no power to withstand a German onslaught. They were, however, very conscious of their own perils and of their need for time to repair the havoc in the High Commands of their armies. In these circumstances, the prospects of Mr. Strang's mission were not exuberant.

The negotiations wandered around the question of the reluctance of Poland and the Baltic States to be rescued from Germany by the Soviets; and here they made no progress. In the leading article of June 13, *Pravda* had already declared that an effective neutrality of Finland, Esthonia, and Latvia was vital to the safety of the U.S.S.R. "The security of such states," it said, was of prime importance for Britain and France, as "even such a politician as Mr. Churchill" had recognised. The issue was discussed in Moscow on June 15. On the following day the Russian press declared that "in the circles of the Soviet Foreign Ministry results of the first talks are regarded as not entirely favourable." All through July the discussions continued fitfully, and eventually the Soviet Government proposed that conversations should be continued on a military basis with both French and British representatives. The British Government, therefore, dispatched Admiral Drax with a mission to Moscow on August 10. These officers possessed no written authority to negotiate. The French Mission was headed by General Doumenc. On the Russian side Marshal Voroshilov officiated. We now know that at this same time the Soviet Government agreed to the journey of a German negotiator to Moscow. The military conference soon foundered upon the refusal of Poland and Rumania to allow the transit of Russian troops. The Polish attitude was, "With the Germans we risk losing our liberty; with the Russians our soul." [3]

* * * * *

At the Kremlin in August, 1942, Stalin, in the early hours of the morning, gave me one aspect of the Soviet position. "We formed the impression," said Stalin, "that the British and French Governments were not resolved to go to war if Poland were attacked, but that they hoped the diplomatic line-up of Britain, France, and Russia would deter Hitler. We were sure it would not." "How many divisions," Stalin had asked, "will France send against Germany on mobilisation?" The answer was: "About a hundred." He then asked: "How many will England send?" The answer was: "Two and two more later." "Ah, two and two more later," Stalin had repeated. "Do you know," he asked, "how many divisions we shall have to put on the Russian front if we go to war with Germany?" There was a pause. "More than three hundred." I was not told with whom this conversation took place or its date. It must be recognised that this was solid ground, but not favourable for Mr. Strang of the Foreign Office.

It was judged necessary by Stalin and Molotov for bargaining purposes to conceal their true intentions till the last possible moment. Remarkable skill in duplicity was shown by Molotov and his subordinates in all their contacts with both sides. As late as August 4, the German Ambassador Schulenburg could only telegraph from Moscow:

From Molotov's whole attitude it was evident that the Soviet Government was in fact more prepared for improvement in German-Soviet relations, but that the old mistrust of Germany

[3] Quoted in Reynaud, *op. cit.*, volume 1, page 587.

persists. My over-all impression is that the Soviet Government is at present determined to sign with England and France if they fulfil all Soviet wishes. Negotiations, to be sure, might still last a long time, especially since the mistrust of England is also great. . . . It will take a considerable effort on our part to cause the Soviet Government to swing about.[4]

He need not have worried: the die was cast.

*   *   *   *   *

On the evening of August 19, Stalin announced to the Politburo his intention to sign a pact with Germany. On August 22, Marshal Voroshilov was not to be found by the Allied missions until evening. He then said to the head of the French Mission:

The question of military collaboration with France has been in the air for several years, but has never been settled. Last year, when Czechoslovakia was perishing, we waited for a signal from France, but none was given. Our troops were ready. . . . The French and English Governments have now dragged out the political and military discussions too long. For that reason the possibility is not to be excluded that certain political events may take place. . . . [5]

The next day Ribbentrop arrived in Moscow.

*   *   *   *   *

We now possess, in the *Nuremberg Documents* and in those captured and recently published by the United States, the details of this never-to-be-forgotten transaction. According to Ribbentrop's chief assistant, Gauss, who flew with him to Moscow: "On the afternoon of August 22, the first conversation between Ribbentrop and Stalin took place. . . . The Reich Foreign Minister returned very satisfied from this long conference. . . ." Later in the day an agreement on the text of the Soviet-German Non-Aggression Pact was reached quickly and without difficulties. "Ribbentrop himself," says Gauss, "had inserted in the preamble a rather far-reaching phrase concern-

4 *Nazi-Soviet Relations*, page 41.
5 Reynaud, *op. cit.*, volume 1, page 588.

ing the formation of friendly German-Soviet relations. To this
Stalin objected, remarking that the Soviet Government could
not suddenly present to their public a German-Soviet declaration of friendship after they had been covered with *pails of
manure* by the Nazi Government for six years. Thereupon
this phrase in the preamble was deleted." In a secret agreement Germany declared herself politically disinterested in
Latvia, Esthonia, and Finland, but considered Lithuania to
be in her sphere of influence. A demarcation line was drawn
for the Polish partition. In the Baltic countries, Germany
claimed only economic interests. The Non-Aggression Pact
and the secret agreement were signed rather late on the night
of August 23.[6]

* * * * *

Despite all that has been dispassionately recorded in this
and the foregoing chapter, only totalitarian despotism in both
countries could have faced the odium of such an unnatural act.
It is a question whether Hitler or Stalin loathed it most. Both
were aware that it could only be a temporary expedient. The
antagonisms between the two empires and systems were mortal.
Stalin no doubt felt that Hitler would be a less deadly foe to
Russia after a year of war with the Western Powers. Hitler
followed his method of "One at a time." The fact that such
an agreement could be made marks the culminating failure
of British and French foreign policy and diplomacy over several years.

On the Soviet side it must be said that their vital need was
to hold the deployment positions of the German armies as
far to the west as possible so as to give the Russians more time
for assembling their forces from all parts of their immense
empire. They had burnt in their minds the disasters which
had come upon their armies in 1914, when they had hurled
themselves forward to attack the Germans while still themselves only partly mobilised. But now their frontiers lay far
to the east of those of the previous war. They must be in oc-

---

[6] *Nuremberg Documents*, Part 1, page 210 ff.

cupation of the Baltic States and a large part of Poland by force
or fraud before they were attacked. If their policy was cold-
blooded, it was also at the moment realistic in a high degree.

The sinister news broke upon the world like an explosion.
On August 21/22, the Soviet Tass Agency stated that Ribbentrop was flying to Moscow to sign a Non-Aggression Pact with
the Soviet Union. Whatever emotions the British Government
may have experienced, fear was not among them. They lost
no time in declaring that "such an event would in no way
affect their obligations, which they were determined to fulfil."
Nothing could now avert or delay the conflict.

*   *   *   *   *

It is still worth while to record the terms of the Pact:

Both High Contracting Parties obligate themselves to desist from
any act of violence, any aggressive action, and any attack on each
other, either individually or jointly with other Powers.

This treaty was to last ten years, and if not denounced by
either side one year before the expiration of that period, would
be automatically extended for another five years. There was
much jubilation and many toasts around the conference table.
Stalin spontaneously proposed the toast of the Fuehrer, as follows, "I know how much the German Nation loves its Fuehrer,
I should therefore like to drink his health." A moral may be
drawn from all this, which is of homely simplicity — "Honesty
is the best policy." Several examples of this will be shown in
these pages. Crafty men and statesmen will be shown misled
by all their elaborate calculations. But this is the signal instance. Only twenty-two months were to pass before Stalin and
the Russian nation in its scores of millions were to pay a frightful forfeit. If a Government has no moral scruples, it often
seems to gain great advantages and liberties of action, but "All
comes out even at the end of the day, and all will come out
yet more even when all the days are ended."

*   *   *   *   *

Hitler was sure from secret interchanges that the Russian Pact would be signed on August 22; even before Ribbentrop returned from Moscow or the public announcement was made, he addressed his Commanders-in-Chief as follows:

We must be determined from the beginning to fight the Western Powers. . . . The conflict with Poland was bound to come sooner or later. I had already made this decision in the spring, but I thought I would first turn against the West and only afterwards against the East. . . . We need not be afraid of a blockade. The East will supply us with grain, cattle, coal. . . . I am only afraid that at the last minute some *Schweinhund* will make a proposal for mediation. . . . The political aim is set further. A beginning has been made for the destruction of England's hegemony. The same is open for the soldier, after I have made the political preparations.[7]

*   *   *   *   *

On the news of the German-Soviet Pact, the British Government at once took precautionary measures. Orders were issued for key parties of the coast and anti-aircraft defences to assemble, and for the protection of vulnerable points. Telegrams were sent to Dominion Governments and to the colonies, warning them that it might be necessary in the very near future to institute the precautionary stage. The Lord Privy Seal was authorised to bring The Regional Organisation onto a war footing. On August 23, the Admiralty received Cabinet authority to requisition twenty-five merchantmen for conversion to armed merchant cruisers (A.M.C.), and thirty-five trawlers to be fitted with Asdics. Six thousand reservists for the overseas garrisons were called up. The anti-aircraft defence of the radar stations and the full deployment of the anti-aircraft forces were approved. Twenty-four thousand reservists of the air force and all the air auxiliary force, including the balloon squadrons, were called up. All leave was stopped throughout the fighting services. The Admiralty issued warnings to merchant shipping. Many other steps were taken.

[7] *Nuremberg Documents*, Part 1, page 173.

*   *   *   *   *

The Prime Minister decided to write to Hitler about these
preparatory measures. This letter does not appear in Mr.
Feiling's biography, but has been printed elsewhere. In justice
to Mr. Chamberlain it should certainly be widely read:

Your Excellency will have already heard of certain measures
taken by His Majesty's Government and announced in the press and
on the wireless this evening.

These steps have, in the opinion of His Majesty's Government,
been rendered necessary by the military movements which have
been reported from Germany, and by the fact that apparently the
announcement of a German-Soviet Agreement is taken in some
quarters in Berlin to indicate that intervention by Great Britain
on behalf of Poland is no longer a contingency that need be
reckoned with. No greater mistake could be made. Whatever may
prove to be the nature of the German-Soviet Agreement, it cannot
alter Great Britain's obligation to Poland, which His Majesty's
Government have stated in public repeatedly and plainly, and
which they are determined to fulfil.

It has been alleged that if His Majesty's Government had made
their position more clear in 1914, the great catastrophe would have
been avoided. Whether or not there is any force in that allegation,
His Majesty's Government are resolved that on this occasion there
shall be no such tragic misunderstanding. If the need should arise,
they are resolved and prepared to employ without delay all the
forces at their command, and it is impossible to foresee the end of
hostilities once engaged. It would be a dangerous delusion to think
that, if war once starts, it will come to an early end, even if a success
on any one of the several fronts on which it will be engaged should
have been secured.

At this time I confess I can see no other way to avoid a catastrophe that will involve Europe in war. In view of the grave
consequences to humanity which may follow from the action of
their rulers, I trust that Your Excellency will weigh with the
utmost deliberation the considerations which I have put before
you.[8]

Hitler's reply, after dwelling on the "unparalleled magnanimity" with which Germany was prepared to settle the

8 *Ibid.*, Part 2, pages 157–58.

question of Danzig and the Corridor, contained the following
piece of lying effrontery:

The unconditional assurance given by England to Poland that
she would render assistance to that country in all circumstances,
regardless of the causes from which a conflict might spring, could
only be interpreted in that country as an encouragement henceforward to unloose, under cover of such a charter, a wave of
appalling terrorism against the one and a half million German
inhabitants living in Poland.[9]

On August 25, the British Government proclaimed a formal
treaty with Poland, confirming the guarantees already given.
It was hoped by this step to give the best chance to a settlement by direct negotiation between Germany and Poland in
the face of the fact that if this failed, Britain would stand by
Poland. Said Goering at Nuremberg:

On the day when England gave her official guarantee to Poland,
the Fuehrer called me on the telephone and told me that he had
stopped the planned invasion of Poland. I asked him then whether
this was just temporary or for good. He said, "No, I shall have to
see whether we can eliminate British intervention." [10]

In fact, Hitler postponed D-Day from August 25 to September 1, and entered into direct negotiation with Poland, as
Chamberlain desired. His object was not, however, to reach an
agreement with Poland, but to give His Majesty's Government
every opportunity to escape from their guarantee. Their
thoughts, like those of Parliament and the nation, were upon a
different plane. It is a curious fact about the British Islanders,
who hate drill and have not been invaded for nearly a thousand years, that as danger comes nearer and grows, they become progressively less nervous; when it is imminent, they are
fierce; when it is mortal, they are fearless. These habits have
led them into some very narrow escapes.

9 *Ibid.*, page 158.
10 *Ibid.*, page 166.

*   *   *   *   *

A letter from Hitler to Mussolini at this time has recently been published in Italy:

Duce,

For some time Germany and Russia have been meditating upon the possibility of placing their mutual political relations upon a new basis. The need to arrive at concrete results in this sense has been strengthened by:

1. The condition of the world political situation in general.
2. The continued procrastination of the Japanese Cabinet in taking up a clear stand. Japan was ready for an alliance against Russia in which Germany — and in my view Italy — could only be interested in the present circumstances as a secondary consideration. She was not agreeable, however, to assuming any clear obligations regarding England — a decisive question from the German side, and I think also from Italy's. . . .
3. The relations between Germany and Poland have been unsatisfactory since the spring, and in recent weeks have become simply intolerable, not through the fault of the Reich, but principally because of British action. . . . These reasons have induced me to hasten on a conclusion of the Russian-German talks. I have not yet informed you, Duce, in detail on this question. But now in recent weeks the disposition of the Kremlin to engage in an exchange of relations with Germany — a disposition produced from the moment of the dismissal of Litvinov — has been increasingly marked, and has now made it possible for me, after having reached a preliminary clarification, to send my Foreign Minister to Moscow to draw up a treaty which is far and away the most extensive non-aggression pact in existence today, and the text of which will be made public. The pact is unconditional, and establishes in addition the commitment to consult on all questions which interest Germany and Russia. I can also inform you, Duce, that, given these undertakings, the benevolent attitude of Russia is assured, and *that above all there now exists no longer the possibility of any attack whatsoever on the part of Rumania in the event of a conflict.*[11]

To this Mussolini sent an immediate answer:

I am replying to your letter which has just been delivered to me by Ambassador Mackensen.

[11] *Hitler-Mussolini Letters and Documents*, page 7.

1. As far as the agreement with Russia is concerned, I completely approve.

2. I feel it would be useful to avoid a rupture or coolness with Japan and her consequent drawing together with the group of democratic states. . . .

3. The Moscow Pact blocks Rumania, and may change the position of Turkey, who has accepted an English loan, but who has not yet signed the alliance. A new attitude on the part of Turkey would upset the strategic disposition of the French and English in the Eastern Mediterranean.

4. About Poland I understand completely the German position and the fact that such a tense situation cannot continue indefinitely.

5. Regarding the practical attitude of Italy in the event of military action, my point of view is the following:

If Germany attacks Poland and the conflict is localised, Italy will give Germany every form of political and economic aid which may be required.

If Germany attacks Poland and the allies of the latter counterattack Germany, I must emphasise to you that I cannot assume the initiative of warlike operations, given the actual conditions of Italian military preparations which have been repeatedly and in timely fashion pointed out to you, Fuehrer, and to von Ribbentrop.

Our intervention could, however, be immediate if Germany were to give us at once the munitions and raw materials to sustain the shock which the French and British would probably inflict upon us. In our previous meetings war was envisaged after 1942, and on this date I should have been ready on land, by sea, and in the air, according to our agreed plans.[12]

From this point Hitler knew, if he had not divined it already, that he could not count upon the armed intervention of Italy if war came. Any last-minute attempts by Mussolini to repeat his performance of Munich were brushed aside. It seems to have been from English rather than from German sources that the Duce learnt of the final moves. Ciano records in his *Diary* on August 27, "The English communicate to us the text of the German proposals to London, about which we are kept entirely in the dark." [13] Mussolini's only need now was Hitler's acquiescence in Italy's neutrality. This was accorded to him.

12 *Ibid.*, page 10.   13 Ciano, *op. cit.*, page 136.

*   *   *   *   *

On August 31, Hitler issued his "Directive Number 1 for the conduct of the war."

1. Now that all the political possibilities of disposing by peaceful means of a situation on the eastern frontier which is intolerable for Germany are exhausted, I have determined on a solution by force.

2. The attack on Poland is to be carried out in accordance with the preparation made for "Fall Weiss" [Case White] with the alterations which result, where the Army is concerned, from the fact that it has in the meantime almost completed its dispositions. Allotment of tasks and the operational targets remain unchanged.

The date of attack — September 1, 1939. Time of attack — 04.45 [inserted in red pencil].

3. In the West it is important that the responsibility for the opening of hostilities should rest unequivocally with England and France. At first purely local action should be taken against insignificant frontier violations.[14]

*   *   *   *   *

On my return from the Rhine front, I passed some sunshine days at Madame Balsan's place, with a pleasant but deeply anxious company, in the old château where King Henry of Navarre had slept the night before the Battle of Ivry. Mrs. Euan Wallace and her sons were with us. Her husband was a Cabinet Minister. She was expecting him to join her. Presently he telegraphed he could not come, and would explain later why. Other signs of danger drifted in upon us. One could feel the deep apprehension brooding over all, and even the light of this lovely valley at the confluence of the Eure and the Vesgre seemed robbed of its genial ray. I found painting hard work in this uncertainty. On August 26, I decided to go home, where at least I could find out what was going on. I told my wife I would send her word in good time. On my way through Paris I gave General Georges luncheon. He produced all the figures of the French and German Armies, and classified the divisions in quality. The result impressed me so much that for the first time I said: "But you are the masters." He re-

14 *Nuremberg Documents,* Part 2, page 172.

plied: "The Germans have a very strong army, and we shall
never be allowed to strike first. If they attack, both our countries will rally to their duty."

That night I slept at Chartwell, where I had asked General
Ironside to stay with me next day. He had just returned from
Poland, and the reports he gave of the Polish Army were most
favourable. He had seen a divisional attack-exercise under a
live barrage, not without casualties. Polish morale was high.
He stayed three days with me, and we tried hard to measure
the unknowable. Also at this time I completed bricklaying the
kitchen of the cottage which during the year past I had prepared for our family home in the years which were to come.
My wife, on my signal, came over via Dunkirk, on August 30.

*   *   *   *   *

There were known to be twenty thousand organised German
Nazis in England at this time, and it would only have been in
accord with their procedure in other friendly countries that the
outbreak of war should be preceded by a sharp prelude of
sabotage and murder. I had at that time no official protection,
and I did not wish to ask for any; but I thought myself sufficiently prominent to take precautions. I had enough information to convince me that Hitler recognised me as a foe. My
former Scotland Yard detective, Inspector Thompson, was in
retirement. I told him to come along and bring his pistol with
him. I got out my own weapons, which were good. While one
slept, the other watched. Thus nobody would have had a walk-
over. In these hours I knew that if war came — and who could
doubt its coming? — a major burden would fall upon me.

END OF BOOK ONE

★

Book Two

THE TWILIGHT WAR

September 3, 1939 — May 10, 1940

1

War

POLAND WAS ATTACKED by Germany at dawn on September 1. The mobilisation of all our forces was ordered during the morning. The Prime Minister asked me to visit him in the afternoon at Downing Street. He told me that he saw no hope of averting war with Germany and that he proposed to form a small War Cabinet of Ministers without departments to conduct it. He mentioned that the Labour Party were not, he understood, willing to share in a national coalition. He still had hopes that the Liberals would join him. He invited me to become a member of the War Cabinet. I agreed to his proposal without comment, and on this basis we had a long talk on men and measures.

After some reflection, I felt that the average age of the Ministers who were to form the supreme executive of war direction

would be thought too high, and I wrote to Mr. Chamberlain
after midnight accordingly:

2.9.39.

Aren't we a very old team? I make out that the six you mentioned to me yesterday aggregate 386 years or an average of over 64!
Only one year short of the Old Age Pension! If, however, you
added Sinclair (49) and Eden (42) the average comes down
to fifty-seven and a half.

If the *Daily Herald* is right that Labour will not come in, we shall
certainly have to face a constant stream of criticism, as well as the
many disappointments and surprises of which war largely consists.
Therefore, it seems to me all the more important to have the
Liberal Opposition firmly incorporated in our ranks. Eden's influence with the section of Conservatives who are associated with
him, as well as with moderate Liberal elements, also seems to me
to be a very necessary reinforcement.

The Poles have now been under heavy attack for thirty hours,
and I am much concerned to hear that there is talk in Paris of a
further note. I trust you will be able to announce our Joint
Declaration of War at *latest* when Parliament meets this afternoon.

The *Bremen* will soon be out of the interception zoné unless the
Admiralty take special measures and the signal is given today. This
is only a minor point, but it may well be vexatious.

I remain here at your disposal.[1]

I was surprised to hear nothing from Mr. Chamberlain during the whole of September 2, which was a day of intense crisis.
I thought it probable that a last-minute effort was being made
to preserve peace; and this proved true. However, when Parliament met in the afternoon, a short but very fierce debate occurred, in which the Prime Minister's temporising statement
was ill-received by the House. When Mr. Greenwood rose to
speak on behalf of the Labour Opposition, Mr. Amery from
the Conservative benches cried out to him, "Speak for England." This was received with loud cheers. There was no
doubt that the temper of the House was for war. I even
deemed it more resolute and united than in the similar scene
on August 2, 1914, in which I had also taken part. In the eve-

[1] Feiling, *op. cit.,* page 420.

ning a number of gentlemen of importance in all parties called
upon me at my flat opposite the Westminster Cathedral, and
all expressed deep anxiety lest we should fail in our obligations to Poland. The House was to meet again at noon the next
day. I wrote that night as follows to the Prime Minister:

2.9.39.

I have not heard anything from you since our talks on Friday,
when I understood that I was to serve as your colleague, and when
you told me that this would be announced speedily. I really do
not know what has happened during the course of this agitated day;
though it seems to me that entirely different ideas have ruled from
those which you expressed to me when you said, "The die was cast."
I quite realise that in contact with this tremendous European
situation changes of method may become necessary, but I feel
entitled to ask you to let me know how we stand, both publicly
and privately, before the debate opens at noon.

It seems to me that if the Labour Party, and as I gather the
Liberal Party, are estranged, it will be difficult to form an effective
War Government on the limited basis you mentioned. I consider
that a further effort should be made to bring in the Liberals, and in
addition that the composition and scope of the War Cabinet you
discussed with me requires review. There was a feeling tonight in
the House that injury had been done to the spirit of national unity
by the apparent weakening of our resolve. I do not underrate the
difficulties you have with the French; but I trust that we shall now
take our decision independently, and thus give our French friends
any lead that may be necessary. In order to do this, we shall need
the strongest and most integral combination that can be formed.
I therefore ask that there should be no announcement of the composition of the War Cabinet until we have had a further talk.

As I wrote to you yesterday morning, I hold myself entirely at
your disposal, with every desire to aid you in your task.

I learnt later that a British ultimatum had been given to
Germany at 9.30 P.M. on September 1, and that this had been
followed by a second and final ultimatum at 9 A.M. on September 3. The early broadcast of the third announced that the
Prime Minister would speak on the radio at 11.15 A.M. As
it now seemed certain that war would be immediately declared

by Great Britain and also by France, I prepared a short speech which I thought would be becoming to the solemn and awful moment in our lives and history.

The Prime Minister's broadcast informed us that we were already at war, and he had scarcely ceased speaking when a strange, prolonged, wailing noise, afterwards to become familiar, broke upon the ear. My wife came into the room braced by the crisis and commented favourably upon German promptitude and precision, and we went up to the flat top of the house to see what was going on. Around us on every side, in the clear, cool September light, rose the roofs and spires of London. Above them were already slowly rising thirty or forty cylindrical balloons. We gave the Government a good mark for this evident sign of preparation, and as the quarter of an hour's notice, which we had been led to expect we should receive, was now running out, we made our way to the shelter assigned to us, armed with a bottle of brandy and other appropriate medical comforts.

Our shelter was a hundred yards down the street and consisted merely of an open basement, not even sandbagged, in which the tenants of half a dozen flats were already assembled. Everyone was cheerful and jocular, as is the English manner when about to encounter the unknown. As I gazed from the doorway along the empty street and at the crowded room below, my imagination drew pictures of ruin and carnage and vast explosions shaking the ground; of buildings clattering down in dust and rubble, of fire brigades and ambulances scurrying through the smoke, beneath the drone of hostile aeroplanes. For had we not all been taught how terrible air raids would be? The Air Ministry had, in natural self-importance, greatly exaggerated their power. The pacifists had sought to play on public fears, and those of us who had so long pressed for preparation and a superior air force, while not accepting the most lurid forecasts, had been content they should act as a spur. I knew that the Government were prepared, in the first few days of the war, with over two hundred and fifty thousand beds for air-raid casualties. Here at least there had been no underestimation. Now we should see what were the facts.

After about ten minutes had passed, the wailing broke out again. I was myself not sure that this was not a reiteration of the previous warning, but a man came running along the street shouting "All Clear," and we dispersed to our dwellings and went about our business. Mine was to go to the House of Commons, which duly met at noon with its unhurried procedure and brief, stately prayers. There I received a note from the Prime Minister asking me to come to his room as soon as the debate died down. As I sat in my place, listening to the speeches, a very strong sense of calm came over me, after the intense passions and excitements of the last few days. I felt a serenity of mind and was conscious of a kind of uplifted detachment from human and personal affairs. The glory of Old England, peace-loving and ill-prepared as she was, but instant and fearless at the call of honour, thrilled my being and seemed to lift our fate to those spheres far removed from earthly facts and physical sensation. I tried to convey some of this mood to the House when I spoke, not without acceptance.

Mr. Chamberlain told me that he had considered my letters, that the Liberals would not join the Government, that he was able to meet my views about the average age to some extent by bringing the three Service Ministers into the War Cabinet in spite of their executive functions, and that this would reduce the average age to less than sixty. This, he said, made it possible for him to offer me the Admiralty as well as a seat in the War Cabinet. I was very glad of this because, though I had not raised the point, I naturally preferred a definite task to that exalted brooding over the work done by others which may well be the lot of a Minister, however influential, who has no department. It is easier to give directions than advice, and more agreeable to have the right to act, even in a limited sphere, than the privilege to talk at large. Had the Prime Minister in the first instance given me the choice between the War Cabinet and the Admiralty, I should, of course, have chosen the Admiralty. Now I was to have both.

Nothing had been said about when I should formally receive my office from the King, and in fact I did not kiss hands till the fifth. But the opening hours of war may be vital with navies. I therefore sent word to the Admiralty that I would take charge forthwith and arrive at six o'clock. On this the Board were kind enough to signal to the Fleet, "Winston is back." So it was that I came again to the room I had quitted in pain and sorrow almost exactly a quarter of a century before, when Lord Fisher's resignation had led to my removal from my post as First Lord and ruined irretrievably, as it proved, the important conception of forcing the Dardanelles. A few feet behind me, as I sat in my old chair, was the wooden map-case I had had fixed in 1911, and inside it still remained the chart of the North Sea on which each day, in order to focus attention on the supreme objective, I had made the Naval Intelligence Branch record the movements and dispositions of the German High Seas Fleet. Since 1911 much more than a quarter of a century had passed, and still mortal peril threatened us at the hands of the same nation. Once again defence of the rights of a weak state, outraged and invaded by unprovoked aggression, forced us to draw the sword. Once again we must fight for life and honour against all the might and fury of the valiant, disciplined, and ruthless German race. Once again! So be it.

*   *   *   *   *

Presently the First Sea Lord came to see me. I had known Dudley Pound slightly in my previous tenure of the Admiralty as one of Lord Fisher's trusted staff officers. I had strongly condemned in Parliament the dispositions of the Mediterranean Fleet when he commanded it in 1938, at the moment of the Italian descent upon Albania. Now we met as colleagues upon whose intimate relations and fundamental agreement the smooth working of the vast Admiralty machine would depend. We eyed each other amicably if doubtfully. But from the earliest days our friendship and mutual confidence grew and ripened. I measured and respected the great professional and personal qualities of Admiral Pound. As the war, with all its shifts and fortunes, beat upon us with clanging blows, we became ever truer comrades and friends. And when, four years later, he died at the moment of the general victory over Italy, I mourned with a personal pang for all the Navy and the nation had lost.

I spent a good part of the night of the third, meeting the Sea Lords and heads of the various departments, and from the morning of the fourth I laid my hands upon the naval affairs. As in 1914, precautionary measures against surprise had been taken in advance of general mobilisation. As early as June 15, large numbers of officers and men of the reserves had been called up. The reserve fleet, fully manned for exercises, had been inspected by the King on August 9, and on the twenty-second various additional classes of reservists had been summoned. On the twenty-fourth an Emergency Powers Defence Bill was passed through Parliament, and at the same time the Fleet was ordered to its war stations; in fact our main forces had been at Scapa Flow for some weeks. After the general mobilisation of the Fleet had been authorised, the Admiralty war plan had unfolded smoothly, and in spite of certain serious deficiencies, notably in cruisers and anti-submarine vessels, the challenge, as in 1914, found the Fleet equal to the immense tasks before it.

* * * * *

I had, as the reader may be aware, a considerable knowledge of the Admiralty and of the Royal Navy. The four years from 1911 to 1915, when I had the duty of preparing the Fleet for war and the task of directing the Admiralty during the first ten critical months, had been the most vivid of my life. I had amassed an immense amount of detailed information and had learned many lessons about the Fleet and war at sea. In the interval I had studied and written much about naval affairs. I had spoken repeatedly upon them in the House of Commons. I had always preserved a close contact with the Admiralty and, although their foremost critic in these years, I had been made privy to many of their secrets. My four years' work on the Air Defence Research Committee had given me access to all the most modern developments of radar which now vitally affected the naval service. I have mentioned how in June, 1938, Lord

Chatfield, the First Sea Lord, had himself shown me over the
anti-submarine school at Portland, and how we had gone to sea
in destroyers on an exercise in submarine-detection by the use
of the Asdic apparatus. My intimacy with the late Admiral
Henderson, Controller of the Navy till 1938, and the discussions which the First Lord of those days had encouraged me to
have with Lord Chatfield upon the design of new battleships
and cruisers, gave me a full view over the sphere of new construction. I was, of course, familiar from the published records
with the strength, composition, and structure of our Fleet,
actual and prospective, and with those of the German, Italian,
and Japanese Navies.

As a critic and a spur, my public speeches had naturally
dwelt upon weaknesses and shortcomings and, taken by themselves, had by no means portrayed either the vast strength of
the Royal Navy or my own confidence in it. It would be unjust
to the Chamberlain Administration and their service advisers
to suggest that the Navy had not been adequately prepared for
a war with Germany, or with Germany and Italy. The effective
defence of Australasia and India in the face of a simultaneous
attack by Japan raised more serious difficulties: but in this case
— which was at the moment unlikely — such an assault might
well have involved the United States. I therefore felt, when I
entered upon my duties, that I had at my disposal what was
undoubtedly the finest-tempered instrument of naval war in
the world, and I was sure that time would be granted to make
good the oversights of peace and to cope with the equally certain unpleasant surprises of war.

*   *   *   *   *

The tremendous naval situation of 1914 in no way repeated
itself. Then we had entered the war with a ratio of sixteen to
ten in capital ships and two to one in cruisers. In those days we
had mobilised eight battle squadrons of eight battleships with
a cruiser squadron and a flotilla assigned to each, together with
important detached cruiser forces, and I looked forward to a
general action with a weaker but still formidable fleet. Now,

the German Navy had only begun their rebuilding and had no power even to form a line of battle. Their two great battle-ships, *Bismarck* and *Tirpitz*, both of which, it must be assumed, had transgressed the agreed Treaty limits in tonnage, were at least a year from completion. The light battle cruisers, *Scharn-horst* and *Gneisenau*, which had been fraudulently increased by the Germans from ten thousand tons to twenty-six thousand tons, had been completed in 1938. Besides this, Germany had available the three "pocket battleships" of ten thousand tons, *Admiral Graf Spee*, *Admiral Scheer*, and *Deutschland*, together with two fast eight-inch-gun cruisers of ten thousand tons, six light cruisers, and sixty destroyers and smaller vessels. Thus there was no challenge in surface craft to our command of the seas. There was no doubt that the British Navy was over-whelmingly superior to the German in strength and in numbers, and no reason to assume that its science training or skill was in any way defective. Apart from the shortage of cruisers and destroyers, the Fleet had been maintained at its customary high standard. It had to face enormous and innum-erable duties, rather than an antagonist.

* * * * *

My views on the naval strategic situation were already largely formed when I went to the Admiralty. The command of the Baltic was vital to the enemy. Scandinavian supplies, Swedish ore, and above all protection against Russian descents on the long undefended northern coastline of Germany — in one place little more than a hundred miles from Berlin — made it imperative for the German Navy to dominate the Bal-tic. I was therefore sure that in this opening phase Germany would not compromise her command of that sea. Thus, while submarines and raiding cruisers, or perhaps one pocket battle-ship, might be sent out to disturb our traffic, no ships would be risked which were necessary to the Baltic control. The German Fleet, as at this moment developed, must aim at this as its prime and almost its sole objective. For the main purposes of sea power and for the enforcement of our principal naval offensive

measure, the blockade, we must of course maintain a superior
fleet in our northern waters; but no very large British naval
forces were, it seemed, needed to watch the debouches from the
Baltic or from the Heligoland Bight.

British security would be markedly increased if an air attack
upon the Kiel Canal rendered that side-door from the Baltic
useless, even if only at intervals.

A year before, I had sent a note upon this special operation
to Sir Thomas Inskip:

October 29, 1938.

In a war with Germany the severance of the Kiel Canal would
be an achievement of the first importance. I do not elaborate this,
as I assume it to be admitted. Plans should be made to do this and,
if need be, all the details should be worked out in their variants
by a special technical committee. Owing to there being few locks,
and no marked difference of sea-level at the two ends of the Canal,
its interruption by H.E. bombs, even of the heaviest type, could
swiftly be repaired. If, however, many bombs of medium size fitted
with time fuses, some set for a day, others for a week, and others
for a month, etc., could be dropped in the Canal, their explosions
at uncertain intervals and in uncertain places would close the Canal
to the movement of warships or valuable vessels until the whole
bottom had been deeply dredged. Alternatively, *special fuses with
magnetic actuation* should be considered.

The phrase about magnetic mines is interesting in view of
what was soon to come upon us. No special action had, however, been taken.

*   *   *   *   *

The British merchant fleet on the outbreak of war was about
the same size as in 1914. It was over twenty-one million tons.
The average size of the ships had increased, and thus there were
fewer. This tonnage was not, however, all available for trade.
The Navy required auxiliary warships of various types which
must be drawn chiefly from the highest class of liners. All the
defence services needed ships for special purposes: the Army
and R.A.F. for the movement of troops and equipment overseas, and the Navy for all the work at fleet bases and elsewhere,

and particularly for providing oil fuel at strategic points all over the world. Demands for tonnage for all these objects amounted to nearly three million tons, and to these must be added the shipping requirements of the Empire overseas. At the end of 1939, after balancing gains and losses, the total British tonnage available for commercial use was about fifteen and a half million tons.

*   *   *   *   *

Italy had not declared war, and it was already clear that Mussolini was waiting upon events. In this uncertainty and as a measure of precaution till all our arrangements were complete, we thought it best to divert our shipping round the Cape. We had, however, already on our side, in addition to our own preponderance over Germany and Italy combined, the powerful fleet of France, which by the remarkable capacity and long administration of Admiral Darlan had been brought to the highest strength and degree of efficiency ever attained by the French Navy since the days of the monarchy. Should Italy become hostile, our first battlefield must be the Mediterranean. I was entirely opposed, except as a temporary convenience, to all plans for quitting the centre and merely sealing up the ends of the great inland sea. Our forces alone, even without the aid of the French Navy and its fortified harbours, were sufficient to drive the Italian ships from the sea, and should secure complete naval command of the Mediterranean within two months and possibly sooner.

The British domination of the Mediterranean would inflict injuries upon an enemy Italy which might be fatal to her power of continuing the war. All her troops in Libya and in Abyssinia would be cut flowers in a vase. The French and our own people in Egypt could be reinforced to any extent desired, while theirs would be overweighted if not starved. Not to hold the Central Mediterranean would be to expose Egypt and the Canal, as well as the French possessions, to invasion by Italian troops with German leadership. Moreover, a series of swift and striking victories in this theatre, which might be obtainable in

the early weeks of a war, would have a most healthy and helpful
bearing upon the main struggle with Germany. Nothing should
stand between us and these results, both naval and military.

*   *   *   *   *

I had accepted too readily when out of office the Admiralty
view of the extent to which the submarine had been mastered.
Whilst the technical efficiency of the Asdic apparatus was
proved in many early encounters with U-boats, our anti-U-boat
resources were far too limited to prevent our suffering serious
losses. My opinion recorded at the time, "The submarine
should be quite controllable in the outer seas and certainly in
the Mediterranean. There will be losses, but nothing to affect
the scale of events," was not incorrect. Nothing of major importance occurred in the first year of the U-boat warfare. The
Battle of the Atlantic was reserved for 1941 and 1942.

In common with prevailing Admiralty belief before the war,
I did not sufficiently measure the danger to, or the consequent
deterrent upon, British warships from air attack. "In my
opinion," I had written a few months before the war, "given
with great humility (because these things are very difficult to
judge), an air attack upon British warships, armed and protected as they now are, will not prevent full exercise of their
superior sea power." However, the deterrents — albeit exaggerated — upon our mobility soon became grave. The air almost immediately proved itself a formidable menace, especially
in the Mediterranean. Malta, with its almost negligible air
defences, presented a problem for which there was no immediate solution. On the other hand, in the first year no British
capital ship was sunk by air attack.

*   *   *   *   *

There was no sign at this moment of any hostile action or
intent upon the part of Japan. The main preoccupation of
Japan was naturally America. It did not seem possible to me
that the United States could sit passive and watch a general
assault by Japan upon all European establishments in the Far

East, even if they themselves were not for the moment involved. In this case we should gain far more from the entry of the United States, perhaps only against Japan, if that were possible, than we should suffer from the hostility of Japan, vexatious though that would be. On no account must anything which threatened in the Far East divert us from our prime objectives in Europe. We could not protect our interests and possessions in the Yellow Sea from Japanese attack. The farthest point we could defend if Japan came in would be the fortress of Singapore. Singapore must hold out until the Mediterranean was safe and the Italian Fleet liquidated.

I did not fear at the moment of the outbreak that Japan would send a fleet and army to conquer Singapore, provided that fortress were adequately garrisoned and supplied with food and ammunition for at least six months. Singapore was as far from Japan as Southampton from New York. Over these three thousand miles of salt water Japan would have to send the bulk of her Fleet, escort at least sixty thousand men in transports in order to effect a landing, and begin a siege which would end only in disaster if the Japanese sea communications were cut at any stage. These views, of course, ceased to apply once the Japanese had occupied Indo-China and Siam and had built up a powerful army and very heavy air forces only three hundred miles away across the Gulf of Siam. This, however, did not occur for more than a year and a half.

As long as the British Navy was undefeated, and as long as we held Singapore, no invasion of Australia or New Zealand by Japan was deemed possible. We could give Australasia a good guarantee to protect them from this danger, but we must do it in our own way, and in the proper sequence of operations. It seemed unlikely that a hostile Japan exulting in the mastery of the Yellow Sea would send afloat a conquering and colonising expedition to Australia. A large and well-equipped army would be needed for a long time to make any impression upon Australian manhood. Such an undertaking would require the improvident diversion of the Japanese Fleet, and its engagement in a long, desultory struggle in Australia. At any moment

a decision in the Mediterranean would liberate very powerful
naval forces to cut invaders from their base. It would be easy
for the United States to tell Japan that they would regard the
sending of Japanese fleets and transports south of the Equator
as an act of war. They might well be disposed to make such
a declaration, and there would be no harm in sounding them
upon this very remote contingency.

The actual strength of the British and German Fleets, built
and building, on the night of September 3, 1939, and that of
the American, French, Italian, and Japanese Fleets on the same
basis, is set forth in Appendix A, Book II. It was my recorded
conviction that *in the first year of a world war* Australia and
New Zealand would be in no danger whatever in their homeland, and by the end of the first year we might hope to have
cleaned up the seas and oceans. As a forecast of *the first year of
the naval war* these thoughts proved true. We shall in their
proper place recount the tremendous events which occurred in
1941 and 1942 in the Far East.

*   *   *   *   *

Newspaper opinion, headed by *The Times,* favoured the
principle of a War Cabinet of not more than five or six Ministers, all of whom should be free from departmental duties.
Thus alone, it was argued, could a broad and concerted view
be taken upon war policy, especially in its larger aspects. Put
shortly, "Five men with nothing to do but to run the war" was
deemed the ideal. There are, however, many practical objections to such a course. A group of detached statesmen, however high their nominal authority, are at a serious disadvantage
in dealing with the Ministers at the head of the great departments vitally concerned. This is especially true of the service
departments. The War Cabinet personages can have no direct
responsibility for day-to-day events. They may take major decisions, they may advise in general terms beforehand or criticise
afterwards, but they are no match, for instance, for a First Lord
of the Admiralty or a Secretary of State for War or Air who,
knowing every detail of the subject and supported by his profes-

sional colleagues, bears the burden of action. United, there is little they cannot settle, but usually there are several opinions among them. Words and arguments are interminable, and meanwhile the torrent of war takes its headlong course. The War Cabinet Ministers themselves would naturally be diffident of challenging the responsible Minister, armed with all his facts and figures. They feel a natural compunction in adding to the strain upon those actually in executive control. They tend, therefore, to become more and more theoretical supervisors and commentators, reading an immense amount of material every day, but doubtful how to use their knowledge without doing more harm than good. Often they can do little more than arbitrate or find a compromise in interdepartmental disputes. It is therefore necessary that the Ministers in charge of the Foreign Office and the fighting departments should be integral members of the supreme body. Usually some at least of the "Big Five" are chosen for their political influence, rather than for their knowledge of, and aptitude for, warlike operations. The numbers, therefore, begin to grow far beyond the limited circle originally conceived. Of course, where the Prime Minister himself becomes Minister of Defence, a strong compression is obtained. Personally, when I was placed in charge I did not like having unharnessed Ministers around me. I preferred to deal with chiefs of organisations rather than counsellors. Everyone should do a good day's work and be accountable for some definite task, and then they do not make trouble for trouble's sake or to cut a figure.

Mr. Chamberlain's original War Cabinet plan was almost immediately expanded, by the force of circumstances, to include Lord Halifax, Foreign Secretary; Sir Samuel Hoare, Lord Privy Seal; Sir John Simon, Chancellor of the Exchequer; Lord Chatfield, Minister for the Co-ordination of Defence; Lord Hankey, Minister without Portfolio; Mr. Hore-Belisha, Secretary of State for War; and Sir Kingsley Wood, Secretary of State for Air. To these were added the Service Ministers, of whom I was now one. In addition it was necessary that the Dominions Secretary, Mr. Eden, and Sir John Anderson as

Home Secretary and Minister of Home Security, though not actual members of the War Cabinet, should be present on all occasions. Thus our total was eleven. The decision to bring in the three Service Ministers profoundly affected Lord Chatfield's authority as Minister for the Co-ordination of Defence. He accepted the position with his customary good nature.

Apart from myself, all the other Ministers had directed our affairs for a good many recent years or were involved in the situation we now had to face both in diplomacy and war. Mr. Eden had resigned on foreign policy in February, 1938. I had not held public office for eleven years. I had, therefore, no responsibility for the past or for any want of preparation now apparent. On the contrary, I had for the last six or seven years been a continual prophet of evils which had now in large measure come to pass. Thus, armed as I now was with the mighty machine of the Navy, on which fell in this phase the sole burden of active fighting, I did not feel myself at any disadvantage; and had I done so, it would have been removed by the courtesy and loyalty of the Prime Minister and his colleagues. All these men I knew very well. Most of us had served together for five years in Mr. Baldwin's Cabinet, and we had, of course, been constantly in contact, friendly or controversial, through the changing scenes of parliamentary life. Sir John Simon and I, however, represented an older political generation. I had served, off and on, in British Governments for fifteen years, and he for almost as long, before any of the others had gained public office. I had been at the head of the Admiralty or Ministry of Munitions through the stresses of the First World War. Although the Prime Minister was my senior by some years in age, I was almost the only antediluvian. This might well have been a matter of reproach in a time of crisis, when it was natural and popular to demand the force of young men and new ideas. I saw, therefore, that I should have to strive my utmost to keep pace with the generation now in power and with fresh young giants who might at any time appear. In this I relied upon knowledge as well as upon all possible zeal and mental energy.

For this purpose I had recourse to a method of life which had been forced upon me at the Admiralty in 1914 and 1915, and which I found greatly extended my daily capacity for work. I always went to bed at least for one hour as early as possible in the afternoon and exploited to the full my happy gift of falling almost immediately into deep sleep. By this means I was able to press a day and a half's work into one. Nature had not intended mankind to work from eight in the morning until midnight without that refreshment of blessed oblivion which, even if it only lasts twenty minutes, is sufficient to renew all the vital forces. I regretted having to send myself to bed like a child every afternoon, but I was rewarded by being able to work through the night until two or even later — sometimes much later — in the morning, and begin the new day between eight and nine o'clock. This routine I observed throughout the war, and I commend it to others if and when they find it necessary for a long spell to get the last scrap out of the human structure. The First Sea Lord, Admiral Pound, as soon as he had realised my technique, adopted it himself, except that he did not actually go to bed but dozed off in his armchair. He even carried the policy so far as often to go to sleep during the Cabinet meetings. One word about the Navy was, however, sufficient to awaken him to the fullest activity. Nothing slipped past his vigilant ear, or his comprehending mind.

2

The Admiralty Task

ASTONISHMENT WAS WORLD-WIDE when Hitler's crashing onslaught upon Poland and the declarations of war upon Germany by Britain and France were followed only by a prolonged and oppressive pause. Mr. Chamberlain in a private letter published by his biographer described this phase as "twilight war"; [1] and I find the expression so just and expressive that I have adopted it as the title for this Book. The French armies made no attack upon Germany. Their mobilisation completed, they remained in contact motionless along the whole front. No air action, except reconnaissance, was taken against Britain; nor was any air attack made upon France by the Germans. The French Government requested us to abstain from air attack on Germany, stating that it would provoke retalia-

[1] Feiling, *op. cit.*, page 424.

tion upon their war factories, which were unprotected. We contented ourselves with dropping pamphlets to rouse the Germans to a higher morality. This strange phase of the war on land and in the air astounded everyone. France and Britain remained impassive while Poland was in a few weeks destroyed or subjugated by the whole might of the German war machine. Hitler had no reason to complain of this.

The war at sea, on the contrary, began from the first hour with full intensity, and the Admiralty therefore became the active centre of events. On September 3, all our ships were sailing about the world on their normal business. Suddenly they were set upon by U-boats carefully posted beforehand, especially in the western approaches. At nine that very night the outward-bound passenger liner *Athenia* of 13,500 tons was torpedoed, and foundered with a loss of a hundred and twelve lives, twenty-eight of them American citizens. This outrage broke upon the world within a few hours. The German Government, to prevent any misunderstanding in the United States, immediately issued a statement that I personally had ordered a bomb to be placed on board this vessel in order by its destruction to prejudice German-American relations. This falsehood received some credence in unfriendly quarters.[2] On the fifth and sixth, the *Bosnia, Royal Sceptre,* and *Rio Claro* were sunk off the coast of Spain, the crew of the *Rio Claro* only being saved. All these were important vessels.

My first Admiralty minute was concerned with the probable scale of the U-boat menace in the immediate future:

Director of Naval Intelligence.   4.IX.39.

Let me have a statement of the German U-boat forces, actual and prospective, for the next few months. Please distinguish between ocean-going and small-size U-boats. Give the estimated radius of action in days and miles in each case.

I was at once informed that the enemy had sixty U-boats and that a hundred would be ready early in 1940. A detailed

[2] See also *Nuremberg Documents, op. cit.,* Part 4, page 267.

answer was returned on the fifth, which should be studied.[3]
The numbers of long-range endurance vessels were formidable
and revealed the intentions of the enemy to work far out in the
oceans as soon as possible.

*   *   *   *   *

Comprehensive plans existed at the Admiralty for multiply-
ing our anti-submarine craft. In particular, preparations had
been made to take up eighty-six of the largest and fastest
trawlers and to equip them with Asdics; the conversion of
many of these was already well advanced. A wartime building
programme of destroyers, both large and small, and of cruisers,
with many ancillary vessels, was also ready in every detail, and
this came into operation automatically with the declaration of
war. The previous war had proved the sovereign merits of convoy. The Admiralty had for some days assumed control of the
movements of all merchant shipping, and shipmasters were
required to obey orders about their routes or about joining
convoy. Our weakness in escort vessels had, however, forced
the Admiralty to devise a policy of evasive routing on the
oceans, unless and until the enemy adopted unrestricted U-boat
warfare, and to confine convoys in the first instance to the east
coast of Britain. But the sinking of the *Athenia* upset these
plans, and we adopted convoy in the North Atlantic forthwith.
The organisation of convoy had been fully prepared, and

[3] *German Submarines*

Type	Tonnage	Numbers in service August 1939	Numbers expected to be in service December 1939	Numbers expected to be in service by early 1940	Estimated radius of action	
					Miles	Days
Coastal	250	30	32	32	4,000	33 at 5 knots
Ocean	500	10	10	23	} 7,200	30 at 10 knots
Ocean	517	9	15	17		
Ocean	712	2	2	..	} 8,400	35 at 10 knots
Ocean	740	8	13	16		
Ocean	1,060	..	2	11	10,000	42 at 10 knots
Ocean	1,028	1 (Built for Turkey		not delivered)	8,000	33 at 10 knots
Grand totals		60	74	99		

shipowners had already been brought into regular consultation
on matters of defence which affected them. Furthermore, instructions had been issued for the guidance of shipmasters in
the many unfamiliar tasks which would inevitably fall upon
them in war, and special signalling as well as other equipment
had been provided to enable them to take their place in convoy. The men of the merchant navy faced the unknown future
with determination. Not content with a passive rôle, they demanded weapons. The use of guns in self-defence by merchant
ships has always been recognised as justifiable by international
law, and the defensive arming of all sea-going merchant ships,
together with the training of the crews, formed an integral part
of the Admiralty plans which were at once put into effect. To
force the U-boat to attack submerged and not merely by gun-
fire on the surface not only gave greater chance for a ship to
escape, but caused the attacker to expend his precious torpedoes more lavishly and often fruitlessly. Foresight had preserved the guns of the previous war for use against U-boats, but
there was a grave shortage of anti-aircraft weapons. It was very
many months before adequate self-protection against air attack
could be provided for merchant ships, which suffered severe
losses meanwhile. We planned from these first days to equip
during the first three months of war a thousand ships with at
least an anti-submarine gun each. This was in fact achieved.

Besides protecting our own shipping, we had to drive German commerce off the seas and stop all imports into Germany.
Blockade was enforced with full rigour. A Ministry of Economic Warfare was formed to guide the policy, whilst the Admiralty controlled its execution. Enemy shipping, as in 1914,
virtually vanished almost at once from the high seas. The German ships mostly took refuge in neutral ports or, when intercepted, scuttled themselves. None the less, fifteen ships totalling
seventy-five thousand tons were captured and put into service
by the Allies before the end of 1939. The great German liner
Bremen, after sheltering in the Soviet port of Murmansk,
reached Germany only because she was spared by the British

submarine *Salmon,* which observed rightly and punctiliously the conventions of international law.[4]

* * * * *

I held my first Admiralty conference on the night of September 4. On account of the importance of the issues, before going to bed in the small hours I recorded its conclusions for circulation and action in my own words:

5.IX.39.

1. In this first phase, with Japan placid, and Italy neutral though indeterminate, the prime attack appears to fall on the approaches to Great Britain from the Atlantic.

2. The convoy system is being set up. By convoy system is meant only anti-submarine convoy. All question of dealing with raiding cruisers or heavy ships is excluded from this particular paper.

3. The First Sea Lord is considering movement to the western approaches of Great Britain of whatever destroyers and escort vessels can be scraped from the Eastern and Mediterranean theatres, with the object of adding, if possible, twelve to the escorts for convoys. These should be available during the period of, say, a month, until the flow of Asdic trawlers begins. A statement should be prepared showing the prospective deliveries during October of these vessels. It would seem well, at any rate in the earliest deliveries, not to wait for the arming of them with guns, but to rely upon depth-charges. Gun-arming can be reconsidered when the pressure eases.

4. The Director of the Trade Division (D.T.D.) should be able to report daily the inward movement of all British merchant ships approaching the island. For this purpose, if necessary, a room and additional staff should be provided. A chart of large size should show at each morning all vessels within two, or better still three, days' distance from our shores. The guidance or control of each of these vessels must be foreseen and prescribed so that there is not one whose case has not been individually dealt with, as far as our resources allow. Pray let me have proposals to implement this, which should come into being within twenty-four hours, and work

4 This submarine was commanded by Lieutenant-Commander Bickford, who was specially promoted for his numerous exploits, but was soon afterwards lost with his vessel.

up later. The necessary contacts with the Board of Trade or other departments concerned should be effected and reported upon.

5. The D.T.D. should also prepare tomorrow a scheme under which every captain or master of a merchant ship from the Atlantic (including the Bay) is visited on arrival by a competent naval authority, who in the name of the D.T.D. will examine the record of the course he has steered, including zigzags. All infractions or divergences from Admiralty instructions should be pointed out, and all serious departures should be punished, examples being made of dismissal. The Admiralty assume responsibility, and the merchant skippers must be made to obey. Details of this scheme should be worked out in personnel and regulations, together with appropriate penalties.

6. For the present it would seem wise to maintain the diversion of merchant traffic from the Mediterranean to the Cape route. This would not exclude the passage of convoys for troops, to which, of course, merchant vessels which were handy might add themselves. But these convoys can only be occasional, i.e., not more than once a month or three weeks, and they must be regarded, not as part of the trade protection, but as naval operations.

7. It follows from the above that in this period, i.e., the first six weeks or two months of the war, the Red Sea will also be closed to everything except naval operations, or perhaps coastal traffic to Egypt.

8. This unpleasant situation would be eased by the deliveries of the Asdic trawlers and other reliefs. Secondly, by the determination of the attitude of Italy. We cannot be sure that the Italian uncertainty will be cleared up in the next six weeks, though we should press His Majesty's Government to bring it to a head in a favourable sense as soon as possible. Meanwhile the heavy ships in the Mediterranean will be on the defensive, and can therefore spare some of the destroyer protection they would need if they were required to approach Italian waters.

9. The question of a breaking-out of any of the five (or seven) German ships of weight would be a major naval crisis requiring a special plan. It is impossible for the Admiralty to provide escorts for convoys of merchant ships against serious surface attack. These raids, if they occur, could only be dealt with as a naval operation by the main Fleet, which would organise the necessary hunting parties to attack the enemy, the trade being cleared out of the way so far as possible till results were obtained.

The First Lord submits these notes to his naval colleagues for consideration, *for criticism and correction,* and hopes to receive proposals for action in the sense desired.

The organisation of outward-bound convoys was brought into force almost at once. By September 8, three main routes had begun to work, namely, from Liverpool and from the Thames to the western ocean, and a coastal convoy between the Thames and the Forth. Staffs for the control of convoys at these ports and many others at home and abroad were included in the war plan, and had already been dispatched. Meanwhile, all ships outward bound in the Channel and Irish Sea and not in convoy were ordered to Plymouth and Milford Haven, and all independent outward sailings were cancelled. Overseas, arrangements for forming homeward-bound convoys were pressed forward. The first of them sailed from Freetown on September 14 and from Halifax, Nova Scotia, on the sixteenth. Before the end of the month regular ocean convoys were in operation, outward from the Thames and Liverpool and homeward from Halifax, Gibraltar, and Freetown.

Upon all the vital need of feeding the island and developing our power to wage war there now at once fell the numbing loss of the Southern Irish ports. This imposed a grievous restriction on the radius of action of our already scarce destroyers:

First Sea Lord and others.   5.IX.39.

A special report should be drawn up by the heads of departments concerned and sent to the First Lord through the First Sea Lord and the Naval Staff upon the questions arising from the so-called neutrality of the so-called Eire. Various considerations arise: (1) What does Intelligence say about possible succouring of U-boats by Irish malcontents in West of Ireland inlets? If they throw bombs in London,[5] why should they not supply fuel to U-boats? Extreme vigilance should be practised.

Secondly, a study is required of the addition to the radius of our destroyers through not having the use of Berehaven or other South Irish anti-submarine bases; showing also the advantage to be gained by our having these facilities.

[5] This referred to a criminal act unconnected with the war.

The Board must realise that we may not be able to obtain satisfaction, as the question of Irish neutrality raises political issues
which have not yet been faced, and which the First Lord is not
certain he can solve. But the full case must be made for consideration.

*   *   *   *   *

After the institution of the convoy system, the next vital
naval need was a safe base for the Fleet. At 10 P.M. on September 5, I held a lengthy conference on this. It recalled many
old memories. In a war with Germany, Scapa Flow is the true
strategic point from which the British Navy can control the
exits from the North Sea and enforce blockade. It was only in
the last two years of the previous war that the Grand Fleet was
judged to have sufficient superiority to move south to Rosyth,
where it had the advantage of lying at a first-class dockyard.
But Scapa, on account of its greater distance from German air
bases, was now plainly the best position and had been definitely
chosen in the Admiralty war plan.

In the autumn of 1914, a wave of uneasiness had swept the
Grand Fleet. The idea had got round, *"the German submarines were coming after them into the harbours."* Nobody at
the Admiralty then believed that it was possible to take a submarine, submerged, through the intricate and swirling channels by which the great lake of Scapa can alone be entered. The
violent tides and currents of the Pentland Firth, often running
eight or ten knots, had seemed in those days to be an effective
deterrent. But a mood of doubt spread through the mighty
array of perhaps a hundred large vessels which in those days
composed the Grand Fleet. On two or three occasions, notably
on October 17, 1914, the alarm was given that there was a U-
boat inside the anchorage. Guns were fired, destroyers thrashed
the waters, and the whole gigantic armada put to sea in haste
and dudgeon. In the final result the Admiralty were proved
right. No German submarine in that war ever overcame the
terrors of the passage. It was only in 1918, after the mutiny
of the German Navy, that a U-boat, manned entirely by officers
seeking to save their honour, perished in a final desperate

effort. Nevertheless, I retained a most vivid and unpleasant
memory of those days and of the extreme exertions we made to
block all the entrances and reassure the Fleet.

There were now in 1939 two dangers to be considered: the
first, the old one of submarine incursion; the second, the new
one of the air. I was surprised to learn at my conference that
more precautions had not been taken in both cases to prepare
the defences against modern forms of attack. Anti-submarine
booms of new design were in position at each of the three main
entrances, but these consisted merely of single lines of net. The
narrow and tortuous approaches on the east side of the Flow,
defended only by remnants of the blockships placed in the
former war and reinforced now by two or three recent additions, remained a source of anxiety. On account of the increased size, speed, and power of modern submarines, the old
belief that the strong tidal streams made these passages impassable to a submarine no longer carried conviction in responsible quarters. As a result of the conference on my second
evening at the Admiralty, many orders were given for additional nets and blockships.

The new danger from the air had been almost entirely ignored.
Except for two batteries of anti-aircraft guns to defend the
naval oil tanks at Hoy and the destroyer anchorage, there were
no air defences at Scapa. One airfield near Kirkwall was available for the use of naval aircraft when the Fleet was present,
but no provision had been made for immediate R.A.F. participation in the defence, and the shore radar station, although
operative, was not wholly effective. Plans for basing two R.A.F.
fighter squadrons at Wick had been approved, but this measure
could not become effective before 1940. I called for an immediate plan of action. Our air defence was so strained, our
resources so limited, and our vulnerable points — including all
vast London — so numerous, that it was no use asking for much.
On the other hand, protection from air attack was now needed
only for five or six great ships, each carrying a powerful anti-
aircraft armament of its own. To keep things going, the
Admiralty undertook to provide two squadrons of naval fighter
aircraft whilst the Fleet was in Scapa.

It seemed most important to have the artillery in position
at the shortest interval, and meanwhile there was nothing for it
but to adopt the same policy of "hide-and-seek" to which we
had been forced in the autumn days of 1914. The west coast
of Scotland had many landlocked anchorages easy to protect
from U-boats by indicator nets and ceaseless patrolling. We
had found concealment in the previous war a good security;
but even in those days the curiosity of a wandering airplane,
perhaps fuelled by traitor hands, had filled our hearts with fear.
Now that the range of aircraft exposed the whole British
Islands at any time to photographic reconnaissance, there was no
sure concealment against large-scale attack either by U-boats or
from the air. However, there were so few ships to cover, and they
could be moved so often from one place to another, that, having
no alternative, we accepted the hazard with as good grace
as possible.

*   *   *   *   *

I felt it my duty to visit Scapa at the earliest moment. I had
not met the Commander-in-Chief, Sir Charles Forbes, since
Lord Chatfield had taken me to the Anti-Submarine School at
Portland in June, 1938. I therefore obtained leave from our
daily Cabinets, and started for Wick with a small personal staff
on the night of September 14. I spent most of the next two
days inspecting the harbour and the entrances with their
booms and nets. I was assured that they were as good as in the
last war, and that important additions and improvements were
being made or were on their way. I stayed with the Commander-in-Chief in his flagship, *Nelson,* and discussed not only
Scapa but the whole naval problem with him and his principal
officers. The rest of the Fleet was hiding in Loch Ewe, and on
the seventeenth the Admiral took me to them in the *Nelson.*
As we came out through the gateway into the open sea, I was surprised to see no escort of destroyers for this great ship. "I
thought," I remarked, "you never went to sea without at least
two, even for a single battleship." But the Admiral replied,
"Of course, that is what we should like; but we haven't got the
destroyers to carry out any such rule. There are a lot of

patrolling craft about, and we shall be into the Minches in a few hours."

It was like the others a lovely day. All went well, and in the evening we anchored in Loch Ewe, where the four or five other great ships of the Home Fleet were assembled. The narrow entry into the loch was closed by several lines of indicator nets, and patrolling craft with Asdics and depth-charges, as well as picket boats, were numerous and busy. On every side rose the purple hills of Scotland in all their splendour. My thoughts went back a quarter of a century to that other September when I had last visited Sir John Jellicoe and his captains in this very bay, and had found them with their long lines of battleships and cruisers drawn out at anchor, a prey to the same uncertainties as now afflicted us. Most of the captains and admirals of those days were dead, or had long passed into retirement. The responsible senior officers who were now presented to me as I visited the various ships had been young lieutenants or even midshipmen in those far-off days. Before the former war I had had three years' preparation in which to make the acquaintance and approve the appointments of most of the high personnel, but now all these were new figures and new faces. The perfect discipline, style and bearing, the ceremonial routine — all were unchanged. But an entirely different generation filled the uniforms and the posts. Only the ships had most of them been laid down in my tenure. None of them was new. It was a strange experience, like suddenly resuming a previous incarnation. It seemed that I was all that survived in the same position I had held so long ago. But no; the dangers had survived too. Danger from beneath the waves, more serious with more powerful U-boats; danger from the air, not merely of being spotted in your hiding-place, but of heavy and perhaps destructive attack!

Having inspected two more ships on the morning of the eighteenth, and formed during my visit a strong feeling of confidence in the Commander-in-Chief, I motored from Loch Ewe to Inverness, where our train awaited us. We had a picnic

lunch on the way by a stream, sparkling in hot sunshine. I felt
oddly oppressed with my memories.

> "For God's sake, let us sit upon the ground
> And tell sad stories of the death of kings."

No one had ever been over the same terrible course twice
with such an interval between. No one had felt its dangers and
responsibilities from the summit as I had or, to descend to a
small point, understood how First Lords of the Admiralty are
treated when great ships are sunk and things go wrong. If
we were in fact going over the same cycle a second time, should
I have once again to endure the pangs of dismissal? Fisher,
Wilson, Battenberg, Jellicoe, Beatty, Pakenham, Sturdee, all
gone!

> "I feel like one
> Who treads alone
> Some banquet hall deserted,
> Whose lights are fled,
> Whose garlands dead,
> And all but he departed!"

And what of the supreme measureless ordeal in which we
were again irrevocably plunged? Poland in its agony; France
but a pale reflection of her former warlike ardour; the Russian
Colossus no longer an ally, not even neutral, possibly to become a foe. Italy no friend. Japan no ally. Would America
ever come in again? The British Empire remained intact and
gloriously united, but ill-prepared, unready. We still had command of the sea. We were woefully outmatched in numbers
in this new mortal weapon of the air. Somehow the light faded
out of the landscape.

We joined our train at Inverness and travelled through the
afternoon and night to London. As we got out at Euston the
next morning, I was surprised to see the First Sea Lord on the
platform. Admiral Pound's look was grave. "I have bad news
for you, First Lord. The *Courageous* was sunk yesterday evening in the Bristol Channel." The *Courageous* was one of our

oldest aircraft carriers, but a very necessary ship at this time. I thanked him for coming to break it to me himself, and said, "We can't expect to carry on a war like this without these sorts of things happening from time to time. I have seen lots of it before." And so to bath and the toil of another day.

In order to bridge the gap of two or three weeks between the outbreak of war and the completion of our auxiliary anti-U-boat flotillas, we had decided to use the aircraft carriers with some freedom in helping to bring in the unarmed, unorganised, and unconvoyed traffic which was then approaching our shores in large numbers. This was a risk which it was right to run. The *Courageous* attended by four destroyers had been thus employed. Towards evening on the seventeenth, two of these had to go to hunt a U-boat which was attacking a merchant ship. When the *Courageous* turned into the wind at dusk, in order to enable her own aircraft to alight upon her landing-deck, she happened, in her unpredictable course, by what may have been a hundred-to-one chance, to meet a U-boat. Out of her crew of 1,260 over 500 were drowned, including Captain Makeig-Jones, who went down with his ship. Three days before another of our aircraft carriers, later to become famous, H.M.S. *Ark Royal,* had also been attacked by a submarine while similarly engaged. Mercifully the torpedoes missed, and her assailant was promptly sunk by her escorting destroyers.

*   *   *   *   *

Outstanding among our naval problems was that of dealing effectively with surface raiders, which would inevitably make their appearance in the near future as they had done in 1914.

On September 12 I issued the following minute:

First Lord to First Sea Lord.   12.IX.39.

Cruiser Policy

In the past we have sought to protect our trade against sudden attack by [means of] cruisers; having regard to the vast ocean spaces to be controlled, the principle was "the more the better." In the search for enemy raiders or cruisers, even small cruisers could play their part, and in the case of the *Emden* we were forced to gather

over twenty ships before she was rounded up. However, a long
view of cruiser policy would seem to suggest that a new unit of
search is required. Whereas a cruiser squadron of four ships could
search on a front of, say eighty miles, a single cruiser accompanied
by an aircraft carrier could cover at least three hundred miles, or if
the movement of the ship is taken into account, four hundred miles.
On the other hand, we must apprehend that the raiders of the
future will be powerful vessels, eager to fight a single-ship action
if a chance is presented. The mere multiplication of small, weak
cruisers is no means of ridding the seas of powerful raiders. Indeed
they are only an easy prey. The raider, cornered at length, will
overwhelm one weak vessel and escape from the cordon.

Every unit of search must be able to find, to catch, and to kill.
For this purpose we require a number of cruisers superior to the
10,000-ton type, or else pairs of our own 10,000-ton type. These
must be accompanied by small aircraft carriers carrying perhaps a
dozen or two dozen machines, and of the smallest possible displacement. The ideal unit of search would be one killer or two three-
quarter killers, plus one aircraft carrier, plus four ocean-going
destroyers, plus two or three specially constructed tankers of good
speed. Such a formation cruising would be protected against submarines, and could search an enormous area and destroy any single
raider when detected.

The policy of forming hunting groups as discussed in this
minute, comprising balanced forces capable of scouring wide
areas and overwhelming any raider within the field of search,
was developed so far as our limited resources allowed, and I
shall refer to this subject again in a later chapter. The same
idea was afterwards more fully expanded by the United States
in their task force system, which made an important contribution to the art of sea warfare.

*   *   *   *   *

Towards the end of the month I thought it would be well
for me to give the House some coherent story of what was
happening and why.

First Lord to Prime Minister.   24.IX.39.

Would it not be well for me to make a statement to the House on the anti-submarine warfare and general naval position, more at length than what you could give in your own speech? I think I could speak for twenty-five or thirty minutes on the subject, and that this would do good. At any rate, when I saw in confidence sixty press representatives the other day, they appeared vastly relieved by the account I was able to give. If this idea commended itself to you, you would perhaps say in your speech that I would give a fuller account later on in the discussion, which I suppose will take place on Thursday, as the budget is on Wednesday.

Mr. Chamberlain readily assented, and accordingly in his speech on the twenty-sixth he told the House that I would make a statement on the sea war as soon as he sat down. This was the first time, apart from answering questions, that I had spoken in Parliament since I had entered the Government. I had a good tale to tell. In the first seven days our losses in tonnage had been half the weekly losses of the month of April, 1917, which was the peak year of the U-boat attack in the first war. We had already made progress by setting in motion the convoy system; secondly, by pressing on with the arming of all our merchant ships; and thirdly, by our counter-attack upon the U-boats. "In the first week our losses by U-boat sinkings amounted to 65,000 tons; in the second week they were 46,000 tons; and in the third week they were 21,000 tons. In the last six days we have lost only 9,000 tons." [6] I observed

6 The following are the corrected figures:
British Merchant Shipping Losses by Enemy Action September, 1939

(Numbers of ships shown in parentheses)

		Submarine (Gross Tons)	Other Causes (Gross Tons)
1st Week	(September 3–9)	64,595 (11)	
2d Week	(September 10–16)	53,561 (11)	11,437 (2) (mine)
3d Week	(September 17–23)	12,750 (3)	
4th Week	(September 24–30)	4,646 (1)	5,051 (1) (surface raider)
	Total	135,552 (26)	16,488 (3)
		152,040 (29)	

In addition there were losses in neutral and Allied shipping amounting to 15 ships of 33,527 tons.

throughout that habit of understatement and of avoiding all optimistic forecasts which had been inculcated upon me by the hard experiences of the past. "One must not dwell," I said, "upon these reassuring figures too much, for war is full of unpleasant surprises. But certainly I am entitled to say that so far as they go these figures need not cause any undue despondency or alarm."

Meanwhile [I continued], the whole vast business of our worldwide trade continues without interruption or appreciable diminution. Great convoys of troops are escorted to their various destinations. The enemy's ships and commerce have been swept from the seas. Over 2,000,000 tons of German shipping is now sheltering in German, or interned in neutral harbours. . . . In the first fortnight of the war we have actually arrested, seized, and converted to our own use, 67,000 tons more German merchandise than has been sunk in ships of our own. . . . Again I reiterate my caution against oversanguine conclusions. We have in fact, however, got more supplies in this country this afternoon than we should have had if no war had been declared and no U-boat had come into action. It is not going beyond the limits of prudent statement if I say that at that rate it will take a long time to starve us out.

From time to time the German U-boat commanders have tried their best to behave with humanity. We have seen them give good warning and also endeavour to help the crews to find their ways to port. One German captain signalled to me personally the position of a British ship which he had just sunk, and urged that rescue should be sent. He signed his message, "German Submarine." I was in some doubt at the time to what address I should direct a reply. However, he is now in our hands, and is treated with all consideration.

Even taking six or seven U-boats sunk as a safe figure,[7] that is one-tenth of the total enemy submarine fleet as it existed at the declaration of war destroyed during the first fortnight of the war, and it is probably one-quarter or perhaps even one-third of all the U-boats which are being employed actively. But the British attack upon the U-boats is only just beginning. Our hunting force is getting stronger every day. By the end of October, we expect to

[7] We now know that only two U-boats were sunk in September, 1939.

have three times the hunting force which was operating at the beginning of the war.

This speech, which lasted only twenty-five minutes, was extremely well received by the House, and in fact it recorded the failure of the first German U-boat attack upon our trade. My fears were for the future, but our preparations for 1941 were now proceeding with all possible speed and on the largest scale which our resources would allow.

*   *   *   *   *

By the end of September, we had little cause for dissatisfaction with the results of the first impact of the war at sea. I could feel that I had effectively taken over the great department which I knew so well and loved with a discriminating eye. I now knew what there was in hand and on the way. I knew where everything was. I had visited all the principal naval ports and met all the Commanders-in-Chief. By the letters patent constituting the Board, the First Lord is "responsible to Crown and Parliament for all the business of the Admiralty," and I certainly felt prepared to discharge that duty in fact as well as in form.

On the whole the month of September had been prosperous and fruitful for the Navy. We had made the immense, delicate, and hazardous transition from peace to war. Forfeits had to be paid in the first few weeks by a world-wide commerce suddenly attacked contrary to formal international agreement by indiscriminate U-boat warfare; but the convoy system was now in full flow, and merchant ships were leaving our ports every day by scores with a gun, sometimes high-angle, mounted aft, and a nucleus of trained gunners. The Asdic-equipped trawlers and other small craft armed with depth-charges, all well prepared by the Admiralty before the outbreak, were now coming daily into commission in a growing stream with trained crews. We all felt sure that the first attack of the U-boat on British trade had been broken and that the menace was in thorough and hardening control. It was obvious that the Germans would

build submarines by hundreds, and no doubt numerous shoals
were upon the slips in various stages of completion. In twelve
months, certainly in eighteen, we must expect the main U-boat
war to begin. But by that time we hoped that our mass of new
flotillas and anti-U-boat craft, which was our first priority,
would be ready to meet it with a proportionate and effective
predominance. The painful dearth of anti-aircraft guns, especially 3.7-inch and Bofors, could, alas, only be relieved after
many months; but measures had been taken within the limits
of our resources to provide for the defence of our naval harbours; and meanwhile the Fleet, while ruling the oceans,
would have to go on playing hide-and-seek.

*   *   *   *   *

In the wider sphere of naval operations no definite challenge
had yet been made to our position. After the temporary sus-
pension of traffic in the Mediterranean, our shipping soon
moved again through this invaluable corridor. Meanwhile, the
transport of the Expeditionary Force to France was proceeding
smoothly. The Home Fleet itself "somewhere in the North"
was ready to intercept any sortie by the few heavy ships of the
enemy. The blockade of Germany was being enforced by similar methods to those employed in the previous war. The
Northern Patrol had been established between Scotland and
Iceland, and by the end of the first month a total of nearly
three hundred thousand tons of goods destined for Germany
had been seized in prize against a loss to ourselves of a hundred and forty thousand tons by enemy action at sea. Overseas,
our cruisers were hunting down German ships while at the
same time providing cover against attack on our shipping by
raiders. German shipping had thus come to a standstill. By
the end of September, some three hundred and twenty-five
German ships totalling nearly seven hundred and fifty thousand
tons were immobilised in foreign ports. Few, therefore, fell
into our hands.

Our Allies also played their part. The French took an important share in the control of the Mediterranean. In home

waters and the Bay of Biscay they also helped in the battle
against the U-boats, and in the central Atlantic a powerful
force based on Dakar formed part of the Allied plans against
surface raiders.

The young Polish Navy distinguished itself. Early in the
war three modern destroyers and two submarines, *Wilk* and
Orzel, escaped from Poland and, defying the German forces
in the Baltic, succeeded in reaching England. The escape of
the submarine *Orzel* is an epic. Sailing from Gdynia when
the Germans invaded Poland, she first cruised in the Baltic,
putting into the neutral port of Tallinn on September 15 to
land her sick captain. The Esthonian authorities decided to
intern the vessel, placed a guard on board, and removed her
charts and the breech-blocks of her guns. Undismayed, her
commanding officer put to sea after overpowering the guard.
In the ensuing weeks the submarine was continually hunted by
sea and air patrols, but eventually, without even charts, made
her escape from the Baltic into the North Sea. Here she was
able to transmit a faint wireless signal to a British station giving her supposed position, and on October 14 was met and
escorted into safety by a British destroyer.

*　　*　　*　　*　　*

In September I was delighted to receive a personal letter
from President Roosevelt. I had met him only once in the
previous war. It was at a dinner at Gray's Inn, and I had been
struck by his magnificent presence in all his youth and strength.
There had been no opportunity for anything but salutations.

President Roosevelt to Mr. Churchill.　　　　　　　　　　11.IX.39.

It is because you and I occupied similar positions in the World
War that I want you to know how glad I am that you are back
again in the Admiralty. Your problems are, I realise, complicated
by new factors, but the essential is not very different. What I want
you and the Prime Minister to know is that I shall at all times
welcome it, if you will keep me in touch personally with anything
you want me to know about. You can always send sealed letters
through your pouch or my pouch.

I am glad you did the Marlborough volumes before this thing started — and I much enjoyed reading them.

I responded with alacrity, using the signature of "Naval Person," and thus began that long and memorable correspondence — covering perhaps a thousand communications on each side, and lasting till his death more than five years later.

3

The Ruin of Poland

The German Plan of Invasion — Unsound Polish Dispositions — Inferiority in Artillery and Tanks — Destruction of the Polish Air Force — The First Week — The Second Week — The Heroic Polish Counter-Attack — Extermination — The Turn of the Soviets — The Warsaw Radio Silent — The Modern Blitzkrieg — My Memorandum of September 21 — Our Immediate Dangers — My Broadcast of October 1.

MEANWHILE, around the Cabinet table we were witnessing the swift and almost mechanical destruction of a weaker state according to Hitler's method and long design. Poland was open to German invasion on three sides. In all, fifty-six divisions, including all his nine armoured divisions, composed the invading armies. From East Prussia the Third Army (eight divisions) advanced southward on Warsaw and Bialystok. From Pomerania the Fourth Army (twelve divisions) was ordered to destroy the Polish troops in the Dantzig Corridor, and then move southeastward to Warsaw along both banks of the Vistula. The frontier opposite the Posen Bulge was held defensively by German reserve troops, but on their right to the southward lay the Eighth Army (seven divisions) whose task was to cover the left flank of the main thrust. This thrust was assigned to the Tenth Army (seventeen divisions) directed straight upon Warsaw. Farther south again, the Fourteenth Army (fourteen divisions) had a dual task, first to capture the important industrial area west of Cracow, and then, if the main

front prospered, to make direct for Lemberg (Lwow) in south-
east Poland.

Thus, the Polish forces on the frontiers were first to be penetrated, and then overwhelmed and surrounded by two pincer
movements: the first from the north and southwest on Warsaw;
the second and more far-reaching, "outer" pincers, formed by
the Third Army advancing by Brest-Litovsk to be joined by
the Fourteenth Army after Lemberg was gained. Those who
escaped the closing of the Warsaw pincers would thus be cut
off from retreat into Rumania. Over fifteen hundred modern
aircraft was hurled on Poland. Their first duty was to overwhelm the Polish air force, and thereafter to support the Army
on the battlefield, and beyond it to attack military installations
and all communications by road and rail. They were also to
spread terror far and wide.

In numbers and equipment the Polish Army was no match
for their assailants, nor were their dispositions wise. They
spread all their forces along the frontiers of their native land.
They had no central reserve. While taking a proud and
haughty line against German ambitions, they had nevertheless
feared to be accused of provocation by mobilising in good time
against the masses gathering around them. Thirty divisions,
representing only two-thirds of their active army, were ready
or nearly ready to meet the first shock. The speed of events
and the violent intervention of the German air force prevented
the rest from reaching the forward positions till all was broken,
and they were only involved in the final disasters. Thus, the
thirty Polish divisions faced nearly double their numbers
around a long perimeter with nothing behind them. Nor
was it in numbers alone that they were inferior. They
were heavily outclassed in artillery, and had but a single
armoured brigade to meet the nine German Panzers, as
they were already called. Their horse cavalry, of which
they had twelve brigades, charged valiantly against the swarming tanks and armoured cars, but could not harm them with
their swords and lances. Their nine hundred first-line aircraft,
of which perhaps half were modern types, were taken by sur-

prise and many were destroyed before they even got into the air.

According to Hitler's plan, the German armies were unleashed on September 1, and ahead of them his air force struck the Polish squadrons on their airfields. In two days the Polish air power was virtually annihilated. Within a week the German armies had bitten deep into Poland. Resistance everywhere was brave but vain. All the Polish armies on the frontiers, except the Posen group, whose flanks were deeply turned, were driven backward. The Lodz group was split in twain by the main thrust of the German Tenth Army; one half withdrew eastward to Radom, the other was forced northwestward; and through this gap darted two Panzer divisions making straight for Warsaw. Farther north the German Fourth Army reached and crossed the Vistula, and turned along it in their march on Warsaw. Only the Polish northern group was able to inflict a check upon the German Third Army. They were soon out-

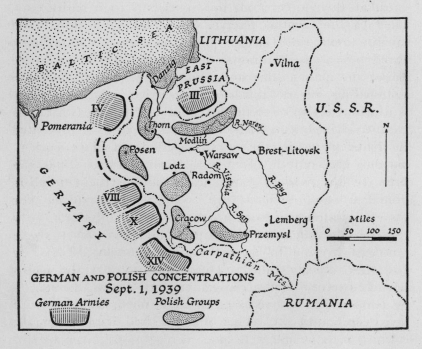

GERMAN AND POLISH CONCENTRATIONS
Sept. 1, 1939
German Armies   Polish Groups

flanked and fell back to the river Narew, where alone a fairly strong defensive system had been prepared in advance. Such were the results of the first week of the Blitzkrieg.

The second week was marked by bitter fighting and by its end the Polish Army, nominally of about two million men, ceased to exist as an organised force. In the south the Fourteenth German Army drove on to reach the river San. North of them the four Polish divisions which had retreated to Radom were there encircled and destroyed. The two armoured divisions of the Tenth Army reached the outskirts of Warsaw, but having no infantry with them could not make headway against the desperate resistance organised by the townsfolk. Northeast of Warsaw the Third Army encircled the capital from the east, and its left column reached Brest-Litovsk a hundred miles behind the battle front.

It was within the claws of the Warsaw pincers that the Polish Army fought and died. Their Posen group had been joined by divisions from the Thorn and Lodz groups, forced towards them by the German onslaught. It now numbered twelve divisions, and across its southern flank the German Tenth Army was streaming towards Warsaw, protected only by the relatively weak Eighth Army. Although already virtually surrounded, the Polish Commander of the Posen group, General Kutrzeba, resolved to strike south against the flank of the main German drive. This audacious Polish counter-attack, called the battle of the river Bzura, created a crisis which drew in, not only the German Eighth Army, but a part of the Tenth, deflected from their Warsaw objective, and even a corps of the Fourth Army from the north. Under the assault of all these powerful bodies, and overwhelmed by unresisted air bombardment, the Posen group maintained its ever-glorious struggle for ten days. It was finally blotted out on September 19.

In the meantime the outer pincers had met and closed. The Fourteenth Army reached the outskirts of Lemberg on September 12, and striking north joined hands on the seventeenth with the troops of the Third Army which had

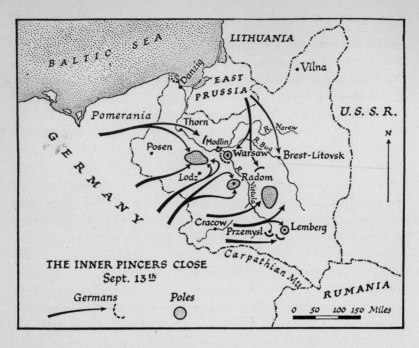

THE INNER PINCERS CLOSE
Sept. 13th

Germans   Poles

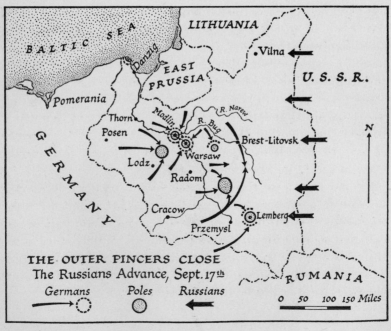

THE OUTER PINCERS CLOSE
The Russians Advance, Sept. 17th

Germans   Poles   Russians

passed through Brest-Litovsk. There was now no loophole of escape for straggling and daring individuals. On the twentieth, the Germans announced that the battle of the Vistula was "one of the greatest battles of extermination of all times."

It was now the turn of the Soviets. What they now call "Democracy" came into action. On September 17, the Russian armies swarmed across the almost undefended Polish eastern frontier and rolled westward on a broad front. On the eighteenth, they occupied Vilna, and met their German collaborators at Brest-Litovsk. Here in the previous war the Bolsheviks, in breach of their solemn agreements with the Western Allies, had made their separate peace with the Kaiser's Germany, and had bowed to its harsh terms. Now in Brest-Litovsk, it was with Hitler's Germany that the Russian Communists grinned and shook hands. The ruin of Poland and its entire subjugation proceeded apace. Warsaw and Modlin still remained unconquered. The resistance of Warsaw, largely arising from the surge of its citizens, was magnificent and forlorn. After many days of violent bombardment from the air and by heavy artillery, much of which was rapidly transported across the great lateral highways from the idle Western Front, the Warsaw radio ceased to play the Polish National Anthem, and Hitler entered the ruins of the city. Modlin, a fortress twenty miles down the Vistula, had taken in the remnants of the Thorn group, and fought on until the twenty-eighth. Thus, in one month all was over, and a nation of thirty-five millions fell into the merciless grip of those who sought not only conquest but enslavement, and indeed extinction for vast numbers.

We had seen a perfect specimen of the modern Blitzkrieg; the close interaction on the battlefield of army and air force; the violent bombardment of all communications and of any town that seemed an attractive target; the arming of an active Fifth Column; the free use of spies and parachutists; and above all, the irresistible forward thrusts of great masses of armour. The Poles were not to be the last to endure this ordeal.

* * * * *

The Soviet armies continued to advance up to the line they had settled with Hitler, and on the twenty-ninth the Russo-German Treaty partitioning Poland was formally signed. I was still convinced of the profound, and as I believed quenchless, antagonism between Russia and Germany, and I clung to the hope that the Soviets would be drawn to our side by the force of events. I did not, therefore, give way to the indignation which I felt and which surged around me in our Cabinet at their callous, brutal policy. I had never had any illusions about them. I knew that they accepted no moral code, and studied their own interests alone. But at least they owed us nothing. Besides, in mortal war anger must be subordinated to defeating the main immediate enemy. I was determined to put the best construction on their odious conduct. Therefore, in a paper which I wrote for the War Cabinet on September 25, I struck a cool note.

Although the Russians were guilty of the grossest bad faith in the recent negotiations, their demand, made by Marshal Voroshilov that Russian armies should occupy Vilna and Lemberg if they were to be allies of Poland, was a perfectly valid military request. It was rejected by Poland on grounds which, though natural, can now be seen to have been insufficient. In the result Russia has occupied the same line and positions as the enemy of Poland, which possibly she might have occupied as a very doubtful and suspected friend. The difference in fact is not so great as might seem. The Russians have mobilised very large forces and have shown themselves able to advance fast and far from their pre-war positions. They are now limitrophe with Germany, and it is quite impossible for Germany to denude the Eastern Front. A large German army must be left to watch it. I see General Gamelin puts it at least twenty divisions. It may well be twenty-five or more. An Eastern Front is, therefore, potentially in existence.

In a broadcast on October 1, I said:

Poland has again been overrun by two of the Great Powers which held her in bondage for a hundred and fifty years, but were unable to quench the spirit of the Polish nation. The heroic defence of Warsaw shows that the soul of Poland is indestructible, and that she will rise again like a rock, which may for a time be submerged by a tidal wave, but which remains a rock.

Russia has pursued a cold policy of self-interest. We could have wished that the Russian armies should be standing on their present line as the friends and allies of Poland instead of as invaders. But that the Russian armies should stand on this line was clearly necessary for the safety of Russia against the Nazi menace. At any rate, the line is there, and an Eastern Front has been created which Nazi Germany does not dare assail. . . .

I cannot forecast to you the action of Russia. It is a riddle wrapped in a mystery inside an enigma; but perhaps there is a key. That key is Russian national interest. It cannot be in accordance with the interest or the safety of Russia that Germany should plant herself upon the shores of the Black Sea, or that she should overrun the Balkan States and subjugate the Slavonic peoples of Southeastern Europe. That would be contrary to the historic life-interests of Russia.

The Prime Minister was in full agreement. "I take the same view as Winston," he said, in a letter to his sister, "to whose excellent broadcast we have just been listening. I believe Russia will always act as she thinks her own interests demand, and I cannot believe she would think her interests served by a German victory followed by a German domination of Europe." [1]

[1] Feiling, *op. cit.*, page 425.

4

War Cabinet Problems

THE WAR CABINET and its additional members, with the Chiefs of the Staff for the three services and a number of secretaries, had met together for the first time on September 4. Thereafter we met daily, and often twice a day. I do not recall any period when the weather was so hot — I had a black alpaca jacket made to wear over only a linen shirt. It was, indeed, just the weather that Hitler wanted for his invasion of Poland. The great rivers on which the Poles had counted in their defensive plan were nearly everywhere fordable, and the ground was hard and firm for the movement of tanks and vehicles of all kinds. Each morning the C.I.G.S., General Ironside, standing before the map, gave long reports and appreciations which very soon left no doubt in our minds that the resistance of Poland would speedily be crushed. Each day I reported to the Cabinet the Admiralty tale, which usually consisted of a list of British merchant ships sunk by the U-boats. The British Expeditionary Force of four divisions began its movement to France, and the Air Ministry deplored the fact that they were not allowed to bombard military objectives in Germany. For the rest, a great deal of business was transacted on the Home Front, and there were, of course, lengthy discussions about foreign affairs, particularly concerning the attitude of Soviet Russia and Italy and the policy to be pursued in the Balkans.

The most important step was the setting-up of the "Land Forces Committee" under Sir Samuel Hoare, at this time Lord Privy Seal, in order to advise the War Cabinet upon the scale and organisation of the Army we should form. I was a member of this small body, which met at the Home Office, and in one single sweltering afternoon agreed, after hearing the generals, that we should forthwith begin the creation of a fifty-five-division army, together with all the munition factories, plants, and supply services of every kind necessary to sustain it in action. It was hoped that by the eighteenth month, two-thirds of this, a considerable force, would either already have been sent to France or be fit to take the field. Sir Samuel Hoare was clear-sighted and active in all this, and I gave him my constant support. The Air Ministry, on the other hand, feared that so large an army and its supplies would be an undue drain upon our skilled labour and man-power, and would hamper them in the vast plans they had formed on paper for the creation of an all-powerful, overwhelming air force in two or three years. The Prime Minister was impressed by Sir Kingsley Wood's arguments, and hesitated to commit himself to an army of this size and all that it entailed. The War Cabinet was divided upon the issue, and it was a week or more before a decision was reached to adopt the advice of the Land Forces Committee for a fifty-five-division army, or rather target.

I felt that as a member of the War Cabinet I was bound to take a general view, and I did not fail to subordinate my own departmental requirements for the Admiralty to the main design. I was anxious to establish a broad basis of common ground with the Prime Minister, and also to place him in possession of my knowledge in this field which I had trodden before; and being encouraged by his courtesy I wrote him a series of letters on the various problems as they arose. I did not wish to be drawn into arguments with him at Cabinets, and always preferred putting things down on paper. In nearly all cases we found ourselves in agreement, and although at first he gave me the impression of being very much on his guard, yet I am glad to say that month by month his confidence and good will seemed to grow. His biographer has borne testimony to this. I also wrote to other members of the War Cabinet and to various Ministers with whom I had departmental or other business. The War Cabinet was hampered somewhat by the fact that they seldom sat together alone without secretaries or military experts. It was an earnest and workmanlike body, and the advantages of free discussion among men bound so closely together in a common task, without any formality and without any record being kept, are very great. Such meetings are an essential counterpart to the formal meetings where business is transacted and decisions are recorded for guidance and action. Both processes are indispensable to the handling of the most difficult affairs.

I was deeply interested in the fate of the great mass of heavy artillery which as Minister of Munitions I had made in the previous war. Such weapons take a year and a half to manufacture, but it is of great value to an army, whether in defence or offence, to have at its disposal a mass of heavy batteries. I remembered the struggles which Mr. Lloyd George had had with the War Office in 1915 and all the political disturbance which had arisen on this subject of the creation of a dominating very heavy artillery, and how he had been vindicated by events. The character of the war on land, when it eventually manifested itself eight months later, in 1940, proved utterly different from that of 1914/1918. As will be seen, however, a vital need in home defence was met by these great cannons. At this time I conceived we had a buried treasure which it would be folly to neglect.

I wrote to the Prime Minister on this and other matters:

First Lord to Prime Minister.   *September* 10, 1939.

I hope you will not mind my sending you a few points privately.

1. I am still inclined to think that we should not take the initiative in bombing, except in the immediate zone in which the French armies are operating, where we must, of course, help. It is to our interest that the war should be conducted in accordance with the more humane conceptions of war, and that we should follow and not precede the Germans in the process, no doubt inevitable, of deepening severity and violence. Every day that passes gives more shelter to the population of London and the big cities, and in a fortnight or so there will be far more comparatively safe refuges than now.

2. You ought to know what we were told about the condition of our small Expeditionary Force and their deficiencies in tanks, in trained trench-mortar detachments, and above all in heavy artillery. There will be a just criticism if it is found that the heavy batteries are lacking. . . . In 1919, after the war, when I was S. of S. for War, I ordered a mass of heavy cannon to be stored, oiled, and carefully kept; and I also remember making in 1918 two twelve-inch Hows. at the request of G.H.Q. to support their advance into Germany in 1919. These were never used, but they were the last word at the time. They are not easy things to lose. . . . It seems to me most vitally urgent, first, to see what there is in the cupboard; secondly, to recondition it at once and make the ammunition of a modern character. Where this heavy stuff is concerned, I may be able to help at the Admiralty, because, of course, we are very comfortable in respect of everything big. . . .

3. You may like to know the principles I am following in recasting the naval programme of new construction. I propose to suspend work upon all except the first three or perhaps four of the new battleships, and not to worry at the present time about vessels that cannot come into action until 1942. This decision must be reviewed in six months. It is by this change that I get the spare capacity to help the Army. On the other hand, I must make a great

effort to bring forward the smaller anti-U-boat fleet. Numbers are
vital in this sphere. A good many are coming forward in 1940,
but not nearly enough considering that we may have to face an
attack by 200 or 300 U-boats in the summer of 1940. . . .

4. With regard to the supply of the Army and its relation to the
air force, pardon me if I put my experience and knowledge, which
were bought not taught, at your disposal. The making by the
Minister of Supply of a layout on the basis of fifty-five divisions at
the present time would not prejudice Air or Admiralty, because
(a) the preliminary work of securing the sites and building the
factories will not for many months require skilled labour; here are
months of digging foundations, laying concrete, bricks, and mortar,
drainage, etc., for which the ordinary building-trade labourers suffice;
and (b) even if you could not realise a fifty-five-division front by the
twenty-fourth month because of other claims, you could alter
the time to the thirty-sixth month or even later without affecting the
scale. On the other hand, if he does not make a big layout at
the beginning, there will be vexatious delays when existing factories
have to be enlarged. Let him make his layout on the large scale,
and protect the needs of the air force and Army by varying the
time factor. A factory once set up need not be used until it is
necessary, but if it is not in existence, you may be helpless if you
need a further effort. It is only when these big plants get into
work that you can achieve adequate results.

5. Up to the present (noon) no further losses by U-boats are
reported, i.e., thirty-six hours blank. Perhaps they have all gone
away for the week-end! But I pass my time waiting to be hit.
Nevertheless, I am sure all will be well.

I also wrote to Doctor Burgin:

First Lord to Minister of Supply.   *September* 10, 1939.

In 1919 when I was at the War Office, I gave careful instructions
to store and oil a mass of heavy artillery. Now it appears that this
has been discovered. It seems to me the first thing you should do
would be to get hold of this store and recondition them with the
highest priority, as well as make the heavy ammunition. The Admiralty might be able to help with the heavy shells. Do not hesitate
to ask.

The reply was most satisfactory:

Minister of Supply to First Lord.   *September* 11, 1939.

The preparation for use of the super-heavy artillery, of which
you write, has been the lively concern of the War Office since the
September crisis of 1938, and work actually started on the recon-
ditioning of guns and mountings, both of the 9.2-inch guns and the
12-inch howitzers, last January.

These equipments were put away in 1919 with considerable care,
and as a result, they are proving to be, on the whole, not in bad
condition. Certain parts of them have, however, deteriorated and
require renewal, and this work has been going on steadily throughout this year. We shall undoubtedly have some equipments ready
during this month, and, of course, I am giving the work a high
priority. . . .

I am most grateful for your letter. You will be glad to see how
much has already been done on the lines you recommend.

*   *   *   *   *

First Lord to Prime Minister.   *September* 11, 1939.

Everyone says there ought to be a Ministry of Shipping. The
President of the Chamber of Shipping today pressed me strongly
for it at our meeting with the shipowners. The President of the
Board of Trade asked me to associate him in this request, which,
of course, entails a curtailment of his own functions. I am sure
there will be a strong parliamentary demand. Moreover, the
measure seems to me good on the merits. The functions are three-
fold:

(*a*) To secure the maximum fertility and economy of freights in
accordance with the war policy of the Cabinet and the pressure of
events.

(*b*) To provide and organise the very large shipbuilding programme necessary as a safeguard against the heavy losses of tonnage
we may expect from a U-boat attack apprehended in the summer
of 1940. This should certainly include the study of concrete ships,
thus relieving the strain on our steel during a period of steel
stringency.

(*c*) The care, comfort, and encouragement of the merchant
seamen who will have to go to sea repeatedly after having been
torpedoed and saved. These merchant seamen are a most important
and potentially formidable factor in this kind of war.

The President of the Board of Trade has already told you that
two or three weeks would be required to disentangle the branches
of his department which would go to make up the Ministry of
Shipping from the parent office. It seems to me very wise to allow
this period of transition. If a Minister were appointed and announced, he would gather to himself the necessary personal staff,
and take over gradually the branches of the Board of Trade which
are concerned. It also seems important that the step of creating
a Ministry of Shipping should be taken by the Government before
pressure is applied in Parliament and from shipping circles, and
before we are told that there is valid complaint against the existing
system.

*   *   *   *   *

This Ministry was formed after a month's discussion and
announced on October 13. Mr. Chamberlain selected Sir John
Gilmour as its first head. The choice was criticised as being
inadequate. Gilmour was a most agreeable Scotsman and a
well-known Member of Parliament. He had held Cabinet office
under Mr. Baldwin and Mr. Chamberlain. His health was
declining, and he died within a few months of his appointment,
and was succeeded by Mr. Ronald Cross.

First Lord to Prime Minister.   *September* 15, 1939.

As I shall be away till Monday, I give you my present thought on
the main situation.

It seems to me most unlikely that the Germans will attempt an
offensive in the West at this late season. . . . Surely his obvious plan
should be to press on through Poland, Hungary, and Rumania to
the Black Sea, and it may be that he has some understanding with
Russia by which she will take part of Poland and recover
Bessarabia. . . .

It would seem wise for Hitler to make good his Eastern connections and feeding-grounds during these winter months, and thus
give his people the spectacle of repeated successes, and the assurance of weakening our blockade. I do not, therefore, apprehend
that he will attack in the West until he has collected the easy spoils
which await him in the East. None the less, I am strongly of
opinion that we should make every preparation to defend ourselves
in the West. Every effort should be made to make Belgium take

the necessary precautions in conjunction with the French and British Armies. Meanwhile, the French frontier behind Belgium should be fortified night and day by every conceivable resource. In particular the obstacles to tank attack, planting railway rails upright, digging deep ditches, erecting concrete dolls, land-mines in some parts and inundations all ready to let out in others, etc., should be combined in a deep system of defence. The attack of three or four German armoured divisions, which has been so effective in Poland, can only be stopped by physical obstacles defended by resolute troops and a powerful artillery. . . . Without physical obstacles the attack of armoured vehicles cannot be effectively resisted.

I am very glad to find that the mass of wartime artillery which I stored in 1919 is all available. It comprises 32 twelve-inch, 145 nine-inch, a large number of eight-inch, nearly 200 six-inch, howitzers, together with very large quantities of ammunition; in fact it is the heavy artillery, not of our small Expeditionary Force, but of a great army. No time should be lost in bringing some of these guns into the field, so that whatever else our troops will lack, they will not suffer from want of heavy artillery. . . .

I hope you will consider carefully what I write to you. I do so only in my desire to aid you in your responsibilities, and discharge my own.

The Prime Minister wrote back on the sixteenth, saying:

All your letters are carefully read and considered by me, and if I have not replied to them, it is only because I am seeing you every day, and, moreover, because, as far as I have been able to observe, your views and mine have very closely coincided. . . . To my mind the lesson of the Polish campaign is the power of the air force, when it has obtained complete mastery in the air, to paralyse the operations of land forces. . . . Accordingly, as it seems to me, although I shall, of course, await the report of the Land Forces Committee before making up my mind, absolute priority ought to be given to our plans for rapidly accelerating the strength of our air force, and the extent of our effort on land should be determined by our resources *after* we have provided for air force extension.

First Lord to Prime Minister.   *September* 18, 1939.

I am entirely with you in believing that air power stands foremost in our requirements, and indeed I sometimes think that it may be the ultimate path by which victory will be gained. On the other hand, the Air Ministry paper, which I have just been studying, seems to peg out vast and vague claims which are not at present substantiated, and which, if accorded absolute priority, would overlay other indispensable forms of war effort. I am preparing a note upon this paper, and will only quote one figure which struck me in it.

If the aircraft industry with its present 360,000 men can produce nearly one thousand machines a month, it seems extraordinary that 1,050,000 men should be required for a monthly output of two thousand. One would expect a very large "reduction on taking a quantity," especially if mass-production is used. I cannot believe the Germans will be using anything like a million men to produce two thousand machines a month. While, broadly speaking, I should accept an output of two thousand machines a month as the objective, I am not at present convinced that it would make anything like so large a demand upon our war-making capacity as is implied in this paper.

The reason why I am anxious that the Army should be planned upon a fifty- or fifty-five division scale, is that I doubt whether the French would acquiesce in a division of effort which gave us the sea and air and left them to pay almost the whole blood-tax on land. Such an arrangement would certainly be agreeable to us; but I do not like the idea of our having to continue the war single-handed.

There are great dangers in giving absolute priority to any department. In the late war the Admiralty used their priority arbitrarily and selfishly, especially in the last year when they were overwhelmingly strong, and had the American Navy added to them. I am every day restraining such tendencies in the common interest.

As I mentioned in my first letter to you, the layout of the shell, gun, and filling factories, and the provision for explosives and steel, does not compete directly while the plants are being made with the quite different class of labour required for aeroplane production. It is a question of clever dovetailing. The provision of mechanical vehicles, on the other hand, is directly competitive, and must be carefully adjusted. It would be wise to bring the army munitions plants into existence on a large scale, and then to let them begin to eat only as our resources allow and the character of the war requires. The time factor is the regulator which you would apply according to circumstances. If, however, the plants are not begun now, you will no longer have the option.

I thought it would be a wise thing to state to the French our intention to work up to an army of fifty or fifty-five divisions. But whether this could be reached at the twenty-fourth month or at the thirtieth or fortieth month should certainly be kept fluid.

At the end of the late war, we had about ninety divisions in all theatres, and we were producing aircraft at the rate of two thousand a month, as well as maintaining a Navy very much larger than was needed, and far larger than our present plans contemplate. I do not, therefore, feel that fifty or fifty-five divisions and two thousand aircraft per month are incompatible aims, although, of course, the modern divisions and modern aircraft represent a much higher industrial effort — everything having become so much more complicated.

* * * * *

First Lord to Prime Minister. *September* 21, 1939.

I wonder if you would consider having an occasional meeting of the War Cabinet Ministers to talk among themselves without either secretaries or military experts. I am not satisfied that the large issues are being effectively discussed in our formal sessions. We have been constituted the responsible Ministers for the conduct of the war; and I am sure it would be in the public interest if we met as a body from time to time. Much is being thrown upon the Chiefs of the Staffs which falls outside the professional sphere. We have had the advantage of many valuable and illuminating reports from them. But I venture to represent to you that we ought sometimes to discuss the general position alone. I do not feel that we are getting to the root of the matter on many points.

I have not spoken to any colleague about this, and have no idea what their opinions are. I give you my own, as in duty bound.

On September 24, I wrote to the Chancellor of the Exchequer:

I am thinking a great deal about you and your problem, as one who has been through the Exchequer mill. I look forward to a severe budget based upon the broad masses of the well-to-do. But I think you ought to couple with this a strong anti-waste campaign. Judging by the small results achieved for our present gigantic expenditure, I think there never was so little *"value for money,"* as what is going on now. In 1918, we had a lot of unpleasant regulations in force for the prevention of waste, which after all was part of the winning of victory. Surely you ought to make a strong feature of this in your Wednesday's statement. An effort should be made to tell people the things they ought to try to avoid doing. This is by no means a doctrine of abstention from expenditure. Everything should be eaten up prudently, even luxuries, *so long as no more are created.* Take stationery, for example — this should be regulated at once in all departments. Envelopes should be pasted up and redirected again and again. Although this seems a small thing, it teaches every official, and we now have millions of them, to think of saving.

An active "savings campaign" was inculcated at the Front in 1918 and people began to take a pride in it, and look upon it as part of the show. Why not inculcate these ideas in the B.E.F. from the outset in all zones not actually under fire?

I am trying to prune the Admiralty of large schemes of naval improvement which cannot operate till after 1941, or even in some cases [when they cannot operate] till after the end of 1940. Beware lest these fortification people and other departmentals do not consume our strength upon long-scale developments which cannot mature till after the climax which settles our fate.

I see the departments full of loose fat, following on undue starvation. It would be much better from your point of view to come along with your alguazils *as critics* upon wasteful exhibitions, rather than delaying action. Don't hamper departments acting in a time of crisis; give them the responsibility; but call them swiftly to account for any failure in thrift.

I hope you will not mind me writing to you upon this subject, because I feel just as strongly about the husbanding of the money power as I do about the war effort, of which it is indeed an integral part. In all these matters you can count on my support, and also, as the head of a spending department, upon my submission to searching superintendence.

*   *   *   *   *

In every war in which the Royal Navy has claimed the command of the seas, it has had to pay the price of exposing immense targets to the enemy. The privateer, the raiding cruiser, and above all the U-boat, have in all the varying forms of war exacted a heavy toll upon the life-lines of our commerce and food-supply. A prime function of defence has, therefore, always been imposed upon us. From this fact the danger arises of our being driven or subsiding into a defensive naval strategy and habit of mind. Modern developments have aggravated this tendency. In the two Great Wars, during parts of which I was responsible for the control of the Admiralty, I have always sought to rupture this defensive obsession by searching for forms of counter-offensive. To make the enemy wonder where he is going to be hit next may bring immeasurable relief to the process of shepherding hundreds of convoys and thousands of merchantmen safely into port. In the First World War I hoped to find in the Dardanelles, and later in an attack upon Borkum and other Frisian islands, the means of regaining the initiative, and forcing the weaker naval power to study his own problems rather than ours. Called to the Admiralty again in 1939, and as soon as immediate needs were dealt with and perils warded off, I could not rest content with the policy of "convoy and blockade." I sought earnestly for a way of attacking Germany by naval means.

First and foremost gleamed the Baltic. The command of the Baltic by a British Fleet carried with it possibly decisive gains. Scandinavia, freed from the menace of German invasion, would thereby naturally be drawn into our system of war trade, if not indeed into actual co-belligerency. A British Fleet in mastery of the Baltic would hold out a hand to Russia in a manner likely to be decisive upon the whole Soviet policy and strategy. These facts were not disputed among responsible and well-informed men. The command of the Baltic was the obvious supreme prize, not only for the Royal Navy but for Britain. Could it be won? In this new war the German Navy was no obstacle. Our superiority in heavy ships made us eager to engage them wherever and whenever there was opportunity. Minefields could be swept by the stronger naval power. The U-boats imposed no veto upon a fleet guarded by efficient flotillas. But now, instead of the powerful German Navy of 1914 and 1915, there was the air arm, formidable, unmeasured, and certainly increasing in importance with every month that passed.

If two or three years earlier it had been possible to make an alliance with Soviet Russia, this might have been implemented by a British battle squadron joined to the Russian Fleet and based on Kronstadt. I commended this to my circle of friends at the time. Whether such an arrangement was ever within the bounds of action cannot be known. It was certainly one way of restraining Germany; but there were also easier methods which were not taken. Now in the autumn of 1939, Russia was an adverse neutral, balancing between antagonism and actual war. Sweden had several suitable harbours on which a British Fleet could be based. But Sweden could not be expected to expose herself to invasion by Germany. Without the command of the Baltic, we could not ask for a Swedish harbour. Without a Swedish harbour we could not have the command of the Baltic. Here was a deadlock in strategic thought. Was it possible to break it? It is always right to probe. During the war, as will be seen, I forced long staff studies of various operations, as the result of which I was usually convinced that they were better left alone, or else that they could not be fitted in with the general conduct of the struggle. Of these the first was the Baltic domination.

*   *   *   *   *

On the fourth day after I reached the Admiralty, I asked that a plan for forcing a passage into the Baltic should be prepared by the Naval Staff. The Plans Division replied quickly that Italy and Japan must be neutral; that the threat of air attack appeared prohibitive; but that apart from this the operation justified detailed planning and should, if judged practicable, be carried out in March, 1940, or earlier. Meanwhile, I had long talks with the Director of Naval Construction, Sir Stanley Goodall, one of my friends from 1911/12, who was immediately captivated by the idea. I named the plan "Catherine," after Catherine the Great, because Russia lay in the background of my thought. On September 12 I was able to write a detailed minute to the authorities concerned.[1]

Admiral Pound replied on the twentieth that success would depend on Russia not joining Germany and on the assurance of co-operation by Norway and Sweden; and that we must be able to win the war against any probable combination of Powers without counting upon whatever force was sent into the Baltic. He was all for the exploration. On September 21, he agreed that Admiral of the Fleet the Earl of Cork and Orrery, an officer of the highest attainments and distinction, should come to work at the Admiralty, with quarters and a nucleus staff, and all information necessary for exploring and planning the Baltic offensive project. There was an apt precedent for this in the previous war, when I had brought back the famous Admiral "Tug" Wilson to the Admiralty for special duties of this kind with the full agreement of Lord Fisher; and there are several instances in this war where, in an easy and friendly manner, large issues of this kind were tested without any resentment being felt by the Chiefs of Staff concerned.

Both Lord Cork's ideas and mine rested upon the construction of capital ships specially adapted to withstand air and torpedo attack. As is seen from the minute in the Appendix, I wished to convert two or three ships of the *Royal Sovereign* class for action inshore or in narrow waters by giving them super-bulges against torpedoes and strong armour-plated decks against air bombs. For this I was prepared to sacrifice one or even two turrets and seven or eight knots' speed. Quite apart from the Baltic, this would give us facilities for offensive action, both off the enemy's North Sea coast, and even more in the Mediterranean. Nothing could be ready before the late spring of 1940, even if the earliest estimates of the naval constructors and the dockyards were realised. On this basis, therefore, we proceeded.

On the twenty-sixth, Lord Cork presented his preliminary appreciation, based, of course, on a purely military study of the problem. He considered the operation, which he would, of course, have commanded, perfectly feasible but hazardous. He

[1] See Appendix B, Book II.

asked for a margin of at least thirty per cent over the German
Fleet on account of expected losses in the passage. If we were
to act in 1940, the assembly of the Fleet and all necessary training must be complete by the middle of February. Time did
not, therefore, permit the deck-armouring and side-blistering of
the *Royal Sovereigns,* on which I counted. Here was another
deadlock. Still, if these kinds of things go working on, one may
get into position — maybe a year later — to act. But in war, as
in life, all other things are moving too. If one can plan calmly
with a year or two in hand, better solutions are open.

I had strong support in all this from the Deputy Chief of
Staff, Admiral Tom Phillips (who perished in the *Prince of
Wales* at the end of 1941 near Singapore); and from Admiral
Fraser, the Controller and Third Sea Lord. He advised the ad-
dition to the assault fleet of the four fast merchant ships of the
Glen Line, which were to play their part in other events.

*   *   *   *   *

One of my first duties at the Admiralty was to examine the
existing programmes of new construction and war expansion
which had come into force on the outbreak.

At any given moment there are at least four successive annual
programmes running at the Admiralty. In 1936 and 1937, five
new battleships had been laid down which would come into
service in 1940 and 1941. Four more battleships had been authorised by Parliament in 1938 and 1939, which could not
be finished for five or six years from the date of order.
Nineteen cruisers were in various stages of construction. The
constructive genius and commanding reputation of the Royal
Navy in design had been distorted and hampered by the treaty
restrictions for twenty years. All our cruisers were the result
of trying to conform to treaty limitations and "gentleman's
agreements." In peace-time vessels had thus been built to keep
up the strength of the Navy from year to year amid political
difficulties. In war-time a definite tactical object must inspire
all construction. I greatly desired to build a few 14,000-ton
cruisers carrying 9.2-inch guns, with good armour against eight-

inch projectiles, wide radius of action, and superior speed to any existing *Deutschland* or other German cruiser. Hitherto the treaty restrictions had prevented such a policy. Now that we were free from them, the hard priorities of war interposed an equally decisive veto on such long-term plans.

Destroyers were our most urgent need, and also our worst feature. None had been included in the 1938 programme, but sixteen had been ordered in 1939. In all, thirty-two of these indispensable craft were in the yards, and only nine could be delivered before the end of 1940. The irresistible tendency to make each successive flotilla an improvement upon the last had lengthened the time of building to nearer three than two years. Naturally, the Navy liked to have vessels capable of riding out the Atlantic swell and large enough to carry all the modern improvements in gunnery and especially anti-aircraft defence. It is evident that along this line of solid argument a point is soon reached where one is no longer building a destroyer but a small cruiser. The displacement approaches or even exceeds two thousand tons, and a crew of more than two hundred sail the seas in these unarmoured ships, themselves an easy prey to any regular cruiser. The destroyer is the chief weapon against the U-boat, but as it grows ever larger it becomes itself a worth-while target. The line is passed where the hunter becomes the hunted. We could not have too many destroyers, but their perpetual improvement and growth imposed severe limitation on the numbers the yards could build, and deadly delay in completion.

On the other hand, there are seldom less than two thousand British merchant ships at sea, and the sailings in and out of our home ports amounted each week to several hundreds of ocean-going vessels and several thousands of coastwise traders. To bring the convoy system into play, to patrol the Narrow Seas, to guard the hundreds of ports of the British Isles, to serve our bases all over the world, to protect the minesweepers in their ceaseless task, all required an immense multiplication of small armed vessels. Numbers and speed of construction were the dominating conditions.

It was my duty to readjust our programmes to the need of the hour and to enforce the largest possible expansion of anti-U-boat vessels. For this purpose two principles were laid down. First, the long-term programme should be either stopped or severely delayed, thus concentrating labour and materials upon what we could get in the first year or year and a half. Secondly, new types of anti-submarine craft must be devised which were good enough for work on the approaches to the island, thus setting free our larger destroyers for more distant duties.

On all these questions I addressed a series of minutes to my naval colleagues:

Having regard to the U-boat menace, which must be expected to renew itself on a much larger scale towards the end of 1940, the type of destroyer to be constructed must aim at numbers and celerity of construction rather than size and power. It ought to be possible to design destroyers which can be completed in under a year, in which case fifty at least should be begun forthwith. I am well aware of the need of a proportion of flotilla leaders and large destroyers capable of ocean service, but the arrival in our fleets of fifty destroyers of the medium emergency type I am contemplating would liberate all larger vessels for ocean work and for combat.

The usual conflict between long-term and short-term policy rises to intensity in war. I prescribed that all work likely to compete with essential construction should be stopped on large vessels which could not come into service before the end of 1940, and that the multiplication of our anti-submarine fleets must be effected by types capable of being built within twelve months, or, if possible, eight. For the first type we revived the name corvette. Orders for fifty-eight of these had been placed shortly before the outbreak of war, but none were yet laid down. Later and improved vessels of a similar type, ordered in 1940, were called frigates. Besides this, a great number of small craft of many kinds, particularly trawlers, had to be converted with the utmost dispatch and fitted with guns, depth-charges, and Asdics; motor launches of new Admiralty design were also required in large numbers for coastal work. Orders were placed to the limit of our shipbuilding resources, including those of Canada. Even so we did not achieve all that we hoped, and delays arose which were inevitable under the prevailing conditions and which caused the deliveries from the shipyards to fall considerably short of our expectations.

*   *   *   *   *

Eventually my view about Baltic strategy and battleship reconstruction prevailed in the protracted discussions. The designs were made and the orders were given. However, one reason after another was advanced, some of them well-founded, for not putting the work in hand. The *Royal Sovereigns*, it was said, might be needed for convoy in case the German pocket battleships or eight-inch-gun cruisers broke loose. It was represented that the scheme involved unacceptable interference with other vital work, and a plausible case could be shown for alternative priorities for our labour and armour. I deeply regretted that I was never able to achieve my conception of a squadron of very heavily deck-armoured ships of no more than fifteen knots, bristling with anti-aircraft guns and capable of withstanding to a degree not enjoyed by any other vessel afloat both air and under-water attack. When in 1941 and 1942, the defence and succouring of Malta became so vital, when we had every need to bombard Italian ports and, above all, Tripoli, others felt the need as much as I. It was then too late.

Throughout the war the *Royal Sovereigns* remained an expense and an anxiety. They had none of them been rebuilt like their sisters the *Queen Elizabeths*, and when, as will be seen in due course, the possibility of bringing them into action against the Japanese Fleet which entered the Indian Ocean in April, 1942, presented itself, the only thought of the Admiral on the spot, of Admiral Pound and the Minister of Defence, was to put as many thousands of miles as possible between them and the enemy in the shortest possible time.

*   *   *   *   *

One of the first steps I took on taking charge of the Admiralty and becoming a member of the War Cabinet was to form a

statistical department of my own. For this purpose I relied
on Professor Lindemann, my friend and confidant of so many
years. Together we had formed our views and estimates about
the whole story. I now installed him at the Admiralty with
half a dozen statisticians and economists whom we could trust
to pay no attention to anything but realities. This group of
capable men, with access to all official information, was able,
under Lindemann's guidance, to present me continually with
tables and diagrams, illustrating the whole war so far as it came
within our knowledge. They examined and analysed with re-
lentless pertinacity all the departmental papers which were
circulated to the War Cabinet, and also pursued all the inquiries which I wished to make myself.

At this time there was no general governmental statistical
organisation. Each department presented its tale on its own
figures and data. The Air Ministry counted one way, the War
Office another. The Ministry of Supply and the Board of
Trade, though meaning the same thing, talked different dialects. This led sometimes to misunderstandings and waste of
time when some point or other came to a crunch in the Cabinet.
I had, however, from the beginning my own sure, steady source
of information, every part of which was integrally related to all
the rest. Although at first this covered only a portion of the field,
it was most helpful to me in forming a just and comprehensible
view of the innumerable facts and figures which flowed out
upon us.

5

The Front in France

IMMEDIATELY UPON THE OUTBREAK, our Expeditionary Army began to move to France. Whereas, before the previous war at least three years had been spent in making the preparations, it was not till the spring of 1938 that the War Office set up a special section for this purpose. Two serious factors were now present. First, the equipment and organisation of a modern army was far less simple than in 1914. Every division had mechanical transport, was more numerous, and had a much higher proportion of non-fighting elements. Secondly, the extravagant fear of air attack on the troopships and landing-ports led the War Office to use only the southern French harbours, and St. Nazaire, which became the principal base. This lengthened the communications of the Army, and in consequence retarded the arrival, deployment, and maintenance of the British troops, and consumed profuse additional numbers along the route.[1]

[1] Advanced parties of the British Expeditionary Force began to land in France on September 4. The First Corps were ashore by September 19, and the Second

469

Oddly enough, it had not been decided before war on which sector of the front our troops should be deployed, but the strong presumption was that it would be south of Lille; and this was confirmed on September 22. By mid-October four British divisions, formed into two army corps of professional quality, were in their stations along the Franco-Belgian frontier. This involved a road-and-rail movement of two hundred and fifty miles from the remote ports which had been closed for landing. Three infantry brigades, which arrived separately during October and November, were formed into the 5th Division in December, 1939. The 48th Division came out in January, 1940, followed by the 50th and 51st Divisions in February, and the 42d and 44th in March, making a total of ten. As our numbers grew we took over more line. We were not, of course, at any point in contact with the enemy.

When the B.E.F. reached their prescribed positions, they found ready-prepared a fairly complete artificial anti-tank ditch along the front line, and every thousand yards or so was a large and very visible pillbox giving enfilade fire along the ditch for machine and anti-tank guns. There was also a continuous belt of wire. Much of the work of our troops during this strange autumn and winter was directed to improving the French-made defences and organising a kind of Siegfried Line. In spite of frost, progress was rapid. Air photographs showed the rate at which the Germans were extending their own Siegfried Line northwards from the Moselle. Despite the many advantages they enjoyed in home resources and forced labour, we seemed to be keeping pace with them. By the time of the May offensive, 1940, our troops had completed four hundred new pillboxes. Forty miles of revetted anti-tank ditch had been dug and great quantities of wire spread. Immense demands were made by the long line of communications stretching back to Nantes. Large base installations were created, roads improved, a hundred miles of broad-gauge railway line laid, an extensive system of buried

Corps by October 3. General Headquarters (G.H.Q.) was set up initially at Le Mans on September 15. The principal movement of troops was made through Cherbourg, with vehicles and stores through Brest and Nantes, and assembly-points at Le Mans and Laval.

cable dug in, and several tunnelled headquarters for the corps
and army commands almost completed. Nearly fifty new airfields and satellites were developed or improved with runways,
involving over fifty thousand tons of concrete.

On all these tasks the Army laboured industriously, and to
vary their experiences, moved brigades by rotation to a sector
of the French Front in contact with the enemy near Metz,
where there was at least some patrol activity. All the rest of the
time was spent by our troops in training. This was indeed necessary. A far lower scale of preparation had been reached when war
broke out than that attained by Sir John French's army a quarter
of a century before. For several years no considerable exercise
with troops had been held at home. The Regular Army was
twenty thousand short of establishment, including five thousand officers, and under the Cardwell system, which had to provide for the defence of India, the greater part of this fell upon
the home units, which in consequence became hardly more
than cadres. The little-considered, though well-meant, doubling of the Territorial Army in March, 1939, and the creation
of the militia in May of that year, both involved drawing heavily upon the Regular Army for instructors. The winter months
in France were turned to good account, and every kind of training programme was woven into the prime work of fortification.
It is certain that our Army advanced markedly in efficiency during the breathing-space which was granted it, and in spite of
exacting toils and the absence of any kind of action, its morale
and spirit grew.

Behind our front immense masses of stores and ammunition
were accumulated in the depots all along the communications.
Ten days' supply was gathered between the Seine and the
Somme, *and seven days' additional north of the Somme.* This
latter provision saved the Army after the German break-through.
Gradually, in view of the prevailing tranquillity, other ports
north of Havre were brought into use in succession. Dieppe
became a hospital base; Fécamp was concerned with ammunition; and in the end we were making use, in all, of thirteen
French harbours.

*   *   *   *   *

The advantage which a Government bound by no law or treaty has over countries which derive their war impulse only after the criminal has struck, and have to plan accordingly, cannot be measured. It is enormous. On the other hand, unless the victory of the aggressors is absolute and final, there may be some day a reckoning. Hitler, unhampered by any restraint except that of superior force, could strike when and where he chose; but the two Western Democracies could not violate Belgium's neutrality. The most they could do was to be ready to come to the rescue when called upon by the Belgians, and it was probable that this would never happen until it was too late. Of course, if British and French policy during the five years preceding the war had been of a manly and resolute character, within the sanctity of treaties and the approval of the League of Nations, Belgium might have adhered to her old allies, and allowed a common front to be formed. This would have brought immense security, and might perhaps have averted the disasters which were to come.

Such an alliance properly organised would have erected a shield along the Belgian frontier to the sea against that terrible turning movement which had nearly compassed our destruction in 1914 and was to play its part in the ruin of France in 1940. It would also have opened the possibility of a rapid advance from Belgium into the heart-centre of German industry in the Ruhr, and thus added a powerful deterrent upon German aggression. At the worst Belgium could have suffered no harder fate than actually befell her. When we recall the aloofness of the United States; Mr. Ramsay MacDonald's campaign for the disarmament of France; the repeated rebuffs and humiliations which we had accepted in the various German breaches of the disarmament clauses of the Treaty; our submission to the German violation of the Rhineland; our acquiescence in the absorption of Austria; our pact at Munich and acceptance of the German occupation of Prague — when we recall all this, no man in Britain or France who in those years was responsible for public action has a right to blame Belgium. In a period of vacillation and appeasement, the Belgians clung to neutrality, and vainly comforted themselves with the belief that they could hold the German invaders on their fortified frontiers until the British and French Armies could come to their aid.

* * * * *

In 1914, the spirit of the French Army and nation, burning from sire to son since 1870, was vehemently offensive. Their doctrine was that the numerically weaker power could only meet invasion by the counter-offensive, not only strategic but tactical at every point. At the beginning the French, with their blue tunics and red trousers, marched forward while their bands played the *Marseillaise*. Wherever this happened, the Germans, although invading, sat down and fired upon them with devastating effect. The apostle of the offensive creed, Colonel Grandmaison, had perished in the forefront of the battle for his country and his theme. I have explained in *The World Crisis* why the power of the defensive was predominant from 1914 to 1916 or 1917. The magazine rifle, which we ourselves had seen used with great effect by handfuls of Boers in the South African War, could take a heavy if not decisive toll from troops advancing across the open. Besides this there were the ever-multiplying machine-guns.

Then had come the great battles of the artillery. An area was pulverised by hundreds and presently by thousands of guns. But if after heroic sacrifices the French and British advanced together against the strongly entrenched Germans, successive lines of fortifications confronted them; and the crater-fields which their bombardment had created to quell the first lines of the enemy became a decisive obstacle to their further progress, even when they were successful. The only conclusion to be drawn from these hard experiences was that the defensive was master. Moreover, in the quarter of a century that had passed, the fire-power of weapons had enormously increased. But this cut both ways; as will later be apparent.

It was now a very different France from that which had hurled itself upon its ancient foe in August, 1914. The spirit of *Revanche* had exhausted its mission and itself in victory.

The chiefs who had nursed it were long dead. The French
people had undergone the frightful slaughter of one and a half
million of their manhood. Offensive action was associated in the
great majority of French minds with the initial failures of the
French onslaught of 1914, with General Nivelle's repulse in 1917,
with the long agonies of the Somme and Passchendaele, and
above all with the sense that the fire-power of modern weapons
was devastating to the attacker. Neither in France nor in Britain
had there been any effective comprehension of the consequences of the new fact that armoured vehicles could be made
capable of withstanding artillery fire, and could advance a hundred miles a day. An illuminating book on this subject, published some years before by a Commandant de Gaulle, had met
with no response. The authority of the aged Marshal Pétain in
the *Conseil Supérieur de la Guerre* had weighed heavily upon
French military thought in closing the door to new ideas, and
especially in discouraging what had been quaintly called "offensive weapons."

In the after-light, the policy of the Maginot Line has often
been condemned. It certainly engendered a defensive mentality; yet it is always a wise precaution in defending a frontier
of hundreds of miles to bar off as much as possible by fortifications, and thus economise the use of troops in sedentary rôles
and "canalise" potential invasion. Properly used in the French
scheme of war, the Maginot Line would have been of immense
service to France. It could have been viewed as presenting a
long succession of invaluable sally-ports, and above all as block-
ing-off large sectors of the front as a means of accumulating
the general reserves or "mass of manoeuvre." Having regard
to the disparity of the population of France to that of Germany,
the Maginot Line must be regarded as a wise and prudent
measure. Indeed, it was extraordinary that it should not have
been carried forward at least along the river Meuse. It could
then have served as a trusty shield, freeing a heavy, sharp, offensive French sword. But Marshal Pétain had opposed this extension. He held strongly that the Ardennes could be ruled out as
a channel of invasion on account of the nature of the ground.

Ruled out accordingly it was. The offensive conceptions of the Maginot Line were explained to me by General Giraud when I visited Metz in 1937. They were, however, not carried into effect, and the Line not only absorbed very large numbers of highly trained regular soldiers and technicians, but exercised an enervating effect both upon military strategy and national vigilance.

The new air power was justly esteemed a revolutionary factor in all operations. Considering the comparatively small numbers of aircraft available on either side at this time, its effects were even exaggerated, and were held in the main to favour the defensive by hampering the concentrations and communications of great armies once launched in attack. Even the period of the French mobilisation was regarded by the French High Command as most critical on account of the possible destruction of railway centres, although the numbers of German aircraft, like those of the Allies, were far too few for such a task. These thoughts expressed by air chiefs followed correct lines, and were justified in the later years of the war, when the air strength had grown ten or twenty-fold. At the outbreak they were premature.

* * * * *

It is a joke in Britain to say that the War Office is always preparing for the last war. But this is probably true of other departments and of other countries, and it was certainly true of the French Army. I also rested under the impression of the superior power of the defensive, provided it were actively conducted. I had neither the responsibility nor the continuous information to make a new measurement. I knew that the carnage of the previous war had bitten deeply into the soul of the French people. The Germans had been given the time to build the Siegfried Line. How frightful to hurl the remaining manhood of France against this wall of fire and concrete! I print in Appendix J, Book II (called "Cultivator Number 6") one kind of long-term method by which I then thought the fire-power of the defensive could be overcome. But in my mind's outlook in the opening months of this Second World War, I did not dissent from the general view about the defensive, and I believed that anti-tank obstacles and field guns, cleverly posted and with suitable ammunition, could frustrate or break up tanks except in darkness or fog, real or artificial.

In the problems which the Almighty sets his humble servants things hardly ever happen the same way twice over, or if they seem to do so, there is some variant which stultifies undue generalisation. The human mind, except when guided by extraordinary genius, cannot surmount the established conclusions amid which it has been reared. Yet we are to see, after eight months of inactivity on both sides, the Hitler inrush of a vast offensive, led by spearpoint masses of cannon-proof or heavily armoured vehicles, breaking up all defensive opposition, and for the first time for centuries, and even perhaps since the invention of gunpowder, making artillery for a while almost impotent on the battlefield. We are also to see that the increase of fire-power made the actual battles less bloody by enabling the necessary ground to be held with very small numbers of men, thus offering a far smaller human target.

*   *   *   *   *

No frontier has ever received the same strategic attention and experiment as that which stretches through the Low Countries between France and Germany. Every aspect of the ground, its heights and its waterways, has been studied for centuries in the light of the latest campaign by all the generals and military colleges in Western Europe. At this period there were two lines to which the Allies could advance if Belgium were invaded by Germany and they chose to come to her succour; or which they could occupy by a well-planned secret and sudden scheme, if invited by Belgium. The first of these lines was what may be called the line of the Scheldt.[2] This was no great march from the French frontier and involved little serious risk. At the worst it would do no harm to hold it as a "false front." At the best it might be built up according to events. The second

2 See map.

line was far more ambitious. It followed the Meuse through Givet, Dinant, and Namur by Louvain to Antwerp. If this adventurous line was seized by the Allies and held in hard battles, the German right-handed swing of invasion would be heavily checked; and if their armies were proved inferior, it would be an admirable prelude to the entry and control of the vital centre of Germany's munition production in the Ruhr.

Since the case of an advance through Belgium without Belgian consent was excluded on grounds of international morality, there only remained an advance from the common Franco-German frontier. An attack due eastward across the Rhine, north and south of Strasbourg, opened mainly into the Black Forest, which, like the Ardennes, was at that time regarded as bad ground for offensive operations. There was, however, the question of an advance from the front Strasbourg-Metz northeastward into the Palatinate. Such an advance, with its right on the Rhine, might gain control of that river as far north as

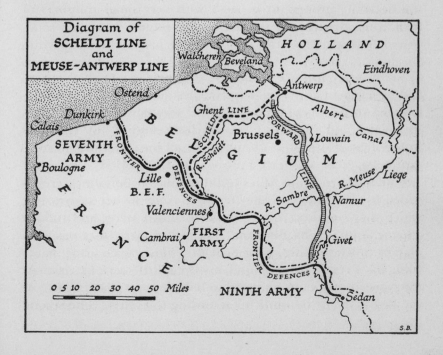

Coblenz or Cologne. This led into good fighting country; and
these possibilities, with many variants, had been a part of the
war-games in the Staff Colleges of Western Europe for a good
many years. In this sector, however, the Siegfried Line, with
its well-built concrete pillboxes mutually supporting one another and organised in depth with masses of wire, was in September, 1939, already formidable. The earliest date at which
the French could have mounted a big attack was perhaps at the
end of the third week of September. But by that time the Polish campaign had ended. By mid-October the Germans had
seventy divisions on the Western Front. The fleeting French
numerical superiority in the West was passing. A French offensive from their eastern frontier would have denuded their
far more vital northern front. Even if an initial success had
been gained by the French armies at the outset, within a month
they would have had extreme difficulty in maintaining their
conquests in the East, and would have been exposed to the
whole force of the German counter-stroke in the North.

This is the answer to the question, "Why remain passive till
Poland was destroyed?" But this battle had been lost some
years before. In 1938, there was a good chance of victory while
Czechoslovakia still existed. In 1936, there could have been
no effective opposition. In 1933, a rescript from Geneva would
have procured bloodless compliance. General Gamelin cannot
be the only one to blame because in 1939 he did not run the
risks which had so erroneously increased since the previous
crises, from which both the French and British Governments
had recoiled.

The British Chiefs of Staff Committee estimated that the
Germans had by September 18 mobilised at least 116 divisions
of all classes, distributed as follows: Western Front, 42 divisions; Central Germany, 16 divisions; Eastern Front, 58 divisions. We now know from enemy records that this estimate was
almost exactly correct. Germany had in all from 108 to 117
divisions. Poland was attacked by 58 of the most matured.
There remained 50 or 60 divisions of varying quality. Of these,
along the Western Front from Aix-la-Chapelle to the Swiss

frontier, there stood 42 German divisions (14 active, 25 reserve, and 3 Landwehr). The German armour was either engaged in Poland or had not yet come into being, and the great flow of tanks from the factories had hardly begun. The British Expeditionary Force was no more than a symbolic contribution. It was able to deploy two divisions by the first and two more by the second week in October. In spite of the enormous improvement since Munich in their relative strength, the German High Command regarded their situation in the West while Poland was unconquered with profound anxiety, and only Hitler's despotic authority, will-power, and five-times-vindicated political judgment about the unwillingness of France and Great Britain to fight induced or compelled them to run what they deemed an unjustified risk.

Hitler was sure that the French political system was rotten to the core, and that it had infected the French Army. He knew the power of the Communists in France, and that it would be used to weaken or paralyse action once Ribbentrop and Molotov had come to terms and Moscow had denounced the French and British Governments for entering upon a capitalist and imperialist war. He was convinced that Britain was pacifist and degenerate. In his view, though Mr. Chamberlain and M. Daladier had been brought to the point of declaring war by a bellicose minority in England, they would both wage as little of it as they could, and once Poland had been crushed, would accept the accomplished fact as they had done a year before in the case of Czechoslovakia. On the repeated occasions which have been set forth, Hitler's instinct had been proved right and the arguments and fears of his generals wrong. He did not understand the profound change which takes place in Great Britain and throughout the British Empire once the signal of war has been given; nor how those who have been the most strenuous for peace turn overnight into untiring toilers for victory. He could not comprehend the mental or spiritual force of our island people, who, however much opposed to war or military preparation, had through the centuries come to regard victory as their birthright. In any case the British Army could

be no factor at the outset, and he was certain that the French
nation had not thrown its heart into the war. This was indeed
true. He had his way, and his orders were obeyed.

*   *   *   *   *

It was thought by our officers that when Germany had completely defeated the Polish Army, she would have to keep in
Poland some 15 divisions, of which a large proportion might
be of low category. If she had any doubts about the Russian
pact, this total might have to be increased to upwards of 30
divisions in the East. On the least favourable assumption
Germany would, therefore, be able to draw over 40 divisions
from the Eastern Front, making 100 divisions available
for the West. By that time the French would have mobilised 72
divisions in France, in addition to fortress troops equivalent to 12
or 14 divisions, and there would be 4 divisions of the British
Expeditionary Force. Twelve French divisions would be required to watch the Italian frontier, making 76 against Germany. The enemy would thus have a superiority of four to
three over the Allies, and might also be expected to form additional reserve divisions, bringing his total up to 130 in the
near future. Against this the French had 14 additional divisions
in North Africa, some of which could be drawn upon, and
whatever further forces Great Britain could gradually supply.

In air power, our Chiefs of Staff estimated that Germany
could concentrate, after the destruction of Poland, over two
thousand bombers in the West as against a combined Franco-
British total of 950.[3] It was, therefore, clear that once Hitler
had disposed of Poland, he would be far more powerful on the
ground and in the air than the British and French combined.
There could, therefore, be no question of a French offensive
against Germany. What, then, were the probabilities of a German offensive against France?

There were, of course, three methods open. First, invasion
through Switzerland. This might turn the southern flank of
the Maginot Line, but had many geographical and strategic dif-

[3] Actually the German bomber strength at that date was 1546.

ficulties. Secondly, invasion of France across the common frontier. This appeared unlikely, as the German Army was not believed to be fully equipped or armed for a heavy attack on the Maginot Line. And thirdly, invasion of France through Holland and Belgium. This would turn the Maginot Line and would not entail the losses likely to be sustained in a frontal attack against permanent fortifications. The Chiefs of Staff estimated that for this attack Germany would require to bring from the Eastern Front twenty-nine divisions for the initial phase, with fourteen echelonned behind, as reinforcements to her troops already in the West. Such a movement could not be completed and the attack mounted with full artillery support under three weeks; and its preparation should be discernible by us a fortnight before the blow fell. It would be late in the year for the Germans to undertake so great an operation; but the possibility could not be excluded.

We should, of course, try to retard the German movement from east to west by air attack upon the communications and concentration areas. Thus, a preliminary air battle to reduce or eliminate the Allied air forces by attacks on airfields and aircraft factories might be expected, and so far as England was concerned, would not be unwelcome. Our next task would be to deal with the German advance through the Low Countries. We could not meet their attack so far forward as Holland, but it would be in the Allied interest to stem it, if possible, in Belgium.

We understand [wrote the Chiefs of Staff] that the French idea is that, provided the Belgians are still holding out on the Meuse, the French and British Armies should occupy the line Givet-Namur, the British Expeditionary Force operating on the left. *We consider it would be unsound to adopt this plan unless plans are concerted with the Belgians for the occupation of this line in sufficient time before the Germans advance. . . . Unless the present Belgian attitude alters and plans can be prepared for early occupation of the Givet-Namur [also called Meuse-Antwerp] line, we are strongly of opinion that the German advance should be met in prepared positions on the French frontier.*

In this case it would, of course, be necessary to bomb Belgian and Dutch towns and railway centres used or occupied by German troops.

The subsequent history of this important issue must be recorded. It was brought before the War Cabinet on September 20, and after a brief discussion was remitted to the Supreme War Council. In due course the Supreme War Council invited General Gamelin's comments. In his reply General Gamelin said merely that the question of Plan "D" (i.e., the advance to the Meuse-Antwerp line) had been dealt with in a report by the French delegation. In this report the operative passage was: "If the call is made in time the Anglo-French troops will enter Belgium, but not to engage in an encounter battle. Among the recognised lines of defence are the line of the Scheldt and the line Meuse-Namur-Antwerp." After considering the French reply, the British Chiefs of the Staff submitted another paper to the Cabinet, which discussed the alternative of an advance to the Scheldt, but made no mention at all of the far larger commitments of an advance to the Meuse-Antwerp line. When this second report was presented to the Cabinet on October 4 by the Chiefs of Staff, no reference was made by them to the all-important alternative of Plan "D." It was, therefore, taken for granted by the War Cabinet that the views of the British Chiefs of the Staff had been met and that no further action or decision was required. I was present at both these Cabinets, and was not aware that any significant issue was still pending. During October, there being no effective arrangement with the Belgians, it was assumed that the advance was limited to the Scheldt.

Meanwhile, General Gamelin, negotiating secretly with the Belgians, stipulated: first, that the Belgian Army should be maintained at full strength, and secondly, that Belgian defences should be prepared on the more advanced line from Namur to Louvain. By early November, agreement was reached with the Belgians on these points, and from November 5 to 14, a series of conferences was held at Vincennes and La Fère, at which, or some of which, Ironside, Newall, and Gort were present. On

November 15, General Gamelin issued his Instruction Number 8, confirming the agreements of the fourteenth, whereby support would be given to the Belgians, "if circumstances permitted," by an advance to the line Meuse-Antwerp. The Allied Supreme Council met in Paris on November 17. Mr. Chamberlain took with him Lord Halifax, Lord Chatfield, and Sir Kingsley Wood. I had not at that time reached the position where I should be invited to accompany the Prime Minister to these meetings. The decision was taken: "Given the importance of holding the German forces as far east as possible, it is essential to make every endeavour to hold the line Meuse-Antwerp in the event of a German invasion of Belgium." At this meeting Mr. Chamberlain and M. Daladier insisted on the importance which they attached to this resolution, and thereafter it governed action. This was, in fact, a decision in favour of Plan "D," and it superseded the arrangement hitherto accepted of the modest forward move to the Scheldt.

As a new addition to Plan "D," there presently appeared the task of a Seventh French Army. The idea of an advance of this army on the seaward flank of the Allied armies first came to light early in November, 1939. General Giraud, who was restless with a reserve army around Rheims, was put in command. The object of this extension of Plan "D" was to move into Holland via Antwerp so as to help the Dutch, and secondly, to occupy some parts of the Dutch islands Walcheren and Beveland. All this would have been good if the Germans had already been stopped on the Albert Canal. General Gamelin wanted it. General Georges thought it beyond our scope; and preferred that the troops involved should be brought into reserve behind the centre of the line. Of these differences we knew nothing.

In this posture, therefore, we passed the winter and awaited the spring. No new decisions of strategic principle were taken by the French and British Staffs or by their Governments in the six months which lay between us and the German onslaught.

6

The Combat Deepens

Peace Suggestions — The Anglo-French Rejection — Soviet Absorption of the Baltic States — My Views on British Military Preparations — Possible Détente with Italy in the Mediterranean — The Home Front — The Sinking of the "Royal Oak" — My Second Visit to Scapa Flow, October 31 — Decision About the Main Fleet Base — Mr. and Mrs. Chamberlain Dine at Admiralty House — The Loss of the "Rawalpindi" — A False Alarm.

HITLER TOOK ADVANTAGE of his successes to propose his peace plan to the Allies. One of the unhappy consequences of our appeasement policy, and generally of our attitude in the face of his rise to power, had been to convince him that neither we nor France were capable of fighting a war. He had been unpleasantly surprised by the declarations of Great Britain and France on September 3; but he firmly believed that the spectacle of the swift and crashing destruction of Poland would make the decadent democracies realise that the day when they could exercise influence over the fate of Eastern and Central Europe was gone for ever. He felt very sure at this time of the Russians, gorged as they were with Polish territory and the Baltic States. Indeed, during this month of October he was able to send the captured American merchantman *City of Flint* into the Soviet port of Murmansk under a German prize crew. He had no wish at this stage to continue a war with France and Britain. He felt sure His Majesty's Government would be very glad to accept the decision reached by him in Poland, and that a peace offer would enable Mr. Cham-

berlain and his old colleagues, having vindicated their honour
by a declaration of war, to get out of the scrape into which they
had been forced by the warmongering elements in Parliament.
It never occurred to him for a moment that Mr. Chamberlain
and the rest of the British Empire and Commonwealth of Nations now meant to have his blood or perish in the attempt.

The next step taken by Russia after partitioning Poland with
Germany was to make three "Mutual Assistance Pacts" with
Esthonia, Latvia, and Lithuania. These Baltic States were the
most vehemently anti-Bolshevist regions in Europe. They had
all broken themselves free from the Soviet Government in the
civil war of 1918 and 1920, and had built up, in the harsh manner in which revolutions are conducted in those regions, a type
of society and government of which the main principle was
hostility to Communism and to Russia. From Riga in particular for twenty years a stream of violently anti-Bolshevik
propaganda had flowed daily by radio and all other channels
to the world. With the exception of Latvia, they had not, however, associated themselves with the Hitlerite Germany. The
Germans had been content to throw them into their Russian
deal, and the Soviet Government now advanced with pent-up
hate and eager appetite upon their prey. These three states had
formed a part of the Tsarist Empire, and were the old conquests of Peter the Great. They were immediately occupied
by strong Russian forces against which they had no means of
effectual resistance. A ferocious liquidation of all anti-Communist and anti-Russian elements was carried through by the
usual methods. Great numbers of people who for twenty years
had lived in freedom in their native land and had represented
the dominant majority of its people disappeared. A large
proportion of these were transported to Siberia. The rest went
farther. This process was described as "Mutual Assistance
Pacts."

* * * * *

At home we busied ourselves with the expansion of the Army
and the air force and with all the necessary measures to
strengthen our naval power. I continued to submit my ideas

to the Prime Minister, and pressed them upon other colleagues as might be acceptable.

First Lord to Prime Minister.   1.X.39.

This week-end I venture to write to you about several large issues.

1. When the peace offensive opens upon us, it will be necessary to sustain the French. Although we have nearly a million men under arms, our contribution is, and must for many months remain, petty. We should tell the French that we are making as great a war effort, though in a different form, as in 1918; that we are constructing an army of fifty-five divisions, which will be brought into action wherever needed, as fast as it can be trained and supplied, having regard to our great contribution in the air.

At present we have our Regular Army, which produces four or five divisions probably superior to anything in the field. But do not imagine that Territorial divisions will be able, after six months' training or so, to take their part without needless losses and bad results against German regular troops with at least two years' service and better equipment; or stand at the side of French troops many of whom have had three years' service. The only way in which our forces in France can be rapidly expanded is by bringing the professional troops from India, and using them as the cadre upon which the Territorials and conscripts will form. I do not attempt to go into details now, but in principle, 60,000 Territorials should be sent to India to maintain internal security and complete their training, and 40,000 or 45,000 Regular troops should *pari passu* be brought back to Europe. These troops should go into camps in the South of France, where the winter weather is more favourable to training than here, and where there are many military facilities, and become the nucleus and framework of eight or ten good field divisions. The texture of these troops would, by the late spring, be equal to those they will have to meet or stand beside. The fact of this force developing in France during the winter months would be a great encouragement and satisfaction to the French.

2. I was much concerned at the figures put forward by the Air Ministry of their fighting strength. They had a hundred and twenty squadrons at the outbreak of war, but this actually boiled down to ninety-six, or barely three-quarters, able to go into action. One usually expects that on mobilisation there will be a large expansion.

In this case there has been a severe contraction. What has happened is that a large number of squadrons have had to be gutted of trained air personnel, of mechanics, or spare parts, etc., in order to produce a fighting force, and that the débris of these squadrons has been thrown into a big pool called the reserve. Into this pool will also flow, if the winter months pass without heavy attack, a great mass of new machines and large numbers of trained pilots. Even after making every deduction which is reasonable, we ought to be able to form at least six squadrons a month. It is much better to form squadrons which are held back in reserve than merely to have a large pool of spare pilots, spare machines, and spare parts. This disparity at the present time with Germany is shocking. I am sure this expansion could be achieved if you gave the word.

3. The A.R.P. (Air Raid Precautions) defences and expense are founded upon a wholly fallacious view of the degree of danger to each part of the country which they cover. Schedules should be made of the target areas and of the paths of flight by which they may be approached. In these areas there must be a large proportion of whole-time employees. London is, of course, the chief [target], and others will readily occur. In these target areas the street-lighting should be made so that it can be controlled by the air wardens on the alarm signal being given; and while shelters should be hurried on with and strengthened, night and day, the people's spirits should be kept up by theatres and cinemas until the actual attack begins. Over a great part of the countryside, modified lighting should be at once allowed, and places of entertainment opened. No paid A.R.P. personnel should be allowed in these [areas]. All should be on a voluntary basis, the Government contenting itself with giving advice, and leaving the rest to local effort. In these areas, which comprise at least seven-eighths of the United Kingdom, gas-masks should be kept at home and only carried in the target areas as scheduled. There is really no reason why orders to this effect should not be given during the coming week.

* * * * *

The disasters which had occurred in Poland and the Baltic States made me all the more anxious to keep Italy out of the war, and to build up by every possible means some common interest between us. In the meantime the war went on, and I was busy over a number of administrative matters.

First Lord to Home Secretary.   7.X.39.

In spite of having a full day's work usually here, I cannot help feeling anxious about the Home Front. You know my views about the needless, and in most parts of the country senseless, severities of these black-outs, entertainment restrictions and the rest. But what about petrol? Have the Navy failed to bring in the supplies? Are there not more supplies on the water approaching and probably arriving than would have been ordered had peace remained unbroken? I am told that very large numbers of people and a large part of the business of the country is hampered by the stinting. Surely the proper way to deal with this is to have a ration at the standard price, and allow free purchasing, subject to a heavy tax, beyond it. People will pay for locomotion, the revenue will benefit by the tax, more cars will come out with registration fees, and the business of the country can go forward.

Then look at these rations, all devised by the Ministry of Food to win the war. By all means have rations, but I am told that the meat ration, for instance, is very little better than that of Germany. Is there any need of this when the seas are open?

If we have a heavy set-back from air attack or surface attack, it might be necessary to inflict these severities. Up to the present there is no reason to suppose that the Navy has failed in bringing in the supplies, or that it will fail.

Then what about all these people of middle age, many of whom served in the last war, who are full of vigour and experience, and who are being told by tens of thousands that they are not wanted, and that there is nothing for them except to register at the local Labour Exchange? Surely this is very foolish. Why do we not form a Home Guard of half a million men over forty (if they like to volunteer), and put all our elderly stars at the head and in the structure of these new formations? Let these five hundred thousand men come along and push the young and active out of all the home billets. If uniforms are lacking, a brassard would suffice, and I am assured there are plenty of rifles at any rate. I thought from what you said to me the other day that you liked this idea. If so, let us make it work.

I hear continual complaints from every quarter of the lack of organisation on the Home Front. Can't we get at it?

*   *   *   *   *

Amidst all these preoccupations there burst upon us suddenly an event which touched the Admiralty in a most sensitive spot.

I have mentioned the alarm that a U-boat was *inside Scapa Flow*, which had driven the Grand Fleet to sea on the night of October 17, 1914. That alarm was premature. Now, after exactly a quarter of a century almost to a day, it came true. At 1.30 A.M. on October 14, 1939, a German U-boat braved the tides and currents, penetrated our defences, and sank the battleship *Royal Oak* as she lay at anchor. At first, out of a salvo of torpedoes, only one hit the bow and caused a muffled explosion. So incredible was it to the Admiral and Captain on board that a torpedo could have struck them, safe in Scapa Flow, that they attributed the explosions to some internal cause. Twenty minutes passed before the U-boat, for such she was, had reloaded her tubes and fired a second salvo. Then three or four torpedoes striking in quick succession ripped the bottom out of the ship. In less than two minutes, she capsized and sank. Most of the men were at action stations, but the rate at which the ship turned over made it almost impossible for anyone below to escape.

An account based on a German report written at the time may be recorded:

At 01.30 on October 14, 1939, H.M.S. *Royal Oak*, lying at anchor in Scapa Flow, was torpedoed by *U 47* (Lieutenant Prien). The operation had been carefully planned by Admiral Doenitz himself, the Flag Officer [submarines]. Prien left Kiel on October 8, a clear bright autumn day, and passed through Kiel Canal — course N.N.W., Scapa Flow. On October 13, at 4 A.M., the boat was lying off the Orkneys. At 7 P.M. — Surface; a fresh breeze blowing, nothing in sight; looming in the half darkness the line of the distant coast; long streamers of Northern Lights flashing blue wisps across the sky. Course West. The boat crept steadily closer to Holm Sound, the eastern approach to Scapa Flow. Unfortunate it was that these channels had not been completely blocked. A narrow passage lay open between two sunken ships. With great skill Prien steered through the swirling waters. The shore was close. A man on a bicycle could be seen going home along the coast road. Then sud-

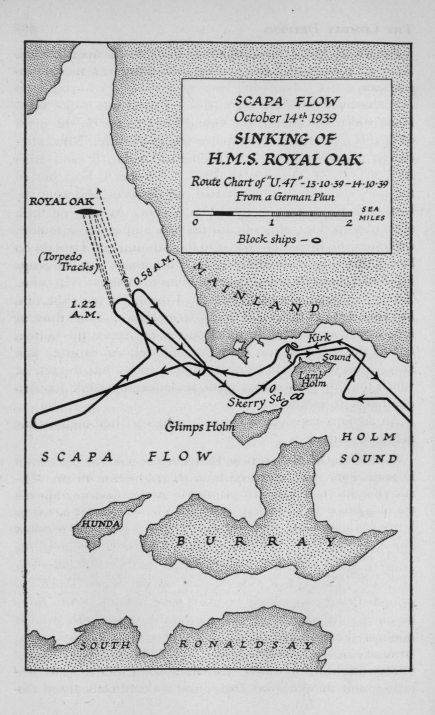

SCAPA FLOW
October 14th 1939
SINKING OF
H.M.S. ROYAL OAK
Route Chart of "U.47" - 13·10·39 - 14·10·39
From a German Plan

0   1   2   SEA
              MILES

Block ships — o

ROYAL OAK

(Torpedo
Tracks)

0.58 A.M.

1.22
A.M.

MAINLAND

Kirk
Sound

Lamb
Holm

Skerry Sd.

Glimps Holm

SCAPA   FLOW

HOLM

SOUND

HUNDA

B U R R A Y

S O U T H   R O N A L D S A Y

denly the whole bay opened out. Kirk Sound was passed. They
were in. There under the land to the north could be seen the
great shadow of a battleship lying on the water, with the great
mast rising above it like a piece of filigree on a black cloth. Near,
nearer — all tubes clear — no alarm, no sound but the lap of the
water, the low hiss of air pressure and the sharp click of a tube
lever. *Los!* [Fire!] — five seconds — ten seconds — twenty seconds.
Then came a shattering explosion, and a great pillar of water rose
in the darkness. Prien waited some minutes to fire another salvo.
Tubes ready. Fire. The torpedoes hit amidships, and there followed a series of crashing explosions. H.M.S. *Royal Oak* sank, with
the loss of 786 officers and men, including Rear-Admiral H. E. C.
Blagrove [Rear-Admiral Second Battle Squadron]. *U 47* crept
quietly away back through the gap. A blockship arrived twenty-
four hours later.

This episode, which must be regarded as a feat of arms on
the part of the German U-boat commander, gave a shock to
public opinion. It might well have been politically fatal to
any Minister who had been responsible for the pre-war precautions. Being a newcomer I was immune from such reproaches in these early months, and moreover, the Opposition
did not attempt to make capital out of the misfortune. On the
contrary, Mr. A. V. Alexander was restrained and sympathetic.
I promised the strictest inquiry.

On this occasion the Prime Minister also gave the House an
account of the German air raids which had been made on October 16 upon the Firth of Forth. This was the first attempt the
Germans had made to strike by air at our Fleet. Twelve or
more machines in flights of two or three at a time had bombed
our cruisers lying in the Firth. Slight damage was done to the
cruisers *Southampton* and *Edinburgh* and to the destroyer
Mohawk. Twenty-five officers and sailors were killed or
wounded; but four enemy bombers were brought down, three
by our fighter squadrons and one by the anti-aircraft fire. It
might well be that only half the bombers had got home safely.
This was an effective deterrent.

The following morning, the seventeenth, Scapa Flow was
raided, and the old *Iron Duke*, now a demilitarised and dis-

armoured hulk used as a depot ship, was injured by near
misses. She settled on the bottom in shallow water and continued to do her work throughout the war. Another enemy
aircraft was shot down in flames. The Fleet was happily absent
from the harbour. These events showed how necessary it was
to perfect the defences of Scapa against all forms of attack
before allowing it to be used. It was nearly six months before
we were able to enjoy its commanding advantages.

*   *   *   *   *

The attack on Scapa Flow and the loss of the *Royal Oak*
provoked instant reactions in the Admiralty. On October 31,
accompanied by the First Sea Lord, I went to Scapa to hold a
second conference on these matters in Admiral Forbes' flagship. The scale of defence for Scapa upon which we now agreed
included reinforcement of the booms and additional blockships
in the exposed eastern channels, as well as controlled minefields and other devices. These formidable deterrents would
be reinforced by further patrol craft and guns sited to cover all
approaches. Against air attack it was planned to mount eighty-
eight heavy and forty light A.A. guns, together with numerous
searchlights and increased barrage-balloon defences. Substantial fighter protection was organised both in the Orkneys and
at Wick on the mainland. It was hoped that all these arrangements could be completed, or at least sufficiently advanced, to
justify the return of the Fleet by March, 1940. Meanwhile,
Scapa could be used as a destroyer-refuelling base; but other
accommodation had to be found for the heavy ships.

Experts differed on the rival claims of the possible alternative bases. Admiralty opinion favoured the Clyde, but Admiral
Forbes demurred on the ground that this would involve an
extra day's steaming each way to his main operational area.
This in turn would require an increase in his destroyer forces
and would necessitate the heavy ships working in two divisions.
The other alternative was Rosyth, which had been our main
base in the latter part of the previous war. It was more suitably placed geographically, but was more vulnerable to air

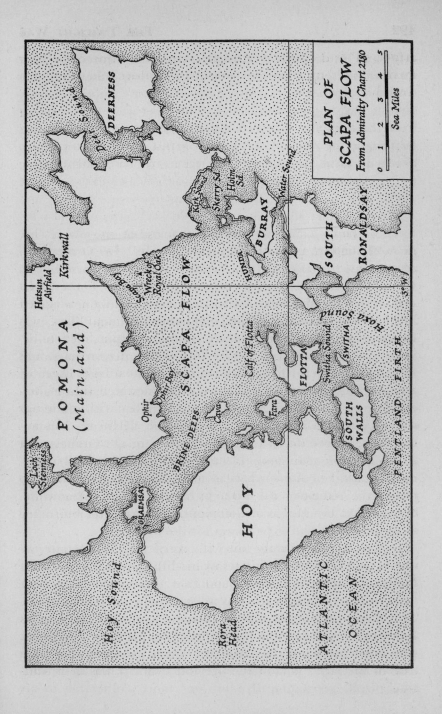

PLAN OF
SCAPA FLOW
From Admiralty Chart 2180

0 1 2 3 4 5
Sea Miles

POMONA
(Mainland)

Loch
Stenness

Hatsun
Airfield

Kirkwall

Deer Sound

DEERNESS

Kirk Sd.
Skerry Sd.
Holm Sd.
Water Sound

BURRAY

SOUTH
RONALDSAY

Scapa Bay
Wreck of
Royal Oak

SCAPA FLOW

HUNDA

Orphir

Orphir Bay

BRINE DEEPS

Cava

Fara

Calf of Flotta

FLOTTA

Switha Sound
Switha
Hoxa Sound

3° W.

HOY

GRAEMSAY

SOUTH
WALLS

PENTLAND FIRTH

Rora
Head

Hoy Sound

ATLANTIC
OCEAN

attack. The decisions eventually reached at this conference were summed up in a minute which I prepared on my return to London.[1]

*   *   *   *   *

On Friday, November 13, my relations with Mr. Chamberlain had so far ripened that he and Mrs. Chamberlain came to dine with us at Admiralty House, where we had a comfortable flat in the attics. We were a party of four. Although we had been colleagues under Mr. Baldwin for five years, my wife and I had never met the Chamberlains in such circumstances before. By happy chance I turned the conversation onto his life in the Bahamas, and I was delighted to find my guest expand in personal reminiscence to a degree I had not noticed before. He told us the whole story, of which I knew only the barest outline, of his six years' struggle to grow sisal on a barren West Indian islet near Nassau. His father, the great "Joe," was firmly convinced that here was an opportunity at once to develop an Empire industry and fortify the family fortunes. His father and Austen had summoned him in 1890 from Birmingham to Canada, where they had long examined the project. About forty miles from Nassau in the Caribbean Gulf there was a small desert island, almost uninhabited, where the soil was reported suitable for growing sisal. After careful reconnaissance by his two sons, Mr. Joseph Chamberlain had acquired a tract on the island of Andros and assigned the capital required to develop it. All that remained to grow was the sisal. Austen was dedicated to the House of Commons. The task, therefore, fell to Neville.

Not only in filial duty but with conviction and alacrity he obeyed, and the next six years of his life were spent in trying to grow sisal in this lonely spot, swept by hurricanes from time to time, living nearly naked, struggling with labour difficulties and every other kind of obstacle, and with the town of Nassau as the only gleam of civilisation. He had insisted, he told us, on three months' leave in England each year. He built a small harbour and landing-stage and a short railroad or tram-

[1] See Appendix E, Book II.

way. He used all the processes of fertilisation which were judged suitable to the soil, and generally led a completely primitive open-air existence. But no sisal! Or at any rate no sisal that would face the market. At the end of six years he was convinced that the plan could not succeed. He came home and faced his formidable parent, who was by no means contented with the result. I gathered that in the family the feeling was that though they loved him dearly they were sorry to have lost fifty thousand pounds.

I was fascinated by the way Mr. Chamberlain warmed as he talked, and by the tale itself, which was one of gallant endeavour. I thought to myself, "What a pity Hitler did not know when he met this sober English politician with his umbrella at Berchtesgaden, Godesberg, and Munich, that he was actually talking to a hard-bitten pioneer from the outer marches of the British Empire!" This was really the only intimate social conversation that I can remember with Neville Chamberlain amid all the business we did together over nearly twenty years.

During dinner the war went on and things happened. With the soup an officer came up from the War Room below to report that a U-boat had been sunk. With the sweet he came again and reported that a second U-boat had been sunk; and just before the ladies left the dining-room he came a third time reporting that a third U-boat had been sunk. Nothing like this had ever happened before in a single day, and it was more than a year before such a record was repeated. As the ladies left us, Mrs. Chamberlain, with a naïve and charming glance, said to me, "Did you arrange all this on purpose?" I assured her that if she would come again we would produce a similar result.[2]

* * * * *

Our long, tenuous blockade-line north of the Orkneys, largely composed of armed merchant-cruisers with supporting warships at intervals, was of course always liable to a sudden attack by German capital ships, and particularly by their two

2 Alas, these hopeful reports are not confirmed by the post-war analysis.

fast and most powerful battle cruisers, the *Scharnhorst* and
the *Gneisenau*. We could not prevent such a stroke being
made. Our hope was to bring the intruders to decisive action.

Late in the afternoon of November 23, the armed merchant
cruiser *Rawalpindi*, on patrol between Iceland and the Faroes,
sighted an enemy warship which closed her rapidly. She believed the stranger to be the pocket battleship *Deutschland* and
reported accordingly. Her commanding officer, Captain Ken-
nedy, could have had no illusions about the outcome of such an
encounter. His ship was but a converted passenger liner with a
broadside of four old six-inch guns, and his presumed antagonist mounted six eleven-inch guns besides a powerful secondary armament. Nevertheless, he accepted the odds, determined
to fight his ship to the last. The enemy opened fire at ten
thousand yards and the *Rawalpindi* struck back. Such a one-
sided action could not last long, but the fight continued until,
with all her guns out of action, the *Rawalpindi* was reduced
to a blazing wreck. She sank some time after dark with the loss
of her captain and two hundred and seventy of her gallant
crew. Only thirty-eight survived, twenty-seven of whom were
made prisoners by the Germans, the remaining eleven being
picked up alive after thirty-six hours in icy water by another
British ship.

In fact it was not the *Deutschland*, but the battle cruiser
Scharnhorst which was engaged. This ship, together with the
Gneisenau, had left Germany two days before to attack our
Atlantic convoys, but having encountered and sunk the *Rawalpindi* and fearing the consequences of the exposure, they abandoned the rest of their mission and returned at once to Germany. The *Rawalpindi's* heroic fight was not therefore in
vain. The cruiser *Newcastle*, near-by on patrol, saw the gun-
flashes, and responded to the *Rawalpindi's* first report, arriving on the scene with the cruiser *Delhi* to find the burning
ship still afloat. She pursued the enemy and at 6.15 P.M.
sighted two ships in gathering darkness and heavy rain. One
of these she recognised as a battle cruiser, but lost contact in
the gloom, and the enemy made good his escape.

The hope of bringing these two vital German ships to battle dominated all concerned, and the Commander-in-Chief put to sea at once with his whole fleet. When last seen the enemy was retiring to the eastward, and strong forces, including submarines, were promptly organised to intercept him in the North Sea. However, we could not ignore the possibility that having shaken off the pursuit the enemy might renew his advance to the westward and enter the Atlantic. We feared for our convoys, and the situation called for the use of all available forces. Sea and air patrols were established to watch all the exits from the North Sea, and a powerful force of cruisers extended this watch to the coast of Norway. In the Atlantic the battleship *Warspite* left her convoy to search the Denmark Strait and, finding nothing, continued round the north of Iceland to link up with the watchers in the North Sea. The *Hood*, the French battle cruiser *Dunkerque,* and two French cruisers were dispatched to Icelandic waters, and the *Repulse* and *Furious* sailed from Halifax for the same destination. By the twenty-fifth fourteen British cruisers were combing the North Sea with destroyers and submarines co-operating and with the battle-fleet in support. But fortune was adverse, nothing was found, nor was there any indication of an enemy move to the west. Despite very severe weather, the arduous search was maintained for seven days.

On the fifth day, while we were waiting anxiously in the Admiralty and still cherishing the hope that this splendid prize would not be denied us, a German U-boat was heard by our D.F. stations making a report. We judged from this that an attack had been made on one of our warships in the North Sea. Soon the German broadcast claimed that Captain Prien, the sinker of the *Royal Oak,* had sunk an eight-inch cruiser to the eastward of the Shetlands. Admiral Pound and I were together when this news came in. British public opinion is extremely sensitive when British ships are sunk, and the loss of the *Rawalpindi,* with its gallant fight and heavy toll in life, would tell heavily against the Admiralty if it remained unavenged. "Why," it would be demanded, "was so weak a ship exposed without effective support? Could the German cruisers range at will even the blockade zone in which our main forces were employed? Were the raiders to escape unscathed?"

We made a signal at once to clear up the mystery. When we met again an hour later without any reply, we passed through a very bad moment. I recall it because it marked the strong comradeship that had grown up between us and with Admiral Tom Phillips, who was also there. "I take full responsibility," I said, as was my duty. "No, it is mine," said Pound. We wrung each other's hands in lively distress. Hardened as we both were in war, it is not possible to sustain such blows without the most bitter pangs.

But it proved to be nobody's fault. Eight hours later, it appeared that the *Norfolk* was the ship involved and that she was undamaged. She had not encountered any U-boats, but said that an air bomb had fallen close astern. However, Captain Prien was no braggart.[3] What the *Norfolk* thought to be an air bomb from a clouded sky was in fact a German torpedo which had narrowly missed its target and exploded in the ship's wake. Peering through the periscope, Prien had seen the great upheaval of water, blotting out the ship from his gaze. He dived to avoid an expected salvo. When, after half an hour, he rose for another peep, the visibility was poor and no cruiser was to be seen. Hence his report. Our relief after the pain we had suffered took some of the sting out of the news that the *Scharnhorst* and the *Gneisenau* had safely re-entered the Baltic. It is now known that the *Scharnhorst* and *Gneisenau* passed through our cruiser line, patrolling near the Norwegian coast, on the morning of November 26. The weather was thick and neither side saw the other. Modern radar would have ensured contact, but then it was not available. Public impressions were unfavourable to the Admiralty. We could not bring home to the outside world the vastness of the seas or the intense exertions which the Navy was making in so many areas. After more than two months of war and several serious losses, we had nothing to show on the other side. Nor could we yet answer the question, "What is the Navy doing?"

[3] See Appendix I, Book II.

7

The Magnetic Mine

November and December, 1939

Conference with Admiral Darlan — The Anglo-French Naval Position — M. Campinchi — The Northern Barrage — The Magnetic Mine — A Devoted Deed — Technical Aspects — Mine-Sweeping Methods (Appendix) — "Degaussing" (Appendix) — The Magnetic Mining Attack Mastered and under Control — Retaliation — Fluvial Mines in the Rhine — "Operation Royal Marine."

IN THE FIRST DAYS OF NOVEMBER, I paid a visit to France for a conference on our joint operations with the French naval authorities. Admiral Pound and I drove out about forty miles from Paris to the French Marine Headquarters, which were established in the park around the ancient château of the Duc de Noailles. Before we went into the conference, Admiral Darlan explained to me how Admiralty matters were managed in France. The Minister of Marine, M. Campinchi, was not allowed by him to be present when operational matters were under discussion. These fell in the purely professional sphere. I said that the First Sea Lord and I were one. Darlan said he recognised this, but in France it was different. "However," he said, "Monsieur le Ministre will arrive for luncheon." We then ranged over naval business for two hours with a great measure of agreement. At luncheon M. Campinchi turned up. He knew his place, and now presided affably over the meal. My son-in-law, Duncan Sandys, who was acting as my Aide, sat next to Darlan. The Admiral spent most of luncheon explaining to

him the limits to which the civilian Minister was restricted by
the French system. Before leaving, I called on the Duke in his
château. He and his family seemed plunged in melancholy, but
showed us their very beautiful house and its art treasures.

In the evening I gave a small dinner in a private room at the
Ritz to M. Campinchi. I formed a high opinion of this man.
His patriotism, his ardour, his acute intelligence, and above
all his resolve to conquer or die, bit home. I could not help
mentally comparing him to the Admiral, who, jealous of his
position, was fighting on quite a different front from ours.
Pound's valuation was the same as mine, although we both
realised all that Darlan had done for the French Navy. One
must not underrate Darlan, nor fail to understand the impulse
that moved him. He deemed himself the French Navy, and
the French Navy acclaimed him their chief and their reviver.
For seven years he had held his office while shifting Ministerial
phantoms had filled the office of Minister of Marine. It was his
obsession to keep the politicians in their place as chatterboxes
in the Chamber. Pound and I got on very well with Campinchi. This tough Corsican never flinched or failed. When
he died, broken and under the scowl of Vichy, towards the
beginning of 1941, his last words were of hope in me. I shall
always deem them an honour.

Here is the statement summing up our naval position at this
moment, which I made at the conference:

Statement to the French Admiralty by the First Lord

The naval war alone has opened at full intensity. The U-boat
attack on commerce, so nearly fatal in 1917, has been controlled
by the Anglo-French anti-submarine craft. We must expect a large
increase in German U-boats (and possibly some will be lent to
them by Russia). This need cause no anxiety, provided that all our
counter-measures are taken at full speed and on the largest scale.
The Admiralty representatives will explain in detail our large
programmes. But the full development of these will not come till
late in 1940. In the meanwhile, it is indispensable that every anti-
submarine craft available should be finished and put in commission.

2. There is no doubt that our Asdic method is effective, and far

better than anything known in the last war. It enables two torpedo-boats to do what required ten in 1917/18. But this applies only to hunting. For convoys, numbers are still essential. One is only safe when escorted by vessels fitted with Asdics. This applies to warships equally with merchant convoys. The defeat of the U-boat will be achieved when it is certain that any attack on French or British vessels will be followed by an Asdic counter-attack.

The British Admiralty is prepared to supply and fit every French anti-submarine craft with Asdics. The cost is small, and accounts can be regulated later on. But any French vessels sent to England for fitting will be immediately taken in hand; and also we will arrange for the imparting of the method and for training to be given in each case. It would be most convenient to do this at Portland, the home of the Asdics, where all facilities are available. We contemplate making provision for equipping fifty French vessels if desired.

3. But we earnestly hope that the French Marine will multiply their Asdic vessels, and will complete with the utmost rapidity all that can enter into action during 1940. After this is arranged for, it will be possible six months hence to consider 1941. For the present let us aim at 1940, and especially at the spring and summer. The six large destroyers laid down in 1936 and 1937 will be urgently needed for ocean convoys before the climax of the U-boat warfare is reached in 1940. There are also fourteen small destroyers laid down in 1939, or now projected, which will play an invaluable part without making any great drain on labour and materials. Total — twenty vessels — which could be completed during 1940, and which, fitted with Asdics by us, would be weapons of high consequence in the destruction of the U-boat offensive of 1940. We also venture to mention as most desirable vessels the six sloop minesweepers laid down in 1936, and twelve laid down in 1937, and also the sixteen submarine-chasers of the programme of 1938. For all these we offer Asdics and every facility. We will fit them as they are ready, as if it were a field operation. We cannot, however, consider these smaller vessels in the same order of importance as the large and small destroyers mentioned above.

4. It must not be forgotten that defeat of the U-boats carries with it the sovereignty of all the oceans of the world for the Allied Fleets, and the possibility of powerful neutrals coming to our aid, as well as the drawing of resources from every part of the French

and British Empires, and the maintenance of trade, gathering with it the necessary wealth to continue the war.

5. At the British Admiralty we have drawn a sharp line between large vessels which can be finished in 1940 and those of later periods. In particular, we are straining every nerve to finish the *King George V* and the *Prince of Wales* battleships within that year, if possible by the autumn. This is necessary because the arrival of the *Bismarck* on the oceans before these two ships were completed would be disastrous in the highest degree, as it can neither be caught nor killed, and would therefore range freely throughout the oceans, rupturing all communications. But France has also a vessel of the highest importance in the *Richelieu,* which might be ready in the autumn of 1940 or even earlier, and will certainly be needed if the two new Italian ships should be finished by the dates in 1940 at which they profess to aim. Not to have these three capital ships in action before the end of 1940 would be an error in naval strategy of the gravest character, and might entail not only naval but diplomatic consequences extremely disagreeable. It is hoped, therefore, that every effort will be made to complete the *Richelieu* at the earliest possible date.

With regard to later capital ships of the British and French Navies, it would be well to discuss these in April or May next year, when we shall see much more clearly the course and character of the war.

6. The British Admiralty now express their gratitude to their French colleagues and comrades for the very remarkable assistance which they have given to the common cause since the beginning of this war. This assistance has gone far beyond any promises or engagements made before the war. In escorting home the convoys from Sierra Leone, the French cruisers and destroyers have played a part which could not otherwise have been supplied, and which, if not forthcoming, would simply have meant more slaughter of Allied merchantmen. The cruisers and *contre-torpilleurs* which, with the *Dunkerque,* have covered the arrival of convoys in the western approaches, were at the time the only means by which the German raiders could be warded off. The maintenance of the French submarines in the neighbourhood of Trinidad has been a most acceptable service. Above all, the two destroyers which constantly escort the homeward- and outward-bound convoys between Gibraltar and Brest are an important relief to our resources, which, though large and ever-growing, are at full strain.

Finally, we are extremely obliged by the facilities given to the *Argus* aircraft carrier to carry out her training of British naval aircraft pilots under the favourable conditions of Mediterranean weather.

7. Surveying the more general aspects of the war: the fact that the enemy have no line of battle has enabled us to disperse our naval forces widely over the oceans, and we have seven or eight British hunting units joined by two French hunting units, each capable of catching and killing a *Deutschland*. We are now cruising in the North Atlantic, the South Atlantic, and the Indian Oceans. The result has been that the raiders have not chosen to inflict the losses upon the convoys which before the war it had been supposed they could certainly do. The fact that certainly one, and perhaps two, *Deutschlands* have been upon the main Atlantic trade routes for several weeks, without achieving anything, makes us feel easier about this form of attack, which had formerly been rated extremely dangerous. We cannot possibly exclude its renewal in a more energetic form. The British Admiralty think it is not at all objectionable to keep large vessels in suitable units ranging widely over the oceans where they are safe from air attack, and make effective and apparent the control of the broad waters for the Allies.

8. We shall shortly be engaged in bringing the leading elements of the Canadian and Australian armies to France, and for this purpose a widespread disposition of all our hunting groups is convenient. It will also be necessary to give battleship escorts to many of the largest convoys crossing the Atlantic Ocean. We intend to maintain continually the northern blockade from Greenland to Scotland, in spite of the severities of the winter. Upon this blockade, twenty-five armed merchant cruisers will be employed in reliefs, supported by four eight-inch-gun 10,000-ton cruisers, and behind these we always maintain the main fighting forces of the British Navy, to wit, the latest battleships, and either the *Hood* or another great vessel, the whole sufficient to engage or pursue the *Scharnhorst* and the *Gneisenau* should they attempt to break out. We do not think it likely in view of the situation in the Baltic that these two vessels will be so employed. Nevertheless, we maintain continually the forces necessary to cope with them.

It is hoped that by a continuance of this strategy by the two Allied Navies, no temptation will be offered to Italy to enter the war against us, and that the German power of resistance will certainly be brought to an end.

The French Admiralty in their reply explained that they were in fact proceeding with the completion of the vessels specified, and that they gladly accepted our Asdic offer. Not only would the *Richelieu* be finished in the summer of 1940, but also in the autumn the *Jean Bart*.

*   *   *   *   *

In mid-November, Admiral Pound presented me with proposals for re-creating the minefield barrage between Scotland and Norway which had been established by the British and American Admiralties in 1917/18. I did not like this kind of warfare, which is essentially defensive, and seeks to substitute material on a vast scale for dominating action. However, I was gradually worn down and reconciled. I submitted the project to the War Cabinet on November 19.

The Northern Barrage
Memorandum by the First Lord of the Admiralty

After much consideration I commend this project to my colleagues. There is no doubt that, as it is completed, it will impose a very great deterrent upon the exits and returns of U-boats and surface raiders. It appears to be a prudent provision against an intensification of the U-boat warfare, and an insurance against the danger of Russia joining our enemy. By this we coop the lot in, and have complete control of all approaches alike to the Baltic and the North Sea. The essence of this offensive minefield is that the enemy will be prevented by the constant vigilance of superior naval force from sweeping channels through it. When it is in existence we shall feel much freer in the outer seas than at present. Its gradual but remorseless growth, which will be known to the enemy, will exercise a depressive effect upon his morale. The cost is deplorably heavy, but a large provision has already been made by the Treasury, and the northern barrage is far the best method of employing this means of war [i.e., mining].

This represented the highest professional advice, and of course is just the kind of thing that passes easily through a grave, wise Cabinet. Events swept it away; but not until a great

deal of money had been spent. The barrage mines came in handy
later on for other tasks.

*   *   *   *   *

Presently a new and formidable danger threatened our life.
During September and October, nearly a dozen merchant ships
were sunk at the entrance of our harbours, although these had
been properly swept for mines. The Admiralty at once suspected that a magnetic mine had been used. This was no
novelty to us; we had even begun to use it on a small scale at
the end of the previous war. In 1936, an Admiralty Committee
had studied counter-measures against magnetic-firing devices,
but their work had dealt chiefly with countering magnetic torpedoes or buoyant mines, and the terrible damage that could
be done by large ground-mines laid in considerable depth by
ships or aircraft had not been fully realised. Without a specimen of the mine, it was impossible to devise the remedy. Losses
by mines, largely Allied and neutral, in September and October
had amounted to fifty-six thousand tons, and in November
Hitler was encouraged to hint darkly at his new "secret
weapon" to which there was no counter. One night when I was
at Chartwell, Admiral Pound came down to see me in serious
anxiety. Six ships had been sunk in the approaches to the
Thames. Every day hundreds of ships went in and out of British harbours, and our survival depended on their movement.
Hitler's experts may well have told him that this form of attack
would compass our ruin. Luckily he began on a small scale,
and with limited stocks and manufacturing capacity.

Fortune also favoured us more directly. On November 22
between 9 and 10 P.M., a German aircraft was observed to drop
a large object attached to a parachute into the sea near Shoeburyness. The coast here is girdled with great areas of mud
which uncover with the tide, and it was immediately obvious
that whatever the object was it could be examined and possibly
recovered at low water. Here was our golden opportunity. Before midnight that same night two highly skilled officers, Lieu-
tenant-Commanders Ouvry and Lewis from H.M.S. *Vernon*,

the naval establishment responsible for developing underwater weapons, were called to the Admiralty, where the First Sea Lord and I interviewed them and heard their plans. By 1.30 in the morning, they were on their way by car to Southend to undertake the hazardous task of recovery. Before daylight on the twenty-third, in pitch darkness, aided only by a signal lamp, they found the mine some five hundred yards below high-water mark, but as the tide was then rising, they could only inspect it and make their preparations for attacking it after the next high water.

The critical operation began early in the afternoon, by which time it had been discovered that a second mine was also on the mud near the first. Ouvry with Chief Petty Officer Baldwin tackled the first, whilst their colleagues, Lewis and Able Seaman Vearncombe, waited at a safe distance in case of accidents. After each prearranged operation, Ouvry would signal to Lewis, so that the knowledge gained would be available when the second mine came to be dismantled. Eventually the combined efforts of all four men were required on the first, and their skill and devotion were amply rewarded. That evening Ouvry and his party came to the Admiralty to report that the mine had been recovered intact and was on its way to Portsmouth for detailed examination. I received them with enthusiasm. I gathered together eighty or a hundred officers and officials in our largest room, and made Ouvry tell his tale to a thrilled audience, deeply conscious of all that was at stake. From this moment the whole position was transformed. Immediately, the knowledge derived from past research could be applied to devising practical measures for combating the particular characteristics of the mine.

The whole power and science of the Navy were now applied; and it was not long before trial and experiment began to yield practical results. Rear-Admiral Wake-Walker was appointed to co-ordinate all technical measures which the occasion demanded. We worked all ways at once, devising first active means of attacking the mine by new methods of mine-sweeping and fuse-provocation; and secondly, passive means of defence for all ships against possible mines in unswept, or ineffectually swept, channels. For this second purpose a most effective system of demagnetising ships by girdling them with an electric cable was developed. This was called "degaussing," and was at once applied to ships of all types. Merchant ships were thus equipped in all our major ports without appreciably delaying their turn-round; in the Fleet progress was simplified by the presence of the highly trained technical staffs of the Royal Navy. The reader who does not shrink from technical details will find an account of these developments in Appendix H, Book II.

* * * * *

Serious casualties continued; the new cruiser *Belfast* was mined in the Firth of Forth on November 21, and on December 4, the battleship *Nelson* was mined whilst entering Loch Ewe. Both ships were, however, able to reach a dockyard port. Two destroyers were lost, and two others, besides the minelayer *Adventure,* were damaged on the east coast during this period. It is remarkable that German Intelligence failed to pierce our security measures covering the injury to the *Nelson* until the ship had been repaired and was again in service. Yet from the first many thousands in England had to know the true facts.

Experience soon gave us new and simpler methods of degaussing. The moral effect of its success was tremendous, but it was on the faithful, courageous, and persistent work of the minesweepers and the patient skill of the technical experts, who devised and provided the equipment they used, that we relied chiefly to defeat the enemy's efforts. From this time onward, despite many anxious periods, the mine menace was always under control and eventually the danger began to recede. By Christmas Day I was able to write to the Prime Minister:

December 25, 1939.

Everything is very quiet here, but I thought you would like to know that we have had a marked success against the magnetic mines. The first two devices for setting them off which we have got into action have both proved effective. Two mines were blown

up by the magnetic sweep and two by lighters carrying heavy coils.
This occurred at Port A [Loch Ewe], where our interesting invalid
[the *Nelson*] is still waiting for a clear passage to be swept for her
to the convalescent home at Portsmouth. It also looks as if the
demagnetisation of warships and merchant ships can be accomplished by a simple, speedy, and inexpensive process. All our best
devices are now approaching [completion]. The aeroplanes and
the magnetic ship — the *Borde* — will be at work within the next
ten days, and we all feel pretty sure that the danger from magnetic
mines will soon be out of the way.

We are also studying the possible varying of this form of attack,
viz., acoustic mines and supersonic mines. Thirty ardent experts
are pursuing these possibilities, but I am not yet able to say that
they have found a cure. . . .

It is well to ponder this side of the naval war. In the event a
significant proportion of our whole war effort had to be devoted to combating the mine. A vast output of material and
money was diverted from other tasks, and many thousand men
risked their lives night and day in the minesweepers alone. The
peak figure was reached in June, 1944, when nearly sixty thousand were thus employed. Nothing daunted the ardour of the
merchant navy; and their spirits rose with the deadly complications of the mining attack and our effective measures for
countering it. Their toils and tireless courage were our salvation. The sea traffic on which we depended for our existence
proceeded without interruption.

*   *   *   *   *

The first impact of the magnetic mine had stirred me deeply,
and apart from all the protective measures which had been
enforced upon us, I sought for a means of retaliation. My visit
to the Rhine on the eve of the war had focused my mental
vision upon this supreme and vital German artery. Even in
September, I had raised discussion at the Admiralty about the
launching or dropping of fluvial mines in the Rhine. Considering that this river was used by the traffic of many neutral
nations, we could not, of course, take action unless and until

the Germans had taken the initiative in this form of indiscriminate warfare against us. Now that they had done so, it seemed to me that the proper retort for indiscriminate sinkings by mines at the mouths of the British harbours was a similar and if possible more effective mining attack upon the Rhine.

Accordingly, on November 17, I issued several minutes of which the following gives the most precise account of the plan:

Controller [and others].

1. As a measure of retaliation it may become necessary to feed large numbers of floating mines into the Rhine. This can easily be done at any point between Strasbourg and the Lauter, where the left bank is French territory. General Gamelin was much interested in this idea, and asked me to work it out for him.

2. Let us clearly see the object in view. The Rhine is traversed by an enormous number of very large barges, and is the main artery of German trade and life. These barges, built only for river work, have not got double keels or any large subdivision by bulkheads. It is easy to check these details. In addition there are at least twelve bridges of boats recently thrown across the Rhine upon which the German armies concentrated in the Saarbrueck-Luxemburg area depend.

3. The type of mine required is, therefore, a small one, perhaps no bigger than a football. The current of the river is at most about seven miles an hour, and three or four at ordinary times, but it is quite easy to verify this. There must, therefore, be a clockwork apparatus in the mine which makes it dangerous only after it has gone a certain distance, so as to be clear of French territory and also so as to spread the terror farther down the Rhine to its confluence with the Moselle and beyond. The mine should automatically sink, or preferably explode, by this apparatus before reaching Dutch territory. After the mine has proceeded the required distance, which can be varied, it should explode on a light contact. It would be a convenience if, in addition to the above, the mine could go off if stranded after a certain amount of time, as it might easily spread alarm on either of the German banks.

4. It would be necessary in addition that the mine should float a convenient distance beneath the surface so as to be invisible in the turgid waters. A hydrostatic valve actuated by a small cylinder of compressed air should be devised. I have not made the calcula

tions, but I should suppose forty-eight hours would be the maximum for which it would have to work. An alternative would be to throw very large numbers of camouflage globes — tin shells — into the river, which would spread confusion and exhaust remedial activities.

5. What can they do against this? Obviously nets would be put across; but wreckage passing down the river would break these nets, and except at the frontier, they would be a great inconvenience to the traffic. Anyhow, when our mine fetched up against them, it would explode, breaking a large hole in the nets, and after a dozen or more of these explosions the channel would become free again, and other mines would jog along. Specially large mines might be used to break the nets. I cannot think of any other method of defence, but perhaps some may occur to the officers entrusted with this study.

6. Finally, as very large numbers of these mines would be used and the process kept up night after night for months on end, so as to deny the use of the waterway, it is necessary to bear in mind the simplification required for mass production.

The War Cabinet liked this plan. It seemed to them only right and proper that when the Germans were using the magnetic mine to waylay and destroy all traffic, Allied or neutral, entering British ports, we should strike back by paralysing, as we might well do, the whole of their vast traffic on the Rhine. The necessary permissions and priorities were obtained, and work started at full speed. In conjunction with the Air Ministry we developed a plan for mining the Ruhr section of the Rhine by discharge from airplanes. I entrusted all this work to Rear-Admiral FitzGerald, serving under the Fifth Sea Lord. This brilliant officer, who perished later in command of an Atlantic convoy, made an immense personal contribution. The technical problems were solved. A good supply of mines was assured, and several hundred ardent British sailors and marines were organised to handle them when the time should come. All this was in November, and we could not be ready before March. It is always agreeable in peace or war to have something positive coming along on your side.

8

The Action off the River Plate

ALTHOUGH it was the U-boat menace from which we suffered most and ran the greatest risks, the attack on our
ocean commerce by surface raiders would have been even more
formidable could it have been sustained. The three German
pocket battleships permitted by the Treaty of Versailles had
been designed with profound thought as commerce-destroyers.
Their six eleven-inch guns, their twenty-six-knot speed, and
the armour they carried had been compressed with masterly
skill into the limits of a ten-thousand-ton displacement. No

single British cruiser could match them. The German eight-inch-gun cruisers were more modern than ours, and if employed as commerce-raiders, would also be a formidable threat. Besides this, the enemy might use disguised heavily armed merchantmen. We had vivid memories of the depredations of the *Emden* and *Koenigsberg* in 1914, and of the thirty or more warships and armed merchantmen they had forced us to combine for their destruction.

There were rumours and reports before the outbreak of the new war that one or more pocket battleships had already sailed from Germany. The Home Fleet searched but found nothing. We now know that both the *Deutschland* and the *Admiral Graf Spee* sailed from Germany between August 21 and 24, and were already through the danger zone and loose in the oceans before our blockade and northern patrols were organised. On September 3, the *Deutschland*, having passed through the Denmark Straits, was lurking near Greenland. The *Graf Spee* had crossed the North Atlantic trade route unseen and was already far south of the Azores. Each was accompanied by an auxiliary vessel to replenish fuel and stores. Both at first remained inactive and lost in the ocean spaces. Unless they struck, they won no prizes. Until they struck, they were in no danger.

The orders of the German Admiralty issued on August 4 were well conceived:

Task in the Event of War

Disruption and destruction of enemy merchant shipping by all possible means. . . . Enemy naval forces, even if inferior, are only to be engaged if it should further the principal task. . . .

Frequent changes of position in the operational areas will create uncertainty and will restrict enemy merchant shipping, even without tangible results. A temporary departure into distant areas will also add to the uncertainty of the enemy.

If the enemy should protect his shipping with superior forces so that direct successes cannot be obtained, then the mere fact that his shipping is so restricted means that we have greatly impaired his supply situation. Valuable results will also be obtained if the pocket battleships continue to remain in the convoy area.

With all this wisdom the British Admiralty would have been in rueful agreement.

*   *   *   *   *

On September 30, the British liner *Clement,* of five thousand tons, sailing independently, was sunk by the *Graf Spee* off Pernambuco. The news electrified the Admiralty. It was the signal for which we had been waiting. A number of hunting groups were immediately formed, comprising all our available aircraft carriers, supported by battleships, battle cruisers, and cruisers. Each group of two or more ships was judged to be capable of catching and destroying a pocket battleship.

In all, during the ensuing months the search for two raiders entailed the formation of nine hunting groups, comprising twenty-three powerful ships. We were also compelled to provide three battleships and two cruisers as additional escorts with the important North Atlantic convoys. These requirements represented a very severe drain on the resources of the Home and Mediterranean Fleets, from which it was necessary to withdraw twelve ships of the most powerful types, including three aircraft carriers. Working from widely dispersed bases in the Atlantic and Indian Oceans, the hunting groups could cover the main focal areas traversed by our shipping. To attack our trade the enemy must place himself within reach of at least one of them. To give an idea of the scale of these operations, I set out the full list of the hunting groups at their highest point on page 514.

*   *   *   *   *

At this time it was the prime objective of the American Governments to keep the war as far from their shores as possible. On October 3, delegates of twenty-one American Republics, assembled at Panama, decided to declare an American security zone, proposing to fix a belt of from three hundred to six hundred miles from their coasts within which no warlike act should be committed. We were anxious to help in keeping the war out of American waters — to some extent, indeed, this was to our advantage. I therefore hastened to inform President

Organisation of Hunting Groups — October 31, 1939

Force	Composition			Area
	Battleships and Battle Cruisers	Cruisers	Aircraft Carriers	
F		*Berwick*		North America and West Indies
		York		
G		*Cumberland*		East coast of South America
		Exeter		
		Ajax		
		Achilles		
H		*Sussex*		Cape of Good Hope
		Shropshire		
I		*Cornwall*	*Eagle*	Ceylon
		Dorsetshire		
J	*Malaya*		*Glorious*	Gulf of Aden
K	*Renown*		*Ark Royal*	Pernambuco-Freetown
L	*Repulse*		*Furious*	Atlantic convoys
X		Two French 8-inch cruisers	*Hermes*	Pernambuco-Dakar
Y	*Strasbourg*	*Neptune*		Pernambuco-Dakar
		One French 8-inch cruiser		

Additional escorts with North Atlantic convoys:

Battleships:	*Revenge*	*Resolution*	*Warspite*
Cruisers:	*Emerald*	*Enterprise*	

Roosevelt that, if America asked all belligerents to respect such
a zone, we should immediately declare our readiness to fall in
with their wishes — subject, of course, to our rights under
international law. We should not mind how far south the
security zone went, provided that it was effectively maintained.
We should have found great difficulty in accepting a security
zone which was to be policed only by some weak neutral; but
if the United States Navy was to take care of it, we should feel
no anxiety. The more United States warships there were
cruising along the South American coast, the better we should
be pleased; for the German raider which we were hunting
might then prefer to leave American waters for the South
African trade route, where we were ready to deal with him.

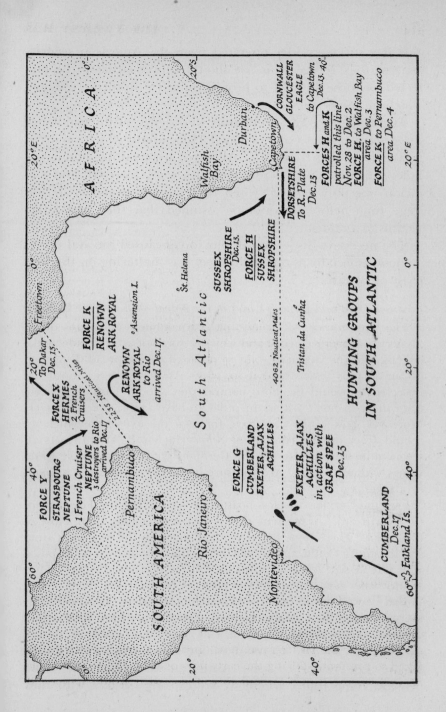

FORCE Y
STRASBOURG
NEPTUNE
1 French Cruiser
NEPTUNE
3 destroyers to Rio
arrived Dec.17

20°
To Dakar
Dec.15.

FORCE X
HERMES
2 French
Cruisers

FORCE K
RENOWN
ARK ROYAL

RENOWN
ARK ROYAL
to Rio
arrived Dec.17.

Freetown

St. Helena

°Ascension I.

2235 Nautical Miles

A F R I C A

20° E

Durban

Walfish
Bay

Capetown

CORNWALL
EAGLE
to Capetown
Dec.15. 40°

GLOUCESTER

FORCES H and K
patrolled this line
Nov.28 to Dec.2
FORCE H. to Walfish Bay
area. Dec.3
FORCE K. to Pernambuco
area. Dec.4

DORSETSHIRE
To R. Plate
Dec.13

FORCE H
SUSSEX
SHROPSHIRE

SUSSEX
SHROPSHIRE
Dec.15.

S o u t h   A t l a n t i c

4062 Nautical Miles

Tristan da Cunha

20°

Pernambuco

SOUTH AMERICA

Rio Janeiro

FORCE G
CUMBERLAND
EXETER, AJAX
ACHILLES

Montevideo

EXETER, AJAX
ACHILLES
in action with
GRAF SPEE
Dec.13

CUMBERLAND
Dec.17

60°° Falkland Is.

40°

HUNTING GROUPS
IN SOUTH ATLANTIC

But if a surface raider operated from the American security
zone or took refuge in it, we should expect either to be protected, or to be allowed to protect ourselves from the mischief
which he might do.

At this date we had no definite knowledge of the sinking of
three ships on the Cape of Good Hope route which occurred
between October 5 and 10. All three were sailing homeward
independently. No distress messages were received, and suspicion was only aroused when they became overdue. It was
some time before it could be assumed that they had fallen
victims to a raider.

The necessary dispersion of our forces caused me and others
anxiety, especially as our main Fleet was sheltering on the west
coast of Britain.

First Sea Lord and Deputy Chief of the Naval Staff.   21.X.39.

The appearance of *Scheer* off Pernambuco and subsequent
mystery of her movements, and why she does not attack trade, make
one ask, did the Germans want to provoke a widespread dispersion
of our surplus vessels, and if so, why? As the First Sea Lord has
observed, it would be more natural they should wish to concentrate them in home waters in order to have targets for air attack.
Moreover, how could they have foreseen the extent to which we
should react on the rumour of *Scheer* in South Atlantic? It all
seems quite purposeless, yet the Germans are not the people to do
things without reason. Are you sure it was *Scheer* and not a plant,
or a fake?

I see the German wireless boast they are driving the Fleet out of
the North Sea. At present this is less mendacious than most of
their stuff. There may, therefore, be danger on the east coast from
surface ships. Could not submarine flotillas of our own be disposed
well out at sea across a probable line of hostile advance? They
would want a parent destroyer perhaps to scout for them. They
should be well out of our line of watching trawlers. It may well be
there is something going to happen, now that we have retired to a
distance to gain time.

I should be the last to raise those "invasion scares," which I combated so constantly during the early days of 1914/15. Still, it might
be well for the Chiefs of Staff to consider what would happen if,

for instance, twenty thousand men were run across and landed, say, at Harwich, or at Webburn Hook, where there is deep water close inshore. These twenty thousand men might make the training of Mr. Hore-Belisha's masses very much more realistic than is at present expected. The long dark nights would help such designs. Have any arrangements been made by the War Office to provide against this contingency? Remember how we stand in the North Sea at the present time. I do not think it likely, but is it physically possible?

*   *   *   *   *

The *Deutschland,* which was to have harassed our lifeline across the Northwest Atlantic, interpreted her orders with comprehending caution. At no time during her two and a half months' cruise did she approach a convoy. Her determined efforts to avoid British forces prevented her from making more than two kills, one being a small Norwegian ship. A third ship, the United States *City of Flint,* carrying a cargo for Britain, was captured, but was eventually released by the Germans from a Norwegian port. Early in November, the *Deutschland* slunk back to Germany, passing again through Arctic waters. The mere presence of this powerful ship upon our main trade route had, however, imposed, as was intended, a serious strain upon our escorts and hunting groups in the North Atlantic. We should in fact have preferred her activity to the vague menace she embodied.

The *Graf Spee* was more daring and imaginative, and soon became the centre of attention in the South Atlantic. In this vast area powerful Allied forces came into play by the middle of October. One group consisted of the aircraft carrier *Ark Royal* and the battle cruiser *Renown,* working from Freetown, in conjunction with a French group of two heavy cruisers and the British aircraft carrier *Hermes,* based on Dakar. At the Cape of Good Hope were the two heavy cruisers *Sussex* and *Shropshire,* while on the east coast of South America, covering the vital traffic with the River Plate and Rio de Janeiro, ranged Commodore Harwood's group, comprising the *Cumberland, Exeter, Ajax,* and *Achilles.* The *Achilles* was a New Zealand ship manned mainly by New Zealanders.

The *Spee's* practice was to make a brief appearance at some point, claim a victim, and vanish again into the trackless ocean wastes. After a second appearance farther south on the Cape route, in which she sank only one ship, there was no further sign of her for nearly a month, during which our hunting groups were searching far and wide in all areas, and special vigilance was enjoined in the Indian Ocean. This was in fact her destination, and on November 15 she sank a small British tanker in the Mozambique Channel, between Madagascar and the mainland. Having thus registered her appearance as a feint in the Indian Ocean, in order to draw the hunt in that direction, her Captain — Langsdorff, a high-class person — promptly doubled back and, keeping well south of the Cape, re-entered the Atlantic. This move had not been unforeseen; but our plans to intercept him were foiled by the quickness of his withdrawal. It was by no means clear to the Admiralty whether in fact one raider was on the prowl or two, and exertions were made, both in the Indian and Atlantic Oceans. We also thought that the *Spee* was her sister ship, the *Scheer*. This disproportion between the strength of the enemy and the counter-measures forced upon us was vexatious. It recalled to me the anxious weeks before the actions at Coronel and later at the Falkland Islands in December, 1914, when we had to be prepared at seven or eight different points, in the Pacific and South Atlantic, for the arrival of Admiral von Spee with the earlier edition of the *Scharnhorst* and *Gneisenau*. A quarter of a century had passed, but the puzzle was the same. It was with a definite sense of relief that we learnt that the *Spee* had appeared once more on the Cape-Freetown route, sinking two more ships on December 2 and one on the seventh.

*   *   *   *   *

From the beginning of the war, Commodore Harwood's special care and duty had been to cover British shipping off the River Plate and Rio de Janeiro. He was convinced that sooner or later the *Spee* would come towards the Plate, where the richest prizes were offered to her. He had carefully thought out the tactics which he would adopt in an encounter. Together, his eight-inch cruisers *Cumberland* and *Exeter,* and his six-inch cruisers *Ajax* and *Achilles,* could not only catch but kill. However, the needs of fuel and refit made it unlikely that all four would be present "on the day." If they were not, the issue was disputable. On hearing that the *Doric Star* had been sunk on December 2, Harwood guessed right. Although she was over three thousand miles away, he assumed that the *Spee* would come towards the Plate. He estimated with luck and wisdom that she might arrive by the thirteenth. He ordered all his available forces to concentrate there by December 12. Alas, the *Cumberland* was refitting at the Falklands; but on the morning of the thirteenth, *Exeter, Ajax,* and *Achilles* were in company at the centre of the shipping routes off the mouth of the river. Sure enough, at 6.14 A.M., smoke was sighted to the east. The longed-for collision had come.

Harwood in the *Ajax,* disposing his forces so as to attack the pocket battleship from widely divergent quarters and thus con-

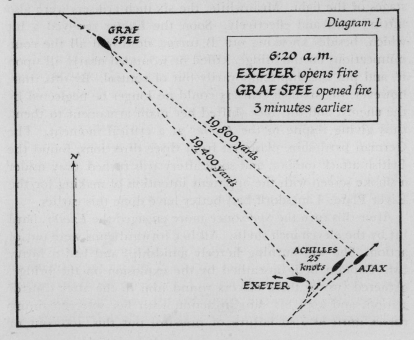

Diagram 1

6:20 a.m.
EXETER opens fire
GRAF SPEE opened fire
3 minutes earlier

fuse her fire, advanced at the utmost speed of his small squadron. Captain Langsdorff thought at the first glance that he had
only to deal with one light cruiser and two destroyers, and he
too went full speed ahead; but a few moments later, he recognised
the quality of his opponents, and knew that a mortal action im-
pended. The two forces were now closing at nearly fifty miles
an hour. Langsdorff had but a minute to make up his mind.
His right course would have been to turn away immediately so
as to keep his assailants as long as possible under the superior
range and weight of his eleven-inch guns, to which the British
could not at first have replied. He would thus have gained for
his undisturbed firing the difference between adding speeds
and subtracting them. He might well have crippled one of his
foes before any could fire at him. He decided, on the contrary,
to hold on his course and make for the *Exeter*. The action,
therefore, began almost simultaneously on both sides.

Commodore Harwood's tactics proved advantageous. The
eight-inch salvos from the *Exeter* struck the *Spee* from the earliest
stages of the fight. Meanwhile, the six-inch cruisers were also
hitting hard and effectively. Soon the *Exeter* received a hit
which, besides knocking out B turret, destroyed all the communications on the bridge, killed or wounded nearly all upon
it, and put the ship temporarily out of control. By this time,
however, the six-inch cruisers could no longer be neglected by
the enemy, and the *Spee* shifted her main armament to them,
thus giving respite to the *Exeter* at a critical moment. The
German battleship, plastered from three directions, found the
British attack too hot, and soon afterwards turned away under
a smoke screen with the apparent intention of making for the
River Plate. Langsdorff had better have done this earlier.

After this turn the *Spee* once more engaged the *Exeter,* hard
hit by the eleven-inch shells. All her forward guns were out of
action. She was burning fiercely amidships and had a heavy
list. Captain Bell, unscathed by the explosion on the bridge,
gathered two or three officers round him in the after control
station, and kept his ship in action with her sole remaining
turret until at 7.30 failure of pressure put this, too, out of

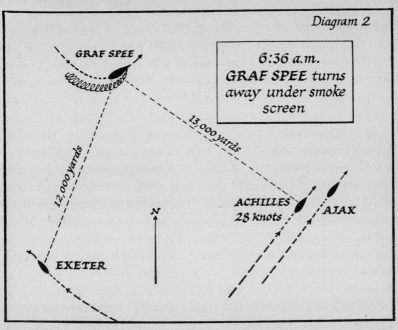

Diagram 2

6:36 a.m.
GRAF SPEE turns
away under smoke
screen

GRAF SPEE

13,000 yards

12,000 yards

ACHILLES
28 knots

AJAX

N

EXETER

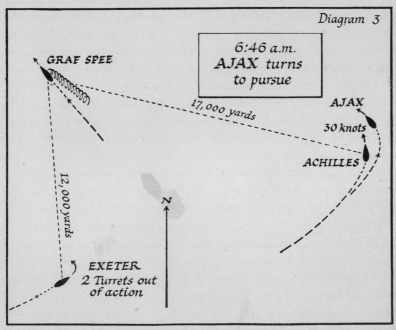

Diagram 3

6:46 a.m.
AJAX turns
to pursue

GRAF SPEE

17,000 yards

AJAX

30 knots

ACHILLES

12,000 yards

N

EXETER
2 Turrets out
of action

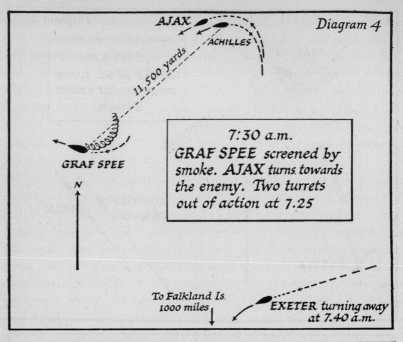

AJAX

ACHILLES

11,500 yards

GRAF SPEE

N

Diagram 4

7:30 a.m.
GRAF SPEE screened by
smoke. AJAX turns towards
the enemy. Two turrets
out of action at 7.25

To Falkland Is.
1000 miles ↓

EXETER turning away
at 7.40 a.m.

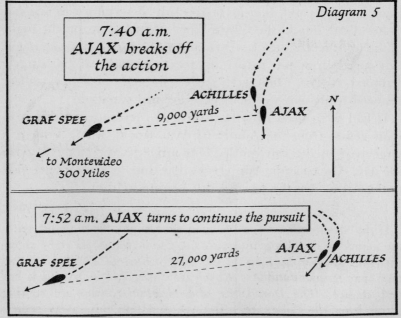

Diagram 5

7:40 a.m.
AJAX breaks off
the action

ACHILLES

GRAF SPEE

9,000 yards

AJAX

N

to Montevideo
300 Miles

7:52 a.m. AJAX turns to continue the pursuit

GRAF SPEE

27,000 yards

AJAX

ACHILLES

action. He could do no more. At 7.40 the *Exeter* turned away to effect repairs and took no further part in the fight.

The *Ajax* and *Achilles*, already in pursuit, continued the action in the most spirited manner. The *Spee* turned all her heavy guns upon them. By 7.25 the two after turrets in the *Ajax* had been knocked out, and the *Achilles* had also suffered damage. These two light cruisers were no match for the enemy in gun-power, and finding that his ammunition was running low, Harwood in the *Ajax* decided to break off the fight till dark, when he would have better chances of using his lighter armament effectively, and perhaps his torpedoes. He, therefore, turned away under cover of smoke, and the enemy did not follow. This fierce action had lasted an hour and twenty minutes. During all the rest of the day the *Spee* made for Montevideo, the British cruisers hanging grimly on her heels with only occasional interchanges of fire. Shortly after midnight, the *Spee* entered Montevideo and lay there repairing damage, taking in stores, landing wounded, transshipping personnel to a German merchant ship, and reporting to the Fuehrer. *Ajax* and *Achilles* lay outside, determined to dog her to her doom should she venture forth. Meanwhile, on the night of the fourteenth, the *Cumberland,* which had been steaming at full speed from the Falklands, took the place of the utterly crippled *Exeter.* The arrival of this eight-inch-gun cruiser restored to its narrow balance a doubtful situation.

It had been most exciting to follow the drama of this brilliant action from the Admiralty War Room, where I spent a large part of the thirteenth. Our anxieties did not end with the day. Mr. Chamberlain was at that time in France on a visit to the Army. On the seventeenth I wrote to him:

December 17, 1939.

If the *Spee* breaks out, as she may do tonight, we hope to renew the action of the thirteenth with the *Cumberland,* an *eight* eight-inch-gun ship, in the place of the six-gun *Exeter.* The *Spee* knows now that *Renown* and *Ark Royal* are oiling at Rio, so this is her best chance. The *Dorsetshire* and *Shropshire,* who are coming across from the Cape, are still three and four days away respectively. It is fortunate that the *Cumberland* was handy at the Falklands, as *Exeter* was heavily damaged. She was hit over a hundred times, one turret smashed, three guns knocked out, and sixty officers and men killed and twenty wounded. Indeed the *Exeter* fought one of the finest and most resolute actions against superior range and metal on record. Every conceivable precaution has been taken to prevent the *Spee* slipping out unobserved, and I have told Harwood (who is now an Admiral and a K.C.B.) that he is free to attack her anywhere outside the three-mile limit. We should prefer, however, that she should be interned, as this will be less creditable to the German Navy than being sunk in action. Moreover, a battle of this kind is full of hazard, and needless bloodshed must never be sought.

The whole of the Canadians came in safely this morning under the protection of the main fleet and [are] being welcomed by Anthony, Massey, and I trust a good part of the people of Greenock and Glasgow. We plan to give them a cordial reception. They are to go to Aldershot, where no doubt you will go and see them presently.

There have been ten air attacks today on individual ships along the east coast from Wick to Dover, and some of the merchant ships have been machine-gunned out of pure spite, some of our people being hit on their decks.

I am sure you must be having a most interesting time at the Front, and I expect you will find that change is the best kind of rest.

From the moment when we heard that action was joined, we instantly ordered powerful forces to concentrate off Montevideo, but our hunting groups were naturally widely dispersed and none was within two thousand miles of the scene. In the north, Force K, comprising the *Renown* and *Ark Royal*, was completing a sweep which had begun at Capetown ten days before and was now six hundred miles east of Pernambuco, and twenty-five hundred miles from Montevideo. Farther north still, the cruiser *Neptune* with three destroyers had just parted company with the French Force X and were coming south to join Force K. All these were ordered to Montevideo; they had first to fuel at Rio. However, we succeeded in creating the impression that they had already left Rio and were approaching Montevideo at thirty knots.

On the other side of the Atlantic, Force H was returning to the Cape for fuel after an extended sweep up the African coast. Only the *Dorsetshire* was immediately available at Capetown and was ordered at once to join Admiral Harwood, but she had over four thousand miles to travel. She was followed later by the *Shropshire*. In addition, to guard against the possible escape of the *Spee* to the eastward, Force I, comprising the *Cornwall, Gloucester,* and the aircraft carrier *Eagle* from the East Indies station, which at this time was at Durban, was placed at the disposal of the Commander-in-Chief, South Atlantic.

* * * * *

Meanwhile, Captain Langsdorff telegraphed on December 16 to the German Admiralty as follows:

Strategic position off Montevideo. Besides the cruisers and destroyers, *Ark Royal* and *Renown*. Close blockade at night; escape into open sea and break-through to home waters hopeless. . . . Request decision on whether the ship should be scuttled in spite of insufficient depth in the Estuary of the Plate, or whether internment is to be preferred.

At a conference presided over by the Fuehrer, at which Raeder and Jodl were present, the following answer was decided on:

Attempt by all means to extend the time in neutral waters. . . . Fight your way through to Buenos Aires if possible. No internment in Uruguay. Attempt effective destruction, if ship is scuttled.

As the German envoy in Montevideo reported later that further attempts to extend the time limit of seventy-two hours were fruitless, these orders were confirmed by the German Supreme Command.

Accordingly, during the afternoon of the seventeenth the *Spee* transferred more than seven hundred men, with baggage and provisions, to the German merchant ship in the harbour. Shortly afterwards Admiral Harwood learnt that she was weighing anchor. At 6.15 P.M., watched by immense crowds, she left harbour and steamed slowly seaward, awaited hungrily by the British cruisers. At 8.54 P.M., as the sun sank, the *Ajax's* aircraft reported: *"Graf Spee* has blown herself up." The *Renown* and *Ark Royal* were still a thousand miles away.

Langsdorff was broken-hearted by the loss of his ship. In spite of the full authority he had received from his Government, he wrote on December 19:

> I can now only prove by my death that the fighting services of the Third Reich are ready to die for the honour of the flag. I alone bear the responsibility for scuttling the pocket battleship *Admiral Graf Spee.* I am happy to pay with my life for any possible reflection on the honour of the flag. I shall face my fate with firm faith in the cause and the future of the nation and of my Fuehrer.

That night he shot himself.

Thus ended the first surface challenge to British trade on the oceans. No other raider appeared until the spring of 1940, when a new campaign opened, utilising disguised merchant ships. These could more easily avoid detection, but on the other hand could be mastered by lesser forces than those required to destroy a pocket battleship.

*   *   *   *   *

As soon as the news arrived of the end of the *Spee,* I was impatient to bring our widely scattered hunting groups home. The *Spee's* auxiliary, the *Altmark,* was, however, still afloat, and it was believed that she had on board the crews of the nine ships which had been sunk by the raider.

First Sea Lord.   17.XII.39.

Now that the South Atlantic is practically clear except for the *Altmark,* it seems of high importance to bring home the *Renown* and *Ark Royal* together with at least one of the eight-inch-gun cruisers. This will give us more easement in convoy work and enable refits and leave to be accomplished. I like your plan of the two small ships anchoring tomorrow in Montevideo inner harbour, but I do not think it would be right to send Force K so far south. Moreover, perhaps so many warships would not be allowed in at one time. It would be very convenient if, as you proposed, *Neptune* relieved *Ajax* as soon as the triumphal entry [into Montevideo harbour] is over; and it would be very good if all the returning forces could scrub and search the South Atlantic on their way home for the *Altmark*. I feel that we ought to bring home all that are not absolutely needed. The Northern Patrol will require constant support in two, or better still three, reliefs from the Clyde as long as we stay there. I agree with Captain Tennant that the German Admiralty will be most anxious to do something to get their name back.

Perhaps you will let me know what you think about these ideas.

I was also most anxious about the *Exeter,* and could not accept the proposals made to me to leave her unrepaired in the Falkland Islands till the end of the war.

First Sea Lord, Controller and others. 17.XII.39.

This preliminary report of damage to *Exeter* shows the tremendous fire to which she was exposed and the determination with which she was fought. It also reflects high credit on the Constructors' Department that she should have been able to stand up to such a prolonged and severe battering. This story will have to be told as soon as possible, omitting anything undesirable [i.e., what the enemy should not know].

What is proposed about repair? What can be done at the Falklands? I presume she will be patched up sufficiently to come home for long refit.

First Sea Lord, D.C.N.S., Controller. 23.XII.39.

We ought not readily to accept the non-repair during the war of *Exeter.* She should be strengthened and strutted internally as far as possible, and should transfer her ammunition, or the bulk of it, to some merchant ship or tender. Perhaps she might be filled up in part with barrels or empty oil drums, and come home with reduced crew under escort either to the Mediterranean or to one of our dockyards. If nothing can be done with her then, she should be stripped of all useful guns and appliances, which can be transferred to new construction.

The above indicates only my general view. Perhaps you will let me know how it can be implemented.

Controller and First Sea Lord.   29.XII.39.

I have not seen the answer to the telegram from the Rear
Admiral, South America, about it not being worth while to repair
Exeter, on which I minuted in the contrary sense. How does this
matter now stand? I gathered from you verbally that we were all
in agreement she should come home and be thoroughly repaired,
and that this need not take so long as the R.A. thought.

What is going to happen to *Exeter* now? How is she going to be
brought home, in what condition, and when? We cannot leave her
at the Falklands, where either she will be in danger or some
valuable ship will be tethered to look after her. I shall be glad to
know what is proposed.

My view prevailed. The Exeter reached this country safely.
I had the honour to pay my tribute to her brave officers and
men from her shattered deck in Plymouth Harbour. She was
preserved for over two years of distinguished service, until she
perished under Japanese guns in the forlorn battle of the
Straits of Sunda in 1942.

*   *   *   *   *

The effects of the action off the Plate gave intense joy to the
British nation and enhanced our prestige throughout the world.
The spectacle of the three smaller British ships unhesitatingly
attacking and putting to flight their far more heavily gunned
and armoured antagonist was everywhere admired. It was contrasted with the disastrous episode of the escape of the *Goeben*
in the Straits of Otranto in August, 1914. In justice to the
admiral of those days it must be remembered that all Commodore Harwood's ships were faster than the *Spee,* and all except
one of Admiral Troubridge's squadron in 1914 were slower
than the *Goeben.* Nevertheless, the impression was exhilarat-
ing, and lightened the dreary and oppressive winter through
which we were passing.

The Soviet Government were not pleased with us at this
time, and their comment on December 31, 1939, in the *Red
Fleet* is an example of their factual reporting:

Nobody would dare to say that the loss of a German battleship

is a brilliant victory for the British Fleet. This is rather a demonstration, unprecedented in history, of the impotence of the British.
Upon the morning of December 13, the battleship started an
artillery duel with the *Exeter*, and within a few minutes obliged
the cruiser to withdraw from the action. According to the latest
information the *Exeter* sank near the Argentine coast, en route for
the Falkland Islands.

* * * * *

On December 23, the American Republics made a formal
protest to Britain, France, and Germany about the action off
the River Plate, which they claimed to be a violation of the
American security zone. It also happened about this time that
two German merchant ships were intercepted by our cruisers
near the coast of the United States. One of these, the liner
Columbus of thirty-two thousand tons, was scuttled and
survivors were rescued by an American cruiser; the other
escaped into territorial waters in Florida. President Roosevelt
reluctantly complained about these vexations near the coasts of
the Western Hemisphere; and in my reply I took the opportunity of stressing the advantages which our action off the Plate
had brought to all the South American Republics. Their trade
had been hampered by the activities of the German raider and
their ports had been used for his supply ships and information
centres. By the laws of war the raider had been entitled to
capture all merchant ships trading with us in the South
Atlantic, or to sink them after providing for their crews; and
this had inflicted grave injury on American commercial interests, particularly in the Argentine. The South American
Republics should greet the action off the Plate as a deliverance
from all this annoyance. The whole of the South Atlantic was
now clear, and might perhaps remain clear, of warlike operations. This relief should be highly valued by the South American States, who might now in practice enjoy for a long period
the advantages of a security zone of three thousand, rather than
three hundred, miles.

I could not forbear to add that the Royal Navy was carrying
a very heavy burden in enforcing respect for international law

at sea. The presence of even a single raider in the North Atlantic called for the employment of half our battle-fleet to give sure protection to the world's commerce. The unlimited laying of magnetic mines by the enemy was adding to the strain upon our flotillas and small craft. If we should break under this strain, the South American Republics would soon have many worse worries than the sound of one day's distant seaward cannonade; and in quite a short time the United States would also face more direct cares. I therefore felt entitled to ask that full consideration should be given to the burden which we were carrying at this crucial period, and that the best construction should be placed on action which was indispensable if the war was to be ended within reasonable time and in the right way.

9

Scandinavia, Finland

The Norway Peninsula — Swedish Iron Ore — Neutrality and the Norwegian Corridor — An Error Corrected — Behind the German Veil — Admiral Raeder and Herr Rosenberg — Vidkun Quisling — Hitler's Decision, December 14, 1939 — Soviet Action Against the Baltic States — Stalin's Demands upon Finland — The Russians Declare War on Finland, November 28, 1939 — Gallant Finnish Resistance — The Soviet Failure and Rebuff — World-Wide Satisfaction — Aid to Finland and Norwegian and Swedish Neutrality — The Case for Mining the Leads — The Moral Issue.

THE THOUSAND-MILE-LONG PENINSULA stretching from the mouth of the Baltic to the Arctic Circle had an immense strategic significance. The Norwegian mountains run into the ocean in a continuous fringe of islands. Between these islands and the mainland there was a corridor in territorial waters through which Germany could communicate with the outer seas to the grievous injury of our blockade. German war industry was mainly based upon supplies of Swedish iron ore, which in the summer were drawn from the Swedish port of Lulea at the head of the Gulf of Bothnia, and in the winter, when this was frozen, from Narvik on the west coast of Norway. To respect the corridor would be to allow the whole of this traffic to proceed under the shield of neutrality in the face of our superior sea power. The Admiralty Staff were seriously perturbed at this important advantage being presented to Germany, and at the earliest opportunity I raised the issue in the Cabinet.

rons and flotillas. It was only natural and it was only right that His Majesty's Government should have been long reluctant to incur the reproach of even a technical violation of international law.

They certainly were long in reaching a decision.

At first the reception of my case was favourable. All my colleagues were deeply impressed with the evil; but strict respect for the neutrality of small states was a principle of conduct to which we all adhered.

First Lord to First Sea Lord and others. 19.IX.39.

I brought to the notice of the Cabinet this morning the importance of stopping the Norwegian transportation of Swedish iron ore from Narvik, which will begin as soon as the ice forms in the Gulf of Bothnia. I pointed out that we had laid a minefield across the three-mile limit in Norwegian territorial waters in 1918, with the approval and co-operation of the United States. I suggested that we should repeat this process very shortly. [This, as is explained above, was not an accurate statement, and I was soon apprised of the fact.] The Cabinet, including the Foreign Secretary, appeared strongly favourable to this action.

It is therefore necessary to take all steps to prepare it.

1. The negotiations with the Norwegians for the chartering of their tonnage must be got out of the way first.

2. The Board of Trade would have to make arrangements with Sweden to buy the ore in question, as it is far from our wish to quarrel with the Swedes.

3. The Foreign Office should be made acquainted with our proposals, and the whole story of Anglo-American action in 1918 must be carefully set forth, together with a reasoned case.

4. The operation itself should be studied by the Admiralty Staff concerned. The Economic Warfare Department should be informed as and when necessary.

Pray let me be continually informed of the progress of this plan, which is of the highest importance in crippling the enemy's war industry.

A further Cabinet decision will be necessary when all is in readiness.

On the twenty-ninth, at the invitation of my colleagues, and

after the whole subject had been minutely examined at the
Admiralty, I drafted a paper for the Cabinet upon this subject
and on the chartering of neutral tonnage which was linked
with it.

Norway and Sweden

Memorandum by the First Lord of the Admiralty

September 29, 1939.

Chartering Norwegian Tonnage.

The Norwegian Delegation is approaching, and in a few days
the President of the Board of Trade hopes to make a bargain with
them by which he charters all their spare tonnage, the bulk of
which consists of tankers.

The Admiralty consider the chartering of this tonnage most important, and Lord Chatfield has written strongly urging it upon
them.

German Supplies of Iron Ore from Narvik.

2. At the end of November the Gulf of Bothnia normally freezes,
so that Swedish iron ore can be sent to Germany only through
Oxelosund in the Baltic, or from Narvik at the north of Norway.
Oxelosund can export only about one-fifth of the weight of ore
Germany requires from Sweden. In winter normally the main
trade is from Narvik, whence ships can pass down the west coast
of Norway, and make the whole voyage to Germany without leaving
territorial waters until inside the Skagerrak.

It must be understood that an adequate supply of Swedish iron
ore is vital to Germany, and the interception or prevention of these
Narvik supplies during the winter months, i.e., from October to
the end of April, will greatly reduce her power of resistance. For
the first three weeks of the war no iron-ore ships left Narvik owing
to the reluctance of crews to sail and other causes outside our
control. Should this satisfactory state of affairs continue, no special
action would be demanded from the Admiralty. Furthermore,
negotiations are proceeding with the Swedish Government which
in themselves may effectively reduce the supplies of Scandinavian
ore to Germany.

Should, however, the supplies from Narvik to Germany start
moving again, more drastic action will be needed.

Relations with Sweden.

3. Our relations with Sweden require careful consideration. Germany acts upon Sweden by threats. Our sea power gives us also powerful weapons, which, if need be, we must use to ration Sweden. Nevertheless, it should be proposed, as part of the policy outlined in paragraph 2, to assist the Swedes so far as possible to dispose of their ore in exchange for our coal; and, should this not suffice, to indemnify them, partly at least, by other means. This is the next step.

Charter and Insurance of All Available Neutral Tonnage.

4. The above considerations lead to a wider proposal. Ought we not to secure the control, by charter or otherwise, of all the free neutral shipping we can obtain, as well as the Norwegian, and thus give the Allies power to regulate the greater part of the sea transport of the world and recharter it, profitably, to those who act as we wish?

And ought we not to extend neutral shipping not under our direct control the benefit of our convoy system?

The results so far achieved by the Royal Navy against the U-boat attack seem, in the opinion of the Admiralty, to justify the adoption of this latter course. This would mean that we should offer safe convoy to all vessels of all countries traversing our sea routes, provided they conform to our rules of contraband, and pay the necessary premiums in foreign devisen. They would, therefore, be able to contract themselves out of the war risk, and with the success of our anti-U-boat campaign we may well hope to make a profit to offset its heavy expense. Thus, not only vessels owned by us or controlled by us, but independent neutral ships, would all come to enjoy the British protection on the high seas, or be indemnified in case of accidents. It is not believed at the Admiralty that this is beyond our strength. Had some such scheme for the chartering and insurance of neutral shipping been in force from the early days of the last war, there is little doubt that it would have proved a highly profitable speculation. In this war it might well prove to be the foundation of a League of Free Maritime Nations to which it was profitable to belong.

5. It is therefore asked that the Cabinet, if they approve in principle of these four main objectives, should remit the question

to the various departments concerned in order that detailed plans
may be made for prompt action.

Before circulating this paper to the Cabinet and raising the
issue there, I called upon the Admiralty Staff for a thorough
recheck of the whole position.

First Lord to the Assistant Chief of the Naval Staff.   29.IX.39.

Please reconvene the meeting on iron ore we held on Thursday
tomorrow morning, while Cabinet is sitting, in order to consider
the draft print which I have made. It is no use my asking the
Cabinet to take the drastic action suggested against a neutral
country unless the results are in the first order of importance.

I am told that there are hardly any German or Swedish ships
trying to take ore south from Narvik. Also that the Germans have
been accumulating ore by sea at Oxelosund against the freezing-up,
and so will be able to bring good supplies down the Baltic via the
Kiel Canal to the Ruhr during the winter months. Are these statements true? It would be very unpleasant if I went into action on
mining the Norwegian territorial waters and was answered that it
would not do the trick.

2. At the same time, assuming that the west coast traffic of
Norway in ore is a really important factor worth making an
exertion to stop, at what point would you stop it?

Pray explore in detail the coast and let me know the point.
Clearly it should be north at any rate of Bergen, thus leaving
the southern part of the west Norwegian coast open for any traffic
that may come from Norway or out of the Baltic in the Norwegian
convoy across to us. All this has to be more explored before I can
present my case to the Cabinet. I shall not attempt to do so until
Monday or Tuesday.

When all was agreed and settled at the Admiralty, I brought
the matter a second time before the Cabinet. Again there was
general agreement upon the need; but I was unable to obtain
assent to action. The Foreign Office arguments about neutrality were weighty, and I could not prevail. I continued, as will
be seen, to press my point by every means and on all occasions.
It was not, however, until April, 1940, that the decision that
I asked for in September, 1939, was taken. By that time it was
too late.

*   *   *   *   *

Almost at this very moment (as we now know), German eyes were turned in the same direction. On October 3, Admiral Raeder, Chief of the Naval Staff, submitted a proposal to Hitler headed "Gaining of Bases in Norway." He asked, "That the Fuehrer be informed as soon as possible of the opinions of the Naval War Staff on the possibilities of extending the operational base to the North. It must be ascertained whether it is possible to gain bases in Norway under the combined pressure of Russia and Germany, with the aim of improving our strategic and operational position." He framed, therefore, a series of notes which he placed before Hitler on October 10.

In these notes [he wrote] I stressed the disadvantages which an occupation of Norway by the British would have for us: the control of the approaches to the Baltic, the outflanking of our naval operations and of our air attacks on Britain, the end of our pressure on Sweden. I also stressed the advantages for us of the occupation of the Norwegian coast: outlet to the North Atlantic, no possibility of a British mine barrier, as in the year 1917/18. . . . The Fuehrer saw at once the significance of the Norwegian problem; he asked me to leave the notes and stated that he wished to consider the question himself.

Rosenberg, the Foreign Affairs expert of the Nazi Party, and in charge of a special bureau to deal with propaganda activities in foreign countries, shared the Admiral's views. He dreamed of "converting Scandinavia to the idea of a Nordic community embracing the northern peoples under the natural leadership of Germany." Early in 1939, he thought he had discovered an instrument in the extreme Nationalist Party in Norway, which was led by a former Norwegian Minister of War named Vidkun Quisling. Contacts were established, and Quisling's activity was linked with the plans of the German Naval Staff through the Rosenberg organisation and the German Naval Attaché in Oslo.

Quisling and his assistant, Hagelin, came to Berlin on December 14, and were taken by Raeder to Hitler, to discuss a political stroke in Norway. Quisling arrived with a detailed plan. Hitler, careful of secrecy, affected reluctance to increase his commitments, and said he would prefer a neutral Scandinavia. Nevertheless, according to Raeder, it was on this very day that he gave the order to the Supreme Command to prepare for a Norwegian operation.

Of all this we, of course, knew nothing. The two Admiralties thought with precision along the same lines in correct strategy, and one had obtained decisions from its Government.

*   *   *   *   *

Meanwhile, the Scandinavian peninsula became the scene of an unexpected conflict which aroused strong feeling in Britain and France, and powerfully affected the discussions about Norway. As soon as Germany was involved in war with Great Britain and France, Soviet Russia in the spirit of her pact with Germany proceeded to block the lines of entry into the Soviet Union from the west. One passage led from East Prussia through the Baltic States; another led across the waters of the Gulf of Finland; the third route was through Finland itself and across the Karelian Isthmus to a point where the Finnish frontier was only twenty miles from the suburbs of Leningrad. The Soviet had not forgotten the dangers which Leningrad had faced in 1919. Even the White Russian Government of Kolchak had informed the Peace Conference in Paris that bases in the Baltic States and Finland were a necessary protection for the Russian capital. Stalin had used the same language to the British and French Missions in the summer of 1939; and we have seen in earlier chapters how the natural fears of these small states had been an obstacle to an Anglo-French Alliance with Russia, and had paved the way for the Molotov-Ribbentrop Agreement.

Stalin had wasted no time; on September 24, the Esthonian Foreign Minister had been called to Moscow, and four days later his Government signed a Pact of Mutual Assistance which gave the Russians the right to garrison key bases in Esthonia. By October 21, the Red Army and air force were installed. The same procedure was used simultaneously in Latvia, and Soviet garrisons also appeared in Lithuania. Thus, the southern road

to Leningrad and half the Gulf of Finland had been swiftly
barred against potential German ambitions by the armed
forces of the Soviet. There remained only the approach
through Finland.

Early in October, Mr. Paasikivi, one of the Finnish statesmen
who had signed the Peace of 1921 with the Soviet Union, went
to Moscow. The Soviet demands were sweeping; the Finnish
frontier on the Karelian Isthmus must be moved back a considerable distance so as to remove Leningrad from the range of
hostile artillery. The cession of certain Finnish islands in the
Gulf of Finland; the lease of the Rybathy Peninsula together
with Finland's only ice-free port in the Arctic Sea, Petsamo;
and above all, the leasing of the port of Hango at the entrance
of the Gulf of Finland as a Russian naval and air base, completed the Soviet requirements. The Finns were prepared to
make concessions on every point except the last. With the keys
of the Gulf in Russian hands the strategic and national security
of Finland seemed to them to vanish. The negotiations broke
down on November 13, and the Finnish Government began
to mobilise and strengthen their troops on the Karelian frontier. On November 28, Molotov denounced the Non-Aggression Pact between Finland and Russia; two days later, the Russians attacked at eight points along Finland's thousand-mile
frontier, and on the same morning the capital, Helsingfors, was
bombed by the Red air force.

The brunt of the Russian attack fell at first upon the frontier defences of the Finns in the Karelian Isthmus. These comprised a fortified zone about twenty miles in depth running
north and south through forest country deep in snow. This
was called the "Mannerheim Line," after the Finnish Commander-in-Chief and saviour of Finland from Bolshevik subjugation in 1917. The indignation excited in Britain, France, and
even more vehemently in the United States, at the unprovoked
attack by the enormous Soviet Power upon a small, spirited,
and highly civilised nation, was soon followed by astonishment
and relief. The early weeks of fighting brought no success to
the Soviet forces, which in the first instance were drawn almost

RUSSIAN ATTACK
ON FINLAND
December 1939

◀— — — December 1939

0   50   100   200 Miles

entirely from the Leningrad garrison. The Finnish Army, whose total fighting strength was only about two hundred thousand men, gave a good account of themselves. The Russian tanks were encountered with audacity and a new type of hand-grenade, soon nicknamed "The Molotov Cocktail."

It is probable that the Soviet Government had counted on a walk-over. Their early air raids on Helsingfors and elsewhere, though not on a heavy scale, were expected to strike terror. The troops they used at first, though numerically much stronger, were inferior in quality and ill-trained. The effect of the air raids and of the invasion of their land roused the Finns, who rallied to a man against the aggressor and fought with absolute determination and the utmost skill. It is true that the Russian division which carried out the attack on Petsamo had little difficulty in throwing back the seven hundred Finns in that area. But the attack on the "Waist" of Finland proved disastrous to the invaders. The country here is almost entirely pine forests, gently undulating and at the time covered with a foot of hard snow. The cold was intense. The Finns were well equipped with skis and warm clothing, of which the Russians had neither. Moreover, the Finns proved themselves aggressive individual fighters, highly trained in reconnaissance and forest warfare. The Russians relied in vain on numbers and heavier weapons. All along this front the Finnish frontier posts withdrew slowly down the roads, followed by the Russian columns. After these had penetrated about thirty miles, they were set upon by the Finns. Held in front at Finnish defence lines constructed in the forests, violently attacked in flank by day and night, their communications severed behind them, the columns were cut to pieces, or, if lucky, got back after heavy loss whence they came. By the end of December, the whole Russian plan for driving in across the "Waist" had broken down.

Meanwhile, the attacks against the Mannerheim Line in the Karelian Peninsula fared no better. North of Lake Ladoga a turning movement attempted by about two Soviet divisions met the same fate as the operations farther north. Against the Line itself a series of mass attacks by nearly twelve divisions was launched in early December and continued throughout the month. The Russian artillery bombardments were inadequate; their tanks were mostly light, and a succession of frontal attacks were repulsed with heavy losses and no gains. By the end of the year, failure all along the front convinced the Soviet Government that they had to deal with a very different enemy from what they had expected. They determined upon a major effort. Realising that in the forest warfare of the north they could not overcome by mere weight of numbers the superior tactics and training of the Finns, they decided to concentrate on piercing the Mannerheim Line by methods of siege warfare in which the power of massed heavy artillery and heavy tanks could be brought into full play. This required preparation on a large scale, and from the end of the year fighting died down all along the Finnish Front, leaving the Finns so far victorious over their mighty assailant. This surprising event was received with equal satisfaction in all countries, belligerent or neutral, throughout the world. It was a pretty bad advertisement for

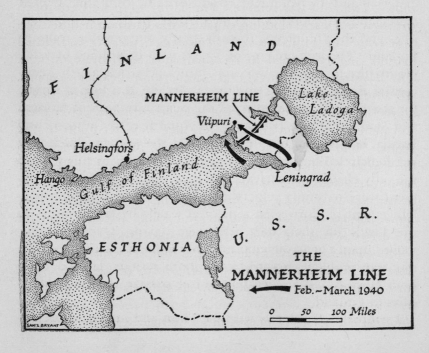

THE
MANNERHEIM LINE
Feb.~March 1940

0   50   100 Miles

the Soviet Army. In British circles many people congratulated
themselves that we had not gone out of our way to bring the
Soviets in on our side, and preened themselves on their foresight. The conclusion was drawn too hastily that the Russian
Army had been ruined by the purge, and that the inherent rottenness and degradation of their system of government and
society was now proved. It was not only in England that this
view was taken. There is no doubt that Hitler and all his generals meditated profoundly upon the Finnish exposure, and
that it played a potent part in influencing the Fuehrer's
thought.

All the resentment felt against the Soviet Government for
the Ribbentrop-Molotov Pact was fanned into flame by this
latest exhibition of brutal bullying and aggression. With this
was also mingled scorn for the inefficiency displayed by the
Soviet troops and enthusiasm for the gallant Finns. In spite
of the Great War which had been declared, there was a keen
desire to help the Finns by aircraft and other precious war
material and by volunteers from Britain, from the United
States, and still more from France. Alike for the munition supplies and the volunteers, there was only one possible route to
Finland. The iron-ore port of Narvik with its railroad over the
mountains to the Swedish iron mines acquired a new sentimental if not strategic significance. Its use as a line of supply
for the Finnish armies affected the neutrality both of Norway
and Sweden. These two states, in equal fear of Germany and
Russia, had no aim but to keep out of the wars by which they
were encircled and might be engulfed. For them this seemed
the only chance of survival. But whereas the British Government were naturally reluctant to commit even a technical infringement of Norwegian territorial waters by laying mines in
the Leads for their own advantage against Germany, they
moved upon a generous emotion, only indirectly connected with
our war problem, towards a far more serious demand upon
both Norway and Sweden for the free passage of men and supplies to Finland.

I sympathised ardently with the Finns and supported all proposals for their aid; and I welcomed this new and favourable breeze as a means of achieving the major strategic advantage of cutting off the vital iron-ore supplies of Germany. If Narvik was to become a kind of Allied base to supply the Finns, it would certainly be easy to prevent the German ships loading ore at the port and sailing safely down the Leads to Germany. Once Norwegian and Swedish protestations were overborne for whatever reason, the greater measures would include the less. The Admiralty eyes were also fixed at this time upon the movements of a large and powerful Russian ice-breaker which was to be sent from Murmansk to Germany, ostensibly for repairs, but much more probably to open the now-frozen Baltic port of Lulea for the German ore ships. I, therefore, renewed my efforts to win consent to the simple and bloodless operation of mining the Leads, for which a certain precedent of the previous war existed. As the question raises moral issues, I feel it right to set the case in its final form as I made it after prolonged reflection and debate.

Norway — Iron-Ore Traffic

Note by the First Lord of the Admiralty

16.XII.39.

The effectual stoppage of the Norwegian ore supplies to Germany ranks as a major offensive operation of war. No other measure is open to us for many months to come which gives so good a chance of abridging the waste and destruction of the conflict, or of perhaps preventing the vast slaughters which will attend the grapple of the main armies.

2. If the advantage is held to outweigh the obvious and serious objections, the whole process of stoppage must be enforced. The ore from Lulea [in the Baltic] is already stopped by the winter ice, which must not be [allowed to be] broken by the Soviet ice-breaker, should the attempt be made. The ore from Narvik must be stopped by laying successively a series of small minefields in Norwegian territorial waters at the two or three suitable points on the coast, which will force the ships carrying ore to Germany to quit territorial waters and come onto the high seas, where, if German, they will

be taken as prize, or, if neutral, subjected to our contraband control. The ore from Oxelosund, the main ice-free port in the Baltic, must also be prevented from leaving by methods which will be neither diplomatic nor military. All these three ports must be dealt with in various appropriate ways as soon as possible.

3. Thus, it is not a question of denying Germany a mere million tons between now and May, but of cutting off her whole winter supply except the negligible amounts that can be got from Gavle, or other minor ice-free Baltic ports. Germany would, therefore, undergo a severe deprivation, tending to crisis before the summer. But when the ice melts in the Gulf of Bothnia the abundant supply from Lulea would again be open, and Germany is no doubt planning, not only to get as much as she can during the winter, but to make up the whole nine and a half million tons which she needs, or even more, between May 1 and December 15, 1940. After this she might hope to organise Russian supplies and be able to wage a very long war.

4. It may well be that, should we reach the month of May with Germany starving for ore for her industries and her munitions, the prevention of the reopening of Lulea may become [for us] a principal naval objective. The laying of a declared minefield, including magnetic mines, off Lulea by British submarines would be one way. There are others. If Germany can be cut from all Swedish ore supplies from now onwards till the end of 1940, a blow will have been struck at her war-making capacity equal to a first-class victory in the field or from the air, and without any serious sacrifice of life. It might indeed be immediately decisive.

5. To every blow struck in war there is a counter. If you fire at the enemy he will fire back. It is most necessary, therefore, to face squarely the counter-measures which may be taken by Germany, or constrained by her from Norway or Sweden. As to Norway, there are three pairs of events which are linked together. First, the Germans, conducting war in a cruel and lawless manner, have violated the territorial waters of Norway, sinking without warning or succour a number of British and neutral vessels. To that our response is to lay the minefields mentioned above. It is suggested that Norway, by way of protest, may cancel the valuable agreement we have made with her for chartering her tankers and other shipping. But then she would lose the extremely profitable bargain she has made with us, and this shipping would become valueless to

her in view of our contraband control. Her ships would be idle, and her owners impoverished. It would not be in Norwegian interests for her Government to take this step; and interest is a powerful factor. Thirdly, Norway could retaliate by refusing to export to us the aluminium and other war materials which are important to the Air Ministry and the Ministry of Supply. But here again her interests would suffer. Not only would she not receive the valuable gains which this trade brings her, but Great Britain, by denying her bauxite and other indispensable raw materials, could bring the whole industry of Norway, centring upon Oslo and Bergen, to a complete standstill. In short, Norway, by retaliating against us, would be involved in economic and industrial ruin.

6. Norwegian sympathies are on our side, and her future independence from German overlordship hangs upon the victory of the Allies. It is not reasonable to suppose that she will take either of the counter-measures mentioned above (although she may threaten them), unless she is compelled to do so by German brute force.

7. This will certainly be applied to her anyway, and whatever we do, if Germany thinks it her interest to dominate forcibly the Scandinavian peninsula. In that case the war would spread to Norway and Sweden, and with our command of the seas there is no reason why French and British troops should not meet German invaders on Scandinavian soil. At any rate, we can certainly take and hold whatever islands or suitable points on the Norwegian coast we choose. Our northern blockade of Germany would then become absolute. We could, for instance, occupy Narvik and Bergen, and keep them open for our own trade while closing them completely to Germany. It cannot be too strongly emphasised that British control of the Norwegian coast-line is a strategic objective of first-class importance. It is not, therefore, seen how, even if retaliation by Germany were to run its full course, we should be worse off for the action now proposed. On the contrary, we have more to gain than lose by a German attack upon Norway or Sweden. This point is capable of more elaboration than is necessary here.

There is no reason why we should not manage to secure a large and long-continued supply of iron ore from Sweden through Narvik while at the same time diverting all supplies of ore from Germany. This must be our aim.

I concluded as follows:

8. The effect of our action against Norway upon world opinion and upon our own reputation must be considered. We have taken up arms in accordance with the principles of the Covenant of the League in order to aid the victims of German aggression. No technical infringement of international law, so long as it is unaccompanied by inhumanity of any kind, can deprive us of the good wishes of neutral countries. No evil effect will be produced upon the greatest of all neutrals, the United States. We have reason to believe that they will handle the matter in the way most calculated to help us. And they are very resourceful.

9. The final tribunal is our own conscience. We are fighting to re-establish the reign of law and to protect the liberties of small countries. Our defeat would mean an age of barbaric violence, and would be fatal, not only to ourselves, but to the independent life of every small country in Europe. Acting in the name of the Covenant, and as virtual mandatories of the League and all it stands for, we have a right, and indeed are bound in duty, to abrogate for a space some of the conventions of the very laws we seek to consolidate and reaffirm. Small nations must not tie our hands when we are fighting for their rights and freedom. The letter of the law must not in supreme emergency obstruct those who are charged with its protection and enforcement. It would not be right or rational that the aggressor Power should gain one set of advantages by tearing up all laws, and another set by sheltering behind the innate respect for law of its opponents. Humanity, rather than legality, must be our guide.

Of all this history must be the judge. We now face events.

* * * * *

My memorandum was considered by the Cabinet on December 22, and I pleaded the case to the best of my ability. I could not obtain any decision for action. Diplomatic protest might be made to Norway about the misuse of her territorial waters by Germany, and the Chiefs of the Staff were instructed to consider the military implications of any possible future commitments on Scandinavian soil. They were authorised to plan for landing a force at Narvik for the sake of Finland, and also to

consider the military consequences of a German occupation of
Southern Norway. But no executive orders could be issued to
the Admiralty. In a paper which I circulated on December 24,
I summarised the Intelligence reports which showed the possibilities of a Russian design upon Norway. The Soviets were said
to have three divisions concentrated at Murmansk preparing
for a seaborne expedition. "It may be," I concluded, "that this
theatre will become the scene of early activities." This proved
only too true: but from a different quarter.

10

A Dark New Year

THE END OF THE YEAR 1939 left the war still in its sinister trance. An occasional cannon-shot or reconnoitring patrol alone broke the silence of the Western Front. The armies gaped at each other from behind their rising fortifications across an undisputed "No-Man's-Land."

There is a certain similarity [I wrote to Pound on Christmas Day] between the position now, and at the end of the year 1914. The transition from peace to war has been accomplished. The outer seas, for the moment at any rate, are clear from enemy surface craft. The lines in France are static. But in addition on the sea we

549

have repelled the first U-boat attack, which previously did not
begin till February, 1915, and we can see our way through the
magnetic-mine novelty. Moreover, in France the lines run along
the frontiers instead of six or seven of the French provinces and
Belgium being in the enemy's hands. Thus I feel we may compare
the position now very favourably with that of 1914. And also I have
the feeling (which may be corrected at any moment) that the
Kaiser's Germany was a much tougher customer than Nazi
Germany.

This is the best I can do for a Christmas card in these hard times.

I was by now increasingly convinced that there could be no
"Operation Catherine" in 1940.

The sending of a superior surface fleet into the Baltic [I wrote to
Pound, January 6], though eminently desirable, is not essential to
the seizure and retention of the iron-fields. While therefore every
preparation to send the Fleet in should continue, and strong efforts
should be made, it would be wrong to try it unless we can see our
way to maintaining it under air attack, and still more wrong to
make the seizure of the iron-fields dependent upon the sending of
a surface fleet. Let us advance with confidence and see how the
naval side develops as events unfold.

And again a week later:

Mr. Churchill to First Sea Lord.   15.I.40.

I have carefully considered all the papers you have been good
enough to send me in reply to my various minutes about "Catherine." I have come reluctantly but quite definitely to the conclusion that the operation we outlined in the autumn will not be
practicable this year. We have not yet obtained sufficient mastery
over U-boats, mines, and raiders to enable us to fit for their special
duties the many smaller vessels required. The problem of making
our ships comparatively secure against air attack has not been
solved. The dive-bomber remains a formidable menace. The
rockets [called for secrecy "the U.P. weapon," i.e., unrotated pro-
jectile], though progressing rapidly towards the production stage,
will not be available in sufficient quantities, even if all goes well,
for many months to come. We have not been able so far to give the
additional armour protection to our larger ships. The political
situation in the Baltic is as baffling as ever. On the other hand,

the arrival of the *Bismarck* in September adds greatly to the scale of the surface resistance to be encountered.

2. But the war may well be raging in 1941, and no one can tell what opportunities may present themselves then. I wish, therefore, that all the preparations of various ships and auxiliaries outlined in your table and marked as "beneficial" should continue as opportunity offers; that when ships come into the dockyards for repair or refit, everything should be done to them which will not delay their return to service. And it would surely be only common prudence, in view of the attitude of Russia, to go on warning our destroyers for service in winter seas. I am glad to feel that we are agreed in this.

*   *   *   *   *

So far no ally had espoused our cause. The United States was cooler than in any other period. I persevered in my correspondence with the President, but with little response. The Chancellor of the Exchequer groaned about our dwindling dollar resources. We had already signed a pact of mutual assistance with Turkey, and were considering what aid we could give her from our narrow margins. The stresses created by the Finnish War had worsened our relations, already bad, with the Soviets. Any action we might undertake to help the Finns might lead to war with Russia. The fundamental antagonisms between the Soviet Government and Nazi Germany did not prevent the Kremlin actively aiding by supplies and facilities the development of Hitler's power. Communists in France and any that existed in Britain denounced the "imperialist-capitalist" war, and did what they could to hamper work in the munition factories. They certainly exercised a depressing and subversive influence within the French Army, already wearied by inaction. We continued to court Italy by civilities and favourable contracts, but we could feel no security, or progress towards friendship. Count Ciano was polite to our Ambassador. Mussolini stood aloof.

The Italian Dictator was not, however, without his own misgivings. On January 3, he wrote a revealing letter to Hitler expressing his distaste for the German agreement with Russia:

No one knows better than I with forty years' political experience
that policy — particularly a revolutionary policy — has its tactical
requirements. I recognised the Soviets in 1924. In 1934, I signed
with them a treaty of commerce and friendship. I, therefore, understood that, *especially as Ribbentrop's forecast about the non-intervention of Britain and France has not come off,* you are obliged to
avoid the second front. You have had to pay for this in that Russia
has, without striking a blow, been the great profiteer of the war in
Poland and the Baltic.

But I, who was born a revolutionary and have not modified my
revolutionary mentality, tell you that you cannot permanently
sacrifice the principles of *your* revolution to the tactical requirements of a given moment. . . . I have also the definite duty to add
that a further step in the relations with Moscow would have catastrophic repercussions in Italy, where the unanimity of anti-Bolshevik feeling is absolute, granite-hard, and unbreakable. Permit me
to think that this will not happen. The solution of your *Lebensraum* is in Russia, and nowhere else. . . . The day when we shall
have demolished Bolshevism we shall have kept faith with both
our revolutions. Then it will be the turn of the great democracies,
who will not be able to survive the cancer which gnaws them. . . .

*   *   *   *   *

On January 6, I again visited France to explain my two
mechanical projects, Cultivator Number 6[1] and the Fluvial Mine
("Operation Royal Marine"), to the French High Command.
In the morning, before I left, the Prime Minister sent for me
and told me he had decided to make a change at the War Office,
and that Mr. Hore-Belisha would give place to Mr. Oliver
Stanley. Late that night, Mr. Hore-Belisha called me on the
telephone at our Embassy in Paris and told me what I knew
already. I pressed him, but without success, to take one of the
other offices which were open to him. The Government was
itself in low water at this time, and almost the whole press of
the country declared that a most energetic and live figure had
been dismissed from the Government. He quitted the War
Office amid a chorus of newspaper tributes. Parliament does
not take its opinion from the newspapers; indeed, it often

[1] See Appendix J, Book II.

reacts in the opposite sense. When the House of Commons met
a week later, he had few champions, and refrained from making any statement. I wrote to him, January 10, as follows:

I much regret that our brief association as colleagues has ended.
In the last war I went through the same experience as you have
suffered, and I know how bitter and painful it is to anyone with
his heart in the job. I was not consulted in the changes that were
proposed. I was only informed after they had been decided. At the
same time, I should fail in candour if I did not let you know that
I thought it would have been better if you went to the Board of
Trade or the Ministry of Information, and I am very sorry that
you did not see your way to accept the first of these important
offices.

The outstanding achievement of your tenure of the War Office
was the passage of conscription in time of peace. You may rest with
confidence upon this, and I hope that it will not be long before we
are colleagues again, and that this temporary set-back will prove
no serious obstacle to your opportunities of serving the country.

It was not possible for me to realise my hope until, after the
break-up of the National Coalition, I formed the so-called
"Caretaker Government" in May, 1945. Belisha then became
Minister of National Insurance. In the interval he had been
one of our severe critics; but I was very glad to be able to bring
so able a man back into the Administration.

*   *   *   *   *

All January the Finns stood firm, and at the end of the
month the growing Russian armies were still held in their positions. The Red air force continued to bomb Helsingfors and
Viipuri, and the cry from the Finnish Government for aircraft
and war materials grew louder. As the Arctic nights shortened,
the Soviet air offensive would increase, not only upon the towns
of Finland, but upon the communications of their armies. Only
a trickle of war material and only a few thousand volunteers
from the Scandinavian countries had reached Finland so far.
A bureau for recruiting was opened in London in January, and
several scores of British aircraft were sent to Finland, some
direct by air. Nothing in fact of any use was done.

The delays about Narvik continued interminably. Although the Cabinet were prepared to contemplate pressure upon Norway and Sweden to allow aid to pass to Finland, they remained opposed to the much smaller operation of mining the Leads. The first was noble; the second merely tactical. Besides, everyone could see that Norway and Sweden would refuse facilities for aid; so nothing would come of the project anyway.

In my vexation after one of our Cabinets I wrote to a colleague:

January 15, 1940.

My disquiet was due mainly to the awful difficulties which our machinery of war conduct presents to positive action. I see such immense walls of prevention, all built and building, that I wonder whether any plan will have a chance of climbing over them. Just look at the arguments which have had to be surmounted in the seven weeks we have discussed this Narvik operation. First, the objections of the economic departments, Supply, Board of Trade, etc. Secondly, the Joint Planning Committee. Thirdly, the Chiefs of Staff Committee. Fourthly, the insidious argument, "Don't spoil the big plan for the sake of the small," when there is really very little chance of the big plan being resolutely attempted. Fifthly, the juridical and moral objections, all gradually worn down. Sixthly, the attitude of neutrals, and above all, the United States. But see how well the United States have responded to our *démarche!* Seventhly, the Cabinet itself, with its many angles of criticism. Eighthly, when all this has been smoothed out, the French have to be consulted. Finally, the Dominions and their consciences have to be squared, they not having gone through the process by which opinion has advanced at home. All this makes me feel that under the present arrangements we shall be reduced to waiting upon the terrible attacks of the enemy, against which it is impossible to prepare in every quarter simultaneously without fatal dissipation of strength.

I have two or three projects moving forward, but all I fear will succumb before the tremendous array of negative arguments and forces. Pardon me, therefore, if I showed distress. One thing is absolutely certain, namely, that victory will never be found by taking the line of least resistance.

However, all this Narvik story is for the moment put on one

side by the threat to the Low Countries. If this materialises, the position will have to be studied in the light of entirely new events. . . . Should a great battle engage in the Low Countries, the effects upon Norway and Sweden may well be decisive. Even if the battle ends only in a stalemate, they may feel far more free, and to us a diversion may become even more needful.

* * * * *

There were other causes for uneasiness. The progress of converting our industries to war production was not up to the pace required. In a speech at Manchester on January 27, I urged the immense importance of expanding our labour supply and of bringing great numbers of women into industry to replace the men taken for the armed forces and to augment our strength:

We have to make a huge expansion, especially of those capable of performing skilled or semi-skilled operations. Here we must specially count for aid and guidance upon our Labour colleagues and trade-union leaders. I can speak with some knowledge about this, having presided over the former Ministry of Munitions in its culminating phase. Millions of new workers will be needed, and more than a million women must come boldly forward into our war industries — into the shell plants, the munition works, and into the aircraft factories. Without this expansion of labour and without allowing the women of Britain to enter the struggle as they desire to do, we should fail utterly to bear our fair share of the burden which France and Britain have jointly assumed.

Little was, however, done, and the sense of extreme emergency seemed lacking. There was a "twilight" mood in the ranks of Labour and of those who directed production as well as in the military operations. It was not till the beginning of May that a survey of employment in the engineering, motor, and aircraft group of industries which was presented to the Cabinet revealed the facts in an indisputable form. This paper was searchingly examined by my statistical department under Professor Lindemann. In spite of the distractions and excitements of the Norwegian hurly-burly then in progress, I found time to address the following note to my colleagues:

Note by the First Lord of the Admiralty.   *May* 4, 1940.

This Report suggests that in this fundamental group, at any rate, we have hardly begun to organise man-power for the production of munitions.

In [previous papers] it was estimated that a very large expansion, amounting to 71.5 per cent of the number engaged in the metal industry, would be needed in the first year of war. Actually the engineering, motor, and aircraft group, which covers three-fifths of the metal industry and which is discussed in this survey, has only expanded by 11.1 per cent (122,000) between June, 1939, and April, 1940. This is less than one-sixth of the expansion stated to be required. Without any Government intervention, by the mere improvement of trade, the number increased as quickly as this in the year 1936/37.

Although 350,000 boys leave school each year, there is an increase of only 25,000 in the number of males under twenty-one employed in this group. Moreover, the proportion of women and young persons has only increased from 26.6 per cent to 27.6 per cent. In the engineering, motor, and aircraft group, we now have only one woman for every twelve men. During the last war the ratio of women to men in the metal industries increased from one woman for every ten men to one woman for every three men. In the first year of the last war, July, 1914, to July, 1915, the new workers drafted into the metal industries amounted to 20 per cent of those already there. In the group under survey which may fairly be taken as typical of the whole metal industry, only 11 per cent have been added in the last ten months.

Admiralty establishments, in which employment has been increased by nearly 27 per cent, have not been considered here, as no figures of the different types of labour are given.

*   *   *   *   *

On January 19, anxieties about the Western Front received confirmation. A German staff-major of the 7th Air Division had been ordered to take some documents to Headquarters in Cologne. Wishing to save time for private indulgences, he decided to fly across the intervening Belgian territory. His machine made a forced landing; the Belgian police arrested him and impounded his papers, which he tried desperately to destroy. These contained the entire and actual scheme for the invasion of Belgium, Holland, and France on which Hitler had resolved. The French and British Governments were given copies of these documents, and the German major was released to explain matters to his superiors. I was told about all this at the time, and it seemed to me incredible that the Belgians would not make a plan to invite us in. But they did nothing about it. It was argued in all three countries concerned that probably it was a plant. But this could not be true. There could be no sense in the Germans trying to make the Belgians believe that they were going to attack them in the near future. This might make them do the very last thing the Germans wanted, namely, make a plan with the French and British Armies to come forward privily and quickly one fine night. I, therefore, believed in the impending attack. But such questionings found no place in the thought of the Belgian King, and he and his Army Staff merely waited, hoping that all would turn out well. In spite of all the German major's papers, no fresh action of any kind was taken by the Allies or the threatened states. Hitler, on the other hand, as we now know, summoned Goering to his presence, and on being told that the captured papers were in fact the complete plans for invasion, ordered, after venting his anger, new variants to be prepared.

It was thus clear at the beginning of 1940 that Hitler had a detailed plan involving both Belgium and Holland for the invasion of France. Should this begin at any moment, General Gamelin's Plan "D" would be put in operation, including the movement of the Seventh French Army and the British Army. Plan "D" [2] had been worked out in exact detail and required only one single word to set it in motion. This course, though deprecated at the outset of the war by the British Chiefs of Staff, had been definitely and formally confirmed in Paris on November 17, 1939. On this basis the Allies awaited the impending shock, and Hitler the campaigning season, for which the weather might well be favourable from April onwards.

During the winter and spring, the B.E.F. were extremely

[2] See Chapter 5, pages 482–483.

busy setting themselves to rights, fortifying their line and preparing for war, whether offensive or defensive. From the highest rank to the lowest, all were hard at it, and the good showing that they eventually made was due largely to the full use
made of the opportunities provided during the winter. The
British was a far better army at the end of the "Twilight War."
It was also larger. The 42d and 44th Divisions arrived in
March and went on to the frontier line in the latter half of
April, 1940. In that month there also arrived the 12th, 23d,
and 46th Divisions. These were sent to complete their training in France and to augment the labour force for all the work
in hand. They were short even of the ordinary unit weapons
and equipment, and had no artillery. Nevertheless, they were
inevitably drawn into the fighting when it began, and acquitted
themselves well.

The awful gap, reflecting on our pre-war arrangements, was
*the absence of even one armoured division in the British Ex-
peditionary Force.* Britain, the cradle of the tank in all its variants, had between the wars so far neglected the development of
this weapon, soon to dominate the battlefields, that eight
months after the declaration of war our small but good army
had only with it, when the hour of trial arrived, the First Army
Tank Brigade, comprising seventeen light tanks and one hundred "infantry" tanks. Only twenty-three of the latter carried
even the two-pounder gun; the rest machine-guns only. There
were also seven cavalry and yeomanry regiments equipped with
carriers and light tanks which were in process of being formed
into two light armoured brigades. Apart from the lack of
armour the progress in the efficiency of the B.E.F. was marked.

*   *   *   *   *

Developments on the French Front were less satisfactory.
In a great national conscript force the mood of the people
is closely reflected in its army, the more so when that
army is quartered in the homeland and contacts are close. It
cannot be said that France in 1939/40 viewed the war with uprising spirit or even with much confidence. The restless in-

ternal politics of the past decade had bred disunity and discontents. Important elements, in reaction to growing Communism, had swung towards Fascism, lending a ready ear to Goebbels' skilful propaganda and passing it on in gossip and rumour. So also in the Army the disintegrating influences of both Communism and Fascism were at work; the long winter months of waiting gave time and opportunity for the poisons to be established.

Very many factors go to the building-up of sound morale in an army, but one of the greatest is that the men be fully employed at useful and interesting work. Idleness is a dangerous breeding-ground. Throughout the winter there were many tasks that needed doing; training demanded continuous attention; defences were far from satisfactory or complete, even the Maginot Line lacked many supplementary field works; physical fitness demands exercise. Yet visitors to the French Front were often struck by the prevailing atmosphere of calm aloofness, by the seemingly poor quality of the work in hand, by the lack of visible activity of any kind. The emptiness of the roads behind the line was in great contrast to the continual coming and going which extended for miles behind the British sector.

There can be no doubt that the quality of the French Army was allowed to deteriorate during the winter, and that they would have fought better in the autumn than in the spring. Soon they were to be stunned by the swiftness and violence of the German assault. It was not until the last phases of that brief campaign that the true fighting qualities of the French soldier rose uppermost in defence of his country against the age-long enemy. But then it was too late.

*   *   *   *   *

Meanwhile, the German plans for a direct assault on Norway and a lightning occupation of Denmark also were advancing. Field-Marshal Keitel drew up a memorandum on this subject on January 27, 1940:

The Fuehrer and Supreme Commander of the Armed Forces wishes that Study "N" should be further worked on under my direct and personal guidance, and in the closest conjunction with the general war policy. For these reasons the Fuehrer has commissioned me to take over the direction of further preparations.

The detailed planning for this operation proceeded through the normal channels.

*   *   *   *   *

In early February, when the Prime Minister was going to the Supreme War Council in Paris, he invited me for the first time to go with him. Mr. Chamberlain asked me to meet him at Downing Street after dinner.

The main subject of discussion on February 5 was "Aid to Finland," and plans were approved to send three or four divisions into Norway, in order to persuade Sweden to let us send supplies and reinforcements to the Finns, and incidentally to get control of the Gullivare ore-field. As might be expected, the Swedes did not agree to this and, though extensive preparations were made, the whole project fell to the ground. Mr. Chamberlain conducted the proceedings himself on our behalf, and only minor interventions were made by the various British Ministers attending. I am not recorded as having said a word.

The next day, when we came to recross the Channel, an amusing incident occurred. We sighted a floating mine. So I said to the Captain: "Let's blow it up by gun-fire." It burst with a good bang, and a large piece of wreckage sailed over towards us and seemed for an instant as if it were going to settle on the bridge, where all the politicians and some of the other swells were clustered. However, it landed on the forecastle, which was happily bare, and no one was hurt. Thus everything passed off pleasantly. From this time onwards I was invited by the Prime Minister to accompany him, with others, to the meetings of the Supreme War Council. But I could not provide an equal entertainment each time.

*   *   *   *   *

The Council decided that it was of first importance that Finland should be saved; that she could not hold out after

the spring without reinforcements of thirty to forty thousand
trained men; that the present stream of heterogeneous volunteers was not sufficient; and that the destruction of Finland
would be a major defeat for the Allies. It was, therefore, necessary to send Allied troops either through Petsamo or through
Narvik and/or other Norwegian ports. The operation through
Narvik was preferred, as it would enable the Allies "to kill
two birds with one stone" [i.e., help Finland cut off the iron
ore]. Two British divisions due to start for France in February should be retained in England and prepared for fighting
in Norway. Meanwhile, every effort should be made to procure
the assent and if possible the co-operation of the Norwegians
and Swedes. The issue of what to do if Norway and Sweden
refused, as seemed probable, was never faced.

A vivid episode now sharpened everything in Scandinavia.
The reader will remember my concern to capture the *Altmark*,
the auxiliary of the *Spee*. This vessel was also a floating prison
for the crews of our sunk merchant ships. British captives
released by Captain Langsdorff according to international
law in Montevideo Harbour told us that nearly three hundred
British merchant seamen were on board the *Altmark*. This
vessel hid in the South Atlantic for nearly two months, and
then, hoping that the search had died down, her captain made
a bid to return to Germany. Luck and the weather favoured
her, and not until February 14, after passing between Iceland
and the Faroes, was she sighted by our aircraft in Norwegian
territorial waters.

First Lord to First Sea Lord.   16.2.40.

On the position as reported to me this morning, it would seem
that the cruiser and destroyers should sweep northward during
the day up the coast of Norway, not hesitating to arrest *Altmark*
in territorial waters should she be found. This ship is violating
neutrality in carrying British prisoners of war to Germany. Surely
another cruiser or two should be sent to rummage the Skagerrak
tonight? The *Altmark* must be regarded as an invaluable trophy.

In the words of an Admiralty communiqué, "certain of His

Majesty's ships which were conveniently disposed were set in
motion." A destroyer flotilla, under the command of Captain
Philip Vian, of H.M.S. *Cossack,* intercepted the *Altmark,* but
did not immediately molest her. She took refuge in Josing
Fiord, a narrow inlet about half a mile long surrounded by
high snow-clad cliffs. Two British destroyers were told to
board her for examination. At the entrance to the fiord they
were met by two Norwegian gunboats, who informed them
that the ship was unarmed, had been examined the previous
day, and had received permission to proceed to Germany, making use of Norwegian territorial waters. Our destroyers thereupon withdrew.

When this information reached the Admiralty, I intervened,
and with the concurrence of the Foreign Secretary, ordered our
ships to enter the fiord. I did not often act so directly; but
I now sent Captain Vian the following order:

February 16, 1940, 5.25 P.M.
Unless Norwegian torpedo-boat undertakes to convoy *Altmark*
to Bergen with a joint Anglo-Norwegian guard on board, and a
joint escort, you should board *Altmark,* liberate the prisoners, and
take possession of the ship pending further instructions. If Norwegian torpedo-boat interferes, you should warn her to stand off.
If she fires upon you, you should not reply unless attack is serious,
in which case you should defend yourself, using no more force than
is necessary, and ceasing fire when she desists.

Vian did the rest. That night, in the *Cossack* with searchlights
burning, he entered the fiord through the ice floes. He first went
on board the Norwegian gunboat *Kjell* and requested that the
Altmark should be taken to Bergen under a joint escort, for
inquiry according to international law. The Norwegian captain repeated his assurance that the *Altmark* had been twice
searched, that she was unarmed, and that no British prisoners
had been found. Vian then stated that he was going to board
her, and invited the Norwegian officer to join him. This offer
was eventually declined.

Meanwhile, the *Altmark* got under way, and in trying to

ram the *Cossack* ran herself aground. The *Cossack* forced her way alongside and a boarding party sprang across, after grappling the two ships together. A sharp hand-to-hand fight followed, in which four Germans were killed and five wounded; part of the crew fled ashore and the rest surrendered. The search began for the British prisoners. They were soon found in their hundreds, battened down, locked in storerooms, and even in an empty oiltank. Then came the cry, "The Navy's here!" The doors were broken in and the captives rushed on deck. Altogether two hundred and ninety-nine prisoners were released and transferred to our destroyers. It was also found that the *Altmark* carried two pom-poms and four machineguns, and that despite having been boarded twice by the Norwegians, she had not been searched. The Norwegian gunboats remained passive observers throughout. By midnight Vian was clear of the fiord, and making for the Forth.

Admiral Pound and I sat up together in some anxiety in the Admiralty War Room. I had put a good screw on the Foreign Office, and was fully aware of the technical gravity of the measures taken. To judge them fairly, it must be remembered that up to that date Germany had sunk 218,000 tons of Scandinavian shipping with a loss of 555 Scandinavian lives. But what mattered at home and in the Cabinet was whether British prisoners were found on board or not. We were delighted when at three o'clock in the morning news came that three hundred had been found and rescued. This was a dominating fact.

On the assumption that the prisoners were in a pitiable condition from starvation and confinement, we directed ambulances, doctors, the press, and photographers to the port of Leith to receive them. As, however, it appeared that they were in good health, had been well looked after on the destroyers, and came ashore in a hearty condition, no publicity was given to this aspect. Their rescue and Captain Vian's conduct aroused a wave of enthusiasm in Britain almost equal to that which followed the sinking of the *Graf Spee*. Both these events strengthened my hand and the prestige of the Admiralty. "The Navy's here!" was passed from lip to lip.

Every allowance must be made for the behaviour of the Norwegian Government, which was, of course, quivering under the German terror and exploiting our forbearance. They protested vehemently against the entry of their territorial waters. Mr. Chamberlain's speech in the House of Commons contained the essence of the British reply:

According to the views expressed by Professor Koht [the Norwegian Prime Minister], the Norwegian Government see no objection to the use of Norwegian territorial waters for hundreds of miles by a German warship for the purpose of escaping capture on the high seas and of conveying British prisoners to a German prison camp. Such a doctrine is at variance with international law as His Majesty's Government understand it. It would in their view legalise the abuse by German warships of neutral waters and create a position which His Majesty's Government could in no circumstances accept.

* * * * *

Hitler's decision to invade Norway had, as we have seen, been taken on December 14, and the staff work was proceeding under Keitel. The incident of the *Altmark* no doubt gave a spur to action. At Keitel's suggestion on February 20, Hitler summoned urgently to Berlin General Falkenhorst, who was at that time in command of an army corps at Coblenz. Falkenhorst had taken part in the German campaign in Finland in 1918, and upon this subject the interview with the Fuehrer opened. The General described the conversation at the Nuremberg Trials.

Hitler reminded me of my experience in Finland, and said to me, "Sit down and tell me what you did." After a moment, the Fuehrer interrupted me. He led me to a table covered with maps. "I have a similar thing in mind," he said: "the occupation of Norway; because I am informed that the English intend to land there, and I want to be there before them."

Then marching up and down he expounded to me his reasons. "The occupation of Norway by the British would be a strategic turning movement which would lead them into the Baltic, where we have neither troops nor coastal fortifications. The success which

we have gained in the East and which we are going to win in the
West would be annihilated because the enemy would find himself
in a position to advance on Berlin and to break the backbone of
our two fronts. In the second and third place, the conquest of
Norway will ensure the liberty of movement of our Fleet in the Bay
of Wilhelmshaven, and will protect our imports of Swedish ore."
. . . Finally he said to me, "I appoint you to the command of the
expedition."

That afternoon Falkenhorst was summoned again to the
Chancellery to discuss with Hitler, Keitel, and Jodl the detailed operational plans for the Norwegian expedition. The
question of priorities was of supreme importance. Would
Hitler commit himself in Norway before or after the execution
of "Case Yellow" — the attack on France? On March 1, he
made his decision: Norway was to come first. The entry in
Jodl's diary for March 3 reads, "The Fuehrer decides to carry
out 'Weser Exercise' before 'Case Yellow' with a few days' interval."

*   *   *   *   *

A vexatious air attack had recently begun on our shipping
all along the east coast. Besides ocean-going vessels destined
for the large ports, there were on any given day about three
hundred and twenty ships of between five hundred and two
thousand tons either at sea or in harbour on the coast, many
engaged in coal transport to London and the south. Only a
few of these small vessels had yet been provided with an anti-
aircraft gun, and the enemy aircraft, therefore, concentrated
upon this easy prey. They even attacked the lightships. These
faithful servants of the seamen, moored in exposed positions
near the shoals along our coasts, were of use to all, even the
marauding U-boat itself, and had never been touched in any
previous war. Several were now sunk or damaged, the worst
case being off the Humber, where a fierce machine-gun attack
killed eight out of the lightship's crew of nine.

As a defence against air attack, the convoy system proved as
effective as it had against the U-boats, but everything was now
done to find some kind of weapon for each ship. In our dearth

of ack-ack guns all sorts of contrivances were used. Even a life-saving rocket brought down an air bandit. The spare machine-guns from the Home Fleet were distributed with naval gunners to British and Allied merchant ships on the east coast. These men and their weapons were shifted from ship to ship for each voyage through the danger zone. By the end of February, the Army was able to help, and thus began an organisation later known as the Maritime Royal Artillery. At the height of the war in 1944, more than thirty-eight thousand officers and men from the regular forces were employed in this task, of which fourteen thousand were found by the Army. Over considerable sections of the east coast convoy route, air fighter protection from the nearest airfields could soon be given on call. Thus the efforts of all three services were combined. An increasing toll was taken of the raiders. Shooting-up ordinary defenceless shipping of all countries turned out to be more costly than had been expected, and the attacks diminished.

Not all the horizon was dark. In the outer seas there had been no further signs of raider activity since the destruction of the *Graf Spee* in December, and the work of sweeping German shipping from the seas continued. During February, six German ships left Spain in an attempt to reach Germany. Only one succeeded; of the remainder three were captured, one scuttled herself, and one was wrecked in Norway. Seven other German ships attempting to run the blockade were intercepted by our patrols during February and March. All except one of these were scuttled by their captains. Altogether by the beginning of April, 1940, seventy-one ships of three hundred and forty thousand tons had been lost to the Germans by capture or scuttling, while two hundred and fifteen German ships still remained cooped in neutral ports. Finding our merchant ships armed, the U-boats had abandoned the gun for the torpedo. Their next descent had been from the torpedo to the lowest form of warfare — the undeclared mine. We have seen how the magnetic-mine attack had been met and mastered. Nevertheless, more than half our losses in January were from this cause and more than two-thirds of the total fell on neutrals.

On the Navy estimates at the end of February, I reviewed the salient features of the war at sea. The Germans, I surmised, had lost half the U-boats with which they had entered the war. Contrary to expectation, few new ones had yet made their appearance. Actually, as we now know, sixteen U-boats had been sunk and nine added up to the end of February. The enemy's main effort had not yet developed. Our programme of shipbuilding, both in the form of escort vessels and in re-placement of merchant ships, was very large. The Admiralty had taken over control of merchant shipbuilding, and Sir James Lithgow, the Glasgow shipbuilder, had joined the Board for this purpose. In the first six months of this new war our net loss had been less than two hundred thousand tons compared with four hundred and fifty thousand tons in the single deadly month of April, 1917. Meanwhile, we had continued to cap-ture more cargoes in tonnage destined for the enemy than we had lost ourselves.

Each month [I said in ending my speech] there has been a steady improvement in imports. In January the Navy carried safely into British harbours, despite U-boats and mines and the winter gales and fog, considerably more than four-fifths of the peace-time average for the three preceding years. . . . When we consider the great number of British ships which have been withdrawn for naval service or for the transport of our armies across the Channel or of troop convoys across the globe, there is nothing in these results — to put it mildly — which should cause despondency or alarm.

11

Before the Storm

March, 1940

MARCH 12 was the long-desired date for the reoccupation and use of Scapa as the main base of the Home Fleet. I thought I would give myself the treat of being present on this occasion in our naval affairs, and embarked accordingly in Admiral Forbes' flagship at the Clyde.

The Fleet comprised five capital ships, a cruiser squadron, and perhaps a score of destroyers. The twenty-hour voyage lay through the Minches. We were to pass the Northern Straits at dawn and reach Scapa about noon. The *Hood* and other ships from Rosyth, moving up the east coast, would be there some hours before us. The navigation of the Minches is intricate, and the northern exit barely a mile wide. On every

side are rocky shores and reefs, and three U-boats were reported
in these enclosed waters. We had to proceed at high speed
and by zigzag. All the usual peace-time lights were out. This
was, therefore, a task in navigation which the Navy keenly
appreciated. However, just as we were about to start after
luncheon, the Master of the Fleet, navigating officer of the flagship, on whom the prime direct responsibility lay, was suddenly
stricken by influenza. So a very young-looking lieutenant who
was his assistant came up onto the bridge to take charge of the
movement of the Fleet. I was struck by this officer, who without any notice had to undertake so serious a task requiring such
perfect science, accuracy, and judgment. His composure did
not entirely conceal his satisfaction.

I had many things to discuss with the Commander-in-Chief,
and it was not until after midnight that I went up onto the
bridge. All was velvet black. The air was clear, but no stars
were to be seen, and there was no moon. The great ship
ploughed along at about sixteen knots. One could just see the
dark mass astern of the following battleship. Here were nearly
thirty vessels steaming in company and moving in order with
no lights of any kind except their tiny stern-lights, and constantly changing course in accordance with the prescribed anti-
U-boat ritual. It was five hours since they had had any observation of the land or the heavens. Presently the Admiral joined
me, and I said to him: "Here is one of the things I should be
very sorry to be made responsible for carrying out. How are
you going to make sure you will hit the narrow exit from the
Minches at daylight?" "What would you do, sir," he said,
"if you were at this moment the only person who could give
an order?" I replied at once: "I should anchor and wait till
morning. 'Anchor, Hardy,' as Nelson said." But the Admiral
answered: "We have nearly a hundred fathoms of water beneath us now." I had, of course, complete confidence, gained
over many years, in the Navy, and I only tell this tale to bring
home to the general reader the marvellous skill and precision
with which what seem to landsmen to be impossible feats of
this kind are performed when necessary as a matter of course.

It was eight o'clock before I woke, and we were in the broad waters north of the Minches, steering round the western extremity of Scotland towards Scapa Flow. We were perhaps half an hour's steaming from the entrance to Scapa when a signal reached us saying that several German aircraft had dropped mines in the main entrance we were about to use. Admiral Forbes thereupon decided that he must stand out to the westward for twenty-four hours until the channel had been reported clear, and on this the whole Fleet began to change its course. "I can easily put you ashore in a destroyer if you care to transship," he said. "The *Hood* is already in harbour and can look after you." As I had snatched these three days from London with difficulty, I accepted this offer. Our baggage was rapidly brought on deck; the flagship reduced her speed to three or four knots, and a cutter manned by twelve men in their life-belts was lowered from the davits. My small party was already in it, and I was taking leave of the Admiral when an air-raid alarm sounded, and the whole ship flashed into activity as all the ack-ack batteries were manned and other measures taken.

I was worried that the ship should have had to slow down in waters where we knew there were U-boats, but the Admiral said it was quite all right, and pointed to five destroyers which were circling round her at high speed, while a sixth waited for us. We were a quarter of an hour rowing across the mile that separated us from our destroyer. It was like in the olden times, except that the sailors had not so much practice with the oars. The flagship had already regained her speed and was steaming off after the rest of her Fleet before we climbed on board. All the officers were at their action stations on the destroyer, and we were welcomed by the surgeon, who took us into the wardroom, where all the instruments of his profession were laid out on the table ready for accidents. But no air raid occurred, and we immediately proceeded at high speed into Scapa. We entered through Switha Sound, which is a small and subsidiary channel and was not affected by the mine-dropping. "This is the tradesmen's entrance," said Thompson,

my Flag Commander. It was in fact the one assigned to the
storeships. "It's the only one," said the destroyer lieutenant
stiffly, "that the flotillas are allowed to use." To make everything go well, I asked him if he could remember Kipling's
poem about

"Mines reported in the fairway, warn all traffic and detain.
'Send up . . .' "

and here I let him carry on, which he did correctly:

"Unity, Claribel, Assyrian, Stormcock, and Golden Gain."

We soon found our way to the *Hood*, where Admiral Whitworth received us, having gathered most of his captains, and I
passed a pleasant night on board before the long round of in-
spections which filled the next day. This was the last time I
ever set foot upon the *Hood*, although she had nearly two
years of war service to perform before her destruction by the
Bismarck in 1941.

More than six months of constant exertion and the highest
priorities had repaired the peace-time neglect. The three main
entrances were defended with booms and mines, and three additional blockships among others had already been placed in
Kirk Sound through which Prien's U-boat had slipped to destroy the *Royal Oak*. Many more blockships were yet to come.
A large garrison guarded the base and the still-growing batteries. We had planned for over one hundred and twenty ack-
ack guns with numerous searchlights and a balloon barrage
to command the air over the Fleet anchorage. Not all these
measures were yet complete, but the air defences were already
formidable. Many small craft patrolled the approaches in
ceaseless activity, and two or three squadrons of Hurricane
fighters from the airfields in Caithness could be guided to an
assailant in darkness or daylight by one of the finest radar installations then in existence. At last the Home Fleet had a
home. It was the famous home from which in the previous
war the Royal Navy had ruled the seas.

*   *   *   *   *

Although, as we now know, May 10 was already chosen for
the invasion of France and the Low Countries, Hitler had not
yet fixed the actual date of the prior Norway onslaught. Much
was to precede it. On March 14, Jodl wrote in his diary:

The English keep vigil in the North Sea with fifteen to sixteen
submarines; doubtful whether reason to safeguard own operations
or prevent operations by Germans. Fuehrer has not yet decided
what reason to give for Weser Exercise.

There was a hum of activity in the planning sections of the
German war machine. Preparations both for the attack on
Norway and the invasion of France continued simultaneously
and efficiently. On March 20, Falkenhorst reported that his
side of the "Weser" operation plan was ready. The Fuehrer
held a military conference on the afternoon of March 16, and
D-Day was provisionally fixed, apparently for April 9. Admiral
Raeder reported to the conference:

. . . In my opinion the danger of a British landing in Norway
is no longer acute at present. . . . The question of what the British
will do in the North in the near future can be answered as follows:
They will make further attempts to disrupt German trade in
neutral waters and to cause incidents in order perhaps to create
a pretext for action against Norway. One object has been and still
is to cut off Germany's imports from Narvik. These will be cut off
at least for a time, however, even if the Weser operation is carried
out.
*Sooner or later Germany will be faced with the necessity of
carrying out the Weser operation.* Therefore, it is advisable to do
so as soon as possible, by April 15 at the latest, since after that
date the nights are too short; there will be a new moon on April 7.
The operational possibilities of the Navy will be restricted too
much if the Weser operation is postponed any longer. The submarines can remain in position only for two to three weeks more.
Weather of the type favourable for "Operation *Gelb*" [Yellow] is
not to be waited for in the case of the Weser operation; overcast,
foggy weather is more satisfactory for the latter. The general state
of preparedness of the naval forces and ships is at present good.

*   *   *   *   *

From the beginning of the year, the Soviets had brought their main power to bear on the Finns. They redoubled their efforts to pierce the Mannerheim Line before the melting of the snows. Alas, this year the spring and its thaw, on which the hard-pressed Finns based their hopes, came nearly six weeks late. The great Soviet offensive on the Isthmus, which was to last forty-two days, opened on February 1, combined with heavy air-bombing of base depots and railway junctions behind the lines. Ten days of heavy bombardment from Soviet guns, massed wheel to wheel, heralded the main infantry attack. After a fortnight's fighting, the line was breached. The air attacks on the key fort and base of Viipuri increased in intensity. By the end of the month, the Mannerheim defence system had been disorganised, and the Russians were able to concentrate against the Gulf of Viipuri. The Finns were short of ammunition and their troops exhausted.

The honourable correctitude which had deprived us of any strategic initiative equally hampered all effective measures for sending munitions to Finland. We had been able so far only to send from our own scanty store contributions insignificant to the Finns. In France, however, a warmer and deeper sentiment prevailed, and this was strongly fostered by M. Daladier. On March 2, without consulting the British Government, he agreed to send fifty thousand volunteers and a hundred bombers to Finland. We could certainly not act on this scale, and in view of the documents found on the German major in Belgium, and of the ceaseless Intelligence reports of the steady massing of German troops on the Western Front, it went far beyond what prudence would allow. However, it was agreed to send fifty British bombers. On March 12, the Cabinet again decided to revise the plans for military landings at Narvik and Trondheim, to be followed at Stavanger and Bergen, as a part of the extended help to Finland into which we had been drawn by the French. These plans were to be available for action on March 20, although the need of Norwegian and Swedish permission had not been met. Meanwhile, on March 7, Mr. Paasikivi had gone again to Moscow;

this time to discuss armistice terms. On the twelfth, the Russian terms were accepted by the Finns. All our plans for military landings were again shelved, and the forces which were being collected were to some extent dispersed. The two divisions which had been held back in England were now allowed to proceed to France, and our striking power towards Norway was reduced to eleven battalions.

* * * * *

Meanwhile, "Operation Royal Marine" had ripened. Five months of intensive effort with Admiralty priorities behind it had brought its punctual fruition. Admiral Fitzgerald and his trained detachments of British naval officers and marines, each man aflame with the idea of a novel stroke in the war, were established on the upper reaches of the Rhine, ready to strike when permission could be obtained. My detailed explanation of the plan will be found in Appendix L, Book II. In March all preparations were perfected and I at length appealed both to my colleagues and to the French. The War Cabinet were very ready to let me begin this carefully prepared offensive plan, and left it to me, with Foreign Office support, to do what I could with the French. In all their wars and troubles in my lifetime I have been bound-up with the French, and I believed that they would do as much for me as for any other foreigner alive. But in this phase of "twilight war" I could not move them. When I pressed very hard, they used a method of refusal which I never met before or since. M. Daladier told me with an air of exceptional formality that "The President of the Republic himself had intervened, and that no aggressive action must be taken which might only draw reprisals upon France." This idea of not irritating the enemy did not commend itself to me. Hitler had done his best to strangle our commerce by the indiscriminate mining of our harbours. We had beaten him by defensive means alone. Good, decent, civilised people, it appeared, must never strike themselves till after they have been struck dead. In these days the fearful German volcano and all its subterranean fires drew near to their explosion point. There were still months of pretended war. On the one side endless discussions about trivial points, no decisions taken, or if taken rescinded, and the rule "Don't be unkind to the enemy, you will only make him angry." On the other, doom preparing — a vast machine grinding forward ready to break upon us!

*　　*　　*　　*　　*

The military collapse of Finland led to further repercussions. On March 18, Hitler met Mussolini at the Brenner Pass. Hitler deliberately gave the impression to his Italian host that there was no question of Germany launching a land offensive in the West. On the nineteenth, Mr. Chamberlain spoke in the House of Commons. In view of growing criticism he revived in some detail the story of British aid to Finland. He rightly emphasised that our main consideration had been the desire to respect the neutrality of Norway and Sweden, and he also defended the Government for not being hustled into attempts to succour the Finns which had offered little chance of success. The defeat of Finland was fatal to the Daladier Government, whose chief had taken so marked, if tardy, action, and who had personally given disproportionate prominence to this part of our anxieties. On March 21, a new Cabinet was formed under M. Reynaud, pledged to an increasingly vigorous conduct of the war.

My relations with M. Reynaud stood on a different footing from any I had established with M. Daladier. Reynaud, Mandel, and I had felt the same emotions about Munich. Daladier had been on the other side. I therefore welcomed the change in the French Government, and I also hoped that my fluvial mines would now have a better chance of acceptance.

Mr. Churchill to M. Reynaud. *March* 22, 1940.

I cannot tell you how glad I am that all has been accomplished so successfully and speedily, and especially that Daladier has been rallied to your Cabinet. This is much admired over here, and also Blum's self-effacing behaviour.

I rejoice that you are at the helm, and that Mandel is with you, and I look forward to the very closest and most active co-operation between our two Governments. I share, as you know, all the anxieties you expressed to me the other night about the general course of the war, and the need for strenuous and drastic measures; but I little thought when we spoke that events would soon take a decisive turn for you. We have thought so much alike during the last three or four years that I am most hopeful that the closest understanding will prevail, and that I may contribute to it.

I now send you the letter which I wrote to Gamelin upon the business which brought me to Paris last week, and I beg you to give the project your immediate sympathetic consideration. Both the Prime Minister and Lord Halifax have become very keen upon this operation ["Royal Marine"], and we were all three about to press it strongly upon your predecessor. It seems a great pity to lose this valuable time. I have now upwards of six thousand mines ready and moving forward in an endless flow — alas, only on land — and of course there is always danger of secrecy being lost when delays occur.

I look forward to an early meeting of the Supreme Council, where I trust concerted action may be arranged between French and English *colleagues* — for that is what we are.

Pray give my kind regards to Mandel, and believe me, with the warmest wishes for your success, in which our common safety is deeply involved.

The French Ministers came to London for a meeting of the Supreme War Council on March 28. Mr. Chamberlain opened with a full and clear description of the scene as he saw it. To my great satisfaction he said his first proposal was that "a certain operation, generally known as the 'Royal Marine,' should be put into operation immediately." He described how this project would be carried out and stated that stocks had been accumulated for effective and continuous execution. There would be complete surprise. The operation would take place in that part of the Rhine used almost exclusively for military purposes. No similar operation had ever been carried out before, nor had equipment previously been designed capable of taking advantage of river conditions and working successfully against the barrages and types of craft found in rivers.

Finally, owing to the design of the weapon, neutral waters would not be affected. The British anticipated that this attack would create the utmost consternation and confusion. It was well known that no people were more thorough than the Germans in preparation and planning; but equally no people could be more completely upset when their plans miscarried. They could not improvise. Again, the war had found the German railways in a precarious state, and therefore their dependence on their inland waterways had increased. In addition to the floating mines, other weapons had been designed to be dropped from aircraft in canals within Germany itself, where there was no current. He urged that surprise depended upon speed. Secrecy would be endangered by delay, and the river conditions were about to be particularly favourable. As to German retaliation, if Germany thought it worth while to bomb French or British cities, she would not wait for a pretext. Everything was ready. It was only necessary for the French High Command to give the order.

He then said that Germany had two weaknesses: her supplies of iron ore and of oil. The main sources of supply of these were situated at the opposite ends of Europe. The iron ore came from the North. He unfolded with precision the case for intercepting the German iron-ore supplies from Sweden. He dealt also with the Rumanian and Baku oilfields, which ought to be denied to Germany, if possible by diplomacy. I listened to this powerful argument with increasing pleasure. I had not realised how fully Mr. Chamberlain and I were agreed.

M. Reynaud spoke of the impact of German propaganda upon French morale. The German radio blared each night that the Reich had no quarrel with France; that the origin of the war was to be found in the blank cheque given by Britain to Poland; that France had been dragged into war at the heels of the British; and even that she was not in a position to sustain the struggle. Goebbels' policy towards France seemed to be to let the war run on at the present reduced tempo, counting upon growing discouragement among the five

million Frenchmen now called-up and upon the emergence
of a French Government willing to come to compromise terms
with Germany at the expense of Great Britain.

The question, he said, was widely asked in France, "How
can the Allies win the war?" The number of divisions, "despite British efforts," was increasing faster on the German side
than on ours. When, therefore, could we hope to secure that superiority in man-power required for successful action in the
West? We had no knowledge of what was going on in Germany in material equipment. There was a general feeling in
France that the war had reached a deadlock, and that Germany
had only to wait. Unless some action were taken to cut the
enemy's supply of oil and other raw material, "the feeling
might grow that blockade was not a weapon strong enough to
secure victory for the Allied cause." About the operation
"Royal Marine," he said that, though good in itself, it could
not be decisive, and that any reprisals would fall upon France.
However, if other things were settled, he would make a special
effort to secure French concurrence. He was far more respon-
sive about cutting off supplies of Swedish iron ore, and he
stated that there was an exact relation between the supplies
of Swedish iron ore to Germany and the output of the German iron and steel industry. His conclusion was that the Allies should lay mines in the territorial waters along the Norwegian coast and later obstruct by similar action ore being
carried from the port of Lulea to Germany. He emphasised
the importance of hampering German supplies of Rumanian
oil.

It was at last decided that, after addressing communications
in general terms to Norway and Sweden, we should lay minefields in Norwegian territorial waters on April 5, and that,
subject to the concurrence of the French War Committee,
"Royal Marine" should be begun by launching the fluvial
mines in the Rhine on April 4, and on April 15 upon the German canals from the air. It was also agreed that if Germany
invaded Belgium the Allies should immediately move into
that country without waiting for a formal invitation; and that if

Germany invaded Holland, and Belgium did not go to her assistance, the Allies should consider themselves free to enter
Belgium for the purpose of helping Holland.

Finally, as an obvious point on which all were at one, the
communiqué stated that the British and French Governments
had agreed on the following solemn declaration:

*That during the present war they would neither negotiate nor
conclude an armistice or treaty of peace except by mutual agreement.*

This pact later acquired high importance.

* * * * *

On April 3, the British Cabinet implemented the resolve of
the Supreme War Council, and the Admiralty was authorised
to mine the Norwegian Leads on April 8. I called the actual
mining operation "Wilfred," because by itself it was so small
and innocent. As our mining of Norwegian waters might
provoke a German retort, it was also agreed that a British
brigade and a French contingent should be sent to Narvik to
clear the port and advance to the Swedish frontier. Other
forces should be dispatched to Stavanger, Bergen, and Trondheim, in order to deny these bases to the enemy.

It is worth while looking back on the stages by which at
last the decision to mine the Leads was reached.[1] I had asked

[1] September 29, 1939. First Lord calls attention of the Cabinet to the value
of Swedish iron ore to the German economy.

November 27, 1939. First Lord addresses a minute to the First Sea Lord asking for examination of proposal to mine the Leads.

December 15, 1939. First Lord raises in Cabinet the question of iron-ore
shipments to Germany.

December 16, 1939. Circulation of detailed memorandum on the subject to
the Cabinet.

December 22, 1939. Memorandum considered by the Cabinet.

February 5, 1940. Detailed discussion of issue in connection with aid to Finland at Supreme War Council in Paris (W.S.C. present).

February 19, 1940. Renewed discussion of mining of Leads in British Cabinet. Admiralty authorised to make preparations.

February 29, 1940. Authorisation cancelled.

March 28, 1940. Resolution of Supreme War Council that minefields should
be laid.

April 3, 1940. Final decision taken by British Cabinet.

April 8, 1940. The minefields laid.

for it on September 29, 1939. Nothing relevant had altered
in the meanwhile. The moral and technical objections on the
score of neutrality, the possibility of German retaliation against
Norway, the importance of stopping the flow of iron ore from
Narvik to Germany, the effect on neutral and world-wide opinion — all were exactly the same. But at last the Supreme War
Council was convinced, and at last the War Cabinet were reconciled to the scheme, and indeed resolved upon it. Once
had they given consent and withdrawn it. Then their minds
had been overlaid by the complications of the Finnish War.
On sixty days "Aid to Finland" had been part of the Cabinet
agenda. Nothing had come of it all. Finland had been
crushed into submission by Russia. Now after all this vain
boggling, hesitation, changes of policy, arguments between
good and worthy people unending, we had at last reached
the simple point on which action had been demanded seven
months before. But in war seven months is a long time. Now
Hitler was ready, and ready with a far more powerful and
well-prepared plan. One can hardly find a more perfect example of the impotence and fatuity of waging war by committee or rather by groups of committees. It fell to my lot in
the weeks which followed to bear much of the burden and
some of the odium of the ill-starred Norwegian campaign, the
course of which will presently be described. Had I been allowed to act with freedom and design when I first demanded
permission, a far more agreeable conclusion might have been
reached in this key theatre, with favourable consequences in
every direction. But now all was to be disaster.

> He who will not when he may,
> When he will, he shall have Nay.

* * * * *

It may here be right to set forth the various offensive proposals and devices which in my subordinate position I put
forward during the "Twilight War." The first was the entry
and domination of the Baltic, which was the sovereign plan if
it were possible. It was vetoed by the growing realisation of

the air power. The second was the creation of a close-action squadron of naval tortoises not too much afraid of the air-bomb or torpedo, by the reconstruction of the *Royal Sovereign* class of battleships. This fell by the way through the movement of the war and the priorities which had to be given to aircraft carriers. The third was the simple tactical operation of laying mines in the Norwegian Leads to cut off the vital German iron-ore supplies. Fourthly comes "Cultivator Number 6": [2] namely, a long-term means for breaking a deadlock on the French Front without a repetition of the slaughter of the previous war. This was superseded by the onrush of German armour turning our own invention of tanks to our undoing, and proving the ascendancy of the offensive in this new war. The fifth was the "Operation Royal Marine," namely, the paralysing of traffic on the Rhine by the dropping and discharge of fluvial mines. This played its limited part and proved its virtue from the moment when it was permitted. It was, however, swept away in the general collapse of the French resistance. In any case it required prolonged application to cause major injury to the enemy.

To sum up: in the war of armies on the ground I was under the thrall of defensive fire-power. On the sea I strove persistently within my sphere to assert the initiative against the enemy as a relief from the terrible ordeal of presenting our enormous target of sea commerce to his attack. But in this prolonged trance of the "Twilight" or "Phoney" war, as it was commonly called in the United States, neither France nor Britain was capable of meeting the German vengeance thrust. It was only after France had been flattened out that Britain, thanks to her island advantage, developed out of the pangs of defeat and the menace of annihilation a national resolve equal to that of Germany.

* * * * *

Ominous items of news of varied credibility now began to come in. At the meeting of the War Cabinet on April 3,

2 See Appendix J, Book II.

the Secretary of State for War told us that a report had been
received at the War Office that the Germans had been collecting strong forces of troops at Rostock with the intention of
taking Scandinavia if necessary. The Foreign Secretary said
that the news from Stockholm tended to confirm this report.
According to the Swedish Legation in Berlin, two hundred
thousand tons of German shipping were now concentrated at
Stettin and Swinemunde with troops on board which rumour
placed at four hundred thousand. It was suggested that these
forces were in readiness to deliver a counter-stroke against a
possible attack by us upon Narvik or other Norwegian ports,
about which the Germans were said to be still nervous.

Soon we learnt that the French War Committee would not
agree to the launching of "Royal Marine." They were in
favour of mining the Norwegian Leads, but opposed to anything that might draw retaliation on France. Through the
French Ambassador Reynaud expressed his regret. Mr. Chamberlain, who was much inclined to aggressive action of some
kind at this stage, was vexed at this refusal, and in a conversation with M. Corbin he linked the two operations together.
The British would cut off the ore supplies of Germany as the
French desired, provided that at the same time the French allowed us to retaliate by means of "Royal Marine" for all the
injuries we had suffered and were enduring from the magnetic
mine. Keen as I was on "Royal Marine," I had not expected
him to go so far as this. Both operations were methods of making offensive war upon the enemy, and bringing to an end the
twilight period from the prolongation of which I now believed
Germany was the gainer. However, if a few days would enable us to bring the French into agreement upon the punctual
execution of the two projects, I was agreeable to postponing
"Wilfred" for a few days.

The Prime Minister was so favourable to my views at this
juncture that we seemed almost to think as one. He asked me
to go over to Paris and see what I could do to persuade
M. Daladier, who was evidently the stumbling-block. I met
M. Reynaud and several others of his Ministers at dinner on

the night of the fourth at the British Embassy, and we seemed in pretty good agreement. Daladier had been invited to attend, but professed a previous engagement. It was arranged that I should see him the next morning. While meaning to do my utmost to persuade Daladier, I asked permission from the Cabinet, to make it clear that we would go forward with "Wilfred" even if "Royal Marine" was vetoed.

I visited Daladier at the Rue St. Dominique at noon on the fifth, and had a serious talk with him. I commented on his absence from our dinner the night before. He pleaded his previous engagement. It was evident to me that a considerable gulf existed between the new and the former Premier. Daladier argued that in three months' time the French aviation would be sufficiently improved for the necessary measures to be taken to meet German reactions to "Royal Marine." For this he was prepared to give a firm date in writing. He made a strong case about the defenceless French factories. Finally he assured me that the period of political crises in France was over, and that he would work in harmony with M. Reynaud. On this we parted.

I reported by telephone to the War Cabinet, who were agreed that "Wilfred" should go forward notwithstanding the French refusal of "Royal Marine," but wished this to be the subject of a formal communication. At their meeting on April 5, the Foreign Secretary was instructed to inform the French Government that notwithstanding the great importance we had throughout attached to carrying out the "Royal Marine" operation at an early date, and simultaneously with the proposed operation in Norwegian territorial waters, we were nevertheless prepared as a concession to their wishes to proceed with the latter alone. The date was thus finally fixed for April 8.

* * * * *

On Friday, April 5, 1940, the Prime Minister addressed the Central Council of the National Union of Conservative and Unionist Associations in a spirit of unusual optimism:

After seven months of war I feel ten times as confident of victory as I did at the beginning. . . . I feel that during the seven months our relative position towards the enemy has become a great deal stronger than it was.

Consider the difference between the ways of a country like Germany and our own. Long before the war Germany was making preparations for it. She was increasing her armed forces on land and in the air with feverish haste; she was devoting all her resources to turning out arms and equipment and to building up huge reserves of stocks; in fact, she was turning herself into a fully armed camp. On the other hand, we, a peaceful nation, were carrying on with our peaceful pursuits. It is true that we had been driven by what was going on in Germany to begin to build up again those defences which we had so long left in abeyance, but we postponed as long as any hope of peace remained — we continually postponed — those drastic measures which were necessary if we were to put the country onto a war footing.

The result was that when war did break out, German preparations were far ahead of our own, and it was natural then to expect that the enemy would take advantage of his initial superiority to make an endeavor to overwhelm us and France before we had time to make good our deficiencies. Is it not a very extraordinary thing that no such attempt was made? Whatever may be the reason — whether it was that Hitler thought he might get away with what he had got without fighting for it, or whether it was that after all the preparations were not sufficiently complete — however, one thing is certain: he missed the bus.

And so the seven months that we have had have enabled us to make good and remove our weaknesses, to consolidate, and to tune up every arm, offensive and defensive, and so enormously to add to our fighting strength that we can face the future with a calm and steady mind whatever it brings.

Perhaps you may say, "Yes, but has not the enemy, too, been busy?" I have not the slightest doubt he has. I would be the last to underrate the [his] strength or determination to use that strength without scruple and without mercy if he thinks he can do so without getting his blows returned with interest. I grant that. But I say this too: the very completeness of his preparations has left him very little margin of strength still to call upon.

This proved an ill-judged utterance. Its main assumption that we and the French were relatively stronger than at the beginning of the war was not reasonable. As has been previously explained, the Germans were now in the fourth year of vehement munition manufacture, whereas we were at a much earlier stage, probably comparable in fruitfulness to the second year. Moreover, with every month that had passed, the German Army, now four years old, was becoming a mature and perfected weapon, and the former advantage of the French Army in training and cohesion was steadily passing away. The Prime Minister showed no premonition that we were on the eve of great events, whereas it seemed almost certain to me that the land war was about to begin. Above all, the expression "Hitler missed the bus" was unlucky.

All lay in suspense. The various minor expedients I had been able to suggest had gained acceptance; but nothing of a major character had been done by either side. Our plans, such as they were, rested upon enforcing the blockade by the mining of the Norwegian corridor in the North, and by hampering German oil supplies from the Southeast. Complete immobility and silence reigned behind the German Front. Suddenly, the passive or small-scale policy of the Allies was swept away by a cataract of violent surprises. We were to learn what total war means.

12

The Clash at Sea

April, 1940

*Lord Chatfield's Retirement — The Prime Minister Invites Me to
Preside over the Military Co-ordination Committee — An Awkward Arrangement — "Wilfred" — Oslo — The German Seizure
of Norway — Tragedy of Neutrality — All the Fleets at Sea —
The "Glowworm" — The "Renown" Engages the "Scharnhorst"
and "Gneisenau" — The Home Fleet off Bergen — Action by
British Submarines — Warburton-Lee's Flotilla at Narvik —
Supreme War Council Meets in London, April 9 — Its Conclu-
sions — My Minute to the First Sea Lord, April 10 — Anger in
England — Debate in Parliament, April 11 — The "Warspite"
and Her Flotilla Exterminate the German Destroyers at Narvik
— Letter from the King.*

BEFORE RESUMING THE NARRATIVE, I must explain the alterations in my position which occurred during the month
of April, 1940.

Lord Chatfield's office as Minister for the Co-ordination of
Defence had become redundant, and on the third, Mr. Chamberlain accepted his resignation, which he proffered freely.
On the fourth, a statement was issued from Number 10 Downing
Street that it was not proposed to fill the vacant post, but that
arrangements were being made for the First Lord of the Admiralty, as the senior Service Minister concerned, to preside
over the Military Co-ordination Committee. Accordingly
I took the chair at its meetings, which were held daily, and
sometimes twice daily, from the eighth to the fifteenth of April.

I had, therefore, an exceptional measure of responsibility but
no power of effective direction. Among the other Service Ministers, who were also members of the War Cabinet, I was "first
among equals." I had, however, no power to take or to enforce
decisions. I had to carry with me both the Service Ministers
and their professional chiefs. Thus, many important and able
men had a right and duty to express their views of the swiftly
changing phases of the battle — for battle it was — which now
began.

The Chiefs of Staff sat daily together after discussing the
whole situation with their respective Ministers. They then
arrived at their own decisions, which obviously became of
dominant importance. I learned about these either from the
First Sea Lord, who kept nothing from me, or by the various
memoranda or *aides-mémoires* which the Chiefs of Staff Committee issued. If I wished to question any of these opinions,
I could of course raise them in the first instance at my Co-
ordinating Committee, where the Chiefs of Staff, supported by
their departmental Ministers whom they had usually carried
along with them, were all present as individual members.
There was a copious flow of polite conversation, at the end
of which a tactful report was drawn up by the secretary in
attendance and checked by the three service departments to
make sure there were no discrepancies. Thus we had arrived
at those broad, happy uplands where everything is settled for
the greatest good of the greatest number by the common
sense of most after the consultation of all. But in war of the
kind we were now to feel, the conditions were different. Alas,
I must write it: the actual conflict had to be more like one
ruffian bashing the other on the snout with a club, a hammer,
or something better. All this is deplorable, and it is one of
the many good reasons for avoiding war and having everything settled by agreement in a friendly manner, with full consideration for the rights of minorities and the faithful recording of dissentient opinions.

The Defence Committee of the War Cabinet sat almost
every day to discuss the reports of the Military Co-ordination

Committee and those of the Chiefs of Staff; and their conclusions or divergences were again referred to frequent Cabinets. All had to be explained and re-explained; and by the time this process was completed, the whole scene had often changed. At the Admiralty, which is of necessity in wartime a battle headquarters, decisions affecting the Fleet were taken on the instant, and only in the gravest cases referred to the Prime Minister, who supported us on every occasion. Where the action of the other services was involved, the procedure could not possibly keep pace with events. However, at the beginning of the Norway campaign the Admiralty in the nature of things had three-quarters of the executive business in its own hands.

I do not pretend that, whatever my powers, I should have been able to take better decisions or reach good solutions of the problems with which we were now confronted. The impact of the events about to be described was so violent and the conditions so chaotic that I soon perceived that only the authority of the Prime Minister could reign over the Military Co-ordination Committee. Accordingly, on the fifteenth, I requested Mr. Chamberlain to take the chair, and he presided at practically every one of our subsequent meetings during the campaign in Norway. He and I continued in close agreement, and he gave his supreme authority to the views which I expressed. I was most intimately involved in the conduct of the unhappy effort to rescue Norway when it was already too late. The change in chairmanship was announced to Parliament by the Prime Minister in reply to a question as follows: "I have agreed, at the request of the First Lord of the Admiralty, to take the chair myself at the meetings of the Co-ordination Committee when matters of exceptional importance relating to the general conduct of the war are under discussion."

Loyalty and good will were forthcoming from all concerned. Nevertheless, both the Prime Minister and I were acutely conscious of the formlessness of our system, especially when in contact with the surprising course of events. Although the Admiralty was at this time inevitably the prime mover, obvious

objections could be raised to an organisation in which one of
the Service Ministers attempted to concert all the operations
of the other services, while at the same time managing the
whole business of the Admiralty and having a special responsibility for the naval movements. These difficulties were not removed by the fact that the Prime Minister himself took the
chair and backed me up. But while one stroke of misfortune
after another, the results of want of means or of indifferent
management, fell upon us, almost daily, I nevertheless continued to hold my position in this fluid, friendly, but unfocused
circle.

* * * * *

On the evening of Friday, April 5, the German Minister in
Oslo invited distinguished guests, including members of the
Government, to a film show at the Legation. The film depicted
the German conquest of Poland, and culminated in a crescendo
of horror scenes during the German bombing of Warsaw. The
caption read: "For this they could thank their English and
French friends." The party broke up in silence and dismay.
The Norwegian Government was, however, chiefly concerned
with the activities of the British. Between 4.30 and 5 A.M. on
April 8, four British destroyers laid our minefield off the entrance to West Fiord, the channel to the port of Narvik. At
5 A.M. the news was broadcast from London, and at 5.30 a
note from His Majesty's Government was handed to the Norwegian Foreign Minister. The morning in Oslo was spent in
drafting protests to London. But later that afternoon, the Admiralty informed the Norwegian Legation in London that
German warships had been sighted off the Norwegian coast
proceeding northwards, and presumably bound for Narvik.
About the same time reports reached the Norwegian capital
that a German troopship, the *Rio de Janeiro,* had been sunk
off the south coast of Norway by the Polish submarine *Orzel,*
that large numbers of German soldiers had been rescued by
the local fishermen, and that they said they were bound for
Bergen to help the Norwegians defend their country against
the British and French. More was to come. Germany had

broken into Denmark, but the news did not reach Norway until after she herself was invaded. Thus she received no warning. Denmark was easily overrun after a formal resistance in which a few soldiers of the King of Denmark's Guard were killed.

That night German warships approached Oslo. The outer batteries opened fire. The Norwegian defending force consisted of a minelayer, the *Olav Tryggvason,* and two minesweepers. After dawn two German minesweepers entered the mouth of the fiord to disembark troops in the neighbourhood of the shore batteries. One was sunk by the *Olav Tryggvason,* but the German troops were landed and the batteries taken. The gallant minelayer, however, held off two German destroyers at the mouth of the fiord and damaged the cruiser *Emden.* An armed Norwegian whaler mounting a single gun also went into action at once and without special orders against the invaders. Her gun was smashed and the Commander had both legs shot off. To avoid unnerving his men, he rolled himself overboard and died nobly. The main German force, led by the heavy cruiser *Bluecher,* now entered the fiord, making for the narrows defended by the fortress of Oskarborg. The Norwegian batteries opened, and two torpedoes fired from the shore at five hundred yards scored a decisive strike. The *Bluecher* sank rapidly, taking with her the senior officers of the German Administrative Staff and detachments of the Gestapo. The other German ships, including the *Luetzov,* retired. The damaged *Emden* took no further part in the fighting at sea. Oslo was ultimately taken, not from the sea, but by troop-carrying airplanes and by landings in the fiord.

Hitler's plan immediately flashed into its full scope. German forces descended at Kristiansand, at Stavanger, and to the north at Bergen and Trondheim. The most daring stroke was at Narvik. For a week supposedly empty German ore ships returning to that port in the ordinary course had been moving up the corridor sanctified by Norwegian neutrality, filled with supplies and ammunition. Ten German destroyers, each carrying two hundred soldiers, and supported by the *Scharnhorst* and *Gneisenau,* had left Germany some days before, and reached Narvik early on the ninth.

Two Norwegian warships, *Norge* and *Eidsvold,* lay in the
fiord. They were prepared to fight to the last. At dawn
destroyers were sighted approaching the harbour at high speed,
but in the prevailing snow-squalls their identity was not at
first established. Soon a German officer appeared in a motor
launch and demanded the surrender of the *Eidsvold.* On receiving from the commanding officer the curt reply, "I attack,"
he withdrew, but almost at once the ship was destroyed with
nearly all hands by a volley of torpedoes. Meanwhile, the
Norge opened fire, but in a few minutes she too was torpedoed
and sank instantly.

In this gallant but hopeless resistance two hundred and
eighty-seven Norwegian seamen perished, less than a hundred
being saved from the two ships. Thereafter the capture of
Narvik was easy. It was a strategic key — for ever to be denied
us.

*   *   *   *   *

Surprise, ruthlessness, and precision were the characteristics
of the onslaught upon innocent and naked Norway. Nowhere
did the initial landing forces exceed two thousand men. Seven
army divisions were employed, embarking principally from
Hamburg and Bremen, and for the follow-up from Stettin and
Danzig. Three divisions were used in the assault phase, and
four supported them through Oslo and Trondheim. Eight
hundred operational aircraft and two hundred and fifty to
three hundred transport planes were the salient and vital feature of the design. Within forty-eight hours all the main ports
of Norway were in the German grip.

*   *   *   *   *

On the night of Sunday the seventh, our air reconnaissance
reported that a German fleet, consisting of a battle cruiser, two
light cruisers, fourteen destroyers, and another ship, probably
a transport, had been seen the day before moving towards the
Naze across the mouth of the Skagerrak. We found it hard at
the Admiralty to believe that this force was going to Narvik. In
spite of a report from Copenhagen that Hitler meant to seize

that port, it was thought by the Naval Staff that the German
ships would probably turn back into the Skagerrak. Nevertheless, the following movement was at once ordered. The Home
Fleet, comprising *Rodney, Repulse, Valiant,* two cruisers and
ten destroyers, was already under steam and left Scapa at 8.30
p.m. on April 7; the Second Cruiser Squadron of two cruisers
and fifteen destroyers started from Rosyth at 10 p.m. on the
same night. The First Cruiser Squadron, which had been embarking troops at Rosyth for the possible occupation of Norwegian ports, was ordered to march her soldiers ashore, even
without their equipment, and join the fleet at sea at the earliest
moment. The cruiser *Aurora* and six destroyers similarly
engaged in the Clyde were ordered to Scapa. All these decisive
steps were concerted with the Commander-in-Chief. In short,
everything available was ordered out on the assumption — which he had by no means accepted — that a major
emergency had come. At the same time the mine-laying operation off Narvik, by four destroyers, was in progress, covered
by the battle cruiser *Renown,* the cruiser *Birmingham,* and
eight destroyers.

When the War Cabinet met on Monday morning, I reported
that the minefields in the West Fiord had been laid between
4.30 and 5.00 a.m. I also explained in detail that all our fleets
were at sea. But by now we had assurance that the main
German naval force was undoubtedly making towards Narvik.
On the way to lay the minefield "Wilfred," one of our destroyers, the *Glowworm,* having lost a man overboard during
the night, stopped behind to search for him and became separated from the rest of the force. At 8.30 a.m. on the eighth,
the *Glowworm* had reported herself engaged with an enemy destroyer about one hundred and fifty miles southwest of West
Fiord. Shortly afterwards she had reported seeing another
destroyer ahead of her, and later that she was engaging a
superior force. After 9.45 she had become silent, since
when nothing had been heard from her. On this it was
calculated that the German forces, unless intercepted, could
reach Narvik about ten that night. They would, we hoped, be

engaged by the *Renown*, *Birmingham*, and their destroyers.
An action might, therefore, take place very shortly. "It was
impossible," I said, "to forecast the hazards of war, but such
an action should not be on terms unfavourable for us." Moreover, the Commander-in-Chief with the whole Home Fleet
would be approaching the scene from the south. He would
now be about opposite Statland. He was fully informed on all
points known to us, though naturally he was remaining silent.
The Germans knew that the Fleet was at sea, since a U-boat
near the Orkneys had been heard to transmit a long message
as the Fleet left Scapa. Meanwhile, the Second Cruiser Squadron off Aberdeen, moving north, had reported that it was
being shadowed by aircraft and expected to be attacked
about noon. All possible measures were being taken by the
Navy and the R.A.F. to bring fighters to the scene. No aircraft carriers were available, but flying boats were working.
The weather was thick in places, but believed to be better in
the north, and improving.

The War Cabinet took note of my statement and invited
me to pass on to the Norwegian naval authorities the information we had received about German naval movements. On
the whole, the opinion was that Hitler's aim was Narvik.

On April 9, Mr. Chamberlain summoned us to a War Cabinet at 8.30 A.M., when the facts, as then known to us, about
the German invasion of Norway and Denmark were discussed.
The War Cabinet agreed that I should authorise the Commander-in-Chief of the Home Fleet to take all possible steps to
clear Bergen and Trondheim of enemy forces, and that the
Chiefs of Staff should set on foot preparations for military expeditions to recapture both those places and to occupy Narvik.
These expeditions should not, however, move until the naval
situation had been cleared up.

* * * * *

Since the war we have learned from German records what
happened to the *Glowworm*. Early on the morning of Monday
the eighth, she encountered first one and then a second enemy

destroyer. A running fight ensued in a heavy sea until the cruiser *Hipper* appeared on the scene. When the *Hipper* opened fire, the *Glowworm* retired behind a smoke-screen. The *Hipper*, pressing on through the smoke, presently emerged to find the British destroyer very close and coming straight for her at full speed. There was no time for the *Hipper* to avoid the impact, and the *Glowworm* rammed her 10,000-ton adversary, tearing a hole forty metres wide in her side. She then fell away crippled and blazing. A few minutes later she blew up. The *Hipper* picked up forty survivors; her gallant captain was being hauled to safety when he fell back exhausted from the cruiser's deck and was lost. Thus the *Glowworm's* light was quenched, but her captain, Lieutenant-Commander Gerard Roope, who commanded, was awarded the Victoria Cross posthumously, and the story will long be remembered.

When the *Glowworm's* signals ceased abruptly, we had good hopes of bringing to action the main German forces which had ventured so far. During Monday we had a superior force on either side of them. Calculations of the sea areas to be swept gave prospects of contact, and any contact meant concentration upon them. We did not then know that the *Hipper* was escorting German forces to Trondheim. She entered Trondheim that night, but the *Glowworm* had put this powerful vessel out of action for a month.

Vice-Admiral Whitworth in the *Renown*, on receiving *Glowworm's* signals, first steered south, hoping to intercept the enemy, but on later information and Admiralty instructions he decided to cover the approaches to Narvik. Tuesday the ninth was a tempestuous day, with the seas running high under furious gales and snowstorms. At early dawn the *Renown* sighted two darkened ships some fifty miles to seaward of West Fiord. These were the *Scharnhorst* and *Gneisenau*, who had just completed the task of escorting their expedition to Narvik, but at the time it was believed that only one of the two was a battle cruiser. The *Renown* opened fire first at eighteen thousand yards and soon hit the *Gneisenau*, destroying her main gun-control equipment and for a time causing her to

stop firing. Her consort screened her with smoke, both ships
then turned away to the north, and the action became a chase.
Meanwhile, the *Renown* had received two hits, but these
caused little damage, and presently she scored a second and
later a third hit on the *Gneisenau*. In the heavy seas the *Renown* drove forward at full speed, but soon had to reduce to
twenty knots. Amid intermittent snow-squalls and German
smoke-screens the fire on both sides became ineffective. Although the *Renown* strained herself to the utmost in trying
to overhaul the German ships, they at last drew away out of
sight to the northward.

*   *   *   *   *

On the morning of April 9, Admiral Forbes with the
main fleet was abreast of Bergen. At 6.20 A.M. he asked
the Admiralty for news of the German strength there, as he intended to send in a force of cruisers and destroyers under Vice-
Admiral Layton to attack any German ships they might find.
The Admiralty had the same idea, and at 8.20 made him the
following signal:

Prepare plans for attacking German warships and transports
in Bergen and for controlling the approaches to the port on the
supposition that defences are still in hands of Norwegians. Similar
plans as regards Trondheim should also be prepared if you have
sufficient forces for both.

The Admiralty sanctioned Admiral Forbes' plan for attacking Bergen, but later warned him that he must no longer
count on the defences being friendly. To avoid dispersion,
the attack on Trondheim was postponed until the German
battle cruisers should be found. At about 11.30 four cruisers
and seven destroyers, under the Vice-Admiral, started for Bergen, eighty miles away, making only sixteen knots against a
head wind and a rough sea. Presently aircraft reported two
cruisers in Bergen instead of one. With only seven destroyers
the prospects of success were distinctly reduced, unless our
cruisers went in too. The First Sea Lord thought the risk to

these vessels, both from mines and the air, excessive. He consulted me on my return from the Cabinet meeting, and after reading the signals which had passed during the morning, and a brief discussion in the War Room, I concurred in his view. We therefore cancelled the attack. Looking back on this affair, I consider that the Admiralty kept too close control upon the Commander-in-Chief, and after learning his original intention to force the passage into Bergen, we should have confined ourselves to sending him information.

That afternoon, strong air attacks were made on the Fleet, chiefly against Vice-Admiral Layton's ships. The destroyer *Gurkha* was sunk, and the cruisers *Southampton* and *Glasgow* damaged by near misses. In addition the flagship *Rodney* was hit, but her strong deck-armour prevented serious damage.

When the cruiser attack on Bergen was cancelled, Admiral Forbes proposed to use torpedo-carrying naval aircraft from the carrier *Furious* at dusk on April 10. The Admiralty agreed, and also arranged attacks by R.A.F. bombers on the evening of the ninth and by naval aircraft from Hatston (Orkney) on the morning of the tenth. Meanwhile, our cruisers and destroyers continued to blockade the approaches. The air attacks were successful, and the cruiser *Koenigsberg* was sunk by three bombs from naval aircraft. The *Furious* was now diverted to Trondheim, where our air patrols reported two enemy cruisers and two destroyers. Eighteen aircraft attacked at dawn on the eleventh, but found only two destroyers and a submarine besides merchant ships. Unluckily the wounded *Hipper* had left during the night, no cruisers were found, and the attack on the two German destroyers failed because our torpedoes grounded in shallow water before reaching their targets.

Meanwhile, our submarines were active in the Skagerrak and Kattegat. On the night of the eighth, they had sighted and attacked enemy ships northward-bound from the Baltic, but without success. However, on the ninth the *Truant* sank the cruiser *Karlsruhe* off Kristiansand, and the following night the *Spearfish* torpedoed the pocket battleship *Luetzow* returning from Oslo. Besides these successes submarines accounted for at least

nine enemy transports and supply ships with heavy loss of life
during the first week of this campaign. Our own losses were
severe, and three British submarines perished during April in
the heavily defended approaches to the Baltic.

*   *   *   *   *

On the morning of the ninth, the situation at Narvik was
obscure. Hoping to forestall a German seizure of the port, the
Commander-in-Chief directed Captain Warburton-Lee, commanding our destroyers, to enter the fiord and prevent any
landing. Meanwhile, the Admiralty transmitted a press report
to him indicating that one ship had already entered the port
and landed a small force. The message went on:

Proceed to Narvik and sink or capture enemy ship. It is at your
discretion to land forces, if you think you can recapture Narvik
from number of enemy present.

Accordingly, Captain Warburton-Lee, with the five destroyers of his own flotilla, *Hardy, Hunter, Havock, Hotspur,* and
Hostile, entered West Fiord. He was told by Norwegian pilots
at Tranoy that six ships larger than his own and a U-boat had
passed in and that the entrance to the harbour was mined. He
signalled this information and added: "Intend attacking at
dawn." Admiral Whitworth, who received the signals, considered whether he might stiffen the attacking forces from his own
now augmented squadron, but the time seemed too short and
he felt that intervention by him at this stage might cause delay.
In fact, we, in the Admiralty, were not prepared to risk the *Renown* — one of our only two battle cruisers — in such an enterprise. The last Admiralty message passed to Captain Warburton-Lee was as follows:

Norwegian coast defence ships may be in German hands: you
alone can judge whether in these circumstances attack should be
made. Shall support whatever decision you take.

His reply was:

Going into action.

In the mist and snowstorms of April 10, the five British

destroyers steamed up the fiord, and at dawn stood off Narvik. Inside the harbour were five enemy destroyers. In the first attack the *Hardy* torpedoed the ship bearing the pennant of the German Commodore, who was killed; another destroyer was sunk by two torpedoes, and the remaining three were so smothered by gun-fire that they could offer no effective resistance. There were also in the harbour twenty-three merchant ships of various nations, including five British: six German were destroyed. Only three of our five destroyers had hitherto attacked. The *Hotspur* and *Hostile* had been left in reserve to guard against any shore batteries or against fresh German ships approaching. They now joined in a second attack, and the *Hotspur* sank two more merchantmen with torpedoes. Captain Warburton-Lee's ships were unscathed, the enemy's fire was apparently silenced, and after an hour's fighting no ship had come out from any of the inlets against him.

But now fortune turned. As he was coming back from a third attack, Captain Warburton-Lee sighted three fresh ships approaching from Herjangs Fiord. They showed no signs of wishing to close the range, and action began at seven thousand yards. Suddenly out of the mist ahead appeared two more warships. They were not, as was at first hoped, British reinforcements, but German destroyers which had been anchored in Ballangen Fiord. Soon the heavier guns of the German ships began to tell; the bridge of the *Hardy* was shattered, Warburton-Lee mortally stricken, and all his officers and companions killed or wounded except Lieutenant Stanning, his secretary, who took the wheel. A shell then exploded in the engine-room, and under heavy fire the destroyer was beached. The last signal from the *Hardy's* Captain to his flotilla was:

Continue to engage the enemy.

Meanwhile, the *Hunter* had been sunk, and the *Hotspur* and the *Hostile*, which were both damaged, with the *Havock* made for the open sea. The enemy who had barred their passage was by now in no condition to stop them. Half an hour later, they encountered a large ship coming in from the sea, which proved to be the *Rauenfels* carrying the German reserve ammunition.

She was fired upon by the *Havock,* and soon blew up. The survivors of the *Hardy* struggled ashore with the body of their Commander, who was awarded posthumously the Victoria Cross. He and they had left their mark on the enemy and in our naval records.

*   *   *   *   *

On the ninth, MM. Reynaud and Daladier, with Admiral Darlan, flew over to London, and in the afternoon a Supreme War Council meeting was held to deal with what they called "the German action in consequence of the laying of mines within Norwegian territorial waters." Mr. Chamberlain at once pointed out that the enemy's measures had certainly been planned in advance and quite independently of ours. Even at that date this was obvious. M. Reynaud informed us that the French War Committee, presided over by the President, had that morning decided in principle on moving forward into Belgium should the Germans attack. The addition, he said, of eighteen to twenty Belgian divisions, besides the shortening of the front, would to all intents and purposes wipe out the German preponderance in the West. The French would be prepared to connect such an operation with the laying of the fluvial mines in the Rhine. He added that his reports from Belgium and Holland indicated the imminence of a German attack on the Low Countries; some said days, some said hours.

On the question of the military expedition to Norway, the Secretary of State for War reminded the Council that the two British divisions originally assembled for assistance to Finland had since been sent to France. There were only eleven battalions available in the United Kingdom. Two of these were sailing that night. The rest, for various reasons, would not be ready to sail for three or four days or more.

The Council agreed that strong forces should be sent where possible to ports on the Norwegian seaboard, and joint plans were made. A French Alpine division was ordered to embark within two or three days. We were able to provide two British battalions that night, a further five battalions within three days, and four more within fourteen days — eleven in all. Any additional British forces for Scandinavia would have to be withdrawn from France. Suitable measures were to be taken to occupy the Faroe Islands, and assurances of protection would be given to Iceland. Naval arrangements were concerted in the Mediterranean in the event of Italian intervention. It was also decided that urgent representations should be made to the Belgian Government to invite the Allied armies to move forward into Belgium. Finally, it was confirmed that if Germany made an attack in the West or entered Belgium, "Royal Marine" should be carried out.

*   *   *   *   *

I was far from content with what had happened so far in Norway. I wrote to Admiral Pound:

10.IV.40.

The Germans have succeeded in occupying all the ports on the Norwegian coast, including Narvik, and large-scale operations will be required to turn them out of any of them. Norwegian neutrality and our respect for it have made it impossible to prevent this ruthless *coup*. It is now necessary to take a new view. We must put up with the disadvantage of closer air attack on our northern bases. We must seal up Bergen with a watched minefield, and concentrate on Narvik, for which long and severe fighting will be required.

It is immediately necessary to obtain one or two fuelling-bases on the Norwegian coast, and a wide choice presents itself. This is being studied by the Staff. The advantage of our having a base, even improvised, on the Norwegian coast is very great, and now that the enemy have bases there, we cannot carry on without it. The Naval Staff are selecting various alternatives which are suitable anchorages capable of defence, and without communications with the interior. Unless we have this quite soon we cannot compete with the Germans in their new position.

We must also take our advantages in the Faroes.

Narvik must be fought for. Although we have been completely outwitted, there is no reason to suppose that prolonged and serious fighting in this area will not impose a greater drain on the enemy than on ourselves.

For three days we were deluged with reports and rumours

from neutral countries and triumphant claims by Germany of
the losses they had inflicted on the British Navy, and of their
master-stroke in seizing Norway in the teeth of our superior
naval power. It was obvious that Britain had been forestalled,
surprised, and as I had written to the First Sea Lord, outwitted.
Anger swept the country, and the brunt fell upon the Admiralty. On Thursday the eleventh, I had to face a disturbed and
indignant House of Commons. I followed the method I have
always found most effective on such occasions, of giving a calm,
unhurried factual narrative of events in their sequence, laying
full emphasis upon ugly truths. I explained for the first time
in public the disadvantage we had suffered since the beginning
of the war by Germany's abuse of the Norwegian corridor, or
"covered way," and how we had at last overcome the scruple
which "caused us injury at the same time that it did us honour."

It is not the slightest use blaming the Allies for not being able
to give substantial help and protection to neutral countries if we
are held at arm's length until these neutrals are actually attacked
on a scientifically prepared plan by Germany. The strict ob-
servance of neutrality by Norway has been a contributory cause to
the sufferings to which she is now exposed and to the limits of the
aid which we can give her. I trust this fact will be meditated
upon by other countries who may tomorrow, or a week hence, *or a
month hence,* find themselves the victims of an equally elaborately
worked-out staff plan for their destruction and enslavement.

I described the recent reoccupation by our Fleet of Scapa
Flow, and the instant movement we had made to intercept the
German forces in the North, and how the enemy were in fact
caught between two superior forces.

However, they got away. . . . You may look at the map and see
flags stuck in at different points and consider that the results will
be certain, but when you get out on the sea with its vast distances,
its storms and mists, and with night coming on, and all the uncertainties which exist, you cannot possibly expect that the kind
of conditions which would be appropriate to the movements of
armies have any application to the haphazard conditions of war
at sea. . . . When we speak of the command of the seas, it does not

mean command of every part of the sea at the same moment, or
at every moment. It only means that we can make our will prevail
ultimately in any part of the seas which may be selected for operations, and thus indirectly make our will prevail in every part of
the sea. Anything more foolish than to suppose that the life and
strength of the Royal Navy should have been expended in cease-
lessly patrolling up and down the Norwegian and Danish coasts,
as a target for the U-boats, on the chance that Hitler would launch
a blow like this, cannot be imagined.

The House listened with growing acceptance to the account,
of which the news had just reached me, of Tuesday's brush
between the *Renown* and the enemy, of the air attack on the
British Fleet off Bergen, and especially Warburton-Lee's incursion and action at Narvik. At the end I said:

Everyone must recognise the extraordinary and reckless gambling
which has flung the whole German Fleet out upon the savage seas
of war, as if it were a mere counter to be cast away for a particular
operation. . . . This very recklessness makes me feel that these costly
operations may be only the prelude to far larger events which im-
pend on land. We have probably arrived now at the first main
clinch of the war.

After an hour and a half the House seemed to be very much
less estranged. A little later there would have been more to tell.

*   *   *   *   *

By the morning of April 10, the *Warspite* had joined the
Commander-in-Chief, who was proceeding towards Narvik. On
learning about Captain Warburton-Lee's attack at dawn, we
resolved to try again. The cruiser *Penelope* with destroyer
support was ordered to attack "if in the light of experience this
morning you consider it a justifiable operation." But while the
signals were passing, *Penelope,* in searching for enemy transports reported off Bodo, ran ashore. The next day (twelfth) a
dive-bombing attack on enemy ships in Narvik Harbour was
made from the *Furious.* The attack was pressed home in terrible weather and low visibility, and four hits on destroyers
were claimed for the loss of two aircraft. This was not enough.

We wanted Narvik very much and were determined at least to clear it of the German Navy. The climax was now at hand.

The precious *Renown* was kept out of it. Admiral Whitworth shifted his flag to the *Warspite* at sea, and at noon on the thirteenth he entered the fiord escorted by nine destroyers and by dive-bombers from the *Furious*. There were no minefields; but a U-boat was driven off by the destroyers and a second sunk by the *Warspite's* own *Swordfish* aircraft, which also detected a German destroyer lurking in an inlet to launch her torpedoes on the battleship from this ambush. The hostile destroyer was quickly overwhelmed. At 1.30 P.M., when our ships were through the Narrows and a dozen miles from Narvik, five enemy destroyers appeared ahead in the haze. At once a fierce fight began with all ships on both sides firing and manoeuvring rapidly. The *Warspite* found no shore batteries to attack, and intervened in deadly fashion in the destroyer fight. The thunder of her fifteen-inch guns reverberated among the surrounding mountains like the voice of doom. The enemy, heavily overmatched, retreated, and the action broke up into separate combats. Some of our ships went into Narvik Harbour to complete the task of destruction there; others, led by the *Eskimo*, pursued three Germans who sought refuge in the head waters of Rombaks Fiord and annihilated them there. The bows of the *Eskimo* were blown off by a torpedo; but in this second sea-fight off Narvik, the eight enemy destroyers which had survived Warburton-Lee's attack were all sunk or wrecked without the loss of a single British ship.

When the action was over, Admiral Whitworth thought of throwing a landing party of seamen and marines ashore to occupy the town, where there seemed for the moment to be no opposition. Unless the fire of the *Warspite* could dominate the scene, an inevitable counter-attack by a greatly superior number of German soldiers must be expected. With the risk from the air and by U-boats, he did not feel justified in exposing this fine ship so long. His decision was endorsed when a dozen German aircraft appeared at 6 P.M. Accordingly, he withdrew early next morning after embarking the wounded from the destroyers. "My impression," he said, "is that the enemy forces in Narvik were thoroughly frightened as a result of today's action. I recommend that the town be occupied without delay by the main landing-force." Two destroyers were left off the port to watch events, and one of these rescued the survivors of the *Hardy,* who had meanwhile maintained themselves on shore.

*   *   *   *   *

His Majesty, whose naval instincts were powerfully stirred by this clash of the British and German Navies in Northern waters, wrote me the following encouraging letter:

                                    BUCKINGHAM PALACE
                                    April 12, 1940

My dear Mr. Churchill,

I have been wanting to have a talk with you about the recent striking events in the North Sea, which, as a sailor, I have naturally followed with the keenest interest, but I have purposely refrained from taking up any of your time, as I know what a great strain has been placed upon you by your increased responsibilities as Chairman of the Co-ordination Committee. I shall, however, ask you to come and see me as soon as there is a lull. In the meantime I would like to congratulate you on the splendid way in which, under your direction, the Navy is countering the German move against Scandinavia. I also beg of you to take care of yourself and get as much rest as you possibly can in these critical days.

                Believe me,
                        Yours very sincerely,
                                    GEORGE R.I.

13

Narvik

FOR MANY GENERATIONS, Norway, with its homely, rugged population engaged in trade, shipping, fishing, and agriculture, had stood outside the turmoil of world politics. Far off were the days when the Vikings had sallied forth to conquer or ravage a large part of the then-known world. The Hundred Years' War, the Thirty Years' War, the wars of William III and Marlborough, the Napoleonic convulsion, and later conflicts, had left Norway unmoved and unscathed. A large proportion of the people had hitherto thought of neutrality and neutrality alone. A tiny army and a population with no desires except to live peaceably in their own mountainous and semi-Arctic country now fell victims to the new German aggression.

It had been the policy of Germany for many years to profess cordial sympathy and friendship for Norway. After the previous war some thousands of German children had found food and shelter with the Norwegians. These had now grown up in Germany, and many of them were ardent

Nazis. There was also a Major Quisling, who with a handful of young men had aped and reproduced in Norway on an insignificant scale the Fascist Movement. For some years past, Nordic meetings had been arranged in Germany to which large numbers of Norwegians had been invited. German lecturers, actors, singers, and men of science had visited Norway in the promotion of a common culture. All this had been woven into the texture of the Hitlerite military plan, and a widely scattered internal pro-German conspiracy set on foot. In this every member of the German diplomatic or consular service, every German purchasing agency, played its part under directions from the German Legation in Oslo. The deed of infamy and treachery now performed may take its place with the Sicilian Vespers and the massacre of St. Bartholomew. The President of the Norwegian Parliament, Carl Hambro, has written:

In the case of Poland and later in those of Holland and Belgium, notes had been exchanged, ultimata had been presented. In the case of Norway, the Germans under the mask of friendship tried to extinguish the nation in one dark night, silently, murderously, without any declaration of war, without any warning given. What stupefied the Norwegians more than the act of aggression itself was the national realisation that a Great Power, for years professing its friendship, suddenly appeared a deadly enemy; and that men and women with whom one had had intimate business or professional relations, who had been cordially welcomed in one's home, were spies and agents of destruction. More than by the violation of treaties and every international obligation, the people of Norway were dazed to find that for years their German friends had been elaborating the most detailed plans for the invasion and subsequent enslaving of their country.

The King, the Government, the Army, and the people, as soon as they realised what was happening, flamed into furious anger. But it was all too late. German infiltration and propaganda had hitherto clouded their vision and now sapped their powers of resistance. Major Quisling presented himself at the radio, now in German hands, as the pro-German ruler of the conquered land. Almost all Norwegian officials refused to serve him. The Army was mobilised and at once began under General Ruge to fight the invaders pressing northwards from Oslo. Patriots who could find arms took to the mountains and the forests. The King, the Ministry, and the Parliament withdrew first to Hamar, a hundred miles from Oslo. They were hotly pursued by German armoured cars, and ferocious attempts were made to exterminate them by bombing and machine-gunning from the air. They continued, however, to issue proclamations to the whole country urging the most strenuous resistance. The rest of the population was overpowered and terrorised by bloody examples into stupefied or sullen submission. The peninsula of Norway is nearly a thousand miles long. It is sparsely inhabited, and roads and railways are few, especially to the northward. The rapidity with which Hitler effected the domination of Norway was a remarkable feat of war and policy, and an enduring example of German thoroughness, wickedness, and brutality.

The Norwegian Government, hitherto in their fear of Germany so frigid to us, now made vehement appeals for succour. It was from the beginning obviously impossible for us to rescue Southern Norway. Almost all our trained troops, and many only half-trained, were in France. Our modest but growing air force was fully assigned to supporting the British Expeditionary Force, to home defence, and vigorous training. All our anti-aircraft guns were demanded ten times over for vulnerable points of the highest importance. Still, we felt bound to do our utmost to go to their aid, even at violent derangement of our own preparations and interests. Narvik, it seemed, could certainly be seized and defended with benefit to the whole Allied cause. Here the King of Norway might fly his flag unconquered. Trondheim might be fought for, at any rate as a means of delaying the northward advance of the invaders until Narvik could be regained and made the base of an army. This it seemed could be maintained from the sea at a strength superior to anything which could be brought against it by land through five hundred miles of mountain territory. The Cabinet heartily approved all possible measures for the rescue and

defence of Narvik and Trondheim. The troops which had been
released from the Finnish project, and a nucleus kept in hand
for Narvik, could soon be ready. They lacked aircraft, anti-
aircraft guns, anti-tank guns, tanks, transport, and training.
The whole of Northern Norway was covered with snow to
depths which none of our soldiers had ever seen, felt, or imagined. There were neither snowshoes nor skis — still less
skiers. We must do our best. Thus began this ramshackle
campaign.

*　　*　　*　　*　　*

There was every reason to believe that Sweden would be the
next victim of Germany or Russia, or perhaps even both. If
Sweden came to the aid of her agonised neighbour, the military
situation would be for the time being transformed. The Swedes
had a good army. They could enter Norway easily. They
could be at Trondheim in force before the Germans. We could
join them there. But what would be the fate of Sweden in the
months that followed? Hitler's vengeance would lay them low,
and the Bear would maul them from the east. On the other
hand, the Swedes could purchase neutrality by supplying the
Germans with all the iron ore they wanted throughout the
approaching summer. For Sweden the choice was a profitable
neutrality or subjugation. She could not be blamed because
she did not view the issue from the standpoint of our unready
but now eager island.

After the Cabinet on the morning of April 11, I wrote the
following minute, which the sacrifices we were making for the
rights of small states and the Law of Nations may justify:

Prime Minister.
Foreign Secretary.

I am not entirely satisfied with the result of the discussion this
morning, or with my contribution to it. What we want is that
Sweden should not remain neutral, but declare war on Germany.
What we do not want is to provide either the three divisions which
we dangled to procure the Finland project, or to keep her fully
supplied with food as long as the war lasts, or to bomb Berlin, etc.,
if Stockholm is bombed. These stakes are more than it is worth

while paying at the present time. On the other hand, we should do everything to encourage her into the war by general assurances that we will give all the help we can, that our troops will be active in the Scandinavian Peninsula, that we will make common cause with her as good allies, and will not make peace without her, or till she is righted. Have we given this impulse to the Anglo-French Mission? If not, there is still time to do it. Moreover, our diplomacy should be active at Stockholm.

It must be remembered that Sweden will say, "Thank you for nothing," about any offers on our part to defend the Gullivare iron field. She can easily do this herself. Her trouble is to the south, where we can do but little. Still, it will be something to assure her that we intend to open the Narvik route to Sweden from the Atlantic by main force as soon as possible, and also that we propose to clean up the German lodgments on the Norwegian coast *seriatim*, thus opening other channels.

If the great battle opens in Flanders, the Germans will not have much to spare for Scandinavia, and if, on the other hand, the Germans do not attack in the West, we can afford to send troops to Scandinavia in proportion as German divisions are withdrawn from the Western Front. It seems to me we must not throw cold water on the French idea of trying to induce the Swedes to enter the war. It would be disastrous if they remained neutral and bought Germany off with ore from Gullivare down the Gulf of Bothnia.

I must apologise for not having sufficiently gripped this issue in my mind this morning, but I only came in after the discussion had begun, and did not address myself properly to it.

There was justice in the Foreign Secretary's reply, by which I was convinced. He said that the Prime Minister and he agreed with my general view, but doubted the method I favoured of approaching Sweden.

April 11, 1940.

From all the information that we have from Swedish sources that are friendly to the Allies, it appears that any representations that can be readily translated in their mind into an attempt by us to drag them into the war will be likely to have an effect opposite to that which we want. Their immediate reaction would be that we were endeavouring to get them to do what, until we have established a position in one or more of the Norwegian ports, we were unable or unwilling to do ourselves. And accordingly the result would do us more harm than good.

*   *   *   *   *

It was easy to regather at short notice the small forces for a Narvik expedition which had been dispersed a few days earlier. One British brigade and its ancillary troops began to embark immediately, and the first convoy sailed for Narvik on April 12. This was to be followed in a week or two by three battalions of Chasseurs Alpins and other French troops. There were also Norwegian forces north of Narvik which would help our landings. Major-General Mackesy had been selected on April 5 to command any expedition which might be sent to Narvik. His instructions were couched in a form appropriate to the case of a friendly neutral power from whom some facilities are required. They contained among their appendices the following references to bombardment:

It is clearly illegal to bombard a populated area in the hope of hitting a legitimate target which is known to be in the area, but which cannot be precisely located and identified.

In the face of the German onslaught, new and stiffer instructions were issued to the General on the tenth. They gave him more latitude, but did not cancel this particular injunction. Their substance was as follows:

His Majesty's Government and the Government of the French Republic have decided to send a field force to initiate operations against Germany in Northern Norway. The object of the force will be to eject the Germans from the Narvik area and establish control of Narvik itself. . . . Your initial task will be to establish your force at Harstad, ensure the co-operation of Norwegian forces that may be there, and obtain the information necessary to enable you to plan your further operations. It is not intended that you should land in the face of opposition. You may, however, be faced with opposition owing to mistaken identity; you will, therefore, take such steps as are suitable to establish the nationality of your force before abandoning the attempt. The decision whether to land or not will be taken by the senior naval officer in consultation with you. If landing is impossible at Harstad, some other suitable locality should be tried. A landing must be carried out when you have sufficient troops.

At the same time a personal letter from General Ironside, the C.I.G.S., was given to General Mackesy, which included the remark: "You may have a chance of taking advantage of naval action and should do so if you can. Boldness is required." This struck a somewhat different note from the formal instructions.

My contacts with Lord Cork and Orrery had become intimate in the long months during which the active discussions of Baltic strategy had proceeded. In spite of some differences of view about "Catherine," his relations with the First Sea Lord were good. I was fully conscious from long and hard experience of the difference between pushing things audaciously on paper so as to get them explored and tested — the processes of mental reconnaissance-in-force — and actually doing them or getting them done. Admiral Pound and I were both agreed from slightly different angles that Lord Cork should command the naval forces in this amphibious adventure in the North. We both urged him not to hesitate to run risks but to strike hard to seize Narvik. As we were all agreed and could talk things over together, we left him exceptional discretion, and did not give him any written orders. He knew exactly what we wanted. In his dispatch he says, "My impression on leaving London was quite clear that it was desired by His Majesty's Government to turn the enemy out of Narvik at the earliest possible moment, and that I was to act with all promptitude in order to attain this result."

Our staff work at this time had not been tempered by war experience, nor was the action of the service departments concerted except by the meetings of the Military Co-ordination Committee, over which I had just begun to preside. Neither I, as Chairman of the Committee, nor the Admiralty were made acquainted with the War Office instructions to General

Mackesy, and as the Admiralty directions had been given
orally to Lord Cork, there was no written text to communicate
to the War Office. The instructions of the two departments,
although animated by the same purpose, were somewhat different in tone and emphasis; and this may have helped to cause
the divergences which presently developed between the military and naval commanders.

Lord Cork sailed from Rosyth at high speed in the *Aurora*
on the night of April 12. He had intended to meet General
Mackesy at Harstad, a small port on the island of Hinney in
Vaags Fiord which, although one hundred and twenty miles
from Narvik, had been selected as the military base. However,
on the fourteenth he received a signal from Admiral Whitworth
in the *Warspite,* who had exterminated all the German destroyers and supply ships the day before, saying: "I am convinced that Narvik can be taken by direct assault now without
fear of meeting serious opposition on landing. I consider that
the main landing-force need only be small. . . ." Lord Cork,
therefore, diverted the *Aurora* to Skjel Fiord in the Lofoten

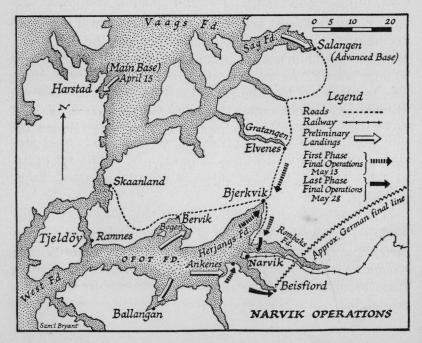

NARVIK OPERATIONS

Islands, flanking the approach to Narvik, and sent a message
ordering the *Southampton* to join him there. His intention
was to organise a force for an immediate assault consisting of
two companies of the Scots Guards, who had been embarked
in the *Southampton,* and a force of seamen and marines from
the *Warspite* and other ships already in Skjel Fiord. He could
not, however, get in touch with the *Southampton* except after
some delay through the Admiralty, whose reply contained the
following sentence: "We think it imperative that you and the
General should be together and act together and that no attack
should be made except in concert." He therefore left Skjel
Fiord for Harstad and led the convoy, carrying the 24th
Brigade, into harbour there on the morning of the fifteenth.
His escorting destroyers sank *U-49* which was prowling
near-by.

Lord Cork now urged General Mackesy to take advantage
of the destruction of all the German naval force and to make a
direct attack on Narvik as soon as possible, but the General
replied that the harbour was strongly held by the enemy
with machine-gun posts. He also pointed out that his
transports had not been loaded for an assault, but only for an
unopposed landing. He opened his headquarters at the hotel
in Harstad, and his troops began to land thereabouts. The
next day he stated that on the information available landing at Narvik was not possible, nor would naval bombardment make it so. Lord Cork considered that with the help
of overwhelming gun-fire troops could be landed in Narvik
with little loss; but the General did not agree, and could find
some cover in his instructions. From the Admiralty we urged
an immediate assault. A deadlock arose between the military
and naval chiefs.

At this time the weather greatly worsened, and dense falls
of snow seemed to paralyse all movements by our troops, unequipped and untrained for such conditions. Meanwhile, the
Germans in Narvik held our ever-growing forces at bay with
their machine-guns. Here was a serious and unexpected check.

*   *   *   *   *

Most of the business of our improvised campaign passed through my hands, and I prefer to record it as far as possible in my own words at the time. The Prime Minister had a strong desire, shared by the War Cabinet, to occupy Trondheim as well as Narvik. This operation, "Maurice," as it was called, promised to be a big undertaking. According to the records of our Military Co-ordination Committee of April 13:

[I was] very apprehensive of any proposals which might tend to weaken our intention to seize Narvik. Nothing must be allowed to deflect us from making the capture of this place as certain as possible. Our plans against Narvik had been very carefully laid, and there seemed every chance that they would be successful if they were allowed to proceed without being tampered with. Trondheim was, on the other hand, a much more speculative affair, and I deprecated any suggestion which might lead to the diversion of the Chasseurs Alpins until we had definitely established ourselves at Narvik. Otherwise we might find ourselves committed to a number of ineffectual operations along the Norwegian coast, none of which would succeed.

At the same time consideration had already been given to the Trondheim area, and plans were being made to secure landing-points in case a larger-scale action should be needed. A small landing of naval forces would take place at Namsos that afternoon. The Chief of the Imperial General Staff had collected a force of five battalions, two of which would be ready to land on the Norwegian coast on April 16, and three more on April 21 if desired. The actual points at which landings were to be made would be decided that night.

General Mackesy's original orders had been that, after landing at Narvik, he should push rapidly on to Gullivare ore-field. He has now been told to go no farther than the Swedish frontier, since, if Sweden were friendly, there need be no fear for the ore-fields, and if hostile, the difficulties of occupying them would be too great.

I also said that:

It might be necessary to proceed to invest the German forces in Narvik. But we should not allow the operation to degenerate into an investment except after a very determined battle. On this understanding I was willing to send a telegram to the French saying

that we hoped and thought that we should be successful in seizing
Narvik by a *coup-de-main*. We should explain that this had been
made easier by a change in the orders which did not now require
the expedition to go beyond the Swedish frontier.

It was decided by the War Cabinet to attempt both the
Narvik and Trondheim operations. The Secretary of State for
War with foresight warned us that reinforcements for Norway
might soon be required from our army in France, and suggested that we should address the French on the point at a very
early date. I agreed with this, but thought it premature to approach the French for a day or two. This was accepted. The
War Cabinet approved a proposal to inform the Swedish and
Norwegian Governments that we intended to recapture both
Trondheim and Narvik; that we recognised the supreme importance of Trondheim as a strategic centre, but that it was
important to secure Narvik as a naval base. We added that we
had no intention that our forces should proceed over the Swedish frontier. We were at the same time to invite the French
Government to give us liberty to use the Chasseurs Alpins for
operations elsewhere than at Narvik, telling them what we
were saying to the Swedish and Norwegian Governments.
Neither I nor Mr. Stanley liked the dispersion of our forces.
We were still inclined to concentrate all on Narvik, except for
diversions elsewhere. But we deferred to the general view, for
which there was no lack of good reasons.

*   *   *   *   *

On the night of the sixteenth-seventeenth disappointing
news arrived from Narvik. General Mackesy had, it appeared,
no intention of trying to seize the town by an immediate assault
protected by the close-range bombardment of the Fleet; and
Lord Cork could not move him. I stated the position to my
Committee as it then appeared.

April 17.

1. Lord Cork's telegram shows that General Mackesy proposes
to take two unoccupied positions on the approaches to Narvik
and to hold on there until the snow melts, perhaps at the end of

the month. The General expects that the first demi-brigade of
Chasseurs Alpins will be sent to him, which it certainly will not
be. This policy means that we shall be held up in front of Narvik
for several weeks. Meanwhile, the Germans will proclaim that we
are brought to a standstill and that Narvik is still in their possession. The effects of this will be damaging both upon Norwegians
and neutrals. Moreover, the German fortification of Narvik will
continue, requiring a greater effort when the time comes. This
information is at once unexpected and disagreeable. One of the
best regular brigades in the Army will be wasting away, losing men
by sickness, and playing no part. It is for consideration whether
a telegram on the following lines should not be sent to Lord
Cork and General Mackesy:

> Your proposals involve damaging deadlock at Narvik and the
> neutralisation of one of our best brigades. We cannot send you
> the Chasseurs Alpins. The *Warspite* will be needed elsewhere,
> in two or three days. Full consideration should, therefore, be
> given by you to an assault upon Narvik covered by the *Warspite*
> and the destroyers, which might also operate at Rombaks Fiord.
> The capture of the port and town would be an important success.
> We should like to receive from you the reasons why this is not
> possible, and your estimate of the degree of resistance to be ex-
> pected on the waterfront. Matter most urgent.

2. The second point which requires decision is whether the
Chasseurs Alpins shall go straight on to join General Carton de
Wiart at or beyond Namsos, or whether, as is easy, they should
be held back at Scapa and used for the Trondheim operation on
the twenty-second or twenty-third, together with other troops available for this main attack.

3. Two battalions of the 146th Brigade will, it is hoped, have
been landed before dawn today at Namsos and Bandsund. The
3d Battalion in the *Chobry* will make a dangerous voyage tomorrow
to Namsos, arriving if all is well about dusk, and landing. The
anchorage of Lillejonas was bombed all the afternoon without
the two transports being hit, and the large 18,000-tonner is now
returning empty to Scapa Flow. If the leading Chasseurs Alpins
are to be used at Namsos, they must go there direct instead of
making rendezvous at Lillejonas.

4. The question of whether the forces now available for the main

attack on Trondheim are adequate must also be decided today. The two Guards battalions that were to be mobilised, i.e., equipped, cannot be ready in time. The two French Foreign Legion battalions cannot arrive in time. A regular brigade from France can, however, be ready to sail from Rosyth on the twentieth. The first and second demi-brigades of the Chasseurs Alpins can also be in time. A thousand Canadians have been made available. There is also a brigade of Territorials. Is this enough to prevail over the Germans in Trondheim? The dangers of delay are very great and need not be restated.

5. Admiral Holland leaves tonight to meet the Commander-in-Chief, Home Fleet, on his return to Scapa on the eighteenth, and he must carry with him full and clear decisions. It may be taken as certain that the Navy will cheerfully undertake to carry troops to Trondheim.

6. It is probable that fighting will take place tonight and to-morrow morning for the possession of Andalsnes. We hope to have landed an advance party from the cruiser *Calcutta,* and are moving sufficient cruisers to meet a possible attack by five enemy destroyers at dawn.

7. The naval bombardment of Stavanger aerodrome will begin at dawn today.

The Committee agreed to the telegram, which was accordingly sent. It produced no effect. It must remain a matter of opinion whether such an assault would have succeeded. It involved no marches through the snow, but on the other hand, landings from open boats both in Narvik Harbour and in Rombaks Fiord, under machine-gun fire. I counted upon the effect of close-range bombardment by the tremendous ship batteries which would blast the waterfronts and cover with smoke and clouds of snow and earth the whole of the German machine-gun posts. Suitable high-explosive shells had been provided by the Admiralty both for the battleship and the destroyers. Certainly Lord Cork, on the spot and able to measure the character of the bombardment, was strongly in favour of making the attempt. We had over four thousand of our best regular troops, including the Guards brigade and marines, who, once they set foot on shore, would become intermingled at close quarters with the German defenders, whose regular troops, apart from the crews rescued from the sunken destroyers, we estimated, correctly as we now know, at no more than half their number. This would have been considered a fair proposition on the Western Front in the previous war, and no new factors were at work here. Later on in this war, scores of such assaults were made and often succeeded. Moreover, the orders sent to the commanders were of such a clear and imperative character, and so evidently contemplated heavy losses, that they should have been obeyed. The responsibility for a bloody repulse would fall exclusively on the home authorities, and very directly upon me. I was content that this should be so; but nothing I or my colleagues or Cork could do or say produced the slightest effect on the General. He was resolved to wait till the snow melted. As for the bombardment, he could point to the paragraph in his instructions against endangering the civil population. When we contrast this spirit with the absolutely reckless gambling in lives and ships and the almost frenzied vigour, based upon long and profound calculations, which had gained the Germans their brilliant success, the disadvantages under which we lay in waging this campaign are obvious.

14

Trondheim

*A Key Objective — The Obvious Plan — "Operation Hammer" —
Attitude of the Commander-in-Chief, Home Fleet — Choice of
Generals — A Chapter of Accidents — Situation on April 14 —
Situation on April 17 — Second Thoughts of the Staffs — Power
of Unopposed Air Force — The Change of Plan — Sir Roger
Keyes' Desires and Credentials — My Report to the Co-ordina-
tion Committee of April 19 — The War Cabinet Accept the
Abandonment of "Hammer" — Urgency of Narvik, April 20 —
General Ismay's Summary.*

TRONDHEIM, if it were within our strength, was of course the
key to any considerable operations in Central Norway. To
gain it meant a safe harbour with quays and docks upon which
an army of fifty thousand men or more could be built up and
based. Near-by was an airfield from which several fighter squadrons could work. The possession of Trondheim would open
direct railway contact with Sweden, and greatly improve the
chances of Swedish intervention or the degree of mutual aid
possible if Sweden were herself attacked. From Trondheim
alone the northward advance of the German invasion from
Oslo could be securely barred. On the broadest grounds of
policy and strategy it would be good for the Allies to fight Hitler on the largest possible scale in Central Norway, if that was
where he wanted to go. Narvik, far away to the north, could be
stormed or reduced at leisure and would all the while be protected. We had the effective command of the sea. As to the

air, if we could establish ourselves firmly on Norwegian airfields, we should not hesitate to fight the German air force
there to any extent which the severely limiting conditions allowed to either side.

All these reasons had simultaneously convinced the French
War Council, the British War Cabinet, and most of their advisers. The British and French Prime Ministers were at one.
General Gamelin was willing to withdraw French or release
British divisions from France for Norway to the same extent
that the Germans diverted their forces thither. He evidently
welcomed a prolonged battle on a large scale south of Trondheim, where the ground was almost everywhere favourable to
defence. It seemed that we could certainly bring forces and
supplies to the scene across the open sea through Trondheim
far quicker than the Germans could fight their way up the
single road and railway line from Oslo, both of which might be
cut behind them by bombs or parties dropped from the air.
The only question was, Could we take Trondheim in time?
Could we get there before the main enemy army arrived from
the south, and for this purpose, could we obtain even a passing
relief from their present unchallenged air domination?

There was a surge of opinion in favour of Trondheim which
extended far beyond Cabinet circles. The advantages were so
obvious that all could see them. The public, the clubs, the
newspapers and their military correspondents had, for some
days past, been discussing such a policy freely. My great friend,
Admiral of the Fleet, Sir Roger Keyes, champion of forcing the
Dardanelles, hero and victor of Zeebrugge, passionately longed
to lead the Fleet or any portion of it past the batteries into the
Trondheim Fiord and storm the town by landings from the
sea. The appointment of Lord Cork, also an Admiral of the
Fleet, to command the naval operations at Narvik, although
he was senior to the Commander-in-Chief, Admiral Forbes,
seemed to remove the difficulties of rank. Admirals of the
Fleet are always on the active list, and Keyes had many
contacts at the Admiralty. He spoke and wrote to me repeatedly with vehemence, reminding me of the Dardanelles and

how easily the Straits could have been forced if we had not been stopped by timid obstructionists. I also pondered a good deal upon the lessons of the Dardanelles. Certainly the Trondheim batteries and any minefields that might have been laid were trivial compared to those we had then had to face. On the other hand, there was the airplane, capable of dropping its bombs on the unprotected decks of the very few great ships which now constituted the naval power of Britain on the oceans.

At the Admiralty the First Sea Lord and the Naval Staff generally did not shrink from the venture. On April 13 the Admiralty had officially informed the Commander-in-Chief of the Supreme Council's decision to allot troops for the capture of Trondheim, and had raised the question with him in a positive manner whether the Home Fleet should not force the passage.

Do you consider [the message ran] that the shore batteries could be either destroyed or dominated to such an extent as to permit transports to enter? If so, how many ships and what type would you propose?

On this Admiral Forbes asked for details about the Trondheim defences. He agreed that the shore batteries might be destroyed or dominated in daylight by battleships provided with suitable ammunition. None was carried at that moment in Home Fleet ships. The first and most important task, he said, was to protect troopships from heavy air attack over the thirty miles approach through narrow waters, and the next to carry out an opposed landing of which ample warning had been given. In the circumstances he did not consider the operation feasible.

The Naval Staff persisted in their view, and the Admiralty with my earnest agreement replied on April 15 as follows:

We still think that the operation described should be further studied. It could not take place for seven days, which would be devoted to careful preparation. Danger from air not appreciably less wherever these large troopships are brought into the danger

zone. Our idea would be that in addition to R.A.F. bombing of
Stavanger aerodrome, *Suffolk* should bombard with high-explosive
at dawn, hoping thereby to put the aerodrome out of business. The
aerodrome at Trondheim could be dealt with by Fleet air-arm
bombers and subsequently by bombardment. High-explosive shells
for fifteen-inch guns have been ordered to Rosyth. *Furious* and
First Cruiser Squadron would be required for this operation. Pray,
therefore, consider this important project further.

Admiral Forbes, although not fully convinced of its sound-
ness, therefore addressed himself to the project in a more
favourable mood. In a further reply he said that he did not
anticipate great difficulty from the naval side, except that he
could not provide air defence for the transports while carrying
out the landing. The naval force required would be the
Valiant and *Renown* to give air defence to the *Glorious,* the
Warspite to bombard, at least four A.A. cruisers and about
twenty destroyers.

* * * * *

While plans for the frontal attack on Trondheim from the
sea were being advanced with all speed, two subsidiary landings
were already in progress designed to envelop the town from
the landward side. Of these the first was a hundred miles to the
north, at Namsos, where Major-General Carton de Wiart, V.C.,
had been chosen to command the troops with orders "to secure
the Trondheim area." He was informed that the Navy were
making a preliminary lodgment with a party about three hundred strong in order to take and hold points for his disembarkation. The idea was that two infantry brigades and a light
division of Chasseurs Alpins should land hereabouts in conjunction with the main attack by the Navy upon Trondheim,
"Operation Hammer." For this purpose the 146th Brigade and
the Chasseurs Alpins were being diverted from Narvik. Carton
de Wiart started forthwith in a flying-boat, and reached
Namsos under heavy air attack on the evening of the fifteenth.
His staff officer was wounded, but he took effective charge on
the spot. The second landing was at Andalsnes, about a

hundred and fifty miles by road to the southwest of Trondheim. Here also the Navy had made a lodgment, and on April 18 Brigadier Morgan with a military force arrived and took command. Lieutenant-General Massy was appointed Commander-in-Chief of all the forces operating in Central Norway. This officer had to exercise his command from the War Office because there was as yet no place for his Headquarters on the other side.

*   *   *   *   *

On the fifteenth, I reported that all these plans were being developed, but the difficulties were serious. Namsos was under four feet of snow and offered no concealment from the air. The enemy enjoyed complete air mastery, and we had neither anti-aircraft guns nor any airfield from which protecting squadrons might operate. Admiral Forbes had not, I said, at first been very keen on forcing his way into Trondheim because of the risk of air attack. It was, of course, of first importance that the Royal Air Force should continue to harass the Stavanger airfield, by which the enemy airplanes were passing northward. The *Suffolk* would bombard this airfield with her eight-inch guns on April 17. This was approved, and the bombardment took place as planned. Some damage was done to the airfield, but during her withdrawal the *Suffolk* was continuously bombed for seven hours. She was heavily hit and reached Scapa Flow the following day with her quarterdeck awash.

The Secretary of State for War had now to nominate a military commander for the Trondheim operation. Colonel Stanley's first choice fell upon Major-General Hotblack, who was highly reputed, and on April 17 he was briefed for his task at a meeting of the Chiefs of Staff held in the Admiralty. That night at 12.30 A.M. he had a fit on the Duke of York's Steps, and was picked up unconscious some time later. He had luckily left all his papers with his staff, who were working on them. The next morning Brigadier Berney-Ficklin was appointed to succeed Hotblack. He too was briefed, and started by train for Edinburgh. On April 19, he and his staff left by air for Scapa. They crashed on the airfield at Kirkwall. The pilot and one of the crew were killed, the rest were seriously injured. Every day counted.

*   *   *   *   *

On April 17, I explained in outline to the War Cabinet the plan which the staffs were making for the main landing at Trondheim. The forces immediately available were one regular brigade from France (twenty-five hundred strong), one thousand Canadians, and about one thousand men of a Territorial brigade as a reserve. The Military Co-ordination Committee had been advised that the forces available were adequate and that the risks, although very considerable, were justified. The operation would be supported by the full strength of the Fleet, and two carriers would be available with a total of about one hundred aircraft, including forty-five fighters. The provisional date for the landing was April 22. The second demi-brigade of Chasseurs Alpins would not reach Trondheim until April 25, when it was hoped they would be able to disembark at the quays in Trondheim.

Asked whether the Chiefs of Staff were in agreement with the plans as outlined, the Chief of the Air Staff said on their behalf and in their presence that they were. The operation was, of course, attended by considerable risks, but these were worth running. The Prime Minister agreed with this view, and emphasised the importance of air co-operation. The War Cabinet gave cordial approval to the enterprise. I did my best to have it carried out.

Up to this point all the staffs and their chiefs had seemed resolved upon the central thrust at Trondheim. Admiral Forbes was actively preparing to strike, and there seemed no reason why the date of the twenty-second should not be kept. Although Narvik was my pet, I threw myself with increasing confidence into this daring adventure, and was willing that the Fleet should risk the weak batteries at the entrance to the fiord, the possible minefields, and, most serious, the air. The ships carried what was in those days very powerful anti-aircraft armament. A group of ships had a combined overhead fire power which few aircraft would care to encounter at a height where bombing would be accurate. I must here explain that the power of an air force is terrific when there is nothing to oppose it. The pilots can fly as low as they please and are often safer fifty feet off the ground than high up. They can cast their bombs with precision and use their machine-guns on troops with only the risk of a chance rifle bullet. These hard conditions had to be faced by our small expeditions at Namsos and Andalsnes, but the Fleet, with its ack-ack batteries and a hundred seaborne airplanes, might well be superior during the actual operation to any air power the enemy could bring. If Trondheim were taken, the neighbouring airfield of Vaernes would be in our hands, and in a few days we could have not only a considerable garrison in the town, but also several fighter squadrons of the R.A.F. in action. Left to myself, I might have stuck to my first love, Narvik; but serving as I did a respected chief and friendly Cabinet, I now looked forward to this exciting enterprise to which so many staid and cautious Ministers had given their strong adherence, and which seemed to find much favour with the Naval Staff and indeed among all our experts. Such was the position on the seventeenth.

Meanwhile, I felt that we should do our utmost to keep the King of Norway and his advisers informed of our plans by sending him an officer who understood the Norwegian scene and could speak with authority. Admiral Sir Edward Evans was well suited to this task, and was sent to Norway by air through Stockholm to make contact with the King at his head-quarters. There he was to do everything possible to encourage the Norwegian Government in their resistance and explain the measures which the British Government were taking to assist them. From April 22 he was for some days in consultation with the King and the principal Norwegian authorities, helping them to understand both our plans and our difficulties.

* * * * *

During the eighteenth, a vehement and decisive change

in the opinions of the Chiefs of Staff and of the Admiralty occurred. This change was brought about, first, by increasing realisation of the magnitude of the naval stake in hazarding so many of our finest capital ships, and also by War Office arguments that even if the Fleet got in and got out again, the opposed landing of the troops in the face of the German air power would be perilous. On the other hand, the landings which were already being successfully carried out both north and south of Trondheim seemed to all these authorities to offer a far less dangerous solution. The Chiefs of Staff drew up a long paper opposing "Operation Hammer."

This began with a reminder that a combined operation involving an opposed landing was one of the most difficult and hazardous operations of war, requiring the most careful and detailed preparations. The Chiefs of Staff had always realised that this particular operation would involve very serious risks; for, owing to the urgency of the situation, there had not been time for the detailed and meticulous preparation which should have been given to an operation of this character and, as there had been no reconnaissance or air photographs, the plan had been worked out from maps and charts. The plan had the further disadvantage that it would involve concentrating almost the whole of the Home Fleet in an area where it could be subjected to heavy attack from the air. There were also new factors in the situation which should be taken into account. We had seized the landing places at Namsos and Andalsnes and established forces ashore there; there were reliable reports that the Germans were improving the defences at Trondheim; and reports of our intention to make a direct landing at Trondheim had appeared in the press. On reconsidering the original project in the light of these new factors, the Chiefs of Staff unanimously recommended a change of plan.

They still thought it essential that we should seize Trondheim and use it as a base for subsequent operation in Scandinavia; but they urged that, instead of the direct frontal assault, we should take advantage of our unexpected success in landing forces at Namsos and Andalsnes and develop a pincer movement on Trondheim from north and south. By this means, they declared, we could turn a venture which was attended by grave hazards into one which could achieve the same result with much less risk. By this change of plan the press reports of our intentions could also be turned to our advantage; for by judicious leakages we could hope to leave the enemy under the impression that we still intended to persist in our original plan. The Chiefs of Staff, therefore, recommended that we should push in the maximum forces possible at Namsos and Andalsnes, seize control of the road and rail communications running through Dombas, and envelop Trondheim from the north and south. Shortly before the main landings at Namsos and Andalsnes, the outer forts at Trondheim should be bombarded from the sea with a view to leading the enemy to suppose that a direct assault was about to take place. We should thus invest Trondheim by land and blockade it by sea; and although its capture would take longer than originally contemplated, our main forces might be put ashore at a slightly earlier date. Finally, the Chiefs of Staff pointed out that such an enveloping operation, as opposed to a direct assault, would release a large number of valuable units of the Fleet for operations in other areas, e.g., at Narvik. These powerful recommendations were put forward with the authority, not only of the three Chiefs of Staff, but of their three able vice-chiefs, including Admiral Tom Phillips and Sir John Dill, newly appointed.

No more decisive stopper on a positive amphibious plan can be imagined, nor have I seen a Government or Minister who would have overridden it. Under the prevailing arrangement, the Chiefs of Staff worked as a separate and largely independent body without guidance or direction from the Prime Minister or any effective representative of the supreme executive power. Moreover, the leaders of the three services had not yet got the conception of war as a whole, and were influenced unduly by the departmental outlook of their own services. They met together, after talking things over with their respective Ministers, and issued *aides-mémoires* or memoranda which carried enormous weight. Here was the fatal weakness of our system of conducting war at this time.

When I became aware of this right-about-turn, I was indignant, and questioned searchingly the officers concerned. It was
soon plain to me that all professional opinion was now adverse
to the operation which only a few days before it had spontaneously espoused. Of course, there was at hand, in passionate
ardour for action and glory, Sir Roger Keyes. He was scornful
of these belated fears and second thoughts. He volunteered to
lead a handful of older ships with the necessary transports into
Trondheim Fiord, land the troops and storm the place, before
the Germans got any stronger. Roger Keyes had formidable
credentials of achievement. In him there burned a flame. It
was suggested in the May debates that "the iron of the Dardanelles had entered into my soul," meaning that on account of
my downfall on that occasion I had no longer the capacity to
dare; but this was really not true. The difficulties of acting
from a subordinate position in the violent manner required
are of the first magnitude.

Moreover, the personal relations of the high naval figures
involved were peculiar. Roger Keyes, like Lord Cork, was
senior to the Commander-in-Chief and the First Sea Lord.
Admiral Pound had been for two years Keyes' staff officer in
the Mediterranean. For me to take Roger Keyes' advice against
his would have entailed his resignation, and Admiral Forbes
might well have asked to be relieved of his command. It was
certainly not my duty in the position I held to confront the
Prime-Minister and my War Cabinet colleagues with these personal dramas at such a time and upon an operation which, for
all its attractiveness and interest, was essentially minor even
in relation to the Norwegian campaign, to say nothing of the
general war. I therefore had no doubt that we must accept
the Staff view in spite of their change of mind, and the obvious
objections that could be raised against their mutilated plan.

I accordingly submitted to the abandonment of "Hammer."
I reported the facts to the Prime Minister on the afternoon of
the eighteenth, and though bitterly disappointed he, like me,
had no choice but to accept the new position. In war, as in life,
it is often necessary, when some cherished scheme has failed,

to take up the best alternative open, and if so, it is folly not to work for it with all your might. I therefore turned my guns round too. I reported in writing to the Co-ordinating Committee on April 19 as follows:

1. The considerable advance made by Carton de Wiart, the very easy landings we have had from Andalsnes and other ports in this southern fiord, the indiscretions of the press pointing to a storm of Trondheim, and the very heavy naval forces required for this operation called "Hammer," with the undoubted major risk of keeping so many valuable ships so many hours under close air attack, have led the Chiefs of Staff and their deputies to advise that there should be a complete alteration of the emphasis between the two pincer attacks and the centre attack; in the following sense: that the main weight should be thrown into the northern and southern pincers, and that the central attack on Trondheim should be reduced to a demonstration.

2. Owing to the rapidity with which events and opinions have moved, it became necessary to take a decision of which the Prime Minister has approved, as set out above, and orders are being issued accordingly.

3. It is proposed to encourage the idea that a central attack upon Trondheim is afoot, and to emphasise this by a bombardment by battleships of the outer forts at the suitable moment.

4. Every effort will be made to strengthen Carton de Wiart with artillery, without which his force is not well-composed.

5. All the troops we have now under orders for "Hammer" will be shoved in as quickly as possible, mostly in warships, at the various ports of the Romsdal Fiord to press on to Dombas, and then, some delaying force being sent southward to the Norwegian main front, the bulk will turn north towards Trondheim. There is already one brigade (Morgan's) ashore beyond Andalsnes with the six hundred marines. The brigade from France and the supporting Territorial brigade will all be thrown in here as quickly as possible. This should enable Dombas to be secured, and the control to be extended to the more easterly of the two Norwegian railways running from Oslo to Trondheim, Storen being a particularly advantageous point. The destination of the second demi-brigade of Chasseurs Alpins, the two battalions of the French Foreign Legion, and the thousand Canadians, can for today or tomorrow be left open.

6. The position of the Namsos force must be regarded as some-what hazardous, but its commander is used to taking risks. On the other hand, it is not seen why we cannot bring decisive superiority to bear along the Andalsnes-Dombas railway, and operate as occasion serves beyond that most important point, the object being the isolation of Trondheim and its capture.

7. Although this change of emphasis is to be deprecated on account of its being a change, it must be recognised that we move from a more hazardous to a less hazardous operation, and greatly reduce the strain upon the Navy involved in "Hammer." It would seem that our results would be equally achieved by the safer plan, and it does not follow that they will be delayed. We can certainly get more men sooner onto Norwegian soil by this method than the other.

8. It is not possible to deprive Narvik of its battleships at the moment when we have urged strenuous action. *Warspite* has therefore been ordered to return [there]. Some further reinforce-ment will be required for Narvik, which must be studied at once. The Canadians should be considered.

9. At the same time, the sweep of the Skagerrak will now become possible to clear away the enemy anti-submarine craft and aid our submarines.

The next day I explained to the War Cabinet the circum-stances in which it had been decided to call off the direct assault on Trondheim, and stated that the new plan which the Prime Minister had approved was, broadly, to send the whole of the 1st Light Division of Chasseurs Alpins to General Carton de Wiart for his attack on the Trondheim area from the north and to send the regular brigades from France to reinforce Brigadier Morgan, who had landed at Andalsnes and had pushed on troops to hold Dombas. Another Territorial brigade would be put in on the southern line. It might be possible to push part of this southern force right forward to reinforce the Norwegians on the Oslo front. We had been fortunate in get-ting all our troops ashore, without loss so far (except of the ship carrying all Brigadier Morgan's vehicles), and the present plans provided for the disembarkation of some twenty-five thousand men by the end of the first week in May. The French had offered two further light divisions. The chief limiting factor was the provision of the necessary bases and lines of communication on which the forces were to be maintained. The bases would be liable to heavy air attack.

The Secretary of State for War then said that the new plan was little less hazardous than the direct attack on Trondheim. Until we had secured the Trondheim aerodrome, little could be done to offset the heavy scale of enemy air attack. Nor was it altogether correct to describe the new plan as a "pincer movement" against Trondheim, since while the northern force would bring pressure to bear in the near future, the first task of the southern force must be to secure themselves against a German attack from the south. It might well be a month before any serious move could be made against Trondheim from this direction. This was a sound criticism. General Ironside, however, strongly supported the new movement, expressing the hope that General Carton de Wiart, who when reinforced by the French would have, he said, quite a large force at his disposal, a large part of which would be highly mobile, might get astride of the railway from Trondheim to Sweden. The troops already at Dombas had no guns or transport. They should, however, be able to hold a defensive position. I then added that the direct assault on Trondheim had been deemed to involve undue risk both to the Fleet and to our landing-parties. If in the course of a successful assault the Fleet were to lose a capital ship by enemy air action, this loss would have to be set against the success of the operation. Again, it was obvious that the landing-parties might suffer heavy casualties, and General Massy took the view that the stake was out of proportion to the results desired, particularly as these could be obtained by other methods. The Secretary of State for War, having justly pointed out that these other methods offered no sure or satisfactory solution, was content they should be tried. It was evident to us all that we had, in fact, only a choice of unpleasant courses before us, and also a compulsion to act. The War Cabinet endorsed the transformation of the plan against Trondheim.

I now reverted to Narvik, which seemed at once more important and more feasible since the attack on Trondheim was abandoned, and addressed a note to my Committee as follows:

The importance and urgency of reaching a decision at Narvik can hardly be overrated. If the operations become static, the situation will deteriorate for us. When the ice melts in the Gulf of Bothnia, at the latest in a month from now, the Germans may demand of the Swedes free passage for their troops through the ore-field in order to reinforce their people in Narvik, and may also demand control of the ore-field. They might promise Sweden that if she agreed to this in the far North, she would be let entirely alone in the rest of the country. Anyhow, we ought to take it for granted that the Germans will try to enter the ore-field and carry succour to the Narvik garrison by force or favour. We have, therefore, at the outside only a month to spare.

2. In this month we have not only to reduce and capture the town and the landed Germans, but to get up the railway to the Swedish frontier and to secure an effective well-defended seaplane base on some lake, in order, if we cannot obtain control of the ore-field, to prevent its being worked under German control. It would seem necessary that at least three thousand [more] good troops should be directed upon Narvik forthwith, and should reach there by the end of the first week in May at latest. The orders for this should be given now, as nothing will be easier than to divert the troops if in the meanwhile the situation is cleared up. It would be a great administrative advantage if these troops were British, but if this cannot be managed for any reason, could not the leading brigade of the Second French Light Division be directed upon Narvik? There ought to be no undue danger in bringing a big ship into Skjel Fiord or thereabouts.

3. I should be very glad if the Deputy Chief of Naval Staff could consult with an officer of equal standing in the War Office upon how this need can be met, together with ships and times. Failure to take Narvik will be a major disaster, and will carry with it the control by Germany of the ore-field.

The general position as it was viewed at this moment cannot be better stated than in a paper written by General Ismay on April 21.

The object of operations at Narvik is to capture the town and obtain possession of the railway to the Swedish frontier. We should then be in a position to put a force, if necessary, into the Gullivare ore-fields, the possession of which is the main objective of the whole of the operations in Scandinavia.

As soon as the ice melts in Lulea in about a month's time, we must expect that the Germans will obtain, by threats or force, a passage for their troops in order that they themselves may secure Gullivare and perhaps go forward and reinforce their troops at Narvik. It is, therefore, essential that Narvik should be liquidated in about a month.

The object of operations in the Trondheim area is to capture Trondheim, and thereby obtain a base for further operations in Central Norway, and Sweden if necessary. Landings have been made at Namsos on the north of Trondheim and Andalsnes on the south. The intention is that the Namsos force will establish itself astride the railway running eastward from Trondheim, thus encircling the Germans there on the east and northeast. The force landed at Andalsnes has as its first rôle the occupation of a defensive position, in co-operation with the Norwegians at Lillehammer, to block any reinforcement of Trondheim from the main German landing at Oslo. The road and railways between Oslo and Trondheim have both to be covered. When this has been achieved, some troops will work northward and bring pressure to bear on Trondheim from the south.

At the present moment our main attention is directed to the Trondheim area. It is essential to support the Norwegians and ensure that Trondheim is not reinforced. The capture of Narvik is not at the present moment so urgent, but it will become increasingly so as the thaw in the Gulf of Bothnia approaches. If Sweden enters the war, Narvik becomes the vital spot.

The operations in Central Norway which are now being undertaken are of an extremely hazardous nature, and we are confronted with serious difficulties. Among these, the chief are:

First, that the urgent need of coming to the assistance of the Norwegians without delay has forced us to throw ashore hastily improvised forces — making use of whatever was readily available.

Secondly, that our entry into Norway is perforce through bases which are inadequate for the maintenance of big formations.

The only recognised base in the area is Trondheim, which is in the hands of the enemy. We are making use of Namsos and

Andalsnes, which are only minor ports possessing few, if any, facilities for unloading military stores, and served by poor communications with the interior. Consequently, the landing of mechanical transport, artillery, supplies, and petrol (nothing is obtainable locally) is a matter which, even if we were not hampered in other ways, would present considerable difficulty. Thus, until we succeed in capturing Trondheim, the size of the forces which we can maintain in Norway is strictly limited.

Of course, it may be said that all Norwegian enterprises, however locally successful, to which we might have committed ourselves would have been swept away by the results of the fearful battle in France which was now so near. Within a month the main Allied armies were to be shattered or driven into the sea. Everything we had would have been drawn into the struggle for life. It was, therefore, lucky for us that we were not able to build up a substantial army and air force round Trondheim. The veils of the future are lifted one by one, and mortals must act from day to day. On the knowledge we had in the middle of April, I remain of the opinion that, having gone so far, we ought to have persisted in carrying out "Operation Hammer," and the threefold attack on Trondheim on which all had been agreed; but I accept my full share of responsibility for not enforcing this upon our expert advisers when they became so decidedly adverse to it and presented us with serious objections. In that case, however, it would have been better to abandon the whole enterprise against Trondheim and concentrate all upon Narvik. But for this it was now too late. Many of the troops were ashore, and the Norwegians crying for help.

15

Frustration in Norway

ON APRIL 20, I had procured agreement to the appointment
of Lord Cork as sole Commander of the naval, military,
and air forces in the Narvik area, thus bringing General
Mackesy directly under his authority. There was never any
doubt of Lord Cork's vigorously offensive spirit. He realised
acutely the danger of delay; but the physical and administrative difficulties were far greater on the spot than we could
measure at home. Moreover, naval officers, even when granted
the fullest authority, are chary of giving orders to the Army
about purely military matters. This would be even more true
if the positions were reversed. We had hoped that by relieving
General Mackesy from direct major responsibility, we should
make him feel more free to adopt bold tactics. The result was
contrary to this expectation. He continued to use every argu-

ment, and there was no lack of them, to prevent drastic action.
Things had changed to our detriment in the week that had
passed since the idea of an improvised assault upon Narvik
town had been rejected. The two thousand German soldiers
were no doubt working night and day at their defences, and
these and the town all lay hidden under a pall of snow. The
enemy had no doubt by now also organised two or three thousand sailors who had escaped from the sunken destroyers.
Their arrangements for bringing air power to bear improved
every day, and both our ships and landed troops endured increasing bombardment. On the twenty-first, Lord Cork wrote
to me as follows:

I write to thank you for the trust you have reposed in me. I
shall certainly do my best to justify it. The inertia is difficult to
overcome, and of course the obstacles to the movements of troops
are considerable, particularly the snow which, on northern slopes
of hills, is still many feet deep. I myself have tested that, and as it
has been snowing on and off for two days the position has not
improved. The initial error was that the original force started on
the assumption they would meet with no resistance, a mistake we
often make, e.g., Tanga.[1] As it is, the soldiers have not yet got
their reserves of small-arms ammunition, or water, but tons of stuff
and personnel they do not want. . . .

What is really our one pressing need is fighters; we are so overmatched in the air. There is a daily inspection of this place, and
they come when there are transports or steamers to bomb. Sooner
or later they must get a hit. I flew over Narvik yesterday, but it was
very difficult to see much. The rocky cliff is covered with snow,
except for rock outcrops, round which the drifts must be deep. It
is snow down to the water's edge, which makes it impossible to see
the nature of the foreshore.

While waiting for the conditions necessary for an attack, we are
isolating the town from the world by breaking down the railway
culverts, etc., and the large ferry steamer has been shelled and
burnt. . . . It is exasperating not being able to get on, and I quite
understand you wondering why we do not, but I assure you that it
is not from want of desire to do so.

[1] The landing at Tanga, near Zanzibar, in 1917.

Lord Cork decided upon reconnaissance in force, under cover of a naval bombardment, but here General Mackesy interposed. He stated that before the proposed action against Narvik began, he felt it his duty to represent that there was no officer or man in his command who would not feel ashamed for himself and his country if thousands of Norwegian men, women, and children in Narvik were subject to the proposed bombardment. Lord Cork contented himself with forwarding this statement without comment. Neither the Prime Minister nor I could be present at the Defence Committee meeting on April 22, as we had to attend the Supreme War Council in Paris on that day. Before leaving I had drafted a reply which was approved by our colleagues:

I presume that Lord Cork has read the bombardment instructions issued at the outbreak of war. If he finds it necessary to go beyond these instructions on account of the enemy using the shelter of buildings to maintain himself in Narvik, he may deem it wise to give six hours' warning by every means at his disposal, including if possible leaflets, and to inform the German Commander that all civilians must leave the town, and that he would be held responsible if he obstructed their departure. He might also offer to leave the railway line unmolested for a period of six hours to enable civilians to make good their escape by that route.

The Defence Committee endorsed this policy, strongly expressing the view that "it would be impossible to allow the Germans to convert Norwegian towns into forts by keeping the civilians in the towns to prevent us from attacking."

* * * * *

We arrived in Paris with our minds oppressed by the anxieties and confusion of the campaign in Norway, for the conduct of which the British were responsible. But M. Reynaud, having welcomed us, opened with a statement on the general military position which by its gravity dwarfed our Scandinavian excursions. Geography, he said, gave Germany the permanent advantage of interior lines. She had 190 divisions, of which 150 could be used on the Western Front. Against these the Allies had 100, of which 10 were British. In the previous war, Germany, with a population of sixty-five millions, had raised 248 divisions, of which 207 fought on the Western Front. France on her part had raised 118 divisions, of which 110 had been on the Western Front; and Great Britain 89 divisions, of which 63 had been on the Western Front, giving a total of 173 Allied against 207 German divisions in the West. Equality had been attained only when the Americans arrived with their 34 divisions. How much worse was the position today! The German population was now eighty millions, from which she could conceivably raise 300 divisions. France could hardly expect that there would be 20 British divisions in the West by the end of the year. We must, therefore, face a large and increasing numerical superiority which was already three to two and would presently rise to two to one. As for equipment, Germany had the advantage both in aviation and aircraft equipment and also in artillery and stocks of ammunition. Thus Reynaud.

To this point, then, had we come from the days of the Rhineland occupation in 1936, when a mere operation of police would have sufficed; or since Munich, when Germany, occupied with Czechoslovakia, could spare but thirteen divisions for the Western Front; or even since September, 1939, when, while the Polish resistance lasted, there were but forty-two German divisions in the West. All this terrible superiority had grown up because at no moment had the once victorious Allies dared to take any effective step, even when they were all-powerful, to resist repeated aggressions by Hitler and breaches of the Treaties.

*   *   *   *   *

After this sombre interlude, of the gravity of which we were all conscious, we came back to the Scandinavian tangle. The Prime Minister explained the position with clarity. We had landed thirteen thousand men at Namsos and Andalsnes without loss. Our forces had pushed forward farther than had been expected. On finding that the direct attack on Trondheim would demand a disproportionate amount of naval force, it had been

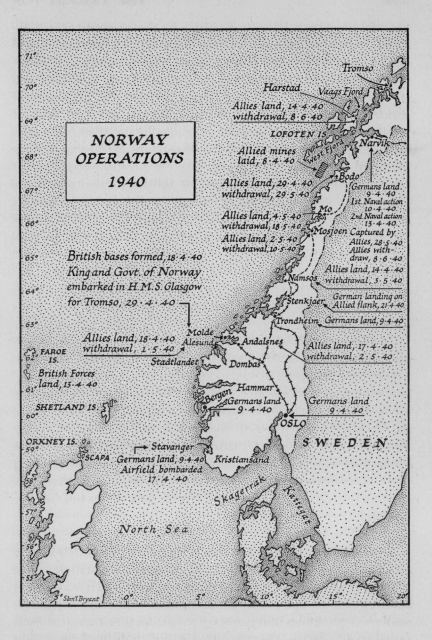

NORWAY
OPERATIONS
1940

Tromso

Harstad
Vaags Fjord
Allies land, 14·4·40
withdrawal, 8·6·40

LOFOTEN IS.

Narvik
Allied mines
laid, 8·4·40

West Fjord

Bodo
Germans land,
9·4·40
1st Naval action
10·4·40
2nd Naval action
13·4·40

Allies land, 29·4·40
withdrawal, 29·5·40

Mo

Allies land, 4·5·40
withdrawal, 18·5·40

Mosjoen Captured by
Allies, 28·5·40

Allies land, 2·5·40
withdrawal, 10·5·40

Allies with-
draw, 8·6·40

British bases formed, 18·4·40
King and Govt. of Norway
embarked in H.M.S. Glasgow
for Tromso, 29·4·40

Allies land, 14·4·40
withdrawal, 5·5·40

Namsos

German landing on
Allied flank, 21·4·40

Stenkjaer

Trondheim Germans land, 9·4·40

Molde
Alesund

Andalsnes

Allies land, 17·4·40
withdrawal, 2·5·40

Allies land, 18·4·40
withdrawal, 1·5·40

Stadtlandet

Dombas

FAROE
IS.

British Forces
land, 13·4·40

Hammar

Bergen
Germans land
9·4·40

Germans land
9·4·40

SHETLAND IS.

OSLO

ORKNEY IS.
SCAPA

Stavanger
Germans land, 9·4·40
Airfield bombarded
17·4·40

Kristiansand

SWEDEN

Skagerrak

Kattegat

North Sea

Sam'l Bryant

decided to make a pincer movement from the north and south instead. But in the last two days these new plans had been rudely interrupted by a heavy air attack on Namsos. As there had been no anti-aircraft fire to oppose them, the Germans had bombed at will. Meanwhile, all German naval vessels at Narvik had been destroyed. But the German troops there were strongly fortified, so that it had not yet been possible to attack them by land. If our first attempt did not succeed, it would be renewed.

About Central Norway, Mr. Chamberlain said that the British Command were anxious to reinforce the troops who had gone there, to protect them against the German advance from the south, and to co-operate subsequently in the capture of Trondheim. It was already certain that reinforcements would be required. Five thousand British, seven thousand French, three thousand Poles, three British mechanised battalions, one British light-tank battalion, three French light divisions, and one British Territorial division were to be available in the near future. The limitation would not be the number of troops provided, but the number that could be landed and maintained in the country. M. Reynaud said that four French light divisions would be sent.

I now spoke for the first time at any length in these conferences, pointing out the difficulties of landing troops and stores in the face of enemy aircraft and U-boats. Every single ship had to be convoyed by destroyers, every landing-port continuously guarded by cruisers or destroyers, not only during the landing, but till ack-ack guns could be mounted ashore. So far the Allied ships had been extraordinarily lucky and had sustained very few hits. The tremendous difficulties of the operation would be understood. Although thirteen thousand men had now been safely landed, the Allies had as yet no established bases, and were operating inland with weak and slender lines of cummunication, practically unprovided with artillery or supporting aircraft. Such was the position in Central Norway.

At Narvik the Germans were less strong, the port far less exposed to air attack, and once the harbour had been secured, it would be possible to land at a very much faster rate. Any forces

which could not be landed at ports farther south should go to
Narvik. Among the troops assigned to the Narvik operation,
or indeed in Great Britain, there were none able to move across
country in heavy snow. The task at Narvik would be not only
to free the harbour and the town, nor even to clear the whole
district of Germans, but to advance up the railway to the Swedish frontier in strength commensurate with any further German designs. It was the considered view of the British Command that this could be done without slowing down the rate
of landing at other ports beyond the point to which it was
already restricted by the difficulties described.

We were all in full agreement on the unpleasantness of our
plight and the little we could do at the moment to better it.
The Supreme War Council agreed that the immediate military
objectives should be:

(a) The capture of Trondheim, and
(b) the capture of Narvik, and the concentration of an adequate
Allied force on the Swedish frontier.

The next day we talked about the dangers to the Dutch and
Belgians and their refusal to take any common measures with
us. We were very conscious that Italy might declare war upon
us at any time, and various naval measures were to be concerted
in the Mediterranean between Admiral Pound and Admiral
Darlan. To this meeting General Sikorski also was invited. He
declared his ability to constitute a force of a hundred thousand
men within a few months. Active steps were also being taken
to recruit a Polish division in the United States.

At this meeting it was agreed also that if Germany invaded
Holland the Allied armies should at once advance into Belgium
without further approaches to the Belgian Government; and
that the R.A.F. could bomb the German marshalling-yards and
the oil refineries in the Ruhr.

*   *   *   *   *

When we got back from the Conference, I was so much concerned at the complete failure, not only of our efforts against

the enemy, but of our method of conducting the war, that I wrote as follows to the Prime Minister:

Being anxious to sustain you to the best of my ability, I must warn you that you are approaching a head-on smash in Norway.

I am very grateful to you for having at my request taken over the day-to-day management of the Military Co-ordination [Committee], etc. I think I ought, however, to let you know that I shall not be willing to receive that task back from you without the necessary powers. At present no one has the power. There are six Chiefs [and Deputy Chiefs] of the Staff, three Ministers, and General Ismay, who all have a voice in Norwegian operations (apart from Narvik). But no one is responsible for the creation and direction of military policy except yourself. If you feel able to bear this burden, you may count upon my unswerving loyalty as First Lord of the Admiralty. If you do not feel you can bear it, with all your other duties, you will have to delegate your powers to a deputy who can concert and direct the general movement of our war action, and who will enjoy your support and that of the War Cabinet unless very good reason is shown to the contrary.

Before I could send it off, I received a message from the Prime Minister saying that he had been considering the position of Scandinavia and felt it to be unsatisfactory. He asked me to call on him that evening at Downing Street after dinner to discuss the whole situation in private.

I have no record of what passed at our conversation, which was of a most friendly character. I am sure I put the points in my unsent letter, and that the Prime Minister agreed with their force and justice. He had every wish to give me the powers of direction for which I asked, and there was no kind of personal difficulty between us. He had, however, to consult and persuade a number of important personages, and it was not till May 1 that he was able to issue the following note to the Cabinet and those concerned.

May 1, 1940.

I have been examining, in consultation with the Ministers in charge of the service departments, the existing arrangements for the consideration and decision of defence questions, and I circulate for the information of my colleagues a memorandum describing certain modifications which it has been decided to make in these arrangements forthwith. The modifications have been agreed to by the three Service Ministers. With the approval of the First Lord of the Admiralty, Major-General H. L. Ismay, C.B., D.S.O., has been appointed to the post of Senior Staff Officer in charge of the Central Staff which, as indicated in the memorandum, is to be placed at the disposal of the First Lord. Major-General Ismay has been nominated, while serving in this capacity, an additional member of the Chiefs of Staff Committee. N. C.

Defence Organisation

In order to obtain a greater concentration of the direction of the war, the following modifications of present arrangements will take effect.

The First Lord of the Admiralty will continue to take the chair at all meetings of the Military Co-ordination Committee at which the Prime Minister does not preside himself, and in the absence of the Prime Minister will act as his deputy at such meetings on all matters delegated to the Committee by the War Cabinet.

He will be responsible on behalf of the Committee for giving guidance and directions to the Chiefs of Staff Committee, and for this purpose it will be open to him to summon that Committee for personal consultation at any time when he considers it necessary.

The Chiefs of Staff will retain their responsibility for giving their collective views to the Government and, with their respective staffs, will prepare plans to achieve any objectives indicated to them by the First Lord on behalf of the Military Co-ordination Committee, and will accompany their plans by such comments as they consider appropriate.

The Chiefs of Staff, who will in their individual capacity remain responsible to their respective Ministers, will at all times keep their Ministers informed of their conclusions.

Where time permits, the plans of the Chiefs of Staff, with their comments and any comments by the First Lord, will be circulated for approval to the Military Co-ordination Committee, and unless the Military Co-ordination Committee is authorised by the War Cabinet to take final decision, or in the case of disagreement on the Military Co-ordination Committee, circulated to the War Cabinet.

In urgent cases it may be necessary to omit the submission of plans to a formal meeting of the Committee, but in such cases the First Lord will no doubt find means of consulting the Service Ministers informally, and in the case of dissent, the decision will be referred to the Prime Minister.

In order to facilitate the general plan outlined above and to afford a convenient means of maintaining a close liaison between the First Lord and the Chiefs of Staff, the First Lord will be assisted by a suitable central staff (distinct from the Admiralty Staff) under a senior staff officer who will be an additional member of the Chiefs of Staff Committee.

I accepted this arrangement, which seemed a marked improvement. I could now convene and preside over the meetings of the Chiefs of Staff Committee, without whom nothing could be done, and I was made responsible formally "for giving guidance and direction" to them. General Ismay, the senior staff officer in charge of the Central Staff, was placed at my disposal *as my staff officer and representative,* and in this capacity was made a full member of the Chiefs of Staff Committee. I had known Ismay for many years, but now for the first time we became hand-and-glove, and much more. Thus the Chiefs of Staff were to a large extent made responsible to me in their collective capacity, and as a deputy of the Prime Minister I could nominally influence with authority their decisions and policies. On the other hand, it was only natural that their primary loyalties should be to their own Service Ministers, who would have been less than human if they had not felt some resentment at the delegation of a part of their authority to one of their colleagues. Moreover, it was expressly laid down in the memorandum that my responsibilities were to be discharged *on behalf of* the Military Co-ordination Committee. I was thus to have immense responsibilities, without effective power in my own hands to discharge them. Nevertheless, I had a feeling that I might be able to make the new organisation work. It was destined to last only a week. But my personal and official connection with General Ismay and his relation to the Chiefs of Staff Committee was preserved unbroken and unweakened from May 1, 1940, to July 27, 1945, when I laid down my charge.

*   *   *   *   *

It is now necessary to recount the actual course of the fighting for Trondheim. Our northern force from Namsos was eighty miles from the town; and our southern force from Andalsnes was one hundred and fifty miles away. The central attack through the fiord ("Hammer") had been abandoned, partly through fear of its cost and partly through hopes of the flanking movements. Both these movements now failed utterly. The Namsos force, commanded by Carton de Wiart, hastened forward in accordance with his instructions against the Norwegian snow and the German air. A brigade reached Verdal, fifty miles from Trondheim, at the head of the fiord, on the nineteenth. It was evident to me, and I warned the staffs, that the Germans could send in a single night a stronger force by water from Trondheim to chop them. This occurred two days later. Our troops were forced to withdraw some miles to where they could hold the enemy. The intolerable snow conditions, now sometimes in thaw, and the fact that the Germans who had come across the inner fiord were like us destitute of wheeled transport, prevented any serious fighting on the ground; and the small number of scattered troops plodding along the road offered little target to the unresisted air power. Had Carton de Wiart known how limited were the forces he would have, or that the central attack on Trondheim had been abandoned — a vital point of which our staff machinery did not inform him — he would no doubt have made a more methodical advance. He acted in relation to the main objective as it had been imparted to him.

In the end, nearly everybody got back exhausted, chilled, and resentful to Namsos, where the French Chasseur Brigade had remained; and Carton de Wiart, whose opinion on such issues commanded respect, declared that there was nothing for it but evacuation. Preparations for this were at once made by the Admiralty. On April 28, the evacuation of Namsos was ordered. The French contingent would re-embark before the British, leaving some of their ski troops to work with our rear guard. The probable dates for leaving were the nights of the first and second of May. Eventually the withdrawal was achieved in a single night. All the troops were re-embarked on the night of the third, and were well out to sea when they were sighted by the German air reconnaissance at dawn. From eight o'clock in the morning to three in the afternoon, wave after wave of enemy bombers attacked the warships and the transports. We were lucky that no transport was hit, as no British air forces were available to protect the convoy. The French destroyer *Bison,* and H.M.S. *Afridi,* which carried our rear guard, were "sunk fighting to the end."

*   *   *   *   *

A different series of misfortunes befell the troops landed at Andalsnes; but here at least we took our toll of the enemy. In response to urgent appeals from General Ruge, the Norwegian Commander-in-Chief, Brigadier Morgan's 148th Infantry Brigade had hastened forward as far as Lillehammer. Here it joined the tired-out battered Norwegian forces whom the Germans, in the overwhelming strength of three fully equipped divisions, were driving before them along the road and railway from Oslo towards Dombas and Trondheim. Severe fighting began. The ship carrying Brigadier Morgan's vehicles, including all artillery and mortars, had been sunk, but his young Territorials fought well with their rifles and machine-guns against the German vanguards, who were armed not only with 5.9 howitzers, but many heavy mortars and some tanks. On April 24, the leading battalion of the 15th Brigade arriving from France reached the crumbling front. General Paget, who commanded these regular troops, learned from General Ruge that the Norwegian forces were exhausted and could fight no more until they had been thoroughly rested and re-equipped.

He, therefore, assumed control, brought the rest of this brigade into action as fast as they arrived, and faced the Germans with determination in a series of spirited engagements. By the adroit use of the railway, which fortunately remained unbroken, Paget extricated his own troops, Morgan's Brigade, which had lost seven hundred men, and some Norwegian units. For one whole day the bulk of the British force hid in a long railway tunnel fed by their precious supply train, and were thus completely lost to the enemy and his all-seeing air. After fighting five rear-guard actions, in several of which the Germans were heavily mauled, and having covered over a hundred miles, he reached the sea again at Andalsnes. This small place, like Namsos, had been flattened out by bombing; but by the night of May 1, the 15th Brigade, with what remained of Morgan's 148th Brigade, had been taken on board British cruisers and destroyers and reached home without further trouble. General Paget's skill and resolution during these days opened his path to high command as the war developed.

A forlorn, gallant effort to give support from the air should be recorded. The only landing-"ground" was the frozen lake of Lesjeskogen, forty miles from Andalsnes. There a squadron of Gladiators, flown from the *Glorious,* arrived on April 24. They were at once heavily attacked. The Fleet air arm did their best to help them; but the task of fighting for existence, of covering the operations of two expeditions two hundred miles apart, and of protecting their bases, was too much for a single squadron. By April 26, it could fly no more. Long-range efforts by British bombers, working from England, were also unavailing.

* * * * *

Our withdrawal enforced by local events had conformed to the decision already taken by the War Cabinet on the advice of the Military Co-ordination Committee with the Prime Minister presiding. We had all come to the conclusion that it was beyond our power to seize and hold Trondheim. Both claws of the feeble pincers were broken. Mr. Chamberlain announced

to the Cabinet that plans must be made for evacuating our
forces both from Namsos and Andalsnes, though we should in
the meanwhile continue to resist the German advance. The
Cabinet was distressed at these proposals, which were, however,
inevitable.

*   *   *   *   *

In order to delay to the utmost the northward advance of
the enemy towards Narvik, we were now sending special companies raised in what was afterwards called "Commando" style,
under an enterprising officer, Colonel Gubbins, to Mosjoen,
one hundred miles farther up the coast. I was most anxious
that a small part of the Namsos force should make their way in
whatever vehicles were available along the coastal road to
Grong. Even a couple of hundred would have sufficed to fight
small rear-guard actions. From Grong they would have to find
their way on foot to Mosjoen. I hoped by this means to gain
the time for Gubbins to establish himself so that a stand could
be made against the very small numbers which the enemy could
as yet send there. I was repeatedly assured that the road was
impassable. General Massy from London sent insistent requests. It was replied that even a small party of French
Chasseurs, with their skis, could not traverse this route. "It
was [seemed] evident," wrote General Massy a few days later
in his dispatch, "that if the French Chasseurs could not retire
along this route, the Germans could not advance along it. . . .
This was an error, as the Germans have since made full use of
it and have advanced so rapidly along it that our troops in
Mosjoen have not had time to get properly established, and it
is more than likely that we shall not be able to hold the place."
This proved true. The destroyer *Janus* took a hundred
Chasseurs Alpins and two light A.A. guns round by sea, but
they left again before the Germans came.

*   *   *   *   *

We have now pursued the Norwegian campaign to the
point where it was overwhelmed by gigantic events. The superiority of the Germans in design, management, and energy were

plain. They put into ruthless execution a carefully prepared
plan of action. They comprehended perfectly the use of the air
arm on a great scale in all its aspects. Moreover, their individual ascendancy was marked, especially in small parties. At
Narvik a mixed and improvised German force, barely six
thousand strong, held at bay for six weeks some twenty thousand Allied troops, and though driven out of the town lived to
see them depart. The Narvik attack, so brilliantly opened by
the Navy, was paralysed by the refusal of the military commander to run what was admittedly a desperate risk. The
division of our resources between Narvik and Trondheim was
injurious to both our plans. The abandonment of the central
thrust on Trondheim wears an aspect of vacillation in the
British High Command for which, not only the experts, but
the political chiefs who yielded too easily to their advice, must
bear a burden. At Namsos there was a muddy waddle forward
and back. Only in the Andalsnes expedition did we bite. The
Germans traversed in seven days the road from Namsos to
Mosjoen, which the British and French had declared impassable. At Bodo and Mo, during the retreat of Gubbins'
force to the north, we were each time just too late, and the
enemy, although they had to overcome hundreds of miles of
rugged, snow-clogged country, drove us back in spite of gallant
episodes. We, who had the command of the sea and could
pounce anywhere on an undefended coast, were outpaced by
the enemy moving by land across very large distances in the
face of every obstacle. In this Norwegian encounter, our finest
troops, the Scots and Irish Guards, were baffled by the vigour,
enterprise, and training of Hitler's young men.

We tried hard, at the call of duty, to entangle and embed
ourselves in Norway. We thought Fortune had been cruelly
against us. We can now see that we were well out of it. Meanwhile, we had to comfort ourselves as best we might by a series of
successful evacuations. Failure at Trondheim! Stalemate at
Narvik! Such in the first week of May were the only results
we could show to the British nation, to our Allies, and to the
neutral world, friendly or hostile. Considering the prominent

part I played in these events and the impossibility of explaining
the difficulties by which we had been overcome, or the defects
of our staff and governmental organisation and our methods
of conducting war, it was a marvel that I survived and maintained my position in public esteem and parliamentary confidence. This was due to the fact that for six or seven years I
had predicted with truth the course of events, and had given
ceaseless warnings, then unheeded but now remembered.

*   *   *   *   *

"Twilight War" ended with Hitler's assault on Norway. It
broke into the glare of the most fearful military explosion so
far known to man. I have described the trance in which for
eight months France and Britain had been held while all the
world wondered. This phase proved most harmful to the Allies. From the moment when Stalin made terms with Hitler,
the Communists in France took their cue from Moscow and
denounced the war as "an imperialist and capitalist crime
against democracy." They did what they could to undermine
morale in the Army and impede production in the workshops.
The morale of France, both of her soldiers and her people,
was now in May markedly lower than at the outbreak of war.

Nothing like this happened in Britain, where Soviet-directed
Communism, though busy, was weak. Nevertheless, we were
still a Party Government, under a Prime Minister from whom
the Opposition was bitterly estranged, and without the ardent
and positive help of the trade-union movement. The sedate,
sincere, but routine character of the Administration did not
evoke that intense effort, either in the governing circles or in
the munition factories, which was vital. The stroke of catastrophe and the spur of peril were needed to call forth the dormant
might of the British nation. The tocsin was about to sound.

16

Norway: The Final Phase

*Immediate Assault on Narvik Abandoned — The Landings in
May — General Auchinleck Appointed to the Chief Military
Command — The Capture of the Town, May 28 — The Battle
in France Dominates All — Evacuation — The Homeward Con-
voys — Apparition of the German Battle Cruisers — The Loss
of the "Glorious" and "Ardent" — The Story of the "Acasta" —
Air Attack on German Ships at Trondheim — One Solid Result
— The German Fleet Ruined.*

I N DEFIANCE OF CHRONOLOGY, it is well to set forth here the
end of the Norwegian episode.

After April 16, Lord Cork was compelled to abandon the
idea of an immediate assault. A three hours' bombardment on
April 24, carried out by the battleship *Warspite* and three cruisers, was not effective in dislodging the garrison. I had asked
the First Sea Lord to arrange for the replacement of the *Warspite* by the less valuable *Resolution,* which was equally useful
for bombarding purposes. Meanwhile, the arrival of French
and Polish troops, and still more the thaw, encouraged Lord
Cork to press his attack on the town. The new plan was to land
at the head of the fiord beyond Narvik and thereafter to attack
Narvik across Rombaks Fiord. The 24th Guards Brigade had
been drawn off to stem the German advance from Trondheim:
but by the beginning of May, three battalions of Chasseurs
Alpins, two battalions of the French Foreign Legion, four
Polish battalions, and a Norwegian force of about thirty-five
hundred men were available. The enemy had for their part

been reinforced by portions of the 3d Mountain Division, which had either been brought by air from southern Norway or smuggled in by rail from Sweden.

The first landing, under General Mackesy, took place on the night of May 12/13 at Bjerkvik, with very little loss. General Auchinleck, whom I had sent to command all the troops in Northern Norway, was present and took charge the next day. His instructions were to cut off the iron-ore supplies and to defend a foothold in Norway for the King and his Government. The new British commander naturally asked for very large additions to bring his force up to seventeen battalions, two hundred heavy and light anti-aircraft guns, and four squadrons of airplanes. It was only possible to promise about half these requirements.

But now tremendous events became dominant. On May 24, in the crisis of shattering defeat, it was decided, with almost universal agreement, that we must concentrate all we had in France and at home. The capture of Narvik had, however, to be achieved both to ensure the destruction of the port and to cover our withdrawal. The main attack on Narvik across Rombaks Fiord was begun on May 27 by two battalions of the Foreign Legion and one Norwegian battalion under the able leadership of General Béthouart. It was entirely successful. The landing was effected with practically no loss and the counter-attack beaten off. Narvik was taken on May 28. The Germans, who had so long resisted forces four times their strength, retreated into the mountains, leaving four hundred prisoners in our hands.

We now had to relinquish all that we had won after such painful exertions. The withdrawal was in itself a considerable operation, imposing a heavy burden on the Fleet, already fully extended by the fighting both in Norway and in the Narrow Seas. Dunkirk was upon us, and all available light forces were drawn to the south. The battle fleet must itself be held in readiness to resist invasion. Many of the cruisers and destroyers had already been sent south for anti-invasion duties. The Commander-in-Chief had at his disposal at Scapa the capital ships

Rodney, Valiant, Renown, and *Repulse.* These had to cover
all contingencies.

Good progress in evacuation was made at Narvik, and by
June 8 all the troops, French and British, amounting to twenty-
four thousand men, together with large quantities of stores
and equipment, were embarked and sailed in three convoys
without hindrance from the enemy, who indeed now amounted
on shore to no more than a few thousand scattered, disorganised, but victorious individuals. During these last days
valuable protection was afforded against the German air force,
not only by naval aircraft, but by a shore-based squadron of
Hurricanes. This squadron had been ordered to keep in action
till the end, destroying their aircraft if necessary. However, by
their skill and daring these pilots performed the unprecedented
feat — their last — of flying their Hurricanes on board the carrier *Glorious,* which sailed with the *Ark Royal* and the main
body.

To cover all these operations, Lord Cork had at his disposal,
in addition to the carriers, the cruisers *Southampton* and *Cov-
entry* and sixteen destroyers, besides smaller vessels. The
cruiser *Devonshire* was meanwhile embarking the King of Norway and his staff from Tromso, and was therefore moving independently. Lord Cork informed the Commander-in-Chief of
his convoy arrangements, and asked for protection against
possible attack by heavy ships. Admiral Forbes dispatched the
Valiant on June 6, to meet the first convoy of troopships and
escort it north of the Shetlands and then return to meet the
second. Despite all other preoccupations he had intended to
use his battle cruisers to protect the troopships. On June 5,
reports had reached him of two unknown ships apparently
making for Iceland, and later of an enemy landing there. He,
therefore, felt compelled to send his battle cruisers to investigate these reports, which proved to be false. Thus, on this
unlucky day our available forces in the North were widely
dispersed. The movement of the Narvik convoys and their protection followed closely the method pursued without mishap
during the past six weeks. It had been customary to send

transports and warships, including aircraft carriers, over this route, with no more than anti-submarine escort. No activity by German heavy ships had hitherto been detected. Now, having repaired the damage they had suffered in the earlier encounters, they suddenly appeared off the Norwegian coast.

The battle cruisers *Scharnhorst* and *Gneisenau,* with the cruiser *Hipper* and four destroyers, left Kiel on June 4, with the object of attacking shipping and bases in the Narvik area and thus providing relief for what was left of their landed forces. No hint of our intended withdrawal reached them till June 7. On the news that British convoys were at sea, the German Admiral decided to attack them. Early the following morning, the eighth, he caught a tanker with a trawler escort, an empty troopship *Orama,* and the hospital ship *Atlantis.* He respected the immunity of the *Atlantis.* All the rest were sunk. That afternoon the *Hipper* and the destroyers returned to Trondheim, but the battle cruisers, continuing their search for prey, were rewarded when at 4 P.M. they sighted the smoke of the aircraft carrier *Glorious,* with her two escorting destroyers, the *Acasta* and *Ardent.* The *Glorious* had been detached early that morning to proceed home independently owing to shortage of fuel, and by now was nearly two hundred miles ahead of the main convoy. This explanation is not convincing. The *Glorious* had enough fuel to steam at the speed of the convoy. All should have kept together.

The action began about 4.30 P.M. at over twenty-seven thousand yards. At this range the *Glorious,* with her four-inch guns, was helpless. Efforts were made to get her torpedo-bombers into the air, but before this could be done, she was hit in the forward hangar, and a fire began which destroyed the Hurricanes and prevented torpedoes being got up from below for the bombers. In the next half-hour she received staggering blows which deprived her of all chance of escape. By 5.20 she was listing heavily, and the order was given to abandon ship. She sank about twenty minutes later.

Meanwhile, her two destroyers behaved nobly. Both made smoke in an endeavour to screen the *Glorious,* and both fired their torpedoes at the enemy before being overwhelmed. The *Ardent* was soon sunk. The story of the *Acasta*, now left alone at hopeless odds, has been told by the sole survivor, Leading-Seaman C. Carter:

On board our ship, what a deathly calm, hardly a word spoken, the ship was now steaming full speed away from the enemy, then came a host of orders, prepare all smoke floats, hose-pipes connected up, various other jobs were prepared, we were still steaming away from the enemy, and making smoke, and all our smoke floats had been set going. The Captain then had this message passed to all positions: "You may think we are running away from the enemy, we are not, our chummy ship [*Ardent*] has sunk, the *Glorious* is sinking, the least we can do is make a show, good luck to you all." We then altered course into our own smoke-screen. I had the order stand by to fire tubes 6 and 7, we then came out of the smoke-screen, altered course to starboard firing our torpedoes from port side. It was then I had my first glimpse of the enemy, to be honest it appeared to me to be a large one [ship] and a small one, and we were very close, I fired my two torpedoes from my tubes [aft], the foremost tubes fired theirs, we were all watching results. I'll never forget that cheer that went up; on the port bow of one of the ships a yellow flash and a great column of smoke and water shot up from her. We knew we had hit, personally I could not see how we could have missed so close as we were. The enemy never fired a shot at us, I feel they must have been very surprised. After we had fired our torpedoes we went back into our own smoke-screen, altered course again to starboard. "Stand by to fire remaining torpedoes"; and this time as soon as we poked our nose out of the smoke-screen, the enemy let us have it. A shell hit the engine-room, killed my tubes' crew, I was blown to the after end of the tubes, I must have been knocked out for a while, because when I came to, my arm hurt me; the ship had stopped with a list to port. Here is something, believe it or believe it not, I climbed back into the control seat, I see those two ships, I fired the remaining torpedoes, no one told me to, I guess I was raving mad. God alone knows why I fired them, but I did. The *Acasta's* guns were firing the whole time, even firing with a list on the ship. The enemy then hit us several times, but one big explosion took place right aft, I have often wondered whether the enemy hit us with a torpedo, in any case it seemed to

lift the ship out of the water. At last the Captain gave orders to
abandon ship. I will always remember the Surgeon Lieutenant,[1]
his first ship, his first action. Before I jumped over the side, I saw
him still attending to the wounded, a hopeless task, and when I
was in the water I saw the Captain leaning over the bridge, take a
cigarette from a case and light it. We shouted to him to come on
our raft, he waved "Good-bye and good luck" — the end of a
gallant man.

Thus perished 1,474 officers and men of the Royal Navy and
forty-one of the Royal Air Force. Despite prolonged search,
only thirty-nine were rescued and brought in later by a Norwegian ship. In addition, six men were picked up by the enemy
and taken to Germany. The *Scharnhorst,* heavily damaged by
the *Acasta's* torpedo, made her way to Trondheim.

While this action was going on, the cruiser *Devonshire,*
with the King of Norway and his Ministers, was about a hundred miles to the westward. The *Valiant* coming north to
meet the convoy was still a long way off. The only message
received from the *Glorious* was corrupt and barely intelligible, which suggests that her main wireless equipment was
broken from an early stage. The *Devonshire* alone received
this message, but as its importance was not apparent she did not
break wireless silence to pass it on, as to do so would have involved serious risk of revealing her position, which in the circumstances was highly undesirable. Not until the following
morning were suspicions aroused. Then the *Valiant* met the
Atlantis, who informed her of the loss of the *Orama* and that
enemy capital ships were at sea. The *Valiant* signalled the information and pressed on to join Lord Cork's convoy. The
Commander-in-Chief, Admiral Forbes, at once proceeded to
sea with the only ships he had, the *Rodney,* the *Renown,* and
six destroyers.

The damage inflicted on the *Scharnhorst* by the heroic
Acasta had important results. The two enemy battle cruisers
abandoned further operations and returned at once to Trondheim. The German High Command were dissatisfied with the

[1] Temporary Surgeon-Lieutenant H. J. Stammers, R.N.V.R.

action of their admiral in departing from the objective which
had been given him. They sent the *Hipper* out again; but it
was then too late.

On the tenth, Admiral Forbes ordered the *Ark Royal* to join
him. Reports showed that enemy ships were in Trondheim
and he hoped to make an air attack. This was delivered by
R.A.F. bombers on the eleventh without effect. On the following morning, fifteen Skuas from the *Ark Royal* made a dive-
bombing attack. Enemy reconnaissance gave warning of their
approach, and no fewer than eight were lost. To add one last
misfortune to our tale, it is now known that one bomb from a
Skua struck the *Scharnhorst,* but failed to explode.

Whilst these tragedies were in progress, the Narvik convoys
passed on safely to their destinations, and the British campaign
in Norway came to an end.

*   *   *   *   *

From all this wreckage and confusion there emerged one fact
of major importance potentially affecting the whole future of
the war. In their desperate grapple with the British Navy, the
Germans ruined their own, such as it was, for the impending
climax. The Allied losses in all this sea-fighting off Norway
amounted to one aircraft carrier, two cruisers, one sloop, and
nine destroyers. Six cruisers, two sloops, and eight destroyers
were disabled, but could be repaired within our margin of sea
power. On the other hand, at the end of June, 1940, a
momentous date, the effective German Fleet consisted of no
more than *one eight-inch cruiser, two light cruisers, and four
destroyers.* Although many of their damaged ships, like ours,
could be repaired, the German Navy was no factor in the
supreme issue of the invasion of Britain.

17

The Fall of the Government

*Debate of May 7 — A Vote of Censure Supervenes — Lloyd George's
Last Parliamentary Stroke — I Do My Best with the House —
My Advice to the Prime Minister — Conferences of May 9 —
The German Onslaught — A Conversation with the Prime
Minister, May 10 — The Dutch Agony — Mr. Chamberlain
Resigns — The King Asks Me to Form a Government — Accession
of the Labour and Liberal Parties — Facts and Dreams.*

THE MANY DISAPPOINTMENTS and disasters of the brief campaign in Norway caused profound perturbation at home, and the currents of passion mounted even in the breasts of some of those who had been most slothful and purblind in the years before the war. The Opposition asked for a debate on the war situation, and this was arranged for May 7. The House was filled with Members in a high state of irritation and distress. Mr. Chamberlain's opening statement did not stem the hostile tide. He was mockingly interrupted and reminded of his speech of April 5, when in quite another connection he had incautiously said, "Hitler missed the bus." He defined my new position and my relationship with the Chiefs of Staff, and in reply to Mr. Herbert Morrison made it clear that I had not held those powers during the Norwegian operations. One speaker after another from both sides of the House attacked the Government and especially its chief with unusual bitterness and vehemence, and found themselves sustained by growing applause from all quarters. Sir Roger Keyes, burning for distinction in the new war, sharply criticised the Naval Staff for their failure to attempt the capture of Trondheim. "When I saw," he said, "how badly things were going, I never ceased importuning the Admiralty and War Cabinet to let me take all responsibility and lead the attack." Wearing his uniform as Admiral of the Fleet, he supported the complaints of the Opposition with technical details and his own professional authority in a manner very agreeable to the mood of the House. From the benches behind the Government, Mr. Amery quoted amid ringing cheers Cromwell's imperious words to the Long Parliament: "You have sat too long here for any good you have been doing. Depart, I say, and let us have done with you. In the name of God, go!" These were terrible words coming from a friend and colleague of many years, a fellow Birmingham Member, and a Privy Councillor of distinction and experience.

On the second day, May 8, the debate, although continuing upon an adjournment motion, assumed the character of a vote of censure, and Mr. Herbert Morrison, in the name of the Opposition, declared their intention to have a vote. The Prime Minister rose again, accepted the challenge, and in an unfortunate passage appealed to his friends to stand by him. He had a right to do this, as these friends had sustained his action, or inaction, and thus shared his responsibility in "the years which the locusts had eaten" before the war. But today they sat abashed and silenced, and some of them had joined the hostile demonstrations. This day saw the last decisive intervention of Mr. Lloyd George in the House of Commons. In a speech of not more than twenty minutes he struck a deeply wounding blow at the head of the Government. He endeavoured to exculpate me: "I do not think that the First Lord was entirely responsible for all the things which happened in Norway." I immediately interposed: "I take complete responsibility for everything that has been done by the Admiralty, and I take my full share of the burden." After warning me not to allow myself to be converted into an air-raid shelter to keep the splinters from hitting my colleagues, Mr. Lloyd George turned upon Mr. Chamberlain: "It is not a question of who are the

Prime Minister's friends. It is a far bigger issue. He has appealed for sacrifice. The nation is prepared for every sacrifice so long as it has leadership, so long as the Government show clearly what they are aiming at, and so long as the nation is confident that those who are leading it are doing their best." He ended: "I say solemnly that the Prime Minister should give an example of sacrifice, because there is nothing which can contribute more to victory in this war than that he should sacrifice the seals of office."

As Ministers we all stood together. The Secretaries of State for War and Air had already spoken. I had volunteered to wind up the debate, which was no more than my duty, not only in loyalty to the chief under whom I served, but also because of the exceptionally prominent part I had played in the use of our inadequate forces during our forlorn attempt to succour Norway. I did my very best to regain control of the House for the Government in the teeth of continuous interruption, coming chiefly from the Labour Opposition benches. I did this with good heart when I thought of their mistaken and dangerous pacifism in former years, and how, only four months before the outbreak of the war, they had voted solidly against conscription. I felt that I, and a few friends who had acted with me, had the right to inflict these censures, but they had not. When they broke in upon me, I retorted upon them and defied them, and several times the clamour was such that I could not make myself heard. Yet all the time it was clear that their anger was not directed against me, but at the Prime Minister, whom I was defending to the utmost of my ability and without regard for any other considerations. When I sat down at eleven o'clock, the House divided. The Government had a majority of eighty-one, but over fifty Conservatives voted with the Labour and Liberal Oppositions, and there was no doubt that in effect, though not in form, both the debate and the division were a violent manifestation of want of confidence in Mr. Chamberlain and his Administration.

After the debate was over, he asked me to go to his room, and I saw at once that he took the most serious view of the sentiment of the House towards himself. He felt he could not go on. There ought to be a National Government. One party alone could not carry the burden. Someone must form a Government in which all parties would serve, or we could not get through. Aroused by the antagonisms of the debate, and being sure of my own past record on the issues at stake, I was strongly disposed to fight on. "This has been a damaging debate, but you have a good majority. Do not take the matter grievously to heart. We have a better case about Norway than it has been possible to convey to the House. Strengthen your Government from every quarter, and let us go on until our majority deserts us." To this effect I spoke. But Chamberlain was neither convinced nor comforted, and I left him about midnight with the feeling that he would persist in his resolve to sacrifice himself, if there was no other way, rather than attempt to carry the war further with a one-party Government.

I do not remember exactly how things happened during the morning of May 9, but the following occurred. Sir Kingsley Wood, Secretary of State for Air, was very close to the Prime Minister as a colleague and a friend. They had long worked together in complete confidence. From him I learned that Mr. Chamberlain was resolved upon the formation of a National Government and, if he could not be the head, he would give way to anyone commanding his confidence who could. Thus, by the afternoon, I became aware that I might well be called upon to take the lead. The prospect neither excited nor alarmed me. I thought it would be by far the best plan. I was content to let events unfold. In the afternoon, the Prime Minister summoned me to Downing Street, where I found Lord Halifax, and after a talk about the situation in general, we were told that Mr. Attlee and Mr. Greenwood would visit us in a few minutes for a consultation.

When they arrived, we three Ministers sat on one side of the table and the Opposition leaders on the other. Mr. Chamberlain declared the paramount need of a National Government, and sought to ascertain whether the Labour Party would serve under him. The conference of their party was in session at

Bournemouth. The conversation was most polite, but it was clear that the Labour leaders would not commit themselves without consulting their people, and they hinted, not obscurely, that they thought the response would be unfavourable. They then withdrew. It was a bright, sunny afternoon, and Lord Halifax and I sat for a while on a seat in the garden of Number 10 and talked about nothing in particular. I then returned to the Admiralty and was occupied during the evening and a large part of the night in heavy business.

*   *   *   *   *

The morning of the tenth of May dawned, and with it came tremendous news. Boxes with telegrams poured in from the Admiralty, the War Office, and the Foreign Office. The Germans had struck their long-awaited blow. Holland and Belgium were both invaded. Their frontiers had been crossed at numerous points. The whole movement of the German Army upon the invasion of the Low Countries and of France had begun.

At about ten o'clock, Sir Kingsley Wood came to see me, having just been with the Prime Minister. He told me that Mr. Chamberlain was inclined to feel that the great battle which had broken upon us made it necessary for him to remain at his post. Kingsley Wood had told him that, on the contrary, the new crisis made it all the more necessary to have a National Government, which alone could confront it, and he added that Mr. Chamberlain had accepted this view. At eleven o'clock, I was again summoned to Downing Street by the Prime Minister. There once more I found Lord Halifax. We took our seats at the table opposite Mr. Chamberlain. He told us that he was satisfied that it was beyond his power to form a National Government. The response he had received from the Labour leaders left him in no doubt of this. The question, therefore, was whom he should advise the King to send for after his own resignation had been accepted. His demeanour was cool, unruffled, and seemingly quite detached from the personal aspect of the affair. He looked at us both across the table.

I have had many important interviews in my public life, and this was certainly the most important. Usually I talk a great deal, but on this occasion I was silent. Mr. Chamberlain evidently had in his mind the stormy scene in the House of Commons two nights before, when I had seemed to be in such heated controversy with the Labour Party. Although this had been in his support and defence, he nevertheless felt that it might be an obstacle to my obtaining their adherence at this juncture. I do not recall the actual words he used, but this was the implication. His biographer, Mr. Feiling, states definitely that he preferred Lord Halifax. As I remained silent, a very long pause ensued. It certainly seemed longer than the two minutes which one observes in the commemorations of Armistice Day. Then at length Halifax spoke. He said that he felt that his position as a peer, out of the House of Commons, would make it very difficult for him to discharge the duties of Prime Minister in a war like this. He would be held responsible for everything, but would not have the power to guide the assembly upon whose confidence the life of every Government depended. He spoke for some minutes in this sense, and by the time he had finished, it was clear that the duty would fall upon me — had in fact fallen upon me. Then, for the first time, I spoke. I said I would have no communication with either of the Opposition Parties until I had the King's commission to form a Government. On this the momentous conversation came to an end, and we reverted to our ordinary easy and familiar manners of men who had worked for years together and whose lives in and out of office had been spent in all the friendliness of British politics. I then went back to the Admiralty, where, as may well be imagined, much awaited me.

The Dutch Ministers were in my room. Haggard and worn, with horror in their eyes, they had just flown over from Amsterdam. Their country had been attacked without the slightest pretext or warning. The avalanche of fire and steel had rolled across the frontiers, and when resistance broke out and the Dutch frontier guards fired, an overwhelming onslaught was

664 THE TWILIGHT WAR

made from the air. The whole country was in a state of wild confusion; the long-prepared defence scheme had been put into operation; the dykes were opened; the waters spread far and wide. But the Germans had already crossed the outer lines, and were now streaming across the causeway which enclosed the Zuyder Zee. Could we do anything to prevent this? Luckily, we had a flotilla not far away, and this was immediately ordered to sweep the causeway with fire, and take the heaviest toll possible of the swarming invaders. The Queen was still in Holland, but it did not seem she could remain there long.

As a consequence of these discussions, a large number of orders were dispatched by the Admiralty to all our ships in the neighborhood, and close relations were established with the Royal Dutch Navy. Even with the recent overrunning of Norway and Denmark in their minds, the Dutch Ministers seemed unable to understand how the great German nation, which, up to the night before, had professed nothing but friendship, and was bound by treaty to respect the neutrality of Holland, so strictly maintained, should suddenly have made this frightful and brutal onslaught. Upon these proceedings and other affairs, an hour or two passed. A spate of telegrams pressed in from all the frontiers affected by the forward heave of the German armies. It seemed that the old Schlieffen Plan, brought up to date with its Dutch extension, was already in full operation. In 1914, the swinging right arm of the German invasion had swept through Belgium, but had stopped short of Holland It was well known then that had that war been delayed fo three or four years, the extra army group would have bee ready, and the railway terminals and communications adapted for a movement through Holland. Now the famous movemen had been launched with all these facilities and with every ci cumstance of surprise and treachery. But other developmen lay ahead. The decisive stroke of the enemy was not to be turning movement on the flank, but a break through the ma front. This none of us or the French, who were in responsib command, foresaw. Earlier in the year I had, in a publishe interview, warned these neutral countries of the fate whic was impending upon them and which was evident from the troop dispositions and road and rail development, as well as from the captured German plans. My words had been resented.

In the splintering crash of this vast battle, the quiet conversations we had had in Downing Street faded or fell back in one's mind. However, I remember being told that Mr. Chamberlain had gone, or was going, to see the King, and this was naturally to be expected. Presently a message arrived summoning me to the Palace at six o'clock. It only takes two minutes to drive there from the Admiralty along the Mall. Although I suppose the evening newspapers must have been full of the terrific news from the Continent, nothing had been mentioned about the Cabinet crisis. The public had not had time to take in what was happening either abroad or at home, and there was no crowd about the Palace gates.

I was taken immediately to the King. His Majesty received me most graciously and bade me sit down. He looked at me searchingly and quizzically for some moments, and then said: "I suppose you don't know why I have sent for you?" Adopting his mood, I replied: "Sir, I simply couldn't imagine why." He laughed and said: "I want to ask you to form a Government." I said I would certainly do so.

The King had made no stipulation about the Government being national in character, and I felt that my commission was in no formal way dependent upon this point. But in view of what had happened, and the conditions which had led to Mr. Chamberlain's resignation, a Government of national character was obviously inherent in the situation. If I had found it impossible to come to terms with the Opposition Parties, I should not have been constitutionally debarred from trying to form the strongest Government possible of all who would stand by the country in the hour of peril, provided that such a Government could command a majority in the House of Commons. I told the King that I would immediately send for the leaders of the Labour and Liberal Parties, that I proposed to form a War Cabinet of five or six Ministers, and that I hoped to let him have at least five names before midnight. On this I took my leave and returned to the Admiralty.

Between seven and eight, at my request, Mr. Attlee called upon me. He brought with him Mr. Greenwood. I told him of the authority I had to form a Government and asked if the Labour Party would join. He said they would. I proposed that they should take rather more than a third of the places, having two seats in the War Cabinet of five, or it might be six, and I asked Mr. Attlee to let me have a list of men so that we could discuss particular offices. I mentioned Mr. Bevin, Mr. Alexander, Mr. Morrison, and Mr. Dalton as men whose services in high office were immediately required. I had, of course, known both Attlee and Greenwood for a long time in the House of Commons. During the eleven years before the outbreak of war, I had in my more or less independent position come far more often into collision with the Conservative and National Governments than with the Labour and Liberal Oppositions. We had a pleasant talk for a little while, and they went off to report by telephone to their friends and followers at Bournemouth, with whom, of course, they had been in the closest contact during the previous forty-eight hours.

I invited Mr. Chamberlain to lead the House of Commons as Lord President of the Council, and he replied by telephone that he accepted and had arranged to broadcast at nine that night, stating that he had resigned, and urging everyone to support and aid his successor. This he did in magnanimous terms. I asked Lord Halifax to join the War Cabinet while remaining Foreign Secretary. At about ten, I sent the King a list of five names, as I had promised. The appointment of the three Service Ministers was vitally urgent. I had already made up my mind who they should be. Mr. Eden should go to the War Office; Mr. Alexander should come to the Admiralty; and Sir Archibald Sinclair, leader of the Liberal Party, should take the Air Ministry. At the same time I assumed the office of Minister of Defence, without, however, attempting to define its scope and powers.

Thus, then, on the night of the tenth of May, at the outset of this mighty battle, I acquired the chief power in the State, which henceforth I wielded in ever-growing measure for five years and three months of world war, at the end of which time, all our enemies having surrendered unconditionally or being about to do so, I was immediately dismissed by the British electorate from all further conduct of their affairs.

During these last crowded days of the political crisis, my pulse had not quickened at any moment. I took it all as it came. But I cannot conceal from the reader of this truthful account that as I went to bed at about 3 A.M., I was conscious of a profound sense of relief. At last I had the authority to give directions over the whole scene. I felt as if I were walking with Destiny, and that all my past life had been but a preparation for this hour and for this trial. Eleven years in the political wilderness had freed me from ordinary party antagonisms. My warnings over the last six years had been so numerous, so detailed, and were now so terribly vindicated, that no one could gainsay me. I could not be reproached either for making the war or with want of preparation for it. I thought I knew a good deal about it all, and I was sure I should not fail. Therefore, although impatient for the morning, I slept soundly and had no need for cheering dreams. Facts are better than dreams.

END OF BOOK TWO

★

APPENDICES

In Appendices, Book II, short titles are frequently used in the memoranda and minutes when addressing members of the Board of Admiralty or heads of departments. For the convenience of the reader the corresponding full titles are tabulated below.

Short Title	Full Title
Controller	Controller and Third Sea Lord
D.C.N.S.	Deputy (or Vice) Chief of Naval Staff
A.C.N.S.	Assistant Chief of Naval Staff
D.N.I.	Director of Naval Intelligence
D.T.D.	Director of Trade Division
D.N.C.	Director of Naval Construction
D.T.M.	Director of Torpedoes and Mining
D.N.O.	Director of Naval Ordnance
D.S.R.	Director of Scientific Research

★

CONTENTS

APPENDICES TO BOOK ONE

APPENDICES TO BOOK TWO

PART I

Appendix A, Book I

A CONVERSATION WITH COUNT GRANDI

September 28, 1935.

Mr. Churchill to Sir Robert Vansittart.

Though he pleaded the Italian cause with much address, he of course realises the whole position. . . .

I told him that since Parliament rose, there had been a strong development of public opinion. England, and indeed the British Empire, could act unitedly on the basis of the League of Nations, and all parties thought that that instrument was the most powerful protection against future dangers wherever they might arise. He pointed out the injury to the League of Nations by the loss of Italy. The fall of the régime in Italy would inevitably produce a pro-German Italy. He seemed prepared for economic sanctions. They were quite ready to accept life upon a communal basis. However poor they were, they could endure. He spoke of the difficulty of following the movements of British public opinion. I said that no foreign ambassador could be blamed for that, but the fact of the change must be realised. Moreover, if fighting began in Abyssinia, cannons fired, blood was shed, villages were bombed, etc., an almost measureless rise in the temperature must be expected. He seemed to contemplate the imposition of economic sanctions which would at first be ineffective, but gradually increase until at some moment or other an event of war would occur.

I said the British Fleet was very strong, and, although it had to be rebuilt in the near future, it was good and efficient at the present moment, and it was now completely ready to defend itself; but I repeated that this was a purely defensive measure in view of our Mediterranean interests, and did not in any way differentiate our position from that of other members of the League of Nations. He accepted this with a sad smile.

I then talked of the importance of finding a way out: "He that ruleth his spirit is greater than he that taketh a city." He replied that they would feel that everywhere except in Italy. They had to deal with two hundred thousand men with rifles in their hands. Mussolini's dictatorship was a popular dictatorship, and success was the essence of its strength. Finally, I said that I was in favour of a meeting between the political chiefs of the three countries. . . . The three men together could carry off something that one could never do by himself. After all, the claims of Italy to primacy in the Abyssinian sphere and the imperative need of internal reform [in Abyssinia] had been fully recognised by England and France. I told him I should support such an idea if it were agreeable. The British public would be willing to try all roads to an honourable peace. I think there should be a meeting of three. Any agreement they reached would of course be submitted to the League of Nations. It seems to me the only chance of avoiding the destruction of Italy as a powerful and friendly factor in Europe. Even if it failed, no harm would have been done, and at present we are heading for an absolute smash.

Appendix B, Book I

MY NOTE ON THE FLEET AIR ARM

WRITTEN FOR SIR THOMAS INSKIP, MINISTER FOR THE CO-ORDINATION OF DEFENCE, IN 1936

1. It is impossible to resist an admiral's claim that he must have complete control of, and confidence in, the aircraft of the battle fleet, whether used for reconnaissance, gun-fire or air attack on a hostile fleet. These are his very eyes. Therefore the Admiralty view must prevail in all that is required to secure this result.

2. The argument that similar conditions obtain in respect of Army co-operation aircraft cannot be countenanced. In one case the aircraft take flight from aerodromes and operate under precisely similar conditions to those of normal independent air force action. Flight from warships and action in connection with naval operations is a totally different matter. One is truly an affair of co-operation only; the other an integral part of modern naval operations.

3. A division must therefore be made between the air force controlled by the Admiralty and that controlled by the Air Ministry. This division does not depend upon the type of the undercarriage of the aircraft, nor necessarily the base from which it is flown. It depends upon the function. Is it predominantly a naval function or not?

4. Most of these defence functions can clearly be assigned. For instance, all functions which require aircraft of any description (whether with wheels, floats, or boats; whether reconnaissance, spotters or fighters, bombers or torpedo seaplanes) to be carried regularly in warships or in aircraft carriers, naturally fall to the naval sphere.

5. The question thus reduces itself to the assignment of any type operating over the sea from shore bases. This again can only be decided in relation to the functions and responsibilities placed upon the Navy. Aircraft borne afloat could discharge a considerable function of trade protection. This would be especially true

in the broad waters, where a squadron of cruisers with their own scouting planes or a pair of small aircraft carriers could search upon a front of a thousand miles. But the Navy could never be required — nor has it ever claimed — to maintain an air strength sufficient to cope with a concentrated attack upon merchant shipping in the Narrow Waters by a large hostile air force of great power. In fact, the maxim must be applied of air force *versus* air force and Navy *versus* Navy. When the main hostile air force or any definite detachment from it is to be encountered, it must be by the British Royal Air Force.

6. In this connection it should not be forgotten that a ship or ships may have to be selected and adapted for purely air-force operations, like a raid on some deep-seated enemy base, or vital centre. This is an air-force operation and necessitates the use of types of aircraft not normally associated with the Fleet. In this case the rôles of the Admiralty and the Air Ministry will be reversed, and the Navy would swim the ship in accordance with the tactical or strategic wishes of the Air Ministry. Far from becoming a baffle, this special case exemplifies the logic of the "division of command according to function."

7. What is conceded to the Navy should, within the limits assigned, be fully given. The Admiralty should have plenary control and provide the entire personnel of the Fleet air arm. Officers, cadets, petty officers, artificers, etc., for this force would be selected from the Royal Navy by the Admiralty. They would then acquire the art of flying and the management of aircraft in the Royal Air Force training-schools — to which perhaps naval officers should be attached — but after acquiring the necessary degree of proficiency as air chauffeurs and mechanics they would pass to shore establishments under the Admiralty for their training in Fleet air arm duties, just as the pilots of the Royal Air Force do to their squadrons at armament schools to learn air fighting. Thus, the personnel employed upon fleet air functions will be an integral part of the Navy, dependent for discipline and advancement as well as for their careers and pensions solely upon the Admiralty. This would apply to every rank and every trade involved, whether afloat or ashore.

8. Coincident with this arrangement whereby the Fleet air arm becomes wholly a naval Service, a further rearrangement of functions should be made, whereby the Air Ministry becomes re-

sponsible for active anti-aircraft defence. This implies, in so far as
the Navy is concerned, that, at every naval port, shore anti-aircraft
batteries, lights, aircraft, balloons and other devices will be combined under one operational control, though the officer commanding would, of course, with his command be subordinate to the
fortress commander.

9. In the same way, the control of the air defences of London
and of such other vulnerable areas as it may be necessary to equip
with anti-air defences on a considerable scale should also be unified
under one command and placed under the Air Ministry. The
consequent control should cover not only the operations, but as
far as may conveniently be arranged, the training, the raising and
administration of the entire personnel for active air defence.

10. The Air Ministry have as clear a title to control active anti-
air defence as have the Navy to their own "eyes." For this purpose
a new department should be brought into being in the Air Ministry, to be called "Anti-Air," to control all guns, searchlights,
balloons and personnel of every kind connected with this function,
as well as such portion of the Royal Air Force as may from time to
time be assigned to it for this duty. Under this department there
will be air force officers, assisted by appropriate staffs, in command
of all active air defences in specified localities and areas.

11. It is not suggested that the Air Ministry or Air Staff are at
present capable of assuming unaided this heavy new responsibility.
In the formation of the anti-air command recourse must be had to
both the older services. Well-trained staff officers, both from the
Army and the Navy, must be mingled with officers of the existing
Air Staff.

N.B. — The question of the recruitment and of the interior administration of the units handed over to the anti-air command for
operations and training need not be a stumbling-block. They
could be provided from the present sources unless and until a more
convenient solution was apparent.

12. This memorandum has not hitherto dealt with *matériel,*
but that is extremely simple. The Admiralty will decide upon the
types of aircraft which their approved functions demand. The
extent of the inroad which they require to make upon the finances
and resources of the country must be decided by the Cabinet, operating through a priorities committee under the Minister for the
Co-ordination of Defence. At the present stage this Minister would,

no doubt, give his directions to the existing personnel, but in the event of war or the intensification of the preparations for war he would give them to a Ministry of Supply. There could of course be no question of Admiralty priorities being allowed to override other claims in the general sphere of air production. All must be decided from the supreme standpoint.

13. It is not intended that the Admiralty should develop technical departments for aircraft design separate from those existing in the Air Ministry or under a Ministry of Supply. They would however be free to form a nucleus technical staff to advise them on the possibilities of scientific development and to prescribe their special naval requirements in suitable technical language to the Supply Department.

14. To sum up, therefore, we have:

First — The Admiralty should have plenary control of the Fleet air arm for all purposes which are defined as naval.

Secondly — A new department must be formed under the Air Ministry from the three Services for active anti-aircraft defence operations.

Thirdly — The question of *matériel* supply must be decided by a priorities committee under the Minister for the Co-ordination of Defence, and executed at present through existing channels, but eventually by a Ministry of Supply.

Appendix C, Book I

A NOTE ON SUPPLY ORGANISATION
JUNE 6, 1936

1. The existing Office of the Minister for the Co-ordination of Defence comprises unrelated and wrongly grouped functions. The work of the Minister charged with strategic co-ordination is different, though not in the higher ranges disconnected, from the work of the Minister charged with: (a) securing the execution of the existing programmes, and (b) planning British industry to spring quickly into wartime conditions and creating a high control effective for both this and the present purpose.

2. The first step therefore is to separate the functions of strategic thought from those of material supply in peace and war, and form the organisation to direct this latter process. An harmonious arrangement would be four separate departments — Navy, Army, Air Force, and Supply — with the Co-ordinating Minister at the summit of the four having the final voice upon priorities.

3. No multiplication of committees, however expert or elaborate, can achieve this purpose. Supply cannot be achieved without command. A definite chain of responsible authority must descend through the whole of British industry affected. (This must not be thought to imply State interference in the actual functions of industry.) At the present time the three service authorities exercise separate command over their particular supply, and the fourth, or planning, authority is purely consultative, and that only upon the war need divorced from present supply. What is needed is to unify the supply command of the three service departments into an organism which also exercises command over the war expansion. (The Admiralty would retain control over the construction of warships and certain special naval stores.)

4. This unification should comprise not only the function of supply but that of design. The service departments prescribe in general technical terms their need in type, quality, and quantity, and the supply organisation executes these in a manner best cal-

culated to serve its customers. In other words, the Supply Department engages itself to deliver the approved types of war stores of all kinds to the services when and where the latter require them.

5. None of this, nor the punctual execution of any of the approved programmes, can be achieved in the present atmosphere of ordinary peacetime preparation. It is neither necessary nor possible at this moment to take wartime powers and apply wartime methods. An intermediate state should be declared called (say) the period of emergency preparation.

6. Legislation should be drafted in two parts — First, that appropriate to the emergency preparation stage, and second, that appropriate to a state of war. Part I should be carried out now. Part II should be envisaged, elaborated, the principles defined, the clauses drafted and left to be brought into operation by a fresh appeal to Parliament should war occur. The emergency stage should be capable of sliding into the war stage with the minimum of disturbance, the whole design having been foreseen.

7. To bring this new system into operation there should first be created a Minister of Supply. This Minister would form a Supply Council. Each member would be charged with the study of the four or five branches of production falling into his sphere. Thereafter, as soon as may be, the existing service sub-departments of supply, design, contracts, etc., would be transferred by instalments to the new authority, who alone would deal with the Treasury upon finance. (By "finance" is meant payments within the scope of the authorised programmes.)

Appendix D, Book I

In time of peace the needs of our small Army, and to some extent of the air force and Admiralty, in particular weapons and ammunition, are supplied by the War Office, which has for this purpose certain Government factories and habitual private contractors. This organisation is capable of meeting ordinary peace-time requirements, and providing the accumulation of reserves sufficient for a few weeks of war by our very limited regular forces. Outside this there was nothing until a few months ago. About three or four months ago authority was given to extend the scope of War Office orders in certain directions to ordinary civil industry.

On the other hand, in all the leading Continental countries the whole of industry has been for some time solidly and scientifically organised to turn over from peace to war. In Germany, of course, above all others, this became the supreme study of the Government even before the Hitler régime. Indeed, under the impulse of revenge, Germany, forbidden by treaty to have fleets, armies, and an air force, concentrated with intense compression upon the perfecting of the transference of its whole industry to war purposes. We alone began seriously to examine the problem when everyone else had solved it. There was, however, still time in 1932 and 1933 to make a great advance. Three years ago when Hitler came into power we had perhaps a dozen officials studying the war organisation of industry as compared with five or six hundred working continuously in Germany. The Hitler régime set all this vast machinery in motion. They did not venture to break the treaties about Army, Navy, and air force until they had a head of steam on in every industry which would, they hoped, speedily render them an armed nation unless they were immediately attacked by the Allies.

What is being done now? Preparation cannot reach a stage of mass deliveries for at least eighteen months from the date of the order. If by ammunition is meant projectiles (both bombs and shells) and cartridge-cases containing propellant, it will be necessary to equip the factories with a certain amount of additional special-purpose machine-tools, and to modify their existing lay-out. In addition jigs and gauges for the actual manufacture must be made. . . . The manufacture of these special machine-tools will have to be done in most cases by firms quite different from those to whom the output of projectiles is entrusted. After the delivery of the special machine-tools, a further delay is required while they are being set up in the producing factories, and while the process of production is being started. Then and only then, at first in a trickle, then in a stream, and finally in a flood, deliveries will take place. Not until then can the accumulation of war resources begin. This inevitably lengthy process is still being applied on a relatively minute scale. Fifty-two firms have been offered contracts. Fourteen had last week accepted contracts. At the present moment it would be no exaggeration to state that the German ammunition plants may well amount to four or five hundred, already for very nearly two years in full swing.

Turning now to cannon: by cannon I mean guns firing explosive shells. The processes by which a cannon factory is started are necessarily lengthy, the special plants and machine-tools are more numerous, and the lay-out more elaborate. Our normal peace-time output of cannon in the last ten years has, apart from the Fleet, been negligible. We are therefore certainly separated by two years from any large deliveries of field guns or anti-aircraft guns. Last year it is probable that at least five thousand guns were made in Germany, and this process could be largely amplified in war. Surely we ought to call into being plant which would enable us, if need be, to create and arm a national army of a considerable size.

I have taken projectiles and cannon because these are the core of defence; but the same arguments and conditions, with certain modifications, apply over the whole field of equipment. The flexibility of British industry should make it possible to produce many forms of equipment, for instance, motor lorries and other kindred weapons such as tanks and armoured cars, and many slighter forms of material necessary for an army, in a much shorter time if that industry is at once set going. Has it been set going? Why should we be told that the Territorial Army cannot be equipped until after the Regular Army is equipped? I do not know what is the position about rifles and rifle ammunition. I hope at least we have enough for a million men. But the delivery of rifles from new sources is a very lengthy process.

Even more pertinent is the production of machine-guns. I do not know at all what is the programme of Browning and Bren machine-guns. But if the orders for setting up the necessary plant were only given a few months ago, one cannot expect any appreciable deliveries except by direct purchase from abroad before the beginning of 1938. The comparable German plants already in operation are capable of producing supplies limited only by the national manhood available to use them.

But this same argument can be followed out through all the processes of producing explosives, propellant, fuses, poison gas, gas-masks, searchlights, trench-mortars, grenades, air-bombs, and all the special adaptations required for depth-charges, mines, etc., for the Navy. It must not be forgotten that the Navy is dependent upon the War Office and upon an expansion of national industry for a hundred and one minor articles, a shortage in any one of which will cause grave injury. Behind all this again lies of course the supply of raw materials, with its infinite complications.

What is the conclusion? It is that we are separated by about two years from any appreciable improvement in the material process of national defence, so far as concerns the whole volume of supplies for which the War Office has hitherto been responsible, with all the reactions that entails, both on the Navy and the War Office. But upon the scale on which we are now acting, even at the end of two years, the supply will be petty compared either with our needs in war, or with what others have already acquired in peace.

Surely if these facts are even approximately true — and I believe they are mostly understatements — how can it be contended that there is no emergency; that we must not do anything to interfere with the ordinary trade of the country; that there is no need to approach the trade unions about dilution of trainees; that we can safely trust to what the Minister of Co-ordination of Defence described as "training the additional labour as required on the job"; and that nothing must be done which would cause alarm to the public, or lead them to feel that their ordinary habit of life was being deranged?

Complaint is made that the nation is unresponsive to the national need; that the trade unions are unhelpful; that recruiting for the Army and the Territorial Force is very slack, and even is obstructed by elements of public opinion. But as long as they are assured by the Government that there is no emergency these obstacles will continue.

I was given confidentially by the French Government an estimate of the German air strength in 1935. This tallies almost exactly with the figures I forecast to the Committee of Imperial Defence in December last. The Air Staff now think the French estimate too high. Personally I think it is too low. The number of machines which Germany could now put into action simultaneously may be nearer two thousand than fifteen hundred. Moreover, there is no reason to assume that they mean to stop at two thousand. The whole plant and lay-out of the German air force is on an enormous scale, and they may be already planning a development far greater than anything yet mentioned. Even if we accept the French figures of about fourteen hundred, the German strength at this moment is double that of our Metropolitan air force, judged by trained pilots and military machines that could go into action and be maintained in action. But the relative strength of two countries cannot be judged without reference to their power of replenishing their fighting force. The German industry is so organised that it can certainly produce at full blast a thousand a month and increase the number as the months pass. Can the British industry at the present time produce more than three hundred to three hundred and fifty a month? How long will it be before we can reach a war-potential output equal to the Germans? Certainly not within two years. When we allow for the extremely high rate of war wastage, a duel between the two countries would mean that before six months were out our force would be not a third of theirs. The preparation for war-time expansion at least three times the present size of the industry seems urgent in the highest degree. It is probable however that Germany is spending not less than one hundred and twenty millions on her Air Force this year. It is clear therefore that so far as this year is concerned we are not catching up. On the contrary, we are falling farther behind. How long will this continue into next year? No one can tell.

*   *   *   *   *

It has been announced that the programme of one hundred and twenty squadrons and fifteen hundred first-line aircraft for home defence would be completed by April 1, 1937. Parliament has not been given any information how this programme is being carried out in machines, in personnel, in organisation, or in the ancillary supplies. We have been told nothing about it at all. I do not blame the Government for not giving full particulars. It would be too dangerous now. Naturally, however, in the absence of any information at all, there must be great anxiety and much private discussion. . . . I doubt very much whether by July next year we shall have thirty squadrons equipped with the new types. I understand that the deliveries of the new machines will not really begin to flow in large numbers for a year or fifteen months. Meanwhile we have very old-fashioned and obsolete tackle.

There is a second question about these new machines: When they begin to flow out of the factories in large numbers fifteen months hence, will they be equipped with all necessary appliances? Take, for instance, the machine-guns. If we are aiming at having a couple of thousand of the latest machines, i.e., fifteen hundred and five hundred in reserve in eighteen months from now, what arrangements have been made for their machine-guns? Some of these modern fighting machines have no fewer than eight machine-guns in their wings. Taking only an average of four with proper reserves, that would require ten thousand machine-guns. Is it not a fact that the large-scale manufacture of the Browning and Bren machine-guns was only decided upon a few months ago?

Let us now try the airplane fleet we have built and are building by the test of bombing-power as measured by weight and range. Here I must again make comparison with Germany. Germany has the power at any time henceforward to send a fleet of airplanes capable of discharging in a single voyage at least five hundred tons of bombs upon London. We know from our war statistics that one ton of explosive bombs killed ten people and wounded thirty, and did fifty thousand pounds worth of damage. Of course, it would be absurd to assume that the whole bombing fleet of Germany would make an endless succession of voyages to and from this country. All kinds of other considerations intervene. Still, as a practical measure of the relative power of the bombing fleets of the two countries, the weight of discharge per voyage is a very reasonable measure. Now, if we take the German potential discharge upon London at a minimum of five hundred tons per voyage of their entire bombing fleet, what is our potential reply? *They* can do this from now on. What can we do? First of all: How could we retaliate upon Berlin? We have not at the present time a single squadron of machines which could carry an appreciable load of bombs to Berlin. What shall we have this time next year? I submit for your consideration that this time next year, when it may well be that the potential discharge of the German fleet is in the neighbourhood of a thousand tons, we shall not be able to discharge in retaliation more than sixty tons upon Berlin.

But leave Berlin out of the question. Nothing is more striking about our new fleet of bombers than their short range. The great bulk of our new heavy and medium bombers cannot do much more than reach the coasts of Germany from this Island. Only the nearest German cities would be within their reach. In fact the retaliation of which we should be capable this time next year from this Island would be puerile judged by the weight of explosive dropped, and would be limited only to the fringes of Germany.

Of course, a better tale can be told if it is assumed that we can operate from French and Belgian jumping-off grounds. Then very large and vital industrial districts of Germany would be within reach of our machines. Our air force will be incomparably more effective if used in conjunction with those of France and Belgium than it would be in a duel with Germany alone.

I now pass to the next stage. Our defence, passive and active, ground and air, at home. Evidently we might have to endure an ordeal in our great cities and vital feeding-ports such as no community has ever been subjected to before. What arrangements have been made in this field? Take London and its seven or eight million inhabitants. Nearly two years ago I explained in the House of Commons the danger of an attack by thermite bombs. These small bombs, little bigger than an orange, had even then been manufactured by millions in Germany. A single medium airplane can scatter five hundred. One must expect in a small raid literally tens of thousands of these bombs which burn through from storey to storey. Supposing only a hundred fires were started and there were only ninety fire brigades, what happens? Obviously the attack would be on a far more formidable scale than that. One must expect that a proportion of heavy bombs would be dropped at the same time, and that water, light, gas, telephone systems, etc., would be seriously deranged. What happens then? Nothing like it has ever been seen in world history. There might be a vast exodus of the population, which would present to the Government problems of public order, of sanitation and food-supply which would dominate their attention, and probably involve the use of all their disciplined forces.

What happens if the attack is directed upon the feeding-ports, particularly the Thames, Southampton, Bristol, and the Mersey, none of which are out of range? What arrangements have been made to bring in the food through a far greater number of subsidiary channels? What arrangements have been made to protect our defence centres? By defence centres I mean the centres upon which our power to continue resistance depends. The problem of the civil population and their miseries is one thing; the means by which we could carry on the war is another. Have we organised and created an alternative centre of Government if London is thrown into confusion? No doubt there has been discussion of this on paper, but has anything been done to provide one or two alternative centres of command with adequate deep-laid telephone connections, and wireless from which the necessary orders can be given by some coherent thinking-mechanism? . . .

Appendix E, Book I

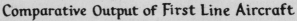

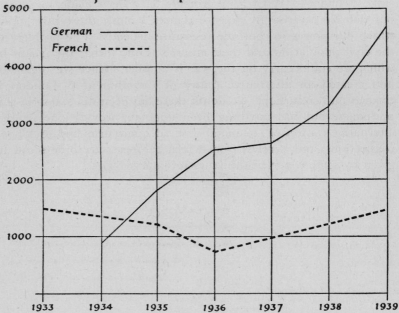

Comparative Output of First Line Aircraft

Note: German figures derived from captured documents; French figures from a French source.

Appendix A, Book II

TABLES OF NAVAL STRENGTH
SEPTEMBER 3, 1939

BRITISH AND GERMAN FLEETS

	British Including Dominions			*German*		
		Building			Building	
Type	Built	completing before 31.12.40	completing after 31.12.40	Built	completing before 31.12.40	completing after 31.12.40
Battleships.	12	3	4(e)	—	2	2(f)
Battle Cruisers.	3	—	—	2	—	—
"Pocket" Battleships.	—	—	—	3	—	—
Aircraft Carriers.	7	3	3	—	1(f)	1(f)
Seaplane Carriers.	2	—	—	—	—	—
Cruisers:						
8 inch.	15	—	—	2	2(g)	1(f)
6 inch or below.	49(a)	13	6	6(h)	—	3(f)
Destroyers.	184(b)	15(d)	17	22	3	13(l)
Sloops.	38	4	—	—	—	—
Escort Destroyers.	—	20	—	—	—	—
Corvettes (including patrol vessels).	8	3(j)	—	8	—	—
Torpedo Boats.	—	—	—	30	4	6(l)
Minesweepers.	42	—	—	32	10	—
Submarines.	58	12	12	57(k)	40(m)	—
Monitors (15 inch).	2	—	—	—	—	—
Minelayers.	7	2	2	—	—	—
River Gunboats.	20	—	—	—	—	—
Trawlers.	72(c)	20	—	—	—	—
Motor Torpedo Boats (including Motor Gunboats, etc.).	27	12	—	17	—	—

(a) Includes 3 ships converted to A-A ship.
(b) Includes ships converted to Escort Vessel (D).
(c) 16 fitted for A-S duties, remainder fitted for minesweeping.
(d) In addition six destroyers building for Brazil were taken over.
(e) Includes *Lion* and *Temeraire* which were later cancelled.
(f) Never completed.
(g) Only one of these, *Prinz Eugen,* was completed.
(h) Includes training-cruiser *Emden.*
(j) In addition fifty-eight corvettes ordered but not laid down.
(k) British estimate at this date was 59 plus one built for Turkey but not delivered. (See Chapter II.)
(l) Under war conditions many of these must be expected to complete in 1940.
(m) Includes all U-boats known to be building or projected on 3.9.39; 58 were actually completed between the outbreak of war and the end of 1940.

UNITED STATES

Strength of Fleet September 3, 1939
(excluding Coastguard Vessels)

Type	Built	Building and projected	Estimated date of completion
Battleships...............................	15	8	1 in 1941 1 in 1942 4 in 1943 2 later
Aircraft Carriers..........................	5	2	1 in 1940 1 later
Aircraft Tenders..........................	13	6	2 in 1941 4 later
Cruisers (8 inch).........................	18	—	—
" (6 inch).........................	18	7(a)	1 in 1939–40 6 in 1943
Destroyers...............................	181(b)	42	11 in 1939 16 in 1940 15 in 1941
Destroyer Tenders........................	8	4	2 in 1940 2 later
Submarines...............................	99(c)	15	4 in 1940 11 in 1941–42
Gunboats (including Patrol Vessels).........	7	—	—
River Gunboats...........................	6	—	—
Minelayer................................	10	1	1940
Minesweepers............................	26	3	1940
Submarine Tenders.......................	6	2	1941
Submarine Chasers.......................	14	16	4 in 1940 12 later
Motor Torpedo Boats.....................	1	19	1939–40

(a) Includes four ships mounting 5-inch guns.   (b) Includes 126 over age.   (c) Includes 65 over age.

FRANCE

September 3, 1939

	Completed	Under construction	Projected date of completion
Battleships...............................	8 (incl. 1 Training Ship)	3	1 in 1940 1 in 1941 1 in 1943
Battle Cruisers...........................	2	—	—
Aircraft Carriers.........................	1	1	1 in 1942
Aviation Transport........................	1	—	—
Cruisers..................................	18	3	—
Light Cruisers (Contre-Torpilleurs)..........	32	—	—
Destroyers (Torpilleurs)....................	28	24	6 in 1940
Motor Torpedo Boats......................	3	6	6 in 1940
Torpedo Boats............................	12	—	—
Cruiser Submarine........................	1	—	—
Submarines (1st Class).....................	38	3	—
" (2d Class).....................	33	10	2 in 1940
Minelaying S-M's.........................	6	1	—
River Gunboats (incl. 2 ex-S-M Chasers)......	10	—	—
Net and Mine Layer.......................	1	—	—
Minelayers...............................	3	—	—
Minesweepers............................	26	7	—
Colonial Sloops...........................	8	—	—
Submarine Chasers........................	13	8	5 in 1940

ITALY

September 3, 1939

	Completed	Under construction	Projected date of completion
Battleships.............................	4	4	2 in 1940 2 in 1942
Cruisers 8 inch...........................	7	—	—
Cruisers 6 inch...........................	12	—	—
Old Cruisers.............................	3	—	—
Cruisers 5.3 inch.........................	—	12	1942–43
Destroyers..............................	59	8	1941–42
Torpedo Boats...........................	69	4	1941–42
Submarines..............................	105	14	{ 10 in 1940 { 4 in 1941–42
Motor Torpedo Boats......................	69	—	—
Minelayers..............................	16	—	—
Sloop...................................	1	—	—
Seaplane Tender.........................	1	—	—

JAPAN

September 3, 1939

		Under construction in 1939	Projected date of completion	Strength on entering war Dec. 7, 1941
Battleships...............	10	2	1 in 1941 1 in 1942	10
Aircraft Carriers...........	6	? 10	1 in 1940 4 in 1941 5 in 1942	11
Cruisers.................	18–8 inch 17–5.5 inch 3 old types	3 or 4	3 in 1940 1 in 1942	18–8 inch 20–5.5 inch 3 old types
Seaplane Tenders..........	2	2	2 in 1942	2
Minelayers...............	5	2	1 in 1939 1 in 1940	8
Destroyers...............	113	20	2 in 1939 10 in 1940 8 in 1941	129
Submarines..............	53	33	3 in 1940 11 in 1941 19 in 1942	67
Escort Vessels............	4	—	—	4
Gunboats................	10	3	2 in 1940 1 in 1941	13
Torpedo Boats...........	12	—	—	—

Appendix B, Book II

PLAN "CATHERINE"

Minute of September 12, 1939

PART I

(1) For a particular operation special tools must be constructed. D.N.C. thinks it would be possible to hoist an "R" [a battleship of the *Royal Sovereign* class] nine feet, thus enabling a certain channel where the depth is only twenty-six feet to be passed. There are at present no guns commanding this channel, and the States on either side are neutral. Therefore there would be no harm in hoisting the armour belt temporarily up to the water level. The method proposed would be to fasten caissons [bulges] in two layers on the sides of the "R," giving the ship the enormous beam of one hundred and forty feet. No insuperable difficulty exists in fixing these, the inner set in dock and the outer in harbour. By filling or emptying these caissons the draught of the vessel can be altered at convenience, and, once past the shallow channel, the ship can be deepened again so as to bring the armour belt comfortably below the waterline. The speed when fully hoisted might perhaps be sixteen knots, and when allowed to fall back to normal draught, thirteen or fourteen. These speeds could be accepted for the operation. They are much better than I expected.

It is to be noted that the caissons afford admirable additional protection against torpedoes; they are in fact super-blisters.

It would also be necessary to strengthen the armour deck so as to give exceptional protection against air bombing, which must be expected.

(2) The caissons will be spoken of as "galoshes" and the strengthening of the deck as the "umbrella."

(3) When the ice in the theatre concerned melts (?) about March, the time for the operation would arrive. If orders are given for the necessary work by October 1, the designs being made meanwhile, we have six months, but seven would be accepted. It would be a great pity to waste the summer; therefore the highest priority

would be required. Estimates of time and money should be provided on this basis.

(4) In principle two "Rs" should be so prepared, but of course three would be better. Their only possible antagonists during the summer of 1940 would be the *Scharnhorst* and *Gneisenau*. It may be taken for certain that neither of these ships, the sole resource of Germany, would expose themselves to the fifteen-inch batteries of the "Rs," which would shatter them.

(5) Besides the "Rs" thus prepared, a dozen mine-bumpers should be prepared. Kindly let me have designs. These vessels should be of sufficiently deep draught to cover the "Rs" when they follow, and be worked by a small engine-room party from the stern. They would have a heavy fore-end to take the shock of any exploding mine. One would directly precede each of the "Rs." Perhaps this requirement may be reduced, as the ships will go line ahead. I can form no picture of these mine-bumpers, but one must expect two or three rows of mines to be encountered, each of which might knock out one. It may be that ordinary merchant ships could be used for the purpose, being strengthened accordingly.

(6) Besides the above, it will be necessary to carry a three months' reasonable supply of oil for the whole expeditionary fleet. For this purpose turtle-back blistered tankers must be provided capable of going at least twelve knots. Twelve knots may be considered provisionally as the speed of the passage, but better if possible.

PART II

(1) The objective is the command of the particular theatre [the Baltic], which will be secured by the placing [in it] of a battle squadron which the enemy heavy ships dare not engage. Around this battle squadron the light forces will act. It is suggested that three 10,000-ton eight-inch-gun cruisers and two six-inch should form the cruiser squadron, together with two flotillas of the strongest combat destroyers, a detachment of submarines, and a considerable contingent of ancillary craft, including, if possible, depot ships, and a fleet repair vessel.

(2) On the approved date the "Catherine" Fleet would traverse the passage by night or day, as judged expedient, using if desired smoke screens. The destroyers would sweep ahead of the fleet, the mine-bumpers would precede the "Rs," and the cruisers and lighter

vessels would follow in their wake. All existing apparatus of paravanes and other precautions can be added. It ought, therefore, to be possible to overcome the mining danger, and there are no guns to bar the channel. A heavy attack from the air must be encountered by the combined batteries of the Fleet.

Note: An aircraft carrier could be sent in at the same time and kept supplied with reliefs of aircraft reaching it by flight.

PART III

It is not necessary to enlarge on the strategic advantages of securing the command of this theatre. It is the supreme naval offensive open to the Royal Navy. The isolation of Germany from Scandinavia would intercept the supplies of iron ore and food and all other trade. The arrival of this Fleet in the theatre and the establishment of command would probably determine the action of the Scandinavian States. They could be brought in on our side; in which case a convenient base could be found capable of being supplied overland. The difficulty is that until we get there, they do not dare; but the three months' oil supply should give the necessary margin, and if the worst comes to the worst, it is not seen why the Fleet should not return as it came. The presence of this Fleet in the theatre would hold all enemy forces on the spot. They would not dare to send them on the trade routes, except as a measure of despair. They would have to arm the whole northern shore against bombardment, or possibly even, if the alliance of the Scandinavian Powers was obtained, military descents. The influence of this movement upon Russia would be far-reaching, but we cannot count on this.

Secrecy is essential, as surprise must play its full part. For this purpose the term "Catherine" will always be used in speaking of the operation. The caissons will be explained as "additional blisters." The strengthening of the turtle-deck is normal A.A. precaution.

I commend these ideas to your study, hoping that the intention will be to solve the difficulties.

                                                                    W. S. C.

Appendix C, Book II

NEW CONSTRUCTION AND RECONSTRUCTION

First Lord to First Sea Lord and Others.   *October* 8, 1939.

1. It is far more important to have some ships to fight with, and to have ships that Parliament has paid for delivered to date, than to squander effort upon remote construction which has no relation to our dangers!

2. A supreme effort must be made to finish *King George V* and *Prince of Wales* by their contract dates. The peace-time habit of contractors in booking orders and executing them when they please cannot be allowed to continue in time of war. Advise me of the penalties that may be enforced, in order that a case may be stated, if necessary, to the Law Officers of the Crown. Advise me also of the limiting factors. I suppose as usual the gun-mountings. It must be considered a marked failure by all concerned if these ships are not finished by their contract dates. I will myself inquire on Friday next into the condition of each of these ships, and will see the contractors personally at the Admiralty in your presence. Pray arrange these meetings from 5 P.M. onwards. It is no use the contractors saying it cannot be done. I have seen it done when full pressure is applied, and every resource and contrivance utilised. In short, we must have *K.G.V.* by July, 1940, and *P. of W.* three months later. The ships we need to win the war with must be in commission in 1940.

Pray throw yourselves into this and give me your aid to smooth away the obstacles.

3. The above remarks apply also to the aircraft carriers. *Illustrious* is to be five months late, and we know what that means. *Victorious* is even to be nine months late. *Formidable* from the 1937 programme is six months late, and *Indomitable* five months late. All these ships will be wanted to take part in the war, and not merely to sail the seas — perhaps under the German flag (!) — after it is over. Let me appeal to you to make this go. The later construction of aircraft carriers will not save us if we are beaten in 1940.

4. Thirdly, there are the cruisers. Look, for example, at the

Dido, which was contracted to be finished in June, 1939, and is
now offered to us in August, 1940. What is the explanation of this
fiasco?

5. We have at this moment to distinguish carefully between
running an industry or a profession, and winning the war. The
skilled labour employed upon vessels which cannot complete
during 1940 should, so far as is necessary or practicable, be shifted
on to those that can complete in 1940. Special arrangements must
be made as required to transfer the workmen from the later ships
to those that are needed for the fighting. All ships finishing in
1941 fall into the shade, and those of 1942 into the darkness. We
must keep the superiority in 1940.

6. The same principles apply even more strongly to destroyers
and light craft; but these seem to be going on pretty well, and I
have not yet had time to look in detail into their finishing dates.
But we most urgently require two new battleships, four aircraft
carriers and a dozen cruisers *commissioned and at work* before the
end of 1940.

W. S. C.

*   *   *   *   *

First Lord to First Sea Lord.   *October* 21, 1939.

I address this to you alone, because together we can do what is
needful.

We must have a certain number of capital ships that are not
afraid of a chance air bomb. We have been able to protect them
by bulges and Asdics against the U-boats. We must have them
made secure against the air. It is quite true that it may well be a
hundred to one against a hit with a heavy air torpedo upon a ship,
but the chance is always there, and the disproportion is grievous.
Like a hero being stung by a malarious mosquito! We must work
up to the old idea of a ship fit to lie the line against whatever may
be coming.

To come to the point. I want four or five ships made into
tortoises that we can put where we like and go to sleep content.
There may be other types which will play their parts in the outer
oceans; but we cannot go on without a squadron of heavy ships
that can stand up to the battery from the air.

I wrote you this morning about the *Queen Elizabeth.* But we
must make at least five other ships air-proof, i.e., not afraid of a

thousand-pound armour-piercing bomb, if by chance it should hit from ten thousand feet. This is not so large a structural rearrangement as might appear. You have got to pull a couple of turrets out of them, saving at least two thousand tons, and this two thousand tons has to be laid out in flat armour of six or seven inches, as high as possible, having regard to stability. The blank spaces of the turrets must be filled with A.A. guns. This means going down from eight guns to four. But surely four fifteen-inch can wipe out *Scharnhorst* or *Gneisenau*. Before the new German battleship arrives, we must have *King George V* and *Prince of Wales*. Let us therefore concentrate on having five or six vessels which are not afraid of the air, and therefore can work in narrow waters, and keep the high-class stuff for the outer oceans. Pull the guns out and plaster the decks with steel. This is the war proposition of 1940.

How are you going to get these ships into dockyards hands with all your other troubles?

Do not let us worry about the look of the ship. Pull the superimposed turrets out of them. Do one at Plymouth, one at Portsmouth, two on the Clyde, and one on the Tyne. These four-gun ships could be worked up to a very fine battery if the gunnery experts threw themselves into it. But, after all, they must bristle with A.A. and they must swim or float wherever they choose. Here is the war *motif* of 1940, and we now have the time.

How all this reinforces our need for armoured ammunition ships, and armoured oilers, is easily seen. In all this we have not got to think so much of a sea action as of sea-power maintained in the teeth of air attack.

All this ought to be put in motion Monday, and enough information should be provided to enable us to take far-reaching decisions not later than Thursday. On that day let us have Controller, D.N.C. and D.N.O. and shift our fighting front from the side of the ship to the top.

*　　*　　*　　*　　*

It looks to me as if the war would lag through the winter with token fighting in all spheres, but that it will begin with mortal intensity in the spring.

Remember no one can gainsay what we together decide.

W. S. C.

Appendix D, Book II

NEW CONSTRUCTION PROGRAMMES

1939-1940

(EXCLUSIVE OF LIGHT COASTAL CRAFT)

I Type	II New Construction Approved Before Outbreak of War	III 1939 War Programmes	IV 1940 War Programmes	V Revised (War) Estimated Completion Dates		VI Actual Completions	
				(a) By End of 1940	(b) By End of 1941 in Addition to (a)	(a) By End of 1940	(b) By End of 1941 in Addition to (a)
Battleships..............	9(a)	—	1(e)	2	2	1	2
Aircraft carriers.........	6	—	—	3	2	2	2
Cruisers, 8-inch.........	—	—	—	—	—	—	—
6-inch and below......	23(b)	6	—	13	7	7	6
Fleet destroyers........	32	16	32	12	28	11 + 6(g)	14
Escort destroyers.......	20	36	30	26	34	25	25
Sloops.................	4	2	20	4	2	2	4
Corvettes..............	61(c)	60	52(f)	88	48	51	70
Submarines.............	12	19	49	22	23	19	19
Minelayers.............	4	—	—	2	2	—	4
Minesweepers..........	20(d)	22	22	10	31	5	20
Trawlers (anti-submarine)..	20	32	100	42	50	30	53

(a) Includes H.M. Ships *Lion*, *Temeraire*, *Conqueror*, and *Thunderer* which were subsequently cancelled.
(b) Includes four ships of 1939 programme not laid down on 3.9.39, two of which were subsequently cancelled.
(c) Includes 58 ordered but not laid down on 3.9.39.
(d) Ordered but not laid down on 3.9.39,
(e) H.M.S. *Vanguard*.
(f) 27 of these were later named frigates.
(g) Six destroyers building for Brazil and taken over.

Appendix E, Book II

FLEET BASES

First Lord to D.C.N.S. and others. 1.II.39.

It was arranged at a conference between the First Lord, the First Sea Lord and the C.-in-C. on *Nelson, October* 31, 1939, that the following arrangements should be made at Fleet bases:

1. Scapa cannot be available, except as a momentary refuelling base for the Fleet, before the spring. Work is, however, to proceed with all possible speed upon

(*a*) blockships in the exposed channels:

(*b*) doubling the nets and placing them specially wherever required. They are to be at least as numerous and extensive as in the last war, plus the fact that the modern net is better. The routine of the gates is to be studied afresh with a view to briefer openings and greater security.

(*c*) The trawler and drifter fleet on the scale used in the Great War is to be earmarked for Scapa, and its disposition carefully considered by Plans Division. However, all these trawlers and drifters will be available for the Forth until it is time to use Scapa as a main base, i.e., not before the end of February, 1940.

(*d*) The work on the hutments is to proceed without intermission.

(*e*) Gun platforms are to be made in concrete for the whole of the eighty guns contemplated for the defence of Scapa. The work on these is to proceed throughout the winter; but the guns will not be moved there or mounted until the spring, when everything must be ready for them.

(*f*) The aerodromes at Wick are to be increased to take four squadrons.

(*g*) The R.D.F. work is to be gone on with, but must take its turn with more urgent work.

Meanwhile, Scapa can be used as a destroyer refuelling base, and the camouflaging of the oil tanks and the creation of dummy oil tanks should proceed as arranged. Staff at Scapa is not to be diminished, but there is no need to add to the oil storage there beyond the 120,000 tons already provided. The men now making the underground storage can be used for other work of a more urgent nature, even within the recent Board decision.

2. *Loch Ewe.* Port A is to be maintained in its present position with its existing staff. A permanent boom and net is to be provided even before the Scapa nets are completed. The freshwater pipe is to be finished and any minor measures taken to render this base convenient as a concealed resting-place for the Fleet from time to time.

3. *Rosyth* is to be the main operational base of the Fleet, and everything is to be done to bring it to the highest possible efficiency. Any improvements in the nets should be made with first priority. The balloons must be supplied so as to give effective cover against low-flying attack to the anchorage below the Bridge. The twenty-four 3.7 guns and the four Bofors which were lately moved to the Clyde are to travel back, battery by battery, in the next four days to the Forth, beginning after the Fleet has left the Clyde. It is not desired that this move should appear to be hurried, and the batteries may move as convenient and in a leisurely manner, provided that all are in their stations at the Forth within five days from the date of this minute. Strenuous effort with the highest priority for the R.D.F. installations which cover Rosyth must be forthcoming. Air Vice-Marshal Dowding is today conferring with the C.-in-C., Home Fleet, upon the support which can be forthcoming from A.D.G.B. The arrangement previously reached with the Air Ministry must be regarded as the minimum, and it is hoped that at least six squadrons will be able to come into action on the first occasion the Fleet uses this base.

D.C.N.S. will kindly find out the upshot of the conference between the C.-in-C. and Vice-Marshal Dowding and report the results. We must certainly look forward to the Fleet being attacked as soon as it reaches the Forth, and all must be ready for that. Thereafter this base will continue to be worked up in every way until it is a place where the strong ships of the Fleet can rest in security. Special arrangements must be made to co-ordinate the fire of the ships with that of the shore batteries observing that a seventy-two-gun concentration should be possible over the anchorage.

4. The sixteen balloons now disposed at the Clyde should not

be removed, as they will tend to mislead the enemy upon our intentions.

I should be glad if D.C.N.S. will vet this minute and make sure it is correct and solid in every detail, and, after obtaining the assent of the First S.L., make it operative in all Departments.

W. S. C.

First Lord to First Sea Lord.   3.I.40.

Scapa Defences

1. When in September we undertook to man the Scapa batteries, etc., the number of Marines required was estimated at 3,000. This has now grown successively by War Office estimates to 6,000, to 7,000, to 10,000, or even 11,000. Of course, such figures are entirely beyond the capacity of the Royal Marines to supply.

2. Moreover, the training of the Royal Marines "hostilities only" men can only begin after March 1, when the necessary facilities can be given by the Army. Nothing has, in fact, been done since September except to gather together the nucleus of officers and N.C.O.s with about eight hundred men. These can readily be used by us either for the Marine striking force or the mobile defence force.

The War Office, on the other hand, have a surplus of trained men in their pools, and seem prepared to man the guns at Scapa as they are mounted at the rate of sixteen a month. As we want to use the base from March onwards, it is certain that this is the best way in which the need can be met.

3. If by any chance the War Office do not wish to resume the reponsibility, then we must demand from them the training facilities from February 1 and their full assistance with all the technical ratings we cannot supply; and also make arrangements for the gradual handing-over of the staff. It is clear, however, that the right thing is for them to do it, and we must press them hard.

4. I do not wish the Admiralty to make too great a demand upon the Army. It would seem that the numbers required could be substantially reduced if certain tolerances were allowed. The figure of thirty men per gun and fourteen per searchlight is intended to enable every gun and searchlight to be continuously manned at full strength, night and day, all the year round. But the Fleet will often be at sea, when a lower scale of readiness could be accepted.

Moreover, one would not expect the guns to be continuously in action for very prolonged attack. If these attacks were made, the Fleet would surely put to sea. It is a question whether the highest readiness might not be confined to a proportion of the guns, the others having a somewhat longer notice.

5. Is it really necessary to have 108 anti-aircraft lights? Is it likely that an enemy making an attack upon the Fleet at this great distance would do it by night? All their attacks up to the present have been by day, and it is only by day that precise targets can be hit.

6. When the Fleet is ready to use Scapa, we must shift a large proportion, preferably half, of the guns and complements from Rosyth. We cannot claim to keep both going at the same time on the highest scale. Here is another economy.

7. It is suggested, therefore, by me that five thousand men should be allotted to the Scapa defences, and that the Commander should be told to work up gradually the finest show of gun-power he can develop by carefully studying local refinements which deal with each particular battery and post.

8. For a place like Scapa, with all this strong personnel on the spot, parachute landings or raids from U-boats may be considered most unlikely. There is, therefore, no need to have a battalion in addition to the artillery regiments. The Commander should make arrangements to have a sufficient emergency party ready to deal with any such small and improbable contingencies.

9. The case is different with the Shetlands, where we should be all the better for a battalion, though this need not be equipped on the Western-Front scale.

W. S. C.

Appendix F, Book II

NAVAL AID TO TURKEY

Note by the First Lord of the Admiralty.   *November* 1, 1939.

The First Sea Lord and I received General Orbay this afternoon, and informed him as follows:

In the event of Turkey being menaced by Russia, His Majesty's Government would be disposed, upon Turkish invitation and in certain circumstances, to come to the aid of Turkey with naval forces superior to those of Russia in the Black Sea. For this purpose it was necessary that the anti-submarine and anti-aircraft defences of the Gulf of Smyrna and the Gulf of Ismid should be developed, British technical officers being lent if necessary. These precautions would be additional to the existing plans for placing anti-submarine nets in the Dardanelles and in the Bosphorus.

We were not now making a promise or entering into any military engagement; and it was probable that the contingency would not arise. We hoped that Russia would maintain a strict neutrality, or even possibly become friendly. However, if Turkey felt herself in danger, and asked for British naval assistance, we would then discuss the situation with her in the light of the Mediterranean situation and of the attitude of Italy with the desire to enter into a formal engagement. It might be that the arrival of the British Fleet at Smyrna would in itself prevent Russia from proceeding to extremities, and that the advance of the British Fleet to the Gulf of Ismid would prevent a military descent by Russia on the mouth of the Bosphorus. At any rate, it would be from this position that the operations necessary to establish the command of the Black Sea would be undertaken.

General Orbay expressed himself extremely gratified at this statement. He said that he understood perfectly there was no engagement. He would report to his Government on his return, and the necessary preparatory arrangements at the bases would be undertaken.

I did not attempt to enter into the juridical aspect, as that would no doubt be thrashed-out should we ever reach the stage where a formal Convention had to be drawn up. It was assumed that Turkey would ask for British aid only in circumstances when she felt herself in grave danger, or had actually become a belligerent.

Appendix G, Book II

THE BLACK-OUT

Note by the First Lord of the Admiralty.   *November* 20, 1939.

I venture to suggest to my colleagues that when the present moon begins to wane, the black-out system should be modified to a sensible degree. We know that it is not the present policy of the German Government to indulge in indiscriminate bombing in England or France, and it is certainly not their interest to bomb any but a military objective. The bombing of military objectives can best be achieved, and probably only be achieved, by daylight or in moonlight. Should they change this policy, or should a raid be signalled, we could extinguish our lights again. It should have been possible by this time to have made arrangements to extinguish the street-lighting on a Yellow Warning. However, so far as night-bombing for the mere purpose of killing civilians is concerned, it is easy to find London by directional bearing and the map, whether the city is lighted or not. There is no need to have the "rosy glow" as a guide, and it would not be a guide if it were extinguished before the raiders leave the sea. But there is not much in it anyway.

2. There is, of course, no need to turn on the full peace-time street-lighting. There are many modified forms. The system in force in the streets of Paris is practical and effective. You can see six hundred yards. The streets are light enough to drive about with safety, and yet much dimmer than in time of peace.

3. The penalty we pay for the present methods is very heavy: First, the loss of life; secondly, as the Secretary of State for Air has protested, the impediment to munitions output, and also work at the ports, even on the west coast; thirdly, the irritating and depressing effect on the people which is a drag upon their war-making capacity, and, because thought unreasonable, an injury to the prestige of His Majesty's Government; fourthly, the anxieties of women and young girls in the darkened streets at night or in

704

blacked-out trains; fifthly, the effect on shopping and entertainments.

I would therefore propose that as from December 1:

(a) Street-lighting of a dimmed and modified character shall be resumed in the cities, towns, and villages.

(b) Motor cars and railway trains shall be allowed substantially more light, even at some risk.

(c) The existing restrictions on blacking-out houses, to which the public have adapted themselves, shall continue; but that vexatious prosecutions for minor infractions shall not be instituted. (I see in the newspapers that a man was prosecuted for smoking a cigarette too brightly at one place, and that a woman who turned on the light to tend her baby in a fit was fined in another.)

(d) The grant of these concessions should be accompanied by an effective propaganda continuously delivered by the broadcast, and handed out to motorists at all refuelling stations, that on an air-raid warning all motorists should immediately stop their cars and extinguish their lights, and that all other lights should be extinguished. Severe examples should be made of persons who, after a warning has been sounded, show any light.

4. Under these conditions we might face the chances of the next three winter months in which there is so much mist and fog. We can always revert to the existing practice if the war flares up, or if we do anything to provoke reprisals.

W. S. C.

Appendix H, Book II

THE MAGNETIC MINE, 1939–1940

A Note on the Measures Against the Magnetic Mine

Although the general characteristics of magnetic firing-devices for mines and torpedoes were well understood before the outbreak of war, the details of the particular mine developed by the Germans could not then be known. It was only after the recovery of a specimen at Shoeburyness on November 23, 1939, that we could apply the knowledge derived from past research to the immediate development of suitable counter-measures.

The first need was for new methods of mine-sweeping; the second was to provide passive means of defence for all ships against mines in unswept or imperfectly swept channels. Both these problems were effectively solved, and the technical measures adopted in the earlier stages of the war are briefly described in the following paragraphs.

Active Defence — Mine-Sweeping Methods

The Magnetic Mine

To sweep a magnetic mine, it is necessary to create a magnetic field in its vicinity of sufficient intensity to actuate the firing mechanism and so detonate it at a safe distance from the mine-sweeper. A design for a mine-destructor ship had been prepared early in 1939, and such a ship was soon brought into service experimentally, fitted with powerful electro-magnets capable of detonating a mine ahead of her as she advanced. She had some success early in 1940, but the method was not found suitable or sufficiently reliable for large-scale development.

At the same time various forms of electric sweep were developed for towing by shallow-draught vessels; and electro-magnetic coils carried in low-flying aircraft were also used, but this method presented many practical difficulties and involved considerable risk to the aircraft. Of all the methods tried, that which came to be known as the L.L. sweep showed the most promise, and efforts were soon concentrated on perfecting this. The sweeping gear consisted of long lengths of heavy electric cable known as tails, towed by a small vessel, two or more of which operated together. By means of a powerful electric current passed through these tails at carefully adjusted time-intervals, mines could be detonated at a safe distance astern of the sweepers. One of the difficulties which faced the designers of this equipment was that of giving the cables buoyancy. The problem was solved by the cable industry, in the first instance by the use of a "sorbo" rubber sheath, but later the method employed for sealing a tennis ball was also successfully adapted.

By the spring of 1940, the L.L. sweepers were coming into effective operation in increasing numbers. Thereafter the problem resolved itself into a battle of wits between the mine-designer and the mine-sweeping expert. Frequent changes were made by the Germans in the characteristics of the mine, each of which was in turn countered by readjustment of the mechanism of the sweep. Although the enemy had his successes and for a time might hold the initiative, the counter-measures invariably overcame his efforts in the end, and frequently it was possible to forecast his possible developments and prepare the counter in advance. Up to the end of the war the L.L. sweep continued to hold its own as the most effective answer to the purely magnetic mine.

The Acoustic Mine

In the autumn of 1940, the enemy began to use a new form of mine. This was the "Acoustic" type, in which the firing mechanism was actuated by the sound of a ship's propellers travelling through the water. We had expected this development earlier and were already well prepared for it. The solution lay in providing the minesweeper with means of emitting a sound of appropriate character and sufficient intensity to detonate the mine at a safe distance. Of the devices tried, the most successful was the Kango vibrating hammer fitted in a watertight container under the keel of the ship. Effective results depended on finding the correct frequency of vibration, and, as before, this could only be achieved quickly by obtaining a specimen of the enemy mine. Once again we were fortunate; the first acoustic mine was detected in October, 1940, and in November two were recovered intact from the mud flats in the Bristol Channel. Thereafter, successful counter-measures followed swiftly.

Soon it transpired that both acoustic and magnetic firing devices were being used by the enemy in the same mine, which would therefore respond to either impulse. In addition, many anti-sweeping devices appeared, designed to keep the firing mechanism inactive during the first or any predetermined number of impulses, or for a given period of time after the mine was laid. Thus, a channel which had been thoroughly swept by our minesweepers, perhaps several times, might still contain mines which only "ripened" into dangerous activity later. Despite all these fruits of German ingenuity and a severe set-back in January, 1941, when the experimental station on the Solent was bombed and many valuable records destroyed, the ceaseless battle of wits continued to develop slowly in our favour. The eventual victory was a tribute to the tireless efforts of all concerned.

Passive Defence — Degaussing

It is common knowledge that all ships built of steel contain permanent and induced magnetism. The resulting magnetic field may be strong enough to actuate the firing mechanism of a specially designed mine laid on the sea bed, but protection might be afforded by reducing the strength of this field. Although complete protection in shallow water could never be achieved, it was evident that a considerable degree of immunity was attainable. Before the end of November, 1939, preliminary trials at Portsmouth had shown that a ship's magnetism could be reduced by winding coils of cable horizontally round the hull, and passing current through them from the ship's own electrical supply. The Admiralty at once accepted this principle; any ship with electric power could thus be given some measure of protection, and whilst pressing on with further investigation to determine the more precise requirements, no time was lost in making large-scale preparations for equipping the Fleet with this form of defence. The aim was to secure immunity for any ship in depths of water over ten fathoms, whilst mine-sweeping craft and other small vessels should be safe in much shallower depths. More extensive trials carried out in December showed that this "coiling" process would enable a ship to move with comparative safety in half the depth of water which would be needed without such protection. Moreover, no important interference with the ship's structure and no elaborate mechanism were involved, although many ships would require additional electric power plant. As an emergency measure temporary coils could be fitted externally on a ship's hull in a few days, but more permanent equipment, fitted internally, would have to be installed at the first favourable moment. Thus, in the first instance there need be little delay in the normal turn-round of shipping. The process was given the name of "degaussing," and an organisation was set up under Vice-Admiral Lane-Poole to supervise the fitting of all ships with this equipment.

The supply and administrative problems involved were immense. Investigation showed that whereas the needs of degaussing would absorb fifteen hundred miles of suitable cable every week, the industrial capacity of the country could only supply about one-third of that amount in the first instance. Although our output could be stepped up, this could only be done at the expense of other important demands, and the full requirements could only be met by large imports of material from abroad. Furthermore, trained staffs must be provided at all our ports to control the work of fitting, determine the detailed requirements for each individual ship, and give technical advice to the many local authorities concerned with shipping movements. All this refers to the protection of the great mass of ships comprising the British and Allied merchant fleets.

By the first weeks of 1940, this organisation was gathering momentum. At this stage the chief preoccupation was to keep ships moving to and from our ports, particularly the east coast ports where the principal danger lay. All efforts were therefore concentrated on providing temporary coils, and the whole national output of suitable electric cable was requisitioned. Cable-makers worked night and day to meet the demand. Many a ship left port at this time with her hull encased in festoons of cable which could not be expected to survive the battering of the open sea, but at least she could traverse the dangerous coastal waters in safety and could be refitted before again entering the mined area.

Wiping

Besides the method described above, another and simpler method of degaussing was developed which came to be known as "wiping." This process could be completed in a few hours by placing a large cable alongside the ship's hull and passing through it a powerful electric current from a shore supply. No permanent cables need be fitted to the ship, but the process had to be repeated at intervals of a few months. This method was not effective for large ships, but its application to the great multitude of small coasters which constantly worked in the danger zone gave much-needed relief to the organisation dealing with "coiling" and yielded immense savings in time, material, and labour. It was of particular value during the evacuation of Dunkirk, when so many small craft of many kinds not normally employed in the open sea were working in the shallow waters round the Channel coasts.

Memorandum by the First Lord of the Admiralty.   15.III.40

Degaussing of Merchant Ships

My colleagues will be aware that one of our most helpful devices for countering the magnetic mine is the demagnetisation or degaussing of ships. This affords immunity in waters of over ten fathoms.

The number of British ships trading to ports in the United Kingdom which require to be degaussed is about 4,300.

The work of degaussing began in the middle of January, and by March 9, 321 warships and 312 merchant vessels were completed. Two hundred and nineteen warships and approximately 290 merchant vessels were in hand on the same date.

The supply of cable, which has up to the present governed the rate of equipment, is rapidly improving; and it is now the supply of labour in the shipyards which is likely to control the future rate of progress.

It would be a substantial advantage if part of the work of degaussing of British ships could be placed in foreign yards. The number of neutral ships engaged in trade with this country is about seven hundred. Neutral crews and in particular the crews of Norwegian ships are beginning to be uneasy about the dangers from enemy mines on the trade-ways to our ports. The importance to us of the safety of these neutral ships and of the confidence of their crews is a strong argument for disclosing to neutral countries the technical information which they require to demagnetise their ships which trade with this country.

Against the substantial advantages of arranging for some British ships to be demagnetised in foreign yards and of extending demagnetisation to neutral ships must be set any disadvantages of a loss of secrecy. If the enemy is informed of the measures which we are taking, he may (a) increase the sensitivity of his mines, or he may (b) mix mines of opposite polarity in the same field. If secrecy could be preserved, its advantage would be to delay these reactions of the enemy. But technical details of our degaussing equipment have had to be given to all ship-repairing firms in this country. Information which has been so widely distributed almost certainly becomes quickly known to the enemy.

Moreover (a) and (b) have the disadvantages to the enemy that —

(a) would make the mines easier to sweep and reduce the damage to non-degaussed ships by placing the explosion further forward or even ahead of the ships; and

(b) reversal of polarity would only be effective against certain ships which are difficult to demagnetise thoroughly, and would also require a sensitive setting of the mine.

The above position has altered since the arrival of the *Queen Elizabeth* at New York and the subsequent publicity given to the subject in the press. The enemy now knows the nature of the protective measures we are taking and, knowing the mechanism of his own mine, it will not be difficult for him to deduce the manner in which degaussing operates. He can therefore now adopt any counter-measures within his power. The press notices have had the further effect of increasing demands for information from neutrals, and to continue to refuse such information conflicts with our general policy of encouraging neutral ships to trade in this country.

It is considered, therefore, by my advisers that we shall not be losing an advantage of any great importance by ceasing to treat the information as secret.

The Admiralty recommend, therefore —

(i) that shipyards in neutral countries be used, if necessary, to supplement resources in this country for the degaussing of British merchant ships;

(ii) that technical information of our methods of demagnetisation be supplied as and when necessary to neutral countries for the degaussing of neutral ships trading with this country.

W. S. C.

Appendix I, Book II

EXTRACT FROM WAR DIARY OF *U.47*

28.11.39
German Time.

1245.	Posⁿ. 60° 25′ N. 01° E.	Masts in sight bearing 120° (true).
1249.	Wind. NNW. 10–9. Sea 8 Cloudy.	I recognise a cruiser of the "London" class.
1334.	60° 24′ N. 01° 17′ E.	Range 8 hm. (Approx. 880 yds.). Estimated speed of cruiser — 8 knots. 1 torpedo fired from No. 3 tube. After 1 min. 26 secs. an explosion heard. I can see the damage caused by the hit, aft of the funnel. The upper deck is buckled and torn. The starboard torpedo-tube mounting is twisted backwards over the ship-side. The aircraft is resting on the tail-unit. The cruiser appears to have a 5° list to starboard, as she disappears on a reciprocal course into a rain squall.
1403.		Surfaced. Set off in pursuit.
1420.		Cruiser again in sight bearing 090°. I dive to close her, but she disappears in another rain squall.
1451.		Surfaced and searched the area but she could not be found.

On 29.11.39 the following entry was made in the war diary of Admiral von Doenitz: "Following the report that *U.47* had torpedoed a cruiser, Propaganda claimed a sinking. From the serviceman's point of view, such inaccuracies and exaggerations are undesirable."

Appendix J, Book II

CULTIVATOR NUMBER 6

Note by the Author

During these months of suspense and paralysis I gave much thought and compelled much effort to the development of an idea which I thought might be helpful to the great battle when it began. For secrecy's sake this was called "White Rabbit Number 6," later changed to "Cultivator Number 6." It was a method of imparting to our armies a means of advance up to and through the hostile lines without undue or prohibitive casualties. I believed that a machine could be made which would cut a groove in the earth sufficiently deep and broad through which assaulting infantry and presently assaulting tanks could advance in comparative safety across No-Man's-Land and wire entanglements, and come to grips with the enemy in his defences on equal terms and in superior strength. It was necessary that the machine cutting this trench should advance at sufficient speed to cross the distance between the two front lines during the hours of darkness. I hoped for a speed of three or four m.p.h.; but even half-a-mile would be enough. If this method could be applied upon a front of perhaps twenty or twenty-five miles, for which two or three hundred trench-cutters might suffice, dawn would find an overwhelming force of determined infantry established on and in the German defences, with hundreds of lines-of-communication trenches stretching back behind them, along which reinforcements and supplies could flow. Thus we should establish ourselves in the enemy's front line by surprise and with little loss. This process could be repeated indefinitely.

When I had had the first tank made twenty-five years before, I turned to Tennyson d'Eyncourt, Director of Naval Construction, to solve the problem. Accordingly I broached the subject in November to Sir Stanley Goodall, who now held this most important office, and one of his ablest assistants, Mr. Hopkins, was put in charge with a grant of one hundred thousand pounds for experiments. The design and manufacture of a working model was completed in six weeks by Messrs. Ruston-Bucyrus of Lincoln. This suggestive little machine, about three feet long, performed excellently in the Admiralty basement on a floor of sand. Having obtained the active support of the Chief of the Imperial General Staff, General Ironside, and other British military experts, I invited the Prime Minister and several of his colleagues to a demonstration. Later I took it over to France and exhibited it both to General Gamelin and later on to General Georges, who expressed approving interest. On December 6, I was assured that immediate orders and absolute priority would produce two hundred of these machines by March, 1941. At the same time it was suggested that a bigger machine might dig a trench wide enough for tanks.

On February 7, 1940, Cabinet and Treasury approval were given for the construction of two hundred narrow "infantry" and forty wide "officer" machines. The design was so novel that trial units of the main components had first to be built. In April, a hitch occurred. We had hitherto relied on a single Merlin-Marine type of engine, but now the Air Ministry wanted all these, and another heavier and larger engine had to be accepted instead. The machine in its final form weighed over a hundred tons, was seventy-seven feet long, and eight feet high. This mammoth mole could cut in loam a trench five feet deep and seven-and-a-half feet wide at half-a-mile an hour, involving the movement of eight thousand tons of soil. In March, 1940, the whole process of manufacture was transferred to a special department of the Ministry of Supply. The utmost secrecy was maintained by the three hundred and fifty firms involved in making the separate parts, or in assembling them at selected centres. Geological analysis was made of the soil of Northern France and Belgium, and several suitable areas were found where the machine could be used as part of a great offensive battle plan.

But all this labour, requiring at every stage so many people to be convinced or persuaded, led to nothing. A very different form of warfare was soon to descend upon us like an avalanche, sweeping all before it. As will presently be seen, I lost no time in casting aside these elaborate plans and releasing the resources they involved. A few specimens alone were finished and preserved for some special tactical problem or for cutting emergency anti-tank obstacles. By May, 1943, we had only the pilot model, four narrow and five wide machines, made or making. After seeing the full-sized pilot model perform with astonishing efficiency, I minuted "cancel and wind up the four of the five 'officer' type, but keep the four 'infantry'-type in good order. Their turn may come." These survivors were kept in store until the summer of 1945, when the Siegfried Line being pierced by other methods, all except one was dismantled. Such was the tale of "Cultivator Number 6." I am responsible but impenitent.

Appendix K, Book II

(Numbers of ships shown in parentheses)

	1939			
	September	October	November	December
U-boats.................	135,552 (26)	74,130 (14)	18,151 (5)	33,091 (6)
Mines...................	11,437 (2)	3,170 (2)	35,640 (13)	47,079 (12)
Surface raider...........	5,051 (1)	27,412 (5)	706 (1)	21,964 (3)
Aircraft.................	—	—	—	487 (1)
Other and unknown causes..	—	—	2,676 (3)	875 (1)
Total (gross tons).........	152,040 (29)	104,712 (21)	57,173 (22)	103,496 (23)

	1940			
	January	February	March	April
U-boats.................	6,549 (2)	67,840 (9)	15,531 (9)	14,605 (3)
Mines...................	61,943 (11)	35,971 (9)	16,747 (8)	13,106 (6)
Surface raider...........	—	—	—	5,207 (1)
Aircraft.................	23,296 (9)	—	5,439 (1)	—
Other and unknown causes..	10,081 (2)	6,561 (3)	1,585 (1)	41,920 (9)*
Total (gross tons).........	101,869 (24)	110,372 (21)	39,302 (13)	74,838 (19)

Grand total (gross tons)......743,802 (172)

* All these ships were sunk or seized by the Germans in Norwegian ports.

Appendix L, Book II

OPERATION "ROYAL MARINE"

Note by the First Lord of the Admiralty.   *March* 4, 1940.

1. It will be possible to begin the naval operation at any time at twenty-four hours' notice after March 12. At that time there will, as planned, be available two thousand fluvial mines of the naval type, comprising three variants. Thereafter a regular minimum supply of one thousand per week has been arranged. The detachment of British sailors is on the spot, and the material is ready. All local arrangements have been made with the French through General Gamelin and Admiral Darlan. These mines will, it is believed, affect the river for the first hundred miles below Karlsruhe. There is always risk in keeping men and peculiar material teed-up so close (four to six miles) to the enemy's front, although within the Maginot Line. The river is reported to be in perfect order this month. It will probably be deepened by the melting of the snows in April, involving some lengthening of the mine-tails; also the flow from the tributaries may be temporarily stopped or even reversed.

2. The air force will not be ready till the moon is again good in mid-April. Therefore, unless our hand is forced by events, it would seem better to wait till then, so as to infest the whole river simultaneously, and thus also confuse the points of naval departure. By mid-April the air force should have a good supply of mines which could be laid every night during the moon in the reaches between Bingen and Coblentz. All mines of both classes will become harmless before reaching the Dutch frontier. Before the end of April it is hoped that a supply of the special mines for the still-water canals may be ready, and by the May moon the mines for the mouths of rivers flowing into the Heligoland Bight should be at hand.

3. Thus this whole considerable mining campaign could be brought into being on the following timetable:

Day 1. Issue of proclamation reciting the character of the

German attacks on the British coasts, shipping, and river mouths, and declaring that henceforth (while this continues), the Rhine is a mined and forbidden area, and giving neutrals and civilians twenty-four hours' notice to desist from using it or crossing it.

Day 2. After nightfall, deposit as many mines as possible by both methods, and keep this up night after night. The supply by that time should be such as to keep all methods of discharge fully employed.

Day 28. Begin the laying of the mines in the still-water canals and river mouths, thereafter keeping the whole process working, as opportunity serves, until the kind of attacks to which we are being subjected are brought to an end by the enemy, or other results obtained.

4. The decisions in principle required are:

(a) Is this method of warfare justified and expedient in present circumstances?

(b) Must warning be given beforehand, observing that the first shock of surprise will be lost? However, this is not considered decisive, as the object is to prevent the use of the river and inland waterways rather than mere destruction.

(c) Should we wait till the air force are ready, or begin the naval action as soon as possible after March 12?

(d) What reprisals, if any, may be expected, observing that there is not natural or economic feature in France or Great Britain in any way comparable with the Rhine, except our coastal approaches, which are already beset.

5. It is desirable that the Fifth Sea Lord, who has the operation in charge, should go to Paris on Thursday, concert the details finally, and ascertain the reactions of the French Government. From the attitude of M. Daladier, General Gamelin, and Admiral Darlan it is thought these will be highly favourable.

W. S. C.

Appendix M, Book II

NAVAL LOSSES IN NORWEGIAN CAMPAIGN
April–June, 1940

German Naval Losses, April–June, 1940
Ships Sunk

Name	Type	Cause
Bluecher...............	8-inch Cruiser..........	Torpedo and gun-fire by Norwegian coast defences, Oslo, April 9
Karlsruhe...............	Light Cruiser...........	Torpedoed by submarine *Truant* in Kattegat, April 9
Koenigsberg.............	Light Cruiser..........	Bombed by Fleet Air Arm, Bergen, April 10
Brummer................	Gunnery Training Ship..	Torpedoed in Kattegat by submarine, April 15
Wilhelm Heidkamp.......	Destroyer..............	Torpedoed. First attack on Narvik, April 10
Anton Schmitt...........	"	
Hans Ludemann..........	"	Destroyed by torpedo or gun-fire. Second
Georg Thiele.............	"	attack on Narvik, April 13 (five of these
Bernd von Arnim.........	"	were damaged in the first attack on April 10)
Wolf Zenker.............	"	
Erich Geise..............	"	
Erich Koellner...........	"	
Hermann Kunne..........	"	
Dieter von Roeder........	"	
Numbers: 44, 64, 49, 1, 50, 54, 22, 13	U-boats...............	Various. Three off Norway. Five in North Sea
Albatross................	Torpedo Boat..........	Wrecked. Oslo, April 9

In addition, three minesweepers, two patrol craft, eleven transports and four fleet auxiliaries sunk.

Ships Damaged

Name	Type	Cause
Gneisenau...............	Battle Cruiser..........	Action with *Renown*, April 9. Torpedoed by submarine, *Clyde*, June 20
Scharnhorst.............	Battle Cruiser..........	Torpedoed by *Acasta*, June 8
Hipper..................	8-inch Cruiser..........	Action with *Glowworm*, April 8
Luetzow.................	Pocket Battleship.......	Action with coastal batteries, Oslo, April 9. Torpedoed by submarine *Spearfish*, Kattegat, April 11
Emden..................	Light Cruiser..........	Action with coastal batteries, Oslo, April 9
Bremse.................	Gunnery Training Ship ..	Action with coastal batteries, Bergen, April 9

In addition, two transports damaged and one captured.

Ships Out of Action During the Whole Period

Name	Type	Cause
Scheer..................	Pocket Battleship.......	Engine repairs
Leipzig.................	Light Cruiser..........	Torpedo damage repairs

GERMAN FLEET AVAILABLE ON JUNE 30, 1940

Type	Effective	Remarks
Battle Cruisers...........	Nil...................	*Scharnhorst* and *Gneisenau* damaged
Pocket Battleships........	Nil...................	*Scheer* under repair. *Luetzow* damaged
8-inch Cruiser............	*Hipper*...............	
Light Cruiser.............	*Koeln, Nuernberg*........	*Leipzig* and *Emden* damaged
Destroyers...............	*Schoemann, Lody, Ihn, Galster*..............	Six others under repair
Torpedo Boats...........	Nineteen..............	Six others under repair. Eight new craft working up

In addition, the two old battleships *Schlesien* and *Schleswig-Holstein* were available for coast defence.

ALLIED NAVAL LOSSES IN THE NORWEGIAN CAMPAIGN
Ships Sunk

Name	Type	Cause
Glorious.................	Aircraft Carrier........	Gun-fire, June 9
Effingham...............	Cruiser...............	Wrecked, May 17
Curlew..................	A.A. Cruiser...........	Bombed, May 26
Bittern.................	Sloop.................	Bombed, April 30
Glowworm...............	Destroyer.............	Gun-fire, April 8
Gurkha.................	"	Bombed, April 9
Hardy..................	"	Gun-fire, April 10
Hunter.................	"	Gun-fire, April 10
Afridi..................	"	Bombed, May 3
Acasta.................	"	Gun-fire, June 8
Ardent.................	"	Gun-fire, June 8
Bison (French)..........	"	Bombed, May 3
Grom (Polish)...........	"	Bombed, May 4
Thistle.................	Submari..e...........	U-boat, April 14
Tarpon.................	"	Unknown, April 22
Sterlet.................	"	Unknown, April 27
Seal...................	"	Mined, May 5
Doris (French)..........	"	U-boat, May 14
Orzel (Polish)...........	"	Unknown, June 6

In addition, eleven trawlers, one loaded and two empty troop transports, and two supply ships sunk.

Ships Damaged (excluding minor damage)

Name	Type	Cause
Penelope.................	Cruiser...............	Grounding, April 11
Suffolk.................	"	Bombed, April 17
Aurora.................	"	Bombed, May 7
Curaçao.................	A.A. Cruiser...........	Bombed, April 24
Cairo..................	"	Bombed, May 28
Emile Berlin (French).....	Cruiser...............	Bombed, April 19
Pelican.................	Sloop................	Bombed, April 22
Black Swan..............	"	Bombed, April 28
Hotspur.................	Destroyer.............	Gun-fire, April 10
Eclipse.................	"	Bombed, April 11
Punjabi.................	"	Gun-fire, April 13
Cossack.................	"	Grounding, April 13
Eskimo.................	"	Torpedo, April 13
Highlander..............	"	Grounding, April 13
Maori..................	"	Bombed, May 2
Somali.................	"	Bombed, May 15

First Lord's Minutes

SEPTEMBER, 1939

First Lord to Secretary and to all Departments.　　　　4.IX.39.

To avoid confusion, German submarines are always to be described officially as U-boats in all official papers and communiqués.

First Lord to D.N.I. and Secretary.　　　　6.IX.39.

1. This is an excellent paper and the principles are approved. However, in the first phase (say, September) when losses may be high, it is important that you show that we are killing U-boats. The policy of silence will come down later. The daily bulletin prepared by Captain Macnamara should, when possible, for the first week be shown to the First Lord, but should not be delayed if he is not available. It is of the highest importance that the Admiralty bulletin should maintain its reputation for truthfulness, and the tone should not be forced. The bulletin of today is exactly the right tone.

2. When Parliament is sitting, if there is anything worth telling, bad or good, the First Lord or Parliamentary Secretary will be disposed to make a statement to the House in answer to friendly private-notice questions.

These statements should be concerted with the Parliamentary Secretary, who advises the First Lord on Parliamentary business. Sensational or important episodes will require special attention of the First Lord or First Sea Lord.

3. Lord Stanhope, as Leader of the House of Lords, should always be made acquainted with the substance of any statement to be made in the House of Commons upon the course of the naval war.

Moreover, the First Lord wishes that his Private Secretary should keep Lord Stanhope informed during these early weeks upon matters in which his Lordship may have been interested. He should not be cut off from the course of events at the Admiralty with which he has been so intimately concerned.

First Lord to D.N.I. (Secret.)   6.IX.39.

What is the position on the west coast of Ireland? Are there any signs of succouring U-boats in Irish creeks or inlets? It would seem that money should be spent to secure a trustworthy body of Irish agents to keep most vigilant watch. Has this been done? Please report.

First Lord to D.C.N.S.   6.IX.39.

Kindly give me report on progress of Dover barrage, and repeat weekly.

First Lord to Controller.   6.IX.39.

1. What are we doing about bringing out old merchant ships to replace tonnage losses? How many are there, and where? Kindly supply lists, with tonnage. Arrangements would have to be made to dock and clean all bottoms, otherwise speed will be grievously cut down.

2. I should be glad to receive proposals for acquiring neutral tonnage to the utmost extent.

First Lord to First Sea Lord, Controller and others.   6.IX.39.

1. It is much too soon to approve additional construction of new cruisers, which cannot be finished for at least two years, even under war conditions. The matter can be considered during the next three months. Now that we are free from all Treaty restrictions, if any cruisers are built they should be of a new type, and capable of dominating the five German 8-inch cruisers now under construction.

2. Ask the D.N.C. at his convenience to give me a legend of a 14,000- or 15,000-ton cruiser carrying 9.2 guns with good armour against 8-inch projectiles, wide radius of action, and superior speed to any existing *Deutschland* or German 8-inch-gun cruisers. It would be necessary before building such vessels to carry the United States with us.

3. The rest of the programme is approved, as it all bears on U-boat hunting and ought to be ready within the year.

4. I shall be very glad to discuss the general questions of policy involved with the Board.

First Lord to Prime Minister.   7.IX.39.

It seems most necessary to drill the civil population in completely putting out their private lights, and the course hitherto followed has conduced to this. But surely the great installations of lights controlled from two or three centres are in a different category.

While enforcing the household black-outs, why not let the controllable lighting burn until an air-warning is received? Then when the hooters sound, the whole of these widespread systems of lighting would go out at once together. This would reinforce the air-raid warning, and when the all-clear was sounded, they would all go up together, telling everyone. Immense inconvenience would be removed, and the depressing effect of needless darkness; and as there are at least ten minutes to spare, there would be plenty of time to make the black-out complete.

Unless you have any objection, I should like to circulate this to our colleagues.

First Lord to Controller. 9.IX.39.

Dates of Completion for Naval Construction: Tabular Statement Prepared by Controller

In peace-time, vessels are built to keep up the strength of the Navy from year to year amid political difficulties. In war-time, a definite tactical object must inspire all construction. If we take the Navies, actual and potential, of Germany and Italy, we can see clearly the exact vessels we have to cope with. Let me therefore have the comparable flotillas of each of these Powers, actual and prospective, up to 1941, so far as they are known. *Having regard to the U-boat menace, which must be expected to renew itself on a much larger scale toward the end of* 1940, the type of destroyer to be constructed must aim at numbers and celerity of construction rather than size and power. It ought to be possible to design destroyers which can be completed in under a year, in which case fifty at least should be begun forthwith. I am well aware of the need of a proportion of flotilla-leaders and large destroyers capable of ocean service, but the arrival in our Fleets of fifty destroyers of the medium emergency type I am contemplating would liberate all larger vessels for ocean work and for combat.

Let me have the entire picture of our existing destroyer fleet, apart from the additions shown on this paper. Until I have acquainted myself with the destroyer power, I will not try to understand the escort vessels, etc.

First Lord to Controller, D.N.C. and others.   11.IX.39.

The following ideas might be considered before our meeting at 9.30 Tuesday, September 12:

1. Suspend for a year all work on battleships that cannot come into action before the end of 1941. This decision to be reviewed every six months. Concentrate upon *King George V, Prince of Wales,* and *Duke of York,* and also upon *Jellicoe* if it can be pulled forward into 1941; otherwise suspend.

2. All aircraft carriers should proceed according to accelerated programme.

3. Concentrate on the *Didos* which can be delivered before the end of 1941. By strong administrative action it should be possible to bring all the present programme within the sacred limit, to wit, ten ships. No new *Didos* till this problem has been solved.

4. *Fijis.* Please, No! This policy of scattering over the seas weak cruisers which can neither fight nor flee the German 8-inch 10,000-ton cruisers — of which they will quite soon have five — should be abandoned. The idea of two *Fijis* fighting an 8-inch-gun cruiser will never come off.[1] All experience shows that a cluster of weak ships will not fight one strong one. (*Vide* the escape of the *Goeben* across the mouth of the Adriatic, August, 1914.)

5. I was distressed to see that till the end of 1940, i.e., sixteen months, we only receive ten destroyers, and only seven this year, and that there is a gulf of nine months before the subsequent six are delivered. However, we have taken over the six Brazilians which arrive during 1940 and mitigate this position. Let us go forward with all these to the utmost. These ships called "destroyers" have strayed far in design from their original rôle of "torpedo-boat destroyers," in answer to the French mosquito flotillas of the nineties. They are really small unarmoured cruisers with a far heavier stake in men and money than their capacity to stand the fire of their equals justifies. Nevertheless, for combat and for breasting ocean billows they have an indispensable part to play.

6. Fast escort vessels: I now learn these are really medium destroyers of a thousand tons. The whole of this class should be pressed forward to the utmost.

[1] The *Fiji* class mounted 6-inch guns. None the less, the 6-inch cruisers *Ajax* and *Achilles* later fought a successful and glorious action with the *Graf Spee* mounting 11-inch guns.

7. We have also the whale-catcher type — but this is 940 tons, which is a great deal where numbers are required. I doubt whether our dollars will enable us to place 40 of these in the United States. It would be much better to supplement them by a British-built programme of another type.

8. I would ask that a committee of (say) three sea-officers accustomed to flotilla work, plus two technicians, should sit at once to solve the following problems:

An anti-submarine and anti-air vessel which can be built within twelve months in many of the small yards of the country; 100 should be built if the design is approved. The greatest simplicity of armament and equipment must be arrived at, and a constant eye kept upon mass production requirements. The rôle of these vessels is to liberate the destroyers and fast escort vessels for a wider range of action, and to take over the charge of the Narrow Seas, the Channel, the inshore Western Approaches, the Mediterranean and the Red Sea, against submarine attack.

I hazard specifications only to have them vetted and corrected by the committee, viz.:

500 to 600 tons.

16 to 18 knots.

2 cannons around 4-inches according as artillery may come
    to hand from any quarter, preferably of course firing
    high angle;

depth-charges;

no torpedoes, and only moderate range of action.

These will be deemed the "Cheap and Nasties" (Cheap to us, nasty to the U-boats). These ships, being built for a particular but urgent job, will no doubt be of little value to the Navy when that job is done — but let us get the job done.

9. The submarine programme is approved as they still have a part to play.

I shall be very grateful if you will give me your views on these ideas, point by point, to-morrow night.

First Lord to First Sea Lord, Controller and others.   18.IX.39.

As it is generally impossible to use the catapult aircraft in the open ocean, but nevertheless they would be a great convenience around the South American continental promontory, the question arises whether landing-grounds or smooth-water inlets cannot be marked down on uninhabited tracts or in the lee of islands, upon which aircraft catapulted from vessels in the neighbourhood could alight, claiming, if discovered, right of asylum. They could then be picked up by the cruiser at convenience. Perhaps this has already been done.

First Lord to First Sea Lord and others.   20.IX.39.

While I greatly desire the strengthening of this place [Scapa Flow] against A.A. attack, and regard it as a matter of extreme urgency, I consider the scale of eighty 3.7-inch guns goes beyond what is justified, having regard to other heavy needs. It is altogether out of proportion to lock up three regiments of A.A. artillery, etc. (comprising 6,200 men) for the whole war in Scapa. Scapa is no longer the base of the Grand Fleet, but only of three or four principal vessels. Alternative harbours can be used by these. The distance from Germany, 430 miles, is considerable. We must be very careful not to dissipate our strength unduly in passive defence.

I approve, therefore, of the additional sixteenth 3.7-inch as a matter of the highest urgency. But I think they should be erected by the Admiralty to avoid the long delays and heavy charges of the War Office Ordnance Board.

The second twenty equipments should be considered in relation to the needs of Malta, as well as to the aircraft factories in England. This applies still more to the full scale of 3.7-inch guns, numbering forty-four. Their destination can only be considered in relation to the future war need.

The light A.A. guns seem to be excessive, having regard to the heavy pom-pom fire of the Fleet. The searchlights and balloons are most necessary, as are also the two Fighter Squadrons. Do we not require a more powerful R.D.F. station? And should there not be an additional R.D.F. station on the mainland?

In this case the urgency of getting something into position counts far more than making large-scale plans for 1940.

Let me have reduced proposals with estimates of time and money, but without delaying action on the first instalments.

Also a report of the A.A. defences of Malta, and also of Chatham.

First Lord to First Sea Lord and others.   21.IX.39.

It was very pleasant to see the aircraft carrier *Argus* in the basin

at Portsmouth to-day. The boats of this vessel have been sent to
the C.-in-C., Home Fleet, but no doubt they could easily be replaced, and various guns could be mounted. We are told that
modern aircraft require a larger deck to fly on and off. In that
case, would it not be well to build some aircraft suitable for the
ship, as these can be made much quicker than a new aircraft
carrier? We ought to commission *Argus* as soon as possible, observing that the survivors of *Courageous* are available. Pray consider
the steps that should be taken to this end. I am told she is a very
strong ship under water, but if not the bulkheads could be shored
up or otherwise strengthened.[2]

First Lord to First Sea Lord and others.   21.IX.39.

D.C.N.S. and I were much impressed with the so-called Actaeon
net against torpedoes, on which the "Vernon" are keen. This net
was introduced at the end of the late war. It is a skirt or petticoat
which is only effective when the vessel is in motion. The "Vernon"
declare that a vessel can steam eighteen knots with it on. The
Laconia is to be tried out with one. The net is of thin wire and
large mesh. It should be easy to make in large quantities very
quickly. I suggest that this is a matter of the highest urgency and
significance. It should be fitted on merchant ships, liners, and also,
indeed, above all upon ships of war having solitary missions without destroyer protection. Could not a committee be formed before
the week is out which would grip this idea, already so far advanced
by the naval authorities, and see whether it cannot be brought into
the forefront of our immediate war preparations? If it is right it
would require a very large scale application.[3]

First Lord to First Sea Lord and others.   21.IX.39.

The importance of using all available guns capable of firing at
aircraft whether on ships in harbour or in the dockyard to resist
an air attack should be impressed upon Commanders-in-Chief of
Home Ports as well as upon officers at lesser stations. The concerting of the fire of these guns with the regular defences should

---

[2] The *Argus* was commissioned and performed valuable service training
pilots for the Fleet Air Arm in the Mediterranean.

[3] Many practical difficulties were encountered in the development of these
nets. The early trials were unsuccessful, and it was not until 1942 that the
equipment was perfected. Thereafter it was fitted in over 750 ships with varying success. Ten ships are known to have been saved by this device.

be arranged. If necessary, the high-angle guns of ships in dry dock should be furnished with crews from the depots, and special arrangements made to supply the electrical power, even though the ship is under heavy repair. There must be many contrivances by which a greater volume of fire could be brought to bear upon attacking aircraft. We must consider the moonlight period ahead of us as one requiring exceptional vigilance. Please consider whether some general exhortations cannot be given.

First Lord to Admiral Somerville and Controller.   23.IX.39.

Let me have at your earliest convenience the programme of installation of R.D.F. in H.M. ships, showing what has been done up to date, and a forecast of future installations, with dates. Thereafter, let me have a monthly return showing progress. The first monthly return can be November 1.

First Lord to First Sea Lord and others.   24.IX.39.

A lot of our destroyers and small craft are bumping into one another under the present hard conditions of service. We must be very careful not to damp the ardour of officers in the flotillas by making heavy weather of occasional accidents. They should be encouraged to use their ships with war-time freedom, and should feel they will not be considered guilty of unprofessional conduct, if they have done their best, and something or other happens. I am sure this is already the spirit and your view, but am anxious it should be further inculcated by the Admiralty. There should be no general rule obliging a court martial in every case of damage. The Board should use their power to dispense with this, so long as no negligence or crass stupidity is shown. Errors towards the enemy, [i.e., to fight,] should be most leniently viewed, even if the consequences are not pleasant.

First Lord to First Sea Lord, D.C.N.S. and D.N.I.   24.IX.39.
(For general guidance.) (Most secret.)

1. Mr. Dulanty is thoroughly friendly to England. He was an officer under me in the Ministry of Munitions in 1917/18, but he has no control or authority in Southern Ireland (so-called Eire). He acts as a general smoother, representing everything Irish in the most favourable light. Three-quarters of the people of Southern Ireland are with us, but the implacable, malignant minority can

make so much trouble that De Valera dare not do anything to offend them. All this talk about partition and the bitterness that would be healed by a union of Northern and Southern Ireland will amount to nothing. They will not unite at the present time, and we cannot in any circumstances sell the loyalists of Northern Ireland. Will you kindly consider these observations as the basis upon which Admiralty dealings with Southern Ireland should proceed?

2. There seems to be a good deal of evidence, or at any rate suspicion, that the U-boats are being succoured from West of Ireland ports by the malignant section with whom De Valera dare not interfere. And we are debarred from using Berehaven, etc. If the U-boat campaign became more dangerous we should coerce Southern Ireland both about coast watching and the use of Berehaven, etc. However, if it slackens off under our counter-attacks and protective measures, the Cabinet will not be inclined to face the serious issues which forcible measures would entail. It looks therefore as if the present bad situation will continue for the present. But the Admiralty should never cease to formulate through every channel its complaints about it, and I will from time to time bring our grievances before the Cabinet. On no account must we appear to acquiesce in, still less be contented with, the odious treatment we are receiving.

First Lord to First Sea Lord and D.C.N.S.   29.IX.39.

While anxious not to fetter in any way the discretion of C.-in-C., Home Fleet, I think it might be as well for you to point out that the sending of heavy ships far out into the North Sea will certainly entail bombing attacks from aircraft, and will not draw German warships from their harbours. Although there were no hits on the last occasion, there might easily have been losses disproportionate to the tactical objects in view. This opinion was expressed to me by several Cabinet colleagues.

The first brush between the Fleet and the air has passed off very well, and useful data have been obtained, but we do not want to run unnecessary risks with our important vessels until their A.A. has been worked up to the required standard against aircraft flying 250 miles an hour.[4]

4 This refers to an incident on September 26 when the Home Fleet was attacked by aircraft in the North Sea, without suffering damage. It was on this

First Lord to Secretary.   30.IX.39

Surely the account you give of all these various disconnected Statistical Branches constitutes the case for a central body which should grip together all Admiralty statistics, and present them to me in a form increasingly simplified and graphic.

I want to know at the end of each week everything we have got, all the people we are employing, the progress of all vessels, works of construction, the progress of all munitions affecting us, the state of our merchant tonnage, together with losses, and numbers of every branch of the R.N. and R.M. The whole should be presented in a small book such as was kept for me by Sir Walter Layton when he was my statistical officer at the Ministry of Munitions in 1917 and 1918. Every week I had this book, which showed the past and the weekly progress, and also drew attention to what was lagging. In an hour or two I was able to cover the whole ground, as I knew exactly what to look for and where.

How do you propose this want of mine should be met?

October, 1939

First Lord to Secretary.   9.X.39.

The First Lord's Statistical Branch should consist of Professor Lindemann, who would do this besides his scientific activities, and a secretary who knows the Admiralty, a statistician, and a confidential typist who is also preferably an accountant. The duties of this branch will be:

1. To present to the First Lord a weekly picture of the progress of all new construction, showing delays from contract dates, though without inquiring into the causes, upon which First Lord will make his own inquiries.

2. To present return of all British or British-controlled merchant ships together with losses under various heads and new construction or acquisition —
   (a) during the week,
   (b) since the war began;
   also forecasts of new deliveries.

3. To record the consumption weekly and since war began of

occasion that the *Ark Royal* was singled out for special attention. The Germans claimed that she had been sunk and the pilot who made the claim was decorated. For weeks afterwards the German wireless reiterated daily the question, "Where is the *Ark Royal*?"

all ammunition, torpedoes, oil, etc., together with new deliveries, i.e., weekly and since the war began, monthly or weekly outputs and forecasts.

4. To keep a complete continuous statistical survey of Fleet Air Arm, going not only into aircraft but pilots, guns and equipment of all kinds, and point out all apparent lag.

5. To present a monthly survey of the losses of personnel of all kinds.

6. To keep records of inquiries and any special papers relating to numbers and strength provided by First Lord.

7. To make special inquiries, analysing for First Lord Cabinet Papers and papers from other Departments which have a statistical character, as requested by First Lord.

As soon as the personnel of the department is settled after discussion with Professor Lindemann, who should also advise on any additions to the above list of duties, a Minute must be given to all departments to make the necessary returns to Statistical Branch (to be called "S") at the times required, and to afford any necessary assistance.

Air Supply

October 16, 1939.

This most interesting paper is encouraging, but it does not touch the question on which the War Cabinet sought information — namely, the disparity between the monthly output of new aircraft, and the number of squadrons composing the first-line air strength of the R.A.F. We were told in 1937 that there would be 1,750 first-line aircraft modernly equipped by April 1, 1938 (see Sir Thomas Inskip's speeches). However, the House of Commons was content with the statement that this position had in fact been realised by April 1, 1939. We were throughout assured that reserves far above the German scale were the feature of the British system. We now have apparently only about 1,500 first-line aircraft with good reserves ready for action. On mobilisation the 125 squadrons of April 1, 1939, shrank to 96. It is necessary to know how many new squadrons will be fully formed during the months of November, December, January, and February. It is difficult to understand why, with a production of fighting machines which has averaged over seven hundred a month since May, and is now running even higher, only a handful of squadrons have been added to our first-line strength, and why that strength is below what we were assured was so reached in April of this year. One would have thought with outputs so large, and pilots so numerous, we should have been able to add ten or fifteen squadrons a month to our first-line air strength; and no explanation is furnished why this cannot happen. Then squadrons of sixteen each, with one hundred per cent reserves, would only amount to 320 a month, or much less than half the output from the factories. The Cabinet ought to be told what are the limiting factors. They should be told this in full detail. Is it pilots or mechanics or higher ground staff or guns or instruments of any kind? We ought not, surely, to continue in ignorance of the reasons which prevent the heavy outputs of the factories from being translated into a fighting-front of first-line aircraft organised in squadrons. It may be impossible to remedy this, but at any rate we ought to examine it without delay. It is not production that is lagging behind, but the formation of fighting units with their full reserve upon the approved scale.

D.S.R., Controller and Secretary.   16.X.39

I am very much obliged to the Director of Scientific Research for his interesting memorandum [on the Admiralty Research Department], and I entirely agree with the principle that the first stage is the formulation of a felt want by the fighting Service. Once this is clearly defined in terms of simple reality it is nearly always possible for the scientific experts to find a solution. The Services should always be encouraged to explain what it is that hurts or hinders them in any particular branch of their work. For instance, a soldier advancing across No-Man's-Land is hit by a bullet which prevents his locomotion functioning further. It is no use telling him or his successor to be brave, because that condition has already been satisfied. It is clear however that if a steel plate or other obstacle had stood between the bullet and the soldier, the latter's powers of locomotion would not have been deranged. The problem therefore becomes how to place a shield in front of the soldier. It then emerges that the shield is too heavy for him to carry, thus locomotion must be imparted to the shield; and how? Hence the tanks. This is of course a simple example.

2. In your list of Branches and Departments very little seems to be allowed for physical investigation, the bulk being concentrated upon application and development. I am therefore very glad to

know that the Clarendon Laboratory will be utilised for this purpose, and I shall be dealing with the paper on that subject later in the day.

First Lord to Controller and others.   18.X.39.

Requisitioning of Trawlers

I have asked the Minister of Agriculture to bring Mr. Ernest Bevin and his deputation to the Admiralty at 4.15 o'clock tomorrow after they have explored the ground among themselves. Let all be notified and an official letter written to the Ministry of Agriculture inviting them here. I will preside myself.

Meanwhile A.C.N.S., D.T.D. and Controller or Deputy-Controller should, together with Financial Secretary, meet together this evening to work out a plan, the object of which is the *Utmost Fish*, subject to naval necessity. The immediate loss arising from our requisition should be shared between ports, and the fact that a port has built the best kind of trawlers must not lead to its being the worst sufferer. Side by side with this equalisation process a type of trawler which can be built as quickly as possible, and will serve its purpose, should be given facilities in the shipyards. As soon as these trawlers flow in, they can either be added to the various ports or else be given to the ports from whom the chief requisition has been made, the equalising trawlers being restored after temporary use — this is for local opinion to decide. It is vital to keep the fish trade going, and we must fight for this part of our food supply as hard as we do against the U-boats.[5]

First Lord to First Sea Lord and D.C.N.S. (Most Secret)   19.10.39.

The Turkish situation has sharpened-up. Suppose Turkey wanted us to put a Fleet in the Black Sea sufficiently strong to prevent Russian military pressure upon the Bosphorus or other parts of the Turkish northern coast, and the Cabinet were satisfied that this might either keep Russia from going to war or, if she were at war, prevent her attacking Turkey, can the Force be found? What is the strength of the Russian Black Sea marine, and what would be sufficient to master them? Might this not be an area where British submarines with a few destroyers and a couple of protecting cruisers all based on Turkish ports would be able to give an im-

---

[5] Throughout the war a special section of the Trade Division dealt with the needs of fishing vessels working round our coasts.

mense measure of protection? Anyhow, the possibility should be studied in all its military bearings by the Naval Staff, and ways and means of finding and maintaining the Force worked out.

Clearly, if Russia declares war upon us, we must hold the Black Sea.

First Lord to First Sea Lord and Controller.   23.X.39.

Before going further into your paper on the Northern Barrage, I should like to know what amounts of explosives are involved, and how these could be provided without hampering the main fire of the Armies. Perhaps the Controller could today discuss this point with Mr. Burgin or the head of his Chemical Department. I do not know what are the limiting factors in this field. I hear predictions that toluene may run short. I presume the output required for the barrage would be far outside the limits of the Admiralty cordite or explosive factories. I suggest that Controller has all this information collected informally, both from the Admiralty and the Ministry of Supply, and that we talk it over on our return.[6]

First Lord to First Sea Lord.   23.X.39.

I should be glad if you would arrange to discuss with the other Chiefs of Staff this morning the question of raid or invasion, having regard to the position of the Fleet and the long dark nights. I frequently combated these ideas in the late war, but now the circumstances do not seem to be altogether the same. I have of course no knowledge of the military arrangements, but it seems to me there ought to be a certain number of mobile columns or organised forces that could be thrown rapidly against any descent. Of course, it may be that the air service will be able to assume full responsibility.

First Lord to First Sea Lord and D.C.N.S.   27.X.39.

Pray consider this note which I wrote with the idea of circulating it to the Cabinet.

It is surely not our interest to oppose Russian claims for naval bases in the Baltic. These bases are only needed against Germany, and in the process of taking them a sharp antagonism of Russian and German interests becomes apparent. We should point out to the Finns that the preservation of their country from Russian in-

[6] See Chapter 7.

vasion and conquest is the vital matter, and this will not be affected
by Russian bases in the Gulf of Finland or the Gulf of Bothnia.
Apart from Germany, Russian naval power in the Baltic could
never be formidable to us. It is Germany alone that is the danger
and the enemy there. There is, indeed, a common interest between
Great Britain and Russia in forbidding as large a part of the Baltic
as possible to Germany. It is quite natural that Russia should need
to have bases which prevent German aggression in the Baltic Provinces or against Petrograd. If the above reasoning is right, we
ought to let the Russians know what our outlook is, while trying
to persuade the Finns to make concessions, and Russia to be content with strategic points.

First Lord to D.C.N.S. and Secretary.   29.X.39.

Arrange for a stand of arms to be placed in some convenient
position in the basement and let officers and able-bodied personnel
employed in the Admiralty building have a rifle, a bayonet and
ammunition assigned to each. Fifty would be enough. Let this
be done in forty-eight hours.

First Lord to General Smuts.   29.X.39.
Personal and Private.

Monitor *Erebus* is ready to sail for Capetown. As you know we
have never considered fifteen-inch guns necessary for defence of
Capetown, but to please Pirow agreed to lend *Erebus* until those
defences were modernised in view of his fear of attack by Japan.
We realise the defences of Capetown remain weak, but the Germans have no battleships, and the only two battle-cruisers they
possess, the *Scharnhorst and Gneisenau,* would be very unlikely to
try to reach South African waters, or if they did so to risk damage
far from a friendly dockyard from even weak defences. Should
they break out, a major naval operation would ensue, and we shall
pursue them wherever they go with our most powerful vessels until
they are hunted down. Therefore, it seems to me you are unlikely
to have need of this ship. On the other hand, she would be most
useful for various purposes in the shallows of the Belgian coast,
especially if Holland were attacked. She was indeed built by
Fisher and me for this very purpose in 1914. The question is therefore mainly political. Rather than do anything to embarrass you
we would do without the ship. But if you let us have her either

by re-loan or re-transfer Admiralty will be most grateful, and would, of course, reimburse Union.[7]

All good wishes.

NOVEMBER, 1939

First Lord to Secretary.   4.XI.39.

The French have a very complete installation in the country for all the business of their Admiralty, and have already moved there. Our policy is to stay in London until it becomes really impossible, but it follows from this that every effort must be made to bring our alternative installation up to a high level of efficiency.

Pray let me know how it stands, and whether we could in fact shift at a moment's notice without any break in control. Have the telephones, etc., been laid effectively? Are there underground wires as well as others? Do they connect with exchanges other than London, or are they dependent upon the main London exchange? If so, it is a great danger.

First Lord to First Sea Lord and others.   9.XI.39.

I am deeply concerned at the immense slowing-down of trade, both in imports and exports, which has resulted from our struggle during the first ten weeks of the war. Unless it can be grappled with and the restriction diminished to, say, twenty per cent. of normal, very grave shortage will emerge. The complaints coming in from all the Civil Departments are serious. We shall have failed in our task if we merely substitute delays for sinkings. I frankly admit I had not appreciated this aspect, but in this war we must learn from day to day. We must secretly loosen-up the convoy system (while boasting about it publicly), especially on the outer routes. An intricate study must be made of the restrictions now imposed, and consequent lengthening of voyages, and a higher degree of risk must be accepted. This is possible now that so many of our ships are armed. They can go in smaller parties. Even across the Atlantic we may have to apply this principle to a certain degree. If we could only combine with it a large effective destroyer force, sweeping the Western Approaches as a matter of course instead of providing focal points on which convoys could be directed, we should have more freedom. This is no reversal or stultification of previous policy, which was absolutely necessary at the outset. It is

7 General Smuts replied that of course he would do as we wished.

a refinement and development of that policy so that its end shall
not be defeated.

First Lord to D.C.N.S. 9.II.39.

It appears to me that St. Helena and Ascension must be made
effectively secure against seizure by landing parties from, say, a
Deutschland. We should look very foolish if we found them in
possession of the two 6-inch guns with a supply ship in the harbour.
I don't feel the garrisons there are strong enough.

First Lord to First Sea Lord. 15.XI.39.

Pray let me have details of the proposed first Canadian convoy.
How many ships, which ships, how many men in each ship, what
speed will convoy take, escort both A-S and anti-raider? Place of
assembly and date of departure should be mentioned verbally.

First Lord to Secretary and A.C.N.S. 16.XI.39.

Have you made sure that the intake of air to Admiralty basement
is secure? Are there alternative intakes in case of the present one
being damaged by a bomb? What would happen in the case of fire
in the courtyard?

There seem to be heaps of rubbish, timber, and other inflammable material lying about, not only in the courtyard, but in some
of the rooms underneath. All unnecessary inflammable material
should be removed forthwith.

First Lord to First Sea Lord. 20.XI.39.

Nothing can be more important in the anti-submarine war than
to try to obtain an independent flotilla which could work like a
cavalry division on the approaches, without worrying about the
traffic or U-boat sinkings, but could systematically search large areas
over a wide front. In this way these areas would become untenable
to U-boats, and many other advantages would flow from the
manoeuvre.[8]

First Lord to First Sea Lord and others. 22.XI.39.

When a sudden emergency, like this magnetic-mine stunt, arises,
it is natural that everyone who has any knowledge or authority in
the matter should come together, and that a move should be got

8 This policy did not become possible until a later phase in the war.

on in every direction. But do you not think we now want to bring into being a special section for the job, with the best man we can find at the head of it working directly under the Staff and the Board? Such a branch requires several subdivisions, for instance, one lot should be simply collecting and sifting all the evidence we have about these mines from their earliest effort on the west coast and interviewing survivors, etc., so that everything is collected and focused.

The second lot would deal with the experimental side, and the "Vernon" would be a part of this. I am told Admiral Lyster is doing something here; he has a plan of his own which he is working, but it is desirable that a general view should prevail.

The third section is concerned with action in the shape of production, and getting the stuff delivered for the different schemes; while the fourth, which is clearly operational, is already in existence.

It is not suggested that this organisation should be permanent, or that all those who take part in it should be working whole-time. It should be a feature in their daily duties, and all should be directed and concerted from the summit.

Pray consider this, and make out a paper scheme into which all would fit.

First Lord to First Sea Lord and others.   23.XI.39.

I approve the appointment of Admiral Wake-Walker to concert the magnetic-mine business. But it is necessary that he should have precise functions and instructions. (1) He will assemble all the information available. (2) He will concert and press forward all the experiments, assigning their priority. (3) He will make proposals for the necessary production. (4) He will offer advice to the Naval Staff upon the operational aspect, which nevertheless will proceed independently from hour to hour under the Naval Staff and the C.-in-C., Nore. In all the foregoing he will of course act under the Board.

2. Let me see a chart of duties divided between these various branches, and make it clear that the officers of the various technical Departments in the Admiralty shall be at Admiral Wake-Walker's service from time to time as may be needed. You will no doubt consult him in making this plan.

3. It is essential that Admiral Drax should be in on all this from

the beginning, and also in touch with C.-in-C., Nore, so that he comes into full understanding and operation from December 1.[9]

First Lord to First Sea Lord and others.   27.XI.39.

1. We must arrive at clear ideas about the Swedish iron ore for Germany. Doubt has been thrown on whether it is important to stop this or not. I am informed by M. of E.W. that on the contrary nothing would be more deadly, not only to German war-making capacity but to the life of the country, than to stop for three or even six months this import.

2. The suggestion has been made verbally to me by the Naval Staff that when Lulea freezes we should violate Norwegian neutrality by landing a force, or perhaps stationing a ship in territorial waters at Narvik. I am opposed to both these alternatives.

3. Pray examine and advise upon a proposal to establish a minefield, blocking Norwegian territorial waters at some lonely spot on the coast as far south as convenient. If the Norwegians will do this themselves, well and good. Otherwise a plan must be made for us to do it. Doubt has been thrown upon our ability to maintain the necessary watch on this minefield, or to intercept vessels laden with ore which go outside it. But this is surely ill-founded. The mere fact that we had laid the minefield and were known to be watching and blockading would deter the ore-ships, and the process would not be too onerous for the C.-in-C., Home Fleet. However, let me have your final view.

4. It must be remembered that in addition to the ore-ships, much merchandise valuable to Germany is coming down the Norwegian Leads. A statement was shown me by the D.N.I. that five ore-ships had already, in November, gone from Narvik to Germany, and that empty ships are going up now to receive the ore. What do the M. of E.W. say to this? We must know what the facts are, and have agreement between the Departments.

5. Meanwhile, the Russians have notified us that their gigantic Arctic ice-breaker is almost immediately to come down the Norwegian territorial waters on her way nominally to Kronstadt. But at the same time we hear that the Russians are hiring this ice-breaker to Germany to break the ice up to Lulea. If this were done, and no other counter-measures taken, the whole flow of ore into Germany would proceed at its present rate of nearly a million tons

[9] See Chapter 7 and Appendix H dealing with the magnetic-mine problem.

a month, thus completely frustrating all our policies. How are we to deal with this? I will make you a suggestion verbally; but meanwhile the Foreign Office must be consulted on the whole position.

First Lord to Secretary. 27.XI.39.

I notice that in the Air Ministry every room is provided with candles and matches for use in emergency.

Pray take steps immediately to make similar provision in the Admiralty.

First Lord to D.C.N.S. and First Sea Lord. 30.XI.39.

I should be glad if you would consider whether it is not possible to add a third vessel to the Australasian escorts. Perhaps the Australians will offer anothers of their cruisers, but if not, cannot we find another 6-inch-gun ship with a catapult? This would leave *Ramillies* freer to engage the enemy, if an attack should be made by surface ships. It enables also scouting to be done far ahead and to the flanks of the convoy, thus giving ample warning. The transportation of the Australian divisions is an historic episode in Imperial history. An accident would be a disaster. Perhaps one of our detached submarines in the Indian Ocean could also help.

DECEMBER, 1939

First Lord to Controller and others. (Secret.) 3.XII.39.

I was much interested in D.C.N.'s remark about the possibility of making a new battleship with the four spare fifteen-inch-gun turrets. Such a vessel would be of the battleship cruiser type, heavily armoured and absolutely proof against air attack. Pray let me have a legend with estimates in money and time. This ship could come in after the *King George V* batch are finished and before *Temeraire* and *Lion*.[10]

First Lord to Secretary, D.C.N.S. and First Sea Lord. 12.XII.39.

1. In view of the danger of surprise attacks at a time when the enemy may expect to find us off our guard, there must be no break or holiday period at Christmas or the New Year. The utmost vigilance must be practised at the Admiralty and in all naval ports. On the other hand, it should be possible between now and February 15 to give a week's leave to almost every officer concerned in staff duties. I am very glad to hear this is being planned at the

10 Plans for this ship went forward. She became H.M.S. *Vanguard.*

Admiralty, and it will, I presume, be imitated as far as possible at the naval ports.

2. Every effort should be made to ease the strain upon the destroyer crews. At Devonport I am told admirable arrangements are made to relieve the flotilla complements as they come in from patrols, and that two or three days' rest in port brings them round in a wonderful manner. Similar arrangements are in force at Rosyth, and Scapa, but I am told that the amenities of Scapa are so much below those of the naval ports that the men are deeply disappointed when their brief spell of rest takes place there. No doubt in some cases this is inevitable, but I trust the whole question will be reviewed with the intention of comforting these crews to the utmost extent that operations will permit.

First Lord to D.C.N.S., Admiral Wake-Walker   24.XII.39.
     (to initiate action) and D.S.R.

I suppose you are already looking ahead to a possible change by the enemy from magnetic mines to acoustic or supersonic. Pray let me have a note at your convenience.

First Lord to Secretary, D.C.N.S. and First Sea Lord.   28.XII.39.

It should be explained to the Foreign Office that the six-mile limit in Italian waters was instituted by the Admiralty as a voluntary and self-denying ordinance at the outset of the war. It was never communicated to the Italians, nor made public to the world. It therefore forms no part of any bargain or agreement. It was simply a convenient guide for British naval authorities at a particular juncture. It has now become onerous, and possibly deeply injurious to the blockade, and in these circumstances the Admiralty would propose as a departmental matter to notify the C.-in-C., Mediterranean, that the three-mile limit only need be observed. They will at the same time renew their injunctions to treat Italian shipping with special leniency, and to avoid causes of friction or complaint with that favoured country.

Let me see draft.

January, 1940

First Lord to Secretary.   4.I.40.

Can anything be done to utilise the canal system to ease the transport of coal, north and south? Pray let me have a note on this at my return.

First Lord to First Sea Lord, Controller, D.T.M.,   12.I.40.
Rear-Admiral A. H. Walker and Professor Lindemann
Operation "Royal Marine"

1. This matter was fully discussed in France with high military authorities, and various arrangements have been made. Captain Fitzgerald and Major Jefferis have seen the necessary people and should now furnish me with reports of their work. The French military men point out that they control the head waters of the Saar and the Moselle, in addition to the Rhine, and that many possibilities are open there. All are convinced that we should not act until a really large supply of the needful is in hand. Not only must the first go-off be on the largest scale at all points, but the daily and weekly supply thereafter must be such as to keep the tension at the highest pitch indefinitely.

2. It is, of course, understood that while all action is to be prepared the final decision rests with the Governments.

3. In all circumstances I am prepared to postpone the date from the February moon to the March moon. Meanwhile, every exertion is to be made to perfect the plan and accumulate the greatest store.

4. A meeting of all concerned will be held in my room on Monday night at 9.30. By this time everyone should be able to report progress and everything should be concerted. I am asking the Secretary of State for Air to be present to hear the reports. These may be individually presented, but those concerned are to consult together in the interval. Above all, any obstacle or cause of undue delay is to be reported, so that the operations can be brought to full readiness as soon as possible. We may be forced to act before the March moon.[11]

First Lord to Admiral Usborne.   13.I.40.
"U.P." Weapon

Your report dated 12.1.40. Everything seems to be going all right except the bombs, which are the only part of this process not under our control. I note that Messrs. Venner have fallen behind in respect of one component of these. But are you satisfied that the Air Ministry have done their part with the bombs?

Pray let me have a special report on the subject, and also let me know whether I should not write to the Secretary of State for Air, asking to have this part of the business handed over to us like the

[11] See Chapters 7 and 11.

rest has been. These U.P. experiments are of immense importance. The whole security of H.M. warships and merchant ships may be enhanced by this development. I am counting on you to make sure that all is concerted and brought forward together, and that we shall go into mass production on a large scale at the earliest moment.

I am sorry that the experiments today with the ejection trials were not completed, though I understand from Professor Lindemann that they were in principle satisfactory.

Pray press on with these with the utmost speed.

I think the time is coming when a report of progress should be furnished to the Air Ministry and the War Office, who have entrusted their interests in this matter to me. Perhaps, therefore, you would prepare a compendious statement, showing position to date and future prospects.[12]

First Lord to First Sea Lord, Controller, D.C.N.S.,   12.I.40.
   Secretary and A.C.N.S.

The First Lord wishes to congratulate all those concerned in dealing with magnetic mines on the success which has so far been achieved.

First Lord to Controller.   13.I.40.

I am very glad to receive your paper on concrete ships. I am not at all satisfied that the idea has been sufficiently explored. Great progress has been made since the last war in ferro-concrete. Quite a different class of workmen and materials would be called into being, and the strain on our ordinary shipbuilding plans proportionately relieved. In these circumstances, I think an effort should be made to make one sea-going ship at once.[13]

First Lord to Naval Secretary.   14.I.40.

Perhaps you will see Mr. Cripps (brother of Sir Stafford Cripps)

---

[12] This minute refers to the unrotated projectile (rocket propulsion), which was then being developed for use against low-flying aircraft. The device consisted of a battery of rockets which, on reaching a predetermined height, released long trailing wires, each carrying a small bomb at the end, and supported by a parachute. An aircraft fouling one of these wires would draw the bomb into its wing, where it would explode.

This device was a stop-gap necessitated by our grievous shortage of short-range weapons. Later on it was superseded by more effective weapons.

[13] The development of concrete ships promised important relief to our vital war industries. It seemed that they could be built quickly and cheaply by types

who had a very good record in the last war and is a brave and able man. There must be many openings in some of our minesweepers.

[ENCLOSURE: *Letter from the Hon. Frederick Cripps asking "could he be used for mine-sweeping?"*]

First Lord to First Sea Lord. 16.I.40.

A.A. Defences of Scapa

Surely it would be better to have a conference as I suggested and talk matters over round a table than that I should have to prepare a paper and raise the matter as a Cabinet issue? The squandering of our strength proceeds in every direction, everyone thinking he is serving the country by playing for safety locally. Our Army is puny as far as the fighting front is concerned; our Air Force is hopelessly inferior to the Germans'; we are not allowed to do anything to stop them receiving their vital supplies of ore; we maintain an attitude of complete passivity, dispersing our forces ever more widely; the Navy demands Scapa and Rosyth both to be kept at the highest point. Do you realise that perhaps we are heading for *defeat?* I feel I must do my duty, even in small things, in trying to secure effective concentration upon the enemy, and in preventing needless dispersion.

First Lord to First Sea Lord. 19.I.40.

Fleet Air Arm — Estimated Cost During the First Twelve Months of the Year

I have been increasingly disquieted about the demand which the Fleet Air Arm involves upon British war-making resources. None the less this estimate is a surprise to me, as I had not conceived how enormous was the charge involved. I have always been a strong advocate of the Fleet Air Arm, in fact I drafted for Sir Thomas Inskip the compromise decision to which he eventually came in 1938. I feel all the more responsible for making sure that the Fleet Air Arm makes a real contribution to the present war in killing and defeating Germans.

2. When some years ago the Fleet Air Arm was being discussed,

of labour not required in normal shipbuilding and would save large quantities of steel. These claims were found on examination to be based on false assumptions and many unforeseen technical difficulties arose. An experimental ship of two thousand tons was built, but was a failure, and although experimental work continued, the use of concrete hulls was only successful in barges up to about two hundred tons.

the speed of carrier-borne and shore-based aircraft was not unequal; but since then the shore-based development has been such as to make it impossible for carrier-borne aircraft to compete with shore-based. This left the Fleet Air Arm the most important duties of reconnaissance in the ocean spaces, of spotting during an action with surface ships and launching torpedo seaplane attacks upon them. However, there are very few surface ships of the enemy, and one can only consider the possible break-out of a German raider or fast battleship as potential targets. Provision must be made for this; but certainly it does not justify anything like this immense expenditure.

3. On the other hand, our air force has fallen far behind that of Germany, and under present conditions the air menace to this Island, its factories, its naval ports and shipping, as well as to the Fleet in harbour, must be considered as the only *potentially mortal* attack we have to fear and face. I am most anxious therefore to liberate the R.A.F. from all ordinary coastal duties in the Narrow Waters and the North Sea, and to assume this responsibility for the Fleet Air Arm, which then, and then alone, would have a task proportioned to its cost and worthy of its quality.

4. Some time ago the Air Ministry were making their way in the world and were very jealous of their sphere, but now that a prime importance has come to them, equal in many ways to that of the Royal Navy, they are much more tolerant; moreover, they are deeply anxious to increase their own disposable strength. They have recently allowed us to form two shore-based squadrons for the Orkneys, etc., and I believe that, with tact and in the present good atmosphere, this principle might be applied all along the east coast. We have, I suppose, an unequalled class of pilots and observers for such purposes, and the advantage to both Services would be unquestionable.

5. I propose, therefore, in principle for your consideration, that a plan should be drawn up by the Fifth Sea Lord, to save one hundred and one hundred and fifty pilots from the Fleet Air Arm, together with mechanics and administrative staff, in order to form six, seven, or eight shore-based naval squadrons, and that the complements of the aircraft-carriers, especially the unarmoured aircraft-carriers, should be reduced as much as is necessary. For reconnaissance in the outer seas we should have to content ourselves with very small complements. When the armoured carriers are complete,

their complement must be considered in the light of the conditions prevailing then in the North Sea. The Fleet Air Arm training schools and other establishments must be rigorously combed to provide these new fighting forces.

6. If the details of this plan are worked out, I would approach the Air Ministry and offer to relieve them of the whole coastal work in Home Waters *without adding to the cost to the public*. We should make a smaller demand on future deliveries for carrier-borne aircraft and ask in return to be given a supply of fighters or medium bombers, perhaps not at first of the latest type, but good enough for short-range action. We should then take over the whole responsibility as a measure of war emergency, and leave the future spheres of the Department to be settled after the war is over.

Pray let me have your thought upon this.[14]

First Lord to D.C.N.S., D.N.I. and Secretary. 31.I.40.

Thirty years ago I was shown Foreign Office confidential books printed on paper so inflammable that they could be almost immediately destroyed. Since then, all this business has advanced. It would be possible to print books on cellulose nitrate, which would almost explode on being lighted. Existing books could be photographed on to this with great facility. Alternatively, or conjointly, these books could be reduced to tiny proportions and read by a small projecting-apparatus. Let a small committee be formed on this question. Pray propose me names. Professor Lindemann will represent me.

First Lord to First Sea Lord and D.C.N.S. 31.I.40.

Pictures have been published in many newspapers of the Australian troops marching through Sydney, etc., before starting for the war. Thus the enemy must know that convoys will be approaching the entrance to the Red Sea and the neighbourhood of Socotra. Although there is no intelligence of any U-boat in the Indian Ocean, how can we be quite sure one has not made its way up from Madagascar, where there was a rumour, to the Red Sea,

[14] This plan was swept away by events. The Fleet Air Arm made its contribution to the R.A.F. during the Battle of Britain. Later the development of the U-boat war taxed to the utmost the resources of Coastal Command which itself drew heavily on Bomber Command to meet its ever-growing commitments.

Later again in 1941 the advent of the "Escort Carrier" type enabled the Fleet Air Arm to play a conspicuous part in the defeat of the U-boats operating beyond the range of normal shore-based aircraft.

and been oiled from some Italian or Arabian port? I must say I should feel more comfortable if anti-submarine escort could be provided from the neighbourhood of Socotra. This could be done by sending the destroyer *Vendetta* from Haifa to rendezvous, say two hundred miles east of Socotra, with the destroyer *Westcott*, which is already following up the convoy from Singapore. The presence of these two Asdic-fitted destroyers would give complete assurance, and only one of them has to go far out of her way.

Pray let me have a note on this.

FEBRUARY, 1940

First Lord to First Sea Lord.   9.II.40.

Legend of Particulars of Third War Emergency Flotilla

Destroyers of 1,650 tons almost amount to small cruisers. These unarmoured vessels with nearly two hundred men on board become as *Grenville* and *Exmouth* have shown, a prize and a target for a U-boat in themselves. In this case the destroyers are within ten tons of the flotilla-leader. By steadily increasing the size and cost of destroyers, we transfer them gradually from the class of the hunters to that of the hunted. It is unsound to place so large a human stake in an unarmoured, highly vulnerable vessel. The length of time in building vessels of this class makes it unlikely they will take part in the present war. What we require are larger numbers of smaller vessels more quickly delivered. It will be necessary to keep the number of these very large destroyers at a minimum. The simplified armament and extra endurance are good features.

First Lord to First Sea Lord (with papers)
        D.G.N.S., D.N.I., Controller and Secretary   11.II.40.
Japanese Strength — N.I.D. 02242/39

1. It is of the greatest importance to form a true opinion about present and prospective Japanese building. Before I can put this case to the Cabinet, I must be satisfied that there is solid evidence of the ability of Japan to construct a navy superior to the present navies of Britain and the United States, built and building. The financial condition of Japan has lamentably deteriorated. She has for two and a half years been engaged in a most ruinous war in China, between one and one and a half millions of Japanese soldiers have had to be maintained in the field. No decisive

progress has been made. On the contrary, it is believed the Chinese are gaining strength. Certainly there is a marked reaction in Japan, and the internal tension is very great.

2. We must look at the kind of statements which are made about their new shipbuilding intentions in the light of these facts. They have to buy a large proportion of their materials for warship construction from over the seas, and this, with the drain of the China war, must greatly affect their foreign exchange. What would be the cost of the programme set out in the First Sea Lord's table in yen, in sterling, and in dollars? It seems to me that they are going into figures of naval expense never attempted before at a time when their finances are rapidly deteriorating.

3. What is their capacity of steel production? What is their consuming power of steel? If my recollection serves me, the Japanese consuming power of steel is in the neighbourhood of three million tons a year, compared to British fifteen and American fifty-four. Yet such a programme as Japan is said to be embarking on would be, and is, a heavy drain on British or American strength. No doubt the heavy building in America and Britain will impose an additional effort on Japan. Whether they can go the pace is quite another question. I do not feel that mere rumours of ships they are said to have laid down form a sufficient basis. Has Major Morton's Branch or Committee which studies the military capacities of enemy or potentially enemy countries been consulted?

In short, I am extremely sceptical of the Japanese power to build a fleet equal to the present built and building fleets of either Britain or the United States.

First Lord to First Sea Lord.   20.II.40.

In view of yesterday's Cabinet decision all preparations should be made to carry out the operation referred to as soon as possible.

Pray let me have your proposals.

I consider the matter is most urgent, as it must be linked with the *Altmark*. The operation being minor and innocent may be called "Wilfred." [15]

First Lord to First Sea Lord and others.   24.II.40.

Let me have an early report on condition of *Exeter* and time

[15] This refers to the mining of the Norwegian Leads. Owing to many political complications referred to in Chapter 11, the operation did not take place until April 8.

likely for her repairs. Every effort should be made to keep the crew together. If *Exeter* repairs take more than three or four months, what are the other cruisers coming along in the interval by which *Exeter's* crew could be taken on with their present captain? In the Army it would be thought madness to break up a unit like this, and I do not see why the same moral consideration should not affect the Navy too.[16]

First Lord to Controller and others.   25.II.40.

Reclassification of Smaller War Vessels

Director of Plan's remark that the terms "destroyer has by association come to imply a particular type of vessel whose principal weapon is the torpedo" ignores the whole story of the destroyer, whose chief function was to destroy the torpedo-boat with superior gun-fire. The idea of destruction is not confined to destruction by torpedo; it may equally be expressed by depth-charges or gun-fire.

I agree with First Sea Lord about the needlessness of repeating the word "vessel," and his wish to simplify all titles to one word.

I should like the word "destroyer" to cover ships formerly described as "fast escort vessels," which are, in fact, medium destroyers. I do not like the word "whaler," which is an entire misnomer, as they are not going to catch whales, and I should like to have some suggestions about this. What is, in fact, the distinction between an "escorter," a "patroller," and a "whaler" as now specified? It seems most important to arrive at simple conclusions quickly on this subject, and enforce them from March 1 on all commands and departments. Let me see a list of the vessels built and building which will fall in the various categories.[17]

MARCH, 1940

First Lord to First Sea Lord and Secretary.   1.III.40.

A plan should be prepared for a battleship concentration in the

---

[16] In Chapter 8 my minutes are recorded dealing with the difficulties which arose over bringing the *Exeter* home after the River Plate action. She now remained under repair for many months.

[17] The "fast escort vessels" became known as "Hunt" class destroyers, as their names were all selected from famous packs of hounds. Large numbers were built and they served with distinction both in the anti-U-boat war and in our amphibious operations. Later ancient names were revived.

The "whalers" became known as "corvettes" and later types were called "frigates."

Escort vessels became "sloops."

Mediterranean (with other craft), supposing trouble should arise
in March. I do not expect trouble; but it would be well to have
all the combinations surveyed in advance.[18]

First Lord to First Sea Lord, Controller and others.   5.III.40.

After the air attack on the Fleet on September 26, we all thought
it most necessary to train the A.A. gunners against faster targets
than those hitherto provided. Ideas were suggested by Professor
Lindemann, experiments were made, and other ideas for flares, etc.,
put forward by the "Vernon." What has happened about all this?
Of course the weather has been terribly against it, but I fear there
have virtually been no practices in Home Waters at high-speed
targets. Five months have passed, and it is very serious if we have
not been able to develop an effective system of fast targets, and
obtain the necessary machines so that the Fleet can work up.

We must have this now that the weather is improving and the
Fleet back at Scapa. An improvement in the gunnery of H.M. ships
is of the utmost importance to their safety.

First Lord to First Sea Lord and Controller.   5.III.40.

Repairing ships is better than new building. A strong effort
should be made to turn this 8,000-ton ship *Domala* into an effective
cargo-carrying bottom immediately she can be seized upon, and
repaired in the plainest way for the roughest work.

2. Are we doing enough about salvage? Let me have a return
of the vessels now beached on our coasts, and a report on the
measures taken to fit them again for sea. The very minimum
should be done to them, compatible to life and navigation. *There
ought to be a tremendous move-on in the salvage and repair departments.* The tonnage working on any given day ranks above the
rate of new merchant shipbuilding.

First Lord to First Sea Lord.   6.III.40.

I think it would be only prudent for you to concert with the

---

[18] As a result of these deliberations the battleship *Warspite* was ordered to
return to the Mediterranean, but with the opening of the Norwegian campaign
she was recalled to Home waters and did not reach the Mediterranean until
May.

Before the Italian declaration of war in June, the *Malaya, Ramillies,* and
Royal Sovereign had also joined the Mediterranean Fleet from convoy duty in
the Atlantic.

French the necessary regroupings of the Allied Fleets, which would be appropriate to a hostile or menacing Italian attitude. Perhaps you will let me know about this on my return.

First Lord to Parliamentary Secretary.   11.III.40.

I am very glad you have had a considerable measure of success in your parleys with the trades unions. Be careful about the "Ministry of Labour Training Centres." As hitherto organised, these have been nothing but quasi-philanthropic institutions to tone-up the unfortunate people in the derelict areas. They have never been organised to make skilled tradesmen out of semi-skilled. In their present condition they are a snare so far as we are concerned. We have got to get competent people to learn new trades. The Minister of Labour has always said that his training centres cannot touch any but the unemployed, meaning thereby the peace-time unemployed. What we have to cater for is a far livelier class who are changing their occupations in consequence of the war.

I think you must rely on training in the dockyards and in special training schools stablished by the Admiralty.

Speak to me about this, as it seems to me to be a serious flaw.

First Lord to First Sea Lord and others.   14.III.40.

Now that we are not allowed to interfere with the Norwegian Corridor, would it not be possible to have one or two merchant ships of sufficient speed, specially strengthened in the bows and if possible equipped with a ram? These vessels would carry merchandise and travel up the Leads looking for German ore-ships or any other German merchant vessels, and then ram them by accident. This is only another development of the "Q" ship idea.

First Lord to D.C.N.S., D.N.I. (*to initiate action*).   22.III.40.
      (*Secret*)

Mr. Shinwell declares that in Vigo there are still a number of German merchant ships, many of whose crews are non-German, and among the Germans many non-Nazis. He suggests that with a little money and some organisation it would be possible to get these crews to take the ships to sea, when they could be picked up by our ships, and those who had brought them out suitably rewarded. Is there anything in this?

First Lord to D.C.N.S. and First Sea Lord.   30.III.40.

*Cutting from D.T. 29.3.40. Twenty Nazi ships get ready to sail
— attempts to run the blockade (Amsterdam, Friday). Elster
reported at Rotterdam.*

The reason why I cut this from the *Daily Telegraph* and asked
my question of the D.N.I. is because an exodus of German ships
from Dutch ports might well be a danger-sign in respect of Holland
herself. I have no doubt the same thought has occurred to you.

First Lord to Secretary.   31.III.40.

*War Cabinet — Sub-Committee on Reserved Occupations.
Note by Treasury.*

While there are nearly 1,500,000 unemployed and no serious
drain of casualties from the Army, I propose to resist the disturbance of Admiralty work by movement of men we need from
the dockyards. The matter must be settled by Cabinet decision.
You should let Sir Horace Wilson know how much I regret I
cannot meet his views.

APRIL, 1940

First Lord to Controller.   1.IV.40.

Where are the facts about the return of the 40 destroyers, which
are in hospital, to their duty? And can anything be done to speed
up new destroyers, especially those of the 40th Flotilla, by leaving
out some of the final improvements and latest additions, which
take so much time? The great aim must be to have the maximum
numbers during these coming summer months. They can go back
to have further treatment when we have a larger margin.

First Lord to First Sea Lord, and others.   4.IV.40.

While I do not see any adverse change in the Italian situation,
I presume that the appropriate Departments of the Admiralty Staff
are at work upon, or have already completed, a plan of naval operations in the Mediterranean against Italy, should she force us into
war with her. We might be asked for this by the Cabinet, and I
should be glad to see it as soon as possible, at any rate during the
course of the next four or five days.

First Lord to Controller.   12.IV.40.

The most intense efforts should be concentrated upon *Hood,* as we may need all our strength to meet an Italian threat or attack. Pray let me have a time-table showing when she will be ready for sea.

First Lord to D.C.N.S.   12.IV.40.

Are there any other Danish islands besides the Faroes which require attention?

Will you also kindly ask the Staff to examine the position at Curaçao, in case Holland should be overrun. The Fourth Sea Lord spoke to me on the oil supplies dependent upon Curaçao Refineries. I should like a short paper upon the subject.

First Lord to Sir James Lithgow.   12.IV.40.

Weekly Statement of Shipyard Workers, dated 9.IV.40.

This report is much more favourable, and for the first time shows a lift on new merchant construction. Altogether we have added fifteen thousand men since February 1, when we took over. Are you satisfied that all arrangements made by the late Parliamentary Secretary are completed, and working satisfactorily? We shall want another thirty thousand men, and the most strenuous efforts must be made to procure them. Can anything else be done now?

Has not the time arrived when you will be ready with your report for the Cabinet, which I rather hoped to have sent them last week? I should like to be able to have it ready for them next week. Will you kindly let me see it in outline first?

First Lord to D.C.N.S.   13.IV.40.

One of the branches under your control should make a careful study of Spanish islands, in case Spain should be drawn into a breach of neutrality.

First Lord to Controller, First Sea Lord and Secretary.   13.IV.40.

Controller's Minute of April 13 about "Hood" [19]

This is a very different story to what was told me when it was proposed to repair this ship at Malta. I was assured that the whole operation would take thirty-five days, and that the ship would never be at more than thirty-five days' notice, and that only for a short time. When I asked the other day how long it would take to

[19] See also First Lord's Minute of April 12 above.

bring *Hood* back into service, I was told fourteen days. I take it, therefore, she has been above twenty days under repair at present, to which must now be added seventeen days more in April and thirty-one in May — total seventy-eight days — or much more than double what I was told before this vital ship was laid up in this critical period. Pray give me an explanation of this extraordinary change. Moreover, after these seventy-eight days there are to be fourteen days repairing her reserve feed tanks — total, therefore, ninety-two days, or more than three months at the most critical period in the war.

The engineer in charge of the *Hood* assured me when I was last at Scapa that they had found out the way to nurse her defective condenser tubes so as to get twenty-seven knots, and that there was no reason why she should not remain in commission and carry on for six months.

I much regret not to have been more accurately informed in view of the Italian attitude.

First Lord to First Sea Lord and others.   14.IV.40.

On the assumption that Narvik falls into our hands in the near future we must consider the uses to which we intend to put it. First we want to make it a convenient oiling-base, where our flotillas acting on the Norwegian coast can refuel at the highest economy. Secondly, we require to ship the masses of ore there to this country in a very active manner.

For these purposes we must have a moderate garrison, say about a thousand Territorial troops. A few efficient A.A. batteries, both high and low ceiling; a well-netted, boomed and perhaps partially mined barrier; and a good supply of oil in tankers. Is there plenty of fresh water?

We must expect sporadic attacks from the air. A few coast-defence guns should be mounted to protect the approaches. The sunken German torpedo boats might perhaps supply some of these. Their salvage and repair must be explored, and the port got working as soon as possible. Some of the working party of Marines now being raised might well be sent to Narvik. There are, I believe, good shops where repairs can be effected. A portion of the staff, I suppose Plans Division, should begin work on this question today and formulate requirements. Our object must be to make Narvik self-supporting and self-defended at the earliest moment after we have it in our power, as we shall want all our stuff lower down the coast. The necessary guns (A.A.) may be taken from A.D.G.B.

First Lord to Civil Lord. 16.IV.40.

Faroes

With your experience and connections in the Department, you should now assume the duty of concerting the action to make the Faroes satisfactory for our purposes. D.C.N.S. will supply you with requirements. Pray make a weekly report. We must have an aerodrome and an R.D.F. at the very earliest moment, together with a certain amount of A.A. defence, and a few coast guns. This will be a very tempting base for a raider.

First Lord to Prime Minister. 18.IV.40.

Commentary on German Report Obtained by the French on Ammunition

It is an error to suppose that an offensive can be maintained merely by the unlimited use of artillery ammunition. The creation of a labyrinth or zone of crater fields becomes itself an obstacle, of great difficulty to the attacking army. The moment must come when the infantry advance into this zone and have to fight hand-to-hand with the defenders. Meanwhile, so far as expenditure of ammunition is concerned, the defence can reserve its power till the enemy's infantry advance, and thus economise to an enormous extent. There is no truth in the statement that "all great offensives always came to a stop solely because the attacking armies did not have sufficient ammunition." The impulse of an offensive dies away as the fighting troops become more distant from their point of departure. They thus get ahead of their supplies, whether ammunition or food. The more they have pulverised the intervening ground with their artillery, the more difficult it is to bring supplies of ammunition, even if they have them in their original forward dumps, up to the fighting troops. It is at such moments that the opportunity to deliver the counter-strokes arises.

Altogether this paper, which is most interesting, gives me the impression of being written by someone high up in the Munitions Department of Germany, who naturally thinks in terms only of shell. Shell is very important, and we are not likely to have too much of it, but there is not the slightest reason for supposing that unlimited artillery ammunition can win victory on a great scale in modern war. The transportation of the ammunition to the guns in the various phases of the battle remains, as heretofore, the limiting factor upon the artillery.

First Lord to Admiral Somerville. 21.IV.40.

Pray give me a short note upon the present position of R.D.F. so far as it concerns the Navy and Coast Defence, showing weak points and anything you wish done to remedy them.

First Lord to First Sea Lord and V.C.N.S. 25.IV.40.

The reason why I am worrying about these minefields on the approaches to Narvik is that now *Warspite* has quitted, and we have an uncocked-up ship in *Resolution* only, this ship might be at a disadvantage in range should *Scharnhorst* or *Gneisenau* turn up one fine morning. Perhaps however it is possible to shelter in a fiord so as to avoid long-range fire, and force action at reduced ranges, or perhaps *Resolution* could be careened. Anyhow, I think it indispensable that we should reach certainty so far as the defence of Narvik from a surface raid is concerned.[20]

(*Action this Day.*)
First Lord to First Sea Lord and others. 28.IV.40.

In view of the bad reports from the Faroes about aircraft or seaplane bases and the fact we must reckon with the Germans all along the Norwegian coast, it seems indispensable that we have a base in Iceland for our flying-boats and for oiling the ships on the Northern Patrol. Let a case be prepared for submission to the Foreign Office. The sooner we let the Icelanders know that this is what we require the better.[21]

First Lord to Sir James Lithgow and Controller. 30.IV.40.

These figures of our shipping gains from the German aggression against Norway and Denmark amount roughly to 750 ships, aggregating 3,000,000 tons. The effect of this upon our shipping and shipbuilding position requires to be considered. Clearly, we have obtained an easement we never foresaw when we embarked upon our present programme. I should be glad to know your reaction, and in particular how the latest paper prepared by Sir James Lithgow is affected.

[20] Our ships were using Skjel Fiord in the Lofoten Islands as an advanced base. This covered the approach to Narvik through West Fiord.
[21] Iceland was occupied by British forces on May 10.

SOME QUESTIONS ABOUT PERSONNEL

First Lord to First Sea Lord, Second Sea Lord, and   18.IX.39.
    Secretary.

I have just approved the message to the Northern Patrol.

About the Newfoundland fishermen: the boatwork of the New-foundlanders was an important thing to render this effective in the stormy winter months. These men are the hardiest and most skilful boatmen in rough seas who exist. They long for employ-ment. Please propose me measures at once to raise one thousand R.N.V.R. in Newfoundland; drafting the necessary letter to the Dominions Office and outlining terms and conditions. They have nothing to learn about the sea, but almost immediately some method of training and discipline could be brought into play. In ten days at the outside this should be working in Newfoundland.

First Lord to Second Sea Lord.   21.IX.39.

In conversation with the Commander-in-Chief, Home Fleet, I have promised to look into the question of providing a theatre and cinema ship for the Home Fleet and Northern Patrol at Scapa.

I think it much more desirable to use a ship than shore facilities. I have in mind the arrangements made for the Grand Fleet during the last war, when S.S. *Gurko* was used.

The ship should contain a large N.A.A.F.I. shop as well as cinema and theatrical facilities, and possibly could be combined with a refrigerator storage ship.

Pray let me have your plans for implementing this most impor-tant adjunct of naval life at Scapa.

First Lord to Second Sea Lord and Secretary. (Secret.)   29.IX.39.

Leakage of Information

This is a proposal to dismiss from the Royal Navy, without trial, without formulating a charge, or even questioning, a petty officer who is identified with half-a-dozen of the same name by the fact that he has very white teeth, and who is reported to have been at a dinner at some unspecified date at which presumably indiscreet talk occurred. There is no suggestion that he was paid money, or that there was any treasonable intention. I do not find in these papers the slightest evidence that could be adduced before any court against this man, nor does the Director of Public Prosecutions. Yet, without being given any chance of defending himself, he is to be cast from the Service at the outset of a great war, with the kind of suspicion hanging over him for the rest of his life of having been a spy or a traitor.

Such processes cannot be allowed. If it is thought worth while to pursue these not very serious though annoying leakages into the sphere of penal action, the man must plainly be charged with some definite offence known to the Naval Discipline Act and brought before a court martial which can alone pronounce upon his guilt or innocence.

With regard to the dockyard employees and others, against whom the evidence is also vague and flimsy, no such procedure is necessary. It might perhaps be permissible, as a matter of administration, to move them about a little.

First Lord to Secretary. 4.X.39.

Let me have a list at once of the branches to which promotion from the lower deck still does not apply. What proportion do these branches bear to the other branches?

First Lord to Second Sea Lord, Parliamentary 7.X.39.
Secretary and Secretary.

Will you kindly explain to me the reasons which debar individuals in certain branches from rising by merit to commissioned rank? If a cook may rise, or a steward, why not an electrical artificer or an ordnance rating or a shipwright? If a telegraphist may rise, why not a painter? Apparently there is no difficulty about painters rising in Germany!

First Lord to Secretary. 7.X.39.

Admirals of the Fleet

This matter does not require verbal treatment. Kindly draft Minutes *f.m.s.* [for my signature] to First and Second Sea Lords in the sense of surmounting the difficulties. I am very clear that the Admirals of the Fleet should remain on the Active List like Field-Marshals, and should not be penalised for winning promotion unduly young. You might explain to the Treasury privately that no money is involved. What is the value of being made Admiral of

the Fleet if it is only to hoist the Union flag for one day and retire
to Cheltenham, writing occasional letters to *The Times?*   •

First Lord to Second Sea Lord and others concerned   14.X.39.
     and Secretary.

There must be no discrimination on grounds of race or colour
[in the employment of Indians or Colonial natives in the Royal
Navy]. In practice much inconvenience would arise if this theoretical equality had many examples. Each case must be judged on
its merits, from the point of view of smooth administration. I
cannot see any objection to Indians serving on H.M. ships where
they are qualified and needed, or, if their virtues so deserve, rising
to be Admirals of the Fleet. But not too many of them, please.

First Lord to First Sea Lord.   24.X.39.

I see no reason to suspend these enlistments or bar the Navy
door to the Dominions in time of war. Most particularly am I
concerned with Newfoundland, about which I have given special
directions. The Newfoundlanders are certainly not to be "left to
find their own way to this country" from Newfoundland. Care and
pains are to be taken to recruit, train and convey to the United
Kingdom as many as possible. I hope we shall get one thousand. I
understand this is in progress, and let me have a report saying
exactly what is being done in Newfoundland.

With regard to the other Dominions, suitable enlistments should
be accepted whether for hostilities only or for permanent service.
These ratings can be trained at the naval ports in the Dominions:
at Sydney, at Halifax and Esquimalt, and at Simonstown. Opportunity will then be given to transport the men in batches to this
country or draft them on to His Majesty's ships visiting the
Dominions.

Pray let a scheme on these lines be put forward with a view to
surmounting the difficulties.

First Lord to Naval Secretary and others concerned.   19.XII.39.
          "Salmon's" War Patrol Narrative

I am in entire accord with the Second Sea Lord's Minute of
yesterday. I shall be most willing to concur in the promotion and
honours proposed, both to the officers and to the men. I await
the proposals of the Sea Lords in respect of the promotion. Naval

Secretary should prepare submissions for the Honours to the King, and, if possible, these should be published, both as to officers and men, before the *Salmon* sails again. Perhaps His Majesty would like himself to see the officer (Lieutenant-Commander Bickford), and conclude the audience by pinning on the D.S.O. Naval Secretary might find out what they think about this at the Palace. It seems probable that similar, though not necessarily the same, awards will be required in the case of the Commander of the *Ursula,* and here again the crew must participate. Every effort must be made to announce the awards to the men at the same time as the officers. The whole of this should be put through in forty-eight hours at the latest.

First Lord to Fourth Sea Lord.   12.XII.39.

I am told that the minesweeper men have no badge. If this is so, it must be remedied at once. I have asked Mr. Bracken to call for designs from Sir Kenneth Clark within one week, after which production must begin with the greatest speed, and distribution as the deliveries come to hand.

Special Entry Cadetship.   8.II.40.

It seems very difficult to understand why this candidate should have been so decisively rejected in view of his high educational qualifications, his Service connections, and his record as set out by his father in his letter of January 4. One has to be particularly careful that class prejudice does not enter into these decisions, and, unless some better reasons are given to me I shall have to ask my Naval Secretary to interview the boy on my behalf, before assuming responsibility for writing to his father as proposed.

First Lord to Secretary.   25.II.40.

Candidate for the Navy Entrance Examination,
November, 1939, who failed

I do not at all mind "going behind the opinion of a board duly constituted," or even changing the board or its chairman if I think injustice has been done. How long is it since this board was re-modelled? I could not help being unfavourably struck with the aspect of the Dartmouth cadets whom I saw marching by the other day. On the other hand I was enormously impressed with the candidates for commission from the ranks who I saw drilling and being trained on the parade-ground at Portsmouth. They were of course much older, but a far finer-looking type.

Not only shall my Naval Secretary see the boy, but I shall hope to have time to see him myself. Who are the naval representatives on the board of selection? Naval officers should be well represented.

Action accordingly.

Let me have a list of the whole board — with the full records of each member and the date of his appointment.

First Lord to First Sea Lord and D.C.N.S. 25.II.40.

I should like *Salmon* to go to Devonport as you suggested as an extra practice submarine for a few months after the severe and distinguished service she has rendered. There would be advantages in having Commander Bickford in the Plans Division of the Admiralty for, say six months, in order to bring them in close and direct contact with the very latest conditions prevailing in Heligoland Bight. This officer seems to me very able, and he has many things today about anti-U-boat warfare which I trust will be gathered at the earliest opportunity.

2. Is there any reason why *Ursula* should not go, on escort to the Norwegian convoy?

3. There may be other vessels which R.A.S. (Rear Admiral Submarines) would say have also had heavy strain. Perhaps this might be looked into later.

4. If the war were general and everybody engaged to the hilt there would be no need to consider these variations of duty. But considering that the peculiar brunt falls upon very few at the present time, and that nothing is comparable to submarine work amid the minefields and all its increasing dangers, I am strongly of the opinion that we should keep a rotation, shifting boats and crews which have had a particularly hard time, or have distinguished themselves, to easier duties, and letting others have a chance of winning renown. Is there any possibility of arranging a certain number of relief crews for submarines, suitable for the Bight so as to divide the strain among a larger proportion of the personnel? I should like this to be studied.

5. Have the men of the *Salmon* and *Ursula* received their medals and honours? The officers have already been decorated. Let special measures be taken to ensure that the men have these rewards before they go to sea again.

First Lord to Second Sea Lord and Fourth Sea Lord.   24.III.40.

Backgammon would be a good game for Wardroom, Gunroom, and Warrant Officers' Mess, and I have no doubt it would amuse the sailors. What happened to the one thousand pounds Lord Rothermere gave me for various kinds of amusements? Is it all expended, and how? I have no doubt I could get some more if necessary. Backgammon is a better game than cards for the circumstances of wartime afloat, because it whiles away twenty minutes or a quarter of an hour, whereas cards are a much longer business.

First Lord to First Sea Lord and Second Sea Lord.   25.III.40.

I see charges of looting preferred against our men in the German press. I should not think it necessary to mention this but for the fact that it has come to my notice that the Captain of the *Altmark's* watch, chronometer, and Iron Cross were stolen, and are now in the hands of some of the sailors as souvenirs. Anything of this kind must be stopped with the utmost strictness. No souvenir of any value can be preserved without being reported and permission obtained. Personal property of enemies may be confiscated by the State, but never by individuals.

First Lord to Second Sea Lord.   7.IV.40.

I have seen the three candidates. Considering that these three boys were fifth, eighth, and seventeenth in the educational competitive examination out of more than ninety successful, 320 qualified, and 400 who competed, I see no reason why they should have been described as unfit for the Naval Service. It is quite true that A has a slightly cockney accent, and that the other two are the sons of a chief petty officer and an engineer in the merchant service. But the whole intention of competitive examination is to open the career to ability, irrespective of class or fortune. Generally speaking, in the case of candidates who do exceptionally well in the examination, the presumption should be that they will be accepted. Similarly, those who do very badly in the educational examination may nevertheless in a few cases be fit to serve. But the idea of rejecting boys at the very top of the list, unless some very grave defect presents itself, is wholly contrary to the principles approved by Parliament.

I am sure if the Committee, when they had these boys before them, had known that they were among the cleverest in the whole list, they would not have taken so severe a view and ruled them out altogether on the personal interview. It seems to me that in future the Committee ought to conduct the interview *after* the examination, and with the results of it before them. Furthermore, it is wrong that a boy should be allowed to sit for examination, with all the stress and anxiety attached to it, when it has already been settled that, even if he is first on the list, he has already been ruled out.

I also feel that there is no need for any mention of a disqualifying standard for interview and record. The Interview Board should also be instructed that they may award different marks to the same candidate for different branches of the Service. It is obvious that a boy may be much more suitable for the Paymaster than the Executive Branch, and the Committee should be able to differentiate accordingly.

There will, of course, be no need for the Interview Committee to see all the candidates. There must be a qualifying educational standard. This is four hundred marks at present, out of a total of 1,350. I notice that all the successful boys in the last examination had well over six hundred marks. Surely it would ease the work of the Interview Committee if the qualifying educational standard were raised?

Pray make me proposals for rearranging the present system so as to achieve the above conditions. Cadetships are to be given in the three cases I have mentioned.

★

Index

INDEX

From Honey to Ashes

Claude Lévi-Strauss

FROM HONEY
to ASHES

Introduction to a
Science of Mythology: 2

TRANSLATED FROM THE FRENCH BY
JOHN AND DOREEN WEIGHTMAN

HARPER & ROW, PUBLISHERS
NEW YORK, EVANSTON, SAN FRANCISCO

FIRST U.S. EDITION

ISBN 06–012589–6

LIBRARY OF CONGRESS CATALOG CARD NUMBER: 72–85209

Contents

Illustrations

Table of Symbols

$\left\{\begin{array}{l}\triangle\\\bigcirc\end{array}\right.$ man
               woman

$\triangle = \bigcirc$ marriage (disjunction of marriage: #)

$\overline{\underset{\triangle \quad \bigcirc}{\quad}}$ brother and sister (their disjunction $\;\sqcap\!\!\!\!/\!\!\!\!\sqcap\;$)

$\begin{array}{cc}\triangle & \bigcirc \\ | & | \\ \triangle & \bigcirc\end{array}$ father and son, mother and daughter, etc.

$\Rightarrow$ transformation

$\rightarrow$ is transformed into ...

$\leftrightarrow$ if and only if ...

$\left\{\begin{array}{l}:\\::\end{array}\right.$ is to ...
               as ...

$/$ contrast

$\left\{\begin{array}{l}\equiv\\\not\equiv\end{array}\right.$ congruence, homology, correspondence
               non-congruence, non-homology, non-correspondence

$\left\{\begin{array}{l}=\\\neq\end{array}\right.$ identity
               difference

$\left\{\begin{array}{l}\cup\\//\end{array}\right.$ union, reunion, conjunction
               disunion, disjunction

f function

$x^{(-1)}$ inverted x

$+, -$ these signs are used with various connotations, depending on the context: plus, minus; presence, absence; first or second term of a pair of opposites.

TRANSLATORS' NOTE

All through the first two volumes of *Mythologiques*, we have translated the plural form *nous*, which is common in academic theses and learned articles in French, as 'I', because this seemed to us to give a more natural style in English. However, for reasons which he explains in the recently published Volume 4, *L'Homme nu*, the author has deliberately avoided the first person singular. To be consistent we must continue to use 'I', but we shall give an additional explanatory note at the appropriate point in Volume 4.

TO MONIQUE

Scriptorum chorus omnis amat nemus, et fugit urbes,
rite cliens Bacchi, somno gaudentis et umbra.

Horace, *Epistles*, II, L. 11,
to Julius Florus

Foreword

The present work, the second in a series devoted to the study of myths, continues the inquiry which was begun in *The Raw and the Cooked*. This being so, I have made a point of restating at the outset, although in a new light, information essential to readers unacquainted with the previous volume, who nevertheless wish to begin confidently on this one. It aims to show that the world of mythology is round, and therefore does not refer back to any necessary starting-point. The reader can begin where he chooses and yet be sure of completing the course, provided he heads always in the same direction and advances patiently and steadily.

Both in France and other countries, the method employed in the first volume and the findings put forward have given rise to much discussion. The time has not yet come, I think, for me to reply to what has been said. Rather than allow the argument to take a philosophical turn which would very soon have a sterilizing effect, I prefer to carry on with my task and add more evidence. Opponents and defenders alike will thus have further documents at their disposal. When the undertaking is almost completed and I have produced all my witnesses and displayed all the exhibits, the case can be heard.

For the time being, then, I will do no more than thank those who have helped me in my task. Jesus Marden dos Santos, director of the *Serviço de Meteorologia do Brasil*, Djalma Batista, director of the *Instituto Nacional de Pesquisas da Amazonia*, Dalcy de Oliviera Albuquerque, director of the *Museu Paraense Emilio Goeldi*, and Mme Claudine Berthe of the *Muséum national d'histoire naturelle* supplied invaluable meteorological or botanical information. Mme Jacqueline Bolens assisted in the assembling of the material from German sources, and translated it. Mlle Nicole Belmont helped me with documentation and illustrations.

TOWARDS HARMONY

*Et encore estandi l'angre sa main tierce foiz et toucha
le miel, et le feu sailli sus la table et usa le miel sanz
faire à la table mal, et l'oudeur qui yssi du miel et
du feu fu tresdoulce.*

'De l'Ystoire Asseneth', p. 10; in *Nouvelles
Françoises en prose du XIVe siècle.*
Bibl. elzévirienne, Paris, 1858

Metaphors inspired by honey are among the oldest in the French language, as well as in others of earlier date. The Vedic hymns often link milk and honey and, according to the Bible, the Promised Land was to flow with both these substances. The words of the Lord are 'sweeter than honey'. The Babylonians regarded honey as the most fitting offering for the Gods, since the latter demanded a food untouched by fire. In the *Iliad*, earthenware jars of honey were used as an offering to the dead. In other contexts, such jars served as repositories for their remains.

For several thousand years now, phrases such as *tout miel* (all honey) and *doux comme miel* (sweet as honey) have been current in Western civilization. Metaphors inspired by the use of tobacco are, on the contrary, recent and easily datable. Littré mentions only two: *cela ne vaut pas une pipe de tabac* (that is worthless) and *tomber dans le tabac* (to fall on hard times). Such slang phrases, many other variants of which could be quoted (cf. Vimaître),[1] can also be found in other languages: in English, 'not to care a tobacco for' means to care very little for somebody or something; and in Portuguese *tabaquear* means to mock or poke fun at someone (Sébillot). Among French sailors, expressions such as *il y aura du tabac* and *coup de tabac* indicate bad weather. *Coquer, fourrer, foutre, donner du tabac* and, more recently, *passer à tabac, tabasser* mean to ill-treat, bully, belabour (Rigaud, Sainéan, Lorédan-Larchey, Delvau, Giraud, Galtier-Boissière and Devaux).

Honey and tobacco are both edible substances yet neither, strictly speaking, depends in any way on cooking. For honey is made by non-human beings, the bees, who supply it ready for consumption, while the most common method of consuming tobacco places the latter, contrary to honey, not on the *hither side* of cooking but *beyond* it. It is not consumed in the raw state, as is honey, nor exposed to fire before consumption, as is the case with meat. It is burnt to ashes, so that the

[1] See Bibliography, pp. 477–92, for full information on this and other titles.

smoke thus released can be inhaled. Now, everyday speech (I am taking my examples chiefly from French, but am convinced that similar observations could be made on the basis of other languages, either directly or by a simple process of transposition) bears out the fact that the expressions *à miel* (with honey, or honey as adjective) and *à tabac* (tobacco, ditto) form a pair, and are used to convey antithetical ideas, which in turn are situated on various levels. I am not forgetting, of course, that some phrases including the word 'honey' constitute border-line cases in which the connotation becomes pejorative: 'honeyed discourse', 'honeyed words', and even *miel* alone, when used as an interjection in French, with the present participle *emmiellant*,[2] a practice which is not simply based on a similarity of sound convenient for young ladies who consider themselves to be well-bred.[3] Far from disregarding these distortions of meaning, I shall explain their existence. But even so, there would seem to be no doubt that, in Western civilization, 'honey' and 'tobacco' phrases stand in opposition to each other. In spite of a certain amount of overlapping, what I would like to call their points of semantic balance are differently placed; the 'honey' phrases are mainly eulogistic, the 'tobacco' phrases on the whole disparaging. They denote respectively abundance and dearth, luxury and poverty; and either gentleness, kindliness and serenity – 'Manare poetica mella', or unruliness, violence or confusion. Perhaps, if we had further examples to hand, we might even say that the former stand in a certain relationship to space (*tout miel* 'all honey'), the latter in a certain relationship to time (*toujours le même tabac* 'always the same old thing').

The sentence which I have used as the epigraph to this Introduction shows that the oppositional relationship we are concerned with existed, in a sense, before the two substances formed a pair. Before tobacco was even known in Europe, the 'honey fire', lit by the supernatural power of the angel, marked out the place of the absent term and anticipated its properties, which had to be those of a correlative and antithetical

---

[2] *C'est un miel* (it's a honey). This is a slang phrase, used by the Parisian lower classes indiscriminately and mostly inappropriately. If they approve of, or admire something, they say '*C'est un miel*'; equally if they go into some foul-smelling place. At the sight of a bloody combat with bare fists or knives, they will say: '*C'est un miel*' (Delvau). '*C'est un miel*: It is very pleasant and (ironically) very unpleasant' (Lorédan-Larchey). This wide semantic range is already present at least by implication in the belief held by the Greeks and Romans, and which was probably Egyptian in origin, that a swarm of bees would inevitably spring from the rotting carcass of a calf which had been asphyxiated in a confined space by the blocking up of its respiratory passages, and whose flesh had been beaten to make it disintegrate without damage to the skin (Virgil, *Georgics*, IV, vv. 299–314, 554–8).

[3] TRANSLATORS' NOTE: *Miel* and *emmiellant* are used euphemistically for *merde* and *emmerdant*.

term of liquid honey, corresponding to it point by point in the complementary scale of the dry, the burnt and the aromatic. The fact that the *Ystoire Asseneth*, from which the example is taken, is most probably the work of a late medieval Jewish author throws a still more curious light on the medieval interpretation, also Jewish nevertheless, of the verse in Leviticus prohibiting the offering of honey on altars, because of the unpleasant smell of burnt honey. At any rate, the discrepancy shows that, in medieval times and perhaps even earlier, honey was a 'marked' term in respect of fumes and smell, which were later to become the essential modes of tobacco. The fact that the oppositional relationship existed before the substances themselves, or at least before one of them, enables us to understand how it was that, as soon as tobacco became known, it combined with honey to form a pair endowed with supreme virtues. In an English play written by William Lily at the end of the sixteenth century (1597) and whose title, *The Woman in the Moone*, is not without analogies in the mythology of the New World, as will be seen in the next volume, the heroine, Pandora, wounds her lover with a sword and, seized with remorse, sends for medicinal herbs with which to dress the cut:

> Gather me balme and cooling violets,
> And of our holy herb nicotian
> And bring withall pure honey from the hive
> To heale the wound of my unhappy hand.[4]

I find this quotation particularly gratifying since it unexpectedly emphasizes the link which, by way of the previous volume, *The Raw and the Cooked*, unites the present work to *The Savage Mind*. (The French title, *La Pensée sauvage*, also means 'The Wild Pansy', a flower closely related to the violets in the quotation.) And it also testifies to a long-established connection in England between honey and tobacco, a connection which still seems to exist on the technical level. We Frenchmen tend to think that English brands of tobacco are closer to honey than our own. We often explain the affinity by imagining, rightly or wrongly, that the pale leaves of English tobacco have been macerated in honey.

Unlike Europe, South America has always been familiar with, and partaken of, both honey and tobacco. It therefore provides an especially rewarding field for the semantic study of the opposition between them, since both diachronically and synchronically, honey and tobacco

[4] Quoted by Laufer, p. 23.

can be observed there side by side over a long period. In this respect, North America seems to stand in a symmetrical relationship to the Old World, since, in recent times, that part of the Continent, apparently, was acquainted only with tobacco, honey having almost completely disappeared, whereas Europe was perfectly familiar with honey at the time when tobacco was introduced as a novelty. I shall return to this problem again later (Vol. III). It follows that tropical America, on which I drew in the previous volume to study the contrast between the two fundamental categories of cooking, the raw and the cooked, which are the constituent elements of the meal, proves also to be an appropriate area for the analysis of a second pair of opposites – honey and tobacco – in so far as these substances offer complementary characteristics; the former being infra-culinary, and the latter meta-culinary. It is along these lines that I propose to continue my research into the mythic representations of the transition from nature to culture. As I develop my inquiry and extend the area of investigation, I shall be able to follow up the previous investigation into the mythic origin of cooking, with an examination of what might be called the *peripheral adjuncts of the meal*.

In doing so, I shall, as always, keep to the plan which is prescribed by the actual contents of the myths. Neither honey, nor tobacco, nor the idea of establishing a connection between them on a logical or concrete level is to be considered as a speculative hypothesis. On the contrary, these themes are explicitly suggested by certain myths, encountered and partially studied in the course of the previous volume. To spare the reader the necessity of referring back to that work, here is a brief recapitulation.

My opening remarks in *The Raw and the Cooked*, the first volume in the series, had, as their starting-point, a story told by the Bororo Indians of central Brazil, relating to the origin of storms and rain (M_1). I began by showing that, without postulating any relationship of priority between this and other myths, it could be reduced to a transformation by inversion of a Ge myth relating to the cooking of food (M_7–M_{12}); the Ge linguistic group is geographically and culturally very close to the Bororo, and the myth exists in different tribal variants. All the myths referred to have as their central theme the story of a bird-nester, marooned at the top of a tree or a rocky cliff as the result of a quarrel with an affine (brother-in-law, sister's husband or father in a matrilineal society). In one instance, the hero punishes his persecutor by sending down rain which puts out domestic fires. In other instances, he brings back to his parents the burning log of which the jaguar was master, thereby procuring cooking fire for the human race, instead of taking it from them.

Noting that in the Ge myths and in a myth belonging to a neighbouring group (Ofaié, M_{14}), the jaguar, master of fire, occupies the position of an affine, since he married a human wife, I established the existence of a transformation which, in its regular form, is exemplified by myths belonging to Tupi tribes adjacent to the Ge: Tenetehara and Mundurucu (M_{15}, M_{16}). As in the previous instance, these myths portray a brother-in-law (or, on this occasion, several) who are 'takers' of women. But the myths with which we are now concerned do not depict an animal brother-in-law who protects and feeds the human hero personifying the group of affines, but describe a conflict between one or several superhuman heroes (demiurges and relatives) and their human affines (sisters' husbands) who refuse them food; as a result of which they changed into wild pigs, or more accurately into tayassuidae of the queixada species (*Dicotyles labiatus*), which did not exist as yet and which the natives consider to be the superior form of game, representing meat in the highest sense of the term.

So, as we move from one group of myths to the next, we see that they depict either a human hero and his relation (by marriage): the jaguar, the animal master of cooking fire; or superhuman heroes and their relations (by marriage): human hunters, the masters of meat. The jaguar, although an *animal*, behaves *courteously*: he gives food to his human brother-in-law, protects him from his wife's spitefulness and allows the stealing of cooking fire. The hunters, although *human*, behave *savagely*: they keep all the meat for their own use, and indulge in unrestrained intercourse with the wives they have been given, without offering any gifts of food in return:

(*a*) [Human/animal hero] $\Rightarrow$ [Superhuman/human heroes]
(*b*) [Animal, courteous brother-in-law $\rightarrow$ eater of raw food]
$\Rightarrow$ [Humans, savage brothers-in-law $\rightarrow$ eaten cooked]

This double transformation is also repeated on the etiological level, since one of the groups of myths deals with the origin of the cooking of food and the other with the origin of meat; the *means* and the *matter* of cooking respectively:

(*c*) [fire] $\Rightarrow$ [meat]

The two groups are not only symmetrical in structure, they also stand in a dialectical relationship to each other: meat had to exist before man could cook it; this meat, which occurs in the myths in the superior form of the flesh of the queixada, was cooked for the first time with the help of the fire obtained from the jaguar, presented in the myths as a hunter of pigs.

Having reached this stage in the demonstration, I was anxious to test its accuracy through one of its consequences. If a Bororo myth (M_1) was transformable into Ge myths (M_7-M_{12}) on the same axis, and if in turn the Ge myths were transformable into Tupi myths $(M_{15,16})$, on a different axis, the whole group could only constitute a closed set, as I had supposed, on condition that there existed other transformations situated possibly along a third axis, and allowing us to move back from the Tupi myths to the Bororo myths which were themselves a transformation of the original myth. Observing a methodological rule to which I remain systematically faithful, I had, then, to subject the two Tupi myths to a kind of filtering process in order to discover what residue, if any, of mythic material had remained unused during the previous operations.

It was at once obvious that there was such a residue and that it consisted of the series of devices used by the demiurge to change his wicked brothers-in-law into pigs. In M_{15}, he ordered his nephew to shut the culprits up inside a prison made of feathers, to which he set fire, with the result that the suffocating smoke brought about their transformation. M_{16} starts off in the same way, except that the demiurge is helped by his son, and that it is the tobacco smoke injected into the feather enclosure which plays the decisive part. A Kayapo-Kubenkranken myth about the origin of wild pigs (M_{18}), and which I had previously shown to be necessarily a derivation from the other two, or from one of them, provided a weak variant of the magic transformation, which in this instance is attributed to the use of a charm made from feathers and thorns. I therefore proposed (RC, p. 101) to arrange the magic methods in the following pattern:

[1](tobacco smoke, M_{16}), [2](feather smoke, M_{15}), [3](feather charm, M_{18})

In addition to the fact that the above arrangement is the only logically satisfying one, since it takes into account both the derivative nature of M_{18} in relation to M_{15} and M_{16} and the simultaneous presence of the smoke in M_{15} and M_{16} and the feathers in M_{15} and M_{18}, it is confirmed by a famous myth of the Cariri Indians, which was transcribed at the end of the seventeenth century by the French missionary Martin de Nantes. The Cariri myth (M_{25}) also explains the origin of wild pigs, which it attributes to the greed of the first men who begged the demiurge to let them taste this hitherto unknown meat. The demiurge took the children off to the sky and changed them into young wild pigs. Henceforth, men would be allowed to hunt the wild pig, but they would be deprived of the demiurge's company. The latter decided to stay in the sky and he arranged for tobacco to take his place on earth. In this myth, therefore, tobacco also plays a decisive role, but in an even more powerful form than in the Mundurucu version (M_{16}): from being a simple magical substance it becomes the hypostasis of a divinity (cf. M_{338}). There is, then, a series in which tobacco smoke is the weak form of personified tobacco, feather smoke the weak form of tobacco smoke, and the feather charm the weak form of feather smoke.

This much having been established, how do the Bororo describe the origin of wild pigs? One of their myths (M_{21}) explains that the animals were once men and that their wives, in order to avenge an insult, served them a stew of prickly fruits. When their throats were scratched by the prickles, the men grunted 'ú, ú, ú . . . ' and were changed into wild pigs, which utter this cry.

This myth has a two-fold claim on our attention. In the first place, the magical role played by the thorns links up with the charm made of feathers *and thorns*, which occurred in M_{18}. When looked at from this angle, it is seen to follow on after M_{18} in the series of magical transformations to which it adds a new variant, without changing the order in which the others had been arranged. But in another respect, the Bororo myth effects a reversal: instead of the incident arising from a quarrel between affines, as it does in M_{15}, M_{16} and M_{18}, it is the result of a quarrel between husbands and wives. For a discussion of this transformation, I refer the reader to the previous volume (*RC*, p. 91) where I showed it to be typical of Bororo mythology. In the present instance, it therefore results from the application of the general rule on which it depends:

(*a*) *In the case of a non-varying message* (in this instance, the origin of wild pigs):

Mundurucu, etc.
$$\left[\triangle \overset{/\!/}{\frown} \bigcirc = \triangle \right] \Rightarrow$$
Bororo
$$\left[\bigcirc \neq \triangle \right]$$

Going one stage further, I felt compelled to ask myself whether there did not exist among the Bororo a myth reproducing the family circumstances depicted by the Mundurucu etc. myths about the origin of wild pigs, while at the same time transmitting, if not the same message, at least a transformed version of the message. I identified M_{20} as such a myth. The chief characters in it are ancestors who used to live in huts made of feathers at some distance from their brother-in-law (their sister's husband), from whom they obtained all they wanted by sending one of their younger brothers to him as a go-between (compare: M_{15}, *nephew as guest*/M_{16}, *son as go-between*).

One day they wanted some honey, but all they obtained was a thick, scummy substance, unfit for eating. This was because, in defiance of the taboos, the brother-in-law had had intercourse with his wife when it was being gathered. The wife herself added insult to injury by spying on her brothers while they were engaged in designing and making shell necklaces and beads. Because of the insult, the heroes built a pyre and threw themselves into the flames, whence they rose again in the form of birds with ornamental feathers. Later cotton, gourds and the urucú were to spring from their ashes (*RC*, pp. 92–3).

The etiological functions of this myth are at once more limited and more broadly significant than those of the Tupi myths, which also take as their starting-point a quarrel between affines; more limited since, as is often the case among the Bororo, the myth is intended to explain the origin not of one or several vegetable or animal species, but of varieties or sub-varieties. At the beginning of the myth, the birds were already in existence, otherwise the heroes could not have lived in huts made of feathers and down. But the birds which rose up from the sacrificial fire had 'prettier and more brightly coloured' plumage. Similarly, the myth makes it clear that the plants which sprang up among the ashes belonged to varieties of superior quality – for instance, a kind of urucú which gave a red unequalled for the dyeing of cotton. This initial limitation of the etiological field is accompanied by yet another. The Bororo myth does not claim to explain how one vegetable or animal species came to be available to the whole human race, or even to the tribe in general, but rather why certain varieties or sub-varieties came to belong to one particular clan or sub-clan. In this respect, the myth is particularly eloquent, not only on the subject of plants but also about the adornments designed by the heroes, and which, before they die, they divide out among the various family groups composing their clan.

Although more limited in these two respects, the Bororo myth can claim to be more broadly significant in a third, since its etiological function is, in a sense, intensified. The Tenetehara and Mundurucu myths with which I would like to compare it deal with the origin of one animal – the pig, in other words with good meat, whereas the Bororo myth deals, on the one hand, with the origin of certain birds with beautiful feathers and, on the other, with the origin of several vegetable products, also of exceptional quality.

But there is more to be said. The animal species the origin of which is traced in the Tupi myths is described purely in terms of food, whereas the animals and vegetables in the Bororo myth are described purely in their relationship to technology. The new birds are distinguished from the others by the ornamental richness of their plumage and none of the new plants have any food value: they serve only for the manufacture of useful articles and ornaments. Although the three myths, M_{15}, M_{16} and M_{20}, undoubtedly have the same starting-point, they develop contrapuntally (see the diagram on p. 26), in accordance with the second rule, complementary to the one on p. 23, and which can now be formulated as follows:

(b) *In the case of a non-varying armature* (here: $(\triangle \quad o = \triangle)$) :

Mundurucu, etc. $\left[\text{ origin of meat } \right] \Rightarrow$ Bororo $\left[\text{ origin of cultural objects } \right]$

I can now summarize the general line of my argument. The myths about the origin of wild pigs are concerned with a kind of meat which the natives put into a superior category, and which is therefore, *par excellence*, the raw material for cooking. It is therefore legitimate, logically, to treat these myths as functions of the myths about the origin of domestic fire, the latter describing the means, the former the matter, of culinary activity. Now, just as the Bororo transform the myth about the origin of cooking fire into a myth about the origin of rain and storms – in other words, of water – we have confirmed that, with them, the myth about the origin of *meat* becomes a myth about the origin of *cultural objects*. Or, to put it another way, in the one instance we have a crude, natural material which is situated on the *hither side* of cooking and, in the other, technical and cultural activity which lies *beyond* cooking.

$$\begin{bmatrix} M_{15}: \\ M_{16}: \\ M_{20}: \end{bmatrix} \begin{array}{l} \text{Giver of} \\ \text{woman or} \\ \text{givers of} \\ \text{women, living} \\ \text{some distance} \\ \text{from brother(s)-} \\ \text{in-law} \end{array} \quad \begin{array}{l} \text{intermediary} \\ \\ \text{role} \\ \\ \text{ascribed} \\ \\ \text{to} \end{array} \left\{ \begin{array}{ll} M_{15}: \text{nephew} & \text{ill-treated by} \\ \quad\text{of giver} & \text{the takers of ...} \\ M_{16}: \text{son of} & \text{is refused meat} \\ \quad\text{giver} & \text{by the takers} \\ M_{20}: \text{younger} & \text{obtains bad honey} \\ \quad\text{brother} & \text{from the taker} \\ \quad\text{of givers} \end{array} \right. $$

//

$$\begin{bmatrix} M_{15}: \\ M_{16}: \text{... previous to} \\ M_{20} \text{... following on} \end{bmatrix} \begin{array}{l} \text{the sexual abuse} \\ \text{of the woman} \\ \text{(women) received} \\ \text{from ...} \end{array} \left\{ \begin{array}{l} M_{15}: \\ M_{16}: \end{array} \begin{array}{l} \text{(men) who then shut them up} \\ \text{in a feather } \textit{prison} \end{array} \right. \\ M_{20}: \text{men who formerly lived} \\ \qquad\quad \text{in a feather } \textit{palace}$$

//

$$\begin{bmatrix} M_{15}: \\ \\ M_{16}: \end{bmatrix} \begin{array}{l} \text{scene} \\ \text{of} \\ \text{bestial} \\ \text{behaviour} \end{array} \begin{array}{l} \text{excessive} \\ \text{intercourse} \\ \text{with the} \\ \text{wives} \end{array} \left[\begin{array}{l} M_{15}: \text{culprits passively smoked out} \\ \qquad \text{by smoke from feathers} \\ M_{16}: \text{culprits passively smoked out} \\ \qquad \text{by tobacco smoke} \end{array} \right] \begin{array}{l} \text{transformed into} \\ \textit{edible} \text{ wild} \\ \text{pigs} \end{array} $$

$$M_{20}: \begin{array}{l} \text{scene of the} \\ \text{invention} \\ \text{of civilized} \\ \text{arts} \end{array} \begin{array}{l} \text{indiscreetly} \\ \text{spied upon} \\ \text{by the} \\ \text{sister} \end{array} \begin{array}{l} \text{self-appointed} \\ \text{victims} \\ \text{burnt on} \\ \text{pyre} \end{array} \begin{array}{l} \text{transformed into birds} \\ \text{with ornamental feathers} \end{array}$$

//

$$\begin{bmatrix} M_{15}: \\ M_{16}: \end{bmatrix} \text{origin of meat, } \textit{food} \text{ of ANIMAL origin} \\ M_{20}: \text{origin (1) of } \textit{adornments} \text{ of ANIMAL origin;} \\ \qquad\qquad \text{(2) of } \textit{non-alimentary} \text{ products of VEGETABLE origin}$$

//

$$\begin{Bmatrix} M_{15} \text{ etc.} \\ -M_{20}: \end{Bmatrix} \begin{array}{l} \text{in so far as} \\ \text{they relate} \\ \text{to a split in} \\ \text{humanity} \end{array} \left\{ \begin{array}{l} \text{partly} \\ \text{moving} \\ \text{towards} \\ \text{culture} \end{array} \left\{ \begin{array}{ll} M_{20}: \text{by obtaining} & \\ \quad\text{adornments} & \equiv \text{CULTURE} \\ \quad \textit{beyond} \text{ cooking} & \\ M_{15} \text{ etc.: by ob-} & \\ \quad\text{taining meat} & \equiv \text{NATURE} \\ \quad\text{on the } \textit{hither} & \\ \quad\textit{side} \text{ of cooking} & \end{array} \right. \right.$$

$$\begin{array}{l} \text{partly} \\ \text{retro-} \\ \text{gressing} \\ \text{to nature} \end{array} \left\{ \begin{array}{ll} M_{20}: \text{by changing} & \equiv \text{SKY} \\ \quad\text{into birds ...} & \text{(cf. } M_1: \text{celestial } \textit{water}) \\ M_{15} \text{ etc.: being} & \equiv \text{EARTH} \\ \quad\text{changed into} & \text{(cf. } M_1\text{--}M_{12}: \text{terrestrial} \\ \quad\text{quadrupeds ...} & \textit{fire}) \end{array} \right.$$

It is easy to show that, with this transformation, the sequence comes full circle and that the group of myths we have been dealing with is, in this respect, cyclical in character. First, we worked out the following transformation:

(*a*) *Ge* $\left[\text{origin of cooking (fire)} \right] \Rightarrow$ *Bororo* $\left[\begin{array}{l} \text{origin of anti-cooking} \\ \text{(fire)} = \text{water} \end{array} \right]$

We then moved on to:

(*b*) *Ge* $\left[\text{origin of cooking fire } (= \textit{means}) \right] \Rightarrow$ *Tupi* $\left[\begin{array}{l} \text{origin of meat} \\ (= \textit{substance}) \text{ for} \\ \text{cooking} \end{array} \right]$

The third and last transformation, which has just been determined, can be expressed as follows:

(c) *Tupi* [origin of meat (cooking substance)] ⇒ *Bororo*
[origin of adornments (*anti-matter* of cooking)]

since we have seen that the adornments came from non-edible parts of animals (shells, feathers) and from plants (gourds, cotton, urucú) which have no use as food. The initial contrast between the means (of cooking) and its opposite, has therefore simply been transformed into a contrast between the substance (for cooking) and its opposite. The Bororo myths always stand in the same relationship to these two pairs of opposites.

All I have said so far was demonstrated in *The Raw and the Cooked* with the help of the same or different arguments. I now propose to deal with a different aspect of these myths, which did not need to be examined in the previous volume, or which was only mentioned incidentally. I established earlier that, in the series of magical means described by the Cariri, Mundurucu, Tenetehara and Kubenkranken myths to explain the transformation of humans into pigs, tobacco was the relevant term. We should not be surprised by the fact that no reference is made to tobacco in the Bororo myth about the origin of cultural objects, since it resembles the Tupi myths as regards its armature, and transmits an inverted message which presupposes a different vocabulary. We thus see the emergence of a new term, which is missing from the other myths: this is honey, the refusal of which, or more precisely the offer of which in the form of a variety of inferior quality, acts as the determining factor in the transformation of the heroes into birds, concurrently with their *sister's* 'incestuous' behaviour, of which the Mundurucu myth presents a symmetrical image, in the form of the excessive copulation of the husbands with their wives (who are the hero's *sisters*).

It will also be remembered that in the Bororo myth about the origin of wild pigs, which is symmetrical with the other, since in this instance, and when it is compared with the Tupi-Ge group on the same theme, the message seems to be identical and the armature inverted, an unpleasant stew (full of thorns) replaces the poor quality honey (lumpy instead of smooth). The magical means in the Bororo myths, which tend towards the moist, thus contrast with the magical means in the Ge-Tupi series (tobacco or feather smoke, feather and thorn charm) which tend towards the dry, a contrast which is congruous with the one between the Bororo myth about the origin of water and the Ge-Tupi myths about the origin of fire, that I took as my starting-point.

In actual fact, the situation is rather more complex, since only one of the two Bororo myths is entirely 'wet': this is M_{21}, in which the disagreement between husbands and wives arises in connection with fishing (fish : aquatic game, forming a triangle with the birds : celestial game in M_{20}, and the pigs : terrestrial game in M_{16} etc.) and ends with the victory of the women, thanks to a preparation of stewed fruit (stewed fruit = *vegetable* ∪ *water*/*fish* = *animal* ∪ *water*). Conversely, the dry plays an essential part in M_{20}, with the pyre on which the heroes deliberately choose to be burnt to death, and which seems to be homologous (although more emphatic in character) with the burning feathers in M_{15}, and the burning tobacco in M_{16}. But, although the terms are undeniably homologous, they are opposed to each other as regards the ultimate purposes for which they are respectively used. The burning on the pyre – of the heroes themselves, and not of a product intended for their consumption – constitutes a double 'ultra-culinary' process, which therefore has a *supplementary* relationship with its result: the appearance of adornments and ornaments which are also 'ultra-culinary', since they fall within the domain of culture, whereas cooking is a technical activity ensuring a transition between nature and culture. In M_{15} and M_{16}, on the contrary, the burning of the feathers and tobacco which is also 'ultra-culinary' in type although to a lesser degree, occurs as a *complementary* process of its result, which is the appearance of meat, a doubly 'infra-culinary' object, since it is at once the natural and preliminary condition for the existence of cooking.

This difficulty having been solved, I am now more free to emphasize the opposition between honey and tobacco which emerges from the myths for the first time at this point, and with which we shall be concerned to the end of this book. The fact that these two terms belong to the same pair of opposites was established by the exclusive presence of one or other in M_{20} and M_{16}, which, for independent reasons, I showed to be reversed as regards their message. It should be added at this point that a term correlative with the 'bad' honey – i.e. the 'bad' stewed fruit – appears in M_{21}, which is identical with M_{16} as regards its message (origin of wild pigs), but reversed as regards its armature

$$\left(\circ \neq \triangle/\overset{\overline{}\,/\!/\,\overline{}}{\triangle} \quad \circ = \triangle \right)$$ and doubly reversed (both as regards armature and message) in relation to M_{20}. Honey and stewed fruit are classed

as vegetable substances (this is obvious as regards the stewed fruit; it will be demonstrated later in the case of honey), both belonging to the category of the moist. 'Bad' honey is defined as being thick and lumpy, in contrast to good honey, which consequently is smooth and runny;[5] the 'bad' stewed fruit is full of prickles, which similarly make it thick and rough to the tongue. Honey and stewed fruit are therefore analogous; and at the same time we know that, in the series of magical means, the prickly stewed fruit comes after the feather and thorn charms in M_{18}, which is a weakened transformation of the feather smoke in M_{15}, which, in turn, stands in the same relationship to the tobacco smoke in M_{16}. Finally, as we have just seen, by broadening the series, it is possible to establish the relationship of correlation and opposition between honey and tobacco.

We thus have fresh evidence of the fact that the system revolves round the central theme of tobacco. Only tobacco worthy of the name unites properties that are normally incompatible. A Bororo myth (M_{26}) about the origin of tobacco or, to be more accurate, of the different species of fragrant leaves smoked by the Indians, describes how the latter, on trying them for the first time, pronounced some to be good and others unpleasant, according to whether the smoke was 'pungent' or not. The terms of the series of magical means whereby men were changed into animals are therefore linked. Tobacco smoke and smoke from burning feathers are both pungent, but one is foul-smelling and the other scented; stewed fruit is tasty (since people eat it in any case) but may be more or less well prepared; smooth to the palate when the prickles have been removed, or extremely prickly; honey, too, can be smooth or lumpy. So there are two kinds of smoke, two kinds of stewed fruit and two kinds of honey. Finally, in the homomorphic myths (those which have the same armature), honey and tobacco are in a relationship of symmetrical inversion.

We now find ourselves faced with an interesting problem. Tropical America offers us, in the first place, a mythological system relating to the origin of cooking, which, according to the groups considered, is presented either directly (origin of fire), or in an inverted form (origin of water). Let us therefore call the direct form of this first system S_1, and the inverted form, S_{-1}, which we shall leave aside for the moment. By turning S_1 back upon itself from the point of emergence of one of

[5] The Umutina invocation to honey – the Umutina are close cousins of the Bororo – clearly brings out the fact that fluidity is one of the main properties demanded: 'To give a lot of honey ... soft, sweet and liquid ... like water. To give honey which flows like river water, sweet as clayey water, and not to give thick honey (pollen)' (Schultz 2, p. 174).

its elements (the episodic appearance of a wild pig), I reconstituted, in *The Raw and the Cooked*, a second mythological system relating to the origin of wild pigs, that is of meat: the substance and pre-condition of cooking, just as fire was the means and instrument of cooking in the first system. The second system, which I will call S_2, I will place arbitrarily to the right of S_1 (since that was the diagrammatic form adopted in *The Raw and the Cooked*, Figure 6, p. 98). This being so, a third system relating to the origin of cultural objects, and symmetrical with S_2 in relation to S_1, will have to be placed to the left of S_1 (since meat and adornments are respectively on the hither side and on the far side of cooking, the origin of which is explained in S_1). The inverted system of S_2 will be called S_{-2}:

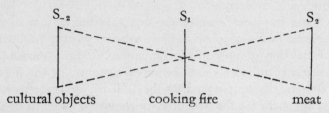

its elements S_{-2} S_1 S_2

cultural objects   cooking fire   meat

Let us confine ourselves for a moment to the examination of what is taking place in the mythic field 'to the right' of S_1. What we see there is S_2, which I previously defined in two ways: it is a mythic system the *aim* of which is to explain the origin of wild pigs, and which uses as a *means* to this end a variety of substances, which I have shown to be combinatorial variants of tobacco smoke. Tobacco therefore emerges in S_2 as an instrumental term. But, just as S_1 (the origin of cooking) inevitably presupposes S_2 (the existence of meat) – since one is the substance used for the other – the use of tobacco as a means in S_2 presupposes its previous existence. In other words, to the right of S_2 there must be a mythological system, S_3, in which tobacco acts as the end and not just the means; which consequently consists of a group of myths about the origin of tobacco; and which, being a transformation of S_2, just as S_2 was a transformation of S_1, ought to reproduce S_1, at least on one axis, so that the group can be considered as closed on that side. Otherwise, it would be necessary to repeat the operation and look for another system, S_4, which would raise a similar query, and so on and so forth until we arrived at a positive answer, or until we lost all hope of succeeding and resigned ourselves to the view that mythology is a genre devoid of redundancy. If this were so, any attempt to create a grammar of mythology would be based on an illusion.

As it happens, I have already isolated the system, S_3, in the previous volume and confirmed that it reproduces S_1. It will suffice to recall that the myths in question are a group of Chaco myths (M_{22}, M_{23}, M_{24}) about the origin of the jaguar (a problem posed by S_1, in which the jaguar appears as master of cooking fire) and of tobacco (a problem posed by S_2). The mere fact that these two terms are found together in the same etiological field is no doubt highly significant. But the most important point is that S_3 does in fact reproduce S_1, since the story follows the same pattern in either case: it tells of a bird-nester (macaws' or parrots' nests) who becomes involved with a jaguar, either male or female (or male in the first instance and subsequently female); either friendly or hostile and, finally, either brother-in-law or wife, i.e. an affine. Furthermore, the myths in S_1 have cooking as their objective – cooking through the medium of 'constructive' fire the function of which is to make meat fit for human consumption. Similarly, the myths in S_3 have tobacco as their objective, through the medium of a destructive fire (the pyre on which the jaguar dies so that the plant springs up from its ashes). This fire is constructive only as regards tobacco, which, unlike meat, has to be burnt (= destroyed) before it can be consumed.

It is therefore clear that to the right of S_2 we have a system, S_3, which transforms it and explains it, while at the same time reproducing S_1, and that consequently the sequence is closed on that side. If we look to the left of S_1, we find S_{-2}, the *purpose* of which is to explain the origin of adornments while using honey as a *means*, and honey is a term which has been independently proved to be symmetrical with tobacco. If the group is in fact closed, we can suppose, not only that there exists to the left of S_{-2} a system S_{-3}, which establishes the existence of honey, as S_3 had already done for tobacco at the other extremity of the field, but which also, as regards content, must reproduce S_1 (although in a different perspective) in a manner symmetrical to the way in which S_3 reproduced S_1. So that S_3 and S_{-3}, each of which reproduces S_1 in its particular fashion, also reproduce each other (see diagram on p. 32).

Let us therefore set out in search of S_{-3}. As far as is known, it was among certain northern Tupi tribes that honey seems to have held the most important place in ceremonial life and religious thought. Like their Tembé relatives, the Tenetehara of Maranhão dedicated their most important festival to honey. It took place every year, at the end of the dry season, that is in September or October. Although it had not been celebrated for very many years, the Indians whom Wagley and Galvão (p. 99) visited between 1939 and 1941 flatly refused to let them hear the honey festival songs because, as they said, the rains had started and to sing out of season might bring down some supernatural punishment upon them.

The festival proper only lasted a few days, but preparations were begun six or eight months in advance. As early as March or April, the

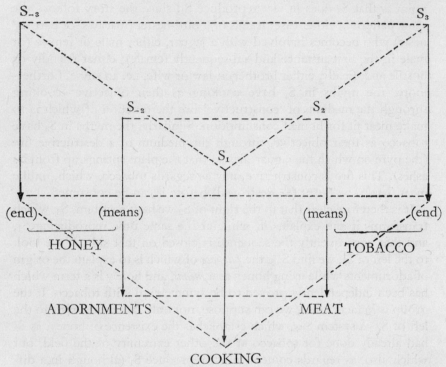

wild honey had to be gathered and stored away in gourds which were hung from the beams of a ceremonial hut, specially built for the occasion. According to the accounts available, there were between 120 and 180 gourds, each one containing more than a litre of honey. They were fastened next to each other and formed from six to eight rows. During the entire period of the honey-gathering, the villagers would assemble every night and sing songs: the women in the ceremonial hut, 'underneath the honey', the men on the dancing arena outside. It appears that the songs referred to different types of game and to the hunting techniques prescribed for each variety. The main purpose of the honey festival was to ensure successful hunting for the rest of the year.

The task of organizing the honey-gathering and the festival fell to an important member of the community, who assumed the title of 'proprietor of the feast'. When he was certain that enough honey had been gathered, he sent messengers to invite the neighbouring villages. Vast quantities of manioc soup and game were prepared and offered to the visitors. Both visitors and hosts greeted each other noisily, but as soon as the newcomers entered the ceremonial hut, the shouts and the sounding of the horns gave way to absolute silence. The men arranged themselves in groups according to their villages, and each group sang in turn. The men of the village which was acting as host were the last to sing. Then the gourds were taken down, but the contents were poured into a large jar and diluted with water before being drunk. The feast continued until all the honey had been consumed. On the morning of the last day, there was a collective hunt, followed by a feast of roasted meat (Wagley-Galvão, pp. 122-5).

There is a myth which explains the origin of the honey festival:

M₁₈₈. Tenetehara. 'The origin of the honey festival'

M_{188}. *Tenetehara. 'The origin of the honey festival'*

One day, Aruwé, a well-known Tenetehara hunter, found a spot where many macaws came to eat seeds from a tree. He climbed into the tree, built a hunting blind and waited. He killed many macaws. When he climbed down from his hunting blind at the end of the day, however, he saw jaguars approaching. He hid again and saw that they came to this tree to collect wild honey. When they left, he returned to his village with the macaws he had killed. He spent the next day hunting from the same tree and with the same excellent luck. He waited until after the jaguars had come and gone before leaving his blind.

One day Aruwé's brother asked him to teach him where to hunt. His brother wanted tail feathers from the red macaw to make decorations for a festival. Aruwé ... instructed him not to climb down until after the jaguars had gone. The brother ... saw the jaguars coming to the tree and, against the advice of his brother, decided to try to kill one. His first arrow missed and the jaguar climbed the tree and killed the brother.

Aruwé waited all one day and all one night for his brother to return. When he did not return he was certain that his brother had been killed by the jaguar. He returned to the spot and saw signs of the battle. He followed the jaguar's tracks which were marked with his brother's blood, until they disappeared at the opening of an

B

ant-hill. Aruwé was a shaman ... he transformed himself into an ant and entered into the hill. Inside he saw many houses: it was the village of the jaguars. Aruwé changed himself into a man again and entered the village in search of his brother. He saw a jaguar woman there who appealed to him. He went with her into her father's house and married her. It was her father who had killed his brother and the father explained how the brother had provoked the jaguars. Aruwé lived with the jaguars for a long time.

Aruwé watched the jaguars leave the village each day for many days and return each day with gourd containers full of wild honey ... At night the jaguar people gathered near the house where they hung the honey and sang beautiful songs unknown to the Tenetehara. Aruwé learned [the dances] and the songs.

Soon afterwards, Aruwé was homesick to see his Tenetehara wife and son. He asked the jaguar people to let him go back to visit them. They agreed on condition that he take his jaguar wife with him. The couple returned to the Tenetehara village. Aruwé asked his jaguar wife to wait outside while he told his Tenetehara wife of his arrival. The Tenetehara wife was happy ... and he stayed a long time. When he went back to the ant-hill his jaguar wife had gone, and she had filled in the entrance of the ant-hill after her. Aruwé returned several times, but he never again found the jaguar village. He taught the Tenetehara how to celebrate the Honey Feast. The Honey Feast as it is celebrated nowadays was taught to the Tenetehara by Aruwé (Wagley–Galvão, pp. 143–4).

Before embarking on a discussion of this myth, I will give the Tembé version (the Tembé are a sub-group of the Tenetehara):

M_{189}. Tembé. 'The origin of the honey festival'

Once upon a time, there were two brothers. One made himself a hide-out at the top of an azywaywa tree, the flowers of which the macaws used to come and eat. He had already killed a great many birds, when two jaguars appeared on the scene carrying gourds which they filled with nectar pressed from the blossom on the tree. For several days running, the hunter watched the animals without daring to kill them, but, in spite of his advice, his brother was less prudent. He shot at the jaguars, without suspecting that they were invulnerable. The animals raised a storm, which shook the tree, bringing down both the hide-out and its occupant, who was killed instantly. They carried off the corpse to the underworld, the entrance of which was as small as an ant hole, and they placed it on a wooden cross standing in bright sunshine.

The hero, after being changed into an ant, came to the jaguars' hut, where vessels full of honey were hanging. He learnt the ritual songs, and every evening he resumed his human form and danced with the jaguars; in the day-time he became an ant again.

When he returned to his village, he told his companions of all he had seen (Nim. 2, p. 294).

The two versions differ only as regards the amount of detail given, and as regards the origin of the honey which, in M_{189}, does not come from bees, but is directly expressed from the yellow flowers of the azywaywa tree, which may be the same as aiuuá-iwa, one of the lauraceae. Whatever the species, this reading is particularly instructive since, unlike our varieties of honey, those found in tropical America do not seem to be extracted mainly from flowers. But the South American Indians, who find honey chiefly in hollow tree-trunks where various kinds of bees make their nests, classify it for this reason as a vegetable. Several Tacana myths (M_{189b}, etc.) describe the unfortunate experience of a monkey, which was cruelly stung when it bit into a wasps' nest, thinking it to be a fruit (H.-H., pp. 255-8). A Karaja myth (M_{70}) tells how the first men, when they emerged from the bowels of the earth, gathered 'great quantities of fruit, bees and honey'. According to the Umutina, the first human beings were created from wild fruits and honey (Schultz 2, pp. 172, 227, 228). The same correlation is found in Europe, among the peoples of antiquity, as is proved by the following quotation from Hesiod: 'At the top of the oak-tree are acorns, in the middle, bees' (*Works and Days*, vv. 232-3) and by various Latin beliefs: in the Golden Age, the leaves of trees secreted honey and bees are still spontaneously generated from foliage and grasses (Virgil, *Georgics*, I, vv. 129-31; IV, vv. 200).

This perhaps explains why the Tupi refer to the bee as iramanha, which Nordenskiöld (5, p. 170; 6, p. 197), following Ihering, takes to mean: 'keeper of the honey' (and not producer). But, according to Chermont de Miranda, the term ira-mya means 'mother of honey'. Barbosa Rodrigues gives iramaña, without any explanatory comment, whereas Tastevin and Stradelli give ira-maia, with the suggestion that the second word is borrowed from the Portuguese *mãe*, 'mother'; Stradelli, however, is not absolutely convinced (see under 'maia, manha'), since his *Vocabulario* mentions a root, manha(na), which has the same meaning as the one proposed by Ihering.

I shall return to this question later. For the moment, it is important to stress the relationship between the Tenetehara and Tembé myths and those in the S_1 group, since it confirms my theory that myths which

Figure 1. Hunting macaws. (A drawing by Riou, based on J. Crevaux, *Voyage dans l' Amérique du Sud*, Paris, 1883, p. 263.)

have honey as their principal theme must reproduce those concerned with the origin of cooking fire, while the latter in their turn are reproduced by the myths about the origin of tobacco (S_3). In all three cases, we are concerned with a bird-nester (or hunter) going after macaws or parrots, and who discovers that one or several jaguars are at the foot of the tree or rock up which he himself has climbed. In all the myths, the jaguar is a relative by marriage, either the husband of a human wife in S_1, a wife who began by being human in S_2, or the father of a jaguar-wife in the myth with which we are now concerned. In S_1 and S_3 the jaguar eats the macaws; in S_{-3} it is the man who eats them. The *two* jaguars in S_1, one masculine and protective, the other feminine and hostile, behave differently towards the *same* man. The *single* jaguar in S_{-2} behaves in equally different ways towards the *two* men: he eats one and gives his daughter to the other. In S_3, where there is only one jaguar and one man, the duality is re-established on the diachronic level, since the jaguar was initially a human wife, who subsequently changed into a man-eating wild beast. The three systems therefore have the same armature consisting of the triad: man (or men), macaws, jaguar(s), whose different behaviour patterns $(+, -)$ unite the following terms in groups of two:

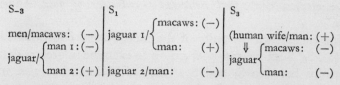

Each mythological system springs from what might be called a dietetic opposition – the raw and the cooked in S_1 (but always with reference to meat): cannibalism and another kind of carnivorous diet (parrots devoured by the woman) in S_3; lastly, in S_{-3}, a carnivorous diet (the man is defined as a killer of macaws) and a vegetarian diet (since we have seen that honey is classed among the vegetable substances). From this point of view, the three systems can be arranged as follows:

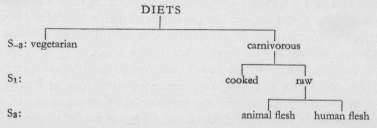

In spite of this seemingly 'open' structure, the group is closed in S_3 and S_{-3}. Of the three systems only S_1 presents a static character: at the beginning, the man is an 'eater of raw food', and the jaguar an 'eater of cooked food', and at the end they simply switch roles. At the beginning of S_{-3}, on the contrary, man is carnivorous and the jaguar vegetarian, and although it succeeds in introducing man to its diet, this is only after it has changed from a vegetarian to a cannibal diet, like the woman who changed into a jaguar in S_3. Symmetrically, the 'cannibalism' of the woman in S_3 (she devours live birds) anticipates and announces her transformation into a jaguar; and as a penalty for having turned man into a food (instead of a consumer of food), the jaguar itself has to undergo the transformation into tobacco: a vegetable food (the situation is congruous with that of consumer of vegetable food in S_{-3}) which must be *reduced to ashes* before being consumed, and is therefore anti-symmetrical with the honey eaten in a *moist* form by the jaguar in S_{-3}. The group is definitely closed, but the closing is dependent on three transformations, which themselves are situated on three axes; there is an identical transformation: *cannibalistic jaguar* $\Rightarrow$ *cannibalistic jaguar*; and two non-identical transformations, both referring to a vegetarian diet : *food consumed* $\Rightarrow$ *consumer of food*, and : *burnt* $\Rightarrow$ *moist*.

Having established the unity of the meta-system constituted by the group $\{S_1, S_3, S_{-3},\}$ we can now go on to examine in greater detail the relationships between S_1 and S_{-3}; my initial intention was, in fact, to discover S_{-3} as a reproduction of S_1. In this limited perspective, I should like to make three remarks:

(1) It is a characteristic of man to be both vegetarian and carnivorous. From the vegetarian point of view, he is congruous with the macaws (which are always described in the myths as being vegetarian birds, thus forming a pair of opposites with birds of prey, cf. *RC*, p. 324). From the carnivorous point of view, man is congruous with the jaguar. From this double relationship of congruence, S_{-3} deduces a third, directly uniting the jaguars and the macaws, which are similar in respect of honey since they frequent the same tree, either with different purposes (a weak form of the rivalry in M_{188}), or with the same purpose in M_{189} where the macaws eat the flowers from which the jaguars express the nectar. The direct congruence between macaws and jaguars (derived from the two other kinds of congruence between men and macaws and men and jaguars, through the application of an argument of the type: our friends are the friends of our friends)[6] might in theory be established in two ways, either by changing the mythical macaws into carnivorous birds, or by changing the mythical jaguars into vegetarians. The first transformation would be in contradiction with the

---

[6] It is clear from this that mythic thought utilizes two distinct forms of deduction. The congruence between man and the macaw in respect of vegetarianism and between man and the jaguar in respect of carnivorousness, are deduced from empirically observed data. On the other hand, the congruence between the macaw and the jaguar, which can be inferred from the other two instances of congruence, is synthetic in character, since it is not based on experience, and is even contrary to observation. Many apparent anomalies in ethnozoology and ethnobotany can be explained, once it is realized that these systems of knowledge juxtapose conclusions arrived at by what we can, in the light of the preceding remarks, call *empirical deduction* and *transcendental deduction* (cf. my article, 'The Deduction of the Crane', in P. and E. K. Matanda, eds., *Structural Analysis of Oral Tradition* [Philadelphia: University of Pennsylvania Press, 1971]).

unequivocal position occupied by the macaws in other myths. The second would only be in contradiction with that occupied by the jaguars if, in S_{-3}, the latter were presented purely and simply as the masters and originators of a vegetable food – honey. But as it happens, the myths belonging to this group make no such statement. M_{189} is careful to distinguish two antithetical ways of eating honey: the way adopted by the macaws, which is *natural*, since they only eat the flowers (which, in a sense are 'raw'), whereas the jaguars gather the honey for a *cultural* purpose: the celebration of the honey festival. The jaguars are not therefore 'masters of the honey', which the macaws also eat (and that men no doubt eat too, although at this period they associated no ritual with the process) but rather 'masters of the honey festival': i.e. initiators of a mode of culture linked furthermore with hunting); and this confirms, rather than disproves, the part played by the jaguar as master of another mode of culture – cooking fire – in S_1.

(2) From the point of view of kinship, a transformation occurs when we move from S_1 to S_{-3}:

$$S_1 \left[\underset{\text{jaguar}}{\triangle} = \underset{\text{humans}}{\overset{\ulcorner \quad \urcorner}{\bigcirc \quad \triangle}} \right] \Rightarrow S_{-3} \left[\underset{\text{humans}}{\triangle} = \underset{\text{jaguars}}{\overset{\ulcorner \quad \urcorner}{\bigcirc \quad \triangle}} \right]$$

In other words, men are givers of women in S_1, and takers in S_{-3}.

This transformation is accompanied by another, which is concerned with attitudes. A remarkable feature of S_1 is the indifference with which the jaguar appears to receive the news of the murder, or wounding, of his wife by the young hero whom he has adopted as his son (*RC*, pp. 81–3). His 'profession of indifference' has an exact parallel in S_{-3}, where the hero is easily convinced that the jaguar who killed his brother did so in legitimate self-defence (M_{188}), or even allows himself to be so charmed by the songs and dances of the honey festival that he forgets his original purpose in coming to visit the jaguars, which was to find or avenge his brother (M_{189}):

$$\Rightarrow S_1 \left[\begin{array}{c} \underset{\text{indifferent}}{\overset{\text{jaguar}}{\triangle}} = \underset{}{\overset{\text{victim}}{\bigcirc}} \\ \underset{\substack{\text{man as} \\ \text{killer}}}{\triangle} \end{array} \right] \Rightarrow S_{-3} \left[\begin{array}{c} \overset{\text{jaguar as}}{\underset{\text{killer}}{}} \\ \triangle \\ \mid \\ \underset{\text{victim}}{\triangle} \quad \underset{\substack{\text{man} \\ \text{indifferent}}}{\triangle} = \bigcirc \end{array} \right]$$

(3) Finally there exists, between S_1 and S_{-3}, one last resemblance which, in this instance too, is accompanied by a difference. In both systems, the jaguar plays the part of an initiator of culture – either in respect of cooking, which requires fire, or in respect of the honey festival, which requires water. Cooked food consumed in the profane manner corresponds to the former, while raw food consumed in the sacred manner corresponds to the latter. It can also be said that, along with cooking (accompanied, in S_1, by bows and arrows and yarn), the jaguar brings material cultural benefits to man. With the honey festival, which among the northern Tupi tribes is the most important and most sacred of religious ceremonies, the jaguar brings spiritual cultural benefits. The transition is a decisive one in both instances but, significantly, in the one case it is from the raw to the cooked (and so definitively constitutive of culture), and in the other from profane rawness to sacred rawness (thereby overcoming the opposition between the natural and the supernatural, but in a non-definitive way, since the rites have to be celebrated afresh every year), and so corresponds to the bridging of wider or narrower gaps:

$$
\overbrace{\underbrace{\text{nature} \qquad\qquad \text{culture} \qquad\qquad \text{supernature}}_{\textit{honey festival}}}^{\textit{cooking}}
$$

*

One final aspect of the meta-system remains to be considered, but it will be more clearly understandable if I first briefly recapitulate what has already been said.

Having obtained S_2 by reversing S_1, we found that there occurred in S_2, according to the group concerned, a breaking-up of the sociological armature which, in the case of a non-varying message (origin of wild pigs), takes the form:  among the Tenetehara and the Mundurucu, whereas among the Bororo it is: $\bigcirc \# \triangle$. When we inquired what message the sociological armature: in the last-mentioned group corresponded to we discovered that it was the origin of ornaments and adornments, i.e. the origin of cultural objects (S_{-2}).

Setting this finding aside for the time being, we embarked on a third stage by pointing out that the jaguar, both as an animal and as the kindly brother-in-law in S_1, was the counterpart of the pigs in S_2 – brothers-in-law (who had been changed) into animals (because) of their spiteful behaviour. S_2, however, was concerned with the origin of pigs. The question was whether or not there existed a system, S_3, which would account for the origin of the jaguars who were the protagonists in S_1. Certain Chaco myths (S_3) met this requirement and it was particularly significant that, within the same story, they should confuse the origin of the jaguar and the origin of tobacco, since this had the effect of closing the circle: in S_1, the jaguar is the means whereby cooking fire ('constructive fire') is obtained; in S_2, tobacco fire is the means whereby pigs are created (since it causes them to appear); finally, in S_3, the funeral pyre (destructive fire) is the means whereby tobacco is created, since it springs from the jaguar's body, of which it is – and no pun is intended – the 'end' (purpose). Now, tobacco fire occupies an exactly intermediary position between cooking fire and the funeral pyre: it produces a consumable substance, but only after it has been reduced to ashes (RC, pp. 83–107). At the same time as the transformation from S_2 into S_3 was being confirmed, we established three points. Firstly, S_3 reproduced S_1 in respect of the code (story of a bird-nester; a triad formed by man, macaws and the jaguar); secondly, S_3 transformed S_1 in respect of the armature, which became $\bigcirc \# \triangle$ instead of

$$\overset{\overline{/\!/}}{\underset{\triangle \quad \bigcirc \; = \; \triangle}{\rule{0pt}{0pt}}}$$; finally, this transformation was identical with the one

we observed in moving from the Tupi myths to the Bororo myth similarly concerned with the origin of pigs.

This being so, a problem arises. If, among the Bororo, the armature

$\bigcirc \# \triangle$ is already used in S_2, and the armature $\overset{\overline{/\!/}}{\underset{\triangle \quad \bigcirc \; = \; \triangle}{\rule{0pt}{0pt}}}$ in S_{-2},

what kind of family relations must these Indians resort to in order to explain the origin of tobacco? As it happens, they present a further instance of a break-up, since we find that they have two different myths relating to the origin of different species of tobacco.

These myths have already been analysed (RC, pp. 103–7), so I shall do no more than give a brief reminder of them here. One, M_{26}, describes how one kind of tobacco (*Nicotiana tabacum*) sprang up from the ashes of a snake, to which a woman had given birth after being accidentally fertilized by the blood of a boa, which her husband had killed while out hunting, and which she was helping to carry home in pieces. The other myth (M_{27}) is concerned with a species of anonaceous plant, of which the Bororo also smoke the leaves and which they call by the same name as real tobacco. These leaves were discovered by a fisherman in a fish's belly; at first, he smoked them only at night and in secret, but his companions forced him to share with them. To punish them for their gluttony in swallowing the smoke instead of exhaling it – thus depriving the spirits of the offering which was their due – the latter changed the men into otters. As regards M_{26}, I showed it (*RC*, p. 103) to be rigorously symmetrical with the Chaco myths about the origin of tobacco (M_{23}, M_{24}). No less significant are the connections between M_{26} and the Bororo myth about the origin of wild pigs (M_{21}), of which we have two versions: the one that has already been summarized, and another, older one, which was transcribed in 1917. In spite of some gaps and obscure passages, it transpires from this version that the women, being jealous of their husbands' success at fishing, agreed to prostitute themselves to the otters, on condition that the otters supplied them with fish. Thus the women could claim to be better at fishing than the men (Rondon, pp. 166–70). The story is the same as in the other version, except that the latter draws a veil over the relationship between the women and the otters, which seem to be prompted by less debauched motives.

Although the theme of the animal as seducer is frequent in South American mythology, we know of hardly any instances in which this particular role is ascribed to otters; it is usually fulfilled by the tapir, the jaguar, the caiman or the snake. The Bororo use the tapir as seducer but humanize it (it is a man whose clan eponym is the tapir, M_2) and we find that, in M_{26}, they use the snake, while at the same time reducing its seductive function to a minimum, since the snake in question is not alive but dead, only a section of its body is concerned, not the whole animal, and the fertilizing of the woman occurs accidentally and without her knowledge, by means of the blood (a polluting, but not a fertilizing, liquid) which drips from the piece of flesh she is carrying. Thus, in this instance, an animal which is normally a seducer has its potency reduced; and, similarly, its victim, the woman, is forgiven a sin, which here appears to be rather an effect of mischance. On the other hand, in their myth about the origin of wild pigs, the Bororo have an exceptional seducer – the otter – which plays a particularly active part with regard to the women, while they show themselves to be doubly vicious: they conclude an obscene bargain with the animals in order to get the better of the men in fishing, whereas in a properly organized society, the men catch the fish and the women merely transport it.

Why otters? In the group of Bororo myths we are now examining, they appear in two contexts. According to M_{27}, a fishing expedition, undertaken by a man, led to the discovery of tobacco through the medium of a fish, which was kept hidden from other men; and the inhaling of the tobacco smoke led to the transformation of men into otters. According to M_{21}, the transformation of the otters into men (= seducers of human wives: the Rondon version, in fact, refers to them as 'men') leads to a fishing expedition, undertaken by women, which deprives the men of fish and causes them to change into pigs, after eating stewed fruit full of prickles. There is, then, a relationship between the *direction* of one transformation: men into otters, or otters into men (in one instance, it is metonymical: it concerns *part* of the men; in the other, it is metaphorical: the otters copulate with the women *like* men) and the contents of the other transformation, relating to a substance which was swallowed when it ought to have been ejected: tobacco or stewed fruit; but either with metaphorical intent (so that the tobacco smoke could assume the *function* of an offering to the spirits) or metonymically (by the spitting out of the prickles which were *part* of the stewed fruit).

If we now remember that, in the Mundurucu myth (M_{16}) about the origin of wild pigs, the inhaled tobacco smoke (which in the Bororo myth changes men into otters) brings about their transformation into pigs (whereas, in the case of the Bororo, the prickly stewed fruit fulfilled this function), we shall be able to understand the reason for the presence of the otters, the masters of fish in the same way as the pigs are masters of terrestrial game (for evidence of this, cf. *RC*, pp. 117–18). The two species are symmetrical, granted the various transformations, which are homologous among themselves, from the *dry* to the *moist*, from *tobacco* to *stewed fruit*, from *hunting* to *fishing*, and finally from *fire* to *water*. The argument can be summarized in the two formulae:

(a) $^{M_{16}}$[men $\Rightarrow$ pigs], $^{M_{27}}$[men $\Rightarrow$ otters] = ^{f}[inhaled smoke]

(b) $^{M_{21}}$[men $\Rightarrow$ pigs] = ^{f}[smoke = stewed fruit], [otters $\Rightarrow$ men]

Having thus – with the help of M_{16} – reduced the codes of M_{27} and M_{21} to a single unit by using their common properties which, in the case of M_{16} and M_{21}, lie in the fact that they are myths of origin about the same animal species: wild pigs, and in the case of M_{16} and M_{27}, that they have recourse to the same agent, tobacco smoke, which, when inhaled, causes the men to be changed into different animal species, we can effect the same reduction by starting with M_{26} which, like M_{27}, is a myth about the origin of tobacco. It is obvious that M_{26} is a transformation of M_{27} and M_{21} in respect of the dry and the moist: the tobacco (in M_{26}) comes from an animal corpse which has been *thrust into fire* instead of being *taken out of water*, as it is in M_{27}. And the resulting substance consists of smoke, which is good on condition that it is *pungent*,[7] and thus contrasts with the *drink* in M_{21}, which the men made the fatal mistake of believing to be good, for the simple reason that they never thought it would be *pungent*.

This two-fold transformation: [*out of water*] $\Rightarrow$ [*into fire*] and [*drink*] $\Rightarrow$ [*smoke*], is a clear inversion, in the body of Bororo mythology, of the transformation governing the transition from the Ge and Tupi myths about the origin of fire to the corresponding Bororo myth (M_1), which we know to be a myth about the origin of water. If we confine ourselves to the Bororo group (M_{21}, M_{26}, M_{27}), which is, in fact, the subject of the present discussion, the transformations which must inevitably command our attention are those correlative to the sociological armature. M_{21} describes a quarrel between husbands and wives about fishing, the women refusing to collaborate with their husbands as carriers of fish, which is the role normally assigned to them in accordance with the rules governing the division of labour between the sexes, and claiming the right to fish on their own account, like the men, and better than the men, a claim which leads them to becoming the otters' mistresses. Everything happens the other way round in M_{26}: the activity is hunting, not fishing, and the women are keen to collaborate with their husbands, since they respond to the whistling set up by the hunters some way from the village, and run to help them to carry the pieces of meat. As I have already pointed out, these docile wives have no trace of perversity. Fate alone is responsible for the fact that in totally non-erotic circumstances, one of them is contaminated, rather than seduced, by a piece of meat.[8] The fact that it is meat from a snake, a phallic animal and a seducer figuring in innumerable myths of tropical America, emphasizes still further that M_{26} is aimed very carefully at neutralizing these characteristics.

[7] M_{26}, which is marvellously explicit on this point, says that when men first encountered tobacco, they 'gathered the leaves and put them to dry; then they rolled them into cigars, which they lit and began to smoke. When the tobacco was strong, they would say: "This one is strong, it is good!" But when it wasn't strong, they would say: "It is bad, it is not pungent." ' (Colb. 3, p. 199.)

TRANSLATORS' NOTE: The French terms used by the author, and which we have translated as 'pungent', are *piquante*, *il pique*, which can also mean 'stinging', 'prickly' and 'sharp' (of a drink).

[8] Cf. *RC*, p. 152, n. 6, in connection with the Bororo horror of blood.

The same kind of neutralization of the quarrel between husbands and wives as that which forms the armature of M_{21} can be observed in M_{27}, although it is expressed in a different way. Let us say that, in M_{26}, the husbands and wives remain but the quarrel disappears, whereas the contrary is true in M_{27}, where the quarrel remains but the husbands and wives disappear. In M_{27}, there is definitely a quarrel, but it occurs between companions of the same sex – whose functions in respect of fishing are alike instead of being complementary. And yet one of them tries to keep for himself the miraculous result of a collective undertaking, and only decides to share it when he is discovered and cannot do otherwise.

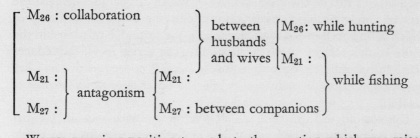

We are now in a position to reply to the question which was raised a little while ago. In order to explain the origin of tobacco, the Bororo who are, as it were, 'short' of an armature, re-use the one that has already served to explain the origin of wild pigs, and which is the same as the one employed by the Chaco tribes for the origin of tobacco: $\bigcirc \mathbin{\#} \triangle$, which can be generalized in the form $\bigcirc / \triangle$, contrasting with $\bigcirc \cup \triangle$. But since this armature already fulfils a different role in their myths, they vary it by taking it as far as it will go in the two possible directions: either they keep the terms and abolish the relationship: $(\bigcirc/\triangle) \Rightarrow (\bigcirc \cup \triangle)$, or they keep the relationship, and abolish the difference between the terms: $(\bigcirc/\triangle) \Rightarrow (\triangle/\triangle)$. So they imagine either collaboration between husbands and wives which is impaired from without by fate, or collaboration between individuals of the same sex which is impaired from within through a perverse action committed by one of them. As there are two solutions, there are two myths explaining the origin of tobacco, and as these solutions are reversed, the myths too are reversed in respect of vocabulary, since one species of tobacco comes from water, the other from fire.

Consequently, the transformation of the sociological armature, which is a feature of the mythical systems as a whole {S_1 (origin of fire), S_{-1} (origin of water), S_2 (origin of meat), S_{-2} (origin of cultural objects or advantages), S_3 (origin of tobacco), S_{-3} (origin of the honey festival)} is not completely exhausted by its canonical expression: $\left[\underset{\triangle \quad o}{} = \triangle \right] \Rightarrow \left[o \neq \triangle \right]$. Beyond $[\bigcirc \# \triangle]$, it can still produce further results. As has been established, the myths approach the disjunction between husbands and wives from two points of view: the techno-economical, since in illiterate societies there is generally a division of labour according to the sexes to bring out the full significance of the matrimonial state; and the sexual. By alternately choosing one or other viewpoint and taking it to its logical conclusion, we obtain a series of sociological terms ranging from the character of the *perverse companion* to that of the *apathetic seducer*, which are parallel denials, the first of a relationship between individuals the entire significance of which is on a techno-economic level, and the second, a relationship the entire significance of which is situated on the sexual level, the seducer being supposedly by definition purely sexual; consequently, one lies *beyond* relationship by marriage, while the other is *on the hither side* of kinship.

This sociological armature, which is refracted twice over and for that reason somewhat blurred in outline, nevertheless remains discernible throughout the Bororo myths relating to the origin of tobacco (without raising any doubts about their transformational relationship with the Chaco myths on the same theme) and it is also found in myths situated at the opposite end of the semantic field, that is in the Tembé and Tenetehara myths dealing with the origin of the honey festival (M_{188}, M_{189}). In both versions, the hero has a brother who turns out to be a *vicious companion*: a fault which brings about his disjunction. The hero then sets off in search of his brother, but he forgets about him almost immediately, on being captivated ($=$ *seduced*) by the songs and dances of the honey festival. Later he is *seduced* by the welcome given him by his own people and forgets his *jaguar/wife*, whom he cannot find anywhere when he sets off to look for her.

Having reached this point in my analysis, I could declare myself satisfied and consider that I had succeeded in bringing all the myths into 'harmony' with each other, like the instruments of an orchestra which, after the confused din of their tuning-up, begin to vibrate in unison, if there did not remain one discordant element in the meta-system that I am using, as it were, as an orchestra in order to play the score which, after a fashion, is constituted by this book. At one end of the semantic field, we find not one but two groups of myths explaining the origin of tobacco: the Chaco myths with a sociological armature [$\bigcirc \neq \triangle$], which explain the origin of tobacco *in general*, for the benefit of *humanity as a whole* (from the latter point of view, the sending out of messengers to the neighbouring villages, referred to in the myths, indicates an outlook which is 'open' to the external world); and then beyond these myths, those of the Bororo, the sociological armature of which presents a doubly refracted image of the preceding armature, and which are about the origin of *particular varieties* of tobacco for the benefit of *specific clans* of a tribal society. It follows that, both as regards object and subject, the Bororo myths have a synecdochic relationship with the Chaco myths: they consider parts of the whole (a part of tobacco and part of the smokers), instead of considering the whole.

But although, at this end of the semantic field, we have too many myths at our disposal, the opposite occurs at the other end, where we have too few. Myths (M_{188}, M_{189}), which I used to make good this deficiency, are not strictly speaking, nor as might have been expected, myths about the origin of honey: they are myths about the origin of the honey *festival* – a social and religious rite and not a natural product, although the natural product is necessarily involved in the ritual. So, at this point, a group of myths about the origin of honey is missing, a group which, as one reads the diagram on p. 32 from right to left, ought to figure immediately before, or to the side of, S_{-3}. If we postulate the existence of such a group, as a working hypothesis, it follows that system S_{-3}, which is concerned with honey, is symmetrically reduplicated by system S_3, which deals with tobacco. Finally, the symmetry between S_{-3} and S_3 must conceal an obvious dissymmetry on another level: the two groups of myths about the origin of tobacco have, as I have said, a synecdochic relationship with each other, a relationship which, if we take the terms in the broader sense, is a form of metonymy. Whereas, if there are any myths about the origin of the honey proper, their relationship with the myths about the origin of honey *festival* must be that of signified to signifier, the actual honey acquiring a significance it lacks as a natural product, when it is gathered and consumed for social and religious purposes. In such a case, the relationship between the two groups of myths would be metaphorical in nature.

Such considerations determine the direction of the inquiry I am now about to undertake.

PART ONE THE DRY AND THE DAMP

Si quando sedem augustam seruataque
mella
thesauri relines, prius haustu sparsus
aquarum
ora foue, fumosque manu praetende
sequacis.

Virgil, *Georgics*, IV, vv. 228–30

1 *The Dialogue Between Honey and Tobacco*

Bees, like wasps, are hymenopterous insects, and several hundreds of species of them, arranged in groups of thirteen families or sub-families, for the most part solitary, are to be found in tropical America. But only the social bees produce honey in sufficient quantities to serve as food: *pais de mel*, 'fathers of honey', is the charming Portuguese description; they all belong to the Meliponidae family, and the *Melipona* and *Trigona* species. Unlike European bees, the Meliponidae are stingless, and they are also smaller in size. But they can be extremely troublesome because of their aggressive behaviour, which explains why one species is known colloquially as *torce cabellos*, 'hair-twister'; and they can cause even greater distress when in their tens, or even hundreds, they fasten onto the face and body of the traveller in order to suck his sweat and his nasal and ocular secretions. This explains the colloquial name for the species *Trigona duckei*: *lambe olhos*, 'lick-eyes'.

The person attacked very soon becomes infuriated by tickling sensations occurring in particularly sensitive spots – inside the ears and nostrils and in the corners of the eyes and mouth – and which it is impossible to put a stop to by means of the sudden movements we normally use to drive insects away. The bees which become heavy and, as it were, drunk with human food seem to lose the desire, and perhaps even the the ability, to fly away. Their victim, weary of beating the air to no purpose, is very soon driven to striking his face, a fatal move, because the squashed, sweat-laden corpses glue the surviving insects to the spot and act as a lure for others, which are attracted by the prospect of a further meal.

The everyday experience I have just described is enough to show that the Meliponidae have a more varied diet than European bees, and do not disdain food of animal origin. More than a century ago, Bates noted (p. 35) that the bees in the Amazonian regions fed not so much on flowers as on the sap from trees and on bird droppings. According to Schwartz (2, pp. 101–8), the Meliponidae are attracted to a great variety of substances, from nectar and pollen to decaying carcasses, urine and excrement. It is, therefore, not surprising that the honey they produce is very different, in colour and consistency as well as in taste and chemical composition, from the honey produced by the *Apis mellifica*. The honey made by the Meliponidae is often very dark, always liquid and slow to crystallize, because of its high water content. Unless it is boiled, which is a possible method of ensuring its preservation, it soon ferments and turns sour.

Ihering, from whom I have borrowed the above details (see his article, 'As abelhas sociaes indigenas') states clearly that sucrose, of which an average proportion of ten per cent is present in the honey of the *Apis mellifica*, is completely absent from the honey made by the Meliponidae, which instead contains levulose and dextrose, but in far higher proportions (30–70 per cent and 20–50 per cent respectively). As levulose has a considerably greater sweetening capacity than sucrose, the many different varieties of honey produced by the Meliponidae have a richness and subtlety difficult to describe to those who have never tasted them, and indeed can seem almost unbearably exquisite in flavour. A delight more piercing than any normally afforded by taste or smell breaks down the boundaries of sensibility, and blurs its registers, so much so that the eater of honey wonders whether he is savouring a delicacy or burning with the fire of love. These erotic overtones do not go unnoticed in the myths. On a more commonplace level, the high sugar content and powerful flavour of the varieties produced by the Meliponidae give honey a status which is not comparable with that of any other food and also mean that it has almost always to be diluted with water before it is eaten.

Certain kinds of honey, which are alkaline in composition, have a laxative effect and are dangerous. This is the case with the honey of a few species of Meliponidae, belonging to the *Trigona* sub-group, and especially the varieties of honey made by wasps (Vespidae), which are said to be equally as 'intoxicating' as the honey of a *Trigona* bee known in the State of São Paulo as *feiticeira*, 'witch', or: *vamo-nos-embora*, 'off we go' (Schwartz 2, p. 126). Other varieties of honey are definitely poisonous; for instance, the honey produced by the wasp known in Amazonia as *sissuira* (*Lecheguana colorada*, *Nectarina lecheguana*), which was probably responsible for the poisoning Saint-Hilaire suffered from (III, p. 150). This occasionally toxic effect can probably be explained by the fact that the insects have fed on poisonous species of flowers, as has been suggested in the case of *Lestrimelitta limão* (Schwartz 2, p. 178).

Be that as it may, wild honey has an attraction for Indians that no other food can equal, an attraction which, Ihering has noted, is tantamount to a passion: '*O Indio ... (e) fanatico pelo mel de pau.*' In Argentina too,

> the greatest diversion and keenest pleasure enjoyed by the rural peon is that of honey-gathering. For a spoonful of honey he is ready to work an entire day around a trunk and often endangers his life. One cannot estimate the risk which people are prepared to take in the mountains for the sake of honey. All that is needed is that a peon observe a small portal of wax or a cleft in a trunk to make him go immediately for a hatchet and to overturn or at the least destroy a beautiful trunk of the most valued species (Spegazzini, quoted by Schwartz 2, p. 158).

Before setting off to gather honey, the Ashluslay of the Chaco bleed themselves above the eyes in order to increase their luck (Nordenskiöld 4, p. 49). The Abipones, who used to live on the borders of Paraguay and Brazil, and whose distant descendants are the Caduveo of the southern part of the Mato Grosso, explained to Dobrizhoffer (Vol. II, p. 15) that they used to pluck their eyebrows very carefully, so that they would have no difficulty in following the flight of an isolated bee as it made its way to its nest: this is a method of locating with the naked eye which we shall encounter shortly in a myth belonging to a neighbouring community (p. 70).

Ihering's comment refers more particularly to *mel de pau*, or 'wood honey', which is found in two forms: in nests stuck to the surface of the trunk or hanging from a branch, and which, according to their appearance, are given picturesque names: 'manioc cake', 'tortoise shell', 'vagina', 'dog's penis', 'gourd' etc. (Rodrigues 1, p. 308, n. 1); or inside hollow trees, where certain species, chiefly the mandassaia bee (*Melipona quadrifasciata*), knead together the wax they secrete and the clay they collect to make various kinds of round 'pots' whose capacity varies from three to fifteen cubic centimetres, and which may be present in sufficient quantity to give a yield of several litres of the most deliciously flavoured honey (Figure 2).

These bees, and other species too perhaps, have been partly domesticated in certain areas. The simplest and most common method consists in leaving a certain amount of honey in the hollow tree in order to induce the swarm to return. The Paressi catch the swarm in a gourd, which they leave near the hut, and several tribes in Guiana, Colombia and Venezuela do the same, or bring back the hollow tree, suitably trimmed, and hang it parallel with the roof beams; or they may even hollow out a trunk specially (Whiffen, p. 51; Nordenskiöld 5, 6).

Mandassaia

Figure 2. Mandassaia bee (*Melipona anthidioides quadrifasciata*) and its nest. (After Ihering, cf. *loc. cit.*, under 'mandassaia'.)

The so-called 'earth' or 'toad' honey (*Trigona cupira*), which is less abundant than wood honey, is found in underground nests, with entrances often beginning a long way from the actual nests and so minute that only one insect at a time can pass through. After hours and days of patient watching in order to locate the entrance, it is necessary to dig for several hours more before obtaining a very meagre quantity of honey – about half a litre.

We can conclude from these various observations that the different kinds of honey in tropical America are found in insignificant or appreciable (but always very uneven) quantities, according to whether they are produced by earth or tree species; and that the tree species include bees and wasps whose honey is as a general rule poisonous; and finally, that the various kinds of bee honey can be either sweet or intoxicating.[1]

This three-fold division, although no doubt too simple to be an accurate reflection of the zoological reality, has the advantage of corresponding to native categories. Like other South American tribes, the Kaingang-Coroado think of bees and wasps as being opposites, bees having been created by the demiurge, and wasps by the deceiver, along with poisonous snakes, the puma and all the animals hostile to man (Borba, p. 22). It must not be forgotten that, although the Meliponidae do not sting (but sometimes bite), the wasps of tropical America include some highly poisonous species. But within this major opposition between bee honey and wasp honey, there exists another opposition, less absolute since it includes a whole series of intermediary stages, between harmless and intoxicating kinds of honey, whether these kinds are produced by different species, or derive from the same honey which varies according to whether it is eaten fresh or fermented: the taste of honey differs with the species and the time at which it is gathered, and may range from extremely sweet to acid and bitter (Schultz 2, p. 175). As we shall see later, the Amazonian tribes make a systematic use of the poisonous kinds of honey in their ritual in order to induce vomiting. The Caingang of southern Brazil consider honey as having two strongly contrasted properties. They regard honey and raw vegetables as being cold foods,[2] the only foods to be given to widowers and widows, who would be in danger of constipation and death if they ate meat or any other cooked food (Henry 1, pp. 181–2). However, other groups of this same population distinguish between two different varieties of beer made from maize: one is a simple extract of maize called 'goifa', and the other, 'quiquy', has honey added to it (this is the only use that this particular community makes of honey). The honey beer, which is 'more intoxicating' than the other sort, is drunk without food and it induces vomiting (Borba, pp. 15, 37).

This two-fold division of honey, which almost everywhere is separated into the categories of the sweet and the bitter, the harmless and

[1] It would perhaps be more accurate to say that they produce a drugged effect, and cause paralysis and depression, whereas wasp honey tends to cause nervous excitement with overtones of gaiety (Schwartz 2, p. 113). But the problems relating to the poisonous nature of the various kinds of South American honey are still far from being definitively solved.

[2] Unlike Mexicans, who classify honey among the 'warm' foods (Roys 2, p. 93).

the poisonous, even among groups who have no knowledge of fermented drinks or do not use honey in their preparation, is clearly illustrated by a Mundurucu myth, which has already been summarized and discussed (*RC*, pp. 267–8). I indicated at the time, however, that I was keeping a version of it in reserve to be examined in a different context. Here it is:

M₁₅₇ᵦ. Mundurucu. 'The origin of agriculture'

In former times, game and cultivated plants were unknown to the Mundurucu. They fed on wild tubers and tree fungi.

It was then that Karuebak, the mother of manioc, arrived and taught men the art of preparing it. One day, she ordered her nephew to clear an area of the forest, and she announced that soon bananas, cotton, caras (*Dioscorea*), maize, the three varieties of manioc, water-melons, tobacco and cane sugar would grow there. She ordered a ditch to be dug in the newly cleared area, and asked to be buried in it. Care should be taken, however, not to walk over her.

A few days later, Karuebak's nephew found that the plants listed by his aunt were growing on the place where she lay; however, he inadvertently walked on the hallowed ground, and the plants at once stopped growing. This determined the size to which they have grown ever since.

A sorcerer, displeased at not having been informed of the miracle, caused the old woman to perish in the hole where she lay. Since she was no longer there to advise them, the Indians ate manikuera raw, not knowing that this particular variety of manioc is poisonous and emetic in that form. They all died, and next morning went up into the sky where they became stars.

Other Indians, who had eaten manikuera first raw and then cooked, were transformed into honey flies. And those who licked the remains of the cooked manikuera became the kind of bees which produce bitter, emetic honey.

The first Mundurucu Indians who ate water-melons also died, since the fruit had been brought by the devil. This is why the Mundurucu call water-melons 'the devil's plants'. The surviving Indians kept the seeds and planted them, and the water-melons which grew from these seeds were harmless.

Since that time people have had no hesitation in eating them (Kruse 2, pp. 619–21. There is an almost identical variant in Kruse 3, pp. 919–20).

The version noted down by Murphy in 1952-3 and which I used in the previous volume is both remarkably similar to, and remarkably different from, those given by Kruse. The similarity lies in the contrast between two types of food, one consisting of the straightforwardly edible plants, and the other of the one or two plants which can be eaten only after undergoing a transformation. In the Murphy version, only timbó is mentioned as belonging to the second category; timbó is the fish poison the Mundurucu grow in their plantations and which, although not directly eaten as food, is consumed indirectly, as it were, in the form of the fish which it allows the Indians to catch in huge quantities. The Kruse versions quote timbó in the list of cultivated plants which were to grow from the body of old mother Karuebak, but do not enlarge upon its characteristics in the way the Murphy version does. Instead, they present two themes: the water-melons which only become edible in the second generation, after the seeds have been planted and cultivated by the Indians themselves, and the manikuera, which is also only suitable for consumption in a modified state, after it has been cooked in order to rid it of its toxicity.

Let us leave the water-melons aside for the moment (we shall come back to them later) and assume that the manikuera in M_{157b} takes the place of the timbó in M_{157}. The first men ate manikuera in three forms: raw, cooked and as left-overs, that is, without unduly straining the wording of the myth, in a rancid state and belonging to the category of the rotten. The eaters of raw manioc were changed into stars. It must be realized that, at the time, 'there was neither sky, nor Milky Way, nor Pleiades,' only mist and hardly any water. Because of the absence of sky, the souls of the dead vegetated under the roofs of the huts (Kruse 3, p. 917).

I have two observations to make in connection with this point. In the first place, the eating of raw poisonous manioc leads simultaneously to the appearance of the sky and to disjunction, for the first time, between the dead and the living. The disjunction in the form of stars is the result of an act of gluttony, since to avoid death, men ought to have postponed their meal instead of rushing at it. Here we find a link with a Bororo myth (M_{34}), which explains the origin of stars by the transformation of children who had been greedy. Now – and this is my second observation – I put forward elsewhere (RC, pp. 240-43) reasons for believing that these stars are the Pleiades. The specific mention of the Pleiades at the beginning of the Mundurucu myth gives weight to this suggestion, which will be given definitive confirmation later in the present volume. We shall in fact see that while the Pleiades represent, as it were, the first term in a series also including sweet honey and bitter honey, certain Amazonian myths associate the Pleiades directly with the poisonous honey which here occupies an intermediary position (that of poisoner) between the change undergone by the men who ate raw (poisoned) manioc and that undergone by those who ate cooked manioc and who are a danger neither to themselves nor to others and consequently occupy a neutral position between two strong positions.[3]

It follows that honey, like fish poison, occupies an ambiguous and equivocal position in the general scheme of vegetable foods. Timbó is both a poison and a means of procuring food; it is not directly edible in one form, but is indirectly edible in another. The distinction, stated explicitly in M_{157}, is replaced in M_{157b} by another more complex distinction, in which honey is both associated with, and opposed to, poison. The substitution of honey for fish poison in two very close variants of the same myth might well have some empirical foundation, since in one region of Brazil – the valley of the Rio São Francisco – the crushed nest of an aggressive species of melipona, which produces a rare and unpleasant-tasting honey (*Trigona ruficrus*), is used as fish poison with excellent results (Ihering, under 'irapoan'). But, apart from the fact that this method of fishing has not been described as existing among the Mundurucu, there is no need to assume that it was once more widespread in order to understand that the qualities attributed to honey by the myths constantly fluctuate between two extremes: either it is thought of as a food, whose richness and sweetness make it superior to all others, and therefore the object of ardent desire; or as a particularly treacherous poison, since the nature and seriousness of its effects are always unpredictable, depending, as they do, on the variety of the honey, where and when it was gathered and the circumstances in which it is eaten. But this imperceptible transition from the category of the delectable to that of the poisonous is not a feature peculiar to

---

[3] The order adopted by the myth: the poisoned > the neutral > the poisoners is puzzling only if the double contrast it observes is not noticed:

$$\begin{cases} raw : \text{mortal} \\ cooked : \text{non-mortal} \end{cases} \begin{cases} \text{fresh } (+) \\ \text{rancid } (-) \end{cases}$$

It is nevertheless remarkable that, in this pattern, the rotten appears as a *terminus ad quem* of the cooked, instead of the raw being the *terminus a quo* of the cooked, as in most of the myths of tropical America. In respect of this transformation, which is probably correlative with certain methods of preparing fermented drinks, cf. RC, pp. 159–60.

South American honey, since it can also be seen as a characteristic of tobacco and other plants with a similar narcotic effect.

Let us begin by noting that the South American Indians count tobacco as a 'food', along with honey and fish-poison. Colbacchini (2, p. 122, n. 4) observes that the Bororo 'do not use a special verb to denote the action of smoking a cigar; they say "okwage mea-ği", "eating a cigar" (literally "with the lips enjoy the cigar"), while the cigar itself is called "ké", "food" '. The Mundurucu have a myth the opening episode of which suggests the same link between tobacco and food:

M_{190}. *Mundurucu*. '*The insubordinate page*'

There lived in the village of Macuparí the chief of which was Karudaiibi, a man named Wakörebö. Now Wakörebö had a wife in the village of Uaradibika, and he went there often to visit her. On one occasion he arrived when the men were all absent and only the women were in the village. He repaired to the men's house and found there a young boy whom he ordered to bring fire to light his cigarette. The boy refused, saying impudently that cigarettes were not food. Wakörebö explained to him that for men cigarettes were food, but the boy still refused to perform the errand. This angered Wakörebö so much that he picked up a stone and hurled it at the boy, striking him in the head and killing him instantly (Murphy 1, p. 108; cf. Kruse 2, p. 318).

In spite of their uneven distribution, the two species of cultivated tobacco – *Nicotiana rustica* (from Canada to Chile) and *N. tabacum* (restricted to the Amazonian basin and the West Indies) – would both seem to have come originally from the Andes, where domestic tobacco had apparently been obtained by the cross-breeding of wild species. Paradoxically enough, it seems that tobacco was not smoked in this region in pre-Columbian times, and that it was originally chewed or taken as snuff. Very soon, however, it was replaced by the leaves of the coca plant. The paradox recurs in tropical America where, even at the present time, some tribes smoke tobacco, while adjoining tribes are unacquainted with it or prohibit its use. The Nambikwara are confirmed smokers, and are hardly ever seen without a cigarette in their mouths, or slipped under a cotton arm-band or into the pierced lobe of the ear. Yet their neighbours, the Tupi-Kawahib, have such a violent dislike for tobacco that they look disapprovingly at any visitors who dare to smoke in their presence, and even on occasions come to blows with them. Such differences are not infrequent in South America, where the use of tobacco was no doubt even more sporadic in the past.

Even in those areas where tobacco is known, it is consumed in very diverse ways. When it is smoked, pipes may be used, or it may be made into cigars or cigarettes; in Panama, the lit end of the cigarette was placed in the mouth of a smoker, who blew the smoke out so that his companions could inhale it through their cupped hands. It seems that, in the pre-Columbian era, the use of pipes was rarer than the making of cigars and cigarettes.

Tobacco was also ground to a powder and sniffed up through the nose, either by one person or two people together (thanks to a small instrument with a bent nozzle which made it possible for the tobacco to be blown into the nostrils of a companion, either in its pure state or blended with other narcotic plants such as *piptadenia*); or eaten in powder form, chewed, or sucked in the form of a sticky syrup, thickened by boiling and evaporation. In several regions of Montaña and Guiana, the Indians drink tobacco after boiling the leaves, or simply leaving them to soak.

The methods of using tobacco may be very varied, but the same is true of the intended result. Tobacco is consumed either individually or collectively: either in solitude, or by two or several people together; and either purely for pleasure or for ritualistic purposes which may have to do with magic or religion. A sick man is sometimes treated by being made to inhale tobacco fumes. Or someone about to be initiated, or to become a priest or healer is purified by being made to imbibe greater or lesser quantities of tobacco juice in order to induce vomiting, followed sometimes by loss of consciousness. Lastly, tobacco is used to make offerings of leaves or smoke by which it is hoped to attract the attention of the Spirits and communicate with them.

And so, like honey, tobacco, the profane use of which allows it to be classed as a food, can in its other functions possess the exactly opposite characteristic: it can act as an emetic and even as a poison. It has been confirmed that a Mundurucu myth about the origin of honey is careful to distinguish between these two aspects. The same is true of a myth about the origin of tobacco, belonging to the Iranxé or Münkü, a small tribe who live in a region to the south of the Mundurucu:

M_{191}. *Iranxé (Münkü). 'The origin of tobacco'*

A man had behaved badly towards another man, who was determined to take his revenge. Using a fruit-gathering expedition as a pretext, the latter got his enemy to climb a tree, and there he left him, after removing the pole that had been used to make the ascent.

The prisoner, who was starving, thirsty and emaciated, caught sight of a monkey and called to it for help; the monkey agreed to bring him some water, but claimed to be too weak to help him get down. A thin, foul-smelling urubu (vulture), succeeded in rescuing him and then took him back to its home. It was the master of tobacco, of which it possessed two kinds, one good and the other poisonous. It presented them to its protégé so that he could learn to smoke the former and use the latter as a means of revenge.

When the hero returned to the village, he gave the bad tobacco to his persecutor who was seized with a fit of giddiness and changed into an ant-eater. The hero went after him and, having come upon him unawares in broad daylight when he was asleep, killed him. He invited his benefactor, the urubu, to eat its fill of the decayed corpse (Moura, pp. 52–3).

The above myth, of which we possess only this one obscure and elliptical version, is extremely interesting on several counts. It is a myth about the origin of tobacco which, as I had already postulated (and confirmed in the case of the Chaco myths on the same subject), reflects myths about the origin of fire: the hero is a fruit-picker (homologous with the bird-nester) stranded at the top of a tree and saved by a fearsome animal (ferocious like the jaguar, or revolting like the urubu) in which the hero bravely places his trust, and which is master of a cultural advantage, as yet unknown to man, that it bestows upon him: cooking fire in the one instance, tobacco in the other, which we know to be a food like cooked meat, although the way in which it is consumed places it beyond cooking.

However, the Chaco myths we used in the construction of system S_3 (origin of tobacco) were in the main a reproduction of the myths in S_1 (origin of fire), whereas M_{191} provides further evidence by being a still closer reflection of S_{-1}: i.e., the Bororo myth about the origin of water (M_1).

Let us begin by establishing this point. It will be remembered that, unlike the Ge myths about the origin of fire, the Bororo myth about the origin of wind and rain (M_1) begins with an incestuous act committed by an adolescent boy who rapes his mother and whose father is resolved on revenge. The Iranxé myth does not refer explicitly to incest, but the expression used by the informant in his dialectal Portuguese, 'Um homem fêz desonestidade, o outro ficou furioso', clearly seems to refer to some kind of sexual misdemeanour, since the normal meaning of the word 'desonestidade' in the inland districts of Brazil implies some act contrary to the rules of decency.

There is nothing in the Ge myths about the origin of fire which corresponds to the helpful monkey episode in M_{191}, but it is reminiscent of the series of three helpful animals in M_1 which help the hero to achieve success in the expedition to the aquatic realm of the souls. The link between the two myths is confirmed when we see that, in M_1, the hero overcomes the presence of water (he succeeds in crossing it), while in M_{191} he overcomes the absence of water, since the monkey brings him some kind of fruit already broken open and full of refreshing juice to alleviate his thirst. When I compared M_1 with a Sherente myth (M_{124}), which also has a thirsty hero who is helped by animals, I showed (*RC*, pp. 205–6) that there was a transformation allowing the transition from the monkey to the pigeon, which occupies a central position among the three helpful animals in M_1.

The jaguar, which plays the main role in system S_1 (M_7–M_{12}), is absent from M_1 and M_{191}. In both cases, it is replaced by the urubu or urubus which come to the hero's aid.

At this point, however, the problem becomes more complex. The urubus in M_1 behave ambiguously: to begin with, they show no pity (and even feed on the hero's flesh), and only later do they behave with compassion (by bringing the hero down to ground level). The same ambiguous behaviour occurs in M_{191}, but this time the animal is the monkey. To begin with, it shows compassion (by quenching the hero's thirst) but later behaves callously (by refusing to take the hero back to the ground). From the point of view of symmetry, the urubu in M_{191} corresponds more closely to the pigeon in M_1 (one is related to air, the other to water) as regards the non-ambiguous nature of their respective behaviour, since the urubu gives the hero tobacco, and the pigeon makes him a present of the rattle, and – as I shall establish later – tobacco and the rattle are linked.

There is no doubt, then, that the transition from one myth to the other is possible, although it can only be effected by means of a series of chiasmi:

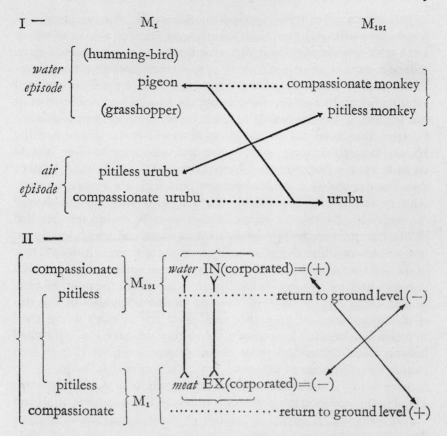

Finally, we can observe one final point of resemblance between M_{191} and M_1. In both myths (and contrary to what occurs in those in system S_1), the hero takes his revenge on his persecutor by transforming *himself* into an animal (a species of deer in M_1) or by changing the *persecutor* into an animal (an ant-eater in M_{191}). The change is either self-imposed or imposed on another, but it always ends with the death of the opponent and his being devoured, either in a fresh or rotten state, by an aquatic/cannibal (M_1) or by an aerial/carrion-eater (M_{191}). A good deal might be said about the deer/ant-eater contrast, since I have established elsewhere that these two species form a pair with the jaguar (which replaces one or other of them in S_1): either diachronically (since mythical deer were man-eating jaguars), or synchronically (since the ant-eater is the opposite of a jaguar). For more details about this two-fold argument, cf. *RC*, pp. 138–9, 188–9.

The fact that the Iranxé version in S_3 and the Bororo version in S_{-1} are so similar in structure raises ethnographical problems to which I can refer only briefly. Until very recently the vast zone stretching to the north-west of what used to be Bororo territory, between the sources of the Tapajoz and those of the Xingu, was one of the least explored areas of Brazil. In 1938–9, when I happened to be near the sources of the Tapajoz, it was impossible to reach Iranxé territory, which was not far from that inhabited by the Nambikwara, because – although the Iranxé themselves were said to be peace-loving – another hostile community, the Beiços of Pau, barred the way (L.-S. 3, p. 285). Since then, contact has been established, not only with the Iranxé, but also with several tribes – the Caiabi, the Canoeiro and the Cintalarga[4] (Dornstauder, Saake 2) – which, if they can be completely studied before they die out, will probably help to transform such ideas as we have at present about the relationship between Bororo culture and that of the Ge tribes, more especially the Tupi farther north. It has long been common practice to consider the Bororo solely from the point of view of their affinities with their western and southern neighbours. But this is chiefly because we knew nothing about the cultures along their northern borders. In this respect, the affinity we have just confirmed between their myths and those of the Iranxé, suggests that Bororo culture was also open to influences from the Amazonian basin.

Since I must, unfortunately, restrict myself to a formal analysis, I shall simply mention two features common to the armatures of M_1 and

[4] This tribe is in the headlines at the time of writing, as can be seen from the following three-column article in *France-Soir* (March 14th–15th, 1965):

120 BRAZILIANS SET UPON BY
INDIANS WITH A TASTE FOR HUMAN FLESH
(From our special permanent correspondent, Jean-Gérard Fleury.)

'Rio de Janeiro, March 13th (by cable). Alarm in Brazil: armed with bows and arrows, Indians of the formidable cannibal tribe known as "broad belts" are besieging Vilh-Na (*sic*: Vilhena?), a village with a population of 120 inhabitants which lies off the Belem–Brasilia road (?).

'An air-force plane has flown over the area to drop antidotes against the curare which the Indians use to poison the tips of their arrows.

'The "broad-belt" Indians, who are traditionally partial to human flesh, recently tried out a new recipe: they grilled a captured *gaucho*, after smearing him all over with wild honey.'

Whether or not this story is of local origin, it provides admirable illustration of the fact that the native South Americans, whether they be peasants of the Brazilian hinterland or Indians, regard honey as an extreme food, since its use in conjunction with that other extreme food, human flesh, represents a peak of horror that ordinary cannibalism would perhaps be incapable of inspiring. The Guayaki of Paraguay, who are cannibals, believe there are two kinds of food which are too strong to be eaten in their pure state – honey, to which they add water, and human flesh, which must be stewed with palm kernels (Clastres).

M_{191}, which help to explain why they are developed in the same way. Both myths are obviously etiological in character. They deal either with the origin of celestial water which puts out domestic fires, thus causing men to regress to a *pre-culinary* state, or rather (since the myth does not claim to explain the origin of cooking) to an *infra-culinary* state; or with the origin of tobacco, that is, a food which has to be burnt before it can be consumed, and whose introduction consequently implies an *ultra-culinary* use of cooking fire. M_1 therefore brings the human race back *to the hither side* of the domestic hearth, whereas M_{191} takes it *beyond*.

Both myths are off-centre in relation to the institution of the domestic hearth, and also resemble each other in another way, which similarly distinguishes them from the myths grouped together in S_1. Etiologically, they run along parallel and complementary lines. M_1 explains simultaneously how the hero becomes *master of fire* (his hearth-fire being the only one not put out by the storm), and his enemy (along with all the other inhabitants in the village) the *victim of water*. M_{191} explains simultaneously how the hero becomes *master of good tobacco*, and his enemy the *victim of bad tobacco*. But in both myths, only the appearance and consequences of the negative term are commented upon at length (involving in each instance the death of the hero's opponent), since, in M_1, the swamp where the piranhas live is a function of the rainy season, just as, in M_{191}, the transformation of the culprit into an ant-eater is a function of the enchanted tobacco, whereas the positive term receives virtually no mention.

But there is more to it than that. The pair of opposites: water $(-)$/fire $(+)$ in M_1 corresponds, as we have just seen, to the pair of opposites tobacco $(-)$/tobacco $(+)$ in M_{191}, and we know already that the latter pair of opposites also exists in the Bororo myths since they distinguish between good and bad tobacco, although the difference is based not on the nature of the tobacco but on the method of consumption:[5] tobacco, the smoke of which is exhaled, establishes a beneficent form of communication with the Spirits (whereas, in M_{191}, it is the consequence of a communication of this kind); tobacco, the smoke of which is *inhaled*, leads to the transformation of humans into animals (otters with very small eyes in M_{27}), which is precisely the fate suffered in M_{191} by the man who eats bad tobacco (he is changed into an ant-eater, an animal which, throughout the length and breadth of

[5] Cf. *RC* where I stressed on several occasions (pp. 143, 194, 272) that Bororo mythology tends to be on the side of culture.

Brazil, is frequently described in myths as a 'blocked' animal, i.e. with no mouth or no anus). In the Bororo myths, good tobacco is linked with fire (it comes from the ashes of a snake) and bad tobacco is linked with water (it is discovered in a fish's belly and causes its victims to be changed into otters, aquatic animals). The correspondence between the myths is therefore fully proved:

Iranxé [tobacco (+) : (−)] :: Bororo [(M₁, fire (+) : water (−)) :: (M₂₆–M₂₇, tobacco (+) : tobacco (−))]

Iranxé $[\text{tobacco } (+) : (-)]$ :: Bororo $[(M_1, \text{fire } (+) : \text{water } (-)) :: (M_{26}-M_{27}, \text{tobacco } (+) : \text{tobacco } (-))]$

Finally, remembering the distinction, congruous with the preceding ones, between good tobacco which is pungent (*qui pique*) and bad tobacco which is not pungent, a distinction that the Bororo myth, M_{26}, introduces as a subsidiary theme, we arrive at the final confirmation of the fact that, like honey, tobacco occupies an ambiguous and equivocal position between food and poison:

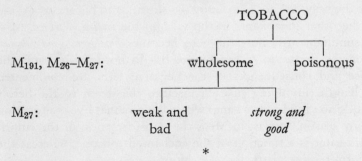

At the beginning of this book, I stressed the doubly paradoxical, yet very real nature, of the contrast in European cultures between tobacco and honey. With us, one term is indigenous, the other exotic; one very ancient, the other barely four centuries old. The existence, in South America, of a correlational and oppositional connection between honey and tobacco is to be explained, it would seem, by precisely opposite reasons. There, honey and tobacco are both indigenous, and the origin of both is lost in the dim and remote past.[6] Honey and tobacco are therefore bracketed together, not as they are in European societies because of an external contrast which underlines their complementary

[6] I am restricting my remarks for the moment to tropical America. The place occupied by honey in the thought and mythology of the Indians of North America raises problems which will be dealt with in a different context. As regards Central America and Mexico, where agriculture was highly developed in the pre-Columbian period, the observation and analysis of still surviving rites has as yet hardly begun, although their rich complexity is hinted at in the few references to them to be found in ancient or contemporary literature.

properties, but rather because of an internal contrast between opposite properties which honey and tobacco each conjugate separately and independently, since – within different registers and on different levels – each seems perpetually to oscillate between two states: that of being a supreme food and that of being a deadly poison. Furthermore, in between these two states can be found a whole series of intermediary forms, and it is particularly difficult to gauge the transitions from one to another since they depend on minute, and often imperceptible, differences relating to the quality of the commodity, the time of the harvest, the quantity consumed or the time which elapses before consumption.

These inherent uncertainties may be accompanied by others. The physiological effect of tobacco is partly that of a stimulant and partly that of a narcotic. Honey too may be a stimulant or a drug. In South America, honey and tobacco share these properties with other natural products or prepared foods. Let us consider first the case of honey. It has already been noted that South American varieties of honey are unstable and that, if they are mixed with water and left for a few days, or even a few hours, they begin to ferment spontaneously. One observer noted this phenomenon during the honey feast of the Tembé Indians: 'The honey, mixed with wax from the comb and soaked in water, ferments in the sun … I was offered some (of this intoxicating drink); although at first I was reluctant to try it, I found it had a sweet and acid taste which was very pleasant' (Rodrigues 4, p. 32).

Whether it is eaten fresh, or in a spontaneously fermented form, honey is, then, akin to the innumerable fermented liquors which South American Indians make with manioc, maize, palm-tree sap or fruit of various kinds. In this connection, it is significant that the deliberate and systematic preparation of a fermented honey drink – let us call it mead, for the sake of simplicity – seems to have existed only to the west and south of the Amazonian basin, among the Tupi-Guarani, the southern Ge tribes, the Botocudo, the Charrua and almost all the Chaco tribes. This crescent-shaped area coincides approximately with the southern limits of beer-making with manioc and maize, while in the Chaco it borders on the zone where beer is made from algaroba (*Prosopis* sp.), which is a local development (Figure 3). It is conceivable then that mead was regarded as a substitute for manioc beer and, to a lesser degree, for maize beer. On the other hand, the map clearly shows another contrasting feature between the southern zone, where mead is predominant, and the discontinuous but essentially northern zones, where what could be called tobacco 'honey' is made, that is, where tobacco is soaked or boiled and then imbibed in a liquid or syrupy form. Just as it is important to distinguish between the two ways of consuming honey, in the fresh or the fermented form, the forms of tobacco consumption, in spite of their great variety, can be reduced to two main categories: tobacco can be consumed dry, when it is taken as snuff or smoked and, in that case, it is similar to several vegetable narcotics: *Piptadenia, Banisteriopsis, Datura,* etc. (with some of which it is occasionally mixed); or else it can be consumed moist, as a kind of jam or potion. It follows that the pairs of opposites which I used at the beginning to define the relationship between honey and tobacco (*cooked/raw, moistened/burnt, infra-culinary/super-culinary,* etc.) express only part of the truth. In reality, the situation is much more complex, since honey can exist in two forms: fresh or fermented; and tobacco, in several forms: burnt or moistened, and in the latter case, raw or cooked. It is to be expected, then, that at the two opposite ends of the semantic field under investigation, the myths about the origin of honey or tobacco, which, as I have already postulated and to some extent verified, are reduplicated in terms of the contrast between 'good' and 'bad' honey, 'good' and 'bad' tobacco, should show a second line of division, situated along a different axis, and determined not by differences affecting *natural properties,* but by differences relating to *cultural customs.* Finally, since on the one hand, 'good' honey is *sweet,* while 'good' tobacco is *strong,* and on the other hand, 'honey' in the literal sense can be eaten *raw,* whereas in most cases tobacco 'honey' is the result of the tobacco having been previously *cooked,* it is to be expected that the transformational relationships between the various types of 'honey' myths and 'tobacco' myths should take the form of a chiasmus.

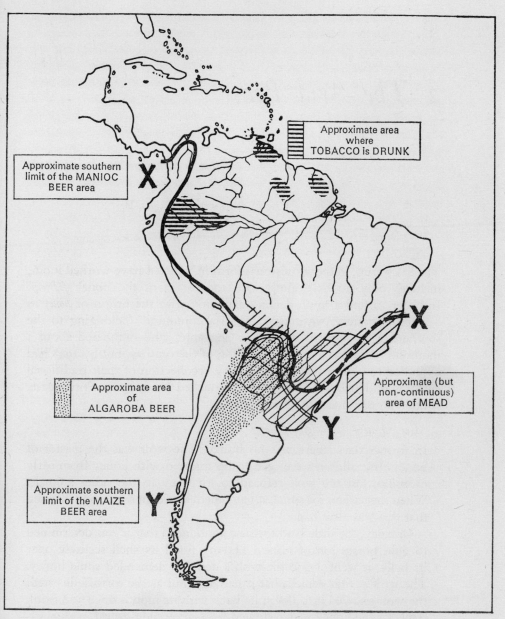

Figure 3. Beer, mead and tobacco liquor in South America. (Redrawn from *Handbook of South American Indians*, Vol. 5, pp. 533, 540.)

2 *The Arid Beast*

*Venit enim tempus quo torridus aestuat aer
incipit et sicco fervere terra Cane.*

Propertius, *Elegies*, II,
XXVIII, vv. 3–4

The S₋₃ group, in the provisional form in which I have worked it out, includes only myths dealing with the origin of the honey *festival*. In order to find a myth dealing explicitly with the origin of *honey* as a natural product, we must refer to a community belonging to the southern Mato Grosso, the Ofaié-Chavanté, who numbered about a thousand individuals at the beginning of the century, but by 1948 had dwindled to a mere handful with little recollection of their traditional customs and beliefs. Their myths, couched in dialectal Portuguese, contain a great many obscure passages.

M_{192}. Ofaié. 'The origin of honey'

In former days, there was no honey. The wolf was the master of honey. Its children were seen to be smeared with honey from early morning, but the wolf refused to give any to the other animals. When they asked for some, it gave them araticum fruits, and claimed that this was all it had.

One day, the little land tortoise announced that it was determined to gain possession of honey. Having fitted its shell securely over its belly, it went inside the wolf's den and demanded some honey. The wolf at first denied that it had any, but as the tortoise insisted, the wolf allowed it to lie on its back with its mouth open and drink freely of the honey which flowed from a hanging gourd.

This was just a trick. Taking advantage of the fact that the tortoise was totally absorbed in its feast, the wolf got its children to gather dead wood to make a fire around the tortoise, in the hope that it could be eaten when it was cooked. But to no avail: the tortoise continued to drink its fill of the honey. It was the wolf which found the intense heat hard to bear. When the gourd was empty, the tortoise calmly got up, scattered the wood cinders, and told the wolf it ought now to give honey to all the animals.

The wolf fled. Under the tortoise's command, the animals cornered it and the prea lit a bush-fire round the place where it had taken refuge. As the circle of fire grew smaller, the animals wondered if the wolf was really there: only a partridge flew out from the flames. But the tortoise, which had continued to watch the spot where the wolf had taken refuge knew that the wolf had changed into a partridge.

So it continued to keep its eyes fixed on the partridge until the bird was out of sight. On the tortoise's orders, the animals rushed off after it. The chase lasted several days. Each time they caught up with the bird, it flew off again. After climbing onto another animal's head to get a better view, the tortoise saw the partridge change into a bee. The tortoise planted a stake to show the direction taken by the bee. The chase was resumed, but just as ineffectively. The animals had by now completely lost heart. 'No, no,' said the tortoise, 'we have been advancing for only three months and we have covered almost half the distance. Look at the stake there, behind you: it is showing us the right direction.' The animals turned round and saw that the stake had changed into a pindo palm tree (*Cocos* sp.).

They continued on and on. Finally, the tortoise announced that they would arrive at their goal the next day. And next day, sure enough, they saw the bees' 'house', the entrance of which was guarded by poisonous wasps. One after another, the birds tried to approach the house, but the wasps attacked them 'by squirting them with their fluid' and the birds fell to the ground in a daze and died. However, the smallest of them, a woodpecker (or a humming-bird?) succeeded in getting past the wasps and taking the honey. 'Well, my son,' said the tortoise, 'now we have some honey. But there is very little of it; if we eat it, there will soon be none left.' It took the honey, gave each animal a cutting (*uma muda*) so that it could make a house for itself and plant the honey. They would come back when there was enough honey for all.

A long time afterwards, the animals began to be anxious about their honey plantations, and they asked the 'maritaca' to go and see what was happening. But the heat in the honey plantations was so intense that the 'maritaca' could not get near. The next animals who agreed to make the attempt preferred to stop on the way: the parrot on a fruit tree (*mangaba*: *Hancornia speciosa*), the blue macaw in a pleasant forest; and they blamed their failure on the scorching heat. Finally, the parakeet flew so high, almost as high as the sky, that it succeeded in reaching the plantations, which were laden with honey.

When the leader of the animals had been informed, he decided to go to the plantations and see for himself. He inspected the houses: many people had eaten the honey they had been given to plant, and so had none left; others had enough, buried at ground level and easy to extract. 'This cannot last much longer,' said the leader; 'we shall soon be without honey. There is very little, in fact, hardly any at all. Wait a little and there will be enough honey for everybody.' In the meantime he had released the bees, which flew away into the forest.

Later, he called the inhabitants together and told them to take their hatchets and set off in search of honey: 'Now the forest is full of all kinds of honey: bora, mandaguari, jati, mandassaia, cagafogo – absolutely every variety. All you have to do is go and look for it, and if you do not care for one particular kind of honey, you can move on to the next tree, where you will find another. You can collect as much as you like; the supply will never be exhausted, provided you only take as much as you can carry away in the gourds and other containers you must take with you. But what you cannot take away must be left where it was for the next time, after you have carefully closed up the opening (made in the tree with an axe).'

Since then, because of this, we have had enough honey. When people go to clear the forest, they find honey. In one tree there is bora honey, in another mandaguari honey and in another jati honey. There is every variety (Ribeiro 2, pp. 124–6).

Although this is a very long myth, I have translated it almost literally, not only because its obscurity is such that any attempt to shorten it would have very soon made it incomprehensible, but also on account of its importance and the wealth of detail it contains. It expresses the standard native doctrine in respect of honey and, for this reason, dictates how all the myths to be examined subsequently should be interpreted. The reader should therefore not be surprised if the analysis of the myth proves to be difficult, and forces me temporarily to disregard certain aspects, and proceed by successive approximations, rather as if it were necessary to stand well back from the myth and reconnoitre it in outline before exploring each detail.

Let us, therefore, go straight to the main point. What is the myth about? It describes the time when animals, man's ancestors, were not in possession of honey, the form in which they first obtained it, and how they gave up this form in favour of the one that men are now familiar with.

It is not surprising that the acquisition of honey should go back to the mythical period when there was no difference between animals and men, since honey is a wild product belonging to the category of nature. As such, it must have become part of the heritage of humanity when men were still living in a 'state of nature', before any distinction was made between nature and culture, or between men and animals.

It is also quite normal that the myth should describe the original honey as a plant, which germinates, grows and ripens. As we have already seen, in the pattern of Indian thought, honey is considered as part of the vegetable kingdom; M_{192} provides fresh confirmation of this.

Nevertheless, we are not dealing here with any ordinary plant, since the first kind of honey was cultivated, and the development outlined by the myth consisted in turning it into wild honey. Here we touch on the essential point, since the originality of M_{192} is that it takes the reverse approach to that adopted by the myths about the introduction of cultivated plants, which I grouped together and studied in *The Raw and the Cooked* under numbers M_{87}–M_{92} (cf., too, M_{108} and M_{110}–M_{118}). These myths refer to a time when men knew nothing of agriculture and fed on leaves, tree fungi and rotten wood before the existence of maize was revealed to them by a celestial woman, who had taken the form of an opossum. The maize was like a tree in appearance, and grew wild in the forest. But men made the mistake of felling the tree, and they then had to share out the seeds, clear the ground for cultivation and sow maize, because the dead tree was not sufficient for their needs. This gave rise, on the one hand, to the different varieties of cultivated species (in the beginning, they had all been together on one tree) and, on the other hand, to the differences between peoples, languages and customs, which occurred when the first men dispersed in various directions.

In M_{192}, everything happens in like manner, but the other way round. Men do not need to learn about agriculture, since, as animals, they are already in possession of it and can apply it to the production

of honey, from the moment the latter falls into their hands. But cultivated honey has two disadvantages: either men do not resist the temptation to devour their honey 'in the blade', or the honey plants grow
well and are so easily harvested – in the same way as plants grown in
fields – that excessive consumption exhausts productive capacity.

As the myth then sets out to demonstrate systematically, the transformation of cultivated honey into wild honey removes these disadvantages and gives men a triple security. First, the bees become wild
and diversify into the various species; this means that there will be
several varieties of honey instead of one. Next, honey will be more
plentiful. Finally, the greed of the honey-gatherers will be limited by
the quantities it is possible to bring back; the excess honey will remain
in the nest, where it will keep until the next gathering. There is, therefore, a three-fold gain – in quality, quantity and lastingness.

There is no doubt where the originality of this myth lies: it is, one
might say, 'anti-neolithic' in outlook, and pleads in favour of an
economy based on collecting and gathering, to which it attributes the
same virtues of diversity, abundance and preservation claimed by most
of the other myths for the reverse outlook, which is a consequence of
humanity's adopting the arts of civilization. And it is honey which
provides the occasion for this extraordinary reversal. In this sense, a
myth about the origin of honey also refers to its loss.[7] Once it becomes
wild, honey is half lost, but it has to be lost in order to be saved. So
powerful is its gastronomical appeal that, were it too easily obtained,
men would partake of it too freely until the supply was exhausted.
Through the medium of the myth, honey is saying to man: 'You would
not find me, if you had not first looked for me.'

We can, then, at this point, make a curious observation, which will
recur later in connection with other myths. In the case of M_{188} and
M_{189}, we were dealing with genuine myths of origin, but they were
not wholly satisfactory, because they related to the honey festival, and
not to honey itself. And now we find ourselves faced with a new
myth concerned with honey proper, but which, in spite of appearances,
is not so much a myth about the origin of honey as about its loss, or
more precisely, one which is intent on transforming an illusory origin

[7] Compare with the following passage (M_{192b}) from the creation myth of the Caduveo:
'When the caracara (a species of falcon and an incarnation of the deceiver) saw the honey
forming in the huge gourds where it was to be had for the taking, he said to Gô-noêno-
hôdi, the demiurge: "No, this is not right, this is not the way it should be, no! Put the
honey in the middle of the tree so that men are forced to dig it out. Otherwise the lazy
creatures will not work" ' (Ribeiro 1, p. 143).

(since the initial possession of honey was tantamount to a lack of honey) into an advantageous loss (men being assured of having honey, as soon as they agree to relinquish it). The succeeding chapters of this volume will throw light on the paradox, which must be accepted as a structural feature of myths with honey as their theme.

Let us now return to the text of M_{192}. The plantations, where the primordial beasts cultivated their honey, had one extraordinary feature: the heat there was so intense that no one could approach, and only after several fruitless attempts did the animals succeed in finding a way in. In order to interpret this episode, we might be tempted to proceed by drawing an analogy with the myths about the origin of cultivated plants which explain that, before men were acquainted with vegetable foods, cooked in accordance with culture, they fed on vegetable matter which had rotted in accordance with nature. If the cultivated honey of the heroic ages is the opposite of the wild honey of today, and if, as has already been established, real honey denotes the category of the moist in correlation with, and in contrast to, tobacco which denotes the category of the burnt, must we not reverse the relationship and move the honey of olden days into the category of the dry and the burnt?

There is nothing in the myths to rule out such an interpretation, but I believe it to be incomplete, because it disregards an aspect of the problem to which, on the contrary, the honey myths constantly call attention. As I have already stressed, honey has several paradoxical features, not the least of which is the fact that, although it has a connotation with humidity in its relationship to tobacco, it is constantly associated in the myths with the dry season, for the simple reason that, like most wild products, honey is gathered and eaten fresh during that season.

There are innumerable indications to this effect. Both the northern Tupi tribes and the Karaja used to celebrate a honey festival which took place during the harvest period, that is, during August (Machado, p. 21). In the province of Chiquitos in Bolivia, wild honey was collected from June to September (d'Orbigny, quoted by Schwartz 2, p. 158). Among the Siriono of lower Bolivia honey 'is most abundant in the dry season, after the flowering of the plants and trees; therefore the drinking bouts (the drink is mead mixed with maize beer) occur during the months of August, September, October and November' (Holmberg, pp. 37–8). The Tacana Indians collect bees' wax during the dry season (H.-H., pp. 335–6). In Guayaki territory in eastern Paraguay there is no clearly defined dry season: there is, however, a cold season, at the beginning of which, in June and July, abundance of honey coincides with the distinctive colouring taken on by a certain creeper (timbó) which is said to be 'pregnant with honey' (Clastres). The Tereno of the southern Mato Grosso, in preparation for their Oheokoti festival at the beginning of April, used to devote a whole month to the gathering of large quantities of honey (Altenfelder Silva, pp. 356, 364).

We have seen that the Tembé and the Tenetehara begin collecting for their honey festival in March or April, that is, at the end of the rainy season (see above, p. 32). The myth we are now dealing with is less explicit, but even so contains two indications to this effect. The last part makes it clear that it is when people go to clear the land for cultivation that they find honey. In central Brazil, clearing operations are carried out after the rainy season, so that the felled wood can dry off for two or three months before being burnt. The sowing and planting are done immediately afterwards so as to take advantage of the first rains. Also, the scorching heat in the place where the cultivated honey is growing is described in terms of the dry season: *la tem secca brava*, 'the drought is severe'. This leads me to conclude that the old honey and the present-day honey are to be thought of not so much as antithetical terms but as terms of unequal force. Cultivated honey was a super-honey: plentiful, concentrated in one area and easy to harvest. And just as these advantages led to corresponding disadvantages, such as eating too much too quickly and using up the supply, so in this context the reference to honey in hyperbolic terms results in equally hyperbolic climatic conditions. Since honey is collected during the dry season, super-honey calls for a hyper-dry season which, like hyper-abundance and hyper-accessibility, means that enjoyment of it is practically ruled out.

The behaviour of the parrot and the macaw provides an argument in support of this second interpretation. They were sent by their companions to look for the honey, but chose to stop, one on a mangaba plant (a savannah fruit, which ripens during the dry season), the other in the refreshing shade of the forest. Both, therefore, lingered on the way in order to take advantage of the last amenities of the rainy season. The attitude of these two birds thus recalls that of the raven in the Greek myth about the origin of the constellation Corvus, which also lingers near seeds or fruit (which would ripen only at the end of the dry season), instead of bringing back the water requested by Apollo.

As a result, the raven is doomed to endure everlasting thirst; previously, he had a splendid voice, but from now on only a harsh croak was to emerge from his parched throat. It should be remembered that, according to the Tembé and Tenetehara myths about the origin of (the) honey (festival), the macaws formerly used to feed on honey, and honey is a dry season 'beverage', like the chthonian well-water in the Greek myth, as opposed to celestial water which is associated with a different period of the year. Perhaps, then, this episode of the Ofaié myth is meant to explain by omission, why the parrot and the macaw, which are fruit-eating birds, do not (or no longer) eat honey, although honey is considered to be a fruit.

I have no hesitation in thus comparing the Indian myth and the Greek myth, since in *The Raw and the Cooked*, I established that the latter was a dry-season myth and, without postulating the existence of some ancient, and unproven, link between the Old and New Worlds, I was able to show that the use of an astronomical coding imposed such strict limitations on mythic thought that it was understandable, on a purely formal level, that the myths of the Old and New World should, in certain instances, reproduce each other either directly or by inversion.

The Ofaié myth presents the 'maritaca's' failure as preceding that of the parrot and the macaw. The meaning of the word 'maritaca' is uncertain; it could be either an abbreviation of 'maritacáca', which means skunk, or a dialectal form of 'maitáca', a small parrot of the genus *Pionus*. It is difficult to be definite, especially since there exists an Amazonian form: 'maitacáca', of the word for skunk (Stradelli 1), which is identical with the name of the bird, apart from the repetition of the last syllable. In support of the theory that the word is a distortion of 'maitáca', it can be pointed out that the Ofaié, in referring to the skunk, seem to use a similar, although slightly different, word: 'jara-tatáca' (M75), frequent evidence of which is found in Brazil (cf. Ihering, under 'jaritacáca, jaritatáca'), and that the other animals in the same sequence are also parrots. As will appear subsequently, the skunk interpretation is not to be ruled out entirely, but the transition maitáca > maritaca is more likely from the phonetic point of view than the loss of the reduplicated syllable, and so it is this interpretation I propose to adopt.

Let us suppose, therefore, that four parrots are involved. It is immediately obvious that they can be classified in several ways. The myth stresses that the parakeet, which was successful in its mission, is the smallest of them: 'Aí foi o periquitinho, êste pequeno, voôu bem alto para cima, quasi chegou no céu ... ' It is, then, because of its small size and lightness that the parakeet can fly higher than other birds of the same species and succeeds in avoiding the scorching heat which prevails in the honey plantations. On the other hand, the macaw which tries just before the parakeet is, as is made quite clear in the text, an 'arára azul' (*Anodorhynchus hyacinthinus*): it therefore belongs to the largest variety of a family which itself includes the biggest of the psittacidae (cf. Ihering, under 'arára-una'). The parrot which has its turn before the macaw is smaller in size than the macaw; and the maitáca, which comes first, is smaller than the parrot although bigger than the parakeet which closes the cycle. So, the three birds which fail are absolutely bigger, and the one which succeeds absolutely smaller, and the first three are graded according to size, so that the major contrast is between the macaw and the parakeet:

bigger: *smaller:*

maitáca < parrot < macaw / parakeet (< maitáca)

It should now be noted that, within the series of bigger birds, the parrot and the macaw form a functional pair: they do not even attempt to carry out their mission and prefer to take refuge, one in the *savannah*, the other in the *forest*, in close proximity to evidence of the recent end of the rainy season: juicy fruits and cool shade, whereas the other two birds are the only ones which definitely brave the drought and testify, one to its 'dry' aspect: the unbearable heat, and the other to its moist aspect: the abundance of honey.

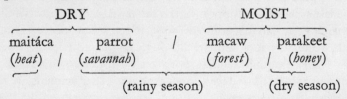

Finally, if we adopt a third point of view, and think in terms of the result of the birds' mission, a different principle of classification becomes evident. Only the first and last birds bring back an actual report on the situation, although one item of information is negative in character (the bird explains that the intense heat makes it impossible to reach the plantations), and the other positive (the abundance of honey is an incentive to the animals to brave the obstacle). On the other hand, the two birds which occupy a middle position (both in size and in the narrative sequence) do not bother to go and see for themselves and merely repeat what has already been said: they therefore bring back no information:

$$\underbrace{\text{maitáca} \ / \quad \underbrace{\text{parrot} \qquad \text{macaw}}_{\text{no information}} \ / \quad \text{parakeet}}$$
$$(-) \qquad (o) \qquad (o) \qquad (+)$$

maitáca / parrot   macaw / parakeet
(−)   (o)   (o)   (+)

no information   real information

I have spent some time over the sequence of the four birds, and for a specific purpose. The analysis of the sequence makes it possible to settle a methodological point. It shows that a sequence which the old mythography would have interpreted as a semantic redundance and a rhetorical device must, like the myth as a whole, be taken absolutely *seriously*. We are not dealing with a gratuitous enumeration, which can be dismissed with brief reference to the mystic connotation of the figure 4 in American thought. No doubt the connotation exists; but it is systematically exploited to build up a multi-dimensional system allowing the combination of synchronic and diachronic attributes, relating in the one case to structure, in the other to events, to absolute properties and relative properties, essences and functions. The demonstration I have just carried out not only throws light on the nature of mythic thought and the mechanism of its operations, by clarifying the procedures it uses to integrate methods of classification, some depending on a concept of continuity and progress (the arranging of animals in order of size, or according to the amount of information supplied, etc.), others on discontinuity and antithesis (the contrasting of largest and smallest, dry and moist, savannah and forest, etc.); it also establishes and illustrates an interpretation. The sequence just deciphered turns out to be more complex than at first appeared, and this complexity makes it possible to understand why birds of the same family which we mistakenly believed to be distinguished only by their size, and solely for the purpose of creating a fairly commonplace dramatic effect (the smallest and weakest succeeds where bigger and stronger birds fail), are also vehicles for the expression of contrasts which, as I have shown on different grounds, are an intrinsic part of the armature of the myth.

I propose, then, to apply the same kind of exhaustive analysis to the part played by two other characters: the prea and the tortoise. But before solving the problem they present, I must draw attention to one particular point.

The episode of the four birds, which relates to the *collecting* of *cultivated* honey, reproduces the scenario of a previous episode which dealt with the *planting* of *wild* honey: in both instances, one or more abortive attempts are made before success is finally achieved. 'Tudo que é passarinho', so birds too, tried to conquer wild honey, but they were prevented from doing so by the wasps, which were guarding it and which savagely slaughtered them. Only the last and smallest of the birds succeeded: 'êste ... bem pequeno, êste menorzinho dêles', and about its identity we unfortunately cannot be certain, since the only version we possess hesitates between the woodpecker and the humming-bird. Whatever the species, the two episodes are obviously parallel.

Now, in the second episode, cultivated honey is passively unattainable because of the heat, just as in the first episode wild honey is actively unattainable because of the wasps. But the wasps' warlike disposition is expressed in a very curious form in the myth: 'They attacked, by squirting out their fluid (*largavam aquela agua dêles*) and the animals fell down in a daze and died.' This episode may seem paradoxical in two respects. First, I have shown (*RC*, p. 314) that there is a contrast between vermin and poisonous insects, congruous with that between the rotten and the burnt, and from this point of view the wasps should not appear as a mode of water, but as a mode of fire (cf. the vernacular term *caga fogo* which corresponds to the Tupi *tataira*, 'fire honey', the name of an aggressive, stingless bee which secretes a caustic fluid: *Oxytrigona*, Schwartz 2, pp. 73–4). Secondly, this particular way of describing the wasps' attack is immediately reminiscent of the way in which certain myths belonging to the same region describe the behaviour of an entirely different animal: the skunk, which squirts its opponents with an evil-smelling fluid – a deadly poison, according to the myths (*RC*, p. 154 n. 9, and M$_{75}$ which is another Ofaié myth; cf., too, M$_5$, M$_{124}$).

Let me recall, then, some of the conclusions that were reached about the skunk in *The Raw and the Cooked*. (1) In both North and South America, this member of the family of the mustelidae and the opossum form a pair of opposites. (2) North American myths expressly associate the opossum with the rotten, the skunk with the burnt. At the same time, the skunk is shown to have a direct affinity with the rainbow and has the power to resuscitate the dead. (3) In South America, on the other hand, it is the opossum which has an affinity with the rainbow (to the extent that, in Guiana, it is called by the same name), and just as the rainbow in South America is credited with lethal power, one of the mythical functions attributed to the opossum is the shortening of human life.

As we move from one hemisphere to the other, the respective functions of the skunk and the opossum would seem to be reversed. In the South American myths, both animals appear as rotten or putrescent creatures. But the opossum has affinities with the dry season and with the rainbow (which initiates a miniature dry season, since it heralds the end of the rainy season), and so, if the total system has any coherence, it should follow that the skunk's South American affinities place it with the rainy season.

Is it conceivable that the mythology of honey may have adapted the very general contrast between the opossum and the skunk for its own purposes, while modifying it along the lines of a more limited contrast between the bee and the wasp, which for obvious reasons would correspond more closely to its needs?

If this hypothesis were true, it would provide us with the key to the anomaly we noticed in the role that the myth assigns to the wasps, and which lies in the fact that the role is coded in terms of water instead of fire. The anomaly would be a result of the implied equation:

(a) wasps$^{(-1)}$ ≡ skunk

In this case, for the *opossum/skunk* contrast to be maintained, the mythology of honey would have to contain by implication the complementary equation:

(b) bee$^{(-1)}$ ≡ opossum

signifying in this instance – since bees are *producers* or *guardians* of honey (see above, p. 35) – that the opossum must be the *consumer* or *stealer* of honey.[8]

As will be seen later, this hypothesis, which I arrived at by means of deductive and *a priori* reasoning, will be fully confirmed by the myths. We can already understand why, in M_{192}, the bees are categorized as dry (the approach to them is 'scorching') and the wasps as moist (the approach to them is 'damp').

[8] In *RC*, *passim*, I emphasized the semantic position of the opossum as a polluting and foul-smelling beast. According to evidence discussed by Schwartz 2, pp. 74–8, it would seem that several meliponae are able to pollute or immobilize their enemies by means of more or less foul-smelling secretions, either for the purposes of attack or in self-defence. On the subject of the smell emitted by the meliponae, and especially the sub-species *Trigona*, cf. *ibid.*, pp. 79–81. It should also be noted that the meliponae practise what entomologists call 'brigandage', either as a full-time or as an occasional activity. It would appear that *Trigona limão* does not collect nectar and pollen from flowers, but simply steals honey from other species (Salt, p. 461).

Most important of all, these provisional findings are indispensable, if we are to make any headway with the analysis of the contents of M_{192}. The opossum does not appear in person in the myth, but the role of stealer of honey which the myth should assign to it by omission, if my hypothesis is correct, is fulfilled by two other animals: (a) the prea (*cavia aperea*) which sets fire to the bushes (cf. M_{56}) and whose function, as has already been suggested on quite different grounds, may be to act as a combinatory variant of the opossum (*RC*, pp. 170, 193, n. 29), since both are on the side of fire and the dry season, one actively as a fire-raiser, the other passively as a sufferer by fire (*RC*, pp. 129, 218, n. 8). (b) The second animal is the land tortoise (jaboti) which unmasks the wolf, master of honey, sees through its series of disguises and finally by sheer tenacity catches up with it at the spot where it had hidden all the honey, after changing into a bee.

It should be recalled at this point that an important group of myths, mostly Amazonian in origin, correlate and contrast the tortoise and the opossum as being imputrescible and putrescible: respectively, master and victim of decay (*RC*, pp. 174–6). The tortoise, even when deprived of food and buried in the ground which has been softened by the first rains, can survive for several months in a damp heat, whereas the opossum cannot withstand such heat, whether it is buried in the ground or in a fish's belly, whence it emerges permanently foul-smelling (*ibid.*). Like the prea, therefore, the tortoise forms the active pole of a pair of opposites, with the opossum as the passive pole: in relation to the dry, the prea is a fire-raiser, the opossum a sufferer by fire; in relation to the moist, the tortoise emerges victorious from the decay which kills the opossum, or for which the opossum has at least to serve as a vehicle. One detail in M_{192} confirms the triple relationship, since the myth, in also describing the tortoise in respect of the dry, uses a new transformation for this purpose: the tortoise *cannot be burnt* (this gives the triangle: fire-raiser/sufferer by fire/impervious to fire), a characteristic which is confirmed objectively by ethnography, since the wolf's trick of trying to cook the tortoise while it was lying on its back is based on a method which may seem barbarous but is still current in central Brazil: the tortoise is so difficult to kill that the peasants cook it alive among the hot wood cinders, with its own shell acting as the cooking-dish; the process may last several hours, because the poor beast takes so long to die.

We have gradually exhausted the subject matter of M_{192}. The only point which still remains to be elucidated is the part played by the wolf, the master of honey and of the araticum fruit. The araticum is a plant of the anonaceae family (*Anona montana* and neighbouring species, or perhaps *Rollinia exalbida*, which is known under the same name) and produces large fruit with farinaceous pulp and an acid flavour. Like honey, it is one of the wild products of the dry season, and so one can easily see how, in the myth, it might play the part of a honey substitute. Whether or not the reference is to the same fruit or to different kinds, this minor doublet is a common feature in the mythology of honey and as such, as we shall see, its interpretation raises no difficulty. Unfortunately, the same cannot be said of the wolf.

The animal referred to as a 'wolf' (*lobo do mato*) seems to be almost always a kind of long-legged, long-haired fox: *Chrysocion brachiurus, jubatus*; *Canis jubatus*, which is found in central and southern Brazil, and consequently in the territory of the Ofaié, who assign a major role to this animal in their myth about the origin of honey. Gilmore's observation (pp. 377–8) that 'all the native Neotropical canids are foxes, with the exception of the bush dog' (*Icticyon venaticus*), is a warning to us to pay particular attention to myths which present a fox as the master of honey, as well as to those which assign this role to other animals in almost identical terms but at the same time maintain an oppositional relationship between the animal which is master of honey and the opossum:

M₉₇. Mundurucu. 'Opossum and his sons-in-law' (extract)

The opossum had one mishap after another with the series of sons-in-law he chose. The daughter then married the honey-eating fox and one day the new husband invited her to take a gourd and go hunting with him. He climbed a tree in which he spied a beehive and called out, 'Honey, honey'. The honey flowed out of the beehive and filled the gourds. When the father tried to emulate his son-in-law, he had no success and he ordered his daughter to leave the fox. (Murphy 1, p. 119. In a different version, the dove, then the hummingbird take the place of the fox, Kruse 2, pp. 628–9.)

M₉₈. Tenetehara. 'Opossum and his sons-in-law' (extract)

The 'honey-monkey' walked through the forest and sucked up honey. When he arrived home, he asked his father-in-law for a knife, and punching a hole in his throat he filled up a gourd vessel with the

Figure 4. The *lobo do mato* or guará. (After Ihering, *loc. cit.*, under 'guará'.)

honey which flowed out. The opossum tried to imitate his son-in-law, and died an instant death, since, unlike the 'honey-monkey', opossums have no pouch in their throat (Wagley–Galvão, p. 153).

M99. Vapidiana. 'Opossum and his sons-in-law' (extract)

The mosquito sucked the honey, then ordered his wife to pierce his body with a needle and honey flowed from his belly. But only blood came from the opossum's belly ... (Wirth 2, p. 208).

These are adequate samples of an extremely widespread type of story, and they illustrate three points. First, the nature of the animal which is master of honey may vary a great deal, from the fox to the mosquito by way of the monkey and birds. Secondly, the role of master of honey often presents a tautological character, the animals being defined as functions of honey, instead of the opposite being the case, so that it may be difficult to identify them: which animal exactly is the 'honey-eating fox'? And the 'honey-monkey', which has a pouch in its throat, is surely an *alter ego* of the guariba monkey, whose hyoid bone is hollow and cup-shaped. Any animal, then, can play the part of master of honey, provided he has an acknowledged capacity for guzzling: in the myths, the dove or the pigeon drink their fill of water (*RC*, p. 204); and it is an observable fact that the humming-bird sucks nectar from flowers and the mosquito blood from other animals, while the howler monkey has a receptacle (actually, a resonator) in his gullet. So the pigeon, the humming-bird and the mosquito fill their bellies, and the monkey fills its gullet. In each instance, the real or supposed organ creates the function (master of honey). Only the fox, which was our starting-point, presents a problem, since it is impossible to discern what anatomical basis there could be in its case. And yet the myth manages to justify its function as master of honey by an external rather than an internal device, which is cultural rather than natural: the fox places gourds at the foot of the hive, and they fill up at his command.

The difficulty raised by the canidae as masters of honey is still further increased by the absence, in the myths we have considered up till now, of an animal which would be better suited to the part, if it is taken in the literal sense and not – as in all the cases we have just looked at – in the figurative sense. I am thinking of the irára (*Tayra barbara*), the vernacular Portuguese and Spanish names for which – papa-mel, 'honey-eater', and melero, 'honey-merchant', speak for themselves. This species of the mustelidae family is a nocturnal forest animal. Although carnivorous, it is very fond of honey as is indicated by its name in *lingua geral*, which is derived from the Tupi word *ira*, meaning honey; and it attacks hives in hollow trees by burrowing through the roots or by tearing at the trunk with its claws. A plant which the Bororo call 'the irára plant' is used in magic rites intended to ensure a good honey harvest (*EB*, Vol. I, p. 664).

The Tacana of Bolivia give the irára an important place in their myths. They contrast it with a honey-stealing fox which, in a story (M_{193}), tears off a piece of the irára's flesh, thus creating the yellow patch which stands out against the irára's black fur (H.-H., pp. 270–76).[9]

[9] The ancient Mexicans used to say of a species with a light-coloured head (*Tayra barbara senex*) that, if the head happened to be yellow, this meant that the hunter would die, whereas if it were white, he would have a prolonged and wretched life. It was an animal of ill-omen (Sahagun, Book XI, Ch. 1 under 'Tzoniztac').

Since this 'fox' has just had its tail pulled off, it might be confused with the opossum, which is often referred to as a fox and which, in both North and South America, is the subject of several myths explaining how its tail became bare. One group of myths (M_{194}–M_{197}) is concerned with the adventures of a pair of twins, the Edutzi, in the land of the animal demons, from among whom they each select a wife. The irára plays a part, either as the father of the two women who are sisters, or as the second husband of one of them, the other being in that case the vampire. In order to shield its daughters from the vengeful Edutzi, the 'melero' changes them into macaws (H.-H., pp. 104–10). These myths will be examined later in a different context. I will say no more about the Tacana for the moment, except to point out that they have a group of myths (M_{198}–M_{201}) which divide the animals into two camps: caterpillar /cricket, monkey/jaguar, cricket/jaguar, fox/jaguar, cricket/melero. In spite of the uncertainty of the terms, which means that, before these myths can be interpreted correctly, the enormous body of material collected by Hissink would have to be sorted out on both the syntagmatic and paradigmatic levels, it would seem that the relevant contrasts are between animals which are respectively large and small, terrestrial and celestial (or chthonian and celestial). Generally speaking, the jaguar is the dominant member in the first camp and the cricket in the second. The melero appears twice in this group of myths either as an intermediary between the two camps, or as the cricket's chief opponent (in place of the jaguar). It is therefore the leader of the chthonian animals. Except when it is fighting the caterpillar, the cricket always wins, since it is helped by wasps which inflict painful stings on its honey-seeking rival.[10] In addition to the monkey and the cricket, the fox and the ocelot figure among the opponents of the jaguar. The fox and the ocelot have a small shaman's drum which also plays a part in the clash between the Edutzi and the melero in the group M_{194}–M_{197}. Sahagun (*loc. cit.*) compares the ocelot with a Mexican variety of the melero.

The presence of the irára or melero in a great number of the myths of eastern Bolivia is especially worthy of remark, since Brazilian and Guiana myths make little mention of this animal. With the exception of a Taulipang myth (M_{135}) about the origin of the Pleiades, which ends with a father and his children deciding to change into an araiuag: 'a quadruped similar to a fox, but with soft, shiny, black fur, a slender body, a round head and a long snout' (K.-G. 1, pp. 57–60), which could well be the irára since 'it likes honey and is not afraid of bees', there are

[10] Cf. the enemies defeated by wasps and hornets in the Popol Vuh.

very few references to it. Moving southwards, we first encounter it in
Amazonia. A short myth (M₂₀₂) contrasts the corupira, the cannibalistic
spirit of the woods, with the honey-eating irára. The irára saves an
Indian from the corupira's claws, after the cunauaru frog (cf. *RC*,
pp. 270–71) has rendered the same service to an Indian woman who,
like the Indian, had stolen the ogre's meal. Thereafter, the ogre was to
eat neither fish nor tatu. He was to eat human flesh, whereas the irára
would continue to live on honey (Rodrigues 1, pp. 68–9).

The Botocudo of the Rio Doce area in eastern Brazil have two myths
about the irára:

M₂₀₃. Botocudo. 'The origin of water'

In olden times, the humming-bird possessed all the water in the
world and the animals had nothing to drink but honey. The humming-bird used to go and bathe every day, and the envious animals
got the wild turkey (mutum: *Crax* sp.) to spy on it, but to no avail.

One day, the entire population was assembled round a fire. The
irára arrived late, because it had been away collecting honey. It asked
for some water in a low voice, and was told: 'There is none.' So it
offered to give the humming-bird honey in exchange for water, but
the latter refused and announced that it was going to have a bath.
The irára followed it and came to the water, which was in a little
hole in the rock, almost at the same time. The humming-bird jumped into the water and the irára did likewise, and splashed about so
vigorously that the water spurted out in all directions, thus giving
rise to streams and rivers (Nim. 9, p. 111).

The author to whom we owe the above myth observes that the same
story is found among the Yamana of Tierra del Fuego, except that the
humming-bird's role is reversed; it discovers the water which is being
jealously guarded by the fox.

M₂₀₄. Botocudo. 'The origin of animals'

In olden times, animals were like humans, and were all friends. They
had enough to eat. It was the irára which had the idea of setting them
at variance with each other. It taught the snake to bite and kill its
victims and the mosquito to suck blood. From that moment they all
became beasts, including the irára, so that no one would recognize
it. The sorcerer who supplied the animals with their food was unable
to remedy the situation. He changed into a woodpecker and his
stone axe became the bird's beak (Nim. 9, p. 112).

These myths prompt several observations. The first myth contrasts the irára, the master of honey, with the humming-bird, the master of water. It has already been observed that in South America honey and water invariably go together, since honey is always diluted before it is consumed. The original situation referred to by the myth, in which the animals in possession of honey have no water, and vice versa, is therefore 'anti-natural', or more accurately 'anti-cultural'. A myth belonging to the Kayua of southern Brazil (M_{62}) describes how the animals challenged each other to a race:

The irára, too, wanted to run in the race. It is said to carry honey on its back. The ema (*Rhea americana*) said to it: 'You will die. You live

Figure 5. The irára (*Tayra barbara*). (After A. E. Brehm, *La Vie des animaux, les Mammifères*, Vol. I, Paris, undated, p. 601.)

on honey. You want to run in the race. There is no water here. You will die of thirst ... I don't drink water, all my friends can run, I will not give them any.' After running in the race and nearly dying of thirst, the dog broke the container carried by the irára and the honey was spilt, to the irára's intense annoyance. Then the ema said to it: 'It is no use being cross, it was done in fun. We don't fight here. Go away.' And it took all the irára's honey from it (Schaden 1, p. 117).

Here too, therefore, the irára is a bad-tempered, unsatisfied animal because it has honey but no water. It is therefore an incomplete master of honey, anxious at times to wrest possession of the water it lacks from an opponent who is in possession of it (M_{203}), at other times in danger of losing the honey it possesses to a rival capable of doing without the water which it, the irára, so acutely lacks (M_{62}). In either case, it cannot accept the *status quo*: hence its role as a deceiving demiurge in M_{204}.[11]

My second observation relates specifically to M_{204}, in which the irára endows snakes with their poison, an effect which Chaco myths (M_{205}, M_{206}) attribute to the action of pimento fire or smoke (Métraux 3, pp. 19–20; 5, p. 68). Encouraged by Cardus' observation (p. 356) that the Guarayu consider tobacco to be an antidote to snake bites, let us take the following equation as a working hypothesis:

$$\text{smoked pimento} = \text{smoked tobacco}^{(-1)}$$

If we now allow that honey without water (= too strong) stands in the same extreme position in relation to diluted honey as pimento smoke does to tobacco, we shall be able to understand how the irára, the master of honey without water, can, in the Botocudo myth, play a part which is easily confused with the part that Chaco myths assign to a kind of smoke, which scorches literally (fire) or figuratively (pimento), in a total system that can be illustrated as follows:

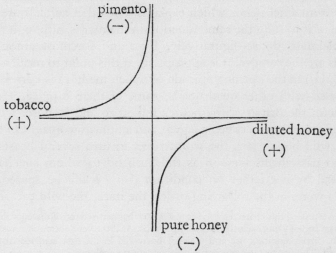

Figure 6. Tobacco, pimento, honey

[11] It is amusing to compare it with Jupiter who plays the same part of deceiving god, lavish with his malice, but niggardly as regards honey:

> *Ille malum virus serpentibus addidit atris*
> *praedarique lupos iussit pontumque moveri*
> *mellaque decussit foliis ignemque removit.*

> (Virgil, *Georgics*, I, vv. 129–31)

The above analogical model[12] is indirectly confirmed by the fact that, in Amazonia, a contrast exists between bad honey, which is known to induce vomiting and is used ritually for this purpose, and good tobacco, which the Tucano of Colombia say came from divine vomits. The first thus appears as the *cause* of vomiting which is intended to establish communication between men and gods, whereas the second appears as the *result* of vomiting, which already constitutes in itself a form of communication between the gods and men. Finally, it will be recalled that in M_{202}, a myth made up of two superimposable episodes, the irára intervenes as a combinatory variant of the cunauaru frog, the mistress of a hunting poison, that is, of an inedible substance which like timbó (cf. above, p. 57) is 'transformed' into game, an edible substance, whereas the irára is in possession of pure honey which, as such, is inedible but which can be transformed (by being diluted) into an edible substance.

The preceding discussion has to some extent served to clarify the mythic position of the irára. Being a master of honey, in the literal sense, the irára cannot fully carry out this function in the eyes of men, since it differs from them in eating honey without water; it therefore suffers from a deficiency which explains why other animals are chosen instead of it to fulfil the same function in the myths, although they can only claim to do so figuratively. First and foremost among these animals are the canidae. It is appropriate at this point to recall a Bororo myth (M_{46}) in the opening episode of which the irára is correlated and contrasted with other quadrupeds, some of them canidae. The myth deals with the origin of the heroes Bakororo and Ituboré, who were born of a marriage between a jaguar and a human woman. On her way to the wild beast's lair, the woman met in turn several beasts which tried to pass themselves off as the husband to whom she had been promised by her father on condition that his life be spared. These animals were, in the following order, the irára, the wild cat, the small

---

[12] I am stressing this characteristic because Leach has accused me of disregarding models of this type and of using exclusively binary patterns. As if the very notion of transformation of which I make constant use and which I borrowed in the first instance from d'Arcy Wentworth Thompson were not entirely dependent on analogy ...

In fact, I constantly have recourse to both types, as the reader may have noticed in connection with a different analysis (p. 79), in which I even tried to combine them. In *The Raw and the Cooked*, there were clear examples of analogical models – e.g. the graphs or diagrams, Fig. 5, p. 90; Fig. 6, p. 98; Fig. 7, p. 107; Fig. 8, p. 194; Fig. 20, p. 335, and the formulae on pp. 163, 199, 249, 250, etc. The same is true of all the diagrams in which the signs + and − denote, not the presence or absence of certain terms, but the *more* or *less* pronounced character of certain polarities which, within a single group of myths, may vary, either directly or inversely.

wolf, the great wolf, the jaguatirica or ocelot and the puma. Having
unmasked them all in turn, the woman finally arrived at the jaguar's
house.

In its way this episode provides a lesson in ethnozoology, since
seven species are set out both in order of size and in relation to their
greater or lesser resemblance to the jaguar. From the point of view of
size, it is clear that

(1) wild cat < ocelot < puma < jaguar;
(2) small wolf < great wolf.

From the point of view of resemblance to the jaguar, the irára and
the jaguar are furthest apart; and the irára is also much smaller than the
jaguar. The most remarkable feature of the series is its miscellaneous
nature in the light of modern taxonomy, since it includes one of the
mustelidae, two canidae and four felidae, in other words animal families
very different both in their anatomy and in their way of life. To mention
only the most superficial of the differences between them, certain
species have spotted or marked coats, while others are all of one colour,
but may be light or dark.

But the fact that this seems to us to be a miscellaneous grouping
does not necessarily mean that it appeared so to the native mind.
Starting with the root iawa, the Tupi form the following nouns by the
addition of suffixes: iawara, 'dog', iawarate, 'jaguar', iawacaca, 'otter',
iawaru, 'wolf', iawapopé, 'fox' (Montoya), thus grouping felidae,
canidae and one of the mustelidae in one and the same category. The
Carib of Guiana used to classify animal species according to a principle
which is far from clear, but in which it would seem that the jaguar's
name, arowa, with the addition of a determinative – tortoise, jacamin
bird, agouti, rat, deer, etc. – was used to designate several kinds of
quadrupeds (Schomburgk, Vol. II, pp. 65–7). Consequently, as I showed
in *The Raw and the Cooked* with regard to ungulates and rodents, to which
the native mentality applies the same principle of classification based
on the oppositional relationship of the long and the short (animals with
tails/animals without tails; long snout/short snout etc.), it would
seem that one of the mustelidae such as the irára must not be radically
separated from animals belonging to different zoological species. In
these circumstances, the fact that the myths assign the role of master
of honey to various members of the canidae family would seem to
arise not so much in connection with one particular species and its
empirical behaviour, as in connection with a very broad ethnozoological

category including not only the irára, which we know from experience to be a master of honey, but also the canidae about which I have yet to show that, from the semantic point of view, they are better fitted to fulfil this role than the irára, even though the available empirical evidence does not qualify them for it as clearly as the irára. But we must also take into account the fact that, in the myths, honey does not appear simply as a natural product: it is heavily overlaid with connotations which, in a sense, have been superimposed upon it. In order to control honey, which has become its own metaphor, a real but incomplete master is less well suited than one who is particularly able to fulfil the function with the required authority, since the myths give the function itself a figurative meaning.

In order to explain the semantic position of the canidae, we must undoubtedly look towards the Chaco. In the myths belonging to this area, the fox occupies a leading position as the animal incarnation of a deceiving god, who occasionally also takes on human form. Among the Chaco myths, there exists a group in which Fox has a positive or negative, but always strongly marked, relationship with honey. I now propose to examine these myths which, so far, have not been studied from this particular point of view.

M_{207}. Toba. 'Fox takes a wife'

After several adventures at the end of which Fox died but came back to life again as soon as there was a slight fall of rain, he arrived at a village in the guise of a handsome young lad ... A girl fell in love with him ... They slept together. The girl, who was in love with him, scratched and tore him with her nails. 'Don't scratch me like that,' cried Fox, 'or I shall leave you. It hurts.' ... Fox cried until his cries were those of a fox and ... the girl left him.

Another girl fell in love with [Fox] and they slept together until morning. Fox said 'I shall go look for some food' ... In the bush he collected sachasandias and empty honey combs. He put them in a bag and returned home. The girl's mother took the bag and hung it on a post. She said, 'I am going to get a gourd and mix water and honey in it and let it ferment. I shall prepare mead for my family. What is left will be for my son-in-law.' ... Fox said to his wife, 'I am going to take a walk and will come later' ... Fox's parents-in-law opened the bag and cried, 'This is not honey, these are sachasandias ... This fellow is not a man ... – he is Fox' (Métraux 5, pp. 122–3).

M_{208}. *Toba. 'Fox in search of honey'*

It is said that one day Fox set out to look for wasp honey (lecheguana). He travelled for a long time with no success, and then met a bird (čelmot), which was also looking for honey and which agreed to accompany him. The bird found large quantities of honey. It climbed trees, kept a watchful eye on individual wasps in order to discover the whereabouts of their nests, and then all it had to do was to take out the honey. Fox tried to do likewise, but without success.

The bird then decided to put a spell on such a lamentable partner. It murmured some magic words: 'May a splinter of wood enter Fox's foot so that he cannot walk!' Hardly had it finished saying this when Fox, jumping down from a tree he had climbed, impaled himself on a pointed stick, and died. The bird (čelmot) went off to quench its thirst in a pond, and returned home without telling anyone what had happened.

There was a slight shower of rain and Fox came back to life. Having removed the stake, he succeeded in finding some honey which he put into his bag. As he was thirsty, he set off in the direction of a pond and jumped in without looking. The pond was dry and Fox broke his neck. Nearby a frog was digging a well. Its stomach was full of water. After a very long time, a man appeared who wanted to drink. He noticed that the pond was dry, that Fox was dead and that the frog's stomach was full of water. He pierced it with a cactus thorn; the water spurted out and spread all around, wetting Fox who came back to life again.

One day when Fox was expecting guests and preparing algaroba beer, he noticed Lizard who was sleeping at the top of a Uchan tree (*Chorisia insignis*). Fox left the beer and begged Lizard to make room for him, explaining that he liked to climb trees and that the only reason he did not usually live in the tree-tops was that he preferred to have company there. Lizard cast a spell: 'When Fox jumps may he tear his stomach!' Fox jumped in order to join Lizard and was ripped open by the thorns on the trunk of the yuchan. As he fell, his intestines came out and caught on the tree and held him suspended in mid-air. 'We shall make these entrails grow,' said Lizard, 'so that men can cut them and eat them.' This was the origin of the creeper called 'Fox Tripes', which Indians eat (Métraux 5, pp. 126–7).

In the Matako version of the same myth (M_{209a}), the deceiver, who is called Takjuaj ('Tawk'wax) hangs his own intestines on the branches of the tree, where they are changed into creepers. He buries his stomach just below the surface of the ground, and it becomes a kind of melon

Figure 7. A South American fox. (After Ihering, *loc. cit.*, under 'cachorro do mato'.)

full of water. His *reyuno*[13] and his heart give rise to the smooth tasi and the prickly tasi and, under the ground, his large intestine is changed into manioc (Palavecino, p. 264).

Métraux divides this group of myths into three distinct narratives, but if we superimpose them one on the other, it is not difficult to see that they all have a common pattern. A food-collecting operation: a search for honey (probably to make mead, cf. M_{207}) or the preparation of some other fermented beverage fails because Fox does not know how to climb trees, or it succeeds only after Fox has fallen from the tree,

---

[13] I have been no more successful than Métraux (5, p. 128) who left the term untranslated, in discovering the meaning of this Spanish word in the local dialect. It obviously refers to a part of the body. But the anatomy of the Matako deceiver is full of surprises, as is shown by the following different version (M_{209b}) of the same myth:
'Tawkxwax climbed a yuchan and fell down head first. As he fell the thorns of the tree tore his body. He removed his stomach from his body and buried it. From it grew a plant (iletsáx), the root of which is very large and full of water. His intestines became lianas. Like a cow, Tawkxwax had two stomachs. With the second he made a plant called iwokanó' (Métraux 3, p. 19).
It is worth noting that in North America myths closely resembling the Chaco ones likewise associate an excessive use, either of parts of the body, or of trees, or plants or wild fruits and the origin of the latter with a deceiver personified by Mink or Coyote (Menomini: Hoffman, p. 164; Pawnee: Dorsey, pp. 464–5; Kiowa: Parsons, p. 42). Among the Iroquois (Hewitt, p. 710), several climbing plants with edible fruit are said to have sprung from the intestines of Tawiskaron, the god of winter. The Ojibwa believe that the demiurge's evil brother underwent the same transformation. In South America itself, the Fox reappears as a clumsy and greedy deceiver in the myths of the Uitoto (Preuss 1, pp. 574–81), and also in those of the Uro-Cipaya on the Andean plateau (Métraux 2).

but in that case the search has made him thirsty and the deceiver, behaving thoughtlessly as always, falls to his death in a waterless pond: water being the indispensable element needed to restore him to life. Fox who is *impaled* in the first episode corresponds, in the second (but with the reverse effect: wet earth instead of dry earth), to the frog whose stomach is *pierced* and, in the third, to the Fox who is disembowelled, not as a result of falling *from high to low*, as in the first two episodes, but by trying to jump *from low to high*. When Fox falls *from high to low*, he is *without honey* (first episode). When he falls to a still lower position (to the bottom of a dried-up pond), he is *without water* (second episode). Finally, when he jumps *from low to high* (third episode) he determines the appearance, *at the half-way mark*, not of honey or water, but of things which bear an extraordinary resemblance to them in the sense that, not being absolutely one or the other, they illustrate approximately the conjunction of both, which were previously in a state of disjunction: honey above in the trees, water below in the pond or in the belly of a frog which is busy digging a well. The conjunction takes the form of plants or wild fruits which, like honey (in the native system of classification), belong to the vegetable realm but, unlike honey, contain water.

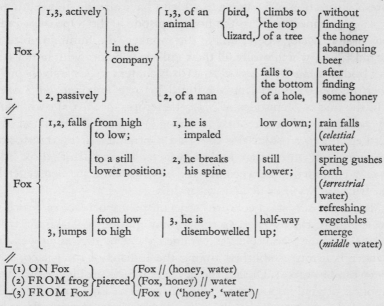

In support of the above summary, it can be pointed out that certain themes occurring in the three episodes correspond to each other exactly. This is especially so in the case of what I would like to call the 'piercing operation': Fox is impaled on a sharp-pointed stick, the frog's stomach is pierced with a cactus spine, Fox is disembowelled by the spikes on the trunk of the yuchan tree. As will be confirmed later, this is a basic theme in honey myths, and we shall obviously have to try to find some explanation for it. But for the time being, I merely wish to emphasize three points.

In the first place, the 'piercing' has to do in each case with a natural vessel: the fox's body or the frog's body, that is – since the fox is the hero of the myth – his *own body* or some *other body*. In the first episode, his own body is a *container without content*: nothing escapes from Fox's impaled body since his stomach is empty (without honey) and he is thirsty (without water). After being restored to life by the rain, which moistens the outside of his dry, still empty and water-seeking body, Fox breaks his spine, thus introducing, by means of his *own body*, the second term of a contrast: *pierced entrails/broken bones*, the first term of which is represented by the body of another – the body of the frog, which, unlike that of Fox, then appears in the form of a *container with content*: it is full of water. This outward materialization of the container, once its internal materialization is out of the question, provides a fresh illustration of a pattern to which I have already drawn attention (p. 85), in connection with the honey episode in the 'Opossum and his sons-in-law' cycle, where, unlike the monkey, the humming-bird and the mosquito, which busily fill their gullets or bellies with honey (their own bodies *container* ∪ *content*), the fox is content to be passively present when the honey is poured into the gourd (his own body *container || content*).

In the first two episodes of M_{208}, therefore, the (fox's) own body is dry and the body of the other (the frog's) is wet. The function of the third episode is to solve this two-fold contradiction: by transforming his own body into other bodies (vegetables and fruit), Fox brings about a conjunction between dry and wet, since the swollen vegetables and fruit are dry outside and wet inside.

My next observation concerns a detail the importance of which will emerge more clearly later. In the second episode of M_{208}, the frog is master of water, because it has obtained water by digging a well. This practice is firmly established among the Indians of the Chaco, where water can be scarce: 'During the dry season, the problem of the water supply is of vital importance to the natives. The Lule and Vilela tribes, who used to live to the south of the Bermejo, dug deep wells or built huge reservoirs. The present-day Lengua have wells between $4\frac{1}{2}$ and six metres deep and about seventy-five centimetres wide. They are so constructed as to allow a man to go down inside by placing his feet in notches cut in opposite sides of the well wall' (Métraux 14, p. 8).

Finally, it is impossible to mention the theme of 'broaching' without reference to its inverted form, which is illustrated in other Chaco myths about Fox, particularly those belonging to the Toba and the Mataco. These myths (discussed in RC, p. 305; M₁₇₅) relate how the deceiver Tawkxwax, or his Toba equivalent Fox, had all the orifices of his body blocked by a wasp or a bee, which I showed – by a very different line of reasoning – to be a frog that had been transformed by inversion of the dry/damp connotations belonging respectively to the two creatures. It is clear that, in this respect, the second episode in M₂₀₈ is a retransformation of M₁₇₅ by means of a three-fold contrast: *dry/wet, closed/open, active/passive*, which can be reduced to the following formula:

$$M_{175}[^1BEE\ ^2which\ ^3blocks] \Rightarrow M_{208}[^1FROG\ ^2which\ is\ ^3pierced$$

corresponding to the fact that, in M₁₇₅, Fox has all the water he could wish for (exteriorized by the bee: in jars) but regards it with contempt, whereas in M₂₀₈ he is deprived of water which he covets because the water is interiorized by the frog (in its body).

Another Toba myth offers a variant of the final episode of M₂₀₈–M₂₀₉:

M₂₁₀. Toba. 'Fox stuffed with honey'

Fox is fishing in the lagoon while Carancho is looking for wasp honey (lecheguana). He finds a great deal, but Fox catches no fish. His entire contribution to the midday meal consists of two poor chumuco birds.[14] Fox is annoyed at his friend's not appreciating the birds, and he refuses the honey on the ground that it is bad. Carancho casts a spell on him: 'May Fox's stomach secrete honey!' Fox does indeed discover that his excrement is full of honey, that his saliva changes into honey as soon as he spits it out, and that he is oozing honey from every pore.

Thereupon, Carancho, having made a good haul of fish, invites Fox to eat some of it. Fox begins by eating heartily, but when Carancho reveals that what he thinks is fish is really honey magically disguised, Fox is so sickened that he vomits. He notices with a certain pride that his vomit changes into water-melons: 'It is as if I were a shaman. Where I vomit, new plants grow!' (Métraux 5, pp. 138–9).

This variant is interesting in two respects. First of all, it illustrates a

---

[14] On these birds as an inferior form of game, see RC, p. 204.

D

connection, already observed among the Mundurucu, between honey and water-melons (cf. p. 57). It will be remembered that the Mundurucu believe water-melons to come 'from the devil', and that they were originally poisonous, until men domesticated and cultivated them so that they became safe to eat. Now Fox, a deceiving divinity, clearly plays the part of a 'devil' in Toba mythology. The Goajiro Indians, who live in the extreme north of tropical America, in Venezuela, also

Figure 8. The carancho bird (*Polyborus plancus*). (After Ihering, *loc. cit.*, under 'carancho'.)

believe the melon to be a 'diabolical' food (Wilbert 6, p. 172). The same is true of the Tenetehara (Wagley–Galvão, p. 145). The diabolical nature of water-melons, which is widely believed in by tribes remote from each other and different both in language and culture, raises a problem that we must try to solve.

At the same time, M_{210} recreates in a clearer and more vigorous form the contrast, already present in M_{208}–M_{209}, between the unlucky fox and its more gifted companion, which was first a bird (the čelmot), then the lizard. The companion in question here is none other than Carancho, i.e. the demiurge (as opposed to the deceiving Fox) who, among the Toba, takes the form of a predatory, carrion-eating, species of falcon, fond of larvae and insects, *Polyborus plancus*: 'It prefers savannah lands and open spaces. It has a slightly pompous gait and when it raises its feathered crest it has a rather noble bearing, which is hardly in keeping with its very plebeian mode of life' (Ihering, under 'carancho').[15] In the myth, the demiurge is a master of fishing and of the search for honey, and Fox is furious at being inferior to him. Sickened by honey, like the corupira in the Amazonian myth, M_{202}, he has to make do with being master of water-melons.

Figure 9. Carácará birds (*Milvago chimachima*). (After Ihering, *loc. cit.*, under 'carácará'.)

It is clear that, in this instance, the water-melons are a substitute for honey and fish. What have these three sources of food in common and in what ways are they different? At the same time, what common features are there between the water-melons (*Citrullus* sp.) which spring up from Fox's vomit and the plants created from his entrails in M_{208}–M_{209}: edible creepers, tasi, manioc, and also, as it happens, the water-melon? Finally, what is the relationship with the fruit of the sachasandia tree, of which Fox is the master in M_{207}?

[15] The carancho is bigger than the carácará, another of the falconidae (*Milvago chimachima*), which plays the part of the deceiver in Caduveo mythology, cf. above, p. 74, n. 7.

Within this group, a special place must be given to manioc, which is the only cultivated plant. But at the same time it is, of all cultivated plants, the one which demands least attention and the one which does not ripen at any set season. Cuttings are planted at the beginning of the rainy season. The ground is weeded from time to time and, several months later, the plants are fully grown: between eight and eighteen months, according to the methods used. From then on, and until the crop is exhausted, they supply edible roots all through the year.[16] Since manioc requires little attention, is capable of thriving in the poorest soil, is always available and is so along with wild plants at times when other cultivated plants have already been harvested, if not eaten, it represents a non-specified source of food which is mentioned together with wild plants with a certain food value. This is because the fact that it can still be eaten during the wild fruit season is more important from the practical point of view of the native diet than its being theoretically included among the cultivated plants.

As for the sachasandia (*Capparis salicifolia*), its fruit has a sinister connotation at least for the Mataco, about whom we know a great deal, since it provides the normal means of suicide, for these Indians seem particularly prone to take their own lives. Poisoning by sachasandia brings about convulsions, foaming at the mouth, irregular beating of the heart, which stops and starts again, contractions of the throat, choking sounds, trembling and jerky contractions accompanied by violent diarrhoea. Finally the victim falls into a coma and dies fairly quickly. Prompt treatment in the form of morphine injections and the administration of an emetic has made it possible to save several Indians, who have later described their symptoms: profound depression, followed by giddiness 'as if the world were turning upside down', which forces them to lie down (Métraux 10).

It is therefore understandable that the sachasandia should figure in the Chaco diet only during periods of shortage. And even then the

---

[16] Whiffen's observation (p. 193) about north-west Amazonia can be generalized: 'Although manioc is planted as a rule just before the heaviest annual rainfall becomes due, there is no part of the year when some of the roots are not ready to gather.'

In support of the preceding remarks, I can also quote the following comments by Leeds (pp. 23-4): 'Thus manioc has no clear peak, is regular over the years, is storable both in raw form and in prepared forms ... is so located as not to permit of a concentration of labour at any one time and needs no massive labour for harvesting because of short harvest periods. Thus, in general, the very nature of manioc as a crop, and the labour requisites for harvesting it, require no centralized authority, and renders it possible and even probable that the management of production or distribution can be carried on without it. The same may be said on the whole, for all the hunting, fishing and gathering harvests.'

fruit must be boiled up five times in fresh water to eliminate the toxins. However, this is also true, although to a lesser extent, of most of the wild plants I have listed.

Several authors (Métraux 14, pp. 3–28; 12, pp. 246–7; Henry 2; Susnik, pp. 20–21, 48–9, 87, 104) have described in detail the cycle of economic life in the Chaco. From November until January or February, the Indians in the Pilcomayo area drink the pods of the algaroba (*Prosopis* sp.), the nourishing fruit of the chanar (*Gourleia decorticans*) and of the mistol (*Zizyphus mistol*) in the form of a lightly fermented beer. This is the period the Toba call 'kotap', which seems to have the same meaning as 'bienestar', when peccaries and coati are plump and plentiful. It is a time of feasts, merrymaking and inter-tribal visits, when bridegrooms-to-be present their future mothers-in-law with bags full of meat.

In February and March, the wild produce already mentioned is replaced by other forms: among agricultural tribes poroto del monte (*Capparis retusa*), tasi (*Morrenia odorata*) and Barbary figs (*Opuntia*) provide an addition to maize, pumpkins and water-melons. As soon as the rains stop in April, any surplus wild fruit is dried in the sun for winter use, and the plantations are made ready.

From the beginning of April to mid-June, shoals of fish swim up the rivers, heralding a season of plenty. In June and July, the streams gradually dry up, fishing becomes difficult and once more the population has to fall back on wild fruit: tasi, which has already been mentioned, and tusca (*Acacia aroma*), both of which ripen between April and September.

August and September are the months of real food shortage, when the Indians live on reserves of dried fruit, with the addition of the naranja del monte (*Capparis speciosa*), cucurbitaceae, bromeliaceae, wild tubers, an edible creeper (Phaseolus?) and the sachasandia fruit already mentioned. Because of their bitter taste, several other varieties of fruit which I mentioned previously – e.g. poroto and naranja del monte – must also be boiled in several changes of water, then dried in the sun after being crushed in a mortar. When water runs short, the Indians drink what has collected at the base of the leaves of the caraguata, one of the bromeliaceae, and chew the fleshy root of one of the euphorbiaceae.

During the dry months, the Indians scatter and lead a nomadic life, after being together in large groups during the festive season to drink algaroba beer and fish along the river banks. Families go off on their own and wander through the woods, looking for wild fruit and game. All the tribes hunt, especially the Mataco who have no access to the rivers. The great collective hunts, which are often carried out with the help of bush fires, take place chiefly during the dry season, although hunting goes on during the rest of the year as well.

The Toba, who call this period Káktapigá, lay stress in their stories on the fact that this is the time when animals are thin and lacking in the fat so necessary in the diet of the hunter. This is the time of 'hunger sickness': the mouth becomes dry and parched, and the flesh of the ema (nandu) provides a bare subsistence. Consequently, influenza is rife and unweaned children and old people die; the staple food is armadillos, and the Indians wrap themselves up well and sleep near their fires ...

It is clear from the preceding details that, although there is no real rainy season in the Chaco, where violent downpours can occur at any period in the year, the rains tend nevertheless to be concentrated between October and March (Grubb, p. 306). All the fox's plants therefore appear to be dry-season foods; this is also true of fish, and of honey which is collected chiefly during the nomadic period. However, the dry season is shown to have, alternatively, two different aspects: it is characterized by plenty and by shortage. All the myths we are dealing with relate to the dry season, which is considered either in its most favourable aspect, which is marked by a plentiful supply of fish and honey (of which, as Métraux stresses (*loc. cit.*, p. 7), Chaco Indians are very fond), or in its poorest and most distressing aspect, since most of the wild fruits gathered during the dry season are poisonous or bitter and require complicated treatment before they are safe to eat. Water-melons, which grow at the beginning of the dry season, are non-poisonous owing to the fact that they are cultivated. Under their hard outer bark, they conceal a copious supply of water and thus allow the last beneficial effects of the closing rainy season to be prolonged right into the dry season. They are a supreme and paradoxical illustration of the contrast between container and content: one being dry, the other wet;[17] and they can be used as an emblem for a deceiving god, who is also paradoxically different outside and inside.

Surely, in its way, the yuchan tree, on whose hard spikes Fox is disembowelled, is not unlike the water-melon and other juicy fruit eaten during the dry season. In Mataco and Ashluslay mythology

---

[17] Kruse's version of M₁₅₇ (p. 56) is most eloquent on this point: 'When the fruit becomes hard, declares the mother of cultivated plants, it will be ready for eating.'

(M_{111}), the yuchan is the tree which, in former times, held all the water in the world inside its swollen trunk, and which supplied men with fish from one year's end to the next. It therefore interiorizes terrestrial water and neutralizes the contrast between the fishing season and the fishless season, just as wild fruits interiorize celestial water and thus neutralize – although only relatively, but nevertheless in an empirically verifiable manner – the contrast between the dry season and the rainy season. Later in the Guiana myths, we shall come across trees which, like the yuchan, belong to the bombax family, and it is hardly necessary to remind the reader that evidence of their being considered as the tree of life is to be found even in ancient Maya mythology. But the fact that the theme also exists in the Chaco, and in the particular form of the tree filled with water and fish, shows that, in this region, it has a peculiar link with the techno-economical substructure: the spiky dryness of the trunk, in an allegorical way, encloses the water, and the water encloses the fish, just as the dry season encloses the special period when fish become more plentiful in the rivers, and also encloses within its duration the ripening period of wild fruit, which encloses water within the volume circumscribed by its hard skin.

Finally, like fish, honey presupposes both water (with which it is diluted to make mead) and dryness. They are mediatory agents between the dry and the wet and at the same time between the high and the low, since during the dry season the dry is atmospheric in nature, hence celestial, and in the absence of rain-water must inevitably come from the earth – that is, from wells. The mediation illustrated by honey and fish is therefore the most ambitious in range, because of the gap between the terms which have to be brought together, and the most rewarding in its results, whether the latter are defined quantitatively (fish, the most plentiful of all foods), or qualitatively (honey, the most delicious of all foods). The fox manages to bring about the same mediation, although at a more mediocre level: however juicy they are, wild fruits do not take the place of water, and they give a great deal of trouble before they can be harvested and rendered fit for consumption. Finally, this makeshift mediation is achieved by the fox at an equal distance between the high and the low – it is half-way up the tree – and through the sacrifice of its middle parts since, anatomically speaking, its entrails are half-way between the high and the low.

3 The Story of the Girl Mad About Honey, Her Base Seducer and Her Timid Husband

a. IN THE CHACO

The first of the honey myths belonging to the Chaco region that we discussed (M_{207}), and in which Fox plays the chief part, hints at the intervention of a feminine partner: the young girl whom Fox seduced after he had disguised himself as a handsome boy, and whom he made a pretence of marrying. A short myth repeats this particular episode: it anticipates, in a condensed form, an important group of myths which it is possible to isolate, once we have recognized the basic pattern outlined in M_{211}, behind the various transformations:

M_{211}. *Toba.* '*Sick Fox*'

On returning from a successful honey expedition, in which he had taken part along with the other villagers, Fox was stung by a poisonous spider. His wife called four famous healers to give him treatment. At this time Fox had human form. As he coveted his sister-in-law, who was prettier than his wife, he insisted that she should act as his nurse. He expected to be able to seduce her when they were alone together. But she would not hear of it, and denounced him to her sister who left her husband in a rage. Fox's behaviour, which was so little in keeping with the malady with which he claimed to be afflicted, finally aroused suspicion and he was unmasked (Métraux 5, pp. 139–40).

Here now are variants of the same myth, but in which the theme is treated at much greater length:

M_212. *Toba. 'The girl mad about honey'* (1)

Sakhé was the daughter of the master of the Water People, and she was so fond of honey she was always begging for it. Irritated by her persistent requests, both men and women replied: 'Get married!' Even her mother, when pestered by the daughter for honey, told her it would be better if she got married.

So the young girl decided to marry Woodpecker, the famous honey-gatherer. He was, as it happened, in the woods with other birds, all busy like himself, piercing holes in the tree-trunks with their beaks in order to reach the bees' nests. Fox pretended to help them but did no more than beat the tree with his stick.

Sakhé inquired where Woodpecker was to be found. As she walked in the direction indicated, she met Fox, who tried to pass himself off as the bird. But his breast was not red, and his bag, instead of honey, contained only dirt. The young girl was not deceived; she continued on her way and finally met Woodpecker, to whom she proposed marriage. Woodpecker showed little enthusiasm, discussed the matter and said he was sure that the young girl's parents would not approve of him. Whereupon she insisted angrily: 'My mother lives alone, and does not want me any more!' Fortunately, Woodpecker had some honey, and she calmed down as she ate it. Finally, Woodpecker said: 'If it is true that your mother has sent you with this intention, I shall not be afraid to marry you. But if you are lying, how could I marry you? I am no fool!' Thereupon he came down from the tree he had climbed, carrying his bag full of honey.

Meanwhile the lazy Fox had filled his bag with sachasandia and tasi fruits, which people fall back on when they can find nothing else. Yet, during the days that followed, Fox deliberately refrained from going back to look for honey with the birds which were dissatisfied with the amount of honey gathered on their first expedition. He preferred to steal the honey he ate.

One day, Woodpecker had left his wife alone in the encampment, and Fox tried to take advantage of the situation. Pretending to have a splinter in his foot which prevented him following his companions, he went back alone to the encampment. Almost immediately on arrival there, he tried to rape the wife. But the latter, who was pregnant, fled into the woods. Fox pretended to be asleep. He felt terribly ashamed.

When Woodpecker returned, he inquired anxiously about his wife, and Fox lied to him, saying that she had just left with her mother. Woodpecker, who was a chief, ordered that a search party should be sent to find her. But the mother was not at home and the wife had disappeared. Woodpecker then shot magic arrows in several directions. Those which saw nothing came back to him. When the third arrow did not come back, Woodpecker knew that it had fallen at the spot where his wife was, and he set off to join her.

Meanwhile, Woodpecker's son (it must be assumed that he had had time to be born and grow up) had recognized his father's arrow. Along with his mother, he went to meet him; they kissed each other and wept for joy. The wife told the husband what had happened.

The wife and child reached the camp first. They handed food round, and the mother introduced the child. But the grandmother, who knew nothing of her daughter's marriage and motherhood, was surprised. 'Well, yes,' explained the daughter, 'you scolded me. I left and got married.' The old woman said not a word, and her daughter too was vexed with her because of being scolded and driven away when she had asked for honey. The child spoke up: 'My father is Woodpecker, a big chief and clever hunter and he knows how to find honey ... Don't scold me, or I'll go away.' The grandmother protested that she had no such intention and was delighted. The child agreed to go and look for his father.

Woodpecker assured his mother-in-law, who was amiability itself, that he was in need of nothing, that he did not want any algaroba beer, and that he could look after himself. He asked the old woman to be kind to her grandson, who would be his heir. He also announced his intention of having other children.

Now, Woodpecker prepared to take his revenge. He accused Fox of having lied about his lame foot. Because of him, the wife had nearly died of thirst in the woods! Fox protested, accused his victim of being over-prudish, and insisted that she had had no grounds for taking fright. He offered gifts, which Woodpecker refused. With the help of his son, he tied Fox up, and the child undertook to cut Fox's throat with his grandfather's knife. For the son had more nerve than the father (Métraux 5, pp. 146–8).

After giving this version of the myth, Métraux draws attention to several variants supplied by his informants; some of them reproduce M_{207}, while others resemble the version published by Palavecino. In this last version, the heroine recognizes Fox by his characteristic stench (cf. M_{103}). Fox therefore stinks like an opossum, but – if we are to go by the Toba myths – less than the skunk, since the latter hunts and kills pigs with its noxious farts, and Fox tries in vain to imitate it (M_{212b}, Métraux 5, p. 128). Once she is married to Woodpecker and lavishly provided with honey, the heroine refuses to give any to her mother. When caught unawares by Fox while bathing, she prefers to change into a capybara, rather than yield to him. From this point onwards, the Palavecino version follows a decidedly different course:

M_{213}. *Toba. 'The girl mad about honey'* (2)

After the failure of his amorous ventures, Fox could not think how to avoid the vengeance of the outraged husband. Since the wife had disappeared, why should he not pretend to be her? So he took on the appearance of his victim and, at Woodpecker's request, undertook to delouse him, a service a wife normally performs for her husband. Fox, however, was clumsy: he injured Woodpecker with his needle, as he tried to kill the lice. Woodpecker's suspicions were aroused, and he asked an ant to bite his so-called wife in the leg. Fox uttered most unfeminine howls, which betrayed his identity. Woodpecker killed him, then, by means of magic arrows, tried to find out where his wife was hiding. After discovering from one of the arrows that she had changed into a capybara, he gave up searching for her, believing that from then on she would want for nothing. After being dried and mummified by the sun, Fox was restored to life by rain and went on his way (Palavecino, pp. 265–7).

Before examining the Mataco variants of the story of the girl mad about honey, I propose to introduce a myth about the origin, not of honey, but of mead, and one which shows how important this fermented beverage was among the Chaco Indians.

M_{214}. *Matako. 'The origin of mead'*

In ancient times there was no mead. An old man tried to make it with some honey ... He mixed the honey with water and left the mixture to ferment for one night. The next day he tasted it and found it very good. The other people did not want to taste the drink as they thought it might be poisonous. The old man said, 'I will drink because I am very old and if I died it would not matter.' The old man drank much of the mixture and he fell down as if dead.

That night he awoke and told the people that the beer was not a poison. The men carved a larger trough and drank all the beer they made. It was a bird who carved the first drum, and he beat it all night, and at dawn he was changed into a man (Métraux 3, p. 54).

The interest of this short myth lies in the fact that it establishes a two-fold equivalence: on the one hand between fermented honey and poison and, on the other, between the trough used for mead and the wooden drum. The first equivalence confirms my previous remarks; the importance of the second will appear at a much later stage, and I shall leave it on one side for the time being. It will be noted that the invention of the trough-drum leads to the transformation of an animal into a human, and consequently that the invention of mead brings about a transition from nature to culture. This was already obvious from my analysis of the myths about the origin of the honey (festival) (M_{188}, M_{189}); at the same time, according to a Botocudo myth which I have already discussed (M_{204}), the irára, master of honey without water (hence non-mead) is responsible for the reverse transformation of humans into animals. Another Matako myth confirms this (M_{215}): whoever eats too much honey without water chokes and is in danger of dying. Honey and water are mutually involved with each other, and one is given in exchange for the other (Métraux 3, pp. 74–5). After stressing the importance of the correlation between honey and water in Mataco thought, we can now embark on the main myths.

M_{216}. *Mataco. 'The girl mad about honey'* (1)

The daughter of the Sun adored honey and the larvae of bees. As she was white-skinned and pretty, she resolved to marry only an expert in the collecting of honey of the ales variety, which is very difficult to extract from hollow trees, and her father told her that Woodpecker would make an ideal husband. She therefore set off to look for him, and went deep into the forest where the sound of axes could be heard.

First, she met a bird which could not probe deep enough to get at the honey, and so she went on her way. Just when she was about to catch up with Woodpecker, she accidentally stepped on a dry branch which snapped under her weight. Woodpecker took fright and flew to the top of the tree that he was busy on. From his high perch, he asked the young girl what she wanted. She explained why she had come. Although she was pretty, Woodpecker was afraid of her. When she asked him for a drink (she knew that Woodpecker always carried a gourd full of water), he began to come down, but he was overcome with fear again and went back up to his retreat. The girl told him that she admired him and wished to have him as her husband. Finally, she persuaded Woodpecker to come down to her, and she was able to quench her thirst and eat as much honey as she wanted. The marriage took place. Tawkxwax was jealous, because he desired the girl; she, however, despised him and told him so. Every evening, when Woodpecker reached the conjugal abode, she gently deloused him with the help of a cactus thorn.

One day, during her menstrual period, she remained behind in the village, and Tawkxwax caught her unawares while she was bathing. She fled, leaving her clothes behind. T. dressed up in them and took on the appearance of a woman, whom Woodpecker believed to be his wife. He therefore asked her to delouse him as usual; but with each movement T. scraped his head. This made Woodpecker angry and aroused his suspicions. He called an ant and asked it to climb between T.'s legs: 'If you see a vulva, that's all right, but if you see a penis, sting him!' The twinge of pain caught T. unawares, so that he lifted up his skirt and revealed his true identity; he received a sound thrashing. After which, Woodpecker went off in search of his wife.

After a while he disappeared too and the sun became anxious as to his fate. Sun started to seek him. He followed his trail until his footprints disappeared in a pool. Sun threw his spear into the water and it immediately dried up. At the bottom were two *lagu* fish, one small and the other large. He managed to make the small one vomit but could find nothing in its stomach. He did the same to the large fish and in its stomach was the woodpecker. The woodpecker came to life and he changed himself into a bird. Sun's daughter disappeared forever (Métraux 3, pp. 34–6).

Another variant in the same collection (M_{217}) relates that Sun had two daughters and fed on aquatic animals – lewo – similar to caymans, the masters of wind, tempests and storms, and which were rainbows in animal form. The story continues along almost identical lines to the preceding version, except that Sun advises his daughter to get married, because he cannot supply her with the quality of honey she prefers. After unmasking the deceiver, Woodpecker kills him, then finds his wife again at her father's house, where she has, in the meantime, given birth to a child. Two days later, Sun asks his son-in-law to go and fish for lewo in the water of a lake. Woodpecker does so, but one of the aquatic monsters swallows him. The young woman begs her father to give her back her husband. Sun discovers the culprit, and orders it to restore its victim to life. Woodpecker flies out of the monster's mouth (*ibid.*, pp. 36–7).

A third version, also Mataco in origin, differs considerably from the previous versions.

M₂₁₈. *Mataco. 'The girl mad about honey'* (3)

In the beginning, animals were men and fed exclusively on bees' honey. Sun's youngest daughter was cross with her father, who was a great leader living on the shores of a lake, because he did not give her enough larvae to eat. On his advice, she set out in search of Woodpecker who, of all the birds, was the best honey-gatherer. Woodpecker's village was a long way away from her father's village. When she arrived at Woodpecker's house, she married him.

At the beginning of the third moon, Takjuaj (= Tawkxwax) arrived at Woodpecker's village, ostensibly to take part in the honey harvest. One day when the honey-gatherers were working a short distance away from the village, he deliberately hurt his foot on a thorn and asked Sun's daughter to carry him to the village on her back. Sitting astride her in this way, he tried to copulate with the young woman from behind. She threw him off angrily and went back to her father, the Sun.

Takjuaj was in an embarrassing situation. What would Woodpecker say when he could not find his wife? Perhaps he would try to take his revenge and kill him? He therefore decided to take on the appearance of his victim [var. he made himself clay breasts and a clay vagina]. Woodpecker returned, gave all the honey he had gathered to the woman he took to be his wife, but from the unusual manner in which Takjuaj set about eating the grub (he threaded it onto a needle) [var. from the manner in which T. deloused him], Woodpecker spotted the deception, and confirmed it by means of an ant which he sent to inspect the nether parts of the false wife [var. when bitten by the ant, T. jumped and his false attributes dropped off]. Woodpecker then beat Takjuaj to death and hid his body in a hollow tree. After which, he set off to look for his wife.

He found her at Sun's house. The latter asked him to go and find him a lewoo, for that was the only food he ate. The monster devoured the fisherman. The wife demanded to have her husband back. Sun went to the lewoo, and forced it to vomit; Woodpecker's soul flew out; from then on Woodpecker became a bird. This is the origin of Woodpeckers, as they are known today (Palavecino, pp. 257–8).

The theme of the deceiver imprisoned in a hollow tree, the importance of which will appear later, is found in another myth in the same collection:

M_{219}. Mataco. 'The stoppered and blocked deceiver'

During the course of his wanderings, Takjuaj noticed a mistol tree (*Zizyphus mistol*), the fallen fruit of which lay strewn on the ground. He started to eat and realized that the food was passing straight through his anus undigested; he coped with this difficulty by means of a cork made from 'pasto' (paste? straw? – cf. M_1). Having put on a little flesh, T. met the nakuó bee (= moro moro, cf. Palavecino, pp. 252–3) and asked it for some honey. The bee pretended to comply with this request, and made him enter a hollow tree full of honey, but lost no time in blocking up the opening with clay. T. remained a prisoner in the tree for a lunar month, until a violent gale tore the tree apart and set him free (Palavecino, p. 247).

This myth is reminiscent of another one (M_{175}; cf. *RC*, pp. 305–11), in which the same deceiver quarrels with a bee or wasp which blocks up all the orifices of his body. Thus the Fox, whether in human form (Mataco) or animal form (Toba), appears in the Chaco myths as a personage whose body serves as the basis for a dialectic of opening and closing, container and content, outside and inside. The piercing may be from the outside (adjunction of feminine attributes), and the closing internal (closing up of the orifices through excess in M_{175}, or through a lack in M_{219}). Fox is pierced before he is blocked up (M_{219}), or blocked up before being pierced (M_{175}): in the one instance, he is a container without any content of its own (when the food passes through his body), in the other, he is the content of another container (the hollow tree in which he is imprisoned). This links up with my previous comments on a Mundurucu myth (M_{97}; cf. above, p. 83) and on other Chaco myths (M_{208}: cf. pp. 93–5).

It is quite clear that the Mundurucu and Chaco myths throw light on each other. In the former, the canidae also play a part: as a Mundurucu hero (M_{220}), Fox ties his enemy Jaguar to a tree-trunk, on the pretext that he is *protecting him from a strong wind* (compare with M_{219}; Fox himself is imprisoned in a tree-trunk – tree = *internal prison/external prison* – from which he is eventually *freed* by a strong wind); a wasp *fails to free* Jaguar (M_{219}: a bee *succeeds in imprisoning* Fox). After which Jaguar, in order to catch Fox, hides in a *hollow tree*, where Fox forces him to betray his presence by making him believe that the hollow tree talks when it is empty, but is silent when it is protecting an occupant: this is a transposition into the acoustic code of the contrast between homogeneous container without content (the case of the talking tree) and non-homogeneous content in the container (the case of the silent tree). The symmetry between the Chaco myths and a Mundurucu myth is continued significantly in the use the latter makes of the well-known theme of the *bicho enfolhado*: the fox finally deceives the jaguar by smearing itself with honey (*external use/internal use*), and then rolling in dead leaves which stick to its body. Thus disguised, the fox succeeds in reaching the river to which the jaguar is trying to deny it access (Couto de Magalhães, pp. 260–64; Kruse 2, pp. 631–2). Thanks to honey (but which he puts to a non-alimentary use) Mundurucu Fox therefore succeeds in getting something to drink, whereas in the Chaco myths Fox, who is very thirsty (through having eaten too much honey), fails to find anything to drink, because the ponds are dry. Another Mundurucu myth (M_{221}), the leading characters of which are the fox and the vulture (that is, the eater of raw food as opposed to the eater of rotten food), transforms the theme of the *bicho enfolhado*: Fox, who is now victim instead of persecutor, smears his body with *wax* (*/honey*) in order to stick feathers on it (*/leaves*). Thus attired, he proposes to *fly in the air* (*/swim in water*) *so as to follow the vulture* (*/to escape from the jaguar*). But the sun melts the wax and Fox crashes to the ground and is killed, whereas, in M_{220}, the water dissolves the honey and Fox manages to survive by swimming to safety (cf. Farabee 4, p. 134). All these transformations bear witness to the fact that we are dealing with a coherent system, the logical frontiers of which follow the geographical frontiers of the Amazon basin and of the Chaco, in spite of the distance between these two areas.

But if this is the case, we are perhaps justified in trying to elucidate one detail in the Chaco myths by a corresponding detail in a Mundurucu myth. It will be remembered that a Mataco variant of the story of the girl mad about honey (M_{216}) describes the latter as being 'white-skinned and very pretty'. Now, in Mundurucu cosmogony, the moon is a metamorphosed young virgin with a very white skin (Farabee, *ibid.*, p. 138; other versions in Kruse 3, pp. 1000–1003; Murphy 1, p. 86). The parallel is all the more significant in that there exists a Guiana belief to the effect that honey runs short during the period of the full moon (Ahlbrinck, under 'nuno' §5, and 'wano' §2). The story of the girl mad about honey might therefore admit of an interpretation in terms of the astronomical code, in which the heroine (whose father, as we already know, is the Sun) could be the incarnation of the full moon, and would be all the more greedy for honey since honey is completely lacking when she is present.

In support of this negative pre-condition, I can quote a variant of M_{218}, but one which is of very remote origin since it belongs to the Pima of Arizona (M_{218b}). Coyote pretended to be wounded and insisted that his sister-in-law should carry him on her back; he took advantage of the situation to copulate with her from behind. This offensive behaviour led to the imprisonment of all the animals: that is, *game was lost* instead of *honey being lost* as in South America. Yet the North American version seems to adhere so closely to the affinity between the two themes that it uses one metaphorically to describe the other: Coyote, the liberator of game, opens wide the prison door and 'out swarmed the deer and other game animals, as pour forth the bees from a newly opened hive' (Russell, pp. 217–18). With or without reference to honey, the Chaco myths we have just examined reappear in North America, from California to the basins of the Columbia and Fraser rivers.

At this point, a further observation should be made. In M_{213}, the girl mad about honey changes into a capybara. Another Mataco version (M_{222}) tells the story of a girl mad about wasp honey, lecheguana, who is changed into a non-identified nocturnal rodent (Métraux 3, p. 57, n. 1). As is well known, the capybara (*Hydrochoerus capibara*), which is also nocturnal (Ihering, under 'capivara'), is the largest living rodent; but another rodent, smaller but still quite large and with the same habits (viscacha, according to the informant: *Lagostomus maximus?*) might well be a combinatory variant of the capybara, especially since the Bororo language, for instance, takes the name of the capybara as a model for the formulation of the names of other rodents: okiwa gives okiwareu, 'similar to the capybara' = rat.

The capybara plays a fairly minor part in the myths of tropical America. Towards the end of this volume, I shall discuss a Tacana myth (M_{302}) which attributes the origin of capybaras to the greed of a woman who had an insatiable passion for meat instead of honey. According to the Warao of Venezuela (M_{223}), the origin of the capybara dates from the transformation of disgreeable and disobedient wives (Wilbert 9, pp. 158–60), terms which are also applicable to the girl mad about honey who continually pesters her family in order to obtain the coveted delicacy.

In the Chaco itself, a cosmological myth ends with a woman being changed into a capybara:

M_{224}. *Mocovi. 'The origin of capybaras'*

In the olden days, a tree called Nalliagdigua reached from the earth right up to the sky. The souls used to climb up from branch to branch until they came to lakes and a river, where they caught large quantities of fish. One day the soul of an old woman could catch nothing, and the other souls refused to give her anything. So the old woman's soul became angry. Having changed into a capybara, she set about gnawing the base of the tree until it fell, to the distress of the entire population (Guevara, p. 62, quoted by L.-N. 6, pp. 156–67).

So, here too, the story is about a frustrated woman. But, in this last transformation, it is easy to recognize the heroine of a Mataco myth about the origin of the Pleiades (M_{131a}): the old woman responsible for the loss of the fish and *honey*, both of which used to be available all the year round, and whose season is henceforth to be marked by the appearance of the Pleiades (*RC*, p. 241 *et seq.*). It is clearly the seasonal nature of the honey harvest that the heroine of the myths takes over, as it were, and for which she assumes responsibility.

This being so, it should also be pointed out that the Vapidiana, who live along the frontier between Guiana and Brazil, refer to the constellation Aries as 'the capybara', and that for them its appearance heralds the planting season, which is also the locust season and the time for hunting the capybara (Farabee 1, pp. 101, 103). No doubt this northern region is a long way away from the Chaco and has a different climate, and the timing of seasonal occupations is not the same in both areas. I shall return to the point later when I shall try to show that, in spite of these differences, the cycles of economic life have something in common.

The rising of Aries occurs two or three weeks before the rising of the Pleiades, whose importance in the economic and religious life of the Chaco tribes is well known. Among the Vapidiana, the triple connotation of Aries also suggests the dry season, when the ground is cleared for cultivation, vast swarms of locusts appear and the capybara is hunted: the animals are more easily spotted when rivers and lakes are low, since they live under water during the day and wait until nightfall to come out to graze on the banks.

I have found no reference to the Aries constellation in the astronomy of the Chaco tribes, of which Lehmann-Nitsche has made a detailed study. But if, on the strength of the oft-proved affinity between the Chaco and Guiana myths, we can accept the fact that the metamorphosis into a capybara contains an implicit allusion to a constellation heralding the dry season, it would be possible to integrate the two aspects, the astronomical one and meteorological one, which we discovered to be characteristic of the Chaco myths relating to the honey harvest. Looked at from this angle, the *diurnal/nocturnal* contrast in M_{222} would merely be a transposition, onto a scale of periodicity even shorter than the other two (daily, instead of monthly or seasonal) of the basic contrast between the two seasons which is, in the last analysis, the contrast between dry and wet:

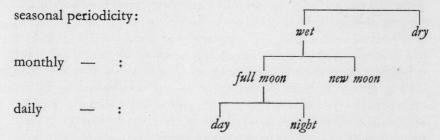

Moreover, among the Toba, the viscacha (which I suggested could be a combinatory variant of the capybara) gives its name to an unidentified constellation (L.-N. 5, pp. 195–6), so that it might be the case that each level retains the features of the other two and differs only in the order of importance it attributes to the three types of periodicity. The three types would, then, be present at each level, one overtly, the other two in a disguised form.

We can now try to get a synthetic view of the whole group of Chaco myths which have as their heroine a girl mad about honey. The heroine's father is the master of aquatic spirits (M_{212}) or the Sun (M_{216}), which feeds on aquatic animals, the originators of rain and storms (M_{217}, M_{218}), and which are assimilated to the rainbow (M_{217}). This initial contrast recalls a famous mythological theme of the Caribbean area (Central America, the West Indies and Guiana): the conflict between the Sun and the hurricane, represented in the day-time by the rainbow and at night by the Big Dipper. There too, the myth is seasonal in character since, in that part of the world, hurricanes occur from mid-July to mid-October, the period during which the Big Dipper disappears almost completely below the horizon (L.-N. 3, *passim*).

On the strength of this connection, let us suppose that, at the beginning of the myths we are examining, the dry, in the person of the Sun, prevails over the wet, represented by the aquatic animals, masters of rain, which form the Sun's diet. Everything, therefore, is taking place in the mode of the dry, and this explains why the heroine is doubly unsatisfied: diachronically speaking, she is the full moon, that is, the wet in the dry, and absence of honey in its presence; but, on the other hand, from the synchronic point of view, the presence of honey, which is associated with the dry season, is not enough; there must be water too, since honey is drunk diluted with water and, from this point of view, honey, although present, is also absent. Honey is a dual substance: diachronically it belongs to the dry; and synchronically it requires water. This is not only true from the culinary point of view; it is also the case as regards the seasonal timetable: in mythical times, according to the Mataco (M_{131a}), men fed exclusively on honey and fish, a link-up which is explained by the fact that, in the Chaco, the period when fish is plentiful lasts from the beginning of April to about May 15th, that is, it is situated right in the middle of the dry season. But as we saw earlier (p. 103), there was a time when all the water and all the fish in the world were permanently available in the hollow trunk of the tree of life. Thus, both the contrast between the seasons and the paradoxical combination, during the dry season, of the 'wet' foods (honey and wild fruits) with the absence of water were neutralized at one and the same time.

In all versions, the heroine can choose between two potential husbands: Woodpecker, a bashful fiancé, but one who possesses the secret of the conjunction between the dry and the wet: even during the search for honey in the dry season, he remains master of an inexhaustible supply of water contained in the gourd which he keeps with him all the time; in fact, he even offers water before honey.[18] In all these

---

[18] The woodpecker's position as master of honey is based on empirical observation: 'Woodpeckers . . . attack nests of stingless bees in the neighbourhood of the flight hole, notwithstanding the fact that the bark is entirely healthy at this point, so that a search on the part of the woodpecker for larvae beneath the bark cannot be offered in explanation of the attack. A few pecks at the trunk of the tree will produce an outpouring of the bees from the nest in numbers to satisfy even a bird's appetite. Numerous specimens of a species of stingless bees were obtained from the stomach of a woodpecker, *Ceophloeus lineatus*, and as it is customary to name a species after its collector, this bee was described as *Trigona (Hypotrigona) ceophloei*. It is said that the jaty bee (*Trigona [Tetragona] jaty*) seals the entrance

respects, the fox is in direct contrast to the woodpecker: he is a brazen seducer, without any honey, which he tries to replace by dirt or by the wild fruits found during the dry season, and without water. Even when he manages to obtain honey, he still has no water and this lack leads to his downfall. The oppositional relationship between the fox and the woodpecker can therefore be given the following simplified expression: (dry — water)/(dry + water).

Between the two, the girl mad about honey occupies an ambiguous position. On the one hand, she is a vixen, since she is without honey and begs for it, or even steals it; yet on the other hand she could be like woodpecker, plentifully supplied with honey and water, if only she could stabilize her marriage with the bird. The fact that she does not do so presents a problem which will be solved later. For the moment, I merely wish to draw attention to a similarity between the heroine of the Mataco myths and the heroine of a short Amazonian myth of uncertain origin, which sheds light on one aspect of the myths I have just been examining. In the Amazonian myth (M_{103}), a young and pretty girl is impelled by hunger to set off in search of a husband. She arrives first of all at the house of the opossum, which she rejects as a husband because it stinks: she also turns down the worm-eating raven (vulture) for the same reason. Finally she comes to the abode of a species of small falcon, the inajé, which feeds her on birds and which she marries. When the vulture or urubu comes to claim the young girl, inajé breaks its skull, and its mother washes the wound with water which is too hot and scalds it. This is why the urubus are bald-headed (Couto de Magalhães, pp. 253–7).

In this myth, as in those belonging to the Chaco, the hunger felt by a young unmarried girl provides, as it were, the source of the action. It is the initial lack, to which Propp refers, which determines the subsequent events in the story. The end, too, is the same: the brazen and foul-smelling seducer is either beaten, maimed or killed (cf. M_{213}). It is true that, in M_{103}, there are three potential husbands instead of two, but this is also the case in M_{216} in which an incompetent bird, which is called čitani in Mataco, is the first to claim the heroine's hand: and in M_{213}, where the same part is played by a bird known as ciñiñi in Toba and, in Spanish, as gallineta (Palavecino, p. 266); it is

---

to its nest with resin to prevent woodpeckers and other birds getting into the nest' (Schwartz 2, p. 96). The woodpecker appears as master of honey in the myths of the Apinayé (Oliveira, p. 83), the Bororo (Colb. 3, p. 251) and Caingang (Henry 1, p. 144), and no doubt of many other tribes.

perhaps a species of wild hen.[19] On this slender basis, I shall try to carry the comparison further:

		Opossum	Urubu	Inajé
M_{103}:	RAW/ROTTEN	−	−	+
	AIR/EARTH:	−	+	+

		Fox	Gallineta	Woodpecker
M_{213}:	HONEY(≡ RAW)/WILD FRUITS(≡ ROTTEN):	−	−	+
	AIR/EARTH:	−	+	+

In the above tables, the signs + and − are assigned respectively to the first and the second term of each pair of opposites. In order to justify the congruence: wild fruits ≡ rotten, we need only observe that the fox does not climb trees (except in M_{208}, where the action leads to its death), and the myths describe it as feeding on fallen wild fruits (cf. M_{219}), which are therefore already damaged, and which must also be the food of the gallineta, since the gallinaceae (supposing the bird belongs to this species) live mostly on the ground, and this particular bird is unable to gather honey, and so resembles the fox in respect of the search for food (but differs from it in being a bird with the power of flight and not an earth-bound quadruped).

The comparison between M_{103} and M_{213} confirms that on two new axes – the raw and the rotten and the high and the low – the fox and the woodpecker are also diametrically opposed to each other. What happens in the myths we are now examining? The story of the heroine's marriage is related in three episodes. Being placed, as we have seen, in an intermediary position between those occupied by her two suitors, she tries to win over one, and is herself the object of an identical attempt by the other. Finally, after her disappearance or metamorphosis, Fox, usurping the heroine's role, tries to win over Woodpecker: this is a ludicrous and non-mediatized union which is bound to come to nothing. From then on, the oscillations between the polar terms become more marked. When forced to flee by Fox, who is the dry in its pure state, the heroine – at least in one version – changes into a capybara, that is, she goes in the direction of water. Executing the opposite movement, Woodpecker goes towards the Sun (*high + dry*), which sends him to fish for sub-aquatic monsters (*low + wet*), from which he escapes only by abandoning his human form and assuming his nature

[19] I put forward my interpretation very tentatively, since Tebboth's Toba Dictionary gives 'carpinteiro (ave)' for chiñiñi. The bird should therefore be regarded as a different species of woodpecker, which is contrasted with the ordinary woodpecker for reasons unknown.

as a bird once and for all: but the bird is the woodpecker, that is, as has already been shown in *RC* (pp. 203–5), and can be directly inferred from its habits, a bird which finds its food under the bark of trees and therefore lives half-way between the high and the low: not a terrestrial bird like the gallinaceae, nor one which haunts the heights of the sky like the birds of prey, but one associated with the atmospheric sky and the middle region where the union of sky and water is effected (*high + wet*). However, a result of this transformation, which is also an instance of mediation, is that there will no longer be any human master of honey. The time is past when 'animals were men and fed exclusively on bees' honey' (M_{218}). This provides further confirmation of the fact, which was remarked upon in connection with other myths, that the mythology of honey is concerned with its loss rather than with its origin.

b. IN THE STEPPES OF CENTRAL BRAZIL

Had we not already, with the help of examples drawn from the Chaco, defined the group of myths which has the girl mad about honey as its heroine, we should no doubt be unable to find it elsewhere. Yet this group also exists in the inland areas of Brazil, and in particular among the central and eastern Ge; but in a strangely modified and depleted form, with the result that certain versions barely hint at the theme of the girl mad about honey, to which they make no more than a brief reference. In other versions it is set in so different a context that it is almost unrecognizable until behind the superficially divergent stories more exhaustive analysis reveals the single basic pattern which re-establishes their unity.

In *The Raw and the Cooked*, I referred to the first part of a myth belonging to the Apinayé and the Timbira and which I will recall now only very briefly, since what we are concerned with at the moment is its continuation. The myths tell of two giant, man-eating eagles, which used to persecute Indians and which two heroic brothers undertook to kill. One Apinayé version, in which only one eagle appears, ends with this happy outcome (Oliveira, pp. 74–5).[20] But another version goes beyond this point.

M_{142}. *Apinayé. 'The killer bird'* (continuation: cf. *RC* pp. 258–9)

After killing the first eagle, the two brothers Kenkutan and Akréti tackled the second. They adopted the same tactics, which consisted

[20] So do the Mehin versions (Pompeu Sobrinho, pp. 192–5; cf. *RC*, p. 258).

in taking turns in coming out into the open, so as to tire the bird which swooped down each time in vain on an elusive prey and had to climb again before making its next attack. But Kenkutan, either through clumsiness or fatigue, was not quick enough to escape from the bird, which cut off his head with one stroke of its wing and returned to its eyrie, where it remained.

Akréti was forced to abandon the fight. He picked up his brother's head, put it on the branch of a tree and set off in search of his fellow-tribesmen, who had fled in order to escape from the cannibalistic eagles. He wandered over the savannah, where he met first of all the sariema tribe (*Cariama cristata*) which had set fire to the brush wood in order to hunt lizards and rats. After introducing himself, he went on his way and met the black araras or macaws [21] which were breaking and eating the nuts of the tucum palm (*Astrocaryum tucuman*) in the burnt savannah. In response to their invitation, he shared their meal and left them. He then went deeper into the forest, where monkeys were gathering sapucaia nuts (*Lecythis ollaria*). They gave him some which he ate with them and, after inquiring of them which road would take him back to his native village, Akréti finally arrived at the water-hole used by the villagers.

Hidden behind a jatoba tree (*Hymenea courbaril*), he caught pretty Kapakwei unawares as she was finishing bathing. He introduced himself, told his story and the two young people agreed to get married.

When evening came, Kapakwei made an opening in the grass wall of the hut near her bed so that her lover could rejoin her in secret. But he was so big and strong that he almost completely destroyed the wall. Having been discovered by Kapakwei's companions, Akréti publicly revealed his identity. He announced that he was going to hunt small birds for his mother-in-law; he actually killed four 'ostriches', which he carried back by their necks as if they were ordinary partridges.

One day, he set off with his wife in order to collect honey from a nest of wild bees. Akréti made a hole in the trunk and told Kapakwei to take out the combs. But she plunged her arm in so far that it became wedged. Saying that he would widen the hole with his axe, Akréti killed his wife and cut her up into pieces, which he roasted. On returning to the village, he offered the pieces of meat to his

---

[21] Nimuendaju, no doubt following the practice of his informants, uses the term in referring to the blue arara or macaw (*Anodorynchus hyacinthinus*); (cf. Nim. 7, p. 187).

relatives. One of the brothers-in-law suddenly noticed that he was eating his sister. Convinced that Akréti was a criminal, he followed his tracks back to the scene of the murder and discovered the remains of his sister, which he gathered up and buried in accordance with the demands of ritual.

The next day, taking advantage of the fact that Akréti wanted to cook *Cissus* (a plant of the grape family, cultivated by eastern Ge) in the glowing embers of a huge communal fire,[22] the women pushed him so that he fell in. An ant-hill sprang up from his ashes (Nim. 5, pp. 173–5).

At first sight, this story seems difficult to understand, since we are not told why the young husband dealt so brutally with his pretty wife, with whom he had fallen in love only a short while before. Also, the ignominious fate meted out to him by his fellow-villagers shows a lack of gratitude on their part, if we reflect that it was he who had rid them of the monsters. Finally, the link with myths in which the heroine is a girl mad about honey seems very tenuous, apart from the fact that honey has a place in the narrative.

It should, however, be noted that the story of a woman caught by the arm in a tree full of honey and who dies in this uncomfortable position is also found not far from the Chaco in the region of the Rio Beni (Nordenskiöld 5, p. 171) and among the Quechua in the north-west of the Argentine (L.-N. 8, pp. 262–6), in whose myth the woman, after being abandoned at the top of a tree laden with honey, changes into a nightjar, a bird which replaces the eagle in some versions of the Ge myth (M_{227}).

But the comparison is even more obvious, if we refer to another version of the myth belonging to the Kraho, a sub-group of the eastern Timbira, who are close neighbours of the Apinayé. The Kraho regard the two episodes – the destruction of the eagles and the hero's marriage – which in Apinayé mythology are run together, as belonging to two separate myths. Have we, then, to explain the contradiction between the great service rendered by the hero to his compatriots and their lack of compassion by an accidental confusion of two myths? To do so would be to disregard an absolute rule of structural analysis: myths do not admit of discussion, they must always be accepted *as they are*. If Nimuendaju's informant included in a single myth episodes which elsewhere

[22] 'Unlike the Sherente and the Canella, the men of the Apinayé tribe participate in the cooking of meat pâtés' (Nim. 5, p. 16).

belong to different myths, this can only mean that the episodes are connected by some link which it is up to us to discover and which is essential for the interpretation of both.

Here, then, is the Kraho myth which clearly corresponds to the second part of M_{142}, while at the same time depicting the heroine as a girl mad about honey:

M_{225}. Kraho. 'The girl mad about honey'

An Indian set off with his wife in search of honey. The tree containing the nest had hardly been felled when the wife, yielding to her craving for honey, and heedless of her husband's pleas to allow him to finish his task, threw herself upon it. He flew into a rage, killed the gluttonous woman, cut up her body and roasted the pieces on hot stones. Then, he made a straw basket into which he put the pieces, and returned to the village. He arrived during the night and invited his mother-in-law and his sisters-in-law to eat what he said was ant-eater meat. The victim's brother arrived on the scene, tasted the meat, and at once recognized what it was. The next morning, they buried the roasted pieces of the young woman, then took the killer off into the savannah. They lit a big fire underneath a tree which they asked him to climb in order to bring down a nest of arapuã bees [*Trigona ruficrus*]. His brother-in-law then shot an arrow at him and wounded him. The man fell; they finished him off by clubbing him to death, after which they burnt his corpse in the red hot ashes (Schultz 1, pp. 155–6).

We are now beginning to understand why the hero of M_{142} killed his wife during a honey-gathering expedition. She too probably displayed excessive greed and had exasperated her husband by her gluttony. But one other point is worthy of attention. In both cases, the wife's relatives, unwittingly, eat the flesh of their daughter or sister, which is precisely the punishment meted out in other myths (M_{150}, M_{156}, M_{159}) to the wife or wives who have been seduced by a tapir and are forced to eat their lover's flesh. This, surely, can only mean that in the group dealing with the girl mad about honey, honey, a vegetable and not an animal entity, plays the part of seducer.

No doubt the development of the story cannot be exactly the same in both instances. The group in which the tapir is the seducer plays on the double meaning of the consumption of food: taken figuratively, it suggests copulation, that is, misbehaviour, but taken in the literal sense it denotes punishment. In the group dealing with the girl mad about honey, these relationships are reversed: in both instances, it is a question of the consumption of food, but in the first case – the consumption of honey – there is also an erotic connotation, as I have already suggested (p. 52) and as is confirmed, along different lines, by the comparison I am now making. The guilty girl cannot be condemned to eat her metaphorical 'seducer': this would be tantamount to gratifying her, since it is exactly what she wishes; and she obviously cannot copulate with a food (however, see M_{269}, where this idea is taken to its logical conclusion). So, the transformation: *literal seducer* ⇒ *metaphorical seducer* inevitably involves two further ones: *wife* ⇒ *parents*, and *wife who eats* ⇒ *wife who is eaten*. The fact that the parents are punished through their daughter is not, however, the result of a purely formal operation. As will be seen later, the punishment is directly motivated and, in this respect, the form and content of the story are interdependent. For the moment, I am merely concerned to point out that these successive inversions lead to another: the wives seduced by the tapir and tricked by their husbands (who make them eat their lover's flesh) take their revenge by deliberately changing into fish (M_{150}); the parents of the wife seduced by honey are tricked by their son-in-law (who makes them eat their daughter's flesh), and they take their revenge by transforming *him* willy-nilly into an ant-hill or by reducing him to ashes, that is, by pushing him in the direction of the dry and of earth, instead of towards the wet and water.

As will become clear later, this demonstration of the semantic position of honey as seducer, which has been carried out with the help of the myths, represents an important achievement. But, before going further, I should add to the Kraho version of the second episode in the Apinayé myth, the other Kraho version which refers directly to the first episode, and then consider the mutual transformational relationships between the three myths.

M_{226}. Kraho. 'The killer bird'

In olden times, in order to escape from the cannibalistic birds, the Indians decided to take refuge in the sky which, in those days, was not so far away from the earth. Only one old man and one old woman, who failed to set off with the rest, remained below with their two grandsons. Being afraid of the birds, they decided to live in hiding in the bush.

The two boys were called Kengunan and Akrey. Before long

Kengunan displayed magic powers which allowed him to assume the forms of all sorts of animals. One day, the two brothers decided to remain in the river until they became strong and agile enough to destroy the monsters. Their grandfather made them a platform underneath the water where they could lie down and sleep; every day he brought them some sweet potatoes on which the two heroes lived [in a Kayapo version, which is very similar to, but less detailed than, the Kraho version, the hiding-place is also under water (Banner 1, p. 52)].

After living in isolation for a long time, they reappeared big and strong, while their grandfather carried out the celebratory rites which marked the end of the young men's period of seclusion. He handed each one a sharpened stick. Thus armed, the brothers proved themselves to be prodigious hunters. At that time, animals were much bigger and heavier than they are now, yet Kengunan and Akrey killed them and brought them back without any difficulty. They pulled out the feathers of the winged creatures they slew, and changed them into birds [id. Kapayo version, Banner 1, p. 52].

It is at this point that the episode of the war against the cannibalistic birds occurs. It differs very little from the summary I have already given in connection with M_{142}, except that it is Akrey and not his brother who is killed and decapitated by the second bird, and his head, which is also placed in the fork of a tree, changes into the nest of an arapuã bee (cf. M_{225}).

Kenkunan avenged his brother by slaying the killer bird. He decided not to go back to his grandparents and to roam the world until he should meet with death at the hands of some unknown people ... During his travels, he encountered, in succession, the tribe of emas (Rhea americana: a small, three-toed ostrich) which set fire to the brush in order to be able to pick up more easily the fallen fruit of the pati palm (Orcus sp.; Astrocaryum according to Nim. 8, p. 73), then the sariema tribe (Cariama cristata, a smaller bird than the preceding one) which used the same tactics in hunting grasshoppers. The hero then left the savannah and entered the forest,[23] where the coati tribe (Nasua socialis) lit fires in order to bring to the surface the earthworms they fed on. The fires which next occurred were those lit by monkeys, which cleared the ground in order to gather the fruit of the pati palm and the jatoba tree (Hymenea cour-

[23] The opposition between chapado and mato, which is employed by the informant, is more accurately an opposition between open country and dense shrub-like vegetation.

baril), then those lit by tapirs looking for jatoba fruit and edible leaves.

Finally, the hero spotted a track which led to a water-hole used by an unknown tribe (the so-called coati people – the Mehin Indians – just as the name of the Kraho Indians means paca people). He remained hidden and watched a 'log' race. Later, he suddenly appeared to a young girl who had come to draw water, and engaged her in a conversation strangely reminiscent of the meeting between Golaud and Mélisande in Maeterlinck's play: 'You are a giant!' – 'I am a man like other men ... ' Kenkunan told his story: now that he had avenged his brother's death, he had but one hope which was to die at the hands of an enemy people. The young girl assured him that her people were well-disposed towards him and Kenkunan made her a proposal of marriage.

After the episode of the nocturnal visit which, as in M_{142}, revealed the hero's stature and physical strength, the latter was discovered by the villagers who greeted him warmly. It was fortunate for them that they did, since Kenkunan, armed only with his spear, displayed his gifts as a hunter. I shall return later to this section of the story.

Single-handed, Kenkunan drove back an enemy people which had encroached on the hunting grounds belonging to his adopted village. He was universally respected and lived to such a great age that it is not certain whether he died finally of sickness or old age ... (Schultz 1, pp. 93–114).

In more than one place, this version compares the childhood of Akrey and Kenkunan with the initiation rites to which young men were subject. The informant is even careful to explain that present-day adolescents spend their period of seclusion in the huts and not under water, but that their sisters or mothers look after them: when it is hot, they wash them with water drawn from the river and fatten them up with lavish quantities of sweet potatoes, cane sugar and yams (*loc. cit.*, pp. 98–9). Among the Apinayé and the Timbira, the close link between myth and ritual is clear from Nimuendaju's commentary. He even notes that the Timbira ritual of the pepyé, that is the young men's initiation ceremony, is the only one to be explained by a myth of origin. In this myth, we find the main features of the Kraho version almost word for word, and I shall restrict myself to noting the differences between them.

M₂₂₇. Timbira. 'The killer bird'

First of all, the myth is more explicit about kinship ties. The old man and old woman are respectively the father and mother of a woman who, along with her husband, was devoured by the cannibalistic bird. The grandparents took charge of the orphans when the other Indians fled.

Akrei and Kenkunan do not spend their period of seclusion underneath the water but on a natural bridge, formed by two huge treetrunks which had fallen across the stream. On these trunks the grandfather built a platform and a waterproof hut, in which the two boys shut themselves away (in this respect, then, the Timbira version reproduces the Apinayé version). When they reappeared after the old man had performed all the ceremonies by himself, including the ritual 'log' race, their hair was so long that it came right down to their knees. Armed with heavy clubs, the brothers killed the first bird, but the second (which was a nightjar, *Caprimulgus* sp.) cut off Akrei's head. His brother placed the head in the fork of a tree near a nest of borá bees (*Trigona clavipes*) which make their nests low down in hollow trees (Ihering, under 'vorá, borá').

Kenkunan went back to his grandparents and told them about his brother's tragic end, then he started off to try to find his fellow-tribesmen. The animals he met told him exactly which way to go. They were, in succession, emas which hunt grasshoppers, lizards and snakes by setting fire to the brush; sariemas who offered him a dish of lizards pounded together with manioc, but which the hero refused, and finally more sariemas, which were fishing with fish-poison, and whose meal he consented to share.

He hid by the spring of the village until he saw approaching the girl engaged to him since infancy. He gave her the flesh of a deer he had killed, then she returned to the village and brought him sweet potatoes.

After the incident of the nocturnal visit during which the hero smashed the hut wall because he was so big and strong, he did not incur the hostility of the men of the village, thanks to his new mother-in-law who had recognized him.

Meanwhile the grandparents had been wandering alone and aimlessly over the savannah. When they came to a mountain which blocked their path, they decided to go round it, the man to the right, the woman to the left, and to meet on the far side. Hardly had they started off on their separate ways when they changed into ant-eaters. Hunters killed the old man, whom they did not recognize in his new form. His wife, weeping bitter tears, waited for him in vain. Finally she went on her way and disappeared (Nim. 8, pp. 179–81).

When we compare these various versions of the same myth, we note that they are on the whole fairly detailed, and also that they differ on precise points. This gives me an opportunity to settle once and for all a methodological question which has perhaps already been puzzling the reader. A short while back, I recalled a rule of structural analysis, which is that a myth should always be accepted *as it is* (p. 121). But on the very same page I may have infringed this rule by proposing to fill in what I said was a gap in the Apinayé version (M_{142}) with the help of the more precise account provided by the Kraho version (M_{225}). To be consistent, ought I not to have accepted the Apinayé version 'as it was' and allowed the episode of the young woman's murder by her husband, which is inexplicable in the context, to remain unaccountable? To overcome this objection, it is necessary to distinguish between two possibilities.

It can happen that myths belonging to different communities transmit the same message, without all being equally detailed or equally clear in expression. We therefore find ourselves in a situation comparable to that of a telephone subscriber who is rung up several times in succession by a caller giving, or repeating, the same message, in case a storm or other conversations may have caused interference with his earlier messages. Of the various messages, some will be relatively clear, others relatively indistinct. The same will be true even in the absence of background noise, if one message is given at great length whereas a second is abridged in telegraphese. In all these instances, the general sense of the messages will remain the same, although each one may contain more or less information, and a person who has heard several may legitimately rectify or complete the less satisfactory ones with the help of the more explicit.

It would be quite a different matter if one were dealing not with identical messages, each of which is transmitting a varying amount of information, but with intrinsically different messages. In this case, the quantity and quality of the information would be of less consequence than the content, and each message would have to be accepted *as it is*. We would be in danger of making the worst kind of miscalculations if, arguing from the quantitative or qualitative insufficiency of each myth, we imagined we could make good the insufficiency by combining separate messages into one single message, which would have no meaning at all, apart from that which the person receiving it might care to attribute to it.

Let us now return to the myths. When and how can we decide whether they represent identical messages, differing only in respect of the quantity or quality of the information transmitted, or whether they are messages conveying irreducible information and cannot be used to complete each other? The problem is a difficult one, and there is no hiding the fact that, in the present state of both theory and method, it is often necessary to settle the matter empirically.

But, in the particular instance with which we are concerned at the moment, we are fortunate in having at our disposal an external criterion which removes the element of uncertainty. We know that the Apinayé and the Timbira-Kraho group, which are both very similar in language and culture, are not really different communities, since their separation dates from a period sufficiently recent for the Apinayé to preserve the memory of it in their legendary tales (Nim. 5, p. 1; 8, p. 6). Consequently, the myths of these central and eastern Ge can not only be legitimately subjected to a formal treatment which brings out their common properties; their structural affinities have an objective foundation in both ethnography and history. The Ge myths form a logical group, primarily because they belong to the same family, and so it is possible to establish a system of genuine relationships between them.

It is therefore legitimate to complete some of these myths with the help of others since, only a few centuries ago at most, they were still indistinguishable. But conversely, the differences which now separate them acquire a greater value, and take on an even greater significance. For if we are dealing with myths which were the same at a relatively recent date historically, omissions or gaps can be explained by the fact that certain details have been forgotten, or certain episodes become blurred; but if the myths contradict each other, there must be some good reason for this.

After completing the myths by means of their resemblances, we must now try to discover the points on which they differ.

They all agree in recognizing the superiority of one brother over the other: one brother is stronger, more adroit, more agile; in M_{226}, he is even gifted with magic powers which allow him to change into various animals. In the Kraho and Timbira versions, the stronger brother is called Kengunan or Kenkunan; and the one who falls victim to the second bird, either through weariness or lack of dexterity, bears the name of Akrey. The Apinayé version is the only one which reverses the roles: at the very beginning of the myth, Akréti shows himself to be a prodigious hunter and a good runner; he is the one who survives the fight with the monster, whereas Kenkutan has his head cut off.

This inversion is the result of another, which itself follows on from the fact that the Apinayé are the only people to identify the hero of the myth with the husband of a woman mad about honey, who does not appear in the Timbira myths and to whom the Kraho devote a completely separate myth (M_{225}). So the Apinayé reverse the respective parts played by the two brothers because, in Apinayé mythology, but not in that of the Kraho and the Timbira, the brother who is victorious over the cannibalistic birds is doomed to come to a sad end. He murders his wife, he is killed and burnt by his relatives, and he is turned into an ant-hill. All this is in complete contrast with what happens to the hero in the Kraho myths, where he enjoys a long and glorious old age – 'like unto himself at last … '[24] we might be tempted to say in order to emphasize that the hero's old age, the ultimate end of which the myth does not even define in concrete terms, constitutes an identical transformation (identical with itself) – and is diametrically opposed (but on a different axis) to what happens in Timbira mythology, where there is, of course, a different transformation (as in Apinayé mythology) affecting not the hero himself but his ancestors, who are changed into ant-eaters (which eat ant-hills) and not into ant-hills (which are eaten by ant-eaters). Between these two transformations, one identical, one different, one passive, one active, there occurs the pseudo-transformation of the murdered woman in M_{225}, whose body is offered to her mother and sisters as if it were ant-eater meat.

Every time the myths specify the genealogical position of the grandparents, they place them in the maternal line of descent. But in all other respects, the versions systematically follow a contrasting pattern of behaviour.

In the Apinayé version (M_{142}), after his brother's death, the hero leaves his grandparents and never sees them again; he sets out in search of his own people and, having found them again, he marries a compatriot who proves to be a disastrous wife.

In the Kraho version (M_{226}), the hero also leaves his grandparents

[24] TRANSLATORS' NOTE: *Tel qu'en lui-même enfin …* the first words of Mallarmé's sonnet on Edgar Allan Poe.

E

and never sees them again, but he sets out in search of a hostile people at whose hands he hopes to die; and although he finally marries a girl belonging to this people, she turns out to be a perfect wife.

Finally, in the Timbira version (M_{227}), the hero is careful to return to his grandparents in order to bid them farewell before setting off to look for his own people, among whom he rediscovers and marries the girl to whom he has been betrothed since childhood. From every point of view, therefore, this last version is the one of the three with the most 'family' feeling:

	M_{142}	M_{226}	M_{227}
grandparents: revisited (+)/abandoned (−)	−	−	+
marriage with: compatriot (+)/foreigner(−)	+	−	+
wife: good (+)/bad (−)	−	+	+

Similarly, a varying fate awaits the remains of the hero's brother – that is, his head: in M_{142}, it is placed in the fork of a tree; in M_{226}, it is placed in the fork of a tree and changed into an arapuã bees' nest; in M_{227}, it is placed in the fork of a tree near a nest of borá bees. M_{142} is difficult to interpret in this respect, for we have no means of knowing whether it is really different or whether something has been omitted: does the head undergo no transformation, or did the informer deliberately omit or disregard this detail? I therefore confine my comparison to the variants M_{226} and M_{227} which, as regards their respective relationships, can be defined in two ways. First, the transformation into a bees' nest is a more strongly emphasized theme than the mere proximity of a head and a nest would seem to indicate. Next, the nest of the arapuã bee is different from the nest of the borá bee: one is a hanging nest and is therefore found outside the tree, the other is inside, in the hollow trunk; furthermore, the nest of the arapuã bees has a relatively higher position than that of the borá bees, which are also called 'tree-bole bees', because they nest close to the ground. Finally, the arapuã are an aggressive species, which produce a rare kind of honey, both inferior in quality and disagreeable in taste (cf. Ihering, under 'irapoã', 'vorá').

In all respects, therefore, M_{226} seems to be a more dramatic version than M_{227}. Furthermore, in this version all the contrasts seem to be amplified – the Indians escape to the sky, the two brothers go and live in seclusion at the bottom of a river, and the hero displays exceptional magic powers. It will be noted, too, that in M_{225} the arapuã nest fulfils an intermediary function: it is a *means* which brings about the death of the hero himself and not a *result* of his brother's death. In the sub-group formed by the two myths about 'the girl mad about honey', this fatal means forms a pair with the one used in M_{142}:

$$\text{means of the hero's death}: M_{142}\left[Cissus\begin{Bmatrix}\text{cultivated}\\\text{cooked}\end{Bmatrix}\right]\Rightarrow M_{225}\left[Arapu\tilde{a}\begin{Bmatrix}\text{wild}\\\text{raw}\end{Bmatrix}\right]$$

I end this list of differences with a brief examination of the episode relating to the hero's various encounters, which can be looked at from various standpoints: the animals encountered, the produce they live on, the hero's acceptance or rejection of their food, and finally, the affinity (often specified by the myths) existing between the animal species and their natural setting, which is either savannah or forest:

	natural setting	animals encountered	food	hero's attitude
(1) M_{142}	savannah ,,	sariema black macaw	lizards, rats; tucum palm nuts	o +
	forest	monkey	nuts of the sapucaia tree	+
(2) M_{226}	savannah ,,	ema sariema	pati nuts; grasshoppers	o o
	forest ,, ,,	coati monkey tapir	earthworms; pati, jatoba; jatoba, leaves	o o o
(3) M_{227}		ema sariema (1) sariema (2)	lizards, snakes, grasshoppers; manioc and lizards; fish	— — +

A steady contrast seems to be maintained between savannah and forest, as well as between animal food and vegetable food, except in M_{227} where the contrast is between terrestrial food and aquatic food:

$$M_{142}, M_{226}: \frac{\text{savannah}}{\text{forest}} \qquad M_{227}: \frac{\text{earth}}{\text{(savannah)}}\Big|\text{water}$$

This divergency brings us back to the root of the matter, that is, to the transformation which takes place in M_{227} (and only in M_{227}): that of the grandparents into ant-eaters, in spite of the extreme consideration shown them by the hero. Consequently, even when the young initiate has no desire to break with his elders, they leave him. The fact that the grandmother alone survives in the form of an ant-eater can no doubt be explained by the belief, which is current from the Chaco (Nino, p. 37) to the north-west of the Amazonian basin (Wallace, p. 314), that large ant-eaters (*Myrmecophaga jubata*) are all females. But what is the significance of the appearance, within the group we are dealing with, of a cycle which centres in such a curious way round the ant-eater? Ant-eaters certainly feed on ant-hills, into which the hero of M_{142} is changed; in M_{225} this same hero offers his wife's flesh to his parents-in-law, claiming that it is ant-eater flesh, and he thus changes them into eaters of this animal, which his grandparents themselves are transformed into in M_{227}.

To solve the enigma, another short myth must be introduced at this point:

M_{228}. Kraho. 'The old woman who changed into an ant-eater'

An old woman one day took her grandchildren to gather puça fruit (unidentified; cf. Nim. 8, p. 73).[25] She took her basket and told them to climb the tree. When the children had eaten all the ripe fruit, they started to gather the unripe fruit which they threw at their grandmother in spite of her protests. When the children were scolded, they changed into parakeets. The old woman, who had no teeth, remained below alone, asking herself: 'What will become of me? What am I going to do now?' She changed into an ant-eater, and went off to dig up ant-hills (*cupim*). Then she disappeared into the forest (Schultz 1, p. 160. Cf. Métraux 3, p. 60; Abreu, pp. 181–3).

This myth has an obvious transformational relationship with the Sherente myth (M_{229}) about the origin of ant-eaters and the padi feast (the wild fruit is generously offered by the ant-eaters instead of being denied them; cf. Nim. 6, pp. 67–8). I shall return to the padi feast later, but here I wish to examine other aspects of the myth.

As in M_{227}, the old woman who changes into an ant-eater is a grandmother abandoned by her grandsons. At the same time, the greedy children who overindulge in fruit and pick them while they are still green, offer a striking analogy with the wife mad about honey, who also consumes her 'corn when it is green', since she devours the honey before her husband has finished collecting it. The greedy children are

[25] According to Corrêa (Vol. II), in the State of Piauhy *pussa* is *Rauwolfia bahiensis*, one of the Apocynaceae.

also reminiscent of the children in a Bororo myth (M_{34}), who are punished for the same misdemeanour. In this myth, the children escape to the sky and change into stars, not parakeets. But these stars are more probably Pleiades, which are sometimes called 'the Parakeets' by South American Indians. Moreover, the fate of the Kraho children is identical with the fate meted out in a Bororo myth (M_{35}) to another greedy child who is changed into a parrot because he swallows scalding fruit: that is 'overcooked', rather than green = 'too raw'. Finally, M_{228} states explicitly that the grandmother is toothless, and this appears to be also the case with the old men in M_{229} before they change into ant-eaters. They give all the fruit of the padi palm they have gathered to their daughter, explaining that they cannot chew it because it is too hard. The grandmother in M_{35} has her tongue cut out, and this makes her dumb like an ant-eater.[26]

There are still further points to be noted. The old woman, who is the victim of her descendants' greed and who changes into an ant-eater, can be compared with the heroine of the Chaco myths which we studied in the first part of this chapter: she was a young woman, not an old one; she changed into a capybara, not an ant-eater, and she was the victim both of her own gluttonous passion for honey in the literal sense, and of metaphorical gluttony (gluttony transposed onto the sexual plane) on the part of a rejected suitor. If, as I suggest, the Kraho myth M_{228} is a weak form of a myth about the origin of the stars of which M_{35} represents the strong form, we can consider it significant that M_{228} should also exist in the Chaco, but as the strong form of a myth about the origin of the stars and more particularly of the Pleiades. The fact can be deduced from M_{131a}, and especially from M_{224} in which the heroine, an old woman who is also a victim of the gluttony of her own family, changes into a capybara. The cycle of transformations is completed by another Chaco myth of Toba origin (M_{230}) which tells how men tried to climb up to heaven in order to escape from a universal fire. Some succeeded and changed into stars; others fell and found shelter in caves. When the fire died down, they came out into the open in the form of various animals; one old man had become a cayman, and an old woman an ant-eater, etc. (L.-N. 5, pp. 195–6).

It follows from my preceding observations that the transformations into ant-eater and capybara act as a pair of opposites. The first is toothless and the other, the largest of the rodents, has long teeth. Throughout

[26] The Caingang-Coroado believe both large and small ant-eaters to be dumb old men (Borba, pp. 22, 25).

the whole of tropical America, the sharp incisors of the capybara are used to make planes and engraving tools, whereas the tongue of the toothless great ant-eater is used as a file (Susnik, p. 41). It is not surprising that a contrast based on both anatomical and technological factors should be systematically exploited. The transformation into one or other animal is a function of gluttony attributable either to the self or the other, and of which kin or affines are guilty. It entails also a triple disjunction along the axes of the high and the low, the dry and the wet, youth and old age. In this last respect, the Timbira version admirably conveys what happens at each initiation: the new age

Figure 10. The fight between the jaguar and the ant-eater. (Redrawn after Nim. 12, Fig. 13, p. 142.)

group takes the place of the one immediately preceding it, and the others do likewise, with the result that the oldest group is excluded from active life, and is forced to take up its position in the centre of the village where it has no more than an advisory capacity (Nim. 8, pp. 90–92).

The contrast between the capybara and the ant-eater is confirmed when we observe that the Mocovi believe the Milky Way to be the ashes of the tree of the world, which was burnt after the old woman turned capybara had cut it down (the Bororo call the Milky Way 'Ashes of stars'). The Tucuna have a myth (M_{231}) in which the ant-eater appears in the form of a 'bag of charcoal' in the Milky Way, i.e. a negative Milky Way: dark on a light background, instead of light on a dark background. The territory of the Tucuna is far removed from that of the Ge, and still farther removed from the Chaco. But the northern Kayapo, who belong to the central Ge group, and the Bororo, who have the Kayapo on one side and the Chaco tribes on the other, have the same myth about the fight between the ant-eater and the jaguar, with exactly the same details, (M_{232a}, b; Banner 1, p. 45; Colb. 3, pp. 252–3): the only difference is the absence of the astronomical coding. But if we can assume that, behind the story of the fight between the ant-eater and the jaguar a latent astronomical code is constantly in operation, and in such a way that the two zones of the Milky Way devoid of stars correspond to the fighting animals, the jaguar gaining the ascendancy shortly after sunset and – since the relative positions are reversed during the night – being overcome before dawn by the ant-eater, we cannot exclude the possibility that the Iranxé myth about the origin of tobacco (M_{191}), in which the vulture replaces the jaguar as the ant-eater's opponent, may lend itself to a similar interpretation. The same could apply to the Timbira myth (M_{227}), which describes how the old man and old woman are changed into ant-eaters while they are walking round a mountain on different sides, and one of them is killed by hunters, while the other continues on its way. This example, too, suggests a nocturnal change which modifies visibility and the respective positions of celestial objects. Finally, if it were legitimate to universalize the Vapidiana identification of the Aries constellation with a capybara, it would seem still more significant that the celestial ant-eater should be a 'non-constellation' close to the Scorpion and – with a discrepancy of about three hours – in phasic contrast with Aries.

It follows from these remarks that, although the Ge myths dealing with the killer bird belong historically to the same family, they belong logically to a group of which they illustrate various transformations. This group is itself a sub-group within a broader system in which the Chaco myths about the girl mad about honey also have their place. We have shown that in the Ge myths, the girl mad about honey fulfils a logical function; whenever she appears, she personifies the *bad marriage* made by the hero, in spite of the fact that he chose his wife from among his *own people*; this is one particular combination within a permutation, the other elements of which are a *good marriage* contracted *among his own people*, and a marriage which is still *better*, although it has been contracted *among strangers*, who may even be presumed to be his enemies. This combinatory system is therefore based on the concepts of local endogamy and exogamy, and it always implies disjunction.

In M_{142} and M_{225}, the hero is unhappily married among his own people, and is disjoined by the individuals who kill him in order to avenge the murder of his wife, the woman mad about honey, and who cause the culprit to be reduced to ashes or changed into an ant-hill, the food of ant-eaters: he is thus turned into a *terrestrial object*. And when, in M_{226}, the hero rushes off in search of enemies at whose hands he can expect only death, this is because his own people have brought disjunction between himself and them by fleeing up into the sky, thus turning themselves into *celestial subjects*. Finally in M_{227}, the hero does all he can *to avoid* disjunction between himself and his own people: he is an attentive grandson, faithful to his own people and to the young girl to whom he has been betrothed since childhood. But to no avail, since his grandparents, to whom he has shown his attachment by his respectful behaviour, are deliberately disjoined from him by changing into ant-eaters, that is, into *terrestrial subjects*. The fact that the axis of disjunction is thus defined by two poles, 'sky' and 'earth', explains why the strongest versions present the initiation as taking place under water, and the weakest (in this respect) at water level. The initiation period is intended to give young men the necessary strength, not to oppose disjunction, from which there is no escape in societies where initiation leads to marriage and matrilocal residence, but to adjust themselves to it, on condition, however, that they make a suitable marriage. This, in fact, is the lesson implicit in the myths, as will be shown later.

Let us begin by sketching the outlines of the meta-group, to which belong both the Ge myths about the killer-bird and those Chaco myths concerned with the girl mad about honey. In the latter, we are concerned with a heroine who is greedy for honey and who is the daughter of Sun, the master of aquatic spirits; the poles of disjunction are therefore sky and water, and more particularly (since I have shown that we are dealing with dry-season mythology) the dry and the wet. The heroine finds herself placed between two suitors: Fox and Woodpecker, one too ardent, the other too retiring, and who later become respectively base seducer and lawful husband. As regards the search for food, they are both in the same category: they represent the gathering of wild produce; only one illustrates its generous aspect: honey and water, the other its meagre aspect: toxic fruits and absence of water. The myth ends with the (temporary) neutralization of Fox, Woodpecker's disjunction in the direction of the sky (where he definitively assumes his bird nature) and the disjunction of the heroine who vanishes, no one knows where, while still quite young or changes into a capybara, an animal belonging to the category of water.

The Apinayé myth (M_{142}) and the Kraho myth (M_{225}) present an inverted picture of the same system. Instead of being the heroine, the girl mad about honey becomes an insignificant adjunct to the hero. The hero reconciles the antithetical functions of Fox and Woodpecker, since the two characters of the *brazen seducer* and the *timid husband* are merged into one, which is that of the *bold husband*. However, the duality is re-established on two levels: on the level of economic functions, since the Ge myths simultaneously introduce hunting and the search for honey, and on that of kinship, since the two affines in M_{213} etc., one timid, the other brazen, are replaced by two relatives, a timid brother and a bold brother.

Corresponding to the heroine who has been changed into a capybara (an aquatic subject with long teeth) is a hero who has been changed into an ant-hill (terrestrial object of a toothless mammal), and one of whose kinsmen, his brother (the counterpart of the heroine's husband, an affine), survives, after being devoured by a celestial monster (whereas the husband was eaten by an aquatic monster), in the form of a round object (his head) placed on a branch where it looks like a bees' nest (the food, situated at the half-way mark, of a bird – the woodpecker of the Chaco myths – which itself belongs to the middle world).

Between these two symmetrical and equally catastrophic versions, the Kraho myth (M_{226}) defines a point of equilibrium. The hero is an accomplished hunter whose marriage has been a success and who attains an advanced age. His 'non-metamorphosis' is indicated by his longevity and by the fact that the myth does not disclose what really happened to him in the end: 'And Kengunan spent his whole life in this village until he was no longer conscious of anything, anything at all. Then he died. And even at that time in the village where he lived, nothing further was known about Kengunan, either whether he died of an illness or of old age. He disappeared and the village remained' (Schultz 1, p. 112). This indeterminate state of permanence contrasts with the irrevocable transformations undergone by the heroine (M_{213}) or the hero (M_{142}), or again with the premature disappearance of the heroine before she has had time to reach an advanced age.

The Timbira version (M_{227}), in its turn, provides a link between the Kraho myth (M_{226}) and the Apinayé-Kraho myths (M_{142}, M_{225}):

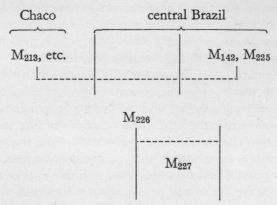

The axis of disjunction is vertical in M_{213} etc. (*sky/water*). It is horizontal in M_{142} (the search for the Indians who have gone far away), vertical in M_{225}, but only faintly stressed (the arapuã's nest in the tree, the red hot ashes below), and reversed in relation to M_{213} (the Sun above, the sub-aquatic monsters below). And whereas M_{226} brings two axes into play: one vertical (the disjunction of the Indians in the sky, while the protagonists remain on earth) the other horizontal (the horizontal disjunction of the hero searching for a distant and hostile people), in M_{227} there is only one horizontal axis of disjunction, and the vertical axis exists only in a latent state (if, as I believe, the transformation of the grandparents into ant-eaters is to be explained in terms of an astronomical coding), and comes last, whereas it occurs at the beginning of M_{226}. We can therefore confirm, in the Ge subgroup, that the Timbira version occupies an intermediary position between the other versions, and this explains the special treatment of the brother's head which is cut off by the bird. It will be remembered that the head is placed on a low branch near a nest of borá bees, whereas in the other versions a nest of arapuã bees, hanging much higher up, is connected with the hero himself (M_{225}) or with his brother (M_{226}), as the means of the death of the one, or the result of the death of the other, as has already been explained.

The Chaco myths dealing with the girl mad about honey and those of central Brazil in which the same character plays a less obvious part, are then part of the same group. Since the former, as we already know, are seasonal in character in that they describe certain kinds of economic activity and one particular period in the year, the same must also be true of the latter. The point needs now to be elaborated.

The territory occupied by the central and eastern Ge forms an almost continuous zone in central Brazil, stretching south approximately from 3–10° of latitude and west from 40–50° of longitude. Within this vast region, climatic conditions are not absolutely uniform: the north-western part borders on the Amazonian basin, the north-eastern part on the famous 'triangle' of drought, where there can be a total absence of rainfall. On the whole, however, the climate in all regions is like that of the central plateau, where there is a contrast between a rainy and a dry season. However, the various Ge tribes do not all adapt to their climatic environment in the same way.

We know something of the seasonal occupations of the northern Kayapo. Their dry season extends from May to October. The natives clear the land at the beginning of the dry season, and burn the wood at the end, by which time it has dried. As the Kayapo fish only with poison, their fishing is restricted to the season when the rivers are low, that is, from the end of July until the beginning of the rainy season. And 'since the operation ... destroys almost all the fish at one go, (it) can only take place once a year in the same river. Fish, therefore, provides only a small fraction of their food, and the fact that it is scarce makes it all the more appreciated' (Dreyfus, p. 30). Game is also scarce: 'sometimes expeditions have to be made very far afield in order to find the meat the Kayapo lack and of which they are extremely fond' (*ibid.*).

At the end of the dry season, game becomes even scarcer and sometimes there is a shortage of agricultural produce. Extra food is obtained by collecting wild fruit. In November and December, the inhabitants of the village set off in different directions to look for piqui fruit, which ripen about this time. The dry months (July to September) correspond, therefore, to a nomadic way of life which continues far into the rainy season for the gathering of the piqui fruit. But this nomadic existence does not necessarily signify a food shortage: the aim of the annual expedition, which always occurs sometime between August and September, is to 'assemble the food required for the great festivities marking the close of the rituals which take place before the rains start, and agricultural work begins again'. When an epidemic strikes the village, the Indians believe that the best remedy is to return to their nomadic existence and that the disease will be driven away if they live in the forest for a while: 'food being more plentiful – they regain strength and return in better physical condition' (*ibid.*, p. 33).

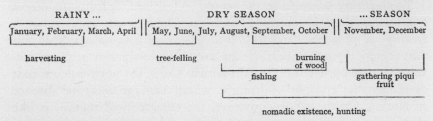

Nimuendaju observes that the prevailing climate in Timbira country is 'noticeably drier than in the adjacent Amazonian area. Unlike the territory farther east and south-east, the country does not suffer the terrors of a drought, yet there is a definite dry season from July until December' (Nim. 8, p. 2). These details do not coincide exactly with the pattern of the ceremonial calendar, which divides the year into two halves, one corresponding in theory to the dry season, from the maize harvest in April until September, the other beginning with the agricultural work which precedes the rains, and occupying the rest of the year (cf. Nim. 3, pp. 62, 84, 86, 163). All the important feasts take place during the ritual period, the so-called dry season, and which consequently is also the period when the Indians lead a settled life. For this reason, and although the information at our disposal is not always clear, it would seem that collective hunts take place during the rainy season (Nim. 8, pp. 85–6). However, mention is also made of hunting savannah birds (emas, sariemas and falconidae) during the dry season, and of collective hunts at the end of each important ceremony (*ibid.*, pp. 69–70). Practically nothing is known about conditions in former times, but it is possible that the spatial contrast between the dry savannah and the strip of forest land bordering the streams and rivers (where fishing takes place and where the plantations are) was as important in native thought as the temporal contrast between the seasons. At any rate, observers seem to have been particularly struck by the former contrast (Nim. 8, p. 1). This may perhaps explain why the contrast between forest animals and savannah animals, which is merely mentioned in the Apinayé and Kraho myths, is concealed in the Timbira version behind another more complex contrast, which gives the following pattern for the respective foods eaten by the animals encountered by the hero:

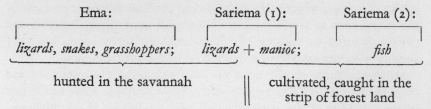

Ema:	Sariema (1):	Sariema (2):
lizards, snakes, grasshoppers;	*lizards + manioc*;	*fish*
hunted in the savannah		cultivated, caught in the strip of forest land

Let us move on now to the Apinayé. 'Anciently, as soon as their clearings were planted, the Apinayé marched into the steppe where they lived the nomadic life of hunters and gatherers until harvest time; only sporadically this or that family would return to the village' (Nim. 5, p. 89). During this period, certain priests had the special task of keeping a jealous watch over the growing plants, which they called 'their children'. Any woman who dared to pick anything from her field before the ban was lifted would be in danger of severe punishment. When the crops were ripe, the priests recalled the villagers from the forest. After a final collective hunt, the families returned to the village, and were at last free to use the produce of their plantations. This moment marked the beginning of the ceremonial period (*ibid.*, p. 90).

If this account of the ancient customs is accurate, what we are dealing with is a rainy season nomadism, since in central Brazil planting takes place at the end of the dry season and the crops ripen a few weeks or a few months later. Thus, the Sherente clear the ground during June and July then burn and plant during August and September, so that germination is helped by the first rains, which follow soon after (Oliveira, p. 394). This rainy-season nomadism, of which we have also found evidence among the Timbira, does not exclude dry-season nomadism, during which hunting also plays an important part, whereas fishing is a far less important activity than is the case in the Chaco. All this suggests that the contrast between the period of plenty and the period of shortage, which is so strongly marked among the Chaco tribes (much more so than the contrast between two kinds of seasons), is expressed by the central Brazilian tribes in socio-economic terms: either in the form of a sacred (ceremonial) period plus a profane period (with no ceremonies) or a nomadic period – collectively devoted to hunting and fruit-picking – plus a sedentary period, mainly taken up with agricultural work. Among the Apinayé, where it appears that agricultural tasks and the occupations associated with the nomadic way of life were carried out during the same months, there was nevertheless a contrast between them; the former, being sacred, were the prerogative of a group of priests, whereas the latter, being profane, were the concern of the population as a whole. The crops grew and ripened during the period devoted to hunting and fruit-picking, but the two kinds of activity were nevertheless considered as being quite distinct.

However, there seems to be no doubt that the Ge myths we are concerned with, like the corresponding Chaco myths, relate to the dry season. The list of the various foods being eaten by the animals encountered by the hero provides an initial indication. All the animal or vegetable products mentioned, whether savannah creatures such as snakes, lizards and grasshoppers, or fish caught during the period when the rivers are running low, or palm or sapucaia nuts or jatobá pods, are typical of the dry season. For instance, this was the season when the Botocudo of eastern Brazil gathered sapucaia nuts, which were an important element in their diet.

Both the Timbira and Apinayé Indians associated the harvesting and gathering of wild produce with the period of nomadic life in the savannah. Nevertheless, the transition from the Chaco myths to the Ge myths is marked by a transformation. In the former, honey and wild fruits are the foods gathered during the nomadic period, while game and honey occupy this position in the latter. But the reason why game replaces wild fruit is immediately obvious: the picking of wild fruit was essentially a feminine occupation among the Ge, but honey was collected by the men (Nim. 5, p. 94; 8, pp. 72–5). As regards the hierarchy of masculine occupations, it can be said that, in the Chaco, the collecting of honey was held to be more important than the picking of wild fruits, just as in central Brazil hunting was considered more important than the collecting of honey:

$$
\begin{bmatrix} \text{CHACO} \\ M_{213} \text{ etc.:} \\ \text{honey} > \text{wild fruit} \end{bmatrix} \Rightarrow \begin{bmatrix} \text{CENTRAL BRAZIL} \\ M_{226}: \quad M_{142}: \\ \text{game} \quad \text{game} > \text{honey} \end{bmatrix}
$$

I have examined the structure of the group from the formal point of view, and I have linked certain transformations occurring within the group to the ecological features of each region, and to various aspects of the material culture of the communities concerned. On these two levels, I have thus succeeded in solving two difficulties that were pointed out by Nimuendaju in connection with the Apinayé version (M_{142}):

Pebkumre'dy (the second phase of the initiation) represents the true initiation for warriors ... The Apinayé link its origin to the same traditional theme that the Canella (= Timbira) associate with their own initiation ritual of the pepyé: the fight between two brothers and a giant falcon. It would seem, however, that the parts played by the brothers are reversed, and I think that the final episode spread down from the north to the Apinayé and that it was added at a later date – I am referring to the story of the man who roasted his wife (Nim. 5, p. 56).

We know, however, that this story is part of the Ge heritage, since it exists as a separate myth among the Kraho Indians. In fact, where Nimuendaju saw two distinct problems, I have shown that there is only one, the different aspects of which throw light on each other. It is because the Apinayé hero (unlike the Kraho or Timbira hero) is destined to meet an ignominious death that his role must be filled by that one of the two brothers who, in the other versions, is killed in his place. It still remains to be explained why this variant requires the presence of the girl mad about honey who becomes the doomed brother's wife. After subjecting these myths to a formal analysis and studying them ethnographically, we must now consider them from a third point of view, namely that of their semantic function.

As I have pointed out on several occasions and have just recalled, the central and eastern Ge regard the fight between the two brothers and the killer-birds as the origin of the young men's initiation ceremony. The initiation rite had a two-fold character. On the one hand, it marked the fact that male adolescents had reached the status of hunters and warriors; thus, among the Apinayé, at the end of the period of seclusion, initiates received ceremonial clubs from their sponsors in exchange for game (Nim. 5, pp. 68–70). But at the same time the initiation rite was a prelude to marriage. In theory at least, the young men were still bachelors. Any young girl who bestowed her favours on one of them before initiation was ruthlessly punished; she was subjected to collective rape by the fully grown men on the day when her lover went into seclusion, and from then on was reduced to the condition of a prostitute. At the close of the initiation period, the young men all got married on the same day, as soon as the ceremony was over (Nim. 5, p. 79).

This was a particularly important event for the men since, like most Ge tribes, the Apinayé were matrilocal. On the day of the marriage, the future brothers-in-law dragged the intended husband out of his maternal hut and led him to their own maternal hut, where his wife-to-be awaited him. Marriage was always monogamous and it was considered to be an indissoluble bond, provided the young woman was a virgin. Each family undertook the responsibility of dealing with the husband or wife, as the case might be, if either should attempt to break the marriage bond. So, the teaching given to the novices every evening all through the initiation period had a distinctly pre-marital aspect: marriage was the main subject for discussion – the instructors explained how to choose a wife 'so as to forestall being fettered to a lazy and faithless woman ... ' (Nim. 5, p. 60).

The same thing was true among the Timbira: 'Formerly, a young man could not marry before completing the cycle of the initiation rites and thus attaining the status of penp, "warrior". At the end of the closing ceremony, the future mothers-in-law walked in parade, leading the young warriors, their prospective sons-in-law, on ropes' (Nim. 8, p. 200 and pl. 40a). All the marriages took place at a collective ceremony at the end of the initiation (*ibid.*, p. 122). The exhortations addressed to the novices never failed to stress the two-fold aim of the rites. During seclusion, the young men were crammed with food, so as to build up strength for competitive sports, hunting and war; not only were they constantly kept in training throughout the entire period of seclusion by means of foot-races and collective hunting expeditions, this was also the time when they were first given the kopó, a weapon half-way between a spear and a club, which is looked upon as being essentially a weapon of war throughout the whole of central Brazil.

The other aspect of the teaching given them related to marriage: how to avoid quarrels and arguments which might set the children a bad example, but also how to detect feminine shortcomings such as flightiness, laziness and untruthfulness. Lastly, the man's duties towards his parents-in-law were enumerated (Nim. 8, pp. 185–6).

The myths provide, as it were, an active commentary on these aspects of the rites. But, according to the versions, certain aspects are singled out and treated in relation to some particular eventuality. Let us look first of all at the Kraho myth about the fight with the killer-bird (M_{226}). It is centred entirely on hunting and war. The hero, Kengunan, is past-master in both these arts, which are to all intents and purposes one and the same, since he does not use bows and arrows for hunting, but only the spear-cum-club, the kopó, which is a weapon of war, although the Timbira use it on exceptional occasions in hunting the ant-eater (Nim. 8, p. 60), a practice which, incidentally, is very much in keeping with the myth's original conclusion (M$_{227}$).

In fact, the major part of the Kraho version consists of an enthusiastic enumeration of the qualities of a good hunter. Without a bow or a dog, he can find game where no one else can: he kills enormous quantities of game, and although the slaughtered animals are very heavy, he carries them without any difficulty. Yet he modestly declares that he has killed nothing, or only an insignificant amount of game, so as to allow his affines the surprise and credit of making the discovery for themselves. His affines only, since he is married and lives in a village belonging to another tribe where he has no blood relations. Above all, by his example, Kenkunan teaches respect for the taboos on which a successful hunt depends. The hunter must not eat the game he himself has killed or, if he eats it, he must at least postpone the act of consumption in two ways which are complementary to each other: in time, by allowing the meat to become cold; and in space, by taking care not to grasp it with his naked hands, but to pick it up on the pointed end of a stick: 'The Kraho', according to the informant, 'do not eat the first animal they have killed; but only if they have killed a lot of the same quality (= species); even then, they do not take the meat in their hands, but pick it up on a pointed stick and allow it to get cold before eating it' (Schultz 1, p. 108).

Among the Ge, therefore, the hunting rites taught to novices during initiation consist chiefly in the practice of discretion. The main object of the married hunter is to provide food for his affines, from whom, the tribe being matrilocal, he is receiving hospitality. He does so generously and modestly, being careful to disparage the game he himself has killed, and to refrain from partaking of it, or to partake of it only very moderately, while keeping the meat at a distance through the use of time and space as mediatory agents.

Now, as we have already observed, the postponement of consumption is a characteristic feature of the rites performed at the honey festival of the northern Tupi tribes, the Tembé and the Tenetehara, who are neighbours of the Ge. Instead of eating the honey immediately, they store it, and the honey, which ferments during the waiting period, becomes a *sacred, shared* beverage. It is shared with the guests from neighbouring villages, and thus helps to strengthen inter-group relations. Yet it is sacred too, since the honey festival is a religious ceremony, the aim of which is to ensure successful hunting throughout the year, and therefore has the same purpose as the Ge hunting rites.

It is possible that a similar distinction existed in the Chaco between the honey collected during the dry season and consumed immediately, and the honey intended for the preparation of mead which, as certain indications suggest, was perhaps kept in reserve, since according to Paucke (1942, pp. 95–6) among the Mocovi,

> the making of mead took place chiefly from November onwards, when the heat was intense. The beverage made from honey and fruit was drunk both day and night and the natives lived in a constant state of intoxication. More than a hundred people would be present at these feasts, which sometimes degenerated into drunken brawls.
>
> In order to prepare the mead, the dried skin of a jaguar or deer was hung up by the corners to form a pouch, into which the honey was poured along with its wax, and then water was added. In the space of three or four days, the mixture fermented naturally in the sun. Young men and bachelors, unless they were of noble birth, were not allowed to drink, and had to be content to act as cup-bearers (*ibid.*, 1943, pp. 197–8).

The weather is cold in the Chaco from July to September. The documents therefore suggest that the collective and ceremonial consumption of mead was also perhaps deferred consumption. At all events, the rites excluded certain categories of men who, like the Ge hunters, although in a different way, were entitled to take part in them only after a certain *point in time*: in this case, after a change in status.

The Caingang of southern Brazil provide a more straightforward illustration of these discriminatory behaviour patterns. One informant has given an illuminating account of an excursion into the forest with two companions in search of honey. Once a tree had been spotted, fires were lit all round it in order to stupefy the bees. Then it was felled and the trunk hollowed out with axes. As soon as the bees' nest was uncovered – 'we take out the layers of the paper-like structure and in our hunger eat the contents raw. They are sweet, rich and juicy. Now we build small fires and lay the cells against them to roast. Having eaten my fill, I receive no more. The two Indians divide the rest, the one who discovered it getting the larger share.' For, to quote the informant, 'honey constitutes a kind of free food. When a nest is discovered, anyone who happens along may share it. No one would think of making a whole meal of honey, but it is a godsend in the middle of the day' (Henry 1, pp. 161–2).

The Suya of the Rio Xingu area are also said to eat honey on the spot where it has been collected: 'All the Indians thrust their hands into the honey and licked it; they ate the combs along with the larvae and the masses of pollen. A small quantity of honey and larvae was kept in reserve and taken back to the camp' (Schultz 3, p. 319).

In contrast to this immediate consumption of fresh honey, which is shared and eaten there and then without ceremony, the Caingang practice deferred consumption in the form of mead intended primarily for affines.

A man and his cousins or brothers decide to make beer for his in-laws. They cut down cedars, hollow them for troughs and go to look for honey. After several days they have enough. They then send their wives for water to fill the troughs. The honey is poured into the water, and the water is heated with hot stones ... The woody stem of a fern called *nggign* is pounded and titrated and the red infusion mixed in the trough. This is to make the beer red; without *nggign*, say the Kaingang, the beer would not ferment. This goes on for days, and then the mouth of the trough is covered with strips of bark and the beer is left standing several days longer. When it begins to bubble, the Indians decide that it is *thô*, intoxicating or bitter, and ready to drink ... (Henry 1, p. 162).

This lengthy preparation, some details of which have been omitted, appears even more complex when it is remembered that the making of the troughs requires huge trees, the felling of which is in itself a long and difficult operation. Moreover, sometimes several of these huge trees had to be felled in order to find one without a crack through which the beer might leak. A whole team of Indians would labour arduously to drag the perfect trunk back to the village, then to hollow out the trough with rudimentary tools, there being a constant danger that a leak might occur during the operation, or worse still, after the beer has started to ferment (*ibid.*, pp. 169–70).

Among the Caingang, then, there were two ways of consuming honey: immediate consumption, without preferential distribution, and in the fresh state; long-deferred consumption, which made it possible to store up an adequate supply and to achieve the conditions necessary for the preparation of fermented honey. Now it will be remembered that, according to the informant, mead is intended for affines. In addition to the fact that the same kind of priority of distribution has a prominent place in the hunting rites in the Ge myths, certain details of the Chaco myths dealing with the girl mad about honey point to a similar conclusion.

On the day after his marriage, the deceiving fox in the Toba myths brings back poisonous fruit and empty combs. But his mother-in-law, who believes the bag to be full of honey, picks it up at once and declares, as a matter of course, that she is going to make mead for all her relatives with the honey gathered by her son-in-law (M_{207}). When Sun's daughter demands a variety of honey he is unable to find, he replies no less spontaneously: 'Get married!' (M_{216}).[27] The theme of marriage as a means of obtaining honey recurs as a leitmotiv in all the myths in this group. Here, too, then, two ways of consuming honey can be distinguished: the woman eats her fill of the fresh honey there and then; at the same time, some honey is kept in reserve and brought back, and this honey is intended for the affines.

We now understand why, in the Chaco myths, the girl mad about honey is doomed to meet with a lamentable end, i.e. is changed into an animal or disappears. Her greed and indiscretion do not provide a sufficient reason, since these defects do not prevent her from making a good marriage. It is only after her marriage that she commits the real crime: she refuses to give her mother the honey collected by her husband. This detail occurs by implication in M_{212}, and in M_{213} it is stressed in a very significant way since, in this version, a mean heroine is changed into a capybara, whereas the heroine of M_{224}, who is old instead of young, also assumes the appearance of a capybara in order to be avenged on her own people for their meanness. Consequently, the misdemeanour committed by the girl mad about honey is that she carries selfishness, greed or spite to the *extent of interrupting the cycle of food-gifts between affines*. She keeps back the honey in order to eat it herself, instead of allowing it to flow, as it were, from her husband who has gathered it to his parents who are entitled to eat it.

We already know that, from the formal point of view, all the myths we have examined so far (whether they belong to the northern Tupi, the Chaco tribes, or the central and eastern Ge), form one group. But now we understand why. All these myths transmit the same message, without necessarily using the same vocabulary or the same grammatical constructions. Some use the active, some the passive, mood. Some

[27] Among the Umutina, too, 'the honey which had been collected was always shared out according to a system based on kinship. The largest share went to the hunter's mother-in-law, and the smallest to his sons, and a little honey was set aside for those who were absent' (Schultz 2, p. 175).

explain what happens when what ought to be done is done; others adopt the reverse procedure and consider the consequences of doing the opposite of what ought to be done. Lastly, since all the myths deal with the question of bringing up young people, the central figure in the story can be a man or a woman: a bad woman who does not even benefit from having a good husband; or a good man who makes a success of his marriage even in a hostile country (but is this not always the situation of a man in a matrilocal society?); or again, a well-bred man who is guilty on three counts: he has chosen a bad woman as his wife, he has rebelled against her and has offended his affines, to whom he offers a kind of 'anti-contribution' in the form of their daughter's flesh.

Within this group, the Ge myths stand out as displaying a characteristic dialectical pattern, for each version examines the instruction given to initiates from a different angle. The hero of the Kraho version, who is a master of war and hunting, makes a success of his marriage through this fact alone, and the successful marriage is, as it were, an additional bonus. He found a good wife, because he was not afraid to seek death at the hands of strangers; and he succeeded in keeping his wife and in reaching an advanced age, because he had won the gratitude of his affines by seeing that they were plentifully supplied with food and by destroying their enemies. The Timbira version reproduces more or less the same pattern, but in a much weaker form, since here the emphasis is shifted: the relevant theme, instead of being the concluding of a marriage, is rather the revoking of a blood relationship (the grandparents are changed into ant-eaters), always in accordance with the rule that even a marriage arranged from childhood and with fellow-countrymen represents a sort of bond which is incompatible with the bond which springs from a blood relationship. As for the Apinayé version, as compared with the other two, it is weaker on four counts: the part of chief protagonist is given to the brother to whom the other versions assign a lower position; the story takes place during a honey-gathering expedition, a more humble form (as compared with hunting) of the search for food during the dry season; the teaching referred to is that relating to the choice of a wife, and not to the conduct of hunting and warfare; finally, and contrary to what happens in the other myths, the hero fails to derive benefit from this teaching, since he marries a wife who is as ill-bred as he is.

Whether explicitly referred to or not, honey plays the part of relevant feature in all the myths. The Chaco myths evolve a theory of honey which contrasts it with other wild and vegetable foods of the dry season. The Ge myths, either overtly or by omission, expound the same theory, basing it on the contrast between honey and game. Among the Ge, only the consumption of game was subject to certain ritualistic prohibitions which caused it to be deferred in time and space, whereas the consumption of honey does not seem to have been controlled by any specific rules. No doubt the Apinayé had a ritual connected with cultivated plants but, with the exception of manioc which has little or no seasonal character, these plants have no place in any mythological cycle definable in relationship to the dry season.

Finally, among the Tembé and Tenetehara, the same theory of deferred consumption is based almost entirely on honey, but only in so far as the deferred consumption of honey is seen as a means of the non-deferred consumption of game: the honey festival is put off until a certain period of the year, in order to ensure successful hunting throughout the whole year.

It follows then that, in the myths of central Brazil, the non-deferred consumption of honey (of which a woman is guilty) is the opposite of the deferred consumption of game (which redounds to a man's credit). In the Chaco, the non-deferred consumption of honey (by a woman) both resembles the non-deferred consumption of wild fruits (i.e. which are still toxic) by both sexes, and forms a contrast with the deferred consumption of honey by a man who does without it himself for the benefit of his affines.

PART *TWO*   THE FEAST OF THE FROG

Et veterem in limo ranae cecinere querellam.

Virgil, *Georgics*, I, v. 378

1 *Variations 1, 2, 3*

In connection with the Ofaié myth about the origin of honey (M_{192}), I pointed out a progressive–regressive movement which I now see is characteristic of all the myths we have studied up till now. The Ofaié myth can be described as a myth of origin in one respect only. For the honey to which it refers bears very little resemblance to the honey with which we are now familiar. This early form of honey had an invariable and uniform flavour, and grew in plantatlons, like the culti-vated plants. As it was within easy reach, it was eaten up when it was barely ripe. Before men could possess honey permanently and enjoy all its different varieties, cultivated honey had to disappear and be replaced by wild honey, which, although available in smaller quantities, is present in an inexhaustible supply.

The Chaco myths illustrate the same theme, more discreetly and less explicitly. In former times, honey was the only food, and it ceased to fulfil this function when the woodpecker, the master of honey, changed into a bird and abandoned human society for good. The Ge myths, on the other hand, transpose the historical sequence into terms of a contemporary contrast between hunting, which is subject to all kinds of rules and is therefore a cultural quest for food, and the collecting of honey, which, being free of all restrictions, suggests a natural means of acquiring food.

We must not be surprised then if, when we move on now to Guiana, we find there as elsewhere myths about the origin of honey, which are also concerned with its loss:

M_{233}. *Arawak. 'Why honey is so scarce now'*

In olden times bees' nests and honey were very plentiful in the bush, and there was one man in particular who had earned quite a repu-tation for discovering their whereabouts. One day while chopping into a hollow tree in order to extract honey from it, he heard a voice from inside calling: 'Take care! You are cutting me!' Opening the tree very carefully he discovered a beautiful woman who told him she was called Maba, 'honey', and who was the Honey-Mother, that is, the Spirit of honey. As she was quite nude, he collected some cotton which she made into a cloth, and he asked her to be his wife. She consented on condition that he never mention her name, and they lived very happily for many years. And, just in the same way that he became universally acknowledged as the best man for finding bees' nests, so she made a name for herself in the way of brewing excellent cassiri and paiwarri. No matter the number of visitors, she only had to make one jugful, and this one jugful would make them all drunk. She thus proved to be a splendid wife.

One day, however, when all the drink was finished, the husband, no doubt slightly intoxicated, went round to his many guests and expressed regret that there was no more liquor. 'The next time', he said, 'Maba will make more.' The mistake had been made and the name of his wife uttered. The woman at once changed into a bee and flew away, although he put up his hands to stop her. And with her, his luck flew away, and since that time honey has always been more or less scarce (Roth 1, pp. 204–5).

Cassiri is a kind of beer made from previously boiled manioc and 'sweet red potatoes', to which is added other manioc that has been chewed by the women and children and impregnated with saliva and cane sugar in order to speed up fermentation, a process which lasts about three days. The preparation of paiwarri is similar, except that this beer is made with previously roasted manioc cakes. It must be consumed more rapidly, since it only takes twenty-four hours to prepare and starts to turn sour after two or three days, unless freshly roasted manioc is added and the other operations repeated (Roth 2, pp. 227–38). The fact that the mother of honey is credited with the preparation of fermented beverages is all the more significant in that the Guiana Indians do not make mead: 'Wild honey may be mixed with water and drunk, but there is no record of it ever having been left to ferment' (*ibid.*, p. 227).

Yet the Indians of Guiana are well versed in the manufacture of fermented liquors from manioc, maize or various fruits. Roth mentions no less than fifteen (2, pp. 227–32). It may well be that fresh honey was sometimes added to the beverage as a sweetening agent. But as evidence of this practice is chiefly found in myths, as will be shown later, the association of fresh honey with fermented beverages can more likely be explained by the intoxicating properties of certain kinds of honey, which make them immediately comparable to fermented beverages. Whether we study the cultures of the Chaco or those of Guiana, the same correlative and oppositional relationship can be noted between fresh honey and fermented beverages, although only fresh honey is present as a constant term, the place of the other term being taken by various kinds of beer made from different substances. Only the form of the contrast is permanent, but each culture expresses it in different lexical terms.

A recent work by Wilbert (9, pp. 90–93) contains Warao variants ($M_{233b, c}$) of the myth that I have just summarized. It makes no mention of fermented beverages. The supernatural wife procures for her husband a delicious kind of water, which is in fact honey, on condition that no one else drinks any of it. But he makes the mistake of handing the gourd to a thirsty companion who is asking for a drink, and when the latter exclaims in astonishment 'But this is honey!' the wife's forbidden name is thus uttered. She pretends to go off to relieve nature, but vanishes, after changing into honey of the mohorohi bees. The man in turn changes into a swarm. The Warao version noted by Roth is very different:

M_{234}. *Warao. 'Honey-bee and the sweet drinks'*

There were two sisters looking after their brother and for whom they were always making cassiri, but even when they tried their best, the drink had no taste; it was never good and palatable. So the man was forever complaining and wishing he could find a woman who could make him a real sweet drink, something like honey!

One day while wandering through the bush and wishing he could find such a woman, he heard footsteps behind him. Turning round, he saw a female who said to him: 'Where are you going? You called Koroha (the honey-bee). That is my name and here I am!' The Indian told her about his own and his sisters' wishes and, when she asked him whether he thought his people would like her, he said he was quite sure they would. Koroha accordingly went home with him. The village people asked her how he had met her, but she was careful to explain to her parents-in-law that she had only come because their son had called her.

She then made the drink. And the way she made it! All she had to do was to put her finger in the water, stir it, and the drink was ready! It tasted sweet, sweet, sweet! And never before had it tasted so good. From that time onward they always had sweet drinks. And on every occasion when her husband was thirsty, Koroha brought him water into which she had dipped her little finger to make it sweet.

But at last the man got tired of all this sweet drink and began to quarrel with his wife, who protested angrily: 'You wanted sweet drinks and you called me to get them for you and now you are not satisfied. You can get them for yourself now!' With this she flew away and ever since then people have been punished by being put to all the trouble of climbing up, and cutting the honey out of the tree, and having to clean it before they can use it for sweetening purposes (Roth 1, p. 305).

It is clear that this myth is a transformation of the preceding one in respect both of kinship ties and the beverages mentioned, although in each instance the drinks are beer and honeyed water. But in each of the two myths a distinction is made between the two drinks. The honey in M_{233} is delicious and the beer perfect – that is, very strong, since it intoxicates even in tiny quantities. In M_{234}, the opposite is the case: the honeyed water is too sweet, and therefore in its way too strong, since it proves to be sickly, while the beer is weak and tasteless. Now, the good honey and good beer in M_{233} are solely the result of a conjugal union; they are supplied respectively by a husband and his wife and are offered only to 'guests', that is to an anonymous group, which remains undefined in respect of kinship.

Unlike the hero of M_{233}, a great producer of honey whose skill has made him universally famous, the hero of M_{234} is defined by his negative features. He is a consumer and not a producer and, what is more, is never satisfied. He is, in a sense, only an incidental character, and the really relevant family relationship compares and contrasts the sisters-in-law, who are producers: the husband's sisters who make the beer too weak, and the brother's wife who makes the syrup too sweet:

$$
\begin{array}{c|c}
M_{233} & M_{234} \\
\begin{array}{ccc}
\overbrace{\quad\quad\quad\quad} & & \\
\bigcirc = \triangle & & (\bigcirc) \\
\text{beer (+)} & \text{honey (+)} & \\
\underbrace{\quad\quad\quad\quad\quad} &
\end{array}
&
\begin{array}{ccc}
\overbrace{\quad\quad\quad\quad} & & \\
\bigcirc = (\triangle) & & \bigcirc \\
\text{honey (−)} & & \text{beer (−)} \\
\underbrace{\quad} & & \underbrace{\quad}
\end{array}
\end{array}
$$

Furthermore, the plentiful supply of honey and the strong beer are treated by M_{233} as positively homologous terms: their coexistence is the result of a conjugal union and itself assumes the outward appearance of a logical union, whereas the (over)-plentiful honey and insipid beer in M_{234} are in a logical relationship of disunion:

$$M_{233} \, [\text{beer} \, (+) \cup \text{honey} \, (+)] \Rightarrow M_{234} \, [\text{beer} \, (-) \, // \, \text{honey} \, (-)]$$

It will be remembered that, among the Caingang, who have mead instead of manioc beer as a fermented beverage, the same terms were combined more simply. Like M_{233}, the Caingang material illustrates a logical union, but one established between fresh sweet honey on the one hand and, on the other, a fermented beverage made from honey and which, according to the Caingang, is of better quality as it is more 'bitter', and which is intended for affines. Whereas the four terms of the Guiana system form two pairs of opposites – *sweet/sickly* for sweetened, non-fermented beverages, and *strong/weak* for the fermented beverages – the Caingang have only two terms forming one opposi- tional relationship between two beverages, which are both made from fresh or fermented honey: *sweet/bitter*. The English language, more clearly than the French, offers an approximate equivalent of this basic contrast in the distinction between *soft drink* and *hard drink*. But in French, we surely have the same contrast, transposed, however, from an alimentary coding to the language of social relationships (the terms of which, moreover, are alimentary in the first place, but are used in a figurative sense) when we correlate and contrast *lune de miel* (honey- moon) and *lune de fiel* or *lune d'absinthe* (sour moon), and thus intro- duce a three-fold contrast between the sweet and the bitter, the fresh and the fermented, total and exclusive conjugal union and its rein- sertion into the pattern of social relationships.

In subsequent chapters, I shall show that these familiar and graphic expressions bring us much closer to the inner meaning of the myths than do formal analyses, although we cannot do without such analyses, if only as a laborious means of justifying the other method which, had it been applied straightway, would have been discredited by its naivety. Formal analyses are indispensable, for they alone make it possible to reveal the logical armature hidden beneath seemingly strange and in- comprehensible stories. Only after this armature has been disclosed can we afford the luxury of returning to 'primary truths', which then appear – but on that condition alone – to merit the double meaning we give to the expression.

The *sweet/sickly* contrast, which is a feature of honey in the Guiana myths, exists elsewhere too, since we have met it in an Amazonian myth (M_{202}) in connection with the story of the ogre who was sickened by honey, and in a Chaco myth (M210), the hero of which is Fox who is crammed with honey, exactly like the unfortunate Indian at the end of M234. This last similarity between characters both of whom stand out as not having any clearly defined relationship to honey, inevitably draws

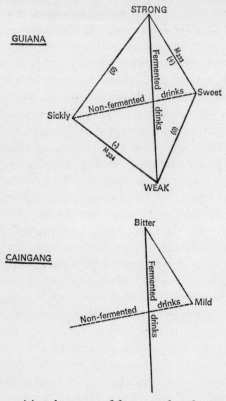

Figure 11. The oppositional system of fermented and non-fermented drinks

attention to another point of resemblance between the Guiana myths and those of the Chaco. The former depict a supernatural creature, the mistress of honey, in the guise of a shy young woman. In M233, where she is completely naked, her first concern is not to offend against modesty: she has to have cotton in order to clothe herself. And, in M234, she is worried about the proposal of marriage, and about the kind of welcome she will receive from her suitor's family. Is he sure that his proposal will meet with approval? As it happens, the woodpecker in the Chaco myths replies to the proposal made to him by the girl mad about honey in exactly the same way and in almost the same terms. It is therefore clear that this diffidence, which the old mythography would no doubt have regarded as a romantic embellishment, constitutes an essential feature of the pattern. When we move from the Chaco to Guiana, it becomes the central theme on which all the other relationships hinge, but which nevertheless preserves the symmetry of the pattern. We note that the Guiana myth, M_{234}, whose hero is a boy mad about honey, provides an exact counterpart to the Chaco myths about the girl mad about honey. The Chaco heroine compares the respective merits of two men: a husband and rejected suitor. The Guiana hero is in the same situation with regard to a wife and sisters. The disappointed suitor – Fox – is rejected because he shows himself to be incapable of supplying good honey, in place of which he offers only toxic fruit (too 'strong'). The sisters drive their brother to marriage because they are incapable of making good beer and can only offer him insipid beer (too weak). In both cases, the result is marriage either with a timid husband, the master of honey, or with a timid wife, the mistress of honey. But the parents of the other spouse are not allowed to enjoy the honey which from now on is in plentiful supply, either because the wife is not sick of it and wants to keep it all for herself, or because the husband is sick of it and does not want his wife to go on producing it. In conclusion, the consumer- or producer-wife changes into an animal – a capybara, or a bee. The following transformations can be noted, as we move for instance from M_{213} to M_{234}:

M_{213}:	M_{234}:
Fox	$\Rightarrow$ Sisters
Woodpecker	$\Rightarrow$ Bee
The Girl mad about honey	$\Rightarrow$ The Boy mad about honey

At this point it must be admitted that the observation I made a little while back raises a problem. If the character acting as the hero in M_{234} is a transformation of the character who is acting as the heroine in M_{213}, how can he also reproduce certain aspects of the character of the Fox? The difficulty will be overcome once I have shown that, in M_{213}, and in the other myths belonging to the same group, there is also a resemblance between Fox and the girl mad about honey, which explains how Fox had the idea of impersonating the heroine in order to deceive the latter's husband (pp. 165, 277).

In order to get to that point, I must first of all introduce a new variant from Guiana. With M_{233} and M_{234} we have by no means exhausted the group of Guiana myths about the origin of honey, all of whose transformations can be generated, that is, whose empirical contents can be deduced, by means of a single algorithm, defined by the following two operations:

It having been accepted that, in the myths of this group, the chief protagonist is an animal, the group can be established if and only if (↔):

(1) *the identity of the animal remains the same in the two consecutive myths, while its sex is reversed;*

(2) *the sex of the animal remains the same in the two consecutive myths, while its specific nature is 'reversed'.*

The homology of the two operations obviously implies the acceptance, as a previously formulated axiom, of the hypothesis that the transformation ($\Rightarrow$) of one animal into another always occurs within a pair of opposites. I have quoted sufficient examples in *The Raw and the Cooked* for the reader to agree with me that this axiom has at least a heuristic value.

Since, in the last version we examined (M_{234}), the chief protagonist was a bee, we shall begin our series of operations with the bee.

a. FIRST VARIATION

$$[\text{bee} \Rightarrow \text{bee}] \leftrightarrow [\bigcirc \Rightarrow \triangle]$$

Here first of all is the myth:

M_{235}. Warao. 'The honey-bee son-in-law'

A man made up a little family party to accompany him on a hunting expedition, leaving his wife and his other two daughters at home. When the hunter and his children had gone far out into the bush, they constructed a shelter in which they camped.

Next day the girl told her father she was indisposed and that she could not build the barbecue and do the cooking, since it was not permissible for her to touch the utensils. The three men went hunting alone, but returned empty-handed. The same thing happened on the succeeding afternoon, as if the young girl's condition were the cause of their bad luck.

Next morning the huntsmen went into the bush, and the girl, who was lying in her hammock in the camp, was somewhat startled on seeing a young man approach and jump in beside her, although she informed him of her condition. She fought and wrestled with him, but the boy held her firmly, assuring her that he had not the slightest intention of troubling her. She learnt that he had been in love with her for a long time, but for the moment his only intention was to rest, and he promised to ask the old man for possession of her later in the proper manner.

So they both lay there quietly in the hammock, discussing their respective prospects and affairs. The young man explained that he was a Simo-ahawara, that is, a member of the bee tribe. Now just as Simo had anticipated, the father was not at all vexed at seeing the stranger in his daughter's hammock. In fact he made not the slightest reference to her even having company.

The marriage took place the following morning and Simo told the three men to remain in their hammocks, as he would make himself responsible for supplying them with food. In an instant he killed a prodigious quantity of game which all three Indians together were unable to raise from the ground, but which he himself brought back without effort. They had plenty to last them for several months. Having dried all the meat, they started on their homeward journey, each one carrying as much as he could. Simo was so strong he carried a load five times heavier than all their loads put together. And yet he speedily caught up with them on the road.

So they all went home together, and Simo took up his residence, as was customary, at his father-in-law's place. After he had finished clearing the land and planting, his wife gave birth to a beautiful baby boy.

Now it was just about this time that his two sisters-in-law were beginning to give trouble. They had fallen in love with him and were always jumping into his hammock, but as fast as they got in he would turn them out. He neither liked nor wanted them, and complained to his wife about their conduct. Of course (as the informant remarks), there was nothing wrong in what his sisters-in-law were trying to do, because among the Warao it is no sin for a man to live with his sisters-in-law as well as his wife.

Every time the three women bathed in the river with Simo minding the baby on the bank, the sisters-in-law would try and dash spray over him. This was very wicked of them, still more so since Simo had warned them that if water should ever touch him it would act like fire, that is, first weaken then destroy him. As a matter of fact, none of the three women had ever seen him bathe: he washed himself in honey just as the little bees do. But only his wife was well aware of the reason for this, since he had told no one else who he was.

F

One day as he was sitting on the bank with the baby in his arms while the three women were washing themselves, the sisters-in-law succeeded in dashing water over him. He at once screamed 'I burn, I burn!', and flying away like a bee into a hollow tree, he melted into honey, and his child changed into Wau-uta, the tree-frog (Roth 1, pp. 199–201).

Let us leave the tree-frog on one side for the time being, since we shall encounter it again later. The theme of the water which burns and melts the bee-man's body can obviously be explained, as Roth observes, by the idea that a person such as the bee-man must be made of honey and wax, the first of which substances dissolves in water, while the other is melted by fire. In support of this theory, I can quote a short Amazonian myth (M_{236}), based on the same theme. After a hunter had been torn to pieces by the birds, the Spirit of the Woods glued the pieces together with wax and warned his protégé that from now on he should not drink anything hot. But the latter forgot about the injunction, the heat caused the wax to melt and his body disintegrated (Rodrigues 1, pp. 35–8).

From the point of view of kinship and the allocation of the various roles, the characters in M_{235} can be divided into three groups, which are easily illustrated by the following diagram:

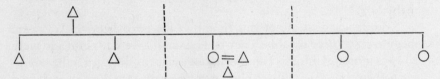

The central group consists of the heroine, her husband who will be turned into honey, and her young son who will also undergo a transformation, but into a frog.

The group on the left, which consists entirely of men, is composed of characters collectively described as unlucky hunters.

The group on the right, which is entirely feminine, comprises the two sisters-in-law. This distribution recalls the one we observed in the Chaco myths which I used in order to constitute the cycle relating to the girl mad about honey. There too we had three groups:

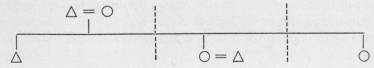

with, in the centre, Fox and the young girl he succeeded in marrying on the pretext that he would provide his parents-in-law with the honey they lacked. The group on the left, then, consists of unlucky honey-gatherers, who have not been supplied with food by their son-in-law (whereas, in M_{235}, it consists of a band of unlucky hunters, who, on the contrary, are plentifully supplied with food by their son-in-law). In both cases, the group on the right consists of one or more sisters-in-law, but only after a further reversal has been effected, since in the one instance, it is the husband who leaves his wife and tries to seduce a sister-in-law who is not at all anxious to follow him, and, in the other, the sisters-in-law who try to seduce a husband who is determined to remain faithful.

The reversal of the erotic relationship that the myth establishes between the affines is therefore itself a function of a two-fold reversal of their alimentary relationship: negative in the one instance, positive in the other; and centring either on honey or meat.

It is remarkable that Bee, in assuming the male sex in M_{235}, should become a supplier of meat (dried meat according to the myth, that is half-way between raw and cooked), whereas in M_{233} and M_{234} in which Bee was a female, she played the part of provider of honey (in a raw form) or beer (in a cooked form). But the fact is that honey, which has an alimentary significance in M_{233} and M_{234}, takes on a sexual connotation in M_{235} (all three are Guiana myths); that is, honey which is always held to be 'seductive' is literally so in the one instance and figuratively so in the other. This transformation within the Guiana group is equally apparent when M_{235} is compared with the Chaco myths, for it is clear that if we move back from the latter to the Guiana myth, the respective functions of the female affines are reversed, at the same time as there is a transition, as regards the 'seductive' connotation of honey, from the literal to the figurative sense. In the Chaco myths, the wife is mad about honey in the literal, and therefore alimentary, sense, and the sister-in-law unintentionally arouses sexual passion in her brother-in-law, Fox. In M_{235}, the opposite happens: the sisters-in-law are mad about honey, but in the figurative sense, since their sister's husband is called 'Honey', and unintentionally arouses sexual passion in them.

But in this respect, they bear a resemblance to Fox, who like them, and as a result of the same amorous approaches, causes the other characters to be changed into animals. From this point of view, the group appears to be over-determined, a circumstance which is in danger of causing some confusion in the table of commutations, where certain terms seem arbitrarily related by multiple connections. I referred to this difficulty earlier, and the time has now come to solve it.

I shall begin by observing that, in M_{235}, there are two sisters-in-law, whereas one would have been enough for the purposes of the narrative. This is also the case in the Toba myths, which I suggested could be interpreted as a reverse transformation of the Guiana myth. Might it not be accepted, as a working hypothesis, that the fact of there being two sisters expresses the ambiguity inherent in a kind of behaviour which can be interpreted in two ways: either in the literal sense, as a search for food, or figuratively, as a sexual quest, since the myth is concerned with the amatory possession of honey (that is, in this case, the possession of a character called 'Honey')? The presence of two sisters-in-law in M_{235} would mean, then, that the common role assigned to them involves two separate aspects. It is as if the purpose of one of the sisters-in-law were to interpret, in the figurative sense, the part played by the Chaco heroine, who was also mad about honey, but honey as food, whereas the other sister-in-law might be said to preserve, in the literal sense, the seductive function assigned to Fox on the sexual level, with the difference that the roles are switched: in the Chaco, Fox trying to seduce his wife's sister; in Guiana, the sisters-in-law trying to seduce Bee, their sister's husband.

This interpretation opens up interesting vistas, when we consider its sociological implications. It suggests a relationship of equivalence between a rhetorical transformation and a sociological transformation:

rhetorical level [literal sense $\Rightarrow$ figurative sense] ::

$$\text{\textit{sociological level}} \begin{bmatrix} \text{seduction of a woman} \\ \text{by a man} \end{bmatrix} \Rightarrow \begin{bmatrix} \text{seduction of a man} \\ \text{by a woman} \end{bmatrix}$$

If it is possible to find other examples confirming this relationship, we shall be able to conclude that, in native thought, the seduction of a woman by a man belongs to the real world, and is the reverse of a symbolic or imaginary procedure. For the moment, I merely put forward the suggestion, pending the time when other myths force me to consider the problems relating to the existence and function of a rhetorical coding (see below pp. 170, 174 ff, 279 ff).

In explaining the duality of the sisters-in-law by the ambiguity of their function, I have at least succeeded in removing the confusion which was threatening to invade the table of commutations, as it may be drawn up on the basis of the Guiana myth. But we have not solved the overall problem, since it is now essential that there should be a duplicated role in the Chaco myths corresponding to the two sisters-in-law in M_{235}. This is a *sine qua non* of the completion of the transformational group.

At this juncture, then, it is appropriate to recall that, in the Chaco myths, Fox plays two parts: his own, first of all, when he tries to marry or seduce the girl mad about honey; and that of the girl herself when he tries to take her place as Woodpecker's wife after her disappearance. Fox is therefore both a man with a sexual passion for women and a girl with an (alimentary) passion for honey, and this, from the diachronic point of view, amounts to a good analytical description of the synthetic attitude attributed by M_{235} to a pair of women (analytically separate on the synchronic level), who are both mad about a man, and mad about 'Honey'.

Therefore Fox's diachronic duality clearly corresponds to the synchronic duality of the two sisters-in-law.

One last comparison must be made. In M_{235}, Bee, who is at first alive, dies after being splashed by water from a river (terrestrial water), which acts upon him as if it were fire. It will be remembered that, in the Chaco myths, Fox, who was dead and dried up as a result of the sun's heat, comes to life again when he is moistened (= splashed) by rain, that is, by celestial water. It is clear, therefore, that if, in the Chaco myths, Fox and Woodpecker are opposites, and that if Woodpecker, the master of honey in the Chaco myths, is congruous with Bee, the master of hunting in the Guiana myth, the Chaco Fox and the Guianese Bee are, not surprisingly, opposites. Each behaves differently towards a young girl who is alone and indisposed: one tries to take advantage of her condition, while the other does not do so. Fox is unlucky in his search for honey; Bee is a miraculous hunter, and is therefore half-way (not only because of his hunting ability but also because of his great strength) between the hero of the Chaco myths and the hero of the Ge myths. But this creates no problems, since we have previously established that the latter myths also stand in a transformational relationship to the Chaco 'honey' myths. But at the same time we see along what a multiplicity of axes we must distribute the transformations which make it possible to move from the Chaco myths to the Guiana myths: *honey/game, male/female, raw/cooked, spouse/affine, literal sense/figurative sense, diachrony/synchrony, dry/wet, high/low, life/death.* The great variety of axes rules out any hope of being able to grasp the group's structure intuitively with the help of diagrams which, in the present instance, would necessitate so many signs and symbols that the reading of them would complicate the explanation rather than simplify it.

b. SECOND VARIATION

$$[\triangle \Rightarrow \triangle] \leftrightarrow [\text{bee} \Rightarrow \text{frog}]$$

In assuming the male sex, Bee also changes from mistress of honey to master of hunting. His new function continues throughout his transformation into a frog, which takes place, as it were, with parity of sex. It will be remembered that the last myth had already prepared the way for this transformation since, at the same time as Bee lost his skill as a hunter and returned to his honey nature, he left a son – therefore a male – who turned into a frog. Consequently, Bee played two parts, one of which was a reversion to his original role as mistress of honey (M_{233}, M_{234}), while the other moved on towards the next transformation, the hero of which is, precisely, a male frog:

M_{237}. *Arawak. 'The story of Adaba'*

There were once three brothers who went out to hunt, taking their sister with them. She was left all alone in the camp while they wandered about in search of game. But they brought back nothing except an occasional powis (wild turkey, Portuguese: 'mutum', *Crax* sp.). This happened for many days.

Close to the camp a tree-frog, Adaba, lived in a hollow tree which contained a little water. One afternoon when the frog was singing 'Wang! Wang! Wang!', the young girl called out to him: 'What are you holloing for? It would be much better if you stopped that noise and brought me some game to eat!' So Adaba stopped holloing, changed himself into a man and went off into the bush. Two hours later he returned with some meat which he told the girl to cook, for her brothers were sure to return with nothing. They were greatly surprised when they did in fact return empty-handed, to see their sister busy barbecuing plenty of meat, and a strange man lying in one of their hammocks! He was a strange man indeed: he had stripes all the way down his thin legs and he wore a lapcloth: otherwise he was quite naked. Having said 'howday' to one another, Adaba asked the three brothers what the result of their hunting expedition had been and told them he would like to inspect their arrows. He burst into a hearty laugh and wiped off the fungus that was growing everywhere on them, and said that, so long as they did not remove this stuff, their arrows would never shoot straight. He then told their sister to spin a fishing line and tie it between two trees. He next told the brothers to take aim at the line, and each brother's arrow stuck into the very centre of the fishing line. Adaba himself had a curious trick in shooting with his arrow: instead of aiming at an animal direct he would point the arrow up into the sky so that in its descent it would stick into the creature's back. The brothers began to learn this method and very soon became such adepts that they never missed anything. They became so proud of themselves and of Adaba that they decided to take him home with them and make him their brother-in-law. Adaba lived a long, long time very happily with their sister.

But one day, the woman insisted on her husband following her to the pond in which she bathed. 'No,' replied Adaba, 'I never bathe in places like this, in ponds. My bathing-place is in the water-holes inside hollow trees.' So the woman dashed some of the water over him and, after doing so three times, she jumped out of the pond and rushed to seize him. But directly she put her hands on him, he turned himself into a frog again and hopped away into the hollow tree where he still is. When the sister came back home again her brothers asked where Adaba was, but all she would tell them was that he had gone away. But they happened to know how and why he had gone away so they beat their sister unmercifully. This, however, did not mend matters because Adaba never came out of the hollow tree again to bring them luck. The three brothers never brought back anything like the quantity of game they used to get when Adaba was present (Roth 1, p. 215).

The Arawak word adaba corresponds to the Tupi: cunauaru and to the Carib kobono-aru, which means a tree-frog (*Hyla venulosa*), able to eject a caustic fluid. A weak variant which is Carib in origin (M_{237b}) refers to the animal by the dialectical form konowaru. In this variant, which comes from the Barama river Caribs of British Guiana, the woman is unmarried and one day expresses her regret at the fact that the frog she hears singing in the bush is not a man: if he were, he would bring her back some game. The wish is no sooner uttered than it is fulfilled. The unlucky hunter mentioned later is a passing stranger, whom Konowaru cures by washing him with urine. Konowaru eventually changes back into a frog, after being splashed by his wife, in spite of his warning (Gillin, pp. 195–6).

In connection with the above variant, it should be noted that, throughout Guiana, the epidermal secretions of tree-frogs are used as a magic ointment by hunters, and their bodies enter into the making of various charms and talismans (Gillin, p. 181; Roth 1, pp. 278–9, 370; Ahlbrinck, under 'Kunawaru'; Goeje, p. 48). Ahlbrinck, who gives a Kalina variant which will be studied later, states that the Kunawaru frog usually lives in a hollow tree and that 'if there is water in the tree, it utters a cry resembling that of a young child: wa ... wa' (*ibid.*). This is clearly the same cry, of which M_{237} and M_{237b} give a phonetic transcription.

The ethnozoology of the cunauaru tree-frog was discussed in *The Raw and the Cooked* (pp. 264–5, 310). I will therefore simply mention two points. In the first place, this particular species lays its eggs in a nest made of cylindrical cells, built in a hollow tree. The cells are fashioned by the animal with resin from the breu branco (*Protium heptaphyllum*). The water which collects in the hollow cavity of the tree rises up into the cells, through the funnel-like opening at their lower end – and covers the eggs. According to popular belief, the resin is secreted by the body of the frog, and it is used as a talisman for fishing and hunting (Tastevin 2 under 'cunawara'; Stradelli 1 under 'cunuaru-icyca').

Zoology and ethnography explain, then, how the bee and the tree-frog came to form a pair of opposites, and how I was able to postulate above, as a theoretical principle, that the transformation of one into the other must inevitably appear as an inversion. Both the bee and the tree-frog do, in fact, make their nests in hollow trees. In both cases, the nest consists of cells, in which the animal lays its eggs, and the cells are fashioned out of an aromatic substance, wax or resin, which the animal secretes or is thought to secrete. It is, of course, untrue that the tree-frog itself produces the resin; it merely collects it and moulds it into shape, but something similar occurs in the case of a great number of meliponae, which build their cells with a mixture of wax and clay, the latter ingredient also being collected.

Although they are alike on all these counts, the bee and the tree-frog nevertheless differ in one essential respect, which constitutes the relevant feature of the contrast between them. The bee belongs to the category of the dry (cf. *RC*, p. 311 and M_{237}: for the bee, water is as fire), whereas the frog belongs to the category of the wet: it needs water inside its nest to make sure that the eggs are protected, so it sings when it finds water, and in the whole of tropical America (as in the rest of the world too) the croaking of the frog is a sign of rain. We can therefore formulate the equation:

$$(\text{bee} : \text{frog}) :: (\text{dry} : \text{wet})$$

Next it must be stressed that myths and rites establish a connection between the tree-frog and success in hunting: 'It is difficult to understand the relationship, except on a basis of some original belief in the divinity of these batrachians, such as we know to have existed in other parts of the Guianas' (Roth 1, pp. 278–9). I hope it was satisfactorily shown in *The Raw and the Cooked* that the connection is to be explained by the cunauaru's ability to emit a toxic fluid, which the native mind associates with the poison used in hunting, and for the preparation of which the venom of dendrobate batrachians is sometimes used (Vellard, pp. 37, 146). As an instance of the emergence of nature within culture, the poison used in hunting or fishing thus has a particularly close affinity with the sociological character of the seducer, and this explains why, in certain myths, poison is the son of the animal which plays the part of seducer (*RC*, pp. 275–81).

As I have established at various points throughout this book, honey too must be placed in the category of seducers: either in the figurative sense, as a substance which inspires quasi-erotic desire, or in the literal sense, whenever honey is used to describe a character who is defined purely in relation to it (like *deficiency of honey* or *abundance of honey*, that is, the girl mad about honey in the Ge and Chaco myths, or Bee in the Guiana myths). It is clear, then, that the transformation of Bee, mistress of honey, into Frog, master of the poison used in hunting, can also be explained in this way.

In M_{237}, Adaba, a marvellous hunter, uses a particular technique of archery: he shoots the arrow into the air and it falls downwards onto the animal, piercing its backbone. This is not a purely imaginary device, since evidence of its use is found among tribes who are extremely expert in archery. The natives of tropical America are not all equally skilled in this respect. I have often had occasion to observe the indifferent performances of the Nambikwara, whereas the Bororo reveal an expertise which struck other observers before me: 'An Indian draws a circle of about a yard in diameter on the ground and stands one pace away from the circumference. He then shoots eight or ten arrows straight up into the air and they all fall inside the circle. Every time we happened to be present during this exercise, we felt that the arrows could not fail to fall on the archer's head; but, confident in his skill, the latter remained motionless where he stood' (Colb. 3, p. 75). In 1937 or 1938, I met a small group of fairly deprimitivized Guarani Indians in the Parana valley who, according to the demonstration they gave us, seemed to practise a similar form of archery, but in their case it was dictated by the weight of their arrows which were iron-tipped or headed with a piece of crudely fashioned iron. These unwieldy missiles had to be used at short range and were given a sharply curved flight.

We must not, therefore, exclude the possibility that experience provided the framework on which the myth embroidered. But the framework in question could hardly be more than a pretext, since the archer in the myth is not so much skilled as endowed with a magic power: he does not calculate the course of his arrows but releases them at random, as is precisely stated in a variant, to one aspect of which I have already referred. In this variant (M_{236}), the Spirit of the Woods enables a hunter to shoot birds without fail and without taking aim, but on condition that he should never let fly in the direction of a flock of birds; if he does, the companions of the slaughtered bird will take revenge. This is what happens when the hero fails to respect the prohibition. He is torn to pieces by the birds, but brought back to life by his supernatural protector who sticks the fragmented body together again with wax (p. 162).

The interest of this variant lies in the very clear distinction it makes between two possible ways of interpreting the idea of 'random shooting'; it can be taken either in the absolute sense of shooting at nothing, or in the relative sense of shooting in the general direction of a group, in which case the uncertainty is not about the *species* of the animal which will be killed, but about which *individual* animal will be killed out of several which all belong to the same, already known, species. As we have already seen, M_{236} can be brought into line with M_{235} on the basis of two homologous pairs of opposites: *water/fire*, *honey/wax*. The comparison with M_{237}, which itself is a transformation of M_{235}, now suggests a further comparison between M_{235} and M_{236}, this time on the rhetorical level. The contrast between the literal meaning and the figurative meaning, which emerged from the analysis of M_{235}, provides an adequate model of the contrast between the two methods of random shooting in M_{236}, one of which is prescribed, the other prohibited. Only the former corresponds to the definition of random shooting as understood in the literal sense, since, in the absence of any kind of target, it represents a genuine instance of randomness. But the latter, in which the target is at once present yet indeterminate, does not have the same degree of randomness although, like the other, it is referred to as random shooting; it can only be random in the figurative sense.

Other aspects of the Adaba myth will be more profitably discussed after I have introduced myths illustrating the next stage in the series of transformations.

c. THIRD VARIATION

$$[\text{frog} \Rightarrow \text{frog}] \leftrightarrow [\triangle \Rightarrow \bigcirc]$$

The third variation, which is illustrated by several myths of major importance, will engage our attention for longer than previous variations.

M_{238}. *Warao. 'The broken arrow'*

There was once a man who had two brothers-in-law. While he was one of the unluckiest of mortals, they invariably returned home with plenty of game. Tired of supplying both him and his wife with food, they decided to lose him away (get rid of him), and instructed him to follow a track leading to the Black Jaguar's lair. At the sight of the monster the Indian fled, but the jaguar pursued him and they both started running round and round an immense tree. The man, who ran faster, just managed to catch up with the animal's hind-quarters and cut off his heels. Black Jaguar was unable to walk at all and sat down. The Indian next shot it through the neck with an arrow, then finished the job with a knife.

Now his two brothers-in-law, knowing well how poor a hunter he was, never doubted that they had seen the last of him. They were thus greatly surprised at his arrival at the house and made excuses for having left him, alleging that there had been a misunderstanding. At first they were unwilling to believe that he had killed Black Jaguar, but the man was so insistent that they all, including their old father, agreed to follow him to the place. When they saw the ogre, the three men were so afraid that the victor had to trample on the carcass before his father-in-law would agree to approach it. As a reward for this doughty deed, the old man gave his son-in-law another of his daughters, his brothers-in-law built him a bigger house and he was henceforth recognized as headman of the village.

But the man was very anxious to have a reputation for being clever in hunting all other animals. He therefore resolved to ask Wau-uta, the tree-frog, to help him. He set out to look for the tree in which she lived and stood below it, calling out to her and begging her to show him all the things he was anxious to learn. It was nearly dark and the frog gave no answer. He continued his entreaties which, when it became quite dark, he interspersed with tears and groans, 'for he knew full well that if he cried long enough, she would come down just as a woman does when, after refusing a man once, she finally takes pity when she hears him weeping'.

As he stood waiting underneath the tree, a whole flock of birds appeared, all arranged in regular order according to size, from the smallest to the largest. One after the other, they pecked his feet with their beaks so as to make him clever in hunting. Wau-uta was beginning to take pity on him, but of course he did not know that. When the birds had finished with him, the rats came in order of their size, to be followed by the acouri, the paca, the deer, the wild pig, then the tapir. As they filed past the Indian, each animal put out its tongue and licked his feet so as to give him luck when hunting its kind. Next came the tigers, from the smallest to the largest, all going through the same performance. Last of all the snakes crept past.

This went on all through the night and it was only at daybreak that it came to a stop, when the man finally ceased his weeping. A stranger came up to him. It was Wau-uta carrying a curious looking arrow: 'So it was you making all that noise last night and keeping me awake! Look down your arm, from your shoulder to your hand!' His arm was covered with fungus and the other was just the same. The man scraped off all the fungus, for that was what had given him bad luck. Whereupon Wau-uta suggested that they should exchange arrows; hers had broken into three or four pieces and had been subsequently spliced. When he tried it in his bow, the man nevertheless succeeded in shooting at a thin vine rope hanging a long way off. Wau-uta explained to him that henceforth he must shoot into the air and in any direction he liked; and the Indian observed that, when it fell, his arrow always stuck into some animal or other: birds first of all, in the same rotation as before, then a rat, an acouri etc., finally the tapir; tigers, snakes in their proper order, exactly in the way the animals had filed past him during the night. When all this was finished, Wau-uta told him he might keep the arrow on condition that he never divulged to anyone that it was she who had taught him to be so good a marksman. Then they said good-bye and parted company.

Our friend returned home to his two wives, and soon gained as great a reputation as a provider of smoked meat as he already bore for his bravery in killing the Black Jaguar. All did their level best to discover the secret of his success, but he refused to tell. So they invited him to a big beer-feast. Drink proved his undoing; he let loose his tongue and divulged what had happened. Next morning, after regaining consciousness, he went to fetch his arrow, the one Wau-uta had given him, but found it replaced by his own. From that time he lost all his luck (Roth 1, pp. 213–14).

There is a long Kalina variant of this myth (the Kalina are a Carib group of Guiana), which provides a perfect transition from M_{237} to M_{238}. In this particular variant (M_{239}), the protecting frog is a male cunauaru, i.e., it is of the same species and sex as Adaba, the hero of M_{237}. But, as in M_{238}, the frog in M_{239} plays the part of protector to an unlucky hunter who is rescued from the cannibalistic Jaguar (instead of killing it); it removes the maleficent fungus from the hunter's arrows (like Adaba, but unlike Wau-uta, who discovers the fungus on the hunter's body) and turns him into a first-class marksman (although there is no question here of any magic arrow).

The rest of the story takes us back to M_{237}: the hero returns to his own people but he has acquired a frog's nature through living with batrachians. So he bathes only in 'frog's water', which is found in hollow trees. His wife is to blame for his coming into contact with water in which human beings wash, and as a result of this, his son and he both turn into frogs (Ahlbrinck, under 'awarupepe', 'kunawaru').

The theme of the animals grouped according to size is still present in this variant, but occurs in a different place, that is, during the hero's stay with the cannibalistic Jaguar. The latter asks him how he uses his arrows, and he replies that he kills animals, which he enumerates according to their different families, at the same time as he displays his arrows one after the other, in each case starting with the smallest animal and working up to the largest. As the size of the animal quoted increases, the Jaguar's laughter grows louder (cf. Adaba laughing when he discovers the fungus on the arrows), for he hopes that his interlocutor is about to name the jaguar and thus provide him with an excuse for devouring him. On coming to the last arrow, the hero names the tapir,[1] and the Jaguar roars with laughter for two hours, thus allowing the man time to escape.

Let us approach the myth from this angle. The entire group to which it belongs describes, alternately, or concurrently, two types of behaviour: verbal behaviour relating to a name which must not be uttered or a secret which must not be betrayed; and physical behaviour relating to bodies which must not be brought into contact with each other. M_{233}, M_{234}, M_{238} and M_{239} (first part) are concerned with verbal behaviour: it is forbidden to utter Bee's name or reproach her for having a bee's nature, to betray Wau-uta's secret or to utter the Jaguar's name. M_{235}, M_{236}, M_{237} and M_{239} (second part) are concerned with physical behaviour: the bee's or the frog's bodies must not be wet with the water human beings use to wash. In all the myths, the theme is always the harmful collocation of two terms, one of which is a living being and, according to the physical or verbal character of the conduct described, the other can be a thing or a word. We can say, then, that the idea of collocation is taken literally in the first instance, and figuratively in the second.

The term which is actively brought into contact with the other can itself have two characteristics. As a word (the proper noun) or as a sentence (the secret), it is compatible with the individual to whom it is applied. 'Bee' is unmistakably the name of the bee, 'Jaguar' that of the jaguar, and it is equally true that Maba and Wau-uta are each responsible for the benefits they confer. But when it is a question of a thing (water in this instance), then it is incompatible with the being with whom it is brought into contact: the kind of water used by humans is antipathetic both to the bee and to the frog.

Thirdly, the contact between the two terms (whether physical or verbal) can be either random or directed, according to circumstances. In M_{233} and M_{238}, the hero utters the forbidden word involuntarily and by accident. In M_{235} and M_{239}, the sisters-in-law or the woman do not know why they must not splash water onto the hero. On the other hand, in M_{239}, the hero lists the animals in order of size, starting with the smallest and working up to the largest, and only in this instance is the maleficent contact avoided. The following comparative table must therefore include this possibility, and it must also take into account the disastrous consequences of the contact, although in this case they would

---

[1] The Dutch original gives *buffel*, buffalo, but this is the term Ahlbrinck uses to denote the tapir, as the translator of the French version observes in a note in the article 'maipuri'.

be expressed as a conjunction (the jaguar would eat the man) and not
by disjunction (the transformation of the supernatural woman or man
into an animal):

	M_{233}	M_{234}	M_{235}	M_{237}	M_{238}	M_{239}
actual/verbal	−	−	+	+	−	+
compatible/incompatible	+	+	−	−	+	−
directed/random	−	−	−	−	−	+
contact: *brought about/avoided*	+	+	+	+	+	+
conjunction/disjunction	−	−	−	−	−	−

The purpose of this summary in diagrammatic form (in which the
signs + and − denote respectively the first and second term of each
pair of opposites) is merely to serve as a temporary guide. It is incomplete, because some myths are only partially present. Having
reached this stage of the analysis, I must now introduce other aspects.
What has already been said by no means exhausts the question of the
contrast between order and randomness. If we go through the series
of myths, we discover that its field of application is much vaster than
the one we have explored up till now, and that it also involves an
additional contrast. At the beginning, we are dealing with two-term
systems: a character and the name he or she bears, an individual and
something he cannot tolerate, then from M_{238} onwards, two individuals who cannot tolerate each other (the hero and the jaguar). So far,
then, the negative relationship constitutes a polarity, just like the positive, and subjectively random, relationship which occurs from M_{236}
onwards between a hunter and his game *on condition that he aims into the
air*, that is, without there seeming to be any foreseeable link between the
behaviour and its result: an animal will no doubt be killed, but the
species to which it belongs will remain unknowable until the result is
achieved. I have already drawn attention to the semi-random nature of
the ultimate behavioural possibilities that M_{236} is careful to forbid:
if the archer shoots in the direction of a flock of birds, the uncertainty
will relate to the identity of the individual bird which will be killed but
not to the species, and so the conditions required by the hypothesis
will no longer be fulfilled. So the other birds swoop down on the culprit and tear him to pieces.

On the other hand, a hunter who was certain of hitting something,
but without knowing exactly what, cannot be considered as a perfect
hunter. It is not enough to be always sure of killing something; he needs
to assert his mastery over the whole range of game. The behaviour of
the hero in M_{238} admirably conveys this compulsion: even the fact of
having killed the cannibalistic jaguar, the supreme form of game, did

not necessarily mean that he was an established hunter: 'He was very anxious to have a reputation for being clever in hunting all other animals, in addition to the glory he had earned in ridding the country of the Black Jaguar' (Roth 1, p. 213). Since M_{236} shows the impossibility of escaping subjectively, and by quantitative means, from the inadequacies of a system of polarity, the solution must be at once objective and qualitative, that is, the subjectively random character of the system (from which, as M_{236} proves, there is no escape) must be counterbalanced by an objective transformation from a polar system to an ordered system.

The transformation of the polar system begins in the first episode of M_{238}. There are still no more than two contrasting terms – on the one hand, the jaguar who is an ogre, and on the other hand, the unlucky hunter who is doomed to become his prey. So what happens? The jaguar chases the hunter round a tree and their respective positions, after being clearly defined to begin with, become relative, since it is no longer certain who is running after whom, who is the hunter and who the hunted. In escaping from his pursuer, the hunter catches up with the animal from behind, and wounds it unexpectedly; all that then remains to be done is to finish it off. Although the system is still confined to two terms, it is no longer a polar system; it has become cyclical and reversible: the jaguar was stronger than the man and the man is stronger than the jaguar.

We have yet to note the transformation, at a later stage, of the two-term system, which is cyclical and not transitive, into a transitive system comprising several terms. This transformation takes place between M_{238} (first part) and M_{239} (first part) and then M_{238} (second part). This interlinking is hardly surprising since we saw that M_{239} overlaps M_{238} and also M_{237}, which is the first of the three in the cycle of transformations.

The first ordered and transitive cycle appears in M_{239} (first part), in the doubly muted form of verbal behaviour the result of which calls for negative expression: the hero *is not* eaten by the jaguar, even though the latter forced him to list all wild animals, each family in turn, beginning with the least important families, and working up from the smallest animal in each family to the largest. As the hero does not mention the jaguar (deliberately or unintentionally, we do not know) the jaguar does not kill the man, in spite of the fact, which is not mentioned in the context, that men usually kill jaguars. The hero's verbal behaviour and the imaginary hunt he mimes for the jaguar's benefit, by presenting all his arrows in turn, are replaced in M_{238} (second part) by real animal behaviour and by a hunt in the literal sense, both of which call into play a complete and ordered zoological system since, in both instances, the animals are arranged in classes, which in turn are graded from the least harmful to the most dangerous, while the animals themselves are graded within each class from the smallest to the largest. The initial contrast, which was the contrast inherent in fatality (whether the latter is negative, in the sense that terms which ought never to have been brought into contact are accidentally juxtaposed, or positive, in the sense that, during the magic hunt, the hunter is always sure of shooting some animal by chance, although it is always one that he had no precise intention of killing), is thus overcome, thanks to the emergence, *in response to a subjectively random intention, of an objectively ordered natural world*. The analysis of the myths confirms that, as I have suggested elsewhere (9, pp. 18–19, 291–3), a belief in the effectiveness of magic presupposes an act of faith in the natural order.

If we come back to the formal organization of the group of myths in question, it is clear that further remarks must now be added to complete those already made. From M_{233} to M_{235} we are dealing with a system involving two terms, the conjunction of which – imaginary if one of the terms is a name or a predicative judgment, real if it is a thing – brings about the irreversible disjunction of the other term, accompanied by negative consequences. In order to overcome the antithesis of the polarity, M_{236} at one point envisages a solution which it admits to be wrong, because the result is a negative conjunction – that of the hunter and the birds, which leads to the hero's death. M_{236} thus appears as a blind alley or a cul-de-sac, in which the literal and figurative meanings, which the earlier myths used alternately, are simultaneously blocked. In this myth, the conjunction between the man and the birds has a physical reality and must be taken in the literal sense; but as I have already shown (p. 171), it results from the fact that the hero chose to interpret the prohibition imposed on him in the figurative sense.

The first part of M_{238} transforms the polar system into a cyclical system without introducing new terms; the transformation takes place in the literal sense, since the two adversaries pursue each other materially around a tree, which is a thing. The pursuit results in a positive conjunction, the implications of which are still limited: the man gets the better of the jaguar. The cyclical and ordered system appears first of all in a verbal and figurative form in M_{239} (first part), in which it is confirmed by a positive disjunction (the man escapes from the jaguar), then in a literal and real sense in M_{238} (second part), where the confirmation is a positive conjunction with general implications: man has become the master of all forms of game.

There is one last aspect we still have to examine: the one relating to the theme of the fungus covering the arrows (M_{237}, M_{239}) or the arms (M_{238}) of the unlucky hunter. Since we know that, in fact, M_{239} illustrates a transformation intermediary between M_{237} and M_{238}, we must suppose that the fungus on the arrows, the instruments used by the hunter, is an initial approximation towards the fungus which directly affects his body, and that the transition from one to the other occurs correlatively with the transition from the still random system of M_{237} to the completely ordered system of M_{238}.

I indicated earlier that Guiana hunters often rub their arms with the secretions of certain species of frogs. The Tucuna in the Rio Solimões area observe a similar practice when undergoing treatment prescribed by a shaman. For this purpose, they use the frothy secretions, which are soluble in water, of a tree-frog with a bright green back and a white stomach (*Phyllomedusa*). When rubbed over the arms, the secretions cause vomiting, which has a cleansing effect. As we shall see further on, several tribes of the Amazonian region have recourse to certain toxic varieties of honey in order to achieve the same result. In the light of this approach, it is possible to consider the fungus referred to in the myths as a representation in reverse of the tree-frog's secretions: the latter ensure success in hunting, the former prevents it; the tree-frog removes fungus and supplies secretions. Furthermore, through a series of transformations, an indirect connection can be detected between the honey which appears at the beginning of the group and the fungus referred to at the end. We have already seen how, from the Chaco myths to the Ge myths on the one hand, and through the series of Guiana myths on the other, honey could be transformed into game; and it is now clear that, if we start with the game which is ensured by means of the frog's secretions, the latter can be changed into fungus which hinders the pursuit of game.

One observation is called for here. In the rites, the frog is the means of obtaining game in the literal sense; it plays this part through the effect of a physical contact between its body and that of the hunter. In the myths, the part played by the frog is retained but it is described in the figurative form, since the virtues of the frog are moral, not physical. This being so, the literal meaning continues to exist, but refers to the fungus which has a physical effect on the hunter's body and which, in a sense, constitutes an inverted frog. This is an important transformation, because it enables us to establish an indirect link between the group we are dealing with and a Tucuna myth, although the only point in common is, it would seem, the theme of the fungus on the hunter's body:

M_{240}. *Tucuna*. '*The mad hunter*'

A bird-catcher set his snares, but every time he went to examine them, he found he had caught nothing but a sabiá bird (a kind of thrush: one of the *Turdidae*). Yet his fellow-hunters used to bring back large birds such as the mutum (*Crax* sp.) and the jacus (*Penelope* sp.). Everyone made fun of the unlucky hunter, who was plunged into deepest gloom by these jests.

The next day, he once again caught nothing but a thrush and flew into a rage. He forced open the bird's beak, broke wind into it, letting it fly away. Almost at once the man went mad, and started to rave. What he said made no sense: 'he talked endlessly about snakes, rain and the ant-eater's neck etc.'[2] He also told his mother he was hungry, and when she brought him food he refused it, insisting that he had only just finished eating. He continued to talk until he died five days later. His corpse, which was stretched out in a hammock, became covered with mould and fungi and continued to utter a stream of nonsense. When they came to bury him, he said: 'If you bury me, fire ants will attack you!' At last they waited no more but buried him while he was talking (Nim. 13, p. 154).

I have transcribed the above myth almost literally because of the interest of the clinical picture it gives of madness. The madness takes the form of verbal behaviour and is expressed by a flood of words and confused utterances, which anticipate metaphorically the mould and fungi with which the corpse of the madman is eventually covered in the literal sense. Like the heroes of the Guiana myths, the madman is an unlucky hunter. But whereas the Guiana heroes claim that they are being victimized and address verbal complaints to the animals, he behaves in a physically aggressive manner towards the animals, and for this he is punished by a metaphorical fungus: madness, which is the *consequence* of his absurd behaviour, whereas his Guiana counterparts got rid of real fungus, which was the *cause* of their enforced inaction.

---

[2] This last feature can be explained, no doubt, by the fact that large ant-eaters seem to have no neck: their head is a direct extension of their body.

In *The Raw and the Cooked*, I emphasized on several occasions that mould and fungi have a special significance in native thought patterns. They are vegetable substances belonging to the category of the rotten, on which men fed before the introduction of the civilized arts of agriculture and cooking. As a vegetable substance, mould is therefore opposed to game, an animal food; moreover, one is rotten, whereas the other is intended to be cooked; finally, the rotten vegetable substance belongs to nature, whereas cooked meat belongs to culture. On all these levels, we see an amplification of the contrast between terms, which in the Guiana myths were initially brought together. M_{233} described the blending (within the range of purely vegetable foods) of honey, a raw, natural food, and beer, a cooked, cultural food. In the case of honey, we can say that nature anticipates culture, since it provides a food which is ready to eat: in the case of beer, it is rather culture which excels itself, since beer is not only cooked but fermented.

In moving from the initial contrast: *raw/fermented*, to the subsequent contrast: *raw/cooked*, the myths are following a regressive course: the rotten is on the hither side of the raw as the cooked is on the hither side of the fermented. At the same time, the gap between the terms has widened, because the initial polarity was concerned with two vegetable terms, whereas the one we have now arrived at consists of a vegetable and an animal term. Consequently, the mediatory nature of the polarity also follows a regressive course.

We now embark on the study of an important Guiana myth, which is extant in several different versions. Although the story is quite different, this myth can be compared to the preceding ones, if we adopt the same angle of approach, since, in it, the frog appears still more clearly as a feminine character.

M_{241}. *Warao. 'The story of Haburi'*

Long ago, there were two sisters minding themselves, for they had no man to look after them. So they were very puzzled to discover one day that starch of the palm tree, ité (*Mauritia*), they had felled the evening before was all ready prepared. Next day the same thing happened, and then it happened again and often so they decided to keep watch. About the middle of the night they saw a manicole palm tree (*Euterpe*) bend gradually over until it touched the cut they had made in the trunk of the ité tree. Both sisters rushed up and caught hold of it, begging it earnestly to turn into a man. It refused at first but, as they begged so earnestly, it did so. He became the husband of the elder of the two sisters and by and by she gave birth to a beautiful baby boy, whom she called Haburi.

The two women had their hunting-ground near two ponds; one of these ponds belonged to them, and so they used to fish there. The other belonged to Jaguar,[3] and they advised the man not to go near it. He did so nevertheless, because the jaguar's pond contained more fish than theirs. But Jaguar came along and, in order to be revenged, he killed the thief. He then took the husband's shape and returned to the spot where the two women were camped. It was almost dark. Jaguar was carrying his victim's basket, which contained the stolen fish. In a coarse, rough voice which surprised the sisters, the false husband told them they could cook the fish and eat it, but that he himself was too tired to share their meal. All he wanted was to sleep, while he nursed Haburi. They brought the child to him and, while the women were eating their dinner, he started to snore so loudly that he could be heard on the other side of the river. Several times in his sleep, he uttered the name of the man he had killed and whom he was pretending to impersonate. The dead man was called Mayara-kóto. This made the women anxious and they suspected some act of treachery. 'Our husband never snored like that,' they said, 'and he never called his own name before.' They gently removed Haburi from the arms of the sleeper, slipping in a bundle of bark in his place. They quickly made off with him, taking with them a wax light and a bundle of firewood.

While going along, they heard Wau-uta, who at that time was a witch, singing and accompanying her song with her ceremonial rattle. The women went on and on, quickly too, for they knew that, once they arrived at Wau-uta's place, they would be safe. In the meantime the jaguar had woken up. When he found himself alone, holding a bundle of bark in his arms instead of a baby boy, he became extremely angry. He changed back into his animal shape and hurried after the fugitives. The women heard him coming and hurried still more. Finally they knocked at Wau-uta's door. 'Who is there?' – 'It is us, the two sisters.' But Wau-uta would not open the door. So the mother pinched Haburi's ears to make him cry. Wau-uta, her curiosity aroused, asked: 'What child is that? Is it a girl or a boy?'

[3] TRANSLATORS' NOTE: In Roth, the animal is referred to as Tiger, which the author has translated into French as Jaguar.

'It is a boy, my Haburi', replied the mother and Wau-uta opened the door immediately and asked them to come in.

When the jaguar arrived, Wau-uta told him she had seen no one, but the beast knew by the scent that she was telling a lie. Wau-uta suggested he should find out for himself by poking his head through the half-open door. The door was covered with thorns, and as soon as Jaguar put his head in, the old woman closed it and killed him. But the sisters began to grieve for their dead husband and cried so much that Wau-uta told them to go and gather manioc in the plantation and make beer, so that they could drown their sorrow. They wanted to take Haburi, but Wau-uta insisted that there was no point in doing so and that she would take care of him.

While the sisters were in the fields, Wau-uta made the child grow by magic into a youth. She gave him a flute and some arrows. On their way back from the plantation, the women were surprised to hear music being played, for they did not remember there being a man in the house when they left. And though ashamed, they went in and saw a young man playing the flute. They asked after Haburi but Wau-uta maintained that the child had run after them as soon as they had left for the field and that she thought he was with them. All this was a lie, because she had made Haburi grow up with the intention of making him her lover. She still further deceived the two sisters by pretending to take part in the search for the little boy, having previously ordered Haburi to say she was his mother, and given him full directions as to how he must treat her.

Haburi was a splendid shot: no bird could escape his arrow, and Wau-uta directed him to give her all the big birds he killed and to give his mother and his aunt all the little ones which he had to pollute first by fouling them. The object of this was to make the sisters so vexed and angry that they would leave the place. But this they would not do: they continued searching for their little child. This sort of thing went on for many days; big birds and dirtied little birds being presented by Haburi to Wau-uta and the two women, respectively.

One day, however, Haburi did miss a bird for the first time, his arrow sticking into a branch overhanging a creek where the otters,[4] the hunter's uncles, used to come and feed. It was a nice, cleared spot and here Haburi eased himself, taking care to cover up the dung

[4] TRANSLATORS' NOTE: Roth has water-dogs, which the author has translated as otters.

with leaves. Then he climbed the tree to dislodge the arrow. Just then the otters arrived and, scenting the air, they at once suspected that their worthless nephew must be somewhere about. They discovered him on the tree branch and ordered him to come down and sit, when they would tell him a few home truths: he was leading a bad life, the old woman was not his mother, and the two younger ones were his mother and aunt respectively. They impressed upon him that it was wicked of him to divide the birds unfairly. He must do exactly the opposite, giving his real mother, the elder of the two sisters, the larger birds and tell her he was sorry and apologize for his wickedness which was due entirely to ignorance on his part.

So Haburi made a clean breast of it to his mother and gave the dirtied little birds to Wau-uta. The latter worked herself into a great passion, told Haburi that he must be mad and blew in his face [in order to drive out the evil spirits, cf. Roth 1, p. 164]; so angered and upset was she that she could eat nothing at all. All through the night she nagged Haburi. But the next morning, the latter again gave the big birds he had shot to his real mother and the dirtied little ones to Wau-uta who gave him no peace. Haburi therefore made up his mind to get out with his mother and aunt.

Haburi built a canoe from bees' wax, but by next morning a black duck had taken it away. He made another little clay canoe, which was stolen by another kind of duck. In the meantime he cut a large field and cleared it so quickly that the women could grow enough manioc for their proposed journey. Haburi would often slip away and make a boat, always with different kinds of wood and of varying shapes, but just as regularly a different species of duck would come and steal them. The last one he made was from the silk-cotton tree and this particular one was not stolen. Thus it was Haburi who first made a boat and who taught ducks to float on the surface of the water, because it was with his boats that they managed to do so. 'Indeed,' the informant comments, 'we Warao say that each duck has its own particular kind of boat.'

What was even more curious was that the next morning the last boat was found to be bigger than it was the night before. Haburi told his mother and her sister to collect all the provisions and put them aboard, while he continued to plant manioc cuttings along with Wau-uta. At the first opportunity, he slipped secretly back to the house, took his axe and his arrows and proceeded down to the waterside, having previously ordered the posts not to talk, for in those days the posts of a house could speak and, if the owner of the house were absent, a visitor could thus find out his whereabouts. Unfortunately Haburi forgot to warn the parrot in the house to keep silent, and when Wau-uta returned, the bird told her which way Haburi had gone.

Wau-uta rushed down to the landing and arrived just in time to see Haburi stepping into the boat to join his mother and aunt. The old woman seized hold of the craft screaming: 'My son! My son! You must not leave me! I am your mother!' and she refused to let go her hold, although they all repeatedly struck her fingers with the paddles and almost smashed them to pieces on the gunwale. So poor Haburi had perforce to land again and, with old Wau-uta, proceeded to a large hollow tree, where bees had built their nest. Haburi made a small hole in the trunk with his axe and told the old woman to go inside and suck the honey. As it happened, she was mad about honey and, although crying very hard at the thought of losing Haburi, she crawled through the little opening, which the latter immediately closed in upon her. And there she is to be found to the present day, the Wau-uta frog, which is heard only in hollow trees. And if you look carefully, you will see how swollen her fingers are from the way in which they were bashed by the paddles when she tried to hold on to the gunwale. If you listen you can also hear her lamenting for her lost lover: Wang! Wang! Wang! (Roth 1, pp. 122–5).

There are other variants of this myth which will be studied later. The reason why I have used Roth's variant first, and given an almost literal translation of it, is because none of the others conveys the myth's astonishing novel-like quality, nor brings out so clearly its originality, dramatic inventiveness and psychological subtleties. In fact, it was not until Rousseau's *Confessions* that French literature had the courage to broach the theme of the young boy taken in by a patroness with ulterior motives, who starts off by playing the mother figure before settling into the role of elderly mistress, while making sure that a certain ambiguity continues to hang over her equivocal sentiments. Madame de Warens was quite a young woman compared with the Guianese frog, who, because of her age and animal nature, has a depressing and repulsive appearance, that the narrator is clearly well aware of. It is stories of this kind (this one is by no means an isolated instance in the American oral tradition, although no other, perhaps, displays such brilliance) which succeed in conveying, in a sudden flash of illumination, the irrefutable feeling that these primitive peoples, whose inventions and beliefs we handle in a rather off-hand manner that would be appropriate only if they were crude productions, are capable of an aesthetic subtlety, an intellectual refinement and a moral sensibility which we ought to approach with scrupulousness and respect. However, I leave it to specialists in the history of ideas and to critics to continue these reflections on the purely literary aspect of the myth, while I turn now to its ethnographical study.

(1) The story begins with a description of the lonely life led by two sisters, who become the wives (they talk about 'our husband') of the supernatural man whose pity they have aroused. It will be remembered that the worst disasters which befell the hero of M_{238} occurred after he obtained a second wife, that the misfortunes endured by the hero of M_{235} sprang from the fact that he had two sisters-in-law, and finally that the heroine of the Chaco myths had the misfortune to have two suitors and that the rivalry between them led to disastrous consequences.

I have already drawn attention to the importance of this duplication which, on the formal level, reflects an ambiguity which seems to me to be an essential characteristic of the symbolic function (L.-S. 2, p. 216). In the myths the ambiguity is expressed by means of a rhetorical code which plays endlessly on the contrast between the thing and the word, the individual and the name he bears, the literal sense and the figurative sense. One version, which unfortunately I have been unable to consult in Paris and which I am quoting from a second-hand source, brings out the dualism of the wives, since the myth (only the initial episode is given here) claims to explain the origin of marriage between one man and two women:

M_{242}. *Arawak. 'The origin of bigamy'*

Two sisters were alone in the world. A man, the first they had ever seen except in their dreams, came down from heaven and explained agriculture, cooking, weaving and all the civilized arts to them. This explains why each Indian now has two wives (Dance, p. 102).

Now, throughout almost the whole of Guiana (and no doubt in other areas too), bigamy implies differentiation in the parts played by the two women. The first wife, who is usually the elder, has certain special duties and privileges. Even if her co-wife is younger and more attractive, the older woman retains her position as head of the household (Roth 2, pp. 687–8). There are no descriptive details about the second wife in the text of M_{241}: she is just a wife. The other one, however, appears in such clearly defined roles as farmer, cook and mother. In bigamy, then, the dualism of the wives is not merely dual, but a polar and orientated system. The second wife is not a reduplication of the first. When she appears, endowed with mainly physical qualities, it is the first one who undergoes a transformation and becomes a kind of metaphor of the wifely function and a symbol of the domestic virtues.

I shall discuss the hero's civilizing role later.

(2) The supernatural husband makes his appearance at the time when the palm trees are being felled for the extraction of starch. About the time when *Mauritia flexuosa* begins to bear fruit, the Warao cut down the tree and split it lengthwise in order to expose the fibrous pith inside. The hollowed out trunk serves as a trough. Water is poured into it, while at the same time the fibrous substance is worked upon, so that a considerable quantity of starch is released. The fibrous particles are extracted then and, when the starch has settled as a deposit, it is put into moulds and the loaves thus obtained are then dried over a fire (Roth 2, p. 216). The other species of palm tree quoted at the beginning of the myth and the foliage of which turns into a man is *Euterpe edulis*, which the Indians cut down in order to facilitate the gathering of the ripe fruit. After softening them in a trough filled with tepid water (boiling water would make them hard), they pound the fruit with a mortar. The mush is drunk while fresh, sweetened with honey and diluted with water (*ibid.*, pp. 233–4).

Since we are dealing here with a myth at the end of which honey plays a decisive part, the customary association between the fruit of the palm tree and honey is all the more reminiscent of the Chaco 'honey' myths, since here, as in the Chaco, we are concerned with vegetable foods which grow wild. Even though the pith would be obtainable during the greater part of the year, the fact that the Indians choose to cut down the trees when they are beginning to fruit, suggests the end of the dry season.[5] The latter is very clearly defined in the Ori-

[5] On the subject of the seasonal fruiting of *Mauritia flexuosa*: 'The tribes ... of the Amazonian area greet the appearance of the ripe fruit with joy. They anxiously await this period of the year in order to celebrate their most important feasts and, at the same time, prearranged marriages' (Corrêa, under 'burity do brejo'). M. Paulo Bezerra Cavalcante, head of the Botany section of the *Museu Paraense Emilio Goeldi*, when consulted about the time of fruiting of several species of wild palm trees, was kind enough to reply (and I take this opportunity of thanking him) that 'according to records made over a period of years, the fruit reaches maturity mostly at the end of the dry season, or the beginning of the rainy season.' According to Le Cointe (pp. 317–32) most of the wild palms in the Brazilian area of Amazonia begin to fruit in February. M. Paulo Bezerra Cavalcante nevertheless gives

noco delta, where the rainfall is at its lowest from September to November, and reaches its maximum in July (Knoch, G 70–75). Besides, in Guiana, palm trees denote the presence of water in spite of drought, like wild fruit in the Chaco, but not in the same way: the Indians consider *Mauritia* and *Euterpe* to be a sure sign of the vicinity of water: when they cannot find water anywhere, they dig near the bases of palm trees (Roth 2, p. 227). Finally, as in the Chaco myths dealing with the origin of mead, the idea of the trough comes to the forefront. The trunk of the *Mauritia* provides a natural trough, in which the Indians prepare the soft damp substance enclosed in this ligneous outer covering which is sufficiently hard for the Warao to use the trunks of the *Mauritia flexuosa* to make the piling for their huts (Gumilla, Vol. I, p. 145). The fruit of the *Euterpe* is also prepared in a trough, but in a *different* trough, not one made from the tree *itself*, that is, the fruit is tipped into an already existing trough, instead of the trough disclosing its contents while it is in the process of being made. So, in the Warao myth, we again encounter the dialectics of container and content, of which the Chaco 'honey' myths first provided an illustration. Now, its reappearance in this new context is all the more significant in that, whereas the Chaco heroine played the part of a girl mad about honey right from the beginning, the heroine of the Haburi myth is an old woman who at the end turns out to be mad about honey and who is imprisoned in a hollow tree, in other words, in a natural trough.

As regards the sections they have in common, the versions recently published by Wilbert (9, pp. 28–44) show a striking similarity to Roth's version. It should, however, be noted that, in Wilbert's two versions, it is the younger of the two sisters who is Haburi's mother, whereas the elder sister has certain masculine characteristics: the myth lays stress on her physical strength and her ability to perform tasks normally carried out by men, such as the felling of palm trees (cf. above p. 180).

In neither of Wilbert's versions is the husband of the two sisters, who is present from the beginning of the story, of supernatural origin. No further light is thrown on the ogre's identity, nor on the reason why, in these versions, he kills the Indian, roasts him and offers the meat to the two women, who recognize the dismembered body of their husband by the penis which has been placed on top of the bundle. In spite of these differences, the ogre's paternal urge is equally stressed:

December for the *Astrocaryum* and *Mauritia* species, November for *Attalea* (whereas Le Cointe gives July, p. 332) and September for *Oenocarpus*. However, these data are not simply transposable to the Orinoco delta where a different climate prevails.

in both the Wilbert versions, as in the Roth version, he asks straight away to be given the baby. The two sisters cover their escape by obstacles magically conjured up from their pubic hair, which they throw behind them as they go. The frog kills the ogre by slashing him with a hacking knife (M_{243}) or by thrusting a lance right through his body from his anus to the tip of his head (M_{244}). The episode of the excrement takes place in the village of the Siawana, in whose cooking-pot Haburi relieves himself (M_{243}), or at the house of Haburi's 'aunt' whose food he also pollutes (M_{244}).

From this point onwards, the Wilbert versions take a distinctly different course. The transformation of Wau-uta into a frog still results from her having eaten honey, but the latter is supplied by the old woman's son-in-law, her daughter's husband, the daughter and her husband being two characters who are introduced for the first time. M_{243} then embarks on an account of further adventures which befall Haburi, and which soon take on a cosmological character. The hero encounters a skull which persecutes him (this episode recurs in one of the myths in Roth's collection and will be examined in a forthcoming volume, where I shall show that it can be interpreted as a reduplication of the frog story), then he shoots an arrow into the ground and discovers the existence of a subterranean world where abundance reigns, in the form of luxuriant palm groves and herds of wild pigs. Haburi and his companions try to reach it but a pregnant woman remains wedged in the passage leading down to it. They push her, her anus gives way and becomes the Morning Star. Those who were behind the pregnant woman were unable to reach the underworld and, as these were the best shamans, men are now deprived of their help which would have considerably improved their lot. The preparing of pith from the palm tree and the acquisition by the animals of their specific characteristics date from this period. The other shorter version (M_{244}) ends with Wau-uta's transformation into a frog. (Cf. also Osborn 1, pp. 164–6; 2, pp. 158–9; Brett 1, pp. 389–90.)

In both the Roth and Wilbert versions, therefore, the extraction of the pith from the palm tree plays a prominent part. In fact, M_{243} is to all intents and purposes a myth about the origin of this culinary process, which coincides with the arrival on earth of the Warao's ancestors, and the definitive organization of the animal kingdom. This aspect would be further confirmed if the Siawana referred to in this version were the same as the Siawani, to whom another myth refers (M_{244b}): a cannibalistic people who were subsequently changed into trees or electric eels, and whose destruction allowed the Indians to become masters of the arts of civilization, foremost among which were the technical skill and utensils which enabled them to prepare the pith of the palm tree (Wilbert 9, pp. 141–5). The importance assigned to this food can be explained if we take into account the fact that 'the moriche palm truly deserves to be called the tree of life of the pre-agricultural Warao. They make use of ten different parts, and have perfected the art of growing it. Most important of all, they consider the pith to be the only food really fit for human consumption, and even worthy of being offered to the gods as a sacrifice. The pith of the moriche palm and fish are linked under the name of nahoro witu, "the true food" ' (Wilbert 9, p. 16).

(3) When they are single, women eat vegetable pith, but once they are married, they have fish too, that is – as we have just seen from the preceding paragraph – their diet is henceforth complete. In a context which is different from the ecological point of view, the Warao group: {starch–fish–honey}, is a substitute for the group {wild fruits–fish–honey} which, as we saw, inspired the Chaco myths.

Now, the fish in question comes from two ponds. So, as in the myths of the same group which have already been studied, we are dealing here with two kinds of water – which are similar from the hydrological point of view, since both are stagnant, but are nevertheless unequal from the alimentary point of view, since one pond contains a lot of fish, the other very little. We can therefore construct the 'two kinds of water' group as follows:

$$M_{235} \left[\begin{pmatrix} \text{bee's 'water'} \\ (= \text{honey}) \end{pmatrix} : \begin{pmatrix} \text{women's water} \\ (\text{running}) \end{pmatrix} \right] :: M_{237} \left[\begin{pmatrix} \text{frog's water} \\ \text{stagnant, high} \end{pmatrix} : \begin{pmatrix} \text{woman's water} \\ \text{stagnant, low} \end{pmatrix} \right]$$

$$:: M_{239} \left[\begin{pmatrix} \text{frog's water} \\ \text{stagnant, high} \end{pmatrix} : \begin{pmatrix} \text{woman's water} \\ ?, \text{low} \end{pmatrix} \right]$$

$$:: M_{241} \left[\begin{pmatrix} \text{women's water} \\ \text{stagnant, fish} (-) \end{pmatrix} : \begin{pmatrix} \text{jaguar's water} \\ \text{stagnant, fish} (+) \end{pmatrix} \right]$$

Honey is not water (except for Bee), but it is stagnant. The myth stresses this feature indirectly by making it clear that the opposite kind of water is running water, unlike all the variants in which the two kinds of water are described as being stagnant, and contrasted in terms of high and low, or of their relative fish content. We can therefore simplify as follows:

$$[\text{stagnant} : \text{running}] :: [\text{high} : \text{low}] :: [\text{fish} (-) : \text{fish} (+)]$$

which gives a horizontal opposition, a vertical opposition, and what could be called an economic opposition.

The *stagnant water/running water* contrast is strongly in evidence throughout the entire American continent, and first and foremost among the Warao. These Indians relate how in former times men obtained their wives from the Spirits of the Waters, to whom they gave their sisters in exchange. But they insisted on the isolation of the women at their menstrual periods, a practice to which the Water Spirits were unaccustomed and to which they strongly objected; since then, the latter have never stopped persecuting them (Roth 1, p. 241). Hence the great number of prohibitions, in particular the one forbidding the washing of the pot-spoons outside the travelling boat either on rivers or at sea. They have to be cleaned in the canoe, otherwise big storms and squalls will arise (*ibid.*, pp. 252, 267, 270). It should be noted in this connection that the Black Jaguar of the myths is supposed to cause thunder by his roaring. Farther south, the Mundurucu made a ritual distinction between running water and stagnant water. The wife of an Indian who owned a trophy head and members of the confraternity of tapirs were not allowed to use the former. Consequently these persons could not bathe in a river: water for washing was brought to them in their homes (Murphy 1, pp. 56, 61).

The Guianese taboo about washing cooking plates and dishes, or about washing them in running water, is also found in the north-west of North America among the Yurok, who stipulate that wooden dishes and greasy hands should be washed in stagnant water, never in running water (Kroeber in Elmendorf, p. 138, n. 78). The rest of the passage suggests that the taboo could be a particular application of a general relationship of incompatibility supposedly existing between food and supernatural beings. In this case, the similarity with the Guianese beliefs would be even more striking, and there would seem to be less risk in using American examples of varying origins in an attempt to explain the nature of the contrast between the two waters.

Among the Twana of Puget Sound, pubescent girls were forced to wash in running water in order to avoid the danger of contamination inherent in their condition (*ibid.*, p. 441). On the other hand, widowers and widows 'had to bathe daily in a pool made by damming a stream or small river ... This practice lasted at least for a lunar month after the burial of the deceased spouse' (*ibid.*, p. 457). The Toba of the Chaco forbade women who had just given birth to bathe in rivers: they were allowed to bathe only in the lagoon (Susnik, p. 158). Just as the Mandan contrasted running water and stagnant water, one being termed 'pure', the other 'impure' because it had no outlet (Beckwith, p. 2), so the Guarani of Paraguay considered running water to be the only 'real' water.

Unlike stagnant water, which is a kind of neutralized water, running water therefore constitutes the 'marked' term. It is more potent and more effective, but at the same time more dangerous, being inhabited by Spirits or being directly linked with them. Metaphorically speaking, we express almost the same idea when we contrast 'spring water' with 'still water'. The Yurok of California force their pubescent girls to feed near waterfalls, where the roar of the river drowns all other noises (Kroeber, p. 45); this is perhaps because they share, with the Cherokee of the south-east of the United States, the belief that noisy water 'talks' and is a medium for a form of supernatural teaching (Mooney, p. 426).

If this way of looking at the problem also applies in the South American myths, as is suggested by the similarity between the beliefs current in the two hemispheres, it follows that running water is prohibited because it might break the tenuous link established between a supernatural person and a human being. Now, we have seen that, from M_{237} onwards, the contrast between stagnant water and running water changes into another kind of contrast – that of relatively high water (since the frog looks for it in hollow trees) and relatively low water (the ponds in which humans bathe). Finally, the transformation is continued in M_{241}. Instead of there being two kinds of water, which are not at the same height, we have two kinds of water which are identical from the vertical point of view, but one of which is harmless and contains few fish, while the other is dangerous and well stocked with fish. The terms of the first contrast are reversed at the same time as this transformation takes place. From M_{235} to M_{239}, the water which was first stagnant, then high, was congruous with a supernatural and beneficent character; the water which was running at first, then low, was congruous with a human and maleficent character. In M_{241}, the reverse is the case, because of the inversion of the signs affecting the supernatural partner which, in this instance, is the Black Jaguar, a cannibalistic monster. Symmetrically, the human character is given a beneficent role. So it is the water which contains only a few fish, and which is weakly stressed in respect of the search for food, which corresponds to the relatively high water where the bee and the frog ought to have continued to bathe, and where man ought to have continued to fish. For, in that case, things would have remained as they were.

This discussion appears to be leading nowhere. Yet without it, we would never have arrived at the preceding hypothesis which, on reflection, is the only one which enables us to discover the armature common to both Wilbert's impressive version and Roth's, which are the most detailed variants of the Haburi myth available. What constitutes the apparent difference between them? Roth's version does not contain the cosmological section. On the other hand, the Wilbert versions do not have the episode of the two ponds. Now, we have just shown that this episode is a transformation of other Guianese myths which belong to the same group as the one we are busy discussing.

But in actual fact, the episode of the ponds and its system of transformations are no more than a falsely anecdotal disguise, barely concealing the cosmological theme which is developed to the full in Wilbert's lengthy version. In the episode of the ponds, the husband of the two sisters gives up safe but poor fishing in a pond which, as we have just seen, corresponds to the stagnant and relatively high water in the myth previously studied, because he prefers good but dangerous fishing in another pond, which corresponds in the same myths to running and relatively low water. Now at the end of the Wilbert version, Haburi and his companions, the forefathers of present-day Indians, make the same choice but on a much larger scale: they give up a quiet and humble life in the upper world under the spiritual guidance of their priests because, in the luxuriant palm groves and herds of wild pigs which they had glimpsed in the underworld, they see a promise of more abundant food. They do not yet know that they can only attain the food after surmounting the great dangers represented by the Spirits of the Waters and the Woods, the most formidable of which is, as it happens, the Black Jaguar.

The supernatural character in Roth's version does no more than reproduce this ancestral behaviour, when, in expectation of better fishing, he allows himself to be drawn towards a kind of water which denotes the low in the system of transformations to which it belongs, in spite of the fact that M_{241} puts it on the same level as the other, which denotes the high by virtue of the same reasoning. In this respect, there is one old version which is perfectly explicit on this point: in the underworld there is a lot of game, but on the other hand water is scarce and Kanonatu, the creator, has to create rain in order to swell the rivers (Brett 2, pp. 61–2). In all the versions, therefore, the main character (or characters) commits a moral transgression which takes the form of a fall. That which the protagonist of M_{241} suffers, since he falls into the clutches of Black Jaguar, is a metaphorical transposition of the physical and cosmic fall which led to the appearance of the first race of human beings. One signifies the other, just as the supernatural character in the first myths in the group is signified by his name (which ought not to have been uttered) and just as the water which splashes him (splashing is a declaration of love in most South American tribes, and especially among the Warao) signifies the physical desire of the sisters-in-law, at the same time as it has a metaphorical value in respect of the leading character, whom water burns *as if* it were fire.

(4) The reader will certainly have noticed that the two sisters in M_{241} are placed in the same situation as the heroine in the Chaco myths (who has a sister herself) that is, between a husband and the latter's rival. In the Chaco, Woodpecker plays the part of the husband who is a food-supplying hero. The Warao husband also supplies food, but fish and not honey. In Guiana fish is a dry-season food, just as honey is in the Chaco (Roth 2, p. 190): fishing is easier when the rivers are low. Moreover, honey reappears at the end of the story.

For the Toba, the husband's rival is Fox, for the Warao, Black Jaguar; in other words, a deceiver in the one instance, and a terrifying ogre in the other. This difference in nature has a parallel on the psychological level. Fox, as we have seen, is 'mad about women'; he is prompted by lust. No such affirmation is made about Black Jaguar in the myth. In fact Black Jaguar begins by behaving in the opposite way from Fox, since he brings the women copious supplies of food: fish in the Roth version, pieces of their husband's roasted flesh in the Wilbert versions. This last detail establishes a similarity between Black Jaguar and the Ge hero, who roasted his wife's corpse and presented it to the latter's parents, because their unfortunate daughter had been too greedy for honey: just as the man who meets the same fate in the Warao myth shows himself to be too greedy for fish. I shall return to this point.

But the main difference between Black Jaguar and Fox is the absence in the former of any erotic motivation. Almost as soon as he arrives at the woman's house, he claims to be tired and his one thought is to sleep, after the baby has been laid in his arms, at his own request. That is the normal behaviour of Indian fathers, whose one idea when they return from hunting is to stretch out in their hammocks and fondle their babies. This detail is important, because it crops up in all versions, and the reason surely is that it throws light on the jaguar's motive, which is diametrically opposed to that of the fox. Just as the latter was 'mad about women', so the jaguar proves to be 'mad about children': what prompts

G

the jaguar is not lust, but a longing for paternity. Having displayed his gifts as a food-supplier to the two women, he settles down to being a dry-nurse to the baby.

Such an attitude seems paradoxical in an ogre, and calls for an explanation. This will be supplied in another chapter where I shall establish definitively a point that was already implicit in the Ge myths, namely, that the area of the group includes a double system of transformations: the one whose development we have been following from the beginning of this book, and another, which cuts across it, as it were, and intersects it exactly at the point we have now reached. It will then be clear that the jaguar behaves in this instance as a food-supplying father, because, in the group which is perpendicular to the one we are studying, he plays the reverse role: that of a seducer who takes mothers away from their children. Another Guianese myth, of which I shall make use later (M_{287}), provides a perfect example of the reversal of roles, since in it the deceived husbands kill Black Jaguar. So if, in M_{241}, the jaguar kills the husband, and not the husband the jaguar, he cannot be a seducer, but must be the reverse (cf. below, pp. 296–303).

As I have not yet reached the stage at which it will be possible to demonstrate this point and construct the meta-system which would integrate both aspects, I prefer to make do for the time being with a different kind of demonstration based on the comparison I have already embarked on between the fox in the Chaco myths and the jaguar in the Guianese myths, and which will be carried out *a contrario*.

Fox is a deceiver. In *The Raw and the Cooked* (pp. 309–10), I pointed out that myths which have this type of character as hero are often constructed like a mosaic, and by reciprocal overlapping of fragments of syntagmatic sequences deriving from different and sometimes opposite myths. The result is a hybrid syntagmatic sequence, the very structure of which conveys, by its ambiguity, the paradoxical nature of the deceiver. If this is so in the case we are concerned with now, we can interpret the character of *ineffectual seducer* as exemplified in Fox as a result of the juxtaposition of two antithetical characteristics, each one attributable to a person who, in his own way, is the reverse of Fox: he is either an *effective seducer*, or the opposite of a seducer, that is a *father*, but a father who (in theory) must in that case prove to be *ineffectual*:

$$\text{DECEIVER} \begin{cases} \text{seducer} \\ \text{ineffectual} \end{cases} \begin{matrix} \diagdown \\ \diagup \end{matrix} \begin{cases} \text{ineffectual, but a seducer}^{(-1)} = \text{father} \\ \text{a seducer, but effectual } (= \text{ineffectual }^{(-1)}) \end{cases} \text{OGRE}$$

With the Warao myth, we discovered one of the two combinations
which define the ogre in contradistinction to the deceiver. And, as I
have already said, we shall encounter the other later; it will be confirmed then that the first was merely a transformation of it. From now
on it is clear that the Fox of the Chaco and the Black Jaguar of Guiana
are in symmetrical contrast to each other, as characters who try to
impersonate their victim with intent to deceive the latter's spouse. Fox
disguises himself as the women he has killed, and Jaguar assumes the
appearance of the man he murdered. After being stung by an ant which
had made certain of his true sex *de visu*, Fox reveals *what he is* by a
physical reaction: he either utters a roar he can no longer disguise, or
pulls up his skirt. Although Jaguar shows himself to be both a good
father and a good husband (unlike Fox, who is extremely clumsy as a
husband), he reveals, morally, *what he is not*: he utters his victim's name.
The incident of the name is therefore a transposition of an episode from
the Chaco myths and gives it a figurative meaning. And it also reflects,
while at the same time reversing it, an incident we have already encountered in other Guianese myths belonging to the same group
(M_{233}, M_{238}). There, the supernatural personage was disjoined from
her human companion when her name was uttered. In the myths we
are discussing now, the humans are disjoined from their supposed
supernatural companion when the latter utters what (since he says it
himself) *cannot be* his name.

(5) The frog is called Wau-uta. That too was the name of the frog
who protected the hunter in M_{238}, and of the tree-frog into which the
hero's baby changed in M_{235}. From a baby turned animal (in the form
of a frog) we move therefore, through the medium of a male, hunting
frog, to a female, bellicose frog (she kills the jaguar) who changes the
baby into an adult. In the preceding instances, the frog belonged to the
cunauaru species, and Roth suggests that Haburi's lecherous protector
was of the same species, especially since the cry is phonetically the same
as that attributed to the cunauaru frog in other myths.

The flight of a woman with her child, both of whom are pursued by
cannibalistic monsters and who find asylum and protection with a frog,
provides the theme of a Mundurucu myth (M_{143}), in which the flight is
also prompted by the wife's recognizing her husband's roasted corpse.
I shall study comparable North American myths in a subsequent
volume.

The Warao myth and the Mundurucu myth are also alike in that the
frog plays the part of shaman in both. A Tucuna myth attributes the

origin of shamanistic powers to the cunauaru. This myth should therefore be quoted, if only to justify, retrospectively, the use we made of observations relating to this tribe in order to throw light on certain Guianese customs:

M_{245}. *Tucuna. 'The origin of shamanistic powers'*

A two-year-old baby girl used to cry continuously every night. Her mother became angered by this and expelled her from the house, and the child went on weeping all by herself, until a cunauaru frog came along and took her away. The little girl stayed with the frog until she reached adolescence, and learned all the magical arts from her protectress, both those which cure and those which kill.

Then she went back to live with humans, among whom sorcery was unknown at that time. When she became very old and unable to look after herself, she asked some young girls to prepare her some food. But the latter did not like her, and refused. During the night, the old woman extracted their leg bones from their bodies. As they could not get up, the girls were forced to watch her as she ate the marrow from their bones, which was her only food.

When the crime became known, the Indians cut the sorceress's throat. She collected the blood which flowed into her cupped hands, blew it towards the sun saying: 'The soul enter into thee also!' Since that time, the soul of the victim enters the body of the killer (Nim. 13, p. 100).

The theme of the whimpering child (see later, p. 378) links the Tucuna myth with a group in which an opossum or a vixen plays the part of abducting animal (*RC*, p. 271, n. 35). The whimpering child who resists 'socialization' remains obstinately on the side of nature and awakens the lust of similarly orientated animals: those who are mad about honey, a natural food, or those mad about women or boys, which are sexual 'foods'. Taking this approach and starting from the frog which was mad about a boy, but still madder about honey, we can establish a link-up with the Chaco girl who was mad about honey and who, in her own way, was a kind of vixen (otherwise the fox would not have attempted to personify her); but at the same time, she was a girl about whom the fox was mad. We shall return later to this instance of reciprocity.

(6) In the Roth version (M_{241}), the frog kills the jaguar by trapping him in the thorny door of the hollow tree in which she lives. The

tactics used by the frog recall those used by characters in certain Chaco myths, who also take refuge in a hollow tree, in order to get rid of a cannibalistic jaguar: through the cracks in the trunk, they thrust lances on which the ogre is fatally wounded (M_{246}; Campana, p. 320), or the theme is reversed and it is the jaguar who, having sunk his claws into the trunk, finds that he cannot break free and is thus at his victims' mercy (Toba: M_{23}). In both instances we are dealing with a female jaguar whose form had been taken by a woman who had killed her husband, whereas the male jaguar of the Guiana myth appeared to the women in the guise of their husband, whom he had killed.

The Chaco myths I have just referred to deal with the origin of tobacco, which springs up from the burnt corpse of the jaguar-woman. After beginning with the contrast between honey and tobacco, and following step by step the cycle of transformations illustrated by the myths about the origin of honey, we now discover that we have come full circle since, at this appreciable distance from our point of departure, we are beginning to discern features which we know to be characteristic of the myths about the origin of tobacco.

And that is not all. The hollow tree which, in the Chaco myths, is used as a refuge against the jaguar, is a yuchan (*Chorisia insignis*), a tree of the bombax family. It is also against the spikes growing on the trunk of the yuchan that the fox is disembowelled in other Chaco myths (M_{208}–M_{209}). Although, according to the sources at our disposal, the cunauaru always seems to choose to live in a tree of a different species (*Bodelschwingia macrophylla Klotzsch* – a tiliacea with scented flowers, the trunk of which becomes hollow when the tree reaches a certain size; Schomburgk, Vol. II, p. 334), the Warao myth appears to refer simultaneously to the physical appearance and the semantic function of the silk-cotton tree in the Chaco myths.

Looking ahead a little, this is an appropriate moment to point out that silk-cotton trees play a part in the myth we are now concerned with. After trying to build a canoe with wax, then with clay, and after experimenting with various different species of tree, the hero achieves his purpose by using the 'silk-cotton tree', which is a member of the bombax family (*Bombax ceiba, B. globosum*). The Warao did, in fact, make use of this wood which, although somewhat soft, proved to be suitable for the building of large canoes capable of taking from seventy to eighty passengers (Roth 2, p. 613). Figure 12 shows a pattern in a string game suggesting the squat and powerful appearance of the tree with its massive trunk.

It is particularly remarkable that Chaco mythology should reflect, on the imaginative level, a real-life aspect of the culture of certain Guianese Indians. The Mataco myth (M246), already referred to, describes how a population which was being persecuted by the jaguar sought refuge inside an ark as high as a house, hollowed out from the trunk of a yuchan tree. But, although the Mataco myth is referring

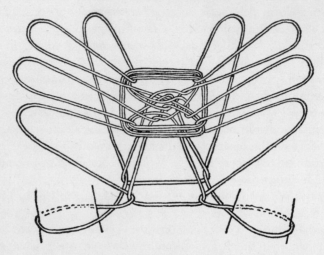

Figure 12. Silk-cotton tree. A pattern in a string game. Warao Indians.
(After Roth 2, Fig. 300, p. 553.)

imaginatively to an aspect of Warao life, in turn this aspect (and its mythical origin as suggested in M241) reverses the original function of the silk-cotton tree as described in the Chaco myths. I recalled further back, when I embarked on this discussion which will be continued in a later chapter, that in the very earliest times a large yuchan tree held all the water and all the fishes of the world in its hollow trunk. The water was therefore in the trunk, whereas the technical operation which changes the trunk into a canoe creates the opposite situation: the tree is in the water. We come back here to the dialectics of container and content and of internal and external, the complexity of which is revealed with exceptional clarity in the series of oppositions (mythical/ mythical, mythical/real, real/mythical) illustrated by the part played by the silk-cotton trees. Either the water and the fish are inside the tree, and human beings outside the tree, or humans are inside the tree, the water outside, and the fish in the water. Between these two extremes, the cunauaru frog's way of life occupies an intermediary position: for it, and for it alone, 'all the water in the world' (since it uses no other) is still in the tree. And when M_{241} presents the canoe made from bees' wax and the one made from the wood of the silk-cotton tree as being diametrically opposed, the explanation surely is that for the bee, which is homologous with the tree-frog along the dry/wet axis (cf. above, p. 168), wax and honey replace the water inside the tree, and are not therefore interchangeable with the tree in its relationship with water.[6]

(7) There is nothing much to be said about the flute and arrows that Wau-uta gives to the boy when he reaches adolescence, except that these are normal attributes of his sex and age, the arrows for hunting, the flute for love-making, since the instrument is used in courting: so it is understandable that the women who hear it in the distance conclude that there is an unknown man in the house. The episode of the otters presents a far more complex problem.

The disgust which the stench of Haburi's excrements arouses in the otters is reminiscent of a belief held by the Tlingit of Alaska, who can hardly be considered as neighbours of the Warao: 'The land otter', they say, 'hates the smell of human excretion' (Laguna, p. 188). The species cannot, however, be the same, because of the distance between the two regions, and their climatic differences. The otters in M_{241} make a collective appearance in the myth and might, because of this, belong to the species, *Lutra brasiliensis*, which lives in groups of ten or twenty, rather than to *Lutra felina* (Ahlbrinck, under 'aware-puya'): the latter is a smaller and solitary species, which the ancient Mexicans believed to possess evil powers and attributes as an incarnation of Tlaloc, being always on the look-out for bathers in order to drown them (Sahagun, Book XII, pp. 68–70, under 'auitzotl').

Yet it is impossible not to see a comparison between the Mexican beliefs and those of Guiana, especially after reading the following

[6] Cf. the knife made from bee's wax, homologous with 'the water which burns like fire' (M_{235}) in: Goeje, p. 127.

In M_{243}, the main contrast is between a canoe made of bone, which sinks to the bottom, and a canoe made from a species of tree called cachicamo. In M_{244}, the contrast is between a canoe made of wood ('sweet mouth wood'), which sinks, and a canoe made from the wood of the cachicamo.

The cachicamo (*Calophyllum callaba*) is a member of the guttifer or clusiaceae family, with a massive trunk (like the silk-cotton tree) and its wood is reputed to be rot-proof. In the Wilbert versions, Haburi also tries the wood of the peramancilla, ohori, ohoru in Warao, that is (Roth 2, p. 82) *Symphonia* sp., *Moronopea* sp., another of the guttiferae, the resin of which was gathered in vast quantities and, among other things, was mixed with bees' wax and used to caulk canoes.

passage from Sahagun: 'When the otter was annoyed – had caught no one, had drowned none of us commoners – then was heard as if a small child wept. And he who heard it thought perhaps a child wept, perhaps a baby, perhaps an abandoned one. Moved by this, he went there to look for it. So there he fell into the hands of the *auitzotl*; there it drowned him' (Sahagun, *loc. cit.*, p. 69).

This particular crying baby, who behaves like a treacherous seducer, is obviously symmetrical with the irritatingly noisy child who appears in M_{245} and other myths. Furthermore, curious echoes of the Mexican belief are found in regions of America where we had already been struck by a similarity of views on the subject of otters. The Tagish Indians of British Columbia, who are akin to the Tlingit both in language and habitat, have associated the Klondike Gold Rush of 1898 with a myth about a certain 'wealth-woman', who is also a frog-woman. Occasionally, at night, the baby she holds in her arms is heard crying. It must be taken from her and not given back to the mother who is doused with urine until she excretes gold (McClellan, p. 123). The Tlingit and the Tsimshian refer in their myths to a 'Lake Woman' who is married to an Indian, gives her sister-in-law a 'coat of riches', and will confer wealth on anyone who hears her baby cry (Boas 2, p. 746; cf. Swanton 2, pp. 173–5). Whether they are otters or frogs, these maternal sirens, whose babies utter the call, drown their victims like the Mexican otters and they share their Guianese sisters' horror of dejecta. Even the association with wealth in the form of precious metals has its Guianese equivalent; surprised at her toilet, the 'Lake woman' of Arawak mythology forgets and leaves behind on the bank the silver comb with which she was combing her hair (Roth 1, p. 242): according to popular beliefs of southern Brazil, Mboitata, the fire-snake, has a passion for iron objects (Orico 1, p. 109).

In Guiana and throughout the Amazonian area, aquatic seducers, whether male or female, often take the form of a cetacean, usually the bôto, or white Amazonian dolphin (*Inia geoffrensis*). According to Bates (p. 309), the bôto was the object of such powerful superstitions that people were forbidden to kill it (cf. Silva, p. 217, n. 47). It was believed that the animal sometimes assumed the shape of a marvellously beautiful woman, who would entice young men down to the water. But if any young man allowed himself to be seduced, she would grasp her victim round the waist and drag him to the bottom. According to the Shipaia (M_{247b}), dolphins are the descendants of an adulterous woman and her lover, who were changed into these animals by the husband – who had been ill-treated as a child – when he found them in a close embrace after prolonged copulation (Nim. 3, pp. 387–8). Nearer to the Warao, the Piapoco of the lower reaches of the Guaviar, a tributary of the Orinoco, believed in evil Spirits who lived by day at the bottom of the water but emerged at night, when they walked about 'screaming like little children' (Roth 1, p. 242).

This variation in the zoological signifier is all the more interesting in that the dolphin itself oscillates between its function as seducer and a diametrically opposite function, which it shares with the otter. A famous Baré myth (the Baré are Arawak living along the Rio Negro) about the doughty deeds of the hero Poronominaré (M_{247}) relates, in one episode, how the dolphin reduced to more modest proportions the hero's penis, which had become excessively swollen as a result of being bitten by the parasites living in the vagina of an alluring old woman (Amorim, pp. 135–8). Now, according to a Mundurucu myth (M_{248}), otters perform the same service for an Indian whose penis has been extended by a frog during copulation (Murphy 1, p. 127). The cry of this frog, of which the myth gives a phonetic transcription, suggests that it was possibly a cunauaru. Another Mundurucu myth (M_{255}), which will be analysed later (p. 206), relates that the sun and moon, as masters of fish, caused a man to revert to infancy; in spite of every kind of stimulation, his penis remained limp (Murphy 1, pp. 83–5; Kruse 3, pp. 1000–1002).

It would seem as if M_{241} were merely consolidating these two stories by expressing them in metaphorical terms: so that he may become her lover more quickly, the frog speeds up the baby Haburi's rate of growth by magical means, and so lengthens his penis. The otters' function, later will be to 'infantilize' the hero by restoring his forgotten youth to him, and by bringing him back to more filial sentiments. Now, otters are also masters of fish. According to Schomburgk (quoted by Roth 2, p. 190) these animals 'have the habit of going to the water and bringing fish after fish to their eating place, where, when a sufficient quantity has been heaped up, they start eating. The Indians turn this peculiarity to their advantage: they carefully stalk the neighbourhood of such place and wait patiently; then as soon as the otter has returned to the water after depositing its booty, they take it away.' So to defecate in such a spot as Haburi does is not only to show that you are a bad fisherman. It is also to relieve nature symbolically in the animals' 'cooking pot': this is the act which the hero commits literally (M_{243}, M_{244}) in the village of the Siawana and in his 'aunt's' house.

Most important of all is the fact that the fishing technique described by Schomburgk and commented on by Wilbert (2, p. 124) is perhaps not unconnected with the way in which Ahlbrinck (under 'aware-puya') explains the Kalina name for the otter: 'the otter is the domestic animal of the spirit of the water; what the dog is to man, so the otter is to the Spirits.' If, by combining all these points, we could conclude that the Guianese Indians consider the otter as a kind of 'fishing-dog', this would give remarkable significance to an Ojibwa myth of North America (to be discussed in the next volume), which retells the story of Haburi almost word for word, and attributes the same infantilizing role to the dog.

It follows from all I have just said that, in spite of the diversity of the species involved, certain beliefs regarding otters persist in the most remote areas of the New World, from Alaska and British Columbia to the Atlantic coast of Northern America, and southwards, through Mexico, as far as the Guiana region. These beliefs, which in each area are adapted to the local species or genera, must be very old. It is possible, however, that empirical observation may have given them a new lease of life here and there. One cannot fail to be struck by the fact that not only the myths, but naturalists as well, acknowledge that these animals, whether they are land or sea-otters, show extraordinary refinement in their habits. Ihering notes (under 'ariranha') that the great South American otter (*Pteroneura brasiliensis*) refrains from eating the heads and backbones of the biggest fish, and there exists a Guianese myth (M$_{346}$) which explains why the otter rejects the claws of crabs. The otter along the Arctic coasts has a very acute sense of smell and cannot tolerate any kind of filth, however minute in quantity, which would impair the insulating properties of its fur (Kenyon).

It is perhaps in this direction that we must look for the origin of that sensitivity to smells which the Indians of both North and South America attribute to otters. But, even if the advances made in animal ethology were to confirm this interpretation, it still remains true that, on the level of the myths, the empirically proved negative connection between otters and excrement becomes part of a combinatory system which operates with sovereign independence and exercises the right to effect different interchanges between the terms of an oppositional system which exists experientially in only one state but of which mythic thought gratuitously creates other states.

A Tacana myth (M$_{249}$) relates that the otter, the master of fish, favoured unlucky fishermen by telling them of the existence of a magic stone, which was buried in his extremely foul-smelling excrement. In order to have a good catch, Indians had to lick the stone and rub it all over their body (H.-H., pp. 210–11). Diametrically opposed to these humans who must not be put off by the otter's foul-smelling excrement are the subterranean dwarfs in Tacana mythology who have no anuses, who never defecate (they feed exclusively on liquids, mostly water) and who are extremely disgusted when they see their first human visitor relieving nature (M_{250}; H.-H., pp. 353–4). These dwarfs with no anuses are an armadillo people who live under the earth, just as the otters live under water. Elsewhere, otters are the subject of similar beliefs. The Trumai (M_{251}) relate how in the old days otters were animals without anuses, which excreted through the mouth (Murphy-Quain, p. 74). This Xingu myth refers back to one of the Bororo myths about the origin of tobacco (for the second time, then, during the analysis of the same myth, the problem of the origin of tobacco appears on the horizon): men who did not exhale tobacco smoke (that is, people who were *blocked* at the top instead of at the bottom) were changed into otters (M_{27}, RC, p. 105), animals which have very small eyes, according to the myth, and which are therefore also blocked and deprived of an opening onto the outside world.

If we now bring all the data together, it is possible to discern the outline of a system in which otters occupy a special place in the mythic series of characters, who are blocked or pierced above or below, or at the front or the back, and whose positive or negative disability may affect the vagina or the anus, the mouth, the eyes, the nostrils or the ears. It is perhaps because they were blocked in former times and knew nothing of the excretory functions that the otters in M_{241} are repelled by human excrement. Yet in a Waiwai myth (M_{252}), the otter is changed from a blocked to a pierced animal, when the twins who are as yet the only living people, undertake to copulate with an otter *per oculos*. The animal protests indignantly that it is not a woman and orders the two brothers to fish for women (congruous therefore with fish), who at that time had toothed vaginas which the twins had to remove so that the women should cease to be impenetrable (Fock p. 42; cf. Derbyshire, pp. 73–4), in other words impossible to pierce. The otter, which is blocked below in Trumai mythology and above in Bororo mythology, and pierced above in Waiwai mythology, undergoes a fourth transformation in Yabarana mythology where it becomes a piercing animal in respect of the low: 'Our informants remembered that the otter was

responsible for menstruation, but they could give no explanation'
(M₂₅₃; Wilbert 8, p. 145):

	Trumaï	Bororo	Waiwaï	Yabarana
blocked/pierced	+	+	—	—
agent/sufferer	—	—	—	+
high/low	—	+	+	—
front/back	—	+	+	+

No doubt, methodical research into South American mythology
would reveal different combinations, or would make it possible, in the
case of the same combinations, to give different definitions of the 'high'
and the 'low' and 'back' and 'front' (cf. *RC*, pp. 135–6). For instance,
a Yupa myth (M₂₅₄ₐ) refers to an otter which was adopted by a fisherman and which kept him supplied with big fish. But the otter refused
to fish for the women. After being *wounded in the head* by its adoptive
father, it bled copiously. To be avenged for this, it abandoned men and
took all the fish along with it (Wilbert 7, pp. 880–81). According to a
Catio myth (M₂₅₄ᵦ), a myocastor (?) *pierces* a man and fertilizes him
(Rochereau, pp. 100–101). For the time being, it is enough to pose the
problem, and I move on straightway to another, of which I shall also
give only a rough outline.

Although the Yabarana informants remembered only vaguely that
their myths established a relationship of cause and effect between the
otter and menstrual periods, they had a very clear recollection of a
story in which an incestuous brother, who is subsequently changed into
a moon, is held responsible for the appearance of this physiological
function (M₂₅₃; Wilbert 8, p. 156). This might be thought to be no
more than a discrepancy between two traditions, the one local, the
other widely known throughout both North and South America, if there
were not numerous proofs of the fact that, in native thought, the moon
and otters are often given similar roles. I have already made a comparison (p. 201) between the otter episode in the Haburi myth and
several Mundurucu myths, on which I must now dwell for a moment.
In M₂₄₈, a hunter allowed himself to be seduced by a cunauaru frog,
which had been changed into a beautiful young woman. But, at the
moment of orgasm, the latter resumed her batrachian form and
stretched her lover's penis by holding it fast in her vagina. When she
finally released the unfortunate hunter, the latter asked the otters for
help, but they, while pretending to put him right, inflicted the reverse

disability on him, that is, they reduced his penis to pitiful proportions. As I have already shown, this story expresses, in literal terms, the one which is told in M_{241} with a figurative meaning: on the one hand, the old frog endows Haburi with a member and appetites far beyond his real age; on the other hand, the otters reverse the situation, and they go even further when they revive the hero's consciousness of his earliest childhood, thus carrying out what can be considered as the first psycho-analytical treatment in history ... [7]

The Mundurucu myth, to which I alluded very briefly, is extra-ordinarily explicit on all these points:

M_{255}. Mundurucu. 'The origin of the suns of summer and winter'

An Indian called Karuetaruyben was so ugly that his wife rejected his advances, and was unfaithful to him. One day, after a collective fishing expedition with fish-poison, he remained alone at the water's edge, sadly reflecting on his lot. The Sun and the Moon, his wife, unexpectedly arrived on the scene. They were very hairy, and their voices resembled the tapir's, and the solitary Indian watched while they threw back into the river the heads and backbones of fish, which were instantly resuscitated.

The two divinities invited Karuetaruyben to tell them his story. To find out if he were speaking the truth, the Sun ordered his wife to seduce him; K. was not only ugly, he was impotent, and his penis remained hopelessly limp. So the Sun transformed K. by magic into an embryo, which he placed in his wife's womb. Three days later she gave birth to a boy, whom the Sun turned into a young man and on whom he bestowed great beauty. When the operation was completed, he made him a gift of a basketful of fish and told him to return to his village and marry another wife, abandoning the one who had deceived him.

The hero had a brother-in-law, a fine upstanding man, who was called Uakurampé. The latter was astounded by the transformation undergone by his sister's husband, and did not rest until he had learned his secret, so that he could imitate it. But when the Moon undertook to seduce him, U. had a normal relationship with her. In order to punish him the Sun had him born again ugly and hunch-backed or according to another version he made him ugly by pulling

---

[7] It is worth recalling that in another, very different part of the New World, the otter plays a didactic role in shamanistic rites of initiation, as is indicated by the joined tongues of man and the animal, depicted on many Haida rattles.

his nose and ears, and 'other parts of the body'. Thereupon he sent him back to his wife, without giving him any fish. According to the different versions, the wife either had to put up with an ugly husband, or she rejected him. 'It is your own fault,' played Karuetaruyben on his flute, 'you were too curious about your mother's vagina ... '

The two heroes became respectively the resplendent sun of the dry season, and the dull, forbidding sun of the rainy season (Kruse 3, pp. 1000–1002; Murphy 1, pp. 83–6).

This myth, of which I have chosen only those aspects which directly concern the present analysis (the others will be dealt with again later), calls for several observations. In the first place, the sun and moon appear as the hairy masters of fishing, and are in this respect congruous with otters; like otters, they respect the heads and backbones of fish, which the otters refrain from eating and which the sun and moon bring back to life again. Secondly, they recognize the hero not by the foul stench of his excrements, as was the case with Haburi, but because of a different physiological disadvantage, namely his impotence, as shown by a penis which remains small and limp in spite of every kind of stimulation. We have here, then, a double modification of the organic code, as compared with M_{241}: in the anatomical category of the low, the front replaces the back, and the reproductory functions supplant the excretory functions; on the other hand, if we make the comparison with M_{255} and M_{258}, we note an extraordinary double inversion. In M_{248}, a penis which had been excessively elongated by the frog was transformed by otters into an excessively shortened penis, whereas in M_{255}, a penis which remained diminutive in the presence of a so-called mistress, soon to be changed into a mother (unlike the frog in M_{241}, a so-called mother soon to be changed into a mistress), was extended to reasonable proportions by the sun. On the other hand, in the same myth, the second hero has a penis which is reasonably long at the beginning, but becomes too long at the end (this at least is what is implied in the Kruse version quoted above.)[8] These various points will be more clearly understood from the table of literal and figurative meanings.

Evidence of the homogeneity of the group can also be found in the names of the hero in M_{255}. Karuetaruyben means 'the red male macaw with the bloodshot eyes', but the hero is also called Bekit-tare-bé, 'the male child who grows fast' (Kruse 3, p. 1001), because his growth is

---

[8] It would be interesting to try and discover whether the Mundurucu myth might not throw some light on the obvious contrast, in the iconography of the gods of the ancient Maya, between the young and beautiful Sun-god and the old, ugly god with the long nose.

magically induced, a fact which creates an additional link with Haburi.

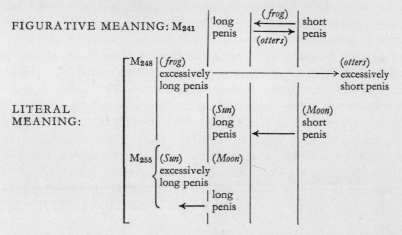

A myth from eastern Bolivia, which is extant in several variants, obviously belongs to the same group:

M_{256}. *Tacana. 'The moon's lover'*

A woman's cotton plantation was pillaged every night. Her husband caught the thieves: they were two celestial sisters, the moon and the morning star.

The man fell in love with the moon, who was very pretty, but she rejected him and advised him to make advances to her sister. Finally she yielded, but she urged upon the man that, before he slept with her, he should weave a large basket. During copulation the man's penis became tremendously long, to such an extent that its owner had to put it in the basket, where it coiled up like a snake, and even protruded over the edge.

Carrying his load, the man returned to the village and related what had happened to him. At night, his penis came out of its basket and wandered off in search of women, with whom it copulated. Everyone was very frightened and one Indian, whose daughter had been attacked, mounted guard. When he saw the penis coming into his hut, he cut off the end, which changed into a snake. The man with the long penis died, and the snake became the mother of the termites which can be heard whistling today. In other versions, the penis is cut by its owner, or by the moon, or by the women who are attacked (Hissink-Hahn, pp. 81–3).

There is, then, a correlatory and oppositional relationship between the *otter/frog* pair, and other homologous pairs: *sun/moon, summer sun/ winter sun* (in M$_{255}$, where the moon is sun's wife) and *morning star/moon* (in M$_{256}$), etc.

Let us now examine the question from a new angle. It will be remembered that, in M$_{241}$, the hero prepared for his escape by inventing the canoe. The first boats he made were stolen by ducks, which at that time could not swim, and which were in fact to acquire the art by using – or, one might say, by fusing with – the canoes made by Haburi. Now there are Chaco myths in which the chief characters are ducks on the one hand, and the sun and the moon on the other. They also contain the theme of the character who is unmasked by the stench of his excrement. In other words, these myths reproduce three different aspects of the Guianese-Amazonian group we have just studied:

M$_{257}$. *Mataco.* '*The origin of moon-spots*'

The sun was hunting ducks. He changed into a duck himself and, armed with a net, dived into the lagoon and pulled the birds under the water. Every time he captured one, he killed it without the other ducks seeing. When he had finished, he shared his ducks out among all the villagers and gave an old bird to his friend Moon. The latter was not pleased, and decided to do his own hunting by using the same method as Sun. Meanwhile, however, the ducks had become suspicious. They defecated and forced Moon who was disguised as a duck to follow suit. Moon's excrements, unlike those of the ducks, were extremely foul-smelling. The birds recognized Moon and attacked him in a body. They scratched and tore his skin until he was almost disembowelled. The spots on the moon are the blue scars left on his stomach by the ducks' claws (Métraux 3, pp. 14–15).

Métraux (5, pp. 141–3) quotes two variants of this myth, one of which, a Chamacoco version, replaces ducks by 'ostriches' (R*hea*); the other, which is Toba in origin, replaces the moon by a deceiving fox. In spite of their dissimilarities, all these myths form one group, of which it is possible to define the armature, while respecting its complexities. Certain myths explain the origin of the spots on the moon, or of the moon itself; in the natural philosophy of the American Indians, this celestial body, especially in its masculine aspect, is considered responsible for menstruation. The other myths also deal with a physiological process, which is the lengthening or shortening of the penis, either in the literal or the figurative sense, and similarly associated with the moon considered in its feminine aspect.

These myths therefore always deal with an event which is definable in relationship to the physiological maturity of the female sex, or the male sex and which, in the latter case, they describe in its positive or its negative aspect. Whether he is impotent or endowed with too short a penis, the man is either symbolically a child or is returning to childhood. And when he moves away from childhood either too far or too abruptly, the extreme character of the change is shown either by an over-long penis, or by excessively foul-smelling excrement. This is surely tantamount to saying that the foul-smelling stools of the male[9] correspond to the same kind of phenomenon as that which, in the case of women, is more normally illustrated by the menstrual flow.

[9] There is a good deal to be said about the semantics of excrement. In a memorable study, Williamson (pp. 280-81) has shown the contrast which exists in the minds of the Mafulu of New Guinea between inedible food remnants and excrements. The polarities are reversed, according to whether the person is an adult or a very young child. Adults pay no heed to their excrements but their inedible food waste, which is unfit for human consumption, has to be carefully preserved for fear it might be snatched away by a sorcerer, and then it is thrown into the river in order to be rendered harmless. In the case of young children, the opposite is true; no attention is paid to the inedible waste from food intended for them, but great care is taken to collect their excrements and put them in a safe place. More recent observations have revealed the existence of special buildings, in which natives of the mountainous regions of New Guinea keep babies' excrements (Aufenanger). It would seem as if waste, whether lying on the hither side or the far side of assimilable food, were an integral part of the consumer, but *ante* or *post factum* according to age. This links up with an interpretation I have given of certain customs practised by the Penan of Borneo, who seem to consider that a young child's food forms an integral part of his person (L.-S. 9, pp. 262-3, n.):

```
                        ADULT
         ┌──────────────┴──────────────┐
    non-assimilable      assimilable        non-assimilable
    parts                parts              parts
                         └──────────────────┬──────────────┘
                                  CHILD
```

Certain facts suggest that South American Indians imagine the same kind of contrast, but shift it from children to the dying who, in relation to the adult in the prime of life, are symmetrical to the new-born. The Siriono of Bolivia collect the vomit and excrement of the very sick in a basket for as long as the death agony lasts. When the dead person is buried, the contents of the basket are emptied near the grave (Holmberg, p. 88). The Yamamadi, who live between the Rio Purus and the Rio Jurua, may perhaps observe the reverse practice, since they build a kind of ramp leading from the hut to the forest: it is, perhaps, the path to be taken by the soul, but perhaps also a way of helping the sick person to crawl outside in order to relieve nature (Ehrenreich, p. 109).

The problem of the semantics of excrement in America should be studied by starting with the contrast between northern myths about a prodigious baby capable of eating its own excrement and the southern versions, in which a no less prodigious baby feeds on menstrual blood (Catio in Rochereau, p. 100). On the other hand, while it may be difficult to separate excrement and the child's body, the same is true of noise: in terms of acoustic

If this hypothesis is true, Haburi, the hero of M_{241}, is following a cycle which is the reverse of that which a girl would follow from birth to puberty. At first a pathological adult, he is restored by the otters to the normality of childhood, whereas a young girl, through the moon's intervention, reaches normal maturity, a phenomenon which is indicated by the onset of monthly periods; these have, however, an intrinsically pathological character, since in native thought menstrual blood is considered as a form of filth and poison. The regressive movement followed by the myth corroborates a feature which I recognized from the beginning as being characteristic of all those belonging to the same group, and which I can now check by a new approach.

So far, I have not discussed ducks. They play a particularly important part in the myths of North America, and to carry out a thorough analysis would involve structuring the system to which they belong with the help of the mythology of both North and South. At the present juncture, such an undertaking would be premature, and so I shall confine myself to the South American context, in order to make two series of observations.

Firstly, in M_{241}, the hero who is the protégé of a frog involuntarily becomes the organizer of a sector of the animal kingdom. Every kind of canoe he invents is stolen from him by ducks of a particular species which, in appropriating the canoe, acquire the ability to swim, as well as their distinctive characteristics. We can thus perceive a direct link between M_{241} and M_{238}, in which another hunter, also the protégé of a frog, involuntarily became the organizer of the animal kingdom, taken this time as a whole. In M_{238}, the entire animal kingdom is graded according to size and family; in M_{241}, we move to one particular animal family, which is divided up into its various species. Between one myth

---

coding, a baby's intolerable cries, which supply the theme of myths I have summarized above (p. 195), are equivalent to foul-smelling excrement. Cries and excrement are therefore mutually interchangeable, by virtue of the basic congruence between din and stench which has already been exemplified in *The Raw and the Cooked*, and to which I shall have occasion to return in other contexts.

This connection supplies an additional piece of information about the semantic position of the otter: because a false adult ejects foul-smelling excrement, the otter sends him back to his mother; because a 'false' child (he has no reason to cry) utters loud howls, the frog, the opossum or the vixen take him away from his mother. We know already, from M_{241}, that the otter and the frog are diametrically opposed, and the preceding observation allows me to generalize the relationship. To carry the analysis further, it would be appropriate to compare the otter with other creatures (more often than not birds) which, in South as well as North America, reveal his true origin to a child who has been carried far away from his own people and brought up by supernatural beings who claim to be his parents.

and the other, therefore, the classificatory impulse diminishes and disintegrates. It remains to be seen why and how.

The natural and zoological organization supplied by M_{238} is the result of a cultural deficiency: it would never have come into being if the hero had not been an inefficient hunter. On the contrary, in M_{241}, it is the result of a cultural acquisition: the art of navigation, the invention of which was necessary so that the ducks could become fused with technical objects – the canoes – to which they owe their present appearance. This conception supposes that ducks are not a part of the animal kingdom in their own right. Having been derived from cultural operations, they provide evidence, at the very heart of nature, of a local regression of culture.

Some readers may suspect me of straining the meaning of the myth. Yet the same theory is found in a Tupi myth from the Lower Amazon (M_{326a}), which will be summarized and discussed later: for the moment, it will be enough to quote one of its themes. Because a taboo was violated, things changed into animals: the basket became the jaguar, the fisherman and his canoe changed into a duck: 'the head and beak came from the fisherman's head, the body from the canoe and the feet from the paddles' (Couto de Magalhães, p. 233).

The Karaja relate (M_{326b}) how Kanaschiwué, the demiurge, gave the duck a clay canoe in exchange for the metal motor-boat which the bird let him have (Baldus 5, p. 33). In the Vapidiana myth about the flood (M_{115}), a duck's beak is changed into a canoe, which enables a family to remain afloat (Ogilvie, p. 66).

Similarly, in a Taulipang myth (M_{326c}), a man is changed into a duck, after being deprived of the magical self-working agricultural implements. If his brothers-in-law had not been responsible for the disappearance of these marvellous tools, men would not have needed to labour in the fields (K.-G. 1, pp. 124–8). The similarity with M_{241} is obvious; in the one instance, the hero creates ducks and then disappears with the arts of civilization; in the other, the hero becomes a duck, when the arts of a 'super civilization' disappear. We shall see that this term is appropriate for the arts which Haburi denies to the Indians, since these are precisely the arts practised by the whites.[10] The comparison of these myths shows, then, that it is not by chance or through some whim on the part of the narrator that, in the first two,

[10] In connection with the re-transformation of the theme of the self-working agricultural implements into that of the revolt of the objects, the negative limit of the moon's ordering function, cf. *RC*, p. 299, n. 11.

ducks appear as canoes which have degenerated into animals.[11] At the same time we can understand why, in a myth the regressive movement of which I have often stressed, the hero's function as the orderer of creation is restricted to a limited field: namely, that in which, according to native thought, creation takes the form of a regression. The fact that the regression occurs from culture to nature raises a different problem, the solving of which I shall postpone for the moment in order to bring the matter of the ducks to a close.

Although ducks are congruous with canoes in respect of culture, in the natural order of things they have a correlatory and oppositional relationship with fish. The latter swim under water whereas the myths we are discussing explain why ducks, in their capacity as ex-canoes, swim on water. In the Mundurucu myths, Sun and Moon catch fish; in the Chaco myths, they fish for ducks. They are fishermen, not hunters, since the myths are careful to explain the technique used: the ducks are caught in a net by a character who has taken on their appearance and who is swimming among them. What is more, this particular form of fishing is carried out from high to low: the captured birds are dragged to the bottom, whereas fishing proper, and in particular the method practised by otters, is carried out from low to high, that is, the fish are taken out of the water and laid on the bank.

M_{241} describes Haburi purely as a bird-catcher. It is only when he misses a bird for the first time that he crouches down to release his excrement on the otters' eating place. This 'anti-fishing' operation, which produces excrement instead of food, is a movement from high to low, like duck-catching, and not from low to high. And it is offensive to the otters, in so far as they are catchers of fish.

It is important therefore to ascertain whether or not there exists a term which has a relationship with fish, correlative with that existing between ducks and canoes. A myth I have already mentioned (M_{252}) supplies such a term and, as it happens, through the agency of the otter. When the twins who know nothing about women try to copulate with an otter through its eyes, the latter explains to them that it is not a woman but that women are to be found in water, where the cultural heroes should fish for them. That the first women were fish or, after quarrelling with their husbands, decided to change into fish is a recurrent theme illustrated in so many myths that there is no need for me to draw up a list. Just as ducks are ex-canoes, so women are ex-fish.

[11] In North America, there is a correlation between ducks and canoes among the Iroquois and the Indians of the Wabanaki group.

Ducks represent a regression from culture to nature, while women constitute a progression from nature to culture, although, in either case, the gap between the two worlds remains extremely small.

This explains why otters, which live on fish, have such ambiguous and equivocal relationships with women. In a Bororo myth (M_{21}), otters act in collusion with women against their husbands, and keep them supplied with fish, on condition that they submit to their desires. Conversely, a Yupa myth, which I have already summarized (M_{254a}), states that the otter caught fish for the Indian who had adopted it, but refused to perform the same service for women. In all the myths, therefore, otters are men, or belong to the male party; this explains why the otter in the Waiwai myth was so indignant when the two simpletons tried to use it as if it were a woman, and started the wrong way round into the bargain.

We have seen that, by inventing the canoe, Haburi created the different species of ducks. He thus imposed order on nature, partially and retroactively. Yet, at the same time, he made a decisive contribution to culture, and one might suppose that the regressive character of the myth would be contradicted by this twist. The old versions quoted by Brett help to solve the difficulty. In Brett's transcription, Haburi bears the name, Aboré, and he is presented as the 'father of inventions'. If he had not had to flee from his aged wife, the Indians would have enjoyed many other fruits of his ingenuity, in particular, woven articles of clothing. One variant mentioned by Roth even relates that the hero sailed away until he finally came to the land of the White men (to the island of Trinidad according to M_{244}) to whom he taught all their arts and manufactures (Roth 1, p. 125). If it is possible to identify Haburi or the Warao Aboré with the god whom the ancient Arawak called Ahibiri or Hubuiri, we should attach a similar kind of significance to Schomburgk's remark that 'this character does not trouble himself about men' (*ibid.*, p. 120). With the exception of navigation, the only civilized art that the natives seem to claim as their own, what the myths are dealing with is undoubtedly the loss of culture, or of a culture superior to their own.

Now, Brett's versions (M_{258}), which are inferior in all respects to those of Roth and Wilbert, have the great advantage of being, in a sense, transversal to the group of Guiana myths and to the group of Ge myths in which the heroine is a girl mad about honey, as in the Chaco myths. Aboré was married to an old frog, Wowtā, which had assumed a woman's form in order to capture him when he was a little child. She was always sending him to look for honey, for which she had a great fondness. Finally, he could stand it no longer and got rid of her by imprisoning her in a hollow tree. After which, he escaped in a wax canoe that he had made in secret. His departure deprived the Indians of many other inventions (Brett 1, pp. 294–5; 2, pp. 76–83).

In concluding this excessively long variation, I must point out that, in its two consecutive parts (illustrated, respectively, by M_{237}–M_{239}, and M_{241}–M_{258}), it has a transformational relationship, worthy of special study, with an important Karaja myth (M_{177}) about unlucky hunters who fell prey to the guariba monkeys, with the one exception of their young brother, who had an ulcer-ridden body and had been rejected by his mother (cf. M_{245}) and fed on refuse by his grandfather. After being cured by a snake, he obtained protection from a frog in exchange for illusory caresses and became a miraculous hunter thanks to throwing-spears given to him by the frog. There was one for each kind of food, and their force had to be diminished by smearing them with ointment, which is the equivalent, then, of a kind of inverted hunting poison. Although the hero had forbidden anyone to touch his magic weapons, one of his brothers-in-law stole the honey throwing-spear (the gathering of honey is here likened to a hunt, whereas in the Ofaié myth, M_{192}, it is likened to agriculture) and by his clumsiness conjured up a monster, who massacred the entire village (Ehrenreich, pp. 84–6). This myth will be discussed in another context and in connection with other versions (cf. below, p. 396).

2 *Variations 4, 5, 6*

d. FOURTH VARIATION

$$[\bigcirc \Rightarrow \bigcirc] \leftrightarrow [\text{frog} \Rightarrow \text{jaguar}]$$

We are now familiar with the character and customs of the cunauaru tree-frog. But I have not previously mentioned the fact that, according to the Tupi of the Amazon valley, this particular frog can be changed into a jaguar, yawaété-cunawarú (Tastevin 2 under 'cunawarú'). Other tribes share the same belief (Surára in Becher 1, pp. 114–15). The Oayana of Guiana call the mythical jaguar – which is blue according to the Tupi, but black in Guiana (cf. M₂₃₈) – Kunawaru-imö, 'Great Cunauaru' (Goeje, p. 48).

The myths make it possible to work out the analysis of this transformation in several stages:

M₂₅₉. *Warao. 'The wooden bride'*

Nahakoboni, whose name means 'he who eats plenty', had no daughter and on becoming old he began to feel anxious about his declining years, since he had neither daughter nor son-in-law to take care of him. He therefore carved a daughter out of the trunk of a plum tree; so skilfully did he cut and carve the timber that he made a wonderfully beautiful young woman, and all the animals came to court her. The old man rejected them all in turn but when Yar, the sun, came forward, Nahakoboni thought he was the kind of son-in-law whose mettle ought to be tried.

He therefore gave him several tasks to perform, the details of which I omit, apart from pointing out that one task reversed the magic technique taught by the frog in M₂₃₈; in this instance, the hero had to reach his target in spite of being ordered to aim into the air (cf. above, p. 172). At all events, the Sun acquitted himself honourably and was given the beautiful Usi-diu (literally: 'seed tree') as his wife. But on trying to prove his love, he discovered he was unable to do so, since Usi-diu's creator, in carving the young girl, had forgotten one essential detail which he confessed himself unable to add. Yar consulted the bunia bird, which promised to help. It allowed itself to be held and nursed by the young girl. Taking advantage of her innocence, it pierced the forgotten opening, from which a snake had first of all to be removed. After that, nothing interfered with the happiness of the two young people.

The father-in-law was greatly displeased that his son-in-law should have taken the liberty of criticizing his work and had called upon the bunia bird to tinker with it. He bided his time, waiting for his revenge to come. When the time for planting came, he destroyed his son-in-law's work several times by means of his 'medicine'; the latter, however, succeeded in cultivating his field with the help of a spirit. In spite of the old man's evil spells, he also finished building a hut for his father-in-law and was at last free to look after his own domestic affairs, and for a long time he and his wife lived very happily together.

One day, Yar decided to set off on a journey westwards. As Usi-diu was pregnant, he advised her to travel at her leisure. All she had to do was to follow his tracks, being careful always to take the right-hand track; in any case, he would scatter feathers on the left, so she could make no mistake. There was no difficulty to begin with, but trouble began when she arrived at a place where the wind had blown the feathers away. Then the unborn babe began to speak and told her which path to follow; it also asked her to gather flowers. While she was stooping, a wasp stung the young woman below the waist. She tried to kill it, missed the insect, but struck herself instead. The unborn babe misinterpreted her action and thought it was being smacked. It became vexed and refused any longer to show its mother which direction to pursue, with the result that the latter went hopelessly astray. She arrived at last at a large house whose only occupant was Nanyobo (the name of a large frog), who appeared to her in the form of a very old and very big woman. Having offered food and drink to the traveller, the frog asked her to clean her head, but to be careful not to put the insects into her mouth because they would poison her. The young woman, overcome with fatigue, forgot the frog's injunction. As was customary among Indians, she placed a louse between her teeth. But no sooner had she done so than she fell dead.

The frog opened up the body and extracted not one child but two:

a pair of beautiful boys, Makunaima and Pia, whom she brought up with great kindness. As the babies grew larger, they began shooting birds, then fish (with arrows) and game. 'You must dry your fish in the sun and never over a fire', the frog told them. Yet she sent them to fetch firewood and, by the time they returned, the fish was always nicely cooked and ready for them. As a matter of fact, the frog used to vomit fire from her mouth and lick it up again before the lads' return, so that there was never a fire burning for them to see. His curiosity aroused, one of the boys changed into a lizard and spied on the old woman. He not only saw her vomit out fire, but watched her take out from her neck a white substance something like the starch of the *Mimusops balata*. The brothers were disgusted by these practices and decided to kill their adoptive mother. They cleared a large field, and left in its centre a fine tree to which they tied her; then surrounding her on all sides with stacks of timber, they set fire to them. While the old woman burnt, the fire which used to be within her passed into the surrounding faggots. These consisted of wood from the hima-heru tree (*Gualtheria uregon*? cf. Roth 2, p. 70) and whenever we rub together two sticks of this same timber we can get fire (Roth 1, pp. 130–33).

Wilbert gives a short version of this myth (M$_{260}$), consisting only of the episode of the wooden bride, Nawakoboni's daughter, whose maidenhead several birds in turn try to break. Some fail because the wood is too hard and are left with bent or broken beaks. Another bird is successful and the young woman's blood fills a cooking pot, where several species of birds come and smear themselves with it; it is at first red but then white, then black. In this way, they acquire their characteristic plumage. The 'ugly bird' came last and that is why its feathers are black (Wilbert 9, pp. 130–31).

This variant calls for one or two comments. The theme of the bride carved out of a tree-trunk is found in very remote regions of the continent: among the Tlingit of Alaska (M$_{261}$), for whom the woman remains dumb, i.e. blocked at the top (high) instead of the bottom (low) (cf. Swanton 2, pp. 181–2),[12] and in Bolivia, where it provides the

[12] I am only quoting the Tlingit as an example. For reasons which will finally emerge in the fourth volume of this series (if it is ever written) [this has now appeared as *L'homme nu* (Paris, 1971)], I would like to draw attention to the special affinities which exist between the myths of tropical America and those of the Pacific coast of North America. But in fact, the theme of the statue or image which comes to life occurs sporadically in North America, in communities as far apart as the Eskimo of the Bering Strait, the Micmac and the Iroquois, the Plains Indians and, to the south, the Pueblo.

subject of a Tacana myth (M_{262}) which has a dramatic ending: the doll which is brought to life by the devil drags her human husband off into the world beyond (H.-H., p. 515). It is found even among the Warao ($M_{236a, b}$), in the form of a story about a young bachelor who carves a woman out of the trunk of a palm tree (*Mauritia*). She supplies him with food which he tries to pass off as refuse, but his companions discover the statue and chop it up (Wilbert 9, pp. 127–9). The kind of tree mentioned in these last myths obviously refers to the 'wooden husband', who appears at the beginning of M_{241}, thus creating an initial link with the other myths in the group.

Elsewhere, an analogy appears, at least on the semantic level, between the 'ugly bird' in M_{260} and the bunia bird in M_{259}, usually referred to as the 'stinking bird' (*Opistho comus*, *Ostinops* sp., Roth 1, pp. 131, 371). The position of this bird in the myths has been discussed elsewhere (*RC*, pp. 185, 205, 269, n. 33), and I shall not return to the subject. On the other hand, it is worth noting how M_{260} develops the bird theme introduced by M_{259}, so that the Wilbert version becomes to all intents and purposes a myth about the differentiation of birds according to species, thus amplifying the episode in M_{241} which is concerned with the different species of ducks. Finally, the Wilbert version links up with a group of myths about the origin of bird plumage (in particular, M_{172}, in which the last bird to arrive, a kind of cormorant, also becomes black). As I showed in *The Raw and the Cooked*, this group can be created by a process of transformation from myths dealing with the origin of hunting- or fishing-poison. Here we find the same armature, but one which results from a series of transformations, the starting-point of which was myths about the origin of honey. It follows that native thought must consider honey and poison to be in some sense homologous and this is borne out by the fact that South American varieties of honey are often poisonous. On the strictly mythical level, the nature of this connection will be disclosed later.

The Wilbert version should also be compared with a Chaco myth we have already studied (M_{175}: *RC*, pp. 305–8) which follows a remarkably similar progression, since in it the birds acquire their distinctive plumage because they open up the apertures in the deceiver's body, and blood spurts out, followed by excrement. As in the Wilbert version, the excrement turns the feathers of an ugly bird black; in this instance, it is the raven.

These parallels would be incomprehensible if they did not reflect some homology between the Toba deceiver or the Mataco fox, and the wooden bride in the Guiana myth. It is impossible to see how this homology could occur, but for the intermediary agency of the girl mad about honey, who, as I have suggested on several occasions (and shall prove conclusively), is herself homologous with the fox or the deceiver. The wooden bride must therefore be a transformation of the girl mad about honey. But we still have to explain how and why. For the moment, it is no doubt advisable to introduce further variants of the Guiana myth, without which it would be difficult to deal with the basic problems.

M264. Carib. 'The frog, the jaguar's mother'

A long time ago, there was a woman who had become pregnant by the sun with twin children, Pia and Makunaima. While they were as yet unborn, they expressed a desire to go and see their father, and asked their mother to travel westwards. They undertook to show her the way, but as she travelled she had to pick pretty flowers for them. So she plucked flowers here and there on the way, but accidentally stumbled, fell down and hurt herself: she blamed her two unborn children as the cause. They became vexed at this and refused to tell her which road she should follow. Thus she took the wrong direction and arrived in an exhausted state at the house of Kono(bo)-aru, the Rain-frog, whose son, the Jaguar, was reputed for his cruelty.

The frog took pity on the woman, and hid her in a cassiri jar. But the Jaguar smelt human flesh, discovered where the woman was hiding and killed her. When he cut up the body, he discovered the twins and handed them over to his mother. She put them first of all in a bundle of cotton: the children grew quickly and reached man's size in a month. The frog then gave them bows and arrows, and told them to go and kill the powis bird (*Crax* sp.), because it was this bird which had killed their mother. The youths therefore went and shot powis and continued shooting them day after day. The last bird they were about to kill told them the truth, and for this reason they spared his life. The two boys were very angry and made themselves new and stronger weapons, with which they killed the jaguar and his mother, the frog.

The two lads now proceeded on their way and arrived at a clump of cotton trees (*bombacaceae*, no doubt), in the centre of which was a house occupied by a very old woman, really a frog, and where they took up their quarters. They went out hunting each day and, on their return, found some baked manioc. They could see no field anywhere about, so they kept a watch on the old woman and discovered that she extracted starch from a white spot on her shoulders. Refusing all food, the brothers invited the frog to lie down on some cotton which they teased out on the floor; then they set fire to it. The frog's skin was scorched so dreadfully as to give it the wrinkled and rough appearance it now bears.

Pia and Makunaima next continued their travels to meet their father. They spent three days at the house of a female tapir. On the third evening, the tapir returned looking very sleek and fat. The boys followed her tracks which they traced to a plum tree. This they shook so violently as to make all the fruit, both ripe and unripe, fall to the ground. The tapir was disgusted to find all her food wasted, beat both boys and cleared off. The boys started in pursuit and tracked her for a whole day. At last they caught up with her and agreed on what tactics they should follow: Makunaima was to wheel round in front and drive the creature back and, as he passed, let fly a harpoon-arrow into it. The rope, however, got in the way of Makunaima as he was passing in front and cut his leg off. On a clear night you can still see them: there is tapir (Hyades), Makunaima (Pleiades), and below is the severed leg (Orion's belt) (Roth 1, pp. 133–5).

The significance of the astronomical coding will be discussed later. In order to link this myth directly with the group about the girl mad about honey, I am going to quote a Vapidiana variation which deals with the origin of Orion and the Pleiades:

M_{265}. *Vapidiana. 'The girl mad about honey'*

One day Banukúre's wife cut off his leg. He went up into the sky, where he became Orion and the belt. In revenge, his brother shut the wicked wife up in a hollow tree, and then he too went up into the sky where he became the Pleiades. The wife was turned into a honey-eating snake (Wirth 1, p. 260).

It is clear that this version, in spite of its brevity, is situated at the point of intersection of several myths: in the first place, the Haburi story, since we may suppose that, like the old frog, the heroine is full of lewd ideas (which prompt her to get rid of her husband). And she is also mad about honey, otherwise she would not agree to go inside a hollow tree and would not change into a honey-loving animal. Moreover, the two myths end with the disjunction of the hero: horizontal disjunction in M_{241}, vertical in M_{243} (but from high to low), and vertical also in M_{265} (this time from low to high). The theme of the woman mad about honey has a more direct link with Brett's version of the myth about Aboré (Haburi), the father of inventions (M_{258}), which presents a kind of short-cut leading back to the Ge myths. The story of the man whose leg is cut off, i.e. the origin of Orion and the Pleiades, which is common to both M_{264} and M_{265}, belongs to a vast group which I was able to touch upon only very briefly in *The Raw and the Cooked*. If this group overlaps with the one whose core I saw as being formed by myths about the girl mad about honey, the reason must be an equivalence between the lewd woman, who allows herself to be seduced by a lover to whom she is too closely related (brother-in-law) or who is too far removed from her (the tapir, which is given a different function in M_{264}), and the woman mad about honey, who behaves with an indecent lack of control towards a food which is also a seducer. This complex relationship will be analysed in greater detail later, but if we are to retain it as a provisional working hypothesis, we must at least have a feeling that the four stages in the disjunction of the cultural heroes, who are separated from a female tapir, after themselves in turn leaving two frogs and being separated from their mother, is to be explained in the long run by the fact that the three animals and the woman herself are just so many combinatory variants of the girl mad about honey. I had already arrived at this hypothesis in connection with the wooden bride, and it should not be forgotten that the mother of the dioscuri in M_{259} was, in the first instance, a wooden bride.

M_{266}. *Macusi. 'The wooden bride'*

The Sun, finding his fish ponds too frequently robbed, set the water-lizard, then the alligator, to watch them. The latter was the thief and continued his old trade. Finally the Sun caught him in the act and slashed him with a cutlass, every cut forming a scale. Alligator begged piteously for his life and in return offered the Sun his daughter in marriage. But he had no daughter and had to sculpt the form of a woman from a wild plum tree. He left it to the Sun to infuse life into her if he liked her, then, as a precautionary measure, hid himself in the water. This habit Alligator has retained up to the present time.

The woman was imperfectly formed, but a woodpecker in quest of food pecked at her body and gave her a vagina. The Sun left her and she set out to look for him. Then follows the incident related in

M_{264}, except that, after killing the jaguar, Pia takes out of his carcass the parts of the body of his mother and makes her whole and alive again. The woman and her two sons find refuge with a frog who draws fire from her body and who scolds Makunaima, when she sees him devouring the live coals, since he has an appetite for fire-eating. Makunaima then prepares to leave. He digs a large canal into which water flows: he makes a canoe, the first of its kind, and gets into it with his mother and Pia. It is from Crane that the brothers learn the art of fire-making by striking a flint, and they also accomplish many other feats. They, for instance, were responsible for causing great waterfalls, by placing huge rocks in the rivers to detain the fishes. They thus became more successful fishermen than the crane. Pia consequently quarrelled with Crane who took up with Makunaima. Finally they separated, and Crane flew away with Makunaima to Spanish Guiana.

Pia and his mother therefore lived alone, travelling together, fishing and seeking fruit, until one day the mother complained of weariness and withdrew to the heights of Roraima. So Pia abandoned the hunt and undertook to teach the Indians the arts of civilization. By him and his teachings we have the Piai men, sorcerer-warriors. Finally Pia rejoined his mother on Roraima where he remained with her for a while. When his time of departure came, he told her that all her wishes would be granted if, while she expressed her wish, she would bow her head and cover her face with her hands. This she still does to the present hour. Whenever she is sad and sorrowful, there arises a storm on the mountain and her tears run in streams down the mountain-side (Roth 1, p. 135).

This version makes it possible to round off the group in two different respects. First of all, it refers back to M_{241}:

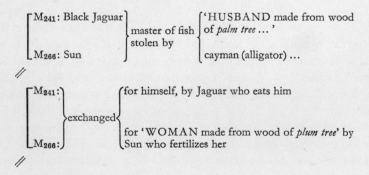

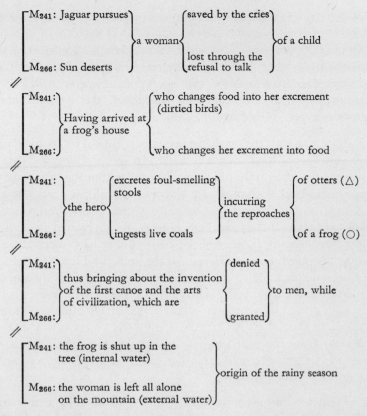

Brett gives an Arawak version (M₂₆₇), in which otters play a distinct part, as they did in M₂₄₁. The otters in the Arawak version destroy the Sun's fish ponds; the cayman tries to do likewise but is caught. To save his life, he has to give a woman to his conqueror (Brett 2, pp. 27–8). In Cubeo mythology, the cayman, the otter and the wooden bride are also linked:

M₂₆₈. *Cubeo. 'The wooden bride'*

Kuwai, the cultural hero, carved a woman out of the trunk of a wahokakü tree. Konéko, the bird (the hero's grandmother, in another version), made her vagina. She was a beautiful woman and Kuwai lived happily with her until one day she was carried off by a spirit, mamüwü. Kuwai sat down on a branch and wept. The otter saw him, asked him what was the matter and took him down to the bottom of the river, where the hero succeeded in winning back his wife.

However, he was chased away by an angry spirit and never came back again.

[In another version, the woman takes a boa as her lover. Kuwai finds them together, kills the snake, cuts its penis into four pieces and gives them to his wife to eat; she thinks they are small fish. On learning that her lover has been murdered, the woman changes back into a tree.] (Goldman, p. 148.)

The story in which the cayman plays a part (M_{269}) refers in all probability to another of Kuwai's wives, since it is specifically stated that this wife was the daughter of an old man of the tribe. One day when she was asleep in her hammock, Kuwai sent Cayman to look for a burning stick with which to light a cigarette. Cayman saw the woman and wanted to copulate with her. In spite of her protests, he succeeded in climbing on top of her. However, she ate the entire lower half of his stomach, including his penis. Kuwai arrived on the scene and told Cayman that he had been warned. He took a small square piece of matting and used it to mend the animal's belly. Then he threw Cayman back into the water, saying: 'It will be your fate always to be eaten' (Goldman, p. 182).

It is clear from the following equations that the two women – the one carved out of a tree, and the other one – are combinatory variants of one and the same myth:

(*a*) W^1 (carried off by a water spirit $\equiv W^2$ (attacked by a cayman);

(*b*) W^1 (seduced by a boa to whom she yields) $\equiv W^2$ (seduced by a cayman whom she resists);

(*c*) W^1 (eats the snake's penis) $\equiv W^2$ (eats the cayman's penis).

On the other hand, the group M_{268}–M_{269} allows us to establish a direct link between M_{266}–M_{267} and M_{241}:

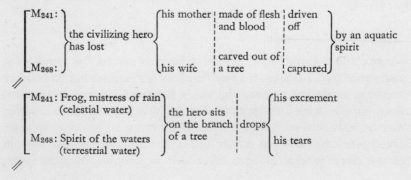

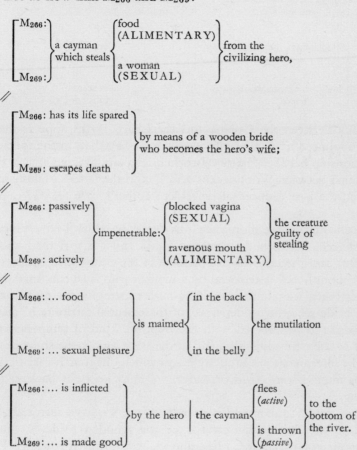

M_{241}:
which arouses the anger of an otter who brings him back
{ to his mother / to his wife }
in order to escape from the aquatic spirit
¦ the civilizing hero disappears

M_{268}:

Let us now link M_{266} and M_{269}:

M_{266}:
a cayman which steals
{ food (ALIMENTARY) / a woman (SEXUAL) }
from the civilizing hero,

M_{269}:

//

M_{266}: has its life spared
by means of a wooden bride who becomes the hero's wife;

M_{269}: escapes death

//

M_{266}: passively
impenetrable:
{ blocked vagina (SEXUAL) / ravenous mouth (ALIMENTARY) }
the creature guilty of stealing

M_{269}: actively

//

M_{266}: ... food
is maimed
{ in the back / in the belly }
the mutilation

M_{269}: ... sexual pleasure

//

M_{266}: ... is inflicted
by the hero | the cayman
{ flees (*active*) / is thrown (*passive*) }
to the bottom of the river.

M_{269}: ... is made good

The loop running between M_{241} and M_{266}–M_{269} is comparatively short because, in respect of both geographical location and of their places in the transformation series, these myths are close to each other. The other loop is much more extraordinary; in spite of the geographical, and what we might call the logical, distance between them, the Macusi myth refers back to the Chaco myths, whose heroine is a girl

H

mad about honey, although this character appears to be absent from the Macusi myth:

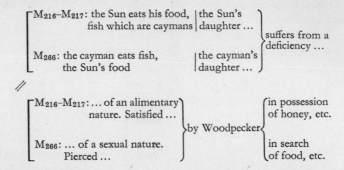

The link between the Guiana and the Chaco myths appears even more pronounced if we take into account the fact that, in the former, the relationship between the two brothers, Pia and Makunaima, is the same as that between Woodpecker and Fox in the latter: Makunaima is, in fact, the base seducer of his elder brother's wife (K.-G. 1, pp. 42–6).

So we encounter once more the equivalence, to which I have several times referred, between the wooden bride and the girl mad about honey. But easy though it is to conceive of the equivalence when the girl mad about honey is replaced by a woman who is equally mad, but about her body, it is difficult to imagine it existing in the case of the wooden bride who, being deprived of the essential attribute of femininity, ought to be afflicted with the opposite kind of temperament. In order to solve this difficulty, and at the same time make some headway in the interpretation of the myths on which this fourth variation is trying to impose some kind of order, we must go right back to the beginning.

The girl mad about honey is greedy. Now, we have seen that, in M_{259}–M_{260}, the father and creator of the wooden bride is called Nahakoboni, which means: the glutton. A glutton for what? For food first of all, no doubt, since some of the trials he imposes on the suitor consist in supplying him with enormous quantities of meat and drink. But this characteristic is not enough wholly to explain his psychological make-up, nor why he feels resentment against his son-in-law for having entrusted the bunia bird with the task of completing the girl he himself was incapable of finishing properly. The text of the myth is most illuminating on this point, provided, as always, that we read it with extreme care, taking each detail as being strictly relevant. Nahakoboni was growing old and needed a son-in-law. Among the Warao, who are a matrilocal tribe, the son-in-law sets up house with his parents-in-law and is supposed to repay them for having been given a wife by contributing labour and food. But in Nahakoboni's view, his son-in-law is not so much his daughter's husband as someone who owes him work and food. The old man wants him *all to himself*, as the mainspring of a domestic family and not the founder of a conjugal family, since what he contributed to the latter as a husband he would inevitably take from the former as son-in-law. In other words, Nahakoboni may be greedy for food, but he is even more so for services to be rendered to him: he is a father-in-law mad about his son-in-law. In the first place, it is essential that the son-in-law should never succeed in discharging his obligations; next – and this is more important – that the girl who has been given in marriage should suffer from a deficiency which, without impairing her mediatory function in the marriage, prevents her father's son-in-law becoming a husband to her. The wife, who is negativized at the outset, offers a striking analogy with the husband of the girl mad about honey, except that in Woodpecker's case the negativity occurs on the psychological level (that is, figuratively), whereas in the girl's case it occurs on the physical level, that is, literally. Anatomically speaking, the wooden bride is not a woman but rather a means whereby her father can acquire a son-in-law. Psychologically speaking, Woodpecker in the Chaco myths is not a man. The idea of marriage fills him with terror and his one concern is about the kind of reception he will be given by his parents-in-law: he is anxious only to be a son-in-law, and as a husband he is 'wooden', if we take the expression this time in its metaphorical sense.

Now, the Chaco myths are careful to present the character of the Sun in two different lights. He is shown first as a father who is unable to supply his daughter with the honey she likes; unable, therefore, to 'satisfy' her in an alimentary sense, just as the father of the wooden bride is unable to give her a sexual outlet. Secondly, the Sun in the Chaco myths is greedy, and so obsessed with one particular kind of food, the lewo fish, similar to cayman, that he sends his son-in-law to his death in order to catch them. This two-fold and fundamental inversion of the Guiana myths, in which a greedy father-in-law puts his son-in-law, the Sun, to the test, can be represented as follows:

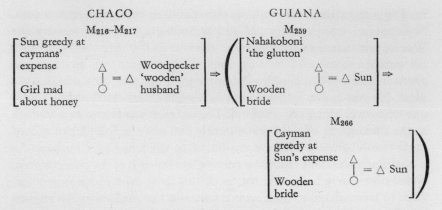

Through the Guiana myths, therefore, we glimpse, in an inverted form, the Chaco myths which were our starting-point: the Sun as father becomes Sun as son-in-law, that is, the relevant kinship bond changes from consanguinity to an affinal relationship. Sun, the examiner, becomes a Sun who is examined. The psychological apathy of the husband changes into the physical apathy of the woman. The girl mad about honey becomes the wooden bride. Lastly, and most importantly, the Chaco myths end with the drying up of the lakes and with the fish-caymans being thrown out of the water, whereas the Guiana myths conclude with the cayman either taking refuge in water, or being thrown back into the water.

I have shown on several occasions that the cayman stands in an oppositional relationship to the otters. The contrast becomes still more marked, if we note that the otters play the part of voluble animals, that is, either instruct or teach, whereas it is generally believed by the Indians of tropical America that caymans have no tongues. The belief is found among the Arawak of Guiana (Brett 1, p. 383), as is testified by the following rhymed text

> Alligators – wanting tongues –
> Show (and share) their father's wrongs.[13]
>
> (Brett, 2, p. 133)

The Mundurucu have a similar kind of story (M_{270}). The cayman was a glutton who devoured his sons-in-law one after the other. In order to save the life of the last son-in-law, the Indians hurled into the

---

[13] This belief is contrary to that held by the ancient Egyptians, who considered that the absence of a tongue added to the alligator's prestige: 'It is the only animal which has no tongue, because the divine word needs neither voice nor tongue' (Plutarch, § XXXIX).

monster's mouth a red-hot stone which burnt up his tongue. Since that time the cayman has been without a tongue and has a stone in its belly (Kruse 2, p. 627).

On the other hand, the otters are the rivals of the Sun in myths in which the latter appears as master of fishing or of fish ponds. In Guiana, as well as in the Chaco, fishing is an activity carried out during the dry season, as is evidenced by information from various sources, and in particular by the beginning of an Arecuna myth: 'At that time, all the rivers dried up and there was a great abundance of fish ... ' (K.-G. 1, p. 40). Conversely, the cayman, which needs water, plays the part of the master of rain in the Chaco myths. Both species are associated with water, but are also opposed to each other in respect of water; one needs a lot of water, the other very little.

In the Waiwai myths dealing with the origin of the Shodewika feast (M_{271}, M_{288}), there is a woman who has a boa as a pet. But she only gives it small rodents to eat and keeps the large game for herself (cf. M_{241}). The snake becomes angry, swallows her up and disappears to the bottom of the river. The husband gets help from the otters, which trap the snake by creating rapids and waterfalls (cf. M_{266}). They extract the woman's bones from the snake's belly and kill it. Its blood turns the river red. The birds come to bathe there and acquire a brilliant plumage, which is, however, made less brilliant again by a subsequent shower of rain against which each species protects itself as best it can. This is how birds came to acquire their distinctive plumage (Fock, pp. 63–5, cf. Derbyshire, pp. 92–3). So, the blood from the snake ($\equiv$ penis, cf. M_{268}) which devoured the woman here plays the same part as the blood of the woman, who was 'devoured' by the bird in search of food (M_{260}), when it accidentally made her a vagina. Although M_{271}, like M_{268}–M_{269}, contrasts the otters with the boa, which is a consumer and not a seducer of the woman, it is worth noting that the Tacana, who often reverse the great mythical themes of tropical America, regard otters and caymans as being in correlation with, rather than in opposition to, each other: they are not opponents but allies (H.-H., pp. 344–8, 429–30).[14]

[14] The crocodile–otter pair also appears in South-East Asia, a coincidence which appears all the more curious when we remember that many other themes are common to America and that part of the world, in particular a story about the marriage of a human and a bee-woman, who lost human form because her husband broke the rule she had laid down about not mentioning her presence (Evans, *text no. 48*). As regards the crocodile–otter pair, cf. also the following: 'They are wicked, incestuous men. They do as the horse does with the snake, the crocodile with the otter, the hare with the fox ... ' (Lafont, *text no. 45*).

The preceding discussion amounts to no more than a preliminary roughing-out of the subject. There is no point in disguising the fact that an exhaustive analysis of the group would raise serious difficulties, because of the multiplicity and diversity of the axes which would be required by any attempt to arrange the myths in order. Like all the other myths of the same group, those we are now considering depend upon rhetorical contrasts. The idea of consumption[15] is taken sometimes in the literal (alimentary) sense, sometimes in the figurative (sexual) sense, and on occasions in both senses at once. This happens in M_{269}, where the woman actually eats her seducer, while he is 'eating' her in the South American meaning of the term, that is, copulating with her. Furthermore, the links between the pairs of opposites are characterized by synecdoche (the cayman eats the fish which *form part* of the Sun's food) or metaphor (the Sun's only food is fish which are *like* caymans). Finally, these relationships, which are sufficiently complex in themselves, can be non-reflexive, but all taken literally or all taken figuratively: or reflexive, one being taken literally and the other figuratively. This situation is illustrated by the strange, partly erotic, partly alimentary marriage between the cayman and the wooden bride in M_{269}. If, for the sake of experiment, we decide to simplify the equations by disregarding contrasts of a metalinguistic nature, it is possible to integrate the most characteristic figures in the Guiana and Chaco myths by means of a diagram:

$$
\text{GUIANA} \left\{
\begin{array}{l}
\text{Cayman: } \triangle \\
\quad\quad\quad\quad\; | \\
\text{Wooden bride: } \bigcirc = \triangle \quad\quad : \text{Sun} \\
\quad\quad\quad\quad\quad\quad\quad\; | \\
\text{Girl mad about honey: } \bigcirc = \triangle : \text{Woodpecker}
\end{array}
\right\} \text{CHACO}
$$

In the Chaco, the Sun feeds at the 'caymans'' expense, and the latter at the expense of Woodpecker, Sun's son-in-law. In Guiana, the cayman feeds at the expense of the Sun and Woodpecker at the expense (but, in actual fact, to the advantage) of the latter's wife: the wooden bride. Finally, among the Cubeo, the cayman and the wooden bride feed (he, metaphorically, she, by synecdoche) on each other. Consequently, from the point of view of the spatial and temporal remoteness of the terms, the gap is greatest in the Chaco myths, and smallest in

[15] TRANSLATORS' NOTE: The author uses the French word *consommation*, which has the two meanings of 'consumption' and 'consummation'.

those of the Cubeo, while the Guiana myths occupy a middle position. Now the Chaco and Cubeo myths are also those whose respective conclusions are most exactly alike, although one gives an inverted picture of the other. At the close of M_{216}, the Sun sends his son-in-law to the lake to fish for fish-caymans, but the latter eat the bird. Sun then dries up the lake with fire, opens the monster's jaw and releases his son-in-law, who is in a sense 'de-eaten'. In M_{269}, the Sun sends the cayman to look for fire (a fire-brand) and his (the Sun's) wife eats him up. Sun closes up the victim's gaping belly and throws the cayman into the water, where, from now on, its fate will be to be hunted and then eaten.

No information is available about cayman-hunting among the Cubeo, but we are better informed in connection with Guiana, where the climatic conditions (in the eastern part at least) are practically the same as those in the Uaupés basin. In Guiana, the cayman is an important source of food; the natives eat both its eggs and its flesh, especially the tail (which is white and very delicately flavoured, as I was able to observe on many occasions). According to Gumilla (quoted by Roth 2, p. 206), the cayman is hunted in winter-time during the rise in the river when fish are scarce. We have less definite information about the Yaruro in the interior of Venezuela: it would seem that the small cayman, *Crocodilus babu*, is hunted all the year round except from May till September, when the main rainy season occurs (Leeds). However, the contrast pointed out by Gumilla between fishing and cayman-hunting seems to be indicated by Petrullo's observation (p. 200) that the Yaruro fish 'when they can find neither crocodiles nor tortoises'.

If it were legitimate to generalize this contrast[16] it would perhaps provide us with an explanation of the inversion which occurs when we move from the Chaco to the Guiana myths. The former are concerned with honey, and honey is gathered during the dry season, which in the Chaco, Guiana and the Uaupés basin is also the fishing season.

The Guiana myths effect a transformation of the Chaco myths along two axes. They state figuratively what the others state literally. And in the last stage at least, the message they transmit is not so much concerned with honey – a natural product, the existence of which testifies to the continuity of the transition from nature to culture – as with the

[16] Without, however, attempting to extend it beyond the Guiana region. The Siriono, who are skilled cayman-hunters but very poor fishermen, carry out both activities chiefly during the dry season (Holmberg, pp. 26–7).

arts of civilization, which provide evidence of the discontinuity between nature and culture, or again of the organization of the animal kingdom into graded species, which establishes discontinuity at the very heart of nature. Now, the Guiana myths lead into cayman-*hunting*, an occupation carried out during the *rainy* season, and as such incompatible with *fishing*, the masters of which are the Sun (also master of the *dry* season) and the otters (homologous with the Sun in respect of water); the otters can therefore be said to be doubly in opposition to the cayman.

However, the first Guiana myths we studied were expressly concerned with honey. We ought, then, to be able to find, at the very heart of the Guiana myths, and expressed with even greater vigour, the transformations which we first noticed when comparing the Chaco myths with certain specimens only of the Guiana myths. In this respect, particular attention must be given to the species of tree used for the carving of the bridegroom in M_{241}, and of the bride in all the others. When the theme appeared for the first time, that is in M_{241} (then in $M_{263a, b}$), the bridegroom or bride came from the trunk of a palm tree: *Euterpe* or *Mauritia*. On the other hand, in M_{259} and M_{266}, it is the wild plum tree which is mentioned (*Spondias lutea*). A great many points of contrast can be noted between these two families.

One includes palm trees, the other anacardiaceae. The trunk of the palm tree is soft inside, whereas the inside of the plum tree is hard. The myths lay great stress on this contrast, particularly the Wilbert versions in which birds twist or break their beaks on the hard wood of the plum tree (M_{260}), whereas the husband's companions have no difficulty in breaking the trunk of the palm tree ($M_{263a, b}$) with their axes. A third point is that, although the Indians eat the fruit of the *Mauritia* palm, it is the starch extracted from the trunk which provides the basic Warao diet. On the other hand, only the fruit of the plum tree can be eaten. Fourthly, the preparation of the starch is a complicated procedure, which is described in great detail in M_{243} because the acquisition of this technique symbolizes the attainment of culture. The palm tree, *Mauritia flexuosa*, exists in the wild state, but the Warao cultivate palm groves so methodically that some observers have claimed that they actually practise 'arboriculture'. It will be remembered that the starch from the palm tree is the only food common to both gods and men. In all these respects, the *Mauritia* palm contrasts with the *Spondias*, since the plum tree grows completely wild and its fruit provides food for both humans and animals, as M₂₆₄ reminds us in the tapir episode.[17] Finally, and most important of all, the edible starch extracted from the trunk of the palm tree (which can easily be split open) maintains a seasonal contrast with the fruit of the plum tree – the trunk of which is hard to pierce.

The contrast is manifested in two ways. First, the trunk of the plum tree is not only hard, it is also believed to be rot-proof. The plum tree is said to be the only tree the tortoise is afraid to have fall on it. With other species, it is just a question of waiting patiently until the wood rots and then the tortoise is free again. The plum tree does not rot; it even goes on producing buds after it has been torn up by the roots, and new branches start growing which imprison the tortoise (Ihering, under 'jaboti'; Stradelli 1, under 'tapereyua-yua'). Spruce (Vol. 1, pp. 162–3), who gives this same member of the anacardiaceae another scientific name: *Mauria juglandifolia* Bth., stresses the fact that 'it possesses great vitality and a stake cut from this wood almost always takes root and grows into a tree'. Now it is well known that, once a palm tree has been felled, or simply had its terminal bud removed, it never grows again.

Secondly, in the case of the *Mauritia flexuosa* (which for the Warao is the most strangely 'marked' palm tree), Roth points out that the extraction of the starch takes place when the tree begins to fructify (2, p. 215). In connection with Roth's observation, I have already noted (p. 186, n. 5) that South American palms bear fruit at the beginning of the rainy season and sometimes even during the dry season. Wilbert, on the other hand, states clearly that the starch is available as a fresh food 'during the greater part of the year' (9, p. 16), but this discrepancy does not necessarily affect the semantic position of palm starch in the myths. It will be remembered that we met with a similar kind of difficulty in connection with Chaco myths, because of the tendency to associate manioc with dry-season foods, although it is available all through the year. Manioc, of course, as I said at the time, being available *even* during the dry season, happens to be more definitely connected with the dry season than with the rainy season, when the various foods available only during this latter period of the year have greater prominence. It is worth noting, in this respect, that the Warao use the same word, aru, to denote both manioc starch and starch from the

---

[17] The contrast between *Spondias* and *Euterpe* is more limited, resulting as it does from the absence of any competition between men and animals. The fruit is gathered while still hard and has to be softened in warm water, as has already been explained.

palm, and that the two products are closely associated in M_{243} and M_{244}.

As regards the ripening of the fruit of *Spondias lutea*, we have precise information concerning the Amazonian region thanks to the excellent commentary with which Tastevin follows up several Tupi myths, to which I shall have occasion to return. The etymology put forward by Tastevin and by Spruce (*loc. cit.*) of the popular name for the wild plum: tapiriba, tapereba; (in Tupi) tapihira-hiwa, 'tapir's tree', seems to me, by reason of its mythic overtones (cf. for instance, M_{264}) more probable than that derived from tapera, 'waste land, deserted area'. The fruit of *Spondias* ripens at the end of January, in other words right in the middle of the Amazonian rainy season (Tastevin 1, p. 247), and in Guiana, at the end of the rainy season (one of two) which lasts from mid-November to mid-February.

So, at the same time as we move from a tree containing an *internal* food inside its *trunk* to another which bears an *external* food on its *branches*, what we might call the meteorological 'centre of gravity' of the myths shifts from the dry to the rainy season: this is a shift similar in nature to the one we were obliged to suppose in order to account for the transition, in the Guiana myths, from the gathering of honey and fishing, which are both dry-season occupations, to cayman-hunting, which is a rainy-season occupation; similar in nature, also, to the shift we observed when comparing the Chaco with the Guiana myths: in the Chaco myths, the *water withdrawn* from the caymans (dry season) is a transformation of *imposed water* (rainy season) in the Guiana myths. Moreover, the arrival of the rainy season is announced explicitly at the end of the Macusi version (M_{266}), and implicitly at the end of the Carib version (M_{264}), since throughout the whole of the Guiana area, the appearance of the Pleiades marks the new year and the beginning of the rains.

A further aspect of the palm/plum pair of opposites is worthy of attention. When the wooden bridegroom or bride comes from the trunk of a palm tree, he or she is a provider of food. They keep their spouses supplied with starch (the bride in $M_{263a, b}$) or with fish (bridegroom in M_{241}), and we know that, from the point of view of the Warao, the starch-fish group constitutes 'real food' (Wilbert 9, p. 16). But when the wooden bride originates from the trunk of a plum tree, she plays the part of mistress and not of provider of food. Furthermore, she is a negative mistress (she cannot be penetrated) rather than a positive provider of food. The axe will destroy the provider of food, but complete the mistress. Symmetrically, although the plum tree is shown to be a source of food (in M_{264}), the food it provides exists only to be denied (to the two brothers, by the tapir).

It is at once obvious that the series of 'wooden brides', when looked at from this angle, is incomplete and must be integrated into the larger group, the study of which was begun in *The Raw and the Cooked*. The star, who is the wife of a mortal in the Ge myths (M_{87}–M_{93}), combines in her person the two roles of impenetrable mistress (because of her chastity) and provider of food (since she introduces cultivated plants, correlative with *Mauritia* which, within the category of wild vegetation, is the equivalent of cultivated plants).[18]

Now, I showed in the previous volume (pp. 179–80) that this particular group of Ge myths could be transformed into a group of Tupi-Tucuna myths, in which the supernatural wife comes from the fruit, fresh or rotten, of a tree. There is, therefore, a whole series of what might be called 'vegetable' wives:

GUIANA	TUPI-TUCUNA	GE
		STAR
		cannibalistic vegetarian
	FRUIT	
	rotten fresh	
TRUNK		
soft hard		
(palm (plum		
tree) tree)		

The central characters are negative mistresses, either psychologically or physically. One is pierced for her own good; the others are raped to their detriment. In both cases, the creature responsible is a god-opossum, a foul-smelling beast, or a bird which is called, precisely, 'stinking one'. It is all the more remarkable that the young girl who begins her human existence in this way should, in the Guiana myths, become the mother of twins who can talk while still unborn, and should be reminiscent of the heroine of a famous Tupi myth (M_{96}): the woman who loses her way because the first child with which she is pregnant refused to guide her, and who arrives at the house of an individual who makes her pregnant with a second child and is subsequently changed into an opossum. So the heroines occupying a middle position

[18] Brett had already pointed out that, among the Warao, the cultivation of the *Mauritia flexuosa* was tantamount to a genuine agricultural activity (1, pp. 166, 175).

are either deflowered or raped by foul-smelling beasts. The heroines occupying polar positions are themselves opossums. This has already been demonstrated in *The Raw and the Cooked* in connection with Star, the wife of a mortal, and we now discover that the situation is repeated at the other end of the axis: like Star, the bride carved from a palm tree is a provider of food. And both are destroyed by their husbands' accomplices: sexually in the case of Star, who is raped by her brothers-in-law; alimentarily in the case of the wooden bride, who is torn to pieces by her lover's companions who want to get at the food inside her.

A separate study of this paradigmatic group, which I have here reduced to its simplest form, but which would reveal other levels when subjected to close investigation, would be worth undertaking for its own sake.[19] I shall limit myself to calling attention to one point. The Guiana myths which have just been analysed (M_{259}, M_{264}, M_{266}), when compared with the rest of South American mythology, reveal a peculiar constructional feature in the sense that their second part – the journey made by the twins' mother – reproduces almost literally the first half of the great Tupi myth I mentioned in the preceding paragraph. This inversion provides additional proof of the fact that the course we have been pursuing from the beginning of this book is taking us round the back, as it were, of South American mythology. This has been clear ever since the reappearance, at the end of my study of the myths about the origin of honey, of the myths explaining the origin of tobacco, to which we were very close at the beginning. But the fact that we now come full circle with the myth about the twins, which has already been encountered twice in the course of our investigation, can only mean that the world of mythology is spherical, in other words, forms a closed system. However, from our present standpoint we are seeing all the major mythical themes on the reverse side. This makes the task of interpreting them more arduous and complex, rather as if we were having to decipher the theme of a tapestry from the intricate tangle of threads at the back, and which blurs a picture that was much clearer when we were looking at it on the right side, as we did in *The Raw and the Cooked*.

But what is the meaning of wrong side and right side in this context? And would the meaning of the two sides not simply have been reversed if I had chosen to begin at the other end? I hope to show that this is not

[19] Starting in particular from the complete text of a Kalapalo myth (M_{47}: in Baldus 4, p. 45), in which the following interesting transformation is to be noted: *woman without vagina* $\Rightarrow$ *woman with piranha fish teeth*, which enable her to eat fish raw.

so. The wrong side and the right side are defined objectively by the native way of looking at the problem, in which the mythology of cooking develops in the right direction, i.e. from nature to culture, whereas the mythology of honey proceeds contrariwise, backwards from culture to nature; in other words, the two courses link up the same points, but their semantic charge is very different and consequently there is no parity between them.

Let us now summarize the fundamental features of this last set of myths. It relates to what might be called *misappropriation of an affine*. The story does not always concern the same kind of relative, and the culprit does not always occupy the same place in the pattern of marriage relationships. The Chaco heroine appropriates for her own use the supplies (of honey) which her husband owed first and foremost to his parents-in-law. Conversely, the greedy father-in-law in the Guiana myth (M_{259}) appropriates for himself supplies which his son-in-law would have owed to his daughter, once he had acquitted himself of his obligations towards the father-in-law. Between the two, and transposing the system of tribute-owing affines from the alimentary to the sexual level, the sisters-in-law in M_{235} try to appropriate for themselves the husband's love for his wife, and the old frog in M_{241} does the same, on the alimentary as well as the sexual plane, with the food supplies the hero owes to his mother, and with the sexual obligations he would have owed to a legitimate wife who would not have been a mistress, and would not have passed herself off as a mother. Consequently a relationship by marriage offers the culprit an opportunity of 'short-circuiting' his parents, his child or his affine. This is the sociological common denominator of the group. But there also exists a cosmological common denominator, the formula of which is more complex. According to whether the chief character is a woman (who fills a pot with the blood from her maidenhead) or a man (who does likewise with his foul-smelling excrement) – both bearing witness to the fact that the attainment of complete femininity or complete masculinity implies retrogression towards filth – a kind of structural order makes its appearance, either on the level of nature (but which gradually becomes weaker), or on the level of culture (but which gradually moves further away). The natural order grows weaker; the discontinuity which it manifests is merely a remnant of some previous richer continuity, since the birds would all have been red if the blood from the deflowering had not left behind a residue of bile and impurities, or if the rain had not washed it off in places. And culture moves upwards (M_{243}) or further into the distance (M₂₄₁, M₂₅₈), since men would have been better provided as regards spiritual help and the arts of civilization if their descent from the upper world had not unfortunately been barred by a woman pregnant with child, or if, because of a frog full of honey, the cultural hero had not been obliged to abandon them. Two females, one big with honey, the other big with child, interrupt, then, the process of mediation which the sexual discharge of blood, or the alimentary discharge of excrement, have on the contrary precipitated.

Nevertheless, in spite of this common armature, differences appear within the group and it is essential that they should be clarified.

Let us first of all compare, from the point of view of their construction, the three myths from the Roth collection, on which the fourth variation is fundamentally based. I mean the Warao myth about the wooden bride (M₂₅₉), the Carib myth about the frog who was the jaguar's mother (M₂₆₄) and, lastly, the Macusi myth about the wooden bride (M₂₆₆).

In the Warao myth, the heroine's adventures unfold according to an admirably regular plan: after being made complete by the bunia bird (who pierces a vagina for her), she is made pregnant by the sun (who fills her). She next swallows the parasite (which also fills her), and the frog empties her corpse of the twins which filled it.

The second and third episodes denote, therefore, a process of filling either from above or from below; one passive, the other active; and as far as the consequences are concerned, the latter is negative (involving the heroine's death), the former positive (since it makes it possible for her to give life).

Now, can it be said that episodes (1) and (4) contrast with the two intervening ones, in so far as they denote a process of emptying as opposed to filling? It seems clear that this is true of the fourth episode, in which the heroine's body is in fact emptied of the children it contained. The first episode, however, which consists of the opening up of the absent vagina, hardly seems comparable to the other in any strict sense.

It is as if mythic thought had been aware of the difficulty and had at once set about solving it. The Warao version introduces an incident, which may seem superfluous, but only at first sight. In order for the heroine to become a real woman, not only has the bunia bird to open her up, but her father has to set to work again (although he has just proclaimed his incompetence) by extracting from the freshly hollowed out vagina a snake which constitutes an additional obstacle to penetration. So the heroine was not just blocked, she was full; and the incident of the snake has no other apparent purpose than to change perforation into evacuation. Once this has been accepted, the construction of the myth can be summarized in the following diagram:

(1) heroine pierced by a bird, allowing evacuation of snake } *passive* { low anterior } heroine emptied (+)

(2) heroine made pregnant by the sun } *passive* { low anterior } heroine filled (+)

(3) heroine ingests a deadly parasite } *active* { high anterior } heroine filled (−)

(4) heroine ripped open by frog } *passive* { low anterior } heroine emptied (−)

If we remember the point, which is expressed in the diagram, that episodes (2) and (4) form a pair (since the frog *empties* the heroine's body of the very children with which the Sun had *filled* her), it follows that episodes (1) and (3) must also form a pair, that is: *snake evacuated from below, passively, with beneficial results | parasite ingested from above, actively, with maleficent results*. From this viewpoint, the myth consists of two superimposable sequences, each formed by two episodes which are in opposition to each other (*heroine emptied | filled : heroine filled | emptied*) and each in contrast to the episode in the other sequence of which it forms the counterpart.

Why this reduplication? We already know one reason, since it has been confirmed on several occasions that the contrast between the literal meaning and the figurative meaning is a constant feature of the group. In this instance, the first two episodes describe figuratively what the last two express literally: the heroine is first of all made 'eatable' (= copulable) in order to be 'eaten'. After which, she is made eatable (killed) in order to be, in fact, eaten in the other versions.

But a careful reading of the myth reveals that the reduplication of the sequences may have another function. It would seem that the first part of the myth – of which, it will be remembered, the Sun is the hero – progresses according to a seasonal cycle, the stages of which are indicated by the tasks imposed on Sun-son-in-law: hunting, fishing, burning, planting, building; whereas the second part, which starts with the Sun's journey westwards, describes a daily cycle. Expressed in this way, the hypothesis may seem unlikely, but a comparison with the other versions will give it some initial confirmation. Later, in a subsequent volume, with the help of other myths, I hope to show the importance of the contrast between seasonal periodicity and daily periodicity and to demonstrate that a close correspondence exists between this contrast and the contrast between the 'styles' in the construction of the narrative.[20]

Finally, and still in connection with M_{259}, it will be noted that, on the etiological level, the myth seems to have one function and one only: that of explaining the origin of a fire-kindling technique by friction.

Let us now consider the way in which the Carib (M_{264}) tell the same story. It will be remembered (p. 219) that they start off straight away with the second part. The daily sequence (the journey in the direction of the Sun) therefore occurs at the beginning. Furthermore, correlatively with the omission of the first part, a new part, dealing with the adventures of the two brothers at the house of another frog, then at the home of a female tapir, is added to the second. There are consequently two parts, and it would seem clear that the one which comes last in the Carib myth, and which is made up of a succession of episodes, recreates the seasonal cycle of hunting, burning and gathering of wild fruits, which start to ripen in January. If this interpretation is correct, the order of the two sequences, the seasonal and the daily, is reversed when we move from the Warao to the Carib version.

The inversion in the order of sequences is accompanied by a complete reversal of the system of contrasts which helped us to define the reciprocal relationships between the four experiences undergone by the heroine. The second experience is now put first, since the story begins when the heroine is pregnant by the Sun, whereas the fourth (the emptying out of the children from the heroine's body) remains unchanged. But between the first and fourth episodes, two new episodes are inserted – (2) the heroine hides in a jar (which she fills), and (3) she is 'emptied' out of this receptacle. This would seem to mean that the Warao version persistently treats the heroine as if she were a 'container', which is alternately emptied (episodes (1) and (4)) and filled (episodes (2) and (3)). On the other hand, the Carib version defines her by means of an oppositional relationship: *container/content*, in respect of which the

[20] Cf. in the meantime my report in the *Annuaire du Collège de France*, 64th year, Paris 1964, pp. 227–30. On the subject of the link between the dry season and the tasks imposed on the son-in-law, see Preuss 1, pp. 476–99.

heroine plays the part of agent or victim, being herself either container or content, with beneficent or maleficent consequences:

$$
\left[
\begin{array}{l}
\quad\text{(1) heroine made pregnant by the sun} \quad\left.\right\}\ \text{container}\quad(+) \\[4pt]
\left[
\begin{array}{l}
\text{(2) heroine filling a jar}\quad\left.\right\}\ \text{content}\quad(+) \\[4pt]
\text{(3) heroine emptied from the jar}\quad\left.\right\}\ \text{content}\quad(-)
\end{array}
\right. \\[12pt]
\quad\text{(4) heroine disembowelled by jaguar}\quad\left.\right\}\ \text{container}\quad(-)
\end{array}
\right.
$$

Now, it is episodes (1) and (4), on the one hand, and (2) and (3), on the other, which form pairs. Within each of the two sequences, the episodes are repeated, provided there is inversion of container and content, whereas, between one sequence and the next, the episodes which correspond to each other form a chiasmus.

The two transformations in mythical structure which we have observed as taking place at different levels, one formal, the other semantic, correspond to a third transformation which occurs on the etiological level. The Carib version merely sets out to explain the origin of certain constellations: Hyades, Pleiades and Orion,[21] which in this region are well known as heralding a change of season. To the ample information I have already given on this subject (RC, pp. 218–19) we can add the evidence supplied by Ahlbrink (under 'sirito'), which relates to Guiana communities who are Carib both in speech and culture: 'When *sirito*, the Pleiad, becomes visible in the evening (in April), thunder can be heard. Sirito is angry because men have cut off one of Ipétiman's (Orion's) legs. And Ipétiman is coming nearer. Ipétiman appears in May.'

Let us accept the fact, then, that M_{264} deals by implication with the beginning of the 'main' rainy season (there are four seasons in Guiana, two wet and two dry), which lasts from mid-May to mid-August. This hypothesis presents two advantages. First of all, it creates a link between the Carib version (M_{264}) and the Macusi version (M_{266}), which deals explicitly with the origin of rain and storms: these are brought about by the heroine's bouts of sadness when her tears stream down the mountain slopes after she has taken up her abode at the top

[21] As does a Tupi variant (M_{264b}) found by Barbosa Rodrigues (1, pp. 257–62), but it refers only to the Pleiades.

of Roraima. Secondly, it is possible to verify objectively, by means of astronomical and climatic references, my earlier hypothesis that the myths now being studied present the reverse side of a pattern, the right side of which we followed in our study of the Ge and Bororo myths in *The Raw and the Cooked*. The attempt to integrate the Ge and Bororo myths, which were seasonal in character, led to the following equation:

a) Pleiades-Orion : Corvus :: dry season : rainy season

We can now verify that, in the Guiana myths, the Pleiades-Orion group heralds the rainy season. What of the Corvus constellation? When it reaches its highest point in the evening in July, it is associated with a divinity responsible for the violent storms which characterize the close of the rainy season (cf. *RC*, p. 231; and in connection with the mythology of storms during the July–October period in the Caribbean Sea and the Big Dipper – the right ascension of which is close to that of the Corvus – L.-N. 3, pp. 126–8); whereas in Guiana also, the rising of Berenice's Hair (which has the same right ascension as the Big Dipper and the Corvus) denotes drought. We thus arrive at the following equation, which is the reverse of the previous one:

b) Pleiades-Orion : Corvus :: rainy season : dry season

This provides a link-up with the Macusi version (M_{266}) which, as we have just seen, deals explicitly with the origin of the rainy season. Furthermore, unlike the two myths we discussed previously, M_{266} has a double etiological function. In so far as it deals with the origin of the rainy season, it coincides with M_{264}: in so far as it explains the origin of fire-kindling by percussion (which the crane teaches to the hero) it coincides with M_{259}.

There are, nevertheless, two differences. The allusion to the rainy season found in M_{266} is *diurnal* (the tears can be seen forming torrents), whereas that in M_{264} is *nocturnal* (certain constellations are visible). And whereas M_{259} describes fire-kindling by *friction* (with two pieces of wood), M_{266} is concerned with fire-kindling by *percussion* (with two stones), a method with which the Guiana Indians are also familiar.

Consequently, as might be expected, M_{266} combines in a single myth episodes which belong by rights to each of the two other versions. It begins with the story of the wooden bride, which is missing from the Carib version, and ends with the twins' adventures after their stay in the frog's house, which are absent from the Warao version. But at the same time it reverses all the details: the father-in-law is put to the test, not the son-in-law; the heroine is pierced by the woodpecker, not by the bunia bird. Although the heroine becomes the prey of the canni-balistic jaguar, she does not die, but is restored to life again. The hero devours the red-hot coals, thus defeating the frog's purpose. It will also be noticed that the Warao bunia is prompted by lust, the Macusi woodpecker by hunger: he therefore eats the heroine in the literal sense. Symmetrically, in the second half of the Macusi version, the jaguar eats her only in the figurative sense, because he dies before he has digested his prey, and because the latter is restored to life almost as soon as she has been drawn out from the animal's belly (cf. above, p. 222).

The synthesis of the Warao and Carib versions, effected by the Macusi version by dint of a great many inversions, reveals that on the return journey we are meeting with myths which are simultaneously con-cerned with the origin of both fire and water, and therefore situated on the same mythological 'latitude' as the Bororo (M_1) and Sherente (M_{12}) myths we encountered on the outward journey, and which were characterized by the same etiological duality. The Macusi version therefore provides a particularly favourable opportunity to take stock of the situation.

The three myths M_{259}, M_{264} and M_{266} are concerned either with the origin of fire on the cultural level (friction or percussion), or with the origin of water on the level of nature (rainy season), or with both together.

Now, before fire was produced by means of cultural devices, it already existed in natural forms: it was vomited up by an animal, the frog, which itself is associated with water. Symmetrically (and on this point the evidence supplied by M_{266} is essential), before water was pro-duced by natural means (rain), it already existed as a cultural achieve-ment, since Makunaima, a veritable engineer of public works, first caused it to rise to the surface in a canal he had dug and in which he launched the first canoe.[22] Now, Makunaima, who devours red-hot coals, is associated with fire just as the frog is associated with water. The two etiological systems are symmetrical. Consequently, in the myths we are studying, the rainy season makes its appearance in the form of a transition from nature to culture. Yet, in the two instances, fire (originally contained in the frog's body) or water (subsequently contained in the mother's body) *both spread* – the former into the trees,

---

[22] The creation myths of the Yaruro also present the digging of rivers to be the necessary pre-condition of the appearance of water (Petrullo, p. 239).

from which sticks are taken to make fire, the latter to the surface of the earth, in the natural hydrographic system (in contrast to the artificial system first created by the demiurge). In both cases, then, we are dealing with a process of dispersion. The fundamentally regressive character of all the myths in the group has been exemplified once again.

How, then, are we to explain the ambiguity of the myths, which is clearly a result of their double etiological function? In order to reply to this question we must look more closely at the character of the crane which, in M₂₆₆, shows the heroes how to produce fire by percussion.

The bird referred to by Roth in English as a *crane* plays an important part in the Guiana myths. As we shall see later (M₃₂₇–M₃₂₈), it is the crane which brings back to man, or enables the humming-bird to bring back, the tobacco which was growing on a reputedly inaccessible island. Now, another Carib myth in Roth's collection (1, p. 192) begins as follows: 'There was once an Indian who was extremely fond of smoking: morning, noon and night he would bring out his little bit of cotton, strike the stones together, make fire and then light his tobacco.' It would therefore seem that, through the intermediary agency of the crane, the device of producing fire by percussion is linked with tobacco.

When it carried the humming-bird to the tobacco island, the crane placed it on the back of its own thighs, and when it relieved itself, the humming-bird's face got dirtied (Roth 1, p. 335); it is therefore a bird inclined towards defecation. Perhaps there is a connection between the crane's connotation with filth and the feeding habits of the great stilt-birds, which live on the dead fish left behind in the river-beds during the dry season (cf. M₃₃₁ and Ihering, under 'jabiru'). During the funeral rites carried out by the Arawak of Guiana, an emblem representing the white crane was solemnly paraded when the small bones of the deceased were being burnt (Roth 2, pp. 643–50). The Umutina call one episode of their funeral ceremonies king-fisher (Schultz 2, p. 262). Lastly, since at least one myth we are dealing with uses an astronomical coding, we should not forget that farther south, among various tribes including the Bororo and the Mataco, part of the Orion constellation bears the name of a stilt-bird, while the West Indian Carib give the name 'the Boatbill' (a kind of small heron) to a star which would appear to be part of the Big Dipper and is supposed to be responsible for thunder and tempests (L.-N., *loc. cit.*, p. 129). If this coincidence is not a pure accident, it provides yet another illustration of the inversion of the pattern of constellations to which I have already drawn attention (p. 242).

Be that as it may, the appearance of the crane in M_{266} as the bird which introduces fire-kindling by percussion (and tobacco in another myth) adds weight to the supposition that myths about the origin of honey in a sense anticipate myths about the origin of tobacco, the characteristic themes of which emerge in succession in the series of transformations: a cannibalistic jaguar killed by a trunk covered with thorns, and otters playing the part of 'blocked' characters (M_{241}). The same transformations might well throw light on the ambiguity of myths which operate simultaneously as myths about the origin of fire (by friction or percussion), and myths about the origin of water (the rainy season and the hydrographic network). For, if it is true, as I hope I have been able to show, that tobacco, when smoked, has an affinity with fire and with honey diluted in water, it becomes comprehensible that myths which deal simultaneously with the etiology of honey and tobacco (and in fact change from one type into the other) manifest the ambiguity I have referred to by allowing us to glimpse the origin of fire, an element which is congruous with tobacco, through – as it were – the origin of water, an element which is congruous with honey. In the Ge myths about the origin of fire (M_7–M_{12}), the jaguar appeared as master of fire and cooked meat at a time when men had to be content with raw meat; and it was the jaguar's human wife who showed canni-balistic tendencies. The Guiana myths reverse all these data, since fire-kindling techniques (and no longer fire itself) are obtained, or invented, in the Guiana myths by human heroes, as a result of their mother having been devoured by a cannibalistic jaguar.

The myths refer to two techniques: friction or gyration, and per-cussion. According to M_{259}, the fire which is now produced by friction was originally the fire *vomited* up by the frog, while M_{266} tells us that it was the crane, a bird to which another Guiana myth attributes a strong tendency to defecate, which instigated fire-kindling by percussion. Between these two myths, a third occupies an intermediary position:

M_{272}. *Taulipang. 'The origin of fire'*

In olden times, when men still knew nothing of fire, there lived an old woman called Pelénosamó. She piled wood up in her hearth and squatted on it. Flames then spurted from her anus and the wood caught fire. She ate her manioc cooked, whereas other people left theirs out in the heat of the sun. A little girl betrayed the old woman's secret. As she refused to give the fire, her arms and legs were bound, she was placed on some wood and her anus was forced open. Whereupon she excreted the fire, which changed into wató (= fire) stones, which make fire when they are rubbed together (K.-G. 1, p. 76 and Vol. III, pp. 48–9).

If we accept the two mythical propositions that fire made by friction was originally vomited, and fire made by percussion excreted, we arrive at the following equation:

$$\text{friction} : \text{percussion} :: \text{mouth} : \text{anus}$$

But in actual fact, further deductions can be made from the material at our disposal, for it lends itself to one in particular which can serve as a test for the method I am using.

It is well known that fire-kindling techniques by gyration (or by friction) have a sexual connotation in various parts of the world, and certainly in South America: the passive wood is said to be female, the stick which is rotated, or moved backwards and forwards, is said to be male. The rhetoric used in the myth transposes this instantly and universally recognizable sexual symbolism by giving it imaginary expression, since the sexual act (copulation) is replaced by a phenomenon relating to the digestive apparatus (vomiting). Furthermore, the female who is passive on the symbolic level becomes active on the imaginary level, and the organs respectively concerned are in one instance the vagina, in the other the mouth, both definable in terms of a contrast between low and high, and both being at the same time anterior (along an axis the other pole of which is occupied by posterior orifices):

symbolical level		imaginary level
O, passive	⇒	O, active
anterior	⇒	anterior
low	⇒	high

In the matter of fire-kindling techniques by percussion, ethnography provides no symbolic representations, the intuitive obviousness and general validity of which are comparable to those we have just mentioned. But M_{272}, reinforced by the recurrent position occupied by the crane in the myths (the old woman who excretes, the bird which excretes, both of them masters of fire-making by percussion), enables us to deduce the unknown symbolism of this technique *from its imaginary expression, which is all we have to go by*. We merely have to apply the same transformation rules as we did in the preceding case, where they were empirically verifiable. We thus obtain the following equations:

imaginary level		symbolical level
O, active	⇒	O, passive
posterior	⇒	posterior
low	⇒	high

Which organ, then, can be defined as posterior and high in a system in which the posterior, low position is occupied by the anus, and the anterior, high position by the mouth? We have no choice; it can only be the ear, as has been demonstrated, moreover, in connection with another problem (RC, p. 136). It follows, therefore, that on the imaginary (that is the mythic) level, vomiting is the opposite correlative of coitus, and defecation the opposite correlative of auditory communication.

It is at once clear how experience confirms the hypothesis obtained by deduction; percussion is noisy, friction is silent. This explains why it was the crane which initiated the former. There is some uncertainty about the identity of the bird Roth refers to as a 'crane'. There are indications in the source-book (Roth 1, pp. 646–7; 2, p. 338) which might lead us to conclude that the bird is a species of heron, and more precisely the bittern (*Botorus tigrinus*). But even if Roth was referring to a heron as a crane, the confusion is a particularly revealing one, for throughout the entire American continent and in other parts of the world too, myths are fond of introducing the crane because of its harsh cry;[23] the ardeidae, too, which might well be the species in question, owe their scientific name, which is derived from *Botorus butor* (bittern), to their cry, which apparently is like the bellowing of an ox or bull, or even of a jungle beast. The fire-kindling technique

[23] The cranes themselves seem to share this view, since an instance is quoted in which one of these birds, on losing its mate, developed a sentimental attachment to an iron bell, the sound of which reminded it of the cry of the absent bird (Thorpe, p. 416).

As regards the harsh call of the crane in the myths of North America, cf. Gatschet (p. 102): 'of all birds the Sandhill crane is the loudest and noisiest.' The Chippewa believe that members of the crane clan have powerful voices and are the tribe's orators (Kinietz in L.-S. 9, p. 154).

As regards China, cf. Granet (p. 504, n. 2): 'The sound of the drum is heard as far away as Lo-yang when *a white crane* [italic in the text] flies right into the Gate of Thunder,' and the reference to the Pi-fang bird, which 'resembles a crane, dances on one foot and produces fire' (p. 526).

It is all the more legitimate to emphasize these parallels since there is an anatomical, hence objective, basis for the crane family's reputation for noise. 'In most species the windpipe is convoluted in the males (not always in the females), entering behind the clavicles into a hollow space in the keel of the sternum' (A. L. Thomson, p. 61).

most prominently connected with noise is, then, the work of a noisy bird.

This technique is as quick as the other method is slow. The double contrast between: *quick*, *noisy*, and *slow*, *silent*, refers back to the more fundamental one, which I emphasized in *The Raw and the Cooked*, between what I called the burnt world and the rotten world; in that context, it was found at the very heart of the category of the rotten, where it was reflected in two modalities, which were respectively the mouldy (slow, silent) and the putrid (quick, noisy), this last modality, in fact, calling for a charivari. So at the same time as we again encounter in the myths the canonical contrast between the origin of water (congruous with the rotten) and that of fire (congruous with the burnt), we note the symmetrical appearance, within the category of burnt, of two cultural modalities: friction and percussion, the respective symbolic positions of which reflect in metonymic language (since it is a matter of two real causes producing the same effect) those which were occupied metaphorically (since the meanings in that case were psychological) by the natural modalities of the mouldy and the putrid, within the category of the rotten. To be convinced of this, we have only to compare the diagram on p. 339 of *RC* with the following one, which is its exact counterpart:

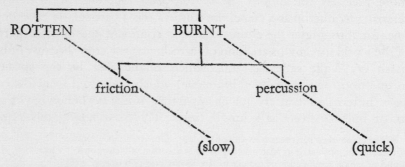

The transition from metaphor to metonymy (or the reverse), which has been illustrated in several places in the preceding pages, and to which I have drawn attention in other works (L.-S. 8, 9, 10), is typical of the development of a series of transformations by inversion when the intermediary stages are sufficiently numerous. Consequently, even in this instance, it is impossible that any real parity should appear between the beginning and the end, except for the inversion which generates the group. The group, being in a state of equilibrium along one axis, shows evidence of imbalance along another axis. This obligatory feature, which is inherent in mythic thought, protects its dynamic force while at the same time preventing it from ever becoming really static. In theory, if not in fact, there is no inertia in myth.

So, we have here an illustration, in the form of a special instance, of the canonical relationship which I described as follows in 1958 (L.-S. 5, p. 252):

$$f_{x(a)} : f_{y(b)} :: f_{x(b)} : f_{(a-1)(y)}$$

It was necessary to quote it at least once more as proof of the fact that I have never ceased to be guided by it since that time.

e. FIFTH VARIATION

$$[\text{jaguar} \Rightarrow \text{jaguar}] \leftrightarrow [\bigcirc \Rightarrow \triangle]$$

In the preceding myths, the frog appeared as the jaguar's mother. I had already tried to solve this ethnozoological paradox in two ways: by showing that the frog and the bee have a correlational and oppositional relationship along an axis the two poles of which are formed by the rainy season and the dry season, and by revealing another correspondence, this time between the bee and the jaguar, since the latter plays the part of master of honey in the Tenetehara and Tembe myths (M_{188}, M_{189}). If the frog is congruous with the wet and the bee with the dry, it is easy to understand that the frog, in its capacity as mistress of celestial water (= the harbinger of the rainy season), could be complementary to the jaguar, whose position as master of fire has been established independently, and which is commutable with the bee.

But why do the northern Tupi look upon the jaguar as a master of honey? Let us go back and consider the four animals which the myths classify simultaneously in respect of both water and honey:

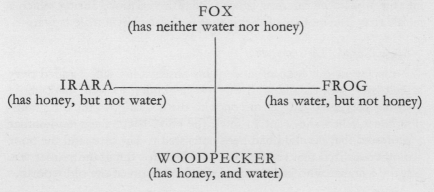

FOX
(has neither water nor honey)

IRARA
(has honey, but not water)

FROG
(has water, but not honey)

WOODPECKER
(has honey, and water)

So:

	water	honey
fox	—	—
irára	—	+
frog	+	—
woodpecker	+	+

Since the frog (in this instance, the cunauaru frog) possesses water, it must be the opposite of the jaguar, which has fire, by virtue of the equation: water = fire$^{(-1)}$ (cf. *RC*, pp. 189–91). Consequently, if the myth undertakes to relate these two animals to honey as well, it can only do so by respecting this major inversion; from which it follows that, since the frog does not possess honey, the jaguar does. This deduction restores the pattern, not only of the Tenetehara and Tembé myths, but also of the Warao myth (M_{235}), which lays down that, in respect of honey, water *is* fire (cf. above, p. 162).

My interpretation suggests that, in these same myths, there is a verifiable correspondence, on a different level, between the frog (the mistress of celestial water) and the cayman, whose semantic position is that of a master of terrestrial water (*RC*, p. 188). The cayman appears in M_{266} as a transformation of the *greedy* old man in M_{259}: and it is also symmetrical with the *greedy* frog in M_{241}: the latter steals the (future) civilizing hero from his mother in order to turn him into a husband capable of satisfying her sexually; the former gives his daughter, who is incapable of satisfying him sexually, to the (future) father of the civilizing hero.

Having clarified the rules governing the transformation of the frog into the jaguar, we can now broach the fifth variation, during which a female frog (the mother of the) jaguar is replaced by a male jaguar.

M_{273}. *Warao. 'The stolen child'*

A man went out hunting and in his absence his wife handed over their baby girl, a child who was just beginning to walk, and whose crying prevented her getting on with the cooking, to the old grandmother. When she went to fetch the child back, the grandmother protested that no child had been entrusted to her care, and the poor mother realized that she had been tricked, for the grandmother was really a jaguar who had assumed the exact form of the old woman.

All their attempts to find the child were fruitless and the parents at last gave up their quest. A few years passed and the parents began to lose things about the house: one day their necklaces, then their cotton garters; one evening all the ité starch vanished, then the bark apron-belt, then the buck-pots ... It was the jaguar who came under cover of night to steal all these things for the little girl to use, for he loved her as if she were his own kith and kin. The jaguar fed her on meat, and when she became a woman he started to lick the menstrual flow of blood, as jaguars and dogs do who like to smell the female organs. The two brothers followed his example, and the young girl found this behaviour very strange indeed.

So she made up her mind to escape and asked how to get back to her own village. The jaguar was suspicious, but she told him that, as he was getting old and would soon die, she surely ought to be returning to her parents. The jaguar, recognizing the force of her argument, was all the more willing to give her the information since he feared that, after his death, his two brothers would eat her up.

When the moment came to make the escape she had planned, she pretended that she could not remove an enormous pot full of meat from the fire, because she could not stand the heat. So without more ado, the jaguar picked up the pot between his paws and, as he held it, she dashed the boiling contents of the pot over him. The creature fell, yelled with pain and died. The two brothers heard his screams but paid no attention, because they thought he must be sporting with his girl. This was certainly not the case, since he had never had inti-mate relations with her.

The young girl ran to the village and made known her identity to her own people. She explained that they must all escape, because the jaguar's brothers would come for revenge and would kill them all. So the Indians got ready to leave, and loosened their hammock-ropes. One young man, a cousin of the young girl, put a heavy whetstone which he would want for sharpening in his hammock. But as he was slinging it over his shoulder in the usual manner, the unprepared-for weight broke his back and he fell down dead. His companions were in such haste to escape that they left his corpse lying there (Roth 1, pp. 202–3).

Roth makes an amusing observation in connection with this myth. When he expressed surprise at the abrupt ending, the old woman who had told him the story replied that when the two jaguars came to the village they found only the corpse there. Hence there was no one left to tell what actually did transpire subsequently.

But if we reverse the argument, the end becomes comprehensible. On arriving at the village, the two jaguars found at least one corpse there, and it may be assumed that they ate it instead of the young girl (whom, according to the myth, they were going to eat if she had stayed with them). To understand the importance of this detail, we need only recall that in the Ge myths about the origin of fire (cooking fire), the jaguar gave cooked meat to men from whom it had received a human wife. Now, here the jaguar has stolen from men (and not received as a gift) a woman who did not become its wife; correlatively, instead of men acquiring cooked animal meat, they give away raw human meat. To be convinced that this is unmistakably the meaning of the ending, which Roth held to be unsatisfactory, we have only to compare term by term the Warao myth and the group of Ge myths about the origin of fire (M_7–M_{12}), while remembering that, like most Ge tribes, the Warao have been claimed to be matrilineal, and that, contrary to what would happen in a patrilineal society, they consider the mother as a kinswoman and not as an affine:

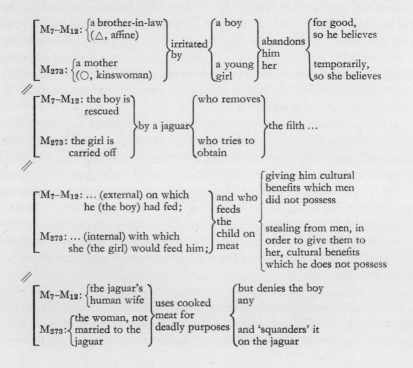

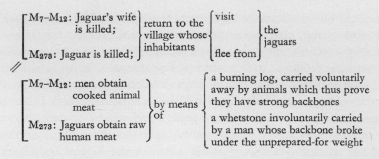

With regard to the last pair of opposites, *stone/burning log*, it will be noted that the stone in question is a whetstone, which is usually moistened before it is used (*water/fire* pair of opposites). Furthermore, it has been shown elsewhere (*RC*, p. 153) that, throughout this entire mythological system, stone is a metaphorical expression of human flesh, whereas the burning log is a metonymic equivalent of cooked meat (cause for effect). So not only the ending of M_{273}, but every single detail, is completely justified.

The preceding table shows M_{273} to be diametrically opposed to the Ge myths about the origin of fire, with which our circular tour around South American mythology began (in *The Raw and the Cooked*). We now find ourselves, therefore, at the opposite pole from our starting-point. Whereas cooking played a doubly conjunctive role in the Ge myths (between sky and earth, and between affines), it appears twice in M_{273}, but always in a disjunctive capacity: it is responsible, in the first place, for a child being abandoned by her mother who is too busy cooking for her husband – and who, consequently, considers her duties as an affine (wife and cook) incompatible with those incumbent on her as kinswoman (mother and nurse); next, it is responsible for the death of the jaguar – which is neither a father nor a husband, but a foster-father; and which dies through being scalded by the contents of a pot, i.e. as the victim of a cook's intentional clumsiness.

But if, instead of casting our minds straight back to our starting-point, we try to retrace our steps slowly, other links emerge which form a series of cross-connections, making it possible to join up M_{273} directly with several of the myths we have already examined. These short-cuts inevitably run through the inside of the sphere; whence it follows that the world of myths is not only round, but hollow.

Since M_{273} is a Warao myth, the jaguar's partiality for the menstrual flow could be satisfactorily explained by a belief, which is peculiar to this tribal group, that supernatural spirits, unlike men, are not disgusted by it (cf. above, p. 190). It is a fact that Warao mythology is fond of describing feminine indispositions. For instance, in M_{260}, the birds dyed their feathers in the blood from the deflowering, and in M_{235} – without going as far as the jaguar in M_{273} – a masculine spirit called Bee has no scruples about lying down with a girl who is unwell: his attitude proves, incidentally, that it is not only in the myths of the northern Tupi that commutation is possible between the jaguar and the bee (cf. above, p. 249).

Nevertheless, the story of M_{273} cannot be entirely explained by reference to Warao views on menstruation. During our investigation we encountered a Tucuna myth (M_{245}), which was also concerned with a girl, weeping because she had been abandoned by her mother, and whom a frog (a transformation of the jaguar, as was shown during the fourth variation) carried off and brought up, and whom she instructed in shamanistic powers. When the girl became a fully grown woman and returned to her own people, she fed exclusively on human marrow. Here we can observe a two-term transformation of the menstrual flow in M_{273}:

(a) M_{273} [jaguar (cannibalistic animal)] $\Rightarrow M_{245}$ [frog (non-cannibalistic animal)]

(b) M_{273} ['cannibalized' heroine   ] $\Rightarrow M_{245}$ ['cannibalizing' heroine   ]

On the other hand, an additional proof of the progressive 'transparence' of the mythology of honey to the mythology of tobacco, which is additional to those I have already given, emerges from another comparison with M_{273}, this time with the Tereno myth about the origin of tobacco (M_{24}). In this myth, which has been summarized and discussed elsewhere (*RC*, p. 100 *ff*) and a Mataco variant (M_{246}, p. 197) of which I had to make use to link up the Warao myths with those of the Chaco, a woman who is subsequently changed into a jaguar (whereas the Warao jaguar began by changing into a woman) tries to poison her husband by feeding him with menstrual blood (unlike the Warao jaguar, who was partial to his 'non-wife's' menstrual blood).

Now, this Tereno myth is one of the very first (with M_{20}) in which we have encountered honey, which plays here (as I showed in the first part of this book) the role of operative factor in the origin of tobacco. This honey is, on each occasion, toxic because of some external reason (the violation of a taboo by the gatherers in M_{20}) or some internal reason (it is mixed with serpents' foetuses in M_{24}). Whether the cause mentioned is psychological or physical, this honey is consequently *filth*. On the contrary, for the jaguar in M₂₇₃, the menstrual blood – filth – is a kind of *honey*. Its behaviour as a jaguar which steals a little girl (who has been abandoned because she cried too much) and which is greedy for her menstrual blood, reproduces the behaviour of the frog in M₂₄₁, who loses no time in offering a home to a little boy (because he cried too much) and who is greedy for the honey he offers her. According to circumstances, greediness brings about or facilitates the escape of the adopted child. And it has been independently established that, in the fifth variation, the jaguar is a transformation of the frog, which is the heroine of the third.

What kind of relationship can there be between honey and menstrual blood? In the first place, they are elaborated substances, like cooked food, but through the action of what might be called 'natural cooking'. In the native system of thought, as has already been explained, honey is produced by a natural form of cooking, which belongs to the vegetable category, and it is clear that the natural form of cooking from which menstrual blood originates belongs to the animal category. We thus obtain a first correlation, to which a second can immediately be added. The jaguar in M₂₇₃, by avoiding any form of physical contact with the kidnapped girl other than the tasting of her menstrual blood, transposes a sexual relationship into alimentary terms. It thus simply reverses the behaviour of the two sisters in M₂₃₅, who tried to 'kidnap' their brother-in-law, because they experienced in sexual terms (enamoured as they were of a man called Honey) a relationship which should have remained on the alimentary level. It must be to confirm the reality of this transformation that the jaguar in M₂₇₃ has two brothers, just as the heroine of M₂₃₅ has two sisters. The two brothers in M₂₇₃ are not content simply with the heroine's menstrual flow; they want to eat her up too. The two sisters in M₂₃₅ are not satisfied with the honey produced by the hero; they want to 'eat' him too, but in the erotic sense.

We can detect a third link between honey and menstrual blood, which relates to a fact I have often stressed (and to which I shall return), namely, that South American varieties of honey are often toxic. In their case, the distance between the categories of the delicious and the poisonous is very short indeed. It is, therefore, not at all surprising that the Warao, who have metaphysical doubts about the merits of the restrictions concerning women who are indisposed (cf. above, pp. 190, 254), should see a connection between honey and the menstrual flow.

One final remark about this myth: when, in the course of the third variation, I mentioned the problem (pp. 208–9) of the menstrual flow (of the woman) and the foul-smelling excrement (of the man), I brought to light the existence of a two-fold movement the parallel nature of which is stressed in the myths. On the one hand, physiological maturation implies a regression to filth which, in terms of auditory coding, is illustrated by the state of the whimpering infant. On the other hand, the emergence of order, whether it be natural or cultural, always results from the disintegration of a higher order, only the remnants of which are retained by humanity. But is this interpretation not contradicted by M_{273}? The heroine is a whimpering baby to begin with, and far from puberty causing her to regress towards filth, it would seem on the contrary to add to her attractions. However, the attractiveness of menstrual blood affects a jaguar, as the myth is careful to point out. 'He was still a jaguar, and continued to do what jaguars and dogs do' (Roth 1, p. 202). What does this mean? Since M_{273} is diametrically opposed to the Ge myths about the origin of cooking, it must be concerned with the origin of the most completely reverse diet: a diet in which animal eats man instead of man eating animal, and in which man is eaten raw whereas the animal is eaten cooked. It is precisely over this horrible scene that the myth discreetly draws a veil, almost before it gets under way. Its aim, therefore, is to explain not the disintegration of an order which has only just been established, but the formation of a disorder which can be integrated in lasting fashion into a mythological system in which the character of the jaguar-cannibal plays a leading part. Consequently, the parallel sequence (that of physiological maturation) must also be reversed. On all counts, the new perspective envisaged by the myth is no less appalling than the previous one.

f. SIXTH VARIATION

$$[\text{jaguar} \Rightarrow \text{jaguar}] \leftrightarrow [\triangle \Rightarrow \bigcirc]$$

Let us look at the myth first of all:

M_{274}. *Arawak. 'The jaguar changed into a woman'*

There was a man justly noted for his skill in hunting wild pigs. He would always succeed in killing five or six, whereas the jaguar who invariably followed on the heels of the pack would catch only one or two. So the jaguar decided to change into a woman, and in this new disguise he approached the hunter and asked him to tell him the secret of his success. 'I have been trained to it since early boyhood,' the latter replied. Then the woman-jaguar expressed her desire to have him for a husband, but he, knowing her true nature, was not too anxious to give a decided answer. She overcame his scruples, however, and together they killed more pigs than it was possible to do singly.

They lived happily together for a long time. She turned out to be an exceedingly good wife, for besides looking after the cooking and the barbecuing, she was an excellent huntress. One day she asked her husband whether he had a father or mother and, on learning that his parents were still alive, she suggested they should pay them a visit, because they must surely think him dead. She knew the way, and offered to act as guide to her husband, but on condition that he promised never to reveal her origin.

So they arrived at the village, taking plenty of pigs with them. The Indian's mother at once wanted to know where his beautiful wife came from. Omitting all mention of the fact that she was really a jaguar, he merely said that he had met her by chance in the forest. Every day husband and wife went out hunting and brought back an extraordinarily large bag. The villagers became suspicious. First of all, the Indian refused to divulge the secret, but his mother became so worried that he at last made a clean breast of it to her. The husband's people made the old woman drunk and forced her to tell the secret. The woman-jaguar, who had heard everything without disclosing her whereabouts felt so ashamed that she fled growling into the bush and was never seen or heard of again. Her poor husband searched the bush in vain, calling out his wife's name, but there never, never came any reply (Roth 1, pp. 203–4).

This myth calls for two comments, one regarding form, the other regarding content.

Let us first of all examine the group of equations which provided the basis for the six variations:

$$(1)\ [\text{bee} \Rightarrow \text{bee}] \leftrightarrow [\bigcirc \Rightarrow \triangle]$$
$$(2)\ [\triangle \Rightarrow \triangle] \leftrightarrow [\text{bee} \Rightarrow \text{frog}]$$
$$(3)\ [\text{frog} \Rightarrow \text{frog}] \leftrightarrow [\triangle \Rightarrow \bigcirc]$$
$$(4)\ [\bigcirc \Rightarrow \bigcirc] \leftrightarrow [\text{frog} \Rightarrow \text{jaguar}]$$
$$(5)\ [\text{jaguar} \Rightarrow \text{jaguar}] \leftrightarrow [\bigcirc \Rightarrow \triangle]$$
$$(6)\ [\text{jaguar} \Rightarrow \text{jaguar}] \leftrightarrow [\triangle \Rightarrow \bigcirc]$$

I

It is clear that the last is not of the same type as the others. Instead of opening up the way to a new transformation, it merely cancels out the immediately previous operation, so that, taken together, equations (5) and (6) produce an identical transformation: one replaced a female jaguar by a male jaguar, while the other changes the male jaguar back into a female jaguar. Just as a dressmaker finishes off her work by tucking in the edge of the material and sewing it underneath to the unseen part to prevent fraying, so the group concludes by turning down the sixth variation over the fifth, like a hem.

Looking now at the content of the myth, we observe that it is not satisfied merely to complete the group at one of its extremities: it takes the group as a totality and turns it into a closed system. After a whole series of transformations, which gradually took us farther and farther away from their starting-point, we have now come back to that point. Provided only we accept the transformation of a bee-woman into a jaguar-woman, M_{274} tells exactly the same story as M_{239} and M_{234}, which provided the 'theme' for the six variations.

In all three myths, the husbands have an identical vocation: the bee's husband is the best honey-gatherer in his tribe, the jaguar-woman's husband has no equal as a hunter, but of pigs only, for he is sometimes outclassed in respect of other kinds of game. Now, if honey is obviously the mediatory term between bee and man, I have explained elsewhere (*RC*, pp. 83–108) why the wild pig (probably *Dicotyles torquatus* in M_{274}, where the species is not made clear; but *D. labiatus* lives in such vast herds that five or six beasts would not represent a very impressive bag) occupies a comparable position between man and jaguar. No doubt the Indian in M_{233} and M_{234} courts the supernatural woman, whereas the reverse happens in M_{274}. But in both instances, the heroines show the same concern for their affines: one before marriage, the other after. I have shown the significance of this feature, which allows us to unite in a single group the Guiana and Chaco myths in which the heroine is characterized in respect of honey (she may be either greedy for, or lavish with, honey), and which therefore provides an additional proof that M_{274} also belongs to this group.

But if the sixth variation simply brings us back to the theme, while demonstrating, through its reduplicative function, that there is no point in looking farther afield, and that the group has been blocked at one of its extremities and is furthermore a closed set, does the static character of the group thus averred not contradict the principle I recalled at the end of the fourth variation, and according to which any mythic transformation should be characterized by an imbalance, which is both a guarantee of its vitality, and a sign that it is incomplete?

In order to solve the difficulty, we should recall the very unusual course we were forced to follow by the series of transformations of the theme. All these myths, we said, deal not so much with origin as with loss. Loss of honey first of all, which in earliest times was available in limitless quantities, and which has now become difficult to find (M_{233}–M_{235}). Then loss of game, which in olden times was abundant but became scarce and widely scattered (M_{237}–M_{239}). Then, according to Haburi's story (M_{241}, M_{258}), culture and the arts of civilization were lost. Haburi, 'the father of inventions', had to abandon men in order to escape from the frog's clutches. Finally came a loss more serious than all the others: the loss of those logical categories without which man cannot conceptualize the contrast between nature and culture, nor overcome the confusion of opposites: cooking fire is vomited, food exuded (M_{263}, M_{264}, M_{266}), and the distinction abolished between food and excrement (M_{273}), as well as between the cannibalistic jaguar's search for food and man's search for food (M_{273}, M_{274}).

Consequently, like a twilight of the gods, the myths describe this inevitable collapse: from a golden age when nature was submissive and generous to man, by way of a sterner age when man was endowed with clear ideas and well-defined contrasts by means of which he was still able to control his surroundings, to a state of gloomy indistinctness in which nothing can be indisputably possessed and still less preserved, because all beings and things are intermingled.

The universal regression towards chaos, so characteristic of the myths we are dealing with, and which is also a falling back into nature explains their ultimately stationary structure. This structure testifies then, but in a different way, to the presence of a built-in gap between the content of the myth and its form: the myths can only depict decadence by means of a stable formal structure, for the same reason that some myths, which try to maintain a state of invariance throughout a series of transformations, are obliged to have recourse to an unbalanced structure. The imbalance is always present but, according to the nature of the message, it is manifested by the instability of the form to adapt itself to the inflections of the content, with regard to which it sometimes falls short: the form is constant if the message is regressive; or which it sometimes overshoots: the form is progressive if the message is constant.

At the beginning of this book, I started from the hypothesis that honey and tobacco form a pair of opposites and that consequently the mythology of honey and that of tobacco must correspond to each other symmetrically. We should now perceive that this hypothesis is not complete since, as regards their respective mythical functions, honey and tobacco entertain more complex relationships with each other. The following chapters will show that, in South America, the function of tobacco consists in restoring what the function of honey destroyed, that is in re-establishing between man and the supernatural that communication which the seductive power of honey (which is none other than that of nature) had caused to be interrupted: 'Tobacco likes listening to myths. According to the Kogi, that is why it grows near houses' (Reichel-Dolmatoff, Vol. II, p. 60). The visible changes which the six variations effected, as it were, under our very eyes therefore resemble the rapid oscillations characteristic of a strip of metal acting as a spring and one end only of which is fixed, while the other, when suddenly released by the breaking of the cable which kept it taut, vibrates in opposite directions before finding its point of rest. Only, here again, the phenomenon unfolds the wrong way round: but for tobacco, which kept it tensed in the direction of the supernatural, culture, reduced to its own resources, can only fluctuate indecisively on either side of nature. After a certain lapse of time, its impetus dies down and its inherent inertia immobilizes it at the one point at which nature and culture are, as it were, in a state of natural equilibrium, and which I have defined as being the honey harvest.

In a sense, therefore, the drama had been enacted and consummated from the very first variation, since it was concerned with honey. The others merely marked out, with ever-increasing precision, the confines of a stage left empty after the play was over. It is therefore of little importance whether they are more or less numerous. Like the chords which end Beethoven's symphonies, and always make us wonder why the composer used so many, and what made him decide not to add still more, they do not conclude a development in progress. The development had already exhausted all its possibilities, but some metalinguistic means had to be found of signalling the end of the message and the signal is obtained by enclosing its last statement in the system (made present for once) of the tones which had contributed, throughout the transmission of the music, to a more faithful rendering of the shades of meaning of the system, by modulating it in several ways.

PART THREE SUMMER IN LENT[1]

Rura ferunt messes, calidi quum sideris aestu
deponit flavas annua terra comas.
Rure levis verno flores apis ingerit alveo,
compleat ut dulci sedula melle favos.
Agricola assiduo primum satiatus aratro
cantavit certo rustica verba pede.
Et satur arenti primum est modulatus avena
carmen, ut ornatos diceret ante Deos.
Agricola et minio suffusus, Bacche, rubenti
primus inexperta ducit ab arte choros.

Tibullus, *Elegies*, I, L.II

[1] TRANSLATORS' NOTE: The French title is *Août en Carême*; the author intends this as an inversion of *arriver comme mars en Carême*, 'to happen as regular as clockwork'. The point is perhaps made clearer in English if *août* is rendered as 'summer'.

1 *Starry Night*

Unlike M_{259} and M_{266}, the Carib version (M_{264}) makes no reference to the origin of fire. The frog does no more than extract flour from a white patch between its shoulders; it neither vomits nor excretes fire and does not perish on a funeral pyre but on a bed of blazing cotton. The fire cannot therefore spread among the trees; its effects are limited to the body of the batrachian, whose scorched skin retains a rough and wrinkled appearance. This absence of an etiological factor, such as is prominent in the parallel versions, is, however, compensated for by the presence of another factor, not mentioned in M_{259} and M_{266}: this is the origin of certain constellations. It will be remembered that the tapir becomes the Hyades, Makunaima the Pleiades and his severed leg the shield of Orion.

A Guiana myth, which probably belongs to the Acawai and that I have already summarized and discussed elsewhere (M_{134}, *RC*, pp. 243–4), says that the Pleiades sprang from the viscera of an Indian, whose brother murdered him in the hope of obtaining his wife. A transition from one version to another is offered by various Guianese myths, and it is all the more plausible in that, in each case, Orion represents the severed member and the Pleiades the rest of the body; the latter, therefore, contains the viscera. In the Taulipang myth (M_{135}), the Pleiades forecast a large catch of fish, as in M_{134}, where the Pleiades correspond only to the viscera. And, in the Arecuna version (M_{136}), the amputation of the hero's limb occurs after he has murdered his grandmother who, like the frog in M_{264}, offered him excreted food. In *The Raw and the Cooked* (pp. 240–46), I discussed at length the symbolical assimilation of the Pleiades to the viscera or the part of the body containing the viscera, pointed out that it occurs in various, widespread localities in the New World and showed that, from the anatomical point of view, the relevant contrast was between: viscera (the Pleiades) and: a long bone (Orion).[2]

[2] Some Guiana variants identify the Pleiades with the head and not with the viscera, but the contrast is maintained in the form: *rounded/lengthy*.

In the Guianese area, then, the Pleiades, represented by the viscera or a part of the body containing the viscera, forecast a plentiful supply of fish. This is not our first encounter with a 'visceral' theme: it also played a part in the cycle of the girl mad about honey. For fuller details, I refer the reader back to Part Two, 2, and shall restrict myself here to mentioning the Toba and Mataco myths (M_{208}, M_{209}) in which the deceiver loses his viscera which change into edible vines, water-melons and wild fruits, or M_{210}, in which vomit (emerging from the viscera in the same way as the latter emerge from the rib-cage and the abdominal cavity) gives rise to water-melons.

In M_{134}, the disembowelling of the hero brings about the appearance of the Pleiades (in the sky) and of fish (in water). In M_{134} (and in the basic myth, M_1), the appearance of aquatic plants (on the surface of the water) is also the result of a disembowelling. Behind these metamorphoses one can discern a two-fold oppositional axis: on the one hand between the high and the low, since the stars float on high 'on the air', as the aquatic plants float down below on the water; and on the other hand between container and content, since water contains fish, whereas water-melons (and, generally speaking, the fruit and vegetables of the dry season) contain water. The disembowelling which determines the origin of water-melons in M_{208}–M_{219}, and the disembowelling which determines the arrival of the fish in M_{134} are all the more comparable in that fishing and the gathering of wild fruit take place chiefly during the dry season. It is true that M_{134} contains no more than a barely perceptible reference to the theme of the girl mad about honey: wishing to be rid of the wife after the husband, the killer Indian persuades her to get inside a hollow tree (i.e. a place where honey would normally be looked for), but under the pretext of catching an agouti (Roth 1, p. 262).[3] Whereas M_{134} does no more than establish a connection between the themes of the viscera and the origin of the Pleiades, the Taulipang (M_{135})

[3] The reference to the agouti is not accidental, since, as we know, in Guianese myths (Ogilvie, p. 65), it alternates with the tapir as master of the tree of life. But not in the same way, apparently: the tapir, the current master of wild fruit, was also master of cultivated plants when the latter, in the wild state, grew on a tree; whereas the agouti, a stealer of cultivated plants, now seems to enjoy a right of priority over them: the Rio Uaupés Indians begin gathering manioc round the outside of the field so as to deceive the agouti living in the adjoining bush, because – they say – it will imagine that there is nothing left to steal (Silva, p. 247). On the other hand, in those myths where the agouti is the first master of the tree of life, he has a grain of maize hidden in his *hollow tooth*, which can be considered as a term standing at the apex of a triangle, the other angles of which are occupied respectively by the *toothed* capybara and the *toothless* ant-eater. It is as if, in mythic thought, the agouti served to link the semantic half-value of the selfish, greedy tapir to another value, of which the capybara and the ant-eater each represent a half.

and Vapidiana (M_{265}) variants – in which the wife is in love with her young brother-in-law, contrary to what happens in M_{134} – associate the theme of the origin of the Pleiades with that of the girl mad about honey: to avenge his mutilated brother, who has been transformed into one of the Pleiades, the hero of M_{135} imprisons the widow, who has insisted on marriage, inside a hollow trunk into which she had imprudently inserted her head in order to eat honey directly from the comb. Whereupon, he transforms himself, along with his children, into an araiuág, a honey-eating animal[4] (cf. above, p. 86), after taking care to set fire to his hut (K.-G. 1, pp. 55–60). It will be remembered that in one of the Chaco myths (M_{219}), the seducer – who, according to another myth, set fire to his village (M_{219b}: Métraux 5, p. 138) – suffers the same punishment as the seductress does here.

Finally, the Arecuna version (M_{136}) combines all three themes: the floating viscera (origin of aquatic plants), the murderous wife who mutilates her husband (transported to the heavens to become the Pleiades), and the punishment of the wife who is shut up in a hollow tree (for having shown too great a greediness for honey).

The recurrence, in the Guianese and Chaco myths, of the theme of the floating or hanging viscera, allows us to apply to the group as a whole a conclusion that I had already entertained through a comparison, in a different context, of certain Guianese myths with the Chaco myths. In all these cases, as can be seen, a relationship through marriage is violated because of uncontrollable covetousness, which may be of an alimentary or sexual nature, but remains identical with itself in either form, since it is directed towards honey as a 'seductive' food or towards a seductive character, who is given the name 'Honey' in several Guianese myths.

In the Chaco version, the relationship between a son-in-law and his parents-in-law is neutralized by too greedy a wife. This is the opposite of the situation in a Guianese myth (M_{259}), where too greedy a father-in-law neutralizes the relationship between his daughter and his son-in-law. In other Guianese myths, a relationship between affines (who are respectively brother-in-law and sister-in-law) is neutralized through the elimination of the husband by his brother (M_{134}), or by his wife (M_{135}). Finally, in M_{136}, which seems out of line when approached in this way, an affine neutralizes a relationship between blood-relatives,

---

[4] But which is not eaten by men, and is therefore 'non-game'. In M_{265} it is the wife who is changed into a honey-eating creature (a snake).

since the son-in-law kills his wife's mother, who has been supplying him with food (whereas, normally, the situation is the reverse). But this inversion of the cycle of services rendered becomes comprehensible when we consider that the food is *excreted*: it is an anti-food which therefore constitutes an anti-service on the part of the mother-in-law. In short, we have arrived at the general transformational system on the basis of an exceptional foodstuff, honey, and an equally exceptional sociological situation, that of the too greedy woman, whether the object of her covetousness is honey (Chaco) or an illicit relationship (Guiana), or both at once (again Guiana).

If we try to see the system as a whole and to determine its basic characteristics, we can say, then, that its peculiarity is the simultaneous exploitation of three codes: an alimentary code the symbols of which are the typical foods of the dry season; an astronomical code which refers to the daily or seasonal movement of certain constellations; thirdly, a sociological code built around the theme of the badly brought up girl who betrays her parents or her husband, but always in such a way as to be incapable of performing the mediatory function in the marriage relationship which is assigned to her by the myth.

Codes 2 and 3 are prominent in the Guianese myths and we have seen that code 1 is doubly present, although in a blurred form: on the one hand, in the connection between the Pleiades and the movement of the fish upstream, and on the other hand, in the final transformation of the heroine, who is at first madly in love with her brother-in-law, into the woman mad about honey. In the Chaco myths codes 1 and 3 are the most obvious, but not only is code 2 discernible in the theme of the fruit and vegetables of the dry season which spring from the trickster's viscera (whereas in Guiana the viscera of the trickster's victim give rise simultaneously to the Pleiades and to fish), the possibility of the existence of an astronomical code is strengthened still further in the case that was considered above (pp. 114–15), in which the heroine, who is transformed into a capybara, represents the constellation of Aries. As it happens, Aries appears slightly before the Pleiades, and the latter slightly before Orion. We are therefore dealing with two pairs of constellations which are slightly dephased as between the Chaco and Guiana. In the case of each pair, the first constellation each time announces the appearance of the second, which is always in the most prominent position. Orion actually occupies an exceptional place in the astronomical code of Guiana, and it is well known that the tribes

of the Gran Chaco attach major importance to the Pleiades and celebrate their return with great ceremonies:

CHACO

Orion > Pleiades > Aries

GUIANA

*

All these details had to be recalled before broaching the essential
problem raised by the analysis of these myths, i.e. the reciprocal con-
vertibility of the three codes. When reduced to its simplest expression,
it can be formulated as follows: what is the common feature uniting
the search for honey, the constellation of the Pleiades and the character
of the badly brought up girl? I shall try to establish a connection
between the alimentary and astronomical codes, then between the
alimentary and the sociological codes and lastly between the sociological
and astronomical codes, and I hope that the triple demonstration will
provide proof of the homology between the three codes.

The most explicit references to the Pleiades are to be found in the
Guianese myths. It is appropriate, then, to begin by establishing the
seasonal calendar for that part of America, as we have already done for
the Gran Chaco and the Brazilian plateau. The task is not an easy one,
since climatic conditions, and particularly the rainfall, vary between the
coast and the interior, and between the western and eastern areas.
The simple contrast between a dry season and a rainy season is hardly
to be found anywhere except in British Guiana and the centre of Venezuela, where the rainfall increases up to July and then falls to its lowest
point in November. To the west of the Orinoco delta, the contrast is
less marked and the rains occur later.[5] On the other side of British

[5] At San Carlos de Rio Negro, Keses distinguishes between a rainy season (from June
to August) and a dry season (from December to March), interlinked by intermediary seasons
which he refers to as the 'rising' or the 'falling' of the waters, and which are marked by
irregular rainfall and violent storms. Also along the Rio Negro, at São Gabriel, i.e. farther
to the south and in Brazilian territory, the rainfall is apparently heaviest from December to
January and then again in May (*Pelo Rio Mar*, pp. 8–9; *Normais*, p. 2). To the west, in the
Uaupés valley, the two periods of slightest rainfall are from June to August and from
December to February (Silva, p. 245). Along the Rio Demini, a tributary flowing into the
Rio Negro on its left bank, Becher (1) distinguishes between two seasons only: rain falls
from April to September and the dry season lasts from October to March. In the territory
of the Waiwai, along the frontier between Brazil and British Guiana, it rains all the year
round; however, Fock singles out two particularly rainy periods, a major one from June
to August and a minor one in December, separated by a relatively dry season from September to November and again from January to February (cf. Knoch, p. G 85). The abundant

Guiana, the pattern is more complex since both seasons divide up into two parts. Since this four-fold rhythm is also observable inland as far as the basins of the Negro and Uaupés rivers (although in these areas rain falls all the year round and the contrasts are less definitely marked), this is the pattern I would like to draw particular attention to (Figure 13).

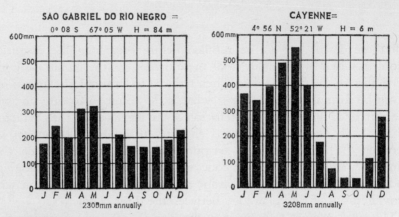

Figure 13. Annual rainfall in Guiana and the Rio Negro basin.
(After Knoch, p. G 85.)

In Guiana, the inhabitants generally distinguish between a 'little dry season' from March to May, a 'big rainy season' from June to September, a 'big dry season' from September to November and a 'little rainy season' from December to February. Since, in fact, rain falls at all periods, this pattern cannot be accepted without certain reservations. The rainfall increases or diminishes according to the time of year but, according to the area under consideration, the driest period occurs between the months of August and September, and this is also the fishing season (Roth 2, pp. 717–18; K.-G. 1, p. 40; Bates, pp. 287–9), as well as the season when various kinds of wild fruit ripen (Fock, pp. 182–4).

The Indians establish connections between the Pleiades and various points in this complex calendar and attribute to the observable conjunctions values which are equally significant although mutually contradictory. The Pleiades, which are still visible in April, in the evenings, on the western horizon, announce the approach of rainstorms

---

information given by such authors as Wallace, Bates, Spruce and Whiffen is not always easy to interpret, because of the relatively short periods they spent in the area, which made it impossible for them to arrive at averages.

(Ahlbrinck, under 'sirito') and when they disappear from sight in May, this is the signal for the recurrence of the rainy season (K.-G. 1, p. 29). They reappear in the mornings in the east in June (or in July at 4 a.m., Fock, *ibid.*) and announce the beginning of the dry season (K.-G., 1, *ibid.*; Crevaux, p. 215) and so determine the beginning of agricultural activities (Goeje, p. 51; Chiara, p. 373). Their rising in the east, in December, after sunset, announces the start of the new year and the return of the rainy season (Roth 2, p. 715). It can thus be seen that the Pleiades are sometimes associated with drought and sometimes with the rainy season.

It would seem that this meteorological ambivalence is reflected on another level too. Whereas they are 'hailed with joy' (Crevaux) on their reappearance in June, the Pleiades can also inspire fear. 'With the Arawaks the Pleiades are called *wiwa yo-koro*, star mother, and they believe that when the Pleiades on their first appearance (in June) are very brilliant or "bad" in fact, the other stars will follow and many people will die in the ensuing year' (Goeje, p. 27). Only through the intervention of a heavenly snake (Perseus) are men saved from mass destruction by the 'death-bearing brilliance' of the Pleiades (*ibid.*, p. 119). According to the Kalina, there were two successive constellations of the Pleiades. The first was swallowed up by a snake. Another snake pursues the second constellation and rises in the east as the constellation is setting in the west. Time will come to an end when the snake catches up with the constellation. But as long as they are in existence, the Pleiades prevent the evil spirits attacking mankind in serried phalanxes: they force them to operate incoherently and piecemeal (*ibid.*, pp. 118, 122–3).

The duality of the Pleiades makes one think immediately of certain phenomena of Andean culture. In the great temple of the sun at Cuzco, there were superposed images on either side of the centre of the altar: on the left, the sun, Venus as the evening star, and the summer Pleiades in their visible form, i.e. 'bright'; on the right, the moon, Venus as the morning star, and the winter Pleiades, hidden behind clouds. The winter Pleiades, which were also called 'the Lord of ripening', were associated with rain and abundance. The summer constellation, 'the Lord of diseases', and more particularly of human malaria, was a harbinger of death and suffering. It was because of this that the 'oncoymita' feast, which marked the appearance of the Pleiades in the spring, included confessional rites, offerings of *cavia* and llamas and anointing with blood (L.-N., pp. 124–31).

On the other hand, Kalina ideas strengthen a theory that has already been put forward about the particularly significant nature of the Orion-Pleiades pair in America and several other areas of the world. I suggested (*RC*, pp. 220–26) that, because of their respective configurations, the two constellations, which are diachronically associated since they rise within a few days of each other, are nevertheless synchronically opposed since the Pleiades are connected with the continuous and Orion with the discontinuous. It follows that the Pleiades can have a beneficent meaning in so far as they are the harbingers of Orion, without relinquishing the maleficent and morbid associations which South American thought attributes to the continuous (*RC*, pp. 279–80) and which only redound to their credit when asserted against evil spirits.

There are more direct proofs of the affinities between the Pleiades and epidemics and poison. According to an Amazonian belief, snakes lose their venom with the disappearance of the Pleiades (Rodrigues 1, p. 221, n. 2). This ambiguity puts the constellation on the same level as honey which, like it, is ambivalent and may be both desired and feared.

In the great myth of origin of the Guarani of Paraguay, the mother of the gods says: 'Under the grass tussocks of the eternal meadows, I have gathered the bees ("eichú", *Nectarina mellifica*) so that they (men) may rinse their mouths with honey when I recall them' (Cadogan 3, p. 95). Cadogan points out that the word 'eichú' refers both to a kind of bee and to the Pleiades. As a matter of fact, the *Nectarina* are wasps (Ihering, under 'enchú') and their honey is often poisonous; it is precisely this honey that the heroine of the Chaco myths is mad about and that the Sun, her father, is incapable of obtaining for her without the help of a husband. This serves to show that, in these myths, the astronomical coding is much more obviously present than could be supposed.

The honey of the *Nectarina*, which has a purifying role in the rites of the southern Guarani, had a similar function in Amazonia, where priests officiating in the cult of Jurupari used it as a vomitive. Stradelli (1, p. 416) translates the expression 'ceucy-irá-cáua' as 'a kind of bee with a very fierce sting; honey which produces heavy vomiting at certain times of the year'. The same author gives the following definition of the expression 'ceucy cipó', 'Ceucy liana': 'a kind of liana, the roots and stems of which, after being pounded in a mortar, are used in the preparation of a potion which is drunk as a purifying agent, on the eve of any feast-day, by the players of sacred musical instruments ...

this drink causes acute vomiting' (p. 415). In Amazonia, the term 'ceucy' (cyucy, ceixu; cf. Guarani: eichú) refers to the constellation of the Pleiades. We can see, then, that from Paraguay to the banks of the Amazon, honey and the Pleiades are interconnected both linguistically and philosophically.

But in Amazonia, what we are concerned with is something quite different from a natural product and a constellation. Ceucy is also the proper name of the heroine of a famous myth, which must now be adduced as evidence:

M₂₇₅. *Amazonia (Tupi). 'The origin of the cult of Jurupari'*

In very remote times, when the world was ruled by women, the Sun, indignant at this state of things, decided to effect a remedy by reforming mankind and submitting it to his law and then choosing a perfect woman, that he could take as his companion. He needed an emissary. He therefore arranged for a virgin named Ceucy to be fertilized by the sap of the cucura or puruman tree (*Pourouma cecropiaefolia*, of the family of moraceae) which streamed over her breasts [or lower down, according to less chaste versions]. The child, who was called Jurupari, took power away from women and restored it to men. To emphasize the latter's independence, he instructed them to celebrate feasts from which women would be excluded, and he taught them secrets to be handed down from generation to generation. They were to put to death any women who learned these secrets. Ceucy herself was the first victim of this pitiless law promulgated by her son who, even today, is still in search of a woman sufficiently perfect to become the wife of the Sun, never yet having found one (Stradelli 1, p. 497).

Many variants of this myth are on record, and some of them are considerably longer. I do not propose to examine them in detail, since they seem to belong to a different mythological *genre* from that of the more popular tales – comparatively homogeneous in tone and inspiration – that I am bringing together here to provide the subject-matter for my investigation. It would seem that some early inquirers in the Amazonian basin, prominent among whom were Barbosa Rodrigues, Amorim and Stradelli, were still able to find esoteric texts belonging to a learned tradition, and comparable in this connection to those discovered more recently by Nimuendaju and Cadogan among the southern Guarani. Unfortunately, we have little or no knowledge of the old native communities which once lived along the middle and lower Amazon. The laconic evidence supplied by Orellana, who sailed down the river as far as the estuary in 1541–2, and still more so the existence of oral traditions, whose extreme complexity, artificial composition and mystical tone suggest that they must be attributed to schools of sages and learned men, argue in favour of a much higher level of religious, social and political organization than anything that has been observed since. The study of these previous documents, which are the remains of a genuine civilization common to the whole of the Amazonian basin, would require a whole volume in itself and would involve the use of special methods in which philology and archaeology (both still in an embryonic state as regards tropical America) would have to play a part. Such a study may one day be possible. Without venturing far into this uncertain territory, I shall merely cull from the different variants miscellaneous points directly germane to my argument.

After Jurupari had ordered, or allowed, his mother's execution, because she had gazed upon the sacred flutes, he sent her up into the sky, where she became the constellation of the Pleiades (Orico 2, pp. 65–6). In the variants current among the tribes along the Rio Branco and the Rio Uaupés (Tariana, Tucano: M_{276a}), the legislator, who is called Bokan or Izy, himself reveals his supernatural origin by means of a myth within the myth, a sort of 'Graal aria', *avant la lettre*. He explains that his father before him was a great legislator named Pinon, the offspring of a secluded virgin who had escaped from her prison to look for a husband and who had been miraculously fertilized by the sun. When she returned to her family with her children, Dinari (as the woman was called) persuaded her son to put an end to the seclusion of girls, but he did not extend this benefit to his sister, Meênspuin, whose hair was adorned with seven stars. As the girl was languishing for lack of a husband, to cure her of this desire and to preserve her virtue, Pinon sent her up into the sky, where she became Ceucy, the Pleiades, and he himself was changed into a snake-like constellation (Rodrigues 1, pp. 73–127; complete text: 2, Vol. II, pp. 13–16, 23–5, 50–71).

Consequently, among the Tupi-Guarani and other populations which have come under their influence, the word 'ceucy' means: (1) a wasp producing poisonous honey which causes vomiting; (2) the constellation of the Pleiades, seen as feminine, sterile, guilty and even perhaps death-dealing; (3) a virgin withheld from the marriage relationship and who is either fertilized miraculously or changed into a star so that she cannot marry.

The triple meaning of the term would be enough in itself to establish the correlation between the sociological, astronomical and alimentary codes, since it is clear that the character of Ceucy is an inversion, on all three levels, of that of the girl mad about honey, as it is illustrated in the Guiana myths. The character in these myths, defying convention and prompted by bestial greed, swallows honey which, in the other context, is vomited up during the process of purification; she is responsible for the appearance of the Pleiades as a fertile, male entity (abundance of fish); finally, she is a mother (often even with several children) who makes a wrong use of marriage by committing adultery with one of her in-laws.

But, in fact, the character of Ceucy is still more complex. We have already seen how it can take a double form: she can be either a miraculously fertilized mother and a breaker of taboos or a virgin forced to turn into a star through the strength of the taboos preventing her marriage. Yet another Amazonian tradition presents Ceucy in the guise of a greedy old woman or of a spirit eternally subject to pangs of hunger:

M_{277}. *Anambé*. '*The ogress Ceucy*'

An adolescent was fishing by the edge of a stream when the ogress Ceucy approached. She saw the boy's reflection in the water and tried to catch it in her net. This made the boy laugh and so revealed his hiding place. The old woman drove him out by means of wasps and poisonous ants, and carried him off in her net to eat him.

The ogress's daughter took pity on the prisoner and set him free.

At first he tried to appease the old woman by weaving baskets which were at once transformed into animals which she devoured (cf. M_{326a}), then he caught enormous quantities of fish for her. In the end, he fled. The ogress pursued him in the form of a cancan bird (*Ibycter americanus?*), and he sought refuge in turn with the honey-gathering monkeys, which hid him in a pot, the surucucú snakes (*Lachesis mutus*), which tried to eat him, the macauan bird (*Herpetotheres cachinans*), which saved him, and lastly the tuiuiú stork (*Tantalus americanus*), which set him down near his village where, in spite of the fact that age had whitened his hair, he was recognized by his mother (Couto de Magalhães, pp. 270–80).

This myth presents a double interest. First, it is recognizably a close variant of a Warao myth (M_{28}), which was summarized and discussed at the beginning of the first volume in this series (*RC,* pp. 109 ff) and which, significantly enough, now that we have been unexpectedly reminded of it, will have to be referred to later for the solution of a problem which it is as yet too early to broach (cf. below, p. 453). This Warao myth (M_{28}) referred to the Pleiades, the Tupi name of which is borne by the ogress in M_{277}: this name explained the origin not only of the Pleiades but also of the Hyades and Orion. In other words, it fulfilled the same etiological function as M_{264} among the Carib of Guiana, a myth which tells of another greedy female who fattens herself up on wild fruit, without leaving any for the hero.

Secondly, the ogress in M_{277}, who *is* the constellation of the Pleiades, provides a transition between the first Ceucy (in M_{275}), who is metaphorically greedy – not for food but for masculine secrets – and the Taulipang heroine in M_{135}, who is greedy for honey in the literal sense in the second part of the myth but who also, from the outset, takes on the character of a metaphorical ogress eager for the caresses of her young brother-in-law and who, through mutilating her husband in an attempt to kill him, determines the appearance of the Pleiades in the form of a male provider of food. The man who is changed into the constellation promises the hero an abundant supply of food: 'Henceforth thou shalt have much to eat!'

Consequently, the Taulipang heroine stands in a metonymical relationship to the Pleiades; the latter are the effect, she is the cause. She thus supplies the hero, unwittingly and in the form of the fish whose arrival is announced by the Pleiades, with the same food as is withheld from the hero in M_{277} by an ogress *named* 'Pleiades' (metaphor)[6] and in M_{28} by an ogress who is the *cause* of the Pleiades (metonymy), in order that they may eat it themselves. These transformations can be illustrated as follows:

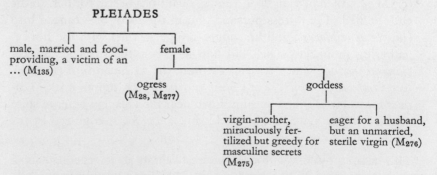

PLEIADES

male, married and food-providing, a victim of an ... (M_{135})

female

ogress (M_{28}, M_{277})

goddess

virgin-mother, miraculously fertilized but greedy for masculine secrets (M_{275})

eager for a husband, but an unmarried, sterile virgin (M_{276})

[6] This confirms yet again that, according to the Indian way of thought, a proper name is a metaphor of the person referred to. (Cf. above, p. 163, and below, p. 328.)

In the diagram, as can be seen, the functions situated at the two extremes (above and to the left, below and to the right) are symmetrical and inverse, whereas the others correspond to intermediary states, with an alternation of the literal and figurative senses at each shift.

I shall now try to establish a direct relationship between the alimentary and sociological codes, and shall begin with an observation. In the Guiana myths, M_{134}–M_{136}, the position of the heroine seems so unstable as to take on diametrically opposed meanings according to the context. In M_{134} she is subject to illicit approaches from her brother-in-law, whereas in M_{135} and M_{136} she is guilty of similar approaches to him. Thus she sometimes appears as a vestal virgin, sometimes as a vividly delineated bacchant.

M_{135}. *Taulipang*. '*The origin of the Pleiades*' (detail)

... Waiúlale (a woman's name) was lying in her hammock. She got up on the arrival of her young brother-in-law (who had been informed by a bird about the barbarous treatment inflicted on his elder brother) and served him with beer and manioc. He asked where his brother was; she replied that he was away gathering fruit. Filled with sadness, the young man lay down and the woman stretched out on top of him. He tried to get up but she held him prisoner in the hammock. Night fell. The accursed woman would not let him out, not even to urinate.

Meanwhile, her husband was screaming with pain in the bush. But she said to the boy: 'Don't bother about your brother! Perhaps he's gone fishing. I'll get out of the hammock when he comes back!' The boy knew everything, having been informed by the bird.

During the night, he pretended to be hungry and asked the woman to fetch him some spicy stew, because he wanted to be rid of her so as to have time to urinate. Then, the wounded man, who had dragged himself as far as the hut, cried out: 'Oh my brother! This woman has chopped my leg off with an axe! Kill her!' The boy asked the woman: 'What have you done to my brother?' – 'Nothing,' she replied. 'When I left him, he was fishing and gathering fruit.' And, although her husband continued to howl with pain outside, she climbed back into the hammock and put her arms so tightly round the boy that he could not move. Meanwhile, the wounded man, who was lying on the ground in front of the hut, was calling: 'My brother! My brother! Help me, my brother!' But the brother could not get out. The wounded man continued to groan until the middle of the night. Then his brother said to him: 'I cannot help you! Your wife will not let me leave the hammock!' She had even closed the door and secured it with ropes. And the boy added, still speaking to his brother: 'I shall avenge you one day! You are out there suffering! One day your wife will have to suffer in the same way!' He struck her, but could not succeed in breaking free (K.-G. 1, pp. 56–7).

Yet it is the same woman, here presented as a ferociously lascivious evil-doer, who, in the Acawai variant (M_{134}), repulses her murderous brother-in-law and behaves as an attentive mother and an inconsolable widow. But this version also takes great care to dissociate her from honey: when the heroine agrees to go into a hollow tree, it is only for the purpose of getting out an agouti. The ambiguity that we have recognized in honey, partly because of its two-fold quality of being both wholesome and poisonous (the same honey having either property according to the circumstances and the season), partly because of its character as a 'ready-made food' which gives it the status of a link between nature and culture, explains the ambiguity of the heroine in the honey myths; she too can be 'entirely natural' or 'entirely cultural', and her unstable identity is a consequence of this ambivalence. For additional proof we must return for a moment to the Chaco myths about the girl mad about honey, from which we started.

It will be remembered that those myths were characterized by the simultaneous presentation of two different plots and the presence of two protagonists. We also saw that the heroine who was mad about honey – so much so, indeed, that she neutralized her husband in his function as a relation by marriage – is reducible to a transformation of the Guiana heroine who is madly in love with her brother-in-law and who – by destroying her husband – neutralizes the relationship by marriage which stands in the way of her illicit designs. The other protagonist in the Chaco myths, Fox or the trickster, combines the two roles: he is both mad about honey and madly in love with his sister-in-law (literally, when she is his wife's sister and metaphorically, when she is the wife of one of his companions). Consequently, the Chaco myths can be arranged in a manner comparable to that shown in the diagram on p. 274, which related to the corresponding Guiana myths:

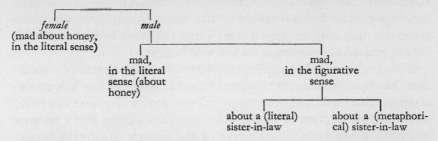

female
(mad about honey,
in the literal sense)

male

mad,
in the literal
sense (about
honey)

mad,
in the figurative
sense

about a (literal)
sister-in-law

about a (metaphori-
cal) sister-in-law

It may be objected that the literal sense of the word 'mad' refers to a mental disorder, with the consequence that the diagram uses it only in the figurative sense. I therefore recall my announced intention of assigning the literal meaning to the appetite for food and the figurative sense to the sexual appetite, throughout the discussion. The opposition *literal/figurative* does not refer to the word 'mad' but to the two forms of madness it serves to designate. That is why I have put a comma after the word 'mad' in each case.

A comparison of the two diagrams suggests several observations. They complete each other, since each applies the dichotomic analysis to only one of the two poles of the sexual contrast: the feminine pole in the first diagram, the masculine pole in the second. The literal and figurative senses, which alternate in one, are consecutive in the other. Lastly, the relationship connecting the masculine pole of the first diagram, or the feminine pole of the second, with the nearest term in either case, is a relationship of contiguity in one instance (the connection between cause and effect) and of resemblance in the other (the man and the woman are similarly mad about honey, in the literal sense).

It emerges from the preceding analysis that, although they are antagonistic to each other in the story, the heroine who is mad about honey and the trickster (whether animal or human in form) are really homologous: they themselves stand in a transformational relationship with each other. This is the basic explanation of the fact that the trickster can take on the appearance of the heroine and attempt to pass himself off as being her. Let us look at this point more closely.

The entire difference between the trickster (who tries to obtain both honey and his sister-in-law) and the heroine (who obtains honey but is obtained by the trickster) is connected with the fact that he is a man – an agent in respect of honey – and she a woman – acted upon in respect of honey – since the honey is transferred from the takers (of women) to the givers through the medium of the woman who establishes this relationship between them. The trickster is without honey; the heroine has honey. The former expresses the honey negatively, the latter positively but only in appearance, since she negativizes honey for others, and uses its presence for her sole benefit.

If the trickster is the negative and masculine embodiment of a situation, whose positive aspect requires a feminine embodiment, it is understandable that he should occasionally take on female disguise: as a man, he is the present cause of absent honey, and can change into a woman in so far as the latter is the cause of the absence of present honey. Therefore, if the trickster takes the place of the vanished heroine, this is because the latter is, at bottom, a female trickster, a vixen.[7] Far from constituting a problem, Fox's female disguise allows the myth to make an implicit truth manifest. The ambiguity of the Chaco heroine, who is seduced but whose character, on another level, fuses with that of her seducer, echoes the ambiguity of her Guiana opposite number.

The same demonstration can be carried out with, as the starting-point, the Ge myths which, as I have said, also stand in a transformational relationship to the Chaco myths, and therefore must have a similar relationship with the Guiana myths.

These myths raised a difficulty: why should a hero, who is chiefly remarkable for his virtues, suddenly appear to be overcome by madness in the Apinayé (M_{142}) and Kraho (M_{225}) versions, where he kills and roasts his wife, so as to offer the unfortunate woman's flesh to her unsuspecting parents? The Guiana parallels make it possible to settle the question through recourse to a different method from that used on the previous occasion, but one which will confirm the original conclusions:

M_{278}. *Warao. 'The story of the man who was changed into a bird'*
There was once an Indian who shared a hut with his wife and her two brothers. One day, when the sky was overcast and there was a threat of rain, he remarked loudly that rain always made him sleep soundly. Whereupon, he lay down in his hammock and rain began to fall. His wife, full of good intentions, asked her brothers to help her to tie her husband up and put him outside. They left him outside in the rain all night long. When he woke at dawn, he said he had

[7] The crying baby, taken care of by a frog in M_{245} and by a frog mad about honey in M_{241}, is looked after by a vixen in other Guiana myths (M_{144}–M_{145}) and also in the myths of Tierra del Fuego (*RC*, p. 271, n. 35).

had a good sleep and asked for his bonds to be untied. He was mad with rage but concealed his anger. To get his own back on his wife, he took her out hunting, and instructed her to gather wood and build a barbecue, because he said he was going to kill an alligator which frequented a neighbouring pool. But as soon as his wife had done what he said, he killed her, cut off her head, carved up the rest of her body and smoked the pieces. He put the meat in a basket which he had woven meanwhile, and which he set down some distance from the village, as was the custom with hunters. Near the basket he drove a stake into the ground on which he propped the victim's head, with its silver brooch still in its nose and its eyes turned in the direction of the village. He brought back with him only the smoked liver, which won him a warm welcome on the part of his brothers-in-law who ate it very eagerly.

The Indian advised them to go to meet their sister because, he said, she was very heavily loaded. When they saw the head, they ran back as fast as they could to the village. The murderer had taken flight in a canoe and had taken care to untie all the others so that they should be washed downstream by the current. The brothers managed to find a boat and set off in pursuit. They had almost caught up with him when he jumped ashore and climbed up a tree, shouting: 'Your little sister is where I left her!' The brothers tried to strike him, but he had already changed into a kind of mutum (one of the gallinae, *Crax* sp.), the cry of which sounds like: 'Here little sister!' (Roth 1, pp. 201–2).

There are several known variants of this myth. In the Kalina version, which is transcribed by Koch-Grünberg following Penard (M$_{279a}$, K.-G. 1, p. 269), the hero was protected in his flight by two birds, *Ibycter americanus* (cf. M$_{277}$) and *Cassidix oryzivora*. After his brothers-in-law caught up with him, they cut off one of his legs and their victim decided to change himself into a constellation: that of Orion, 'which calls for the sun and supports it'. Ahlbrinck (under 'peti') gives other versions, one of which (M$_{279b}$) identifies the protective birds as *Crotophaga ani* and *Ibycter americanus*. The episode in which they occur will be discussed in the next volume. For a general comparison, the reader can refer to K.-G. 1, pp. 270–77. A Warao version (M$_{279d}$) ends with a massacre (Osborn 3, pp. 22–3).

It is not surprising that one of the gallinae should occur as a combinatory variant of a constellation, since I have already pointed out the 'nocturnal' character of these birds (*RC*, p. 204). In M_{28}, the shield of Orion is referred to as 'mother of the tinamidae' (Roth 1, pp. 264–5). Unfortunately we do not know whether the particular species that M_{279a} refers to is the one 'which sings regularly at two-hourly intervals throughout the night, with the result that the mutum is, for the natives, a kind of forest clock' (Orico 2, p. 174), or the one whose cry is heard at dawn, but in either case the calling of the bird can be interpreted as an appeal to the sun. On the other hand, the suggestion, in the last lines of M_{279a}, that Orion might be a nocturnal counterpart of the sun and a 'support' for it, raises the problem of the diurnal and nocturnal celestial phenomena which are correlated in the Indian way of thinking. The problem has already been encountered and partly solved in a particular instance: the connection between the rainbow and a dark area of the Milky Way (*RC*, pp. 246–7). But, for the time being, nothing would justify our extending the same argument to the sun and the whole, or part, of Orion. I shall show the same prudence in my treatment of Ahlbrinck's intriguing observation (*loc. cit.*) that the name of the hero of M_{279b} is that of a pervert.

Other myths belonging to the same area identify the mutum with the Southern Cross instead of Orion, because, according to Schomburgk (in: Teschauer, *loc. cit.*; cf. Roth 1, p. 261), one species (*Crax tomentosa*) begins to sing at the beginning of April, just before midnight, which is the time when the constellation reaches its highest point. This is why the Arecuna Indians call it paui-podolé 'the father of the mutum' (K.-G. 1, pp. 61–3, 277). Roth also mentions a constellation in the shape of a woman's severed leg, which the tinamidae greet with calls when it appears on the horizon before dawn (1, p. 173). But the birds are no longer the same in this case. However, at the period when the Southern Cross reaches its highest point before midnight, Orion is still visible on the western horizon a little after sunset. The bird heard at this time could, then, be associated with one or the other constellation.

It was not because of the astronomical implications that I introduced this group of myths, but for another reason. As it happens, the myths explicitly embody a grammatical contrast that I felt it was indispensable to have recourse to for the formulation of a hypothesis which is now seen to have been objectively justified, since M_{278} and $M_{279a, b}$, etc. tell, *ipsis verbis*, the story of a woman who has drawn the hatred of her husband upon herself *for having understood in the literal sense something that he had intended in the figurative sense*. Ahlbrinck's text is particularly clear on this point: 'There was once an Indian. One day he declared: "With rain like this I shall sleep well tonight." His wife misunderstood the remark and said to her brother: "My husband is stupid. He wants to sleep out in the rain." When night fell, the brothers tied the husband in his hammock and put him out in the rain. The next morning, he was as white as a sheet and absolutely furious ... ' (*loc. cit.*, p. 362).

We thus observe, on the rhetorical level, the final incarnation of a character who first appeared on the culinary level. The fault of the girl mad about honey lay in her exorbitant greed, which brought about the desocialization of a natural product, and caused it to be consumed immediately, whereas consumption ought to have been deferred so that the honey could be used in the exchanges between groups of affines. Still on the culinary level, the Ge transposed the situation from honey to meat, the consumption of which is postponed in this group by means of several taboos. The transformation of alimentary behaviour into linguistic behaviour which is brought about by M_{278}–M_{279}, implies then that, according to Indian thinking, the literal sense corresponds to an immediate 'consumption of the message' by natural means, and the figurative sense to a postponement of consumption, by cultural means.[8]

This is not the end of the matter. The story told by the Guiana myths confirms the link I have already established (pp. 122 *ff*) between the homologous Ge myths and the famous group of myths in which the heroine, or heroines, after being seduced by a tapir, must eat (= consume in the literal sense) the penis or the meat of the animal with which they have copulated (= that they consumed in the figurative sense). A comparison with M_{279} proves that the rule for the transformation of one group into another is even simpler than I suggested (diagram, p. 282).

If we broaden the paradigm so as to include, on the one hand, the Ge heroine in M_{142} and M_{225}, who is killed because of her greediness (for honey) and offered as meat by her husband to his affines and, on the other, the affine (mother-in-law) in M_{136} who is also killed, although for exactly opposite reasons – since she is the contrary of a greedy person: she produces fish, but by excretion, which turns them into an anti-food – we obtain a generalized system in which the relationship by marriage takes on opposite properties according to whether the

[8] A short Cavina myth (M_{279e}) tends in the same direction, since it tells how a woman changed into a monkey after scalding her little brother, whom she had thought fit to put in the boiling pot after her mother had instructed her to wash him with very hot water (Nordenskiöld 3, p. 389).

affine in question is male or female. For a woman, the male affine may be a human (according to culture) or an animal (according to nature): for a man, the female affine may be a wife (according to nature) or a mother-in-law (culturally, since the son-in-law has no physical relationship with her, only a moral one).[9] If, in this male philosophy, one of the

	CODE	FAULT COMMITTED BY THE WOMAN	PUNISHMENT
M_{156}–M_{160} (tapir as seducer)	alimentary	understanding figuratively what ought to have been understood literally	/eat/ an... .../illegitimate/... .../natural/... .../'taker'/
M_{278}–M_{279}	linguistic	understanding literally what ought to have been understood figuratively	/be eaten by/... .../legitimate/... .../cultural/... .../'givers'/

women forgets the lack of parity between the sexes, the woman's metaphorical food will be her real food, the daughter will become the food of the mother, or, alternatively, the mother will, metonymically, 'anti-feed' her son-in-law and will be killed like her daughter.

The myths proclaim that the primary cause of this truly pathological distortion of the marriage relationship is an exorbitant greediness for honey. From M_{20} onwards – in which a too passionate couple, by their lust, corrupted the honey and made it unfit for use in the system of exchanges between brothers-in-law – by way of M_{24}, which reverses this pattern both on the alimentary and the sociological levels – since honey, polluted in a different and more serious way, brings about the break between the two members of an incompatible couple – in every case the myths comment persistently on the irreconcilability between the private relationship of the two spouses (i.e. the natural aspect of marriage) and their role as mediators in a relationship cycle corresponding to its social aspect.

The fox in the Chaco myth succeeds in seducing the girl; but he cannot become a son-in-law, since he is incapable of supplying his parents-in-law with honey. And the woman mad about honey in the

[9] Except, of course, in the case of a polygamous union with a woman and her daughter by a previous marriage, a practice which is not unknown in South America (L.-S. 3, p. 379), particularly in Guiana. However, the myths upon which I am basing my present argument belong to the Carib and Warao tribes, among whom the mother-in-law taboo was strictly observed (Roth 2, p. 685; Gillin, p. 76).

myths of the Gran Chaco and central Brazil, who is clever enough to find a husband, prevents him from also becoming a son-in-law and a brother-in-law, since she proposes to use for her own consumption the honey which would have enabled him to assume his position as an affine. In each case, then, the heroine is a lustful appropriator of the provisions intended for the system of exchanges between affines; and since honey is a natural product which she prevents from fulfilling a social role, she brings down the matrimonial relationship, as it were, to the level of physical union. The myths, in referring to her sad fate, thus utter a sociological condemnation (translated, however, into the terms of an alimentary code) of that *abuse of nature*, which we tolerate if it is short-lived, and which we describe in the terms of the same code, since we call it 'honeymoon'.

However, there is a difference. In our figurative speech, the 'honeymoon' refers to the short period during which we allow the bride and bridegroom to be exclusively concerned with each other: 'The evening and part of the night are devoted to pleasure; and in the day-time the husband reiterates vows of eternal love or describes in detail the delightful future that lies ahead' (*Dictionnaire des proverbes*, under 'lune de miel'). On the other hand, the (French) expressions 'lune de fiel' and 'lune d'absinthe'[10] denote the period when disagreement may begin as husband and wife take their place again in the pattern of social relationships. For us, then, honey is totally on the side of sweetness; it lies at one end of an axis at the opposite pole from bitterness or sourness, symbolized by gall and wormwood, which therefore appear as antitheses of honey.

According to the South American way of thinking, on the contrary, the opposition between sweetness and sourness is inherent in honey itself. This is partly because of the empirical distinction between bee honey and wasp honey, which are respectively wholesome and toxic in the fresh state; and partly because of the transformation undergone by bee honey, which becomes bitter when fermented, and proportionately more bitter as the process is more complete (cf. above, pp. 147–8). This attribution of ambivalence to honey occurs even in communities where mead is unknown. Thus, in Guiana, maize, manioc or wild fruit beer, which is normally bitter, is sweetened through the addition of fresh honey. And in the southern mead-drinking communities, mead is referred to as being bitter, but in comparison with fresh honey. The pole of 'fermentation' is therefore represented either

[10] TRANSLATORS' NOTE: the moon of bile or gall; the wormwood moon.

by honey beer, which is bitter, or by bitter beer to which honey has not been added; the idea of honey remains present, positively or negatively, whether honey is referred to explicitly or is unmentioned.[11]

Consequently, as occasion requires, honey can be raised above its natural condition in two ways. On the sociological level, and without undergoing any physico-chemical transformation, honey fulfils a special role as the substance most appropriate for use in the system of exchanges between affines. On the cultural level, and after undergoing a physico-chemical transformation, fresh honey, which was immediately consumable without the performance of any ritual ceremonies, is changed, by fermentation, into a religious beverage the consumption of which is postponed. In one instance, honey is *socialized*; in the other, it is *culturalized*. The myths choose one formula or the other, according to the techno-economic infrastructure, or combine them, if the infrastructure so allows. Correlatively, the character whom we first encountered in the form of the woman mad about honey is defined in terms of one or other of these two dimensions; sometimes, she is properly socialized (her marriage is satisfactory), but culturally deficient (she does not allow the honey time to ferment) and desocializes her husband; sometimes she is basically a-social (in love with her brother-in-law and murders her husband) but doubly in keeping with

---

[11] The Machiguenga, a Peruvian tribe living in the region of the Rio Madre de Dios, use the same term for sweet and salty. They have a myth (M_{280}) about a supernatural being 'as sweet as salt' whose husband was always licking her. Exasperated by this, she changed him into a bee (siiro), and bees still have a great liking for human sweat.

The woman took as her second husband an Indian whom she fed on boiled fish. Surprised at being given such an abundance of food, the man spied on his wife and discovered that she brought forth the fish from her womb (cf. M_{136}), and this disgusted him. When he complained, his wife changed him into a humming-bird, which feeds on nectar from flowers and on spiders. She turned herself into a block of salt from which, since then, the Indians have got their supplies (Garcia, p. 236).

The myth shows that in a culture which does not distinguish between the flavours of salt and honey:

(1) the bee-woman of M_{233}–M_{234} becomes a salt-woman;
(2) the heroine is exasperated by her husband's greediness, instead of the husband being exasperated by his wife's generosity;
(3) the husband, not the wife, is changed into a bee;
(4) the wife is a consumer of sweat (salty) instead of being a producer of honey (sweet).

Moreover, the absence of any linguistic opposition between two flavours which are confused in the same sense category (the category of the tasty, no doubt) goes hand in hand with the fusion of the two characters who, elsewhere, are kept distinct: the bee-woman who feeds her husband on a positive substance which she secretes (honey), and the mother of the woman greedy for honey, who feeds her son-in-law on a negative substance, which she excretes (fish). An analysis of the myths about fish in North and South America would prove quite easily that, according to the Indian way of thinking, salt – a mineral yet comestible substance – stands at the point of intersection of food and excrement.

her culture, since Guiana is not a mead-drinking area and there is no reason why honey should not be consumed immediately.

The third item in my programme was the establishment of a direct correlation between the sociological and astronomical codes. To achieve this, I shall begin with a rapid review of the common features of the story of the woman mad about honey, as it occurs in the Chaco, Ge and Guiana myths, as well as in the Amazonian myth about Ceucy.

In her various incarnations, the woman mad about honey retains the same character, although it is displayed sometimes in her table-manners and sometimes in her amorous behaviour: she is *ill-bred*. The myth about Ceucy and the variants found in the Uaupés area all appear to be concerned with the definition of a particularly stern *female educational system*, a system which demands the execution of any unfortunate female who, voluntarily or accidentally, has been guilty of gazing upon the musical instruments used in the men's rites. The Rio Uaupés version (M_{276}) brings this point out very clearly since it mentions no less than three codes promulgated by successive legislators and which enumerate the various stages of the female initiation cere-monies: the obligatory shaving off of body hair, the fasting which must follow confinement, and the strict fidelity, discretion and reserve that they must maintain in their relations with their husbands, etc. (Rod-rigues 2, pp. 53, 64, 69–70).

On the other hand, it should not be forgotten that, among the eastern and central Ge tribes, the story of the woman mad about honey belongs to the mythological cycle connected with the initiation rites of young men. These tales are meant as a preparation not only for military endeavour and productive labour, but also marriage; and they serve this edifying purpose by giving a description of an ill-bred woman for the benefit of inexperienced males. The myth about Ceucy operates in the same way, since it provides a single reason for the disabilities to which women are subject and those rites which are a male privilege. On all essential points, the disabilities and the prerogatives are, in fact, complementary.

The third volume in this series will complete the demonstration of the fact that this is an absolutely basic feature of the myths we are now considering, and that those myths shed light on a decisive stage in human thought, which is attested in innumerable other myths and rites the world over. It is as if, in bringing about the mystic submission of women to their authority, men had, for the first time but in a still symbolical way, grasped the principle which would one day allow them to solve the problems created by the numerical dimensions of society; as if, in subordinating one sex to the other, they had evolved a blueprint of the genuine, but as yet inconceivable or impracticable solutions, such as slavery, which would involve the subjection of certain men to the dominion of other men. We should not be misled by the *Malheurs de Sophie*[12] flavour of the story of the woman mad about honey. In spite of its apparent insipidity, which explains the scant attention the myth has so far attracted, its single central character is representative of the destiny of half of the human race, at that fatal point when it became subject to a disability the consequences of which have still not entirely disappeared and which – as the myths hypocritically suggest – might have been avoidable if an intemperate young woman had been able to control her appetite.

Let us rest content, for the time being, with having lifted a corner of the veil covering this dramatic situation, and let us proceed with the comparison. In one group of myths, the heroine briskly swallows the honey, whereas in the other she bears the name of a poisonous honey, which is no sooner eaten than it is vomited up. The Guiana variants present her as a maleficent creature who, operating from without, determines the appearance of the Pleiades in their male, food-providing role. The Ceucy cycle, on the contrary, shows her as being herself determined as the Pleiades, in their feminine form to which the Guiana Indians attribute a sinister significance. The beneficent character is linked with the abundant catches of fish obtained by the Indians through the use of poisonous plants, and the maleficent character with epidemics which kill human beings in large numbers. By way of this connection, the apparently anomalous conclusion of M_{279d} (above, p. 279), which tells of a fratricidal struggle in the course of which 'many Indians died', resumes its place in the group, at the same time as it can be added, as a further example, to the myths of the same type (M_2, M_3), which I was able to use in *The Raw and the Cooked* (pp. 279–81) for the precise purpose of demonstrating the homologous nature of fishing with poison and epidemics.

It will be remembered that the South American myths associate the rainbow, or the rainbow serpent, with the origin of fish poison and epidemics, because of the maleficent character attributed in native

[12] TRANSLATORS' NOTE: *The Misfortunes of Sophia*, a famous children's story by the Comtesse de Ségur.

thought to chromaticism, in the sense of the realm of small intervals. By means of a simple variation in the distance separating the terms, this realm can give rise to another, that of large intervals, which manifests itself on three levels of unequal extent: the universal discontinuity of living species, the havoc caused by diseases which produces a thinly scattered population, and the parallel effect on the fish population of the technique of poisoning (*RC*, pp. 256–81). The grouped, but apparently haphazard, arrangement of the stars forming the constellation of the Pleiades puts the latter, together with the rainbow, into the category of the continuous (*RC*, pp. 222–6): being similar to a fragment of the Milky Way that might have got lost in the sky, the constellation is symmetrical to the fragment of dark sky which happens, by accident, to be in the middle of the Milky Way and which, as I showed (*RC*, pp. 246–7), fulfils the role of nocturnal counterpart of the rainbow. Hence a triple transformation:

$$\begin{bmatrix} continuous \\ diurnal \end{bmatrix} \quad 1 \left(\frac{chromatic\ light}{achromatic\ light} \right) \Rightarrow \begin{bmatrix} continuous \\ nocturnal \end{bmatrix} \quad 2 \left(\frac{illuminated}{dark} \right) \Rightarrow 3 \left(\frac{dark}{illuminated} \right)$$

Moreover, we have seen (pp. 81–271) that there is a direct affinity between the first term (rainbow) and the last (Pleiades), provided we take into account the double contrast: *diurnal/nocturnal* and *daily/seasonal*. Both of them announce the cessation of rain, during a period either in the day or the year. We might almost say that the rainbow is, on a more restricted temporal scale, a diurnal constellation of the Pleiades.

I shall conclude the comparison of the two myth cycles (woman mad about honey and Ceucy) by pointing out that, in the Guiana-Amazonian versions, the first heroine is a married woman and a mother, whereas the other is a secluded virgin whom her own brother changes into a constellation in order to protect her virtue.

If we approach the matter from this angle, it becomes essential to widen the comparison. We know of a myth cycle whose heroine is equidistant from the other two: she is married but chaste, and is raped by her husband's brother or brothers. I am referring to Star, the wife of a mortal (M_{87}–M_{92}) who, in all other respects as well, is a simultaneous transformation of the woman mad about honey and Ceucy:

(1) She is a girl who is *too well bred* and who agrees to be a wetnurse, not a wife.

(2) She vomits up maize, the prototype of *cultivated plants*, in the

face (M_{88}) or even into the mouth (M_{87a}) of her husband, instead of snatching the honey from his mouth (woman mad about honey) or being herself honey that is vomited up (Ceucy); nor must we forget that, according to Indian thought, honey is identified with *wild fruit*.

(3) Star comes down spontaneously from the sky to marry a human, whereas Ceucy represents the opposite case of a heroine who, against her will, is changed into a star *to prevent her* marrying a human, while the woman mad about honey – who is perhaps changed into a star in the Chaco myths for *having been a bad wife* to a future human (since she only allowed him to be a husband and not a son-in-law) – herself changes her husband into a star in the Guiana versions because, wishing to replace him by his brother, she condemns him to be merely an affine, not a husband.

(4) Finally, Star appears in the first instance as a food-provider, like the Pleiades in their masculine form, then as a bringer of death, like the constellation in its feminine form. Star performs the first function when she appears to men for the first time, and the second when she is on the point of leaving them – in a sense, then, at her 'rising' and her 'setting'. She thus represents an inversion of the significance of the Pleiades for the Guiana Indians, since the food-supplying constellation, which announces the arrival of the fish, seems to be the one which is visible in the evening on the western horizon, and this would seem to imply that the Pleiades are death-dealing at the time of their rising.

All these transformations, which allow us to integrate the cycle about Star, the wife of a mortal, into the group we are considering, involve an important consequence. We know that Star is an opossum, a forest animal in the first place in its food-supplying capacity and then a savannah animal in its capacity as a polluted and polluting creature, which brings death to men, after bringing them life through revealing cultivated plants to them (*RC*, pp. 164–88). Now it so happens that the character of the opossum is also expressed in terms of the astronomical and alimentary codes, to which I now return in completing the cycle of the demonstration. From the astronomical point of view, the opossum shows an affinity with the Pleiades since, according to a Rio Negro myth (M_{281}; cf. *RC*, p. 218, n. 8), the opossum and the chameleon chose the day of the first rising of the Pleiades to cauterize their eyes with pimentoes and to expose themselves to the beneficent action of the sun. But the opossum burnt its tail, which has remained hairless ever since (Rodrigues 1, pp. 173–7). Moreover, in Guiana the opossum has the same name as the rainbow (*RC*, pp. 249 *ff*), a fact which provides an additional confirmation of the equation on p. 287.

Secondly – and this is more important – the myths establish a link between the opossum and honey, as I shall show in two ways.

In one version at least of the famous Tupi myth about the twins (Apapocuva, M_{109}), the opossum plays the part of a food-supplying mother; after the death of their mother, the elder of the two boys does not know how to get food for his brother. He appeals to the opossum who, before acting as wet-nurse, is careful to clean the evil-smelling secretions from her breast. To thank her for this, the god provides her with a marsupial pouch and promises her that she will give birth without pain (Nim. 1, p. 326; Mundurucu version in Kruse 3, Vol. 46, p. 920). The southern Guarani have a variant of this myth, in which the opossum's doubtful milk is replaced by honey:

M_{109b}. *Parana Guarani. 'Honey as nourishment'* (extract)

After the murder of their mother, the elder of the twins, Derekey, did not know what to do with his brother, Derevuy, who had nothing to eat and was crying with hunger. Derekey began by trying to re-constitute the body of the dead woman, but his little brother hurled himself onto the scarcely formed breasts so voraciously that he undid Derekey's work. Then the elder boy discovered honey in the trunk of a tree and brought his brother up on it.

The bees belonged to the mandassaia or caipota variety (a sub-species of *Melipona quadrifasciata*, the honey of which is particularly sought after). When the Indians find a bees' nest of this kind, they never eat the larvae and they leave enough honey for them to live on. They do so as a mark of gratitude to the bees who fed the god (Borba, p. 65; cf. Baré, Stradelli 2, p. 259; Caduveo, Baldus 2, p. 37).

As a whole, and particularly in its conclusion, the episode offers such a close parallel with M_{109} that we may conclude that the food-supplying opossum and the bees stand in a transformational relation-ship with each other. This is brought out still more clearly by an earlier episode in the same myth, which also occurs in most other versions. At a time when it must be supposed that the opossum was still without a marsupial pouch, the mother of the twins herself behaves as if she had one, since she converses with her child or children although they are still in the womb. Communication is interrupted – in other words, the womb ceases to fulfil the same role as a marsupial pouch – after

K

an incident which is related in the following terms in M_{109b}: 'The child in the womb asked his mother to give him some flowers. She was picking them here and there when she was stung by a wasp which was sipping honey ... ' (Borba, *loc. cit.*, p. 64). A Warao version (M_{259}), in spite of its geographical remoteness and the difference in language and culture, scrupulously preserves this reading: 'The mother had already picked several red and yellow flowers, when a wasp stung her below the waist. She tried to kill it, missed it, and struck herself. The child in the womb felt the blow and thought that it had been aimed at him; he was annoyed, and refused to continue to guide his mother' (Roth 1, p. 132; cf. Zaparo in Reinburg, p. 12).

Consequently, just as the real opossum, a good wet-nurse, is congruous with bees' honey, so the figurative opossum, who is a bad nursing-mother, is congruous with the wasp, whose honey is sour, if not poisonous. Not only does this analysis reveal a first connection between the opossum and honey; it also supplies an explanation, additional to the one I have already given on p. 236, of the recurrence of the myth about the twins in an apparently very different cycle, the starting-point of which is the origin (or the loss) of honey.

For the purposes of the second demonstration, I must refer to a series of myths which was partially examined in *The Raw and the Cooked* (M_{100}–M_{102}) and earlier in the present work (pp. 81, 82), and in which the tortoise is contrasted now with the tapir, now with the cayman or the jaguar, or again with the opossum.[13] In these stories, the tortoise or the opossum, or both of them, are buried by an opponent, or voluntarily bury themselves, to prove how well they can withstand hunger.

It is unnecessary to go into the details of the myths with which we are mainly concerned here, because they make use of seasonal points of reference: the periods of the year when such and such varieties of wild fruit are plentiful. I mentioned this (pp. 234 *ff*) in connection with plums, *Spondias lutea*, which ripen in January–February, at a time when the rain-soaked earth is already soft enough for the tapir to tread the tortoise into the ground. The latter succeeds in breaking free at the end of the rainy season, when the ground has become a quagmire (M_{282}; Tastevin 1, pp. 248–9). The same author supplies a variant which must be given more attention, since it illus-

[13] TRANSLATORS' NOTE. Here, and in the subsequent discussion, the author uses the masculine article, *le sarigue*, for the male or when the sex is not specified, and the feminine, *la sarigue*, whenever the female sex is indicated.

trates a type of myth to be found all the way from central Brazil to Guiana:

M_{283a}. *Amazonia (Teffé area). 'The tortoise and the opossum'*

One day, the opossum stole the tortoise's flute. The latter wanted to go after him, but being unable to run fast enough, changed its mind, obtained some honey and smeared its anus with it, after hiding its head in a hole.

The opossum noticed the gleaming honey and thought it was water. He put his hand in, licked his fingers and realized his mistake. But since the honey was delicious, the opossum applied his tongue to it. At that moment, the tortoise nipped its buttocks together and the opossum was caught. 'Let go of my tongue!' he cried. The tortoise only agreed to do so after recovering its flute.

On another occasion, the opossum challenged the tortoise to a contest, to see which of them could remain buried the longest without food. The tortoise was the first to try and it remained until the plums were ripe and began falling from the trees. Then it was the turn of the opossum who proposed to remain buried until the wild pineapples were ripe. When a month had gone by, the opossum wanted to come out, but the tortoise told him that the pineapples had hardly begun to swell. Two further months went by and the opossum stopped answering. He was dead and only flies came out when the tortoise opened the hole (Tastevin, *loc. cit.*, pp. 275–86).

Tastevin points out that the tortoise is the female (yauti) of the species *Testudo tabulata*, which is bigger than the male (karumben). Throughout the Amazonian area, the male and female of each species of tortoise seem to have different names; these are, in the case of *Cinesteron scorpioides* (?), yurari (f.) and kapitari (m.), and in the case of *Podocnemis* sp., tarakaya (f.) and anayuri (m.).

The origin of the tortoise's flute is the subject of another myth:

M_{284}. *Amazonia (Teffé area). 'The tortoise and the jaguar'*

After the tortoise had killed the tapir by biting its testicles (M_{282}), it could not prevent the jaguar coming to claim its share of the feast. Indeed, the jaguar took advantage of the fact that the tortoise was away looking for wood, to steal all the meat, leaving only its excrements in exchange.

The tortoise went after it and encountered monkeys who helped it to climb up into the tree where they were gathering fruit. Then they left it.

The jaguar happened to pass and asked tortoise to come down. The latter asked the jaguar to close its eyes, dropped onto its head and broke its skull.

When the jaguar's carcass had rotted away, the tortoise took a shin-bone, turned it into a flute and played on it, singing: 'The jaguar's bone is my flute. Fri! Fri! Fri!'

Another jaguar came on the scene, and thought that the tortoise was threatening and challenging it. The tortoise was not successful in persuading it that it had misheard the words of the song. The jaguar made a bound, but the tortoise hid in a hole and deceived the jaguar into thinking that a foot, which was still visible, was a root. The jaguar set a toad to watch, but the tortoise blinded it with sand and took flight. When the jaguar came back, it dug up the ground in vain and consoled itself by eating the toad (Tastevin, *loc. cit.*, pp. 265–8; Baldus 4, p. 186).

By means of a transformation of this myth, it would be easy to work our way back to M_{55} (cf. *RC*, pp. 126–7). However, I shall leave this to be done by someone else, in case it should take me off in a very different direction from the one I am now proposing to follow and bring me up against the enormous problem of the mythical origin of musical instruments. As will be seen later, I shall not entirely succeed in avoiding the problem. This would certainly be a very rewarding direction in which to investigate, and it would lead us back to M_{136}, in which a mutilated hero, rising up into the sky, plays on a flute which produces the sound: tiu! tiu! tiu! (K.-G. 1, p. 57), whereas, in another story, the tortoise celebrates its victory over its opponents by crying: weh! weh! weh! and clapping its hands (M_{101}). In most of the myths of the tortoise cycle, the bone flute (which should, perhaps, be contrasted with the bamboo flute) seems to symbolize a disjunction (cf. below, p. 139).

But let us return to M_{283}, which uses other contrasts: between the tortoise and the opossum and between plums and pineapples. We know from M_{282} that plums ripen in the rainy season; it follows that the burial of the tortoise lasts from the end of the dry season to the rainy season, during the time of year when, as the myth points out, the plum trees flower, produce fruit and then shed this fruit. Consequently, the burial of the opossum must take place during the other part of the year and, as it must come to an end when the pineapples are ripe, this event must coincide with the end of the dry season. Tastevin gives no information on this point, but since I remember picking very juicy wild pineapples on the lower slopes of the Amazonian basin in August–September 1938, I think the supposition is well-founded. In the north-western part of the Amazonian basin pineapples are especially plentiful in October, which corresponds to the driest period, and this is the time of the so-called 'pineapple-feast' (Whiffen, p. 193).

The fasting contest inspired by the contrast between plums and pineapples follows on from another episode, which it reproduces in part; this is the flute-stealing episode, during which – according to the myth – the tortoise does not succeed in smearing its opponent with resin (Tastevin, *loc. cit.*, pp. 276, 279, 283) or wax (Couto de Magalhães, p. 20 of the *Curso*; the Tupi word is iraiti and, according to Montoya, who discusses the homophonous term in Guarani, the etymological meaning is 'honey-nest'), but does in the end succeed with honey. Thus we arrive at the diagram:

(1) wax   honey
(2) plums   pineapples

in which the left-hand column groups together entities in regard to which the opossum is in a strong position, while the right-hand column shows those in regard to which it is in a weak position: it is unable to resist honey, or unable (so far) to resist pineapples. Why are the terms themselves grouped in pairs? Like plums, wax makes it possible to hold out from the rainy to the dry season; it is the vehicle appropriate to the route leading from wet to dry: we know this from the story of Haburi or Aboré, the inventor of the first canoe which was made, precisely, of *wax*, and that men were ordered to copy henceforth in wood by 'the father of inventions' (Brett 2, p. 82). For what is a canoe, if not a means of overcoming the wet with the dry? Honey and pineapples make it possible to carry out the reverse movement, from the dry to the wet, since these are the kinds of wild fruit gathered during the dry season, as is indicated, in the case of honey, by the beginning of the verse transcription of the myth about Aboré:

Men must hunt for wild bees while the sun says they may

(Brett, *loc. cit.*, p. 26)

This is not all. Certain variants of M_{283}, in which the cayman plays the part of the flute-stealer, instead of the opossum, contain a feature exactly corresponding to the final detail in M_{283}: to oblige the cayman to give back the flute, the tortoise hides in a hole, showing only its honey-smeared behind 'from which, from time to time, there flew out a bee: zum ... ' (M_{283b}, Ihering, under 'jaboti'). There is thus a correspondence between the tortoise whose body has been 'changed into honey' and gives off bees, thus triumphing over the opossum, and the tortoise in the second part of the myth which gets the better of the opossum once and for all, because the latter's body has changed into rottenness, which is giving off flies ('meat flies', not 'honey flies'). In other words, honey makes the tortoise superior to the opossum, and rottenness makes the opossum inferior to the tortoise. As it happens, the opossum[14] is an evil-smelling creature, whereas the tortoise, a hibernating animal, is thought to be impervious to decay (*RC*, pp. 176–7).

What are we to conclude from these myths? The group I previously examined transformed the opossum's milk into honey and the marsupial into a bee; but on condition that the opossum first cleansed itself of the rottenness that is produced naturally by its body. Here, the opossum undergoes a reverse transformation: it is entirely assimilated to rottenness, but, in the last resort, because it first allowed itself to be seduced by honey. Yet it was able to resist wax, which represents the dry, non-perishable part of the bees' nest, whereas honey (because of the contrast that the myth establishes between the two terms) represents the wet, perishable part. The threat from wax therefore causes the opossum (*le* sarigue) to vary in a direction contrary to its nature as an evil-smelling creature, while the attraction of honey impels it in a direction in conformity with its nature, which it indeed carries to the logical limit by becoming carrion. On the one hand, honey stands in a position intermediary between wax and rottenness, thus confirming its ambivalent nature, which I have frequently emphasized. On the other hand, this ambivalence brings honey close to the opossum (*la* sarigue), which is also ambivalent in its two-fold capacity as a marsupial, i.e. a good wet-nurse, and as an evil-smelling creature. Once it is cured of this defect, the opossum tends in the direction of honey, with which it is confused through their resemblance; it becomes a wonderfully appropriate udder, producing milk as sweet as honey. When it is ravenous for honey and seeks to fuse with it, but this time by direct contact – so direct, indeed, that it plunges its tongue into the tortoise's behind – the opossum is the opposite of a wet-nurse, and since this

[14] TRANSLATORS' NOTE: The author now reverts to the feminine gender, *la sarigue*.

first attribute disappears, the other expands to the point of taking over entirely. This is precisely what the Tupi-Guarani myth-cycle about the twins is expressing in its way, since the opossum (*le* sarigue) occurs twice. First, as we have seen, as a female and in a food-supplying capacity. And later, as a man called 'opossum', who has a purely sexual role (cf. M_{96}). While the female opossum is careful to wash, her masculine counterpart stinks (cf. M_{103}).

The group that we have now considered over its whole extent comes to a close, then, on a homologous relationship between the Chaco fox and the Tupi-Guarani opossum (*le* sarigue). In the Chaco myths, the daughter of the Sun, who is abandoned by her husband when she is unwell, and whom Fox tries vainly to seduce, corresponds to the wife of the Sun, who is abandoned in a pregnant state by her husband and seduced by Opossum. Opossum is a false husband who passes himself off as the real one, Fox a false husband who passes himself off as (the wife of) the real one, and both of them give themselves away, the first by his animal stench (when he is claiming to be a human or a different animal), the second by his masculine roughness (when he is claiming to be a woman). It was therefore not entirely a mistake on the part of some early writers to apply to the opossum (*le* sarigue) the Portuguese word for fox: *raposa*. As the problem was expressed in native thought, there was an implication that one animal might be a combinatory variant of the other. They are both connected with the dry season, equally greedy for honey and, in their masculine form, endowed with the same lewd appetites; they only differ when they are considered *sub specie feminae*: the opossum (*la* sarigue) can become a good mother if it can rid itself of a natural attribute (its stench), whereas the fox, even when provided with artificial attributes (a false vagina and false breasts), only succeeds in being a grotesque wife. But is this not because Woman, eternally doomed to be opossum and fox,[15] is unable to overcome her self-contradictory nature and reach that perfection which, were it conceivable, would only serve to put an end to Jurupari's quest?

[15] As was shown on pp. 277–8, the Chaco heroine who is seduced by a fox is herself a vixen; and we have also seen (pp. 289–90) that the Tupi-Guarani heroine is, as it were, a female opossum *avant la lettre*, later to be seduced by a male opossum.

2 *Noises in the Forest*

In Indian thought, the idea of honey covers a multitude of ambiguities; first, because honey appears to have been 'cooked' by the processes of nature; then because of its various properties of being sweet or sour, wholesome or poisonous; and lastly because it can be consumed in either the fresh or the fermented form. We have seen how this substance which radiates ambiguity in all its aspects, is itself reflected in other, equally ambiguous, entities: the constellation of the Pleiades, which is alternatively male or female, food-supplying or death-dealing; the opossum (f.), an evil-smelling mother; and Woman herself, who cannot be counted on to remain a good mother and a faithful wife, since there is always a danger that she may turn into a lewd and murderous ogress, unless she is reduced to the condition of a secluded virgin.

It has also been noted that the myths are not content merely to express the ambiguity of honey by means of semantic equivalents. They also have recourse to meta-linguistic devices, when they make play with the duality of proper names and common nouns, metonymy and metaphor, contiguity and resemblance, the literal sense and the figurative sense. M_{278} establishes a link between the semantic and rhetorical levels, since the confusion between the literal and figurative meanings is specifically attributed to a character in the myth and is the mainspring of the action. Instead of affecting the structure of the myth, it is incorporated into the substance of the story. However, when a woman, who in the end is killed and eaten, makes the mistake of understanding in the literal sense something that was said figuratively, she is behaving in a fashion symmetrical to that of the tapir's mistress, whose mistake is to give the figurative meaning of copulation to that form of eating which normally can only be understood in the literal sense: i.e. the actual eating, by man, of the game he has caught. Her punishment consists in being obliged to consume, in the literal sense, i.e. to eat, the tapir's penis which she thought she would be able to consume figuratively.

But why, in some cases, must the woman eat the tapir, whereas in others she herself is eaten? I have already given a partial answer to this question (p. 123). We can go into it more deeply, however, by means of the distinction between the semantic and rhetorical codes. If we remember that the myths constantly oscillate between two levels, the symbolic and the imaginary (cf. above, p. 246), the preceding analysis can be summarized with the help of an equation:

[*symbolical level*]   [*imaginary level*]
   (swallowing of honey) :   (cannibalism within
                                    the family) ::

[*symbolical level*]   [*imaginary level*]
   (swallowing of the tapir) :   (copulation with
                               the tapir) ::
                    (literal sense) : (figurative sense)

Within the framework of this total system, the two mythic sub-groups – indicated by (*a*) in the case of the tapir-seducer and (*b*) in the case of the woman mad about honey – are each devoted to a local transformation:

(*a*) [*figurative* consumption of the tapir] ⇒ [*literal* consumption of the tapir]

(*b*) [*literal* consumption of honey] ⇒ [cannibalism within the family, as *figurative* consumption]

I now propose to introduce a new contrast: *active/passive*, corresponding to the fact that, in the tapir-seducer cycle, the woman is metaphorically 'eaten' by the tapir (for reasons of symmetry, since it has already been established that it is she who eats him literally), whereas in the woman-mad-about honey cycle, the heroine, who has been actively guilty of empirically observable greed, but a greed which in this instance *symbolizes* her lack of breeding, becomes the passive object of a cannibal family meal, the concept of which is entirely *imaginary*. This gives:

     (*a*) [figurative, passive] ⇒ [literal, active]
     (*b*) [literal, active] ⇒ [figurative, passive]

If, as I postulated, the two cycles stand in a complementary relationship to each other, it is essential that, in the second case, the woman, and not some other protagonist, should be eaten.

Only by understanding the myths in this way is it possible to find a common denominator for all the stories about the woman mad about honey, whether – as in the Chaco versions – she is literally greedy for the substance, or whether the myths describe her in the first place as wanting an affine (M_{135}, M_{136}, M_{298}) or an adopted child (M_{245}, M_{273}), and sometimes both at once (M_{241}, M_{243}, M_{244}; M_{258}) by carrying the idea of the honeymoon to its logical conclusion, as has been illustrated, in modern times, by Baudelaire, through a multiplication of the relationships with the loved one:

> *Mon enfant, ma sœur*
> *Songe à la douceur*
> *D'aller la-bas vivre ensemble!*

> (My child, my sister
> Think of the delight
> Of going away to live there together!)

Once it is unified in this way, the woman-mad-about-honey cycle is consolidated by that of the tapir-seducer, which makes it possible to explain the fact that they intersect empirically. Both of them contain the theme of the character who is dismembered and barbecued and then served up to his unsuspecting family, like any ordinary game.

However, at this stage in the argument, we come up against a two-fold difficulty. It would be a waste of time to purify the substance of the myths by showing that some can be assimilated to others by the operation of transformation rules, if the effort thus expended brought to light cleavages within myths which, on a less sophisticated approach, had displayed no such complexity. Now, as it happens, while we were fusing together the characters of the tapir-seducer and the woman mad about honey in the melting-pot, each seemed to be displaying a dual nature which had not before been immediately perceptible; the simplification achieved on one level is thus in danger of being lost on another.

Let us consider first the character of the tapir. In its erotic activities, it is a representation of nature as seducer, congruous with honey. Its sexual potency, attested by an enormous penis, the size of which is amply stressed in the myths, is comparable, in the alimentary code, only with the seductive power of honey, for which the Indians have a veritable passion.

The relationship of complementarity that we discovered between the cycle of the tapir-seducer and that of the woman mad about honey shows that, according to the Indian way of thinking, honey fulfils the role of alimentary metaphor and corresponds to the sexuality of the tapir in the other cycle. Yet, when we look at the myths in which the tapir is presented as a subject in terms of the alimentary (not the sexual) code, its character is reversed: it is no longer a lover who fully satisfies his human mistress and sometimes feeds her by giving her an abundance of wild fruit, but a selfish and greedy creature. Consequently, instead of being congruous with honey as in the first instance, it becomes congruous with the woman mad about honey who, in her relationship with her parents, displays the same selfishness and greed.

According to several Guiana myths, the tapir was the first master of the food-tree and guards the secret of its location (cf. M_{114} and RC, pp. 184–8). And it will be remembered that, in M_{264}, the twins Pia and Makunaima each in turn take refuge with two animals which can be termed 'anti-food-suppliers'. The frog is so through over-abundance, since it produces a plentiful supply of food, which is really excrement; the tapir is so by default, when it conceals the location of the wild plum tree from the heroes and fattens itself on the fallen fruit.

The tapir's mistress displays exactly the same divergence. On the alimentary level, she is a bad wife and a bad mother who, being absorbed by her passion, neglects to cook food for her husband and to suckle her child (M_{150}). But, sexually speaking, she is a glutton. Consequently, far from complicating our task, the duality peculiar to the principal actor in each cycle confirms my thesis; since this duality is always of the same type, it confirms rather than contradicts the homology I postulated. This homology is certainly displayed through a relationship of complementarity: on the erotic level, the tapir is prodigal, while its human mistress is greedy; on the alimentary level, it is the tapir which is greedy, whereas its mistress, who displays a prodigal attitude towards it in one version (M_{159}), elsewhere has a negligent approach which shows that, for her, the alimentary area is 'unmarked'.

The woman-mad-about-honey cycle and the tapir-seducer cycle, when consolidated by each other, form then a meta-group the outlines of which correspond, on a larger scale, to the pattern I evolved in the second part on the basis of only one of the two cycles. The existence of the rhetorical and erotico-alimentary dimensions on the level of the meta-group was sufficiently brought out in the preceding discussion

for further emphasis upon it to be unnecessary here. But the astronomical dimension is also present, and the tapir-seducer cycle refers to it in
two ways.

The first reference is, no doubt, implicit. Outraged by the fact that
their husbands have compelled them to eat the flesh of their lover, the
women decide to leave home and change into fish (M_{150}, M_{151}, M_{153},
M_{154}). In these versions, which are all Amazonian, we are dealing with
a myth about the origin or plentifulness of fish, a phenomenon that
the myths of the Guiana-Amazonian area ascribe to the Pleiades.
Consequently, in this sense, the tapir-seducer, like the Pleiades, is
responsible for the abundance of fish. The parallel between the animal
and the constellation is strengthened if we remember that the constellation of the Pleiades, i.e. Ceucy in the myths of the Tupi Amazonians, is a secluded virgin who was changed into a star by her brother
the better to preserve her virginity (M_{275}). As it happens, the Mundurucu
(who are Tupi Amazonians) say that the tapir-seducer is an incarnation
of Korumtau, the son of the demiurge, who was forced by his father to
take on this animal form because, as a secluded youth, *he had lost his
virginity*. Such, at least, is the continuation of M_{16}, the beginning of
which is to be found in *RC*, pp. 57, 85.

The preceding deduction is directly confirmed by the Guiana myths
belonging to the tapir-seducer cycle, and this shows, incidentally, that
Roth was too hasty in supposing that some European or African influence must be responsible for the fact that, in both the Old and the
New Worlds, Aldebaran is compared to the eye of some large animal,
tapir or bull (Roth 1, p. 265):

M_{285}. Carib (?). 'The tapir-seducer'

An Indian woman, who had been married only a short while, one
day met a tapir which courted her passionately. It said it had assumed
animal form in order to approach her more easily when she went out
into the fields, but that if she agreed to follow it eastwards to the
point where sky and earth meet, it would resume its human shape
and marry her.

The animal put a spell on her and the young woman made a show
of helping her husband to gather avocado pears (*Persea gratissima*).
While he was climbing up the tree, she chopped off one of his legs
with an axe and ran away (cf. M_{136}). Although he was bleeding profusely, the wounded man managed, by magic, to change one of his
eyelashes into a bird, which went to fetch help. The hero's mother

arrived on the scene in time. She took care of her son and he recovered.

Using a crutch, the lame husband set off in search of his wife, but the rain had obliterated all her tracks. However, he succeeded in catching up with her by following the trail of avocado plants which had sprung up in the places where she had eaten the fruits and thrown away the stones. The woman and the tapir were together. The hero shot the animal to death with an arrow and cut off its head. Then he asked his wife to return with him, otherwise he would pursue her eternally. The wife refused and hurried on with her lover's spirit still after her and her husband behind them both. When they reached the edge of the earth, the woman threw herself into the sky. On a clear night she can still be seen (the Pleiades), with the Tapir's head (the Hyades: the red eye is Aldebaran) close behind and the hero (Orion, with Rigel indicating the upper part of the sound limb) – all three in pursuit (Roth 1, pp. 265–6).

The reference to avocadoes and avocado stones raises a problem which will be dealt with in the next volume. Here I shall restrict myself to pointing out: (1) the parallel between this myth and M_{136}, in which another dissolute wife chops off her husband's leg; (2) the fact that both myths are concerned with the origin of the Pleiades, considered separately or in relation to neighbouring constellations. In one case, the body of the mutilated husband becomes the Pleiades, and his leg the shield of Orion; in the other case, the woman herself becomes the Pleiades, the tapir's head the Hyades, and Orion represents the husband (minus his severed leg) (cf. M_{28} and M_{131b}). The tapir-seducer myth is therefore using an astronomical code to convey a message which is hardly different at all from that of the myths about the origin of the Pleiades belonging to the same area.

But it is the sociological code in particular which is worthy of attention. It proves more clearly than the others the complementary nature of the two cycles, while at the same time integrating them into the much greater whole which is being investigated in this series of volumes. The woman mad about honey in the Guiana myth (M_{136}), and the tapir's mistress who figures in other myths, are both adulterous wives; but they are so in two different ways, which illustrate the extreme forms that the crime of adultery can assume: it may be committed with a brother-in-law who represents the nearest temptation, or with a forest animal representing the most remote temptation. The animal is a manifestation of nature, whereas the brother-in-law, whose closeness is the result of a connection by marriage and not of a blood relationship, which would be biological, is a purely social manifestation:

(tapir : brother-in-law) :: (remote : close) :: (nature : society)

This is not all. Readers of *The Raw and the Cooked* will no doubt remember that the first group of myths I introduced (M_1–M_{20}) – and what I am saying here is, in a sense, only a continuation of my commentary – were also concerned with the problem of relationships by marriage. But between those myths and the ones I am now considering, there is obviously a major difference. In the first group, the affines were chiefly wives' brothers or sisters' husbands, i.e. givers and takers respectively. In so far as every marriage relationship implies collaboration between these two categories, we were dealing with mutually unavoidable brothers-in-law whose action had an organic character and whose conflicts were therefore a normal expression of life in society.

In the second group, on the contrary, the affine is not an inevitable partner, but an optional competitor. Whether the brother-in-law is seduced by the wife or whether he himself plays the role of seducer, he is always a brother of the husband, i.e. a member of the social group whose existence is not essential to the marriage relationship, and who therefore figures as a contingent detail in the domestic pattern. Among the instructions given by the Baniwa to their young men on initiation is the rule 'not to go after their brothers' wives' (M_{276b}). If we take a theoretical view of society for a moment, it is clear that, to be sure of obtaining a wife, each man must be able to dispose of a sister, but he is under no obligation to have a brother. As the myths explain, a brother can, in fact, be a handicap.

Admittedly, the tapir is an animal, but the myths turn it into a 'brother' of the man, since it deprives him of his wife. The only difference is that whereas the human brother, through the mere fact of his existence, is automatically part of the pattern of relationships caused by marriage, the tapir makes a sudden and unexpected incursion into the pattern, simply by virtue of his natural attributes; he is a pure seducer, i.e. a socially void entity (*RC*, p. 276). In the social interplay of marriage relationships, the intrusion of the human brother-in-law is accidental,[16] but that of the tapir amounts to a scandal. But whether the

[16] The same is true of the homologous sister-in-law, i.e. the sister of the wife who figures in the Chaco (M_{211}) and Guiana myths (M_{235}), of which – as I have shown – the myths

myths are concerned with the consequences of a *de facto* situation, or with those resulting from the subversion of a *de jure* situation, what they are dealing with, as I have suggested, is undoubtedly a pathological state of the marriage relationship. There is, then, a distinct gap between them and the myths that I used as my starting-point in *The Raw and the Cooked*. The first myths, which were centred on the fundamental realities of cooking (instead of on honey and tobacco – each, in their different ways, culinary paradoxes), dealt with the physiology of the marriage relationship. Just as there can be no cooking without fire and meat, the marriage relationship cannot be established without wives' brothers and sisters' husbands, who are totally significant brothers-in-law.

It may be objected that fire and meat are not necessary conditions of cooking to the same degree; it is certainly impossible to cook without fire, but lots of other things besides game may be put into the pot. However, it should be noted that the pattern of marriage-relationships in which the brother, or brothers, of the husband figure as pathogenic elements, first appeared in connection with the cycle about Star who married a mortal, which dealt with *the origin of cultivated plants* (M_{87}–M_{92}), i.e. with something logically earlier than the origin of cooking, and which is even specifically stated in one myth (M_{92}) to have come before cooking (RC, p. 167).

Cooking is a mediatory process of the first order between (natural) meat and (cultural) fire, whereas cultivated plants – which are already in their raw state the result of a mediation between nature and culture – are subjected by cooking only to derivative and partial mediation. The ancients understood this distinction, since they thought that agriculture involved a form of cooking. Before the seed was sown, the up-turned clods of earth had to be cooked, 'terram excoquere', through exposure to the sun's heat (Virgil, *Georgics*, II, v. 260). Thus, the actual cooking of cereals was a secondary culinary process. It is true that wild plants may also be used as food but, unlike meat, many of them can be eaten raw. They therefore constitute an indefinite category, hardly suitable for the purposes of a demonstration. This mythic demonstration, when carried out with the *cooking* of meat and the *cultivation* of food plants as simultaneous starting-points, leads, in the first instance, to the achievement of culture and, in the second instance, to the achievement of society; and the myths assert that the latter came after the former (RC, pp. 185–8).

---

about the husband's brother are a transformation. In the tapir-seducer cycle, transformation may also give a seductress-figure (M_{144}, M_{145}, M_{158}).

What must we conclude from this? Like cooking considered in its pure state (the cooking of meat), the marriage relationship considered in its pure state – i.e. involving brothers-in-law purely as giver and taker[17] – expresses the essential interconnection, in native thought, between nature and culture. On the other hand, the myths suggest that the birth of a neolithic economy, involving an increase in the number of communities and the diversification of languages and customs (M_{90}) gave rise to the first difficulties in social life, through population growth and a more haphazard composition of family groups than the beautiful simplicity of the models[18] would have allowed. This is precisely what Rousseau said 200 years ago in his *Discours sur l'origine de l'inégalité*, and I have often drawn attention to his profound ideas, which have been unfairly criticized. The evidence supplied by the South American Indians, and that I have shown to be implicitly present in their myths, cannot, of course, be accepted as an authoritative re-habilitation of Rousseau's views. But it not only indicates a remarkable connection between modern philosophy and these strange stories which, at first sight, would hardly seem capable of such a lofty in-terpretation; we should also be wrong to forget that when mankind, in reflecting upon itself, finds itself prompted to make the same sup-positions, in spite of the extraordinarily different circumstances from which they spring, there is a great probability that the repeated con-vergence of thought with an object which is also its subject, reveals some essential aspect, if not of the history of mankind, at least of human nature with which that history is bound up. In this sense, the diversity of the paths by which Rousseau and the South American Indians – the first consciously, the second unconsciously – were led to make the same speculations about a very remote past, doubtless proves nothing about that past, but it does prove a great deal about man. If man is such that, in spite of the diversity of times and places, he cannot

[17] One always looks upon himself as the incarnation of culture, while the myths relegate the other to the category of nature; in terms of the culinary code, this gives a master of cooking fire and, according to circumstances, sometimes a consumer of raw meat (the jaguar in M_7-M_{12}), sometimes game which is to be cooked (the wild pigs in M_{16}-M_{19}). The equation:

$$\text{(giver : taker)} :: \text{(cooking fire : meat)}$$

was analysed in *RC*, pp. 83-107.

[18] Therefore, these models must be essentially paleolithic in inspiration. This is not to assert, but merely to accept as a possibility, that the Indian conceptions of the marriage relationship, as they are expressed in the rules about exogamy and in the preferences for certain types of relations, go back to such a remote period in the life of mankind. I have touched on this problem in a lecture: 'The Future of Kinship Studies', *Proceedings of the Royal Anthropological Institute of Great Britain and Ireland for 1965*, pp. 15-16.

escape the obligation to entertain similar ideas about how he came into being, his genesis cannot have been in contradiction with that human nature indirectly expressed in the recurrent ideas that men, in various parts of the world, have formulated about their past.

Let us now return to the myths. We have seen that, on the level of the meta-group formed by the tapir-seducer and the woman-mad-about-honey cycles, there survives an ambiguity that had already occurred on humbler levels. Since we are dealing therefore with a structural characteristic of the meta-group, it is appropriate to pay particular attention to one of its modalities which, at first sight, seems to occur only in the tapir-seducer cycle, where it uses the resources of an acoustic code that I have not yet had occasion to consider.

Almost all the myths about a heroine who allows herself to be seduced by an animal – usually a tapir, but sometimes also a jaguar, a snake, a cayman and, in North America, a bear – carefully describe the way in which the woman sets about summoning her lover. In this respect, they can be divided into two groups, according to whether the woman pronounces the animal's name and thus addresses a personal invitation to him, or whether she is content to send an anonymous message which often consists in tapping on a tree-trunk or on a calabash-bowl placed upside down on the water.

Let me give some examples of myths belonging to the first group. Kayapo-Kubenkranken (M_{153}): the tapir-man is called Bira; Apinayé (M_{156}): the cayman's mistresses cry: 'Minti! Here we are!' Mundurucu (M_{49}): the name of the serpent-seducer is Tupasherébé; (M_{150}): the tapir-seducer appears when the women call him by his name, Anyo-caitché; (M_{286}): the hero is in love with a female sloth and calls to her 'Araben! Come to me!' (Murphy 1, p. 125; Kruse 2, p. 631). The future Guiana amazons (M_{287}) call the jaguar-seducer by his name, Walyarimé, which later becomes their rallying cry (Brett 2, p. 181). The tapir in M_{285} tells the woman to whom he is paying court, that his name is Walya (*ibid.*, p. 191). The serpent in a Waiwai myth (M_{271}, M_{288}), which is reared by a woman as a domestic pet, is called Pétali (Fock, p. 63). The cayman-seducer in the Karaja myth (M_{289}) is called Kabroro; the women make him a long speech, to which he replies since, in those days, caymans knew how to talk (Ehrenreich, pp. 83–4). The Ofaié myth (M_{159}) does not mention any name for the tapir, but his mistress calls him with the term 'Benzinho, o benzinho', literally 'blessed little one'. The Tupari myths on the same theme (M_{155}) say that the women summoned the tapir 'with a seductive call' and that, later, 'they repeated the same words' (Caspar 1, pp. 213–14). Sometimes these proper names are no more than the ordinary word for the animal used as a vocative (M_{156}, M_{289}) or as a surname (M_{285}, M_{287}).

The second group includes myths belonging in some cases to the same tribes. Kraho (M_{152}): the woman calls the tapir by striking the trunk of a buriti palm tree. Tenetehara (M_{151}): a tree-trunk, or (M_{80}), where the animal is a big snake, a calabash (Urubu) or by stamping her foot (Tenetehara). To summon their lover, the Mundurucu mistresses of the snake (M_{290}) strike a half-gourd that has been placed upside down on the water: pugn ... (Kruse 2, p. 640). Similarly in Amazonia (M_{183}), to call the rainbow-snake from out of the water. In Guiana (M_{291}), the two sisters call their lover, the tapir, by putting their fingers in their mouths and whistling (Roth 1, p. 245; cf. Ahlbrinck, under 'iriritura'). There is also a whistling call in the Tacana myths, but it is produced by the tapir- or snake-seducer (H.-H., pp. 175, 182, 217); I shall return to this inversion later (see below, pp. 330–31).

It would be easy to add other examples to this list. Those already given are enough to establish the existence of two types of call in relation to the animal acting as seducer. These types are clearly contrasted, since they can be summarized as either linguistic in nature (proper name, common noun used as a proper name, seductive words), or sonorous but non-linguistic (striking gourds, trees or the ground; whistling).

At first sight, we might be tempted to explain the dualism by reference to customs which are known to exist elsewhere. Among the Cubeo on the river Uaupés, the tapir (which the Indians say they have hunted only since they have had guns) is the only variety of large game: 'The hunters keep watch near a stream, where the ground contains salt. The tapir goes there in the afternoons, always following a customary route, and it leaves deep tracks in the muddy earth. Among the maze of these deep pathways fresh tracks and fresh dung are the signs of current use. A man who has seen a fresh track reports it. The hunters go out to kill a tapir who has already been observed, so that they may speak of him in personal terms' (Goldman, pp. 52, 57). When I was with the Tupi-Kawaib in the Rio Machado area, I myself took part in a hunt in which the tapped-out call was used: to make the wild pigs, jaguars or tapirs believe that wild fruit was falling from a tree and so head them into an ambush, the natives struck the ground with a stick at regular intervals: poum ... poum ... poum ... The peasants of central Brazil call this *batuque* hunting (L.-S. 3, p. 352).

In the most favourable hypothesis, these methods may have inspired the stories in the myths, but they do not provide a satisfactory interpretation of them. Admittedly the myths refer to hunting (men hunt the tapir), but their starting-point is different; the gourd call, which is the most frequent tapped-out call, does not correspond to any known practice; then the two types of call stand in opposition to each other, and it is the opposition which has to be explained, not each particular call.

Although the two types are contrasted, each independently has a connection with one or other of the two forms of contrasting behaviour, the function of which I discussed in relation to the Guiana myths about the origin of honey (M_{233}–M_{234}). To attract the animal lover (who is also an evil-doer), either his name has to be pronounced or something must be struck (ground, tree, gourd placed on the water). In the myths I have just referred to, on the other hand, to hold the benefactor (or the benefactress) back, his or her name must not be pronounced and the object must not be struck (in this instance, it is the water with which the seductresses try to splash him). The myths furthermore make it clear that the benefactor or benefactress are not sexual seducers, but modest, reserved and even shy individuals. We are thus dealing with a system involving two forms of linguistic behaviour, speaking and not speaking, and two forms of non-linguistic behaviour, with a positive and a negative significance. According to the particular case, the values of the two forms of behaviour are inverted within each pair; the behaviour homologous to that which attracts the tapir drives away honey, the behaviour homologous to that which holds back the honey does not attract the tapir. At the same time, it should not be forgotten that, whereas the tapir is a sexual seducer, honey is an alimentary seducer:

To effect a conjunction with the sexual seducer:	*To prevent disjunction from the alimentary seducer:*
(1) pronounce his name	(1) avoid pronouncing his name
(2) strike (something)	(2) do not strike (the water)

However, I pointed out that, in the animal-seducer cycle, the tapped-out call is sometimes replaced by a whistled call. In order to carry the analysis further, we must therefore also determine its position in the system.

Like the Indians of the Uaupés river (Silva, p. 255, n. 7) and the Siriono of Bolivia (Holmberg, p. 23), the Bororo communicate with each other at a distance by means of a whistled language, which, far from being limited to a few conventional signals, seems to be a thorough transposition of articulate speech, and so can be used for the transmission of the most varied messages (Colb. 3, pp. 145–6; *EB*, Vol. I, p. 824). It is referred to in a myth:

M₂₉₂ₐ. Bororo. 'The origin of the names of the constellations'

An Indian, accompanied by his little boy, was hunting in the forest, when he noticed a dangerous sting-ray in the river and promptly killed it. The child was hungry and asked his father to cook the sting-ray. The father agreed only grudgingly, because he wanted to carry on fishing. He lit a small fire and, as soon as there were a few embers, he placed the fish on them, after wrapping it in leaves. Then he went back to the river, leaving the child near the fire.

After a while, the boy thought the fish was cooked and called his father. The latter, who was some distance away, shouted to the boy to be patient, but the boy called again and the father, by now thoroughly irritated, came back, took the fish from the fire, saw that it had not yet finished cooking, threw it in his son's face, and went off again.

Burnt and blinded by the embers, the boy began to cry. Strangely enough, echoing cries and murmurs came from the forest. The father took flight in terror, while the child, crying more loudly still, grasped a bokaddi sprout (= bokaddi, bokwadi, jatobá tree: *Hymenea* sp.) which he addressed as 'grandfather' and which he asked to rise in the air and lift him up. At once, the tree began to grow, while a terrible noise could be heard at the base of the trunk. This was caused by the Spirits (kogae) who never left the tree. By now the boy was up in the branches and, from his place of refuge there, he saw that, whenever a star or a constellation rose during the night, the Spirits hailed it by its name in the whistled language. The boy was careful to memorize all the names, which had previously been unknown.

Taking advantage of a moment of inattention on the part of the Spirits, the boy begged the tree to grow small again, and as soon as he could jump to the ground he ran off. It was from him that men learned the names of the constellations (Colb. 3, pp. 253–4).

We do not know much about the Spirits (kogae), except that an unidentified plant, which is used as a hunting talisman, as well as a reed instrument, are referred to by means of a phrase which includes the word kogae, but no doubt in the second case this is because of a connection between this particular family of Spirits, the decoration peculiar to the musical instrument and the badegeba cebegiwu clan of the Cera moiety (cf. *EB*, Vol. I, pp. 52, 740). Because of this uncertainty, and also to avoid overburdening the discussion, I shall not indicate the series of fairly simple transformations which would bring us back directly from M_{292a} to M_2, i.e. almost to our original starting-point[19] (see the table below).

Let us merely note – since the point will be needed later – that the relevant transformation seems to be:

$$M_2 \qquad\qquad M_{292}$$
$$(\text{filth}) \Rightarrow \qquad (\text{noise})$$

a young boy accompanying $\begin{cases} M_2\text{: his mother} \\ M_{292a}\text{: his father} \end{cases}$ witnesses $\begin{cases} M_2\text{: an aggression which turns into }\textit{sexual}\text{ consummation} \\ \\ M_{292a}\text{: a }\textit{threat}\text{ of aggression which does }\textit{not}\text{ turn into }\textit{alimentary}\text{ consumption} \end{cases}$

//

[19] To justify this sudden back-reference, I should point out that the Bororo consider the sting-ray as the metamorphosis of an Indian exasperated by the jeers showered on his son by the child's young friends (Colb. 3, pp. 254–5). This myth (M_{292b}) consequently belongs to the 'vindictive father' group, which also includes M_2, M_{15}–M_{16} and M_{18}, and in which the changing of the self into a poisonous ray (skate?) corresponds to the changing of other people into wild pigs, and of the tapir into an 'other' (cf. *RC*, pp. 214–18, 278–9). It can be shown that, in both North and South America, the ray's tail represents an inverted seductive penis. For South America, cf. M_{247} (the episode in which the tapir *hostile to the hero-seducer* is killed through being impaled on the barb of a ray, Amorim, p. 139), and the Chipaya myth (M_{292c}) about a man who dies while copulating with a ray-woman, through being pierced by her barbs (Nim. 3, pp. 1031–2). The Warao of Venezuela compare the sting-ray to a young woman (Wilbert 9, p. 163). According to the Baniwa, the ray sprang from Jurupari's placenta (M_{276b}). In the Karaja myths, the sting-ray is part of a system which includes the piranha fish and the dolphin, associated respectively with the toothed vagina and the seductive penis (cf. Dietschy 2). For North America, the chief reference is the myths of the Yurok and other Californian tribes, who compare the ray to the female genital system (the body is the womb and the tail the vagina). According to one myth (M_{292d}), Lady-Skate is an irresistible seductress who captures the demigod during copulation by catching his penis between her thighs and thus succeeds in removing him once and for all from the human world (Erikson, p. 272; Reichard, p. 161). Such is also the ultimate fate of the demiurge, Baitogogo, the hero of M_2.

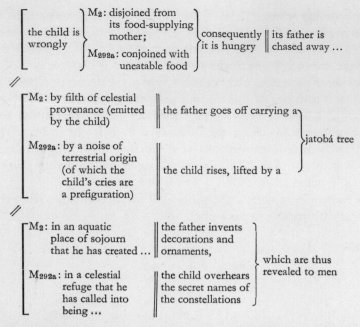

The child in M_2 who, after being changed into a bird, pollutes its father with the excrement that it drops on his shoulder (*from above*), in M_{292} disturbs him (*from a distance*) by untimely calls. The young hero of M_{292} therefore provides a further illustration of the crying baby that we have already encountered in M_{241}, M_{245}, and whom we shall meet again later. At the same time, the *droppings* (excretion) of a very *small* bird, falling from *above*, change into an *enormous* tree which causes the father to go *far away*; symmetrically, the *tears* (secretion) of a *small* child are changed into an *enormous* noise which causes the father to go *far away* and the child himself to rise to a *high* position. The filth in M_2 plays the part of primary cause in the appearance of water, which occupies an extraordinarily ambiguous place in Bororo culture: the water poured over the temporary grave speeds up the decay of the flesh, and thus engenders corruption and filth; yet when the bones have been washed, painted and decorated, they are finally immersed in a lake or a river which serves as their last resting place, since water is the abode of souls, and the condition and means of their immortality.

The whistled language seems to share the same ambiguity on the acoustic level: it belongs to spirits who produce a terrifying din (I have just shown that this din is congruous with filth; in *The Raw and the Cooked* it was established that noise, in the form of 'charivari', was congruous with moral 'corruption'); and yet, although the whistled language is closer to noise than to articulate speech, it conveys information that articulate speech could not have transmitted since, at the time of the myth, men did not know the names of the stars and the constellations.

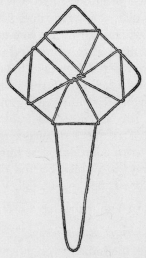

Figure 14. The sting-ray. A figure in a string game. Warao Indians. (Taken from Roth 2, Fig. 318, p. 543.)

Consequently, following M₂₉₂ₐ, the whistled language is something more and better than a language. Another myth also explains in what way it is better but, this time, it would seem, because it is something less:

M₂₉₃. Bororo. 'Why corn-cobs are thin and small'

There was once a Spirit named Burékoïbo whose maize fields were incomparably fine. This Spirit had four sons, and he entrusted the task of planting to one of them, Bopé-joku. The latter did his best and every time the women came to gather maize, he would whistle: 'fi, fi, fi', to express his pride and satisfaction. And indeed, Burékoïbo's maize was very enviable, because of its heavy grain-loaded cobs ...

One day, a woman was gathering maize, while Bopé-joku was whistling away gaily, as usual. She was doing the work rather roughly and she cut her hand on one of the cobs she was picking. Upset by the pain, she insulted Bopé-joku and complained about his whistling.

Immediately, the maize, the growth of which depended on the Spirit's whistling, began to wither and dry on the stalk. Since that time, and because Bopé-joku took his revenge, maize no longer grows of its own accord, but men have to cultivate it by the sweat of their brows.

However, Burékoïbo promised them that he would grant a good harvest on condition that, at sowing time, they blew upwards in the direction of heaven, while uttering prayers to him. He also ordered his son to visit the Indians at this time and to ask them about their work. Any who answered rudely would have only a poor harvest.

Bopé-joku set off and asked each farmer what he was doing. They replied in turn: 'As you see, I am getting my field ready.' The last punched him in the ribs and insulted him. Because of this man's action, maize is not of as fine a quality as before. But any Indian who hopes to gather corn-cobs 'as big as bunches of the fruit of the palm tree', always prays to Burékoïbo and offers the Spirit the first fruits of his field (Kruse 2, pp. 164–6; *EB*, Vol. I, pp. 528, 774).

The Tembé, a northern Tupi tribe, have a very similar myth:

M₂₉₄. Tembé. 'Why manioc is slow in growing'

There was a time when the Indians were not acquainted with manioc. Instead they cultivated camapú. One day when an Indian was preparing the ground for planting, the demiurge Maíra appeared and asked him what he was doing. Rather impolitely, the man refused to reply. Maíra left him, and all the trees surrounding the little clearing fell onto it and covered it with their branches. The man was furious and set off in pursuit of Maíra, with the intention of killing him with his knife. As he could not find the demiurge, he tried to work off his rage on something by throwing a gourd into the air and attempting to hit it before it fell. But the attempt misfired, the knife pierced his throat and he died.

Maíra came across another man, who was weeding his camapú plantation and who answered courteously when the demiurge asked him what he was doing. Whereupon the demiurge changed all the trees around the field into manioc plants and taught the man how to plant them. Then he accompanied him to his village. They had hardly got there when Maíra told the man to go and harvest the manioc. The man hesitated and pointed out that the planting had just been completed. 'All right,' Maíra said, 'you will not have manioc until next year.' And he went off (Nim. 2, p. 281).

Let us begin by clarifying the problem of camapú. The Guarayu, who are Tupi-Guarani belonging to eastern Bolivia, have a myth (M$_{295a}$) which tells how the wife of the Great Ancestor ate nothing but cama á pu; but this did not seem a substantial enough diet and so he created manioc, maize and the banana-vegetable, *platano* (Pierini, p. 704). In another myth (M$_{296}$), the Tenetehara, who are related to the Tembé, say that men used to live on kamamô, a solanaceous forest plant (Wagley–Galvão, pp. 34, 132–3). It is not certain that kamamô and

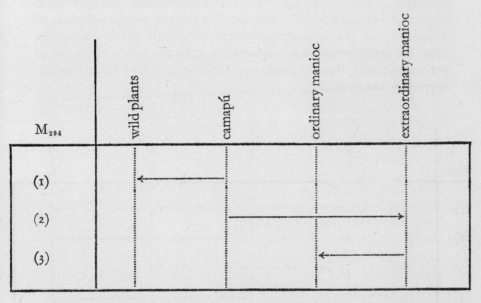

camapú are different names of the same plant, since Tastevin (2, p. 702) refers to camamuri and camapú respectively as being different plants. But camapú (*Psidalia edulis*, Stradelli 1, p. 391; *Physalis pubescens*) is also a solanaceous plant, the semantic position of which is made clearer by a Tucuna myth (M$_{297}$), which states that camapú are the first fruits to grow spontaneously around the edges of plantations (Nim. 13, p. 141). Camapú is therefore a vegetable food at the point of intersection of wild and cultivated plants, and it is such that man can push it towards nature or culture, according to whether or not he uses violent or temperate language. Similarly, a myth common to the Chimane and the Mosetene (M$_{295b}$) explains that wild animals are former human beings guilty of discourteous behaviour (Nordenskiöld 3, pp. 139–43).

When it is looked at in this light, the Tembé myth is seen to contain three sequences: the insults which bring about the transformation of the garden into fallow land and therefore of the camapú into wild plants; the polite speech which transforms the camapú into extraordinary manioc; and lastly the words of distrust which transform extraordinary manioc into ordinary manioc (see table on p. 313).

The Bororo myth comprises four sequences which cover a wider semantic field since, from the point of view of the linguistic means employed, the whistled language lies beyond polite speech and, from the point of view of the agricultural results obtained, the absence of maize is less than a harvest of camapú. We can also note a difference of division within the semantic field common to both myths: M_{293} contrasts the insult which is an exclamation with the insult in lieu of an answer, whereas M_{294} contrasts two types of insulting reply, one explicit, the other veiled:

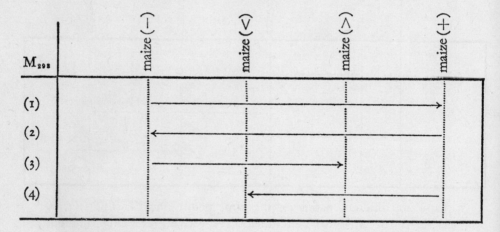

Whatever the accuracy of these shades of significance, which would repay closer analysis, the two myths stand in close parallel since they establish a correlation between acoustic behaviour and agricultural procedures. At the same time, if we take note of the fact that M_{293} is based on a major contrast between insults and the whistled language, and M_{294} on an equally major contrast between insults and polite speech (whereas M_{292a} uses only one contrast, between noise and the whistled language), we can distinguish four types of acoustic behaviour which are arranged in the following order:

1	2	3	4
noise	*insulting speech*	*polite speech*	*the whistled language*

but which nevertheless close a cycle since, as we have seen, whistling, in other contexts, occupies an intermediary position between articulate language and noise.

It will also be noted that all these myths refer to the loss of a miraculous form of agriculture, of which present-day agriculture is only the residue. In this sense, they reproduce the armature of the myths about the origin of honey, which also refer to such a loss and attribute it similarly to immoderate linguistic behaviour: the pronouncing of a name that should not have been uttered, and a consequent displacement of language in the direction of noise, whereas propriety would have required it to move towards silence. This allows us to glimpse the possibility of a still more extensive system, which can be made more definite through the analysis of another myth:

M_{298}. *Machiguenga*. '*The origin of comets and meteorites*'

There was once an Indian who lived with his wife and a son by a previous marriage. Being worried about what might happen between the boy and his step-mother when he was absent, the Indian decided to marry off his son, and went to a distant country to find him a wife. This country was inhabited by cannibal Indians who captured him and tore out his entrails to grill and eat them. Nevertheless he managed to escape.

Meanwhile the woman was planning to poison her husband, because she was in love with her step-son and wished to live with him. She therefore prepared a foul stew (*menjunje de bazofias*) and let ants get into it so as to poison it with their venom. But the man was a sorcerer and he guessed what she was plotting. Before returning, he sent on ahead a messenger spirit in the form of a little boy who said to the wife: 'What are you plotting against my father? Why do you hate him? Why do you want to kill him? Listen to what has happened to him: his intestines have been eaten and, although you cannot tell by looking, he has nothing in his belly. To make him fresh intestines, you must prepare a potion with a piece of mapa [a cultivated root, Grain, p. 241], cotton thread and calabash pulp.' Having said this, the messenger disappeared.

A few days later, the Indian arrived, exhausted by his journey. He asked his wife to give him something to drink, and she provided him with a beverage made from istéa (manioc beer). He at once began to lose blood and his belly was no more than a gaping wound. Terrified by this spectacle, the wife ran off and hid herself in a hollow tree (panáro: unidentified), which stood in the middle of the garden. The Indian, mad with pain, wanted to kill his wife and cried: 'Where are you? Come out, I will not hurt you!' But the wife was afraid and did not move.

In those days, edible plants could speak, but their pronunciation was indistinct. The man asked manioc and magana [*platano*, Grain, *loc. cit.*] 'where their mother was hiding', and as the plants did not reply, he tore them up and threw them into the bush. Ea, a cultivated root [Grain, *loc. cit.*], did its best to tell him, but it spoke so badly that he could not understand what it was saying. He ran in all directions, while his wife looked on from her hiding place.

In the end, the disembowelled man went back into his hut, picked up a bamboo cane and set it alight by striking the ground with a stone. He made himself a tail out of it and, looking up at the sky, said to himself: 'Where should I go? I shall be comfortable up there!' He soared up, transformed into a comet. Meteorites are the drops of incandescent blood from his body. Sometimes he snatches up corpses and turns them into comets like himself (Garcia, pp. 233–4).

This very important myth is worthy of attention from several points of view. In the first place, it is a myth about the origin of comets and meteorites, i.e. of erratic celestial bodies which, unlike the stars and constellations in M_{292a}, cannot be identified and named by the Indians. I have shown that M_{292} is a transformation of M_2, and it is clear that M_{298} is also part of the same group: it begins with an incest like M_2, and, like M_{292}, tells about a hero 'with a hollow stomach', although the expression has to be understood literally or figuratively, according to the circumstances: M_{298} has a disembowelled father, M_2 and M_{292} a famished son.

The father in M_{298}, who tries to kill his incestuous wife, comes back from afar, having lost vital organs which are an integral part of his being. The father in M_2, who has killed his incestuous wife, goes far away, loaded down with the weight of a tree which is a foreign body. This *solid* tree is a *consequence* of the murder of the incestuous woman who, in M_{298}, escapes being murdered by *means* of a *hollow* tree. M_{298} is intended to explain the cosmic anomaly caused by the existence of erratic planets. M_{292} and M_2, on the other hand, complete the order of the world: M_{292} does so on the cosmological level by enumerating and naming the celestial bodies, and M_2 on the sociological level by introducing the decorations and ornaments which make it possible to

enumerate and name the clans and sub-clans (cf. *RC*, pp. 50–55).[20]
Lastly, in both cases, human mortality plays a part, since it appears
sometimes as the means, sometimes as the substance, of the introduction of a social order (M_2) or cosmic disorder (M_{298}).

So far we have looked at the matter from the point of view of the
hero. But the heroine of M_{298} is also an old acquaintance, since she
makes us think simultaneously of two characters, whom I have already
shown to be one and the same. First, the adulterous and murderous
wife of several Chaco myths who, in the Tereno version (M_{24}), poisoned
her husband with her menstrual blood, just as the Machiguenga woman
proposes to do with kitchen refuse impregnated with venom. The
contrast *internal filth/external filth* is echoed by another in the myths:
the Tereno heroine is caught in a pit (M_{24}) or, according to other versions, in a hollow tree (M_{23}, M_{246}). Another hollow tree serves not as a
trap, but as a refuge, for the Machiguenga heroine. Consequently,
according to whether the body of the heroine is, or is not, a receptacle
for poison, another receptacle acts as a shelter for her victims or
herself. And, in the latter case, she meets her doom outside (M_{23}) or
finds salvation inside (M_{298}). I used the recurrence of the hollow-tree
theme previously to connect the story about the jaguar-woman who,
under the influence of stinging[21] honey (the cause of her transformation), was responsible for the creation of tobacco with the story about
the woman mad about honey who triumphs over the jaguar thanks to
a hollow and thorny tree (externally stinging) but changes into a frog
through being imprisoned in a hollow tree full of honey (and therefore internally sweet).

The woman mad about honey is also incestuous, either with her
adopted son (M_{241}, M_{243}, M_{244}; M_{258}) as in the case of the Machiguenga
heroine, or with a young brother-in-law (M_{135}–M_{136}). Also like the
Machiguenga heroine, she plots to kill her husband; but at this point,

---

[20] I have already shown, by another line of reasoning, that M_2 belongs to the tapir-
seducer cycle (*RC*, p. 272, n. 36; p. 309 of the present volume) which, as we know, belongs
to the same group as the woman-mad-about-honey cycle.

Although this is beyond my present scope, it would be appropriate to study certain
North American parallels of M_{298}: e.g. the Pawnee myth which says that meteors sprang
from the body of a man whose enemies killed him and *ate up his brains* (Dorsey 2, pp. 61–2),
and certain details in the Diegueño and Luiseño myths about meteors. Generally speaking,
the treatment of meteors rests on a series of transformations:

dismembered body ⇒ severed head ⇒ emptied skull ⇒ disembowelled body

which call for special study.

[21] The honey in M_{24} is stinging, in two senses: literally, since the husband has mixed
young snakes in with it; and figuratively, since it causes itching.

the devices used are inverted in a very striking way which proves, if proof were needed, how narrow is the margin of creative invention in the myths.

The woman uses a knife in one case and poison in the other. By means of a knife, the Guiana heroine amputates her husband and thus reduces his body to the part containing the entrails (in connection with this interpretation, cf. above, p. 263). By means of poison, or at least the combinatorial variant of poison which consists of a non-remedy given instead of the prescribed remedy, the Machiguenga heroine causes her husband's body to remain disembowelled. In the Guiana myths (M_{135}, M_{136}), the entrails become the Pleiades, an extremely significant constellation for the Indians in the area. In the Machiguenga myth, the entrails become comets or meteors, which belong to an opposite category, because of their erratic nature. The Pleiades, in their masculine form, provide men with fish as food. The comet, in its masculine form, deprives mankind of edible plants and feeds on men, by taking toll of corpses.

A final detail will serve to complete this reconstruction. The Machiguenga hero, to turn himself into a comet, attaches to his behind a bamboo cane which he has set fire to by striking it with a stone. The Taulipang hero, while transforming himself into the Pleiades, holds a bamboo flute to his lips and plays upon it continuously: 'tin, tin, tin', as he rises up into the sky (K.-G. 1, p. 57). Since this is a bamboo flute, it stands in a relationship of correlation and opposition, not only with the *bamboo* in the Machiguenga myth, which is struck (and the importance of which will be explained later), but also with the bone *flute* of which the tortoise in M_{283}–M_{284}[22] is so proud, and with the non-instrumental whistling of the agrarian god in M_{293}; and lastly, in M_{292}, with the naming of the stars by means of the whistled language.[23]

Moreover, the Arawak of Guiana have a rite, about which it would be interesting to know more and which brings together all the inter-related elements I have just been enumerating, since it deals simultaneously with agriculture, the rising of the Pleiades and the two forms of linguistic behaviour that can be more conveniently referred to from

[22] As I do not propose to deal with this second aspect, I shall merely say here that it would be appropriately interpreted on the basis of an episode in M_{276}; the transformation of the bones of Uairy, the ant-eater, into musical instruments, cf. Stradelli 1, under 'mayua'; Uairy had revealed the secret of the masculine rites to women (cf. above, p. 272).

[23] It will be noted that, in M_{247}, the whistling of the sloth in the silence of the night is contrasted with the song that the animal tried to address to the stars when it was still capable of utterance (Amorim, p. 145).

now on as 'the whistled call' and 'the tapped-out reply':[24] 'When towards morning the Pleiades become visible the dry season is imminent, Masasikiri starts his journey and comes to warn the people it is time to prepare their fields. He makes a whistling sound to which he owes his nickname Masakiri (*sic*). When people hear him at night, they strike their cutlasses with something, which makes a sound like a bell; in this way they thank the spirit for his warning' (Goeje, p. 51).[25] Thus the return of the Pleiades is accompanied by an exchange of acoustic signals, the contrast between which has some formal resemblance to that between the two fire-producing techniques, friction and percussion, which I showed to have a relevant function in connection with the myths of the same area (p. 246). 'The tapped-out reply' is, in fact, a percussive noise like the other one; and, in M_{298}, it causes the object that is struck to take fire. And so there is probably nothing arbitrary about the fact that the Guiana myths about the origin of the Pleiades (which is thought of in the first place as a departure conditioning their early return) reverse the whistled call and the tapped-out call along three axes: the knife strikes instead of being struck; the reply is whistled instead of the call, but at the same time is expressed by a tune on the flute, in which the whistling of the Arawak and Bororo agrarian gods can display all its possibilities. If this suggestion is correct, it can be extended to the Tembé myth (M_{294}) in which the ill-bred farmer accidentally kills himself by trying to pierce (his knife strikes, instead of being struck, as is the polite form of reply to the god among the Arawak of Guiana) a freshly picked gourd (which is full and non-resonant and therefore in exact contrast to the sonorousness of a similar gourd dried and emptied). Lastly, it should not be forgotten that while, in most of the myths, the tapir is summoned by a tapped-out call, the Indians compare its cry to a whistle (M_{145}, RC, p. 303). In some cases, too, whistling is used to attract it (Ahlbrinck, under 'wotaro' § 3; Holmberg, p. 26; Armentia, p. 8).

Having thus found that a belief of the Arawak of Guiana provides us with an additional reason for incorporating the Machiguenga myth into the group at present under examination, it is doubtless appropriate at this point to recall that the Machiguenga themselves

[24] TRANSLATORS' NOTE: *appel sifflé*: *réponse cognée*; *cogner* is 'to strike hard, to thump, to bang'.

[25] According to P. Clastres (who gave me the information personally), the non-agricultural Guayaki believe in a trickster-spirit, who is master of honey and armed with an ineffectual bow and arrows made of ferns. This spirit announces his approach by whistling and is driven away by noise.

belong to a large group of Arawak-speaking Peruvian tribes. Together with the Amuesha, Campa, Piro, etc. they constitute an apparently archaic stratum of population which settled in the Montaña area at a very remote period.

Let us now return to myth M_{298}, which defines a form of linguistic behaviour on the part of plants towards men, instead of on the part of men towards plants (M_{293}, etc.), but which, in the latter respect, can be completed with the help of another Machiguenga myth. As this is a very long myth, I shall cut down the summary to a minimum except in the part directly concerned with my argument.

M_{299}. Machiguenga. 'The origin of cultivated plants'

In olden times, there were no cultivated plants. Men ate potters' clay which they cooked and swallowed, as hens swallow, because they had no teeth.

It was Moon who gave men cultivated plants and taught them how to masticate. He did so by instructing an indisposed young girl, whom he visited secretly and eventually married.

On several occasions, Moon caused his human wife to be fertilized by a fish, and she gave birth to four sons: the sun, the planet Venus, the sun of the lower world and the nocturnal sun (which is invisible, but provides the stars with their light). This fourth son was so hot that he scorched his mother's womb and she died while giving birth to him.[26]

Moon's mother-in-law upbraided him and said that, after killing his wife, it was only left for him to eat her. However, Moon succeeded in resuscitating her, but she was now disgusted with life on earth and decided to leave her body and betake her soul to the lower world. Moon was deeply distressed and, having been challenged by his mother-in-law, ate the body after painting the face red, thus inventing a funeral rite which still persists. He found human flesh delicious. Thus, through the fault of the old woman, Moon became a corpse-eater, and decided to go far away.

His third son elected to live in the lower world. He is a weak,

[26] In connection with a 'burning baby', who is the son of the sun, cf. Cavina in Nordenskiöld 3, pp. 286–7, and Uitoto in Preuss 1, pp. 304–14, where the burning sun consumes his adulterous mother who is trying to join him in the sky. This group will be discussed in another volume in connection with the North American parallels. Without going into details, we can accept the fact that the mother whose entrails are scorched by the baby to whom she is giving birth (the nearest imaginable relative) is a transformation of the disembowelled father or the man who has had his brains knocked out (by distant enemies); cf. p. 317, n. 20.

maleficent sun, which sends rain when the Indians are clearing the ground, to prevent them burning the tree stumps. With his other sons, Moon went up into the sky. But the last born was too hot; so much so that on earth he caused stones to split. His father settled him in the firmament, but so high up that we can no longer see him. Only the planet Venus and the sun now live near their father, the Moon.

Moon constructed a trap in a river and it was so efficient that it caught all the corpses floating downstream.[27] A toad kept watch and every time a corpse was caught, it informed Moon by repeatedly croaking 'Tantanaróki-iróki, tantanaróki-iróki', literally: 'the toad tantanaróki and its eye'. Then Moon would hurry to the scene and kill the corpse (*sic*) by beating it with a club. He would cut off the hands and feet and roast and eat them. The rest he would change into a tapir.

Only the daughters of Moon are left on earth; these are the plants cultivated by the Indians and their staple diet: manioc, maize, banana-vegetable (*Musa normalis*), sweet potatoes, etc. Moon continues to take a watchful interest in these plants which he created and which, for this reason, call him 'father'. If the Indians spoil or throw away manioc, scatter the peelings or clean it badly, the manioc-daughter weeps and complains to her father. If they eat manioc by itself or merely seasoned with pimentoes, the daughter becomes angry and says to her father: 'They give me nothing. They leave me all alone, or they give me nothing but pimento, which is so hot I cannot stand it.' On the other hand, if the Indians are careful not to waste any manioc and to put all the peelings into one place where it is forbidden to walk, then the daughter is pleased. And when manioc is eaten with meat or fish, which are superior foods, she says to her father: 'They are treating me well. They give me everything I want.' But what she likes best of all is to be made into beer, which is enriched with saliva and well fermented.

The other daughters of Moon have similar reactions to the treatment they receive from men. Men can hear neither their weeping nor their expressions of satisfaction, but try to please them, because they know that if the daughters were made unhappy, Moon would call them up to him and men would have to feed on earth, as they used to do (Garcia, pp. 230–33).

---

[27] The Machiguenga throw their dead, unceremoniously, into the river (Farabee 2, p. 12).

L

Since Rivet discovered resemblances in vocabulary between the Bororo language and the Otuké dialects of Bolivia in 1913, it has been generally accepted that Bororo culture may have affinities with that of other South American tribes living in the western areas. A comparison between M₂₉₃ and M₂₉₉ does a great deal to strengthen this hypothesis, since the two myths show striking analogies with each other. They both deal with the origin of cultivated plants and with the rites governing either their production (Bororo) or their consumption (Machiguenga). Five agrarian gods are associated with the origin of these rites: a father and his four sons. The Bororo myth does not mention the mother, while the Machiguenga myth eliminates her at an early stage. According to the Machiguenga, the father is the moon, and his sons 'the suns'; and the *Enciclopédia Boróro* points out, in connection with two summaries of a variant of M₂₉₃ which will be given in the eagerly awaited second volume, that the father, Burékoïbo, is none other than the sun, Méri (Espirito denominado tambem Méri', *loc. cit.*, under 'Burékoïbo; cf. also *loc. cit.*, p. 774). In both myths, the third sun acts as a specialist in agricultural activities, either as a help (Bororo) or a hindrance (Machiguenga). However, this slight divergency is still less pronounced than at first appears since, in the Bororo myth, this sun explicitly punishes disrespectful farmers by sending them bad harvests, while the Machiguenga myth implies that the rains which occur during the slash-and-burn process, and thus cause bad harvests, may be a punishment visited upon disrespectful consumers.

The third son in the Machiguenga myth, the sun of the lower world, is a maleficent, chthonian spirit. In the Bororo myth, the third son is called Bopé-joku, from Bopé: evil spirit (cf. *EB*, under 'maeréboe': Os primeiros [espíritos malfazejos] são chamados comumente apenas bópe, assim que esta forma, embora possa indicar qualquer espírito, entretanto comumente designa apenas espíritos maus', p. 773). The meaning of joku is obscure, but we may note that the same sounds occur as part of the name, jokûgoe, of a species of bee which makes its nest below ground or in abandoned ant-hills (*EB*, Vol. I, under 'jokûgoe'). It does not yet seem possible to draw any conclusions from the names of the other sons in the Bororo myth, apart perhaps from the fact that the eldest's name: Uarudúdoe, corresponding to that of the Machiguenga eldest son (Puriáchiri, 'he who warms'), suggests an analogous derivation from waru > baru 'heat' (cf. Bororo barudodu 'warmed-up').

In the Machiguenga myth, there is no mention of the whistled language which, according to the Bororo, used to ensure the spontaneous growth of the miraculous maize. But, at the other end of the semantic field, the Machiguenga go further than the Bororo, since they do not rule out the possibility that cultivated plants may disappear completely if they are badly treated:

harvest:	superlatively good	good	bad	non-existent
$\lceil$ M$_{293}$	whistled language	polite language	insulting language	
$\lfloor$ M$_{299}$		polite treatment		harmful treatment

We observe, then, as between the Bororo and the Machiguenga myths, a remarkable transformation from the more or less polite language spoken to the plants to a more or less elaborate form of cooking in which these same plants are used. There could be no better expression of the fact that, as I have often suggested (L.-S. 5, pp. 99–100; 12, *passim*), cooking is a language in which each society codes messages which allow it to signify a part at least of what it is. I have already demonstrated that, of the various forms of linguistic behaviour, insulting language is the one which approximates most closely to noise, so much so, indeed, that the two forms of behaviour appear to be interchangeable in many South American myths, as well as in the European tradition, as is attested in France by commonsense observation and numerous turns of phrase. I had occasion, in *The Raw and the Cooked*, to establish a direct homology between bad cooking and noise or din (RC, p. 293):[28] we can now see that there is a homology between refined language and more elaborate cooking. It is therefore easy to define the problematical term indicated by x in the equation on p. 311 of the preceding volume: if, in the myths, noise or din corresponds to an abuse of cooked food, this is because it is itself an abuse of articulate speech. The conclusion was predictable, and the remainder of this book will complete the proof.

However, in one way, the Bororo and Machiguenga myths, instead of echoing each other, complete each other. According to the Bororo, man could speak to plants (by means of the whistled language) at a time when the latter were personal beings, capable of understanding such messages and growing spontaneously. Now, communication has

[28] Cf. in French the double meaning of such words as 'gargote' (low-class – and therefore noisy(?) – eating-house, where the food is bad) and 'boucan' (barbecue : din). In support of the equivalence already established between the eclipse and anti-cooking (RC, pp. 296–9), we can, in the present context, refer to the Botocudo belief that eclipses come about when the sun and the moon quarrel and insult each other. They then become black with rage and hate (Nim. 9, p. 110).

been interrupted, or it is carried on through the medium of an agrarian god who speaks to man, and who is answered by men well or badly. The dialogue takes place, then, between the god and men, and plants are no more than the occasion of the dialogue.

In the Machiguenga myths, the opposite is the case. Plants, being the daughters of the god and therefore personal beings, converse with their father. Men have no means of intercepting these messages: 'Los machiguengas no perciben esos lloros y regocijos' (Garcia, p. 232); but since they are being talked about, they are the occasion of the exchange of messages. However, the theoretical possibility of a direct dialogue existed in mythic times, when the comets had not yet made their appearance in the sky. But, at that time, plants were only half-persons, with the gift of speech but so indistinct in utterance that they were unable to use it for purposes of communication.

When completed one by another, the myths are seen, then, to form a total, multi-axial system. The Salesians point out that the Bororo whistled language has two main functions: to ensure communication between speakers who are too far away from each other to conduct a normal conversation; or to prevent eavesdropping by outsiders, who understand the Bororo language but are unacquainted with the secrets of the whistled speech (Colb. 3, pp. 145–6; *EB* Vol. I, p. 824). This mode of communication is, therefore, both broader and more restricted. It is a super-language for the actual speakers but an infra-language for outsiders.

The language spoken by plants has exactly opposite characteristics. When it is addressed directly to man, it is an incomprehensible muttering (M_{298}), whereas when it is used clearly, it by-passes man. He cannot hear it, although it is entirely concerned with him (M_{299}). The whistled language and indistinct speech therefore form a pair of contrasts.

The absence of a multinote flute among the Bororo is all the more remarkable in that they are capable of making fairly complex wind instruments, such as horns and clarinets consisting of a tube with a reed and a sound-box, but which, like the flutes, produce only a single note. No doubt this ignorance on their part (it is, more probably, the result of a prohibition) should be related to the exceptional development of the whistled language: in other communities, the multinote flute is chiefly used for the transmission of messages. We have abundant evidence on this point, especially from the Amazon valley where hunters and fishermen used flute-tunes as leitmotiv to announce their

Bororo, M_{292}:·

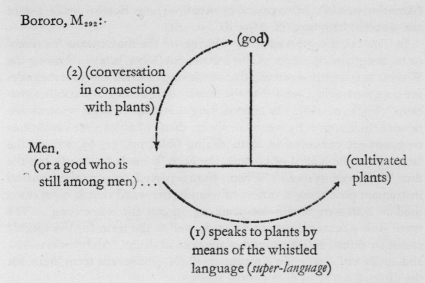

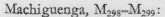

Machiguenga, M_{298}–M_{299}:

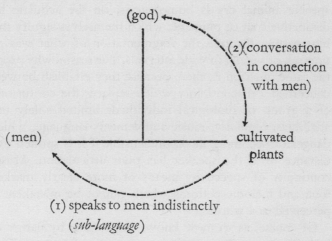

Note: It will be observed that the Bororo whistled language is a *super-language* for the speakers and an *infra-language* for outsiders. Correspondingly, the plant language in M_{298}–M_{299} is an *infra-language* for the speakers (M_{298}) but a *super-language* for outsiders (M_{299}).

return, the outcome of the expedition and the nature of the catch (Amorim, *passim*). In comparable situations, the Bororo make use of the whistled language (cf. M_{26}; *RC*, p. 103).

In Tucano, the expression for playing on the flute means 'to weep' or 'to complain' by means of this instrument (Silva, p. 255). Among the Waiwai 'it is worth observing that much suggests that the flute melodies are programmatic ... and that the music itself describes various situations' (Fock, p. 280). On approaching a strange village, visitors announce their arrival by means of short, sharp whistles; but invitations to guests are conveyed by flute-playing (*ibid.*, pp. 51, 63, 87). In the language of the Kalina of Guiana, the horn 'is made to shout', but the flute 'is allowed to speak'. 'When a flute is played, or any other musical instrument producing a variety of sounds, the word that is most often used is *eruto* – to obtain language or speech for something ... The word *eti* is a personal proper name, as well as the term for the specific call of an animal and the sound of the flute or drum' (Ahlbrinck, index; and under 'eti', 'eto'). An Arecuna myth (M_{145}) uses the term 'flute' for the distinctive cry of each animal species.

These assimilations of meaning are important because, as I showed in *The Raw and the Cooked*, and precisely in connection with M_{145}, the specific animal cry is homologous, on the acoustic level, with the distinctive coat or plumage, which themselves signify the introduction into nature, through the fragmentation of what was originally continuous, of a realm of wide intervals. The reason why proper names have the same function is, then, because they establish between the persons concerned a discontinuity which replaces the confusion characteristic of a group of biological individuals limited solely to their natural attributes. Similarly, music supplements language, which is always in danger of becoming incomprehensible if it is spoken over too great a distance or if the speaker has poor articulation. Music corrects the continuity of speech by means of more clearly marked contrasts of tone and melodic patterns which cannot be mistaken, since they are perceived as a whole.

Of course, as we now know, language is by nature discontinuous, but this is not the way it is conceived of in mythic thought. It is, incidentally, a remarkable fact that the South American Indians are chiefly concerned to exploit its plasticity. The existence, in various places, of dialects peculiar to each sex proves that Nambikwara women are not alone in their tendency to distort words to make them incomprehensible, and to prefer, instead of clear utterance, indistinct mutterings comparable to those of the plants in the Machiguenga myth (L.-S. 3, p. 295). The Indians of eastern Bolivia 'like to borrow foreign words, with the result ... that their language is constantly changing; the women do not pronounce the consonant s but always change it into an f' (Armentia, p. 11). More than a century ago, Bates noted (p. 169) in connection with the Mura, among whom he had lived: 'When the Indians, both men and women, talk together, they seem to delight in inventing new pronunciations and in distorting words. Everybody laughs at these slang inventions, and the new terms are often adopted. I have observed the same thing during long sailing trips with Indian crews.'

An amusing comparison with these remarks is to be found in a letter, full of Portuguese words, that Spruce wrote from a Uaupés village to his friend Wallace, who was by that time back in England: 'Don't forget to tell me how you are progressing in the English language and whether you can already make yourself comprehensible to the natives ... ' Wallace gives the following explanatory commentary:

> When we met at São Gabriel ... we had noticed that we were quite incapable of conversing together in English, without using Portuguese words and expressions which amounted to about a third of our vocabulary. Even when we made up our minds to speak only in English, we succeeded in doing so only for a few minutes and with difficulty and as soon as the conversation became animated or it was necessary to recount an anecdote, Portuguese reasserted itself! (Spruce, Vol. I, p. 320).

Such linguistic osmosis, with which travellers and expatriates are well acquainted, must have played a considerable part in the evolution of the American languages and in the linguistic conceptions of the natives of South America. According to a Kalina theory noted by Penard (in Goeje, p. 32): 'vowels change quicker than consonants, because they are thinner, swifter, more liquid than the resistant consonants, but in consequence their *yumi* close themselves sooner, which means they return to their source more rapidly.[29] Thus words and languages are unmade and remade in the course of time.'

If language belongs to the realm of short intervals, it is understandable that music, which substitutes its own order for linguistic

[29] The meaning of the word *yumi* is obscure. It has been diversely translated as 'spirit' or 'father'; cf. Penard's discussion of the use of the term in Ahlbrinck, under 'sirito'. In the context, *yumi* seems to convey the idea of a cycle. On the meaning of *yumi* and its uses, cf. Goeje, p. 17.

confusion, should appear as *masked speech*, endowed with the two-fold function that is assigned to masks in non-literate societies: the concealment of the individual wearing the mask, who is at the same time given a higher significance. Like proper names which are tantamount to metaphors of the individual, since each proper name transforms an

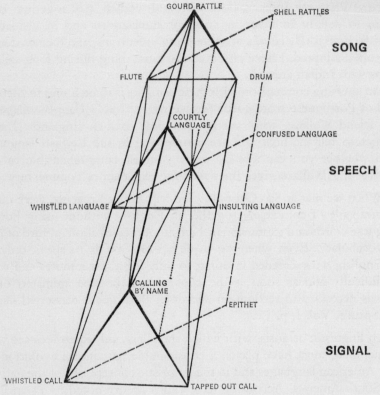

Figure 15. The structure of the acoustic code

individual into a person (L.-S. 9, pp. 284–5), a melodic phrase is a metaphor of speech.

I cannot take this analysis any further, nor do I wish to, since it raises the enormous problem of the relationship between articulate language and music. In any case, the preceding pages are adequate to indicate the general economy of the acoustic code, the existence and function of which is made manifest by the myths. The properties of this code will only appear gradually, but to make them more easily intelligible, I think it advisable at this point to give an approximate account of them, in the form of a diagram which can, as need arises, be made more precise, extended or modified (Figure 15).

The terms of the code are distributed over three levels. At the bottom are the various types of call addressed by the adulterous woman or women to the tapir-seducer (or to other animals acting as combinatory variants of the tapir): calling by name, the whistled call or the tapped-out call. They establish a connection between a human and another creature, which belongs totally to nature in its double capacity as an animal and a seducer. These three types of acoustic behaviour therefore constitute *signals*.

The middle level includes various kinds of linguistic behaviour: the whistled language, polite speech and insulting speech. This speech occurs during a dialogue between one or more men and a divinity who has assumed human shape. This is not, of course, true of the whistled speech as it is ordinarily used, but in the two Bororo myths in which it plays a part (M_{292}, M_{298}), it allows access from the cultural level (that of articulate speech) to the supernatural level, since gods or spirits use it to communicate with supernatural plants (those which once grew spontaneously) or with stars, which are supernatural beings.

Lastly, the three types of musical instrument on the highest level are connected with singing, either because they sing themselves or accompany singing, an activity which contrasts with spoken speech in the same way as the latter contrasts with a system of signals.

In spite of (or because of) its provisional nature this diagram calls for a number of observations.

First, I have established a correlation between the rattle and the drum and contrasted both of them with the flute, although the first two instruments have so far appeared only sporadically in the myths and, as it were, in a veiled form. The rattle has occurred through its reversed transformation in M_{294}: the fresh, full gourd (instead of a dry, empty one) which the hero tries (in vain) to catch on the point of his knife, in the manner of a cup-and-ball, whereas the rattle consists of a gourd threaded on a stick to which it is permanently attached. As for the drum, which I dealt with in connection with a linguistic commentary on the Kalina word 'eti', signifying the sound of the flute and the drum (p. 326), it has been obscurely present since the beginning of this volume. It is the wooden drum, made of a hollowed-out tree-trunk, split on one side, i.e. an object of the same type as the hollow tree which serves as a natural receptacle for honey and which acts as a shelter or a trap in several myths. A Mataco myth (M_{214}) expressly links the wooden drum with the hollowed-out tree-trunk which serves as a trough for the preparation of mead: 'The Indians hollowed out a larger trough and drank all the beer. It was a bird which made the first drum. It banged on it all night, and then, in the morning, turned into a man' (Métraux 3, p. 54). The full significance of this connection will soon become clear. As for the semantic position of the rattle, it will be elucidated at a later stage in the discussion.

Secondly, it was suggested above that the confused speech (addressed to the human hero by the plants in the Machiguenga myth, M_{298}) stands in direct contrast to the whistled language (spoken to the plants by the god in human shape in the Bororo myth, M_{293}, which has been shown to be symmetrical with the other). I have therefore set confused speech some distance behind the other forms of linguistic behaviour, since it is an infra-language inadequate for purposes of communication. But at the same time, its position is equidistant from those of polite speech and insulting speech, which is in keeping with the dramatic point of M_{298}: the plants, which try to initiate an impossible dialogue, want to be polite; but the recipient of the message thinks it is insulting, since he takes his revenge by tearing up the plants and eliminating them from the garden.

The question immediately arises whether there are any intermediate terms between the two extreme levels, the position of which is homologous to that occupied by confused speech on the middle level. It does in fact seem to be the case that the myths and rites provide terms which fulfil the required conditions. In the tapir-seducer cycle, the heroine sometimes calls the animal by uttering an epithet which may be either the ordinary word for the animal raised to the dignity of a proper name or a qualifying adjective solely expressive of the speaker's state of mind. Both kinds of term can lead to confusion: in one case, it is not clear whether the animal is being addressed as a person or named as an object; and in the other case, the identity of the addressee remains undetermined.

The ambiguity inherent in the epithet, whatever the type it belongs to, contrasts it with the whistled call, whose ambivalence has, on the contrary, an iconic character (in the sense in which Peirce used the adjective): the whistle which summons the tapir is a physical reproduction of the animal's own call. As we saw on p. 305, the Tucuna myths replace the whistled call by a whistled announcement. Consequently, the epithet has its proper place on the lower level of the diagram, between calling by name (when the animal has a genuine proper name) and the tapped-out call, but a little way back from both because of its ambiguity.

Passing now to the upper level, I would like to observe that South American organology includes a musical instrument, the position of which is equally ambiguous: the shell-rattles attached to dancers' legs or to a stick which is banged on the ground. From the mythological point of view, these rattles, made of nutshells or animals' hooves threaded on a string and which produce a jangling noise when they strike each other, are similar to the true rattle which produces its noise through the banging about of seeds or pebbles inside a gourd. But from the functional point of view, the shell-rattles are more closely related to the drum, since their movement – which, moreover, is less controlled than that of the hand-held rattle – is the indirect result of the stamping of the legs or the beating of the stick. Therefore, the action of the shell-rattles, which is intentional and discontinuous in its cause but haphazard in its result, is situated some way back, like confused speech; but, for the reasons that have just been given, it is equidistant from the wooden drum and the gourd-rattle.

The preceding analysis is indirectly confirmed by certain ideas about shell-rattles peculiar to the Uitoto. Shell-rattles play a considerable part in their dances, together with the flute and the drum, and are supposed to represent living creatures, especially insects: dragon-flies, wasps and hornets (Preuss 1, pp. 124–33, 633–4), which produce an ambiguous buzzing sound that is coded differently in different areas, sometimes in terms of singing, sometimes in terms of the tapped-out call (*RC*, p. 295, n. 5).

Lastly, between the three levels of the diagram, there is obviously a complicated network of cross-connections, some parallel with each other, others oblique. Let us look first at the parallel connections, each of which corresponds to a ridge of the prism. Moving upwards along one ridge, and according to a scale of increasing intensity, we find the tapped-out call, insulting language and the noise of the drum, which are the types of acoustic behaviour with the most definite affinity to noise, although it should not be forgotten that the drum manages to be, simultaneously, the most sonorous and the most linguistic term in the series: 'The wooden drums of the Boro and the Okaina ... are used to transmit messages about the dates, places and purposes of feast-days. The drummers do not seem to use a code; they try rather to represent the sounds of the words by means of the drums, and the Indians always told me that they made the words with the drum' (Whiffen, pp. 216, 253).

Along the second ridge, we find successively the whistled signal, the whistled language and the sound of the flute. This series indicates the transition from a monotone whistling to modulated whistling and then to a whistled melody. This is, then, a musical axis which is defined by the concept of tonality.

Along the third ridge are grouped essentially linguistic forms of behaviour, since calling by name is a signal made by means of a word (in this, it contrasts with the other two) and polite speech, as the myths indicate, corresponds to the most completely linguistic use of language (in contrast to insulting speech, of course, but also in contrast to whistled speech which, as we have seen, is a super-language on one level, but an infra-language on another). As for the rattle, it is, of all musical instruments, the one with the most definite linguistic function. No doubt the flute speaks, but what it utters is mainly the language of men who 'give' it the power of speech (cf. above, pp. 324–6). And although it is true that the shell-rattles and the drum transmit divine messages to men: 'the bell says its words out loud to men, here on earth' (Preuss, *loc. cit.*), this function is exercised concurrently with the different one of transmitting messages as between men: 'The sound of the drum is a summons to others' (*ibid.*). And how much more eloquent divine speech is when transmitted by a rattle, painted as a likeness of the face of the god! (Zerries 3, *passim*). According to the linguistic theories of the Kalina to which I have already referred, the phonemes of language are present on the surface of the gourd-rattle: 'The circle, encompassing six radii, is the symbol of the vowels *a, e, i, o, u*, with the *m*; ... The rattle represents the globe and the stones in the rattle are the fundamental ideas, and the outside of the rattle is the harmony of speech sounds, etc.' (Goeje, p. 32).

Let us now consider the oblique connections. In the body of the prism represented by the diagram, four diagonals form two isosceles tetrahedra which interpenetrate. The one pointing upwards has, at its angles, all three varieties of call and the rattle, i.e. four terms which, as we shall see, are interlinked by a double connection of correlation and opposition. Without anticipating part of the demonstration to be given later, it will be enough to indicate here that the effect of the calls is to make an animal, a natural creature, appear within human society (and with unfortunate results, since a loss of women ensues). The rattle, on the contrary, determines the appearance of supernatural beings, spirits or gods, with a happy outcome for society.

The other tetrahedron pointing downwards has the three musical instruments at its base, while its fourth angle, after passing through the level of articulate speech, represents calling by name, which is, as it happens, the most linguistic form of call. This pattern refers back to some remarks that I made earlier (pp. 327-8). I said that music is the metaphorical transposition of speech, just as a proper name serves as a metaphor for the biological individual. The four terms thus regrouped are therefore those which function as metaphors, while the four others have a metonymical function: the rattle is the god reduced to his head, and the vocalic aspect is missing from the partial language he utters, the affinities of which are entirely with consonants, since it consists of micronoises; as for the calls, they are reduced, but in a different way, to a part or a moment of speech. Only on the middle level do the metaphorical and metonymical aspects balance each other; naturally enough, on this level we find speech in its literal sense and in three different modalities, in each of which it is entirely present.

3 *The Return of the Bird-Nester*

A long investigation into the mythology of honey has led me to establish within the framework of a wider system, which I have done no more than sketch in rough outline, a relationship of correlation and contrast between what I have found it convenient to term 'the tapped-out call' and 'the whistled call (or reply)'. But, as a matter of fact, 'the tapped-out call' ought to have attracted my attention a long time ago, and precisely in connection with one of the first myths about honey that I happened to discuss.

Let us go back, then, to p. 100 of *The Raw and the Cooked*. The Tereno Indians, who are southern Arawak living in the north-west of the Gran Chaco where the frontiers of Bolivia, Paraguay and Brazil meet, have a myth (M_{24}) about a man who discovers that his wife is poisoning him with her menstrual blood. He goes in search of honey, and mixes it with the flesh of snake embryos taken from the body of a female which has been killed at the foot of a tree which was also occupied by bees. After imbibing the mixture, the woman changes into a jaguar and pursues her husband who, to escape from her, takes over the role of the bird-nester in M_1 and M_7–M_{12}. While the ogress is chasing the parrots he has thrown down to her, the man leaves the tree and runs off in the direction of a ditch, into which his wife falls and kills herself. Tobacco springs up from her corpse.

I introduced this myth and its Mataco (M_{22}) and Toba-Pilaga (M_{23}) variants to demonstrate the existence of a cycle leading from destructive fire (of a jaguar) to tobacco, from tobacco to meat (by way of M_{15}, M_{16}, M_{25}) and from meat to cooking fire, that is, constructive fire, obtained from the jaguar (by way of M_7–M_{12}). This cycle therefore defines a closed set, in which the agents are the jaguar, the wild pig and the bird-nester (*RC*, pp. 83–107). In so doing, it was not necessary to emphasize a detail in M_{24}, which must now be brought to the fore, in the light of the remarks that have just been made: the hero knocks

his sandals one against the other[30] 'in order to find honey more easily';
in other words, he addresses a 'tapped-out call' to honey, and as a result
obtains not only honey but also a snake. We may now ask what the
symbolic significance of this practice can be. As we shall see, echoes of it
can be found in other myths, although it would seem that it cannot be
directly corroborated from the available data.

Several myths found among the Tacana of eastern Bolivia, and
partially used at the beginning of this study (M_{194}–M_{197}) are concerned
with the quarrels between two divine brothers, the Edutzi, and meleros
(in Brazil, irára, *Tayra barbara*), each of whom carries a little drum which
makes a noise whenever they (male or female) are beaten. To rescue his
daughters from such ill-treatment (which is, however, well deserved,
since the daughters betray their divine husbands, either in their
capacity of wives or cooks), the melero turns them into macaws.
This is the origin of the ritual drum of the Tacana priests, which is made
with irára skin and beaten during religious rites to establish communication with the Edutzi (H.-H., pp. 109–10). Here again, then, we find
a link between the search for honey, of which the meleros are masters,
as their Spanish name indicates,[31] and a variety of the tapped-out call.

Whether or not the great linguistic and cultural group to which the
Tacana belong is connected with the Arawak family – the question
still remains unsettled – it nevertheless occupies a significant position
between its northern and western Arawak-speaking neighbours and
the remains of an old settlement to the south and the east, of which the
Tereno are the last survivors. Everything seems to indicate that the
Tereno myth just referred to formed a connecting link between certain
typical Chaco myths relating to the origin of tobacco and a group of
Tacana myths in which the hero becomes a bird-nester but which – as
far as one can tell in the case of myths that have been in contact with
Christianity for more than three centuries – are concerned rather with
the origin of hunting and cooking rites. In this connection, the Tacana
myths refer back to the Ge myths which were studied in Part One
(3 *b*.), and the heroine of which is a woman mad about honey, a role
which falls to the hero's wife in the Tereno myth. The affinity between
the Tacana and the Ge myths is also confirmed by the episode, which
crops up here and there, about the origin of the ant-eater replacing the

[30] Most of the Chaco tribes are in the habit of using sandals with wooden or leather
soles.

[31] In some Spanish-speaking areas, the ant-eater, to which we shall shortly have occasion
to refer again, is also called melero, 'honey-merchant', or colmenero 'bee-keeper' (Cabrera
and Yepes, pp. 238–40).

origin of the jaguar (Chaco), or the origin of the jaguar's eating habits (Ge myths about the origin of cooking fire, M_7–M_{12}), since it has been independently established (*RC*, pp. 189–91) that the animals are inverted within the group of two.

M_{300a}. *Tacana*. '*The story of the bird-nester*'

An Indian, who was a poor hunter but an expert farmer, lived with his wife and her mother and brothers. His in-laws treated him badly because he never brought home any game. However, he supplied them with manioc, maize and bananas.

One day, his brothers-in-law made him climb a tree, ostensibly to collect macaws' eggs; then they cut the liana he had used to hoist himself up and left him, after striking the roots of the tree to bring out from the hollow trunk the ha bacua, 'parrot-snake' (*Boa constrictor*), which lived there, in the confident hope that it would devour their victim.

Huddled at the tip of a branch (or hanging from the severed liana), starving and exhausted, the man nevertheless held off the snake's attacks for a whole day and night (other versions say three, eight or thirty days). He heard a noise *which at first he thought was being made by someone looking for honey* (my italics), but which in fact was being produced by the wood-spirit, Deavoavai, striking the roots of the big trees with his powerful elbows (or with his club) to bring out the boas which were his staple diet. The spirit shot an arrow which turned into a liana. The man used it to get down from the tree, but he was worried about what his rescuer might do to him. Deavoavai then killed the snake and, carrying the enormous mass of meat, went home, after inviting the man to accompany him.

The spirit lived under the roots of a big tree. His house was full of meat and his wife (a tapir or a frog, according to the versions) asked him to agree to relieve his protégé of the indolence which prevented him being a good hunter, and which the spirit drew out from his body in the form of evil-smelling exhalations or a soft mass (according to the versions).

Deavoavai presented the hero with inexhaustible supplies of food. He added a dish specially intended for the wicked in-laws and composed of fish (that the spirit had caught with timbó or by striking his legs with the backs of his hands), mixed with fat from the serpent's heart. Through eating this maleficent food they were transformed first into macaws and then into ha bacua, macaw-snakes, which

Deavoavai killed and ate on the following days (H.-H., pp. 180–83; second version, pp. 183–5: it limits the group of in-laws to the two brothers).

Before going on to examine a third and more complex version, I think it will be useful to clear the ground by means of a few remarks.

That the Tacana and Tereno myths are akin to each other cannot be doubted. In both cases the story deals with a hero who is ill-treated (physically or mentally) by an affine (his wife) or affines (his wife's mother and brothers) and who, in admittedly different circumstances, finds himself reduced to the position of a bird-nester persecuted by an ogre (jaguar or snake). In one instance, the transformation of the affine into an ogre is the result of eating a mixture of honey and snakes; in the other instance, the eating of a mixture of fish and snake-fat brings about the transformation of the affines into snakes of the same species as the ogre. The tapped-out call plays its part in every case: to obtain honey, and the little snakes into the bargain; to obtain fish which, when mixed with snake's fat, take the place of honey; and to obtain big snakes. The text of the Tacana myth strengthens the connection still further since the spirit Deavoavai's tapped-out call is at first attributed by the hero to someone looking for honey (which is actually the case in the Tereno myth). But had the noise been made by an ordinary person looking for honey, the hero would not have been rescued from his desperate situation, which demanded supernatural intervention. It follows that Deavoavai, the master of the forest (H.-H., p. 163), the initiator of techniques and rites (*ibid.*, pp. 62–3), is tantamount to a super-honey-seeker and therefore that the macaw-snakes he is looking for are themselves on the same level as a honey raised to the highest power. Conversely, with less power, the Indian honey-seeker is in the position of a master of the forest.

A Toba myth (M301) tells of a giant snake which is attracted by the noise made by honey-seekers bursting open hollow tree-trunks with their axes. It demands that they should pour fresh honey into its mouth, and then devours them. This snake announces its arrival by means of a loud noise: brrrumbrrummbrum! (Métraux 5, p. 71). This noise, as it is written in the source-text, makes one think of bull-roarers, a point I shall return to. Similarly, the ogre-snakes in the Tacana myth cry or whistle as they approach, and they are also excited by the rustling of the foliage when the wind rises. Throughout all these descriptions, then, the contrast between the tapped-out call and the whistled reply or call is maintained, within the wider framework of a contrast between discontinuous and continuous noise.

The Tacana myth, a transformation of the Tereno myth, is also a transformation of the one about the bird-nester (M_1). As I am tempted to put it, in this rapid aerial survey (necessary for the purposes of this volume), of the mass of mythic material which was reviewed in the opposite direction in the previous volume, we have clearly passed directly above M_1, in approaching the other myth. M_1 and M_{300a} have the same starting-point: a conflict between affines (in the first case, a father and a son, since Bororo society is matrilineal), and the second case, a wife's brothers and a sister's husband (thus respecting the Ge transformations of M_1, but by dint of reversing the roles, since it is now the sister's husband, not the wife's brother, who plays the part of the bird-nester):

	The bird-nester:	*His persecutor:*
Bororo (M_1):	wife's son	mother's husband
Ge (M_7-M_{12}):	wife's brother	sister's husband
Tacana (M_{300a}):	sister's husband	wife's brother

This 'transformation within a transformation' is accompanied by another in the unfolding of the narrative; this other transformation brings out a contrast between the Tacana myth and the Bororo and Ge myths, as might be expected, since the Tacana are patrilineal, unlike the Bororo-Ge group (with the exception of the Sherente, with whom the predictable transformation is observable along another axis, cf. *RC*, pp. 194–5). Consequently, the different sociological coding of the Bororo and Ge myths, when looked at from this angle alone, does not express a true opposition.

Both in the Bororo myth and in the Ge myths, the hero, who has climbed to the top of a tree or a rock, or who has got half-way up a rock-face, cannot come down again because his companion has removed the pole or ladder that he used to climb up. The events in the Tacana myth are much more complex: with the help of a liana, the hero has reached the top of a big tree; his companion then climbs up another liana or a smaller tree nearby and, from this vantage point, cuts the first liana at a height from which it is impossible for his victim to jump to the ground; then he comes down again and, according to one version, even goes to the trouble of chopping down the tree by means of which he has performed the misdeed. A third version combines the two concepts: first the hero climbs to the top of a palm tree from which he can reach a liana that he uses to get to the top of a taller tree; where-upon his brother-in-law makes his return impossible by chopping down the palm tree.

It would seem, then, that the Tacana myth aims at confusing the simple relationship established by the Bororo and Ge myths between the two men: one above, the other below; and that, to achieve this end, it invents a complicated process by which one of the protagonists remains up above, while the other almost reaches the same level and then comes down again. This cannot be a random effect, because the main versions are all very particular about the point. Moreover, the theme is taken up again and developed in the following episode, where the hero tries to avoid the snake, which climbs up the tree to get at him, by coming as far as possible down the severed liana, so that he is now, relatively speaking, at a lower level than his new persecutor.[32]

A group of transformations is now immediately obvious, but they differ as between the Bororo myth and the Ge myths.

In the Tacana, as in the Bororo myth, the hero owes his safety to a liana that he has, however, put to opposite uses: either he has hoisted

[32] It is no doubt this inversion which allows the Tacana myths to link the bird-nester theme with that of the visit to the underground world. One version (M_{300b}) tells the story of an Indian who was so lazy that his brother-in-law (his wife's brother) grew tired of supplying him with food and decided to get rid of him. He therefore got him to climb *down a liana* into an armadillo's hole, ostensibly to catch the animal; then he blocked up the entrance and went off. The armadillo accepted the man's presence, and introduced him to the Idsetti deha, a community of dwarfs without anuses, living exclusively on soup and the smell of food. The hero – either because he did not manage to provide the dwarfs with the missing orifice, or because the dwarfs were disgusted by the sight of him defecating and by the foul smell – persuaded the armadillo to take him back to his own people. Before doing so, the armadillo taught him a method of hunting which consisted in plunging into a pot of boiling water, and coming out through the bottom at the same time as the water. The hunter then found himself in a land stocked with game, where all he had to do was to kill the animals and roast the meat, which his wife then withdrew from the pot, after he had re-emerged from it. The wicked brother-in-law tried to imitate him, but since he did not possess the magic comb given by the armadillo, he was scalded to death (H.-H., pp. 351–5).

It will be noted that the hero of the Bororo myth, M_1, is a bird-nester, whose fundament is devoured by vultures, so that he is incapable of retaining the food he has swallowed: he is an (excessively) pierced person, whereas the hero of M_{300b}, who excavates the armadillo's hole, is both a piercing agent and himself (well) pierced, in comparison with the dwarfs, who are (excessively) stopped up. The transformation of boiled into roast meat or, to put it more accurately, the mediation of roast meat by way of boiled meat, raises problems that cannot be tackled at this stage.

himself to the top of the rock-face (the top of the top) or he has clung to the lower extremity (the bottom of the top). In spite of this difference, the use of a liana establishes a definite kinship between the two myths, and one is even tempted to suppose they have a common origin, since one episode is practically identical in both, although the syntagmatic sequence does not seem to make it inevitable.

The Bororo hero, who has no fundament and cannot digest food after being attacked by the vultures, remembers a tale told him by his grandmother and in which the same difficulty was overcome by means of an artificial posterior made of vegetable pulp. In a version, of which I shall shortly give a summary (M_{303}), the Tacana hero remembers stories told him by his grandmother about the appropriate ways of calling for the help of the wood-spirit, which eventually sets him free. Consequently, in both cases, a form of behaviour which is anal in the one instance and oral in the other is introduced as an effect of another myth, told by a grandmother. This narrative device is sufficiently unusual to imply the existence of an actual, and not simply a logical, kinship between the Bororo and Tacana myths.

Moreover, the analysis can be carried further in this direction. When I compared M_1 with other Bororo myths, I put forward the suggestion that the hero was a 'self-confined person', i.e. a boy approaching the age at which it is customary for young Indians to join male society, and who refused to leave the feminine and maternal environment. Let us compare this with the original failing of the Tacana hero. In a community where, it would seem, agriculture proper was a female activity (Schuller; Farabee 2, p. 155, in connection with the Tiatinagua, who are a sub-group of the Tacana family), he was an inefficient hunter but an expert farmer: he thus assumed a feminine role, and disappointed the expectations of his affines who, from the functional point of view, obtained nothing more (and above all nothing different) from him than what they had got previously from the woman whom they had made over to him. The myth confirms this interpretation by supposing matrilocal residence, which is contrary to the ethnographic reality (Farabee 2, p. 156).

Another Tacana myth deals with the symmetrically opposite possibility of a woman who tries to take on a masculine role:

M_{302}. *Tacana. 'The woman mad about meat'*

There was once a woman who wanted to eat meat, but her husband was a poor hunter and always came back empty-handed. She therefore decided to go hunting on her own and she went off after a stag, which she chased for several days without catching up with it, and which was really a man in animal form. The latter tried to convince the woman, as her husband had done when he attempted to dissuade her from going hunting, that deer were too fast for her; and he then made her a proposal of marriage. But the woman decided to go back home, although the deer-man told her she would never get there.

Actually, she continued her hunting expedition which had already lasted, not three days, as she thought, but three years. The deer-man caught up with her, pierced her with his antlers and left her corpse lying. A jaguar ate her flesh, except for the skin, which changed into a thick cluster of marsh plants. The lice in her hair became wild rice, and from her brain sprang termites and ant-hills.

The man, who at first had been amused by his wife's pretensions, eventually went to look for her. As he was travelling, he met several birds of prey, who informed him of the fate which had overtaken the unfortunate woman. Henceforth, they added, whenever a human being passed an ant-hill surrounded by marsh grasses, he would hear the termites whistling. In spite of the advice given him by the birds, the man insisted on pursuing his quest. He came to a big river, was carried away by the current, and his body was buried in the mud. From his corpse sprang two capybaras, a male and a female, which gave off a powerful stench. This was how these animals came into being (H.-H., pp. 58–9).

This myth has a two-fold interest. In spite of the very great geographical distances involved, it allows us to establish a link between Chaco (Toba, M_{213}; Mocovi, M_{224}) and Venezuelan myths (Warao, M_{223}), about one, or several frustrated (or) disobedient women, who are subsequently changed into capybaras. Admittedly, in this case, it is the husband who is transformed into an aquatic animal, whereas the woman is changed into aquatic plants (to which – for reasons which remain to be discovered – are added the whistling termites of the marshes).[33] The Bororo myth about the bird-nester (M_1) helps us to understand this divergency in the transformational system.

[33] The metamorphosis is always a punishment for excess: in this case, a woman has tried to act the man; in another case (M_{256}), a man tries to take advantage of his long penis to behave like a superman and, in a third, a child displays shocking cruelty (H.-H., pp. 81–3, 192–3).

Indeed – and this is the second point – the myths correspond to each other partially since, in both cases, an affine (wife or father) betrays his or her function by abandoning a husband or a son, and suffers the same punishment: pierced by the antlers of a stag, devoured by cannibalistic animals (jaguar or piranha fish), and the remains (peripheral, in the case of the skin, lice and brain, central in that of the viscera) give rise to marsh plants. And while the Tacana myth makes a capybara out of the man disjoined from his huntress-wife (although he was obstinately trying to find her, in spite of the advice given by the birds), it does so after the fashion of another Bororo myth (M_{21}), in which fisher-women, disjoined from their husbands (and who wish to remain so), change the latter into pigs. The Tacana woman refuses to yield to the advances of the stag-man, although he would have supplied her with meat. In one version of M_{21}, Bororo women receive supplies of fish from otters, which are really men, for having yielded to their advances (Rondon, p. 167).

When I compared the Bororo and Ge myths about the origin of wild pigs in *The Raw and the Cooked*, a transformation of a sociological nature enabled me to reduce the differences between them. The potential line of division which, in the Ge myths, runs between the brother and the married sister, is to be found, in the Bororo myths, between the wife and the husband:

$$[\text{Ge}](\triangle \overset{\#}{\frown} \circ = \triangle) \Rightarrow [\text{Bororo}] (\bigcirc \ \# \ \triangle)$$

If it were legitimate to postulate, on the basis of the Tacana myths, the existence of a little known social structure which seems to be no longer observable in fact, this would give us a third type of empirical situation among the Tacana, and one which would overlap with the other two. At the root of this situation there would be, instead of a state of tension, an urge to come together neutralizing the technological differences between the sexes: the man wants to be a plant-grower, like his wife; the wife wants to hunt like her husband. This desire to blur distinctions no doubt results in a cleavage, but a transformed one, since in this instance (M_{300a}) it occurs between a sister's husband and a wife's brother, the latter objecting to the fact that the wife's husband is a mere replica of the wife herself:

$$M_{300a}\left[\triangle \overset{\#}{\frown} (\bigcirc) = \triangle\right] \Rightarrow M_{302}\left[\text{game} \ // \ (\triangle) \equiv \bigcirc\right]$$

(For the transformation: *brother-in-law* ⇒ *game*, cf. RC, pp. 83–92).

A comparison of the pairs of animals used respectively by M_{21} and M_{302} brings out very clearly the ambiguity of the Tacana attitude about the opposition between the sexes, since the animals concerned are mixed entities:

Bororo (M_{21}) : fish			pigs
Tacana (M_{302})	capybaras ‖	deer	

The fish caught by the Bororo women in M_{21} are entirely connected with water, while the pigs into which their husbands are transformed are entirely connected with land, and may even be considered as chthonian animals. But the capybaras, which are amphibious rodents, illustrate the union of (terrestrial) water and earth; whereas the deer, considered as feminine animals by the Bororo (Colb. 1, p. 23), the Jivaro (Karsten 2, p. 374), the Mundurucu (Murphy 1, p. 93), the Yupa (Wilbert 7, p. 879) and the Guarani (Cadogan 4, p. 57), etc. – in this respect, too, in opposition to the pigs, which are masculine animals[34] – have an affinity with the sky and illustrate the union of earth and air. Perhaps the same explanation would be valid for the fact that the Tacana ogre, who replaces the Ge jaguar in the bird-nester myths, is also a mixed entity, a parrot-snake, which effects a union between earth and air and, like the deer in M_{302}, is faced with an opponent who is sometimes a man, sometimes a woman, but in either case always unwilling to give up the opposite attribute.

All these suppositions are what one might call mythico-deductive in nature; they depend upon a critique, in the Kantian sense of the word, of a body of myths in connection with which I am inquiring in what conditions they might have been produced by a supposedly unknown social structure; I am not, incidentally, under the illusion that they might be a mere reflection of that structure. But although we know very little about the ancient institutions of the Tacana, it is possible to find in them a degree of indirect confirmation of these suppositions, which gives the latter at least some likelihood of being true.

The tribes of the Tacana group practised a double initiation ceremony for boys and girls, involving ritual mutilation intended, it would seem, to stress an equivalence between the sexes in spite of their

[34] However, the form of the contrast is not constant, since the Kogi look upon pigs and armadillos as feminine animals, because they root about in the earth as if they were doing agricultural work (Reichel-Dolmatoff, Vol. I, p. 270).

apparent diversity. The same bamboo knife was used to cut the frenum of the penis in boys and to pierce the hymen in girls (Métraux 13, p. 446). Misbehaviour was punished by the parallel methods of exposure to ants, in the case of women, and to wasps, in the case of men (H.-H., pp. 373-4). And although Cavina women were forbidden to look upon idols or ritual objects, they enjoyed the rare privilege of playing the flute, while the men sang (Armentia, p. 13). This tendency towards sexual equality in the matter of ritual coincides with the interchangeability of the sexes to which the Tacana myths seem, in some obscure way, to aspire.

Also, it may well be that this particular form of dualism, as it finds expression in different ways in the rites and myths, is to be explained by the geographical situation of the Tacana (and their neighbours of the Panoan linguistic group) at the point of intersection of the lower cultures of the tropical forest with those of the Andean plateau. Although the myths we have considered so far have many points in common with those of the Chaco and central Brazil, they also differ from them through the presence, in the Tacana versions, of a divine protagonist, a member of a pantheon with no equivalent among the tribes of the lower cultures, and some of the gods of which even bear Quechua names. In the seventeenth century, there were still objects of Peruvian origin in the square temples erected in isolated spots by the Tacana (Métraux, loc. cit., p. 447).

Because of the role that these divine beings are called upon to play, all the mythic functions are, as it were, moved one stage up; but this general upward shift does not involve any disturbance in the functions themselves, which must continue to be ensured. The Tacana myths get out of the difficulty, we might say, by making two half-terms correspond to a function. Let us consider, for instance, the following transformation: the macaws eaten by the jaguar (in the Ge myths: M_7–M_{12}) are changed into snakes eaten by a divine being (in the Tacana myths: M_{300a}, M_{303}), who therefore exemplifies the Tacana transformation of the Ge jaguar as an imaginary ogre and real saviour. This group is not homogeneous, since the transformation of the macaws into snakes is an *episode which is internal* to the Tacana myth, whereas the transformation of the jaguar into a divine being is the result of an *external operation* carried out on the myth with the help of the Ge myths. To get over the difficulty and obtain a real relation of equivalence between the myths, it has to be accepted that, because of the intervention of a divine protagonist in the Tacana series, the correspondence should be established between three Tacana terms and two Ge terms, according to the formula:

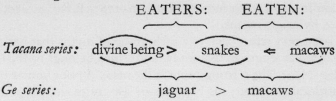

EATERS: EATEN:

Tacana series: divine being > snakes ⇐ macaws

Ge series: jaguar > macaws

As it happens, in the Tacana series, the divine being is a snake-eater and the snake a man-eater, although the humans who are changed first into macaws and then into snakes are themselves eaten by the divine being. In the Ge series, the jaguar replaces the snake (as a potential ogre) and behaves like the divine being (a real saviour), and the macaws are eaten by the jaguar in the same way as the macaw-snakes are by the divine being in the Tacana myths.

This may be the fundamental reason why the Tacana snakes must, logically, be mixed entities: snakes and birds. As snakes, they invert one term of the Ge myths (because of their subordination to a term superior to their own), and as macaws they reproduce the other term. But the main point is the renewed verification of the fact that structural analysis can be a help in historical reconstruction. Tacana specialists agree that these Indians may be of eastern origin: this would mean that they came from the area of the lower cultures and only at a later stage were exposed to Andean influence which imposed its pantheon on an older basis of belief. My interpretation tends in exactly the same direction. It may be added, on the strength of the first difference I noted between the Bororo myth and the Tacana myth with a bird-nester hero, that the complicated process resorted to by the second myth to ensure the isolation of the hero would be easily explicable if it were the result of a transformation of the corresponding episode in the Bororo and Ge myths. The complication, which is made inevitable by the respecting of an additional obligation, would appear gratuitous and incomprehensible if it were the effect of a transformation operating in the reverse direction.

Let us now return to our starting-point, i.e. M_{300a}, about which we already know that it is a transformation of three myths or groups of myths: $\{M_1\}$, $\{M_7-M_{12}\}$, $\{M_{22}-M_{24}\}$, to which we can now add a fourth group $\{M_{17}, M_{161}\}$, because of the double theme of the transformation into a great hunter of an unhappy hero, who is a prisoner at the top of a tree, from which he manages to get down thanks to a liana (which is also a *ficus* in the Tacana myths, H.-H., p. 178; cf. RC, p. 180, n. 20), produced by magic means.

This last aspect refers back to a fifth group of myths that has already been analysed at length in this study, and which belongs to the Guiana area (M_{237}–M_{239}). The starting-point is the same. A poor hunter is living in a matrilocal situation; his brothers-in-law try to get rid of him by delivering him up to a cannibalistic monster. A supernatural protector in the shape of a frog (like the wife of the supernatural protector in one of the Tacana versions) relieves him of the rottenness (stench, in the Tacana myths) which is causing his ill-luck, and presents him with miraculous arrows (which are shot without the archer taking aim, in the Guiana versions, or have blunt points in the Tacana myths). Therefore, whereas the bird-nester is a master of water in the Bororo myths and a master of cooking in the Ge myths, with the Tacana he becomes – like the Guiana hero – a master of hunting on whom depends the very existence of cooking, which requires meat as its material and fire (for roasting) and water (for boiling) as its means.

One version of the Tacana myth about the bird-nester brings out this new function very clearly. I shall skip the first part, which is a fairly exact reproduction of M_{300a}, and shall merely point out that in this version the divine protector is called Chibute. From the point of view that concerns us, this difference can be neglected since Chibute, the son of Deavoavai's sister and a monkey-man (H.-H., pp. 158–62) forms, with his maternal uncle, a semi-dioscuric pair, the terms of which are easily interchangeable: 'Although they are present in the Tacana pantheon as separate characters, Chibute and Deavoavai are, in this context, complementary and have the same semantic function, so that it is legitimate to use the hyphened name Chibute-Deavoavai to refer to the double personage' (*ibid.*, p. 178). After the hero's mother-in-law has consumed the maleficent food and has changed into a snake, ha bacua, her husband, accompanied by his sons, goes to look for her:

M_{303}. *Tacana. 'The education of boys and girls'*

The three men lost their way and, when they encountered some wild pigs, the sons followed the animals and changed into similar ones. The hero's father-in-law continued his search. He became so hungry that he ate his left arm. Suddenly Chibute appeared, chided him for his unkindness and told him that he would never again live among

humans but would be done to death by them. He would be changed
into a giant ant-eater, would wander aimlessly about the earth,
would live without a wife and would engender and bring forth his
children alone.

Moved by his wife's tears, the hero now set out after his parents-
in-law. Chibute showed him the old woman who had been transformed into a snake and was doomed to die of starvation, as well as
the ant-eater – showing him how to kill it, not with a bow and
arrows, but by clubbing it to death. The hero then expressed the
desire to learn how to hunt, and Chibute taught him how to make a
bow from the part of the trunk of the yellow chima palm tree which
faces east,[35] as well as a bow-string and two kinds of arrows. And the
man became the most proficient of hunters.

He in turn instructed backward pupils, with the help of Chibute.
In the case of this second generation, the god abolished certain
restrictions of a magical nature (the rule about making no more than
two arrows a year) but introduced others of a technical nature. The
myth thus moves from the art of hunting as a supernatural gift to
its age-old practice, which is surrounded by all sorts of precautions
and refinements that the myth describes too minutely for it to be
possible to reproduce them in any detail here. I summarize: nocturnal
bathing in water perfumed with the leaves of the emarepana shrub
(unidentified), the scent of which will spread through the forest,[36]
obligatory shooting of the first game sighted and the presentation
of the stomach to the instructor's wife, while the rest of the meat goes

[35] In connection with a similar rule observed by the Yurok in California, who made
their bows only of yew and from the part of the trunk facing uphill, according to some
sources, or towards the river, according to others, Kroeber comments with amused
condescension: 'This is exactly the kind of unpredictable restriction that Indians like to
impose upon themselves' (in Elmendorf, p. 87, n. 10). But even today, in France, the basket-
weavers of the Limousin know that the pliability of chestnut wood varies according to
whether the trees grow in hollows or on slopes, or on slopes with different exposures
(Robert, p. 158). In a rather different context, men whose job it is to float logs downstream
say that the wood tends to drift towards the banks during the full moon but remains in
midstream at the time of the new moon (Simonot, p. 26, n. 4). We may not understand the
reasons underlying a particular piece of lore, but this is not a reason for classifying it
automatically as a superstition.

[36] The Tunebo used a scented root to attract deer, and the Cuna used a plant called bisep
for the same purpose (Holmer–Wassen, p. 10). Indian hunters in Virginia rubbed their bodies
with angelica root, 'the hunting root', and, contrary to their usual practice, approached
from upwind, in the conviction that the smell would attract the deer (B. G. Hoffman). In
this case, too, the practice seems to be a positive technical device rather than a magic rite.
This can hardly be true, however, of the Sherente habit of piercing little boys' ears and
threading light wood sticks through them, with the intention of making the boys good
hunters and immunizing them against disease.

to the aged parents of the hunters. The latter never offer meat to the instructor himself but go to help him on his plantation ...

The young hunters had two sisters, the elder of whom seemed so attractive to the hero's son that he wanted to marry her. Chibute, after being again ritually summoned by means of the call: huu! huu! which the Indians utter using their hands as a speaking-trumpet, explained that the suitor should make a pile of wood in front of the hut of his future parents-in-law, and that the girl should take wood from it, if she wanted to signify agreement. The marriage was performed according to a ritual prescribed by Chibute, and a detailed description of which is to be found in the myth.

When the woman was pregnant, her father-in-law taught her how to ascertain the sex of the child in advance and what to do to ensure an easy birth and a lusty man-child. The myth enumerates other recommendations or prohibitions, the purpose of which is to make sure that the baby does not cry continuously, sleeps at night, has no bumps on its head, etc. I again summarize: bathing in water to which juice of the rijina liana (unidentified) has been added; refraining from eating the meat of the red howler monkey (in the case of the mother), of the jaguar or the tail of the black howler monkey (in the case of the child), and from touching the blue eggs of a forest bird or the soles of the coati's feet (in the case of the child). Next come precepts about the making of arrows, hunting procedures, clues for finding one's way in the forest and the cooking of game (roast red meat, stewed pig's stomach).[37]

Also through the medium of the hero, Chibute next taught the young couple how to spin, weave and make pottery scoured with the burnt bark of the caraipé tree (one of the chrysobalanae; cf. Whiffen, p. 96, n. 3).

[With reference to the whistling termites in M_{302}, it is interesting to note that the husband must *whistle* as he cuts the wood from which the stem of the spindle is to be made and that, for the spindle to rotate more quickly, the board on which it rests must be covered by the woman with the ashes of an ant-heap that the husband has previously set fire to.]

After Chibute had advised them to summon the spider to give

---

[37] This different way of treating the viscera links up with a remark by Whiffen about the tribes in the region between the Rio Issa and the Rio Japura. 'It is beast-like, in their opinion, to eat the liver, kidneys and other intestines of animals, though these may be made into soup or hot-pot' (p. 130, cf. also p. 134). The parts of the animal unworthy of being roasted or smoked can still be consumed provided they are boiled.

spinning lessons to the young woman, he himself taught her how to construct a loom with its various accessories, to prepare vats of dye and to cut and sew clothes for both sexes. He also said that the hunter should adorn himself with certain feathers, carry a game-bag containing the conglomerations of hair, pebbles and fat found in the stomachs or livers of several big animals, take great care to bury the liver of the wild pig on the spot where it had been killed (so that other individuals of the same species would return there) and to make the Master of pigs an offering of a woven pouch decorated with symbols, so that he would not take his herd away but would leave it in the salt-licks where the hunters could kill a lot of animals.[38]

The passage about hunting comes to an end with the description of various signs predicting success or failure. After which, the god discusses fishing, which demands a bow and featherless arrows, made with appropriate raw materials and according to the appropriate methods. There is a lengthy disquisition on dams, nets, the preparation of fish-poison and the transport and cooking of fish. Finally, the myth ends with technical advice for the perfect hunter: daily bathing, archery practice on ant-hills (but only when the moon is waxing); forbidden foods (pig's brains, turtle's liver) or recommended foods (the brains of the *Ateles* and *Cebus* monkeys, pucarava and turtle hearts, eaten raw); correct manners (never to eat the remains of meals left in the pots); the proper way to prepare and carry one's hunting gear; body paintings, etc. The myth ends by saying that Chibute added a great many other instructions that the hero was to pass on to his son and his descendants (H.-H., pp. 165–76).

And this is only part of the complete list! Even in its fragmentary form, this myth contains more ethnographical information than an actual observer could collect during a stay of several months or even years in a tribe. Each single rite, prescription or prohibition would be worthy of a critical and comparative study. I shall give only one example which I have chosen because it is more directly relevant to the present analysis than some of the others.

To determine the sex of an unborn child, the god tells the parents to compare their dreams. If they have both dreamed about a round object, such as the fruit of a genipa (*Genipa americana*), a motacú (a palm tree: *Attalea* sp.) or an assaï (another palm tree: *Euterpe oleracea*),

[38] This passage confirms a deduction in *RC*, p. 108, where I suggested that the pig was thought of simultaneously as meat and as master of meat. Identical rules about hunting existed among the Yuracaré.

they will have a son. The child will be a daughter if their dreams were concerned with a long object, such as a manioc root or a banana.

The free association of ideas characteristic of our culture would no doubt give the opposite result: round for a girl, long for a boy. It is easy to verify the fact that, generally speaking, the sexual symbolism of the South American Indians, whatever the lexical terms it uses, is in general homologous with that of the Tacana and therefore contrary to ours. Here are a few examples relating to the sex of the unborn child. According to the Waiwai of Guiana, if the parents hear the woodpecker whistling, swis-sis, the baby will be a boy; but if the bird is tapping, tororororo, it will be a girl (Fock, p. 122; cf. Derbyshire, p. 157). In Ecuador, the Catio tease a praying mantis: if it responds by putting forward both front legs, a girl is to be expected, whereas one leg indicates a boy (Rochereau, p. 82). This symbolism can be compared with the sexual classification of the Amazonian wooden drums: the big drum producing low notes is female, while the little, high-pitched one is male (Whiffen, pp. 214–15).[39] We thus have a series of equivalences:

female : male :: long : round :: tapped :
          whistled :: whole : half :: big : little :: deep : shrill

In *The Raw and the Cooked* (p. 130), I brought out a contrast, inherent in the feminine sex, between elongated and rounded vulvae. But if it is remembered that the Mundurucu myth to which we were referring declares that the (M_{58}) pretty vulvae are the roundest ones (Murphy 1, p. 78), we arrive at the following proposition:

(*desirable woman*) more : less :: (*vulva*) round : elongated

which appears to contradict the preceding one, unless we bear in mind the latent feeling of repulsion for the female body, common among South American Indians, so that it is only desirable to them, or even tolerable, when, in respect of its odour and physiological functions, it falls short of the full manifestation of all its potentialities (*RC*, pp. 182–3, 269–71).

[39] The method of the Caingang-Coroado, which is less symbolical and more rationalized, is closer to our systematization. They hold out a club to the small ant-eater; if the animal takes it, the child will be a boy; if not, a girl (Borba, p. 25). I do not claim that the equation given above is valid for the symbolism of all tribes. For instance, the Umutina seem to be an exception, since they divide up the fruits of the bacaba do campo palm tree (*Oenocarpus* sp.) into 'male' and 'female' according to whether they are respectively long or short (Schultz 2, p. 227: Oberg, p. 108), and the Baniwa attribute 'flattened' arms to men, 'round' arms to women (M_{276b}). But it is precisely these differences in the representational systems which deserve closer study than they have so far received.

The first series of equivalences can no doubt be simplified, if we consider that the contrast between whistled and tapped echoes the other acoustic contrast between shrill and deep notes; but there remains the problem of why women are thought of as being more 'substantial' than men, if we can sum up the differences in a colloquial term. It would seem, in this connection, that the South American Indians think more or less along the same lines as the native tribes in the mountains of New Guinea, who base a strongly marked distinction between the sexes on the belief that female flesh is distributed 'vertically' along the bones, whereas male flesh is set 'horizontally', i.e. at right-angles to the axis of the bone. This anatomical difference is supposed to explain why women mature more quickly than men and marry on an average ten years earlier and, even in adolescence, can contaminate with their menstrual blood boys who remain particularly vulnerable at that age, since they have not yet been admitted to the social and psychological status of manhood (Meggitt, pp. 207, 222, nn. 5, 6).

In South America, too, a *longitudinal/transversal* contrast, formulated in different terms, was used to express differences of authority and status. Among the ancient tribes of the Rio Negro area, a chieftain could be recognized by the fact that he wore a cylinder of hard stone, pierced lengthwise, i.e. along its axis, whereas the pendants worn by ordinary people, although also cylindrical, were pierced crosswise. We shall encounter this distinction again later; it has some analogy with the difference between the dance sticks of the southern Guarani, which are hollow or solid according to the sex of the performer. It is logical to look upon a cylinder which has been pierced lengthwise as being comparatively more hollow than a similar cylinder which has been pierced across and whose mass therefore remains almost solid.

After giving this one example of the wealth and complexity of the commentaries that might be made on any of the beliefs, customs, rites, prescriptions and prohibitions listed in M_{303}, let us now consider the myth from a more general point of view. We saw that it is a transformation not only of the groups $\{M_1,\}$, $\{M_7-M_{12}\}$, $\{M_{22}-M_{24}\}$, $\{M_{117}$ and $M_{161}\}$, but also of the Guiana group $\{M_{237}-M_{239}\}$. This is not all, since, after noting in passing the fleeting reference to $\{M_{15}-M_{18}\}$ (the transformation of the wicked brothers-in-law into wild pigs), we must now examine the last transformation illustrated by the Tacana myth: that of the group of Ge myths $\{M_{225}-M_{228}$ and $M_{232}\}$, which, as the reader will remember, also deals with the origin of the ant-eater and the training of boys as hunters and (or) warriors.

In *The Raw and the Cooked*, I established an implicit transformational relationship (through the medium of M_5, itself a transformation of M_1) between one myth of this group (M_{142}) and the bird-nester myth, by means of an equivalence between the horizontal disjunction (*upstream-downstream*) and the vertical disjunction (*sky-earth*) of their respective heroes (*RC*, pp. 257–9). If we now move from the Ge myths to the Tacana myths, in which we find the bird-nester image in an undistorted form, we are still obeying the imperative which obliges us to go over the same ground in the opposite direction.

The Ge and Tacana heroes, after their voluntary or involuntary, horizontal or vertical, aquatic or celestial, disjunction, encounter ogres: various species of falcon in the Ge myths, parrot-snakes in the Tacana ones. Since the contrast between birds of prey and parrots is constant in the South American myths, in the form: *flesh-eating, fruit-eating* (birds), the ethnozoological system common to the two groups of myths would be complete if the Ge falcons could be classified as Herpetotheres, the group of snake-eaters, in the same way as the Ge and Chaco jaguars are parrot-eaters. But in at least one version, one of the birds is a *Caprimulgus*, not a falcon, and in other cases the particular kind of falcon remains unspecified.

Be that as it may, in all cases the cannibalistic animals answer to a tapped out call, which comes either, in the Tacana myths, from the hero's enemies (and then from the helpful god) or, in the Ge myths, from the hero himself (cf. also M_{177} in Krause, p. 350, where the hero beats the water: ton, ton, ton … to cause the arrival of the killer eagles). In some cases, one or both grandparents change into ant-eaters (M_{227}, M_{228}, M_{230}), in other cases, the father, or the father and mother of the hero's wife, undergo the same fate (M_{229}, M_{303}). On pp. 132–5 I discussed the following contrasts or transformations:

(*a*) capybara (*long teeth*) | ant-eater (*toothless*);
(*b*) grandparents $\Rightarrow$ ant-eaters (*eaters of ant-hills*);
   hero's head $\Rightarrow$ ant-hill;
   parents-in-law $\Rightarrow$ eaters of ant-eaters.

A comparable group can be found among the Tacana:

   father-in-law $\Rightarrow$ ant-eater (M_{303});
   wife's brain $\Rightarrow$ ant-hill (M_{302});
   hero's parents $\Rightarrow$ eaters of ant-eaters (M_{303});

in connection with two myths M_{302} and M_{303}, one of which deals with the origin of the capybara, the other with the origin of the ant-eater.

Finally, in both the Tacana group and the Ge group, one myth (M_{226}, M_{303}) stands out from the others and is tantamount to a treatise in initiation. But a difference becomes apparent at the same time and it will provide the solution to a methodological and theoretical difficulty, to which the reader's attention must first be drawn.

In conducting the inquiry which has been in progress since the beginning of the previous volume, I have proceeded as if I were scanning the whole mythological field, beginning at an arbitrarily chosen point and moving methodically this way and that, up and down, from right to left and from left to right, in order to reveal certain types of relationships between myths situated consecutively along the same line or between those below or above each other on different lines. But in either case a distinction has to be drawn between the scanning operation itself and the myths it successively or periodically illuminates and which are the object of the operation.

However, in the case of M_{303}, it is as if the relationship between the operation and its object had been reversed, and in two ways. First, the scanning movement which was originally horizontal suddenly appears to be vertical. Secondly – and more importantly – M_{303} is to be defined as a group of exceptional points in the mythological field, and its unity as an object becomes intangible outside the scanning operation itself, which links the points together in its indissoluble movement: the scanning movement therefore represents the mythic substance of M_{303} and the points touched upon the series of operations to which we are subjecting it:

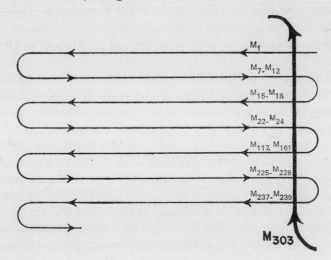

M

The first explanation that comes to mind when we try to account for this two-fold inversion, which is both geometrical and logical, is that a mythic system can only be grasped in a process of becoming; not as something inert and stable but in a process of perpetual transformation. This would mean that there are always several kinds of myths simultaneously present in the system, some of them primary (in respect of the moment at which the observation is made) and some of them derivative. And while some kinds are present in their entirety at certain points, elsewhere they can be detected only in fragmentary form. Where evolution has gone furthest, the elements set free by the decomposition of the old myths have already been incorporated into new combinations.

In one sense, this explanation is obvious since it depends on facts that can hardly be denied: the myths break down and, as Boas said, new myths are made out of their remains. However, it cannot be entirely satisfactory because, clearly, the primary or derivative character that we might thus be led to attribute to a given myth would not belong to it intrinsically, but would be chiefly a function of the order of presentation. As I showed in *The Raw and the Cooked* (pp. 1–6), this order cannot be other than arbitrary, since the myths cannot be judged in advance but give a spontaneous clarification of their reciprocal relationships. Therefore, had I decided to study M_{303} first, for reasons every bit as contingent as those which led me to give the number 1 to the Bororo myth about the bird-nester, M_{303} and not M_1 would have displayed the peculiar properties I am now discussing. Besides, this is not the first time we have encountered them. In connection with other myths (such as M_{139}), I had to bring into play conceptions such as intersection, cross-section and juxtaposition of armatures (*RC*, pp. 252–5).

The difficulty of the problem arises, then, from the necessity of taking two different perspectives simultaneously into account. The historical perspective is absolute and independent of the observer, since we must accept as a fact that a cross-section made at any point in the material of the myths always has a certain degree of diachronic thickness because this material, a heterogeneous mass from the historical point of view, is a conglomeration of elements which have not evolved at the same rate and cannot therefore be said to come before or after. The other perspective is that of structural analysis, but the analyst knows that, wherever he starts from, he will, after a time, inevitably come up against a relationship of uncertainty as a result of which any myth examined at a late stage in the inquiry is at once a local transformation of the myths immediately preceding it and a complete totalization of all or part of the myths included in the field of investigation.

This relationship of uncertainty is no doubt the price that has to be paid for trying to understand a closed system: at first, it is possible to learn a great deal about the nature of the relationships between the elements of a system, the general economy of which remains obscure; and in the end, relationships which by now have become redundant do more to provide information about the general economy of the system than to bring to light new types of connections between the elements. It would seem, then, that we can never know the two things at once and that we have to be satisfied with collecting information related either to the general structure of the system or to the special links between certain of the elements, but never to both at once. And yet, one kind of knowledge necessarily precedes the other, since it is impossible to inquire directly into the structure without being previously acquainted with a sufficient number of relationships between the elements. Consequently, whatever the starting-point chosen in practice, the nature of the results will change as the inquiry progresses.

But, on the other hand, it is impossible that those results should be entirely and exclusively subject to the internal limitations of structural analysis. For, if this were so, the primary or secondary character of myths belonging to very real societies would have only a relative value, and would depend on the perspective chosen by the observer. One would therefore have to give up all hope of using structural analysis to arrive at historical hypotheses. Or rather, such hypotheses would be no more than optical illusions doomed to be dispelled, if not to be reversed, whenever the mythologist chose to lay out his material differently. But, in several instances, I have put forward interpretations while at the same time claiming that, since they were irreversible, or reversible at too great a cost, they made it possible to assert, not merely relatively but absolutely, that of two given myths one represented an earlier, the other a later, stage in a transformation which could not have occurred in the opposite direction.

To try to overcome the difficulty, let us consider M_{303} in its relationship to all the other myths or groups of myths of which it is a transformation. No doubt it strikes us as being simultaneously a particular item in the group of three transformations and as an exceptional expression of the group, which it summarizes within itself as much as, or more than, we can manage to complete the group with its help. This paradoxical situation is a result of the multi-dimensional nature of the mythic field, which structural analysis explores, and at the same time establishes, by executing a spiral movement. A series, which is at first linear and recoiled upon itself, develops into a surface which in turn engenders a volume. Consequently, the first myths studied are little more than a syntagmatic chain, the message of which is to be decoded by reference to paradigmatic sets that the myths, at this stage, have not yet supplied, and which must be sought outside the mythic field, that is in ethnography. But later, and as the inquiry, through its catalysing action, brings into focus the crystalline structure of the field and its volume, a two-fold phenomenon occurs. On the one hand, the paradigmatic relationships internal to the field increase in number much more rapidly than the external relationships, which indeed reach a ceiling, as soon as all the available ethnographical information has been assembled and utilized, so that the context of each myth consists more and more of other myths and less and less of the customs, beliefs and rites of the particular population from which the myth in question derives. On the other hand, the distinction between an internal syntagmatic chain and an external paradigmatic set, which was clear at the outset, tends to disappear both in theory and in practice since, once the mythic field has been brought into being, the arbitrarily chosen axis along which the exploration is carried out, defines not only the series serving – according to the requirements of the moment – as a syntagmatic chain, but also the cross-connections which, at every point in the series, function as paradigmatic sets. According to the perspective adopted by the analyst, any series can therefore serve as a syntagmatic chain or a paradigmatic set, and the initial choice will determine the (syntagmatic or paradigmatic) character of all the other series. This, in fact, is the phenomenon that has been illustrated in the course of the analysis of M_{303}, since the syntagmatic chain formed by this myth can be changed into a paradigmatic set for the interpretation of any of the myths of which it is a transformation, while those myths in their turn would form a paradigmatic set capable of throwing light on M_{303}, if we had begun our inquiry from the opposite end.

All this is true, yet it leaves out of account an aspect of M_{303} which differentiates it absolutely from the other myths with which I have compared it, although at the present stage of the discussion I cannot suggest any historical or logical cause for the difference and therefore must not let myself be put off by the antinomy of structure and event.

All the myths that I have recognized as belonging to the same group as M_{303} refer to the education either of boys or of girls, but never of both together (or if, like M_{142} and M_{225}, they do so, it is to make the special, and therefore equally restrictive, suggestion of a similar *lack* of education). From this point of view, M_{303} introduces an innovation, since it consists of a co-educational treatise equally valid for the Emile of the Ge family and the Sophie[40] of the Guiana-Amazonian tribes.

This original feature in M_{303} confirms, in the first place, the hypothesis about the reversibility of the sexes in the Tacana institutions and way of thinking that I arrived at by purely deductive means.[41] Among these particular Indians, the admission of boys and girls to adulthood is not the result of the ritual establishment of a differential gap between the sexes, leading to a permanent belief that one is superior to the other. On the contrary, the two sexes graduate together, by means of an operation which minimizes their anatomical differences and of simultaneous instruction in the absolute necessity of collaboration (for instance, the husband is involved at several points in the making and the use of the spindle, although spinning is a female occupation).

Secondly, there is a difference between M_{303} and the other myths I have put in the same group: M_{303} is both like them and goes beyond them. The other myths consider only one aspect of a problem which, in theory, has two, whereas M_{303} tries to juxtapose both aspects and put them on the same level. It is therefore more complex, logically, and is, rightly so, a transformation of more myths than any one of the others is. We can carry the argument further: in so far as the mythology of honey, which we have used as a guiding-line, has a badly brought up

[40] TRANSLATORS' NOTE: Emile and Sophie are the pupils in J.-J. Rousseau's educational treatise, *Emile*.

[41] M_{303} provides a particularly striking illustration of this reversibility in the episode about the transformation of the father-in-law into an ant-eater which thereafter will live alone, without a mate, and will conceive and bring forth its young on its own. A common belief in South America, from the Rio Negro (Wallace, p. 314) to the Chaco (Nino, p. 37), is that there is no such thing as a male ant-eater and that the females impregnate themselves, without help from any other agent. The link between the Tacana myth and those of the Guiana area is further strengthened by the transformation of the sons of the father-in-law into pigs, since, because of a stripe on its coat, the Kalina call the giant ant-eater 'the father of the collared peccaris' (Ahlbrinck, under 'pakira'). Whatever may be the force of this last detail, the Tacana transformation of the female ant-eater, capable of conceiving independently, into a male capable of conceiving and producing young, certainly shows that the Tacana ascribe an equivalence to the sexes, which makes them commutative both ways with the same facility.

I have not found the belief in the single-sexed ant-eater among the Toba, but it is indicated indirectly by the fact that even today, when they come across the droppings of the giant ant-eater in the course of a hunt, they change their course, being convinced that the animal leads a solitary life and that there can be no other game near it (Susnik, pp. 41–2).

girl as its protagonist, as soon as it changes into a mythology of hunting, the heroine becomes a hero, a well (or badly) brought up boy. We thus arrive at a meta-group, the terms of which are transformable into each other, depending on the masculine or feminine values of the chief character and the type of techno-economic activity referred to. But all these myths remain, as it were, in the state of semi-myths, which are still to be synthesized by the fitting of their respective series into the framework of a single myth which would aim at filling the gap (since an education specially conceived for one sex could only appear as a lack to the other) by resorting to the third solution of an equal education for all, given as far as possible in common. This is precisely the Tacana solution, which may have been put into practice in the ancient way of life and, in any case, imagined in their myths and justified by them.

We do not know what type of historical evolution would explain this empirically observed fact of the coexistence of opposite educational principles in different parts of tropical America. Does the mixed solution adopted by the Tacana (and perhaps by their Panoan neighbours who, according to Greenberg's recent classification, belong to the same macro-Panoan linguistic family) represent a more ancient form, which split up to produce the masculine initiation rites of the Ge and the feminine-biased ones of the tribes of the Guiana-Amazonian area (and, to a lesser degree, of the Chaco)? Or have we to adopt the opposite hypothesis of a reconciliation or synthesis of conflicting traditions achieved by the Tacana and the Pano, in the course of a migration from west to east? Structural analysis cannot solve such problems. But at least it has the merit of raising them and even of suggesting that one solution is more plausible than another, since my formal comparison of an episode in M_{303} with the corresponding episode in M_1 and M_7-M_{12} led to the conclusion that the Tacana myth may be derived from the Bororo-Ge myths but that the opposite hypothesis gives rise to enormous difficulties. This being so, the co-educational ideal of the Tacana may result from an attempt to adapt an eastern tradition of masculine initiation to a western tradition which laid the chief stress on female education. The attempt may have led to the revision of myths belonging to one or other of the two traditions so that they could be integrated into a single system, although the reciprocal transformational character of these myths suggests that they themselves arose, by differentiation, from a more ancient source.

PART FOUR THE INSTRUMENTS OF DARKNESS

Nunc age, naturas apibus quas Iuppiter ipse
addidit expediam, pro qua mercede canoros
Curetum sonitus crepitantiaque aena secutae
Dictaeo caeli regem pavere sub antro.

Virgil, *Georgics*, IV, vv. 149-52

1 *Din and Stench*

The general remarks I have just made must not cause us to lose sight of the problem which brought us back to the Tereno myth about the bird-nester (M_{24}), and which led us to compare it with the Tacana myths on the same theme (M_{300}–M_{303}). It was a question of understanding the recurrence in these myths of a 'tapped-out call', addressed in other myths to the tapir, an animal seducer, but here addressed to honey, a food which is also seductive, but which is replaced in the Tacana myths (although the link can always be discerned) by a devouring animal, the macaw-snake. Were we in need of a comparison outside Tacana mythology to confirm the group's unity, it would be amply supplied by the Tereno myth which combines the three terms: honey, snake and macaw, in order to arrive at the notion of a destructive kind of honey (by the addition of snake meat), leading to the transformation of the female consumer into a devouring jaguar – a devourer, as it happens, of macaws or parrots – and men too, whereas in the Tacana myth, it is the man (a bird-nester) who is in the position of macaw-eater.

This Tereno myth, in which honey is raised to a negative power by the addition of snake meat and functions as a means, sets out to explain the origin of tobacco, which lies on the far side of honey, just as menstrual blood (which the woman uses to poison her husband) lies on the hither side of honey. I have already referred on many occasions to the polar system constituted by tobacco and honey, and I propose to return to it later. As for the contrast between honey and menstrual blood, we have already encountered it in myths which assign variable values to the relationship between the two terms: these values may approximate to each other, when the master of honey is a male character who is not put off by a young girl who is indisposed (M_{235}); they are reversed, while still remaining far removed from each other, at the end of the series of transformations which led us from the character of the girl mad about honey (or about her own body) to the jaguar which was chaste but mad about menstrual blood (M_{273}).

Another link is observable between the Tereno myth and a group of Tacana myths to which I have referred on several occasions (M_{194}–M_{197}). In M_{197}, the daughters of the irára (the 'melero', an animal master of honey) fed their husbands on a beer into which they mixed their excrement; therefore, like the heroine of the Tereno myth, they behaved as their husbands' poisoners. When he discovered his wife's criminal machinations, the Tereno Indian set off in search of honey, the instrument of his revenge, and he knocked the soles of his sandals together in order to find it more easily. Having similarly become aware of the situation, the Tacana husbands beat their wives, thus causing the little wooden drums they had attached to their wives' backs to sound: pung, pung, pung (M_{196}).[1] On hearing this sound, and in order to prevent them being so ill-used, their father changed the women into macaws:

poison:	tapped-out call:	consequence of vengeance:
M_{24}: menstrual blood	cause (of means) of vengeance	woman changed into (jaguar) eater of macaws
M_{197}: excrement	result (of means) of vengeance	women changed into macaws

A more direct link exists between menstrual blood, excrement and honey. In M_{24}, the husband gives his wife poisoned honey in exchange, as it were, for the menstrual blood he receives from her; in M_{197}, the cook exchanges (with herself) the excrement she mixed with the beer, for the honey she should normally have used.

Consequently, however obscure the episode of the 'tapped-out' call may still appear, its presence in the Tereno myth, which is corroborated by other myths, does not seem to be explicable by exceptional or fortuitous causes. Nor would it seem to be explicable as a relic of some technical device (making a noise to drive off the swarm) or magical practice (anticipatory imitation of the sound of the honey gatherer's axe after he has located the swarm), since such interpretations, having no ethnographical foundation, are inapplicable to the 'tapped-out call' as we have found it described by the Tacana, in a mythic context which has undergone transformation.

If the honey-gatherer's gesture of knocking his sandals together cannot be explained by accidental causes, nor by some technical or magical purpose directly linked with his search, what place can the use of an improvised instrument of noise have in the myth? In an attempt to solve this problem, which does not merely involve an ap-

[1] The Kalina of Guiana also use the skin of the irára to cover small-sized drums (Ahlbrinck, under 'aira').

parently insignificant detail in a very short myth, but also raises by implication the whole question of the theory of calls and, beyond that, the theory of the whole system of musical instruments, I propose to introduce two myths belonging to the Tucuna Indians who live on the banks of the Solimões river, between 67–70° longitude west, and whose dialect is now classed with that spoken by the more northerly Tucano:

M304. Tucuna. 'The family which was changed into jaguars'

An elderly man and his wife set off, along with other men, for an unknown destination, perhaps for the other world. The old man taught his companions how to shoot an arrow at the trunk of a tururi tree. No sooner had the arrow touched the tree than a layer of bark came away from the entire length of the trunk. Each person chose a piece of bark, and, after hammering it out to make it bigger, painted black spots on it to look like the jaguar's markings, and put it on. Having thus transformed themselves into jaguars, the hunters roamed the forest massacring and eating Indians. But others discovered their secret and resolved to exterminate them. They killed the old man while he was attacking them, disguised as a jaguar. His wife heard them utter the murderer's name. Disguised as a jaguar, she ran after him and tore him to pieces.

The old woman's son had two children. One day the old woman accompanied her son and other hunters to a place where envieira trees grew. These are fruit-bearing trees on which toucans feed. Each hunter chose a tree and climbed up it in order to kill the birds with his blow-pipe. Suddenly, the old woman appeared in the shape of a jaguar and devoured the dead birds which had fallen at the foot of the tree up which her son had climbed. After she had gone, the man came down and picked up the remaining birds. He then tried to climb back up the tree, but a thorn got caught in his foot and he bent down to remove it. At that moment the old woman leapt on his neck and killed him. She took out his liver, wrapped it in some leaves and took it back to her grandsons, claiming that it was a tree fungus. The children, however, who had become suspicious because of their father's absence, looked in the pot and recognized a human liver. They followed their grandmother into the forest, saw her change into a jaguar and devour their father's corpse. One of the boys plunged a spear, the tip of which was made from a wild pig's tooth, into the ogress's anus. She fled, and the children buried their father's remains in an armadillo's burrow.

They had already returned to their house when the old woman arrived, moaning. On their feigning concern, she explained that she had hurt herself when she fell on a tree stump in the plantation. The children, however, examined the wound and saw that it had been caused by the spear. They lit a big fire behind the house and found a hollow trunk of an ambaúva tree, one end of which they split lengthwise so that the two wooden tongues banged noisily against each other when they threw the trunk onto the ground. They thus caused such a terrible din that the old woman came out of the house, enraged that so much noise should be made in the vicinity of a sick person. They at once seized hold of her and threw her into the fire where she was burnt alive (Nim. 13, pp. 147–8).

Before analysing this myth, I shall give a few explanations of a botanical and ethnographical nature. Three kinds of tree are mentioned in M₃₀₄: tururi, envieira and ambaúva. The first name, which does not correspond to any clearly defined species, refers to 'several species of *Ficus* and artocarpus' (Spruce 1, p. 28); the inner layer of bark is used for making clothes and receptacles. Envieira (envira, embira) probably refers to the *Xylopia*, the fibrous bark of which is used in the making of mooring ropes, splices and shoulder-belts, and which produces aromatic seeds of which the toucans are very fond, according to the myth, and which the Kalina of Guiana use to make necklaces (Ahlbrinck, under 'eneka', 4, §c). The ambaúva or embaúba, which means literally 'non-tree' (Stradelli 1, under 'embayua'), or as French foresters would say *faux-bois*,[2] is a *Cecropia*. The Tupi name covers several species of which the most often quoted is *Cecropia peltata*, the drum tree (Whiffen, pp. 134, n. 3; 141, n. 5), thus called because its naturally hollow trunk lends itself to the making of drums, as well as dance sticks and horns (Roth 2, p. 465). Finally, the fibrous bark of the *Cecropia* makes stout ropes (Stradelli, *loc. cit.*).

The myth therefore introduces a triple pattern of trees, all used to make clothes and utensils from bark, and one of which, since it is hollowed out by nature, also supplies the raw material for several musical instruments. Now the Tucuna, who make the cylinder of their (skin) drums from embaúba wood (Nim. 13, p. 43), closely associate music and the masks of pounded bark, which play an important part in their festive celebrations, and the making of which they have carried

---

[2] TRANSLATORS' NOTE: Littré's dictionary defines *faux bois* as branches which do not produce fruit and cannot be used for ornament. The term implies trees without any commercial value.

to a high degree of excellence. We may already suppose that M_{304} poses a special problem (but one which for the time being remains obscure) in connection with the making of bark masks and costumes. This aspect becomes more obvious when it is recalled that, at the end of the celebrations, the visitors, who had been disguised in tunics made from the bark of the tururi tree, and decorated with fringes made from the tururi or envira (envieira) tree which almost reached the ground, handed these tunics over to their hosts in exchange for gifts of smoked meat (Nim. 13, p. 84). Now, in the myth too, the fact of wearing a bark tunic which turns him into a jaguar puts the hunter into the position of an acquirer of meat: human, not animal, meat, of course; but the bark, which provides the raw material for the tunic, belongs also to a category which is exceptional in its own way, since it was obtained by magical means, that is, was 'hunted' and not torn from the tree, and was immediately available in the form of long strips, instead of having to be laboriously peeled off the trunk (Nim. 13, p. 81).

Making allowances for the geographical distance, the regular pattern of the transformations which make it possible to move from the Tucuna myth to the Chaco myths (M_{22}–M_{24}) about the origin of the jaguar and tobacco is quite striking:

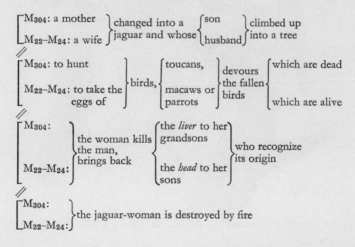

In order to interpret correctly the episode in M_{304}, in which the hero, whose foot has been pierced by a thorn, is killed by the jaguar while trying to remove the cause of the trouble, it must be recalled that, in M_{246}, which belongs to the same group as M_{22}–M_{24}, the ogress turned jaguar perishes on a tree-trunk which bristles with thorn-like spears (they are changed back into thorns in M_{241}, just as the ogress in M_{24} dies as a result of ingesting *strong* (*stinging*) honey, which makes her itch all over). It is also worth noting that, while the heroine of M_{24} poisons her husband with menstrual blood, the heroine of M_{304} brings back their father's liver to her grandsons. South American Indians

Figure 16. Toucans. (A drawing by Valette, after Crevaux, *loc. cit.*, p. 82.)

believe that the liver is an organ formed from coagulated blood and that, in women, it acts as a reservoir for menstrual blood.

In order to arrive at a satisfactory interpretation of the other transformations, it would be essential to elucidate the semantic position of toucans. This is no easy undertaking because the birds appear very infrequently in the myths. I shall do no more than suggest a theory, without claiming that it can be definitively established.

Several species of the *Rhamphastos* family are referred to as toucans. Their chief characteristic is an enormous beak which is, at the same time, very light in weight because it is porous under its horny tegument. Toucans prefer to hop from branch to branch rather than fly. Their feathers are almost entirely black, except over the breast where they are brilliantly coloured, and consequently much sought after for the purposes of ornamentation. These feathers have been prized by others besides the Indians; the ceremonial coat which belonged to Pedro II, Emperor of Brazil, and which can still be admired in the Rio de Janeiro museum, is made from the yellow, silky feathers of the toucan.

The ornamental use of feathers suggests a comparison between the toucan and the parrot and the macaw, but it is in partial contrast to the latter birds in respect of diet. The psittacidae are fruit-eating, the toucan is omnivorous and eats indiscriminately fruit, seeds and small animals, such as rodents and birds. M_{304} mentions that the toucan is particularly fond of aromatic seeds. The fact that in German it is called: *Pfefferfresser*, 'pepper-eater', is less surprising than Ihering (under 'tucano') is inclined to believe, especially since Thevet (Vol. II, p. 939a, b) refers to the toucan as a 'pepper-eater', which propagates pimentoes through the seeds in its droppings.

So far, within the range of bird species, we have consistently met with a major contrast between the psittacidae and the aquilinae (true eagles do not exist in South America). The preceding remarks about the toucan suggests that it occupies an intermediary position between these two polar terms: it can be carnivorous, like birds of prey, and part of its body is covered with feathers as brightly coloured as those of the parrot.[3] But it is obviously the subsidiary opposition between macaws and toucans which should occupy our attention, since it is the only one which plays a part in the group of myths we are studying. In this con-

[3] In support of this statement, I can quote an extract from the Vapidiana myth about the origin of death (M_{305a}). The toucan was the demiurge's pet bird and, when its master's son died, it wept so much that its plumage lost its colour: 'Has not the grief of years and the rivers of tears which he has shed dissolved some of the gaudy colours of orange and black, red and green, and left a ring of faded blue round each eye the width of the nail of a small finger?' (Ogilvie, p. 69). In respect of its plumage, the toucan thus appears as a faded parrot.

In Guiana, the small toucan seems to be subject to a taboo comparable to the one relating to opossum meat among the Ge (*RC*, p. 169): according to the Kalina, anyone who eats the flesh of this bird will die 'while still in full beauty', or as we would say, in the prime of life (Ahlbrinck, under 'Kuyakén').

nection, the toucan's fondness for the aromatic seeds of the envieira tree would seem to be the relevant feature in M_{304}.

One of the myths about the origin of honey, which we studied at the beginning of this book, describes the adventures of an Indian, who was also attacked by jaguars while robbing the nests of macaws, which feed on flowers containing sweet nectar (M_{189}). Now, we know of a myth in which the toucan plays a leading role, most probably after it has been given an exaggeratedly large beak as a punishment for greediness (Métraux 2, p. 178, n. 1). In this particular myth (M_{305b}), a honey-gatherer, thanks to the toucan's advice, succeeds in killing the demiurge Añatunpa (by lighting a fire on the back of his neck), who had offered all the honey-gatherers as food to Dyori, the ogre (Nordenskiöld 1, p. 286). So, while in M_{188}–M_{189} jaguars are changed into honey-gatherers, in M_{305b} a honey-gatherer is changed into a jaguar (which also attacks its opponents' necks). At the same time, the macaws which are being hunted are changed into a helpful toucan, a transformation which could perhaps be explained by the respective association of the macaw with sweet food and of the toucan with highly flavoured food. All the terms in M_{304} would thus reproduce those used in M_{22}–M_{24}, but would give them greater emphasis.

These remarks would be of little interest if they did not help to throw light on other aspects of the problem. In the table on p. 365 I compared only the central parts of the myths, leaving out the beginning of M_{304}, which dealt with the origin of the ability to be transformed into a jaguar, and the end of M_{23}–M_{24} (M_{22} does not contain this episode) which dealt with the origin of tobacco. Now, in these last myths, tobacco comes into existence through the jaguar, just as in M_{304} the jaguar comes into existence, as it were, through the invention of the bark tunics. The wearing of bark tunics and the absorption of tobacco are two ways of entering into communication with the supernatural world. The misuse of one of these methods brings about a woman's death by burning in M_{304}. The death of a woman by burning causes the appearance of the other method in M_{23}–M_{24}, but, according to M_{24} (cf. also M_{27}), initially as a misuse: the first men to possess tobacco wanted to smoke in isolation, that is, without sharing with others, or without trying to communicate with the spirits.

Whereas tobacco smoke sends out a courteous invitation to kindly spirits, according to another Tucuna myth (M_{318}), which will be studied later, it was thanks to the asphyxiating smoke of the pimento that men were able to exterminate a race of evil, cannibalistic spirits and examine them at leisure. The bark tunics which have been made since then were modelled on the appearance of these spirits and make it possible for men to embody them. The initiation ceremony for young girls, at which the visitors arrive in disguise and pretend to attack and destroy their hosts' houses, symbolizes a fight waged by humans to protect the young adolescent girl from the spirits which threaten her during this critical period of her life (Nim. 13, pp. 74, 89). It is clear, then, which path we have to follow if we are to re-establish a complete correspondence between the Tucuna myth (M_{304}) and the Chaco myths about the origin of tobacco. Pimento smoke is the opposite of tobacco smoke, but since it was, in a sense, given to the supernatural spirits in exchange for bark tunics (since these were obtained thanks to the application of pimento smoke), it also represents them in reverse, and the mystic use of bark tunics is therefore, ideologically speaking, on a par with the use of tobacco.

There still remains the problem of the recurrence, which is less surprising than it first appeared, of a noise-making instrument of the clapper type in M_{24} and in M_{304}. The instrument in M_{24} was a makeshift device used for locating honey, which in turn is the instrument of the ogress's successive metamorphoses, culminating in her death by burning. The noise-maker in M_{304} leads the ogress straight to the same fire. But in this case we are dealing with a real instrument, although it has no equivalent in Tucuna organology – in spite of the fact that the latter is one of the most varied in South America – and one which belongs to a type so rare in this part of the world that Izikowitz's classic work (pp. 8–9), under the heading 'clappers' – 'pieces of wood banged one against the other', gives only two references, one of which is doubtful, while the other refers to the imitation of a bird call. It would seem, then, that the Tucuna myth is referring to an imaginary instrument, the making of which it describes very carefully.[4]

The instrument nevertheless exists, if not among the Tucuna, at least among the Bororo, where it has exactly the same shape, although they make it from bamboo and not from the hollow trunk of the embaúba tree. In the Bororo dialect, the instrument is called parabára, a term which also denotes a kind of small white goose, because, according to EB (Vol. I, pp. 857–8), of the resemblance between the cry of the bird and the rattle of the bamboo canes. This is not a convincing explanation, because the popular name of *Dendrocygna viaduta*, irerê, is

[4] An instrument of the same type, but which is used as a catapult, has been reported among the Tucuna, the Aparai, the Toba and the Sherente (Nim. 13, p. 123, n. 23).

also interpreted as being an onomatopoeic term, although the comparison of this bird's cry with a whistle (Ihering, under 'irerê') does not make it sound much like a series of dry rattling noises.

There is some doubt, too, about the place and function of the parabára in Bororo ritual. According to Colbacchini (2, pp. 99–100; 3, pp. 140–41), these instruments, which are made from bamboo poles split longitudinally over a length of thirty to fifty centimetres and which, when shaken, produce sounds which are differently pitched according to the size of the cut, are used at the investiture ceremony for the new chief, which always coincides with funeral rites. The new chief is an incarnation of the hero, Parabára, the inventor of instruments of the same name, and he sits down on the grave while dancers of both sexes make a circle round him, shaking the bamboo poles which they finally lay on the grave. The parabára figures among the gifts presented to the new chief (who always comes from the Cera moiety) by members of the other, Tugaré, moiety.

The *Enciclopédia Bororo* states clearly that the celebration of the parabára rite is a privilege enjoyed by the Apiboré clan belonging to the Tugaré moiety. The individuals officiating at the ceremony, who personify the parabára Spirits, enter the village at the west side, each one holding in both hands a long, split bamboo cane; they move in the direction of the grave, walk round it several times, and then sit down, while the leader of the ritual, who is called Parabára Eimejera (and who is not a village chief in process of being enthroned, as was indicated in the previous sources), announces his arrival to the members of both moieties, to the accompaniment of the crackling sound of the bamboos. When he has finished, the others lay the bamboos on the grave and go away (*EB*, Vol. I, under 'aroe-etawujedu', p. 159).

Since the *Enciclopédia* does not mention the parabára in connection with the investiture of chiefs, it is probable that, because this ritual had to be performed at the same time as a funeral ceremony, the Salesian Fathers first of all thought they should associate with the one what rightfully belonged to the other. A funeral ceremony, unaccompanied by an investiture, has been observed and photographed in a village on the Rio São Lourenço (not the village in which I stayed thirty years ago, but in the same area, which is a long way from the region controlled by the missions). About a fortnight after the temporary burial on the main plaza of the village, dancers attired in ceremonial dress and personifying mythical beings inspected the corpse to see if the decomposition of the flesh had reached a sufficiently advanced stage. Several times they reached a negative conclusion, which is a necessary procedure if the ceremonies are to follow their proper course. One of the dancers, whose body was smeared with white clay, ran round the grave calling to the soul of the dead man to come out. Meanwhile, other men shook split bamboo canes, which made dry rattling noises (Kozák, p. 45).[5]

It is probable that the dancer smeared with clay personified the aigé, a frightening-looking aquatic monster, whose cry is imitated by the bull-roarers. If, as the source suggests, the object of his dance was indeed to invite the dead man's soul to leave the grave, hence the village, in order to follow the mythic beings into the world beyond, the rattling of the parabára could hasten or salute this disjunction, which is also (according to the point of view one adopts) a conjunction. I shall not attempt to go any further in the interpretation of Bororo ritual, since the second volume of the *Enciclopédia Boróro*, which may perhaps include a hitherto unknown myth about the origin of the parabára, has not yet appeared. I merely note that, according to information given to Nordenskiöld, the Yanaigua of Bolivia use an instrument of the clapper type in certain ceremonies (Izikowitz, p. 8). The Tereno of the southern part of the Mato Grosso also have a dance which involves knocking together sticks (*bate pau* in Portuguese), but its meaning is unknown (Altenfelder Silva, pp. 367–9). A festive ceremony performed by the Kayapo-Gorotiré, and which they refer to as men uêmôro, but which is also called *bate pau* by the neighbouring peasants, has been observed recently. The young men form a file two deep and move round in a ring, knocking together sticks about fifty centimetres long. The dance lasts all night, and ends with their copulating with a very young woman, who is 'mistress of the feast' and who has inherited this duty through the women on the paternal side of her

[5] Like the Bororo, several small tribes of southern California have an extremely complex burial ritual, the purpose of which is to prevent the deceased coming back among the living. It includes two dances, called respectively 'twirling' and 'to extinguish the fires'. During the latter, the shamans stamp out the flames with their feet and hands, and in both dances they knock sticks together (Waterman, pp. 309, 327–8 and Pl. 26, 27; Spier 1, pp. 321–2).

Now, California is without any doubt the area in which instruments of the parabára type are most prevalent; they are found from the Yokuts in the south as far north as the Klamath, who live in the state of Oregon (Spier 2, p. 89). The parabára is referred to as a 'clap rattle', or a 'split rattle' by American ethnographers, and its presence has also been recorded among the Pomo (Loeb, p. 189), the Yuki and the Maidu (Kroeber, pp. 149, 419 and Pl. 67). The Nomlaki (Goldschmidt, pp. 367–8) make it from elder-wood, which can play the part of the bamboo in temperate regions. Kroeber (pp. 823, 862) declares the instrument to be typical of central California, where it is supposed to be used only for dances and never for puberty rites or shamanistic ceremonies. Among the Klamath, who may have taken it over from the tribes along the river Pit farther south, its use is probably limited to the 'ghost dance', a messianic cult which appeared about 1870 (Spier 2, *loc. cit.*).

family: she inherits it from one of her father's sisters and passes it on to a daughter of one of her brothers. It stands to reason that this woman cannot claim to be a virgin. Therefore, in accordance with the Kayapo custom, she is only entitled to a second-class marriage. Yet the rite of *bate pau* is performed at those rare and much sought after marriages in which the bride, who is still under the age of puberty, is officially a virgin (Diniz, pp. 26–7). It is possible that the southern Guarani used the same type of noise-making instruments in their rites, since the Mbya describe an important divinity as holding two sticks, one in each hand and shaking them and knocking them together. Schaden (5, pp. 191–2), who gives the information, suggests that the two crossed sticks are perhaps the origin of the famous Guarani cross, which made such a powerful impression on the old missionaries.

The Uitoto believe that, when they stamp with their feet, they are establishing contact with their chthonian forefathers, who came up to the earth's surface in order to watch the feasts given in their honour, and which they themselves celebrate with 'real' words, whereas men speak by means of musical instruments (Preuss 1, p. 126). A Mataco myth (M_{306}) relates that, after the fire which destroyed the earth, a small bird, tapiatson, beat its drum near the burnt branch of a zapallo (*cucurbita* sp.) tree, as the Indians do when the algaroba (*Prosopis* sp.) ripens. The trunk started to grow and became a fine leafy tree which offered the protection of its shade to the new race of men (Métraux 3, p. 10; 5, p. 35).

This myth brings us extraordinarily close to M_{24}, in which the knocking together of the sandals was intended to hasten the conjunction of the hero and another wild 'fruit': honey. In Tacana mythology, another bird, the woodpecker – whom we know to be a master of honey – taps with its beak on a woman's earthenware pot in order to guide her husband who has lost his way (M_{307}; H.-H., pp. 72–4; cf. also the Uitoto myth in Preuss 1, pp. 304–14). In M_{194}–M_{195}, the same conjunctive role is played by the woodpecker, whether he brings a husband back to his wife or helps the divine brothers to return to the supernatural world. It would be interesting to compare more closely the conjunctive function of the tapping in M_{307} with that fulfilled in the Guarani creation myth (M_{308}) by the crackling of seeds as they burst in the fire with an explosive force capable of transporting the younger of the divine brothers to the other side of the water where his elder brother already is (Cadogan 4, p. 79; Borba, p. 67). I shall merely draw attention to the problem, and to the triple reversal of the same theme among the Bororo (M_{46}): brothers are blinded by the noisy explosion of their grandmother's bones which have been thrown into the fire, and recover their sight in water (*disj./conj.*; *animal/vegetable*; *in the water/over the water*; Kalapalo variant (M_{47}): the two brothers are respectively sun and moon, and the younger, having had his nose torn off by one of his grandmother's bones which shot out of the fire 'where they danced and made a clicking noise', decided to go up into the sky; cf. *RC*, pp. 123, 171). To be complete, the study of this theme should include references to North American sources, such as the Zuni myth about the winter ritual in which men regain possession of game which has been stolen by ravens thanks to the noisy explosion of a handful of salt that has been thrown into the fire (M_{309}; Bunzel, p. 928).[6]

So a series of discontinuous noises, which take a great variety of forms, such as tapping or drumming, the knocking together of pieces of wood, the crackling of objects in fire, or the rattling of split poles, play an obscure part in ritual and in mythic narratives. The Tucuna, one of whose myths put me on the track of the Bororo parabára, although the Tucuna themselves are unacquainted with this instrument, knock sticks together in one set of circumstances at least. It is well known that these Indians attach great importance to the puberty rites for girls. As soon as a girl detects signs of her first period, she takes off all her ornaments, hangs them in an obvious place on the posts of her hut and goes off to hide in a nearby bush. When her mother arrives, she sees the ornaments, realizes what has happened and sets off to look for her daughter. The latter replies to her mother's calls by striking two pieces of dry wood together. The mother then loses no time in erecting a partition around the young girl's bed and takes her there after nightfall. From that moment the girl remains in seclusion for two or three months without being seen or heard by anyone except her mother and her paternal aunts (Nim. 13, pp. 73–4).

This reference to the Tucuna provides a suitable opportunity for introducing another myth which is essential for any further discussion of M_{304}:

M_{310}. *Tucuna. 'The jaguar who ate children'*

Peti, the jaguar, had been killing children for a long time. Every time he heard a child crying because it had been left alone by its parents,

[6] The Timbira have a dance accompanied by handclapping which is intended to keep away the harvest parasites (Nim. 8, p. 62). The Pawnee women of the Upper Missouri used to beat the water noisily with their feet at the time of planting and harvesting beans (Weltfish, p. 248).

the animal assumed the form of the mother, carried the little one off and said to it: 'Press your nose against my anus!' He then killed his victim with an emission of intestinal gas, after which he ate it. Dyai, the demiurge, decided to assume the form of a child. Armed with his sling, he sat down at the edge of a path and started to cry. Peti arrived on the scene, put him on his back and ordered him to press his nose against his anus. Dyai, however, was careful to turn his face away. The jaguar went on breaking wind, but to no purpose. Every time he broke wind, he ran faster. Some people he met asked him where he was taking 'our father' (the demiurge). Realizing whom he was carrying on his back, Peti asked Dyai to get down, but the latter refused. The animal went on his way and, passing through a cave, reached the other world. All the time he kept begging Dyai to go away.

The jaguar was ordered by the demiurge to return to the place where they had met. Here there was a muirapiranga tree, the trunk of which had a hole with very smooth sides pierced through it. Dyai forced the jaguar's fore-legs into the hole and secured them firmly. Grasping his dance stick, a hollow bamboo cane, with his hind legs which stuck out on the other side, the animal started to sing. He called on the bat to come and wipe his bottom. Other demons, also members of the jaguar clan, came running up to him in turn and gave him food. Today, you can still sometimes hear the din they make at the place called naimèki, in a small patch of secondary forest near an old plantation ... (Nim. 13, p. 132).

This myth adds a fourth tree, the muirapiranga or myra-piranga, literally, 'red wood' tree, to the botanical trio mentioned in M304. This tree, which belongs to the leguminous family and the *Caesalpina* species, is none other than the famous '*bois de braise*' from which Brazil got its name. Being very hard and fine-grained, it can be used for many purposes. The Tucuna combine it with bone to make drumsticks (Nim. 13, p. 43). The Tucuna skin-drum is certainly of European origin, and another musical instrument appears in the myth, where it forms a counterpart to the split hollow trunk in M304: this is the dance stick, ba:'ma, the use of which is confined to the jaguar clan and perhaps a few other clans; it is a long bamboo cane (*Gadua superba*) which may measure up to three metres. The upper extremity is split to form a groove roughly thirty centimetres long, which represents an alligator's jaw with or without teeth according to whether the instrument is said to be 'male' or 'female'. Below the jaw is a tiny demon's mask, and shell-rattles and ornaments made of falcon's feathers are fastened all the way down the cane. These instruments are always found in pairs, one male, one female. The players face each other and strike the ground at an oblique angle while crossing their bamboo canes. Since the inner dividing membranes have not been removed, the sound produced is very weak (Nim. 13, p. 45).[7]

I have already put together, in a single group, the Tembé-Tenetehara myths about the origin of honey (the honey festival) (M_{188}–M_{189}), the Chaco myths about the origin of tobacco (M_{23}–M_{24}, M_{246}) and the myth explaining the origin of bark tunics (M_{304}, which reverses the true origin myth, as will be seen later). This operation was the result of a triple transformation:

(a) jaguars: peace-loving ⇒ aggressive
(b) birds: macaws, parrots, parakeets ⇒ toucans
(c) bird food: sweet flowers ⇒ aromatic seeds

The transformational relationship which we are about to note between M_{304} and M_{319} makes it possible, without further explanation, to strengthen the link uniting the Chaco and Tucuna myths. For if, as is already obvious, the musical instrument in M_{310} is a transformation of the one in M_{304}, they both refer back to the hollow trunk (transformed into an empty ditch in M_{24}), which in M_{23}, M_{246} acts as a place of refuge for the victims of the cannibalistic jaguar and which causes the latter's death. This can be expressed as the following transformation:

M_{23}, M_{246} M_{304} M_{310}
(hollow tree) ⇒   (split trunk) ⇒   (hollow bamboo)

This group of transformations is homogeneous as regards musical instruments: the split trunk and the hollow bamboo are both instruments of noise, and I have confirmed in another context that, in the Chaco myths, homology exists between the hollow trunk, the trough for making mead and the drum (pp. 107–8). I shall return to this aspect.

[7] Very faint too, no doubt, is the noise, compared to a 'muffled roar', made by the Bororo when they beat the ground with rolls of matting in order to tell their wives and children that the aquatic monsters, aigé, have gone, and that they can safely come out of the huts where they are hiding. It should be noted that the actors personifying the aigé try to knock down the boys who are in process of being initiated and the latter are held up by their sponsors and masculine relatives, because if they fell this would be a very bad omen (EB, Vol. I, pp. 661–2). This episode would seem to be an almost literal transposition of certain details of the Tucuna initiation ceremony for girls (Nim. 13, pp. 88–9).

Let us now superimpose M_{304} and M_{310} one upon the other. At first glance a complex network of relationships appears: for while the syntagmatic sequences of both myths are reproduced in the usual way through certain transformations, they create at one point at which they meet a paradigmatic set which is equivalent to part of the syntagmatic sequence of a Bororo myth (M_5) which, as I showed at the very beginning of the previous volume, is a transformation of the key myth (M_1). It is as if my inquiry were following a spiral pattern and, after reverting to its starting-point, were now momentarily resuming its forward movement by inflecting its curve along a previous course (see table opposite).

Consequently, according to the standpoint we take, either M_{304} is linked to M_{310}, or each one is linked separately to M_5; or the three myths are all interlinked. If we ventured to form the Chaco myths about the origin of the jaguar and (or) tobacco into one 'archimyth' (just as linguists talk of 'archi-phonemes'), we would obtain another series parallel to the previous series:

a wife and mother changed into a jaguar	devourer of husband and children	poisoner of her husband with menstrual blood	perishes *in* a ditch or *on* a hollow tree-trunk bristling with spears (or is held prisoner by its claws which have become embedded in the tree)

So we come back to the problem, already discussed, of the mutual reversibility of a syntagmatic sequence formed by a single group, and a syntagmatic set obtained by cutting a vertical section through the superimposed syntagmatic sequences of several myths, interlinked by transformational relationships. In the present instance, however, we can at least catch a glimpse of the semantic basis of a phenomenon only the formal aspect of which has so far been examined.

It will be remembered that M_5, whose syntagmatic sequence would seem here to cut across that of other myths, explains the origin of diseases which, in a maleficent and negative sense, ensure the transition from life to death, and establish a conjunction between life here below and life in the world beyond. This is clearly the meaning of the other myths, for tobacco fulfils a similar function in a beneficent and positive sense, as does also in M_{310} the use of the dance stick (the reference may even be to its origin), a fact which can be verified in the Tucuna ritual since, in this instance, we are dealing with a real instrument. The imaginary instrument in M_{304} (but which actually has a real place in American organology) fulfils a reverse function, that is,

M_5

An unfriendly grandmother tries to kill her grandson

puts its arm into a pierced tree

The children bury their dead father in an armadillo's burrow

receives a spear thrust which pierces her anus

When dead, she is buried in an armadillo's burrow

under pretext of feeding the child on anti-food (intestinal gas)

under pretext of feeding grandchildren with anti-food (fungus)

devours child

M_{310}: A jaguar changed into a mother

M_{304}: A grandmother changed into a jaguar

it is disjunctive, not conjunctive. Nevertheless this function, like the other one, is beneficent and positive. It is not exercised against demons, who have been put to the service of man, thanks to the bark tunics which imitate their physical appearance, as in the ritual, or – according to M_{310} – against a demon who is effectively caught in a tree-trunk which grips his wrists as in manacles; it is exercised against demons who, through an excessive use of trees with bark, have got completely out of hand; they are not semblances of demons conjured up by men, but men changed into real demons.

We have, then, at our disposal a fairly solid basis for extending the comparison beyond the central zone formed by the three myths M_5, M_{304} and M_{310}, and for attempting to incorporate certain aspects, peculiar to other myths whose position at first sight appears marginal. Let us look first of all at the opening episode of the crying baby in M_{310}, since we are well acquainted with this small personage. Already, in connection with other incidents, I have made considerable progress towards understanding the part he plays, and so the reader will perhaps more readily forgive me if I indulge in a rapid excursion into a more remote region of mythology, where the character of the whimperer is more clearly discernible, because he plays a leading role there. I shall not try to justify my action, and I admit that it is irreconcilable with a sound use of structural method. I will even refrain from using as an argument, in this very special case, my deep conviction that Japanese mythology and American mythology, each in its own way, are using sources which go right back to paleolithic times and which were once the common heritage of Asiatic groups later disseminated throughout the Far East and the New World. Without putting forward any such hypothesis, which would in any case be unverifiable in the present state of knowledge, I shall merely plead extenuating circumstances: only very rarely do I allow myself this kind of digression and, when I do, the apparent divergence is meant to act as a short cut for the establishment of a point which could have been made by a different method, but a much slower and more laborious one, and one more exhausting for the reader.

M_{311}. Japan. 'The crying "baby"'

After the death of his wife and sister Izanami, the god Izanagi divided the world between his three children. To his daughter

Amaterasu, the sun, who had been born from his left eye, he gave the sky. To his son, Tsuki-yomi, the moon, who had been born from his right eye, he gave the ocean. And to his other son Sosa-no-wo, who had been born from his nasal mucus, he gave the earth.

At this time Sosa-no-wo was in the prime of life, and had grown a beard eight hands long. Yet he neglected his duties as master of the earth, and spent his time weeping, wailing and fuming with rage. He explained to his anxious father that he was crying because he wanted to follow his mother to the Nether Land. So Izanagi was filled with detestation of his son and drove him away.

For he himself had tried to see his dead wife again, and he knew that she was just a swollen and festering corpse, and that eight kinds of Thunder Gods rested on her: one each on her head, chest, stomach, back, buttocks, hands, feet and vagina ...

Before departing to the other world, Sosa-no-wo obtained his father's permission to say good-bye to his sister Amaterasu in the sky. But once he got there, he lost no time in defiling the rice-plantations, and Amaterasu was so shocked that she decided to shut herself up in a cave and deprive the world of her light. As a punishment for his misdeeds, her brother was banished for ever to the other world, which he reached after many trials and tribulations (Aston, Vol. I, pp. 14–59).

It would be interesting to compare this concentrated fragment of a fairly lengthy myth with certain South American tales;[8]

M86a. Amazonia. 'The crying baby'

Yuwaruna, the black jaguar, had married a woman whose one thought was to seduce her husband's brothers. This vexed the latter, who killed her, and since she was pregnant they opened up the corpse, whence emerged a little boy who leapt into the water.

He was captured with some difficulty, but never stopped crying and howling 'like a newly born baby'. All the animals were summoned to amuse him, but the little owl was the only one able to soothe him by revealing to him the mystery of his birth. From then on, the child's one thought was to avenge his mother. He killed all the jaguars one after the other, then rose into the sky where he became the rainbow. It is because the sleeping humans did not hear

---

[8] And North American ones, too; e.g. the following passage in a myth belonging to the Dené Hare, which will be referred to again in the next volume: 'From his union with his sister, Kuñyan (the demiurge) had a son who sulked and cried all the time' (Petitot, p. 145).

his calls that their life-span was shortened from that time onwards (Tastevin 3, pp. 188–90; cf. *RC*, pp. 161–3).

The Chimane and the Mosetene have an almost identical myth (M₃₁₂): a child, after being abandoned by his mother, never stopped crying. His tears changed into rain which he himself succeeded in bringing to an end when he took the form of a rainbow (Nordenskiöld 3, p. 146). Now in the Nihongi chronicles too, Sosa-no-wo's final banishment to the other world is accompanied by torrential rain. The god asks for some form of shelter but his request is refused. As a protection, he invents the broad-brimmed hat, and the water-proof coat of green straw. This is why no one is allowed to enter the house of a person thus attired. Before he reaches his last abode, Sosa-no-wo kills a deadly snake (Aston, *loc. cit.*). In South America, the rainbow *is* a deadly snake.

M₃₁₃. *Cashinawa*. 'The crying baby'

One day a pregnant woman went off to fish. Meanwhile a storm broke out, and the baby she was carrying in her womb disappeared. A few months later, it appeared in the form of a quite big child, who cried persistently and gave no one any peace day or night. He was thrown into the river, which dried up the instant his body came into contact with it, while he himself disappeared up into the sky (Tastevin 4, p. 22).

Basing his arguments on a similar Peba myth, Tastevin suggests that this one may refer to the origin of the sun. It will be remembered that a Machiguenga myth (M₂₉₉) mentions three suns: the sun we are familiar with, the one in the underworld and the one in the nocturnal sky. In the beginning, the latter was a red-hot baby who caused his mother to die in giving birth to him, and whom his father, the moon, had to banish from the earth to avoid it being burnt up. The second Sun, like Sosa-no-wo, went to join his dead mother in the underworld where he became a master of maleficent rain. Unlike the corpse of Sosa-no-wo's mother, which was repellent, the corpse of the chthonian sun's mother was so appetizing that it provided the substance of the first cannibalistic meal.

Whether Japanese or American, all these myths closely follow an identical pattern. The crying child is a baby who has been abandoned by his mother, or has been born posthumously, which simply means that the desertion occurred earlier; or he may consider he has been unjustly abandoned, even though he has already reached an age at which a normal child no longer demands constant parental care. This excessive longing for conjunction with the family, which the myths usually situate on a horizontal plane (when it is the result of the mother's absence) involves in every case a vertical disjunction of the cosmic type: the crying child goes up into the sky where he creates a *rotten* world (rain, defilement, the rainbow as a cause of diseases, loss of immortality); or, in symmetrical variants, in order *not to* create a *burnt* world. That at least is the pattern followed by the American myths, which is duplicated and reversed in the Japanese myth in which it is the crying god who goes away, since his second disjunction takes the form of a journey. Notwithstanding this difference, we have no difficulty in recognizing, behind the character of the whimpering child, that of the anti-social hero (in the sense that he refuses to become socialized) who remains obstinately attached to nature and the feminine world: the same hero who, in the key myth, commits incest in order to return to the maternal fold, and who in M_5, although of an age to join the men's house, remains secluded in the family hut. By a quite different line of argument, we had reached the conclusion that M_5, a myth explaining the origin of diseases, was concerned by implication with the origin of the rainbow, the cause of diseases (*RC*, pp. 246–50). We now have additional confirmation of this inference, thanks to the newly discovered equivalence between the secluded boy and the crying baby, whom the myths consider to be the origin of the same meteoric phenomenon.

Before working out the consequences of this connection, we must dwell for a moment on one episode in M_{310}: the episode in which the bat comes to wipe the jaguar's bottom. As will be recalled, the latter was very fond of crying babies and asphyxiated them with his intestinal gases. It is not easy to work out the position of bats in the myths, since there is usually very little information regarding the species. Now, in tropical America, there are nine families and a hundred or so species of bats, all different in size, appearance and eating habits: some eat insects and some fruit, while others (*Desmodus* sp.) suck blood.

We may well speculate, then, about the reason for the transformation, illustrated by a Tacana myth (M_{195}), of one of the 'melero's' two daughters (who, in M_{197}, are multi-coloured macaw-women) into a bat: either the bats referred to feed on nectar, as is sometimes the case, or live in hollow trees like bees, or there is some entirely different reason for the transformation. In support of the link-up, it should be pointed out that in a Uitoto myth (M_{314}), in which the theme of the girl mad about honey makes a fleeting appearance, honey is replaced by cannibalistic bats (Preuss 1, pp. 230–70). Generally speaking, however, these animals are chiefly associated in the myths with blood and the orifices of the body. Bats drew the first burst of laughter from an Indian because they did not know about articulated speech and could only communicate with humans by tickling them (Kayapo–Gorotiré, M_{40}). Bats came out of the abdominal cavity of an ogre who devoured young men (Sherente, M_{315a}; Nim. 7, pp. 186–7). The vampires *Desmodus rotundus* sprang from the blood of the family of the demon Aétsasa; this family was massacred by the Indians whom the demon was decapitating in order to shrink their heads (Aguaruna, M_{315b}; Guallart, pp. 71–3). A demon bat was married to a human and was furious because she refused to give him something to drink. So he cut off the Indians' heads and piled them up in the hollow tree where he lived (Mataco, M_{316}; Métraux 3, p. 48).

The Kogi of the Sierra de Santa Marta, in Colombia, believe that there is a more definite link between bats and menstrual blood. In order to find out if one of their number is indisposed, women ask: ' "Has the bat bitten you?" Young men say that a young girl who has begun to menstruate is a woman, because she has been bitten by the bat. On top of every hut, the priest places a small cross made of thread, which represents both the bat and the female organ' (Reichel-Dolmatoff, Vol. I, p. 270). The Aztecs have the same sexual symbolism but in a reversed form, since they believe that the bat came from Quetzalcoatl's sperm.[9]

What has all this to do with the present argument? *The bat which is generally held responsible for a bodily aperture and a discharge of blood, is transformed, in M_{310}, into an animal responsible for closing a bodily aperture and for the reabsorption of excrement.* This threefold transformation assumes its full significance when we note that it is applied to a jaguar and, what is more, to a jaguar which kidnaps crying children. For we are perfectly familiar with this ogre: we came across him first in a Warao myth (M_{273}) where, in the form of a grandmother (a mother in M_{310}, but a retransformation of the jaguar-grandmother in M_{304}), a jaguar carried off a weeping child and, when the little girl grew up, fed on her menstrual blood (instead of breaking wind with a view to killing the child and feeding on her). Consequently, the jaguar in M_{273} behaves

---

[9] According to an Australian belief, bats spring from the foreskin when it is cut off at the time of the initiation ceremony, and the animal also denotes death (Elkin, pp. 173, 305).

towards a human as if he were a bat, whereas in M_{310} the bat adopts towards the jaguar a form of behaviour which is in correlation and opposition to the behaviour he would have adopted, had the jaguar been a human being.

Now, M_{273} belongs to the same group of transformations as the myths about the origin of honey. M_{310}, on the other hand, belongs to the same group of transformations as the myths about the origin of tobacco. In making the transition from honey to tobacco, we thus confirm the following equation:

(a) (*menstrual blood*)   (*excrement*)
        [jaguar : unwell girl] ::   [bat : jaguar]

which brings us back to a point which might have been learnt independently from a comparison between M_{273} and M_{24} (a myth about the origin of tobacco, in which a jaguar-woman poisons her husband with her menstrual blood):

(b) (*origin of honey*)   (*origin of tobacco*)
       [menstrual blood : food] ::   [menstrual blood :
                                        excrement]

In other words: honey establishes conjunction between extremes, whereas tobacco creates disjunction between intermediary terms by consolidating adjacent terms.

After this interlude about the bat, we can return to the crying baby.

The Tucuna myths M_{304} and M_{310} have two themes in common – cannibalism and filth: in M_{304}, the jaguar-grandmother tries to pass off her son's liver – an internal organ congruous with blood, and more particularly with menstrual blood – for a tree fungus, also an antifood (*RC*, pp. 167, 175, 176); in M_{310}, a jaguar usurping a mother's role, forces the child to breathe in the gases it emits from its dungsoiled rear. But, whether they feed on human flesh or menstrual blood, or whether on the contrary they administer rotten substances as food, the Warao and Tucuna jaguars belong to the great family of animals with a passion for childish bawlings, which also includes the fox and the frog; the latter is also greedy for young flesh, but in the metaphorical sense since, beyond the crying baby, she coveted the adolescent whom she intended to turn into her lover.

By taking this approach, we come back to the equivalence, which had already been confirmed in a different way (p. 310) between cries – that is, din – and filth. These terms are interchangeable, according to whether the myth adopts an acoustic, alimentary or sexual coding. The problem raised by the theme of the crying baby boils down to asking why a given myth chooses to code, in acoustic terms, a mytheme – the character of the secluded boy – which, in other myths, is coded by means of actual incest (M_1) or symbolic incest (M_5).

The problem remains unsolved as regards such myths as M_{243}, M_{245} and M_{273}. In the present instance, however, a possible answer can be discerned. The two Tucuna myths about the cannibalistic jaguar give a prominent place to musical instruments, one imaginary, the other real, but which, because of their semantic function and organological type, form a pair of opposites. The instrument in M_{304}, which I compared to the Bororo parabára, is just a naturally hollow part of tree-trunk which has been split lengthwise, and which is made to reverberate by striking it on the ground at an oblique angle or by throwing it on the ground. The ensuing noise is supposed to keep away from human society a being who is himself human, but has changed into a demon. The instrument in M_{310}, a dancing stick manipulated by the captive jaguar, consists of a bamboo cane (the bamboo is a graminacea which neither South American Indians nor botanists classify as a tree), also naturally hollow, which is made to reverberate when struck against the ground while being held in a vertical position. The use of this instrument allows the jaguar to achieve a result symmetrical with that which has just been attributed to the clapper. The dancing stick establishes conjunction between a demoniacal being who has changed into a human being, and other demons: it draws the latter towards men, instead of driving the former away from men.

That is not all. The dancing stick itself has a two-fold correlational and oppositional relationship with another musical instrument, which had accompanied us discreetly from the beginning of this book and which was apparent in the background of the myths about the origin of honey: I am referring to the drum, an instrument also made from a hollow tree-trunk, to which the myths attribute a great variety of uses: it may be a place where bees nest, or a trough in which mead is prepared, a wooden drum (a transformation of the trough according to M_{214}), a place of refuge for victims of the cannibalistic jaguar and a trap for this same jaguar, as well as for the girl mad about honey ... The wooden drum and the dancing stick are both hollow cylinders, one short and squat, the other long and narrow. The drum passively receives blows from sticks or a hammer, the bamboo cane comes to life when manipulated by a performer whose gestures it amplifies and prolongs, making them reverberate right into the passive ground. The clapper is, therefore, in contrast both with the dancing stick and the drum, since the latter are hollow all the way down, whereas it is split from the outside, crosswise, but only down to a certain point. The drum and the dancing stick are also in contrast to each other, in so far as they can be respectively wider or narrower, shorter or longer, the object or the subject of the action.

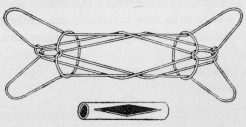

Figure 17. Honey or the hollow tree. A pattern from a Warao string game. (After Roth 2, Fig. 288, p. 525.)

In this triangular pattern, the major contrast is the one between the drum and the clapper, as can be indirectly inferred from a Warao myth, of which we need quote only one episode:

M_{317}. *Warao. 'One of Kororomanna's adventures'*

One day, an Indian called Kororomanna killed a guariba monkey. In trying to return to the village, he lost his way and had to spend the night in an improvised shelter. But he soon realized that he had chosen a bad place in which to camp, for it was right in the middle of a pathway frequented by the demons. You can always distinguish a Spirit road by the noise made by the demons occupying the trees alongside it, for they are always striking the branches and trunks, and producing short, sharp crackling noises.

It was not at all pleasant for Kororomanna, especially as the monkey's body was beginning to swell with all the noxious gases inside. In spite of the smell, he was obliged to keep the carcass near him and to watch over it with a stick, for fear the Demons might steal it from him. At last he fell asleep, only to be wakened again by the demons knocking on the trees. He had a sudden desire to mimic them, and every time they struck a tree he struck the monkey's belly with his stick. Every time he struck the animal there came a resonant *Boom, Boom*, just like the beating of a drum (the Warao use the hides of guariba monkeys to cover the ends of their skin drums).

N

Their curiosity having been aroused by these extraordinary noises, which were much louder than any they could make themselves, the demons at last discovered Kororomanna, who was roaring with laughter at hearing a dead animal break wind so vigorously. The leader of the demons regretted that he could not make such a splendid noise for, unlike ordinary mortals, spirits have no proper posteriors, but just a red spot: they are therefore blocked below. Nevertheless, Kororomanna agreed to split the spirit's hind-quarters. But he drove in his bow with such force that the weapon transfixed the whole body, and even pierced the unfortunate spirit's head. The demon cursed Kororomanna for having killed him, and swore that his fellow-Spirits would avenge his death. Then he disappeared (Roth 1, pp. 126–7).

This episode is taken from a very long myth and confirms the existence of the contrast between the drum, a human instrument (even endowed here with an organic nature), and the 'demoniacal' noise of sticks being struck or knocked together.[10] The dancing stick therefore must be situated between these two: it is a ritual instrument which can summon spirits, like the bark tunics which, in M_{304}, are contrasted with the clapper of the parabára type.

At this point, I would like to interpolate a few remarks on the subject of the dancing stick.

The southern Guarani believe that there is a major contrast between the stick of authority, the symbol of power and a masculine emblem, which is cut from the heart of the *Holocalyx balansae*, and the bamboo dancing stick, which is a female emblem (Cadogan 3, pp. 95–6). The masculine musical instrument is, consequently, the gourd-rattle. This contrast, which is often exemplified in literature, is illustrated most convincingly by a plate in Schaden's work, *Aspectos fundamentais da cultura guarani* (Pl. XIV in the first edition), which shows a row of five Kaiova Indians (one a small boy) holding the cross in one hand and the rattle in the other, followed by four women each one of whom is striking the ground with a piece of bamboo.[11] It would seem that,

[10] As described in the Warao myth, the noise made by the demons is not unlike the noise attributed to the jaguar by reliable observers: 'The jaguar betrays its presence by making a very characteristic series of sharp crackling noises as it nervously twitches its ears, which gives a kind of muffled version of the sound made by castanets' (Ihering, under 'onça'). According to a tale from the Rio Branco region, the jaguar makes a noise at night because its feet are shod, whereas the tapir walks barefoot and silently (Rodrigues 1, pp. 155–6).

[11] The Tacana of Bolivia call the arrow made from (hollow) bamboo 'female', and the one made from (solid) palm wood 'male' (H.-H., p. 338).

among the Apapocuva as well as among the more northerly Guarayu, the dancing stick is used for the special purpose of helping the cultural hero or the tribe as a whole to ascend into the sky (Métraux 9, p. 216). We may thus suppose the existence, among the southern Guarani, of a triple pattern of instruments, only two of which are musical instruments with additional functions: the stick of authority, which is used to assemble the men (north of the Amazon this is also the social function of the wooden drum), the rattle which brings the gods down to men, and the dancing stick which takes men closer to the gods. I have already mentioned Schaden's theory, according to which the Guarani wooden cross is supposed to represent two sticks which were once separate and knocked against each other. Finally, the Guarani contrast between a solid stick, the emblem of masculine authority, and the hollow tube, the feminine liturgical instrument, is reminiscent of the contrast (p. 351) made for sociological purposes by certain Amazonian tribes, between cylinders of hard stone which are used as pendants, according to whether they have been pierced lengthwise (and are hollow) or crosswise (and are solid).

We thus see emerging a dialectic of the hollow and the solid, in which each term is illustrated by several modalities. I have done no more than indicate certain themes and point to some possible lines of research, chiefly in order to enable us to grasp more easily the way in which the dialectic operates within the myths. Now, in their respective conclusions, the myths do much more than contrast musical instruments which are reducible to hollow tubes or solid sticks. The instrument introduced at the end of each myth has a peculiar relationship with a 'mode of the tree', which is defined at another point in the narrative.

In M_{304} and M_{310}, one or several trees are subjected to certain clearly defined operations. Trees (but only one tree to begin with) are stripped of their bark in M_{304}; in M_{310}, one tree has a hole in it. So a tree-trunk which has been stripped lengthwise is contrasted with one which has been pierced crosswise. If we complete this contrast with the one already noted between the musical instruments which appear in the two myths, and which are also 'made from trunks', we arrive at the following four-term pattern:

	M_{304}:	M_{310}:
trees :	stripped trunk	pierced trunk
percussion		
instruments :	split trunk	hollow trunk

It is obvious that this pattern of relationships forms a chiasmus. The pierced trunk and the split trunk correspond to each other, in the sense that each has an aperture perpendicular to the trunk's axis, but median in one instance and terminal in the other, and either internal or external. The symmetrical relationship linking the stripped trunk and the hollow trunk is more straightforward, since it can be reduced to an inversion of outside and inside: the tree which has been stripped of its bark remains as a cylinder with a solid interior and nothing outside, whereas the bamboo consists of an unbroken external envelope, containing only a hollow, that is, nothing:

STRIPPED TRUNK   BAMBOO

That the two-fold contrast: *empty external | solid internal*, and: *empty internal | complete external* is an invariable characteristic of the group can be clearly seen from the way in which M_{310} attempts to reverse the 'true' origin of bark masks, as it is described in a third Tucuna myth:

M_{318}. *Tucuna. 'Origin of bark masks'*

Once upon a time demons used to live in a cave. They went on a spree and attacked a village by night. They stole all the stocks of smoked meat, killed all the inhabitants, then dragged the corpses back to their den in order to eat them.

Meanwhile a party of visitors arrived at the village. They were astonished to find it deserted and followed the tracks of the gruesome procession, which led them to the mouth of the cave. The demons tried unsuccessfully to attract the intruders, but the Indians withdrew and went back home.

Another group of travellers were camping in the forest; among them was a pregnant woman who gave birth to a child. Her companions decided to stay where they were until she was strong enough to continue the journey. They were short of game, however, and had to go to sleep with empty stomachs. In the middle of the night they heard the characteristic gnawing of a rodent. It was an enormous paca (*Coelogenys paca*), which they surrounded and killed.

They all ate the paca meat, with the exception of the woman who had just given birth and her husband. The next morning the men went off to hunt leaving the mother and baby in the camp. The woman suddenly saw a demon coming towards her. He told her that the paca they had killed the night before was his son, and that the demons were coming to avenge his death. Those who had not partaken of the flesh must, if they wanted to save their lives, climb a tree of a certain species, stripping off the bark as they went up.

When the hunters returned, no one believed her story; they even made fun of her. And when, on hearing the hunting-horns and howls of the demons, she tried to warn her companions, the latter were so deeply asleep that even the red-hot resin which she dropped onto them from her torch failed to waken them. She bit her husband who finally got up and followed her like a sleepwalker. Holding the child, they both climbed the tree which the woman had taken care to locate, and tore off the bark as they climbed. When day dawned, they came down from their place of refuge and went back to the camp: there was no one left, the demons having slaughtered all the sleeping Indians. The couple returned to the village and related what had happened.

On the advice of an old sorcerer, the Indians planted a great many pimentoes. When these were ripe, they gathered them and deposited them near the demons' cave, the entrance of which they blocked with trunks of the paxiuba barriguda (a palm tree with a swollen trunk: *Iriartea ventricosa*), except in one place where they lit a big fire. They threw in enormous quantities of pimentoes, so that the smoke penetrated into the cave.

Soon a terrible din could be heard. The Indians allowed those demons who had not taken part in the cannibalistic feast to come out. But all those who had eaten human flesh perished in the cave: they can still be recognized by the red streak across their masks. When the noise stopped, and after Yagua, a slave who had been sent ahead as a scout, had been killed by a few surviving demons, the Tucuna went inside the cave and carefully noted the characteristic appearances of the various species of demons, which are reproduced today in the bark tunics (Nim. 13, pp. 80–81).

A detailed analysis of this myth would take me too far from my present theme, but I would just like to draw attention to the bark-stripping episode. A young mother ($\neq$ the old grandmother in M_{304}) and her husband, who have respected the food restrictions to which they are both subject after childbirth (Nim. 13, p. 69) ($\neq$ the elderly canni-balistic couple in M_{304}), succeed in escaping from the cannibalistic demons ($\neq$ in changing into cannibalistic demons, M_{304}), by stripping off the bark of a tree as they climb, i.e. as they move *from low to high*: whereas the humans, who turned into demons in M_{304}, achieved this result by stripping off bark *from high to low*. The major contrast on pp. 387–8 remains unchanged, and the inverted symmetry of M_{304} and M_{318} (the demons are either uncontrolled or tamed through wearing bark tunics) is dependent on an additional contrast, which has obviously been introduced for the sake of the argument: This is the contrast in the direction in which the tree is stripped, downwards or upwards.

Since the myth refers to a real-life technique, we can determine what the Indian method of bark-stripping was. According to Nimuendaju, who observed and described the Tucuna, it is done neither downwards nor upwards. The Indians fell the tree, cut off a suitable portion and hammer the bark until it is loosened from the trunk. After which they remove the bark by turning it inside out like a glove: or, more usually, they cut it lengthwise to obtain a rectangular piece which is easier to work than a cylindrical shape (Nim. 13, p. 81).[12] The Arawak of Guiana seem to employ the same technique (Roth 2, pp. 437–8), and perhaps invented it (Goldman, p. 223). As regards the techno-economical substructure, both myths, then, seem to be equally irrelevant. One is not 'truer' than the other, but since they are concerned with two com-plementary implications of a ritual which, if it is taken seriously, ex-poses the spectators (not to mention the participants) to certain danger – for what would happen if the demons impersonated by the masked dancers suddenly recovered their evil energy? – they had to invent an imaginary technique which, unlike the real-life technique, admits of opposite methods of procedure.

With the help of real or imaginary instruments, the myths, if appropriately arranged, seem to offer us the spectacle of a vast group of trans-

[12] However, Nimuendaju mentions a downwards stripping technique which is used only in the case of the matamatá tree (*Eschweilera* sp.), and which M_{304} applies to the tururi (*Comatari* sp?). Cf. Nim. 13, pp. 127, 147, n. 5.

formations covering the various ways in which a tree-trunk or a stick can *be hollow*: it can have a natural or an artificial cavity or a longitudinal or a transversal orifice; it can be used as a bee-hive, a trough, a drum, a dance stick, a bark pipe, a clapper, or a cang (a portable pillory) ... Musical instruments occupy a middle position in the series, between the objects at the two opposite extremes which take the form either of a kind of shelter, such as the hive, or of a trap, such as heavy wooden manacles. And we can say that the masks and musical instruments are themselves, each in their own way, shelters or traps, and sometimes even both at the same time. The clapper in M_{304} acts as a trap for the jaguar-demon; the jaguar-demon in M_{310}, who is caught in heavy wooden manacles, obtains the protection of his fellow-demons thanks to the dancing stick. The bark mask-like costumes, the origin of which is described in M_{318}, act as shelters for the dancers who wear them, while at the same time enabling the wearers to catch and harness the power of the demons.

From the beginning of this study, I have been constantly referring to hollow trees, used either as shelters or traps. In the myths about the origin of tobacco, the first function predominates since the people persecuted by the cannibalistic jaguar take refuge in a hollow tree. The second function prevails in the myths about the origin of honey where the fox, the girl mad about honey or the frog are imprisoned in a similar cavity. But the hollow tree only becomes a trap for these characters because it has first of all been a place of refuge for bees. Inversely, the hollow tree, which provides a providential shelter for the victims of the jaguar, in the myths about the origin of tobacco, is changed into a trap in which the jaguar perishes in trying to break through.

It would therefore be more accurate to say that the theme of the hollow tree provides a synthesis of two complementary aspects. This constant characteristic becomes even more obvious when we observe that the myths always use the same kind of trees, or trees of different kinds which are nevertheless alike in several significant aspects.

All the Chaco myths I have examined refer to the yuchan tree, the hollow bark of which shelters the children or the fellow-villagers of the woman turned jaguar, is used to make the first trough for mead, and becomes the first drum; it is in such a trunk that the demon-bat piles up the severed heads of its victims, and that the fox mad about honey is imprisoned or disembowelled, etc. The yuchan tree, in Spanish: *palo borracho*, is in Brazilian Portuguese, *barriguda*, 'the pot-bellied tree'.

It belongs to the silk-cotton tree family (*Chorisia insignis* and similar species), and has three main features – a swollen trunk, which gives it a bottle-like appearance, a profusion of long hard spikes and a white silky down which is gathered from its flowers.

The tree which acts as a trap for the girl mad about honey is more difficult to identify. We are given precise details about the species only in the extreme case in which the cunauaru, or tree-frog, is an embodiment of the heroine: this frog lives in the hollow trunk of Klotzsch's *Bodelsschwingia macrophylla* (Roth 1, p. 125), which is not a silk-cotton tree like the *Ceiba* and the *Chorisia*, but, if I am not mistaken, one of the tiliaceae. In South America, this family includes trees which provide lightweight wood and often have hollow trunks, like the bombax tree, one species of which (*Apeiba cymbalaria*) provides the Bororo with the bark that they beat and turn into loin-cloths for their women (Colb. 3, p. 60). It would seem, therefore, that the native ethnobotanical system groups into one big family trees similarly characterized by their light-weight wood and their frequent transformation into hollow cylinders, whether this transformation occurs naturally and inside the tree, or artificially and outside the tree as a result of human industry which, as it were, empties a bark tube of its trunk.[13] Within this large family particular attention should be paid to the bombax trees, since they play a leading part in the Guiana myths belonging to the same group as all those we have studied up till now:

M319. Carib. 'The disobedient daughters'

Two young girls refused to accompany their parents who had been invited to a drinking party. They remained alone in the family hut where they were visited by a demon who lived in the hollow trunk of a neighbouring tree – a ceiba tree. The demon shot a parrot with an arrow and asked the young girls to cook it. They were only too ready to oblige.

When the dinner was over, the demon slung up his hammock and called on the younger girl to join him. But not feeling so inclined, she sent her sister instead. During the night she heard strange noises and growls, which she first of all thought were caused by their love-making. However, the din grew louder so, after blowing up the fire, she went over to see what was happening. Blood was trickling from the hammock where her sister lay dead, pierced by her lover.

---

[13] Madame Claudine Berthe, an ethnobotanical specialist, has kindly pointed out that several modern botanists class the bombax family with the tiliaceae, or very close to them.

The girl now guessed who he really was and, in order to escape a similar fate, she hid herself under a heap of buck-corn which lay rotting in a corner, all covered with mildew. To make assurance doubly sure, she further warned the Spirit of the Rot that, if he allowed the demon to come and catch her, she would never supply him with any more corn. As it happened, the Spirit was so busy eating the corn that he did not reply to the demon's questions. The demon was unable to find the young girl's hiding place and, now that dawn was beginning to break, he had to hurry back to his home.

It was not until midday that the young girl dared to emerge from her hiding place. She rushed out to meet her people, who were returning from the drinking party. After being informed of what had happened, the parents gathered twenty basketfuls of pimentoes, tipped them round the tree and set fire to them. The demons were asphyxiated by the smoke and came tumbling down from the tree one after the other in the shape of guariba monkeys. Finally, the killer appeared and the Indians clubbed him to death. The younger sister obeyed her parents from that time onward (Roth 1, p. 231).

The armature of the above myth is clearly similar to that of the Guiana myths about the girl left alone in the camp while her people went hunting or visiting neighbours (M_{235}, M_{237}). But whereas in those myths the Spirit was a chaste provider of food and respectful of menstrual blood, the Spirit in this myth is lustful, bloodthirsty and a killer. In all the myths in this group which have a male hero, mildew plays a fatal role and is the cause of disjunction between the hunter and his game. In the present myth, where the leading character is a woman (and is looked upon as game from the demon's point of view), mildew is a protection covering the victim's and not the persecutor's body. The heroine in M_{235} chooses seclusion because she is unwell, and therefore a source of rot, whereas the two heroines in M_{319}, who have no legitimate reason for refusing to accompany their parents, are merely prompted by a spirit of insubordination. So, instead of telling the story of a well-behaved girl who is given honey as a reward, M_{319} tells the story of a disobedient girl who is avenged by the stinging smoke from the pimentoes.[14] Within this group, the two extremes of which I have just described, and which are characterized by a radical inversion of

[14] According to the Tucuna, the Spirit of the ceiba tree inflicts arrow wounds on women who are unwell: and bathing in water in which pimentoes have been cooked is the best antidote for any pollution due to menstrual blood (Nim. 13, pp. 92, 101).

all the themes, it is appropriate to place another myth occupying a middle position:

M_{320}. Carib. 'The origin of tobacco'

A man saw an Indian with agouti paws disappearing into a ceiba tree. He was a nature-spirit. Wood, pimentoes and salt were piled round the tree and then set alight. The Spirit appeared to the man in a dream, and told him to go in three months' time to the place where he, the Spirit, had died. He would find a plant growing among the ashes. By soaking its broad leaves, he could prepare a drink to induce trances. It was during his first trance that the man learnt all the secrets of the healer's art (Goeje, p. 114).

According to a myth from the same source (M_{321}; Goeje, p. 114), the man visited by the Spirit was someone who had refused to help in preparing the fire and he was given tobacco as a reward for his compassion. Whether or not we should place the Spirit who is thus helped between the helpful Spirit in M_{235} and the unhelpful Spirit in M_{319}, it is clear that the Carib myth about the origin of tobacco closes a cycle, since the masculine character with agouti's feet (a vegetarian rodent and a perfectly harmless animal) whose ashes give rise to tobacco for drinking, after he himself has been caught in the trap of the hollow ceiba tree, links up directly with the female character in M_{24}, whose head first of all, and then her body, takes on the appearance of the jaguar, a carnivorous and dangerous animal whose ashes give rise to tobacco for smoking, after its unsuccessful attempt to kill its victims who had taken refuge in the hollow trunk of a silk-cotton tree. The circle has been completed, but only at the cost of certain transformations, which must now be examined.

In all these myths, the tree appears as an invariant term, and the fascination of native thought, from Guiana to the Chaco, with the silk-cotton family, cannot be entirely explained by such objective and noteworthy characteristics as their swollen trunks, lightweight wood and the frequency of an internal cavity. The Carib do not fell the ceiba tree (Goeje, p. 55), because, not only in their territory, but from Mexico to the Chaco, this tree has a supernatural counterpart – the tree of the world, which contains within its hollow trunk primeval water and fish, or the tree of paradise ... Keeping to the method I have used up till now, I propose not to embark on these problems of mythic etymology which, in this particular instance, would necessitate extending the inquiry to the myths of Central America. Since the ceiba tree, or trees of similar species, constitute the invariant terms of the group we are concerned with, to determine their meaning we need do no more than compare and contrast the complexes of mythical contexts in which they happen to appear.

In the Chaco myths about the origin of tobacco, the hollow trunk of a silk-cotton tree is used as a place of refuge; in the Guiana myths about the origin of tobacco, it serves as a trap. But the hollow tree has a dual role in the Guiana myths in which the heroine is a girl mad about honey (whether directly or by transformation): sometimes it is a place of refuge and sometimes a trap, and occasionally both within the same myth (e.g. M_{241}). On the other hand, a secondary contrast emerges between honey which is found inside the tree, and the pimento smoke which rises up all round it.

Having evolved this first series, we can confidently construct a second. In M_{24}, the honey made bitter by the addition of young snakes has the same relationship with smoked tobacco as the stinging pimento smoke in M_{320} with a kind of 'tobacco honey':[15]

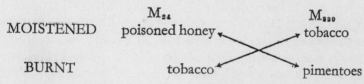

$$M_{24} \qquad\qquad M_{320}$$

MOISTENED   poisoned honey   tobacco

BURNT   tobacco   pimentoes

At the same time as one circle is completed, the transfer of tobacco from the category of the burnt to that of the moistened creates a chiasmus. Two consequences ensue. First, we sense that the mythology of tobacco is two-fold, according to whether the tobacco is smoked or drunk, and according to whether its consumption is associated with the profane or the sacred, just as we had observed, in connection with the mythology of honey, the creation of a duality through the distinction between fresh and fermented honey. Secondly, we see once again that when the armature is retained, the message changes: M_{320} reproduces M_{24}, but deals with a different kind of tobacco. Mythic deduction always has a dialectical character: it moves in spirals, and not in circles. When we think we are back at our starting-point, we are never absolutely and completely there, but only in a certain respect. It would be more accurate to say that we are moving vertically over the place we set out from. But whether we are moving at a higher or a lower level,

[15] In the preparation of which salt plays a part, which explains how it comes to be mentioned in M_{321}.

there is an implied difference representing the significant discrepancy between the initial myth and the terminal myth (the adjectives being taken in a sense relating to distance covered). Finally, according to the viewpoint adopted, the discrepancy can be situated on the level of the armature, the code or the vocabulary.

Let us now look at the sequence of animals. I shall not go back over the correlational and oppositional relationship between the extreme terms, the frog and the jaguar, since this relationship has already been clarified (p. 249). But what is there to be said about the middle pair formed by the guariba monkeys in M_{319} and the agouti in M_{320}? The agouti is a rodent (*Dasyprocta aguti*), and the egotistical master of the fruit of the tree of life in the Guiana myths (cf. p. 264, n. 3). The guariba or howler monkey (*Alouatta* sp.) is a producer of filth: metaphorically, by virtue of the correlation between din and corruption, which has been demonstrated in other ways (p. 310); and literally, since the howler monkey is an incontinent animal which drops its excrement from the tops of trees, unlike the sloth which can control itself for several days and takes the trouble to climb down to the ground in order to defecate regularly in the same place (Tacana, M_{322}–M_{323}; H.-H., pp. 39–40; cf. *RC*, p. 315).[16] The Waiwai, who are a Carib tribe living along the frontier between British Guiana and Brazil, imitate various animals in the dances performed during their Shodewika festival. The dancers, dressed as howler monkeys, climb up onto the cross-beams of the collective hut and squat there, pretending to discharge banana skins onto the heads of the spectators (Fock, p. 181). This means that the agouti and the howler monkey are a pair of opposites, one being a monopolizer of food, the other a dispenser of excrement.

The part of demon-game which is assigned to the howler monkey in the Guiana myths re-emerges almost unchanged in an important Karaja myth (M_{117}), which I have so far referred to only briefly. This is a particularly appropriate point at which to return to it, since it will lead us back by an unexpected route to the problem of the clapper; its hero belongs to the family of 'unlucky hunters' who appear in M_{234}–M_{240}, and so to the group of the girl mad about honey.

M_{177a}. *Karaja*. 'The magic arrows'

Two great howler monkeys lived in the forest, killing and eating hunters. Two brothers tried to destroy them. On their way, they met a

---

16 The contrast between the howler monkey and the sloth was the subject of one of my annual lecture courses at the Collège de France, cf. *Annuaire*, 65th year, 1965–6, pp. 269–70.

toad-woman who promised to teach them how to overcome monsters, but on condition that they took her as their wife. The brothers jeered at her and continued on their way. Soon they perceived the monkeys, armed, like themselves, with throwing-spears. A fight began, but both brothers were wounded in the eye and died.

A third brother lived in the family hut. His body was covered with sores and ulcers, and only his grandmother was prepared to look after him. One day, while hunting birds, he lost an arrow and tried to find it again. It had fallen into a snake's lair. The reptile came out, questioned the boy and learnt of his unhappy condition. To effect a cure, he made him a present of some black ointment, about which he was to tell no one.

He was soon better, and resolved to avenge his brothers' death. The snake gave him a magic arrow, and advised him not to reject the toad-woman's advances. In order to satisfy her, he need only simulate coitus between the poor creature's fingers and toes.

This the hero did, and in exchange was advised to let the monkeys shoot first and, when his turn came, to aim at the eyes. The dead animals remained hanging from the branches by their tails, and a lizard had to be sent to unfasten them.

The hero then went to thank the snake. The latter gave him some magic arrows which could kill and bring back all varieties of game, and which could even gather the fruits of the forest, including honey and many other things. There were as many arrows as there were animal species and different kinds of food, and also, in a gourd, a substance to be smeared on the arrows so that they should not hit the hunter too hard on returning.

With the help of the snake's arrows, the hero could now obtain all the game and fish he wanted. He got married, built a hut and cleared the ground for a plantation. But although he had urged his wife not to entrust his arrows to anyone, she allowed herself to be tricked by her own brother. To begin with, the latter shot successfully at wild pigs and fish, but forgot to smear the arrow used for gathering honey; as it came back to him, it changed into a huge head with a great many jaws all bristling with teeth. The head threw itself upon the Indians and killed them.

Alarmed by the cries, the hero ran back from his plantation and succeeded in driving the monster away. Half the village had perished. When informed of the tragedy, the snake said that it was irreparable.

He invited his protégé to a pirarucu (*Arapaimua gigas*) fishing party, and told the Indian not to forget to tell him, should one of his daughters happen to push him. This is precisely what happened, but the hero forgot the snake's instructions. The latter changed into a pirarucu fish, and the man likewise. When the Indians caught them both, the snake managed to escape through a hole in the net, but the fish-man was dragged up onto the bank, where a fisherman tried to club him to death. The snake came to the rescue, helped him to get out of the net and restored him to his human shape. He explained to him that he had been punished because he had said nothing when the young girl touched him (Ehrenreich, pp. 84–6).

Krause (pp. 347–50) gives two variants of this myth ($M_{117b, c}$). The episode of the pirarucu fishing expedition does not occur in these myths or, if it does, in a scarcely recognizable form. I therefore simply refer the reader to Dietschy's interesting discussion (Dietschy 2) while at the same time pointing out, for the benefit of anyone anxious to make a complete study of the myth, that the conclusion is similar to that of M_{78}. Other differences relate to the hero's family. He is abandoned by his parents and entrusted to his grandfather who feeds him on refuse and fish-bones. In M_{177a} he marries his aunt. The two variants add another victory to the one over the monkeys: the hero vanquishes two birds of prey, after provoking them by striking the water: tou, tou ... (cf. M_{226}–M_{227}). This detail, which is common to the myths of the eastern Ge, suggests that in both cases we are dealing with a foundation myth relating to the initiation ceremony for boys which, among the Karaja, also took place in several stages (Lipkind 2, p. 187).

The interest of the myth lies in the many references linking it up with the Ge and the Guiana tribes (M_{237}–M_{239}, M_{241}–M_{258}), in particular to the Kachúyana, since, as has already been stressed, M_{177} reverses the myth about the origin of curare belonging to the Kachúyana community (M_{161}) by introducing (although with reference to fights with hostile, ill-intentioned howler monkeys) the idea of *inverted poison*, in the form of an ointment, the purpose of which is to weaken the magic arrows, so that, on the return flight, their full force should not be directed against the hunter. It is interesting to note that these super-arrows bring the collecting of wild food produce and honey into the same category as hunting, so that the myth treats these foods as game. The present state of knowledge about the Karaja does not allow us to attempt an explanation, which could be no more than speculative. Lastly, in treating the spaces between the fingers and toes as if they were real orifices, M_{177} refers back to certain Chaco myths, in which the heroine is also a batrachian (M_{175}), and to a Tacana myth (M_{324}) which likewise contains this theme.

The Krause versions modify Ehrenreich's version in one respect, which seems to me to be of vital importance. The snake (or the protector in human form in $M_{177b, c}$), instead of giving the hero magic arrows (which in fact are throwing-spears), presents him with two equally magical instruments: a wooden projectile called obiru, and an object made from two sticks of canna brava (a member of the anonaceous family), one light, one dark, stuck together with wax over their whole length, and decorated at one end with black feathers. This instrument is called hetsiwa.

When he strikes (*schlägt*) these objects or waves them in the air, the hero creates a great wind. Uohu snakes (the word also means 'wind' or 'arrow') suddenly appear and go inside the hetsiwa. Then the wind brings fish, wild pigs and honey, which the hero shares out among the villagers, keeping only the remains to eat with his mother. One day, while he is away fishing, a child gets hold of the obiru, conjures up the snakes, but is unable to make them go back into the hetsiwa. The snakes (or winds) run wild and kill all the people in the village, including the hero, who cannot control the monsters without the help of the obiru. The slaughter puts an end to the human race (Krause, *loc. cit.*).

Among the Karaja, the obiru and the hetsiwa, unlike the Tucuna clapper in M_{304}, actually exist and are known to be in current use. The obiru is a dart shot by means of a spear-thrower. M_{177} suggests that this weapon may have been used in former times for monkey-hunting, but in the early twentieth century it had become a plaything and, in the form in which it has been observed, most probably borrowed from tribes in the Xingu (Krause, p. 273, Figure 127). The hetsiwa, a purely magical object used for warding off rain, presents problems of interpretation which are extremely complex because of the unevenness in size and difference in colour of the two sticks; it also presents linguistic problems. The thicker stick, which is painted black, is called kuoluni, (k)woru-ni, a word meaning electric fish, according to Krause and Machado, but which, in this particular instance, Dietschy (*loc. cit.*) is inclined to link with the general term (k)o-woru, 'magic'. The composition of the name of the slender, whitish stick nohõdémuda is doubtful, except that the element nohõ signifies penis.

According to Krause, Indians also use the term hetsiwa for a magic object made of wax, which is used for casting spells and which represents an aquatic creature that he believes to be the electric fish. Dietschy gives very convincing evidence to prove that it is the dolphin. I nevertheless hesitate to reject outright the supposed symbolical affinity between the first kind of hetsiwa, or the black stick which is one element of it, and the electric fish. In the Karaja language, the latter has the same name as the rainbow, that is, a meteoric phenomenon which, like the magic object, puts an end to rain. The use of the hetsiwa, which is strangely reminiscent of the club-spear employed by the Nambikwara to cut and dissipate storm clouds, also has a link with a more northerly Arawak myth, in which the electric fish fulfils the same function:

M_{325}. *Arawak. 'The marriage of the electric fish'*

An old sorcerer had such a beautiful daughter that he had difficulty in finding a husband worthy of her. He rejected a succession of suitors, including the jaguar. Finally, Kasum, the electric fish (*Electrophorus electricus*, a gymnotus or electric eel), appeared and boasted of his great strength. The old man jeered at him, but after touching the suitor and feeling the violence of the shock, he changed his mind and accepted him as his son-in-law, at the same time giving him the task of controlling thunder, lightning and rain. When storms approached, Kasum divided the clouds, some to the right, some to the left, and drove them respectively southwards and northwards (Farabee 5, pp. 77–8).

The comparison is interesting because of the role assigned to fish in the mythology of the Karaja, who depend almost entirely on fish for their food. The pirarucu made its appearance at the end of M_{177a}. This enormous fish, the only one the Karaja catch in a net (Baldus 5, p. 26), is in this respect unlike all the other species, which are caught with poison, and unlike the snake which, according to M_{177a}, easily escaped through the mesh net. There is a second dichotomy, which corresponds to this initial one between the snake and the pirarucu fish. One Karaja myth (M_{177d}) attributes the origin of pirarucu fish to two brothers who were tired of their wives and who changed into fish (*Arapaima gigas*). One was eaten by storks because it was soft (therefore rotten: cf. M_{331}); the other, which was as hard as stone, survived and became the laténi mask, which terrifies women and children (Baldus 6, pp. 213–15; Machado, pp. 43–5). These men who were disappointed in human love and who changed into pirarucu fish are an inversion of the woman, or women, in the tapir-as-seducer cycle, who were passionately in love with an animal and who changed into fish which, in general terms, are in contrast to the special category formed by the pirarucu.

But let us return to the hetsiwa. If we compare Ehrenreich's and Krause's versions of M_{177}, we discover that almost always two types of objects are involved. The obiru or obirus are used in $M_{177a, b}$ to 'call' game and honey, whereas, it is the function of the magic ointment, according to M_{177a}, and the function of the hetsiwa, according to M_{177b}, to neutralize the dangers inherent in this call. Provided we disregard M_{177c} (a very abbreviated version in which the hetsiwa combines both functions), it follows that the hetsiwa in M_{177b} plays the same part as the ointment in M_{177a}, which is an inverted poison.

Now the hetsiwa is itself an inverted instrument in comparison with the clapper in M_{304}, or the parabára: the two sticks of which it is made and which are fixed together over their whole length *cannot be* struck one against the other. This is by no means a unique instance. It is illustrated in a very similar form among the Sherente whose culture is, in certain respects, remarkably similar to that of the Karaja. Nimuendaju (6, pp. 68–9, Pl. III) describes and illustrates a ritual object called wabu, of which the Indians make four models, two large ones, wabu-zauré, and two small ones, wabu-rié, for the feast of the great ant-eater (cf. above, p. 132). Each one consists of two stems of burity palms (*Mauritia*) painted red and fixed together by means of projecting pegs. At either end of the upper peg hangs a very long tassel, made of bark fibres. The four wabu-bearers accompany the masked dancers to the place at which the feast is held, then divide off into pairs, one of which takes up its position to the east, the other to the west, of the dancing area.

Information is unfortunately lacking about the significance of the wabu and their function in the ritual. But their physical resemblance to the hetsiwa is all the more striking since there are two kinds of wabu, one large, one small, and since Krause (Figure 182a, b) illustrates two types of Karaja ritual instruments made of sticks fixed together.

In the present state of knowledge, the theory according to which the hetsiwa and the wabu represent, as it were, immobilized clappers, must be put forward with extreme prudence. Yet the existence of similar conceptions among the ancient Egyptians gives it a certain credibility. I am well aware that Plutarch's evidence is often suspect. I therefore make no claim to be restating authentic beliefs since, as far as I am concerned, it is of scant importance whether the imagery to which I am about to refer originated among reliable Egyptian sages, among a handful of Plutarch's informants, or in Plutarch's own mind.

In my view, the only point worthy of attention is that, after I had noted on several occasions that the intellectual processes evidenced in Plutarch's work presented a curious similarity to those I was deducing from South American myths, and that, consequently, in spite of the

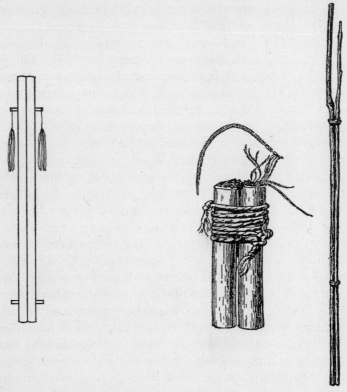

Figure 18 (*left*). Diagram of a wabu. (After Nim. 6, Pl. III.)
Figure 19. The two hetsiwa. (After Krause, *loc. cit.*, p. 333.)

time gap and geographical distance, I had to admit that in both instances human minds had worked in the same way, a new convergence should emerge in connection with a hypothesis I would not have dared to put forward, had it not made the comparison justifiable.

Here then is Plutarch's text:

Moreover, Manethus says that the Egyptians have a mythical tradition in regard to Jupiter, that because his legs were grown together he was not able to walk and so for shame tarried in the wilderness;

but Isis, by severing and separating those parts of his body, provided him with means of rapid progress. This fable teaches by its legend that the mind and reason of the god, fixed amid the unseen and invisible, advanced to generation by reason of motion. The sistrum, a metallic rattle, also makes it clear that all things in existence need to be shaken, or rattled about, and never to cease from motion but, as it were, to be waked up and agitated when they grow drowsy and torpid. They say that they avert and repel Typhon by means of the sistrums, indicating thereby that when destruction constricts and checks Nature, generation releases and arouses it by means of motion (Plutarch's *Moralia. Isis and Osiris,* 376).

Is it not extraordinary that the Karaja, whose magical practices and the problems they raise have led us to Plutarch, should have evolved a story completely symmetrical with his? They say that Kanaschiwué, their demiurge, had to have his arms and legs tied to prevent him from destroying the earth by floods and other disasters, as he would have done had his movements been unrestricted (Baldus 5, p. 29).[17]

In spite of its obscurity, the Greek text introduces a clear contrast between, on the one hand silence and immobility symbolized by two limbs normally separate yet welded together, and on the other movement and noise, symbolized by the sistrums. As in South America, unlike the first term, only the second term is a musical instrument. As in South America also, this musical instrument (or its opposite) is used to 'divert or drive away' a natural force (or it is used to attract it for criminal purposes): in one instance, it is Typhon, that is, Seth; in the other, the tapir or snake as seducers, the snake-rainbow associated with rain, rain itself or the chthonian spirits.

The sistrum proper is not a musical instrument which is widely known in South America. Among the Caduveo, I found sistrums corresponding to the description already given by other observers. They were

---

[17] In the same way, it would also be appropriate to re-examine the famous episode of Aristeus (Virgil, *Georgics,* IV) in which Proteus (who corresponds to Plutarch's Typhon) has to be bound hand and foot during the dry season: '*Iam rapidus torrens sitientis Sirius Indos*', in order to make him consent to show the shepherd how to find honey again, after it has been lost as a result of the disappearance of Eurydice, the mistress, if not of honey like the heroine of M233–M234, undeniably mistress of the honeymoon! Eurydice, who is swallowed by a monstrous sea-serpent (*ibid.,* v. 459), is an inversion of the heroine of M326a who was born from a sea-serpent and who rejected a honeymoon, in the days when animals had the gift of speech, and therefore would not have had any use for an Orpheus.

made of a forked stick with the two branches joined by a string on which were threaded a few discs once carved from bone or shell, but nowadays made of metal. A similar instrument exists among the Yaqui of north Mexico. No other instances of it are known in America (Izikowitz, pp. 150–51).

But, in the absence of the sistrum, we have at our disposal another basis of comparison between the mythical representations of the New World and the Old. The reader will no doubt have noticed that a curious analogy exists between the means employed for the tapped-out call in the South American myths: a resonator made from a gourd or tree-trunk which is struck, sticks which are knocked against each other, or clappers, and a liturgical complex belonging to the Old World, known as the instruments of darkness. The origin of these instruments, and their use from the Thursday to the Saturday of Holy Week, presents a great many problems. As I cannot claim to participate in a complex discussion which lies outside my competence, I shall merely refer to one or two generally accepted points.

It would seem that fixed bells in churches did not make their appearance until rather late, about the seventh century. Their enforced silence from the Thursday to the Saturday of Holy Week does not seem to be recorded before about the eighth century (and then only in Rome). At the end of the twelfth and beginning of the thirteenth century, the restriction appears to have spread to other European countries. But the reason for the bells remaining silent, and for them being replaced temporarily by other sources of noise, is not clear. Their alleged journey to Rome, which accounted for their temporary absence, may be no more than an *a posteriori* explanation, founded moreover on all kinds of beliefs and imaginative suppositions connected with bells: they were thought to be animate, vocal beings, capable of feeling and acting, and fit for baptism. In addition to summoning the congregation to the church, bells had a meteorological, and even a cosmic, function. Their reverberations drove storms away, dispelled clouds and hail, and destroyed evil spells.

According to Van Gennep, whom I have followed so far (t. I, Vol. III, pp. 1209–14), the instruments of darkness which replace the bells include the hammer, the hand rattle, the clapper or hand-knocker, a kind of castanets called '*livre*', the matraca (a flat slab of wood with two moveable plates attached to either side which strike it when it is shaken) and the wooden sistrum on a string or a ring. Other instruments, such as the *batelet* and huge rattles, were quite complicated pieces of apparatus. In theory, all these devices had a definite function, but in actual practice they often overlapped: they were used to make a noise inside the church or out, to summon the congregation in the absence of bells, or to accompany the collecting of alms by children. There is, also, some evidence that the instruments of darkness may have been intended to represent the marvels and terrifying noises which occurred at the time of the death of Christ.

In the case of Corsica (Massignon), wind instruments are mentioned (the marine horn, the wooden whistle, or more simply the making of a whistling noise by blowing between the fingers), together with various percussive instruments or devices: the beating of the altar and benches in churches, the smashing of planks with clubs, the use of hand-knockers, clappers and hand rattles of various types, one of which was called raganetta, 'rainette' (tree-frog), while another made from reeds was a sort of improved parabára, with one of the blades of split bamboo replaced by a cogged wooden wheel. The name 'tree-frog' is also found in other areas.

In France, the instruments of darkness included ordinary objects: metal pots and pans which were beaten, wooden clogs which were used for hammering on the ground, wooden mallets which were used for striking the ground and other objects; sticks with split ends or bundles of branches used in the same way; hand-clapping; and lastly musical instruments of various kinds: some with a solid wooden resonator (the knocker, the hand rattle, the clapper, the board hammered by means of an attachment and the sistrum); others made of metal (big bells, little bells and rattles) or with a membrane (the spinning, friction drum); or vibrating wind instruments (dry and wet whistles, horns, shells, hunting horns, hooters and oboes).

In the High Pyrenees, the author who gives the above classification studied the making and use of a spinning friction drum, called toulou-hou (Marcel-Dubois, pp. 55–89). An old tin with the bottom knocked out, or a cylindrically shaped piece of bark, serves as a resonator: the drum is left open at one end, while a piece of sheepskin or a bladder is secured over the other to act as a membrane. A loop of string is threaded through two holes pierced in the centre. The loose ends are fixed by means of a slip knot round a grooved stick, which is used to work the instrument. After smearing the groove with saliva, the performer grasps the handle and causes the instrument to rotate. The string vibrates and produces a kind of throbbing noise described as 'humming' or 'squeaking', according to whether the string is made of twine or horsehair.

The literal meaning of toulouhou is hornet or bumble-bee. But in other areas the instrument is called after different animals, which may be insects (the grasshopper or cicada) or batrachians (the tree-frog or toad). The German name *Waldteufel*, 'wood demon', is even reminiscent of the Warao myth (M₃₁₇), in which the bush spirits regret that they are so inadequately provided with musical instruments.

Although the ritual stipulates that the bells should remain silent from the Collect during mass on the Thursday before Good Friday to the Gloria on the following Saturday (Van Gennep, *loc. cit.*, pp. 1217–37; Marcel-Dubois, p. 55), it would seem that the Church has always been opposed to the instruments of darkness and has tried to restrict their use. For this reason, Van Gennep accepts the view that their origin lies in folklore. Without deciding whether or not the din made by the instruments of darkness survives as a relic of neolithic or even paleolithic customs, or whether its occurrence in widely scattered areas merely shows that man, when confronted with the same situations, reacts with the help of symbolic representations suggested to him, or perhaps even forced upon him, by the underlying processes which control his thought the world over, we can accept Van Gennep's prudently formulated thesis, and can even quote a parallel instance in support of it:

In China, every year about the beginning of April, certain officials called Sz'hüen used of old to go about the country armed with wooden clappers. Their business was to summon the people and command them to put out every fire. This was the beginning of the season called Han-shih-tsieh, or 'eating cold food'. For three days all household fires remained extinct as a preparation for the solemn renewal of the fire, which took place on the fifth or sixth day after the winter solstice. The ceremony was performed with great pomp by the same officials who procured the new fire from heaven by reflecting the sun's rays either from a metal mirror or from a crystal on dry moss. Fire thus obtained is called by the Chinese heavenly fire and its use is enjoined in sacrifices: whereas fire elicited by the friction of wood is termed by them earthly fire, and its use is prescribed for cooking and other domestic purposes ... This annual renewal of fire was a ceremony of very great antiquity in China ... since it dates from (at least) two thousand years before Christ (Frazer 4, quoting various sources: Vol. 10, p. 137). Granet (pp. 283,

514) twice briefly mentions this rite, with reference to the *Tcheou li* and the *Li ki*.

I have mentioned this old Chinese custom (which has parallels both in the East and the Far East), because it is relevant in more than one respect. In the first place, it seems to follow a relatively simple and easily discernible pattern: in order to seize fire *from above* and bring it down *here below*, there must be an annual conjunction between the sky and the earth. This, however, is a hazardous and almost sacrilegious undertaking, since celestial fire and earthly fire are governed by a relationship of incompatibility. The extinction of terrestrial fires, which is heralded or ordered by clappers, functions therefore as a necessary pre-condition. It creates the required vacuum, which allows the conjunction of celestial fire and the earth to take place without dangerous consequences. The misgivings I inevitably feel at having had to look so far afield for a term of comparison are to some extent allayed by an obvious comparison between the old Chinese rite and a recent ceremony practised by the Sherente Indians, which I have already analysed, and whose importance regarding the problems we are concerned with was indicated in *The Raw and the Cooked* (pp. 289–91, 314). Among the Sherente, too, the rite concerned the renewal of fire, which was preceded by the extinction of domestic fires and by a period of mortification. The new fire had to be obtained from the sun, notwithstanding the danger men exposed themselves to in going near it or in bringing it near to them. The same contrast is also to be observed between celestial fire, which is sacred and destructive, and terrestrial fire, which is profane and constructive, since it is the fire used in the home. To complete the comparison, we would no doubt need to discover the use of wooden clappers among the Sherente. There is no evidence of their being present, but at least we know that these Indians possess a ritual instrument, the wabu, which we recognized, for reasons very different from those that concern us at present, as being an inverted clapper (p. 401). Most important of all, the Sherente ritual of the great fast gives pride of place to another kind of noise-maker – supernatural wasps which reveal their presence to those officiating by a characteristic hum: ken! – ken! – ken-ken-ken-ken! (*RC*, p. 315, n. 19). Now, whereas the Chinese tradition refers only to the clapper, and the Sherente tradition to the wasps, we have seen that, in Europe, the rotating friction drum – which, in the Pyrenees, is called by a name signifying 'bumblebee' or 'hornet' – appears as one of the instruments of darkness alongside the clapper, and can even replace it.

Let us now proceed further with this attempt to work out a mythic and ritual pattern which, as we are beginning to suspect, may be common to cultures very remote from each other, and to very different traditions. Like archaic China and certain Amero-Indian societies, Europe, until quite recently, celebrated a rite involving the extinguishing and renewal of domestic fires, preceded by fasting and the use of the instruments of darkness. This series of events took place just before Easter, so that the 'darkness' which prevailed in the church during the service of the same name (*Tenebrae*), could symbolize both the extinguishing of domestic fires and the darkness which covered the earth at the moment of Christ's death.

In all Catholic countries it was customary to extinguish the lights in the churches on Easter Eve and then make a new fire sometimes with flint or with the help of a burning-glass. Frazer brings together numerous instances which show that this fire was used to give every house new fire. He quotes a sixteenth-century Latin poem in a contemporary English translation, from which I take the following significant lines:

On Easter Eve the fire all is quencht in every place,
And fresh againe from out the flint is fecht with solemne grace.

*

Then Clappers ceasse, and belles are set againe at libertée,
And herewithall the hungrie times of fasting ended bée.

In England, the bells were silent from Maundy Thursday until midday on Easter Sunday, and were replaced by wooden clappers (Frazer, *loc. cit.*, p. 125). In several parts of Europe, the return of plenty was also symbolized by 'gardens of Adonis', which were prepared as Easter approached (Frazer 4, Vol. 5, pp. 253 *ff*).

The plenty which now returned had not just been absent since Maundy Thursday; its loss went back much further, to the day following Shrove Tuesday to be precise. As regards acoustic symbols and their relationship to food, three periods can be distinguished. The instruments of darkness accompanied the final weeks of Lent, that is the period in which the hardships of fasting were most acutely felt, since they had lasted longer. The bells rang out once more on Easter Sunday to mark the end of this Lenten period. But before it even began, an exceptional and unrestrained use of bells had summoned the population to make the most of the last day of plenty: the bell rung on the morning of Shrove Tuesday was known in England as the *pancake bell*. The gastronomic excesses for which it was the signal, and indeed rendered almost obligatory, are illustrated in the following picturesque popular ballad of 1684:

> But hark I hear the pancake bell,
> And fritters make a gallant smell;
> The cooks are baking, frying, boyling,
> Carving, gourmandising, roasting,
> Carbonading, cracking, slashing, toasting.

(Wright and Lones, p. 9; cf. pp. 8–20)

In connection with France, Van Gennep rightly insists on the culinary and ceremonial aspect, which is too often disregarded by theorists, of the Carnival-Lent cycle. But in the popular mind it has always been considered to be sufficiently important for Shrove Tuesday, or the first Sunday in Lent, to be called after the dishes associated with them: *jour des crêpes* or *crozets* (Pancake Day) in the case of Shrove Tuesday, *dimanche des beignets* or *bugnes* (Fritter Sunday) or Carling Sunday (fried peas) in the case of the first Sunday in Lent. At Montbéliard, typical Shrove Tuesday dishes were *pelai* (millet) or *paipai* (rice pudding) in the morning, and in the evening pork, ham, pig chaps or *bon-jésus* (a sort of black-pudding) with pickled cabbage. Elsewhere the Shrove Tuesday repast usually differed from other meals in that it comprised vast quantities of meat of all kinds, certain cuts being set aside specially for this particular day and prepared according to more elaborate recipes than those used for other meals. Clear meat soup, which was also used in ritual sprayings, gruel, pancakes fried in a greased pan, fritters fried in fat or oil were typical Shrove Tuesday dishes. In France, the obligatory making of pancakes is found only in the northern third of the country (Van Gennep, t. I, Vol. III, pp. 1125–36 and map XII).

If, after noting the Church's hostility towards customs it has always condemned as pagan in order to deprive them of the Christian overtones with which Europe has vainly endeavoured to endow them, we try to discover a form common to these American, Chinese and European examples, chosen from among a host of others listed by Frazer which would have served equally well, we arrive, in short, at the following conclusion:

A comprehensive inquiry into the place and function of the mythology of honey in tropical America drew our attention to an acoustic custom, which at first sight appears to be inexplicable. I am referring to the noise made by the knocking together of the honey-gatherer's sandals (M24).[18] In our search for terms of comparison, we encountered first the clapper in M304, which was probably an imaginary instrument, but which put us on the track of real-life instruments of the same type, whose existence in South America had passed almost unnoticed. Whether real or imaginary, these instruments are the equivalent, both from the organological and symbolic points of view, of the instruments of darkness of the European tradition, which had parallels in China, as is proved by an ancient rite.

Before proceeding further, I would like to discuss a point of organology. The European instruments of darkness include vibrating instruments with a solid body, as well as vibrating wind instruments. This then removes the objection to my interpretation which was constituted by the dual nature of the calls addressed to the animal-seducer by the heroine in a great many South American myths. These calls are either tapped out on the convex side of half a gourd placed on a watery surface, a tree-trunk or the ground, or they are whistled in imitation of the animal's cry. European ethnography notes the occurrence of the same ambiguity, sometimes in one particular place and on a clearly specified occasion. In Corsica, 'children armed with sticks beat vigorously on church pews, or, putting two fingers in their mouths, they see who can whistle the loudest. They represent the Jews hounding Christ' (Massignon, p. 276). I shall have more to say about this comment (p. 412).

This is not all. Throughout the present study, it has been noted that, in the minds of the Indians, myths about the origin of honey were associated with the dry season – or, in the absence of a dry season – with a period in the year also denoting scarcity. To this seasonal coding can be added another, acoustic in nature, and certain modalities of which I am now in a position to specify.

The conjunction of the honey-gatherer with the object of his search – a substance which is entirely on the side of nature, since cooking is not necessary in order to render it edible – or the conjunction of the woman

[18] A possible analogy that comes to mind is the use of charivari to prevent swarms of bees flying away. The custom is mentioned by many writers of antiquity listed by Billiard (2, pp. 382–3), and is perhaps still practised in certain areas. But as Billiard observes, 'some people thought the noise pleased the bees, others on the contrary that they were frightened by it.' Agreeing with Layens and Bonnier (pp. 148–9), he expresses the opinion 'that it (the custom) is of no use' or rather that its only purpose is publicly to affirm the rights of the pursuer, 'which is perhaps the only plausible explanation for this time-honoured custom' (Billiard 1, year 1899, no. 3, p. 115). As will appear later, charivari in connection with bees can only be interpreted as a particular instance of the application of the instruments of darkness.

with an animal seducer, whose position is semantically the same as that of honey, an alimentary seducer, are both in danger of causing total disjunction of the human character and culture, i.e. society. It should be emphasized, incidentally, that the concept of the disjunctive conjunction is not a contradictory one, since it refers to three terms, the second of which is joined to the first by the same operation which causes its disjunction from the third. This taking over of one term by another at the expense of a third (cf. *RC*, pp. 286–9) is given acoustic expression in M_{24} in the form of the knocking together of the sandals, just as another Chaco myth (M_{301}) exemplifies the reverse operation, that of conjunctive disjunction, by means of an exactly opposite noise: the brrumbrrrummbrum! of the snake as it prepares to swallow the honey-gatherers, after consuming the honey it has extorted from them.

When I quoted this myth (p. 337), I noted that the snake's cry was reminiscent of the noise of the bull-roarers. South American myths are certainly not the only ones in which a relationship of congruence between the snake and the penis can be observed, but they systematically exploit its full resources when, for instance, they illustrate a correlational and oppositional relationship between the snake, which is 'all penis', and its human mistress, who is 'all womb': a woman who can contain within her womb her lover or her grown child, and whose other orifices are wide open, releasing menstrual blood and urine and even peals of laughter (cf. *RC*, pp. 124 *ff*). Of this basic pair, the tapir with the 'big penis' and the opossum with the 'big womb' (either directly in the form of a good nurse, or figuratively in the form of an adulterous woman) are simply a combinatory variant in which the terms are less clearly defined (cf. *RC*, pp. 255–6).

The fact that observations made in Melanesia and Australia led Van Baal to suggest independently a phallic interpretation of the symbolism of bull-roarers strengthens still further my own conviction that the tapped-out call of the Tereno honey-gatherer and the roaring of the Toba snake form a pair of antithetical terms. I started from the hypothesis that the former was congruous with the tapped-out or whistled call of the tapir's mistress, and the latter with the sound of the bull-roarers. This hypothesis is now given support by the identification of the former with a call, addressed by a woman with a 'big vagina' (in the metaphorical sense) to an animal which is literally endowed with a large penis, and by the identification of the latter with a warning given to women (who, however, in this instance are pursued only to be more effectively driven away) by the bull-roarer, which is a figurative penis.

Consequently, in the one instance, the power of nature conjoins the sexes to the detriment of culture: the tapir's mistress is lost to her lawful husband, and sometimes the whole female race is lost to society. In the other instance, the power of culture disjoins the sexes, to the detriment of nature which prescribes their union; temporarily at least, family links are broken in order to allow human society to be formed.

Let us return for a moment to the Pyrenees. The toulouhou revolves around an axis, like the bull-roarer, and the two instruments are alike as regards the sound they produce, although they are very different from the organological point of view. In ritualistic practices, however, the toulouhou plays a part similar to the one I have just attributed to the bull-roarer by a purely deductive process but which is confirmed by innumerable instances observed in South America (Zerries 2), Melanesia and Australia (Van Baal) and Africa (Schaeffner). The use of the toulouhou is restricted to boys who use it before and during the Good Friday mass in order to frighten women and girls. Now the bull-roarer exists among Pyrenean communities, but never as an instrument of darkness. In the Labourd and Béarn areas, it is a carnival instrument, or else it is used to keep mares away from the sheep-folds (Marcel-Dubois, pp. 70–77). On the organological level, then, the contrast is maintained between the bull-roarer and the instruments of darkness, although on the symbolic level the function assigned to the bull-roarer by illiterate societies is, in a European society, dissociated from the bull-roarer and linked with the instrument of darkness it most resembles. In spite of this minor difference, on which it would be interesting to have specialist opinion, the basic contrast remains and can be formulated in the same terms. When used outside the church and before mass, the toulouhou, unlike the other instruments of darkness, has the same function as the bull-roarer. Its aim is to disjoin women (who are thus conjoined with nature) from the society of men (culture), men being then free to assemble on their own within the sacred precincts. But when it is used inside the church during mass, concurrently with the other instruments of darkness, its function is inseparable from theirs which is (if I may be allowed to generalize on the basis of Mlle Massignon's interpretation of the Corsican data) to symbolize the conjunction of Christ's enemies (nature) with the Saviour, who is then in a state of disjunction with culture.

Let us leave the bull-roarer for the time being and look again at the two-fold coding, seasonal and acoustic, of the group we were discussing. Let us take the seasonal coding first. It can be observed all over the world; in its real form, in South America, where there is an objective contrast between two periods of the year: one characterized by scarcity, the other by plenty; in a conventional form (but which is no doubt a ritualistic expression of an actual experience) in Europe, where Lent can be seen as a period of deliberate scarcity; finally in a quasi-potential form, in Ancient China, where the period of 'eating cold food' hardly lasted for more than a few days. But, in spite of being merely potential, the Chinese contrast is conceptually the most powerful since it is between absent fire and present fire, and the same is true of the Sherente contrast. Elsewhere in South America, the contrast is between a period of plenty and a period of scarcity, which is lived through at length without being necessarily simulated during a longer or shorter space of time. We find the same contrast in Europe, but transposed into the form of a contrast between the days on which meat is eaten and the Lenten period. Consequently, as we move from China to Europe, the major contrast is weakened:

[present fire/absent fire] ⇒ [meat/meatless]

and as we move from the New World (with the exception of one or two instances, such as that of the Sherente) to the Old World, the contrast becomes progressively slighter, since the five or six days of 'eating cold food' in China, or the even smaller number of days which make up the Christian triduum, correspond in miniature form to the longer period which, in Europe, lasts throughout the whole of Lent, from the end of Shrove Tuesday until Easter Sunday. If we disregard these differences and some possible repetitions, the underlying system can be reduced to three pairs of opposites of diminishing magnitude which can be arranged in a logical order, without the correspondences between their respective terms being obliterated:

$$\begin{cases} \text{absent fire} \\ \text{present fire} \begin{cases} \text{scarcity} \\ \text{plenty} \begin{cases} \text{meatless} \\ \text{meat} \end{cases} \end{cases} \end{cases}$$

Whether we are dealing with the absence of fire among the Ancient Chinese and the Sherente, or the period of scarcity in other parts of South America, or the absence of fire coinciding with the culminating point of Lent in the European tradition, it is clear that these various combinations of circumstances have certain features in common:

cooking is abolished either literally or symbolically; during a period varying in length from a few days to a whole season, direct contact is established between humanity and nature, as during the mythic age when fire did not yet exist and men had to eat their food raw, or after a brief exposure to the rays of the sun, which at that time was close to the earth. However, this immediate conjunction of man with nature can itself take two forms; either nature leaves man in the lurch and shortages which had at first been bearable become more acute until a state of famine is reached; or it yields a lavish supply of substitute foods, such as wild fruits and honey, in a natural instead of a cultural form (which only cooking would justify). These two possibilities, which are functions of an immediacy conceived in the negative or the positive mode, correspond to what I referred to in *The Raw and the Cooked* as the rotten world and the burnt world. And the world certainly is burnt symbolically, or is theoretically in danger of being burnt, when, by means of a burning-glass or a mirror (Old World) or by the presentation of fibres to the fire-bearing messenger of the sun (New World), men try to bring celestial fire back to earth in order to relight the fireless hearths. Similarly, that superlative kind of honey which is supposedly achieved by cultivation creates conditions of unbearable heat in the place where it grows (M_{192}). Conversely, we observed that wild, therefore natural, honey, and its metaphorical counterpart, the animal-seducer, carry with them a threat of decay.

Having reached this stage of the demonstration, I must check whether there is not a univocal correlation between the tapped-out (or whistled) call, and, on the one hand, the noise of the bull-roarers and, on the other, the burnt world and rotten world. The whole of the preceding argument would seem to establish, not only that each of these pairs of opposites is relevant in itself, but also that they are mutually concordant. However, we are about to see that serious complications arise at this point.

Let us take the case of the Bororo. They have an instrument of darkness, the parabára, and they also possess the bull-roarer. There is no doubt at all that the latter connotes the rotten world. The bull-roarer, which the Bororo call aigé, mimics the cry of a monster of the same name which is supposed to live in rivers and marshlands. The animal appears in certain rites, in the form of a dancer who is encased in mud from head to foot. The future priest learns of his vocation during a dream in which the aigé embraces him, without his experiencing fear or revulsion either at the monster's smell or at the stench of decayed corpses (Colb. 3, pp. 130, 163; *EB*, Vol. I, under 'ai-je' and 'aroe et-awaraare'). It is much more difficult to arrive at a definite conclusion regarding the symbolism of the parabára, about which practically nothing is known. The imaginary instrument in M₃₀₄, which belongs to the same family, is used to entice a demon out of the hut, i.e. to cause disjunction between him and the inhabitants of the village, and bring about conjunction with the fire in which he is to perish. On the strength of certain observations which I described on p. 370, we might be tempted to attribute the same significance to the Bororo rite of the parabára, since it features in practices which would seem to be intended to make sure that the soul has finally left the temporary grave prepared for it in the centre of the village. But it is only in the myths that the Bororo end on a funeral pyre. In real life, the bones of the dead, after being washed so as to remove all traces of flesh, are thrown into the river.

It follows that the contrast between the bull-roarer and the parabára reflects not so much the opposition between the rotten world and the burnt world as two possible procedures in relationship to the rotten world. The aigé, which is heralded by the noise of the bull-roarers, emerges from water, whereas the soul, which is conditioned by the rattle of the parabáras, moves towards water. But the water is not the same in both instances. The water in which the aigé lives is muddy and stinks of decayed corpses, whereas the bones which have been cleaned, painted and decorated with feathers cannot possibly pollute the clear waters of the lake or river into which they are dropped.

In the case of the Sherente, whose myths are strikingly symmetrical with those of the Bororo (*RC*, pp. 192–5), and present, in terms of fire, problems which the Bororo myths express in terms of water, the bull-roarer is not the voice of a Spirit who is about to appear, but the call which summons him to appear. The Spirit is celestial, not aquatic. He personifies the planet Mars, the companion of the Moon, just as Venus and Jupiter are the companions of the sun (Nim. 6, p. 85). It would seem, then, that the Sherente bull-roarer is associated with the least 'fiery' mode of the sky, and the Bororo bull-roarer with the most 'putrid' mode of water. As it happens, the Sherente also define the two modes of the sky, one diurnal, the other nocturnal, in relation to water. During the ceremonies of the Great Fast, the priests of Venus and Jupiter offer the performers clear water in bowls made from gourds (respectively *Lagenaria* and *Crescentia*), whereas the priests of Mars offer soiled water in a bowl decorated with feathers (Nim. 6, p. 97). This gives the following equivalences:

Bororo   *Sherente*

(dirty water : clean water) ::   [(night : day) ::
                                       (dirty water : clean water)]

This is a revealing formula, in that the 'long night' described by so many South American myths certainly refers to the rotten world, just as the myths about the universal fire refer to the burnt world. This being so, are we not forced to the conclusion that it is the bull-roarer, not the clapper, which plays the part of instrument of 'darkness' in America, whereas the other instrument belongs to a contrasting category which we have been unable to identify? As we move from the Old World to the New, only the form of the contrast seems to remain constant, while the content appears to be reversed.

Nevertheless, it is impossible to be satisfied with this solution, since there is an Amazonian myth connecting darkness with an instrument which has no doubt been imagined but which, from the organological point of view, is closer to the clapper or rattle than to the bull-roarer:

M_{326a}. *The Tupi of the Amazon. 'The origin of night'*
In former times, night did not exist. It was daylight all the time. Night slept beneath the waters. Animals did not exist either, for things themselves had the power of speech.

The daughter of the Great Snake had married an Indian, who was master of three faithful servants. 'Go away,' he said to them one day, 'for my wife refuses to sleep with me.' But it was not their presence which embarrassed the young woman. She wanted to make love only at night. She explained to her husband that her father held night prisoner, and that he should send his servants to fetch it.

When they arrived in a canoe at the abode of the Great Snake, the latter handed them a tightly closed nut of the tucuman (*Astrocaryum tucuman*) palm, and told them not to open it under any pretext. The servants re-embarked and were soon surprised to hear a noise coming from the nut: ten, ten ... xi, like the sound of crickets and little toads which sing at night. One servant wanted to open the nut, but the others were opposed to the idea. After a good deal of discussion and after they had travelled a long way from the Great Snake's abode, they eventually all assembled in the middle of the canoe where they lit a fire and melted the resin sealing the nut. At once night fell and all things that were in the forest changed into quadrupeds and birds; those in the river became ducks and fish. The basket turned into a jaguar, the fisherman and his canoe became a duck: the man's head acquired a beak; the canoe became the body, the oars the feet ...

The darkness covering the world made it clear to the Snake's daughter what had happened. When the morning star appeared, she decided to separate night from day. With this end in view, she changed two balls of thread into birds – the cujubim and the inhambu [respectively of the cracidae and tinamidae families and which sing at regular intervals during the night or to greet the dawn; in connection with these 'bird-clocks', cf. *RC*, p. 204, n. 3]. As a punishment, she changed the disobedient servants into monkeys (Couto de Magalhães, pp. 231–3; cf. Derbyshire, pp. 16–22).

This myth raises some complex problems. Those relating to the trio of servants will be discussed in the next volume. For the time being, I am chiefly concerned with the three-fold contrast which provides the armature of the myth. The contrast between day and night is obvious, and implies two others: first, between the conjunction and the disjunction of the sexes, since day enforces the latter and night is the pre-condition of the former; then, between linguistic behaviour and non-linguistic behaviour: when there was continuous daylight, everything had the power of speech, even beasts and objects, and it was at the precise moment when night made its appearance that things became dumb and animals became unable to express themselves except by inarticulate cries.

Now, in the myth, the first appearance of night is the result of imprudent behaviour on the part of servants, who are playing on an instrument which is literally one of the instruments of darkness, since it contains darkness and since darkness escapes when the aperture is unsealed and is spread abroad in the form of noisy, nocturnal animals – insects and batrachians – which are precisely those the names of which denote the instruments of darkness in the Old World: the frog, the toad, the cicada, the grasshopper, the cricket, etc. The theory that a category corresponding to our European instruments of darkness might exist among the mythic symbols of the New World is given definitive confirmation by the presence, among these symbols, of an instrument which is precisely an instrument of darkness in the literal sense, whereas, the similar instruments in Western mythology can only be given the appellation in a figurative sense.

o

But, if the instrument of darkness in M$_{326a}$ is connected with night, and if night appears in the myth as a necessary pre-condition for the union of the sexes,[19] it follows that the instrument associated with their disunion, the bull-roarer, must by implication be linked with daylight, which fulfils the same function. This would give us a four-fold correlation between night, the union of the sexes, non-linguistic behaviour and the instrument of darkness, contrasting term for term with the correlation between daylight, the disunion of the sexes, universalized linguistic behaviour and the bull-roarer. Apart from the fact that it is difficult to see how the bull-roarer could denote a form of linguistic behaviour, this way of presenting the problem merely reverses the difficulty we encountered in connection with the Bororo and the Sherente. I concluded that, among these Indians, the bull-roarer related to night, and this, in the perspective of a general interpretation, put the instruments of darkness (which we found to be in opposition to the bull-roarer) on the side of daylight. And now, the more normal linking up of the instruments of darkness with night would seem to involve relating the bull-roarer to day, and this contradicts everything we have accepted so far. The situation must therefore be examined more closely.

M$_{326a}$ does not mention the bull-roarer. It does, however, refer to a period when night was guarded by a great snake (whose cry is believed by the Toba to resemble that of the bull-roarer) and when it 'slept beneath the waters' (like the aquatic monster which the Bororo call aigé, 'bull-roarer', and whose cry the bull-roarer imitates). We also know that, in almost every region where the bull-roarer exists, its function is to cause the disjunction of the female sex, and to put women back into the category of nature, outside the sacred and socialized world. Now M$_{326a}$ is a myth belonging to the northern Tupi, that is, to a culture and a region whose mythology describes the great snake as a phallic being in whom all the attributes of virility were concentrated at a time when men themselves had none. They were unable to copulate with their wives, and were obliged to request the services of the snake. This state of affairs came to an end when the demiurge cut the snake's body up into pieces, which he then used to endow each man with the mem-

---

[19] But not in all respects. Although night is a necessary pre-condition for sexual communication, by a compensatory movement which is intended to restore the balance, night would seem to forbid linguistic communication between the partners. Such, at least, is the case among the Tucano, who allow conversation between people of opposite sexes during the day-time, but only between people of the same sex at night (Silva, pp. 166–7, 417). Individuals of opposite sexes can exchange either words or caresses, but not both at the same time, since this would be considered an abuse of communication.

brum virile he lacked (M_{80}). Consequently Tupi mythology presents the snake as a (socially) disjunctive penis, a view which had already been forced upon us by the function and symbolism of the bull-roarer. And this also is the function assumed by the Great Snake in M_{326a} in its capacity as a misbehaving father and not as a corrupt seducer: he gives away his daughter but he does not relinquish night, and without night the marriage cannot be consummated. In this respect, M_{326a} links up with a group of myths we have already studied (M_{259}–M_{269}), in which another aquatic monster presents the man it has accepted as its son-in-law – and who, in certain versions, happens to be none other than the sun, that is, daylight – with a wife who is incomplete and therefore impossible to penetrate: a girl without a vagina, symmetrical with the men without penises in M_{80}, and the reverse of the girl with the (symbolically) over-large vagina in the tapir-as-seducer cycle, the tapir being an animal with a large penis, which I showed on p. 411 to be a combinatory variant of the great snake, which is 'all penis', and which brings us back to our starting-point.

I will leave it to others to explore the complexities of this link-up, for as soon as we pause to examine mythic connections we discover that the pattern they form is so densely interwoven that the investigator who tries to grasp all the details despairs of ever making any headway. But, given the fact that the structural analysis of myths is still in a rudimentary stage, I think it preferable (since a choice has to be made) to forge ahead and mark out a path, even though we are uncertain of our aims, rather than opt for the slow and sure procedures which will one day make it possible for others to follow the same road at an even pace, and to catalogue the riches found along it.

If the comparisons just made are legitimate, we can perhaps now glimpse a possible way out of our difficulties. Let us, then, relate the bull-roarer to night of which it is the master, in the guise of the snake; and let us accept the fact that the instrument of darkness is also related to night. But the night in the one case is not exactly the same as the night in the other. They are alike only in being excessive. The night of the bull-roarer avoids daylight, whereas the night of the instrument of darkness invades daylight. It follows, strictly speaking, that neither of these 'nights' is in opposition to daylight, but rather to the empirically proved alternation in which day and night, far from being mutually exclusive, are united by a reciprocal mediatory relationship: day mediatizes the transition from night to night, and night the transition from daylight to daylight. If the terms 'night' are removed from this periodic sequence which has an objective reality, only day is left, culturizing nature, as it were, in the form of an improper extension of linguistic behaviour to animals and things. Conversely, if the terms 'day' are removed from the sequence, only night is left, naturalizing culture by the transformation of the products of human industry into animals.

The problem which was holding us up can be solved, once we recognize the operative value of a three-term system: day on its own, night on its own, and the regular alternation of the two. The system comprises two simple terms and one complex one consisting of a harmonious relationship between the first two. It provides the framework within which myths of origin, whether concerned with the origin of day or night, divide up into two distinct kinds, according to whether they place day or night at the beginning of the existing alternation. We can therefore distinguish between myths with a nocturnal preliminary and myths with a diurnal preliminary. M_{326a} belongs to the second category. The initial choice has an important consequence in that it necessarily gives precedence to one of the two terms. In the case of myths with a diurnal preliminary, which are the ones we are concerned with here, there was only day in the first instance, and although night existed, it was in a state of disjunction from daylight and remained, as it were, behind the scenes. This being so, the other possibility can no longer materialize in an exactly symmetrical form. Day was formerly where night was not; and when night replaces it (before their regular alternation is established) it can only do so by taking over where day was *before it*. We can thus understand why, by virtue of this hypothesis, the 'long day' is the result of an *initial state* of disjunction, and the 'long night' the result of a *subsidiary act* of conjunction.

On the formal level, these two situations correspond clearly to those I previously distinguished as the rotten world and the burnt world. But from the moment of my evolving this distinction, something happened in the myths. Almost imperceptibly, they moved from a spatial field to a temporal scale and, what is more, from the notion of absolute space to that of relative time. My third volume will be almost entirely devoted to the theory of this major transformation. For the time being, I am concerned merely to bring out a limited aspect of it.

In the absolute space referred to by the myths about the origin of cooking, the high position is occupied by the sky or the sun, and the low position by the earth. Before cooking fire appeared as a mediatory term between these two extremes (uniting them, while at the same time maintaining a reasonable distance between them), their relationships were inevitably characterized by imbalance: they were too near to each other or too far away from each other. The first possibility relates to the burnt world, which connotes fire and light; the second to the rotten world, which connotes darkness and night.

But M_{326a} is situated in relative time, where the mediatory term is not a being or a distinct object standing between two extreme terms. The mediation consists rather in the equilibrium between terms which are not intrinsically extreme, but which can become extreme as a result of the deterioration of the relationship linking them together. If the myth under consideration has a diurnal preliminary, the remoteness of night, that is, its disjunction from day, ensures the reign of light, and its proximity to (or conjunction with) day ensures the reign of darkness. Consequently, according to whether the myth is thought of within the context of absolute space or of relative time, the same signifieds (conjunction and disjunction) will call for opposite signifiers. This reversal is, however, no more relevant than that of the names of the notes of a scale, as a result of a change in the key-signature. In such a case, what counts in the first place is not the absolute position of the notes on, or between, the lines, but the key-signature inscribed at the beginning of the stave.

The bull-roarer and the instrument of darkness are the ritual signifiers of a disjunction and a conjunction, both non-mediatized, which, when transposed into a different tessitura, have as their conceptual signifiers the rotten world and the burnt world. The fact that the same signifieds, in so far as they consist of relationships between objects, can, when these objects are not the same, admit of contrasting signifiers, does not mean that these contrasting signifiers have a signified/signifier relationship with each other.

In formulating the above rule, I am merely extending to the domain of mythic thought De Saussure's principle of the arbitrary character of the linguistic sign, except that the field of application of the principle here acquires an additional dimension, because of the fact (to which I have already drawn attention elsewhere, L.-S. 9, p. 31) that, where myth and ritual are concerned, the same elements can equally well play the part of signified and signifier, and replace each other in each function.

In spite of, or because of this complication, mythic thought is so respectful of this principle that it is careful to assign quite distinct semantic fields to the bull-roarer and the instrument of darkness (which, from the formal point of view, constitute a pair). Why is it the bull-roarer's function, almost the whole world over, to drive women away? Is it not because it would be practically impossible for the bull-roarer to signify disjunction between night and day – the reign of daylight in the middle of night – unlike the instrument of darkness, which brings about conjunction between them? Of this conjunction, the eclipse provides at least one empirical illustration, and when we consider 'darkness' from this viewpoint it appears as a particular kind of eclipse, marked by a particular kind of charivari (*RC*, pp. 286–9). The use of the bull-roarer does more than just reverse this relationship; it transposes it by removing all the feminine terms in the periodic sequence of matrimonial unions. And is it not for this reason that the sequence presents, on the sociological level, an equivalent of the cosmological sequence formed by the regular alternation of day and night?

$$\left(\begin{array}{cccc} \vert & \ulcorner\vert & \ulcorner\vert & \ulcorner \\ \triangle = \bigcirc & \triangle = \bigcirc & \triangle = \bigcirc & \triangle = \bigcirc \end{array} \text{etc.} \right)$$
$$\equiv \text{(day-night, day-night, day-night, day-night, etc.)}$$

We can say, then, that society, temporarily reduced by the bull-roarer to its masculine elements after the isolation and removal of the feminine elements, is like the course of time reduced to day only. Conversely, the Kayapo, who do not seem to have bull-roarers (Dreyfus, p. 129), use the knocking together of sticks to signify a set of circumstances which is symmetrical with that associated elsewhere with the bull-roarer: in their case, they are concerned with establishing the conjugal bond between a man and a woman, and with promiscuity rites (cf. above, p. 371). Lastly, while the instruments of darkness can denote conjunction between day and night, and between the sexes too, we already know that they denote the union of the sky and the earth. In this last respect, it would be interesting to study the part assigned to clappers and similar instruments during the festivities which greet the return of the Pleiades. I shall return later to the Chaco ceremonies, merely pointing out at this point, that, on the north-west coast of North America, rattles (used only for the winter ritual) are replaced by clappers for the spring festival, called meitla, at which the Kwakiutl wear an ornament representing the Pleiades (Boas 3, p. 502; Drucker, pp. 205, 211, 218; cf. also Olson, p. 175 and Boas 2, pp. 552–3).

2 *The Harmony of the Spheres*

It follows from what has gone before that the bull-roarer and the instrument of darkness do not effect conjunction or disjunction pure and simple. We ought rather to say that the two instruments effect conjunction *with* the phenomena of conjunction and disjunction: they conjoin the social group or the world at large to the possibility of one or other of these relationships, the common feature of which is that they exclude mediation. If the acoustic code forms a system, a third type of instrument must therefore exist, denoting the act of mediation.

We know what this instrument is in the European tradition, which establishes a complex network of relationships between the instruments of darkness and bells, according to whether the latter are absent or present and, if present, whether they are marked or unmarked:

INSTRUMENTS / OF DARKNESS /		(BELLS:
marked/unmarked...absent		/present)
Shrove Tuesday................*Lent*...........*(triduum)*		*Easter Sunday*

I propose to show, first of all, that in South America the gourd rattle or rattles (for they are normally found in pairs) represent the instrument of mediation; next, that just as the instruments of darkness appeared as being linked with honey, an excellent food for the tropical 'Lent' represented by the dry season, rattles have a symmetrical relationship with tobacco.

M₃₂₇. *Warao. 'The origin of tobacco and of the first medicine-man'*

An Indian had been living with a woman for a long long time; she was very good at making hammocks but could not bear a child. So he took a second wife by whom he had a child called Kurusiwari. The youngster used constantly to bother the step-mother as she was weaving her hammocks, and prevented her getting on with her work. One day she roughly pushed the child aside. He fell and cried, then left the house unnoticed even by his parents, who were lying together in a hammock, with their minds no doubt on other things.

It was late in the day when his presence was missed. His parents set out to look for him and found him in a neighbour's house playing with some other children. The father and mother explained their errand and entered into an animated conversation with their hosts. When the Indian and his wife finally finished talking, not only had their own child disappeared once more, but one of the children of the house, Matura-wari, was nowhere to be seen. The same thing happened in a third house, with the same result. The two boys had gone, taking with them a third child called Kawai-wari.

It was a case now of six parents searching for three infants. At the end of the first day the third couple abandoned the search, and at the end of the second day the second couple did likewise. In the meantime, the three children had wandered on and on and had made friends with the wasps, which in those days talked but did not sting. It was these children that told the black ones to sting people, and the red ones to give them fever in addition.

It was when the children arrived at the sea-shore that the first pair of parents caught up with them. By this time they had grown into big boys. When the parents begged them to return home, the leader of the three, the boy who had been lost from the first house, refused, saying that his step-mother had ill-treated him and that his parents had paid no attention to him. Both father and mother implored him with tears to return, but all he would promise was that he would appear if they built him a temple (Spirit-house) and 'called' him with tobacco. Thereupon, the three boys crossed the seas and the parents returned to the village, where the father started building the prescribed Spirit-house. He burnt pappaia leaves, cotton leaves and coffee leaves, but all in vain: there was no 'strength' in any of them. But in those days men knew nothing of tobacco, which grew on an island in the middle of the sea. The island was called 'Man-without', because it was peopled entirely by women. The sorrowing father sent a gaulding bird (*Pilerodius*) to fetch some of the tobacco seed: he never returned, and the other sea-birds he sent all met with the same fate. They were all killed by the woman guarding the tobacco field.

The Indian went to consult his brother who brought him a crane. The bird went to roost down near the sea-shore so as to have a good start the following morning. A humming-bird asked him what he was doing, and suggested that he should go instead. In spite of the crane's efforts to dissuade him, the humming-bird set off at dawn. When the crane sailing majestically along met the humming-bird, he saw him struggling in the water in great danger of drowning. The crane picked him up and placed him on the back of his own thighs. Now, this position was all very well for the humming-bird so long as no accident occurred, but when the crane commenced to relieve himself, the humming-bird's face got dirtied (cf. M₃₁₀). He decided to take to the wing again and arrived at the island well ahead of the crane. The latter agreed to wait while the humming-bird went to fetch the seeds. Since he was small and swift in flight, the watchwoman failed to kill him.

The two birds, who now had the wind behind them, flew together until they reached the village where the humming-bird delivered the seed to the crane's master, who handed them to his brother, telling him how to plant the tobacco, then how to cure the leaves and choose the bark to make the cigarettes. He also sent him to collect gourds but kept only the one which had grown on the east side of the tree (cf. p. 347 and n. 35). The man then started singing to the accompaniment of the rattle. His son and the other two lads appeared. They were now the three Spirits of tobacco and always came in answer to the call of the rattle. For the father himself had become the first medicine-man, all through his great grief at losing his child and longing so much to see him once more (Roth 1, pp. 334–6).

Another Warao myth on the same theme can be treated as a variant of the previous one:

M₃₂₈. *Warao. 'The origin of tobacco and of the first medicine-man'* (2)
An Indian called Komatari wanted some tobacco which, at that time, grew on an island out at sea. He first of all approached a man who lived alone on the shore and whom he mistakenly took to be the master of tobacco. A humming-bird joined in their conversation and suggested going to fetch some tobacco leaves. But he made a mistake and brought back tobacco flowers. So the man who lived on the shore set off for the island and succeeded in eluding the people who were keeping watch over the tobacco. He came back with his corial full of leaves and seeds, with which Komatari filled his basket. The stranger took leave of Komatari, but refused to give his name. He said the other would find it out for himself when he became a medicine-man.

Komatari refused to share the tobacco with his companions. He hung the leaves under the roof of his house and left them in charge of the wasps. The latter allowed themselves to be bribed by a visitor who offered them fish and who stole some of the tobacco leaves. Komatari noticed that some tobacco leaves were missing and drove away all the wasps except one particular kind, which he made his watch-men. Then he cleared a small area in the forest and planted his tobacco.

From four Spirits, whom he met in turn but who all refused to tell their names, he obtained the calabash tree, feathers and cotton-twine which were to decorate the first rattle, and the stones which would make it reverberate. Warned by the hero that the finished rattle would be used to destroy them, the Spirits took their revenge by causing diseases. But to no avail; thanks to the rattle, Komatari cured all the sick people, except one man whose condition was too serious. It would ever be thus: some patients would be saved, others could not be saved. Of course, Komatari now knew the names of all the Spirits. The first one he met who procured the tobacco seeds for him was called Wau-uno (Anura in Arawak) 'White Crane' (Roth 1, pp. 336–8).

These two myths, which deal with the origin of shamanistic powers, clearly consider them from two complementary points of view: the summoning-up of the guardian Spirits, or the expulsion of the evil spirits. The bird (*Pilerodius*) which, in M_{327}, failed to bring back the tobacco is the embodiment of one of the Spirits responsible for diseases (Roth 1, p. 349). In both cases, conjunction or disjunction is brought about through the mediation of the rattles and tobacco. It can already be seen that, as I forecast, the two terms are linked.

In both myths, the crane and the humming-bird form a pair, and the respective significance of each bird is reversed according to whether the myth considers shamanism in the one light or the other. The humming-bird is superior to the crane in M_{327}, but inferior in M_{328}. Its inferiority is shown in its naive preference, which is in keeping with its nature, for tobacco flowers rather than tobacco leaves or seeds. On the other hand, the superiority it shows in M_{327} is acquired only at the cost of a denial of its own nature. Normally, it is associated with dryness (*RC*, pp. 205–6) and a pleasant smell (Roth 1, p. 371), but the humming-bird in M_{327} is in danger of drowning and has its face spattered with dung. The 'tobacco road' leads through excrement. In recalling this fact, M_{327} testifies to the objective reality of the progression which led us from honey (itself bordering on excrement and poison) to tobacco. In short, we took the same road as the humming-bird, and the gradual transformation of myths about the origin of honey into myths about the origin of tobacco, a transformation the various stages of which have been described throughout the present work, is reduplicated on a small scale in the Guiana myths which change the smallest bird from a *honey-eater* into a *tobacco-producer*.

Of the two Warao myths, M_{327} is certainly the more complex, and I propose to follow it rather than M_{328}. Two women play an important part in it: one is a skilful weaver, although sterile, while the other is fertile. In Tacana mythology, which I have often compared with the mythology of the northerly regions of South America, female sloths married to humans make the best weavers (M_{329}; H.-H., p. 287). The same point is made in the Waiwai myth about the origin of the Shodewika festival (M_{388}): in former times, only Indians and sloths (*Choloepus*) knew how to make fibre costumes (Fock, p. 57 and n. 39, p. 70).

How are we to explain the attribution of such a talent to the sloth, whose habits hardly predispose it for such an activity? No doubt because the usual position of the sloth, hanging upside down from a branch, is reminiscent of a hammock. Myths about the origin of sloths confirm that the resemblance has not passed unnoticed: they describe the sloth as a transformed hammock, or as a man lying in a hammock (M_{330}, Mundurucu, Murphy 1, p. 121; M_{247}, Baré, Amorim, p. 145). But two significant features in M_{327} enable us to carry the interpretation still further: on the one hand, no explicit reference is made to the sloth; on the other hand, the woman who takes its place as an expert weaver forms a pair with another woman, about whom no details are given except that she is fertile.

I have already explained above (p. 396) that the sloth is a very small eater and only defecates once or twice a week, on the ground and always in the same place. Such habits were bound to attract the attention of the Indians, who consider the control of the excretory functions to be of paramount importance. Commenting on the native custom of inducing vomiting on awakening in order to eliminate all the food which has remained in the stomach overnight (cf. *RC*, p. 241), Spruce (Vol. II, p. 454) notes that 'Indians are less keen to defecate first thing in the morning than to empty their stomachs of food. On the contrary, everywhere in South America, I have noticed that Indians who have a hard day's work in front of them and not much to eat, prefer to postpone evacuation until nightfall. They are better than white men at controlling their natural functions, and seem to respect the maxim which an Indian from San Carlos expressed to me in very approximate Spanish: *Quien caga de mañana es guloso*, 'the man who has his bowels opened in the morning is a glutton.' The Tucano takes a broader, metaphorical view of the connection, when they forbid the canoe- or net-maker to have his bowels opened before the object he is working on is finished, for fear that it might be holed (Silva, p. 368 and *passim*).

In this area, as in others, to yield to nature is to be a bad member of society. This being so, it can happen, at least in the myths, that the being most able to resist nature, will *ipso facto* be the most gifted in respect of cultural aptitudes. The retention which takes the outward form of sterility in the skilful weaver in M_{327} transposes into a different register – that of the reproductive function – the retention characteristic of the sloth on the eliminatory level. The first wife who suffered from genital constipation, although she was a good weaver, is in contrast to the second wife whose fertility seems to be offset by indolence, since she is shown disporting with her husband during the day.[20]

These observations necessitate two further comments. First, it has already been noted that, as regards defecation, the sloth stands in opposition to the howler monkey, which releases its droppings at any moment from the tops of trees. As its name implies, this monkey howls, but mostly when there is a change of weather:

> *Guariba na serra*
> *Chuva na terra*

> When the guariba monkey is heard in the hills,
> there will be rain in the land

is a popular saying (Ihering, under 'guariba'), which is in keeping with the Bororo belief that this species of monkey is a Spirit of rain (*EB*, Vol. I, p. 371). Now, a sudden fall in temperature also makes the sloth come down to the ground to defecate: 'When the wind blows, the sloth walks,' is an Arawak saying (Roth 1, p. 369), and a naturalist (Enders, p. 7) obtained stools regularly every five days from a sloth in captivity by moistening its hind-quarters with cold water. Conse-

[20] The ancients also believed there was a connection between the state of being a weaver and amorous capabilities: but they thought of it as being directly proportional, not in inverse ratio: 'The Grecians described Women-Weavers to bee more hot and earnestly luxurious than other women, because of their sitting trade without any violent exercise of the body ... I might likewise say of these that the same stirring which their labour so sitting doth give them, doth rouze and sollicit them ... ' (Montaigne, *Essays*, trans. John Florio, Vol. III, Ch. XI).

quently, the howler monkey and the sloth are 'barometric' animals, the one honouring this state by its excretions, the other by its howls. As a mode of din, the howling is a metaphorical transposition of filth (cf. p. 209, n. 9, p. 310).

This is not all. Howler monkeys cry noisily and in groups at sunrise and sunset. The sloth is a solitary animal which at night-time emits a faint musical cry 'like a penetrating whistle, beginning on D sharp above middle C and holding true for several seconds' (Beebe, pp. 35–7). According to an old author, the sloth cries 'ha, ha, ha, ha, ha, ha' at night (Oviedo y Valdes in Britton, p. 14). However, the description suggests that the animal in question may be the *Choloepus* and not the *Bradypus*, that is, the large and not the small sloth, to which the other observation referred.

If we take into account the fact that, according to the Tacana myths (M_{322}–M_{323}), any attack on a sloth engaged in the normal exercise of its eliminatory functions would cause a universal conflagration – a belief which, as we saw, is echoed in Guiana (cf. *RC*, p. 315, n. 19), where it is thought that any such attack would expose humanity to the perils resulting from the conjunction of celestial fire with the earth – it is tempting to detect, behind the acoustic aspect of the contrast between the howler monkey and the sloth, one of which is endowed with a 'terrifying' cry, according to the Acawai (Brett 2, pp. 130–32), while the other is doomed to a discreet whistle, according to a Baré myth (Amorim, p. 145), the contrast between the bull-roarer, a 'howling' instrument, and the instruments of darkness.

We now come to the second point, which takes us back to the actual text of the Guiana myths about the origin of tobacco. As it has just been elucidated, the nature of the opposition between the two women in M_{327} brings the first wife, who is sterile and gifted purely from the cultural viewpoint, into contrast with the girl mad about honey in the Chaco and Guiana myths. The second woman is homologous to the latter, since she too shows herself to be lascivious and fertile (cf. M_{135}). On the other hand, and as is normal when we move from myths about the origin of honey to myths about the origin of tobacco, the position of the whimpering child, the term common to both groups, is radically reversed. In one group, he is driven out because he is crying, in the other, he is crying because he has been driven out. In the first instance, it is the woman who can be assimilated to the girl mad about honey who drives him out, because she is exasperated by his crying: in the other instance, the woman whose role is in opposition to that played by the girl mad about honey is responsible, whereas the woman whose role is analogous remains indifferent to the child's crying. Finally, whereas the 'normal' crying baby remains near the house, calling for its mother until some animal, congruous with the girl mad about honey – a vixen or a frog – carries it off, its counterpart in M_{327} chooses to go off of its own accord and makes friends with the marabunta wasps.

This generic name is too vague to allow us to affirm that the marabunta wasps belong to a honey-producing species, and thus are in opposition to the animal abductors which the myths present as greedy consumers of honey. But it is possible to demonstrate the point in another way. Let us note, first of all, that M_{327} and M_{328}, in which wasps play almost identical parts, deal with the origin of shamanism. Now the Guiana sorcerer possesses a special power over wasps. He can drive them all out by knocking with his fingers against the nest, without a single wasp stinging him (Roth 1, p. 341).[21] I have already drawn attention to the existence among the more southerly Kayapo of a ritual battle with wasps.

According to M_{327} and M_{328}, wasps became poisonous because of their very close relationship with shamans or their guardian Spirits. The transformation which was brought about by the whimpering child in M_{327} and by the hero in M_{328} reproduces the transformation that a Botocudo myth (M_{204}) attributes to the irára, an animal which is particularly fond of honey. We thus rediscover a contrast between wasps – which have undergone a transformation through a character replacing the irára in the Botocudo myth – and the abducting animals, which are moreover honey-eaters, that is, congruous with the irára in certain conditions that have already been mentioned (p. 249).

This comparison takes us quite a long way back, but we find ourselves even further back once we have noticed that M_{327} attributes man's lack of tobacco to the unmarried women who keep watch over it on an island; they are Amazons, and 'mad about tobacco'. Now, several

21 But before doing so, he draws his fingers under his armpits. The Tucano do likewise, when they discover a wasp's nest. 'The smell drives the wasps out and the Indians seize the nest full of larvae; the nest acts as a plate, flour is tipped into it and eaten with the larvae' (Silva, p. 222, n. 53). The Cubeo dialect (Goldman, p. 182, n. 1) associates body hair and tobacco: 'body hair' is pwa, and underarm hair is called pwa butci, 'tobacco-hair'. The same Indians carry out a ritual burning of cut hair; they burn it in the same way as tobacco for smoking is burnt.

Guiana myths and one or two Ge myths connect the origin of Amazons with the separation of the sexes which followed on the murder of the jaguar or the cayman (combinatory variants of the tapir-seducer), which the women had taken as lovers (M_{156}, M_{287}). I have established that these women are themselves a variant of the girl mad about honey, transposed into the terminology of the sexual code. The myths we are now dealing with confirm this: on leaving their husbands, the Apinayé Amazons carry off the ceremonial axes; those in the Warao myths have sole control of tobacco which, like the axes, is a cultural symbol. In order to be conjoined with the tapir, the cayman or the jaguar – i.e. with nature – the adulterous women have recourse either to the *tapped* gourd or to the proper *name* of the animal which they imprudently *reveal*. Symmetrically, the Warao shaman's supernatural power is expressed by the rattle which is a *shaken* gourd, and by the *name* of the Spirits whose secret he has *penetrated*.

The Warao myths about the origin of tobacco contain an episode which takes us even further back, right back in fact to the beginning of our inquiry. The humming-bird's flight across a vast stretch of water to fetch tobacco growing on a supernatural island, and so that tobacco can be linked with rattles, refers back to M_1, in which we encountered the same theme for the first time, in the form of a quest, also under-taken by the humming-bird which also went to a supernatural island to fetch, not tobacco, but the rattles themselves – musical instruments which the hero must not cause to sound if he is to be successfully disjoined from the Spirits; whereas in the Warao myth, men are only able to summon the good Spirits and drive away the bad, as they wish, if they cause the instruments to sound.

A superficial study might lead to the assumption that the humming-bird's quest constitutes the only element common to both M_1 and M_{327}. But in fact the analogy between the two myths goes much deeper.

It follows from the interpretation I have already suggested of the character of the crying baby that the latter reproduces the hero of M_1 in terms of the acoustic code. Both refuse to be disjoined from their mothers, although they express their attachment by different means – one by vocal the other by erotic behaviour, passive in the first case, active in the second. The little boy in M_{327} is a whimpering child, but reversed, and so we can expect him to behave in a reverse manner to the hero of M_1. The latter is loath to join the men's house, loath therefore to become an adult member of society. The child in M_{327} shows a precocious interest in cultural activities, particularly those carried out by women, since he keeps on interrupting the making of hammocks, which is a feminine occupation.

Both heroes are boys; one is already quite grown-up, although his incestuous behaviour indicates moral infantilism; the other is still very young but his independence of spirit makes him reach physical maturity at a very early age. In each case, the father has two wives – the child's mother and a step-mother. In M_1, the child is conjoined with the mother, in M_{327} he is disjoined by the step-mother. The conjugal pair in M_{327} corresponds to the incestuous pair in M_1; the grievances of the son, whose filial rights have been encroached upon by the father, correspond to the grievances of the father, whose conjugal rights have been encroached upon by the son. It will be noted that, whereas in the Bororo myth the father complains that his son has supplanted him in an amorous capacity (and therefore as an adult), the son in the Warao myth complains that his parents are too amorously engaged with each other to pay attention to his crying.

The outraged father in M_1 tries first of all to bring about his son's death in water, but three helpful animals aid the boy, thus forming a counterpart to the three children in M_{327} who choose to cross the sea. It will be objected that the hero of M_{327} is one of these three children, whereas the hero in M_1 obtains the help of three animals without being fused with any one of them. This means that there are four characters in M_1, against three in M_{327}. But because of their inverted symmetry, a two-fold difficulty would arise if the two myths were to follow a parallel course. On the one hand, the hero of M_1 returns physically to his own people, whereas the hero in M_{327} comes back 'in spirit' only. On the other hand, the former *brings back* rain and storms, which are therefore to be the *consequence* of his return, whereas the tobacco *fetched* from a long way away is the cause of the latter's return. In the interests of symmetry the same character in M_{327} must be at one and the same time absent (since he has to be brought back) and present (since he has a mission to perform).

M_{327} solves the difficulty by reduplicating the roles. In the first part, a small child acts as the hero; in the second part, a small bird takes over the role. But if, as I am suggesting, the humming-bird is a doublet of the hero, it is clear that even in the first part, where one character virtually assumes both roles, the four characters in M_1, that is one child and three animals (one of which is a humming-bird), must correspond to the three children (one of whom will be changed into a humming-bird) since, in respect of M_{327}, the child and the humming-bird count as one character:

| M_1 | : (boy) | humming-bird | pigeon | grasshopper |
| M_{327} | : boy[1] | (humming-bird) | boy[2] | boy[3] |

In the rest of the story, the hero in M_1 undergoes vertical disjunction while collecting the eggs of macaws, which (M_7–M_{12}) cover him with their droppings. The hero of M_{327}, in the course of his horizontal disjunction, forms an alliance with wasps, which he turns into a poisonous species. This gives a four-fold contrast:

(*macaws/wasps*), (*hostility/friendliness*), (hero = OBJECT in respect of filth/SUBJECT in respect of poison)

The contrast between poisonous insects and filth-producing birds enabled me (*RC*, p. 315, n. 19) to effect a transformation between a Parintintin myth (M_{179}) and the Ge variants of the bird-nester myth (M_7–M_{12}), which deal with the origin of (terrestrial) cooking fire, whereas M_1, which is a transformation of these myths, deals with the origin of (celestial) water. I have just transformed another myth into M_1 and it can be observed that the initial twist shown by M_1 in relation to M_7–M_{12} is maintained in the new transformation as follows:

(*a*) M_7–M_{12} (origin of fire) ⇒ M_1 (origin of water)
(*b*) M_{179} (object of poison) ⇒ M_7–M_{12} (object of filth)
(*c*) M_1 (enemy of macaws) ⇒ M_{327} (friend of wasps)
(*d*) M_{327} (subject of poison) ⇒ M_7–M_{12} (object of filth)

Taking into account the dislocation referred to above and which, in M_{327}, results in the partial overlapping of two episodes which are consecutive in M_1, I now propose to examine the sequence in M_{327} devoted to the humming-bird's journey.

The sequence can be divided into three parts: (1) the humming-bird sets out alone, falls into the water and is nearly drowned; (2) the crane rescues it and places it between its thighs, where it continues its journey in safety, even though its face is bespattered with dung; (3) the humming-bird sets off alone once more and finally gains possession of tobacco.

A word, first of all, on the subject of the crane. In spite of the uncertainty regarding the species thus referred to in the Guiana myths,
I have been able to establish (p. 247) that the bird in question is a wader
with a shrill cry, which produces din, and metaphorically, filth, as the
part it plays in M_{327} corroborates in its own way. But while waders are
a source of noise and metaphorical producers of filth, in real life they
have a correlational and inverted relationship with filth, in their capacity
as carrion-eaters with a fondness for dead fish (cf. p. 244). Since they
represent the *oral resorption* of filth, they are thus closely linked with the
sloth, which, as we have seen, is given to *anal retention* in those myths
in which it appears. The Ipurina, who believe the sloth to be their
ancestor, relate that at the beginning of time storks used to collect
filth and decaying matter all over the world in order to boil it in a solar
pot and subsequently eat it. The pot overflowed, spilling boiling water
which destroyed all living beings except the sloth, which managed to
climb to the top of a tree and repeopled the earth (M_{331}; Ehrenreich,
p. 129; cf. Schultz 2, pp. 230–31).[22] This story throws light on an
episode of a Jivaro origin myth, in which the sloth plays the same role
as ancestor of the human race. For the reason why the heron stole the
two eggs, one of which was to give birth to Mika, the future wife of
Uñushi, the sloth (M_{332}, Stirling, pp. 125–6) was surely that, for the
Jivaro, as for the tribes of north-western Amazonia and Guiana, birds'
eggs come into the category of prohibited foods, because of their
'foetal and therefore impure character' (Whiffen, p. 130; cf. Im Thurn,
p. 18), which makes them congruous with filth. An Aguaruna variant
(M_{333a}) seems to confirm this: according to it, the sun emerged from an
egg which had been taken by the ogre Agempi from the corpse of the
woman he had killed, and which was subsequently stolen by a duck
(Guallart, p. 61). According to a Maquiritaré myth (M_{333b}; M. Thomson, p. 5), two of the four eggs removed from the entrails of Moon,
the hero's sister, were rotten.

As carrion-eaters, aquatic birds play, in respect of water, a part which
is closely homologous to that which the myths attribute to vultures in
respect of land. We can therefore suppose the existence of a correspondence between the three episodes of the humming-bird's journey in

---

[22] The tree in question belongs to the malvaceae family, which according to
modern botanical systems is closely related to the tiliaceae and silk-cotton trees (cf.
p. 392, n. 13). This gives a transformation of internal beneficent water into external
maleficent water, which I refrain from discussing, to avoid prolonging the demonstration.

M_{327} and the three stages of the hero's adventures in M_1. This gives:

$$
\begin{bmatrix} M_1: \\ M_{327}: \end{bmatrix}
\left.\begin{array}{l} \text{hero} \\ \text{vertically} \\ \text{disjoined} \end{array}\right\}
\left\{\begin{array}{l} \text{above,} \\ \\ \text{below,} \end{array}\right.
\text{on the axis: sky}
\left\{\begin{array}{l} \text{earth} \\ \\ \text{water} \end{array}\right.
$$

$/\!/$

$$
\begin{bmatrix} M_1: \text{vultures} \\ \\ M_{327}: \text{crane} \end{bmatrix}
\text{helpful}
\left\{\begin{array}{l} \textit{after devouring} \text{ the hero's} \\ \textit{foul-smelling} \text{ posterior}^{23} \\ \\ \textit{before defecating} \text{ onto the } \textit{face} \text{ of} \\ \text{the } \textit{sweet-smelling} \text{ 'hero'} \end{array}\right.
$$

*

So, throughout the paradigmatic set formed by myths M_1–M_{12}, which I dealt with at the beginning of my inquiry, there exist two mythologies of tobacco. The one, which I was able to illustrate by taking examples mainly from the Chaco, looks for the means of tobacco in the notion of terrestrial and destructive fire, in a correlational and oppositional relationship with cooking fire, which is also terrestrial but at the same time constructive, and the origin of which is outlined in the Ge myths (M_7–M_{12}). The other mythology of tobacco, which we encountered in the Warao myths, looks for the means of tobacco, in the notion of dominated terrestrial water (the ocean that the birds succeed in crossing), which is in correlation and opposition to celestial and dominating water (rain and storms), the origin of which is dealt with in the Bororo myth (M_1).

The two mythologies of tobacco therefore occupy symmetrical positions with regard to the initial paradigmatic set (see Figure 20 on p. 436); there is, however, one difference: the relationship between the Warao myths and M_1 presupposes a transformation with a double twist – *terrestrial/celestial dominated/dominating* water – whereas the relationship of the Chaco myths to the M_7–M_{12} group is a simpler one – *dominated/dominating* terrestrial fire – requiring only one twist. Let us dwell on this point for a moment.

At the beginning of this book, I analysed and discussed a myth belonging to the Iranxé, geographically close to the Bororo, which, in a very simple way, transformed a myth about the origin of water (M_1) into a myth about the origin of tobacco (M_{191}). So, in the Warao

[23] Since the humming-bird is by nature sweet-smelling, while in M_1 the urubus were attracted by the stench of decay emanating from the dead lizards which the hero had fastened onto his person. The reduplication: lizard, urubu-vultures in M_1, as respectively passive and active modes of decay, has its equivalent in M_{327} with the reduplication, 'gaulding bird' and crane; these are two waders associated with decay and which fail in their mission, one passively, the other actively.

myths, we are dealing with a transformation once removed. The disparity can be explained if we take certain cultural factors into account. Throughout tropical America south of the Amazon, i.e. in the areas inhabited by the Iranxé, the Bororo and the Chaco tribes, the consumption of tobacco in the form of an infusion or decoction was

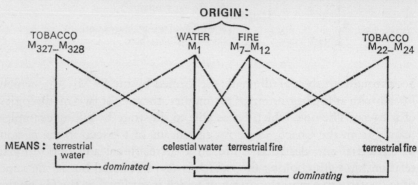

Figure 20. Pattern of relationships between myths dealing with smoked tobacco (right) and myths dealing with tobacco as a drink (left)

unknown. If we disregard tobacco-chewing, which occurred only sporadically, we can say that, in this area, tobacco was only smoked; and this makes it congruous with fire rather than with water. However, within the sub-category of smoked tobacco, I pointed out an instance of reduplication which, on the mythical level, took the form of a distinction between 'good' and 'bad' tobacco (M_{191}), or between a good and a bad use of tobacco (M_{26}, M_{27}). M_{191} even appears as being essentially a myth about the origin of bad tobacco.

As for M_{27}, it is a myth about the origin of the bad use of tobacco which in this case (and in contrast to M_{26}) comes from water. So, to the contrast between the nature of tobacco and its use (the use belonging to the category of culture), there corresponds a contrast between two kinds of relationship which tobacco can have with water, one being metaphorical (a transformation affecting certain myths), the other metonymical (the aquatic origin of tobacco, according to the myth). The relationship to water constitutes the invariant aspect, as if certain myths originating in an area where tobacco is not drunk, established the reality of the absent custom by distinguishing two varieties of smoking tobacco, or two ways of smoking them, of which one, in different ways, is always congruous with water.

The interest of these observations extends beyond the purely formal.

They no doubt contribute in no small measure to the process of reduction I am engaged upon, since they allow certain myths to be assimilated to other myths, and thus, with the help of a small set of universally applicable rules make it possible to simplify a picture, the complexity and confusion of which might at first appear discouraging. But in addition to providing a further illustration of a method, the use of which the reader may think I am extending unduly, they afford a clearer vision of the history of American communities and of the concrete relationships between them. The fact that myths belonging to very different tribes reveal an obscure knowledge of customs, evidence of which is only to be found outside their traditional habitat, proves that the distribution and state of these tribes in recent times tell us little or nothing about their past. The analysis of South American myths shows that the various communities, unconsciously no doubt, 'know' too much about each other for us not to conclude that their present distribution was preceded by different distributions, which were the result of innumerable mixings of races and cultures occurring throughout the ages. The differences we can observe between cultures and the geographical remoteness from each other of the inhabitants are not facts possessing any intrinsic significance; still less do they offer evidence in support of any historical reconstitution. These superficial differences merely reflect a weakened image of a very ancient and complex process of development, at the point where it was suddenly arrested by the discovery of the New World.

The preceding remarks will help us to overcome a difficulty raised by the analysis of the Warao myths. In accordance with their geographical origin, I assigned them to the mythological area of drunk tobacco. The distribution area of this mode of consumption, which is bounded to the south by the Amazon, presents a discontinuous aspect, with clearly marked breaks: 'The Uapés Indians smoke enormous cigars, but none of the tribes south of the Japura smoke their tobacco; it is only licked' (Whiffen, p. 143). This licking tobacco is macerated, crushed and thickened with manioc starch so as to form a kind of syrup. The actual drinking of tobacco, after soaking or boiling, is met with from the Jivaro to the Kagaba (Preuss 3, No. 107, 119), in the Montaña, and in three areas of Guiana: the Lower Orinoco, the upper reaches of the Rio Branco and the Maroni area.

Yet the Warao myths seem to be referring to smoked tobacco. M_{327} underlines this fact on two occasions: first, when the hero's father unsuccessfully burns the leaves of various plants in place of the missing tobacco; and secondly when his brother teaches him how to make a cigarette with the tobacco brought back by the humming-bird. It is well known that the cultural position of the Warao is something of an enigma. The fact that they have temples, and an organized religion with a hierarchy of priests and medicine-men, would seem to point to Andean influences. On the other hand, the groups living on the central part of the Orinoco delta have a very rudimentary culture, linking them to so-called 'marginal' tribes, and they do not consume tobacco (Wilbert 4, pp. 246–7). Whether we choose to regard them as a regressive group or as survivors from some archaic state, we cannot but be puzzled by discordant details, which prompt us to look elsewhere, among the tribes of central Guiana, for a possible term of comparison with the Warao myths:

M₃₃₄. Arecuna. 'The origin of tobacco and other magic drugs'

A small boy had taken his four young brothers into the forest. They met djiadjia birds (unidentified) whose cry means: 'farther on, farther on!' Although they had taken food with them, the children had not eaten and they tried to kill the birds which could be easily approached. However, none was caught and as the children pursued their quarry farther and farther into the forest, they finally reached the plantation where the servants of Piai'man, the master of tobacco, worked. Terrified by the arrows, the servants asked the children to be careful not to put their eyes out. These servants, who were birds, changed into humans so that the children could have them as parents and consent to live with them.

But Piai'man claimed the children, because the djiadjia birds, which had enticed them so far, belonged to him. He undertook to turn them into medicine-men, and gave them daily doses of an emetic beverage. The children remained in isolation in a small house where the women could not see them, and vomited into a waterfall, 'to absorb its sounds', and into a large canoe. After absorbing all sorts of preparations made from the bark, or 'souls' of various trees, the children, who had become very thin and had lost consciousness, were finally given injections of tobacco juice through the nostrils and forced to undergo a painful ordeal which consisted in the threading of fine string made of human hair through their noses and out again at the mouth, by way of the back of the throat.

Towards the end of the initiation, two of the children violated a taboo, with the result that they lost their eyes and were changed into nocturnal Spirits. The three others became skilled medicine-men and grew old alongside their master. They were quite bald when the latter sent them back to their village. They had difficulty in getting their parents to recognize them. Vexed at being considered too old by a young woman whom they desired, they turned her to stone and changed the members of their own family into Spirits. These are the Spirits who now make the medicine-men's tobacco grow in ten days, without there being any need to plant it.[24] There are three varieties of this tobacco. It is very strong (K.-G. 1, pp. 63–8).

This myth introduces the theme of water in a rather discreet form – the novices absorb the voices of the waterfall which, because of their different heights, seem like the voices of three singers – but everywhere else in Guiana, tobacco and rattles are constantly associated with water, both among the Arawak and the Carib tribes. The former relate (M335) how chief Arawânili obtained from Orehu, the goddess of the waters, the gourd tree, pebbles from the bottom of the sea (to put in the rattle) and tobacco, thanks to which he would be able to fight Yauhahu, the evil Spirit responsible for death (Brett 2, pp. 18–21). In Carib mythology (M336), Komanakoto, the first medicine-man, one day heard voices coming from the river; he dived in and saw beautiful women who taught him their songs and presented him with tobacco, as well as with the gourd-rattle complete with its pebbles and handle (Gillin, p. 170). The Kalina fill their rattles with little black and white pebbles found in water (Ahlbrinck, under 'püyei', § 38).

Otherwise, there is no doubt about the analogy with M327. Three children, or five children reduced to three, are voluntarily disjoined from their parents and travel towards the land of tobacco, being enticed there, or helped there, by birds. The land of tobacco is an island in mid-ocean, watched over by keepers; or it is a clearing in the forest cultivated by slaves. According to whether the master of tobacco is a man or a woman (or a group of women), he is welcoming or hostile. However, it should be stressed that, in the former instance, the man has a wife who tries to counteract his zeal as an initiator; 'she did not want to bother with the children'. If she had had her way, the master of tobacco would never have succeeded in obtaining it for them. Each time he tries to gather tobacco up the mountain, she manages to force him to return before he has achieved his purpose. Later in the story,

[24] Among these mauari spirits figure the Amazons who are the mistresses of tobacco in M327 (cf. K.-G. 1, p. 124).

another woman shows the same hostility towards the heroes when they become old men, by refusing to give them, not tobacco (which they already possess) but water.

Now it is obvious that the Arecuna myth refers to drunk tobacco, and to other narcotics taken orally. Although these narcotics are very numerous (the myth mentions fifteen or so), I am tempted to reduce them to three basic kinds corresponding to the three children, since several Guiana specialists agree that it is possible to distinguish three types of medicine-men, associated respectively with tobacco, pimentoes and the takina or takini tree (Ahlbrinck, under 'püyei' § 2; Penard in Goeje, pp. 44–5). This tree could be *Virola* sp., one of the myristicaceae family, which yields several narcotic substances (cf. Schultes 1, 2). According to a Kalina informant, the active principle of the takini is found in the milky sap which is administered to novices and is said to induce terrible delirium (Ahlbrinck, *ibid.*, § 32). Consequently, in spite of the single reference to smoked tobacco, which could be explained as being a result of distortion due to the peculiar position occupied by the Warao within the group of Guiana cultures, the presence of three children in M_{327} and several demons in M_{328} would seem to warrant the attaching of these two myths to a Guiana group about the origin of narcotic beverages, including tobacco soaked in water.

There remains a final series of remarks to be made, tending towards the same conclusion. The heroes of the Guiana myths about the origin of tobacco are children. After being disjoined from their parents, who become the initiators of shamanism by the example they set (M_{328}, M_{334}) or by the rules they lay down (M_{327}), they finally become Spirits, who only appear to men when the latter make them offerings of tobacco. We recognize here a pattern already encountered at the beginning of the previous volume, with the famous Cariri myth about the origin of tobacco (M_{25}). In that myth, the children were disjoined vertically (in the sky, and not horizontally, on land or water) and lived thereafter with a Tobacco Spirit, who had formerly shared the company of humans, but could no longer be summoned except by means of offerings of tobacco. Whereas the Warao Spirit of tobacco is a child, his Cariri counterpart is an old man. The Arecuna Spirit occupies an intermediary position between the two: he is a child who grows up, becomes old and turns bald.

The Cariri myth deals with both the origin of tobacco and that of wild pigs, into which the children are changed by the Tobacco Spirit.

I accounted for the link by showing that the myth could be inserted in a paradigmatic group about the origin of wild pigs, in which tobacco smoke plays the operative role (cf. above, p. 22). So, within the body of myths of tropical America, we can isolate an ordered series which forms a relatively closed set; the ashes of a funeral pyre give rise to tobacco (M_{22}–M_{24}, M_{26}); tobacco when burnt determines the appearance of meat (M_{15}–M_{18}); in order to render the meat edible, men obtain fire from a male jaguar (M_7–M_{12}), the feminine counterpart of which is none other than the victim who perished on the fire (M_{22}–M_{24}).

In these instances, we are concerned exclusively with smoked tobacco, as is borne out on the one hand by ethnography – the communities in which these myths originated consume tobacco in this way – and on the other by formal analysis, since these myths, in order to be arranged in this pattern, must be read, as it were, in the 'fire clef'. In *The Raw and the Cooked* (pp. 107–8), I formulated rules which made it possible to transpose the group into the 'water clef'. However, in so doing, I was merely providing a means of translating it, without establishing the actual existence of a second closed group in which water occupies, with regard to fire, a place symmetrical with that occupied by tobacco.

Supposing such a group does exist, it must be a reflection of the other in the 'water' category of M_7–M_{12}, that is, tending towards M_1, because of the transformational relationship which links these myths:

(*Origin of cooking*)
$$[M_7\text{–}M_{12} : \text{FIRE}] \Rightarrow [M_1 : \text{WATER}]$$

The water, of which M_1 traces the origin, is celestial water or, more exactly, water from tempests or storms and which puts out cooking fire: it is, then, 'anti-cooking', or 'anti-fire'. Now we know that the myths suppose a close relationship between tempests, storms and wild pigs. Thunder keeps watch over the animals; it rumbles when men hunt too freely and kill more game than they need. I have already given several examples of this relationship (*RC*, pp. 208–10); it would not be difficult to find many others scattered throughout the mythic texts. (See Figure 21, p. 442.)

If wild pigs, which supply the best meat, the highest form of cooking matter, are protected from the abuses of cooking by tempests and storms, functioning in the system as 'anti-cooking', the symmetrical group we are looking for can only exist if and when we discover a term which forms a counterpart to tobacco smoke, and, with regard to tempests and storms, has a reverse relationship from that existing between tobacco smoke and wild pigs. Tobacco smoke causes the appearance of the pigs; its counterpart must therefore cause the disappearance of tempests and storms.

Ethnography satisfies this deductive requirement. It is well known that among the northern Kayapo a divinity called Bepkororoti personifies storms (*RC*, pp. 207–10). Certain individuals called Bebkororoti

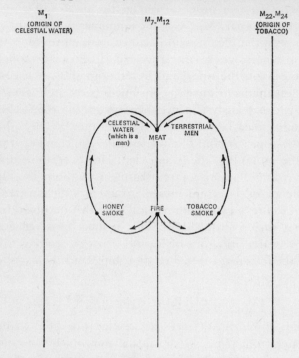

Figure 21. The pattern of relationships between myths about the origin of water, fire and tobacco

mari intercede with him on behalf of the tribe. For this purpose they use burnt bees' wax, which causes the tempest to abate (Diniz, p. 9). This is not an isolated example, as the following Guayaki invocation shows: 'He made smoke with the wax of the Choá bees in order to drive away the celestial jaguar. They struck the trees with their bows, they rent the earth with their axes, they made the smell of the choá wax rise into the sky' (Cadogan 6). When it thunders, according to the Umutina, this means that a Spirit is coming down to earth to look for honey for the celestial people; but he himself does not eat any (Schultz 2, p. 224). No doubt, in one instance, the reference is to a solar eclipse and not to a storm. But a storm is a weak form of an eclipse, and the Guayaki myth offers the additional interest of associating smoke from bees' wax with acoustic operations, to which must be added the explosion made by dry bamboo canes when thrown into the fire (Métraux-Baldus, p. 444), a noise which, as a strong manifestation of the sound of instruments of the parabára type, links up 'honey smoke' with the instruments of darkness, just as 'tobacco smoke' is linked with rattles.

In the interests of brevity, I will refrain from discussing a Uitoto myth, the length and complexity of which would justify a separate study (M_{337}). I merely mention in passing that this myth comes back to tobacco by means of a double twist: tobacco water and not smoke causes the transformation of humans into wild pigs; and the transformation punishes a hostile attitude to lightning which, at that time, was a pretty tame little creature (Preuss 1, pp. 369–403). I will also leave aside Tastevin's too fragmentary observations (4, p. 27; 5, p. 170) on the Cashinawa myths about the transformation of men into wild pigs, after they had consumed tobacco juice out of spite because a young girl did not want to marry any of them. The girl, after being left on her own, takes care of the Spirit of Tobacco, brings him up and eventually marries him; he is the ancestor of the Cashinawa (M_{338a}; cf. M_{19}, RC, p. 103). Symmetrically, in a Shipaia myth (M_{338b}), a couple who remain stuck to a nest of irapuã bees, whose honey they have been unable to ingest, are transformed into wild pigs (Nim. 3, pp. 1011–12).

On the other hand, we must pause to look at a Warao myth which, by substituting rattles for tobacco smoke, reverses both the origin and loss of wild pigs. I drew attention to this myth in *The Raw and the Cooked* (p. 85, n. 2).

M_{17}. *Warao. 'Why wild pigs are scarce'* (RC, Index of Myths: *the origin of wild pigs*)

A man, his wife and his two sons had gone to a drinking party, leaving their two daughters alone in the house, where they had chosen to remain in order to make beer from manioc and sweet potatoes (cassiri). They were visited by a Spirit, who gave them a fresh supply of food and spent the night with them without troubling either of them.

The parents came back and the daughters were unable to keep their adventure secret. The father, who was still fairly befuddled as a result of having been at the drinking party the evening before, insisted on the visitor coming back and, although he had not the slightest idea who he was, offered him his elder daughter in marriage. The Spirit took up his abode with his parents-in-law, and proved to be a good husband and son-in-law. Every day he brought back game, and also taught his parents-in-law how to hunt the wild pig. For they did not know what a wild pig really was. Until then, they had killed only birds which they believed to be pigs. The Spirit only had to shake his rattle and the wild pigs came rushing up.

Time passed. A child was born to the young couple and the husband moved his own property into his father-in-law's house. Among his property, which he had hitherto kept in the bush, were four rattles decorated with feathers, which he kept for hunting. There was a pair of rattles for each kind of wild pig, one savage, the other timid: one was used to call the beast, the other to drive it away. Only the Spirit was allowed to touch them, otherwise, as he explained, trouble would ensue.

One day, while the Spirit was in the fields, one of his brothers-in-law succumbed to temptation and borrowed the rattles. But he shook the one for the savage pigs. The beasts came rushing up, tore the baby to pieces and ate it. The other members of the family, who had escaped into the trees, shouted for help. The Spirit came running up and shook the rattle which drove the beasts away. He was so angry at his brother-in-law's disobedience and at the baby's death, that he decided to leave. From then on, Indians found it hard to get food (Roth 1, pp. 186-7).

This myth about the loss of wild pigs respects the armature of the Tenetehara (M_{15}), Mundurucu (M_{16}) and Kayapo (M_{18}) myths about the origin of pigs, while reversing all the terms. A sister's husband feeds wives' brothers, instead of the latter refusing him food. In all instances, the needy brother-in-law or brothers-in-law are bird-hunters, who are unable to obtain unaided the two existing kinds of pig (M_{17}) or the single type – in this case, the most timid – which existed at that time. The appearance of the savage species, whether absolute or relative, is the result of an abuse, committed in this case by the wife's brothers, in the other myths by the sisters' husbands: an acoustic (cultural) abuse of the rattles, or a sexual (natural) abuse of the wives. In consequence of which, the child is killed by the pigs, driven out or transformed; the savage pigs appear or disappear, and hunting becomes profitable or difficult.

Nevertheless, the Warao myth is more methodical than those belonging to the same group in its exploitation of the dichotomic principle which established an initial contrast between the two species of pig. One species represents a reward for the hunter, the other a punishment, when he makes excessive use of means which ought to be employed in moderation. Since this aspect is omitted from the Tenetehara and Mundurucu versions, we can say that, for the Warao, savage pigs punish the immoderate hunter, a role assigned by the other myths to tempests and storms, which are the pigs' avengers. The dichotomy is extended to rattles, of which there are two pairs, the terms of each pair fulfilling contrasting functions. But the two species of pigs are themselves in contrast to each other, and the four rattles form a functional chiasmus: those which are used to attract the timid species or to drive away the savage species have a positive connotation, which contrasts with the negative connotation of the two others, used to drive away the timid species (although harmless) or to attract the savage species, with the consequences already described. In terms of rattles, these antithetical values reproduce those assigned respectively by other tribes to tobacco smoke and honey smoke, one causing the appearance of pigs (which create tempests and storms), the other driving away tempests and storms (thus making possible an abusive treatment of the pigs).

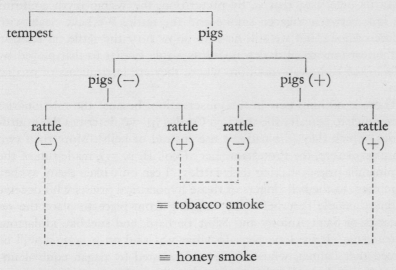

(—) wrong species of pig, wrong rattle (used to attract wrong species, and drive away right species)
(+) the reverse

Finally, and this is my third comment, the narrative of the Warao myth is linked to a paradigmatic set which has already been discussed and the initial term of which was supplied by myths dealing with the loss of honey (M_{233}–M_{239}). In changing from a myth about the origin of wild pigs to a myth about their loss, M_{17} effects two operations. One consists in substituting modes of the rattle (which are antithetical to each other) for the equally antithetical modes of smoke; in other words, it brings about a transfer from the culinary code to the acoustic code. On the other hand, within the culinary code itself, the Warao myth changes a myth about the loss of honey into a myth about the origin of meat (which thereby becomes a myth about its loss). Having been freed by the first operation, smoked tobacco becomes qualified by the second (the internal transformation of the culinary code) to occupy in Warao mythology, as is shown by M_{327}, the place allocated in other myths to drunk tobacco. The contrast between smoked tobacco and drunk tobacco reproduces, within the category of tobacco, the opposition between tobacco and honey, since in northern Amazonia, according to the locality, drunk tobacco or toxic honey are used for the same purificatory purposes.

So in its own way, that is, by preterition, the Warao myth confirms the link between tobacco smoke and the rattle. We have dealt with tobacco smoke, but we still have to show how the rattle, in relation to the instruments of darkness, fulfils a role similar to that played by bells in the European tradition, where they are instruments of mediation.

There is nothing new in this observation, because the missionaries were quick to perceive the analogy. Cardus (p. 79) describes the gourd-rattles 'which they (the natives) use instead of bells'. More than two centuries before, the Protestant, Léry (Vol. II, p. 71), made fun of the Tupinamba priests shaking their rattles: 'I can only liken them, as they were then, to the bell-ringers of those hypocritical priests who deceive ordinary people here below by carrying from place to place the reliquaries of Saint Antony and Saint Bernard, and suchlike idolatrous instruments.' If we look back to what was said on p. 403, it will be agreed that Lafitau, who was more interested by pagan equivalents, was not mistaken when he compared rattles and sistrums.

It was not the only function of the rattles to call and summon worshippers. Through them, the Spirits voiced and made known their oracles and commands. Certain models were constructed and decorated in such a way as to represent faces, while others even had movable jaws. It has been suggested that, in South America, the rattle may have derived from the idol, or the idol from the rattle (cf. Métraux 1, pp. 72–8; Zerries 3). The only point we need remember is that, both from the linguistic point of view and because of their personalization, rattles are related to bells, which were described as *signa* by Gregory of Tours, were received into the Church like new-born babies, and given god-fathers and god-mothers as well as a name, with the result that the blessing ceremony could be normally treated as baptism.

There is no need to have recourse to the Popol Vuh to find evidence of the universality and antiquity of the link between the gourd-rattle and the human head. Several South American languages form the two words from the same root: iwida- in Arawak-Maipuré, -Kalapi- in Oayana (Goeje, p. 35). In Cubeo masks, the skull is represented by half a gourd (Goldman, p. 222); and Whiffen was no doubt echoing the native way of thinking when he compared (p. 122) the 'bare skulls gleaming white like so many gourds on a string'. The Cashinawa Spirit of thunder, who is bald (Tastevin 4, p. 21), has a homologue in the Toupan of the ancient Tupi, who often spoke through the medium of the rattle: 'When it is shaken, they think that Toupan is talking to them,' in other words 'the one who causes rain and thunder' (Thevet, Vol. II, pp. 953a, 910a). In this connection, it will be recalled that bells were supposed to 'tame' natural calamities.

The sacred rattle, a transmitter of messages, seems very far removed from the half-gourd placed on the water and tapped, the prototype of the instrument of darkness used by the heroine to summon the animal-seducer. And far removed it no doubt is, since one instrument ensures mediated and beneficent conjunction with the supernatural world, the other non-mediated and maleficent conjunction with nature, or (since the absence of mediatization always presents these two complementary aspects, cf. *RC*, p. 294), brutal disjunction from culture and society. Yet the distance which separates these two types of instruments does not exclude their being symmetrical; it even implies that they are. The pattern of Indian thought conceals an inverted image of the rattle which makes it possible for it to fulfil the other function.

According to the first missionaries, the Peruvians believed (M_{339}) that, in order to charm and capture men, the devil used gourds which he caused to bob alternately on and under the water. Any unfortunate person who tried to grasp them, and who was a prey to strong desire, was enticed

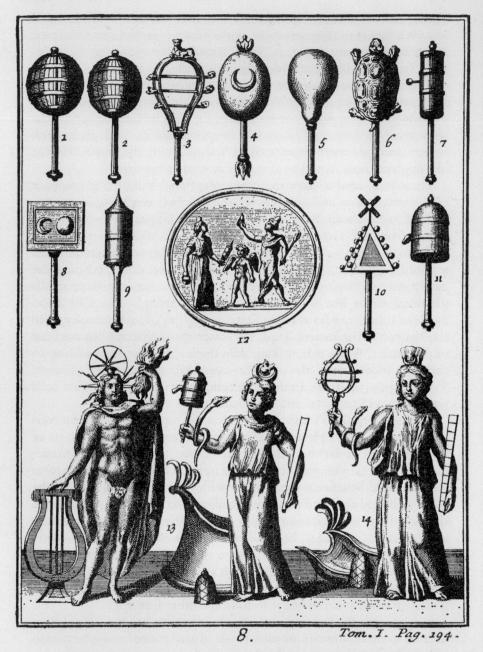

Figure 22. Ancient sistrums and American rattles. (After Lafitau, t. I, p. 194.)

a long way away from the shore and finally drowned (Augustinos, p. 15). It is remarkable that this strange notion, which seems to reflect a hallucination or a phantasm, is also found in Ancient Mexico. In Book XI of his *General History*, which deals with 'terrestrial things', that is, zoology, botany and mineralogy, Sahagun describes (M340) a water-snake, called xicalcoatl, with a dorsal appendage in the form of a richly ornamented gourd, which is used to lure men. The animal allows only the decorated gourd to emerge above the surface. 'Indeed it makes it desirable as if it were going carried by the water.' 'And an ignorant one with avarice, with covetousness, considers that it has been shown to him, and that he merits a very good gourd bowl; then he descends into the water. When he wishes to take it, it only goes drifting away; he goes to follow it there: little by little it makes him reach for it in the depths of the water. Thereupon the water churns up: it foams over him so that there he dies. The serpent's body is black, only its back is intricately designed like a gourd vessel' (Sahagun, Part XII, pp. 85–6).

The same theme occurs here and there from Mexico to Peru. A Tumupasa myth (M341) relates that a boy, a deaf-mute who had been unjustly beaten by his father, set off towards the river, carrying a gourd for drawing water which he had slung across his back. However hard he tried to dive into the water, the gourd made him float on the surface. So he took it off, sank to the bottom and changed into a snake (Nordenskiöld 3, p. 291). A Uitoto myth (M342) describes a battle between the Spirits of the gourd trees and the first men. The latter perished in a flood which spared no one, not even two fishermen who were swept along by the current when they tried to seize hold of a small pottery jar which was floating on the water and eluding their grasp. According to another myth (M343), the conflict which gave rise to the flood occurred on the occasion of the marriage of a Spirit of the waters to a shy young girl, the daughter of the 'Gourd-man' and who was called 'Gourd-under-water' (Preuss 1, Vol. I, pp. 207–18).[25]

[25] An ancient Colombian rite is no doubt linked to the same group, but unfortunately its mythic context is not known: 'They used to practise the following superstitious custom to find out whether children were going to have happy or unhappy lives. At weaning time, a small coil of esparto grass was prepared with, inside it, a piece of cotton dampened with the mother's milk. Six young men, all good swimmers, went to throw it into the river. Then they in turn dived into the water. If the coil disappeared below the surface before they reached it, they would say that the child in question would be unhappy. But, if they had no difficulty in retrieving it, they believed that the child would be very lucky' (Fr P. Simon in Barradas, Vol. II, p. 210).

P

Whether ancient or contemporary, all the myths establish a relationship of incompatibility between gourds and water. Like the sacred rattle, the gourd is by nature 'in the air', hence 'outside water'. The union between the gourd and water, symbolized by the water-snake's appendage, or by the marriage of a gourd-girl with a Spirit of the waters, is diametrically opposed to the contradictory idea – since a gourd usually floats (M_{341}) – of a receptacle *full of air* and *in water*. This, of course, relates to the dried gourd, from which a rattle can be made. Evidence of the contrast between a fresh gourd and a dried gourd in respect of water is found in a Ge myth which, like the Uitoto myth, considers Sun, the demiurge, as being the protector of gourds or gourd-men: either he tries to rescue them from the flood by providing them with poison intended for the Spirits of the water (M_{343}), or (M_{344a}) he prevents Moon, his mother, from gathering gourds, before they are ripe, from a plantation in a clearing made by the snail.[26] According to this myth, which belongs to the Apinayé, the demiurges, Sun and Moon, threw their (*fresh*) gourds into the water, where they instantly changed into humans. When the flood came, some humans managed to stay afloat on a raft which was equipped with (*dried*) gourds as buoys; these men became the ancestors of the Apinayé. Others were carried along by the flood, and gave rise to various other communities. Those who had taken refuge in the trees became bees and termites (Oliveira, pp. 69–71; cf. Nim. 5, pp. 164–5). The contrast between the fresh gourd and the rattle has already been encountered in another myth (M_{294}).[27]

The contrast between the serpent and the gourd-receptacle, which the myths regard as a complete antithesis, is therefore primarily a contrast between the wet, long, solid and soft, and the dry, round, hollow and hard. But this is not all. Whereas the dried gourd supplies the material for a musical instrument, the rattle, the snake (as I showed on p. 418) provides the 'material' of the bull-roarer, which reproduces

[26] 'When the Indian women have planted the gourd tree, they afterwards strike themselves with the hands on the breasts in the belief that thus the fruit of the gourd tree will grow large like the breasts of the women. When the tree has grown big the Canelos women are in the habit of hanging the shells of the forest snail (called churu) upon its branches, in order that it shall bear large and abundant fruit' (Karsten 2, p. 142).

[27] It may be wondered whether the Apinayé myth does not, in its turn, reverse the more widespread South American version, of which a good example is found among the Maipuré of the Orinoco (M_{344b}). In this myth, humanity is reborn from the fruits of the *Mauritia* palm, which are thrown from the top of the tree by the survivors of the flood. This would give a pair of opposites – *gourd*/(palm) *fruit* – congruous, on the acoustic level, with the organological pair *gourd-rattle*/*shell-rattle*.

its cry. In this sense, the snake-gourd illustrates the contradictory union of the bull-roarer and the rattle, or, more accurately, it is the bull-roarer in the guise of the rattle. There is another Chaco myth which, when compared with the Tereno myth (M_{24}) – in which the hero sounds a clapper, an instrument of darkness, in order to find honey more easily – seems to suggest that the same relationship of incompatibility exists between the rattle and the instrument of darkness. In this Toba myth, which I have already made use of (M_{219b}), Fox takes advantage of the absence of the villagers, who are away looking for honey, to set fire to the huts. The Indians are very angry, kill Fox and cut his body up into pieces. Carancho, the demiurge, takes possession of the heart in order to go 'where he hopes to find honey'. The heart protests and declares that it has become a ceremonial rattle: it bounces like a ball, and the Indians give up looking for honey (Métraux 5, p. 138). Consequently, just as the instrument of darkness in M_{24} helps in the search for honey, the transformation of the heart into a rattle has the opposite effect.

There is a group of Guiana myths which I do not propose to analyse in detail, so as to avoid embarking on an examination of the 'rolling head' theme, the study of which would require a whole volume to itself. These myths (M_{345}–M_{346}) belong to the unlucky brother-in-law group which has already been dealt with. Ill-treated by his wife's brothers, because he did not bring back any game, a hunter obtains possession of magical objects which make him a master of hunting and fishing, provided he uses them in moderation. His brothers-in-law spy on him, steal the objects, use them immoderately or clumsily and bring about a flood in which the hero's son perishes; fish and game disappear. According to some versions, the hero changes into a 'rolling head' and attaches himself to the neck of the vulture, which thus turns into a two-headed bird; according to others, he becomes the father of wild pigs (K.-G. 1, pp. 92–104).

The first two magical objects of which the hero takes possession are of particular interest for our inquiry. One is a small gourd, which he must only half fill with water. This causes the river to run dry and all the fish can be picked up. The water returns to its normal level when the contents of the gourd are emptied back into the river bed. The brothers-in-law steal the gourd and make the mistake of filling it to the top. The river overflows, and carries away the gourd as well as the hero's child, who is drowned. However allusive the text of this myth may be, it is certainly linked to the Tumupasa and Uitoto myths I have already quoted, and beyond them to Peruvian and Mexican beliefs, because, according to the other version we know of, the gourd belongs in the first place to the otter, which is a Water Spirit. In this version, the lost gourd is swallowed by a fish and becomes its air-bladder, i.e. an – internal, not external – organ, symmetrical with the Mexican serpent's dorsal appendage.

The second magical object is an oar, which later becomes a joint of the crab's claw. The hero uses it to churn up the water near the bank, and the river dries up below the point where the water had been disturbed. The brothers-in-law imagine they will obtain better results if they stir up the water where it is deep. As on the previous occasion, the river overflows and carries away the magic object. From the organological point of view, the two objects are connected, one to a gourd-receptacle: i.e. a rattle; the other to a beater or clapper: i.e. an instrument of darkness. But each, within its category, admits of only one limited mode of use: the gourd must be only partially filled, in other words, the water *it contains* must be shallow, like the water into which the oar is plunged, that is, which *contains it*. Otherwise, the instruments instead of being beneficent become maleficent. The line of demarcation does not run between the rattle and the instrument of darkness, but between two possible methods of using each type of instrument:

	RATTLE (*mediation present*)	INSTRUMENT OF DARKNESS (*mediation absent*)
moderate use of one or other (*mediation present*)		
immoderate use of one or other (*mediation absent*)		

Unlike the rattle, the gourd which is half-full of water is only half-full of air; unlike the clapper, the oar is a stick which is struck not against another stick but on water. So the two magic objects in M_{345}–M_{346} represent, in respect of water, a compromise similar in type to that which characterizes their use. This observation leads on to the consideration of a further point.

According to whether the gourd is more or less full, the water it contains makes more or less noise as it is tipped into the river. Similarly, the oar makes more or less noise according to whether it is shaken at a greater or lesser distance from the bank. The myths are not explicit about this acoustic aspect of the various kinds of behaviour towards water. But it is very apparent from Amazonian beliefs, which are found even in Guiana: 'Take care not to ... leave your gourd lying upside down in the boat: the gurgling noise made by the air as it comes out from underneath the gourd when water enters it, has the power to make the Bóyusú (a large water snake) appear immediately; this is an encounter people are on the whole anxious to avoid' (Tastevin 3, p. 173). What I said in *The Raw and the Cooked* (p. 294) about the word *gargote* and the fact that it had an acoustic connotation before acquiring a culinary one, will have prepared the reader for the fact that the same consequences can also follow from unclean cooking methods: 'You must not ... throw pimentoes into the water, nor tucupi (manioc juice) containing pimento nor remains of food seasoned with pimento.[28] The Bóyusú would not fail to stir up waves, bring about a storm and cause the boat to sink. So, when a fisherman draws in to the bank to spend the night in his boat, he does not wash the plates that evening: to do so would be much too dangerous' (Tastevin, *ibid.*).

Similarly in Guiana you must not spill fresh water into the canoe, or wash the pot spoon in the river, or plunge the pot directly into the river either to draw water, or in order to clean it, otherwise big squalls and storms will arise (Roth 1, p. 267).

These culinary restrictions, which are also acoustic restrictions,[29] have their equivalent on the linguistic level, and this confirms the homology of the meta-linguistic contrast between the literal meaning and the figurative meaning with the contrasts relating to other codes. According to the Guiana Indians, there is no surer way of offending the Water Spirits and thereby getting caught in storms, and being shipwrecked or drowned than to utter certain words, most of which are of foreign origin. Thus, instead of arcabuza, 'gun', Arawak fishermen must say kataroro, 'foot', and instead of perro, 'dog', kariro, 'the toothed one'. Similarly, they are careful not to refer to certain things by their right names, but by paraphrases: 'that which is hard' is rock, 'the beast with a long tail' the lizard. It is also dangerous to name little

[28] 'Spirits (p. 182) ... burnt tortoise shell' (p. 183), i.e. everything with a strong smell or taste. To act differently would be to 'throw pimento in his (Bóyusú's) eyes. Hence his fury, and those terrifying storms accompanied by torrential rain, which immediately punish any such reprehensible act' (*ibid.*, pp. 182–3).

[29] And, as such, take us straight back to the crying baby by a much shorter loop than the one I have chosen to follow: 'A pregnant woman tries not to make any noise as she works; for instance, she avoids knocking the gourd-bowl against the inside of the jar when she goes to draw water. Otherwise, her unborn son will cry all the time' (Silva, p. 368).

islands and streams (Roth 1, pp. 252–3). If, as I have tried to show in the course of this book, the literal meaning connotes nature, and the metaphorical meaning culture, a system which puts metaphors and paraphrases, careful cooking, moderate noise or silence into one category, and the word 'raw', dirtiness and din into the other, can be declared coherent. Especially since the gourd, which includes within itself all these aspects, acts at one and the same time as speaker (in its capacity as a rattle), culinary utensil (as spoon, scoop, bowl or water bottle), and as a source of intentional or involuntary noise, either because it is used as a resonator for the tapped-out call, or because air rushes in when water pours out.

We come back, then, to the gourd which made its first appearance in *The Raw and the Cooked* in a very unusual role. A Warao myth (M_{28}) tells of an ogress who wears half a gourd as a head-dress, which she often removes and throws into the water in such a way as to make it spin like a top. Then she stands and watches it for a long time.

When I analysed the myth (*RC*, pp. 109–11, 116–20 and *passim*), I left aside this detail, which now takes on greater importance. It should be noted, in the first place, that, among certain tribes at least, it is to some extent a reflection of actual behaviour. Apinayé women 'invariably take with them a gourd-bowl when they go off into the savannah. When empty, this receptacle is usually placed on their heads like a cap, and it is used as a container for anything worth keeping. Men never observe this custom ... A young child's hair would fall out if his parents ate agouti meat, or if the mother put a gourd of the *Crescentia* species on her head instead of one of the *Lagenaria* species, which involves no risk' (Nim. 5, pp. 94, 99).

We have already encountered, among the Sherente, a contrast between *Crescentia* and *Lagenaria*, subsidiary to the one between the gourd receptacle and the receptacle made of some indeterminate substance – and not of earthenware, as I inadvertently stated (*RC*, p. 291) – but perhaps of wood, since bowls made of *Spondias* wood figure among the characteristic emblems of the Sdakran moiety (Nim. 6, p. 22), which is associated with the planet Mars, personified by an officiant who proffers muddy water in a bowl. The two species of gourd which contain clear water are associated, one (*Lagenaria*) with the planet Venus, the other (*Crescentia*) with the planet Jupiter. These two planets are in contrast to each other in so far as one is 'big' (suffix: -zauré) and male (M_{138}), the other 'small' (suffix: -rié) and female (M_{93}). The Jupiter myth describes this planet in the form of a miniature woman whom her husband hides, precisely, in a gourd. The contrast between Mars on the one hand, and Venus and Jupiter on the other, corresponds among the Sherente to the contrast between the moon and the sun (Nim. 6, p. 85). The Apinayé distinguish between the two demiurges thus named according to the good or bad use they make of gourds (M_{344}), which in this case belong to the *Lagenaria* species (Oliveira, p. 69). By uniting the Apinayé and Sherente beliefs, we arrive at the following tentative pattern:

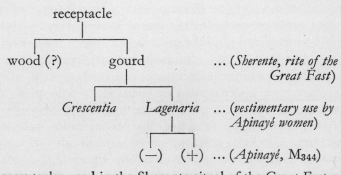

The receptacles used in the Sherente ritual of the Great Fast contain respectively unclean water (which is rejected) and clean water (which is accepted); the gourds used by the Apinayé women can serve both as receptacles and head-dresses if they belong to the *Lagenaria* species, but as receptacles only if they belong to the *Crescentia* species; the latter are, then, just as unacceptable as headgear as soiled water is unacceptable as a beverage. And, when Sun and Moon throw *Lagenaria* gourds into the water, the latter are changed into human beings, who are either successes or failures. Logically, all the terms along the oblique line to the left should have a lunar and nocturnal connotation, and those along the oblique line to the right a solar and diurnal connotation, and this, in the only case where this relationship has not been independently proved, has the following implication:

Crescentia : *Lagenaria* :: (moon, night) : (sun, day).

In order to carry the process of reconstruction further, we would have to know more about the respective positions of *Crescentia* and *Lagenaria* in technology and ritual, and be surer of the interpretation of the Apinayé terms formed from the root gó (Timbira Kō-): gócráti, *Crescentia*, gôrôni, *Lagenaria*, and gôtôti, the ceremonial rattle. Almost everywhere in South America, except perhaps in the Chaco, ceremonial rattles seem to have been made, in former times, from *Crescentia*.

There is some uncertainty in the matter, however, since the American origin of *Lagenaria* remains debatable.

I propose, therefore, to examine the restrictions concerning the gourd as headgear from a more general point of view, and as they can still be observed in Amazonian folk-lore: 'Children usually wash in the house by taking water from a pail with a gourd and pouring it over their bodies. But if they happen to put the scoop over their heads, the mothers at once utter a warning, for it is said that a child who puts a gourd on his head will be ill-mannered, slow to learn and stunted. The same prejudice applies to the empty flour basket ... ' (Orico 2, p. 71). The coincidence is all the more curious since the second use of the gourd described by M₂₈ also exists among Amazonian peasants: 'When someone swallows a fish-bone and chokes on it, the plates (usually made from gourds) must be spun; this is enough to remove the obstruction' (*ibid.*, p. 95). Now, the heroine of M_{28} is a greedy female who devours raw fish. On this precise point, folk-lore and mythic reference converge. In the other instance, the relationship is rather one of symmetry: an Amazonian boy who puts a gourd on his head will not grow; the Apinayé child, whose mother commits the same offence, will become bald – i.e. he will grow old before his time. Baldness being very rare among the Indians, a more accurate expression of the native way of thinking would no doubt be to say that the first child will remain 'raw', whereas the other will 'rot'. There are, in fact, a great many myths which give this explanation for the loss of body hair or hair from the head.[30]

In order to classify the transformations undergone by the gourd, we have, then, at our disposal a double coding system, culinary and acoustic, which frequently combines the two aspects. Let us begin by considering the ceremonial rattle and its inverted form, which I described as the 'diabolical gourd'. One produces sounds, the other is silent. The first enables men to catch the Spirits, who come down into the rattle and speak to men through it; the second enables the Spirits to capture men. And this is not all. The rattle is a container of air, contained in air; the diabolical gourd is a container of air, contained in water. The two instruments are therefore in opposition to each other

---

[30] A man became bald through having lived inside the belly of the great snake, which had swallowed him (Nordenskiöld 1, p. 110: Choroti 3, p. 145: Chimane), or through having touched the rotten corpses in the monster's entrails (Preuss 1, pp. 219–30: Uitoto). Chthonian dwarfs become bald because human excrement fell on their heads (Wilbert 7, pp. 864–6: Yupa). The theme of the person who becomes bald after being swallowed is found even on the north-west coast of North America (Boas 2, p. 688).

in respect of the container, which is either air or water. One introduces the supernatural into the world of culture; the other – which is always described as being elaborately decorated – seems to cause culture to emerge from nature, symbolized in this instance by water.

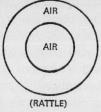

(RATTLE)

(DIABOLICAL GOURD)

Next come four modalities which, still through the agency of the gourd, illustrate the same number of logical operations which have to do with both air and water. The call tapped out on a bowl which has been turned over and placed on the surface of the water, thus causing air to be enclosed inside the gourd by the pressure of water, forms a contrast with the gurgling noise made by the gourd, full of water, as it empties, thus involving the exclusion of water by air:

(TAPPED-OUT CALL.)

(GURGLING GOURD)

These two operations, although reversed in relationship to each other, produce a noise which is caused either by air or water. The other two operations are similarly reversed but silent, either relatively (very little water is poured out gently, near the bank) or absolutely (the gourd is made to spin). The first puts half water and half air in the gourd $(M_{345}-M_{346})$; the second excludes all water from the gourd and includes no air in the water. This can be shown diagrammatically as follows:

(GOURD AS FISHING CHARM)

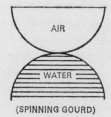

(SPINNING GOURD)

In spite of their formal aspect, which would almost justify recourse to a Boole-Venn kind of algebra to give it adequate expression, these operations have clearly defined, and in each case unambiguous, relationships with the mythology of cooking. Let us examine the last four operations I have just listed. The first devolves upon the mistress of the tapir or of the snake-seducer who, in her eagerness to rejoin her lover, neglects her duties as nursing mother and cook, thus annihilating the art of cooking. The second operation, also connected with the snake – but which has become a devouring monster instead of a seducer – results from a form of cooking which over-manifests its presence by scattering its refuse without thought or care. This gives the following opposition:

(*a*) *non-existent cooking/exorbitant cooking*

The third operation allows the person who performs it to replenish a cooking-pot which had remained empty through his fault. It therefore confers a practical existence on fish and meat, which are themselves pre-conditions of the practical existence of cooking. The fourth operation, which is equally beneficent, cancels out a disastrous consequence of cooking: that which results from an over-greedy eater choking himself. The two noisy operations are therefore connected with anti-cooking, characterized by deficiency or excess; the two silent operations belong to cooking, one of them ensuring the desired means towards it, while the other palliates a foreseen and dreaded consequence:

(*b*) *positive means of cooking obtained/negative consequence of cooking eliminated*

There still remains to be interpreted one last use of the gourd. It is a permissible use for Apinayé women, provided the gourd is a *Lagenaria*, but taboo if it is a *Crescentia* and, in the case of either species, taboo also for children, among the peasant communities of Amazonia. In M_{28}, it is attributed to a supernatural creature.

At first glance, the use of the gourd as a head-dress has no place in a system in which we have found no other vestimentary symbols. Only much later, in the fourth volume of the present series, do I intend to show that this new code is homologous with the culinary code, and to put forward rules for their mutual conversion. At this point, it is enough to stress the *anti-culinary* connotation of the use of a utensil as an article of clothing, the final detail in an ogress's portrait which, if it were imitated by humans, would transfer them from the category of consumers of cooked and prepared food into that of the raw substances which are put into the gourd to be eaten later. On either side of the central category of the cooked, and along two axes, beliefs and myths express, then, by means of the gourd, several antithetical ideas relating either to cooking which is *present*, by establishing a contrast between its positive conditions (meat and fish) and its negative consequences (choking on ingested food); or to cooking which is *neglected* by default (negative) or through excess (positive); or finally, in the *absence* of cooking or in consequence of its symbolic rejection, to the two modes of anti-cooking constituted by the raw and the rotten.

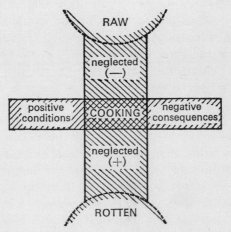

Figure 23. The system of culinary operations

*

Consequently, as the field of inquiry widens and as new myths force themselves upon our attention, myths which were studied a long while back re-emerge and throw into prominence certain of their details, previously neglected or unexplained, but which now appear like pieces of a puzzle that have been put to one side until the gaps in the almost completed pattern reveal the shapes of the missing parts and their inevitable positions; then, when the last piece has been fitted into place, we are vouchsafed – like an unexpected gift or additional bonus – the hitherto undecipherable meaning of some vague shape or indefinite colour, whose relationship to the neighbouring shapes and colours eluded comprehension, whichever way we tried to think of it.

This may be the case with a detail in a myth (M_{24}) I have often referred to in the course of this book; however, it is so tiny a detail that I did not even include it in my summary of the myth (*RC*, p. 100). The hero, a Tereno Indian and a honey-gatherer, is a victim of the machinations of his wife who is slowly poisoning him by mixing her menstrual blood with the food she prepares for him: 'After he had eaten, he walked with a limp and had no zest for work' (Baldus 3, p. 220). After being informed of the cause of his infirmity by his young son, the man sets out to look for honey; and it is at this point that he takes off his sandals made of tapir hide and knocks the soles together 'to find honey more easily'.

So, the hero of M₂₄ is lame. This detail might seem pointless, if limping did not happen to have a very conspicuous place in Tereno ritual. The most important of the Tereno ceremonies took place towards the beginning of April, to celebrate the appearance of the Pleiades and to ward off the dangers of the dry season, then about to begin. After assembling the participants, an old man, facing in succession to the east, the north, the west and the south, proclaimed himself the ancestor of the chiefs of the four cardinal points. Then he raised his eyes to the sky and begged the Pleiades to send rain, and to spare his people from war, disease and snake-bites. When he had finished his prayer, the other persons present set about making a great din which lasted until daybreak. The next evening, at sunset, in preparation for festivities which lasted the whole night through, musicians took up their positions in the four or six huts which had been built for them in the dancing area. The next day was given over to often brutal contests between opponents belonging to opposite moieties. When these were finished, and when everybody had assembled in the chief's hut, a musician, ornately dressed and holding a stag's antlers in his right hand, limped towards a previously chosen hut. He knocked the antlers against the panels of the door and, still limping, returned to the spot he had come from. The owner of the hut came out and asked what was wanted of him. He was asked to give an ox, a cow or a bull, which had been acquired jointly by the community. He then handed over the animal, which was forthwith killed, roasted and eaten (Rhode, p. 409; Colini in Boggiani, pp. 295–6; cf. Altenfelder Silva, pp. 356, 364–5; Métraux 12, pp. 357–8).

In Vancouver Island, an old woman would pretend to limp when she went to throw into the sea the bones of the first salmon, after it had been ritually consumed by children (Boas in: Frazer 4, Vol. 8, p. 254). It is well known that, along the north-west coast of the Pacific, the salmon, which constitute the natives' staple diet, arrive each year in the spring (L.-S. 6, p. 5). All the myths belonging to this region of Northern America associate limping with seasonal phenomena. Winter can be vanquished and spring made to come only by a crippled girl (M347: Shuswap; Teit, pp. 701–2). A child with twisted legs causes the rain to stop (M348: Cowlitz; Jacobs, pp. 168–9) or the sun to shine (M349: Cowlitz and other Salish coastal tribes; Adamson, pp. 230–33, 390–91). A lame man brings back the spring (M350: Sanpoil-Nespelem; Ray, p. 199). Moon's lame daughter marries the new moon; henceforth the weather would be less warm, because the Sun would move (M351: Wishram; Sapir, p. 311). And I end this brief list with a Wasco myth, which brings us back to our starting-point (cf. M3), since it describes a cripple who was the only dead man capable of coming to life again and of remaining among the living; since then, the dead have no longer been able to come to life again, like the trees in spring (M352: Spier–Sapir, p. 277).

The northern Ute of the Whiterocks region (Utah) performed a 'limping dance', sanku'-ni'thkap, the symbolism of which had been forgotten by the time its characteristic movements and the songs and music which went with it, came to be recorded. This exclusively feminine dance imitated the gait of a person limping with the right leg and dragging it along so as to bring it into line with the left, every time the left foot took a step forward. The dancers, who were about a hundred in number, formed two parallel lines about ten yards or so apart, and faced west, the direction in which the drummers had taken up their positions and, behind them, the singers. Each file moved towards the musicians, then swerved round and came back. The drums beat out a characteristic rhythm, peculiar to this dance, each drummed note being slightly out of phase with the note as sung. A contrast could be observed between the 'drumbeats, which recur with mechanical regularity, and the voice, which has a varying accent and rhythm' (Densmore, pp. 20, 105, 210).

Ritual limping has also been noted in the Ancient World where it was similarly linked with seasonal changes. In Britain, the bundle of sheaves which a farmer, who had finished his own harvest, would set up in his neighbour's field where there was still corn standing, was called the 'Crippled Goat' (Frazer 4, Vol. 7, p. 284). In certain parts of Austria, it was customary to give the last sheaf to an old woman who had to limp on one foot as she took it home (*ibid.*, pp. 231–2).

The Old Testament describes a ceremony for overcoming drought, which consisted in dancers limping round the altar. A Talmudic text suggests that in Israel, in the second century A.D., the limping dance was still used to obtain rain (Caquot, pp. 129–30). As with the Tereno, it was a question of bringing a dry period to an end – '*tardis mensibus*', to quote Virgil's expression (*Georgics*, I, v. 32) – as is the general wish in the country districts of Europe once the harvest has been gathered in.

In archaic China, all the themes we have successively encountered in the course of this book were associated with the limping dance. First of all, it had a seasonal character, which is admirably expounded by Granet. The dead season, which was also the season of the dead, began with the arrival of hoar-frost. This put an end to agricultural occupations, which had been carried out in anticipation of the winter drought during which men were confined to the villages: everything had at that time to be closed up for fear of plagues. The instrument used at the Great No, a winter feast, which was chiefly or exclusively masculine, was the drum. It was also the festival of ghosts, celebrated for souls 'who, since they no longer received any form of worship had become maleficent Beings' (Granet, pp. 333–4). These two aspects are found among the Tereno, the chief purpose of whose funeral rites was to cut the bridges between the living and the dead, for fear the latter should come back to torment the former, or even to abduct them (Altenfelder Silva, pp. 347–8, 353). Yet the feast held at the beginning of the dry season was also an invitation to the dead, who were roused by calls to come and visit their relatives (*ibid.*, p. 356).

The ancient Chinese believed that with the arrival of the dry season the earth and sky ceased to communicate (Granet, p. 315, n. 1). The Spirit of drought was personified by a little bald woman[31] with eyes at the top of her head. While she was present, the sky refrained from sending rain, so as not to harm her (*ibid.*, n. 3). Yu the Great, the founder of the first royal dynasty, inspected the cardinal points and caused thunder and rain to return. Just as bells proclaim the coming of autumn and hoar-frost (*ibid.*, p. 334), the instruments of darkness, which we have already discussed (p. 407), forecast the first rumblings of thunder and the arrival of spring (*ibid.*, p. 517). The Chang dynasty was founded thanks to Yi Yin, who sprang from a hollow mulberry

31 Hills and rivers are the first to suffer from drought. It deprives hills of their trees, i.e. their hair, and rivers of their fish, which are their people (Granet, p. 455). This is a symmetrical inversion of the concept of baldness found in South American myths (cf. above p. 456, n. 30). The same word, *wang*, means mad, deceitful, lame, hunchbacked, bald and Spirit of drought (Schafer).

tree, the tree of the east and the rising sun. The hollow tree, perhaps originally a mortar, was used to make the most precious of all musical instruments, a drum shaped like a trough and beaten with a stick. The hollow mulberry and paulownia trees (i.e. one of the *moraceae* – like the American *Ficus* – and a member of the family of *scrophulariaceae*) were cardinal trees associated respectively with the east and north (*ibid.*, pp. 435–44 and 443, n. 1). The founder of the Yin dynasty, T'ang the victorious, fought against drought. Yu the Great, on the other hand, the founder of the Chang dynasty, managed to check the flood which Kouen, his father, had been unable to control. These two heroes were half-paralysed, therefore hemiplegic, and they limped. 'Yu's step' is an expression used for a way of walking in which 'the steps (of each foot) never project beyond each other' (*ibid.*, p. 467, n. 1 and pp. 549–54; Kaltenmark, pp. 438, 444).

The Chinese legend is reminiscent of a Bororo myth I summarized at the beginning of the previous volume and to which I have just referred again (M₃). The hero, who is lame, escapes from the flood and repeoples the earth, which has been laid waste by the baleful sun, by beating on a fish-shaped drum, kaia okogeréu, that is, a wooden mortar hollowed out by fire and with an ovoid base (*EB*, Vol. I, under 'kaia', 'okogeréu').[32] According to a Karaja myth (M₃₅₃), whose link with the previous myths (M₃₄₇–M₃₅₂) is obvious in spite of the geographical distance between them, the sun, the moon and the stars all had to have a leg broken, so that they would limp and move slowly. Otherwise men would not have enough time, and work would be too hard (Baldus 5, pp. 31–2).

To my knowledge, the American data have never before been compared with the information relating to the Ancient World that I have just briefly mentioned. It is clear that, in both contexts, we are dealing with something more important than a mere recurrence of limping. Limping is everywhere associated with seasonal change. The Chinese data seem so close to the facts we have studied in this book that even the brief account I have given involves a recapitulation of several themes, such as the hollow tree, which is a trough and drum, sometimes

---

[32] Perhaps we should also compare Yu the Great, who sprang from a stone, with one of the Edutzi gods of Tacana mythology (M₁₉₆). Edutzi, who was first imprisoned in a stone cavern 'at a time when the earth was still soft', then freed by a squirrel which gnawed through the wall, married a human by whom he had a son resembling a stone. After assuming human shape, the son married, and he slung over his wife's back a little wooden drum which reverberated every time he beat her (H.-H., p. 109). The theme seems to be Arawak in origin (cf. Ogilvie, pp. 68–9).

serving as a place of refuge and sometimes as a trap; disjunction between sky and earth, as well as their conjunction, mediated or non-mediated; baldness as a symbol of imbalance between the dry element and the wet element; seasonal periodicity; and finally the contrast between bells and instruments of darkness symbolizing respectively extreme abundance and extreme scarcity.

Whenever these phenomena occur, either together or separately, it would seem, then, that they cannot be explained by particular causes. For instance, the limping dance of the ancient Jews cannot be accounted for by Jacob's dislocated hip (Caquot, p. 140), nor that of Yu the Great, the master of the drum, by the fact that, during the classical period, Chinese drums rested on a single foot (Granet, p. 505). Unless we accept the fact that the ritual of the limping dance goes back to paleo-lithic times and was part of the common heritage of the Ancient and the New World (a theory which would solve the problem of its origin but leaves its survival unaccounted for), a structural explanation alone can throw light on the recurrence in such widely differing periods and regions, but always within the same semantic context, of a custom whose strangeness is a challenge to the speculative mind.

It is precisely because of the remoteness of the American phenomena, which makes it unlikely that they can have been influenced by some obscure link with customs elsewhere, that it is possible to re-open the question. In the present instance, the observations are unfortunately too few and fragmentary for us to draw a definite conclusion from them. I propose merely to sketch out a theory, without concealing the fact that it must remain vague and uncertain, as long as we are lacking in further information. But if, always and everywhere, the problem is how to *shorten* one period of the year to the advantage of another – either the dry season to hasten the arrival of the rains, or the reverse – may not the limping dance be seen as a reflection, or more accurately as a diagrammatic expression, of the desired imbalance? A normal gait, characterized by the regular alternation of the left and right feet, is a symbolical representation of the periodicity of the seasons; supposing there is a desire to give the lie to this periodicity in order to extend one season (for instance, the salmon months) or to shorten another (the hardships of winter, 'the slow months' of summer, extreme drought or torrential rain), a limping gait, resulting from an inequality in length between the two legs, would supply a suitable signifier in terms of the anatomical code. Incidentally, it is in connection with calendar reform that Montaigne embarks on a discussion of lameness. 'Two or three yeares are now past since the yeare hath beene shortened tenne days in France. Oh how many changes are like to ensue this reformation! It was a right removing of Heaven and Earth together ... '[33]

By quoting Montaigne in support of an interpretation of customs occurring in scattered regions of the globe and about which he knew nothing, I am well aware of taking a liberty which some people may consider to cast a doubt on my whole method. It would be appropriate to dwell on this point for a moment, especially since the problem of comparison and its legitimate limits is discussed with remarkable lucidity by Van Gennep, precisely in connection with the Carnival–Lent cycle which is at the centre of the argument.

After emphasizing the need to state the geographical location of rites and customs, in order to resist the temptation to reduce them to certain hypothetical common denominators – as he would no doubt have accused me of doing – Van Gennep goes on: 'What in fact happens is that so-called common customs turn out not to be common.' This being so, there arises the question of the differences; 'If we accept the fact that carnival-like customs, in most cases, go no further back than the early Middle Ages, with very few instances of survival from the Greco-Roman, the Gallo-Celtic or the Germanic, we may well wonder why, since the Church everywhere banned the same forms of licence and prescribed the same forms of abstentions, rural communities everywhere did not adopt the same attitudes.' Have we to suppose that these attitudes have simply disappeared? But where they were already absent at the beginning of the nineteenth century, there is rarely evidence in ancient sources that they were once present. The hypothesis of survival comes up against the same kind of difficulty: 'Why should certain ancient pagan customs, whether classical or barbarian, have been handed down and preserved in some regions, and not in others, when the whole of Gaul was subjected to the same administrative system, the same religions and the same invasions?'

The agrarian theory put forward by Mannhardt and Frazer is just as unsatisfactory. 'Everywhere in France, at dates which vary according to altitude and climate, winter comes to an end and spring is reborn: can it be that the people of Normandy, Brittany, Poitou, Aquitaine, Gascony and Guyenne took no part in this rebirth which, according to

---

[33] Montaigne, *Essays*, trans. John Florio, Vol. III, Ch. XI. The late Brailoiu made a study of a very common irregular rhythm in popular music, the bichronous rhythm, based on a ratio of 1 to 2/3 or 3/2, and variously called 'limping', 'clogged' or 'jolting'. These adjectives and Montaigne's comments bring us back to the observations I made on pp. 401–3.

the agrarian theory, was the determining cause of the ceremonies of the Cycle?'

'Lastly, Westermack's general theory which stresses the sacred, hence prophylactic and multiplicatory, character of certain days, does not help us much either: we have only to transpose the terms of the preceding question to ask why the French throughout France did not all in the same way regard the days around the spring equinox as being alternately maleficent or beneficent.' And Van Gennep concludes: 'A solution certainly exists. The one usually accepted is that the annual date is of no importance and that different communities chose at random to hold their ceremonies at the equinox or the solstice. This moves the difficulty back a stage without solving it' (Van Gennep, t. I, Vol. III, pp. 1147–9).

It might be thought that the method I have followed, since it involves comparisons between customs originating in both the Old and the New World, puts me in an even worse category than Van Gennep's predecessors. Were they not less blameworthy in looking for the common origin of French customs, and even trying to reduce them to an archaic model, which was, however, much closer in time and space than the models with which I have ventured to compare them? Yet I do not think I am at fault, since to compare me with the theoreticians rightly criticized by Van Gennep would be to fail to recognize that I am not apprehending the facts at the same level. By bringing together, after analyses which in every instance are localized in time and place, phenomena between which there was previously no apparent link, I have given them additional dimensions. And, what is more important, the enrichment, which is evident from the multiplication of their axes of semantic reference, brings about a change of level. As their content gradually becomes more detailed and more complex, and as the number of their dimensions is increased, the truest reality of the phenomena is projected beyond any single one of these aspects with which we might at first have been tempted to confuse it. Reality shifts from content towards form or, more precisely, towards a new way of apprehending content which, without disregarding or impoverishing it, translates it into structural terms. This procedure gives practical confirmation of a statement I made in a previous work: 'it is not comparison that supports generalization, but the other way round' (L.-S. 5, p. 21; translated by Claire Jacobson and Brooke Schaepf).

The errors condemned by Van Gennep all derive from a method which disregards this principle or is unaware of it. But when it is applied systematically and care is taken, in each particular case, to define all its consequences, we find that none of these cases is reducible to any one of its empirical aspects. So if the historical or geographical distance between the various phenomena under consideration is too great, it would in any case be futile to try to link one aspect with others of the same kind, and to claim that a superficial analogy between aspects, whose meaning has not been thoroughly and independently elucidated by internal criticism, can be explained as an instance of borrowing or survival. The analysis of even a single instance, provided it is properly carried out, leads us to mistrust pronouncements such as the one made by Frazer and accepted by Van Gennep (*ibid.*, p. 993, n. 1): 'The idea of a period of time is too abstract for its personification to have been achieved by the primitive mind.' Without discussing the particular phenomena the two authors were thinking of, I shall confine myself to the general principle and declare that nothing is too abstract for the primitive mind, and that the further back we go towards the common and essential conditions of the exercise of all thought, the truer it is that these conditions take the form of abstract relationships.

It is enough to have raised the issue, since I do not propose at this point to embark on a study of the mythical representations of periodicity, which will be the subject of the next volume. In moving now towards the conclusion of the present work, let us simply take advantage of the fact that the Chinese theme of the hollow mulberry tree refers us back to that other hollow tree which occupies such an important place in the Chaco myths about the origin of tobacco and honey that were discussed at length at the beginning. We saw the hollow tree first as a natural hive for South American bees, the 'hollow thing' (as the Ancient Mexicans used to say), as is also, in its own way, the rattle. But the hollow tree was also the primeval receptacle containing all the water and all the fish in the world, and the mead trough which could be changed into a drum. As a receptacle filled with air, or water, or pure honey or honey diluted with water, the hollow tree, in all these modalities, acts as a mediatory term in the dialectic of container and content, the extreme terms of which, in equivalent modalities, belong either to the culinary code or to the acoustic code; and we know that these two codes are linked.

The fox is better qualified than any other character to bring out the significance of these multiple connotations. When imprisoned in a hollow tree (M_{219}), the fox is like honey; when crammed full of honey, which is consequently enclosed within it, the fox is like the tree (M_{210}); when it slakes its thirst with water which fills its stomach, later changed into a water-melon, it contains within its body an internal organ which contains the water (M_{209}). In the series of foods illustrated by these myths, fish and water-melons are not only symmetrical because they belong respectively to the animal and vegetable kingdoms: considered as dry-season foods, fish is food enclosed in water, and the water-melon (especially in the dry season) is water enclosed in a food. Both are in contrast to aquatic plants, which are *on* the water and, by maintaining a relationship of contiguity between the dry element and the wet element, define them by mutual exclusion rather than by mutual inclusion.

A homologous, and similarly triangular, system can be discerned in connection with the hollow tree. The naturally hollow tree is in contrast to the tree which has been stripped of its bark. But, since one consists of a longitudinal cavity enclosed within a solid, and the other of a cavity longitudinally excluded by a solid, they are both in contrast to the tree which is bored and holed transversally, just as the clapper stick of the parabára type is split transversely; it is not surprising, then, that the clapper stick should be in correlation and opposition to two musical instruments, which in turn present the same contrast as the hollow tree and the stripped tree: the drum, which is itself a hollow tree, comparatively squat and broad and with a thick outer casing, and the dance stick, which is also hollow, but not a tree, and comparatively longer and less broad, and with a thin outer casing; one is associated with sociological and horizontal conjunction (the summoning of guests from neighbouring villages), the other with cosmological and vertical conjunction (causing the ascension of the worshippers towards the Spirits), while the clapper stick is used to disjoin the Spirits horizontally by driving them away from humans.

The six main modes of the gourd that I have listed assemble these culinary and acoustic contrasts around an object, which is a receptacle like the hollow tree, transformable like the tree into a musical instrument, and capable of acting as a hive. The table on p. 469 will avoid the necessity of a lengthy commentary.

In diagram form, the gourd system, with its six terms, can be illustrated more satisfactorily than it was in the incomplete and provisional sketches on pp. 456–7 (see Figure 24, p. 470).

The three left-hand terms imply silence and the three right-hand terms noise. The symmetry between the two terms in the middle position is obvious. The four terms occupying the outside positions form a chiasmus, at the same time as they are horizontally united as pairs. Terms (1) and (2) endow the gourd's shell with a relevant function, which is either to establish within itself a union between air and water, or to create disunion between the air inside and the air outside. In (5), the shell does not prevent a union between the air (inside) and the air (outside). In (6), where the shell fulfils the same function with regard to air as it does in (2), it does not ensure the same union between air

culinary triads		triad of the hollow tree	acoustic triads	
gourds:	foods:		noise-makers:	gourds:
fishing charm (M₃₄₅)	fish	hollow tree	drum	rattle
diabolical gourd (M₃₃₉–M₃₄₀)	water-melon	tree stripped of bark	dance stick	gurgling gourd
spinning gourd (M₂₈)	aquatic plants	bored tree	clapper stick	tapped gourd

and water as in (1). Consequently, in (2) and (5), air is disjoined or conjoined in respect of air; in (1) and (6), air is conjoined to water, with or without the action of the shell.

Figure 24, as the culminating point of the present work, calls for certain comments. In *The Raw and the Cooked*, my main theme was South American myths about the origin of cooking, and it led me, in the end, to more general remarks about charivari as a mode of din, and eclipses as the equivalent, on the cosmological level, of the upsetting of affinal, i.e. social, relationships. The present work, which has dealt with the mythology of honey and tobacco, has moved away from cooking in order to investigate the consumable substances peripheral to the meal. This is because of the relative positions of honey and tobacco: the former lies on the hither side of cooking, in the sense that nature offers it to man in the state of an already prepared food and concentrated nutriment, which only needs to be diluted, while the latter lies beyond cooking, since smoked tobacco has to be more than cooked; it has to be burnt before it can be consumed. Just as the study of cooking led us to a discussion of charivari, so the study of the substances surrounding cooking, also obeying what I am inclined to call the curvature of mythological space, has had to deflect its course in the direction of another custom, the widespread distribution of which has also been brought home to us; this is the use of the instruments of darkness, an acoustic modality of din and which also have a cosmological connotation since, wherever they are found, their use is associated with a change of season.

In this instance too, the link with economic and social life is clear. First, because the myths of cooking are concerned with the presence or

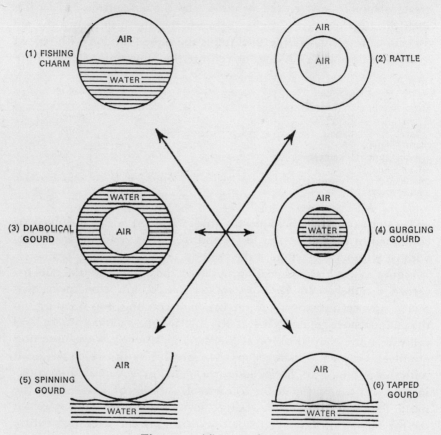

Figure 24. The gourd system

absence of fire, meat and cultivated plants *in the absolute sense*, whereas the myths about the substances surrounding cooking deal with their *relative* presence or absence, in other words, with the abundance or shortage characteristic of one or other periods of the year. Next, and this is the main point, as I have shown (p. 302), the myths about the origin of cooking relate to a physiology of the marriage relationship, the harmonious functioning of which is symbolized by the practice of the art of cooking, whereas, on the acoustic and cosmological levels, charivari and eclipses refer to a social and cosmic pathology which reverses, in another register, the meaning of the message conveyed by the introduction of cooking. Symmetrically, the myths about the circumstances surrounding cooking elaborate a pathology of the marriage relationship, the embryo of which is symbolically concealed in culinary and meteorological physiology: this is because, just as the marriage relationship is constantly threatened 'along its frontiers' – on the side of nature by the physical attractiveness of the seducer, and on the side of culture by the risk of intrigues between affines living under the same roof – cooking, too, because of the availability of honey or the discovery of the use of tobacco, is in danger of moving entirely in the direction of nature or of culture, although hypothetically it should represent their union.

This pathological condition of cooking is not simply linked with the objective presence of certain types of food. It is also a function of the alternation of the seasons which, by being characterized, as they are, sometimes by abundance and sometimes by shortages, allow culture to assert itself, or force mankind to move temporarily closer to the state of nature. Consequently, whereas, in one case, culinary physiology is reversed so as to become a cosmic pathology, in the other case, culinary pathology looks for its origin and objective basis in cosmic physiology, that seasonal periodicity which is distinguished by its regularity and is part of the given nature of things, unlike eclipses which, at least according to the native way of looking at them, are non-periodic accidents.

It would have been impossible to unravel the complexities of this problem if we had broached it simultaneously at all levels; in other words, if, like someone deciphering a text on the basis of a multilingual inscription, we had not understood that the myths transmit the same message with the help of several codes, the clues of which are culinary – that is techno-economic – acoustic, sociological and cosmological. However, these codes are not strictly equivalent to each other, and the myths do not put them all on the same footing. The operational value of one of them is superior to that of the others, since the acoustic code provides a common language into which the messages of the techno-economic, sociological and cosmological codes can be translated. I showed in *The Raw and the Cooked* that cooking implies silence and anti-cooking din, and that this was the case for all the forms that might be assumed by the contrast between a mediated relationship and a non-mediated relationship, independently of the conjunctive or disjunctive character of the latter. The analyses contained in the present book confirm this finding. While the myths about the origin of cooking establish a simple contrast between silence and noise, those concerned with the substances surrounding cooking go more deeply into the contrast and analyse it by distinguishing between several of its modalities. This being so, we are no longer dealing with din, pure and simple, but with contrasts within the category of noise, such as those between continuous and discontinuous noise, modulated or non-modulated noise, and linguistic or non-linguistic behaviour. As the myths gradually widen and specify the category of cooking, which was originally defined in terms of presence or absence, they widen or specify the fundamental contrast between silence and noise, and introduce between these two opposite poles a series of intermediary concepts which mark out a frontier that I have done no more than reconnoitre, taking great care not to cross it in either direction, so as not to find myself venturing into two foreign fields: the philosophy of language and musical organology.

Last but not least, it is necessary to emphasize a formal transformation. If any reader, exasperated by the effort demanded by these first two volumes, is inclined to see no more than a manic obsessiveness in the author's fascination with myths, which in the last resort all say the same thing and, after minute analysis, offer no new opening but merely force him to go round in circles, such a reader has missed the point that a new aspect of mythic thought has been revealed through the widening of the area of investigation.

To work out the system of the myths about cooking, I had to make use of oppositions between terms which practically all referred to tangible qualities: the raw and the cooked, the fresh and the rotten, the dry and the wet, etc. But now, the second stage of my analysis reveals terms which are still contrasted in pairs but whose nature is different in that they refer less to a logic of qualities than to a logic of forms: empty and full, hollow and solid, container and contents, internal and external, included and excluded, etc. In this new instance, the myths still proceed in the same way, that is, by the establishment of simultaneous correspondence between several codes. The reason why tangible representations, such as the gourd and the hollow trunk, play the central role that I have illustrated, is that, in the last resort, these objects in practice fulfil several functions, and the functions are homologous: as a ceremonial rattle, the gourd is an instrument of sacred music, used conjointly with tobacco, which is seen in the myths as an inclusion of culture in nature; but, as a receptacle for food and water, the gourd is a non-sacred cooking utensil, a container intended to hold natural products, and therefore an appropriate illustration of the inclusion of nature in culture. The same is true of the hollow tree which, as a drum, is a musical instrument whose sound acts as a summons and is therefore eminently social, and which, as a receptacle for honey, is part of nature if the honey is fresh and enclosed within it, and part of culture if the honey, instead of being in a naturally hollow tree, has been put to ferment in an artificially hollowed out trunk.

All my analyses show – and this is the justification for their number and monotonousness – that the demarcative features exploited by the myths do not consist so much of things themselves as of a body of common properties, expressible in geometrical terms and transformable one into another by means of operations which constitute a sort of algebra. If this tendency towards abstraction can be attributed to mythic thought itself, instead of being, as some readers may argue, wholly imputable to the theorizing of the mythologist, it will be agreed that we have reached a point where mythic thought transcends itself and, going beyond images retaining some relationship with concrete experience, operates in a world of concepts which have been released from any such obligation, and combine with each other in free association: by this I mean that they combine not with reference to any external reality but according to the affinities or incompatibilities existing between them in the architecture of the mind. We know, as it happens, that just such a dramatic change took place along the frontiers of Greek thought, when mythology gave way to philosophy and the latter emerged as the necessary pre-condition of scientific thought.

But, in the case with which we are now concerned, we cannot speak of progress. First of all, because the change-over, which actually took place in Western civilization, has never occurred among the South American Indians. Secondly, and more importantly, because the logic of qualities and the logic of forms that I have distinguished on the theoretical level, in fact belong to the same myths. It is true that, in this second volume, I have presented a great many new documents, but they are not different in kind from those that I analysed previously: they are myths of the same type, belonging to the same tribes. They have allowed us to move forward from one kind of logic to another, but this progress does not result from some new and different contribution to be found in them. It would be truer to say that the new material has acted on the myths already discussed in the fashion of a photographic developer, bringing out latent, but hidden, properties.

By obliging me to broaden my perspective in order to embrace a greater number of myths, those newly introduced have replaced one system of connections with another, but this does not abolish the original system, since we only have to reverse the operation to make it reappear. If we did so, we should, like an observer adjusting his microscope in order to ensure greater magnification, see the previous pattern reappear as the field of vision was reduced.

The lesson to be drawn from the South American myths is then of specific value for the resolving of problems relating to the nature and development of thought. If myths belonging to the most backward cultures of the New World bring us to this decisive threshold of the human consciousness which, in Western Europe, marks the accession to philosophy and then to science, whereas nothing similar appears to have happened among savage peoples, we must conclude from the difference that in neither case was the transition necessary, and that interlocking states of thought do not succeed each other spontaneously and through the working of some inevitable causality. No doubt, the factors which determine the formation and the respective growth-rates of the different parts of the plant are present in the seed. But the 'dormancy' of the seed, that is, the unforeseeable time which will elapse before the mechanism begins operating, does not depend upon its structure, but on an infinitely complex pattern of conditions relating to the individual history of each seed and all kinds of external influences.

The same is true of civilizations. Those which we term primitive do not differ from the others in their mental equipment but only by virtue of the fact that nothing in any mental equipment ordains that it should display its resources at a given time or utilize them in a certain direction. The fact that, on one occasion in human history and in one place, there occurred a pattern of development which we see, perhaps arbitrarily, as being the cause of subsequent events – although we cannot be sure of this, since there is not and never will be any term of comparison – does not give us authority to transmute one historical occurrence, which can have no meaning beyond its actual happening at that place and in that time, into a proof that such a development should be demandable in all places and at all times. If such were the case, it would be too easy to conclude that, wherever such an evolution has not taken place, its absence is to be explained by the inferiority or inadequacy of societies or individuals (L.-S. 2).

In stating the claims of structural analysis as vigorously as I have done in this book, I am not therefore rejecting history. On the contrary, structural analysis accords history a paramount place, the place that rightfully belongs to that irreducible contingency without which necessity would be inconceivable. In so far as structural analysis, going beyond the apparent diversity of human societies, claims to be reaching back to common and fundamental properties, it abandons the attempt to explain, not of course particular differences which it can deal with by specifying in each ethnographical context the non-varying laws according to which they are being produced, but the fact that these differences, which are all potentially possible at the same time, do not all occur in practice and that only some of them have actually occurred. To be valid, any investigation which is entirely aimed at elucidating structures must begin by submitting to the powerful inanity of events.

Paris, May 1964 – Lignerolles, July 1965

Bibliography

In the numbered entries, works already listed in the Bibliography of the preceding volume retain their original numbers; works appearing here for the first time are added at the end of the entry, regardless of date of publication.

ABBREVIATIONS:

ARBAE	*Annual Report of the Bureau of American Ethnology*
BBAE	*Bulletin of the Bureau of American Ethnology*
Colb.	Colbacchini, A.
EB	Albisetti, C. and Venturelli, A. J., *Enciclopédia Boróro*
H.-H.	Hissink, K. and Hahn, A.
HSAI	*Handbook of South American Indians*
JAFL	*Journal of American Folklore*
JSA	*Journal de la Société des Américanistes*
K.-G.	Koch-Grünberg, Th.
L.-N.	Lehmann-Nitsche, R.
L.-S.	Lévi-Strauss, C.
Nim.	Nimuendaju, C.
RC	Lévi-Strauss, C., *The Raw and the Cooked*, London, 1970
RIHGB	*Revista do Instituto Historico e Geographico Brasileiro*
RMDLP	*Revista del Museo de la Plata*
RMP	*Revista do Museu Paulista*
SWJA	*Southwestern Journal of Anthropology*
UCPAAE	*University of California Publications in American Archaeology and Ethnology*

ABREU, J. Capistrano de. *Rã-txa hu-ni-ku-i. A Lingua dos Caxinauas*, Rio de Janeiro, 1914.

ADAMSON, T. 'Folk-Tales of the Coast Salish', *Memoirs of the American Folk-Lore Society*, Vol. XXVII, 1934.

AHLBRINCK, W. 'Encyclopaedie der Karaiben', *Verhandelingen der Koninklijke Akademie van Wetenschappen te Amsterdam, afdeeling Letterkunde Nieuwe Reeks Deel 27*, 1, 1931 (French translation by Doude van Herwijnen, mimeograph, Institut Géographique National, Paris, 1956).

ALTENFELDER SILVA, F. 'Mudança cultural dos Terena', *RMP*, n.s., Vol. 3, 1949.

ALVAREZ, J. 'Mitologia ... de los salvajes huarayos', *27ᵉ Congrès International des Américanistes*, Lima, 1939.

AMORIM, A. B. de. 'Lendas em Nheêngatu e em Portuguez', *RIHGB*, t. 100, Vol. 154, Rio de Janeiro, 1928.

ARMENTIA, N. 'Arte y vocabulario de la Lengua Cavineña', ed. S. A. Lafone Quevedo, *RMDLP*, t. 13, 1906.

ASTON, W. G. (ed.). 'Nihongi. Chronicles of Japan from the Earliest Times to A.D. 697', *Transactions and Proceedings of the Japan Society*, London, 2 vols., 1896.

AUFENANGER, H. 'How Children's Faeces are Preserved in the Central Highlands of New Guinea', *Anthropos*, t. 54, 1–2, 1959.

AUGUSTINOS. 'Relación de idolatria en Huamachuco por los primeiros — ', *Informaciones acerca de la Religión y Gobierno de los Incas* (Colección de libros y documentos referentes a la Historia del Peru, t. II), Lima, 1918.

AZA, J. P. 'Vocabulario español-machiguenga', *Bol. Soc. Geogr. de Lima*, t. XLI, 1924.

BALDUS, H. (2) *Lendas dos Indios do Brasil*, São Paulo, 1946.

——. (3) 'Lendas dos Indios Tereno', *RMP*, n.s., Vol. 4, 1950.

——. (4) (ed.) *Die Jaguarzwillinge. Mythen und Heilbringersgeschichten Ursprungssagen und Märchen brasilianischer Indianer*, Kassel, 1958.

——. (5) 'Kanaschiwuä und der Erwerb des Lichtes. Beitrag zur Mythologie der Karaja Indianer', *Sonderdruck aus Beiträge zur Gesellungs-und Völkerwissenschaft, Festschrift zum achtzigsten Geburtstag von Prof. Richard Thurnwald*, Berlin, 1950.

——. (6) 'Karaja-Mythen', *Tribus, Jahrbuch des Linden-Museums*, Stuttgart, 1952–3.

BANNER, H. (1) 'Mitos dos indios Kayapo', *Revista de Antropologia*, Vol. 5, No. 1, São Paulo, 1957.

——. (2) 'O Indio Kayapo em seu acampamento', *Boletim do Museu Paraense Emilio Goeldi*, n.s., No. 13, Belém, 1961.

BARRADAS, J. Perez de. *Los Muiscas antes de la Conquista*, 2 vols., Madrid, 1951.

BARRAL, B. M. de. *Guarao Guarata, lo que cuentan los Indios Guaraos*, Caracas, 1961.

BATES, H. W. *The Naturalist on the River Amazon*, London, 1892.

BECHER, H. (1) 'Algumas notas sôbre a religião e a mitologia dos Surára', *RMP*, n.s., Vol. 11, São Paulo, 1959.

——. (2) 'Die Surára und Pakidái. Zwei Yanonámi-Stämme in Nordwestbrasilien', *Mitteilungen aus dem Museum für Völkerkunde in Hamburg*, XXVI, 1960.

BECKWITH, M. W. 'Mandan-Hidatsa Myths and Ceremonies', *Memoirs of the American Folklore Society*, Vol. 32, New York, 1938.

BEEBE, W. 'The Three-toed Sloth', *Zoologia*, Vol. VII, No. 1, New York, 1926.

BILLIARD, R. (1) 'Notes sur l'abeille et l'apiculture dans l'antiquité', *L'Apiculteur*, 42nd–43rd year, Paris, 1898–9.

——. (2) *L'Agriculture dans l'Antiquité d'après les Géorgiques de Virgile*, Paris, 1928.

BOAS, F. (2) 'Tsimshian Mythology', *31st ARBAE*, Washington, D.C., 1916.

——. (3) 'The Social Organization and the Secret Societies of the Kwakiutl Indians', *Reports of the United States National Museum*, Washington, D.C., 1895.

BOGGIANI, G. *Os Caduveo*. Translated by Amadeu Amaral Jr., São Paulo, 1945 (Biblioteca Histórica Brasileira, XIV).

BORBA, T. M. *Actualidade Indigena*, Coritiba, 1908.

BRAILOIU, C. *Le Rythme aksak*, Abbeville, 1952.

BRETT, W. H. (1) *The Indian Tribes of Guiana*, London, 1868.

——. (2) *Legends and Myths of the Aboriginal Indians of British Guiana*, London [1880?].

BRITTON, S. W. 'Form and Function in the Sloth', *Quarterly Review of Biology*, 16, 1941.

BUNZEL, R. L. 'Zuni Katcinas', *47th ARBAE* (1929–30), Washington, D.C., 1932.

BUTT, A. 'Réalité et idéal dans la pratique chamanique', *L'Homme, revue française d'anthropologie*, II, 3, 1962.

CABRERA, A. 'Catalogo de los mamiferos de America del Sur', *Revista del Museo Argentino de Ciencias Naturales, Zoologia* 4, 1957–61.

CABRERA, A. L. and YEPES, J. *Mamiferos Sud-Americanos*, Buenos Aires, 1940.

CADOGAN, L. (1) 'El Culto al árbol y a los animales sagrados en la mitologia y las tradiciones guaraníes', *America Indigena*, Mexico, D.F., 1950.

——. (2) *Breve contribución al estudio de la nomenclatura guaraní en botánica*. Asunción, 1955.

——. (3) 'The Eternal Pindó Palm, and other Plants in Mbyá-Guaraní Myths and Legends', *Miscellanea P. Rivet, Octogenario Dicata*, Vol. II, Mexico, D.F., 1958.

——. (4) *Ayvu Rapyta. Textos míticos de los Mbyá-Guaraní del Guairá*, São Paulo, 1959.

——. (5) 'Aporte a la etnografia de los Guaraní del Amambás Alto Ypané', *Revista de Antropologia*, Vol. 10, Nos. 1–2, São Paulo, 1962.

——. (6) 'Some Animals and Plants in Guaraní and Guayaki Mythology', MS.

CAMPANA, D. del. 'Contributo all'Etnografia dei Matacco', *Archivio per l'Antropologia e l'Etnologia*, Vol. 43, fasc. 1–2, Firenze, 1913.

CAQUOT, A. 'Les Danses sacrées en Israel et à l'entour', *Sources orientales VI: Les Danses sacrées*, Paris, 1963.

CARDUS, J. *Las Misiones Franciscanas entre los infieles de Bolivia*, Barcelona, 1886.

CASCUDO, L. da Camara. *Geografia dos Mitos Brasileiros*, Coleção Documentos Brasileiros 52, Rio de Janeiro, 1947.

CHERMONT DE MIRANDA, V. de. 'Estudos sobre o Nheêngatú', *Anais da Biblioteca Nacional*, Vol. 54 (1942), Rio de Janeiro, 1944.

CHIARA, V. 'Folclore Krahó', *RMP*, n.s., Vol. 13, São Paulo, 1961–2.

CHOPARD, L. 'Des Chauves-souris qui butinent les fleurs en volant', *Science-Progrès La Nature*, No. 3335, March 1963.

CIVRIEUX, M. de. *Leyendas Maquiritares*, Caracas, 1960, 2 parts (Mem. Soc. Cienc. Nat. La Salle 20).

CLASTRES, P. *La Vie sociale d'une tribu nomade: les Indiens Guayaki du Paraguay*, Paris, 1965 (typescript).

COLBACCHINI, A. (1) *A Tribu dos Boróros*, Rio de Janeiro, 1919.

——. (2) *I Boróros Orientali 'Orarimugudoge' del Mato Grosso, Brasile* (Contributi Scientifici delle Missioni Salesiane del Venerabile Don Bosco, 1), Torino [1925?].

——. (3) Cf. next entry:

COLBACCHINI, A. and ALBISETTI, C. *Os Boróros Orientais*, São Paulo–Rio de Janeiro, 1942.

CORRÊA, M. Pio. *Diccionario das Plantas uteis do Brasil*, 3 vols., Rio de Janeiro, 1926–31.

COUMET, E. 'Les Diagrammes de Venn', *Mathématiques et Sciences humaines* (Centre de Mathématique sociale et de statistique E.P.H.E.), No. 10, Spring 1965.

COUTO DE MAGALHÃES, J. V. *O Selvagem*, 4th edn., São Paulo–Rio de Janeiro, 1940.

CRÉQUI-MONTFORT, G. de and RIVET, P. 'Linguistique bolivienne. Les affinités des dialectes Otukè', *JSA*, n.s., Vol. 10, 1913.

CREVAUX, J. *Voyages dans l'Amérique du Sud*, Paris, 1883.

DANCE, C. D. *Chapters from a Guianese Log Book*, Georgetown, 1881.

DEBRIE, R. 'Les Noms de la crécelle et leurs dérivés en Amiénois', *Nos Patois du Nord*, No. 8, Lille, 1963.

DELVAU, A. *Dictionnaire de la langue verte*, Paris, new edn., 1883.

DENSMORE, F. 'Northern Ute Music', *BBAE 75*, Washington, D.C., 1922.

DERBYSHIRE, D. *Textos Hixkaryána*, Belém-Para, 1965.

Dictionnaire des proverbes, Paris, 1821.

DIETSCHY, H. (2) 'Der bezaubernde Delphin von Mythos und Ritus bei den Karaja-Indianern', *Festschrift Alfred Bühler, Basler Beiträge zur Geographie und Ethnologie. Ethnologische Reihe*, Band 2, Basel, 1965.

DINIZ, E. Soares. 'Os Kayapó-Gorotíre, aspectos soció-culturais do momento atual', *Boletim do Museu Paraense Emilio Goeldi*, Antropologia, No. 18, Belém, 1962.

DIXON, R. B. 'Words for Tobacco in American Indian Languages', *American Anthropologist*, Vol. 23, 1921, pp. 19–49.

DOBRIZHOFFER, M. *An Account of the Abipones, an Equestrian People*, transl. from the Latin, 3 vols., London, 1822.

DORNSTAUDER, J. 'Befriedigung eines wilden Indianerstammes am Juruena, Mato Grosso', *Anthropos*, t. 55, 1960.

DORSEY, G. A. (2) *The Pawnee; Mythology* (Part 1), Washington, D.C., 1906.

DREYFUS, S. *Les Kayapo du Nord. Contribution à l'étude des Indiens Gé*, Paris-La Haye, 1963.

DRUCKER, Ph. 'Kwakiutl Dancing Societies', *Anthropological Records*, II, Berkeley, 1940.

EB: ALBISETTI, C. and VENTURELLI, A. J., *Enciclopédia Bororo*, Vol. 1, Campo Grande, 1962.

EHRENREICH, P. 'Beiträge zur Völkerkunde Brasiliens', *Veröffentlichungen aus dem Kgl. Museum für Völkerkunde*, t. II, Berlin, 1891. (Portuguese translation by E. Schaden in *RMP*, n.s., Vol. 2, 1948.)

ELKIN, A. P. *The Australian Aborigines*, 3rd edn., Sydney, 1961.

ELMENDORF, W. W. 'The Structure of Twana Culture', *Research Studies, Monographic Supplement, No. 2*, Washington State University, Pullman, 1960.

ENDERS, R. K. 'Observations on Sloths in Captivity at higher Altitudes in the Tropics and in Pennsylvania', *Journal of Mammalogy*, Vol. 21, 1940.

ERIKSON, E. H. 'Observations on the Yurok: Childhood and World Image', *UCPAAE*, Vol. 35, Berkeley, 1943.

EVANS, I. H. N. *The Religion of the Tempasuk Dusuns of North Borneo*, Cambridge, 1953.

FARABEE, W. C. (1) 'The Central Arawak', *Anthropological Publications of the University Museum*, 9, Philadelphia, 1918.

——. (2) 'Indian Tribes of Eastern Peru', *Papers of the Peabody Museum, Harvard University*, Vol. X, Cambridge, Mass., 1922.

——. (4) 'The Amazon Expedition of the University Museum', *Museum Journal, University of Pennsylvania*, Vol. 7, 1916, pp. 210–44; Vol. 8, 1917, pp. 61–82; Vol. 8, 1917, pp. 126–44.

——. (5) 'The Marriage of the Electric Eel', *Museum Journal, University of Pennsylvania*, Philadelphia, March 1918.

FOCK, N. *Waiwai, Religion and Society of an Amazonian Tribe*, Copenhagen, 1963.

FOSTER, G. M. 'Indigenous Apiculture among the Popoluca of Veracruz', *American Anthropologist*, Vol. 44, 3, 1942.

FRAZER, J. G. (3) *Folk-Lore in the Old Testament*, 3 vols., London, 1918.
——. (4) *The Golden Bough. A Study in Magic and Religion*, 13 vols., 3rd edn, London, 1926–36.

GALTIER-BOISSIÈRE, J. and DEVAUX, P. *Dictionnaire d'argot*. Le Crapouillot, 1952.

GARCIA, S. 'Mitologia ... machiguenga', *Congrès International des Américanistes*, 27th session, Lima, 1939.

GATSCHET, A. S. 'The Klamath Indians of Southwestern Oregon', *Contributions to North American Ethnology*, II, 2 vols., Washington, D.C., 1890.

GILLIN, J. 'The Barama River Caribs of British Guiana', *Papers of the Peabody Museum* ... Vol. 14, No. 2, Cambridge, Mass., 1936.

GILMORE, R. M. 'Fauna and Ethnozoology of South America', *HSAI*, Vol. 6, *BBAE 143*, Washington, D.C., 1950.

GIRAUD, R. 'Le Tabac et son argot', *Revue des Tabacs*, No. 224, 1958.

GOEJE, C. H. de. 'Philosophy, Initiation and Myths of the Indian of Guiana and Adjacent Countries', *Internationales Archiv für Ethnographie*, Vol. 44, Leiden, 1943.

GOLDMAN, I. 'The Cubeo. Indians of the Northwest Amazon', *Illinois Studies in Anthropology*, No. 2, Urbana, 1963.

GOLDSCHMIDT, W. 'Nomlaki Ethnography', *UCPAAE*, Vol. 42, No. 4, Berkeley, 1951.

GOUGENHEIM, G. *La Langue populaire dans le premier quart du XIXe siècle*, Paris, 1929.

GOW SMITH, F. The Arawana or Fish-Dance of the Caraja Indians, *Indian Notes and Monographs, Mus. of the American Indian, Heye Foundation*, Vol. II, 2, 1925.

GRAIN, J. M. 'Pueblos primitivos – Los Machiguengas', *Congrès International des Américanistes*, 27th session, Lima, 1939.

GRANET, M. *Danses et légendes de la Chine ancienne*, 2 vols., Paris, 1926.

GREENHALL, A. M. 'Trinidad and Bat Research', *Natural History*, Vol. 74, No. 6, 1965.

GRUBB, W. Barbrooke. *An Unknown People in an Unknown Land*, London, 1911.

GUALLART, J. M. 'Mitos y leyendas de los Aguarunas del alto Marañon', *Peru Indigena*, Vol. 7, Nos. 16–17, Lima, 1958.

GUEVARA, J. 'Historia del Paraguay, Rio de la Plata y Tucuman', *Anales de la Biblioteca*, t. V, Buenos Aires, 1908.

GUMILLA, J. *Historia natural ... del Rio Orinoco*, 2 vols., Barcelona, 1791.

HENRY, J. (1) *Jungle People. A Kaingáng Tribe of the Highlands of Brazil*, New York, 1941.
——. (2) 'The Economics of Pilagá Food Distribution', *American Anthropologist*, n.s., Vol. 53, No. 2, 1951.

HÉROUVILLE, P. d'. *A la Campagne avec Virgile*, Paris, 1930.

HEWITT, J. N. B. Art. 'Tawiskaron', in 'Handbook of American Indians North of Mexico', *BBAE 30*, 2 vols., Washington, D.C., 1910.

HISSINK, K. and HAHN, A. *Die Tacana, I. Erzählungsgut*, Stuttgart, 1961.

HOFFMAN, B. G. 'John Clayton's 1687 Account of the Medicinal Practices of the Virginia Indians', *Ethnohistory*, Vol. 11, No. 1, 1964.

HOFFMAN, W. J. 'The Menomini Indians', *14th ARBAE*, Washington, 1893.

HOFFMANN-KRAYER, E. *Handwörterbuch des Deutschen Aberglaubens*, 10 vols., Berlin and Leipzig, 1927–42.

HOHENTHAL Jr, W. D. (2) 'As tribos indígenas do médio e baixo São Francisco', *RMP*, n.s., Vol. 12, São Paulo, 1960.

HOLMBERG, A. R. 'Nomads of the Long Bow. The Siriono of Eastern Bolivia', *Smithsonian Institution, Institute of Social Anthropology, Publication No. 10*, Washington, D.C., 1950.

HUDSON, W. H. *The Naturalist in La Plata*, London, 1892.

HOLMER, N. M. and WASSEN, S. H. (2) 'Nia-Ikala. Canto mágico para curar la locura', *Etnologiska Studier*, 23, Göteborg, 1958.

IHERING, H. von. (1) 'As abelhas sociaes indigenas do Brasil', *Lavoura, Bol. Sociedade Nacional Agricultura Brasileira*, Vol. 6, 1902.

——. (2) 'As abelhas sociaes do Brasil e suas denominações tupis', *Revista do Instituto Historico e Geografico de São Paulo*, Vol. 8 (1903), 1904.

IHERING, R. von. *Dicionário dos animais do Brasil*, São Paulo, 1940.

IM THURN, E. F. *Among the Indians of Guiana*, London, 1883.

IZIKOWITZ, K. G. 'Musical and Other Sound Instruments of the South American Indians. A Comparative Ethnographical Study', *Göteborgs Kungl-Vetenskaps-och Vitterhets-Samhälles Handligar Femte Följden*, Ser. A, Band 5, No. 1, Göteborg, 1935.

JACOBS, M. 'Northwest Sahaptin Texts', *Columbia University Contributions to Anthropology*, Vol. XIX, Part 1, 1934.

KALTENMARK, M. 'Les Danses sacrées en Chine', *Sources orientales VI: les Danses sacrées*, Paris, 1963.

KARSTEN, R. (2) 'The Head-Hunters of Western Amazonas', *Societas Scientiarum Fennica. Commentationes Humanarum Litterarum*, t. 7, No. 1, Helsingfors, 1935.

KENYON, K. W. 'Recovery of a Fur Bearer', *Natural History*, Vol. 72, No. 9, November 1963.

KESES, M., P. A. 'El Clima de la región de Rio Negro Venezolano (Territorio Federal Amazonas)', *Memoria, Sociedad de Ciencias Naturales La Salle*, t. XVI, No. 45, 1956.

KNOCH, K. 'Klimakunde von Südamerika', in *Handbuch der Klimatologie*, 5 vols., Berlin, 1930.

KOCH-GRÜNBERG, Th. (1) *Von Roroima zum Orinoco. Zweites Band. Mythen und Legenden der Taulipang und Arekuna Indianer*, Berlin, 1916.

KOZÁK, V. 'Ritual of a Bororo Funeral', *Natural History*, Vol. 72, No. 1, January, 1963.

KRAUSE, F. *In den Wildnissen Brasiliens*, Leipzig, 1911.

KROEBER, A. L. 'Handbook of the Indians of California', *BBAE, 78*, Washington, D.C., 1925.

KRUSE, A. (2) 'Erzählungen der Tapajoz-Mundurukú', *Anthropos*, t. 41–4, 1946–9.

——. (3) 'Karusakaybë, der Vater der Mundurukú', *Anthropos*, t. 46, 1951; 47, 1952.

LABRE, A. R. P. 'Exploration in the Region between the Beni and Madre de Dios Rivers and the Purus', *Proceedings of the Royal Geographical Society*, London, Vol. XI, No. 8, 1889.

LAFITAU, J. F. *Mœurs des sauvages américains comparées aux mœurs des premiers temps*, 4 vols., Paris, 1724.

LAFONT, P. B. *Tólò i Djvat, Coutumier de la tribu Jarai* (Publication de l'École française d'Extrême-Orient), Paris, 1961.

LAGUNA, F. de. 'Tlingit Ideas about the Individual', *SWJA*, Vol. 10, No. 2, Albuquerque, 1954.

LAUFER, B. 'Introduction of Tobacco in Europe', *Leaflet 19, Anthropology, Field Museum of Natural History*, Chicago, 1924.

LAYENS, G. de and BONNIER, G. *Cours complet d'apiculture*, Paris, Libr. gén. de l'enseignement (no date).

LEACH, E. R. 'Telstar et les aborigènes ou "La Pensée sauvage" de Claude Lévi-Strauss', *Annales*, November–December, 1964.

LE COINTE, P. *A Amazonia Brasileira: Arvores e Plantas uteis*, Belem-Pará, 1934.

LEEDS, A. *Yaruro Incipient Tropical Forest Horticulture. Possibilities and Limits*. See Wilbert, J., ed., *The Evolution of Horticultural Systems*.

LEHMANN-NITSCHE, R. (3) 'La Constelación de la Osa Mayor', *RMDLP*, t. 28 (3rd series, t. 4), Buenos Aires, 1924–5.

——. (5) 'La Astronomia de los Tobas (segunda parte)', *RMDLP*, t. 28 (3rd series, t. 4), Buenos Aires, 1924–5.

——. (6) 'La Astronomia de los Mocovi', *RMDLP*, t. 30 (3rd series, t. 6), Buenos Aires, 1927.

——. (7) 'Coricancha. El Templo del Sol en el Cuzco y las imagenes de su altar mayor', *RMDLP*, t. 31 (3rd series, t. 7), Buenos Aires, 1928.

——. (8) 'El Caprimúlgido y los dos grandes astros', *RMDLP*, t. 32, Buenos Aires, 1930.

LÉRY, J. de. *Histoire d'un voyage faict en la terre du Brésil*, ed. Gaffarel, 2 vols., Paris, 1880.

Lévi-Strauss, C. (o) 'Contribution à l'étude de l'organisation sociale des Indiens Boróro', *JSA*, n.s., t. 18, fasc. 2, Paris, 1936.

——. (2) *Les Structures élémentaires de la parenté*, Paris, 1949.

——. (3) *Tristes Tropiques*, Paris, 1955.

——. (5) *Anthropologie structurale*, Paris, 1958.

——. (6) 'La Geste d'Asdiwal', *École pratique des hautes études, Section des Sciences religieuses*, Annuaire (1958–9), Paris, 1958.

——. (8) *Le Totémisme aujourd'hui*, Paris, 1962.

——. (9) *La Pensée sauvage*, Paris, 1962.

——. (10) *The Raw and the Cooked*, London, 1970 (*RC*).

——. (11) *Race et histoire*, Paris, 1952.

——. (12) 'Le triangle culinaire', *L'Arc*, No. 26, Aix-en-Provence, 1965.

Lipkind, W. (2) 'The Caraja', *HSAI, BBAE 143*, 7 vols., Washington, D.C., 1946–59.

Loeb, E. 'Pomo Folkways', *UCPAAE*, Vol. 19, No. 2, Berkeley, 1926.

Lorédan-Larchey. *Nouveau Supplément au dictionnaire d'argot*, Paris, 1889.

Machado, O. X. de Brito. 'Os Carajás', *Conselho Nacional de Proteção aos Indios. Publ. no. 104, annexo 7*, Rio de Janeiro, 1947.

McClellan, C. 'Wealth Woman and Frogs among the Tagish Indians', *Anthropos*, t. 58, 1–2, 1963.

Marcel-Dubois, C. 'Le toulouhou des Pyrénées centrales', *Congrès et colloques universitaires de Liège*, Vol. 19, *Ethno-musicologie*, II, 1960.

Massignon, G. 'La Crécelle et les instruments des ténèbres en Corse', *Arts et Traditions Populaires*, Vol. 7, No. 3–4, 1959.

Medina, J. T. 'The Discovery of the Amazon', transl. by B. T. Lee, *American Geographical Society Special Publication no. 17*, New York, 1934.

Meggitt, M. J. 'Male-Female Relationships in the Highlands of Australian New Guinea', in J. B. Watson, ed., *New Guinea, the Central Highlands, American Anthropologist*, n.s., Vol. 66, No. 4, part 2, 1964.

Métraux, A. (1) *La Religion des Tupinamba*, Paris, 1928.

——. (3) 'Myths and Tales of the Matako Indians', *Ethnological Studies 9*, Göteborg, 1939.

——. (5) 'Myths of the Toba and Pilagá Indians of the Gran Chaco', *Memoirs of the American Folk-Lore Society*, Vol. 40, Philadelphia, 1946.

——. (8) 'Mythes et contes des Indiens Cayapo (groupe Kuben-Kran-Kegn)', *RMP*, n.s., Vol. 12, São Paulo, 1960.

——. (9) *La Civilisation matérielle des tribus Tupi-Guarani*, Paris, 1928.

——. (10). 'Suicide Among the Matako of the Argentine Gran Chaco', *America Indigena*, Vol. 3, No. 3, Mexico, 1943.

——. (11) 'Les Indiens Uro-Čipaya de Carangas: La Religion', *JSA*, Vol. XVII, 2, Paris, 1935.

——. (12) 'Ethnography of the Chaco', *HSAI, BBAE 143*, Vol. 1, Washington, D.C., 1946.

——. (13) 'Tribes of Eastern Bolivia and Madeira', *HSAI, BBAE 143*, Vol. 3.

——. (14) 'Estudios de Etnografía Chaquense', *Anales del Instituto de Etnografía Americana. Universidad Nacional de Cuyo*, t. V, Mendoza, 1944.

MÉTRAUX, A. and BALDUS, H. 'The Guayakí', *HSAI, BBAE 143*, Vol. 1, Washington, D.C., 1946.

MONTOYA, A. Ruiz de. *Arte, vocabulario, tesoro y catacismo de la lengua Guarani* (1640), Leipzig, 1876.

MOONEY, J. 'Myths of the Cherokee', *19th ARBAE*, Washington, D.C., 1898.

MOURA, José de, S.J. 'Os Münkü, 2a Contribuição ao estudo da tribo Iranche', *Pesquisas, Antropologia no. 10*, Instituto Anchietano de Pesquisas, Porto Alegre, 1960.

MURPHY, R. F. (1) 'Mundurucú Religion', *UCPAAE*, Vol. 49, No. 1, Berkeley–Los Angeles, 1958.

MURPHY, R. F. and QUAIN, B. 'The Trumaí Indian of Central Brazil', *Monographs of the American Ethnological Society*, 24, New York, 1955.

NIMUENDAJU, C. (1) 'Die Sagen von der Erschaffung und Vernichtung der Welt als Grundlagen der Religion der Apapocúva-Guarani', *Zeitschrift für Ethnologie*, Vol. 46, 1914.

——. (2) 'Sagen der Tembé-Indianer', *Zeitschrift für Ethnologie*, Vol. 47, 1915.

——. (3) 'Bruchstücke aus Religion und Überlieferung der Šipaia-Indianer', *Anthropos*, t. 14–15, 1919–20; 16–17, 1921–2.

——. (5) 'The Apinayé', *The Catholic University of America, Anthropological Series, no. 8*, Washington, D.C., 1939.

——. (6) 'The Šerente', *Publ. of the Frederick Webb Hodge Anniversary Publication Fund*, Vol. 4, Los Angeles, 1942.

——. (7) 'Šerente Tales', *JAFL*, Vol. 57, 1944.

——. (8) 'The Eastern Timbira', *UCPAAE*, Vol. 41, Berkeley–Los Angeles, 1946.

——. (9) 'Social Organization and Beliefs of the Botocudo of Eastern Brazil', *SWJA*, Vol. 2, No. 1, 1946.

——. (13) 'The Tukuna', *UCPAAE*, Vol. 45, Berkeley–Los Angeles, 1952.

NINO, B. de. *Etnografía chiriguana*, La Paz, 1912.

NORDENSKIÖLD, E. (1) *Indianerleben, El Gran Chaco*, Leipzig, 1912.

——. (3) *Forschungen und Abenteuer in Südamerika*, Stuttgart, 1924.

——. (4) 'La Vie des Indiens dans le Chaco', translated by Beuchat, *Revue de Géographie*, Vol. 6, 3rd part, 1912.

——. (5) 'L'Apiculture indienne', *JSA*, t. XXI, 1929, pp. 169–82.

——. (6) 'Modifications in Indian Culture through Inventions and Loans', *Comparative Ethnographical Studies*, Vol. 8, Göteborg, 1930.

Normais Climatológicas (Ministerio da Agricultura, Serviço de Meteorologia), Rio de Janeiro, 1941.

Normais Climatológicas da área da Sudene (Presidência da Républica, Superintendência do Desenvolvimento do Nordeste), Rio de Janeiro, 1963.

OBERG, K. 'Indian Tribes of Northern Mato Grosso, Brazil', *Smithsonian Institution, Institute of Social Anthropology*, Publ. no. 15, Washington, D.C., 1953.

OGILVIE, J. 'Creation Myths of the Wapisiana and Taruma, British Guiana', *Folk-Lore*, Vol. 51, London, 1940.

OLIVEIRA, C. E. de. 'Os Apinayé do Alto Tocantins', *Boletim do Museu Nacional*. Vol. 6, No. 2, Rio de Janeiro, 1930.

OLSON, R. L. 'The Social Organization of the Haisla of British Columbia', *Anthropological Records II*, Berkeley, 1940.

ORBIGNY, A. d'. *Voyage dans l'Amérique méridionale*, Paris and Strasbourg, Vol. 2, 1839–43.

ORICO, O. (1) *Mitos amerindios*, 2nd edn, São Paulo, 1930.

——. (2) *Vocabulario de Crendices Amazonicas*, São Paulo-Rio de Janeiro, 1937.

OSBORN, H. (1) 'Textos Folklóricos en Guarao', *Boletín Indigenista Venezolano*, Años III–IV–V, Nos. 1–4, Caracas, 1956–7 (1958).

——. (2) 'Textos Folklóricos en Guarao II', *ibid.*, Año VI, Nos. 1–4, 1958.

——. (3) 'Textos Folklóricos Guarao', *Anthropologica*, 9, Caracas, 1960.

PALAVECINO, E. 'Takjuaj. Un personaje mitológico de los Mataco', *RMDLP*, n.s., No. 7, *Antropologia*, t. 1, Buenos Aires, 1936–41.

PARSONS, E. C. (3) 'Kiowa Tales', *Memoirs of the American Folk-Lore Society*, Vol. XXVII, New York, 1929.

PAUCKE, F.: *Hacia allá y para acá (una estada entre los Indios Mocobies)*, *1749–1767*, Spanish translation, Tucumán-Buenos Aires, 4 vols., 1942–4.

Pelo rio Mar – Missões Salesianas do Amazonas, Rio de Janeiro, 1933.

PETITOT, E. *Traditions indiennes du Canada nord-ouest*, Paris, 1886.

PETRULLO, V. 'The Yaruros of the Capanaparo River, Venezuela', *Anthropological Papers no. 11*, *Bureau of American Ethnology*, Washington, D.C., 1939.

PIERINI, F. 'Mitología de los Guarayos de Bolivia', *Anthropos*, t. 5, 1910.

PLUTARCH. 'De Isis et d'Osiris', *Les Œuvres morales de –* , translated by Amyot, 2 vols., Paris, 1584.

POMPEU SOBRINHO, Th. 'Lendas Mehim', *Revista do Instituto do Ceará*, Vol. 49, Fortaleza, 1935.

PREUSS, K. Th. (1) *Religion und Mythologie der Uitoto*, 2 vols., Göttingen, 1921–3.

——. (3) 'Forschungsreise zu den Kagaba', *Anthropos*, t. 14–21, 1919–26.

RAY, V. F. 'The Sanpoil and Nespelem', *Reprinted by Human Relations Area Files*, New Haven, 1954.

REICHARD, G. A. 'Wiyot Grammar and Texts', *UCPAAE*, Vol. 22, No. 1, Berkeley, 1925.

REICHEL-DOLMATOFF, G. *Los Kogi*, 2 vols., Bogotá, 1949–50 and 1951.

REINBURG, P. 'Folklore amazonien. Légendes des Zaparo du Curaray et de Canelos', *JSA*, Vol. 13, 1921.

RHODE, E. 'Einige Notizen über dem Indianerstamm der Terenos', *Zeitschrift der Gesell. für Erdkunde zu Berlin*, Vol. 20, 1885.

RIBEIRO, D. (1) 'Religião e Mitologia Kadiuéu', *Serviço de Proteção aos Indios*, Publ. 106, Rio de Janeiro, 1950.

——. (2) 'Noticia dos Ofaié-Chavante', *RMP*, n.s., Vol. 5, São Paulo, 1951.

RIGAUD, L. *Dictionnaire d'argot moderne*, Paris, 1881.

RIVET, P. Cf. CRÉQUI-MONTFORT, G. de and RIVET, P., *and* ROCHEREAU, H. J. and RIVET, P.

ROBERT, M. 'Les Vanniers du Mas-Gauthier (Feytiat, près de Limoges) depuis un siècle', *Ethnographie et Folklore du Limousin*, No. 8, Limoges, December, 1964.

ROCHEREAU, H. J. and RIVET, P. 'Nociones sobre creencias, usos y costumbres de los Catios del Occidente de Antioquia', *JSA*, Vol. 21, Paris, 1929.

RODRIGUES, J. Barbosa. (1) 'Poranduba Amazonense', *Anais da Biblioteca Nacional de Rio de Janeiro*, Vol. 14, fasc. 2, 1886–7, Rio de Janeiro, 1890.

——. (2) *O Muyrakytã e os idolos symbolicos. Estudo da origem asiatica da civilizacão do Amazonas nos tempos prehistoricos*, 2 vols., Rio de Janeiro, 1899.

——. (3) 'Lendas, crenças e superstições', *Revista Brasileira*, t. X, 1881.

——. (4) 'Tribu dos Tembés. Festa da Tucanayra', *Revista da Exposicão Anthropologica*, Rio de Janeiro, 1882.

RONDON, C. M. da Silva. 'Esbôço grammatical e vocabulário da lingua dos Indios Boróro', *Publ. no. 77 da Comissão ... Rondon. Anexo 5, etnografia*, Rio de Janeiro, 1948.

ROSSIGNOL. *Dictionnaire d'argot*, Paris, 1901.

ROTH, W. E. (1) 'An Inquiry into the Animism and Folklore of the Guiana Indians', *30th ARBAE* (1908–9), Washington, D.C., 1915.

——. (2) 'An Introductory Study of the Arts, Crafts and Customs of the Guiana Indians', *38th ARBAE* (1916–17), Washington, D.C., 1924.

ROYDS, Th. F. *The Beasts, Birds and Bees of Virgil*, Oxford, 1914.

ROYS, R. L. (1) 'The Ethno-botany of the Maya', *Middle Amer. Research Ser. Tulane University*, Publ. 2, 1931.

——. (2) 'The Indian Background of Colonial Yucatan', *Carnegie Institution of Washington*, Publ. 548, 1943.

RUSSELL, F. 'The Pima Indians', *26th ARBAE* (1904–5), Washington, D.C., 1908.

SAAKE, W. (1) 'Die Juruparilegende bei den Baniwa des Rio Issana', *Proceedings of the 32nd Congress of Americanists* (1956), Copenhagen, 1958.

——. (2) 'Dringende Forschungsaufgaben im Nordwestern Mato Grosso', *34ᵉ Congrès International des Américanistes*, São Paulo, 1960.

SAHAGUN, B. de. *Florentine Codex. General History of the Things of New Spain.* In 13 parts. Transl. by A. J. O. Anderson and C. E. Dibble, Santa Fé, New Mexico, 1950–63.

SAINÉAN, L. *Les Sources de l'argot ancien*, Paris, 1912.

SAINT-HILAIRE, A. F. de. *Voyages dans l'intérieur du Brésil*, Paris, 1830–51.

SALT, G. 'A Contribution to the Ethnology of the Meliponidae', *The Transactions of the Entomological Society of London*, Vol. LXXVII, London, 1929.

SAPIR, E. 'Wishram Texts', *Publications of the American Ethnological Society*, Vol. II, 1909.

SCHADEN, E. (1) 'Fragmentos de mitologia Kayuá', *RMP*, n.s., Vol. 1, São Paulo, 1947.

——. (4) *Aspectos fundamentais da cultura guarani* (1st edn in Boletim no. 188, Antropologia, no. 4, Universidade de São Paulo, 1954; 2nd edn, São Paulo, 1962).

——. (5) 'Caracteres especificos da cultura Mbüá-Guarani', nos. 1 and 2, *Revista de Antropologia*, vol. II, São Paulo, 1963.

SCHAEFFNER, A. 'Les Kissi. Une société noire et ses instruments de musique', *L'Homme, cahiers d'ethnologie, de géographie et de linguistique*, Paris, 1951.

SCHAFER, E. H. 'Ritual Exposure in Ancient China', *Harvard Journal of Asiatic Studies*, Vol. 14, Nos. 1–2, 1951.

SCHOMBURGK, R. *Travels in British Guiana 1840–1844*, translated and edited by W. E. Roth, 2 vols., Georgetown, 1922.

SCHULLER, R. 'The Ethnological and Linguistic position of the Tacana Indians of Bolivia', *American Anthropologist*, n.s., Vol. 24, 1922.

SCHULTES, R. E. (1) 'Botanical Sources of the New World Narcotics', *Psychedelic Review*, 1, 1963.

——. (2) 'Hallucinogenic Plants in the New World', *Harvard Review*, 1, 1963.

SCHULTZ, H. (1) 'Lendas dos indios Krahó', *RMP*, n.s., Vol. 4, São Paulo, 1950.

——. (2) 'Informações etnográficas sôbre os Urn utina (1943, 1944 e 1945)', *RMP*, n.s., Vol. 13, São Paulo, 1961–2.

——. (3) 'Informações etnográficas sôbre os Suyá (1960)', *RMP*, n.s., Vol. 13, São Paulo, 1961–2.

SCHWARTZ, H. B. (1) 'The Genus Melipona', *Bull. Amer. Mus. Nat. Hist.*, Vol. LXIII, 1931–2, New York, 1931–2.

——. (2) 'Stingless Bees (Meliponidae) of the Western Hemisphere', *Bull. Amer. Mus. Nat. Hist.*, Vol. 90, New York, 1948.

SÉBILLOT, P. 'Le Tabac dans les traditions, superstitions et coutumes', *Revue des Traditions Populaires*, t. 8, 1893.

SETCHELL, W. A. 'Aboriginal Tobaccos', *American Anthropologist*, n.s., Vol. 23, 1921.

SILVA, P. A. Brüzzi Alves da. *A Civilização Indigena do Uaupés*, São Paulo, 1962.

SIMONOT, D. 'Autour d'un livre: "Le Chaos sensible", de Theodore Schwenk', *Cahiers des Ingénieurs agronomes*, No. 195, April, 1965.

SPEGAZZINI, C. 'Al través de Misiones', *Rev. Faculdad Agr. Veterinaria*, *Univ. Nac. de La Plata*, Series 2, Vol. 5, 1905.

SPIER, L. (1) 'Southern Diegueño Customs', *UCPAAE*, Vol. 20, No. 16, Berkeley, 1923.

——. (2) 'Klamath Ethnography', *UCPAAE*, Vol. 30, Berkeley, 1930.

SPIER, L. and SAPIR, E. 'Wishram Ethnography', *University of Washington Publications in Anthropology*, Vol. III, 1930.

SPRUCE, R. *Notes of a Botanist on the Amazon and Andes …* , 2 vols., London, 1908.

STAHL, G. (1) 'Der Tabak im Leben Südamerikanischer Völker', *Zeit. für Ethnol.*, Vol. 57, 1924.

——. (2) 'Zigarre; Wort und Sach', *ibid.*, Vol. 62, 1930.

STEWARD, J. H. and FARON, L. C. *Native Peoples of South America*, New York-London, 1959.

STIRLING, M. W. 'Historical and Ethnographical Material on the Jivaro Indians', *BBAE 117*, Washington, D.C., 1938.

STRADELLI, E. (1) 'Vocabulario da lingua geral portuguez-nheêngatu e nheêngatu-portuguez, *etc.*', *RIHGB*, t. 104, Vol. 158, Rio de Janeiro, 1929.

——. (2) 'L'Uaupés e gli Uaupés. Leggenda dell' Jurupary', *Bolletino della Società geografica Italiana*, Vol. III, Roma, 1890.

SUSNIK, B. J. 'Estudios Emok-Toba. Parte 1ra: Fraseario', *Boletín de la Sociedad científica del Paraguay*, Vol. VII-1962, Etno-linguistica 7, Asunción, 1962.

SWANTON, J. R. (2) 'Tlingit Myths and Texts', *BBAE 39*, Washington, D.C., 1909.

TASTEVIN, C. (1) *La Langue Tapïhïya dite Tupï ou N'eêngatu*, etc. (Schriften der Sprachenkommission, Kaiserliche Akademie der Wissenschaften, Band II), Vienna, 1910.

——. (2) 'Nomes de plantas e animaes em lingua tupy', *RMP*, t. 13, São Paulo, 1922.

——. (3) 'La Légende de Bóyusú en Amazonie', *Revue d'Ethnographie et des Traditions Populaires*, 6e année, No. 22, Paris, 1925.

——. (4) 'Le fleuve Murú. Ses habitants. – Croyances et mœurs kachinaua', *La Géographie*, Vol. 43, Nos. 4–5, 1925.

——. (5) 'Le Haut Tarauacá', *La Géographie*, Vol. 45, 1926.

TEBBOTH, T. 'Diccionario Toba', *Revista del Instituto de Antropologia de la Univ. Nac. de Tucumán*, Vol. 3, No. 2, Tucumán, 1943.

TEIT, J. A. 'The Shuswap, *Memoirs of the American Museum of Natural History*, Vol. IV, 1909.

TESCHAUER, Carlos S. J. *Avifauna e flora nos costumes, supersticões e lendas brasileiras e americanas*, 3rd edn, Porto Alegre, 1925.

THEVET, A. *Cosmographie universelle illustrée*, 2 vols., Paris, 1575.

THOMPSON, d'Arcy Wentworth. *On Growth and Form*, 2 vols., new edn, Cambridge, Mass., 1952.

THOMPSON, J. E. 'Ethnology of the Mayas of Southern and Central British Honduras', *Field Mus. Nat. Hist. Anthropol. Ser.*, Vol. 17, Chicago, 1930.

THOMSON, M. 'La Semilla del Mundo', *Leyendas de los Indios Maquiritares en el Amazonas Venezolano, Recopiladas por James Bou, Presentadas por –*. Mimeograph.

THOMSON, Sir A. Landsborough (ed.). *A New Dictionary of Birds*, London, 1964.

THORPE, W. H. *Learning and Instinct in Animals*, new edn, London, 1963.

VAN BAAL, J. 'The Cult of the Bull-roarer in Australia and Southern New-Guinea', *Bijdragen tot de taal-, land- en Volkenkunde*, Deel 119, 2e Afl., The Hague, 1963.

VAN GENNEP, A. *Manuel de Folklore français contemporain*, 9 vols., Paris, 1946–58.

VELLARD, J. *Histoire du curare*, Paris, 1965.

VIANNA, U. 'Akuen ou Xerente', *RIHGB*, t. 101, Vol. 155, Rio de Janeiro, 1928.

VIMAÎTRE, Ch. *Dictionnaire d'argot fin-de-siècle*, Paris, 1894.

VIRGIL. *Géorgiques*, text edited and translated by E. de Saint-Denis, Paris, 1963.

WAGLEY, Ch. and GALVÃO, E. 'The Tenetehara Indians of Brazil', *Columbia Univ. Contributions to Anthropology*, 35, New York, 1949.

WALLACE, A. R. *A Narrative of Travels on the Amazon and Rio Negro*, London, 1889.

WATERMAN, T. T. 'The Religious Practices of the Diegueno Indians', *UCPAAE*, Vol. 8, No. 6, Berkeley, 1910.

WEISER, F. X. *Fêtes et coutumes chrétiennes. De la liturgie au folklore* (French translation of *Christian Feasts and Customs*, New York, 1954), Paris, 1961.

WELTFISH, G. *The Lost Universe*, New York, 1965.

WHIFFEN, Th. *The North-West Amazons*, London, 1915.

WILBERT, J. (2) 'Problematica de algunos métodos de pesca, *etc.*', *Memorias, Sociedad de Ciencias Naturales La Salle*, Vol. XV, No. 41, Caracas, 1956.

——. (3) 'Los instrumentos musicales de los Warrau', *Antropológica*, No. 1, pp. 2–22, Caracas, 1956.

——. (4) 'Rasgos culturales circun-caribes entre los Warrau y sus inferencias', *Memorias, Sociedad de Ciencias Naturales La Salle*, t. XVI, No. 45, 1956.

——. (5) 'Mitos de los Indios Yabarana', *Antropológica*, No. 5, Caracas, 1958.

——. (6) 'Puertas del Averno', *Memorias, Sociedad de Ciencias Naturales La Salle*, t. XIX, No. 54, 1959.

——. (7) 'Erzählgut der Yupa-Indianer', *Anthropos*, t. 57, 3–6, 1962.

——. (8) *Indios de la región Orinoco-Ventuari*, Caracas, 1953.

——. (9) 'Warao Oral Literature', *Instituto Caribe de Antropologia y Sociologia, Fundación La Salle de Ciencias Naturales*, Monograph No. 9, Caracas, 1964.

WILBERT, J. (ed.) *The Evolution of Horticultural Systems in Native South America. Causes and Consequences, A Symposium*, Caracas, 1961.

WILLIAMSON, R. W. *The Mafulu. Mountain People of British New Guinea*, London, 1912.

WIRTH, D. M. (1) 'A mitologia dos Vapidiana do Brasil', *Sociologia*, Vol. 5, No. 3, São Paulo, 1943.

——. (2) 'Lendas dos Indios Vapidiana', *RMP*, n.s., Vol. 4, São Paulo, 1950.

WRIGHT, A. R. and LONES, T. E. *British Calendar Customs. England*, Vol. II. *Fixed Festivals, Jan.–May Inclusive* (Publ. of the Folklore Society, CII), London, 1938.

ZERRIES, O. (2) 'The Bull-roarer among South American Indians', *RMP*, n.s., Vol. 7, São Paulo, 1953.

——. (3) 'Kürbisrassel und Kopfgeister in Südamerika', *Paideuma*, Band 5, Heft 6, Bamberg, 1953.

Index

Index of Myths

Numbers in boldface indicate complete myth

1. Myths listed in numerical order and according to subject-matter

a. New Myths

2. Myths listed by tribe

Index